AMA MANAGEMENT HANDBOOK

Edited by Russell F. Moore

American
Management
Association, Inc.

International standard book number: 0-8144-5212-4

Library of Congress catalog card number: 77-135671

Seventh Printing

Board of Editors

Managing Editor

Contributors

DAVID P. ADAMS, Manager, Peat, Marwick, Mitchell & Co.

JAMES E. AHRENS, Vice President and General Manager, Pride Products Company

RAYMOND O. ANDERSON, Assistant to the Director of Research, Honeywell, Inc.

STEPHEN S. BAIRD, Plastic Reliability and Technology Consultant, Quality and Reliability Assurance Components Group, Texas Instruments, Incorporated

KENNETH A. BAKER, President, COMSI, Inc.

STEPHEN P. BARTHOLF, Assistant Vice President—Administrative Services, Horace Mann Educators Corporation

PETER A. BENOLIEL, President, Quaker Chemical Corporation

CHARLES J. BERG, JR., Director, Work Measurement & Clerical Cost Control, Naremco Services, Inc.

DONALD W. BERRY, Vice President, C. B. Lilly, Incorporated

RALPH A. BOLTON, Manager, Systems Contracting, The Carborundum Company

EUGENE BOSHES, Chairman of the Board, Environmental Research & Development, Inc.

RONALD BROWN, Management Consultant

ELIAS BUCHWALD, President, Burson-Marsteller

CHESTER BURGER, President, Chester Burger & Co., Inc.

J. CLARK BURKE, Manager of Security and Office Services, The F. & M. Schaefer Brewing Company

WILLIAM F. BURKE, President, Sanborn Aviation Associates, Inc.

WILLIAM C. BYHAM, Management Development Specialist, J. C. Penney Company, Inc.

JERRY CANTOR, President, Cantor Associates Systems Consultants Inc.

LOUIS M. CARAS, Vice President—Purchases, Gilman Paper Company

ARLO E. CARNEY, Director of Purchases, Belden Corporation

ROBERT B. CARTER, JR., Senior Consultant, Peat, Marwick, Mitchell & Co.

JOHN P. CHIPMAN, Director of Personnel & Labour Relations, Dominion Glass Company Limited

HAMILTON L. CLARK, Assistant to the Controller, MGD Graphic Systems, North American Rockwell

DAVID COE, Chairman of the Board, Moss-Coe International Corporation

GORDON A. COLEMAN, Superintendent, Maintenance, South Point (Ohio) Plant, Allied Chemical Corporation

WILLIAM COPULSKY, Director, Commercial Department, W. R. Grace & Co.

RODERICK S. COWLES, Director of Quality Control, E. R. Squibb & Sons, Inc.

JOSEPH G. COWLEY, Managing Editor, The Research Institute of America, Inc.

GRAEF S. CRYSTAL, Consultant, Towers, Perrin, Forster & Crosby, Inc.

WALTER H. DIAMOND, Manager, Peat, Marwick, Mitchell & Co.

GEORGE S. DOMINGUEZ, Product Group Manager, Geigy Dyestuffs, Division of Geigy Chemical Corporation

L. FRANK EDELBLUT, Director of Materials Management, E. R. Squibb & Sons, Inc.

ROBERT L. FEGLEY, Manager—Public Issues and Customer Research, General Electric Company

KENNETH U. FLOOD, Professor of Logistics, University of Missouri, Columbia

FREDERICK V. FORTMILLER, President, Fortmiller Associates, Inc.

RICHARD D. FRANK, Director of Executive Development, Abraham & Straus

RANDOLPH K. FUSSELMAN, Purchasing Services Manager, J. C. Penney Company, Inc.

VINCENT N. GANNON, Senior Vice President, Hill and Knowlton, Inc.

ROBERT P. GIBBONS, Principal, Touche, Ross & Co.

HOWARD T. GO, President, Interscience Management Corporation

R. MICHAEL GOFFREDO, Director, Management Services, E. R. Squibb & Sons, Inc.

MARILYN J. GOWIN, Manager, Arthur Andersen & Co.

CHARLES E. GRAVES, Employee Relations Consultant

EDWARD J. GREEN, President, Planning Dynamics, Incorporated

JAMES L. GREENE, Vice President and Secretary, American Reserve Corporation

DUNCAN S. GREGG, Director of Purchasing, Kaiser Aluminum & Chemical Corporation

ALFRED GROSS, Professor of Marketing and Chairman, Department of Business Administration, New York University

WILLIAM J. GUYTON, Vice President, A. T. Kearney & Company, Inc.

MACK HANAN, Hanan & Son, Management Consultants

LEE HIRST, Director of Public Relations, The Sperry and Hutchinson Company

ROBERT A. HOLZBACH, Associate, A. T. Kearney & Company, Inc.

ROBERT S. HOLZMAN, Professor of Taxation, Graduate School of Business Administration, New York University

MASAAKI HOTTA, Hotta Management Consultant

DONALD E. HOWARD, Manager, Project Services, Olin Corporation

W. ASQUITH HOWE, Professor of Accounting, Temple University

VINCENT E. HUETHER, Director of Purchasing, Ethicon, Inc.

CHARLES W. HULTMAN, Professor and Chairman, Department of Economics, University of Kentucky

VICTOR R. KENNEDY, JR., Vice President, Marketing, Blue Cross and Blue Shield of Texas

EVELYN KONRAD, President, Evelyn Konrad Associates

HAROLD KOONTZ, Mead Johnson Professor of Management, Graduate School of Business Administration, University of California, Los Angeles

SAMUEL A. KRASNEY, President, John DeNigris Associates, Inc.

BURTON E. LAMKIN, Deputy Director for Library Services, National Agricultural Library, United States Department of Agriculture

CHARLES E. LAWSON, Foreign Exchange Manager, International Banking, Bank of Montreal, Head Office

WILLIAM T. LIFLAND, Partner, Cahill, Gordon, Sonnett, Reindel & Ohl

HARRY A. LUND, Assistant Secretary, Irving Trust Company

WILLIAM J. MCBURNEY, JR., President, Market Development Services (New York)

GEORGE G. MCCONEGHY, General Auditor, The Seeburg Corporation

ROBERT E. MCCOY, Vice President—Manufacturing, McCreary Tire & Rubber Company

JOHN J. MCCREA, Corporate Vice President, Simkins Industries, Inc.

WILLIAM A. MACCREHAN, JR., Manager, Quality Control Engineering, Weapons Department, Westinghouse Electric Corporation

EDWIN C. MCMANUS, Director, Employee Benefits, The Singer Company

P. W. MALONEY, Consultant in Personnel Administration

KENNETH B. MARBLE, Marketing Services Manager, A. B. Dick Company

DONALD E. MILLER, Credit Manager, Eastern Area, Crown Zellerbach Corporation

WILLIAM N. MITCHELL, Partner Emeritus (Deceased), A. T. Kearney & Company, Inc.

HARRY J. MOORE, IBM Director of Manufacturing Services, International Business Machines Corporation

STANLEIGH H. MORRIS, President, Environmental Research & Development, Inc.

ALAN G. NEGUS, Executive Vice President, Naremco Services, Inc.

WALTER F. O'CONNOR, Partner, Peat, Marwick, Mitchell & Co.

JOSEPH F. O'HORA, President, ISD Incorporated

MICHAEL A. OLSON, Attorney, Dorsey, Marquart, Windhorst, West & Halladay

GEORGE M. PARKS, Associate Professor of Industry and Operations Research, Wharton School, University of Pennsylvania

ROBERT F. PEARSE, Professor of Behavioral Sciences, College of Business Administration, Boston University

ARTHUR G. PEARSON, Executive Assistant—Division Director Material, North American Rockwell

MICHAEL PRICHARD, Attorney, Dorsey, Marquart, Windhorst, West & Halladay

CARL J. PRITCHARD, Special Representative, Computer Systems Division, RCA Corporation

ROBERT A. PRITZKER, President, The Marmon Group

ERWIN RAUSCH, President, Didactic Systems, Inc.

MICHAEL N. ROLFE, Associate, A. T. Kearney & Company, Inc.

DAVID W. ROSS, President, Ross Associates, Inc.

DAVID K. ROWE, Corporate Vice President—Industrial Relations, The Macke Company

BERNARD G. RYLE, Director of Research, AMP Incorporated

RICHARD W. SAUNDERS, Partner, Arthur Andersen & Co.

O. GLENN SAXON, Director of Corporate Communications, The Singer Company

JOHN L. SCHWAB, President, John L. Schwab & Associates

JOHN T. SHANAHAN, JR., Partner, Peat, Marwick, Mitchell & Co.

DONALD L. SHAWVER, Professor of Marketing, University of Missouri, Columbia

ROBERT A. SHIFF, President, Naremco Services, Inc.

ELLIS W. SMITH, Vice President—Finance and Treasurer, Reliance Electric Company

JAMES H. SMITH, Treasurer, Coe Laboratories, Inc.

ROBERT L. SMITH, JR., Vice President, Automation & Planning, Blue Cross and Blue Shield of Texas

CHARLES F. STAMM, Manager, Management Services, Touche, Ross & Co.

LEONARD STATEMAN, Vice President, Naremco Services, Inc.

RICHARD J. STEELE, President, Richard Steele and Partners, Inc.

S. DAVID STONER, Manager, International Consulting Office (U.S.), Towers, Perrin, Forster & Crosby, Inc.

GEORGE C. STRYKER, Material Handling Engineer, Westinghouse Electric Corporation, Lamp Division; Consultant

ALAN L. SUMMERS, Assistant Cashier, First National City Bank

H. W. ALLEN SWEENY, Treasurer-Controller, International Standard Brands Incorporated

WALTER L. SYKES, Manager, Plant Engineering and Maintenance, Raytheon Company

CURTIS W. SYMONDS, President, Financial Control Associates

WILLIAM T. THORNHILL, Vice President, The First National Bank of Chicago

FRED M. TRUETT, Chairman of the Board (Retired), Southwestern Drug Corporation

DAVID B. UMAN, Manager of Business Planning, Leasco Data Processing Equipment Corporation

JERROLD G. VAN CISE, Partner, Cahill, Gordon, Sonnett, Reindel & Ohl

RAYMOND VILLERS, Professor, Graduate School of Business Administration, Pace College; Consultant, Rautenstrauch and Villers

WORTH WADE, Author, Publisher, Advance House, Publishers

A. JOHN WARD, President, Management Research & Planning, Inc.

RAY M. WARE, Professor of Economics, Transylvania University

MAX J. WASSERMAN, Consulting Economist; Visiting Lecturer, Kentucky State College

ERNEST H. WEINWURM, Professor Emeritus, De Paul University; Lecturer, San Fernando Valley State College

LEO G. B. WELT, President, Welt International Management Service

RICHARD E. WETTLING, Director of Compensation, Anderson, Clayton & Co.

DONALD G. WILSON, Vice President, Research & Engineering, P. R. Mallory & Co., Inc.

W. McCORMICK WILSON, Manager—General Services, United States Steel Corporation

JOHN L. WOOD, Senior Vice President, Daggett Associates

CHURCH YEARLEY, Vice Chairman of the Board, The First National Bank of Atlanta

RICHARD A. YOUNG, Director of Equal Opportunity, American Optical Corporation

Preface

For nearly 50 years, the American Management Association has played a central role in the development of managerial competence and in the growing acceptance of management as a profession. Increasingly, during these years, it has seemed that students and practitioners might welcome a special sort of guide to the profession; in brief, a single volume that would provide sound, comprehensive, authoritative information on the best contemporary thinking and usage.

The idea of encapsulating in one reference source the policies and procedures favored by successful organizations in a wide range of businesses and industries is, of course, by no means new. There have been excellent handbooks in such individual areas of management as finance, marketing, production, foreign trade, and public relations. There have been very few, however, that consistently sought to view management as a whole. And, of these few, some have been little more than uneven collections of essays which, for the most part, failed completely to convey those interrelationships of the various management processes that are so essential to their understanding.

What happens in the marketing division of a company, for example, is certain to have an impact on what happens, or is likely to happen, in the manufacturing division—and it goes without saying that these activities will affect the company's financial affairs. The ultimate effect will be reflected in the profit-and-loss statement, and this will have an influence on dividend policy, which, in turn, will set the tone of the public relations director's communications to stockholders.

The *Handbook*, then, seeks throughout to make these functional interrelationships clear. It has been compiled—and is offered—as a practical aid to the application of present-day management theory in areas that perhaps are less than familiar to the reader. It is designed specifically to help him solve those inevitable problems, faced by every manager, that cut across functional boundaries. Aimed primarily at the needs of middle and upper management, the book will probably find its greatest use among management generalists as opposed to specialists.

The orientation of the material is practical. At the same time, underlying principles are clearly set out for the interested manager at whatever level. Students of management, whether in undergraduate schools, graduate courses, company training centers, or self-improvement programs, should find the volume invaluable.

The goal in compiling the *AMA Management Handbook* was to assemble a body of factual information that would constitute a solid foundation for management as, ideally, it is or should be practiced today. Each of the major line and staff disciplines—that is, research and development, manufacturing, finance, personnel, administrative services, marketing, and all the others entrusted to sizable company divisions or departments—was allotted a separate section in the book. Then, with the book's basic concept and its organizational pattern thus determined, associate editors were designated for the individual sections.

The associate editors undertook the difficult task of outlining the broad subject-matter areas to be included in their respective sections and, after editorial meetings in which the principal headings were arrived at, specifying the content in considerable detail. It was at this point that the extent to which management processes are interrelated became most obvious. Whether a subject properly belonged in one section or another was many times difficult to decide, particularly since practice differs from organization to organization. If, under the circumstances, a certain residue of duplication persists, it is inherent in the nature of the book. In any case, the detailed index will help the user to get the information he needs quickly and painlessly.

Once the book's contents had been agreed upon, the search for contributing authors began. Here the aim was to find both practicing managers and outstanding specialists who were known to be authorities in their fields. Two criteria were set up: Not only must contributors be intimately involved in management and alert to current trends and techniques, but they must also be able to communicate these effectively within the format and space limitations imposed upon them.

In short, the *Handbook* has been a collaborative effort. Its more than 140 associate editors and contributors have all had extensive, firsthand experience that has enabled each of them to provide a concise, readable, dependable view of his specialty. Many are top corporate executives; others are members of professions closely allied to management: economists, lawyers, accountants, bankers, educators, and consultants.

Not only is the list of associate editors and contributors convincing proof that the *Handbook* is the work of men well qualified for the task, but its appearance at this time is peculiarly appropriate. For, in it, a sincere effort has been made to crystallize the kind of management thinking that is increasingly needed to handle today's complex and demanding managerial assignments.

The multiple challenges facing American management in this second half of the twentieth century are the greatest in its history. They run the gamut from personnel through research, engineering, finance, production, and marketing, and recently they have more and more involved societal relationships. And the practice of management is a dynamic thing; yesterday's skills often do not meet today's needs—much less those just emerging over the horizon. Take only the problem of assuring adequate personnel, above all at managerial levels. Experienced executives are sharply aware of the pressing need to keep managerial personnel up to date—a need that can only become more acute as America's innovative technology continues its exponential growth. Indeed, "executive obsolescence" may be no mere threat but an existing condition. In one company, where the problem has been recognized and steps have been taken to attract and retain the talent on which corporate survival depends, the average age of the key producers may be no more than 29 or 30. In another, the complacent president of 58 has yet to realize his failure to build management reserves for the future—with potentially catastrophic results for the firm.

Then there is the flood of legislation relating to equal opportunity that by now is familiar to virtually everyone with responsibilities in the employment area. The voices of minority groups join in an inescapable crescendo as they push for equality in matters of hiring, pay scales, and managerial posts. By way of example, the U.S. Department of Justice has for the first time filed suit against a large manufacturer, and the union that represents its employees, to stop alleged discrimination against women. And, almost simultaneously, a U.S. district court has ruled that an employer cannot deny a job to an applicant simply because he has been arrested, and the company in question has been enjoined from using or even obtaining the police records of prospective employees.

And so it goes, too, in marketing. Like their counterparts in personnel, marketing executives are faced with far-reaching change. They have felt the impact of the television commercial, the growth of franchising and of leasing as marketing devices, and the increased vocalism of consumer groups demanding everything from greater auto safety to changes in labeling. They have come to be newly aware of the significant marketing/finance interface, and—as in practically every phase of company operations—they have seen the computer used (or, sometimes, abused) to support managerial decision making.

But problems like these, although they may seem to have exerted even greater pressure on the manager in the past few years, are not entirely unfamiliar. Moreover, it must be acknowledged that the computer and EDP, improved communications, the findings of the behavioral scientists, and the many other tools and techniques described here have given managers access to the know-how they must have to withstand this pressure. Yet there is another vast area—less well charted in management literature—in which problems of staggering dimensions are now being posed. These are the problems arising out of man's socio-economic relationships. To the company president or other responsible executive, they take the form of questions that are overwhelming in their urgency: To what extent am I justified in diverting corporate funds that might otherwise be paid out to the owners as dividends and using them to train hard-core unemployed? To clear slums? To eliminate pollution? Where does the obligation of the economy's public sector end and that of private business enterprise begin? What, really, is the proper role of the top corporate officer in relieving the stresses that are proving so divisive and debilitating in our American society? How can he best appraise the costs of alternative courses in a period of delicate balance between inflation and recession? How is he to utilize with maximum efficiency the resources at his command—money, materials, equipment, people, technology—when the only certainty appears to be uncertainty?

This list of the problems which American managers confront in the daily conduct of their businesses could be extended indefinitely. But these same managers and their predecessors have been largely responsible for doubling this nation's output of goods and services in the past quarter century. They *can* solve the problems that surround them now—and they must, if they are to continue successfully to guide the American genius for productive effort. That this volume, in a small way, may assist these managers in their all-important decision making, or speed the solution of an operating problem, or provide fresh insight into some facet of a broader issue confronting company management, is the hope of the *Handbook's* editors, associate editors, and contributors alike.

The American Management Association is truly grateful to the associate editors who from the start determined the organization and content of the book, read the completed typescript, helped to integrate the separate articles, and made numerous valuable suggestions throughout the work of preparation. Thanks are due, as well, to the contributors who supplied the actual text and to the many other individuals and organizations that supplied material and offered useful advice. In addition, a number of publishers generously gave permission to reprint copyrighted material, and their cooperation is hereby acknowledged.

Special mention must be made of the signal contributions to this volume of Ellen Benson. She assumed major responsibility for supervising and coordinating the mammoth task of editing and checking the bulky manuscript and seeing it through the various stages of production. Under her direction, Mary M. Stanton copyedited the entire book, Kathleen Tappen bore the brunt of the proofreading, and D. J. Duffin prepared the index.

RUSSELL F. MOORE

Contents

Section 1

General Management

CONTENTS

Management Objectives

Organization

Policies

Long-Term Planning

Short-Term Planning

Controls

Organization Development

Evaluating Results

PRINCIPLES OF MANAGEMENT—1

The principles of management are essentially a group of concepts generated by experience and responsible research and expressed by a wide variety of business schools in terms of personal disciplines and operating techniques. Although the terminology describing them (not to mention the very classification of their functions) is not always consistent, they tend in the main to lay down guidelines for the basic activities of planning, organizing, coordinating, controlling, and appraising. Competence in these functions, if one wishes to use a measuring rod of modern management, constitutes the complement of skills and insights deemed necessary for satisfactory managerial performance.

Many sophisticated companies, concerned with the healthy growth of their management manpower—a concern which is prerequisite to the achievement of future organizational goals—have made training in the principles of management mandatory. However, experience thus far suggests that training cannot stand alone. To get these principles translated into practice requires a proper climate and the sustained motivation derived only where examples are set at the highest levels.

Attempts to document the authenticity of these principles, beginning with the classic Western Electric experiments, have not been wanting, and on the whole they have proved their value. However, it is worth pointing out that some sincere attempts to give them authority have foundered on attitudes and orientations associated in the minds of many people with what has become tagged as "old line thinking." Close scrutiny of this issue however, fails to give complete support to this assumption.

Many young people coming on the business scene also find these principles hard to assimilate. Current thinking holds that the answer lies in understanding one's self and in ability to relate to others. Though alternative opinions certainly exist, there appears to be something to this position. The swift growth and general popularity of sensitivity training have thrown a great deal of light on the reasons why some individuals make poor managers; in almost every case they are violating the principles. Sensitivity training is not always painless, but it has caught the fancy of many reputable firms and distinguished business practitioners, who have accorded it acceptance as it appears to open the mind to the principles of management and thereby improves one's basic management skills.

Planning

The planning function has received increasing attention in recent years, although informally it has been an active component of most successful businesses since their inception. The growing complexity of the national economy has placed mounting stress on the role of formal planning and endowed it with an economic significance too formidable to ignore.

As a rule, two factors need to be considered. First, for most companies planning requires the evaluation of several diverse elements, which in not a few cases requires intensive training and experience in order to make serious judgments. Second, students of human dynamics have found that the people who are expected to carry out the planning must take part in its inception, a finding that has led to the widespread application of management by objectives. This technique enables managers not only to have a voice in future activities but to draw upon their intimate knowledge of their own operations for contributions to corporate growth; it has stimulated many individuals to seek opportunities for improvement in their own work areas—areas which management at higher levels often cannot observe or evaluate.

Corporate planning begins with certain desired objectives arising out of management's energy and imagination and tempered by serious and authoritative analysis of factors that might circumscribe company resources and capabilities. Guidelines for comprehensive corporate planning have been published by various practitioners and interested scholars, not all of whom agree; however, there is enough concurrence to spell out some directives for general use.

First, the company planning function is essentially the president's job. Because of the complexity of the factors, the president may delegate the study and interpretation of data to others. He may consult with his operating committees, departments, or staff positions designed to coordinate the planning process. He may also talk with knowledgeable outsiders, but responsibility for approving the final plan is his.

Second, planning should be both short- and long-range. One and five years are the traditional projections; the five-year plan is adjusted and advanced as each short-term or yearly plan throws light on additional factors or trends.

Third, planning for growth should not exceed capacity for growth. Setting unrealistic objectives breeds skepticism in employees and often places growth itself in jeopardy.

Fourth, a plan unrealized though conscientiously followed should not be regarded as a failure. Valuable lessons can be gained from such experiences, notably in the area of more circumspect evaluation of obstructive elements and perhaps in the proper use of company facilities and capabilities.

Though tools for management planning tend to be tailored to the needs of individual companies, beginners will find notable assistance in discovering their best procedure by utilizing a common control sheet, which among other things helps determine the priority of steps to be taken. Such a sheet might be set up with six headings running from left to right across the top of the paper, as shown in Exhibit 1.1.

The first heading is *Step*, and in the column below it are lines, numbered 1, 2, 3, 4, and so on, whose purpose is to enumerate the order of efforts.

The second heading is *Item*. This column lists actions to be taken or problems to be looked into, set up in their proper sequence. This ranking is valuable because certain actions may not be meaningful until other actions have been taken, and problems as a rule are either root or ancillary. Root problems should be settled first because they may be generating the ancillaries.

The third heading is *Objectives*, and this column shows the results desired. It is important that entries be as quantitative as possible. Statements such as "10 percent increase in share of market" or "10 percent reduction in turnover" assist later in a clear evaluation of the plan's success.

The fourth heading is *Plan of Action*. This column presents the approach decided upon and the personnel and facilities required.

The fifth heading is *Controls*, and in this column are the reporting and measuring steps agreed upon to detect unanticipated problems and to observe the rate of progress.

The final column is headed *Timing;* it shows terminal dates set up for completing the steps. Though specific dates are always helpful, experience has led many people to feel that some reasonable latitude is justified for steps subjected to foreseeable but unfamiliar complications. Such statements as "9 to 12 months" or "$1\frac{1}{2}$ to 2 years" are not uncommon here.

Planning, of course, can only contribute to success; it cannot insure it. Planning is, however, a primary function and should be given the attention it merits. Since it demands a high degree of conceptualization, it has by nature a subjective side, and care must be taken that planning does not reflect only the experiences and biases of those who have been assigned to the task. Satisfactory objectivity can often be achieved by the proper selection of planning committees and by accepting open expression from all those who will be participating in the plan itself.

Organizing

Organizing is usually the step that determines the actualization and success of a business. In business, accomplishments are only meaningful if they come with the appropriate investments of time and energy, not to mention money. Getting things done "somehow" is rarely sufficient for survival in a competitive economy.

Organization as a subject in itself is not well understood by many managers,

Exhibit 1.1
CONTROL SHEET

Step	Item	Objectives	Plan of Action	Controls	Timing
1.					
2.					
3.					
4.					
5.					
6.					
7.					
8.					
9.					
10.					

possibly because they feel that putting things and people where they will be convenient when needed constitutes organization. Some simply organize themselves and then allow "the team" to organize around them. This often results in an enormous loss of efficiency.

Organization is primarily concerned with the most efficient relationships between people and functions. Not only the mechanics but the dynamics of an organization will play a role in its suitability for achieving business ends. By mechanics is meant the positioning of people and functions in a company as shown on an organization chart. Dynamics refers to the feelings people have about the structure they are asked to work in and the impact of these feelings on their work.

Most businesses are organized along functional lines and are reorganized only as the necessity to do so arises. This is a wasteful practice. Alert management, mindful that organization is one of the easiest victims of historic precedent, protects itself by carrying out continual reviews.

Organizing a business is similar to organizing a managerial activity; both must lead to a profitable return on the total investment made or both are failures.

Organizing for a specific business activity requires assessing the demands of the activity in terms of time, talents, and facilities. Money may or may not be a clear-cut consideration, but in any case it is related to the other three, and as a rule they are consistent factors.

TIME

One of the easiest issues to lose sight of in complex business activities is time, and experienced executives therefore make time budgeting prerequisite to taking any significant action. Deadlines are not necessarily inducements to speedy action. They can be useful checkpoints, keeping interested personnel aware of what should be accomplished and alert to any subtle loss of momentum. Whether sound or not, a judgment should be made on the time required for any proposed business project. Experience may prove that the allotted time was unrealistic, but such measures serve to keep the issue of time alive.

TALENT

Decisions concerning the assignment of personnel should be in observance of the fact that effective organization requires compatibility between assignment and capability. To assign people because of convenience or political considerations or simply for the reason that they are presently unassigned is equivalent to saying the business is operating without any standards of selection. There are companies that have departments composed of 20 people who turn out less work than their competitors do in a similar department staffed with fewer than half that number. Indiscriminate selection of people for a business activity is bound to have the same results as indiscriminate selection of tryouts for a team competing in a league where rivals demand talent.

FACILITIES

Facilities and their proper utilization are major concerns of a skilled executive. The improper or inappropriate use of facilities can easily deprive a company of a return on its capital investment. The best and most versatile computer in the world is a bad investment if it is poorly programmed. Duplicating equipment loses its efficiency if complicated procedures circumscribe its use or if it is placed where it is not easily accessible. Excessive floor space is a needless extravagance where it is not required for company image or very heavy traffic. In organizing for a business activity, care should be taken to see that facilities and personnel are in comfortable proximity to each other and that a knowledge of the economics involved in the use of company equipment is shared by all.

Coordinating

Coordinating is probably the area where the skills of leadership are put most severely to the test. Insight into the skills of delegation and communication becomes essential, and a capacity to anticipate problems born of poor interaction between people can determine ultimate results.

COMMUNICATION

In spite of all the discussion about communication, it is an element in business that is not adequately comprehended by the average executive. Gaps in communication tend to preoccupy subordinates with speculation and can lead to erroneous and destructive guessing. Information that comes too late or from the wrong source rarely serves its objective. The question of status is involved in information, and people do not easily forgive lapses that seem to belie their own importance. Keeping the staff informed is a major responsibility, and its significance goes well beyond the mere transmission of information. It is directly connected with people's estimation of their leadership and, in the end, with their will to work.

DELEGATION

Delegation is a means by which subordinate strength is fruitfully utilized. Delegation is not merely giving someone something to do; it is also giving him the authority to do it. To give someone something to do and then tell him how to do it is to create a lackey. To give someone something to do but stand over him while he is doing it is to waste time, for thus two people are involved in an operation that clearly requires only one. But for the superior to give someone something to do, explaining his own experience with the operation and the objectives for which it is performed, and telling him that henceforth he has the authority to perform it, is to delegate. This allows another human being to bring his talents, insight, creativity, and energy into the common fight against the company's problems. The man who understands how to use other people's talents could command an army with ease. The one who does not so understand would not be able to manage the smallest business.

It is simple to keep this principle in mind if one recalls the saying that there has never been a subordinate who was not in some way superior to his superior. People who lack the humility to accept this idea may sooner or later have the experience of an executive who, upon hearing the thought expressed, sprang to his feet and stormed, "None of my subordinates is superior to me!"—and was asked quietly, "Have you thought about patience?"

Coordinating requires an understanding of these dynamic matters, and there is little hope for the manager who cannot grasp them. Here, perhaps, is the area where management development should most concern itself, for it is the area where least progress in personal skills has been made.

Controlling

Controlling is the short rein that keeps business activities from wandering from their primary intent and keeps the manager aware of the productivity of his operation. It takes many forms, but all worthwhile controls are based upon previously agreed-upon standards. They are of most assistance when arranged on regular time intervals such as monthly or quarterly periods, and they should be as quantitative as possible to discourage any inclination toward subjective interpretations.

Some controls are based upon limiting negative results. For instance, quality control in production may indicate that rejects must not exceed 4 percent of total units processed; or in sales management may establish that customer complaints shall not exceed 2 percent of active accounts in a given territory. These are valuable controls, but they offer little insight to static situations or problems which may be limiting activities. For this, checkpoints must be set up to reveal volume and growth.

Many companies set up control centers for profits, budget variances, and personnel turnover. These are particularly valuable for large organizations, for where they are properly situated, they can pinpoint trouble areas before matters get out of hand and serious losses are incurred.

Perhaps the most widely discussed and significant control has to do with personal performance. Standards of performance for management in industry have received considerable acceptance and in some industries have become part of the management method, partly because of the immense value they carry for the individual to whom the standards apply. The normal approach to the use of this crucial tool is to work up a job description that both superior and subordinate understand and upon which they agree, and from this point the standards of performance are derived. In as many cases as possible the standards are quantitatively expressed. Typical quantitative expressions would be such as the following: "will have all reports in by *the first day* of the month"; "will make 25 canvassing calls per quarter"; "will not exceed budget by *2 percent*." In personal performance appraisal, quantitative standards limit a superior's subjectivity, a troublesome factor that has long been a problem in gaining acceptance for appraisals.

This control of personal performance has paid valuable dividends from both the company's and the individual's point of view. For the company it provides assurance that the man who is meeting his standards is a real and measurable asset. For the individual it provides a road map and a set of guidelines to what constitutes a good job. A man who is meeting his standards can feel secure in the knowledge that he is making a real contribution and deserves his superior's respect.

Appraising

Appraising is the long rein on operations and personnel. It is usually carried out at intervals sufficient to permit perspective on the individual. Six months to a year is the typical interval between appraisals for most firms. Appraising overall results is both the measuring rod and the point of departure for planning. Here direction of growth, success in personal development, and the large-picture approach to operations in general are reviewed and studied.

In the matter of operations, innovations in the field that merit installation or the retooling demands of a new and more desirable product mix can be considered and an appropriate budget set up. In sales, advertising, and public relations, measures that are felt, on the basis of past experience, to be most effective for the coming annual sales offensive can be agreed upon. In research, basic efforts can be evaluated and programs set up to work toward marketable products. These are steps that most companies are familiar with, although a surprising number of firms have no formal approach and as a result changes are made only when serious developments make it necessary—which is, as a rule, too late.

PERSONNEL APPRAISAL

Much attention has been given in recent years to the appraisal of personnel and its value to management manpower inventories and planning. The problem of people has long been recognized as the problem of business, and this recognition has grown in meaning. The proper climate and leadership of an organization are management responsibilities, and nowhere does this come into sharper focus than in the use made of personnel appraisals.

Appraisal forms should be simple, geared to the standards of performance, and regarded as positive tools designed to guide and encourage growth. The use of these forms is manifestly a matter for special caution. Appraisal sessions should be held in a private and mutually convenient spot, and the individual should be allowed to review his own form.

All line management required to conduct appraisal sessions should receive instruction in coaching and counseling. "Quickie" courses and management advisories are of little value. An effort spanning a year or two is normally required for adequate skill.

Care should be taken that appraisers practice and understand the basic steps of coaching: explanation, demonstration, application, and follow-up. In the case of counseling they should be given conscientious and thorough training in the nondirective techniques as well as some background material on the role and origin of attitudes. Organizations whose line management cannot counsel effectively should regard this as alarming. High turnover (particularly among strong people) and lower productivity are the inevitable consequences of this deficiency, not to mention the critical problem of tomorrow's management.

Appraising personnel effectively is the only known road to effective manpower planning. Charts in color showing high and low performers as well as identified potential have made themselves indispensable to productive training and development work. "Shotgun" training is not only wasteful but can become an irritant for many employees, reducing interest and arousing mute criticism. A chart showing each individual's training needs allows training directors to arrange for and offer curriculums in the company's problem areas, and as a result get the necessary return on the company's training dollar.

The manpower inventory chart is a cardinal tool, and much has been achieved by it. Most companies find that plexiglass charts, with boxes representing personnel and filled in by mastic tapes of the appropriate colors, provide great flexibility in evaluating and classifying results.

After each appraisal period the chart can be photographed, setting up a sequence for several years. When one year is compared with the next, any progress in personnel development will be apparent. Groups that do not show adequate progress may require higher management review of their leadership. With this comprehensive approach, back-up management can also be arranged for and promotions can be based on a wider selection of candidates, many of whom—because of inconspicuous assignments or geographic factors—would not otherwise be known.

Principles in Review

Too often the learning approach toward the principles of management is a brief and academic affair. Individuals are given a few spirited lectures, asked to read a book or two, perhaps sent off to a seminar, and the job is regarded as done. Such measures, while often helpful, are a far cry from the real demands of the situation. This is a matter of total effort by a management that is totally aware of the issues. Management should remember that proper observance of these principles has become a competitive weapon and companies innocent of their importance are paying a price.

The best results appear to be realized when top management agrees to sit down and review its own operating philosophy and techniques. These are rarely ego-serving sessions, and enlightened presidents initiating them have learned to take emerging problem issues in small bites. Needless to say, if the president is taking this step merely as "window dressing" to satisfy a director's or stockholder's interest in progressive management, it will lead to hidden cynicism and will be worse than no effort at all.

Once top management understands and applies the principles, success at the lower levels becomes markedly simplified. This is not to say that conscientious effort will not be needed, but it is much easier for a subordinate to learn a system of management if he is living under a superior who practices it than if he has difficulty in reconciling what he sees about him with what he has been asked to do.

Collectively, the principles of management add up to a philosophy which holds that management is getting things done through other people in a way that wins acceptance and provides increasingly productive results. Those who have concerned themselves with the nature of the future say there are only uncertain prospects for management groups that cannot succeed in doing this.—*D. W. Ross*

PRINCIPLES OF MANAGEMENT—2

Over the past 50 years management practitioners and theorists have evolved a number of principles or concepts relating to the practice of effective management in the business organization.

Historical Development

Some of the early management principles were evolved during the era of large manufacturing operations; consequently, there was strong emphasis on planning, organizing, controlling, and motivating from a manufacturing perspective. In a single plant with geographical centralization, production planning and control, and assembly-line methods, it is much easier to practice a logical and systematic management approach than in a large, decentralized, multiproduct and multinational corporation. Some of the relatively static concepts evolved during this era are not directly applicable to today's business firm operating in a complex technical and social environment.

A broader approach came from the study of large firms as they changed to meet new competitive challenges under new marketing situations. Alfred Chandler (*Strategy and Structure*, Massachusetts Institute of Technology Press, 1962) traced the long-range adaptation of formal organizational and management structure in four companies: Du Pont, General Motors, Standard Oil (New Jersey), and Sears Roebuck. Chandler's book deals with changes made in managerial practices and principles to enable the firms to grow and improve profits in a changing economic environment. Studies of this type are called business policy studies.

New Trends

The most recent trend in developing managerial principles deals with new technologies arising out of automation, cybernetics, information systems transmission at high speeds, and computer analysis of complex data.

Bertram Gross, a writer on management philosophy and techniques (*Organizations and Their Managing*, The Free Press, 1964), points out that this trend is associated with such newer areas as statistical decision making, operations research, evaluation and control of complex technical systems, human relations, benefit-cost analysis, and systems analysis design and management.

Gross predicts that organizational management of the future will center on "a dynamic people-resource system operating in specific locations in space and time." He contends that effective understanding of managerial principles rests upon such key areas as (1) certain unpleasant facts of life in organizations (the inevitability of conflict, the imperatives of power, and the persistence of time-honored administrative fallacies); (2) environmental turbulence (rapid changes in customer, supplier, governmental, and social requirements); (3) structural complexities (internal conflict, tension, and change as inescapable parts of complex organizational systems); (4) the multidimensionality of performance (output production, resource utilization, ethical codes of behavior); (5) the delicacy of guidance processes (complex and dynamic communications, planning, activating, evaluating, and decision making); and (6) learning improbabilities (difficulties of teaching and learning new and complex managerial techniques in a rapidly changing world).

Gross notes that managers will have to be both knowledgeable and discriminating in the selection and utilization of the new theories because the proponents will probably make exaggerated claims about their worth. He feels that these new techniques "will probably continue in the future as in the past to be initiated in a burst of grandiose claims of 'breakthroughs' and exaggerated application to irrelevant situations. . . . New labels—even more flamboyant than such older phrases as 'scientific management,' 'administrative science,' and 'management science'—will be used in high-pressure sales talks to obtain funds. . . . Thus, in the 1970's even more than in the past, the effect of the new management techniques on many organizations—particularly those lacking the capacity to test new claims, take new risks, and coordinate new specialists—could easily be greater unmanageability."

In this part of the discussion management principles are considered from two viewpoints: that of relative perspective—that is, the theoretical schools of their creators; and their probable current utility in the real world of the professionally managed business organization.

Schools of Management Theory

Harold Koontz classified the literature on management principles in six different schools ("The Management Theory Jungle," *Journal of the Academy of Management*, December 1961). He pointed out that, whereas early writing on management principles came from experienced practitioners, more recent writings tend to come from academic theorists, some of whom have had no direct experience in organizational management. Koontz's six groupings are briefly described here.

THE MANAGEMENT PROCESS SCHOOL

The management process school looks on management theory as a way of organizing practical management experience. It holds that management practice can be improved through research, empirical testing of principles, and teaching the fundamentals involved in the management process.

THE EMPIRICAL SCHOOL

Writers of the empirical school see management or "business policy" as involving the study and analysis of business organizational cases. They report the systematic study of the experience and techniques of successful managers.

THE HUMAN BEHAVIOR SCHOOL

Also known as the behavioral sciences approach, the human behavior school applies psychological and sociological theories, methods, and techniques to the study of intrapersonal and interpersonal aspects of managing.

THE SOCIAL SYSTEMS SCHOOL

Advocates of the social systems approach seek to identify the nature of the cultural relationships of the various social groups in the organization. They attempt to show how these dynamics relate to management in terms of the direction of the firm's social systems.

THE DECISION THEORY SCHOOL

Decision theory concentrates on studying rational approaches to decision making in the company. Along with analyzing the organizational decision-making process, adherents of this school have recently moved toward a broad view of the enterprise as a social system.

THE MATHEMATICAL SCHOOL

The mathematical approach is advocated by theorists who feel that if management, organization, planning, and decision making are logical processes, they may be capable of expression in mathematical symbols, relationships, and models. As Koontz sees it, the key question here is whether mathematics is a tool of the larger management process or whether much of the process will be eventually reducible to mathematical formulas.

Koontz insists that management principles and theory should be related to the real world of business organization and management. He sees management as "the art of getting things done through and with people in *formally organized groups,* the art of creating an environment in such an organized group where people can perform as individuals and yet cooperate toward attainment of group goals, the art of removing blocks to such performance, the art of optimizing efficiency in effectively reaching (organizational) goals."

The Management Process and Organizational Culture

When business organizations were relatively small and simple, the general manager could usually direct the firm's efforts in person; at most he required the assistance of only a few key subordinate managers. However, as organizations grew in size and complexity, specialization of functions and sheer size required the establishment of organizational units and subunits.

At various periods organizations received overall management direction by men trained primarily in finance, law, engineering, selling and marketing, and science. Many of these men managed primarily from the frame of reference of their technical specialty. They acquired basic management skills through practicing management.

This top organization management developed its general management philosophies and practices largely on the firing line. The management of an entire firm rather than a functional, specialized part of the business gradually evolved a set of practical operating principles and maxims. As Alfred Chandler (*Strategy and Structure*) noted, these operating principles eventually were transformed into the theories and practices of the early professional managers.

During the past 20 years these professional management principles have been taught as a guiding and integrating core of management practices to a new generation of professional managers. Graduate schools of business and professional management associations are in the forefront of this movement.

Behavioral scientists define "organizational culture or climate" as "the sentiments, attitudes, beliefs, and practices of management which define organizational relationships, responsibilities, and permitted actions." The following discussion will perhaps clarify this interrelationship.

"AUTHORITY-OBEDIENCE" MANAGING

Early business organizations were generally managed (in terms of owner-managers and hired-employees relationships) with a combination of authoritarianism and paternalism. Family-owned entrepreneurial firms using relatively simple technologies and operating in local markets for labor, materials, and customers generally used what Alfred Marrow (*Behind the Executive Mask,* American Management Association, 1964) has termed the authority-obedience style of managing.

In this type of management owner-managers directed the operations of the firm's employees in a relatively unilateral way. The employees, many of whom possessed a degree of "trade" or "craft" skill, practiced these skills in an organizational setting to provide the company's products. In such firms the formal educational gap between the owner-manager and his subordinate employees was such that employees tended to carry out orders without too much questioning of either the source or the logic of the company's authority system.

As new machines and new power sources brought the industrial revolution, the old craft-skill hierarchies were broken down to fit the new manufacturing processes. A generation of semiskilled and unskilled factory workers who usually performed their individual tasks on an assembly line grew up to man the new machines. Because of the engineering logic of production cycles, most of the workers performed repetitive tasks in making only a small part of the finished product.

THE BUREAUCRATIC APPROACH

When business organizations became even larger and more complex, the opportunity for close individual contact between owner-managers and employees was reduced. The authoritarian-paternalistic pattern gave way to increased functional specialization. In addition many layers of middle and lower management were introduced for the purpose of coordinating organizational efforts. The result was a bureaucratic approach to organizational structure. Within the bureaucratic structure, technical specialists did the engineering of processes and methods. Hourly employees were expected to work at machine-paced speeds on small units of the total production.

Huge factories employing thousands of men gave the management process an impersonal, bureaucratic flavor. This trend toward managerial bureaucracy coincided with the shift away from craft unions, whose members were carpenters, bricklayers, pipe fitters, and the like. The new pattern of unionism became the industrial union, in which an entire industry (steel, aluminum, and automobile manufacturing, for example) was organized into one large "international" union in Canada and the United States. All manufacturing, clerical, and in some cases technical and engineering employees in one industry belonged to the same union.

Industrial unionism gave unionized employees much greater bargaining power. Strikes and work stoppages, used as bargaining techniques, could be maintained much more effectively than in the old days of the craft unions. The American political and economic climate of the depression of the 1930's encouraged collective bargaining between unions and management concerning wages, working conditions, and fringe benefits.

The shift in organizational climate from the entrepreneurial to the bureaucratic firm was a change from authoritarian-paternalistic, employer-employee relationships to relationships that were primarily impersonal and oriented to rules and precedents. Seniority and length of service became important factors in obtaining promotions and gaining wage increases. Individual differences in employee productivity had little to do with rewards and promotions.

Employees who worked in the bureaucratic climate tended to feel treated as a number or a time card rather than an individual. Work assignments were impersonally made by foremen, who often received them from production schedulers and other technical specialists. Grievances or complaints regarding individual employee treatment were handled by the union-management grievance process established in the labor contract negotiated on a mass basis. The prevailing philosophy of employees in this managerial climate was to do enough work to stay out of trouble and rely on the union to protect them from the arbitrary and impersonal handling of work problems by management.

The basic employee relations philosophy of the period was based on large-scale organization, assembly-line technology, and semiautomated, machine-paced operations. Employers (many had become professional managers and were no longer owners) of large organizations whose stock was widely held by the public typically went through three distinct phases in the management of their firms in relation to the growth of large, powerful industrial unions.

Reaction to unionization. The first phase involved fighting to keep the unions from gaining the power to resist managerial decision making. Industrialists fought unionization and resented the "disloyalty" of employees who joined unions.

The second phase was one of accommodation to union power. During World War II and afterward, many unions required (with the approval of the Federal Government) that all workers in a plant pay union dues under a "maintenance of membership" ruling. Later, all employees were required to belong to the certified union in order to work. Still later, the unions acquired "check-off" privileges (whereby employers were required to deduct dues from members' paychecks and send the money to union headquarters). With the advent of the union shop and the check-off, union security was no longer an issue, and management policy changed to one of adjustment to the unions' role in negotiations and grievances. This policy dictated that management should bargain hard to protect management prerogatives and keep costs down. In addition contract terms were to be strictly adhered to.

The third stage, now taking place, is one of joint problem solving. Both management and unions realize that many issues affecting employees lend themselves to joint decision making so that each side stands to gain something ("win-win"). In these situations union-management teams try to work out the best solutions to common problems rather than attempt to solve the problems on a "win-lose" power basis.

INTRODUCTION OF KNOWLEDGE WORKERS

As business organizations have become more technically sophisticated, there has been an influx of "knowledge workers"—specialists who operate and maintain complex systems. Employees at all levels tend to be less semiskilled or unskilled. There are more engineers, scientists, and technical specialists. Expertise is required for a variety of functions.

Because of the trend toward democratization in American society, plus higher education levels, the organizational expectations of knowledge worker employees are different from the expectations of the less skilled production workers of the past. Managerial philosophy and practice, particularly in regard to organizational relationships, will undoubtedly change to meet these new requirements.

Today's professionally managed organization is moving away from both the old authoritarian-paternalistic and the bureaucratic-impersonal relationships of the past. The current trend is toward more involvement of employees in goal setting and decision making. This is accomplished through the use of management by objectives, more team planning, and more joint problem solving on the part of superiors and subordinates.

HUMAN RELATIONS

In relation to managerial philosophy the shift in organizational climate can be viewed in a variety of ways. George Strauss, management theory analyst, characterizes the human relations movement of the past 20 years as a trend toward power equalization ("Some Notes on Power Equalization," *The Social Science of Organizations,* Harold J. Leavitt, ed., Prentice-Hall, 1963). Strauss sees a reduction in the power and status differential between supervisors and subordinates as "a continuing reaction against the emphasis of programmed work, rigid hierarchical control, and high degrees of specialization which were characteristic of Taylorism and traditional organizational theory."

NEED FOR CHANGE

Kenneth Boulding, an economist, relates the need for changing managerial philosophies to the rapid growth of more complex technology (*The Meaning of the Twentieth Century,* Harper & Row, 1964). Boulding argues that the changes in the U.S. economy and society require rethinking of both economic and organizational efforts if Americans are to take full advantage of the improvements in the standard of living that a properly utilized science might bring to all. He urges concentration on improving organizational systems as a way of solving the problems that will be caused by the rapid depletion of natural resources of energy (coal, oil, gas). The development of new organizations and the discovery of new technologies are required to offset this depletion.

Taking a sharp look at past and present managerial practices and principles in the United States, Peter Drucker (*The Age of Discontinuity,* Harper & Row, 1969) says:

> It is in this field of management that we have done the most work during the last half-century. We had never before faced the task of organizing and leading large knowledge organizations. We had to learn rapidly. No one who knows the field would maintain that we yet know much. Indeed, if there is any agreement in this hotly contested area, it is that tomorrow's organization structures will look different than any we know today.

> Yet work in management is by now no longer pioneering. What is taught under this name in our universities may be 90 percent old wives' tales— and the rest may be procedure rather than management. Still, the main challenges in the area are sufficiently well known. . . . We know, for instance, that we have to measure results. We also know that with the exception of business, we do not know how to measure results in most organizations.

Organizational Relationships

Drucker (*Age of Discontinuity*) states, regarding organizational power and authority:

> The legitimacy of organizational power and of organization-managements —whether of government agency, of hospital, of university, or of business— is, therefore, a problem. It is the political problem of the society of organizations. . . . The comparison of management, whether in business, in the university, the government agency or in the hospital, with a true "government," which is done so entertainingly in *Management and Machiavelli,* is, therefore, half-truth. The managements of modern social institutions (including the government agency that administers, for example, a post office) are not "governments." Their job is functional rather than political. . . . It is also highly desirable to bring these "members" (employees at all levels) as far as possible into the decision-making process. . . . But in the areas that directly affect standards, performance, and results of the institution, the members cannot take over. There, the standards, the performance, and the results must rule them. What is done, and how, is largely determined by what outsiders (customers) want and need.

BASES OF AUTHORITY

In order to accomplish organizational tasks and purposes within an organization of any size or complexity, it is necessary to set up some hierarchy of authority, power, decision making, and administering rewards and punishments for individual behavior in the accomplishment of organizational goals. As Drucker points out, it is both intelligent and important to bring employee members of the organization in on decision making and problem solving whenever they are likely to be affected by the results of such decisions.

However, the employee-participation philosophy of management makes necessary certain costs and benefits trade-offs, as do all aspects of management. In researching these factors Ralph Stogdill (*Managers, Employees, Organizations,* Ohio State University Bureau of Business Research, 1965) found that participation did affect group attitudes but not always group productivity. Norman Maier (*Principles of Human Relations,* John Wiley & Sons, Inc., 1962) believes that when it is important that a management decision have high acceptance on the part of employees—that is, that they implement it well—more participation is indicated than when the decision has to be a high-quality decision. (High-quality decisions are often best made by technical specialists.)

The inverted pyramid. Gross (*Organizations*) points out that the typical concept of organizational authority as being a simple pyramid does not fit the facts of modern corporations. Rather, superimposed on the traditional pyramid of formal organizational authority is an upper pyramid. In corporate life the upper pyramid of final authority consists of the stockholders, the board of directors, and the board executive committee.

Stockholders. The stockholders of corporations, through their ownership of voting stock shares, are the ultimate holders of organizational authority.

Board of directors. Stockholders exercise this authority through a board of directors. Frequently, this board operates through subcommittees that interlock with the chief operating officers of the company. Individual members of working boards of directors of many companies often have major policy assignments that are delegated to them by the board.

Company officers. The company president elected by the board usually occupies the position of either chief executive officer (responsible to the board for long-range policy) or chief operating officer (responsible to the chief executive officer for day-to-day conduct of company business). The president generally has under him a number of vice presidents. Some vice presidents are corporate officers and may serve on the board of directors. In some cases other vice presidents (usually designated as divisional vice presidents) have operating authority but may not be involved in top corporate policy making. In very complex organizations the office of the president concept is evolving. Under this concept two or more executives jointly handle the duties assigned to the president.

Starting at or just below the president level (depending on the organization's size and complexity) are the men at the top as defined in the traditional organizational pyramid.

Divisional managers. Divisional managers (who may or may not hold the divisional vice presidential title) are charged with the operation of company profit centers. With the trend toward decentralization that came with large and complex organizations, a divisional profit-center manager generally has all the organizational components necessary to reach a profit in his unit—(sales, manu-facturing, staff services, and so forth).

"REAL LIFE" VARIATIONS

Although organizational theory holds that authority and power flow from the top to bottom in a superior-subordinate chain of command, in real organizational life there are often important variations.

The multiple hierarchy. Although members of organizations theoretically have only one boss, in complex organizations it is often true that in the downward flow of authority two or more lines—not just one—converge upon one subordinate. Some organizational members may have "functional," "technical," or "professional" authority over other organizational members who are subordinate to them only under certain circumstances (for example, the corporate medical director, who has professional authority over plant medical personnel in professional matters).

Polyarchy. Polyarchy is another form of deviation from the standard hierarchy of authority; it develops in complex organizations. Increased specialization brings coordinate responsibility relationships. Such relationships develop outside of the traditional superior-subordinate relationships. (A committee of peers assigned the task of controlling and reducing a company's wage and salary costs is an example of this type of relationship.)

Delegation of authority. Superiors are expected to delegate authority adequate to complete assignments when they give a task to a subordinate; however, there are many factors that enter into such delegation. The first factor has to do with the superior's managerial style (his philosophy and technique of dealing with subordinates). Authoritarian managers typically reserve power and authority to themselves. "Middle of the road" managers attempt to delegate authority commensurate with power but are often ambivalent and anxious about letting go of power for fear it will weaken their security position in the organization. Newer techniques of management by objectives and goal setting that have recently been developed are utilized by more secure and mature managers—not only to delegate necessary authority and power but also to make the superior a team partner in helping the subordinate solve the problems which stand in the way of the subordinate's successful accomplishment of the task.

Another key variable in delegation of responsibility and authority lies in the subordinate's personality and managerial style. In entrepreneurial organizations subordinates are more concerned about pleasing the key power-figure than they are about risk-taking initiative. They have learned that to displease the authoritarian boss can mean getting fired. Such bosses are apt to evaluate a subordinate's performance more on the basis of loyalty to the boss than on objective results that the subordinate might obtain on the basis of initiative, judgment, and risk taking.

Subordinates who work within a bureaucratic organizational climate often learn that it is more important for their promotion—and survival—to follow organizational rules and procedures than it is to have outstanding profit accomplishments.

In both the entrepreneurial and the bureaucratic types of organizations employees often operate under mixed motives, more concerned to maintain their organizational position or advance within the power structure than to make a maximum contribution to organizational goals. This is because they have learned through experience that although some top managements talk about rewarding ability and results, they are subjective and arbitrary in actually granting promotions and salary increases.

Management and Motivation

As pointed out by Koontz, a number of theories of management philosophy are currently available. Two schools of theory, the human behavior school and the social systems school, deal particularly with the motivational effect of different styles and philosophies of management on employees.

THEORIES AND THEORISTS

The names of a number of prominent management theorists have become associated with the various schools.

Chester Barnard and cooperation. In trying to find an explanation underlying the management process, Chester Barnard, sometimes referred to as "spiritual father of the social systems school," evolved a theory of cooperation. This theory defines "a formal organization" as "any cooperative system in which there are persons able to communicate with each other, and who are willing to contribute action toward a conscious common purpose."

Herbert Simon and systems. Simon, whose name is also associated with the social systems school of management theory, sees organizations as "systems of interdependent activity, encompassing at least several primary groups and usually characterized at the level of consciousness of participants by a high degree of rational direction of behavior toward ends that are objects of common knowledge."

Harry Levinson and the psychological contract. Long associated with the industrial psychiatry program of the Menninger Clinic, Levinson has published a number of studies relating to efforts of workers to achieve a satisfactory interdependent relationship with the company, comfortable interpersonal relationships with fellow workers, and ability to cope with organizational change. He sees the mutual expectations of workers and the company as forming a "psychological contract" worked out through reciprocal agreements.

GROUP THEORIES

Two other members of the social systems school placed particular emphasis on the influence of group behavior on employee motivation and productivity.

Elton Mayo. Mayo was one of the pioneer researchers on the effect of group norms and controls on the productivity of individual employees. Early studies at the Hawthorne Works of the Western Electric Company laid the foundation for awareness of the impact of small-group behavior in business organizations.

Rensis Likert. Likert developed a number of group-related theories. One theory dealt with the effect of "employee-centered" versus "task-centered" supervisors on work-group productivity. Another dealt with the supervisor as a "linking pin" between his supervisor's group (of which he is a peer member) and his own work group (of which he is the head) in transmitting tasks down the organizational hierarchy. More recently Likert has developed the "four stages" theory of managerial philosophy and practice; the stages proceed from authoritarian through bureaucratic to dynamic managerial styles. Likert and his associates are studying the relationship between the four styles of management and employee morale and productivity in organizations.

VALUE THEORIES

Argyris, Blake, and Mouton, three other management theorists whose work was primarily related to the human behavior and social systems schools of management theory, look at the problem of meshing individual needs and strivings with organizational goals and realities.

Chris Argyris. As Strauss points out ("Some Notes"), Argyris and others have developed the "personality versus organization" hypothesis regarding human motivation in industry. In Strauss's view this theory assumes "a basic dichotomy between the individual employees' needs and the desire of business organizations to program individual behavior and to reduce individual discretion."

Strauss summarizes the view of Argyris and his associates as follows: "The only healthy solution is for management to adopt policies which promote intrinsic job satisfaction, individual development, and creativity, according to which people will willingly and voluntarily work toward organizational objectives because they enjoy their work and feel that it is important to do a good job."

In analyzing this theoretical approach Strauss makes two key points. The first is that "it is a prescription for management behavior, and implicit in it are strong value judgments. With its strong emphasis on individual dignity, creative freedom, and self-development, this hypothesis bears all the earmarks of its academic origin.

"Professors place high value on autonomy, inner direction, and the quest for maximum self-development."

Strauss's second point is that these value theories may not hold up in real-life organizational situations. He concludes: "I shall suggest, first, that it [the hypothesis] contains many debatable value judgments, and, second, that it ignores what Harold Leavitt has called 'organizational economics.' I shall conclude that a broad range of people do not seek self-actualization on the job—and that this may be a fortunate thing because it might be prohibitively expensive to design some jobs to permit self-actualization."

Robert Blake and Jane Mouton. In *The Managerial Grid* (Gulf Publishing Company, 1964) Blake and Mouton expand the Ohio State University two-factor model of supervisory behavior (initiating structure and extending consideration into a five-factor model of managerial style). They believe that in this model it is possible to reconcile task- or production-centered objectives (often associated with authoritarian managerial styles) with people-centered objectives (associated with the human relations "personality versus organization" styles).

The authors postulate a "9,9" managerial style or philosophy which would set difficult organizational goals and expect high performance. However, this managerial style would also actively involve all members of the organization (usually, on a group basis in a joint problem-solving, joint goal-setting approach to determining and reaching organizational objectives).

THEORY X AND THEORY Y

Although it can be categorized under both the human behavior school and the "personality versus organization" school of management, Douglas McGregor's Theory X and Theory Y model of managerial philosophy and style has had such a distinctive impact upon managerial thinking that it deserves separate treatment.

McGregor started with Abraham Maslow's need-hierarchy theory of human behavior, which holds that motivation to work is governed by a hierarchy of needs. In ascending order these are physical, safety, social, egoistic, and self-actualizing needs. The need-hierarchy concept assumes that a higher, less basic need does not provide motivation unless all lower, more basic needs are met. However, *once each basic need is met,* it no longer motivates. At that point the worker looks for the satisfaction of the need on the next higher level.

The Theory X philosophy holds that by rigidly structuring work, taking decision making and initiative away from the worker, and forcing him to do a small repetitive task, bureaucratic management makes the worker apathetic, indifferent toward organizational goals, and in general dissatisfied with his job. In other words typically assembly-line work, with its lack of challenge, demotivates the worker. Management then (wrongly) assumes that workers (in terms of their inner needs and motivations) are "by nature" shiftless, irresponsible, and untrustworthy. Management then builds additional control systems to police this worker behavior.

Theory Y management philosophy, on the other hand, assumes that workers are "by nature" capable of being ambitious, trustworthy, creative, and energetic, but that management must restructure the managerial and work situation in order to tap these underlying motivations to produce. In the affluent society most of the workers' physical, safety, and social needs are met through such benefits as pensions, unemployment insurance, and union-negotiated wage rates; therefore, the egoistic and self-actualizing needs must be challenged through job enlargement and less bureaucratic (or authoritarian) supervisory styles if workers are to be expected to produce more.

If Peter Drucker (*Age of Discontinuity*) is right about the current shift away from less skilled workers to technically trained scientists, engineers, and technical-specialist knowledge workers, Theory Y managerial philosophy may prove more effective as time goes on. Drucker assumes that knowledge workers will expect, demand, and get more in the way of individual job satisfaction and challenge than their less skilled counterparts of the industrial era 1900–1950.

MANAGEMENT THEORY IN PRACTICE

In the everyday operating life of an organization a variety of management theories is often used in practice. In producing units of an organization (particularly in such industries as retailing, where the day's sales contribute directly toward profits), unit management is often directive, authoritarian, and highly oriented toward immediate action. This is particularly true in a store—for example—operated by a small cadre of trained managers who supervise a large number of part-time high school students whose primary interest is in the money they receive rather than the work itself. The same is true in many manufacturing operations where costs are closely watched and where scrap rates, excess costs, or other variations from project plan can easily be monitored by those next above in the managerial hierarchy.

Mackenzie and dynamic management. R. Alec Mackenzie ("The Management Process in 3D," *Harvard Business Review,* November-December, 1969) has created a visual model of the management process in action. His model centers around the management of ideas, things, and people. Under "ideas management" fall planning, forecasting, scheduling, budgeting, policies, and procedures. "Things management" includes organizing machines and materials for efficient functioning. "People management" includes areas of management practice that are usually classified within a larger category such as leadership, motivation, or communication.

Top management planning. Depending on the size of the organization, top management policy and general direction tend to be made on the basis of long-range planning and definition of organizational objectives. Some organizations have elaborate staff planning groups, as in the styling and marketing divisions of large automobile firms. However, top management policy is generally arrived at ultimately through a combination of the planning function of the chief executive officer and his staff specialists with the implementing function of the chief operating officer and his assistants.

Middle management commitment to plans. If the company is to get much more than a mechanical "walk through" in terms of compliance with top management's directives, the key members of middle management need to know enough about a plan (1) to make it work intelligently and (2) to develop personal belief and commitment to the plan's soundness and scope. Although many large entrepreneurial and bureaucratic organizations operate with minimal middle management understanding and commitment to overall operating plans, the tendency is more and more to involve middle management in appropriate planning phases. This is particularly true in the installation of complicated new systems that middle management must operate if they are to succeed.

Evolution of Management Styles

In terms of organizational theory, as described by Blake and his associates (*Corporate Darwinism,* Gulf Publishing Company, 1966), management styles typically correspond to the three historic phases of the development of industry.

In the entrepreneurial phase the founder of a new firm runs pretty much a one-man show. He makes all the key decisions, gives all the chief orders and directives, and directs, cajoles, rewards, and punishes his subordinates on a relatively subjective and personal basis. "Management by crisis" is the hallmark of this marginal style.

In the bureaucratic phase the successful entrepreneur finds that as his organization grows it is necessary to bring in forecasting, systems planning, controls, and functional specialists to assist in research and development, manufacturing, sales, and personnel work. Many present-day organizations founded by an inventor-entrepreneur have a bureaucratic and systems overlay. However, underneath, it is found that the founder-entrepreneur makes all the key decisions. His whims and subjective feelings dictate much of the policy.

The classical bureaucratic organization is a somewhat ponderous maze of systems and functions with little ability to adapt to changing conditions. However, some bureaucratic organizations could be classed as scientific management bureaucracies where modern techniques speed up the traditionally slow and cumbersome bureaucratic decision-making processes and enhance the organization's flexibility and risk-taking capacity.

The dynamic or professionally managed organization seeks to take the "pluses" of both the entrepreneurial organization and the bureaucratic firm and mold them into a fast-moving organization that does not have the serious "minuses" usually associated with both types of organizations.

Entrepreneurial pluses include flexibility, risk taking, and speed of decision making. Bureaucratic pluses include planning, the use of systems, controls, and budgets. Thus the dynamic organization uses the professional management tools of: (1) defining organizational goals; (2) a "venture management" (planned and analytical risk taking) approach to new product development and new business opportunities; (3) flexible planning in which assumptions underlying plans are clearly stated; (4) financial engineering—the creative and far-sighted use of money as a resource; (5) management by results rather than by subjective impression or opinion; (6) candid, two-way discussion between superior and subordinate regarding the behavior of each as it relates to attaining organizational goals and completing organizational tasks; and (7) career-planning efforts made to help subordinates achieve maximum self-development and individual satisfaction within the framework of organizational objectives.

Such techniques as operations research studies of the probable relative effectiveness of managerial decision alternatives and the use of applied behavioral sciences concepts to improve communication, manage conflicts, and promote individual and team job motivation are other hallmarks of today's dynamically managed company.

Contemporary Management Methods

As Boulding, Drucker, and Gross have each pointed out in looking ahead to technological changes forecast for the remaining years of the twentieth century, management methods will have to change markedly if they are to keep pace with the evolution of technology and science in the years ahead.

All indications point to organizations employing highly sophisticated technologies which will be operated by well-trained knowledge workers. Herman Kahn's forecasts of life in the year 2000 (Kahn and Wiener, *The Year 2000,* The Macmillan Company, 1967) indicate that about 20 percent of the population may be able, with highly automated equipment, to produce all the goods and services required by the total population. This could in turn lead to drastic life-style changes: People might study until age 30, work in a business, governmental, or social organization until age 50; then return to a life of leisure.

In the immediate present, a number of managerial methods show promise for increasing both individual satisfaction and organizational productivity.

TEAM MANAGEMENT

In team management as defined by Robert Blake and his associates, the manager works with his subordinates as a group or team. Goals are jointly set and progress toward targets becomes the joint responsibility of all team members. When this approach works, it reduces individual competitiveness and increases communication, mutual understanding and respect, and joint effort. The skills of team management require a reorientation on the part of the manager who has been trained to supervise subordinates on a one-to-one basis.

MANAGEMENT BY OBJECTIVES

Increasingly, professional management requires that top corporate management set quantifiable and difficult, but attainable, objectives and direct the organization toward the accomplishment of these objectives. When properly used, this technique eliminates—or reduces—the problems of both entrepreneurial management by crisis and bureaucratic management by rules and past practices.

PROFIT CENTERS

With more sophisticated accounting methods and computer data processing speeds, it is possible to set up organizational units on a profit-center basis. Theoretically, each profit center has its own set of defined goals plus the men, materials, and machinery resources required to attain these goals; hence each profit center can be measured in terms of its relative performance effectiveness.

TEMPORARY SYSTEMS

In complex organizations with sophisticated technologies, temporary systems are increasingly set up to solve short-range problems. A technical group may be pulled together to find solutions to crucial problems. When the problems have been solved, the group disbands and each member returns to his organizational home base. In flexible organizations, temporary systems members are thus required to form rapid, positive, task-oriented organizational relationships to get a specific job done. When the job is completed, these relationships end.

PROJECT MANAGEMENT

One type of temporary system is project management. Under this concept a team of specialists is formed and directed by a project manager who is responsible for project goal completion. When the project has been completed, the project team disbands. Some projects last for several years, and in such a case a relatively permanent set of organizational relationships tends to be built up. However, in the case of short-term projects, such a group has all the interpersonal and organizational characteristics of any other temporary system.

MANAGEMENT BY EXCEPTION

In this version of management by objectives, plans and goals are set up by superior and subordinate in advance. So long as the work is going according to plan or is within acceptable variance limits, the superior does not concern himself with its administration; he leaves that in his subordinate's hands. The superior re-enters the situation only when some exception to the plan, of a magnitude great enough to warrant his attention and action, has occurred.

—R. F. Pearse

MANAGEMENT OBJECTIVES

Objectives have received more attention in recent years than any other aspect of management, but most of the literature is obsolete in the light of present conditions. When the environment changes, it is necessary to revise techniques that are significantly affected by the environment; the astronauts, for example, had to modify their method of walking on earth so they could walk on the moon. We are living in a complex, rapidly changing environment. Economists agree that there have never been so many important, unpredictable events. Only three things about the future are known with certainty: It will not be like the past; it will not be like former expectations of the future; and the rate of change will be faster than ever before. Major changes in the managerial environment have had a tremendous impact on the way objectives are formulated, established, and achieved.

In the past, managers operated on a dual premise: that (1) the future would be substantially like the past (therefore, objectives could be established by the extrapolation of past performance); and that (2) it was possible to predict the future with accuracy (therefore, objectives could be based on rigid forecasts). Since this premise is no longer valid, it becomes increasingly important to develop ways that will enable managers to get better results in spite of the fact that they cannot predict the future with accuracy. Under these circumstances planning is not only more difficult and important; it requires a different technique. Methods that are based on past performance or static forecasts induce rigidity and are a detriment to progress. Better results can be achieved through a system of feedback and revision that will make it possible to optimize performance in a changing environment.

Definitions and Premises

Much confusion has been created by using a variety of terms—"goals," "targets," "bogeys," and "objectives"—in referring to desirable future results. Some authors state that objectives are the overall results and goals are merely steps on the way; others say the opposite is true. This semantic confusion may be minimized by simply agreeing on the following points:

1. Since the terms "objectives," "goals," and "targets" refer to desirable future results, they may be called objectives.

2. Both short- and longer-term results (objectives) are interrelated in the following respects:

    a. They tend to compete for allocation of resources, and there is a dangerous tendency to sacrifice longer-term results for short-term gains.

    b. Short-term objectives must be compatible with longer-term objectives, and it is usually difficult—frequently impossible—to achieve the longer-term results unless the short-term are accomplished.

3. All types of organizational objectives (financial, marketing, and personnel, for example) are also interrelated in the following ways:

    a. They tend to compete for the allocation of resources, and there is a dangerous tendency to give a higher priority to financial than to personnel management, to recruiting than to training, to quantity than to quality, to tangible than to intangible matters.

    b. For optimum results, all objectives must be compatible. The objectives of lower echelons must support the objectives of higher echelons, and it is usually difficult—frequently impossible—to achieve broader, higher objectives unless subordinate objectives are coordinated.

4. It is not only impossible to forecast future objectives with accuracy; it is not even possible to evaluate objectives until the premises have been identified. Future objectives cannot be planned until a hypothesis (model) of the expected has been created, and the members of a management team cannot establish coordinated objectives unless they share the same hypothesis.

5. Future objectives are not only dependent on developments beyond the manager's control; they can only be accomplished if adequate resources—men, money, material, time, and know-how—are provided in the right quality, quantity, time, and place. An objective without essential resources is not an *objective;* it is a *delusion.*

6. From the preceding groundwork it is evident that an objective is a temporary estimate of a desirable future result that cannot be predicted with accuracy, that requires a willing expenditure of resources, and that is believed to be attainable.

7. Certain matters related to objectives are frequently confused with them:

    a. Mission or *purpose* is the basic reason for the existence of the organization.

    b. Policies are broad statements of general intent that tell what is permitted or expected; *procedures* are more specific instructions that tell how it is to be done.

    c. Programs and *projects* are courses of action that must be carried out to achieve the objectives that are deemed desirable.

    d. Strategy is the compatible combination of policies, objectives, and programs that will enable the manager to accomplish optimum results in the circumstances that he believes will prevail.

    e. An *assumption* is a temporary estimate of a very important probable development that cannot be predicted with accuracy, that is subject to no significant control, and that will have major impact on future activities and results. Objectives and assumptions are similar in that both relate to the future and hence cannot be predicted with accuracy; but assumptions pertain to developments beyond the manager's control, while objectives refer to results to be achieved through his own efforts. In practice it is not possible to determine whether an objective is good until the assumptions have been clarified.

Under the conditions previously stated, it is necessary for the manager to create an environment and a process to formulate plans, decisions, and objectives that will minimize the degree to which he is taken by surprise; provide a better method of reaching and revising agreement with whomever he must reach agreement to modify his activities, resource requirements, schedules, or objectives; and help him optimize performance in a changing environment.

Assumptions and Objectives

Since it is impossible to plan for the future (formulate objectives) without first creating an estimate (assumption) of what may happen, there will always be an opportunity or a problem whenever there is a deviation from the anticipated result. It is therefore important to have a process that helps to anticipate, detect, identify, and measure the deviation. In the past both assumptions and objectives were usually expressed in two ways—general and specific. But a third way, the dynamically quantified method, is infinitely superior to the general or specific because of the precision with which a deviation can be detected and the opportunity or problem identified. The dynamically quantified assumption is expressed in precise figures on a chart or graph over periods of time (years, months, weeks) with historical approach, current status, and future estimates. Consider, for example, the three methods of expressing an assumption about the automobile market. In this case the general assumption is that the market will be off a little next year. The specific assumption is that it will be off 8 percent over the next 12 months. The dynamically quantified assumption is that, since over the past year the automobile market was X units by month and the situation at the end of the last month was Y units, the current estimate is that (with due regard for seasonal fluctuations) the market will be Z units each month for the next year.

Following the same procedure, the objectives in another example may be expressed as follows: The general objective is to increase sales of gidgets a little next year. The specific objective is to increase sales of gidgets by 10 percent over the next 12 months. The dynamically quantified objective is expressed in the same manner as the dynamically quantified assumption—in precise figures on a chart or graph covering periods of time with historical approach, current status, and future estimates. Dynamically quantified objectives, expressed in precise estimates, not only enable the manager to detect the deviation; they also provide a compatible series of short-term objectives on the way to the end result. This is especially desirable from a psychological as well as managerial point of view because it establishes a series of progressive accomplishments and facilitates constructive supervision while there is time for remedial action.

In practice it cannot be determined whether one's objectives are good unless they are expressed within the framework of relevant assumptions. Moreover, to be compatible, all objectives formulated within an organizational unit must use the same relevant assumptions. It is absolutely impossible to plan without using assumptions.

Profitability and Key Result Areas

The navy has an old saying, "Men do what is inspected, not what is expected." Managers tend to function in this manner. If optimum results are to be accomplished, quantified objectives must be established in the most important areas of responsibility and backed up with effective measurement and adequate incentives.

In the past it was customary for objectives to be imposed from the top, but a rapidly growing volume of well-documented evidence conclusively proves that when proper environment has been established with appropriate guidelines, managers will consistently propose more "reaching" objectives than they are willing to accept when objectives are imposed from the top. Whether objectives are proposed from the bottom or imposed from the top, every manager should have a set of well-balanced objectives in the key result areas where he is expected to produce important results.

With previous planning methods there was no clear distinction between assumptions beyond the manager's control and objectives achieved through his effort, and neither was expressed in a dynamically quantified manner that made it easier to detect deviations from the anticipated results so that surprise could be minimized, agreement revised, and performance optimized in the light of new developments. Under those circumstances planning was more rigid and managers tended to hold the number of objectives to a minimum. Now there is a growing recognition that it is desirable for managers to establish a set of well-balanced objectives representing all the important areas in which they must produce effective results in order to accomplish their mission. Furthermore, these objectives must be compatible with other commitments, coordinated with the objectives of their associates, and integrated to support the objectives and fulfill the purpose of the organization.

The basic concepts of profitability and key result areas were first published by Peter Drucker (*The Practice of Management,* Harper & Row, 1954). They were later developed into a consistent philosophy for the advanced management program of General Electric Company and have now been adapted for effective use by a wide variety of well-managed companies because they provide a basic frame of reference for a practical system of management by objectives. The fundamental concept in this philosophy establishes profitability as the basic objective of management; it has been selected to emphasize the desirability of achieving longer-range, enduring results rather than sacrificing ultimate gain for short-term profits.

PROFITABILITY

Profitability can be interpreted properly as gain from the activity and thus becomes universal in its application to all managerial situations. This is what the citizens want from their government, the President of the United States wants from the Department of Defense, the stockholders want from the corporation, the board of directors wants from the company president, the president wants from the department heads, and the manager wants from his subordinates. The concept of profitability also works in reverse. This is what the customer wants from the producer, the employee from his supervisor, and the community from the company.

The responsibility of the manager is to provide profitability not only for the stockholders but for all interested parties who have a legitimate claim to gain from the enterprise. Since the continued existence of the business is dependent upon its ability to satisfy the customer, the manager's first responsibility is to provide profit—in both a broad and a specific sense—to the customer; otherwise, he will have no customer and ultimately no business.

It is difficult to set any order of priority as to who should get first preference among the other interested parties, but it may be illuminating to review what actually happens. The supplier is near the head of the line, for as long as the business is solvent he will be paid for his materials and services regardless of whether the business generates a profit for the stockholders. Similarly, the employees receive not only wages but also vacations, pensions, other fringe benefits, and a high degree of job security, regardless of net profits. The local government gets its cut regardless of profit, while the Federal Government, acting more like a partner, waits until profit has been made and then takes half. In a very real sense management has a trusteeship responsibility. The American system of enterprise tends to provide greatest profit to the stockholders of the well-managed companies that provide the greatest gain for all.

KEY RESULT AREAS

According to the original concept, seven key result areas are so essential to the success of an enterprise that if any one area is totally neglected over a period of time, the enterprise will lose its profitability. Moreover, the ability of a company to grow and prosper at a faster rate than its major competitors is dependent upon its ability to develop a combination of strengths in the key result areas that exceeds that of its major competitors.

Since management must achieve effective performance in all the key result areas to attain its major objective, it becomes highly important to take the following action with regard to each key area: evaluate capabilities and opportunities; establish measurable, dynamic objectives; develop adequate programs of action; delegate authority, responsibility, and accountability as close as practical to point of execution; provide reliable information (intelligence) at the time and place of decision; provide resources in right quality, quantity, time, and place; and establish control by exception with adequate feedback.

This brief introduction explains why the concepts of profitability and key result areas are an important frame of reference for a practical system of management by objectives supported by dynamic methods of planning and control. Such an approach is particularly necessary in an organization with several decentralized and diversified programs or profit centers because it provides a consistent pattern which makes it much easier to coordinate, evaluate, and consolidate the planning, execution, and control. The seven key result areas are described here with suggestions for establishing dynamic objectives.

Customer satisfaction. The ability of any company to grow and prosper is directly dependent upon its ability to satisfy its customers. If a company wishes to increase its share of market—to grow faster than the growth of the market—it is usually necessary to take business away from somebody else, which generally means that the company must provide superior customer satisfaction. This key result area includes the entire field of marketing effectiveness: customer acceptance, product style and performance, cost/price relationships, product knowledge and service, brand loyalty, and prestige. Dynamically quantified objectives may include annual sales volume, share of market, size of order, repeat sales, and warranty expense. Sales figures can be broken down by product, industry, market, country, territory, and type.

Productivity. If a competitor can outproduce his competition, he can usually outprice it. Productivity pervades almost all aspects and functions of a business, from warehouse helpers to top executives. Dynamic objectives may include any meaningful ratios of output to input, ranging from sales per salesman to dollars of operating profit to dollars of payroll.

Innovation. There is nothing desirable about anything new unless it is also better. This area is obviously applicable to product development, but other types of innovation may be equally valuable—accounting procedures, computer applications, recruiting and training methods, and management concepts or techniques. In the average company there is no place where greater profit can be made in a shorter period of time with smaller cost and less risk than improving the effectiveness of management; thus any true innovations in management will be especially valuable. One important dynamic objective would be the percent of sales from new products. If meaningful symptoms or indicators that measure progress or results cannot be found, dollars or effort spent for the purpose of achieving innovation (R&D expenditures, for example) may be measured; but there must be follow-up to make sure that results are eventually obtained.

Resources. A great many factors are applicable to the creation, conservation, and use of resources in all functions of management. Dynamic objectives may include inventories, receivables, equity, debt, buildings, land, patents, and licensing.

Management development and performance. Most company presidents agree that the most important bottleneck preventing them from achieving their future objectives is the inability to develop managerial capabilities. Since the problem is so general and so urgent, it is highly desirable to evaluate strengths, weaknesses, and opportunities; establish dynamic objectives; and develop specific programs of action to achieve acceptable results on schedule. Dynamic objectives may include a wide variety of recruitment and training objectives; money or effort spent to improve management (training projects and budgets); or a specified percent of managers who achieve their standards of performance.

Employee attitude and performance. During the past 20 years the No. 1 problem in business and industry has changed. No longer the featherbedding of the blue-collar worker, the problem has now become the energetic stupidity of the "eager beaver" manager who is spending time, effort, and money on projects that never should have been started in the first place. Nevertheless, there is still great opportunity to improve productivity and profits through the improvement of employee attitude and performance. Dynamic objectives may include the reduction of turnover, absenteeism, time lost through accidents, and time lost through work stoppages and training budgets.

Public responsibility. Although the American way of life is based on the effective performance of the private sector, current reports indicate that the private sector is not performing effectively enough to gain the intelligent and enthusiastic support of a majority of the people. Such a situation is dangerous in a democratic society. This problem will not be solved by well-intentioned but generally ineffective efforts to teach economic theory to the public. Nor is it possible for business organizations such as the National Association of Manufacturers (NAM) or the U.S. Chamber of Commerce to do the job for management, although they may help clarify the nature and urgency of the problem and provide general guidance. Much progress has been made in the past 25 years, but the general environment has changed so extensively that many recent developments are not really responsive to the situation. This whole area needs extensive re-examination, but meanwhile every company and company executive must accept a higher degree of individual responsibility. Dynamic objectives may include percent of fair-share givers to the United Fund; employment of employable handicapped; and executive participation as officers or directors of trade associations, chambers of commerce, and school boards. Of course, the most important public responsibility of a business is to grow and prosper so it can continue to satisfy customers, employ people, pay taxes, and contribute to the health and growth of the general economy.

Applying the basic concept. According to a recent survey, the standard key result areas have been adapted by more than 250 companies as the basic pattern for their corporate planning. Recognizing the importance of effective performance, management should formulate dynamically quantified objectives in each of these areas and develop effective programs of action to see that adequate results are accomplished.

In applying the basic concept at subordinate levels (divisions, departments, functions) each manager must identify the most important areas in which he is expected to produce significant results. For example, the director of personnel might list recruiting, training, employee communications, compensation, and industrial relations; the vice president of marketing might identify his own areas as product development, marketing research, advertising and sales promotion, sales, and field service. When agreement has been reached regarding the areas of responsibility, the manager should formulate dynamically quantified objectives in each.

Criteria for Objectives

The next step is to identify the criteria that will enable the manager to determine whether his objectives will be effective for purposes of management by objectives.

SUITABILITY

The first question is of primary importance: Is the objective suitable? If accomplished, would it take one in the right direction? Is it relevant, and does it support the purpose and mission of the organization? Is it compatible with other established objectives? Can it be coordinated with other objectives at the same level and integrated to support the objectives of the next higher echelon? Unless the answers to these questions are in a resounding affirmative, objectives should either be modified or discarded immediately to avoid frustration and wasted resources. The following illustration emphasizes the importance of suitability. The manager of a grocery store has the objective of increasing his sales 20 percent next year. His clerk suggests that he buy the gas station next door. This is economically feasible; but if he doesn't want to enter the gasoline business, it is not a suitable objective because it does not take him in the direction he wants to go. Special care and attention should always be given to any objective or supporting program that tends to change the nature of a business.

FEASIBILITY

Although there is much to be said in behalf of courage, enthusiasm, and the "old school try," these attributes may cause more harm than good if they permit emotion to overrule common sense or encourage the commitment of time, effort, and money to objectives that are unattainable. The establishment of objectives involves decision making, and the quality of decisions cannot consistently rise above the quality of the information on which the decisions are based. The best guide and safeguard to the feasibility of an objective or program is a set of carefully devised, dynamically quantified assumptions. Whenever there is a sales objective that increases faster than the market potential, the question should always be asked, "Whom are you going to take the business from—and how?" Don't count on taking market share from the weakest competitor.

ACCEPTABILITY

The establishment of objectives requires that management be willing and able to provide the essential resources in the right quality and quantity, at the right time and place, and at the right cost. More planning and objective setting get off the track on this score than any other factor. To get a reliable answer to the question of acceptability, it is necessary for the persons responsible for the formulation and acceptance of the objective to have a clear and reliable estimate of the resource requirements. Once again it is essential to examine and evaluate the objective within the framework of dynamically quantified assumptions with regard to those very important probable developments over which management has no control, such as the growth of the market; the health of the economy; the cost of money, materials, and manpower; the effect of regulations or legislation; the changing attitudes and requirements of customers; and competitive strategy and tactics.

VALUE

"Good management" has been defined as "the effective use of resources to accomplish most important objectives." No healthy organization has enough resources to support every objective that is suggested. This is another reason why sound objectives must cascade down from the top within a frame of clearly defined strategy supported by policy guidelines. To get sound answers to the essential questions (Is the objective worth the price? Is it the best buy for the money?), a basic system of cost effectiveness that can be applied to the analysis and evaluation of all major objectives and programs is required.

ACHIEVABILITY

Achievability is substantially different from feasibility. For an objective to be theoretically possible is one thing; to be able to accomplish it is another matter. Results are often disappointing because of failure to discriminate between the objective that may be feasible for someone and the objective that is achievable by the manager. It is also important to determine, before approval is granted and resources are allocated, how it would be achieved.

MEASURABILITY

All the factors in the measurement of progress must be weighed: quantification, in terms of quality, quantity, time, and cost; and dynamic quantification, in terms of historical approach, current status, and future estimate. A further question concerns the possibility of reaching agreement on the method of measurement so that the responsible person can exercise control and minimize the need for externally imposed control.

ADAPTABILITY AND FLEXIBILITY

It should be possible to modify the objective in response to unforeseen developments so that performance can be optimized in the changing environment. Adaptability and flexibility have become much more important with the rapid increase in rate, type, and volume of change.

COMMITMENT

Regardless of whether objectives are proposed from the bottom or imposed from the top, once agreement has been reached, there should be firm commitment on both sides to provide the resources and to accomplish the result.

Modification of Objectives

The first five criteria outlined previously are essential; the other three are highly desirable. An objective is not a truly good objective (and should be neither proposed nor approved) unless it meets essential standards. This is usually recognized in a well-managed company at the time the objectives are formulated; but if unexpected developments occur, the objectives may no longer meet those criteria, and in that event the eighth criterion—commitment—should also be abrogated. It is unwise to continue firm commitment to an objective that is no longer suitable, feasible, acceptable, valuable, or achievable.

In the past, objectives were tied to previous performance or rigid forecasts, and there was no realistic relationship between results and resource requirements. Under these circumstances two common practices caused much resentment, resistance, and frustration, and many bad results: (1) The boss "held the feet to the fire," and once objectives were agreed upon, they were never changed. (2) There were "reaching objectives" to inspire the troops, but more conservative objectives were reported to higher authority; resources were allotted only to attain the lower level.

If both assumptions and objectives are formulated and maintained on the basis of the best available information and expressed in a dynamically quantified manner, they can and should be modified when there is a significant deviation in the anticipated result.

The Task Ahead

During recent years there has been a growing, insistent demand for decentralization and participation throughout the world. It has made a significant impact on the business world, and its influence is bound to increase. In spite of much talk about management by objectives, the results generally have been disappointing. To get better results, management must realize the degree to which recent developments have changed the nature of management requirements; create an environment conducive to intelligent and enthusiastic participation; provide a process that makes it possible to achieve effective delegation without abdication; recognize that management by objectives must start at the top; identify the objectives of this new practice of management and the problems that will be created thereby; develop courses of action to achieve the objectives and solve the problems; do what is necessary to gain the acceptance and support of all persons who are affected by or involved in the change in management requirements; place greater emphasis on effectiveness than on efficiency, and on results than on activity; and manage by objectives rather than delusions.—*E. J. Green*

ORGANIZATION

Organization is the means by which all group enterprises are given socially acceptable purposes and made capable of efficient operation. Two basic conditions always make it important: numbers of participants and diverse operations. A one-man business or even one employing half a dozen or more seldom requires much thought on organization. Under the circumstances, participants are intimately acquainted, probably possess a close community of interest in their joint enterprise, and readily contrive a method of working together. Even when their number is considerably larger, if the task to be performed is not very complicated, organization may require only that attention be given to devising some simple system for enforcing discipline.

As the group becomes larger and its members are less intimately acquainted, it inevitably comes to include individuals differing in temperament, skills, upbringing, attitudes toward each other, personal loyalties, ambitions, and frustrations, influenced in each case by social contacts and relationships on the job and in off hours. As operations evolve also, the tasks to be performed soon begin to manifest recognizable differences.

Diversity of personnel, associated with diversity of operations, soon makes division of labor essential if order is to prevail. It is the essence of organization to reconcile these disparate human resources with the various technologies involved in the operations to be performed.

The desired structure never evolves spontaneously through the voluntary efforts of participants. Correct organization is always initiated by those who eventually emerge from the group as management. Satisfactory levels of technical competence in their individual specialties, coupled with reasonable willingness to subordinate personal inclinations to the interests of the group, are the human resources of which organizations are built; but little of significance actually happens until someone from the outside sets the guideposts to follow.

Basic Elements

The elements of every acceptable solution of the organization problem, reduced to simplest terms, include the following: (1) a recognized source of executive authority capable of taking charge and securing the cooperation of participants in a harmonious team effort; (2) the availability of a sufficient roster of executive manpower desirous of promoting the objectives assumed for the enterprise; (3) precise identification of the operations to be performed and a matching of these with the skills required to assure intended results; and (4) a structure assigning specific individuals to specific tasks and providing a system for securing disciplined action.

INFORMAL ORGANIZATION

Acceptance of the necessity to cooperate, even though it requires of every participant real restraint on what may be his personal preferences, is the chief ingredient of what is meant by the "informal organization" of any group. The personal examples set by various members of the group, who regardless of their official positions (or lack of them) come to be accepted as leaders worthy of imitation by their associates, are of great importance in achieving this. The capacity to influence associates—sometimes called authority of leadership, as distinguished from authority of position possessed by the formal or official members of the executive hierarchy—is an intensely personal thing. It is not especially dependent upon delegations of authority from higher up. It is based upon mutual confidence; upon respect for one's superiors and in turn for one's associates; upon loyalty to the system of authority under which all must work if order is to prevail.

No management can afford to underestimate these subtle influences, which are present in every group of men of goodwill. They can be undermined and turned into a destructive influence by insensitive and clumsy handling on the part of those who possess authority of position only in the formal organization. When the latter themselves also win authority of leadership, however, it becomes a potent builder of morale.

A stage full of prima donnas, no matter how competent they are as individual artists, can never render a symphonic production as the composer conceived it without the guiding hand and sensitivity of the conductor. The acclaim naturally due the conductor for an outstanding performance, or the coaching staff of a champion football team, for example, is never misplaced. It is the understanding, discipline, and direction of the officially authorized leadership as well as the skill and goodwill of the players derived from the crucial informal organization within the group that combine to yield desired results.

FORMAL ORGANIZATION

The formal process of organization includes both analysis and synthesis. The complex of operations to be performed must be examined in detail, but their individual significance depends primarily upon how they contribute to the intended overall purpose. The first step, therefore, in designing an organization is to have a clear conception of its intended objectives. Organization is always a means to some end. Knowing what is to be done, naturally, must precede knowing how to do it. The elements in this required complex of operations must then be pulled apart, as it were, identifying each constituent task capable of explicit definition and expert performance by specialists. These specialized parts must in turn be restructured—united in compatible group efforts; provided with effective channels of communication between one another; integrated in a harmonious team effort by common objectives and policies, unequivocal directives, control and intelligence systems of various sorts, and central guidance and authority.

Specialization and its practical limits. Actually, in almost any operation—no matter how simple or complicated it may be—this process of subdivision can easily be carried to absurd limits. It ordinarily needs to be subjected to critical scrutiny long before ultimate limits are reached. Overspecialization creates its own problems—usually much sooner and more positively in the mental tasks of executives than in simpler clerical and manual crafts.

The proliferating specialists tend eventually to get into each other's way; individual tensions and frustrations accumulate; channels of communication become clogged, slowing down the natural flow of information between closely related jobs; the achievement of reasonable coordination which comprises the very heart of management's responsibility becomes increasingly difficult. The goals of optimum efficiency in organization thus always require those in authority, when delegating responsibilities to their subordinates, to strike some approximate balance between diminishing economies offered by further specialization and the diseconomies resulting from these mounting burdens of coordination.

To achieve this balance never requires discovering and applying some precise mathematical formula but usually does require considerable experimentation before an acceptable structure is achieved. Organization is never an exact science. It is based on few immutable principles. It is subject in every situation to many variables in personnel and local conditions, and must in final analysis be judged by the practical test that "it works." It depends in particular upon the intuitive skill of those in authority in prejudging the exact pattern of operations under which key subordinates can work best, each in his own sphere and with each other.

Multiple-dimension structure. The resulting structure of management includes divisions of executive labor in several dimensions. It is pyramidal in form, with the apex representing the position of the chief executive in whom the total authority of management is centered. From this point, successive delegations of authority extend outward and downward from level to level in a hierarchy until the highly important dividing line between management and nonmanagement is reached at the last level of supervision occupied by foremanship.

As organizations become large and impersonal, the strategic position occupied by foremen sometimes tends to be underrated at the very time top management is farther and farther removed from the work force. Foremen subjected to callous and indifferent treatment from above eventually become so disgruntled that it need not cause surprise if these attitudes are presently reflected in the work force. The foremen actually occupy the outposts of management and as such require special treatment. The precious quality of teamwork in an organization depends upon deliberately cultivating a sense of belonging, from top to bottom of the structure.

Sources and Nature of Managerial Authority

The special quality required of officialdom occupying each level in the hierarchy is possession of authority consistent with the measure of responsibility and accountability expected of that level. In private business enterprises, the ultimate internal source of this authority rests with the ownership as possessors of property rights. Owners in simple, one-man proprietorships or partnerships usually can and do act in the additional role of managers. In corporate organizations, in contrast, this soon becomes totally impractical.

Stockholders, by their numbers, their inability to keep informed concerning detailed problems of the management (if not, indeed, lack of personal competence to make significant contributions to sensible solutions), and their generally declining interest in corporate affairs other than profits are prevented from direct participation in management. As individuals, they are unable to influence managerial decisions except as participants in a majority acting under normal parliamentary procedures.

Unless extraordinary emergencies in these matters occur, participation in management policy insofar as an individual stockholder is concerned tends to be limited to deciding whether to continue his investment when dissatisfied and to somewhat perfunctory voting for or against a slate of directors which he has had little, if any, personal part in proposing.

FUNCTIONS OF DIRECTORATE

Boards of directors, ostensibly selected by stockholders acting as a group subject to corporate charter and by-law provisions, legally possess all the prerogatives of management even though, as individuals acting alone, they have no such mandate. There are, in fact, compelling practical reasons why directors no more than stockholders can themselves undertake to perform the continuous and comprehensive responsibilities of management.

The intermittent schedules on which boards convene to transact company business discourage the intensely concentrated and uninterrupted attention that is essential for successful performance of many phases of managerial work. Most outside directors have also other, quite likely equally compelling interests that prevent, still further, more than intermittent preoccupation with their company's problems. The fact that boards must meet and, like stockholders, act as a group is of itself inconsistent with many of the most critical aspects of creative managerial performance.

Practical limitations on board action. Boards, subject to these limitations, still perform invaluable functions in representing their constituents—the stockholders—by setting overall objectives, approving plans and programs of operation, formulating general policies, offering advice and counsel, and even upon occasion disciplining their managerial representatives. No other agency in the organizational structure can perform these specific duties as well. Planning what in general terms is to be done in an enterprise is naturally a group activity consistent with the general ground rules under which directors are compelled to operate.

Executive accountability. Experience proves unmistakably that final responsibility for seeing that what is planned is actually done usually is best vested in a single executive. There is then no question as to personal accountability for results. This basic obligation to hold someone accountable when things go wrong is extremely difficult to enforce where a group acts jointly in executive capacities, whether it be a board of directors, a commission, or a mere committee. Divided responsibility so far as individual members of the group are concerned readily suggests personal alibis when things go wrong.

It is almost a universal rule that the executive authority vested officially in the board of directors must be delegated to a chief executive officer who occupies the apex of the managerial pyramid. A sound if homely observation in such matters is credited to President Truman, who in characterizing his high office said, "The buck stops here." To have it otherwise would almost certainly create endless confusion and backbiting in management.

DIVISION OF POWERS

Corporate complexities often result in what seems superficially to be some sharing of this heavy burden in the chief executive office—as, for example, by a chairman and president respectively. The actual allocation of duties between these two usually depends on their individual interests, experience, and competence; their respective seniority; or possibly upon any one of a number of face-saving considerations which inevitably must be dealt with in the internal politics of every organization. In some instances, each is a veritable powerhouse in his own right who nevertheless has learned to work harmoniously with the other. Sometimes, in contrast, one or the other is reduced largely to acting as a mere figurehead who, it has been decided, must receive official if largely fictional recognition in the interest of promoting harmony in high places in the organization.

Arrangements in the high command may vary, as circumstances require, anywhere between one extreme wherein the chairmanship is largely honorary and possibly confined merely to presiding at board meetings, with the president designated officially as chief executive officer, to the other extreme with the chairman designated as chief executive officer and the president as second in command, occupying a distinctly subordinate position with whatever specific responsibilities the chairman chooses to assign him.

Unless the division of powers at this level is carefully worked out and understood in advance, such contrivances involving dual allocations of authority may become a source of weakness rather than of strength. If, for instance, the second in command is relegated to the dubious position of an assistant to his superior .officer—"without portfolio," so to speak—his position, provided he has real executive potential, can become extremely frustrating. When long continued, it is not likely to fit him eventually to occupy the position of first in command, which ought to be one of the chief reasons for setting up the relationship in the first place.

A rational division of powers between these two should qualify both to be members of the board so that this body may have without obstruction the benefit of both their views respecting operations. The fact remains that one must be designated as chief executive officer and act as such. Much confusion in the deliberations of the board is avoided if it can thus look to one man and hold him finally accountable for results. Subordinates, also, should never be left in doubt on this point. Knowing who is boss in any critical situation is the first requirement of discipline.

Delegation of Authority

The chief executive officer, as operations take on greater and greater complexity, must devise some efficient means of sharing authority with subordinates. This is the prime factor in organization based upon systematic divisions of executive responsibility. The basic decisions involved in initial planning of the organization include the answers to these questions: Who is to be granted authority in a given set of circumstances? What kind of authority shall be delegated? What limits shall be placed upon its exercise? This necessity of authority delegation to subordinates represents unquestionably the most important test of executive competence.

ERRORS IN DELEGATION

There are always two ways to delegate authority: a right way and a wrong one. If subordinates are left in doubt as to what is expected of them but will be censured if their performance is unsatisfactory, their personal potential for growth as executives is quickly undermined. If their instructions are so ambiguous—so limiting and circumscribed by detailed precautions as to leave them without discretion—little has been accomplished by delegation. Subordinates who are permitted no opportunities for personal decisions never become ready for promotion. When reduced merely to carrying out or transmitting to still lower levels orders and instructions which they had no part in making, this minor role of relaying messages from above is largely wasted effort. Their own creative abilities should instead be utilized in interpreting and adapting communications to local conditions which, because of proximity, they very likely see and understand more clearly than does their distant boss who issued the order in the first place.

Every executive who works through subordinates must take care that their jobs are worth doing even at the risk they may occasionally make mistakes, else they will never prove worthy successors when eventually one becomes a candidate for promotion or replacement.

CORRECT DELEGATION

Executives in every good organization try to permit their subordinates to share in decision making appropriate to their respective levels in the organization structure. Authority thus delegated must be respected and protected, else the goal of effective teamwork soon becomes a myth.

The first requisite in correct delegation of authority is to state clearly what is expected of the recipient in his own job and how these duties fit into the general plan. A clear understanding of the organizational relationships within which he must work is fundamental. Without specific instructions, encroachment on the spheres of fellow workers and disruptive rivalries soon appear.

To permit any member of management for lack of specific ground rules to reach for power wherever his own interests and urges prompt him to do so—or to retire in a protective shell when too timid to resist aggression by more forceful associates—is bound to end in trouble.

There are always definite areas in every executive job where the incumbent should have the right to act on his own discretion. These need to be spelled out. In other matters that need to be clearly understood, his authority is limited to recommendations subject to review and approval by superiors or associates on his own level before initiating action.

The correct rule in such matters is stated quite succinctly in the U.S. Army Field Service Regulations in the caution to those delegating authority to avoid "trespassing upon the province of the subordinate." Orders, the warning continues, "should contain everything beyond the intended authority of the subordinate but nothing more."

This is best observed when delegation of authority states clearly the results expected without inhibiting restrictions on the choice of means for achieving results.

DECENTRALIZED AUTHORITY AND
CENTRALIZED CONTROL

The ultimate goal in delegating authority is to achieve a *decentralization of authority* to the lowest levels in the organization at which competence can be made available to deal with the matters in question. The aim is to insure a judicious distribution of executive authority so that no level becomes overburdened or has too little to do.

The opposite—overcentralization at focal decision-making centers—congests communications and delays decision-making processes.

Difficulties of decentralization. Many influences and human contrivances in every organization tend to defeat this ideal. Instead of decentralization, they result in excessive concentration of executive power. Many executives, strong in other respects, are poor delegators when it comes to divesting themselves of power they have possibly fought for and received from above. They fancy that no one is as competent as they themselves; that the issues in question are too important to be entrusted to subordinates. They rationalize by such arguments their own appetites for power and, by denying subordinates the right to decide issues that they should be able to undertake, eventually undermine the self-confidence and enthusiasm of subordinates in exercising the meager authority they already possess.

Thus, each locus of executive power tends to be subtly subjected to forces that both push and pull permission to decide, even in relatively unimportant matters, to higher levels. Eventually, these maldistributions of power throughout the structure result in serious breakdowns of performance.

Importance of centralized control. Emphasis upon need for decentralized authority must be counterbalanced by maintaining adequate centralization of control. One without the other leads to chaos.

An orderly process of authority delegation always assumes that authority, responsibility, and accountability are coextensive and inseparable. Authority imposes the necessity of deciding actions impersonally and objectively for the organization. For this, the recipient must in turn accept responsibility and be held accountable for results. It is always implied that should things go wrong, he himself must be accountable to his superior for preventive action before it is too late to set them right. He cannot expect to satisfy his superior by complaining that his own subordinates failed him by misrepresenting what was actually happening. His superior will be within his rights to insist that it is precisely the negligent one's business to see that his own subordinates in the chain of command are reliable; that he does know when things go wrong; that he has already set about correcting the situation.

Such precautions up and down the line of command facilitate centralized control and bring it within the range of possibility for management to achieve what, in the vernacular, is called "running a tight ship."

Organization Structure

The specific form of organization employed in any enterprise is dependent on local conditions, company purposes and policies, available personnel, scale of operations, and diversity or similarity of services offered the company's customers. There are, in consequence, truly no precise structural guidelines to be followed without deviation in setting up an organization. All businesses have many problems in common that lead to similarities in the forms of internal specialization. But each business unit is, in many respects, distinctly an individual.

It is always unwise to assume that because a particular structural form seems to have been effective in one instance and at a particular point in time it is likely to prove equally advantageous in another.

The chief variable to be contended with is, of course, the people themselves. It is impossible to set up an ideal structure, for the obvious reason that perfectly adaptable persons are never available for all positions in any organization. All have weaknesses that if not recognizable immediately are sure to come to the surface in some time of emergency. Every organization is thus perforce a compromise. Management must try to take full advantage of the strong points in each individual executive's make-up but build into the structure protective devices against individual weaknesses and personal bias.

BASIS OF DEPARTMENTATION

Total responsibility for operations vested in the chief executive officer must, of necessity, be parceled out to subordinates on some systematic basis. These first-line executives must repeat the process to their subordinates, each in terms of the special responsibilities he has been assigned, and so on downward from level to level throughout the vertical structure. The method selected for making these assignments in any given instance provides the basis of departmentation.

Various factors always influence the choice of bases best adapted to local circumstances. One of the most obvious of these, typically employed at the first level by the chief executive, is to assign responsibility in terms of functions; that is, to persons in charge of finance, production, procurement, distribution, control activities, personnel administration, and similar delegations to whatever extent seems to be required. All these functions represent technical distinctions demanding special training, experience, aptitude, and expertise of a high order from the executive manpower to whom they are assigned. Incumbents chosen because of these special qualifications are empowered to formulate uniform corporate policies and programs in their respective bailiwicks. They are expected to insist that these pronouncements be enforced throughout the organization. This usually makes functional specialization, to some degree at least, the preferred basis of departmentation immediately beneath the office of chief executive.

Each of these functionaries is recognized as the company's major authority in his particular field. And because they are experts and individualists, departmental rivalries disruptive of company harmony occasionally arise.

Minor personal frictions are to be expected among closely associated individualists. A wise central management quickly recognizes the symptoms and brings them under control. Indeed, they can sometimes be put to good account by encouraging friendly competition. The danger is that they should ever get out of hand! Overheated tempers among the players quickly obscure team objectives and presently cause discontented customers.

When operations become diverse, other bases of departmentation, in any event, make their appearance. If, for example, distinct families of products, new and unfamiliar manufacturing techniques, new plants remote from headquarters, special customer groups, unique methods of sale, or similar factors requiring individualized treatment develop, these readily become the logical bases for delegating authority to subordinates. A divisionalized type of organization thus begins to emerge.

Advantages of divisionalization. The creation of divisions, whether at the first level or farther down the line if more appropriate, has the advantage of establishing centers of coordination at these points which supplement that in the office of chief executive. Operations in each such division are certain to be delegated functionally beneath divisional headquarters; so the advantages of technical specialization are not lost—merely moved to lower levels and in each case restricted to local divisional affairs.

Activities in different divisions, embracing plants or groups of similar plants, stores or groups of stores, or even subsidiary companies, are readily measurable in terms of individual earning power; localized incentives can more easily be devised to provide motivation to divisional personnel; operating performance can be compared from division to division, thus simplifying still further the appraisal and control of operations.

Functional departments, in contrast, offer no such opportunity for comparison. How, for instance, are the relative efficiencies of the controller, the production manager, or the executive in charge of marketing to be compared? The convenient profit test applies to none of these, since no one of the group is responsible, single-handed, for generating profits.

Divisions provide even greater advantages as more fertile training grounds for future top management talents. Functional specialists, even when they eventually become the head men in their departments, by the nature of their vocation, become more and more proficient experts, to be sure, but often at risk of not developing ample understanding of the interrelations of their own field with those of other equally important fields. As "specialists" they sometimes have difficulty, when promoted out of their fields, in bridging the transition to becoming "generalists," which is the prime requirement of successful chief executives. An excellent marketing man, an engineering genius, or a financial expert may fail completely to live up to expectations when suddenly promoted to general manager. He has been raised as a partisan and continues to be a partisan in his new environment. His chances of success are likely to depend in considerable measure upon whether his company at that particular time needs in its executive leadership the unique talents and experience his past training has fitted him to render.

Division managers, in contrast, have already been schooled as "generalists" in management. Other things being equal, their promotion to the top spot in the organization often finds them less uncertain as to how to proceed in their new position of enlarged responsibilities.

It has often been observed that large-scale enterprises of the future may face their most critical problem in how to raise able general executive leadership if the chief source of recruits is among executives who have spent their lives thus far as specialists in one function of operations. Emphasis on division management, which unquestionably is a trend as modern business institutions become more complex, provides an alternate solution to this vexing problem.

HORIZONTAL STRUCTURE OF MANAGEMENT

The basis of departmentation is concerned with the horizontal structure of management. Functional departments often predominate at the first level immediately beneath the chief executive because the involved technologies of modern business call for expert treatment. But still another factor has made its appearance in modern business.

Diversification of products, of markets, of methods of reaching different types of customers, has become commonplace. In the current urge to merge in loosely federated conglomerates, orderly management could in many instances scarcely be maintained except by continuing the former organizations of the merged. Companies thus acquired are frequently continued as quasi-independent subsidiaries, operating under their own divisional management and accountable only to a holding type of overall parent company management.

Division managers, sometimes even called presidents, report directly to the chief executive office.

Eventually, perhaps, some combination of divisions and major functional departments emerges, providing in the latter (for instance) central management of finance, personnel administration, research and development, or other corporate activities.

There are especially cogent reasons for centralizing, for the entire corporation, control of these functions. Financial policies and administration, for example, are primarily of corporate rather than merely of divisional scope. Personnel administration has become important to management chiefly because employees have, through organization, increased their bargaining power relative to that of management. Where union organizations include within their jurisdictions the employees of several divisions, the personnel function must·in self-defense be administered by management on a corporate basis. Research and development, in some respects—to cite still a third example—may be administered efficiently on divisional lines, but it also is related to long-term company survival and in these areas must be directed on a corporate rather than on a fragmented divisional basis.

Whatever combination of functional specialties and divisional operations seems most workable at a given level, it is certain that in no organization is one of these bases of departmentation a complete substitute for the other. When local circumstances make it advisable at the first level of delegated powers to favor a divisional pattern of organization, at the second level and possibly subsequent levels functional departments will certainly be needed to reap the advantages of technical specialization in managerial activities.

Span of authority. The span of authority of any executive is measured by the number of subordinates he permits to report to him directly. Most observers are inclined to insist that this number should be strictly limited in the interests of effective administration. Sometimes it is even contended that this should rarely exceed four or five. Unquestionably, there can be too many, and unless real resistance is offered, the number gradually increases until eventually it gets completely out of hand.

Practical limits, however, are reasonably flexible. The effective span of authority, in fact, always depends on several local conditions:

1. The supervisory skills of the executive himself are doubtless one of the most important conditions. Men with facile minds, who have acquired the knack of intense powers of concentration, decisiveness, and facility in shifting mental gears from one problem to another, can permit more varied demands upon their attention without excessive strain or impaired quality in their decisions than can others who perhaps have equal judgment but more plodding mental habits.

2. The general level of intelligence of subordinates is a factor. Less competent subordinates require more supervision.

3. The physical office layout has a bearing on the issue. All managerial responsibilities require some face-to-face encounter if healthy communication is maintained. If time of supervisor and supervised is wasted by office inconvenience, the potential performance of both suffers.

4. Finally, the general complexity of the subject matter ordinarily dealt with is important. If relative performance in the several reporting units is readily measurable and comparable, the effective span of authority can be increased accordingly. The manager of operations in a chain store organization, for example, can quite comfortably supervise the activities of a number of store managers, which would be totally impractical if they represented instead unlike functions.

Divisional organizations, for this reason, ordinarily make possible much longer spans of executive authority than are practicable when the units supervised are as unlike as are typical functional departments.

VERTICAL STRUCTURE OF MANAGEMENT

In the pyramidal structure of organization, as in all geometric figures, two ruling dimensions govern: the horizontal and the vertical. Given a figure of constant area or volume, these dimensions vary inversely in relation to each other; the longer the horizontal, the shorter the vertical dimension.

The horizontal dimension represents, at each level in the hierarchy, the span of authority; the vertical dimension represents, in contrast, the line of command.

The line of command is measured by the number of "communication centers" through which the directives of the chief executive pass in being transmitted to the working level at the base of the pyramid. But this line of command is a two-way street, providing also the channel through which the "intelligence services" flow from below to above concerning what is being accomplished on the firing line.

The quality of administration depends on how adequate these two-way communications prove to be. If messages in either direction are delayed, inaccurately reported, or garbled by incompetent screening and interpretation, the effectiveness of supervision deteriorates and the performance of those supervised declines for lack of instruction and guidance. And the chances of these misadventures greatly increase when the line of command is needlessly lengthened.

The ideal structure is thus a "flat" organization, in which the average span of authority is as extended as practicable without impairing contacts between those at each level and their immediate bosses. The line of command from top to bottom of the structure thus tends to be shortened with improved communication in both directions. Divisional organizations are much more adaptable in this respect than those in which functional departments predominate.

Division of executive labor. Successive levels in the line of command in every well-regulated organization have different responsibilities respecting the common subject matter with which they deal. Top executives, if they are not to become overburdened, must focus their attention upon the generalities of management. They must entrust to more numerous associates at lower levels the responsibility for specifics comprising the voluminous details of day-to-day affairs.

The higher the level, the more executive attention must be concentrated upon setting goals, establishing policies, and seeing that acceptable standards have been provided as guidelines to operations. Above all—since top executive influence can be exerted only through people—their selection, training by example, encouragement, and discipline must be the continuing preoccupation at these exalted levels.

Responsibilities at lower levels, on the other hand, are appropriately centered upon meeting goals, following policy precedents, maintaining standards, instructing subordinates in their assigned tasks, and getting daily work schedules completed on time and in order.

Without this judicious distribution of managerial authority throughout the line of command, long-term plans and the insistent demands of organizational hygiene which must be attended to, if at all, by top management are neglected for want of time. The joy of accomplishment at lower levels also disappears in the presence of needless interference by fussy supervision from above.

LINE AND STAFF STRUCTURE OF MANAGEMENT

Complexities in modern business serve to emphasize still further another type of specialization within the managerial group.

Responsibility for executive decisions must be centered in the line of command as means of clarifying accountability for these decisions. But how to decide correctly is the problem. Modern informational systems reinforced by mysterious electronic data processing installations have suddenly brought within reach enormous masses of carefully distilled factual evidence bearing upon executive decisions.

Operating these systems is the work of experts. It has given new importance to the staff structure of management. It requires gathering pertinent facts; digesting and recasting them in understandable form; relating indicated conclusions to decision-making processes.

These activities culminate in recommended action to line executives. Staff personnel do not and cannot properly substitute for the line in making these decisions. They typically operate as groups, whereas decision accountability must be exacted of single executives empowered to decide. But adequate staff work does result in exposing different points of view; in reconciling conflicting evidence; in clarifying options available to those who ultimately must decide what is to be done. It serves to minimize the chances of error in these decisions.

Functional and line authority.   Staff personnel are endowed with functional authority, so called because as individuals they typically act from restricted functional points of view. As groups, they are expected to iron out differences and come to defensible conclusions which they can recommend for action. Functional authority is thus advisory, in contradistinction to line authority of executives in the direct line of command. The latter ostensibly carries with it powers of enforcement.

These subtle distinctions often have resulted in relegating staff men, no matter how competent and influential, to the role of second-class executives. Many men who have been trained in the line, when transferred to staff responsibilities suddenly are bewildered as to how to make their influence recognized. Staff men also, if they possess feelings of inadequacy, often insist that if only they possessed authority their importance would immediately be recognized.

Actually, these distinctions have little reality. Staff men must exert their authority through powers of persuasion, not compulsion. But so also must the line executive if his influence is to be much recognized. Both line and staff executives are likely to be most persuasive when the positions they choose to defend unmistakably possess the ring of truth. Their convictions must be effectively communicated if they are to prove persuasive.

COORDINATION AND COMMUNICATION

Good organization is always a by-product of effective informational interchange. When communication breaks down, organizations invariably go into decline.

Many formal and informal mechanisms have been designed to secure coordinated effort through keeping everyone adequately informed. Formal communication of management's desires is chiefly conveyed to the organization through three devices of one sort or another:

1. *Policies:* principles or rules of action set up by management for the guidance of the organization. These pronouncements, usually based on precedents, need to be sufficiently flexible to be adjusted to local variations in operations. Their underlying purpose is to induce uniformity in performance. They serve to communicate management's desired corporate image.

2. *Standards:* types or models with which management expects conformity of things—products, methods, costs, budgets, working instructions, or whatever is best controlled by comparison with accepted models established as the result of systematic planning and study.

3. *Procedural manuals:* detailed instructions specifying how to perform involved, repetitive operations requiring the participation of different members of the organization. They establish order. Participation by different departments follows in proper sequence, and in each case intended end results are more readily realized.

Informal communication is never more effective than in face-to-face encounters between various members of the organization who need to know each other. This is the purpose of committees, interdivisional and departmental meetings, and the almost interminable conferences that occupy so much time in every organization. This time is never wasted if the meeting is well disciplined, observes a significant agenda, and includes only those who should be there; and if deliberations are, in the end, brought into focus by a good point-by-point summarization.

Supervisors often make the mistake of assuming that they have communicated because they have issued a written order, and they wonder why nothing happens. Actually, such messages usually need to be not only written but read, listened to, and discussed. Men usually respond when they see clearly why the message is important to the one issuing it. This is the reason why well-directed conferences are important.

Organization Maintenance

It is a truism that organizations are dynamic, not static. Each is made up of people who at some time must be succeeded by others if the enterprise is to continue.

Charts and job descriptions serve to characterize the organization at a given moment; but unless these are regularly updated, they become obsolete. Actually, if organization charts are to serve the purposes of top management adequately, the following three types should be maintained:

1. *The existing organization.* This chart will seldom be ideal from a functional standpoint, as discussed earlier, because it will reflect the strengths and weaknesses and accompanying checks and balances for present incumbents.

2. *The ideal organization.* This chart should show the basic organizational objectives of the enterprise toward which work should be directed when changes are made in current incumbents and responsibilities.

3. *The potential organization.* This chart depicts at a glance the current evaluation of each present incumbent. Is he promotable? Acceptable? Unsatisfactory? Does he have a suitable successor? It is this third chart that should motivate the chief executive officer to institute changes before they occur as a result of "natural causes."

Such vital statistics on an organization, rarely developed in adequate detail, would permit as consistent attention to maintaining the irreplaceable organization as sometimes is devoted to the transient brick and mortar properties of the enterprise.

An organization thus tenderly cared for would probably never, with passing years, have to seek outside its borders for adequate top executive replacements.

—*W. N. Mitchell*

POLICIES

Policy is one of the most misunderstood and misused tools of management. Its confused and largely inaccurate use has caused uncertainties in managing and inconsistencies in decision making, particularly by middle and lower-level managers.

Fundamentally, policies are guides to thinking in decision making. Their task is to delimit an area within which a decision may be made and to assure that a decision will contribute to the attainment of objectives and desired plans. Policies are thus a type of plan, since they are expected to guide decisions for future action. Too often, policies are regarded as "written on stone," and the old cliché that "we do not know why we do it, it is just our policy" is too often true.

The essence of a policy is, then, discretion. The area of discretion in decision making allowed by a policy may be broad, or it may be narrow. Its boundaries may be sharp but are more likely to be somewhat indistinct. Thus a company might have a policy that the customer is always right; this implies a wide degree of discretion but hardly one so broad that a manager would be expected to give away the company to satisfy a customer. Or the discretion may be narrow, as when a company has a policy of buying from the lowest of three qualified bidders; in this case the discretion would extend only to the question of who is a qualified bidder.

The test of discretion is essential in order to separate policies from rules and procedures, two types of plans (since they control future action) with which policies are often confused. Rules are requirements for a given action or nonaction, and a pure rule cannot imply discretion. Procedures are likewise chronological sequences of required actions. In the case of policies people are expected to think. But in the case of rules and procedures, if the rules and procedures are correctly conceived and applied, people are not expected to think.

The Role of Policies

The principal task of policies is to give consistency to decisions while still allowing different decisions on different sets of facts to be made. Policies thus furnish the framework for plans. There is consequently a close relationship between policies and delegation of authority. The very idea of delegation implies that the recipient of organizational authority has discretion in making decisions. But if decisions are to have needed consistency and if, as made by many persons, they are to contribute to a company's objectives and support other decisions and plans, the decision maker needs guidelines.

Policies also have the advantage of helping predecide issues without repetitive laborious research. For example, a contributions policy that states that a company will consider only contributions to national charities for health and education and to local charities of the same nature within the immediate area served by its plants and offices can avoid the time-consuming task of giving detailed consideration to every one of the thousands of worthy causes for which aid is solicited.

The Variety of Policies

In a typical enterprise the variety of policies is legion. Not only do policies have a hierarchy usually consistent with the organization structure; they also apply to and arise from the many functions of an enterprise.

It is sometimes thought that there are a policy level and an administrative level of management. Although it is true that most policies are made at the top and upper levels of management because they are designed to guide decisions of subordinates, it is likewise true that even lower levels of management may make some policy.

The hierarchy of policy can be seen in the typical structure of new product development policy. The overall company policy may be to pursue product development in fields with certain characteristics, and supporting policies may be developed for market research, market testing, laboratory research, and tying in production and development.

Policies are also related to certain functions—such as sales and finance, or to a given project—such as those dealing with a given product line. In classifying policies in a business, one usually finds that they revolve around the areas of product (kind or type, number and variety of new products, quality versus price), marketing (channels of distribution, type of customer, kind of price, and sales promotion), production (buy or make, fixed or temporary tooling, size of production run), finance (owning versus leasing, sources of funds, dividends), personnel (promotion from within versus open competition for positions, executive compensation, employee benefits), and public relations (amount and kind of public information, contributions).

How Policies Are Made

To understand the nature of policies better, it may be well to consider how they arise. They are naturally made by someone, but by whom is not always clear.

The most logical source of policy is that originated by managers, particularly top management, for the express purpose of guiding their subordinates in their decision making. The logic of so doing follows from the nature of policy and the understandable desire to have planning decisions of subordinates fit into a preconceived framework so as to assure the orderly and efficient attainment of objectives.

In practice perhaps most policy stems from the appeal for decisions in exceptional cases up the hierarchy of managerial authority. If an occasion arises where a manager does not know how a decision may be made, he may appeal to his superior for an answer. As appeals are carried upward and decisions made, a kind of common law develops. Precedents develop and become guides for future managerial decisions.

As can be seen, there is a danger that policies so made will become uncoordinated, aimless, and confused. Executives may be making policies without intending to do so. Some people—those close to the decisions made or immediately affected by them—may understand the policy; others may not. Decisions made in one circumstance may be used as policy for decisions made in a completely dissimilar situation.

However, appealed policy can be consistent and foresighted. If a manager knows when he is making policy, and particularly if he follows his new decision with a clear publication of written policy, appealed policies may be completely accurate and effective. However, when a manager finds himself constantly making policy by appeal, he may well ask himself whether he has left too large an area of policy making to chance and whether his subordinates understand the policy he has made.

To a great extent policy is being externally imposed on the enterprise, notably by government, trade unions, and trade associations. Whether in the form of direct regulation, competition of government enterprises, or the contractual conditions imposed by the government as a customer, the result is to prescribe many elements of a company's policy. Strong national unions have also imposed many policies on managers that they might not otherwise make. Also, a large number of national and local trade associations have had their effect on the policies of a business enterprise. And there are other groups—church, school, social, and charitable organizations—that have tended to impose policies on an enterprise.

Some policies are inferred from actions taken. A company may have a policy of producing only high-quality merchandise; but if employees see the company making shoddy products, the real policy will soon be inferred. In making policy, actions do speak louder than words.

Guidelines for Effective Policies

The following guidelines may be kept in mind in making policies effective:

1. *Make sure that policies reflect objectives and plans.* In view of the job of policies to guide decision making and give a consistent structure to plans, policies that do not make the attainment of enterprise objectives more effective and efficient are inadequate.

2. *Policies should represent a consistent pattern.* An ineffective marketing program would surely result if a company tried to support simultaneously, for a given product and market, a policy of vigorous price competition and a policy of attempting to gain product differentiation by heavy advertising.

3. *Policies should be sharply distinguished from rules and procedures.* As pointed out previously, in the case of policies the decision maker is expected to think, albeit within bounds, but in the case of rules and procedures he is not expected to exercise discretion.

4. *Policies must be looked upon as subject to change.* Too often policies are looked upon as something unchangeable and sacrosanct. To be sure, a few policies such as those based on common codes of honesty and decency are unchangeable. But most policies, being guides for future action, must remain flexible to reflect the changes required by future conditions.

5. *Policies should be in writing.* Putting a policy in writing does not necessarily make it clear, but a policy that cannot be put in writing is at best an unclear one. The difficulty of communicating intentions and desires is reduced by precise communication in writing. Furthermore, the very act of writing policies has a way of eliminating fuzziness and inconsistency.

6. *Policies should be taught.* No manager may ever assume that even a carefully written policy is always understood. People have a way of putting their own interpretation on any written statement; the effective manager will therefore take every opportunity to teach the meaning of policy. He can do this in many ways: through answering questions, through review of the decisions that subordinates make, through staff meetings, even through casual conversations.

7. *Policies should be controlled.* Policies have a way of being misinterpreted or becoming obsolete. To avoid these results, regular reviews of policies and their application should be made to ascertain whether they are up to date, whether they are complete, whether they support or hamper the attainment of goals and plans, whether they are understood, whether managers are actually being guided by them in their decision making, and whether managers regard them (rightly or wrongly) as straitjackets interfering with sound action.

—Harold Koontz

LONG-TERM PLANNING

Business managers are responsible for utilizing the resources of an enterprise so as to optimize return on investment and the long-term growth of that investment. In order to accomplish this objective, the resources of the enterprise must be deployed in such a fashion as to take maximum advantage of opportunities. Every business organization operates on a plan, whether the plan is formally articulated or informally understood; and every plan, whatever its quality, attempts to enable an enterprise to focus on market needs and marshal the necessary resources to meet them.

Definition

For the purposes of this discussion a distinction is made between long-term and operational planning. The focus is on the long term and as such entails the establishment of objectives, plans, and programs over an extended period (generally, in excess of one year). Operational planning, on the other hand, is concerned with the short term (one year or less), in which the necessary factors in planning are well known, variables are minimal, and objectives are specific. It is extremely important to realize that long-term planning essentially establishes a dialog within an organization. At a given time corporate objectives and strategies may be opened for review and revision, and this carries the clear implication that operating goals and programs can and should be subject to change. Although a long-term plan should focus the energies of an organization on an integrated approach to the attainment of goals, it should not do so at the expense of losing flexibility and responsiveness to opportunities in a changing marketplace.

Corporate Objectives

Effective planning must take place within the context of basic corporate objectives. All organizations have such objectives, whether or not they are formally stated. Of course, in undertaking long-term planning activity, it is necessary that corporate objectives be articulated in as precise a fashion as possible. If this has not been done previously, a useful way to go about it is to undertake what is known as a stakeholders' analysis. The stakeholders in a business enterprise are the stockholders, employees, customers, suppliers, and the community. In a good number of cases financial institutions also may be considered stakeholders, depending upon the make-up of the company's capitalization and its line of business.

It is advisable to bring a number of people into a stakeholders' analysis. A useful technique is to assign the task in parts to those who have immediate responsibilities and contact with a particular set of stakeholders as well as those who might bring a fresh perspective. Marketing and financial executives, for instance, might undertake the analysis pertaining to customers, while the directors and manufacturing executives turn their attention to the community. Of course, all managers should be encouraged to submit their ideas in any area, and this should be so in all phases of long-term planning.

It is not difficult to see that basic corporate objectives can be evolved and developed naturally from such an analysis. As an example, one company (chemicals) states its basic objectives for stockholders as "to insure a profitable return and long-term growth of their investment"; and, for employees, "to provide fair wages, economic security, pleasant, safe working conditions, and opportunities for career advancement commensurate with individual skills and qualifications." These statements of the chemical company are of necessity general in nature in order to maintain durability and flexibility. This does not mean, however, that basic corporate objectives should not be subject to challenge and review. Additionally, there is need for specificity in statements, indicating the manner by which basic objectives will be achieved.

Inputs for Planning

A great number of diverse inputs are needed in order to evolve a meaningful long-term plan.

EXTERNAL FACTORS

Each business enterprise operates within an environment external to its own existence. Knowledge of present environment and future trends is crucial to the planning function. At the very least, the following four important environmental factors should be studied:

1. *The economy.* Trends in the economy and their effect on markets and financial resources must be given consideration.

2. *Market position.* This entails consideration of the total present and future markets, the present and future share of the market, and the nature of competitive trends and threats.

3. *Technology.* With rapidly emerging and changing technology old markets disappear and new ones come into being. The knowledge of technological developments is a necessary input to long-term planning.

4. *Government policies.* Changes in economic and fiscal policies of the government can have a strong impact upon individual enterprises and business in general. These factors, along with the Justice Department's activity in the antitrust field, must be studied and understood. For many businesses the government is also an important customer.

INTERNAL FACTORS

Each segment of an enterprise has a unique view of the organization. With basic corporate objectives in mind, a number of separate preliminary goals can and should be generated. These in turn become planning issues which must be analyzed, preliminarily accepted or rejected, placed in some order of priority, and preliminarily coordinated—all with a view to supplying internal inputs for a long-term plan. The marketing department, for example, may wish to pursue a new product line or market, while research and development feels that its efforts should follow entirely different lines. Still a third consideration is that financial resources are limited and can support activity in only one or the other area. All inputs of this kind are necessary in developing options and evolving a long-term plan.

RESOURCE ANALYSIS

As planning issues are generated, an analysis must be made of present and future capabilities to respond with such necessary resources as manpower, facilities, product development, and finances. This is not a complete list, but it does give an indication of the type of internal appraisal that must take place.

HISTORICAL OPERATING TRENDS

A study of historical operating trends is most important to the evolution of a long-term plan. Financial models can be built by the use of past trends; depending upon the nature of the business, these models can be made in considerable detail by being broken down into product lines, markets, and/or subsidiary operations, and operating and cash flow projections can be generated.

Formulating a Plan

The procedures and techniques used within an organization to generate and maintain a long-term planning capability are far from precise. Discussed here are the more important approaches found through experience to optimize the success of a long-term planning effort.

TOP MANAGEMENT INVOLVEMENT

The planning activities in any organization must have the full support and involvement of its chief executive officer, for in essence he is the chief planner. There is a tendency among managers to subordinate planning considerations to day-to-day responsibilities; but the higher the manager, the less he can afford to do so. Top management must give priority to planning and insist that it be given attention by all members of middle management throughout the organization.

PARTICIPATIVE APPROACH

An organization obtains the necessary attention of its managers to the planning activity by earnestly seeking the ideas and opinions of all members of management, thus establishing a positive tone and enabling the periodic solicitation and generation of planning ideas. This is often referred to as the participative approach. It recognizes the unique view each manager has of an organization by virtue of his particular position and involvement and sets a premium on his ideas as meaningful inputs to planning.

CORPORATE STRATEGIES

Statements of corporate strategy amplify basic objectives and are a necessary prerequisite for long-term planning. To be sure, corporate strategies must be subject to intensive review and change, but at any given time they should be well articulated and accepted by the organization at large. If a business is undertaking long-term planning for the first time, it becomes top management's responsibility to evolve corporate strategy in a number of different areas. Among these areas might be finance, marketing, R&D, manufacturing, management development, and corporate development.

There can be a number of other areas, depending on the nature of the business. The formulation of these strategies, while remaining a top management responsibility, should be openly discussed and reviewed with members of middle management.

MODEL BUILDING

With the inputs previously described and the statements and/or revisions of basic corporate objectives and strategies in hand, various projections (models) can be constructed. Preliminary financial operating and cash flow projections can now be further refined through the utilization and study of the resource analyses and planning issues. Models can be prepared to reflect projected manpower requirements and marketing, manufacturing, and product development activities. In each of these areas several models can be generated, reflecting alternate courses of action possible through consideration of the planning issues.

APPRAISAL OF ALTERNATIVES

After a number of alternatives have been generated, it becomes necessary to undertake the selective process leading to an integrated overall plan. There is no easy, pat approach to this procedure. The preparation of rough five-year forecasts to reflect alternatives in the following manner has been found useful: (1) the momentum line forecast, a projection of future operations based on historic trends and current operations; (2) the corporate objective or development line forecast, based on the utilization of planning issues that represent future opportunities in keeping with present organization objectives, strategies, and capabilities; (3) the corporate potential line forecast, a projection resulting from reponse to all opportunities as identified in the submitted planning issues.

A comparison of these forecasts will serve to identify gaps and will give members of top and middle management a better picture of alternatives. Through open, round-table discussions both "on and off campus," an overall plan can be generated within the parameters of available resources.

FORM OF PLAN

The final plan can take physical form in a number of ways. In a sense the actual publication of a plan can be anticlimactic in that it never represents the ideal or is completely acceptable to all members of the organization. It should be recognized that a rough, incomplete plan, as long as it has been prepared with care and general participation, is better than no plan at all. At the very least the following should find expression in a long-term corporate plan: corporate objectives; corporate strategies; major programs (corporate development, administration, marketing, R&D, and manufacturing); manpower forecasts; and finance (operating, cash flow, and capital expenditure projections).

It will be noted that no specific period for a long-term plan has been mentioned. Again, this becomes an individual determination, but certainly a long-term plan should cover three years' operations at a minimum. The longer the projection, the more it will be based on trends rather than a programmed response to known data and variables. As long-term planning capabilities are developed, the inclusion of programs covering short- and long-term operations in segments of the business may be highly desirable.

Implementation of Plan

The implementation of a plan is directly dependent upon the skill and effectiveness of an organization's management group. If the enterprise has operated previously without a long-term plan, the effectiveness of management will be obviously enhanced when such a plan has been developed.

BOARD APPROVAL

Because a long-term plan will call for the commitment of corporate resources, it must have the approval of the board of directors. Presumably, the board will have approved the basic objectives of the corporation. With this as a starting point and with well-prepared, reasonable financial forecasts, board approval should not be difficult to obtain. In the final analysis the chief executive officer plays the vital role. As he is the chief planner and thus a primary architect of the plan, approval is tantamount to a vote of confidence, although the board may suggest modifications for consideration.

ORGANIZATIONAL ACCEPTANCE

Since all segments of the organization should have participated in the preparation of the plan, their acceptance of it should be assured. Not all individuals will regard it with complete satisfaction, but on balance it should be acceptable. The plan should be published and, as far as possible, should be put in the hands of all managers with a view to their particular areas of responsibility. Management should make an intensive effort to encourage response, discussion, and challenges to the plan. This represents the start of the recycling process and the regeneration of planning issues. Greater acceptance for long-term corporate planning activity will be developed through this type of approach.

REVIEWING AND RECYCLING THE PLAN

Ideally, sound long-term planning will sharpen an organization's ability to evolve more precise short-term operational plans. These in turn should be subject to periodic (monthly or quarterly) review against stated operating objectives and budgetary targets. Planning issues, tied in with budgeting and operational planning procedures, should be solicited annually from the organization at large. At that time the review of basic corporate objectives and strategies and the preparation of new input data should take place. In this manner the long-term plan is recycled annually in conjunction with operational planning. Long-term planning is a never ending and challenging task.—*P. A. Benoliel*

SHORT-TERM PLANNING

Today's business decisions are made upon future expectations. Depending upon how far these decisions can be dependably projected into the future, they are referred to as long-range, intermediate, or short-range plans. The length of time covered in future projections depends upon the nature of the business, the rapidity of technological change, the defined business expectations, and the motivations and abilities of those responsible for making today's decisions about the future.

In every long-range plan, regardless of projected length, there is a short-range plan. It is the plan of immediate action as of a predetermined time—the today, followed by the tomorrow, the remainder of the month, and the 11 months following. It is the year of action, of fulfillment, and the final test of executive vision, courage, and business activity. It is the final year of every long-range plan, the culmination and the realization of all the business decisions which will have exerted an influence upon the final anticipated outcome of calculated risk taking.

The Annual Profit Plan

Happily, the year is also the beginning of each long-range plan—growth in action—and as such represents a period of temporary coalescence in the decision continuum of time. From this evolves a precise blueprint of the plans and policies that define how management is to achieve the growth objectives and profit goals it has previously set for itself. This definitive blueprint is commonly referred to as the short-term or annual profit plan. It is developed in considerable detail and articulated in quantitative terms. It is the budgeted operations program to which each manager will adhere as closely as possible while still leaving room to meet unforeseen contingencies quickly and effectively, thus providing for change. However, significant differences between budget and results must still be justified.

It follows, then, that with each formulation of a long-range plan there is an accompanying short-range plan representing the bridge to the future. Both plans must be thoroughly evaluated, together and separately, lest the imminence of the short-term plan eclipse the importance of decisions affecting longer-range plans or goals.

BASIC ASSUMPTIONS AND GROUND RULES

It should also follow that each plan is predicated upon very similar assumptions. Plans (1) are realistic, attainable, and conducive to the highest levels of efficiency; (2) make clear distinctions between the general and the specific and are based upon relevant internal and external factors, with emphasis upon their applicability to the short- or to the longer-range plan; (3) offer alternate decision choices formulated in precise detail, each describing its own plans and goals; (4) are formalistic, clearly understood, conducive to easy control, and are expressed in financial or quantitative terms; and (5) identify individuals who are responsible for their implementation and are time-phased, indicating when and how they are to be administered.

The short-term plan, then, is an operative plan defining goals in writing and clearly indicating how these goals are to be carried out, thus representing the control function. For control to be effective, the short-term plan must be translated into dollars, units of production, and other measurements of precision. These measurements are the necessary actions taken to assure that all the agreed-upon objectives are being achieved. They include evaluating managerial performance, comparing actual performance against decisions made against standards, goals, objectives, policies, and other limitations. Deviations are analyzed, and appropriate actions are taken to authorize or correct them. Continuing surveillance on actions taken with respect to deviations frequently provides valuable refinements in future planning.

Where the short-range operating plan provides the written goals and objectives along with the means by which they shall be achieved, the annual profit plan, expressed quantitatively and in commonly understood units (dollars, production, and hours), becomes the basis for the budget for the period defined by the short-range plan, which is normally one year.

Budgeting

Budgeting is that part of the managerial function which concerns planning and control. Budgeting further facilitates the control of the short-range plan in that it involves all members of management, compelling them to participate in setting functional objectives and to contribute to higher-level objectives—profits, growth, and resources development. Budget discipline facilitates the measurement of performance compared with these goals and objectives by the use of verifiable facts and figures on a periodic basis. Budgeting, or profit planning, in addition to performing the primary short-range control, provides high utility in the following aspects: (1) providing a basis for reassessing the basic validity of existing organization relationships, goals, objectives, and even product or service lines; (2) requiring lengthy lead time in preplanning, enhancing cooperation, effectiveness, and synergism; (3) orienting management to a profits-and-results awareness in its decision-making experiences; (4) enhancing awareness of detail and thoroughness in follow-up, and bringing about heightened respect for historical records and their use in the planning process; (5) managing by objectives—to check progress in achieving objectives, coordinate teamwork of subordinates more effectively, identify areas where hard savings can be realized or where inefficiencies exist, facilitate the measurement of subordinate performance, and bring about a more realistic subordinate-supervisory ratio; (6) making the most economical use of manpower along with the other factors of production; (7) clearly defining organizational relationships and identifying relationships of authority and responsibility; (8) analyzing external influences in the business, social, and political areas as they affect the company; and (9) studying marketplace considerations and influences which ordinarily would affect only marketing-oriented managers.

Annual profit planning therefore represents a disciplined managerial control function through the use of budgeting systems. Before examining the different types of budgets, it is necessary to point out some of the limitations of budget utilization.

Budgets do not take the place of good business judgment. They represent commitments based upon the best honest evaluation possible and formulated with the sincere intent to live up to them.

Sales budgets, the basis of annual profit planning, must be steadfastly realistic in their estimates. Unsound reasoning or misinterpretation here will cause losses and waste all down the line. Equally important is the setting of realistic and attainable objectives and standards. Budgets cannot be made too tight; they must provide for change. Standards must be justified. Because the annual profit plan represents "plans in action" and because the budgets represent the control instrumentation, frequent readings must be made on them and deviations from standards must be constantly followed up. Corrective actions must be taken to adjust back to standard, and records must be made to avoid similar deviations in future budgetary planning.

Formulating a budget is one thing; obtaining top management approval is another. Each manager responsible for budget formulation is in effect competing with every other manager for a limited amount of existing company resources (dollars, facilities, and man-hours). It is the prudent manager who works closely with the budget director and who can clearly justify his requirements up to that fine line beyond which credibility breaks down and irrationality provokes a turndown from the chief executive.

A Comprehensive Budget Program

The annual profit plan is but one component of a comprehensive budget program. The other components consist of the long-range plan extending a set number of years into the future; the variable expense budget, which provides cost formulas for budgeting manufacturing, distribution, and administrative expenses; supplementary statistics, which provide break-even analysis by department and product and for the overall operations; and budget reports for management, which show comparisons of actual to budgeted costs, revenue, assets, liabilities, and equities indicating profit-expectation achievement. The program also includes analysis of deviations from budget to determine causes and recommend corrective actions that must be taken.

Upon returning to the annual profit plan and breaking it down into its constituent parts, two main divisions are immediately apparent: the operating budget and the financial budget.

OPERATING BUDGET

The operating budget consists of two subsections relating to revenues and expenses. The first subsection is the budget income statement, which is composed of a master income statement, an income statement by responsibilities, and one by products. The second subsection refers to an income statement supporting schedules. In this subsection is found the heart of profit planning and control: the sales budget, by geographic region, time periods, and product; the production budget, consisting of production quotas and inventory schedules; a materials budget for production; a procurement budget showing how the materials are to be most economically purchased; a direct labor budget; and a manufacturing overhead expense budget covering service and production departments.

Sales budget. The sales budget is the first step in the formulation of the annual profit plan. It will show projected sales by month, by product line, and by geographic areas. For companies doing government work, details of sales and profit may be broken down by contracts. It is also possible to show sales projections to the end of the year as "firm" business (signed orders), as "likely" (the details of the bid have still to be formalized), or as "potential" (the company plans to bid for the business along with competitors). This budget is initiated by regional sales managers and unified by the vice president of sales, who is responsible for the overall sales budget.

Production budget. The production budget logically follows from a soundly reasoned sales budget; it indicates how many of the products by unit will be manufactured to meet customer requirements as shown in the sales budget. The production budget also determines the amount of the product and parts that should be held in inventory. This budget is initially put together by the manufacturing division managers. They are responsible for the direct materials budget, which indicates the amount of the different types of raw material that go into the product required in the production budget. The vice president of manufacturing consolidates these budgets and is responsible for obtaining approval for them.

Procurement budget. The procurement budget, which includes the inputs from the direct materials budget, can now be made up. The purchases budget responsibility includes the proper economies and timing of purchases to be budgeted in accordance with inventory policy and the estimating of the planned unit purchase price for each type of raw material.

Direct labor budget. The direct labor budget is also the responsibility of the manufacturing division managers; it is predicated upon the planned production as shown in the production budget. Direct labor data are expressed in standard labor hours and anticipated average wage rates. The budget format is normally set up by product line and department responsibility. Essentially, this budget provides management with expected direct labor cost.

Manufacturing overhead expense budget. The manufacturing overhead expense budget is based upon the production budget and the building services allocation, which includes the expenses of factory and home office buildings, maintenance, and repairs. The manufacturing overhead expense budget also includes such expense items as supervisors' salaries, indirect labor, utilities, supplies, depreciation, insurance, taxes, and wages. The responsibility for the initial formulation of this budget is that of the manufacturing division managers and covers not only the factory divisions as production centers but also the activities that perform product and customer service functions.

Inventory budget and budgeted cost of goods sold. At this point fairly accurate determinations can be made concerning inventory budgets and the budgeted cost of goods sold. The inventory budget is based upon the cost of purchases, direct labor and material, and overhead expenses. From these data can be determined the budgeted value of final inventories for raw materials, work in process, and finished products. The budgeted cost of goods sold can now be determined from the preceding budgets and is calculated by the budget director who consolidated the supporting budgets.

Administrative expense, distribution, and appropriation budgets. The three remaining subbudgets that complete the operating budget are the administrative expense budget, which covers each administrative department, personnel, and manpower; the distribution expense budget; and the appropriations budget covering advertising, research, and so forth. These budgets are prepared by the appropriate operating heads and are their responsibility.

The operating budget thus provides the basis for the compilation of the financial budget, which will complete the annual profit plan.

FINANCIAL BUDGET

The financial budget consists of a budgeted balance sheet showing how the operations plan will affect the company's basic resources and liabilities. It also includes the budget-sheet supporting schedules showing cash flow, receivables, inventory, capital expenditures, and depreciation. Each of these is set up in budget format.

SETTING AND INSTALLING BUDGETS

The setting of budgets is often a continued problem, especially in companies that have widely scattered operating divisions and in newly formed conglomerates. The reason seems to be that distance begets autonomy, autonomy engenders individualism, and individualism often results in "maverick" resistance to central control methods and procedures. For the budget director the setting of budgets is, first, largely a matter of education and then a matter of initial application—usually, to capital expenditures, factory overhead expense, or sales budgeting. With full and continued backing of the company president, a budget director will need about three years for the budget experience to become routine in an organization that has been unaccustomed to budgetary discipline. Budgeting systems can rarely be superimposed on one organization from another in a wholesale manner. Annual profit planning must be tailored to the new conditions existing in the new organization, meeting the needs of the operations and projected at the level of sophistication of the operating executives. Even in companies where the principles and practices of budgeting are understood, a wise budget controller will approach each new budgeting period or each budgeting revision session as if the whole management team had to be re-educated in the intricacies of rational budgeting.

BUDGET REVISION

Budget revisions vary in magnitude and organizational scope. Revision that is drastic (and costly to accomplish) can result from strikes, fires, storms, breakdowns in production equipment, and abrupt downturns in the economy. Relatively minor changes can be made necessary by misinterpretation of conditions in the marketplace. Quarterly budget reviews are the custom in most companies; at the time of the review adjustments can be made to realign planning with objectives. Monthly budget reviews give each operating head an opportunity to spot trends that, if not corrected, could lead to costly deviations from budget. If the deviations are beyond reasonable explanation, budget revision will probably be required. In any case, budgets should not be regarded as inflexible but, rather, as plans that can be adjusted within reason and when circumstances warrant.

REVIEWING AND ANALYSIS

Review and analysis procedures take different forms, but each represents a significant aspect of control. In the broad sense these are monthly and quarterly comparisons of actual results with budgeted goals and objectives. More specifically, monthly performance reports can be developed to show variations between actual performance and the budget; significant variations should be studied with emphasis on determining the underlying causes rather than giving woeful concern to the results.

CORRECTIVE ACTION

Corrective action, if required, depends largely upon the underlying causes. If the variation (favorable or unfavorable) is slight, a conference with the responsible manager may be all that is needed. Clerical errors could fall in this category. However, a significant variation many times leads back to a management decision that in turn could be traceable to a misunderstanding or to a deliberate decision to deviate from policy or from the annual profit plan. This could well result in an on-the-spot investigation or a special audit and could lead to the removal of the manager from his position. On the other hand, serious variations could result from uncontrollable factors as in the case of strikes, fires, and storms. Often, the underlying causes are not immediately apparent and will require variance analysis in one or more functional areas. Variance analysis has a wide application in financial reporting and is chiefly found in the following: methods studies of variations between performance in a given period and performance in a prior base period; studies of variations between performance and base standard costs; and studies of variations between performance and budgeted goals which are considered as a base of comparison. Variance analysis can therefore be utilized in most budget situations. The essential purpose of this corrective measure and close budget reviews returns the manager to his original starting point in short-term planning: It is primarily to correct his course of action in the achieving of set goals and objectives.

OBJECTIVES AND LONG-TERM PLANS

Budgets and objectives are linked in a relationship of management planning to achieve defined end objectives and control the act of achievement in an orderly, systematic, and cost-effective manner. The relationship of budgets to long-term plans and forecasts assures that today's decisions on events three, five, or ten years in the future will have a higher probability of occurring in accordance with the original decisions. This approach leads the manager to a position from which he is able to make more of the right "risk" decisions than he could make without the discipline of budgeting in his annual profit-planning approach to short-term plans.—*D. K. Rowe*

CONTROLS

One of the most difficult functions of modern management is the proper control of many fast-action situations occurring simultaneously. The manager often finds himself "greasing a squeaking wheel" rather than determining which wheels will be squeaking in the future and performing preventive maintenance before the wheel begins to squeak. In the rush to get a project under way or accelerate a lagging project, he tends to forget his training and proceeds by instinct although fully realizing that he has neglected to provide the proper control mechanism to give him early warning that a problem exists and help him diagnose the problem.

Some managers instinctively provide for a control mechanism in all their planning. Others work hard at providing proper controls. Still others neglect them completely and find themselves continually "fighting brush fires" and dealing with critical situations, never quite understanding how this could happen to them.

Unfortunately, there is no pat answer to development of controls, since controls must be tailored to each particular task. Numerous traditional controls have grown up as integral parts of accounting systems, payroll systems, inventory systems, and sales reporting systems which have developed over a period of time. Continued changes in management techniques and ways of doing business have created control problems that have not all been effectively solved. Quite often a manager will depend upon a traditional control that is not sensitive enough to be of help in the particular situation in which he finds himself; thus even traditional controls must be continually scrutinized to make certain they are sensitive enough to meet the control requirements of a particular activity.

Some managers have taken the position that when they know the qualities of the people they manage and properly utilize the strengths of these people, they do not have to concern themselves with control. The assumption that a human being will always react the same way in a given situation is dangerous; time has shown that this is not the case. The use of proper controls at measured milestones in any project checks on the total progress of the project and tends to permit evaluation of the project itself rather than the performance of individuals.

Definition

Controls can be developed in varying degrees of sophistication depending upon the activity for which they are designed. Basically, a control consists of a comparison between an actual situation and a planned situation.

Modern management techniques require three elements in any management activity: (1) a plan that states the goal; (2) a method of achieving the goal—an implementation procedure that has checkpoints from beginning to end; and (3) a series of comparisons to be performed at each of the checkpoints. These comparisons are made by comparing measured quantities of time, money, and manpower in the actual situation with the estimated quantities in the plan. Any deviation from the plan in either direction indicates a potential problem: It is possible that the planning was not correctly done, and the likelihood of achieving the desired goals becomes questionable. In the event that the plan is found to be sound, the implementation procedure is incorrect. In either case remedial action must be taken immediately to increase the likelihood of success of the project. No matter how complicated the control system, the basic element is a simple comparison of planned versus actual for the measurable quantities of the project.

Purpose of Controls

The obvious purpose of control is to insure ultimate success of an activity. Properly planned controls not only permit the early discovery of problems or deviations from the plan; they also provide sufficient information to permit analysis of the extent and cause of the deviation from the plan. Properly designed controls provide indicators sufficient to permit the manager to quickly assess corrective measures to be taken and to assess the reduced probability of success of the total project if corrective measures are unavailable. For example, if an activity were planned to be accomplished by four men in one year, controls would be provided to permit a monthly assessment of the progress to date. In the event of deviation from the plan, there should be sufficient information in the designed controls to permit the projection of additional manpower required or provide an alternate completion date when such manpower is not available. The manager must be in a position to determine the net effect of the situation at hand.

Design of Controls

There are no hard and fast rules for the proper design of controls in a given situation. The controls necessary to monitor an activity properly will depend upon the complexity of the activity and the experience and capacity of the persons planning, managing, and controlling the activity.

In some activities where progress is very rapid and is highly related to the mechanical and mental dexterity of the persons performing the activity, measurements must be taken hour by hour and immediately compared with the plan. In other activities where the pace is more leisurely, measurements can be taken daily, weekly, or even monthly. In still other activities measurements will be made at various preset milestones, thus permitting assessment of a project phase by phase as it moves to completion.

Because control is a tool of management, its application will vary from manager to manager, and in fact it will usually be designed to point to the manager's known management weakness. For example, if the manager is known to be lax in cost control, a great number of the controls of the plan will be oriented to measure project cost. If the manager is noted for bringing in projects late, the designed controls will be heavily time-oriented. It is a wise manager who has the ability and insight to know his weaknesses and provide in his planning for proper measurement of the factors most likely to create problems.

Kinds of Control

One of the most common controls in all areas of business is the budget. Comparison of performance with budget extends from the lowest element of management to the top level. While the president of a corporation looks at his corporate budget, the department manager looks at his departmental budget—each seeking to control and each dependent upon the other. The department manager is dependent upon the proper budgeting of resources between departments, and the president is dependent upon the proper utilization of those resources by the user departments. The operating budget is probably the most widely used control mechanism in business today. The same techniques used in dollar budgeting can be carried into the other resources which a manager has at hand and can serve as a pattern for all control. Departmental operating budgets permit each manager to assess his operation in light of projected operating conditions. Proper study of the information contained in a departmental operating budget permits the manager to make adjustments to assure compliance with the budget.

A condensed comparative profit-and-loss statement gives management a quick look at the health of a business. A comparison of profits with projected profits gives an overall picture of the corporate activities for the covered period. Cash flow analysis permits the comptroller to monitor the cash flow of his corporation and the president to assess the actual versus the planned situation. A monthly report of orders received permits the sales manager to compare results with the sales plan and make adjustments as necessary to assure achievement of the plan. A monthly report of shipments, together with reports showing unfilled orders and inventory turnover, provides for continued assessment of product availability and flow and permits changes to be made in production schedules if unexpected trends begin to develop.

Recent years have seen the emergence of a series of controls, some of which are highly complex and mathematical in nature, which permit the continued monitoring of progress in new product development. As an activity increases in technological complexity, so must the control system increase in complexity in order to properly compare actual progress with planned progress.

From time to time, standard control procedures indicate new problem areas. When this occurs, it is often necessary to design and implement a series of special controls in order to pinpoint the problem area. Once the problem area has been defined and corrected, special controls may be eliminated or integrated into the standard control procedure for the activity.

It should be kept in mind that any project, no matter how small, must have some kind of control mechanism designed to assure its success. An uncontrolled project is a dangerous thing because it may require the full attention of a manager when his attention should be directed to other areas.

Responsibility for Controls

It is the responsibility of each manager to establish and maintain the controls required to assure successful completion of the tasks within his scope of responsibility. In large or highly complex activities it is often necessary to assign to other individuals the continuous monitoring and comparison of the actual progress of the task with its planned progress. However, the work of these individuals does not relieve the assigned manager of his controls responsibility; it simply assists him in performing this aspect of his total responsibility.

The mere presence of controls does not assure the ultimate success of an activity, just as the presence of a fire extinguisher does not assure the prevention of a fire. One of the manager's major responsibilities is that of continual monitoring of the various control parameters designed into the activity he is managing. Although he may delegate the day-to-day comparisons to assistants, the ultimate responsibility for success of the project rests squarely on the shoulders of the manager of that project.

Controls and Management by Exception

The continued development and expanded use of the technique of management by exception has brought an ever increasing need for effective, efficient use of control. The manager who has designed and effectively utilized controls can devote his efforts to solving the problems detected by the control system; he will not spend his time and talents in searching for and worrying about problems that do not exist. The concentration of a manager's ability in known problem areas permits true management by exception. The concept of management by exception is based on the assumption that measurements are available to detect exceptions and bring them to the notice of management. Without a proper control system, management by exception cannot possibly function.

—*R. L. Smith, Jr.*

ORGANIZATION DEVELOPMENT

Organization development (OD) is the use of group dynamics and related social psychology techniques to assist an organization in examining its technical systems and social relationships problems so as to develop better solutions. In business organizations the goals of planned change and OD are to assist in profit and performance improvement leading to planned growth.

This approach differs from operations research (OR) and from the traditional approach of outside management consultants. Whereas OR is performed by a team of specialists using mathematical techniques to arrive at "optimal" solutions, OD is a facilitating technique. It is designed to assist members of the organization in diagnosing their own problems and developing their own solutions.

In the early days of OD, the practitioner sometimes referred to himself as a change agent. An aura of mystique surrounded his use of interpersonal and intergroup dynamics skills. Now that professional management courses in group dynamics, conflict resolution, planned change, and OD are offered by graduate schools of business and management associations, this mystique has fortunately disappeared.

The OD specialist assists management through improving two-way, problem-solving communication; uncovering interpersonal blocks to organizational effectiveness; and guiding, supporting, and encouraging organization members as they work through the process.

The Nature of OD

During the past century the United States has moved rapidly from a rural agricultural economy into a complex urban technology whose business organizations are characterized by tremendous size, diversity, and complexity.

CHANGES IN EXTERNAL ENVIRONMENT

Some of the major environmental changes in which modern business organizations must operate involve the following:

1. *Science and technology.* New breakthroughs in man's fundamental knowledge of the universe have resulted in the evolution of a sophisticated machine technology.

2. *Cybernation.* The joining of cybernetic feedback systems, including computers, with automation has produced highly automated manufacturing and distribution systems.

3. *Human rights.* Moving from an economy of scarcity into an economy of abundance has produced vast changes in political and social values, beliefs, and expectations regarding the human condition.

CHANGES IN BUSINESS ORGANIZATIONS

The years from 1870 to 1930 saw the evolution of large organizations in the steel, mining, petroleum, and automotive industries. Vertical integration changed small manufacturing, processing, or selling companies into great corporations equipped with complete raw material, manufacturing, and selling capabilities.

Henry Ford I's development of automotive assembly-line techniques and Alfred Sloan's refinements of Du Pont's administrative, organization, and control systems at General Motors were key steps in the evolution of the modern manufacturing corporation.

The depression years brought further changes in business organizations. The Federal Government extended its economic controls. Large, industrywide labor unions sprang up in the steel, automotive, coal, and petroleum processing and electrical manufacturing industries. Both big government and big unions challenged the power of business organizations to install major changes unilaterally.

America went from depressionary deflation into World War II inflation and all-out production. Winning the war required major changes in business operating methods. The same period saw the rapid acceleration of scientific and technological discovery and invention.

The growth of the conglomerate organizational structure in business, with diversified products and services operated by one corporate head, is a recent development.

NEED FOR ORGANIZATIONAL CHANGE

As business became larger and more complex, changes in either its technical or its social systems (relationships, status, and rewards) had to be carefully planned and coordinated.

Technical and social system changes before 1939 were usually made by engineering and technical specialists who used the scientific management concepts developed by Frederick W. Taylor and his associates.

Resistance to change. As long as change was introduced so slowly as not to threaten either job security or ingrained work habits and was accompanied by pay increases, employees tended to see it as helpful. During the depression era, however, the control powers of the Federal Government and of large industrial labor unions limited the right of business management to introduce unilateral change. In addition, middle and lower levels of management, as well as employees, began to resist some changes. Resistance usually took the form of minimal cooperation and commitment to make the new systems or methods work profitably.

BEHAVIORAL SCIENCES CONTRIBUTIONS

Behavioral scientists have actively contributed to organizational behavior and management theory in recent years. Kurt Lewin, a German refugee social psychologist, taught at a number of American universities. In this country he continued his earlier small-group dynamics research, generally working in classroom situations.

In 1939 Alfred Marrow, a social psychologist and president of Harwood Manufacturing Company, asked Lewin and his associates to conduct a series of small group studies in the Harwood plants. These studies indicated that employees accepted planned changes best when they had a consultative and participative voice in determining some aspects of the way the changes were to be installed. Significant improvements in acceptance of change and in productivity were associated with participative change installation (Marrow, *Making Management Human,* McGraw-Hill Book Company, 1957).

After Lewin's death some of his former associates established the University of Michigan's Institute for Social Research. This organization has conducted a number of studies, over the years, which analyze the effectiveness of various planned change and OD techniques. In general these findings also indicate that consultative and participative management techniques (which are used in OD) produce both better employee understanding and more profitable company operation after change has been installed (Rensis Likert, *The Human Organization,* McGraw-Hill Book Company, 1967).

W. Lloyd Warner and Burleigh Gardiner of the University of Chicago, as well as Reinhard Bendix, Robert Dubin, and Leonard Sayles, were among the prominent anthropologists and sociologists who contributed to modern understanding of group and organizational change processes from the behavioral sciences standpoint.

Sensitivity training. In 1947 the National Training Laboratories (NTL) conducted its first sensitivity training workshop. These programs give theoretical understanding and skill practice in self-awareness, interpersonal interaction, and group dynamics. Many of Kurt Lewin's former associates have been key leaders in these programs.

Robert Blake, Robert Lefton, Robert Morton, and Robert Pearse have each developed task-oriented and business-related variations of the original NTL unstructured "T-Group" learning workshops.

[Blake's managerial grid and corporate Darwinism concepts are described under "Principles of Management—2" (pages 1·20 and 1·22); the contributions of a number of other behavioral scientists are also discussed (page 1·19).]

Large-scale industrial OD programs. In 1957 a large petroleum corporation used a team composed of a staff behavioral scientist and a communications consulting organization to assist line management in installing a series of major changes related to cost reduction and profit improvement in three of the company's refineries. The primary OD technique used was the employee attitude survey and feedback, plus assistance to top management in handling the group dynamics problems that the changes produced. In two of the three refineries the behavioral sciences contribution seems to have been a significant one with respect to the final results.

Following the petroleum company's OD program, a number of studies reporting behavioral sciences applications in planned change and OD situations have been published. Until recently the criteria for evaluating the success of an application tended to be testimonial and subjective in nature, and short-range rather than long-range viewpoints were taken. However, one new study recently published links hard data (cost, productivity, and profit improvement figures) with specific technical and social systems changes in a manufacturing plant over a four-year period (Marrow, *Management by Participation,* Harper & Row, 1967).

Lyndall Urwick ("Have We Lost Our Way in the Jungle of Management Theory?" *Personnel,* May-June 1965) has criticized some behavioral scientists on the ground that they downgrade the contributions of other management specialists and for "what can only be described as a take-over bid by some representatives of the so-called 'behavioral sciences' to be the main, if not the sole, source of knowledge about managing. As a result, the semantics of the subject is in a great state of confusion."

CURRENT OD THEORIES

The Blake corporate Darwinism model (see page 1·22) has its critics, but it can be useful to businessmen who seek to improve the effectiveness of their organizations. Because it is described in economic rather than social psychological terms, it is more readily understandable than some of the other theories.

Richard Beckhard, another specialist in OD, defines it as "planned organizationwide effort managed from the top to increase organizational effectiveness and health through planned intervention in the organization's processes using behavioral science knowledge" (*Organization Development—Strategies and Models,* Addison-Wesley, 1969).

PURPOSES AND GOALS

In conceptualizing their purposes and goals, some OD theorists lean heavily on the group dynamics and social psychological terminology developed when the movement began. The reader should note that Blake's *entrepreneurial, mechanistic-bureaucratic, dynamic* organizational model framework overlaps the theoretical statements that follow.

When OD was a relatively esoteric art, the OD practitioner had to struggle through the planning and change process pretty much alone. Now that many managers have been exposed to sensitivity training, conflict resolution, and organizational change seminars, the steps in OD become practical management action sequences. Often, the OD specialist consults with trained line and staff managers in the company in setting up the change program.

Theoretically stated, the purposes and goals of OD are as follows:

1. *Changing managerial strategies.* In practice this usually means helping an organization move from an entrepreneurial or bureaucratic management style into the professionally managed dynamic style.

2. *Improving ways of working.* Older management styles produced power politics, competitive striving within the company, and bureaucratic fumbling. Improved communication and teamwork through planned change and OD increase profits and organizational efficiency.

3. *Changing the organizational climate or culture.* The OD program aims at reducing hostility, individual power plays, and internal friction. The dynamic climate challenges employees to contribute their best efforts to overall organizational goals.

4. *Adapting to the new environment.* Entrepreneurial and mechanistic-bureaucratic organizations do not adapt rapidly enough to new technical and social conditions. Slow response time is costly, sometimes even fatal.

5. *Changing the communication-influence pattern.* Swift two-way communication and delegated decision-making authority are "musts" today because the older methods can no longer do the job. As George Strauss and others have written, power equalization (the reduction of one-man domination and control) is one of the key features of the world today. Subordinates who have good ideas are encouraged to express them. Influence is no longer from the top down; *what is right* becomes more important than *who is right*.

STRATEGY AND TACTICS

OD theorists see an OD program as progressing through a series of definable steps or stages as follows:

Diagnosis. The OD practitioner (now often in conjunction with trained company managers) analyzes surface and underlying interpersonal and organizational problems. He frequently uses some form of employee survey and feedback program to do this.

Strategy planning. The important question is what steps should be taken initially to involve key members of the organization in analyzing their own problems so that the process generates enough internal support to keep the program going. It is vital that the OD specialist not be seen as manipulating the organization at this stage.

Education, orientation, and training. By his own behavior in interacting with members of the organization the OD specialist tries to set up a "role model" of objective problem solving, candid two-way communication, and positive solutions to problems of conflict and power. Increasingly, he gets help in the education and training steps by sending managers to training courses outside the company. However, when the situation warrants it, he may also do in-house training, either on his own or in conjunction with other OD practitioners.

Which units of the organization should be concentrated on during the early stages is another important OD strategic and tactical question. Choices here lie in focusing on (1) individuals, (2) subsystems, and (3) the total system. Individuals may be given counseling or may be sent to courses in sensitivity training, leadership skills, decision making, or even general management, depending on their needs. The term "subsystems" refers to a part (section, department, or other) of a total organization. The initial problem that the OD practitioner is called in to help on is often located in a part of the organization. A total system is a complete operating unit (plant, division, or company). The OD man tries to start where initial efforts offer the greatest chance of helping the organization ultimately to improve its effectiveness in operations and profitability.

EVALUATING OD PROGRAM RESULTS

Ideally, OD program results should be evaluated by a qualified independent research team uninvolved in the planned change program. Since this procedure is both costly and time-consuming, only two OD industrial organization studies have been published in which it was followed. Most evaluation reports are written by the OD practitioner himself and/or a member of management taking part in the change program. Unfortunately, short-range claims plus a degree of subjectivity and testimonial enthusiasm tend to crop up in this type of evaluation. In reading such reports, the professional manager has to distinguish between enthusiasm for the OD practitioner's honest effort and programs that actually help to reduce costs and improve organizational effectiveness and profit.

L. Greiner has published analyses of several planned change programs ("Patterns of Organizational Change," *Harvard Business Review*, May-June 1967). Though admitting a lack of hard data in defining measures of success, Greiner found the following crucial factors operating in those studies which seemed successful:

1. *Strong internal and external pressure.* The organization has been under strong internal and external pressure to change for some time.

2. *Entrance of new man.* A new man with a reputation for ability to introduce improvements comes in, either as the top executive or as a consultant working closely with the top man. This new man encourages top management to analyze its problems closely and brings in new ideas about ways to solve these problems.

3. *Top management interest.* Top management becomes intensely interested in problems and in finding solutions that can be put in on a planned change basis.

4. *A pilot run.* The new ideas are tried in a small portion of the organization before being installed on an organizationwide OD basis.

Personnel Management Techniques

The OD specialist functions as an internal or external consultant who uses behavioral sciences techniques to facilitate problem solving and planned change. The bulk of the actual work is done by members of the organization. Business organizations have developed a number of professional management techniques that expedite the OD process during the past 20 years. These techniques came from practical line and staff executives working in business and government rather than from the behavioral sciences.

Techniques such as long-range planning, management by results, goal setting, and more accurate measures of individual and organizational performance are now available. They are being increasingly taught to professional managers by university graduate schools of business and by professional management associations. Manpower planning and manager development are two of the most useful of these new techniques for implementing portions of an OD program.

MANPOWER PLANNING

Available manpower-planning techniques include (1) a skills inventory of management and technical skills currently possessed by individuals in the company; (2) evaluation of employee growth potential through testing and appraisal; (3) short- and long-range manpower requirement estimates tied in with the company long-range profit plan; and (4) implementation of these manpower-planning steps through developing a personnel staff capable of hiring, training, and assisting line management in promoting the right number of managers who possess the right skills available at the right time.

MANAGERIAL DEVELOPMENT

With the rapid increase of technical and administrative skills required to keep a complex organization operating and growing, managerial development can no longer be left to chance. The company must have a planned program aimed at upgrading, "retreading" (updating key employees in new technologies and administrative methods), and encouraging individual self-development. More than one organization has had to postpone growth because of lack of managers ready to direct new units.

Personnel techniques used in the manager development process include (1) developing job descriptions that spell out responsibilities, requirements, and key relationships in writing; (2) superior-subordinate joint goal setting, in which the two individuals jointly determine the employee's personal results goals that are tied in with overall company goals for a specific period of time; (3) setting performance standards with which to measure performance results; and (4) programming the subordinate's career development activities. These include self-development efforts (reading, lectures, and the like) plus on-the-job training assignments that turn the man's job into a career progression program. Needless to say, career-oriented job assignments must be meshed with the operating realities of the company. However, the operating realities cannot be allowed to interfere with the manager's career development to a point where the company lacks an adequate number of properly trained and experienced managers to meet its planned growth requirements.

Finally, a number of internal company training programs and public training and manager development programs are available to improve manager skills.

—*R. F. Pearse*

EVALUATING RESULTS

The evaluation of results is a continuing part of the management cycle. The process starts with planning; proceeds to organizing, operating, and controlling; and then provides a feedback of information by which the overall results may be analyzed and evaluated. The cycle is then repeated; the prior results become the basis for revised plans and objectives or the improvement or redirection of operating controls. The process of evaluation takes place at all levels of management, from the supervisory level of task-oriented operating detail to the top management level of policy making and strategic planning. Within the management hierarchy the evaluation of results is largely nonfinancial at the supervisory levels of operational control, dealing primarily with such measurements as units of production, productivity per worker, material efficiency, and so forth. As the level of managerial responsibility increases, however, the evaluation of results becomes more and more financially oriented, since finance itself is the common language of business. At the general management level the attention of management should be directed to the basic financial measurements of the company as a single business entity. It should not concern itself with the mass of operating detail for which responsibility has been delegated and from which the overall results have been determined.

Financial Evaluation

Successful business management is measured in terms of profitable operations rather than on the subordinate accomplishments of production efficiency, sales volume, or new product development. Profitable operations in turn are measured in a variety of ways, each of which recognizes the need to relate the dollars of profit earned to some supporting structure that is assumed to have provided the means of earning the profit dollars themselves.

EARNINGS ON SALES

One of the most commonly used financial measurements in the evaluation of results is the ratio of earnings to sales, usually expressed as a percentage of the net book earnings after taxes measured against the net dollar volume of sales recorded for the same fiscal period. The resulting percent-to-sales ratio is often compared to prior periods, as well as to current forecasts and budgets, and provides a useful measure of trends in the cost-volume-price relationship. It is, however, only a partial measurement of overall financial results, since it does not relate to the capital investment required to support the operating levels of sales and production volume on which the earnings are based. For this reason it falls short of providing any proper evaluation of the economic health or true earning power of the company and cannot be used as an overall measurement of results.

EARNINGS PER SHARE

A second measure—one that begins to move in the direction of relating earnings to investment—is the evaluation of financial results expressed in terms of the dollars and cents earned per share of common stock. This is accomplished by taking the net book earnings after taxes (less provision for dividends on the preferred stock, if any) and dividing by the average number of shares of common outstanding during the period. Widely used in annual reports and in statements issued for quarterly earnings, the earnings-per-share evaluation usually carries with it a comparison of similar earnings in prior periods and is essentially an evaluation from the investor's rather than from the managerial point of view.

Since the earnings-per-share evaluation does not relate to either the use of long-term debt or to the normal increase of the equity investment in the business resulting from earnings retained in the business, it fails to provide any indication or evaluation of the economic productivity of the total capital employed. In essence it offers simply a quantitative report of the increase (or decrease) in earnings as measured against the common shareholders' original equity investment. As such it does not answer the question of what the per-share earnings should have been to meet the profit requirement generated by the total amount of capital employed in the business. Since earnings-per-share reports can and frequently do have substantial impact on the short-term market price of the common stock, responsible management will find a need to provide both itself and its shareholders with an additional means of financial evaluation as a standard measure of operating efficiency.

RETURN ON EQUITY

In a third measurement of evaluation the net book earnings after taxes are expressed as a percent of the total equity investment or net worth of the company. This evaluation moves further in the direction of relating total earnings to total investment, since it is based on present rather than original equity investment by the shareholder. It thus takes into account the increase in retained earnings or reinvestment of earnings not paid out to the shareholder in the form of dividends. Return on equity will normally present a much more moderate picture of annual growth in earnings than that implied by the earnings-per-share report and possibly for this very reason is frequently given a secondary role in the evaluation and reporting of financial results. Of the two it more accurately reflects the effectiveness of management in earning an adequate rate of return on the funds employed than would the apparent results reported on a per-share basis. Since it fails to take into account the use of total capital invested in the business, however, it does not provide a complete evaluation of financial performance in companies that also employ long-term debt as a part of the capital structure.

RETURN ON ASSETS

A fourth method frequently used in evaluating the overall results of the business is that of expressing the net book figure of earnings after taxes as a percent of the total assets employed. This moves well beyond the evaluation of return on equity, since the total assets of the business are supplied by all the sources of capital, including debt. As such it provides a much more valid measurement of the effectiveness and capability of management, since the earnings are now related to the total investment required to support the business.

The one minor weakness remaining in an evaluation of financial results based on return on assets is the fact that such a measurement ignores the management of current debt, suggesting that all assets have a common cost and hence should yield a common rate of return. In a typical business a substantial portion of the total assets employed will be provided by trade creditors—assets represented by current debt in the form of accounts payable, accrued payroll, accrued taxes, and the like. The cost of this source of temporary capital is inherent in the cost of goods and services provided and does not represent risk capital on which an adequate rate of return must be earned for the investor. Good management of current debt will therefore take full advantage of the payment terms offered by creditors and employ as large a percentage of total assets from this source as possible. As this is done, the rate of return on total assets will tend to go down even though management has enhanced the true return on invested capital.

RETURN ON INVESTED CAPITAL

The one measurement that fully evaluates the earning power of a business from the managerial point of view is the rate of return on invested capital. This evaluation of financial results by top management recognizes that (*a*) all capital has a cost; (*b*) the total cost of total capital employed—regardless of its source—must be commensurate with the composite risk at which the capital is employed; and (*c*) to be truly profitable, a company must recover all of its costs, including the cost of capital.

This approach places a qualitative measure on the evaluation of earnings, a measure which can be expressed as the minimum rate of return required to fulfill management's obligation to the investor. Although the risk and hence the cost of capital will vary from industry to industry and from company to company within a given industry, a composite of the average industrial risk indicates a figure of 10 percent as the minimum after-tax earnings rate on total capital employed. This concept measures the total stream of earnings against the total amount of invested capital, including the long-term debt as well as the equity investment in the business. Since the book figure of net earnings after taxes has already been charged with the interest on long-term debt—and since total capital has a common risk and a common cost—the net interest cost must be added back to the reported book earnings to provide a measure of total earnings against total capital.

The rate of return on invested capital not only meets the requirement of a complete evaluation of financial results; it also provides management with a focal point from which subordinate evaluations may be developed.

RETURN ON INVESTMENT

The management and evaluation of return on invested capital in larger companies must ordinarily be implemented by the delegation of authority to individual profit centers within the corporate structure. To be effective, such delegation of authority must carry with it responsibility and accountability for the management of investment as well as for the management of profit. This is accomplished by translating the corporate objective for a net after-tax rate of return on total invested capital into the contributing pretax rate of return required from one particular segment of the business. Since capital itself in any business exists only at the corporate level or for the entire business as a single entity, the management of a portion of the capital at the profit-center level can be related to the management of specific assets under the control of the profit-center management. In like fashion the operating results at the profit center are typically measured in terms of profit contribution—a second partial measurement that merely contributes to the recovery of common overheads at the corporate level before net profit or net earnings after taxes can be ascertained.

The bringing together of these two subelements—pretax profit contribution measured against controllable assets—provides a measure known as return on investment (ROI). Although often used loosely to describe the return on assets or return on equity at the corporate level, it plays an important role when properly used as a subordinate evaluation and serves as a standard measure of performance for each subdivision of the business. Since the pretax rate of return at this level will usually appear substantially higher than might appear necessary to middle management, it becomes the task of top management to develop such objectives as a completely integrated part of the overall evaluation of return on invested capital for the company as a whole.

Nonfinancial Evaluation

Although the financial evaluation of results by management must be placed first, since the end objective of business is the profit goal itself, the financial evaluations can by no means stand alone as the sole criterion of success. There is a quality as well as a quantity in earnings, and supporting measurements are needed to indicate both the strength and the probable continuity of the reported profits. These supplementary measurements are essentially nonfinancial in nature but form a critical part of the overall evaluation of results.

SALES GROWTH

On the premise that it is impossible for a company to stand still in business (it is either growing or going backward), the rate of sales growth is one of the most fundamental measurements in support of the financial evaluations. With the constant growth in population and the corresponding annual rates of increase in the gross national product, the demand for goods and services presents a broad picture of ever expanding markets. Lack of sales growth—standing still—therefore represents a gradual decline in both the size and eventual earning power of the company. An apparently profitable rate of return on invested capital for the current period would not, for example, signal the downturn that might be expected in the future that would be clearly indicated by a lack of sales growth.

As in the primary financial evaluation of results, some standard of performance is required to measure satisfactory results in the marketplace. The most commonly accepted yardstick is the share of market or percentage of sales to the total industry served.

SHARE OF MARKET

Where a definable and measurable market for a company's product exists, the percentage of current sales to the total market can usually be evaluated both in terms of the physical volume of goods sold and in terms of the net dollar volume of sales. Long-range growth plans of a company are usually expressed in terms of increasing penetration or larger share of the market. As a minimum the dollar growth in annual sales volume must normally be sufficient to hold the market share as a constant. As an optimum the sales growth in an expanding market should be compounded by capturing a larger percentage of the total volume available.

As a nonfinancial evaluation the share of market measurement thus provides a sort of secondary support to both the rate of sales growth and the current financial rate of return, since it projects probable trends somewhat further into the future.

CUSTOMER RELATIONS

Evaluations of sales growth and share of market alone do not always suffice as reliable indicators of business strength in the marketplace. In the short term a substantial increase in both the dollar volume of sales and the level of market penetration might be made to the detriment of longer-term growth or stability. An additional evaluation is often needed to support the quality of the sales trend —a measurement of customer satisfaction or dissatisfaction with quality, prices, terms of sale, or services. This can best be measured in terms of canceled orders, customer returns, claims for adjustments, or possibly in the collection of receivables. All of these factors, taken in the aggregate, provide an evaluation of the marketing effort that in many ways is a more sensitive barometer of probable future results than the measure of recorded shipments or net book earnings themselves.

NEW PRODUCT DEVELOPMENT

Along with other measurements the future earning power of a company will also be indicated by the rate of new product development—or, conversely, by the rate of obsolescence of its existing products or product lines. A substantial gain, for example, in market share might simply indicate that a particular product was approaching the end of its life cycle and that competition had merely withdrawn in favor of a new or improved product. While this type of evaluation must be subjective to a certain extent, the rate of new product development is measurable and tends to lend further support to the longer-range assessment of future earning power.

CAPITAL INVESTMENT

Capital investment in this sense is the rate at which funds are being invested in capital expenditures for land, buildings, and equipment. Although financial in nature, it is not reflected directly in the current operating results and is thus essentially a subordinate type of evaluation that serves to measure both the quality of present earnings and the probability of improved earnings in the future.

As a rule of thumb most companies plan the annual budget for capital expenditures at a level at least equal to the total of depreciation charged against income for the period. Where this is true, it means that the company is at least replacing the book value of its investment in productive assets—presumably, with more modern equipment that will either serve to increase capacity or reduce operating costs, or do both. Failure to reinvest the total depreciation, on the other hand, may be viewed as a general indication of the eventual obsolescence of productive capacity with attendant rising costs for maintenance and repair, which would lead to a gradual erosion of profits.

EMPLOYEE RELATIONS

The evaluation of both the financial and nonfinancial aspects of the business must include an appraisal of employee attitudes throughout the organization. Management ability and experience, as well as the productivity and skills of the hourly worker, are substantial assets of the business—assets which are not valued or even listed on the balance sheet. Mismanagement of these assets will show up in records of absenteeism, turnover, wage demands or strikes, or in other similar factors reflecting employee attitudes. The evaluation of successful results in this area becomes the task of evaluating morale, a process both difficult and vital to an evaluation of management itself.—*C. W. Symonds*

Section 2

Administrative Services

CONTENTS

Scope and Organization

Systems Management

Management Science

Electronic Data Processing

Computer Time-Sharing and Utilities

Communications Networks

Archives and the Company Library

Office Services

Reproduction: Copying, Duplicating, and Printing

Business Aircraft Operations

Motorcar Fleet Operations

Real Estate Management

SCOPE AND ORGANIZATION

"Administrative services" is a relatively new name for a large and diversified group of staff services used by administrative management to support other activities of the business enterprise. Neither the group nor the label is as yet clearly defined, but better understanding will evolve as more organizations regroup, under administrative services, functions that are presently assigned elsewhere. It is almost certain that additional supportive functions will develop, some of which will be assigned to this group for administration; these will include, for example, organization planning and development and sensitivity training.

Already clearly within the functional area of administrative services are the familiar, well-established subfunctions formerly identified with office services, including mail and messenger services, office equipment and supplies procurement and maintenance, reproduction (copying-duplicating), stenographic and typing pool, and telecommunications. This group of services is usually managed by an executive with the title of office services manager or office manager, although other titles will be found in use today.

Current Developments

Following World War I and further accelerated by World War II, the use of other types of services has become much more general in all kinds of enterprises. These services include electronic (automated) data processing, systems and procedures (systems management), and forms control and records management. Those more common, earlier additions are currently being supplemented by such techniques as management information systems and services; management science applications for planning, decision making, and control; and work measurement and standards.

Still other staff service opportunities—and management challenges—are found within the developing area of administrative services, including the company library with automated information retrieval, the layout and planning of facilities, maintenance management, motorcar and aircraft fleet operations, printing (in-plant), project management, and real estate management.

The management of this expanding group of services, it is evident, must also be in a period of transition and growth. It is certain that to remain qualified as managers, presently qualified office services managers must anticipate changes by preparing for them. This requires preparation, not only to utilize new technologies effectively but also to manage a greater variety of functions. Managerial growth will depend greatly upon improved ability to plan, organize, and control the service activities for which responsibility is assigned.

Organization

The larger organizations or groups of functions that provide administrative services are increasingly being managed by executives who have one of the following titles: vice president of administrative services, director of administrative services, or manager of administrative services. The size and complexity of the total organization are major factors that affect the stature of the executive and his reporting relationships in the structure of management. A vice president will usually report to the operating head, the president, the executive vice president, or a senior vice president. A director or manager of administrative services will report, more often than not, to some functional vice president such as administration or finance. Groups of services within administrative services (for example, office services) are designated as departments or sections (in some cases, divisions) and usually are headed by managers.

Despite constantly shifting organization patterns in business, government, and other enterprises, it is predicted that administrative services will become a clearly defined group of distinct functions, all having the common characteristics of staff service. This is happening because of the pressures of size, complexity, and pace for better services and better management of them. This movement is being furthered by modern management's preparing in advance to meet the foreseeable needs of the future.

Information and Training Sources

Except for literature identified with the existing, discrete types of services in common use today, coverage of the whole broad field of administrative functions and services in one source is rare. Treatment of some of the subfunctions mentioned previously will be found in the journals and other publications of such associations as: the Administrative Management Society, Data Processing Management Association, Society for the Advancement of Management, Society for Management Information Systems, and the Association for Systems Management (formerly Systems and Procedures Association). The Administrative Management Society has established the AMS Professional Accreditation Program to promote growth and development among administrative managers.

In the electronic data processing (EDP) field there are many sources of information and training, including hardware, software, and applications journals, and diploma and degree courses of study, as well as training seminars. Consultants in this field are providing a great deal of training in EDP technology and management. Some few universities are establishing courses and, here and there, a curriculum in management information systems.

The intention in this section of the handbook is to inform management at all levels on the nature and scope of each subfunction. Despite the authoritative experiences from which each treatment is drawn, however, the reader is cautioned that much more could have been said on each topic. It will also be necessary to recognize that only generalized guidelines could be provided and consequently adaptation to each different situation will be required. It is believed and hoped, however, that the reader will find much that is immediately available and applicable to help him solve problems or plan for the future.

Staff Support

When properly planned, implemented, and managed, the staff services and support provided by administrative services will assist management at all levels to do its own job better. Staff support includes expert consulting help to utilize available and evolving management sciences; the development and application of tools and techniques for planning, operating, measuring, and reporting on line and staff operations; assistance in the development and application of essential procedures and disciplines throughout the organization; securing, recording, and processing raw data into useful management information for guidance in making more effective decisions; and competent operation of a variety of services commonly needed throughout the organization.—*W. M. Carrithers*

SYSTEMS MANAGEMENT

Understanding and applications of the systems concept have broadened substantially in recent years. Heretofore restricted mainly to technical areas, the concept has expanded into new fields, especially those related to business enterprises. Management has become a major user with considerable benefit.

The Systems Concept

The *Random House Dictionary of the English Language* (unabridged edition, New York, 1966) lists 16 definitions of the term "systems." They are distinct from each other but can be assembled in three meaningful groups.

The first group of definitions emphasizes the general meaning: assemblage or combination of different things such as parts, knowledge, or thoughts that form some sort of unitary whole. This is the meaning generally associated with the term in discussion of a communication system; the system of a particular knowledge such as philosophy; a system of government, of measurement, or of classification. In all these instances there are a number of individual items or parts with something in common that can be identified in what may be called a systematic manner and thus combined into a complex or system.

The second group of definitions connects systems with specific sciences or techniques, such as biology, chemistry, mathematics, or astronomy.

The third group relates systems to living creatures, including human beings.

Reference is either to a combination, such as human personality, or to human activities, including business organizations. They in turn characteristically consist of a number of subsidiary systems, among which the information system is of particular interest in the present context. This system is the basis of management and control systems. Of special importance also are managerial decision-making systems.

SIGNIFICANCE OF SYSTEMS CONCEPT

The modern systems concept emphasizes the comprehensiveness of complex activities and their impact on the organizations that manage them. The objective is to cover a specific situation or problem in its entirety from beginning to end. This is a novel approach in contrast to traditional processes. It happens often that only the initial parts of a problem are investigated and evaluated, while no attention is given to events at a later stage that can have a decisive effect on the problem as a whole and determine its eventual success or failure. If there had been an investigation of the whole problem initially, the decision made originally might have been different and of higher quality. Similar techniques are often used to get approval for a project when only the initial expense or investment is taken into account and no mention is made of outlays that will arise later. Another example of insufficient investigative effort is the consideration of only the cost of construction of an asset without the cost to operate and maintain it.

A means for dealing with complexities. Companies are growing in size for technological reasons and in order to make optimum use of resources through conglomerate companies. Moreover, management has to take into consideration more and more factors, especially in such areas as regulation by governmental agencies and attention to social responsibilities. Thus it becomes increasingly difficult to keep the major business goals in mind. The systems concept offers an approach to assist management in dealing with all these factors. The concept was tried originally in manufacturing for the defense and space industries when the efforts of many thousands of companies had to be coordinated to get the final products completed on schedule. New techniques, such as the Program Evaluation and Review Technique (PERT), were developed and proved very helpful. Their aim was to encompass the whole problem (effort) until the desired final result was secured.

Management purposes. The same concept is now being accepted for many management purposes. Two principles are the most important: first, to consider the problem as a whole from all angles and through to the final conclusion, whatever it may be; second, to make the total problem manageable by breaking it down into a number of subsidiary problems, each of them to be solved separately but in accordance with predetermined schedules to avoid delays and loss of time. Management should make use of this relatively new approach whenever opportunities arise.

ORGANIZATION BY SYSTEM

In our society, by necessity, the activities of all people are highly organized or systematized. We are forced continuously to operate within various systematic frameworks that are parts of the overall social system to which we belong. We cannot escape the pressures exercised upon us by those organized systems even if we would like to escape from time to time.

Each organization of people represents a separate system. It is a governmental system if it is the result of legislation or executive order; or, otherwise, it is a private, voluntary system. The latter may be profit-directed or not-for-profit oriented. The principles of the organizational system are similar, if not identical, in all cases with the exception of most governmental organizations.

Business system. A business system can be represented by a circle, with the order-giving management at the beginning of the cycle and the order-receiving operating parts of the organization at various points on the semicircle from top to bottom, as shown in Exhibit 2.1. The total cycle reflects the information and communication system, which is an integrated part or subsidiary system of the whole business system. Reports flow from the operating levels upward on the other semicircle to management as feedback information on what is happening (or has happened) at those levels. This permits management to arrive at further decisions based on evaluations of the information received on the actual performance compared with management plans and instructions.

Subsidiary systems. The business system can be looked at as a whole system with a number of subsidiary systems which are either functional systems (sales, operations, personnel, and so forth) or information and communication systems. Both types are essential for the survival of the business organization. The subsid-

Exhibit 2.1
BUSINESS SYSTEM

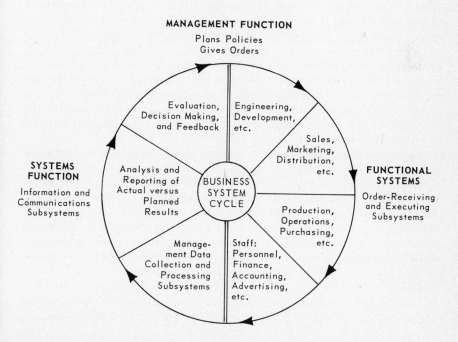

MANAGEMENT FUNCTION
Plans Policies
Gives Orders

SYSTEMS FUNCTION
Information and Communications Subsystems

Evaluation, Decision Making, and Feedback

Engineering, Development, etc.

Sales, Marketing, Distribution, etc.

Analysis and Reporting of Actual versus Planned Results

BUSINESS SYSTEM CYCLE

Production, Operations, Purchasing, etc.

FUNCTIONAL SYSTEMS
Order-Receiving and Executing Subsystems

Management Data Collection and Processing Subsystems

Staff: Personnel, Finance, Accounting, Advertising, etc.

iary system of particular interest in the present context is called the systems function (in the more restricted meaning of the term) and has responsibility for setting up and maintaining the communication and information systems that support and monitor the functional systems.

Organizing the Systems Function

The mission of the systems function in a business organization is to design, install, and maintain the information and communication processes essential for the effective operations of the business. In recent years it has become increasingly common to recognize these activities as a separate function on the organization chart.

SCOPE AND PLACEMENT

Earlier, it had been the practice to assign the systems function in a random manner to whoever was able to perform it at that particular time, usually to a representative of the accounting department or within the controller's organization. This arrangement is still widely found, especially in smaller organizations; yet it has many disadvantages and should be avoided as far as possible. It is recognized that in smaller companies a person may be assigned the systems function on a part-time basis if necessary, but he should be kept on that assignment for the sake of continuity and to accumulate experience.

Division of function. By tradition the information function has been divided into two groups, one in the operating department (operations) and the other usually associated with the accounting activities (staff). In the former the industrial engineers have charge of accumulating data, and they also interpret reports related to operations. The staff information activities, which are mainly concerned with documents and data received from others (especially operations) as well as the accounting department, are assigned to a separate group that is usually called the systems department. Today there is a strong trend toward the label "management information systems department." The traditional division of the information function is unfortunate, but it is strongly entrenched in most organizations and therefore it is difficult to change. Every effort should be made, as long as this arrangement exists, to encourage close liaison between the operations and the staff systems groups and further to support activities that may lead to eventual unification as the desired goal.

Systems function in the organization. Henceforth, this discussion will be limited to the concept and scope of the systems department within the boundaries previously indicated. There continue to be differing opinions on the proper location of the department in the company organization table. As stated earlier, there has been a historical relationship between the systems function and the accounting department, resulting from the fact that a large part of the data is processed by this department, which also prepares a large share of the most important reports for the rest of the organization. Now, however, significant changes are being brought about by the introduction of EDP systems in many companies. The work of the computer (EDP operations) department, including the important programming activities, is closely related to that of the systems function. Moreover, there is a growing tendency to separate the work of the computer from that of the accounting department where it often originated. This has led to the organization of an "independent" information department, combining the systems and computer activities, which logically reports to a member of top management such as the executive or administrative vice president. This information department may eventually include all company data processing activities, even those currently performed by industrial engineers.

Relationship to other functions. The situation of the systems function is typically that of a staff department operating at the corporate level on a companywide basis, sometimes with representation at the divisional level as well. This results in some of the usual problems of coordination with the operating and other staff functions, especially where the other functions, prior to the establishment of the corporate group, did their own systems work—often the case in the accounting department. The systems function, unavoidably, will overlap and to some extent interfere with the "exclusive jurisdiction" of other functions. Such other individual functions are mainly interested in their own problems and give little if any attention to those of the organization as a whole. The systems department, on the other hand, operates from a companywide viewpoint which will sometimes conflict with those of individual departments. The systems department will have to strive for a position that will be acceptable to all, even unrelated groups, at least to some extent. Arrangements need to be made to eliminate differences of opinion that cannot be settled by mutual agreement but require executive decisions to adjudicate. One type of difference that often requires executive decision concerns which problems shall be assigned to the systems function for first attention and in what sequence other projects shall be assigned to follow. A special, close relationship is required with the internal audit function which through its fieldwork determines whether the existing procedures are being properly carried out. Audit reports should alert the systems department to existing systems deficiencies or to lack of observance; these need to be investigated further and appropriately followed up for correction with the assistance of responsible management.

Staffing and Operating the Systems Function

Quality rather than quantity should be the watchword in dealing with all personnel problems of the systems function. The systems department should be just large enough to handle the work load for which it is responsible. All of its members should be of high caliber, and service in the department should be accepted as a special opportunity and distinction; therefore, the selection of the staff, and especially its head, should be made with great care. Recruitment should not be considered only a matter for the personnel department but should also be of concern to top management.

EDUCATIONAL BACKGROUND

The staffing problem continues to be particularly difficult as a result of the long-term, severe shortage of qualified people, as well as the inability of educational institutions thus far to develop enough well-trained people to fill these pressing needs. Very few of the collegiate schools of business make training in information systems a requirement of their curriculums in business administration; most of the graduates have only minimum (if any) knowledge of this important field, and thus the necessary training will have to be done on the job in the traditional apprenticeship way. A great deal of training is currently going on in the computer area. However, most of these graduates have received a very narrow kind of training with a bare minimum of systems information despite the close relationship of the two areas. Until recently, most systems positions have been filled by individuals with an accounting background. Unfortunately, most accountants lack the basic prerequisites, both in knowledge and attitudes, for satisfactory work in the field of information systems. Some efforts have been made to select people with a background in industrial engineering who are more familiar with the principles of systems analysis.

SELECTING THE MANAGER

The choice of a man to head the department will usually be the decisive step in determining the success of the function. The requirements are very broad and thus hard to satisfy. Under present circumstances, only rarely will a company have a man on its staff who can fill the position. Therefore, it will be necessary to go to the outside to find a suitable person, yet this will be exceedingly difficult because of the current shortage. Consulting firms and equipment manufacturers can be good sources of supply, as well as companies with a successful systems installation. In any event, substantial salary and benefits will have to be offered to the person who fills the requirements. These requirements are of two principal types. The first, and more obvious, is a knowledge of the field of information systems with its many specialties. No one can be expected to be an expert in all of these specialties, but the department head should have a reasonably good knowledge of them. The second requirement is in the area of human relations. It is absolutely essential that the person selected to be manager be able to get along well with people—the executives of the company, many of whom have considerable seniority and prestige, as well as his own staff that he will have to both direct and educate. At the same time he will need to give his staff a free hand as far as possible to handle their assignments. Also, the introduction of many types of new equipment which the systems expert has to be able to evaluate has made the manager's job even more difficult. Last, but certainly not least, it must be realized that the systems manager will be the adviser to top management in his field; and he will have an important part in many major decisions, including investments in expensive equipment with high potential obsolescence.

SELECTING THE STAFF

The department head should have a major hand in the selection of staff, and therefore staffing should be done after the manager has been appointed. To benefit from existing experience, every effort should be made to select people from the ranks of the company. Sometimes the new manager will bring in some of his experienced former associates or assistants who will form the backbone of the department. In this case it will be easier to take people from the company with no previous training or experience, since there will be more time to train them for doing the lower-level work, at least. Inexperienced outsiders would have to be trained from the very beginning, both in systems techniques and company background. Qualifications required by staff members are generally less broad than those of the manager but have additional depth in special areas such as computer programming and operations research.

PREROGATIVES OF THE MANAGER

In order to discharge his responsibilities properly, the department manager should have authority to decide on the detailed schedule of work to be done in the systems department. It may have been necessary for the manager to obtain guidance in the form of priorities, especially when there is an overload situation with more urgent demands than can be met, within desired time frames, with existing manpower and other resources. Many managers continue to operate on the "fire brigade" principle whereby they are required to interrupt constantly the regularly scheduled activities to take care of special or emergency situations or an assignment imposed by the order of some high-ranking official who is not aware of the existing work load. To the greatest degree possible the manager should be master in his own house. His orderly schedules and procedures should be disturbed only in cases of genuine emergency. Many studies (analytical projects) undertaken by the department can cover an extended period of time; if they are interrupted frequently, there may be added costs, and total value may be impaired. The department manager also should have the right to draw upon or negotiate for the services of specialists from other functions of the company or to use the temporary services of consultants when the skills required by a situation are not available on his own staff. In this regard employees who have served in the systems department and moved to other positions can be of considerable value.

Problem Solving and Decision Making

The most important managerial application of the systems concept is in problem solving and decision making. These are management's principal responsibilities and its most complex ones. In discharging these responsibilities, management should welcome whatever assistance it can get. Systems analysis, in what is probably the most significant step forward in many years, provides highly valuable help to management in problem solving

THE SCIENTIFIC METHOD

The tremendous successes of the physical sciences in discovering nature's secrets and applying them for human benefit have their roots in a technical approach known as the scientific method. It is surprising that this approach was not applied to the solution of managerial problems until quite recently with the advent of systems analysis.

Systems analysis. The specific, unique characteristic of the scientific approach to problem solving is the use of a logical, step-by-step process which makes it possible to describe and define in detail the procedures that led to the final result and thus to retrace those procedures by following the descriptions (documentation). This is in striking contrast to the traditional approach using only individual judgment and often after only superficial examination. Even when the steps followed in arriving at the solution were the same as those used in the scientific approach, the difference is that all the processes occurred in the problem solver's mind and thus were not subject to review or retracing as can be done in the scientific approach. A number of other advantages are derived from the systematic procedure. An important one is that it compels the problem solver to prepare a formal, written record of all his activities in reaching his conclusions. He will have to do this even if the solution actually came to him informally and suddenly, as well may have been the case. Indeed, many very important discoveries have resulted from this informal occurrence; yet, the problem solver still had to follow the rules of scientific analysis in tracing and describing every step that led to his solution.

The following steps are usually considered necessary to define and analyze a problem, using the scientific method: (1) Select the problem; (2) define the problem; (3) select proper measures to quantify the problem; (4) determine (secure) all the facts necessary for the solution; (5) determine relevant functional relationships, together with tentative alternative solutions; (6) test potential solutions on actual situations under controlled (laboratory) conditions; (7) describe (document) procedures followed to solution in order to permit retracing and evaluation; (8) consider nonquantitative (qualitative) factors when relevant to modify the solution.

Following pages contain explanations of the foregoing definition and analysis phases, but because of lack of space and the infinite variety of possibilities, the solution development, testing, and implementation phases are not given detailed presentations here.

PROBLEM SELECTION

The initial step in problem solving is the selection procedure. Since, ordinarily, the number of problems is virtually unlimited, appropriate selection procedures are essential to achieve maximum cost/value relationships.

Selection considerations. Management tends to select problems which, when solved, promise results that will increase profits within a reasonable time. Problems that do not offer payback opportunities are usually deferred or never approached except in cases of dire need (breakdown situations). Solutions to problems that do not appear to have adequate payback potential within one business may nevertheless be packaged and sold to many businesses by service bureaus and software houses, or will sometimes be left to nonprofit organizations (government agencies, foundations, and other official or private enterprises). The time factor has a significant impact on the selection process. There is the question of how long management can afford to wait for results. The period may be quite extended in the technological field. (For example, Du Pont is known to have spent some 20 years in developing nylon.) Large corporations and sometimes individuals or small groups do engage in long-term research, but business management in general will be reluctant to embark on an extended search for the solution to this kind of problem.

Approval authority. Many organizations encourage everybody in management to make suggestions. These proposals will then be evaluated by committees which select those that appear to have the most merit from the company's point of view. In practice a large share of the proposals originate with the professional staffs. Approval authority is usually spread among the management levels. Thus, plant and department heads may have the authority to approve smaller amounts of time and money to analyze problems than do division managers. Top management, of course, has unlimited authority within economic limits or as established by the board of directors. In summary, management at the proper level must become more willing and more expert in order to assign importance priorities to systems analysis projects so as to insure that resources and costs are applied for maximum return; also, this will relieve the systems department manager of the onus of alleged favoritism when he makes the selection without guidance from others in management.

DEFINING THE PROBLEM

It has truly been said that to be able to define the problem is to have achieved one-half of the solution. Without proper definition efforts may be directed toward some different objective or issue and valuable effort wasted.

The person preparing the definition must be certain of what he wishes to accomplish. He must try very hard to make the definition as detailed and clear as possible to preclude any possibility of misunderstanding caused by uncertain or ambiguous language. The more distinctly the segments of the definition are set forth, the easier it will be to accumulate all the proper facts without doing work that is not essential. As far as practical the definition should be developed in cooperation with those who will have to develop the solution. It may become necessary to make adjustments in the wording of the definition to meet the requirements of techniques which have to be used in order to arrive at the solution as efficiently and economically as possible; for example, the use of management science techniques often forces a finer breakdown of the definition than would otherwise be necessary.

QUANTIFICATION

Systems analysis uses quantitative data as its primary tool; thus the required information must be presented in quantitative terms. Every possible effort therefore should be made to define the problem in such a manner as to permit the application of quantitative analysis. However, serious obstacles may be encountered in this aim, or there may be important managerial problems that do not lend themselves easily to the quantitative approach. Outstanding among the latter are problems related to human attitudes and abilities; nevertheless, efforts are often made to find quantitative solutions to the problem of the performance and abilities of employees as a basis for selection among several individuals.

This procedure may be highly desirable in order to exclude or at least minimize personal bias that may affect the evaluation process, but management should use caution in evaluating the results of these "forced" quantifications.

GATHERING THE FACTS

Every problem is determined by parameters and limits that will have an impact on its solution, and therefore it is essential to collect initially all the relevant information; however, this obvious requirement is all too often disregarded or minimized. The reasons are easy to understand: Gathering facts costs time and money, and management does not like either time or cost expenditures.

Time or cost. Managers are often impatient if answers to pressing questions are not immediately given or if, because of delays, the answer loses much or all of its usefulness. There may be strong pressures for shortcuts to reduce the time. Management must be aware that these attitudes, more often than not, will have an unfavorable effect on the solution of the problem. Even if there is sufficient time to collect all the necessary information, costs may be a limiting factor. There may be a decision that no more than X dollars can be spent in a particular case; such a decision will have an effect similar to that of setting a time limit. Despite these potentially adverse effects, management must have the authority to set limits, especially financial ones, in connection with problem solving just as in the case of any other expenditure. It has the responsibility to evaluate the benefits from a particular solution in relation to the cost of getting it. In some instances an answer involving even a considerable margin of error will be adequate in a particular situation. A complete answer may not be required, and therefore it would be wasteful to attempt to get it, even at relatively small cost. Thus it is impossible to establish an overall rule of procedure; each case must be decided on its merits.

Diminishing return. In connection with fact gathering there exists something like a law of diminishing return. Assume that 75 percent of the information desired can be collected at a given cost. To increase the percentage to, say, 85 percent may increase the cost by perhaps 30 to 40 percent, and the rate will be even higher if an attempt is made to reach a 90 percent or greater coverage. The reason is that the bulk of the required information will usually be already available or can be obtained with little additional effort or expense, but beyond that special efforts are required and the cost may go up at a disproportionate rate. Much will depend on the techniques used in gathering the additional data.

Sources of facts. To find and determine the proper sources of the facts is an issue of considerable importance that influences both time and cost considerations. The sources may be external, internal, or the two in combination. Many sources of external information, both official and private, are available; in most cases existing data will be used, but the company may decide to make its own surveys and investigations (for example, in connection with market research, location studies, or selection of a particular kind of equipment). Internal data will be found mainly in statistical and accounting records and reports, many of which will have been collected in accordance with existing laws or private contractual agreements. To facilitate the use of existing information for problem-solving purposes, attention should be given to a format that permits easy recovery of the data. This work has been greatly facilitated by the memory devices of electronic computer systems.

Presenting the facts. The selection of procedures for presenting the information is determined to a significant extent by technical considerations; therefore, it will be affected by changes in techniques, which recently have been frequent. For example, the growing use of electronic computers has substantially expanded the use of numerical presentation instead of the traditional narrative. This is because numbers are accommodated more economically than words by the computers: moreover, numerical codes are more versatile than words, if proper legends are furnished for decoding.

A number of devices for recording and presenting information are in general use by business organizations especially: words (narratives), numbers, flow charts, graphs, pictures, and special symbols. Historically, the narrative form was most frequently used through documents to be filed away for the future. Certain types of information are presented by numbers exclusively (like accounting data), others mainly by numbers and graphs (like statistical data). The different techniques serve their particular purposes; thus graphic presentation permits easy recognition of comparisons and changes, but it is quite limited when an attempt is made to explain them. In this case the narrative presentation is much preferred. In some instances a variety of techniques is used—for example, in corporate reports to stockholders to serve different types of readers.

Flow charts are a method of presentation of particular importance to the systems specialist. They have also gained wide acceptance for purposes of computer language. A distinction is made between general flow charts which describe the flow of information for a whole function and special flow charts which indicate in detail every step and work station activity.

FUNCTIONAL RELATIONSHIPS

Each problem or situation is the combined result of many factors, and systems analysis requires their identification as far as possible. Two separate activities are required: identification of the factors and determination of their quantitative relations.

Fixed and variable factors. Fixed factors are not affected over the short range by changes in the volume of operations and therefore cannot be controlled by management. Variable factors can be manipulated by management. On the basis of all this information, a model of the problem can be constructed that permits management to evaluate various alternatives of action.

Mathematical models. The factual relationships previously mentioned can be represented in terms of algebraic equations. Inserting the actual numerical data in the equations enables management to predetermine the effects of different decisions on profits and make other important forecasts of information with considerable accuracy. Evaluations of this kind have been commonly used informally by businessmen for a long time, although they were limited to a few variables and subject to the shortcomings of limited manipulation. The use of electronic computers permits the application of simulation techniques which can serve as the equivalent of laboratory experiments in the natural sciences. Any number of alternatives and variables can be tested, and the results will serve as guides for management decisions. Increased use of these novel techniques can be anticipated as managers become more familiar with their problem-solving value.

NONQUANTITATIVE DATA

The limitations of systems analysis based solely on quantitative data have always been a significant factor in accounting, which is restricted to quantitative input data (money). Many efforts have mistakenly been made to limit the analysis to this kind of information. Nonquantitative data are often called irrelevant, or else it is erroneously presumed that increases and decreases in such factors will cancel out.

There is no doubt that these data can be of substantial significance; they should never be disregarded for problem-solving purposes. The question is how they can be determined in a satisfactory manner. First of all, systems analysis is fully applicable for identifying the relevant factors, and therefore should be used for all types of data. Second, a substitute must be found for the numerical data to be inserted into the algebraic equations. Estimates based on individual judgment have to be used for this purpose. Management must be alert to the distinction in use between the data that are based on actual measurements and those that are the result of judgment, but this should not mean that the latter data should not be given their proper weight in solving problems and making decisions.

INFORMATION SYSTEMS FUNCTION

The principles of systems analysis are equally applicable to the problems of the systems function and to managerial problem solving. The task of designing, introducing, and operating the information system is the responsibility of the systems function. The problems it has to face are as complex as those of management, which has a vital interest in observing and reviewing the work of the systems function. It must be assured that every part of the organization, especially every executive who controls any activity, receives all the information at the right time and of the quality he needs to perform his responsibilities. These are indispensable prerequisites for successful operation of the business.

Functional flow. Each procedural activity of the enterprise originates and at the same time consumes information. It transmits data needed by other parts and receives data needed for its own activities from still other parts. The principle of the balance between input and output, which dominates most systems, is not valid in this instance. One particular activity may transmit more information than it receives and needs. The opposite may be true in the case of another activity which requires more information than it supplies to others in the organization. The responsibility of the systems function is only to establish a satisfactory information system for the company. In order to do this, the systems function must examine the other functions to determine the kinds and amounts of information they need and which they can get from other functions. It is the job of the systems function to develop the best possible balance and flow among many conflicting circumstances.

Layout flow. Once the type and amount of information required for all activities and functions have been finally determined, the systems function has to design a flow of information that will be meaningful and economical. The layout of this information flow will have to be reconciled to a considerable degree, despite the capabilities of electronic display and processing, with the physical layout of the various parts of the organization. This flow should be as straightforward as possible; it should avoid time-consuming backward or circular flows. To achieve the best results the information-flow layout should be determined at the same time and in conjunction with the physical layout of all the company functions and activities; it could therefore even be a matter of concern to the architects who design factories and office buildings. This will also be important in connection with devices to speed up the flow of documents and data—for example, adequate wiring, telephone-cable conduit, aisle space for mail carts, and the like. Advances in electronic technology should provide substantial increases in capabilities.

Job breakdown. A highly important but difficult problem for the systems function is how to break down the work flow into appropriate assignments for individual employees who have a part in the information flow. Although an ever increasing part of the work is performed by machines, there is still a great deal for individuals to do. This probably will be the more sophisticated part of the work, requiring considerable training and a good understanding of the meaning of the procedures to be performed, once the bulk of routine work has been taken over by automatic equipment. The systems experts have to make sure that employees are assigned only those tasks that they are fully equipped to perform satisfactorily. Their work loads should be adequate to keep them busy yet not so large as to force them to resort to low-quality work, as happens so often on assembly lines. Another highly important task is to achieve cooperation between department heads and systems experts, especially in the assignment of work to individual employees. The former will be inclined to strive for more employees and therefore lower individual work loads, while the systems experts, who are considering the organization as a whole, will drive for maximum efficiency and economy. The issue of adequate training can also be a critical one. The redistribution of work assignments may be necessary from time to time, especially when there is a change of employees performing specific tasks and when the new employees may not be well fitted for their assignments. Disagreements and arguments must be expected in this connection, and the desired cooperation will often be difficult to attain; top management will sometimes need to intervene and arbitrate so that progress is not impeded by delays in reaching agreement. Further discussion of the systems function and its management may be found in a number of textbooks, including that of W. M. Carrithers and E. H. Weinwurm (*Business Information and Accounting Systems,* Charles E. Merrill Books, Inc., 1967).

Forms Design and Control

The information system of the enterprise provides the means (channels) for the flow of the information. The medium used by these channels to carry the informational contents has been traditionally the forms, sheets of paper on which the data are posted by hand or mechanical equipment (typewriter, printing devices, and the like), and this is still the most widely used method of transmitting information. However, there is a trend that may lead eventually to the total or partial displacement of the traditional method; it is the introduction of electromagnetic devices. Although the information retained magnetically is invisible to the human eye, there are a number of tangible advantages in this new approach. Among the most significant are (1) the enormous density with which a very large amount of information can be packed on a minimum of surface space and (2) the ease and speed with which the information can be made available (retrieved) to the user. The beginnings of a mixed system in which forms and electronics are used side by side can be observed at the present time, but this technique is still in an early stage.

FORMS FUNDAMENTALS

Forms are the principal means of communication both within the organization and as liaison with customers, suppliers, and other outside agencies. External forms also serve to present an image of the company, and therefore public relations considerations enter into the questions of design and performance. Another principal advantage of forms is the possibility of reducing the amount of information that has to be prepared for transmittal; all the repetitive information can be placed on the form in advance and thus does not have to be added each time or transmitted separately. Form flow charts are valuable in describing how the forms carry the information within the organization. The charts also indicate the particular tasks to be performed at individual workplaces and possibly the time required to complete the task. The form flow charts can be coordinated with the regular systems flow charts. The two charts may also be combined to show how the various forms will be used to accomplish a particular kind of information activity. The importance of forms problems will grow with the size of the organization, probably at an accelerated rate. The larger the company, the greater the need for more extensive communications. There certainly is an increased need for information represented by the forms for purposes of internal communications.

FORMS RESPONSIBILITIES

The systems function is responsible for coordinating the control of forms. These particular problems have become so complex that a special subfunction has been evolved. It has become a separate, full-time job in larger companies but should be considered as a special assignment on a part-time basis even by smaller companies. However, forms problems concern all parts of the organization. Other functions, in their own activities, are significantly affected by the kind and number of forms they have to handle. Therefore, close cooperation between the personnel having staff responsibility for forms and the users is essential. Management has to consider the basic policies related to the forms function, especially in (1) deciding on the emphasis to be given outside forms in the light of public relations; (2) supporting all efforts to maintain full control over uses and costs of forms; and (3) deciding on changes that involve substantial investment in equipment.

Suggestions for new forms or changes in existing ones may come from all the people in the organization. New forms in general result from procedural changes initiated by the systems function. Before a new form is designed, it must be determined that the intended purpose cannot be achieved by using or perhaps adapting an existing form. This is always the preferred procedure; only if it is found to be impractical, should the introduction of a new form be considered.

FORMS DESIGN

Maximum efficiency at lowest cost will always be the general principle. However, interpretation and application of the principle are difficult in view of conflicting considerations that often have to be reconciled in some fashion. This is primarily the responsibility of the person in charge of forms.

The person who proposes the design of a new form must give a full description of the data that will be presented in the form, as well as indicate the flow of the form within the information system. The design itself is a technical job for the specialist. He must, however, cooperate closely with the future users of the form to develop a design that will meet their requirements. This may be a difficult and time-consuming job. Differences that cannot be decided at this level will have to be brought to the attention of the head of the systems function and to the executives in charge of the user departments affected for final determination.

The well-designed form presents all the needed information (that is, it is spaced for recording it) in a manner as convenient as possible for those who will prepare the data and those who will use them. Many techniques have been introduced, especially by the forms manufacturers, to make designs as efficient as possible. The device to be used to fill in the data must be given special consideration. Certain data may be especially emphasized or, alternatively, omitted on various copies of the form. Cost considerations will affect the forms design; the more complex the design, the more expensive it will be. This is important in deciding on color schemes, kind and weight of paper stock, carbons for copies, and other factors. The designer must be familiar with the many reproduction techniques that have greatly increased and improved in recent years; the selection will influence the design and will be affected by the intended use.

FORMS CONTROL

Costs and utilization of the forms represent a significant part of overhead costs and operating expenses; management therefore must be interested in close control of these expenses. These control activities include the following principal factors: (1) centralization of all related activities to the greatest extent possible; (2) control of procurement and inventories; (3) emphasis on simplification of design and utilization, avoidance of duplication; (4) pressure for elimination of unnecessary forms and unnecessary use of forms; (5) pressure for lowest costs of materials and duplication; (6) study of possible savings from the introduction of new techniques.

Totally effective control of forms is impractical unless all related activities are concentrated in a single location or function. This is contrary to the actual practice of many companies. Therefore, strong management support is essential to overcome opposition from executives who want to maintain their own independent control of the forms used in their areas. However, the person or persons in charge must maintain closest cooperation with all forms user groups.

Those in charge of forms control must have complete information about the forms in use by the company; therefore, samples of all the forms must be collected as the initial step of the control procedure. Although this would appear to be a simple task, it may not be, and considerable difficulties can be expected. To make it effective, all procurement of forms must be controlled by the centralized authority; this refers to both the forms ordered from outside suppliers and those prepared internally. Newer reproducing techniques such as departmental copier-duplicators have promoted the latter, and this has made effective controls more difficult to maintain. No exception from this rule of centralized procurement should be permitted.

CLASSIFICATION AND ANALYSIS OF FORMS

The forms collected must be classified and analyzed. A folder for each form and one for each kind of information flow must be set up; into these all related forms have to be placed. The folder will provide a complete history of the form from its original introduction. Attention must be given to keeping the folder current at all times. Then each form must be carefully analyzed to determine whether it should be continued, merged with another form, or changed. The effort should always be toward reduction of the number of current forms, an important factor in cost reduction. Similar forms may have been developed by different departments independently without one knowing what the other was doing. The results of these analyses must be discussed with all the interested executives. Differences which cannot be resolved at this level have to be settled in the manner indicated earlier in connection with forms design. These discussions must be handled with great care to avoid disenchantment with the program within the company.

PROCUREMENT AND INVENTORY CONTROL

The two activities of procurement and inventory control are closely related; there has to be sufficient inventory available to bridge the gap until suppliers fill the orders received. Problems arise from the centralization of procurement. The analysis of orders may take some time. Later ordering may be a way to get around these analyses but should not cause undue delays. If more time is required for completion of the analysis, a small order should be put through and the decision as to continuation of the form postponed temporarily. This is the best alternative under those conditions. The purpose of the analysis is twofold: first, to determine whether there have been changes in conditions since the last procurement order; and, second, to make a constant effort toward elimination or changes in existing forms. Without a continuing effort there is danger that present forms will be reordered in a routine fashion without analysis.

COST CONSIDERATIONS

Reduction in the number of existing forms is one of the most effective means of cost reduction. The use of the same form for additional purposes permits larger orders and appropriate discounts. A large portion of the cost of forms is in the setting up of the design of the form as a fixed expense independent of the number of copies printed; doubling the order will increase total cost comparatively little but substantially reduce the cost per unit. On the other hand, there is danger of excess inventories resulting from large orders, which may become useless when there is a change in existing procedures. The order quantity therefore should not be considered just a routine matter but should be the result of careful attention to all the factors. Another important cost factor is space. Each additional form requires some space and related cost; it may be comparatively small in an individual case and not be given any attention. But the cost will grow as the number of new forms increases, and the savings from reduction or elimination of forms can be significant. Attention should also be given to the alternatives of outside procurement and preparation by the facilities available in the company. Costs should be compared and appropriate action taken. Bids from several suppliers should be requested in order to test the cost charged by the present outside or inside supplier.

INVESTIGATING NEW TECHNIQUES

The field of data processing is in a state of transition; new techniques are announced almost daily. Management should see to it that personnel responsible for forms give close attention to new developments and evaluate them for possible adoption by the company. Unless there is review and change, there is danger that existing procedures will be continued more or less automatically, regardless of their merits, under changing conditions.

Manuals of Procedures

The success of the information system as a means of transmitting data within the organization and to the outside depends on an effective system of communications between the systems function and all the parts of the company which have to cooperate in making the system a reality. The principal means of implementing this communications system are procedures prepared by the systems function. They convey the designs developed by the systems function to those who have to execute them.

STANDARD OPERATING PROCEDURES

Each company may develop its own format of procedures for internal communication. However, a common format has emerged gradually which is known as the standard operating procedure (SOP); it contains all the information in detail needed by the operating groups affected by a specific procedural design.

The presentation shall be in a simple, nontechnical form that can be readily interpreted by those who have to follow the procedure in their daily work.

MANUALS

The systems function is responsible for preparing procedures for all the company functions. Most of these procedures are of concern only to specific parts of the organization. Procedures that affect a particular function are collected in a manual. For example, the accounting manual will include all the procedures that deal with this particular function. Others will deal with purchasing, payrolls, personnel, and all the other functional areas. This arrangement makes it easier to get an overall view of the relevant procedures pertaining to a particular function. Individual departments will have on file the manuals that affect their activities. A complete set of all the current manuals will be kept by the systems function and others in need of the complete information—the internal auditors, for example.

RESPONSIBILITY FOR PROCEDURES

The preparation of procedures is a principal task of the systems function. The test of its effectiveness is the extent to which its procedures, which reflect the design of the information system developed by the systems function, are accepted by the whole organization as a guide for day-to-day practices. Many information systems which appear to be of high quality are in fact of little or no value, since their application by the organization is merely spotty. The most important means of accomplishing the desired aim of an effective information system is close cooperation between the systems function and all the other functions in the organization. The systems function operates from a companywide viewpoint, but the individual functions possess experience based on extended practice which must be taken into account by those who are preparing procedures; therefore, this has to be a joint venture of all the functions involved in a particular activity. An important part of this process is the responsibility of the systems function to see to it that everyone affected by a new procedure is fully instructed as to his part in carrying it out. Thus the systems function has important educational responsibilities that should never be disregarded, as is not infrequently the case when it is taken for granted that the mere issuance of a new procedure instruction in writing is all that is required from the systems function.

CONTROLS

Instructions are not self-enforcing; consequently, as a general rule, every SOP must contain provisions for its enforcement. As a matter of principle, compliance is the responsibility of supervision in the organizational units that use the SOP. This should be clearly stated and understood. It is important to the systems function that procedures are faithfully carried out; hence SOP's should incorporate checking and other control measures whenever possible. In practice, adequate enforcement results most often from two additional measures: (1) The internal audit function should test and report on the effectiveness of supervision in discharging its enforcement responsibilities; and (2) the level of management above the tested supervisors must take corrective administrative action when the need is indicated. The activities of internal auditors have been expanded to include "procedural adherence auditing" to help insure compliance with existing procedures by means of audit reports directed to upper levels of management, which must then insist upon remedial action. Also in practice, one of the most effective measures that can be taken by the systems function to insure compliance is to involve the operating (user) organizations in the development and maintenance of the SOP's.

Consultation Services

The use of consultants by management has been growing rapidly. This indicates that their services have been found to be a valuable form of assistance when management has to deal with increasingly diversified and complex situations. In earlier and simpler times managers themselves were expected to be experts experienced in all areas of the business that were important to the success of the enterprise. Partnerships and closely held corporations had the varieties of necessary experience represented in their owner-managers, who were able personally to control the work of the employees by means of their broad experience. This rather comfortable situation no longer prevails. Management is constantly faced with new complexities. Even many years of experience are no longer sufficient for the adequate evaluation of the new, specialized developments or for control of the specialists who do work which the company managers only dimly understand, if at all. It is here that the consultant performs a highly important task to assist and supplement management in its decision-making responsibilities.

OUTSIDE AND INSIDE CONSULTANTS

Many consulting organizations now offer high-quality specialized services which are in ever increasing demand. The greatest value of these outside consultants is in their broad experience with numerous organizations; however, their knowledge of the specific problems of the company engaging their services is limited. Thus it happens frequently that their advice, although it may be objectively correct, does not fit the peculiar conditions of the company. These deficiencies can be remedied by the use of internal consultants, who can be expected to know both the inside and the outside and thus can do much better work than outsiders. Of course, only large organizations can afford to retain highly qualified experts on a permanent basis; but, if they do so, it is likely to be worthwhile.

CONSULTANTS IN THE SYSTEMS FUNCTION

It was mentioned earlier that the systems function has been split up into a number of subfunctions, each of them requiring a kind of knowledge and experience which only a full-fledged specialist could acquire and be expected to demonstrate. This is the principal reason for the frequent use of consultants in the information systems field. Even large companies that can afford to employ a complete group of trained and experienced specialists on a full-time basis will retain outside consultants from time to time to review highly complex and/or major investment situations when it appears to be appropriate to check on the company's own experts. Other companies that have only a small staff of systems experts and few if any real specialists will depend completely on outside consultants for analyses that are beyond the capacity and experience of their own full-time staffs. In most instances these outside consultants will render highly valuable services; however, the limitations already discussed must be kept in mind when management has to make its final decisions.—*E. H. Weinwurm*

RECORDS AND REPORTS MANAGEMENT

Business organizations are groaning under the load of records they seem to need in order to operate. A recent estimate has it that U.S. business firms store some trillion pieces of paper in file drawers and that Federal, state, and local governments easily double that amount.

Even if such figures are not subject to ready verification, it is beyond question that all businesses, even the smallest ones and especially the growing number of service companies, must keep more and better records than ever before. They must do so not only to comply with the ever growing multiplicity of governmental regulations and information requirements but also to provide the prompt and accurate transaction information needed for sheer survival in a continually more complex and competitive business environment. In addition to operational paperwork, our burgeoning technology has stepped up the need to deal with an overwhelming tide of technical and scientific information which doubles every ten years, approaching an estimated 250 million pages annually. Advanced computer systems—despite the ultimate goal of having all transaction and reference information stored on magnetic tape or other memories subject to instant audio or visual retrieval—have not stemmed the paper tide. On the contrary, in the age of information technology, computer systems seem to have added to the flood. Producers of manual and mechanized record-keeping systems have been finding the demand for their products expanding at a rate never experienced before.

Scientific records and reports management has thus become an area of prime management concern, not only because of the growing expense in the manipulation of the documents and records themselves but also because, in this age of integrated information processing, the function can no longer safely be delegated to far-down-the-line supervision.

In the process of checking into information needs and establishing proper records controls, the magnitude of costs incurred under uncontrolled, "growed like Topsy" systems is usually startling. In surveys of hundreds of companies, for example, Naremco (National Records Management Council) has found at least 5 to 10 cubic feet of records for every employee; in large office operations, a minimum of one file station for every three employees; less than 25 percent of current office records under any kind of continuing control; personnel wasting 20 to 30 percent of their time simply looking for information—not analyzing or using it, just trying to find it!

Opportunities

Reductions in space, storage facilities, and paper usage alone will produce sizable savings quite aside from operational improvements achieved by streamlined information storage and retrieval. For example, a broadcasting company—an early advocate of scientific records management—reported a saving of $41,000 only 12 weeks after initiating an organized record-keeping program. It had reduced 33 million pieces of paper to half that amount and had sold 40 tons of paper as waste. But this was only part of the story: The company had, for the first time, a planned program of continuous records control and a current index pinpointing every record in each of its locations, with official guidelines on what records to keep, how long to keep them, and where, with maximum efficiency in prompt information retrieval.

A more recent example concerns only the marketing department of one of the world's largest advertising agencies, where 350 file drawers of information were spread through the offices. Management was concerned about poor and incomplete marketing reports, time and expense of preparation, and gaps in available information. Basic source data were carefully assembled, screened, and evaluated, and the entire collection was reduced to 50 file drawers of marketing intelligence—after which advanced techniques of indexing and information retrieval were applied. (Incidentally, Naremco surveys have revealed that 20 percent of available filing equipment in offices is normally used not for information but for housing blank forms and stationery supplies.)

RECORDS IMPROVEMENT INDEX

A simple index can be set up to indicate the effectiveness of a records control program. Taking the total accumulation of records at the start of the program as 100 percent, the records improvement index shows what percentage has been destroyed as useless and what percentage (representing those with lower access requirements) has been transferred to a records center, where ready reference can still be achieved but with a great reduction of clutter within using offices. Exhibit 2.2 shows indexes achieved in representative programs.

Scientific Records Management

Hereafter, where the meaning is clear, the term "records" will be used in this subsection to denote all filed documents—forms, correspondence, reports, and library and other information reference materials. A program of records management covers three major areas.

1. *Records creation* prevents unnecessary reports, forms, and other documents from being produced and includes an initial audit and weeding-out program to clear operating facilities of excess papers by eliminating those that have outlived their usefulness. It pinpoints records subject to limited reference (or

retained for historical or legal reasons only) for transfer to less expensive central records and storage facilities in accordance with records-retention and disposal controls.

2. *Records processing* streamlines the procedures for record keeping and information retrieval.

3. *Records retention and disposal* sets up policies, procedures, and schedules for the disposition of records not required for continuing operations. It formulates safeguards and procedures for destruction of unneeded records and pinpoints the location of retained records, arranging for access or copies as required. It also covers policies and arrangements for the storage and protection of vital records against hazards of nature, enemy attack, and the like.

TIE-IN WITH
MANAGEMENT INFORMATION SYSTEM

It is obvious that records management does not operate in a vacuum. With the modern trend to integrated management information systems, and with forms, records, reports, and information storage and retrieval governed by increasingly sophisticated computer systems, the basic planning of the function must mesh in with and be influenced by decisions made with respect to such related functions as systems management (including forms control), management science, electronic data processing, computer time-sharing and utilities, and communications networks; and, of course, the physical aspects of records retention and retrieval tie in with such functions as archives, reproduction, and telecommuni-

Exhibit 2.2
GAINS FROM SCIENTIFIC RECORDS MANAGEMENT AT REPRESENTATIVE INSTALLATIONS

Organization	Records Destroyed (Percent)	Records Transferred to New Records Center (Percent)	Records Improvement Index (Percent)
Large city administration	47	26	73
Broadcasting network	46	21	67
Electric storage battery company	23	27	50
Natural gas company	28	37	65
Aircraft company	20	33	53
Metalworking company	69	7	76
Electric motor company	9	69	78
Paper company	44	21	65

Source: Studies and surveys of National Records Management Council.

cations. The locus and form of organization of records management will depend upon the degree to which these related and collateral functions are developed.

Records Creation

Regardless of the size or nature of a specific business, the important thing is the initiation of control over the production of paperwork *before* the fact. It is assumed that a reasonably effective system of paperwork flow has been established and that office methods have been subject to work simplification and other methods improvement analyses. Thus the analyst here is not considered to be responsible for the total systems needs covered elsewhere. However, he will check to find out whether operations have been recently reviewed and whether a formalized control over forms design and use exists—and he will make his own spot check to assure that there are no obvious inefficiencies and duplications in operational paperwork. (For example, if a large number of people—either in one department or in many different locations—are working on the same basic data, any improvement in the form or other paper being used will save significant time in aggregate; and if forms are combined or if changes are made in the location where file copies are retained, significant savings in file handling and space can be achieved.)

The analyst will raise further questions as to the documentation need for information records and reports in use: whether they should go to a recipient in the first place and—importantly—whether they should be retained there, and if so, for how long.

In short, whether the analyst is making a detailed audit himself or working in conjunction with systems people, he will satisfy himself that each form, each report, each generation of new paper has been reviewed in detail. Is each department receiving only the information it needs, or is it clogged with superfluous data input from which it must extract what it needs? Is the department generating what seem to be unnecessary forms and reports? Who has requested or authorized them? What does the recipient do with the information contained in the form and report he used? The goal is to eliminate every unnecessary paper, form, and report coming into a department, generated in a department, and leaving a department. (An important technique here is for the analyst not to ask an executive or worker *whether* he needs a certain form or report. Reluctance to change or a feeling of self-importance predisposes the one who is questioned to a "yes" answer. It is better to ask what information *is needed* to do the job, and *why* information that is apparently superfluous should still come to that particular work station.)

VOLUME OF FILES

With the problem of paper generation reasonably under control, attention can be turned to the volume of paper that should be retained—and where. Detailed policies and procedures tie in with decisions arrived at as a result of the records-processing and records-retention phases of the program, and will of course be influenced by procedures established with respect to central versus departmental files or by the use of "administrative substations." However, it is usually possible at this point to earmark substantial volumes of never- or little-used records for destruction or transfer.

What should the volume of active records be if there is assumed an efficient combination of departmental and central filing of transaction documents—that is, documents that do not include information reports and library documents? While needs will obviously differ for different companies, certain rule-of-thumb ratios may be mentioned, based on research and on the experience of Naremco-surveyed operations. Thus, for general industrial operations, one cubic foot of records for each employee; for government agencies or companies subject to detailed governmental regulation (public utilities, airlines, and the like), five cubic feet of records for each employee; for specialized clerical operations (accounting, purchasing, and so forth), ten to fifteen cubic feet per employee.

Records Processing

An organization's records and information resources fall into two broad categories: transaction documents and reference documents.

TRANSACTION DOCUMENTS

Orders, invoices, checks, active correspondence with customers and suppliers, and the like are transaction documents. Experience shows that these usually comprise over 75 percent of the total record load. Here files can be arranged numerically or alphabetically and present no special retrieval problems. But they do call for modern equipment that provides rapid access, ease of expansion, and adequate protection.

For large volumes of transaction documents, numerous electrical-mechanical, pushbutton-operated systems are available that will rapidly select and present to an operator trays containing desired sections from many thousands of sets of records or from as many as a million cards. However, with today's improvements in manual equipment such as hanging files, fine-guiding capabilities through ingenious numbering systems, and visible indexing, administrative managers can increase the speed of long-established filing methods by as much as 300 to 400 percent.

REFERENCE DOCUMENTS

Reports, research data, marketing information, brochures, legal documents, and the like are reference documents. While comprising in bulk the smaller percentage of filed information in most organizations, they represent by far the greatest problem in terms of prompt and comprehensive information retrieval. It is in this area that some of the most spectacular microfilm, electronic retrieval, and cathode ray display equipment has been developed in recent years. However, by the use of indexing methods, tremendous improvements can be effected by manual methods or by manual methods supplemented by simple devices.

PARALLEL NUMBERING AND ALPHABETIZING

Many transaction record systems, especially if associated with computer processing, will benefit by a numbering system that maintains true alphabetical access to operation files, along with having all entries in numerical sequence. In one widely used system of this sort, names are applied to numbers, rather than numbers to names, through a zigzag arrangement of numbers preprinted on forms supplied by the company that developed the system. Gaps are provided between numbers in prearranged blocks to permit alphabetic insertion of new names without disturbing the numerical order. The zigzag pattern of the preprinted numbers visually locates the numerical midpoint between two previously assigned names when a new name must be entered. A check digit also can be assigned to make possible accuracy checks on input to automated systems.

SUBJECT CLASSIFICATION

In conventional filing, reference documents are arranged either in straight alphabetic form (the "dictionary" file) or by subject ("functional" filing). The latter is usually "hierarchical" (major subjects are divided into subordinate subjects). Thus operational reference and report files such as "Accounting and Finance" will be broken into first-level subdivisions such as "Accounts Payable," "Accounts Receivable," "Budgets," and so forth. The "Budgets" file may be broken into second-level subdivisions—"Budgets—Plants," for example.

When subject files increase in scope and depth of subdivisions, filing and retrieval will be improved by accompanying indexes, especially if the physical files themselves are decentralized. Two indexes are required: a "Classification Guide" and an "Alphabetic Guide" (sometimes termed "Relative Index"). The first is like the table of contents of a book, with numerical code entries for each classification and subclassification, in order. The second, like the index at the back of a book, lists all classification terms and key words in alphabetic order with accompanying codes.

INVERTED INDEXING

Reference files have always created headaches. With conventional multiple cross-indexing, almost endlessly proliferating, even a passable job of anticipating possible look-up approaches is difficult. Alphabetic or subject classification or simple numbering sequences of documents presents serious limitations because of the many subjects a single document or report may cover. One thousand reports can easily give rise to ten or twenty thousand index cards.

A powerful technique for overcoming these handicaps, one that lends itself to simple manual retrieval as well as being especially adaptable for punched-card or computerized search, is inverted indexing, also referred to as concept coordination. The flexibility and control are all in the indexing. The documents themselves are simply given consecutive address numbers and filed by those numbers, although for some subject areas it may be convenient to keep like documents together by assigning blocks of numbers.

The inversion consists of turning the whole idea of indexing around. Instead of the documents themselves being indexed and arranged (although a straight alphabetic card list of all books or reports—for example—as well as of authors can be maintained separately), the information that is indexed is a set of basic concepts (also called descriptors or uniterms) selected with a view to probable look-up. A card for each basic concept or term contains the addresses of all documents in the file bearing on that particular aspect of a subject. The cards are filed alphabetically. Since documents are numbered consecutively, there is no awkward problem of squeezing a new document in between others in tight locations. Because many of the same basic concepts are treated in numerous documents, the concept cards will be only a fraction of the number of total documents on file, although the actual number, of course, is arbitrary and depends upon the refinement or depth desired in look-up.

Broad information retrieval requests will be handled by producing all the documents (or, preparatory to that, simply a list of their titles) found on the applicable concept card—for example, "Tires." But if information is wanted on

Exhibit 2.3

INVERTED INDEXING CONCEPT

1968 GUIDE TO NYLON CORD AUTOMOBILE TIRES		Document Number 482
		Location

LOCATOR TERMS				PROPER NAMES	
Tires				B. F. Goodrich Co.	
Cord					
Nylon					
Automobile					

Trace Card

QUERY: What do we have in our files on tires?
(To satisfy a broad reference request for everything in the files, one uniterm card would be consulted.)
REPLY: There are 27 documents on tires, as follows —
(List titles from log of sequential document entry, or supply actual documents or possibly abstracts.)

TIRES									
0	1	2	3	4	5	6	7	8	9
1490	231	482	1463	914	215	816	1157	1148	719
		1622	1623	1004	425	1626	1437	1778	819
				1464	555	1156	1697		1149
				1624	905				1159
					1125				

Concept or Uniterm Card

Key words from each document are entered on a trace card, as shown on the top, and then posted to appropriate uniterm cards, shown at the bottom. Documents are numbered and filed consecutively. Entry on uniterm card is by *last* or *terminal* digit, to facilitate look-up; no more than ten columns are required.

automobile tires—as distinguished, say, from airplane tires—only those documents are produced whose addresses appear on both the concept card "Automobiles" and the concept card "Tires." If the request is narrowed to "Nylon Automobile Tires," only the smaller number of documents will be produced whose addresses appear on all three applicable concept cards. (See Exhibit 2.3.) The key-word or uniterm approach lends itself to automatic indexing and abstracting, but the writers of documents (if titles only are scanned) must be instructed to write meaningful titles, or an editor must do so.

PIECEMEAL MECHANIZATION AND AUTOMATION

When the classification and indexing needs of the information system are properly thought through, the pacing of mechanization and stages of automation will proceed almost automatically as required.

Edge-punched cards. Edge-punched cards can be used for an inverted indexing system, with quick manual retrieval of all cards that are edge-punched for all the concepts demanded by a specific search.

"Peek-a-boo" devices. The next step up—but still manual—is the use of so-called peek-a-boo devices. A single card, for example, is devoted to a concept. A hole drilled in the card, positioned by numbered coordinates on a matrix, identifies the address of a pertinent document. Ten thousand addresses can be identified on one card. When separate cards, each for a different concept, are superimposed, those holes in the entire stack through which a beam of light is visible identify all the documents relevant to the search.

Aperture cards. Microfilmed documents can be combined with tabulating cards—the so-called aperture cards. These are then susceptible of high-speed search and retrieval by punched-card processing or computer methods or by special rapid access and retrieval units.

Computerized information storage and display. Most computer manufacturers now offer television-like units for remote computer query and response. With such terminals, anyone (even without computer competence) can query a computer on an associated keyboard terminal and get an instantaneous answer in the form of text—or charts or drawings—thrown on the screen. Systems are available in which the display (for example, drawings or charts) can be corrected or updated at the receiving end by use of "light pencils" on the display screens. Systems which will provide hard copy in addition to visual display can also be installed.

Mechanical-electronic systems. Systems are available that combine the push-button mechanical retrieval previously mentioned with closed-circuit television transmission of the documents retrieved. An important advantage here, of course, is that the document itself does not leave the information center and that more than one viewer can consult the same document at the same time.

ADMINISTRATIVE SUBSTATION

A recent development in office planning, which goes beyond records management but is of great interest in connection with that function, is the administrative substation. This is a compact work zone set up to handle many of the paperwork and clerical activities ordinarily scattered through a number of offices. It acts as a local library, copy duplicating center, mail room, stationery and supply depot, secretarial services unit, messenger service center, and archival records and information center.

The significance of such satellite centers to records management is indicated by results of studies of the National Records Management Council showing a total of 20 to 25 percent of available filing cabinet space used to store and hoard blank forms, stationery supplies, and nonrecord items from coffee urns to Christmas decorations; total volume of blank forms alone dispersed at work stations exceeding the total available in the central stationery storeroom by 150 percent; books and library resources spread through offices exceeding the total holdings of the central company library by 300 percent—resources which are not cataloged or indexed (to say nothing of unnecessary duplication).

Archival records and information. The substation can be linked to all other substation file areas as well as to central information files; thus it is both a branch and a central information center. Locally, it can microfilm material for reference on reader-printers and also store hard copy. Through the use of lateral files, special filing equipment is not needed for books, file folders, computer printouts, stationery supplies, and blank forms. Separate cabinets, shelves, and transfer cases are replaced by a single, flexible office module.

Records Retention and Disposal

A comprehensive records-retention schedule is not only sound management but also serves as an important legal safeguard. This is a timetable showing how long and where to keep each type of record.

LEGAL REQUIREMENTS

Assembling data on all legal requirements to answer individual company needs is a huge but straightforward job. Naremco maintains a complete index to every Federal record-keeping requirement. The *Federal Register,* compiled by the National Archives of the United States, daily reports laws and regulations bearing on the retention of business records and consolidates the information in yearly supplements. The Financial Executives Research Foundation (FERF) compiles information on state government and Canadian requirements on records retention as well as requirements of the U.S. Government.

No statutes of limitations bar criminal prosecution, and records that might protect the company against criminal action, while theoretically having a possible use indefinitely, will have to be considered in the light of the cost of storage versus the risk of their ever being needed.

INDIVIDUAL COMPANY EXPERIENCE

Legal requirements are not the sole criterion. The company's own administrative experience must be considered in the decision as to how long to keep a specific record. Thus legal requirements may show a six-year statute of limitations on an accounts-receivable document, but on the basis of past experience the company may take a calculated risk and discard the record within two, three, or four years.

Many records have no direct relation to the various statutes or regulations for which schedules must also be drawn up in the retention program. These will require a study of actual usage—the frequency and purpose of reference. This analysis will also indicate the length of time such records should remain at the scene of operations for active reference and when they should be transferred to a records center—and how long they should be kept there before destruction.

THE RECORDS CENTER

If a separate records center is planned, as distinguished from vault storage for nonaccess retention or for protection of vital records, four factors must be considered: shelving, cartons, indexing, and access.

Shelving. Space-saving shelves, preferably of metal, should be installed for cartons of records. Twelve cartons can be stored satisfactorily on a 32-inch by 42-inch shelf.

Cartons. Corrugated cardboard containers of 10-inch by 12-inch by 15-inch size are usable for letter- or legal-size documents.

Index. Records should be indexed as they are boxed for storage. Each box should have a number designating the permanent location it occupies in the records center. An inventory sheet showing the records contained in the box should also be included.

Access system. A system should be set up for obtaining records or information from the center, with detailed procedures for finding material rapidly and returning it to its proper place after use.

RECORDS PROTECTION

The advent of the nuclear age heightened interest in records protection. However, statistics show that each year two other disasters take a dreadful toll of human lives and destroy millions of dollars of property: fire and flood. These must be considered of actually more immediate importance than a nuclear holocaust.

Nuclear disaster. The most common practice in protecting records against nuclear destruction is to store vital records in specially designed locations within a reasonable distance from the company's headquarters. Storage facilities employed include vaults well below ground level or in the side of a mountain. In addition, vaults of banks in small towns well away from a prime target area are used.

Fire. Protection of valuable records from loss by fire varies from elaborate sprinkler systems to specially constructed safes with added insulation protection. If records are stored in a warehouse or in any normal building, sprinkler systems can be installed. However, consideration must be given to possible damage from water. Tests have shown that documents kept in uninsulated metal containers are literally baked to cinders under intense heat. Wood is of course extremely combustible. However, laboratory tests have demonstrated that double-thickness corrugated cardboard cartons, protected by watchmen and a sprinkler system, are about as good protective containers as any practically available.

Flood. Watertight compartments are of course available for vital records, and there usually are some storage areas available on very high ground away from the headquarters location.

Protection methods. Where a company does not have a vital records center, it can secure protection by making certain that duplicate copies of records are kept in two or more separate and dispersed locations. For example, in a multi-plant company, a plant may retain an original record and send a copy to the home office.

When records have been designated as vital but have infrequent reference use, the most effective protection is to send the original to a vital records center. Or a duplicate of a record can be made for the vital records center by microfilm or fast copy reproduction.

Guidelines for priority. While the importance of some documents will vary according to the nature of the business, certain priority guidelines for records protection can be established. Thus the key factors in establishing the degree to which records may be considered vital are as follows: (1) information needed to resume company operations after a disaster; (2) data required to re-establish the legal and financial status of the company; (3) records that fulfill obligations to stockholders, employees, and outside interests; and (4) records that involve products, prices, and the technical know-how related to products. All of these factors are related to the overriding consideration of assuring the continuity of the business in the event of disaster.

Integrated Information Network

Records management is assuming a vital management role—structuring and managing a companywide information network. This information network under the most advanced concept is a management service designed to provide, at a single point of inquiry, access to all records, information, and data anywhere in the company, including selected outside sources such as subscription information services, outside "data banks," and the like. The network links available information resources—customer and product information, technical information, market and financial information, and the like. The format of information resources linked to the network ranges from original documents to tab cards, to tapes, to "real-time" computerized information systems both in-house and on-line, to the newer "public utility" type of data processing service centers.

Given this burgeoning of functions and responsibilities, it is not to be wondered that there is at this time no clear-cut pattern of organizational position and reporting for the records management function—beyond the fact that it is being increasingly recognized as having grown far beyond the status of a short decade ago. A survey, conducted jointly in 1966 by the Administrative Management Society and *Dun's Review,* definitely highlighted the growing awareness that information is a vital resource of any business. More than 30 percent of the companies surveyed had an information manager position, and of these, 36 percent reported directly to the president. Today the percentages are undoubtedly higher. But whether or not a company recognizes information management by formal title, the records management function will increasingly assume integrated information management responsibilities.—*R. A. Shiff*

WORK SIMPLIFICATION

"Improvement," it has been aptly said, "is a journey, not a destination." At any given time there may be a "one best way" of doing something—to use the phrase made famous by Frank B. Gilbreth, one of the early pioneers of scientific management. However, just around the corner there is probably a still better way of doing it. The final destination is never reached, but the journey is all-important. It is this continuing questioning and improving the way in which work is done, by all who are involved in the specific tasks at hand, that are the subject matter of the philosophy, program, and techniques subsumed under the term "work simplification."

Background

The careful, systematic scrutiny and analysis of industrial tasks by breaking them down into their elements and studying and timing each element separately began with the pioneering work of Frederick W. Taylor ("the father of scientific management") at the Midvale Steel Company, Philadelphia, in the 1880's.

From Taylor's work and that of others who worked with him and came after him, there developed a whole new discipline of industrial engineering, embracing tighter methods of production and inventory control, scientific cost accounting, statistical quality control, and the host of other techniques that make possible the efficient management of complex, ramified industrial operations.

In the early 1930's, after some four decades of increasing sophistication of manufacturing methods, a breakthrough occurred that was destined to bring cost savings to countless firms—savings ranging from thousands to millions of dollars a year in a single company, and all without any additional capital investment in plant or equipment. The breakthrough was the introduction of a new concept—work simplification—by Allan H. Mogensen, a young industrial engineer on the editorial staff of *Factory* who was also engaged in consulting work. Mogensen's contribution consisted not in the development of new engineering or manufacturing principles but rather in the psychological approach of inspiring the entire working force—reaching them through their supervisors—to make a concerted attack on costs by taking a new look at the way work was being done and then, by applying some readily learned techniques of work charting and analysis, coming up with suggestions for improvements.

First use of the term "work simplification" is actually attributed to Professor Erwin H. Schell of the Massachusetts Institute of Technology (MIT), who has been closely associated with Mogensen's work over the years. It was Mogensen, however, who put the philosophy and techniques together into a unified, teachable program for implementation by supervisors and other key personnel. His approach was sensationally successful, and in 1937 he met the demand for more "spreading the gospel" by opening the first of his now famous work simplification conferences held annually at Lake Placid, New York.

The interest in and effectiveness of work simplification have never abated. Recently, almost forty years after the launching of the concept, *Supervisory Management* quoted the work simplification coordinator of a lumber company's regional plant to the effect that a program there saved $120,000 in its first year. The same publication reported savings by other companies, in a recent year, ranging from $1 million to $6,665,000.

Work simplification, which began in manufacturing operations, is now applied wherever work is done: in offices, in retailing, in construction, and even in the medical profession in the streamlining of surgical techniques.

Philosophy

The philosophy of work simplification is expressed in the definitions advanced by some of the well-known practitioners in the field. Mogensen himself, in his early proselytizing, would define work simplification as "the organized application of common sense to finding better and easier ways of doing every job, from eliminating waste motion in minor hand operations to complete rearrangement of plant layout." Every employee, he would insist, was to be taught to ask "Why?" about everything he did, and to be encouraged to use initiative in suggesting savings of time, energy, and material.

The late W. C. Zinck, an industrial engineer and early Mogensen disciple at Lake Placid, in his *Dynamic Work Simplification* (Reinhold Publishing Corporation, 1962) defines the concept as follows:

> Work simplification is an organized, common-sense attack upon the way in which work is done now, with a view to doing it better. It makes use of the techniques of method improvement, but it goes beyond a series of techniques. Work simplification "stretches the mind" by introducing and solidifying a new concept of what is *useful* work. It changes habits of thinking about what must be considered as *waste* work. . . . The *why* of work simplification is to enable every employee, but especially the foreman and direct supervisor, to help improve the competitive position of the company in its industry.

The Veterans Administration, in *Work Simplification,* defines its subject in these terms:

> It is the continuous, organized application of common sense in the search for better and easier ways of doing work. It is a well-planned approach to problem solving. It is the application of *creative thinking* to problem solving. It is the do-it-yourself approach to work improvement. It encourages the free flow of ideas from bottom to top.

Note the emphasis on employee and supervisory participation. Mogensen was asked by a *Factory* interviewer, 21 years after the first Lake Placid conference, "What is it about work simplification that makes it so successful while other methods programs flop?" His reply was:

> Work simplification *always* introduces the human element, is always designed for foreman and employee participation. This isn't true of many methods improvement programs. All too often they put the emphasis on "experting" and give only lip service to employee considerations.

Techniques

The basic premises and techniques of work simplification programs as applied to factory operations are indicated here. Special procedures and adaptations in the later development of office work simplification are discussed farther on in this contribution.

WORKING THROUGH SUPERVISORS

The objective of work simplification is to put the spotlight on individual departments. Most companies have central staff departments manned by industrial engineers and methods and systems people and other professionals whose job it is to make the large plantwide or companywide studies and recommendations that cut across departmental lines. A work simplification program complements the work of the professionals by training and motivating the departmental supervisors to look for improvement possibilities, within their own departments, which the professionals can't search out because they do not have the supervisor's familiarity with the details of his everyday departmental operation. The program also calls for supervisors to cooperate with the full-time methods people on projects affecting their departments and to sell changes called for by such projects to their departmental personnel.

REDUCIBLE WASTE

From the very beginning of a work simplification program the idea is hammered home to supervisors that all reducible waste in a department must be eliminated. The following three basic types of waste recognized by industrial engineers in analyzing processes and operations are stressed (usually, they cannot be entirely eliminated, but every effort must be made to reduce them to a minimum):

1. *Waste in transportation* can result when anything—a product or part, a document, or a person—is moved from one place to another. In an operation analysis, this can be the needless movement of a hand or other body part.

2. *Waste caused by delay or storage* occurs when something remains in one place awaiting further action. This can be a piece of material in a tote pan waiting to be worked on, a subassembly waiting for final scheduled assembly, a letter in an "outgoing" box, a man idle while a machine is finishing a cut, or a clerk idle while waiting for papers to process.

3. *Waste following inspection* occurs when something has been checked or verified but not corrected.

The foregoing are waste because they do not add value to the product being worked on. A certain amount of transportation is of course necessary, and temporary storage or delay may be unavoidable; but the idea is to take a new look to see how much has been taken for granted—has not actually been perceived. Similarly, inspection may have been thought of as constructive because it does not allow faulty work to get by, but actually it adds no value; it simply catches something that was done wrong earlier.

In addition to the foregoing recognizable wastes, Zinck (*Dynamic Work Sim-*

plification) isolated a fourth, recognized only by its absence: failure to use known faster devices. Simple auxiliary tools or devices, mechanization, or the ultimate—complete automation—can reduce the waste of transportation, delay-storage-idle, and inspection to a minimum, and their cost must be weighed against the cost advantages thus achieved.

In work simplification analysis, an operation is explicitly defined: It occurs when something is being changed, or added to or taken away from another object, or arranged or prepared for another operation or for transportation, storage, or inspection. An operation also occurs when information is given or received and when planning or calculating is done. Obviously, an operation itself is a waste if it is dispensable and should be eliminated.

EMPHASIS ON "WHY?"

The next main point of emphasis in work simplification is to take nothing for granted—to challenge everything that is being done in the department. The fact that something has been done in a certain way for a long time is considered to be an argument that there is probably a better way of doing it. Every process and operation is viewed with a fresh look and subjected to searching questions that probe into *what, where, when, who, how,* and *why*—with the accent on *why* because that can be asked about all of the others.

Involved in the answers to the *why* questions are the following improvement questions:

1. *What can be eliminated?* Why is it being done in the first place? Is it an absolute "must"?

2. *What can be combined?* Can an inspection be done along with an operation? Can two operations be done as one (perhaps with a known faster device)? Can one person do two tasks in the same time period (for example, one operator tending two machines; a receptionist doing preliminary file sorting)?

3. *What should be changed?* Will improved motions or rearranged workplace speed output? Again, should a known faster device be applied?

4. *Should sequence of operations be changed?* Changes in sequence may eliminate or reduce operations that add no value, as well as transportations, delays, storages, and inspections.

5. *Should work allocation be changed?* Why is *this* person doing it?

CHARTING TECHNIQUES

It has proved highly effective to have supervisors learn how to use certain work simplification charts for detailed analysis of departmental processes and operations singled out for potential improvement. Standardized symbols are used, usually on preprinted chart forms on which are also entered, along with the symbols, terse descriptive statements about the elements of the work being studied. The purpose of the charting is to make sure that all elements of the work and their sequence are kept in mind when improvement possibilities are sought. And in addition, such charting drives home to the supervisor how startlingly few are the actual value-adding operations; it makes elements of waste never noticed before stand out like sore thumbs. The standardized work simplification symbols in current use are shown in Exhibit 2.4.

In factory operations three basic charts are used: the process analysis chart, the man-machine chart, and the operation analysis chart. Portions of samples of each of these types, shown in Exhibit 2.5, illustrate the technique. The actual size of the forms is 11 by 16¼ inches. Value-adding operations may be shaded to make them stand out. The forms shown are typed for reading convenience; in practice the supervisors fill them in by hand. All elements of the work are tersely described.

The process analysis chart, sometimes referred to as the flow process chart, is the one most commonly used in office work simplification; it is shown in greater detail in Exhibit 2.6. After a supervisor has devised a way to improve a process or an operation, he is asked to chart the new method in the same fashion. In this way he documents the improvement in specific terms, thus enabling him to sell his idea to management and to the workers affected by the proposed changes.

The process analysis. The charted process analysis provides a record in chronological sequence of all the elements of work done on a piece as it goes through a series of operations in the department in a defined process that changes it in some way or assembles or disassembles it from something. In a factory, this could be a piece going through an assembly department, or through plating, or some other process involving a series of operations. In an office it could be a record of what happens to a requisition from the time it comes into a supply office to the time it is filled and filed. The purpose of the chart is to highlight the wastes of transportation, delay-storage-idle, and inspection between the opera-

Exhibit 2.4

WORK SIMPLIFICATION SYMBOLS

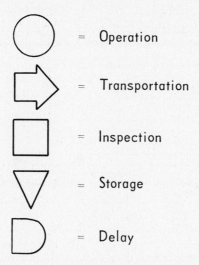

○ = Operation

⇨ = Transportation

□ = Inspection

▽ = Storage

D = Delay

NOTE: Some work simplification programs use one symbol ▽ for Delay-Idle-Storage, and a small circle, approximately half the diameter of Operation, for Transportation.

Exhibit 2.5

PORTIONS OF FACTORY WORK SIMPLIFICATION CHARTS

Reprinted from W. C. Zinck, "Work Simplification," in *The Encyclopedia of Management*, Carl Heyel, ed., Reinhold Publishing Co., 1963; with permission of Van Nostrand Reinhold Co.

PROCESS ANALYSIS

◯ AN OPERATION ◯ A TRANSPORTATION ▽ A DELAY-STORAGE-IDLE ☐ AN INSPECTION

WHAT IS BEING DONE? **WHERE** IS IT BEING DONE? **WHEN** IS IT DONE? **WHO** IS DOING IT? **HOW** IS IT BEING DONE? **WHY** IS IT DONE?

ELEMENT NO.	DESCRIPTION – GIVE ALL DETAILS ALL YOU WILL KNOW ABOUT THE PROCESS FOR YOUR IMPROVEMENT ANALYSIS ARE THE FACTS YOU RECORD HERE WHILE ACTUALLY OBSERVING THE PROCESS	SYMBOL	DISTANCE in feet	TIME in minutes	NOTES – DATA – SKETCHES Things to Check For IMPROVEMENT POSSIBILITIES
1	Regular Pork Trimmings (40%) in truck in Cooler No. 21, where it had been placed in storage by trucker during hog cut operation.	▽			Tub 28 x 57 x 23 deep Capacity 1000 lb. approx.
2	Truck grasped by grinder and grinder-helper from Department 15 – Sausage.	◯			Why not taken directly to cooler No. 9?
3	Truck pushed to grinder in meat preparation room of Sausage Department. Two men needed on account of the unevenness of the floors and weight of truck.	◯	375		Grinder secures pork when needed. Two tubs are ground ahead of the frankfurter emulsion grinding operation.
4	Truck released by grinder and helper in position at grinder work area.	◯			Will not a tub each of Regular and Jowl Trimmings do just as well, and grind as needed?
5	Till forked into grinder.	▽			Grinder head has 3/16" grid. Grinder is Buffalo 78B, John E. Smith's Sons Co.
6	Pork Trimmings forked from truck and tossed into bowl of grinder by grinder.	●		9	Grinder bowl is a bit too high – making the forking a bit awkward.

MAN-MACHINE ANALYSIS

◯ AN OPERATION ◯ A TRANSPORTATION ▽ IDLE ☐ AN INSPECTION

ELEMENT NO.	DISTANCE	MAN WHAT – HOW – WHY RECORD HERE THE FACTS AND THE KEY POINTS OF WHAT YOU ACTUALLY SAW THE MAN DO	ELEMENT SYMBOL	VALUE ADDING TIME MAN	VALUE ADDING TIME MACHINE	ELEMENT SYMBOL	MACHINE RECORD HERE WHAT THE MACHINE DID
		NAME Luther W_____, Jr.		CYCLE TIME 20 Sec.			TYPE .... Grinding Machine
							SPECIFICATIONS 12" Wheel, Bonded
							TOOL-JIG-FIXTURE DATA 12" Level Plate
1		Turns body to left.	◯			▽	Idle
2		Picks up casting.	◯				
3	18"	Carries casting to level plate.	◯				
4		Checks casting legs on plate.	◯				
5	12"	Carries casting to grinding machine.	◯				
6		Grinds casting legs.	●	2	2	●	Grind

OPERATION ANALYSIS

DIE MAKER FILE

	LEFT HAND					RIGHT HAND		
ELEMENT	DISTANCE	DESCRIPTION OF ELEMENT	SYMBOL	VALUE ADD'G TIME	VALUE ADD'G TIME	SYMBOL	DESCRIPTION OF ELEMENT	DISTANCE	ELEMENT
1		Picks up insert.	◯			▽	Holds file.		1
2	12"	To filing position.	◯			◯	To insert.	12"	2
3		Holds insert.	▽		20	●	Files insert at hole to remove rough edge.		3

Exhibit 2.6

PROCESS CHART

	PRESENT		PROPOSED		DIFFERENCE		PROJECT:		NUMBER:	PAGE	OF
	NO.	TIME	NO.	TIME	NO.	TIME					
◯ OPERATIONS							PHASE:				
⇨ TRANSPORTATION							CHART BEGINS:				
☐ INSPECTIONS											
D DELAYS							CHART ENDS:				
▽ STORAGES							CHARTED BY:			DATE:	
DISTANCE TRAVELED		FT.		FT.		FT.					

ANALYZE: IMPROVEMENT:

WHAT? WHY? WHERE? WHEN? WHO? HOW?   ELIMINATE – SIMPLIFY – COMBINE – CHANGE

STEP NUMBER	DETAILS OF (PRESENT/PROPOSED) METHOD	REF. HAND P. MACH. COLLATE FILE OTHER TRANSP. INSPEC. DELAY STORE	DISTANCE	QUANTITY	TIME
		®ⒽⓂ©ⒻⓍ⇨☐D▽			
		®ⒽⓂ©ⒻⓍ⇨☐D▽			
		®ⒽⓂ©ⒻⓍ⇨☐D▽			
		®ⒽⓂ©ⒻⓍ⇨☐D▽			
		®ⒽⓂ©ⒻⓍ⇨☐D▽			
		®ⒽⓂ©ⒻⓍ⇨☐D▽			
		®ⒽⓂ©ⒻⓍ⇨☐D▽			
		®ⒽⓂ©ⒻⓍ⇨☐D▽			
		®ⒽⓂ©ⒻⓍ⇨☐D▽			
		®ⒽⓂ©ⒻⓍ⇨☐D▽			
		®ⒽⓂ©ⒻⓍ⇨☐D▽			
		®ⒽⓂ©ⒻⓍ⇨☐D▽			
		®ⒽⓂ©ⒻⓍ⇨☐D▽			
		®ⒽⓂ©ⒻⓍ⇨☐D▽			
		®ⒽⓂ©ⒻⓍ⇨☐D▽			
		®ⒽⓂ©ⒻⓍ⇨☐D▽			
		®ⒽⓂ©ⒻⓍ⇨☐D▽			
		®ⒽⓂ©ⒻⓍ⇨☐D▽			
		®ⒽⓂ©ⒻⓍ⇨☐D▽			
		®ⒽⓂ©ⒻⓍ⇨☐D▽			
		®ⒽⓂ©ⒻⓍ⇨☐D▽			
		®ⒽⓂ©ⒻⓍ⇨☐D▽			
		®ⒽⓂ©ⒻⓍ⇨☐D▽			
		®ⒽⓂ©ⒻⓍ⇨☐D▽			
		®ⒽⓂ©ⒻⓍ⇨☐D▽			
		®ⒽⓂ©ⒻⓍ⇨☐D▽			
		®ⒽⓂ©ⒻⓍ⇨☐D▽			
		®ⒽⓂ©ⒻⓍ⇨☐D▽			

tions that *add value*. It focuses attention on the time expended for make-ready, moving, and waiting. After the process chart has been analyzed, some operations may be eliminated or changed in a way made obvious by the mere process of charting. Others may be subject to detailed analysis, utilizing the other two charts. Note that the analyst follows *one* piece or document through all of its operations. In complex operations the travel would proceed through several departments; and in highly complex operations—for example, following various components through their operations to the completion of a final assembly— separate process charts for separate components would merge into process charts for subassemblies, ending with one at the end for the final assembly.

The man-machine analysis. As shown in Exhibit 2.5, the man-machine analysis applies the same charting technique to the study of a man-machine operation after (*a*) the process analysis confirms that the operation is indeed necessary at that point, and (*b*) preliminary observation and the questioning attitude indicate that there may be rewards in studying the operation in detail. Note that in this case the preprinted charting form contains parallel columns, one for the man and one for the machine. This serves to emphasize idle time or nonvalue-adding travel or inspection or operation on the part of the one while the other may be performing constructive work.

The operation analysis. The charting of the operation analysis puts the magnifying glass on the operator himself. Note that the process analysis has not looked inside any of the value-adding operations, and the man-machine analysis is a broad, overall observation of the operator's activity, in relation to the machine-controlled operations, to see if anything can be done to reduce his idle time, handling time, make-ready time, and so forth. Now (assuming that the questioning attitude indicated improvement possibilities) the operation analysis concentrates on the detailed right-hand and left-hand activities of the operator (including, of course, bench workers and others not associated with a particular machine). The same charting technique is used (Exhibit 2.5), this time with parallel columns for the right and the left hand respectively.

MOTION ECONOMIES

With respect to operation analyses, work simplification programs drill the supervisors in the basics of motion study, leaving the refined time studies, micromotion analyses, "therblig analysis," and the like to the professionals. These techniques of motion study are still basically those developed by Frank Gilbreth.

Gilbreth developed 22 basic principles of motion economy. These may be found in texts on industrial engineering, specifically in Zinck (*Dynamic Work Simplification*), but the following seven are the ones commonly stressed in work simplification training of supervisors in plants (and the first two of these may be applied in many office applications):

1. Tools, materials, and controls should be located around the workplace, as close in front of the worker as possible. (The area covered by the sweep of the extended arm is considered the maximum normal working area, and that covered by the sweep of the forearm is considered the optimum working area).

2. Tools and materials should be prepositioned wherever possible.

3. Drop deliveries should be used wherever possible.

4. Gravity feed bins and containers should deliver the material as close to point of use as possible.

5. Motions of the arms should be in opposite and symmetrical directions, and should be made simultaneously, for maximum rhythm.

6. Use of the hand as a holding device should be avoided.

7. Hands should be relieved of all work that can be performed more advantageously by the feet or other parts of the body. (Foot treadles are an example.)

SENSE OF ACHIEVEMENT

Experience has shown that supervisors and key people who have been properly motivated and given instruction in the relatively simple charting techniques and elementary industrial engineering principles involved will begin to produce money-saving, profit-increasing ideas almost immediately. The eye-opening effect of the charts in highlighting wastes in operations that have been going on unchallenged for years is dramatic. As soon as a supervisor really "sees" how work is being done in his department, possibilities for improvement will inevitably occur to him.

In this connection, a point early driven home by Mogensen is that the company's professional methods man or outside consultant who is spark-plugging and coordinating a work simplification program will frequently see that an improvement suggestion advanced by a supervisor applying the techniques he has been teaching could actually be made much more effective by application of additional industrial engineering expertise. However, he should refrain from improving the improvement but do everything possible to secure the implementation of the supervisor's idea and to see that the supervisor's coworkers hear about it. The sense of achievement thus imparted will pay handsome dividends in the form of further ideas; and soon the supervisor himself will realize that additional refinements of his idea are possible, and he will come voluntarily to the professional when he needs help.

Office Work Simplification

The basic philosophy and techniques of plant work simplification are directly transferable to the improvement of office operations. Because of the nature of office operations, the process analysis or flow process chart will be found to be most applicable. On the other hand, especially in large offices with many routine, repetitive operations, the use of the operation analysis chart will lead to improvements in the development of efficient work areas, the prepositioning of forms and other supplies, the use of standardized sequences and procedures, and the like.

PLACE IN ORGANIZATION

As with the plant work simplification program, the primary objective is to focus the searchlight and the magnifying glass on departmental operations—again, through the enlistment of the enthusiasm of supervisors and key personnel and their training in the elementary techniques involved.

It is assumed that the company has a staff office methods or systems and procedures department and that one of its professionals or an outside consultant will spark the program, provide the necessary training, and coordinate the results. Thus the development of companywide information systems and systems management, records management and control, large-scale projects (such as studying the feasibility of substituting a central files system or a stenographic pool), detailed work measurement studies, and the like, is the province of the professionals and not part of a departmental work simplification program. However, large-scale companywide projects may be the outgrowth of suggestions stimulated by departmental work simplification analyses. Moreover, the techniques of analysis here discussed are usable in these larger studies. For example, the process flow diagrams used in studies leading to the installation of electronic data processing systems are similar to the flow process charting used in work simplification, although different symbols are used.

CHARTING AND ANALYSIS TECHNIQUES

Six basic charting and analysis instruments are used in office work simplification: the activity list, the task list, the work distribution chart, the process chart, the operation analysis chart (where called for), and the work count.

Because office operations over the years have not been subject to the intense industrial engineering analysis applied to factory operations, the office supervisor does not as a rule start out on a high plateau of balanced-load work areas. Moreover, office personnel as a rule perform a wide variety of tasks rather than a single repetitive machine operation or the completion of a craft function, as in manufacturing. Accordingly, office work simplification, after initial indoctrination on the need to eliminate waste, starts out by having the supervisor prepare the first three of the six charting and analysis instruments to give him a bird's-eye view of all the activities in his unit and the contribution of each employee to each activity. These enable him to take the first broad cut at his improvement problem.

The activity list. All the major activities of the department or unit are entered on an activity list. A large department will require activity lists prepared by the separate sections. Each activity is consecutively numbered for future cross-reference to the task list.

The task list. The supervisor gives each employee a simple form on which to draw up his task list. After entering identifying information (name, position, section, and department), the employee lists all the specific tasks for which he is responsible, together with his rough estimate of the number of hours per week spent on each. (See Exhibit 2.7.) The supervisor, of course, checks all task lists for accuracy. Tasks that do not occur regularly every week are listed separately, then averaged out and prorated on the task list. In the column headed "Quantity" the employee lists his estimate of the number of times he completes each task each week. (If an employee is unsure of the number of hours per week he spends on an activity, he can be supplied a separate form for a week or so on which to record—say, for 15-minute intervals—the starting and stopping times on all the tasks he performs, together with a record of interruptions.) The column headed "Posted to Activity Number" is used by the supervisor later in preparing the work distribution chart. The supervisor, in consultation with his employees, is responsible for resolving any discrepancies that may appear between the tasks entered in the collection of task lists and his activity list.

The work distribution chart. A summary sheet is made up from the two preceding lists. (See Exhibit 2.8.) Major activities are listed down the left-hand column, followed by an entry of total man-hours spent on each activity. Succeeding columns across the page are allocated, one to each employee in the department. Note that these are subheaded "Tasks"; they permit the posting of total hours spent by each employee on each major activity broken down by individual tasks associated with that activity. These individual task entries must, of course, add up to the total for each major activity.

Applying the questioning attitude to the work distribution chart enables the

Exhibit 2.7

TASK LIST FOR WORK DISTRIBUTION CHART

Reprinted from Department of the Army Pamphlet No. 20-300.

NAME:	WORKING TITLE:	GRADE OR RANK:
Paul Smith	Chief Clerk	Sgt. First Class

ORGANIZATION:	SUPERVISOR:	DATE:
Personnel Branch Assignment Section	Maj. Wilson	25 Oct. 1970

TASK NO.	DESCRIPTION	POSTED ON W/D CHART TO ACTIVITY NO.	HOURS PER WEEK	WORK UNITS AND/OR VOLUME (OPTIONAL)
1.	Assemble strength and requirements data used in the assignment of enlisted personnel.		12	
2.	Check officer personnel rosters and records to make certain that each individual file is complete.		10	
3.	Answer routine inquiries on personnel assignment received by phone — refer questions to section chief.		6	25
4.	Study and review special case studies of assignment problems to make certain all data are available.		3	
5.	Keep time and attendance records for section personnel.		4	6
6.	Prepare operating and administrative reports for the Branch and Division.		2	3
7.	Review administrative reports from other sections in the Branch, and indicate pertinent portions to Section Chief.		3	
	Total		40	

Exhibit 2.8

EXAMPLE OF A WORK DISTRIBUTION CHART

Reprinted from Department of the Army Pamphlet No. 20-300.

ORGANIZATION UNIT CHARTED: Assignment Section
[x] EXISTING ORGANIZATION   [ ] RECOMMENDED ORGANIZATION
CHARTED BY: Major Wilson
APPROVED BY:

WORK DISTRIBUTION CHART

ACTIVITY NUMBER	ACTIVITY	Recommended Org. WORK COUNT	Recommended Org. HOURS PER WEEK	J. K. Wilson — Section Chief (Grade M) TASKS	WC	Hrs	Paul Smith — Chief Clerk (Grade Sgt) TASKS	WC	Hrs	Wm. Chase — Strength Analyst (GS 7) TASKS	WC	Hrs	Miss Hall — Order Clerk (GS 5) TASKS	WC	Hrs	Miss Brown — Steno (GS 4) TASKS	WC	Hrs
1.	Assignment of enlisted personnel.	100	53	Allocates replacements to units.	100	7	Assembles strength and requirements data.		7	Recommends allocations.		14	Prepares and proofreads transfer orders.	100	7	Proofreads orders.	100	7
				Allocates levies from higher authority.		5												
2.	Assignment of officer personnel.	50	49	Studies requirements against authorizations.		4	Checks rosters and records for completeness.			Recommends allocations.		8	Prepares and proofreads transfer orders.	50	4	Proofreads orders.	50	5
				Review assignments allocations.		5												
				Approves orders.	50	3												
3.	General inquiry and information Service.		34	Conference with commanders and staff officers.		3	Answers routine inquiries by phone.		3	Presents studies to other branch officials.	25	6	Routine inquiries on status of orders.	10	5	Prepares records of branch conferences.		6
				Review and sign letters of inquiry.		1												
4.	Specific case studies and requirements analysis.		48	Continuing survey of long-range requirements.		3	Reviews case studies.		3	Statistical analysis of unit strength.		3	Furnish data on personnel or orders.	12	6	Dictation and transcription of case studies.		8
				Review case studies.		2				Studies scarce MOS categories.		6						
5.	Administration and supervision.		39	Conference with branch personnel.		1	Time and attendance records.		1	Staff conference.		4	Staff conference. Prepare weekly summaries of transfers.		2	Records of staff conferences.		4
				Prepare budget staff conference.		4 2	Prepare administrative reports.		2									
6.	Miscellaneous activities.		17				Analyzes reports from other sections.		2	Security inspections.		3	Special messenger service.		4	Phone directory, office SOP, etc.		2
	TOTALS (Manhours)		240			40			40			40			40			40

Handwritten annotations: "Process Chart?" "Most Time?" "Properly, need skills?" "Tasks spread too thinly?" "Misdirected effort?" "Unrelated task?" "Misdirected effort?"

¹ Work Count data are optional.

ANALYSIS: WHAT TAKES THE MOST TIME?...IS THERE MISDIRECTED EFFORT?...ARE SKILLS USED PROPERLY?...ARE THERE TOO MANY UNRELATED TASKS?...ARE TASKS SPREAD TOO THINLY?...IS WORK DISTRIBUTED EVENLY?

supervisor to determine where major work imbalances exist and which activities offer potential if subjected to process chart and possibly operation chart analysis. Here are representative key questions: What activities are taking the most time? Are these the ones that *should* take the most time? Does there appear to be misdirected effort? Is excessive time spent on relatively unimportant or unnecessary tasks? Are some employees performing too many unrelated tasks? (Overcrowded columns in the work distribution sheet may be a clue). Are some tasks spread too thinly? (The repetition of the same task in several columns may be a sign that too many employees are doing the same task.) Is work distributed evenly? Do the jobs of some employees look thin when compared with those of others?

The process chart and operation analysis chart. The philosophy and techniques of these charts are the same in office work simplification as previously described for factory operations. Exhibits 2.9 and 2.10 show a process analysis at the Department of the Interior. Here the supervisor, in a campaign to make everyone waste-conscious, had all his employees study one or more of their operations and chart them. The illustrations cover the requisitioning of a rubber stamp. "Before and after" charting dramatizes improvements. The employee charted the paperwork in detail, writing down every separate clerical action, the distance traveled by the papers, and elapsed times. He noted a total of 21 different elements of operations, transportations, inspections, and storages, requiring a total travel of 261 feet and a total time of 117 minutes. Application of purposeful thought, calling for combinations, eliminations, and simplifications, enabled him to cut the work elements to 16, the travel to 116 feet, and the time to 86 minutes—representing more than a 25 percent reduction in processing time.

Flow process charting may, of course, result in suggestions for a new office layout for streamlined paper handling and human traffic, as well as in improved operations.

The work count. The work count is for volume analysis, and the work count sheet is an auxiliary instrument to the work distribution chart and the flow process chart. The first concentrates on the *division* of work; the second, on the *sequence* of work; and the third, the work count, completes the picture by showing the supervisor *how much* is done, and helps schedule the work of his unit. A process chart, for example, will show where work piles up awaiting decisive action. The work count helps show up just how serious the situation is quantitatively and points the way to breaking the bottleneck. The work count sheet can be a simple form, as shown in Exhibit 2.11, although in some instances it is combined with the task list (Exhibit 2.12).

Management Climate

A brief treatment of work simplification must devote so much space to even minimal coverage of the techniques that there is danger of not elaborating sufficiently on underlying philosophy. It cannot be overstressed that the power of work simplification lies in tapping the resources of enthusiasm and initiative on the part of supervisors and key people and, through them, the enthusiasm and initiative of the entire working force. It is not "just another methods improvement program," and it definitely does not replace the continuing, systematic work of the systems and procedures and methods specialists.

Exhibit 2.9

PROCESS ANALYSIS, OFFICE OPERATION, PRESENT METHOD

FORM DI-701	**UNITED STATES** **DEPARTMENT OF THE INTERIOR** **BUREAU OF:** PROCESS CHART	Number 45	Page No. 1	No. of Pages 1
		Instructions: See reverse side before starting study		

Process Charted		SUMMARY FOR ENTIRE PROCESS					
Form DI-1, Requisition, for rubber stamps		ACTIONS	PRESENT		PROPOSED		DIFFERENCE

			No.	Time	No.	Time	No.	Time
Charted By	Date	○ Operations	7	26 min.				
James Nullag	Oct. 27, 1970	⇨ Transportations	6					
		☐ Inspections	2	20½				
Organization		▽ Storages	5	71				
Supply Office		Distance Traveled (Feet)	261					

STEP NUMBER	DETAILS OF [X] PRESENT METHOD [ ] PROPOSED	OPERATION	TRANSPORTATION	INSPECTION	STORAGE	DISTANCE IN FEET	QUANTITY (WORK COUNT)	TIME NEEDED min.	COMMENTS AND ANALYSIS
1	Arrives in supply office with sample sheets attached.							5	
2	Incoming date stamped on requisition.								Combine with step 5?
3	To requisition clerk.					75			Requisition clerk and files are in a room separate from purchase order clerk and supply officer.
4	In incoming box.							15	
5	Applies requisition number.								
6	Requisition recorded on register.							2	Why? Would supply office file suffice?
7	To purchase order clerk.					65			
8	In incoming box.							15	
9	Checks source of supply and schedule for pricing.							20	
10	Computes cost.							10	
11	Prepares purchase order.							10	Could form letter replace purchase order to transmit sample sheet to vendor?
12	Assembles requisition sample sheets, and purchase order.							2	
13	To supply officer.					30			
14	In incoming box.							30	
15	Supply officer approves and signs.							½	
16	To requisition clerk.					85			
17	In incoming box.							5	
18	Requisition clerk completes record on register.							2	
19	Action copies dispatched.								
20	Supply office copies to file clerk.					6			
21	Filed.							1	

Exhibit 2.10

PROCESS ANALYSIS, OFFICE OPERATION, IMPROVED METHOD

FORM DI-701

**UNITED STATES
DEPARTMENT OF THE INTERIOR
BUREAU OF:**

PROCESS CHART

Number	Page No.	No. of Pages
45	1	1

Instructions: See reverse side before starting study.

Process Charted		SUMMARY FOR ENTIRE PROCESS						
Form DI-1, Requisition, for rubber stamps		ACTIONS		PRESENT		PROPOSED		DIFFERENCE	

		ACTIONS	No.	Time	No.	Time	No.	Time
Charted By	Date	◯ Operations	7	26	6	16	1	10 min
James Nullag	Oct. 27, 1970	⇨ Transportations	6	–	4	–	2	–
		☐ Inspections	2	20½	2	20½	–	–
Organization		▽ Storages	6	71	4	50	2	21
Supply Office		Distance Traveled (Feet)	261		116		145	

STEP NUMBER	DETAILS OF ☐ PRESENT ☐ PROPOSED METHOD	OPERATION	TRANSPORTATION	INSPECTION	STORAGE	DISTANCE IN FEET	QUANTITY (WORK COUNT)	TIME NEEDED min.	COMMENTS AND ANALYSIS
1	Arrives in supply office with sample sheet attached.	◯	⇨	☐	▼			5	
2	To requisition clerk.	◯	◼	☐	▽	30			Placed in same room with purchase order clerk and supply officer.
3	In incoming box.	◯	⇨	☐	▼			15	
4	Date received and requisition number stamped on requisition.	●	⇨	☐	▽				
5	Requisition clerk checks source of supply and schedule for pricing.	◯	⇨	◼	▽			20	
6	Computes cost.	●	⇨	☐	▽			10	
7	Enters cost on all copies of requisition.	●	⇨	☐	▽			1	
8	Completes form letter.	●	⇨	☐	▽			2	Requires only the date, requisition No., vendor's address, and supply officer's signature.
9	Assembles form letter and sample sheet.	●	⇨	☐	▽			1	
10	To supply officer.	◯	◼	☐	▽	40			
11	In incoming box.	◯	⇨	☐	▼			30	
12	Supply officer approves requisition and signs letter.	◯	⇨	◼	▽			½	
13	Action copies dispatched.	◯	◼	☐	▽				
14	Requisition recorded on register.	●	⇨	☐	▽			2	
15	Supply office copies to file clerk.	◯	◼	☐	▽	46			
16	Filed.	◯	⇨	☐	▼				
		◯	⇨	☐	▽				
		◯	⇨	☐	▽				

Management must show that it is wholeheartedly behind the program and that it will not only maintain an open mind on suggestions for improvement from anyone and everyone but will also solicit suggestions.

The program should be sparked and coordinated by one of the company's staff professionals in industrial engineering or systems work or by a competent outside consultant. Whoever he is, he must possess a zeal for the work and be able to make his enthusiasm contagious.

Sources of Information

The annual Lake Placid work simplification conferences have been mentioned. Many colleges and universities offer extension courses and special seminars on the subject, as do numerous management consulting firms and professional management associations.

Despite the proven success of work simplification in varied applications, there was for many years no definitive text on the subject—although, of course, numerous articles appeared in the professional and trade press, notably in *Factory,* Mogensen's original forum. (This publication's name was later changed to *Factory Management and Maintenance* and, more recently, to *Modern Manufacturing.*) Zinck's *Dynamic Work Simplification* filled the gap in the literature; this text goes amply into the philosophy as well as the techniques. Zinck's contribution during his years as a work simplification consultant lay in perfecting ways to bring supervisors and key production workers to appreciate the true meaning of waste and to come up with suggestions for getting rid of it.

A documentary series of articles by Herbert F. Goodwin (*Factory Management*

Exhibit 2.11

WORK COUNT SHEET

NAME:				POSITION:		
DEPARTMENT/SECTION:				PREPARED BY:		DATE:
TIME			TASK DESCRIPTION			UNITS PRODUCED
START	STOP	ELAPSED				

Exhibit 2.12

TASK LIST

ORGANIZATION UNIT:					PROJECT:		NUMBER:	PAGE	OF
NAME:					TITLE:			DATE:	

TIME	TASK	QTY.	INTER. LETTER	INTER. QTY.	TASK NO.	DESCRIPTION	TOTAL TIME	TOTAL UNITS	UNIT TIME	HOURS PER WEEK
:00					1					
:15										
:30					2					
:45										
:00					3					
:15										
:30					4					
:45										
:00					5					
:15										
:30					6					
:45										
:00					7					
:15										
:30					8					
:45										
:00					9					
:15										
:30					10					
:45										
:00					11					
:15										
:30					12					
:45										
:00					13					
:15										
:30					14					
:45										
:00					15					
:15										
:30					INTERRUPTIONS					
:45					A					
:00					B					
:15					C					
:30					D					
:45					E					
					F	TOTALS:				

and Maintenance, July 1968) has been reprinted by that publication as a separate 36-page brochure which features interviews with Mogensen, Dr. Lillian M. Gilbreth, Professor Erwin H. Schell, and Professor David B. Porter, all of whom were active in the movement and in the Lake Placid conferences. This brochure also delves into the philosophy and approach of work simplification.

R. E. Steere, Jr. (*Office Work Simplification,* Vol. XXX of the *Complete Management Library,* Prentice-Hall, Inc., 1963) goes thoroughly into the techniques of fact gathering and charting and does not dwell upon the exhortatory and motivational aspects which are the heart of work simplification. On techniques, however, this book is excellent.—*A. G. Negus*

WORK MEASUREMENT AND STANDARDS

White-collar workers in this country exceed the number of blue-collar and farm workers combined, according to the Bureau of Labor Statistics (BLS). Furthermore, the rate of expansion of the white-collar force is increasing rapidly— about four new white-collar jobs are generated for each blue-collar and farm worker job eliminated.

Need for Measurement

At the current time, approximately 80 percent of factory production jobs are covered by performance standards, but less than 5 percent of the white-collar work force has been measured. Numerous client studies indicate that clerical, secretarial, and administrative employee performance is only about 60 percent effective. This means that 40 percent of administrative costs are not being channeled into useful work. It is particularly significant during a period of reduced profit margins coincident with a tight labor market.

The problem is serious in manufacturing but especially acute in service industries, banks and insurance companies, investment firms, and merchandising businesses, since clerical cost is one of their largest items of operating expense and thus can have a substantial effect on net profits.

Arbitrary budget cuts and use of historical data or statistical yardsticks for cutbacks are not always the best solution. Often, the most efficient operations are hurt most and the least efficient are barely touched. There is need for a more scientific and equitable method of determining optimum personnel output with minimum manpower needs. Supervisors require more up-to-date detailed and factual data upon which to plan, schedule, and control their work and manpower so that management can be assured that each organizational unit is operating effectively with the minimum staff necessary to meet the desired level of service and quality.

GUIDELINES AND QUESTIONS

This subsection is designed to provide management with guidelines to highlight effectiveness of performance of the office organization and staffing levels needed; improvement (or lack of improvement) in productivity; sources of trouble spots; capacity of the office organization; and relative accomplishments, economies, or efficiencies effected in office areas.

Executives ponder over answering such questions as the following: What is a fair day's work? How should an uneven work flow be scheduled? Is the organization of the office the best, considering characteristics of the work? Can savings be realized by reducing work content requirements? Are employees spending sufficient time on the skills for which they are being paid? How much is it costing to provide prompt service to customers, and is continuing such a policy worthwhile? Why has a new method or procedure not produced its hoped-for savings? How long does it take before a new employee earns his way? What portion of office expense should be borne by the various company products or lines? What should the office performance level be? Are all positions equitably compensated in relation to the duties required of each job?

The answers to these and other vital questions can be obtained by the application of a modern work measurement program to all clerical, secretarial, and administrative personnel who are employed in highly repetitive tasks—for example, accounts payable and traffic coding—during the workday.

Benefits of a Work Measurement Program

It is not unreasonable to expect a return of at least $3 annually for each $1 invested in a clerical work measurement program. Also, the expense of installing such a program is a one-time, nonrecurring item, whereas the savings continue year after year. What should management expect as the immediate, tangible results of work measurement? There are several possible objectives, not always equally important to every company. Is management interested only in cost reductions? Rather, the program's usefulness should be determined by other factors such as these: (1) better internal control of work scheduling and individual work assignments; (2) improved service to customers by cutting down elapsed time for processing office work; (3) more effective budgeting, forecasting, and planning of manpower; (4) more accurate allocation of expenses to products or customers; (5) a better basis for evaluating method changes; (6) a basis for making organization changes, especially if relocation of offices is being considered; (7) a basis for changes in personnel policies, such as the installation or revision of a job-evaluation plan, or the preparation or rewriting of job descriptions; (8) a service to operating management in providing more accurate facts for future action.

Before starting any work measurement program, it is essential to determine what management expects of the program and how its success will be judged. No work measurement program can be effective without the complete understanding and full support of all levels of management. Often, too much emphasis is placed on methods and techniques rather than purpose.

Operations and Techniques in Work Measurement

Effective work measurement planning involves three basic operations: an analysis of the clerical work; the establishment of a standard time allowance for each task; and the establishment of a reporting system to provide management with a comparison of actual time used versus standard time, or effectiveness measurement.

Many techniques are used in setting standards: Some are detailed and technical (engineered) and produce precise standards; others can be performed without engineering or time study background (nonengineered) or training. When it is impractical—for reasons of time, cost, or internal operating conditions—to use more precise methods, nonengineered standards may provide a satisfactory answer.

Regardless of the technique employed, work units must be carefully selected to be certain they are indicative of the amount of effort required, and that an increase or decrease in their volume will require a proportionate increase or decrease in the manpower needed. The counts of these units of work should be maintained at key points, preferably at the point where the work enters or leaves the work station. (See Exhibit 2.13 for graphic description of a typical work measurement study.)

WORK ANALYSIS

In order to collect information on a particular job, a number of techniques can be employed. Four basic methods of data collection are logs, work sampling, stopwatch studies, and predetermined time standards.

Logs (time records).   Each employee keeps a diary of how his time is spent during a supervised test period and records his time and volume as the work is processed. The results are summarized and analyzed prior to setting standards by statistical means. This technique supplies a wealth of detail about the distribution of the time of all employees, including nonproductive time. The data permits the development of unit times and unit costs with a fair degree of accuracy. Reasons for departure from standard performance can be easily identified. The results offer greater accuracy than standards based on past production records and estimates. The technique is relatively simple; training is minimum; it can be particularly useful on high-volume, repetitive work. However, it is time-consuming, both in gathering data and analyzing them. It is therefore relatively costly. It is more upsetting to employees than other techniques because of the high amount of employee participation in keeping the daily logs. Accuracy must be carefully watched and checked. Results are sufficiently accurate to permit the use of the standards in effectiveness reporting and other work measurement uses, such as scheduling work, leveling the work load, and planning manpower needs.

Work sampling.   The work sampling technique consists of observing, at random times during the day, a group of employees and noting what they are doing. Statistically, if enough observations are taken, the results will tend to be sufficiently close to the actual time spent by the employees on their various duties. The observer also notes idle time, personal time, and time away from the desk or workplace.

Work sampling furnishes a quick, relatively inexpensive result with very little interruption of work operations. It furnishes a factual and reasonably accurate analysis of work load distribution and is useful in cost allocation. Studies can be made without special skill or training of observers. The degree of accuracy or

Exhibit 2.13

PERFORMANCE STANDARDS STUDY

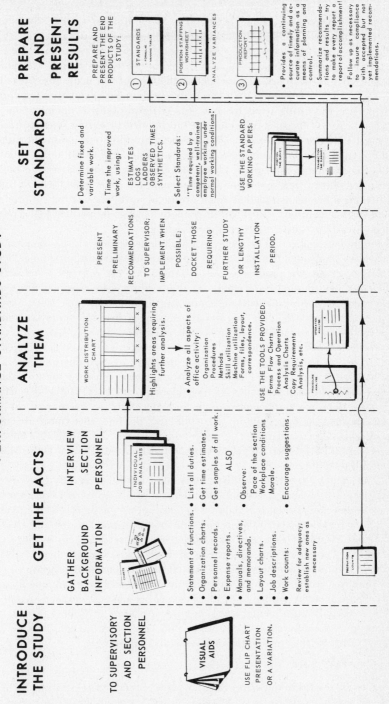

INTRODUCE THE STUDY

TO SUPERVISORY AND SECTION PERSONNEL

USE FLIP CHART PRESENTATION OR A VARIATION.

VISUAL AIDS

GET THE FACTS

GATHER BACKGROUND INFORMATION

• Statement of functions.
• Organization charts.
• Personnel records.
• Expense reports.
• Manuals, directives, and memoranda.
• Layout charts.
• Job descriptions.
• Work counts:
• Review for adequacy; establish new ones as necessary

INTERVIEW SECTION PERSONNEL

INDIVIDUAL JOB ANALYSIS

• List all duties.
• Get time estimates.
• Get samples of all work.

ALSO

• Observe:
   Pace of the section
   Workplace conditions
   Morale.
• Encourage suggestions.

ANALYZE THEM

WORK DISTRIBUTION CHART

Highlights areas requiring further analysis.

• Analyze all aspects of office activity:
   Organization
   Procedures
   Methods
   Skill utilization
   Machine utilization
   Forms, files, layout, correspondence.

USE THE TOOLS PROVIDED:
   Forms Flow Charts
   Process and Operation Analysis Charts
   Copy Requirements Analysis, etc.

PROCEDURE ANALYSIS

OPERATION ANALYSIS

PRESENT PRELIMINARY RECOMMENDATIONS TO SUPERVISOR; IMPLEMENT WHEN POSSIBLE; DOCKET THOSE REQUIRING FURTHER STUDY OR LENGTHY INSTALLATION PERIOD.

SET STANDARDS

• Determine fixed and variable work.
• Time the improved work, using;
   ESTIMATES
   LOGS
   LADDERS
   OBSERVED TIMES
   SYNTHETICS.

• Select Standards:
   "Time required by a competent, well-trained employee working under normal working conditions."

USE THE STANDARD WORKING PAPERS:

OPERATION TIME SURVEY

TRANSACTION TIME SUMMARY

PRODUCTION COUNTS

PREPARE AND PRESENT RESULTS

PREPARE AND PRESENT THE END PRODUCTS OF THE STUDY:

① STANDARDS
   FORMULAE
   HAVING TABLES

② POSITION STAFFING WORKSHEET
   |X|X|X|X|X|
   ANALYZE VARIANCES

③ PRODUCTION REPORT

• Provides a continuing source of timely and accurate information as a means of planning and control.

• Summarize recommendations and results — try to make every report a report of accomplishment!

• Follow up as necessary to insure compliance with accepted but not yet implemented recommendations.

reliability obtained is claimed to compare favorably with standards obtained by other techniques. In fact, the reliability can be increased, if desired, by increasing the number of observations. When leveled for normal work pace, the results are substantially the same as those obtained by more precise timing techniques.

It is not practical, however, to take a sampling of too many fine breakdowns of a job, such as motions of each hand and eye. It is better suited to broad operations, such as posting items on a ledger, retrieving records on microfilm rolls, assembling, and the like. Therefore, it can be used in setting standards for cost control, planning manpower needs, measuring group effectiveness, and gathering information for taking corrective action. Sampling lacks detail and is unsatisfactory for situations requiring it. It does not provide the raw material to build up a predetermined time system or standard time file. It is most useful in quickly obtaining a breakdown of time spent on useful work, personal or nonproductive time, or for identifying work which properly belongs to another job. There are many situations where these results are enough.

Stopwatch studies. The stopwatch technique is one of the simplest, least expensive, and most flexible to use, but it requires trained personnel. Experienced observers can produce excellent results that are consistent and accurate. This requires training in leveling and adjusting for work pace and for extraneous elements. It is particularly useful on large-volume, repetitive work. However, use of the stopwatch must be carefully considered because employees generally are antagonistic toward it and can become resentful.

Predetermined time standards. The several systems using predetermined time values accept the premise that the time necessary to perform fundamental motions in work is constant. Therefore, all such systems construct the unit times or work standards from the times for basic motions comprising the work operations or tasks. The main difference in the several systems is the manner in which each classifies the basic motions and establishes the level that constitutes normal or acceptable performance. The better-known systems are: Methods-Time Measurement (MTM), Work Factor, Master Clerical Data (MCD), and Office Manning Control (OMC).

The data in any one of these systems are consistent at all times. Personal judgment of the analyst is eliminated. The speed of application is an asset. The time to develop standards is reduced by substituting a synthesis of the operation for an actual time study. This is especially useful in preplanning and estimating the time required for a new or changed procedure before it is adopted and installed. The initial cost of learning to apply these values is high. It includes formal training of analysts prior to starting the measurement program.

Employee acceptance varies considerably. In general, the technique is suitable for high-volume, repetitive tasks where manual or physical motions predominate. Where there is much mental computation and reading, it is more difficult to use and convince employees of the validity of the time—even though there are values for reading, writing, mental calculations, and eye-focusing.

CHOOSING THE TECHNIQUE

Each of the techniques described has some specialized role to play in clerical work measurement. None is sufficient by itself, nor applicable to all types of tasks, any more than any one type of office machine can perform all nonmanual operations.

An integrated system can be developed which best suits the operating problems, management practices, and profit objectives. One would certainly use predetermined time values for measuring identical operations in branch offices performing similar work, where a high degree of comparability, for control purposes, is desired. Where jobs are multi-duties, the log would be most useful in allocating the time spent on each task. And so on with each of the available measuring techniques.

This can best be summarized by weighing the various techniques against a set of criteria as shown in Exhibit 2.14.

Exhibit 2.14

EVALUATION OF WORK MEASUREMENT TECHNIQUES

Criteria	Historical Records and Logs	Work Sampling	Stopwatch Timing	Predetermined Time Standards
1. Speed: time required to measure and establish standards	One to four weeks of logging plus summarization	Two to four weeks of observation plus summarization	Fast	Fast
2. Training and skill required: technicians, supervisors	Little	Little	Heavy, including rating	Lengthy
3. Cost: technician, employee time, equipment, etc.	Inexpensive	Inexpensive	Inexpensive	Costly
4. Technical requirements: simplicity, ease of use	Simple	Simple	Complex	Complex
5. Accuracy: Subjective versus objective; degree of distortion	Fair accuracy	Fair accuracy	Very accurate	Very accurate
6. Acceptability: employee, supervisor	Acceptable	Acceptable	Least acceptable	Acceptable if understood by supervisor
7. Interruption of work operations	Little	None	Little	Some supervisor participation
8. Applicability: routine versus nonrepetitive; physical, clerical, professional	Routine and professional	Routine and professional	Routine	Routine
9. Savings: how quickly; how much	Intermediate 10-15 percent	Slow — 8 percent	Fast 15-30 percent	Fast 15-30 percent
10. Usability: in scheduling production; evaluating performance	Fair	Fair	Excellent	Excellent
11. Reporting requirements: difficulty of furnishing data and using reports	Simple	Simple	Complex	Most complex

PROGRAM RESPONSIBILITY

The job of developing and installing a work measurement program may be handled by line management, a staff department in the company, or an outside consultant.

The managers of various line activities may be given the assignment as part of a management development program, with emphasis on the need to improve individual and group production. Guiding principles may be laid down for installing a simple, nonengineered form of measurement.

If a staff department within the company is to develop the program, it may be either the industrial engineering department already engaged in plant time study, or a central office methods department (if one exists), or a department reporting to the controller.

Alternatively, an outside consultant may be called in—a management engineer who has specialized training and experience in methods analysis and work measurement techniques.

Factors to Be Considered in Basic Planning

The approach to the work measurement program must be designed to achieve maximum understanding, acceptance, and participation (as well as optimum savings and other benefits) throughout the company. Important activities to be included in the program's development are the following:

1. *Presenting and thoroughly discussing the program with all levels of management* at the outset, insuring maximum participation and support.

2. *Training selected individuals within the company as analysts* to carry out the program, guiding them through the pilot studies, and demonstrating results so that they can extend the program companywide on their own. Cover all modern measurement techniques providing analysts with the capability to measure nonroutine as well as routine jobs. This gives the analysts the flexibility to achieve greater savings and other benefits in a much shorter time.

3. *Emphasizing systems and procedures improvements* and creating many worthwhile by-product operating and service improvements during the course of the project.

4. *Insuring that close working relationships are maintained between analysts and supervisors during the study.* In this way the supervisors become a real part of the program, contributing many ideas for improvement. As a result, acceptance of change is readily obtained.

Major Phases in Installing a Program

There are three major phases in carrying out a work measurement program: getting it off to a good start; conducting pilot studies to equip analysts to install the program; and extending the program companywide.

INTRODUCTORY STEPS

Several important introductory steps are to be taken at the outset of the program's development: defining company objectives, developing a master plan for the company, selecting analysts, providing orientation for management personnel, and training the analysts.

Defining company objectives. Definitions of company objectives normally focus on the following key factors: (1) cost reduction; (2) operating improvements; (3) service improvements; (4) stronger existing management programs; (5) better management of people; (6) more effective use of the clerical, secretarial, and administrative staff; and (7) reassurance to employees that there will be no "headhunting."

Developing a master plan for the company. Six determinations to be made in developing a master plan are as follows: (1) the organizational units and jobs to be covered; (2) the relationships between this program and others such as data processing, systems development, budget planning, and supervisory development; (3) an appropriate name for the program; (4) the organization of the program and the number of analysts to be staffed; (5) the selection of the units best suited for pilot studies; and (6) the schedule for completing the companywide program.

Selecting analysts. It is essential that the right people be selected—individuals who have analytical ability, sound and mature judgment, and the personality traits necessary to gain acceptance. The knowledge and experience gained through this program provide excellent management training and development opportunities.

General orientation for management personnel. It is most important to gain management understanding and support at all levels at the outset. This will be accomplished through orientation sessions for managerial personnel covering the program's objectives and scope, the general approach and technique, the benefits expected, and the role and responsibilities management must assume to insure that the program is successful. These should be one-session meetings. Initially, they should include all top officers and the officers and supervisors of the pilot study area. It is desirable to cover orientation for all officers and supervisors in the company as soon as possible. Visual aid materials should be used for this purpose.

Classroom training for analysts. After analysts have been selected, they are provided with intensive classroom training in work measurement techniques. The training places heavy emphasis on systems improvements, methods analysis, mechanization opportunities, and improved work organization and scheduling. With this training, analysts are equipped to use the analysis and measurement techniques best suited to each type of work as the program is extended companywide. In classroom training, practical company examples should be used to illustrate improvements and the best uses of the various techniques. It is recommended that representatives from related areas (personnel, training, budgeting, and cost accounting, for example) sit in on the classroom training. The supervisors of the initial pilot study areas should also attend, to the extent that their duties permit, thus receiving maximum exposure to the techniques at the outset.

PILOT STUDIES

Following the classroom training, pilot studies are conducted to equip analysts to install the program companywide; the most important aspects of the work are covered.

Training analysts on the job. During the pilot studies, analysts work full time through the completion of selected pilot study areas, demonstrating how improvements are developed and installed. Thus they learn the best way to determine which work measurement technique to use; analyze and improve methods; set standards; and secure approval and acceptance of changes. They also learn how to reschedule work, level work load, establish staffing formulas, introduce effectiveness reporting, and—most important—how to work with supervisors and management and gain employee acceptance.

An important factor is that of gaining the full acceptance of management, supervisors, and employees, since methods change and standards involve the human equation. For this reason, the analysts should be coached on how to deal with people and how to gain maximum acceptance of all good ideas for improving existing systems, methods, and effectiveness.

Supervisory orientation and development. Provide first-line supervisors with a full understanding of the program and its objectives. Instruct them in the techniques used by the analysts so that they can work closely with the analysts in developing and installing methods and procedures improvements. Also, acquaint them with work measurement techniques so that they will understand and appreciate the accuracy and fairness of the standards established by analysts and use them effectively. Place considerable emphasis on the supervisory responsibility for planning, scheduling, and controlling work and raising the level of effectiveness. Get maximum participation during these sessions.

Supervisory orientation and training are achieved through a series of two-hour sessions—about five in number—scheduled so that the subjects covered coincide with the stages of their studies. These sessions are in addition to the close daily working relationships between analysts and supervisors. In this approach, supervisors regard work improvement as their program, and they start to think like members of management. If the pilot studies are handled in the right way, the supervisors of these areas can become the program's best salesmen throughout the company.

Effectiveness reporting and reports to management. Effectiveness reporting is established in each organizational unit studied so that management will know how effective each area of the company is (actual performance against standards). It must be tailored to the needs of each organizational unit. Reports are therefore designed to meet the managerial needs of each organizational segment. The simplest, least time-consuming report format is the most desirable.

Also important is a simple status report to keep management periodically advised of progress and results from the total program. This is also an effective way for management to follow through and insure that the savings identified and agreed to at the completion of each study are eventually realized as attrition takes place.

EXTENDING THE PROGRAM COMPANYWIDE

Following the completion of the pilot studies and other steps previously enumerated, plans are reviewed for extending the program companywide. The trained analysts will assume full responsibility for completing the program on their own, following a definite schedule of installation.

EFFECT ON EMPLOYEES

It is important to dispel the idea that work measurement will result in "head-chopping." Most employees will fear the possible results of work measurement, despite all assurances to the contrary, and this can destroy the effectiveness of the program. Most companies installing work measurement adopt a policy of reducing personnel through normal attrition and turnover-transfer, voluntary resignation, or promotion. Only by anticipating the fears of employees and explaining the company policy on reduction of personnel can management insure a smooth installation.

Savings and Other Benefits

The many benefits resulting from a comprehensive work improvement and measurement program include the following: (1) a sounder basis for planning and budgeting manpower needs; (2) more effective control of personnel costs; (3) improved scheduling; (4) improved methods, procedures, and systems; (5) improved service to customers; (6) more accurate costing of services; (7) improved supervisory skills; (8) better utilization of employee skills; (9) improved salary administration; and (10) cost reduction.

Experience in developing and implementing work measurement programs in many companies shows that a reasonable target is a job reduction of 15 percent. It is estimated that between 80 and 85 percent of all administrative personnel can be covered in companies of 15 administrative personnel or more. It is safe to expect a minimum return of $3 annual savings for every $1 spent to install a program. The savings shown on the pilot studies alone will point up this expectation. Personnel savings are always achieved through attrition.

—*Leonard Stateman and C. J. Berg, Jr.*

PROJECT MANAGEMENT

The concept of project management is neither new nor unique. Project management is actually an outgrowth of the committee and task force organizational concept. In the military, for instance, it is customary to assign new projects and problems to a group of persons who are expected to have the best qualifications and expertise to achieve the successful completion of the project. The project management concept has the advantage that it is organized to bring together persons with the qualifications most suitable for the successful achievement of specific objectives.

The need for a project management type of organization arises from the realization that the conventional organization, based on functional lines, frequently lacks the ability for a quick response and a unified approach. In a conventional organization the responsibility for the successful accomplishment of a project is frequently fragmented among a company's general management, contract administrators, manufacturing, engineering, and other functional areas. In the continuously changing business world of rapid technological advances and changing sociological conditions, timely response and flexibility of management action are matters of corporate survival. A form of management is required that can cut across functional lines to assure a unified and concentrated approach to the solution of problems and the accomplishment of specific objectives.

Application Areas

The project management concept is usually applied to new areas of development or where fast management response and action are required. In some cases management has no choice but to accept the project management concept if it wants to do business with (for example) the Department of Defense (DOD) and the National Aeronautics and Space Administration (NASA). In commercial business the project management concept is usually applied when new products or devices are involved. Essentially, whenever a company is embarked on (1) a new business activity, (2) the introduction or creation of new products or services, or (3) the correction of critical problems within the company, the concept will be found useful.

The project management concept has the advantage that the responsibility for a project is not fragmented among the functional departments as in a conventional organization. The responsibility and accountability for the successful completion of a project are, instead, clearly defined. The need for a project management type of organization increases in proportion to the size and complexity of the project.

Place in Organization Structure

The project management organization has an independent status and cuts horizontally across the functional organization. In the organizational hierarchy a project manager, to be effective, should have the same status and be at the

Exhibit 2.15

MATRIX ORGANIZATION

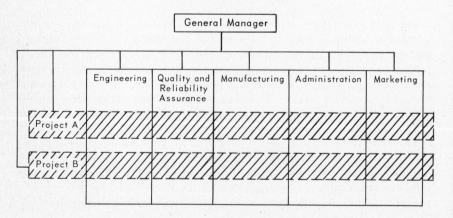

same management level as the managers of the functional departments. This is illustrated in the so-called matrix organization (Exhibit 2.15).

A characteristic of project management is its one-time-through nature. Usually, after successful completion of the project, the project organization is either dissolved or continues as (for example) a new product group and cost center. Usually, the members of the project organization are recruited from the functional departments for the duration of the project. This is a major source of management problems if members of the project organization still retain their reporting responsibility to the functional managers. Preferably, performance appraisal for pay raises and promotion should be made by both the project manager and the functional line manager.

The internal project organization should include the functions that have to be performed by management (Exhibit 2.16).

CHARACTERISTICS OF PROJECT MANAGER

The project manager must be, above all, an achiever. He is actually a general manager in miniature, confronted by problems of administration, accounting, engineering, manufacturing, customer relations, and many others; he must, then, have a broad and versatile background. Not surprisingly, project managers are frequently promoted to the general manager's position. Contrary to many theoretical dissertations on the desired characteristics of a project manager, the fact remains that management almost invariably chooses a person who has a reputation for getting things done. One could describe the ability to get things done by saying that a good project manager is able to exercise good judgment, motivate and coordinate effectively, and have a thorough understanding of management, operational, and scientific engineering principles and practices.

RECRUITING PROJECT TEAM

It is axiomatic that a job must be occupied by the best man available. Usually, the project team is recruited from the functional organization—which is naturally reluctant to lose its best personnel. The project manager must create an incentive for the functional line manager to overcome this handicap. A frequently and successfully used argument is that by having a competent representa-

Exhibit 2.16
EXAMPLE OF PROJECT ORGANIZATION

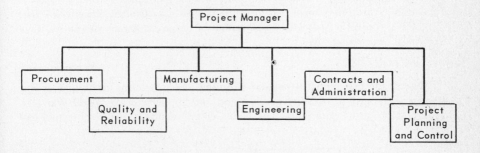

tive on the project team, the functional department will have greater authority and influence over the project. While recruiting the project team, the project manager should bear in mind that he should staff his organization to meet the objectives of the project. The project organization usually must perform the major activities of planning and scheduling, coordinating and controlling, engineering, manufacturing and assembly, quality and reliability assurance, and procurement.

The staffing of the project organization depends on the size and complexity of the project. Constraints on the availability of manpower and/or funding may limit project organization membership to a part-time basis. It may also necessitate the use of one person to cover more than one activity. With this in mind, the choice of a project member should be based first on past professional performance but also, definitely, on the person's ability to grow professionally in more than one discipline.

Modus Operandi of Project Management

The scope and depth of project management's responsibility, authority, and accountability are generally defined by the general manager or the chief executive of an organization. The project manager is usually requested to operate within the framework of existing organization procedures, facilities, and functions. If he cannot execute his responsibilities within these constraints, the general manager will adjust the constraints within the bounds of corporate policy.

The project manager must define his objective (*what* is to be done) and relate it to *how* and *when* it is going to be done within the allocated budget. To accomplish the successful completion of a project, the project manager has to define the tasks to be performed; establish the schedules and expenditure rates associated with these tasks; develop a manpower and facilities plan; develop and define the project organization and its relationships with the other functional departments; staff and designate responsibility and authority to members of the organization; and establish methods and procedures for performance and cost appraisals to assure visibility and management control.

The modus operandi of project management is usually incorporated in a project directive, which should be accompanied by an overall project plan.

Program Planning, Scheduling, and Controlling Techniques

With increased project scope and complexity, the planning, organizing, coordinating, and controlling of a project become a very complex task. Several techniques have been developed that meet the project management objective of visibility and control to improve the allocation of resources among alternative ways to attain project objectives.

GANTT CHARTS

One of the first and still popular planning and scheduling techniques is the Gantt chart introduced by Henry L. Gantt and applied during World War I to the fabrication of munitions. The Gantt chart essentially depicts the progress achieved for a task against the scheduled calendar time, and in the form indicated as follows:

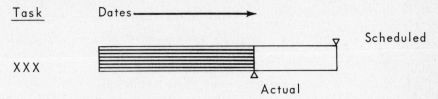

Individual tasks or orders are described on the left-hand portion of the chart, while the scheduled times for the accomplishment of the task are plotted horizontally against the calendar scale. The Gantt chart does not explicitly show manpower and other loads and interrelationships between individual tasks. Its use today is in research and development oriented programs, well-established production programs, and programs which have relatively simple, straightforward tasks.

CPM/CPS

The Critical Path Method (CPM), or Critical Path Scheduling (CPS), was originally developed for use in industry in 1957 and 1958. Its first application was in scheduling construction and maintenance of plants and buildings. Although CPM and PERT (Program Evaluation and Review Technique) have a great deal of similarity, they were independently developed. PERT was developed by the U.S. Navy's Special Projects Office. The CPM method is based on the premise that the activities of a project are executed in a well-defined sequence. The interrelationships between tasks or jobs are indicated by arrows, which also carry a single time estimate for completion of each activity, as shown in the accompanying diagram:

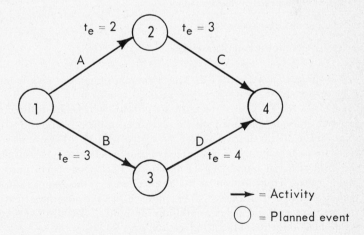

$$T_E \text{ (node 4)} = 7 \text{ days}$$

$$T_L \text{ (node 2)} = (7 - 3) = 4 \text{ days}$$

$$T_L \text{ (node 3)} = (7 - 4) = 3 \text{ days}$$

where:

t_e = expected duration time associated with each activity,

T_E = expected time to reach an event if all the activities prior to it are completed in the expected time for each (T_E = sum of t_e's),

T_L = latest time allowable for an event.

The following are key terminology of the CPM method:

1. *Critical path:* that sequence of activities that impose the most rigid time constraint in the completion of the project (in the foregoing example, *B* and *D*).

2. *Slack time:* the amount of leeway available in reaching an event—that is, $T_L - T_E$ (always zero on the critical path).

(For a more detailed discussion of CPM, see the Manufacturing section of this handbook, page 6·157).

PERT

In addition to the many similarities between CPM and PERT, there are also significant differences. The expected time (t_e), for instance, is computed on the basis of three time estimates:

$$t_e = \frac{t_o + 4t_m + t_p}{6}$$

where:

t_o = optimistic completion time,

t_m = most likely completion time,

t_p = pessimistic completion time.

A logical extension of PERT/Time, where a program is mainly monitored on a time basis, is PERT/Cost, where progress against both time and cost is monitored. In a PERT/Cost system, all activities that generate a direct cost to the program must be indicated on the network or their relationships defined. Because of the administrative burden associated with PERT/Cost, its use in industry is frequently limited to a modified version where cost is broken down only to the level of major tasks. Another version of PERT uses "man units" instead of "time units." Thus, instead of in "elapsed weeks," the completion of an event is indicated by "man weeks." This approach has the advantage that it indicates the manpower requirements to perform the project. (Detailed coverage of PERT is provided in the Manufacturing section, page 6·157).

LINE OF BALANCE

The line of balance (LOB) technique was developed in industry and successfully applied by the U.S. Navy in World War II as a graphical method to evaluate achievement against scheduled performance. The LOB method employs the following elements: the cumulative contract objective chart, which indicates on a calendar-time basis the number of units to be completed or shipped; a progress chart, which indicates the planned and actual activity status of the project at a given time period; and a production plan, which indicates the activities to be performed against a time-to-completion basis.

(For a further explanation of LOB, see G. T. Mundorff and William Bloom, "Managing a Development Program," *Technical Publication No. PB171841,* U.S. Department of Commerce, 1969.)

PPBS

In the mid-1960's the Planning-Programming-Budgeting System (PPBS) was developed; it introduced the systems analysis and cost effectiveness and benefit approach. Its application is chiefly on large and complex projects. The PPBS technique basically revolves on establishing the relationship between (1) effectiveness of the approach and (2) cost of the approach, and on determining the best trade-off between these two parameters. Essentially, PPBS consists of the following steps: defining the problem; determining the key factors of the problem; generating alternative approaches to solve the problem; developing cost-effectiveness relationships for each alternative; and selecting the alternative that yields the optimal cost effectiveness.—*H. T. Go*

MANAGEMENT SCIENCE

The terms "management science" (MS) and "operations research" (OR) are used almost interchangeably in industry and government circles. There is certainly no general agreement on their formal definitions, much less on their differences. Both are generally concerned with the quantitative description of complex business problems and the solution thereof by analytical methods. Both MS and OR, typically, attempt to look at business systems. One commonly quoted definition states that they are concerned with the application of science, through interdisciplinary teams, to problems of organization, planning, and control from the manager's point of view. MS is sometimes thought to be the more "applied" of the two, while OR is more concerned with mathematical methodology. Any distinction, though, must be arbitrary and the terms will be used interchangeably here. In any case they are primarily concerned with decision making—the selection between alternatives—in complex systems of men, money, machines, and materials. They are not distinguished by the kind of problems they study but rather by how they study them. The emphasis is on bringing the power, logic, and rationality of mathematics to bear on operational problems.

Management Science Approaches

Management science approaches are future-oriented. Emphasis is placed on analyzing the classic management question, "What would happen if . . .?" This question could be completed by such phrases as (1) "plant capacity is added," (2) "credit terms are changed," (3) "this advertising program is used," (4) "this product mix is made," and the like.

DISTINGUISHING CHARACTERISTICS

The philosophy of the MS approach is described by three characteristics.

Systems approach and suboptimization. The first distinguishing characteristic of MS is the so-called open-systems approach, which can be described as the executive point of view. The key here is the attempt to avoid systems suboptimization, wherein a lower-level subsystem is optimized to the detriment of the overall system. The open-systems approach would, for example, be less concerned with the design of new materials handling equipment for a given warehouse and more concerned with whether the warehouse should exist at all in the company's overall logistics system. A ready example of the need for the systems approach in the manufacturing area (pictured in Exhibit 2.17) would be the planning of production rates to meet highly seasonal demands.

In general, production costs could be minimized by setting constant production rates so that costs of changing production levels could be avoided. If production costs were the only ones to be considered, it is highly likely from an overall, company point of view that the production system would be suboptimized, be-

Exhibit 2.17
EXAMPLE OF A BALANCE PROBLEM

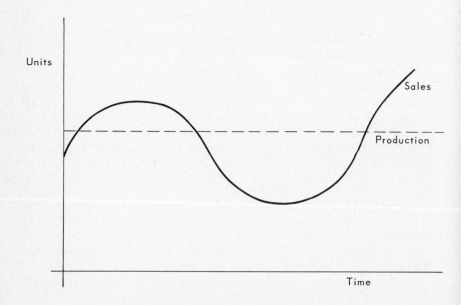

cause excessive costs would be incurred by carrying inventory or by possible lost sales as a result of out-of-stock conditions. The OR approach would be to develop a minimized mathematical expression for total system costs that would include inventory, marketing, distribution, and investment costs as well as production costs.

The methods of OR/MS are designed to look at individual operations in their entirety—that is, to include their relationships with other departments and functions. If the operation of many small units of a corporation were to be individually optimized and little or no attention paid to their interrelationships, when the units were put all together, the overall company system (if it could work at all) would not be optimally designed.

Interdisciplinary team. The second distinguishing characteristic is that of the notion of an interdisciplinary approach to a given problem. It is impossible to tell in advance which scientific discipline is likely to be most profitable in determining solutions to complex management problems. Having the various scientific disciplines represented on a project team will help insure that no profitable avenues of attack are neglected.

The modeling process. The third and perhaps most important characteristic is that the basic approach of these disciplines is to look at management systems by means of models. Usually, an attempt is made to develop a mathematical model, but this is by no means the only possibility. The model is the result of an abstraction process. It is not, should not be, and cannot be an exact duplication of reality. In general a model consists of a set of hypotheses concerning the real world that will transform events into consequences. The modeling process is a well-accepted management tool in many functional business areas, although the concept of a mathematical model is a somewhat newer development. Graphic or schematic models such as an organization chart, a process flow chart, a Gantt scheduling chart, or a PERT network are common examples. There are also familiar examples of physical or analog models such as scale models, mock-ups, and pilot plants.

MATHEMATICAL MODELS

The approach of MS is to take this abstraction process one step further by constructing a mathematical model to give a precise formulation of the interrelationship between operational variables. The management scientist attempts to construct a mathematical model of the performance of a system as a function of the controllable and uncontrollable variables that impact on that system. The basic idea is to abstract the physical situation to a mathematical model, perform various mathematical and optimization operations on the model, and then, with the proper interpretation, translate the mathematical results back to the physical setting. The process itself is not new, as the same thing is done with schematic and physical models. What is new is the application of the power and rigor of mathematics to problems where the number of variables, both controllable and uncontrollable, is so large that the unaided human decision maker cannot possibly analyze the system in its entirety.

Deterministic models. Mathematical models themselves may be conveniently divided into two types. The first of these types, called deterministic, is appropriate for problems where the interrelationships between the operational variables are known or are assumed to be known with certainty. Some examples would be discounted cash flow models for investment planning, the linear programming application discussed in the Manufacturing section of this handbook (page 6·150), and the CPM model (page 6·158).

Stochastic models. The second type of model, called stochastic, is applicable when these interrelationships are known only with probability distributions. In these models probability theory explicitly enters into the analysis. Examples are the queueing theory model and the newsboy problem discussed in the Manufacturing section (pages 6·153 and 6·155). Both types of models can lead to exceedingly complex analyses, considering the very large number of operational variables that must be analyzed if a system is to be looked at in its entirety. However, the process is no more complex than the decision itself, and the mathematical model development will lend an explicit formulation to the problem structure.

Usefulness of the model approach. The necessity for a precise formulation of problem objectives and constraints is one of the principal advantages of the MS approach even if no formal mathematics is employed. Practitioners of PERT and CPM techniques, for instance, claim that much of the advantage to be gained from these approaches comes from the detailed planning necessary to construct the models and that the mathematical manipulations are of secondary importance. The same could be said of many queueing-theory formulations where the model structure itself provides an extremely useful way to think about such flow problems even if the mathematical analysis is too complex, expensive, or time-consuming.

Problem structure and content. Much of the emphasis in the study and practice of OR/MS is directed toward methodological matters and techniques. It has been found that problems in a wide variety of content or functional management areas have these same underlying mathematical forms or structures. That is to say, there is transference from one physical setting to another. Were this not the case, it would be necessary to develop unique mathematical models for each application, but it has been found that the same models are useful in many applied areas. In other words, with these models it is possible to change the nouns and keep the verbs the same to extend the applications into new problem areas. The problem form or structure will be the same, but its content will be different; and in the sense that the mathematics does not care what nouns are used, the same models may be employed.

TECHNIQUES AND METHODOLOGY

No attempt can be made in the scope of this subsection to present an exhaustive listing of the various kinds of models or successful applications of the approach. Some of the more important ones therefore will be briefly described and some representative applications suggested.

Statistical methods. A wide variety of statistical techniques has been developed for use in analyzing management problems. Some of the most common applications relate to quality control; others are for problems of parameter estimation, such as determining the arrival rate in a queueing problem, and for hypothesis testing, such as determining whether or not a manufactured lot is acceptable according to some quality criterion. Regression analysis for sales forecasting and retail store location, exponential smoothing for forecasting inventory requirements, analysis of variance and factor analysis for the determination of optimum plant operating conditions, and the Markov process, which has found application in market research, hospital planning, and reliability engineering, are other examples. These techniques are based on mathematical probability principles utilizing a combination of objective fact and subjective judgment. Some of the more common analytically tractable probability distributions are the binomial and normal distributions, which find much application in quality control work, and the Poisson and exponential distributions, which form the basis for much mathematical queueing theory. Subjective probability judgments can also be handled within the framework of Bayesian statistical decision theory.

Inventory models. Models of this type are useful for analyzing operational problems in all aspects of materials management, including purchasing, inventory control, and distribution. Basically, two types of balance problems are of interest. The external balance problem is concerned with the trade-offs associated with planning production rates and inventory control subject to sales considerations. Internal balance problems are concerned with process design, shop scheduling, and assembly-line balancing.

Allocation. By far the most commonly used model in this area is the linear programming model. Applications are many and varied in virtually all management functions where there is concern for planning how to make the best use of scarce resources in situations where there are many alternative uses. Other mathematical programming models are available in certain situations where some of the assumptions of the linear programming model are violated. Stochastic models can be used when some of the input data are known only with probability distributions, and certain quadratic programming models can be used when the linearity assumption for the objective function is not reasonable.

So-called dynamic programming models may be used when a businessman is concerned with making plans now to maximize returns from future events, the outcome of which are not forecastable with certainty. Perhaps the most common business application is in inventory analysis where a program must be developed to balance production ability, inventory levels, and uncertain sales requirements at minimum cost. In certain applications where linear programming could otherwise be used, it is necessary to restrict the optimum program to be stated in terms of integer-valued variables only. So-called integer programming techniques have been developed to handle certain classes of these problems.

Risk analysis. Stochastic models have been developed under this general heading primarily to analyze investment opportunities where costs and payoffs are uncertain. The basic idea is to apply Monte Carlo methods (see the Manufacturing section, page 6·155) to an appropriately formulated return-on-investment model.

When a businessman says he is taking a calculated risk, rarely does he mean that he has really calculated anything particularly interesting about the risks he is facing. It is usually nothing more than a justification for "seat of the pants" decision making. Since most risk notions can be stated in the formal language of probability theory, these techniques provide a method to incorporate risk measures explicitly. Basically, precise measures of the uncertainty or variance of future payoffs and rates of return are provided for the decision maker, whereas traditional techniques were concerned only with expected values.

Game theory. First developed in the 1940's and closely related to linear programming, game theory is concerned with the analysis of competitive situations in management, economics, warfare, and other areas of conflicting interest.

Cost benefit analysis. Increased emphasis in both government and industry on concepts of program management has led to the development of new techniques for evaluating alternative investment opportunities, especially when payoffs can often not be stated in terms of dollar returns.

Search theory. Originally developed during World War II for application to problems in antisubmarine warfare, search theory mathematical techniques have found application in a variety of other problem areas, including the detection of forest fires.

Replacement. Replacement models are concerned with determining optimal replacement strategies for parts, components, and subsystems that are subject to wear, deterioration, and failure. Some so-called engineering economy models are of this type, and others find their primary application in the field of reliability engineering.

Queueing or waiting-line models. This very important class of mathematical models, useful for analyzing problems in discrete traffic flow, is discussed in detail in the Manufacturing section (page 6·153). In many applied problems the resulting models are so complex that analytical solutions are impossible and the analyst must use simulation techniques. Several special computer programming languages, including SIMSCRIPT and GPSS (General Purpose Simulation System), have been developed to make this approach more feasible and readily available.

Space does not permit more detailed explanations of these and other available management science techniques. For more detailed descriptions and explanations the reader is referred to a number of excellent sources on OR and MS methodology; for example, F. S. Hillier and G. J. Lieberman, *Introduction to Operations Research,* Holden-Day, Inc., 1967; S. B. Richmond, *Operations Research for Management Decisions,* The Ronald Press Company, 1968; and Daniel Teichroew, *An Introduction to Management Science—Deterministic Models,* John Wiley and Sons, Inc., 1964.

Solution Approaches

Many of the mathematical models developed by OR and MS can be solved analytically and optimal policies formulated and decisions determined by purely mathematical means. The linear programming model, certain queueing models, and the PERT model are examples. No experimentation is necessary, and answers can be developed in a deductive way, simply by analyzing the relationship of symbols.

In other problems, either because the mathematical relationships are too complex or because appropriate solution techniques have not yet been developed, it is necessary to use simulation techniques for problem solving and the development of appropriate decision rules. Simulation has been described as the experimental part of OR and the management sciences. Since experimentation in the real world is time-consuming, risky, and expensive, the management scientist would prefer to conduct his experiments on a model of the physical system under study. An example of such experimentation is the newsboy problem of previous reference. Optimum decision rules can be developed in this way without the necessity of trial-and-error experimentation in the real world. These techniques can be applied to many problems in inventory theory, queueing theory, PERT, and a host of other dynamic problem representations.

BUSINESS GAMES

Business games are a special type of simulation, where actual business decision-making situations can be compressed into short time spans for training and development and for experimentation and policy determination without risk. Some are classified as top management games; others concern themselves with only one or more functional areas; all are based on the concept of constructing a model of the business situation under study and moving it through time so that future decisions in the simulated environment are based on feedback in the form of operating results from prior decisions.

The familiar case study is a special example of a static business game where decisions are made at only one point in time. More realistically, these games are dynamic in that a set of decisions at one point in time is influenced by what happened before and in turn influences subsequent sets of decisions. A particular game may be deterministic in the sense that there is a single certain outcome for any particular set of player decisions, or it may be probabilistic in that there are several alternative outcomes. It may be predetermined in that its outcome, either deterministic or probabilistic, for a particular simulated company at any stage is determined as soon as that company has chosen its strategy, or it may be competitively interdependent in that one company's outcome depends on the strategy of others. (That is, the competition is for the same market, and strategies regarding price or advertising will trigger competitive reactions.)

The usefulness of these games as a training mechanism is hotly debated, but there is no doubt that they are widely used in management development activities. Some of the problems are as follows: (1) The level of abstraction may be too high; (2) certain qualitative influences are omitted; (3) there may be illegitimate transfer of certain aspects of the game play to the real world which are either irrelevant or harmful; and (4) behavior exhibited by the participants is different when the real risks are absent.

Proponents claim that this kind of simulation exercise can have great benefit by forcing involvement on the part of the participants without the risks of real-world experimentation. Such games are said to re-emphasize for executives the need for coordination, communication, and control. It is also asserted that they provide an additional intuitive knowledge of the decision-making environment in which a firm operates and force the systems point of view on the participants.

If these simulation games are rich in the sense that they realistically describe a business environment, there is also little doubt that they have been enthusiastically received by many educators and businessmen. In the abstraction process they are a step closer to the real world than other types of simulation in that, through the feedback mechanisms provided, the human decision maker remains a part of the environment. Enthusiasts also claim that there is much to be learned about the behavioral aspects of the decision-making process by observing the game participants in action. Such knowledge could be gained in the real world only with considerable risk and expense, if at all.

Management's Responsibility

The impact of OR and the management sciences has been a major one in many management decision-making areas. New applications are forthcoming at an exponential rate. The objective of insuring better and more profitable solutions to critical and complex problems while preventing costly errors caused by inadequate planning is being met increasingly through the use of the methods of science in management. Successful application depends critically on the interest and understanding of top management, as well as willingness to make an investment in the future with delayed payoff. The expenditures required for a successful OR/MS activity, both in personnel and in computers, are not insignificant. The payoffs, however, have been and can be vital for survival and growth.

A manager need not be a specialist in these areas, but he must become sufficiently informed to evaluate and appraise proposed MS applications to his operations. He must be sufficiently aware of the limitations and assumptions of any modeling process, for to accept blindly is nothing short of management abdication. More importantly, however, today's manager must be prepared to take advantage of whatever new ideas, techniques, and methodologies can assist him in his increasingly complex task of decision making. To do less than this is to stagnate.—*G. M. Parks*

ELECTRONIC DATA PROCESSING

The terminology of data processing is filled with ambiguity. The first objective here, therefore, will be to clarify the meaning of the term "electronic data processing," analyzing it word by word.

The words "data" and "information" are often used interchangeably. For the purposes of this discussion, however, data are considered to be facts, and information is considered to be meaningful data. "Data processing" can be defined as "the recording, classifying, sorting, calculating, summarizing, storing, and retrieving of data to provide useful information."

Since the beginning of recorded time, various methods have been used for processing data. Historically, this development can be traced from recording information on clay tablets, through the use of parchment scrolls, and finally to the use of quill pens and paper—all manual methods.

Attempts at mechanizing data processing date from the development of the first practical adding machine in the 1800's, followed by a slow evolution to what are presently known as accounting and bookkeeping machines. Initially, these were either adding machines redesigned to accept ledger cards or typewriters with adding-machine attachments.

The next major development in data processing came with the introduction of the unit record or punched card by Dr. Hollerith about 1890. This method requires the use of several specialized machines to manipulate cards containing the data into usable information.

The most recent, of course, and perhaps the most important development is electronic data processing, or EDP. As data processing is the manipulation of data into useful information, EDP is the manipulation of data performed electronically rather than manually, mechanically, or electromechanically.

A computer, the electronic configuration that processes data, consists of several pieces of equipment: (1) an *input device* to feed data into the computer; (2) a *control unit* to direct the actions of the computer; (3) an *arithmetic-logic* unit to perform operations on the data; (4) two types of *storage units,* main and auxiliary—main storage (core storage) for immediate access, and auxiliary storage (tape or disk units) for mass data storage; (5) an *output device* to move the manipulated data and information out of the computer.

To use the computer, detailed, step-by-step instructions (programs) are required. These are stored in the main memory or storage unit and direct the control unit in the performance of specific job steps.

In summary, EDP is the utilization of a computer composed of input, control, arithmetic-logic, storage, and output devices to perform at electronic speed the basic operations of recording, classifying, sorting, calculating, summarizing, storing, and retrieving data to develop meaningful information.

Benefits from EDP

With the substantial investment required in equipment and support personnel, managers are understandably interested in the benefits that can be obtained from an EDP installation. These benefits must be examined from two (separate, but closely aligned) viewpoints: (1) "What will EDP do for me as an individual?" and (2) "What will EDP do for the organization?"

BENEFITS TO THE INDIVIDUAL

The executive who allows himself to become too enmeshed in operating details soon loses his perspective and thus becomes decreasingly effective in his role as manager.

Perhaps the most valuable benefit that comes to an individual from EDP is freedom from detail. It results from his ability to identify and separate clerical elements from the nonclerical positions. This freedom is made possible by careful analysis of position requirements and assignment of routine tasks to a computer. The individual thus becomes more effective because he is free to devote more time to the necessary management activities of planning and control while having to deal only with exceptions on a day-to-day basis.

It is difficult to set a value on this type of benefit because there are no adequate measuring devices to determine the increase in an individual manager's contribution as a result of more effective planning.

BENEFITS TO THE ORGANIZATION

It is generally accepted among EDP professionals that one of the greatest benefits available to an organization from EDP comes not from the speed and accuracy of the computer but rather from the planned systems development that must precede utilization of the computer.

Analysis and systems development. Because the machine is incapable of following any except the simplest, most detailed instructions, it forces the organization to set down precisely just what the computer should do and how it should do it. This process frequently uncovers areas in the organization where activities are being conducted in ways inconsistent with corporate objectives.

In order to utilize the computer to full advantage, assignments of responsibility and authority should be analytically examined. This analysis must be related to the overall effort and interactions between groups necessary to accomplish tasks. Communication lines between functional areas must also be examined and, if necessary, reestablished.

Information as a resource. Organizations that truly benefit from the computer are those that realize how it can materially affect the way they conduct their businesses. An organization that treats information as a vital resource of the business and utilizes the computer to provide information that is meaningful, accurate, and timely to the people who need it is one that can reap the greatest benefits.

A word of caution must be introduced at this point. It is not sufficient that meaningful, accurate, and timely information be provided; the management of the organization must be trained to use the new information effectively. An information-oriented management team is needed to insure that the benefits are actually realized by the organization.

Extension of management capability. The manager can utilize the speed and accuracy of the computer to assist in decision making. Utilizing the techniques of MS and OR (see page 2·68), he can reduce the uncertainty and increase the probability of making correct decisions.

Most of the various MS techniques can be performed manually. However, practical limitations on the time required to process large quantities of data and the use of complex mathematics severely—and often totally—limit effective utilization of these techniques in any but a computer environment. EDP permits the manager to utilize these techniques more effectively.

Management decision making. Executive-level decisions must often be made in the framework of a time limitation. Business opportunities may exist for only a short period of time and are thereafter lost. The speed with which an executive can react in such situations determines the ability of the organization to capitalize on the opportunity. His success in making timely and correct decisions in each case depends largely on the quantity and accuracy of the information provided to him within the available time frame.

The ideal situation is one in which, as questions requiring decisions arise, the manager can query the computer to determine alternative courses of action. This is made possible by a new development referred to as interactive systems, where man and machine communicate directly via a terminal and carry on a dialog making use of MS techniques.

One very important thing that EDP can do for a manager is to handle the daily routine tasks quickly and accurately. This frees valuable time for decision making and enables him to devote more attention to the important activities of planning and managing his function.

Placement and Organization of EDP Function

Placement and organization of the EDP function are subjects that deserve and receive considerable attention in management circles. Many factors and considerations must be taken into account when making the placement decision. It is appropriate to trace the development of the function in a typical organization in order to understand its placement.

HISTORICAL DEVELOPMENT OF EDP

EDP as a management tool had its origin in the accounting area in most business organizations. This was a natural evolution from the processing of accounting information using accounting and bookkeeping machines and, later, unit record equipment. Knowledge acquired with the use of unit record equipment provided a logical transition when computers were introduced.

First- and second-generation equipment. Typical applications converted to EDP during the first two generations of computer equipment were generally limited to the financial accounting area, probably for the following reasons:

1. Management did not then sufficiently understand the full potential of the computer and thought of it only as a replacement for the unit record equipment.

2. Technical personnel of the time did not really have a management viewpoint. They were primarily interested in the technical characteristics of the equipment rather than the more sophisticated business applications.

3. The highly structured nature of accounting meant that essentially all the business systems work was already complete for conversion from lower-order equipment to a computer. All that was required was the programming of existing unit record applications.

Third-generation equipment. With the introduction of third-generation equipment, the capabilities of the computer to perform nonaccounting tasks became more generally understood and accepted in most companies. As a result the problem for the EDP function has changed from trying to gain management acceptance of its efforts to having to obtain priority ranking of many work requests from all functions in the organization.

As it became increasingly apparent that the computer was more than a faster method of processing accounting data, forward-looking management recognized that, to effectively utilize the computer, consideration would have to be given to its proper placement in the organization.

PLACEMENT CONSIDERATIONS

Considerations that management must evaluate when attempting to determine the proper placement of the EDP function in the organization are detailed in AMA Research Study 92, *Organizing for Data Processing*. They are (1) the traditional style and philosophy of management in the company; (2) "the state of the art" within the company—length of time computers have been in use, extent of EDP capability within the company, size and adequacy of the data base on which the computer can work, and degree of acceptance of the computer as a management tool by company executives; (3) the need for computer application and the extent to which such applications are required on a companywide, interfunctional basis; (4) the availability of competent leadership to head up the computer complex wherever it is located.

PLACEMENT TRENDS

Two significant trends in the placement of the EDP function are developing: One is toward centralization, the other toward independent status.

Centralization. AMA Research Study 92 cites the following three important factors in a trend toward centralization of the EDP function:

1. There is increasing management demand for companywide information. Corporate management must have information with which to compare the effectiveness of the various divisions or profit centers. Without a common basis for gathering, processing, and measuring that information, it is difficult to compare or evaluate actual operations because of variations in reporting techniques.

2. Few companies can afford multiple, independent EDP installations scattered throughout the various divisions. Not only are the hardware costs significant, but the duplication of personnel required to operate the equipment makes this a very expensive method of organization. Centralized hardware also minimizes the traditional problem of EDP equipment underutilization.

3. Organizations are experiencing great difficulty in locating and retaining qualified, experienced EDP personnel. A centralized EDP facility eliminates the need for duplication of skills. It allows the people who are most qualified to utilize their talents for the benefit of the whole company.

Independent status. Because of the expanded capability of computer hardware and the increasing skill of systems personnel in designing computer-based systems, managerial demand for EDP services has increased beyond the ability of the EDP function to satisfy all requests in most companies—a dilemma that has caused many organizations to review critically the traditional placement of the EDP function.

In many companies this review is resulting in a move to independent status either on the same level as the other functions or reporting to top management in a staff capacity, thus enabling the EDP function to evaluate requests in a more objective manner because it is not influenced by pressures resulting from a reporting relationship.

ORGANIZATION

The organization of a function is best understood if the activities performed within that function are clearly understood. This is particularly true in EDP because of the mystery that has traditionally surrounded the function and because of the increasing specialization required as the field becomes more complex. The activities typically required in an EDP function can be classified in six main categories: problem solving, computer application, programming analysis, programming, operations, and technical support and control.

Problem solving. When a user has requested assistance, an investigation must be undertaken to understand the situation that led to the request, and action must be taken to define the problem of the user. After the problem has been defined, the problem solver and the user must agree to a course of action that will provide a satisfactory solution and then proceed to develop the solution. It is important to note at this point that interest is not in determining *how* to utilize a computer to solve the problem but in determining *what* is required to solve the problem.

Computer application. After the problem has been defined and solved, the method to be used in implementing the solution can be considered. If a computer provides a valid means, it must now be determined how to utilize it to best advantage. At this time technical EDP decisions are made regarding the processing techniques to be used, and the development of program specifications is completed.

Programming analysis. The tasks assigned to the computer must be analyzed in detail to determine the program's approximate size, estimated running time, and relative complexity, and assigned to a qualified programmer.

Programming. The various programs must now be logically developed in detail, coded, and tested to insure that they will work under all possible conditions.

Operations. After the system has been tested, the programs are turned over to an operating group in EDP for routine operation.

Technical support and control. Several specialized activities are becoming increasingly important to the operation of an EDP function: computer software analysis, computer schedule preparation, computer tape/disk library control, and input/output data control.

Assignment of activities. Depending on organization size, the various required activities may be assigned to individuals in different ways. It must be kept in mind, however, that no matter how they are grouped and assigned, all must be completed in order to have a successful operation.

Many organizations that can afford specialization have recently been structuring their systems and data processing departments according to the required activities previously listed. Typical titles for such specialization are as follows: business system analyst (problem solving); computer system analyst (computer application); lead programmer (programming analysis); programmer (programming); and lead operator (operations). A smaller organization that cannot afford this degree of specialization may group the activities; thus the titles and the activities covered might be: systems analyst (problem solving and computer application); programmer (programming analysis and programming); and operator (operations). There are many other possible arrangements, and each organization must decide what is best for it after a thorough analysis of its particular needs.

PRECISE DESCRIPTION AND DOCUMENTATION

The establishment of additional positions to take advantage of specialized labor resolves one problem but introduces another—the problem of communication. The ideas that each person develops in a work assignment must be transmitted to the next person or group in the work sequence.

In order to facilitate communication in a highly specialized organization structure, it is necessary to have both well-defined position descriptions, indicating who is responsible for the various activities, and standard practice instructions covering not only what work is required but how it is to be accomplished.

The success of a project (the typical assignment in the EDP function) depends on how well the various team members work as a group. For the team to function well, each member must know precisely what he is to do, what the others' duties are, and what steps are required to bring the project to successful conclusion. Departmental standard practices become a very important part of the control mechanism required in this environment.

In smaller organizations the formal documentation process is frequently ignored because of pressure of time to get a job done and because it is not absolutely necessary in order to have a job move from one stage to another. One man may do the problem solving, computer application, and program analysis. Since he has done all these things himself, he may feel that documentation of each step would be a waste of time because he knows all about the project. If management allows the project to progress to completion without adequate documentation, however, it risks the possibility that the company would be deprived of all or most of the essential information about the project in case the man left the job.

Staffing the EDP Function

Staffing the EDP function with qualified personnel and retaining them is one of the most difficult tasks confronting the EDP manager. Some of the factors contributing to this situation are the shortage of qualified people, the absence of adequate measuring and evaluation techniques, and the high mobility of people within the industry.

ANALYSIS OF SKILLS

The first step in the staffing process must be a thorough analysis of the skills needed for each activity.

1. *Problem solving* requires the ability to sift through the symptoms in order to pinpoint the real problem and identify its underlying cause. The problem

solver must have an analytical mind, a management viewpoint, and skills in other areas of systems work besides EDP.

2. *Computer application* requires expert knowledge of EDP equipment and the ability to translate, when necessary, the solution proposed by the problem solver into an effective, computer-based application.

3. *Programming analysis* requires thorough knowledge of programming, ability to conceptualize program complexity and size, and talent for training other programmers.

4. *Programming* requires the ability to formulate detailed logic steps and convert them to a computer language.

5. *Operation* requires the technical and mechanical skill to operate the computer and related equipment.

It can be readily understood that the skill requirements for each of the activities vary and may use different types of individuals.

SOURCES OF STAFF

Sources of personnel will vary with the company, depending greatly on geographic location. The important point is that without a defined work environment it is nearly impossible to recruit the most appropriate individuals.

Use of Outside Services

Companies often find it advantageous to go outside their own EDP organization to supplement their efforts. Three general types of outside organizations can be of service in the EDP environment: technical specialists (commonly called software houses), equipment manufacturers, and general business consultants. In recent years there has been some blending of these three organizations into a single one formed along broad lines.

Software houses generally provide technical personnel, for a fee, to write specific programs such as prewritten application programs, "utility" programs, or system control programs. The software house may also provide specific application design and development assistance. The latter may be accomplished by means of systems analysts and programmers who, at the direction of the client, will analyze, design, develop, and/or install operating systems.

Equipment manufacturers generally offer support of a technical nature to a customer. Their advice or support may or may not be application-oriented; typically, it is related to the improvement of specific equipment operations and/or the use of provided software programs. If the manufacturer has played a major role in the equipment configuration design, he may also provide programming and/or business system design assistance. Although the manufacturer does not always charge clients directly for these services, the equipment purchase or rental charges provide for such involvement. The trend is toward separate, direct charges for such services.

General business consultants generally offer three types of service to clients for a fee. First, they can help establish an environment in which management personnel become aware of—and responsive to—required changes in business methods. Second, they can help identify problems and recommend appropriate solutions. Third, they can provide implementation assistance. Frequently, they provide all three services during a single client engagement.

GUIDELINES

When outside services are to be used, it is necessary to establish and maintain an effective working relationship. This can best be accomplished by (1) insuring that the objectives, scope, and specifications of the work are clearly defined and understood; (2) insuring the establishment of and agreement to a formal work plan and time schedule; (3) insuring the establishment of a proper level of participation and involvement between the client personnel and the outside service organization; (4) determining where the work is to be performed—on site, whenever possible; (5) insuring the establishment and actual use of a formal project progress reporting method that specifies the interval of reporting and identifies management checkpoints.

Available Controls for EDP Activities

Control of the activities of an organization implies the ability to measure performance against established goals or plans. For the EDP function, goals or plans may be represented in various ways. Among them are the following:

1. A formal, written statement identifying the objectives of the organization, its nature of organization, its placement in the company, and its scope of operations.

2. Establishment of time standards which identify the time required to perform various tasks in the EDP department. Time standards can be used in two ways: (a) to establish work schedules based on common time increments for specific tasks; and (b) to provide a quantitative basis against which an individual's performance can be measured.

3. Definitions of work practices, stating how individuals are to complete the tasks and the documentation to be prepared before the tasks are considered complete. Work practices definitions also represent a qualitative basis for measuring individual performance.

4. Preparation of work schedules that state when specific events will start and when they are expected to be completed. Monitoring actual progress against these schedules permits decisions concerning future allocation of manpower to be made to insure on-time completion. Work schedules can be established with the use of time standards. Performance against work schedules may be used as one of the measures of the efficiency of the EDP management group.

Information needed to control the various activities of the systems and EDP function will vary with the organizational placement of the individual receiving the information. The control information needs of a vice president of information services are significantly different from those of a project leader or one of the departmental managers. For this reason the subject of control is viewed as being a level-by-level affair as follows:

1. The first level pertains to managers within the EDP activity, such as a systems manager, a programming manager, or an operations manager. Generally,

these individuals will report to an executive with a title such as director of information services.

2. The second level pertains to the director of information services. Generally, this individual will report directly to the chief executive officer or someone reporting to the chief executive officer.

3. The third level pertains to the chief executive officer or an immediate subordinate.

FIRST-LEVEL CONTROL

The first level of management control of the EDP function is at the managerial level. Without control information at this level, higher-level information provided is of questionable value. The types of control needed at this level are briefly described in the following paragraphs:

Work practices.   In the data processing operations area, work practices definitions are needed to guide personnel in the performance of their daily tasks. Typical work practices instructions inform personnel how to maintain equipment; handle and store punched cards, magnetic tape, magnetic disks, paper stock, and unit record control panels; prepare and maintain input/output schedules; and control and distribute output reports.

In the computer system area, work practices should describe the way in which personnel are expected to analyze and design computer-based systems or subsystems, prepare and maintain programming specifications, prepare and maintain data processing operations documentation, and report project progress.

In the programming area, work practices should describe the way in which personnel are expected to code and test programs, document programs, and report project progress.

Manpower reports.   Manpower reporting, consisting of a daily personnel-time reporting system, is a useful management tool. From such a system the department manager is able to do the following:

1. Develop personnel efficiency reports by comparing the actual performance reported against established time standards. The manager can also compare performance between individuals in the department, since all are measured against the same time standards.

2. Develop progress information about projects. As time is reported against specific projects, it can be accumulated by project and compared against the budgeted time.

3. Modify existing time standards to fit existing personnel and environment characteristics.

Monthly project status.   Each first-level manager should be required to prepare monthly a status report for each project in his department. This report should contain the following types of information: (1) amount of resources utilized to date, actual and budgeted; (2) tasks behind schedule, with an explanation of what is being done to make up lost time; (3) actual costs or time applied to date compared with budgeted costs on time to date; (4) percent of project completed.

With the awareness that such a reporting system generates, managers can effectively schedule personnel to meet problems or can take action to forestall problems. Project scheduling and control become acts of management control rather than reactions to crisis.

Equipment utilization. Within the data processing operations area, equipment and personnel utilization reports permit the operations manager to judge operation efficiency, personnel utilization, equipment utilization, and equipment capacity capabilities. This type of reporting, when properly constructed, also provides valuable insight into time wasted because of reruns and excessive time used for program test purposes. Information of this type is valuable for making available additional capacity by correcting poor work practices. In a "charge out" environment, this type of information also provides the basis for billing users for work performed.

Performance to published schedules. Operations management requires a record of actual production compared with the planned monthly published schedule. Deviations can be investigated, discussed with appropriate individuals whether inside or outside the department, and corrective action initiated.

SECOND-LEVEL CONTROL

The next level of control is exercised by the manager of information services or an executive with an equivalent job title. In some organizations this individual may be called the data processing manager. Whatever his title, he is actively responsible for all the identifiable activities within the systems and EDP function.

Monthly progress meetings. The most common control technique is the formal monthly progress meeting, at which reports from the programming manager and computer systems manager are discussed. The operations manager should present the following types of information:

1. Monthly utilization data by machine type.

2. Various ratios which identify utilization relationships. Among these ratios would be the following:

   a. *Total metered production to total paid hours.* This ratio measures the equipment efficiency rate and reflects the efficiency of the operating environment, systems sophistication, and responsibility for accuracy. Operations management should strive to maintain a 95 percent level.

   b. *Total metered production to total power-on hours.* This ratio measures the productive throughput related to scheduled or power-on time and reflects the efficiency of the operating environment, systems sophistication, user appreciation, and responsibility for accuracy, effectiveness of the customer engineer responsible for the installation, and effectiveness of scheduling and planning. Operations management should strive to maintain an 80 percent level.

Manpower plans. Each department manager should prepare quarterly a forecast of manpower requirements for the next 12 months; this forecast should identify the types of personnel required by month. In the case of computer systems or programming personnel, the manpower requirements should be identified and associated with projects in progress or expected to start in the next 12 months. The respective department managers should use this quarterly forecast to support requests for staff additions, deletions, or changes in the mix of personnel.

Monthly expense statements. The director of management information services or the manager should be provided with monthly expense statements for each of his operating entities. These statements should identify, by expense account classification, actual expenses compared to budgeted expense levels. This type of reporting will indicate problem areas in which corrective management action is called for.

Department audits. The other approach to control that the management information services manager may exercise, although not commonly used, is an audit of the various functions. The audit is used most efficiently in organizations where work practices have been established.

One of the difficulties in performing an audit is that, frequently, internal auditors have not been sufficiently trained in EDP practices and techniques. Therefore, very few internal audit groups are qualified to perform meaningful, comprehensive EDP audits. As a result there is a growing tendency for companies that recognize the need for such a service to turn to consulting firms to perform the audit and evaluate the operation.

Department profit-and-loss statement. In companies that charge for EDP services a monthly department statement for profit and loss should be prepared. It may not take the traditional accounting format, but it should indicate the period's actual revenues (even if the charges are only memo transactions) received versus the actual expenses incurred, as well as budgeted income and expenses.

THIRD-LEVEL CONTROL

The control exercised at the third level is largely of a qualitative nature.

Priority assignments. Control can be exercised over the assignment of resources by taking part in the establishment of priority of projects to be undertaken. This insures that EDP resources are being utilized for projects and activities that best support the achievement of the objectives of the organization.

Project-review meetings. Participation in project review also provides a means for control at the third level. Answers to questions such as the following provide an insight into project status: Where does the project stand against schedule? Why does the project stand where it does? What obstacles, if any, are preventing further progress?

Senior executive participation in review sessions generally provides the systems and EDP personnel with a management perspective of the project, decisions to eliminate obstacles and enhance project progress, and direction for further progress on the project.

User satisfaction. The executive should ascertain the level of satisfaction that the EDP organization currently provides user organizations. This information can be secured by soliciting from user personnel the reasons for the reported level of satisfaction.

Reports of high levels of satisfaction should be passed on to management information services management with encouragement to continue the good work.

Reports of low levels of satisfaction should prompt a meeting between EDP and user management personnel to identify existing problems and their causes, and together the two groups should develop satisfactory and feasible solutions to the problems.

Unless the EDP function is controlled, there will be a drain of resources without corresponding beneficial results in the organization's information handling or profit capabilities. The result of an uncontrolled environment will be a source of personal dissatisfaction to technical personnel and to users of the service, causing the gradual but certain decay of the function.

Hardware and Software

In the current literature much has been written about the hardware and software explosion. However, before the subject is discussed here, the terms "hardware" and "software" should be defined.

DEFINITIONS

"Hardware" refers to the mechanical and/or electrical components of a computer obtained by sale or rental from equipment manufacturers or leased from a third party.

"Software" generally refers to computer programs that provide the instructions for the machines to operate. Software can be classified into one of three categories as follows: (1) *application programs,* such as payroll or order invoicing programs, designed to process data related to specific business activities; (2) *utility programs,* such as language compilers or translators, sorts, or merges, which enhance the equipment's ability to process data; (3) *system control programs,* such as system supervisor programs, which are necessary for the practical use of third-generation computers.

HARDWARE SELECTION

It is important to consider the relationship of the applications to be processed to the equipment's capabilities when selecting equipment. Hardware should never be ordered without a complete, in-depth understanding of anticipated uses or applications. For this reason the user must be in a position to provide detailed specifications of the anticipated applications to prospective vendors so that appropriate equipment may be recommended.

Equipment specifications.   The company should provide all prospective vendors with an equipment specification containing the following:

1. A letter of transmittal inviting vendors to submit a proposal for data processing equipment. The letter identifies the proposal's due dates, number of copies required, and the required equipment delivery data. The transmittal letter should contain information about planned applications and their objectives.

2. Some background information about the company, such as sales volume, industry position, and scope of operations.

3. Graphic representations of the applications being considered in the form of a flow chart of the activities to be performed in each application.

4. Input, output, and stored record contents—a description of each record, its

expected processing volume, the fields making up the records, and the size of each field.

5. Logical rules that must govern how the data are to be processed.

6. Response-time requirements for each application.

7. Sample layouts for each report.

8. Information to be included in the vendor's proposal, such as hardware and software support, cost, and delivery date.

Consideration can also be given to providing prospective vendors with a sample problem representative of the type of problem the vendor's equipment will process in the proposed application. The use of sample problems has the advantage of providing a common basis for evaluating the relative merits of each vendor's ability to satisfy the requirements.

Selection criteria. Verification that a certain vendor's equipment proposal is the most responsive to the specifications and is the best available equipment should be made before any equipment is selected. Certainly each proposal should be evaluated against the following criteria, as a minimum.

1. Is the equipment planned for release, or is it presently in the field?

2. How broad and responsive to need is the software support that will be provided? What will it cost?

3. How closely can the equipment comply with the response-time requirements set forth in the specification?

4. What are the related costs associated with obtaining the equipment? There are several types of costs to be considered: (*a*) lease, buy, or rental charges; (*b*) conversion costs of existing system; (*c*) development costs of new system as a function of familiarity with programming languages offered; (*d*) insurance and maintenance costs; (*e*) transportation and installation costs of new equipment; (*f*) training costs for operators and programmers.

5. What is the delivery capability of the manufacturer in meeting installation ,requirements?

6. What is the growth potential of the equipment without substantial reprogramming? This growth potential is often called upward capability.

7. What is the availability of trained people to operate and program the equipment in the geographic area in which the machine will be installed?

8. What are the space and site requirements needed to install the equipment?

9. What is the equipment back-up capability available in the area in which the machine will be installed?

10. What kind of test facilities can the vendor provide?

In the last analysis, the equipment and source selected should be those which best meet the requirements as set forth in the specifications.

SOFTWARE SELECTION

To return to the definition of software: It becomes evident that software selection occurs in two general time frames, each of which has different considerations. The first occurs during the equipment selection process. The number of decisions required during the first frame is quite limited. This can be attributed to three factors.

1. Very few vendors, if any, offer a wide selection of system control programs for any single piece of hardware.

2. The installation of new equipment is frequently accomplished in a technical environment where EDP personnel do not have sufficient technical knowledge about the new equipment to make an intelligent selection of "utility programs." As a result the selection of utility programs during this time frame means, "Give me all the sorts, merges, language translators, and compilers which you (the vendor) can supply." Perhaps, if there has been previous experience, the selection of a prime programming language to be used may be decided upon.

3. Finally, because both the operation and the staff functions of the EDP organization are generally so preoccupied with the initial equipment installation and perhaps the first applications, consideration of applications programs during this time frame is probably nonexistent. Other than the decision of the programming language to be used, very little software selection is made during equipment selection and installation. It is not until the second time frame, after the technical knowledge has been gained and preoccupation with the equipment has been passed, that software selection becomes a major issue of importance.

Equipment specifications. The contents of specifications developed for software are dependent on the type of software needed. Specifications developed for application programs are different in content from specifications developed for utility programs or for system control programs. Regardless of the type of software being considered, the user must prepare the specifications clearly in terms understood by the supplier, be it an equipment manufacturer or software house.

Specifications for the application-program category of software must provide the same type of information that would be provided to the in-house programming staff. Typically, specifications of this type would include the following: input/output requirements, logic tables, decision rules, master files organization, processing records format, response-time requirements, and flow diagrams.

Specifications for utility programs are more difficult to develop because of their high level of technical sophistication. These specifications must identify the objectives of the software, how it is going to be used, and who is going to use it.

Selection criteria. Criteria for selecting software would include answers to the following questions: What is the previous history of the sources in supplying the software? Are the users satisfied? Is the software being offered as a standard package, or will it be tailored to the company? If tailored to the company, will the work be performed on site or at the supplier's place of business? How much support will be provided after the package is installed? Will on-site assistance be provided for training the company's personnel? Will maintenance changes be made by the supplier, once the program is installed, or will company personnel be responsible for all changes? How difficult will it be to have company personnel maintain the package?

Perhaps the most significant consideration in selecting software is determining the advantages that it will provide. When price and performance are competitive, the logical hardware or software supplier to be chosen is the one who will work best with company personnel and who will support them during each phase of the conversion to the new equipment or software package.

Techniques to Make EDP More Productive

Various techniques can be used for increasing the productivity of the EDP function. If the term "increasing productivity" is accepted as meaning "increasing the level of meaningful work successfully accomplished within a functional area with a static level of resources utilized," different techniques should be used for each of the EDP functions. For example, increased productivity in the operations department is identifiable with improved equipment productivity, whereas increased productivity in the systems or programming department is reflected in schedule improvement in terms of project completion.

OPERATIONS DEPARTMENT

Increased productivity in the operations department can be brought about by employing improved programming techniques and utilizing management techniques. Improved programming techniques include multiprogramming, spooling, job stream, and multiple-shift usage.

Until the advent of third-generation computers, data were processed in a batch mode; that is to say, a single job was started and processed and taken down, and the same process was continuously repeated. The technique of batch processing was characterized by relatively low utilization of peripheral equipment, core memory, and central processing units, with a long interval of set-up times between jobs.

Multiprogramming. For computer users who have equipment capable of processing in a multiprogramming mode and are experiencing near-capacity utilization of the equipment, consideration should be given to employing multiprogramming rather than getting more or bigger equipment. Operating in a multiprogramming environment implies multiple-program processing during the same time interval. Multiprogramming permits an environment in which two or more programs can be processed within the same central processing unit of the computer at the same time. The two basic objectives of multiprogramming are to improve utilization through sharing the capabilities of the same central processing unit and to provide greater throughput by eliminating redundant set-up time.

Spooling. For users who have the proper input/output devices, consideration should be given to spooling. Spooling is a technique in which printed output is read onto a magnetic tape or disk for printing at some later time instead of being printed directly on the printer. Spooling permits the use of satellite printers, since all the data have been formatted. Another advantage of spooling is that multiple reports can be "printed" (stored) in queue on the magnetic tape or disk and then, with a smaller computer or at some advantageous time, the data are printed out by report, one after another.

Job stream. Job stream is a technique used to reduce the time of delay between successive processes. Job stream permits operations personnel to "load or stack" the computer with a number of jobs that can be run without operation intervention; therefore, the operator can concentrate on loading the input/output devices prior to each process, thus reducing the delays. Job stream also provides the operator with additional efficiencies through its operator communication and response commands.

Multiple-shift equipment utilization. Multiple-shift equipment utilization should also be considered in making EDP operations more productive. To schedule computer operations around the clock is not unusual, but such scheduling of the support operations, such as data control and data conversion, is not as common. Input or output bottlenecks can often be reduced—if not eliminated— by the installation of multishift key punch and/or data control operations.

Schedules. The productivity of the operations department can also be improved by the use of input and output schedules. Two types of schedules must be considered. One type is concerned with source data input. All input data are scheduled to arrive in the data center at a specific time which is expressed in terms of day of week or day of month, and time of day. This fixes responsibility, and not only in the EDP function; it also establishes a level of responsibility within the user departments.

The second type of schedule to be considered is an equipment processing schedule, prepared monthly and identifying output required by day. On a weekly basis the monthly schedule is recast one week "out" in advance, identifying by small increments of time what is to be processed during each day. These detailed schedules must be understood and complied with by data processing and user personnel. One of the most important aspects is the reporting of actual performance against the schedule. Deviations must be analyzed to determine causal factors. Corrective action by management must follow to improve the probability of meeting future schedules.

SYSTEMS AND PROGRAMMING DEPARTMENT

In the programming function, consideration should be given to modular programming as a means of increasing productivity. In modular programming, programs are made of small pieces or subroutines written once, usually stored in computer memory, and used in other programs as appropriate. The program is developed accordingly without having to be completely written each time. Other techniques to be used for increasing the productivity of the system and programming function are the installation of and compliance with standard work practices and performance standards. There should be standard work practices for programming and for computer system analysis and design.

Regular training of computer systems analysts and programmers can do much to increase the productivity of the function. Training may be conducted off-site by trade associations, formal training institutions, or professional societies, or on-site by equipment manufacturers and company employees. Formal training sessions conducted on a schedule can provide the basis for the introduction of new standard work practices and performance standards. These sessions may also provide a forum for department personnel to gain poise and confidence in the technique of public speaking.

Return on the EDP Investment

The concept of estimating the return on investment (ROI) for each proposed major expenditure that a company is considering and then selecting those which, on the basis of the analysis, offer the greatest potential return is an appealing one to most managements. There is, however, considerable difficulty in applying the concept to all investment decisions because of the problems involved in quantifying the various factors in the equation.

ROI EQUATION

The two elements of the equation are the investment the company must commit to the item and the return the company can realistically expect from the item. Of the two, the investment is the easier to calculate for EDP equipment.

INVESTMENT FACTORS

Included in investment determination are several important elements.

1. *Equipment cost.* This is relatively straightforward if the equipment is purchased; but if it is rented or leased, the periodic payments must be converted to a present value by accepted conventional methods.

2. *Program cost.* This is the cost of program development and testing. It does not include program maintenance.

3. *Operating cost.* Except for initial, one-time, or "learning curve" expense, operating cost is not considered as part of investment.

4. *Other costs.* Consideration must be given to the inclusion of other costs such as training and one-time site preparation costs.

NET RETURN FACTORS

The calculation of the real return from an EDP installation is much more difficult, considering the present state of the art in the development of precise techniques for measuring the value of information. The return can be approximated, however, if the following procedure is utilized.

First, list and quantify all identifiable, tangible returns, such as reduction in inventory carrying costs, increase in utilization of production facilities, and reduction of people and related overhead costs.

Second, from the quantified tangible gross return, calculate and deduct the cost of personnel to operate the equipment, space charges and other overhead elements, maintenance, depreciation (if equipment is owned) or equipment rental, and operating supplies.

Then, list all of the intangible items and have a knowledgeable management person estimate a dollar amount for each. Examples are improved customer service, ability to make faster decisions, and improved information for decision making.

VALUE OF ROI IN EDP

Owing to the imprecise nature of the measures of return, the estimated ROI figure should be used only as a guideline, not as the sole criterion for making a "go—no go" decision for the installation of EDP equipment.

It must be recognized that computer-based systems may be necessary to achieve desired improvements in management's effectiveness. Therefore, the decision to install a computer should probably be based on a combination of available ROI data and the business judgment of the management as to both the intangible impact on the organization's effectiveness and the anticipated effect of this improvement on the company's ability to achieve its objectives.

—R. A. Holzbach and M. N. Rolfe

COMPUTER TIME-SHARING AND UTILITIES

The concept of computer time-sharing is a very simple one. Modern high-speed computers can process the work so fast that several users can "access" a single computer simultaneously. Because he is subject to no noticeable delay, each user seems to be the only one using the computer. In actuality, at any one point in time, on all but a very few time-sharing computers (which are called multiprocessing computers), his work is indeed the only work being handled by the computer's central processing unit (CPU)—the part that does the actual computing—for a second or two ("time slice"). Then, whether the task is completed or not, the computer stops work on its present job, stores it, and goes on to the work of another user. Finally, the computer returns to pick up the partially completed task of the first user exactly where it left off. The whole concept is feasible because, in the batch processing mode, the CPU is less than fully utilized. It is idle between jobs and often when the data and programs are fed into the machine and when results are printed.

In practice, almost all time-shared computers are accessed via telephone lines by remote terminals at the user's location. These terminals, through which the user types or "inputs" programs and data into the computer and receives printed output, are said to be "on-line" to the computer; to date they have been almost invariably either Teletypes or modified typewriters. This situation is about to change as many new terminals, including portable and television-like cathode ray tube devices, are being released.

Time-sharing can also be said to be "real-time" in that the user can receive the results of his program within the time framework needed to make a decision. In fact, time-sharing systems can be used to analyze the results from on-going mechanical processes and control them.

There is idle time even on time-shared computers. Thus a new concept is being implemented: the computer utility—that is, simultaneous use of the same computer for on-site batch, remote batch, and time-shared processing. A complex hierarchy controls time allocation; but in general, time-sharing has the highest priority, with the leftover time parceled among the two batch modes.

The acceptance of time-sharing by scientists and businessmen has been phenomenal. The first successful commercial time-sharing was offered in 1965. In 1970 the revenues of all time-sharing vendors are expected to total about $250 million. Over the next five years, time-sharing revenues should about double every year. At the moment, however, the industry has overreacted to this potential; severe overcapacity exists, and it is expected that several vendors will fail or else be forced to merge.

Uses of Time-Sharing

Determining which tasks belong on time-sharing and which should be done by batch processing is relatively easy. Time-sharing is always available; thus jobs requiring a quick turnaround are ideally suited to this medium. It is uneconomical to set up short runs on the batch processing computer; these should usually be done on time-sharing. However, present terminals are relatively slow input/output devices. Thus time-sharing is best suited to jobs that require little data entry and generate short responses. Finally, tasks requiring interaction between the user and the computer are best suited to time-sharing.

Selecting a Time-Sharing Service

Each time-sharing system has its own peculiarities; several are very important in choosing a time-sharing service.

APPLICATIONS PACKAGES

The most rapidly growing area of the time-sharing field is that of applications software—predesigned (canned) programs for solving standard problems. Using one of these programs to achieve a solution to a problem, a user needs no programming experience—merely sufficient facility with a terminal to enter data. To date, the usage of applications packages has been most disappointing. Many of the programs have not been designed by specialists in their respective fields but by time-sharing vendors who misunderstood the needs of their customers.

Many customers have signed a time-sharing contract solely on the basis of a cursory study of the applications packages available, only to be sadly disappointed when the time came to apply the software to the problem at hand. Only a very careful study of the applications documentation will enable the user to decide if the programs will solve his particular problems.

Two developments promise significantly to improve the usefulness of canned time-sharing software.

Programs authored by users. Several firms are now releasing their proprietary programs as part of the library of commercial time-shared vendors. Usually, some sort of royalty is paid to the author of the programs. The principal advantages of these programs are that their usefulness has been proved by usage within the author's institution and that they have been documented by someone who understands the jargon of the user.

Modular programs. To increase flexibility, programs are now being written as standardized components called modules or subroutines, which the user combines to solve a particular problem. Thus the user must be able to do more than simply enter data but theoretically does not need to have acquired sufficient programming skills to write a complete program.

To date, this scheme has not proved satisfactory for the nonprogrammer. To combine the modules currently available requires a good programming background. However, the time savings that programmers have achieved through the use of modules are very significant. With better documentation and the reprogramming efforts that are being undertaken, it will become easier to combine the modules.

PROGRAMMING LANGUAGES

No matter how refined canned software becomes, sooner or later all users find they have some applications that they must program themselves. Thus careful consideration must be given to the programming languages available. Languages should be suited to both the application at hand and the programming skill of the users. A check should be made to determine if the diagnostics (program error messages) are clear and to the point.

The most popular language is FORTRAN. This language is very versatile; however, it is not easy for a novice who is not technically oriented to master. One major advantage of FORTRAN is its compatibility with batch processing applications. As with all languages, the quality of FORTRAN varies widely among vendors.

The second most used language is one of the simplified languages designed especially for time-sharing—Dartmouth's BASIC. BASIC is easily learned in one day and is most popular among individuals who occasionally must write programs. In its fully expanded form, BASIC has almost all of the important features of FORTRAN. Because it is less complex than FORTRAN, programs written in BASIC are frequently cheaper to run.

An editor is a command system or language that enables a user to make major modifications to the coding of a program by typing a few characters into the terminal. A powerful but easy-to-use editing system is extremely valuable when writing or modifying programs or data.

In addition, more than a dozen special-purpose languages are available on different systems.

SYSTEM COMMANDS

In general, system command languages are of two types: English words (easy to remember) and abbreviations (quick to use). Light users prefer the former; heavy users like the latter.

CUSTOMER SUPPORT SERVICES

The finest time-shared computer in the world is worthless unless the customer knows how to use it. Time-sharing vendors vary widely in the amount and quality of customer service they offer. All vendors supply documentation in the form of user manuals. Some of these manuals are very excellent; many are incomprehensible. Many vendors will train customer personnel not only in the use of the terminal but also in several programming languages. Some vendors will write a customer's programs for him. Finally, the value of good customer assistance personnel is not to be overlooked. Questions arise very frequently, especially when an individual is just beginning to use time-sharing.

PROGRAM SIZE

Computers vary immensely in the size of programs they will handle—in terms of both source and object code. Some vendors have devised methods of overlaying the same area or core and chaining or linking programs together, which eliminate these constraints for some applications. However, these features are often difficult to program around and expensive to use. Although it is desirable to use the largest system possible, it is usually wasteful of the computer's resources and thus more expensive to use a large computer for small programs.

MACHINE SPEED

For high-compute programs a high-speed CPU ("number cruncher") is needed; otherwise, answer output is very slow. However, cost considerations prevent using a high-speed computer for low-compute programs.

FILES

Data stored in the computer, if they are not an integral part of a program, are called a file. There are two basic types of storage: random and sequential. In a random file, by using an address, it is possible to jump about and directly access the desired item. In a sequential file, the items must be accessed one after another in the order in which they have been placed in the file. For large data files, the random access method has definite cost and time savings.

SECURITY

Because an individual's proprietary programs and data share the same CPU and storage facilities as those of the other users, most vendors have constructed elaborate security systems (validation procedures) to guard against unauthorized access. In general, these systems have worked adequately, and there have been few known breakdowns in security.

SYSTEM LOAD

A system that is supporting too many users will have slow response time. A user should test for this at the hours of peak utilization—about 10:30 A.M. and 3:30 P.M.

RELIABILITY

Needless to say, a system that is under repair ("down" or "crashed") often and for long duration is not of much use. In addition, some systems become "confused" more easily than others. Many of the industry's reliability problems stem not from the hardware but from the complex monitor (governor) that controls the actual time-sharing operation. With use, these "bugs" are usually worked out of a system. Thus it is usually unwise to subscribe to a service that is offering time-sharing under new controlling software.

Recognizing that reliability problems will never be completely overcome, some systems have built-in recovery features that retain a user's work even if the system crashes. Thus, when the system comes up, the user may pick up exactly where he left off.

COST CONSIDERATIONS

The pricing of time-sharing services is an extremely complex subject, and it will probably become even more so as some vendors realize that profitability may never be achieved at current rates and attempt disguised price increases. Currently, some services can be used for a total cost of less than $5 an hour. The average is probably about $25 an hour.

Basically, there are three kinds of charges associated with the use of time-sharing.

Terminal connect fee.   Most vendors charge a fee for the use of one of the computer's ports (phone outlets). For example, each hour that a terminal is on-line may cost from $5 to $15.

Central processor fee.   There is often a fee that varies according to the amount of work the computer is required to perform over a given time period. This fee is usually charged per second of usage of the CPU. Charges for a central processing second can be very deceiving, for larger central processors do many times more work in one second than smaller ones. In addition, vendors using the same equipment often calculate central processor utilization differently. The only way to approximate the cost of running a particular application on any service is to run a bench-mark program (a standardized program similar to the application at hand).

Storage fee.   There is almost always a charge for storing programs on-line. This charge is often stated in cents per 1,000 characters. Several types of storage (disk, drum, data cell, and so on) are available to a vendor. In general, the cost is higher the faster a program or data file can be retrieved from storage. Usually, there is a quantity discount for storing a large data base.

Other charges.   The overall pricing plans for time-sharing vary widely. Initiation fees, monthly minimums, or quantity usage discounts may be incorporated in a pricing plan. Some vendors charge all kinds of special fees for services that other vendors include free. A recent innovation that is proving to be very expensive for many a user is a surcharge computed according to the number of characters that are entered into or received by his terminal. Some vendors eliminate one or two of the three basic charges and adjust the others accordingly. Thus, for example, a user might try to run all his high-compute programs on a system with no CPU charge and all his low-compute programs on one with no terminal connect charge. Phone charges are another consideration; toll-free dial-up service is extremely important. In short, there is no substitute for careful analysis, including bench-marking several systems with programs much like those the user expects to run. Unfortunately, to design and convert bench-mark programs that are adequate samples of a firm's overall time-sharing usage to run on each service is very time-consuming.

PRECAUTIONS

In many cities there are more than a dozen vendors offering time-sharing. If a user does not require local dial-up service, he can select from over a hundred. The quality of service varies widely. The choice is not only difficult; an error can be costly. Converting programs from one system to another is time-consuming. Two steps can minimize the chance of an error: Before signing a contract, a user should thoroughly test the system during a trial period; moreover, a prospective subscriber should arrange to confirm his conclusions with several of a vendor's present subscribers.

Using Time-Sharing Effectively

One of the most difficult dilemmas facing an executive is how to maximize the value received per dollar of time-sharing expenditure. Few large institutions have solved this problem successfully. Often, a user finds that he has subscribed to a time-sharing service without any knowledge that other departments in his company are also using time-sharing. Moreover, in many cities where there might be a dozen or more services from which to select, it is very difficult for an inexperienced user to choose the system that best fills his needs—both in terms of cost performance and in system capabilities.

ESTABLISHING A COORDINATOR

The need to establish a time-sharing coordinator (an in-house time-sharing consultant) cannot be overstated. This individual should be selected from among the firm's time-sharing users rather than from the EDP department, which sometimes regards any time-sharing activity as an uncontrollable infringement upon its domain. Moreover, because their work usually does not involve time-sharing usage, EDP personnel lack the first-hand experience which can be so valuable in advising a new time-sharing user. The time-sharing coordinator should be familiar with a firm's batch processing capabilities so that computer work that is not suited to time-sharing will be channeled to the EDP group.

Duties of coordinator. The prime responsibility of the coordinator should be liaison between the various vendors and both present and potential time-sharing users. He should be prepared to advise users on the merits of the various services, to order terminals, and to obtain time-sharing subscriptions. However, the coordinator should be regarded only as a consultant; the user must be permitted to make the final selection of his system. Vendors should be informed that all contact with the individual users is to be channeled through the coordinator.

As the cost performance of the various services fluctuates widely with each application, through the use of a coordinator a large user of time-sharing will get the work done not only with greater efficiency but also with markedly lower expenses.

IN-HOUSE TIME-SHARING

As an institution's time-sharing billing grows to five figures per month, consideration is frequently given to possible cost savings through the establishment of an in-house time-sharing system. To date, few firms have established such systems, principally because the potential savings are largely illusory, for two reasons.

First, most time-sharing vendors are operating at a loss, and this situation is expected to continue for the next several years; yet these vendors achieve economies of scale that few time-sharing users could hope to equal. Second, the assumption is frequently made that all of a firm's time-sharing usage will be moved in-house. Several factors make this very difficult to accomplish. One in-house system cannot possibly have all the features of the systems of several time-sharing vendors. It is usually not economically justifiable to duplicate a vendor's application packages and data bases. Systems that are available at low rental are not large enough to handle a firm's largest programs. Users are often reluctant to learn a new system and convert software that is already operational.

However, institutions that are spending over $50,000 per month and whose billing is expected to grow rapidly through the development of new programs may reap substantial benefits from the establishment of an in-house system. In some instances the advantages derived from custom-tailoring a time-shared computer to an institution's particular applications are very meaningful, particularly if a computer is to be dedicated solely to a single, very large application.

Several time-sharing vendors have recently expanded into the business of operating time-sharing computers for other firms, either on the vendor's or the subscriber's premises. This arrangement frequently overcomes many of the problems associated with user-operated in-house systems.—*A. L. Summers*

COMMUNICATIONS NETWORKS

Ever since the Civil War—for more than 100 years—businessmen have employed electrical communication to improve service to customers, reduce operating costs, and maintain surveillance and control over dispersed operations. Advances in the technology of communication, transmission, processing, and application have permitted larger, more complex, and more widely dispersed operations to be effectively managed.

Voice, data, mail, and messengers are all part of a total communications network. Their commonality of function suggests that they should be under a single manager—a vice president, director, or manager. While mail and messengers will continue to be vital economic elements of a total communications system, the need for current operating information processed and ready for application is causing an explosive growth in the use of electrical communication.

Electrically transmitted information has, through general usage, evolved in two categories—data transmission, which is associated with the language of machines; and voice transmission, which is associated with human language. Some people consider voice as a form of data transmission. The two forms, voice and data, employ a common communication linkage and should therefore be planned simultaneously. (See "Telecommunications," page 2·129.)

Effective computerized communications, which this subsection considers, are divided into two areas—essentials and elements. These are the areas that management will have to review and evaluate to provide a reasonable balance between the operational requirements, the state of the art, and economic considerations.

Essentials of an Effective Computerized System

The essentials of an effective computerized communications system are distribution, volume, language, urgency, accuracy, expandability, dependability, discipline, and security.

DISTRIBUTION

Data distribution is basically of four types: collection, dissemination, message switching, and inquiry and response. Each of these types was employed long before computers became available. Data collection, as the name implies, means the gathering of data from many sources by messenger, mail, or electrical transmission into a central storage location for subsequent processing. The flow of data is usually one-way, from many locations to one location. Data dissemination, on the other hand, is the one-way transmission of data, usually from one location to many locations. Message switching is the transmission of data from one location to one or more other locations through a central handling and control point. It is two-way transmission, both receiving and transmitting. Inquiry and response compose the transmission of data from a single location to a central location; the message is immediately processed, and a reply is transmitted from the central location. It is a two-way transmission. There are several variations within the four types; interactive time-sharing is a form of inquiry and response. The effective system should provide the type or combination of types of data distribution required between all local and dispersed locations.

VOLUME

Data volume is the amount of data transmitted between any two locations. It is usually stated as the number of messages or transactions transmitted during a specified period (hour or day), multiplied by the average number of characters per message. The designer of a computerized communications system must evaluate the throughput capability of the total system to insure that peak volumes are handled as well as the total volume. While the rate of transmission and the operating capability of a system may be listed in terms of bits per second ("bits" is a coined word—"bi" from *bi*nary and "ts" from digi*ts*), the only effective measure of throughput is the number of text characters or message content that is handled in a given period of time. It should be noted that electrical or electromechanical terminals require extra characters for control that vary by the type of equipment, codes (language), and control procedures used. These added characters decrease throughput capability. Each element of the total system also has an effect on the total throughput.

System designers will recognize that increasing the number of cards that a terminal can handle will not provide an equivalent increase in throughput unless all elements of the system can handle the increased rate. Similarly, a terminal printer that can print 400 lines per minute may have no greater throughput capability than one that prints 300 lines per minute if the balance of the system can support only the 300-line-per-minute rate.

LANGUAGE

Language in relation to the electrical transmission of information is used in two ways: first, in terms of the physical form (machine or natural language); and second, in terms of the code used to transmit or record the data.

The natural physical form of input and output is characterized by its ready usability by humans. The keyboard, tone-calling phone, hard copy (handwritten, printed, and graphic), and soft copy as displayed on a cathode ray tube are examples of natural language.

Machine physical form is characterized by reading and recording techniques which can be readily interpreted only by machines. Punched cards and paper tape; imprinted, magnetic ink characters; embossed or punched tokens and badges; magnetic cards, tape, and disk; and microfilm and electrical storage components such as magnetic cores are examples of physical forms that store the machine language.

There can be, of course, combinations of the human and machine physical forms of language on the same documents. A common example is the interpreted punched card. Management expects that system designers will evaluate the physical form required against the operational requirement.

Many codes are used for documents, transmission, and processing. Codes for transmission and recording information vary in relation to the number of code elements (also called levels or bits) used to define a character, the order in which the levels or bits are transmitted, and the assignment of the characters to each particular combination of levels or bits. Each conversion of one code to another adds additional cost and time—admittedly slight, under certain conditions—to the total system. The standard code today is the *American Standard Code for Information Interchange* (ASCII). This 1968 code provides for a possible 128 character representations and control functions. (For a complete list of standards used in data communication, contact the American National Standards Institute, 1430 Broadway, New York, N.Y. 10018.)

Also commonly used in data transmission is the five-level Baudot code used with many teleprinter systems, the six-level binary coded decimal (BCD), an extension of the Hollerith punched-card code, the six-level Teletypesetter code, the seven-level field data code used by the military forces, and the two out of eight parallel codes used for tone dialing. Each of the codes mentioned has a number of variations. Terminals can transmit only to terminals having identical codes unless a conversion (usually by a processor) is performed.

URGENCY

When is the information required? The fact that data are to be transmitted by electrical methods immediately indicates a degree of urgency that cannot be satisfied by mail or messenger. In an electrical transmission system a certain amount of queueing is always present. The amount of queueing and resultant delay that can be tolerated is an essential element of the effective system. Even if the data are not urgent, the amount of delay in completing a transaction may be a waste of personnel time. Systems should be designed to handle the maximum amount of data that must be transmitted during a peak period of time, or the system may come to a complete halt. To insure that the system will not stop due to overload, certain systems can be designed to place restraints on terminals transmitting to the processor.

Transmission scheduling and priorities assigned to various types of messages are two ways in which peak loads can be reduced. Alternate or overflow techniques are also employed in certain private line systems to handle occasional peak loads. The system must be designed to provide the information on-time, or in-time, for the user; to provide the information earlier may add unnecessary costs, but delayed delivery may be intolerable.

If the electrical transmission is connected to a computer and data are to be immediately processed or journal recorded for later processing, the system is considered on-line. If the transmission is to be recorded on a terminal other than the processor for subsequent processing, the transmission is considered off-line. It is noted, as a precaution, that many off-line systems cannot be connected to an on-line system because of some incompatibility.

In general, the volume of information is the determining factor in determining the rate of transmission rather than the time it takes for a transaction to travel from one location to another.

ACCURACY

Errors in a computerized communications system occur in the human input and in the elements of communication. Human input contributes by far the greatest percentage (estimated at 90 to 99 percent by some authorities) of errors to the system. In the elements of the system, errors occur in the terminals, the modems (the modem is a device to modulate and demodulate signals), the communication linkage, and the central processing equipment.

Errors in the terminals, processing equipment, and modems are not common and when present are usually repetitive and easily detected or are caused by a complete malfunction of the unit. Communication linkage errors are the most difficult type to detect and avoid. Statistically, the number of bits in error will average one in 10,000 to 100,000 bits transmitted; however, as the rate of transmission increases, it can be expected that the error rate will increase.

Many types of error detection and correction codes and methods are employed in the transmission of data. The two most common are vertical and horizontal parity checks. Detected errors can be displayed so that manual correction can be made through requesting retransmission, or they can be handled in a method to cause automatic retransmission. The addition of the vertical parity bit with automatic correction will result in an average of one undetected error in every million transmitted.

The addition of the horizontal parity and the additional character with correction will result in an average of one undetected error in every 10 million transmitted. In some systems highly redundant self-correcting codes are used so that retransmission is not required; since these will affect throughput and their cost is high, they are rarely used.

The effect and cost of an error must be evaluated before error controls are considered. The effect of an error in a human-language text (numbers excluded) or a few misspelled words in a data base would probably be negligible. However, the effect of loading a program in a computer with transmission line errors can be very costly. Once an error is detected in the system within the levels deemed appropriate, procedures must be established to correct the errors. Recovery of the correct data can be expensive even if it is done manually. Data captured and entered into the system as close to the source as possible are usually the most accurate. Additional methods are available for the checking of data: Among these are the various types of check digits, format checking, and validity checking, which can be performed by the central processor.

EXPANDABILITY

The computerized communications system can be expected with reasonable certainty to grow, not only because of the volume brought by increased business but also as a result of the requirements dictated by new system applications. It is essential, therefore, that the system be implemented to provide for a modular growth over the time period (years) that the system is expected to remain functional. Conversion or replacement of a computerized communications system is involved and costly. Management expects systems designers to evaluate not only the expandability caused by growth but also the ability to handle increased line speeds and different terminals as the state of the art advances.

DEPENDABILITY

The reliability of a total system is of paramount concern not only to the user but also to all organizations that supply either hardware or services for the system. Reliability in excess of 99 percent on the average can be expected from individual parts of the system. Taken collectively, the total system reliability will be somewhat less. Failures of parts will occur.

One technique to improve system reliability is the use of back-up or standby equipment to be switched into service in the event of failure. Another technique is operating redundancy, splitting the load between two or more facilities so that in the event of failure at least one part of the system can be kept functioning even though total throughput will have been reduced. In communications linkages the switched message network provides automatic back-up of circuits or channels, and private line systems often use this dialed network as back-up. Manual methods, including voice transmission, may also back up the electrical system if properly evaluated.

The degree of reliability required is a function of the amount of outage that can be tolerated and related economic considerations.

DISCIPLINE

Any communications system requires that certain operations and controls be performed in a prescribed manner. Failure to comply with procedures results in missed or repeated transmissions, requires additional equipment and facilities, and results in higher overall costs. It is recognized that equipment suppliers continually improve equipment and procedures to make actions by personnel more automatic and less susceptible to error; nevertheless, proper and continuous training and supervision of operators are essential to an effective system. Certain systems in which the general public or a selected portion of the public is involved may require provisions for manual intervention by a human operator or supervisor to assist in expeditious handling of the communications.

SECURITY

Computerized communications systems should consider two forms of security. The purpose of the first is to prevent unauthorized use of or access to all or selected types of information. This can be accomplished through employing private controlled channels or lines for connections, selective calling by the processor, codes or keys employed by the user, and similar means. The second type of security required is usually encountered when employing an unattended terminal on the switched-message networks. It is possible for calls to be misdirected and the information lost when either transmitting or receiving. Automatic devices have been developed for certain terminals and materially reduce the chances that data transmission will go astray.

COSTS

The essential requirement of management is to make sure that systems designers have evaluated the essentials and elements of alternative computerized communications systems on the basis of costs and values to be realized. Increase in volume will necessarily increase costs, as will increased speed of transmission. Under certain conditions two slow-speed circuits and associated terminals will be able to handle the volume at a lower cost than one high-speed channel and terminal. Error detection and correction add additional costs to the system; however, if manual correction of the data is required at a later time, the costs may be even higher. Back-up and alternate methods add increased costs but must be evaluated against lost production or orders. Baudot code, because of its simplicity, may produce the highest throughput but can also be the most expensive when correction or double transmission is required for accuracy.

Elements of an Effective Computerized System

The elements of a computerized communications system are the terminals, modems, linkage, multiplexors or concentrators, controllers, and the processor, including data base and software. The essential requirement of all the elements is compatibility, both electrical and language.

TERMINALS

The selection of the terminal is probably the most critical in the process of communications network design. After an economic evaluation of all factors the selection of the terminal reduces the number of complex variables that must be considered.

Terminals may be divided into five broad categories: (1) natural-language, general-purpose; (2) natural-language, special-purpose; (3) machine-language, general-purpose; (4) machine-language, special-purpose; and (5) combinations.

Natural-language, general-purpose terminals are typewriter-type devices with either printer (hard copy) or cathode ray tube (soft copy) and tone-calling telephones with voice response and (coming in the future) voice recognition.

Natural-language, special-purpose terminals are created for a specific industry —for example, bank teller terminals, stock quote, and educational terminals.

Machine-language, general-purpose terminals include paper tape and card punches and readers, and magnetic tape and cards.

Machine-language, special-purpose terminals are generally data-collection terminals, token or badge readers, or merchandising tag readers.

The selection of the terminal will involve the people who operate it, the application, throughput, the communications linkage over which it will operate, and the processor and software with which it will work. All elements of the system must be compatible.

Considering that the largest number of errors are introduced into the computerized communications system by the terminal operator, probably the most significant factor that the systems designer has to consider is the human aspect— the man-machine relationship. Consideration of this factor should include the following: The operator is encouraged to do the right thing and is prevented or discouraged from doing the wrong thing; there are adequate status lights so that the operator knows the status of the terminal and the system, but these are limited to necessary functions so as not to be discouraging to the new operator; the terminal provides an easy means for the operator to self-test and isolate trouble, but service points and adjustments are screened or made not available to the operator; the keyboard is designed with a separate numeric section for those who are familiar with the 10-key accounting machine and for the novice (however, if the operator is an experienced key punch operator, the keyboard also contains an included 10-key numeric section); the terminal is light in weight and easily portable, if moving is a requirement, since the law in some states prohibits women from moving items that weigh more than 25 pounds; operator controls and functions should be easily available and usable, but inadvertent use is discouraged; control keys can be easily distinguished from general operational keys; formatting and tabulation are of rapid and positive assistance to the operator; characters and graphics displayed are easily read and, if soft-display, free from flicker to reduce operator fatigue; output copy is clear, easily read, and suitable for reproduction; control functions are not printed or displayed; the operator's position is comfortable and no body strains are imposed; noise, glare, flicker, and sharp edges are reduced and are approved by Underwriters Laboratories; and the operator is encouraged to follow communications rules or discipline. It will be noted that many authorities find little to recommend upper and lower case over upper case alone as far as accuracy of reading is concerned; lower-case capability is desirable if a document will be used for intercompany business purposes.

In addition to the man-machine relationships the system designer would be expected to consider the following application features: the maximum number of characters to be displayed at one time; the maximum number of documents and characters to be entered at one time; the need to refer back to previous output or hard copy versus soft copy; the number of characters or symbols required in the output and the need for multiple standard formats for the operator to complete; the need for graphics on input and output; the need for unattended operation; the requirement for auxiliary input and output devices connected to the main terminal; and the requirement for stand-alone or multiple installations.

Management should also require designers to consider the communications compatibility and other factors, which include the following: confirmation with the approved standards for language, transmission rate, and interfacing; if the terminal is to be used on international communications, the imposition of special requirements if the terminal is to operate on both primary and alternate services; the method of coupling to the communications linkage (direct, acoustic, data access, private, and dialed facilities); the requirement for full or half duplex lines; the use of standard control procedures; the proven dependability for the type of service and locations intended; the maintainability of the terminal and an established maintenance organization. The terminal should be easily moved, for relocation is inevitable, and both communications and power should terminate in a plug; terminals secured for off-line use should be capable of future connection to an on-line system; and the terminal should be supported by constantly maintained and updated software.

MODEMS (DATA SETS)

Modems provide the interface between the terminal and the linkage. The transmission channel at one time was a pair of wires that connected one terminal with another. The extension of the hard wires permitted the digital signals to be transmitted in a simple on-or-off manner. Transmission channels today are generally derived from the use of carrier equipment on a pair of wires and from microwave radio systems which do not pass the simple direct current. It is therefore necessary to have a modulator to convert the signals used at a terminal to a form of alternating current which can be transmitted. The term "demodulate" denotes the reconversion of the signal from the communication channel to a signal which can be used by the receiving terminal. (The word "modem" is a contraction of "*mo*dulator-*dem*odulator.") Modems are selected on the basis of the terminal and communication channel (linkage) and the desired rate of transmission. Equipment manufacturers usually stipulate the type of modem required by their equipment.

Data sets or modems also make feasible a number of other control functions providing interaction between the terminals, the linkage, and (when used) the central switching facilities of the switched-message network (dialed). Auxiliary units provided by the telephone company provide additional control capabilities. An example is the automatic calling unit, which will permit the processor to dial communication circuits automatically without human intervention.

LINKAGE

Linkage is the electrical path that permits the transmission of information between two or more points. It may be provided in one of three ways: by common carrier; by quasicommon carrier such as railroad, pipe line, gas and electric utility, and airline and trucking associations; or by the user. By far the most used method because of cost is the common carrier, both domestic and international.

The service offerings of the common carrier are divided into two main categories: switched or common-user facilities, over which most of the data are transmitted; and private-line or full-period facilities.

The switched facilities are usually paid for on a timed-use basis, while the cost of private lines is charged at flat rates regardless of the amount of use. Costs for services vary with use (intrastate, interstate, or international) and are subject to change. The common carrier should be contacted for exact pricing. Also, it should be recognized that, in addition to the normal monthly recurring charges, certain facilities include a one-time installation or nonrecurring charge. The choice between private-line and switched facilities for data transmission is a matter of comparing costs. The prime consideration in making the choice is the number of transactions and the length of the transmission or holding time. Private-line facilities are available all the time; if dialed or switched facilities are used, the additional time for dialing must be taken into consideration. In addition to the two main categories, available facilities are also classified as narrow-band, voice-band, and wide-band.

Narrow-band switched facilities. Two domestic services are available: TELEX, supplied by Western Union, and TWX, supplied by the telephone companies. (TWX is in process of being acquired by Western Union.) TELEX relies on the five-level Baudot code and is generally a combined terminal and line service, although with adapters other equipment may use the network. The system permits international connection to similar services in other countries. TELEX service is limited to 50 bits per second or 6.6 characters per second. TWX employs either the five-level Baudot or the eight-level ASCII, and like TELEX is generally a combined terminal and line offering. Under certain restraints and with adapters, other terminal equipment may be connected. The system also provides for international connection through services provided by the international carriers. TWX service, depending on terminals selected, may transmit at either 45.45 bits per second or six characters per second, or 110 bits per second or ten characters per second. Both services are available for completely unattended operation.

Voice-band switched facilities. The telephone company common carriers offer most of these services through the familiar switched-voice or -message network. Western Union offers a similar service via its broad band exchange service, but it is limited to selected major cities. In addition to the standard long-distance, station-to-station service (direct distance dialing, or DDD), the telephone industry also offers wide area telephone service (WATS), which is generally available on an interstate basis. Wide area telephone service permits calls to be placed or received for the transmission of data within selected service areas (bands) by means of special access lines that are connected to the exchange network. The entire adjacent United States is divided into six service areas extending outward from the local state. Service may be secured for all or one of the bands, and each service area added includes the previous area or areas. In most states WATS is also available on a statewide basis or a seventh band.

OUTWATS permits calls to be made or data to be sent and received within the service areas selected. INWATS permits calls to be received from the calling party at no charge for sending or receiving data. Full-time service on both INWATS and OUTWATS is available on a flat monthly basis regardless of the number or length of calls. Measured-time service is available generally for ten hours' service at any time during the month. The service is accumulated by fractions of minutes and any additional time is charged at an hourly rate.

Voice-band services permit the transmission of data at rates up to and beyond 10,000 bits per second and are satisfactory for the transmission of redundant data, such as facsimile, at these speeds. For digital data the current practical limit on the switched-voice networks appears to be between 3,200 and 4,800 bits per second, or between 400 and 600 characters per second. The most commonly used speeds are 1,200 and 2,000 bits per second or 120 and 250 characters per second.

Wide-band switched facilities. The availability of wide band (50,000 bits per second) has been greatly restricted because of a number of complex problems. The service is currently available only on an experimental basis in four selected cities. Both the Bell System and Western Union are contemplating expansion of this offering when requirements indicate the need.

Narrow-band private-line facilities. The telephone companies and Western Union provide a group of facilities that permit transmission at rates up to 150 and 180 bits per second, respectively. These channels differ in their carrying capability of bits per second and are priced accordingly. Rates are based on tariff-calculated airline miles per month and on a sliding scale so that the longer the circuit, the lower is the rate per mile per month.

Voice-band private-line facilities. The telephone companies and Western Union provide a basic voice-band channel [$4KH_z$ (4,000 cycles per second) nominal, 300-3,000 H_z (300-3,000 cycles per second) usable] for the transmission of voice or data on a full period or flat monthly basis. The calculation of rates is similar to that of narrow-band facilities, but rates are somewhat higher in price. Service may be on a point-to-point basis, many points to many points on a switched basis, or may be a single line on a multipoint basis (party line), with approximately 35 locations as the practical limit. Multipoint service under computer control is usually referred to as selective calling and involves polling and calling. Narrow-band private-line facilities may also be multipointed.

Private-line facilities may be conditioned at extra cost with balancing equipment to permit greater rates of transmission and better error-performance. Transmission speeds on private lines are similar to speeds on the voice network; the two most commonly used speeds are 1,200 and 2,400 bits per second, 120 and 300 characters per second, respectively, although 4,800 bits or 600 characters per second is increasing in use. Higher speeds mean higher costs.

Group pricing for private-line facilities is also available. Series 8000 provides for 12 voice channels, Series 5700 for 60 channels, and 5800 for 240 channels. The cost of channels thus derived is usually less on a per-mile basis than individual Series 2000 or 3000 voice channels.

Wide-band private-line facilities. Wide-band facilities can generally be treated as special cases of Telepak, in which the Series 2000 or 3000 voice-band services are grouped for a single circuit. Series 8000 channels can be arranged for transmitting up to 50,000 bits per second, and Series 5700 can be arranged for transmitting up to 230,400 bits per second.

MULTIPLEXORS AND CONCENTRATORS

The voice channel, which is the basic channel of the telephone industry, can be divided so that more than one message or signal can be sent over the channel simultaneously. Two primary types of multiplexing systems permit a number of low-speed terminals to be used over a voice-band line: time division and frequency division. Frequency division (the more common) can divide a voice-band line into 12 to 24 narrow-band channels, depending on the rate of transmission. Time-division systems may nearly double this number or provide a combination of channels for cathode ray terminals and teletypewriters. Frequency division is the more flexible and provides (depending on design) a higher-derived channel reliability.

Concentrators are basically of two types. Circuit concentrators permit a number of terminals and their associated channels to be switched on a demand-use basis to one or more similar channels. Message concentrators permit a number of terminals and associated channels of the same or lower capacity to be connected to one or more of the same or higher-capacity channels. Both systems depend on the fact that all terminals are not busy all the time and can share one or more common communications channels.

THE CONTROLLER

The communications control unit (controller) provides the interface between the linkage and the processor or, indirectly, the terminal and the processor. Management's role is to assure that designers evaluate the performance of the controller and its effect on the total system. The controller may be exceedingly simple, or it may be a complete processor capable of handling all communications functions, including message switching. Generally, the controller should be expected to provide complete line coordination and control functions automatically. Further, it should be capable of transferring characters from the line to the processor with minimum interruption of the basic processor. Controllers can maintain complete status of the lines and connected circuits, reporting changes to the processor as required. Consideration should also be given to having the controller provide for code conversion, speed conversion, and the multiplexing and scanning of lines. Trade-offs exist in the quantity and type of lines handled and in the functions performed by the controller and the processor.

PROCESSOR AND DATA BASE

The heart of the on-line system is the data base, especially if inquiry and response type functions are performed. Proper keys and indexes must be included to allow random access devices to be quickly addressed for necessary information. In addition, management must insure that the systems design provides the necessary equipment for communications programs storage and journal recording of messages and statistics for recovery operations, as well as the queueing or temporary storage of messages awaiting processing or transmission. Management should further determine that designers insure that the size and speed of the processor are capable of handling anticipated peak traffic loads and are capable of expansion to meet scheduled growth. The processor memory may also include other teleprocessing functions. Indicative of these functions are the following: code conversion tables, which convert one machine language to another machine language, such as ASCII to Baudot; message routing tables, employed in message switching to define destination or alternate from analysis of the header of the message; line and terminal table, which defines to the processor the type of terminal and network, permitting unlike terminals on different linkages to communicate through the proper use of the code conversion and routing tables; and input/output buffer areas, which serve as temporary storage areas for messages during transition from the terminal to the processor and vice versa.

SOFTWARE

Whether a system is a conventional on-line system or a time-sharing system, it is essential that the processor have a resident executive program that will perform an interrupt analysis, monitor input and output, provide allocation and scheduling of memory and storage, and provide access to the data base. Management should also insure that system designers consider the methods and trade-offs of servicing lines and terminals; the type of input/output buffering; input and output queues; verifying commands and demand for interrupts; creating and maintaining polling and calling tables, automatic answering, and calling; code translation; and provision of control characters. Communications software should also provide for the journal recording of messages; the recording of transaction or volume statistics; checking formats and validity; and procedures for sequence numbering of messages and time stamping of messages. Other program elements include terminal-control procedures, verifying terminal identification, header analysis, and interacting with users' programs. It is certain that malfunctions will occur; therefore, consideration should be given to shutdown and restart procedures and transfer to back-up equipment or alternate equipment.

Other Considerations

In addition to the essentials and elements of communications, such factors as the installation of the system, its management, the use of consultants, and the role of the common carrier should be evaluated.

INSTALLATION

Implementation of a computerized communications system is much the same as in any major systems project. The key factors are an adequate system definition or specification, assignment of appropriate project or implementation management with defined responsibility and control, realistic scheduling (PERT/Time), and training of personnel. Detailed descriptions should be provided for system operation and configuration, compatible equipment, data traffic, and throughput. Implementation should also plan for irregularities and outages that occur in a system. The normal communications system requires operator disciplines; not only should an initial training program be prepared but a continuing program must be organized as well. A caution should be noted: Major terminal systems should be phased into an on-line system and not cut-over. Training should be immediately prior to operator use. The roles of the various equipment suppliers should be defined, especially where fault isolation and repair are concerned.

MANAGEMENT

It is again suggested that the people who are responsible for data and voice communications should be directed by the same vice president, director, or manager. Also, owing to the commonality of programming, communications or conventional programmers and analysts should report to the same executive. The requirement for operators for the central processing is recognized and provided. Consideration should also be given to the use of communications operators and supervisors for large systems. The complexity of the total communications network and system, together with anticipated malfunctions, requires the ability to isolate troubles quickly and provide for restoration. The communications operator is almost a necessity if service is being provided to the general public. It is assumed that the requirements for adequate staffs of personnel, programmers, and analysts are understood. While equipment suppliers provide general communications programs, the user of the systems must supply his own application programs.

CONSULTANTS

There are three sources of outside consulting service—the common carrier, the equipment supplier, and the independent consultant. The common carrier consultant does not require any fee, and his services are related to providing communications equipment and services. Therefore, in principle he cannot be viewed as detached. Whether or not he actually is detached is a function of the individual himself and his company's policies. With the increasing role of data communication in business, it is also increasingly difficult to find representatives who are competent in this subject. It is even more rare to find people competent in both voice and data, and this applies to all three sources of outside consulting.

The equipment supplier can generally provide a broader and more complete consulting service, if for no other reason than to maintain a competitive edge. In some cases, however, fees will be charged. When the supplier is providing only terminal equipment, he can be expected to be more detached about interconnecting facilities, except to the extent that his equipment influences or dictates facility design. In matters relating directly to his company's product, his judgment is, theoretically, not the result of independent evaluation or study.

The independent consultant has, in principle, no vested interest other than to do a good job. His next job depends on all past jobs, and he must serve well to insure his economic security. In communications consulting there are two reimbursement arrangements—straight fee and contingent fee. Under straight fee the consultant performs for a fixed rate, either per diem or lump sum, for a specific project. Under contingency fee on existing systems, the consultant performs for a percentage of the cost savings he produces. In principle the latter is not an objective approach likely to produce best results for the client.

Management should consider outside consulting service if there does not exist sufficient technical ability within the systems staff; when there is a temporary peak load or a particularly complex situation; or when there is a major project or system change where an independent analysis, separate from the management staff, is justified as insurance.

The selection of an outside consultant will be made on the basis of the following: an appraisal of his qualifications, drawn from academic and business background; evidence of current technical competence; a check of performance on similar problems with his client list; the type of negotiation for fee and description of services to be rendered; and the potential rapport and communications capabilities of the prospective consultant.

COMMON CARRIERS

The primary communications common carrier in the continental United States is the American Telephone and Telegraph Company (the Bell System), which owns all or part of 24 associated operating companies, the Long Lines Department for interstate communications, and the Western Electric Company (the manufacturing arm). The Bell System provides, in addition to terminals and communication linkages, a wide range of auxiliary communications devices and services. Providing interconnecting service in certain geographical areas are the independent telephone companies; the largest is the General Telephone System. The services offered by the independents are generally similar to those provided by the Bell System. Also providing terminals and other communications facilities and service is Western Union. This organization also provides nationwide services.

There are three primary international common carriers: RCA Global Communications; ITT World Communications; and Western Union, International. International data communications similar to those supplied in the United States are furnished only by these carriers. It is suggested that management contact these organizations to insure technical compatibility before selecting equipment that may connect to overseas facilities.—*C. J. Pritchard*

ARCHIVES AND THE COMPANY LIBRARY

Historical information relevant to the development of a corporation and organized for permanent preservation comprises the business archives. The company library (sometimes called an information or media center) is an important element in the overall information management process.

Archives

Archives provide invaluable information that reflects industry and community development. They can also provide facts of importance for legal disputes involving the infringement of patents and copyrights for which there is no other source for verification.

A modern archival program is relatively new for businesses; originally, the term applied to the records of government agencies. However, in recent years the increased interest of families and companies in archives has stimulated the growth of such collections in businesses. Two factors are crucial to a successful archives program: First, the program must have the full support and backing of top management; second, the program must have a clearly defined mission supported by delineated goals and statements of scope.

PLANNING

Planning for archives begins with a team effort, the archivist, and top management. Corporate management involvement in the planning, implementation, and operation of archives is emphasized. The professional librarian in the company often serves as the archivist. The team should formulate the broad parameters of the archives program, determining the types of information, data, samples, and artifacts to be included and identifying sources. A close working relationship is required by the team, since funding and much of the materials to be channeled into archives will be supplied by team members.

Early in the planning stage consideration must be given to the type of user the archive is to serve. Is it to be a working collection? Will it contain proprietary information? May individuals outside the company use the archives? Decisions on each of these questions and many more must be made by the team. The answers will aid in deciding the budget necessary to provide the staff, equipment, and space for establishing and maintaining the archives program. Initially, the team may want the advice of a consultant for orientation and guidance. Once the archives program has been resolved, the president—or chairman of the board or a vice president—should continue to work closely with the archivist to exchange counsel and to assure cooperation from other organizational elements.

USES AND USERS

The importance of an archives program to a company is reflected by its use. Its value is not totally derived from direct tangible benefits to the company. Many indirect benefits and the company's responsibility to society must be considered. The users of the company archives generally are in four categories: the public, scholars, researchers, and company employees.

Businesses are an integral part of our society. Company executives are frequently involved in activities where their influence is reflected at the community, state, national, and international levels. These executives are appointed to high government posts, on loan from their companies, to perform assignments of distinction and merit. Through the interweaving of business and society the public will use company archives to identify the effects the company has had on the development of the community and to obtain background information on personalities in the company.

Scholars look to archives as a source for piecing together historical facts that contribute to today's institutions and morality. Understanding and interpreting history with reasonable accuracy entails tracing knowledge to its original setting; thus the socioeconomic environment in which a company, its founder, and company executives strived or failed shows how the personalities of the men and the company were formed and the forces through which they survived.

To the researcher the company archives are significant in determining the development of an area, a region, or an industry. They show the impact of technology through inventions and patents. They show trends in labor, pinpointing new skills, professions, and the educational changes necessary to meet tomorrow's labor market. They provide information showing situations that might lead to favorable business conditions.

The internal use of a company archives collection is unlimited. It helps preserve the corporate memory. Decisions on new policy, product lines, labor disputes, legal allegations, publications, and exhibits can be well served and guided by business records of the past. Business archives primarily support the administrative functions, including technical administration and public relations and communications organizations. Archive records relieve top company executives of the need to depend solely on memory for knowledge of the company's experience. Through archival records, changes in a company over a long period of time can be compressed and identified, whereas recognition of long-term change may escape the notice of individuals. Archives support the seasoned executive and are a vital tool for the new executive.

CHARACTERISTICS

Some clarification of the differences between library, archive, and records management programs may be necessary. There are similarities among the programs at different levels of function and operation in that each program is concerned with information management—that is to say, the collection, organization, storage, and retrieval of information. The chart shown in Exhibit 2.18, however, differentiates among certain of the characteristics of these programs. This information is provided to caution management that an archives program should not be carelessly made a mere adjunct to the library or the records management organization. Archives have unique program objectives and unique standards of value for identifying the relevance of information.

SOURCE AND CONTENT

Sources for business records must be established with sufficient procedures to provide for the continuous flow of items to archives. To identify these sources, preparation is necessary to acquire an understanding of the organization, the administrative hierarchy, and the roles and responsibilities of organizational components. Personal files and the records management organization are excellent sources for archival information. Items received from these sources must be screened to decide whether they have any historical significance. If they have, they are processed into archives. Items placed in archives should be controlled through a carefully planned retention schedule providing for the preservation of items of permanent value and the disposal of items of transitory value. Agreements should be negotiated between archives and donors of records. Ideally, the archivist should have the option to manage gifts from donors. (This encompasses the prerogative of discarding records of no historical significance and

Exhibit 2.18

CHARACTERISTICS CHART

	Archives	Libraries	Records Management
Raison d'etre	Produced or accumulated with organic relationship to company	Economic, research, and cultural	Institutional value
Function	History of company	Satisfy company information needs	Controls internal records
Character of function	Receiving agent	Collecting agent	Control agent
Nature of acquisitions	Historical significance	Company program needs	Company policy
Sources for acquisitions	Individuals	Publishers, gifts, exchanges	Organizational entities
Name of files	Accessions	Acquisitions	Records
Selection	Selects items in the aggregate	Selects and evaluates single items	Not applicable
Processing	Cataloging Indexing	Descriptive and subject cataloging Indexing	Labeling
Cataloging	Describes aggregate units — entire unit is treated	Describes discrete and indivisible items by data elements (author, title, and so on)	Not applicable
File organization	Names of persons Subject Accession number Geographic	Library classification scheme	Chronological Straight number Middle digit Terminal digit
Announcement	Limited	Heavy	None
Retention	Permanent preservation	Periodic weeding — shifts with company	Retention schedule
Users	Public Scholars Researchers Company employees Other libraries	Company employees Other libraries	Company employees

replacing superseded records.) A collection of manuscripts deposited in archives is expected to remain intact, although it may be withdrawn. The agreement should protect the archivist from legal action in case of damage to the material; it should describe the archivist's responsibility and role in regard to the gift. In the case of a deposit collection, the agreement should contain a termination date for the return of the material to the donor.

The content of archives in companies varies as much as the companies the archives represent. Each company's archives program will have its own set of goals, and these goals account for the variety in scope of the records acquired. Examples of types of records that have value for business archives are numerous: books; maps; sound recordings; documents relating to the history of the company; organization charts, pictures, photographs, and other audiovisual materials; machine-readable records; minute books of board meetings; company directives; house organs; public relations brochures; employee publications; catalogs; old contracts and agreements and awards; financial records; samples of old inventory records and forms; selected personnel records; summaries of sales figures; sales manuals; and the correspondence and speeches of senior executives. The files and correspondence of the founder of the company provide an invaluable base for the archives collection. Selected files from middle management should be included, since they have a direct bearing on the implementation of policy, product lines, and company goals. Oral history tapes as appropriate should be prepared in interviews with senior employees and executives and friends of these executives, and perhaps old-timers in the neighborhood. A governing principle in selecting and preserving business records for historical purposes is to select material that will yield accurate and reasonably complete information about every phase of the business—production, distribution, management, finances, personnel, accounting, plant engineering, and research.

FILE ARRANGEMENT

The organization and handling of business archives vary according to use, type of materials, and outstanding agreements or policies for administering the collection or portions of it. An archivist may use several different techniques in organizing a collection. Some business archives are divided into active and inactive files. To optimize the utilization of space and manpower, active files are established for items in constant use. Inactive files are maintained for records that do not receive heavy use. Space requirements determine whether the inactive files will be located on-site or housed at a remote location. A system for the charging out of specific documents is required.

Whether the files should be centralized or decentralized or be managed as a combination of the two will vary among companies. Large, decentralized corporations may find it expedient to decentralize active files to its principal offices initially and then incorporate them into a centralized file for permanent preservation. Some deciding factors for types of files are size of operation, distance of users from files, turn-around time necessary for service, and type of operation. Centralized control and procedures should be provided for the handling of decentralized records before they are received by the central archives depository.

A telecopier may be used to transmit information among decentralized offices in a company.

The experience of the librarian in providing reference services to company officials affords a good backdrop for identifying patterns for organizing archival materials. These materials may be arranged by title, key word or name classification, date, or accession number. Some material may be cataloged and indexed according to modified library processes.

PROTECTION AND STORAGE FACILITIES

To draw up criteria for the systematic disposition of materials that no longer meet archival requirements is an important first step in planning the archives program. A retention schedule for materials is important to the effective management of business archives.

Fire, dampness, mutilation, and disintegration of paper and ink are hazards to archival materials. All records should be stored in a fireproof building, preferably one that has temperature and humidity controls. The records should be protected from dust, dirt, excessive light, and unnecessary handling. Equipment for housing the materials and protecting them must be purchased: corrugated and metal containers and file boxes, cabinets, and cases. Special equipment will be needed for audiovisual, sound, and computer media materials. Special containers for storing archival materials are also on the market.

It may be appropriate to bind, laminate, or microfilm materials to provide extra protection for fragile and rare items. Microfilm is used to prevent wear and tear of the original. In some instances the original is disposed of, depending on the value of the material. Microfilm offers an excellent means for safeguarding materials and also for disseminating duplicate copies of materials within a decentralized company. Microfilm reduces on-site space requirements, and it can easily be incorporated into a mechanized information storage and retrieval system. Generally, it will not be necessary to purchase photographic equipment, since convenient and economical services are available in most cities. Other equipment requirements are a microfilm reader/printer, a hard-copy reproducer (this could be a wet or electrostatic process), a laminating machine, and a tape recorder.

Companies often use a secondary off-site storage facility for vital records. This facility is frequently a subterranean cave that safeguards the company records in the event of national emergency or disaster. Separate files are also required for proprietary and classified information that is not to be used immediately by outside persons or, in some cases, is to be used by only a selected few company officials.

Progress in technology, especially in the fields of computers, microphotography, micromation, and telecommunications, has provided both opportunities and problems for the archivist. The problems are further compounded by the mobility of executives. Transactions that formerly would have been carried out by correspondence are now conducted by telephone or telegraph, or at an informal business luncheon or dinner. Records formerly prepared on ledgers now appear on computer magnetic tapes or disks. These technologies will be useful tools for the archivist, but they will introduce new demands and procedures for the acquisition, organization, and use of business archives.

There is no prescribed time for a company to begin an archives program. Ideally, it should begin before valuable materials are destroyed. Companies that do not have an archival program should give immediate attention to establishing one. Small firms may choose to begin the archives program as an adjunct to another organizational entity. Large companies should implement their archives program with all possible speed.

PROFESSIONAL RESOURCES

Organizations that may serve as sources of further information on business archives are as follows: the Records Management Council; the Society of American Archivists; the Special Libraries Association, Business and Finance Division; and the National Industrial Conference Board (NICB).

The Company Library

The emphasis of the library is determined by the nature of the company. A single source for information, regardless of format or media, simplifies services and communications. Unnecessary fragmentation of a company's information resources dissipates the usefulness of the service and arouses frustration among employees who need information.

SERVICES AND MATERIALS

Services are critical to the utilization of information resources. Circulation of materials, reference, announcement bulletins, the distribution of tables of contents, interlibrary loans, copying, routing of periodicals, literature searching, bibliographies, information retrieval, selective dissemination of information, and translations are examples of services that may be provided. Many services are possible, but wise decisions must be made to keep them in concert with changing company needs and to assure that the benefits to the company are commensurate with the cost.

Materials in the library collection may include books, journals, security-classified materials, technical reports, memorandums and notebooks, patents, clippings, specifications, speeches, films, and other forms of information. Forms may vary from printed pages to film or magnetic tape. Libraries grow exponentially; therefore, the librarian must continuously monitor its growth and development.

Pertinent information must be collected and organized for use. To be utilized efficiently, library materials must be cataloged, classified, and indexed. Either the Dewey or the Library of Congress classification system is recommended for use, since both of these systems classify the universe of knowledge. Few original classification systems succeed, and they seldom justify the effort.

MANAGING THE LIBRARY

The management of the library determines its dynamics and its effectiveness. The librarian is responsible for assuring top management of an effective, responsive program. The librarian should have administrative and technical responsibility for organizing, planning, and operating the library. Effective communications and feedback between the users and the librarian are imperative, and an advisory group or library committee often serves as liaison. Consideration of the librarian as a member of the company team is an aid to communications.

Many factors affect library planning—type of business, users, size, and availability of other library resources in the community. The Special Libraries Association Consultation Service is available to businesses desiring initial advice on establishing a new library.

Library planning includes hiring a qualified librarian who will participate in defining mission and objectives, formulating an acquisition policy (which should consider the proximity of other libraries for borrowing materials of peripheral relevance), and determining service requirements. Since library performance and benefits to the company are reflected through the effectiveness of the librarian in meeting library goals, careful planning of the library is crucial.

Technological achievements optimize library services. Mechanical, electronic, and manual tools are used to process, control, reproduce, and distribute information. Through time-sharing, computers are used for retrieving citations to documents and for automating library operations. The emergence of computerized data banks and information networks enables libraries to substitute computers for manual processes. The use of microfilm systems, telefacsimile, and teletypewriters in libraries is increasing.

A company library serves as a catalyst. One new idea resulting from an answer to a reference question can offset the cost of library service for many years. A successful company library can begin a new dimension of benefits for a business.—*B. E. Lamkin*

OFFICE SERVICES

The office services function covers a wide range of activities that include the development of policies and standards for the many kinds of office equipment and supplies needed to sustain and support the major effort of the parent company; the planning and execution of space utilization; the development and management of an internal mail and communications system; the organization of maintenance operations; the guidance of "people pools" (including reception duties for many areas); various clerical, copying, and part-time operations; and a long list of other supporting operations.

Equipment and Supplies

The almost infinite variety of available office equipment and supplies has a tendency to confuse the mind, and it also creates unlimited opportunities for the mismanagement of equipment funds. This profusion requires that a well-conceived, properly delineated set of policies and standards be created.

POLICIES AND STANDARDS

The purpose in creating policies and standards is to help responsible management get the greatest return for the dollars spent. There are many manufacturers of a like piece of equipment, which makes it impossible for the line officer or clerk to be conversant with the capabilities of each piece of equipment, its ability to withstand the treatment that it will be exposed to, the maintenance requirements, the trade-in possibilities, and the compatibility with other equipment in use by the parent organization—and still have time to perform his primary function.

Policies and standards become a "must" for economic reasons as well, in that a particular type of equipment may lend itself to the needs of one company better than another. The policies and standards should be developed around the functions of all departments within the corporation. The various tasks should be listed, and the machines that perform the necessary work should be sought out. Once the machines with the required capabilities have been identified, the equipment should be listed for procurement by the purchasing department. This procedure establishes the normal standard on which the acquisition of a given piece of equipment is based. Standards for supplies may be primarily established, although the considerations will be different.

Once the required standards have been established, the policies of the corporation need to be published. All personnel given delegated authority to requisition should be informed that centralized purchasing is to be followed and that all requisitions (using an approved form) should be directed to the purchasing agent. The requisition should include specifications to meet the need for any specialized functions.

A major advantage of creating policies to govern the requisitioning of equipment lies primarily in the buying power created by volume purchasing. If ten typewriters are purchased at one time or within one time period, rather than singly, the possibility of obtaining a quantity discount is greatly increased. The requirement to use standardized equipment also creates the opportunity to shift personnel from department to department without the necessity of retraining on unfamiliar equipment. A further advantage of standardization is that as equipment becomes required in one area of the corporation and is unused in another department, it is possible to transfer the unused equipment.

One disadvantage in the use of standardization and centralized purchasing is that equipment manufacturers often make changes in their products that are desirable in a department where needs have changed, yet the using group may not become cognizant of the change without direct contact with the supplier. This problem, however, usually appears in specialized areas of effort and becomes a situation which the system must be designed to detect and handle on an exception basis.

COOPERATIVE EFFORTS

A most important cooperative effort to implement policies and standards is between the purchasing agent and the systems staff and between the purchasing agent and building management. These standards can be and should be developed after study by the systems people. The equipment specified should satisfy the need created by the job to be done as defined by the systems staff. The purchasing agent should seek out available equipment to meet the specifications. The systems staff in turn may need to modify the system to fit the available equipment in an effort to produce the required end result with the least total corporate expenditure for labor and equipment. After the proper balance of method and equipment has been worked out, the findings are translated into a standard for equipment, which is then purchased at the best price.

The same cooperative effort is necessary for building maintenance services and equipment. Cooperative effort must be created in order to find the best products and services for maintaining the building and providing equipment, fixtures, furniture, and supplies for all needs, including lighting, environment control, and communications.

EQUIPMENT

Evaluation of equipment must be done continuously on both owned and leased assets to detect unsatisfactory performance of items previously listed as acceptable. Many items are purchased in such small quantities that it is practically impossible to perform a definitive evaluation of the equipment; thus it becomes necessary to depend upon outside evaluation sources. Independent studies of many types of equipment and supplies are available.

The procurement of equipment always creates the problem of "buy or lease" for the purchasing agent. A good guideline is the length of time that an item will be in use; a short duration points to leasing, as do the possibilities of early obsolescence. Expensive maintenance requirements would cause the user to consider a lease, especially where this essential service is incorporated. A large capital outlay may make it mandatory to lease. On the other hand, the total expenditure incurred by a lease program or anticipated life of the equipment may be so large as to completely offset the advantages of leasing; at this point it becomes desirable to purchase the item. The decision to buy or lease, then, must be based on the availability and cost of capital, the duration of the need, obsolescence, and maintenance.

Once the decision has been made, definite savings can be derived through contracts with suppliers. An established price on a product or service calling for a definite delivery time, with penalty clauses when feasible, if in the form of a contract, does much to reduce surprises on orders and thus makes the planning of the user far more accurate. The creation of the contract documents can be greatly enhanced by making use of the manufacturer's specifications to accurately describe the desired item.

FIXTURES

The acquisition of lighting fixtures, floor coverings, and draperies is usually included in space planning. The requirements are determined by the supervisor of space layout and planning on smaller projects. Larger projects involving construction, including these items, should always be planned by a registered architect or engineer. The procurement of these items normally takes place through the bidding and contracting processes with the general contractor or subcontractor at the time of development of the required space.

The requirements for lighting fixtures are determined on the basis of the work to be performed in the area, the desirable intensity of lighting, the size of the space to be lighted, and the refinement of the space involved. Floor coverings and draperies should be selected according to the needs of the desired environment and the need for external light control and accoustical control. As in the case of equipment, policy guidelines and standards are useful.

FURNITURE

The procurement of furniture begins with the expression of need from a department executive which is translated into specific use requirements, thus dictating the selection of equipment. The function of the majority of the work stations is the same, which simplifies the preparation of specifications. Once the specifications are prepared, bids are taken from suppliers; they are based on minimum annual usage with the stipulation that the supplier maintain a minimum monthly quantity for delivery when required.

The delivered furniture is directed to areas for which updating has been indicated. If a department that has an older style of furniture requests additional furniture, it is often supplied with matching items from a department that is being updated. This makes it possible to maintain like equipment within a department, creating continuity of appearance and eliminating departmental personnel jealousies.

SUPPLIES

Printed materials should be controlled by a perpetual inventory system, thus insuring immediate delivery of items that must be specially manufactured. Stationery items can be contracted for on an annual basis and a minimum quantity maintained on company shelves, using the visual inventory control method. All these items should be procured by the company through specifications to bidders. The specifications can be supplied by the storeroom manager or office services manager and should include manufacturer's name and the quality and quantity desired for the items. Nonstandard items are procured from suppliers who can demonstrate and provide the material needed at competitive prices.

Withdrawal of supplies is accomplished by means of a supply requisition which is sent to the supply department. The items are pulled by a stock clerk and placed in an internal mail department pick-up station, properly marked with delivery location by attaching the original requisition to the order. Charging the order to the user is usually done only on special nonstandard items or on large quantities. The cost of accounting for standard items in reasonable quantities often exceeds their value and is a questionable practice.

Most supplies are expendables and are therefore treated as expense items. The equipment and fixtures are accounted for in the perpetual equipment inventory, are given a depreciation schedule, are capitalized if above an established minimum, and appear in the balance sheet. As equipment is removed from service, the capital assets inventory clerk notifies the accounting department so that the necessary changes can be made.

Layout and Planning

The function of layout and planning for an office falls into two basic categories. The first is space utilization; equipment workflow, storage needs, communication needs, interdepartmental and intradepartmental space relations, and future growth are considered. The second is interior design, in which the major factors are environmental and psychological.

The starting point for space utilization is a survey, by department, of all work stations and supporting equipment in use. Next, a projection of how long each department will stay in the location being planned must be made, and in the course of this activity it becomes necessary to project work station needs for the future. Expansion (and reduction) must be considered at this point, particularly if other departments are involved and even if no immediate remedial action is possible.

STANDARDS

Once the current and projected operating requirements are known by the space designers, a set of standards for office sizes and work station space requirements can be made. Office size will be determined by the level of management of the occupant and the physical limitations imposed by the structure and the use of space. The space allocation for work stations is dependent on the size and types of the equipment used. Telephone and convenience outlets must be included.

After the inventory has been completed, the relationship of work stations has been studied, and the relationship of the department to other departments has been considered, it is possible for a drafting staff (in conjunction with the project or building engineer) to start placing the various elements in a layout. When a new building or larger space is required, it is advisable to engage professionals expert in space utilization and environmental development and coordinate their efforts with the work of the project architects and engineers. On smaller projects the function of space utilization and environmental development may be accomplished by using department supervisors, employees with good color sense, and the knowledge of the various contractors. Final approval of the layout will often be at top management level.

MOVING

When the layout of the work stations has been accomplished and all electrical, telephone, and special features have been approved, and after it has been determined that installation is possible, it becomes necessary to plan the actual moving of the equipment, as well as the purchasing of new equipment when indicated.

The first element to consider in the moving process is the projected completion date of construction in the area to be occupied. After this has been determined and after allowance has been made for contingencies, the purchasing of new equipment must be undertaken, as it may take a long time to acquire needed items. When the delivery date of the new equipment has been established, the moving date for materials in stock can be set. To minimize workflow interruptions, moving schedules must be carefully set and faithfully adhered to.

An orderly move requires planning. Desks, chairs, wastebaskets, typewriters, adding machines, dictating equipment, and all other equipment belonging to a work station should be given the same number, which should be indicated on the floor layout and chalked or signed on the floor in the exact location. If several departments are to be moved at the same time, or if several floors are to be utilized, color coding is useful. If removal of the contents of a desk is required because it is necessary to up-end the desk in moving, the contents should be packed in a box that has the same number as the desk. The drawers should be taped shut to avoid damage in transit. If all work station equipment is properly numbered and placed, there will be no need to readjust seats, reprogram equipment, or train employees in the use of unfamiliar equipment. During the move there should be a supervisor who is familiar with all elements of the move to direct the movers regarding location of equipment and to answer questions about items overlooked during planning stages.

Mail and Messenger Services

Major concerns in developing an efficient mail room are proper location, careful description of duties, and the creation of workable schedules. The mail room should be located in an area of easy access for incoming and outgoing bulk mail. Access through a large door near a driveway becomes a "must," to make possible the transfer of large sacks of mail and packages from delivery trucks to and from the building without having to go through difficult corridors and around tight corners. The location must be in an area where there is access to a freight elevator, passenger elevator, or record lift (automatic, dumb-waiter type of elevator) if the building to be served is a multiple-story building. If one has the opportunity of planning a mail room in a new building of several stories, the record lift concept should be carefully considered; it can provide round-the-clock, instantaneous delivery of mail from the mail room to the various floors above.

EQUIPMENT

The equipment used in the mail room must include a sufficient number of tables for bulk sorting purposes; pigeonhole or bag sorting equipment; scales; postage meters; hand trucks for carrying bulk mail; packaging equipment, including roll-paper racks and tape and string dispensers; and an assortment of scissors, knives, pens, pencils, and other stationery supplies. If internal mail deliveries are to be made by messenger, the mail room manager needs to determine the type of carrying equipment—baskets, pushcarts with sorting baskets, or hand trucks. In some special cases, carrying equipment may include conveyor belts, vacuum tubes, or trolley baskets.

DUTIES

The duties in most mail room operations include receipt of incoming mail and sorting for distribution; receipt of outgoing mail and preparation of it for postal service; preparation of packages and bulk mail for delivery to the post office; internal (and, in some cases, external) messenger service; creation and maintenance of company mailing lists; collating, stuffing, stamping, and zip-code sorting of branch office mailings, as well as bulk mailings; and continuous study of new methods, equipment, and processes for improving the company mail system.

SCHEDULING

The schedules developed by the mail room manager and supervised by him depend on the normal company office hours. It is desirable to pick up or receive incoming mail from the post office sufficiently early that sorting can be accomplished and delivery of first-class mail can be made at the earliest possible hour after the beginning of normal office hours. The length of time necessary to accomplish this, of course, depends on the amount of mail received. The number of stations to which the mail must be delivered also enters into the scheduling of the first mail delivery. Schedules for the remaining deliveries and collections of the day are usually dictated by the required frequency of deliveries, the local post office schedule, and a study of the amount of mail that must be handled so that outgoing mail boxes do not become crowded. Another factor in scheduling is size of work force and related costs.

It may be desirable to have hourly mail delivery of internal mail; as a result, the collection of mail for the postal service at the same time may be not only possible but advisable. The final outgoing postal service mail collection of the day should be made as near the end of clerical office hours as possible. Early collections help reduce peak loads, since most clerical activities are completed near the end of the normal workday. This tendency creates a large mail collection at the end of the day and consequently necessitates additional mail room personnel or a longer sorting period at the end of the day. Incoming mail should be picked up at the post office if a regular post office delivery schedule does not fit into the operations of the company. Generally, if the mail is picked up by company mail room personnel, it can be sorted and ready for internal delivery well in advance of the normal delivery time of the post office. The mail received should be sorted promptly—by department and individual, if so addressed.

U.S. MAIL

Outgoing mail operations should be going on continuously, starting with the first mail pickup of the day. As mail is received from various departments on pick-up, it should have postage affixed and be sorted by zip code, if received in an envelope. Periodically, during the course of the day, it is advisable to deliver this outgoing mail to the U.S. Post Office in order to avoid the huge mail pile-up that occurs toward the end of the day. Many companies request that correspondence to field locations or branch offices be sent to the mail room without being enclosed in an envelope. When it arrives at the mail room, it is sorted by field office and placed in a folder so that, at the end of the day, all the mail going to that branch office can be gathered and sent out in one envelope. This usually reduces the mail cost.

Many corporations that have large bulk mailings find it desirable to have the bulk mailings collated, folded, and stuffed by means of automatic equipment. If this is done during periods when incoming mail is at a minimum, it is possible to keep the workflow of the department at a more constant level.

INTERDEPARTMENTAL MAIL

The interdepartmental mail system is usually operated by the same messengers or personnel who handle the U.S. mail. Usually, it should be picked up and delivered at the same time as the U.S. mail. All company personnel who receive it regularly should be assigned a mail station. The mail station numbering system should be easily understood, thus eliminating long training periods for new mail room personnel. Mail to be sent from one station to another should be enclosed in a special envelope with many address or mail station number blocks printed on the face so that it can be reused numerous times.

FIELD AND SUBSIDIARY LOCATIONS

Most field locations have, as their prime mail service, the U.S. mail. It therefore becomes necessary to make a careful study of delivery times from the home office locations to the various field offices, as well as the return mail, so that mail can be delivered to the post office in time to meet official dispatch hours. If this is not done, mail which normally takes a day or two for delivery may take three or four, thus causing a slowdown in the overall operation.

In some cases where there is a large quantity of material going to a field or subsidiary office, it may be desirable to operate a company delivery service. Quite often, this can be faster than the U.S. mail or parcel delivery services. Such a service does, however, need to be carefully studied to determine that the additional expense of operating is warranted.

POST OFFICE LIAISON

Many frustrations and delays can be eliminated by having a continuous liaison with the post office. A continuing effort to find out the ways in which problems can be eliminated for the post office by additional work in the office mail room often results in better service from the Post Office Department. Such continuing liaison will also keep one well informed of new methods and processes used by the post office, and these new methods often have application within the company mail room. Furthermore, close liaison with the Post Office Department will keep one fully informed of current postal regulations and scheduling, thereby avoiding many problems that could result from not being up to date. It is both costly and embarrassing to have to rerun an entire bulk mailing because of being unaware of a current regulation.

CONTROLLING COSTS

It is very easy to let mail cost get out of hand, because unit charges are usually quite small. Often, department managers feel that to allow small mail charges to go unnoticed will offset the expense of policing them. This, however, is not true when one is dealing with hundreds or thousands of units of mail every day. One of the best ways to control these costs is through the use of postage meters, mail scales, and unit-counting devices. The most important precaution is to have a postage scale that is accurate; mail with insufficient postage is usually caught by the Post Office Department, and additional charges are added to make up for the deficit as well as for the work involved. Another excellent cost control is determining the class of mail that is to be used for various types of mailings. Mail that does not need immediate delivery can often go at the third-class rate and can be handled under bulk procedures. This generates considerable savings.

Maintenance Management

Most offices have such a quantity of equipment and property to maintain that it is practically impossible to have one person who is capable of performing the maintenance on all equipment. It therefore becomes necessary to have a maintenance manager who keeps a complete listing of all types of equipment that need maintenance, creates schedules for preventive maintenance, and hires the necessary in-plant maintenance technicians, as well as arranging for specialized technical assistance from the outside.

SCOPE

The areas to which a maintenance manager must direct his attention are the building grounds, the building exterior and interior, floors, walls, all the mechanical and electrical systems, the shifting of interior walls during space replanning, and—in some cases—maintenance scheduling for all typewriters, adding machines, and the vast amount of other equipment necessary for the operation of an office.

AREAS OF RESPONSIBILITY

Buildings that have large garden areas surrounding them need to be maintained by a crew headed up by at least one individual who has something beyond the qualities of leadership: a "green thumb." Most successful building gardens and grounds are tended with a great deal of loving care—mixed in, of course, with horticultural know-how. If the grounds of the building are not properly maintained, the visitor to the building may question the quality of the business operations conducted within.

The exterior of the building is equally important from a public relations standpoint. It is also the first line of defense against the elements. Exteriors of buildings need to be inspected periodically in order to insure that all construction elements are in good shape and not deteriorating, that seams are properly sealed against water and dust, that windows are kept clean in order to help assure proper light levels on the inside, and that the equipment to maintain the outside of the building is properly kept. The interior of a building, including the day-to-day maintenance of floors, walls, restrooms, lunchrooms, stairways, elevators, and private offices, needs constant supervision and attention in order to maintain a pleasant atmosphere as well as a safe and healthy one. The frequency of cleaning should be set by the building maintenance supervisor.

All buildings, including new ones, need constant repair and alteration. Many repairs are necessitated by the fact that the furniture is rearranged in a room and the convenience outlets need to be moved or changed. Most offices can keep several tradesmen or mechanics busy most of the time, attending to these problems. Special arrangements to have telephones installed or moved will require ample advance notice.

SCHEDULES

Contemporary architecture demands that most new buildings be fully equipped with air conditioning and heating equipment that will maintain a constant heat level year round. This equipment must be properly maintained, as the efficiency of workers drops severely when they are too hot or too cold. It is desirable to have a preventive maintenance schedule for each mechanism. This should include all fans, fan motors, condensers, damper motors, pumps, and electronic control equipment. The frequency of adjustment, cleaning, and lubricating is greatly dependent upon the age of the equipment and the recommendations of the manufacturer. Preventive maintenance and inspection of all elevators is a law in most states. Proper maintenance of elevators may prevent a disaster and at the very least will permit more productive use of time by employees if they do not have to waste time in riding inefficient elevators.

The scheduling of all maintenance should be accomplished by the maintenance manager and should be faithfully adhered to. The schedules for daily maintenance by in-plant employees as well as outside contractors should be checked for promptness and efficiency. The maintenance manager should outline emergency procedures for each piece of equipment within the operation and keep them in a file in a location where maintenance personnel have access to it. These procedures should outline in the simplest form the action that should be taken in the event of failure, fire, or other hazardous situations.

People Pools

Most companies have people pools, whether or not they are organized and operated as such. The smallest group that operates as a pool is a single individual who performs typing tasks for several managers or executives. At the other end of the spectrum is a stenographic pool composed of a number of people who provide services to many others.

PURPOSE

The purpose of creating people pools is to avoid duplication of effort on like tasks and consequently realize a considerable cost reduction. There are many communicators in offices who have need to send out only a few letters per day and consequently need the services of a secretary but cannot possibly keep the secretary busy continuously. By having a single secretary work for several letter writers, it is possible to perform the task with one person instead of several.

People pools should not be limited to stenographic services. Pools created to meet peak clerical loads in a department or to supply temporary assistance during vacations or absences are also useful. Most companies will experience peak-load problems at various times during the year but generally will not have a peak period in all departments at the same time. It is folly to provide sufficient workers to handle peak loads on a full-time basis, as many of these people will be supernumerary during average or slack periods. The training of clerical people for a common type of work function necessary in all departments makes it possible to shift these people from one department to another according to the work demand. This is generally more acceptable than hiring temporary help as needed, since a people pool would have personnel familiar with the philosophy of the company and the work rules and regulations.

ORGANIZATION

The organization of people pools varies from company to company, depending on the type of work to be performed. It is possible to organize on a companywide basis, a departmental basis, an independent service bureau basis, and (within these categories) a centralized or decentralized basis. Generally, the type of tasks to be performed within a company dictates whether a people pool is to be established on a companywide or a departmental basis. A company that needs legal, management, and medical stenographic services may find it extremely difficult to have the same group of people perform these tasks for all departments. Problems can arise because the terms inherent in each of these areas differ widely; consequently, it would be difficult for one person to be familiar with all the usages. This would point toward a stenographic pool formed on a departmental basis rather than on a companywide basis. If, however, there is a strong need for each of these services, it is possible to place specialized stenographers in a pool and have them work purely in their specialties.

The problem of centralization versus decentralization is often solved by the size of the operation. It may be far faster to have decentralized stenographic pools in the areas where several buildings are involved. It may also be less expensive to have several small pools rather than one large pool. The decision to centralize or decentralize will be dictated by the expense of installation and the required speed of services.

SKILLS

The skills needed in most people pools are the ability to operate dictating and transcribing equipment, to take and transcribe shorthand, to type, to proofread, to operate copying equipment, to perform normal clerical operations, and in some cases to operate calculators for computational purposes. With all these skills in a pool situation, it is possible to handle these tasks for a good many people who need them sporadically.

People pools also make it possible to use employees who are interested in working only part time. If it is desirable to have the work of eight stenographers during the course of the day, it is possible for 16 workers to perform this work on a half-day basis, since a thorough knowledge of a specific job is not usually necessary in people pools. By employing part-time employees it also becomes possible to obtain workers with higher skills, since there are many women who cannot work full time because of family commitments but have excellent qualifications and would like to work on a part-time basis.

RECRUITING AND TRAINING

The recruiting and training of these people should be based on the fact that the task they perform is a complete task even though they work only part time. Many women may have worked for the company at an earlier date but had to leave because of pregnancy and would now like to return to work for shorter hours. The names of these people should be listed in personnel records. The full-time workers in a people pool may well be recruited from the line departments where they may already be working as stenographers. Their knowledge would be useful in that they would not have to be retrained to the peculiarities of the company as would new workers. If there are specialized services to be performed by a people pool, it is highly advisable to have several people who understand each specialty so that it will always be covered in the event of sickness or vacation. A continuous cross-training of persons who perform a particular specialty in the peculiarities of another specialty helps to cover for emergency needs and helps train new supervisors in the event that they are needed.

Reception

The reception function is one of great importance, as this is often the first introduction of the company to the general public. An ill-mannered, unkempt, or gruff receptionist can often undo a good deal of the work of a public relations department. It is imperative that a building receptionist be an attractive, well-mannered, neatly dressed, intelligent person who is well acquainted with the basic operations of the company.

The locations where reception duties are normally performed include the entrance of the building, an area near the elevator service on each floor, and one within each department on a floor. As the area covered by the receptionist diminishes, so do the amount of traffic and the need for receptionist duties. Often, a floor receptionist will perform duties for one of the departments or for the services department. A departmental receptionist is usually a person whose prime duties are those of a secretary or clerk, or the operator of a small telephone switchboard.

RECEPTIONIST'S DUTIES

The duties performed by the receptionist at the building entrance are normally those of greeting all incoming guests and acting as an information center for guests and personnel. The greeting function requires a friendly person because the receptionist can often placate an irritated customer and perhaps create a respect for the company through the demonstration of her own enthusiasm.

Security requirements often make it necessary to have all visitors sign in and sign out and to check identification of company personnel. This function is frequently served by the receptionist or (in some cases) a guard who is secondarily a receptionist. The receptionist must have a working knowledge of all departments of the company and all personnel therein, as many times a visitor knows what his problem is but does not have the vaguest idea who or what department should solve it. Thus the receptionist can announce to the appropriate person or persons the name of the guest and the purpose of his visit. The duties of a receptionist may extend into the evening hours and in this case they are primarily the duties of a night watchman and secondarily those of a receptionist.

Many offices combine the duties of the receptionist with the tasks of the telephone operator, personnel clerk, typist or secretary, or other functions that allow the receptionist to stay in one place while performing her tasks. The receptionist who has only receptionist duties most often reports to the building manager or office services director. The receptionist who performs other functions will normally report to the department head who supervises those functions.

One of the rare, incidental activities that receptionists may become engaged in is assistance in emergencies inside the building. The receptionist needs to be well acquainted with emergency procedures and should be carefully trained for them. It is desirable that the receptionist report to a building manager, as he will be knowledgeable about what to do in an emergency (for example, designating the best procedure in case of personnel injury or a fire).

COSTUMES AND UNIFORMS

Many companies require that their building receptionists wear uniforms to identify their function. Uniforms reflect company "personality"; they should be distinctive in appearance but not spectacular. Companies that do not provide uniforms require that the receptionist be well dressed, neat, and well groomed but not extravagantly so. Here again, the company image must be reflected in the clothing that the receptionist wears at work.

Special Facilities

Most offices have facilities in the nature of reception areas, special meeting rooms, conference rooms, lounges, canteens, and cafeterias. Special facility areas usually fall under the management of the office services director.

RECEPTION AREA

Most reception areas require comfortable seating units; tables for the display of magazines, literature, and instructional information; and tables for decorative purposes. The lighting should be pleasant, adequate but not bright, and as decorative as possible. Magazines and literature should be kept tidy, and the magazines should be current. There are some cases, however, where literature of special interest to the office is desirable, and it need not have a current publication date.

BOARD AND CONFERENCE ROOMS

Many offices need special rooms for the board of directors as well as staff conference rooms. Such rooms usually are equipped with large, attractive center tables and comfortable chairs and are carpeted and well lighted so that it is possible to conduct meetings of lengthy duration and still maintain physical comfort for the participants. The use of these rooms varies from company to company and is based upon the needs of top management. The scheduling of such rooms depends upon the prime purpose of the room (board meetings or periodic staff meetings). Board rooms should be equipped with audio and visual aids, light-control devices, good ventilation and climate control, and adequate ash trays and attractive accessories.

The need for conference rooms has grown as the group decision method of management has gained in popularity. It is generally necessary to have a conference room available to each department or, at most, two departments. The conference rooms should be in an area away from noise and heavy traffic but centrally located for the prime users. Equipment includes light control, chalk boards, pin-up boards, telephone, chalk, and pencils and paper. If board rooms are not used by general management personnel, it may be advisable to provide audio and visual capabilities for the conference room. Scheduling of the conference room can often be handled easily by posting a weekly calendar on the door of the room and allowing scheduling on a first-come, first-served basis.

LOUNGES

Some states require that employers provide lounge areas in conjunction with women's restrooms. Many employers, however, do not merely comply with the legal requirements but also provide lounge areas for all employees. Standard equipment includes chairs, coffee tables, small dining tables and chairs, coffee and cold-drink vending machines, and sometimes sandwich and hot-food vending machines. The use of such lounges is generally limited to company "break" periods, lunch hours, other scheduled rest periods, and emergency usage for sick employees.

Telecommunications

The telecommunications of a corporation are a main link with customers, sources of supply, and problem solvers. Because of the immense demand on telecommunications, continuous study of the needs of the company and the ever changing types of equipment available is necessary.

The general types of telecommunications are voice, message, and data transmission. Voice communications are the telephone, PBX operations, mobile telephones, public address systems, intercommunication systems, conference hook-ups through the telephone, and closed-circuit television. Message communications are various Teletype operations and facsimile transmission. Data transmission includes the sending and receiving of data from one computer device to another via telephone lines. (See "Communications Networks," page 2·96.)

USAGE POLICY

The type of communications device to be used must be determined by the requirements. Telephone communications may be on a long-distance or local basis and may be used for intercommunication systems, conference hook-ups, and mobile telephones. The type of long-distance usage may be either wide area telephone service or per-call, long-distance telephone charging.

Policies on internal communications are usually governed by the need of the worker at the work station. Telephone calls within the community are normally allowed by most companies but kept to a minimum, as far as possible. The use of long-distance calling and WATS must be carefully controlled and often requires scheduling. Companies that make use of WATS lines may find it desirable to maintain complete control of the use of these lines from the switchboard. This practice often reduces the misuse by a given department.

The use of Teletype messages and facsimile transmission messages is generally dictated by the required speed of delivery, the length of the message, and the availability of the receiver. The need for a hard copy or permanent record also enters into the selection of these methods of communication.

Data transmission can often be accomplished in the evening and early morning hours over long-distance lines. Usage policies of data transmission are usually devised by the data processing operations department.

ORGANIZATION

The organization of the telecommunications function generally requires a manager, supervisors for the various types of communications, and a sufficient staff to operate the equipment. The manager's prime responsibility is to establish priorities for the various departments for the use of the communications devices. It is also his responsibility to insure that schedules of use are created and adhered to and that proper records of use are kept, so that it is possible to make an intelligent survey of use and future needs. The supervisors of the various functions govern the day-to-day records of use and see to it that personnel are properly trained for their stations and that each station is manned as needed. Since most telecommunication devices are the prime source of information and access to the company, it is most important that these devices be manned at all times during company hours. It is therefore necessary that a sufficient number of back-up people for each device be trained and that the prescribed proficiency level be maintained.

FACILITIES

Switchboard operations should be located in an area with a low level of noise and where there is little possibility of interference by other company personnel. The switching equipment, if on the premises, should be located preferably in a dry basement where access by telephone repair personnel is possible.

Message centers, including telephone and Teletype operations, may be located at the switchboard and controlled by switchboard personnel or may be in a separate location if the message center is a sufficiently large operation.

The use of communications consultants is a necessary service; most companies do not have as thorough a knowledge of available equipment as the telephone representatives. Continuous liaison with telephone company representatives keeps telecommunication managers abreast of changes, new products, and improvements in current methods.—*S. P. Bartholf*

REPRODUCTION: COPYING, DUPLICATING, AND PRINTING

Copying, duplicating, and printing equipment is so widely used in offices for rapid communications that its sheer proliferation presents a special challenge to the modern administrative manager. He must provide the most complete and efficient information communication system possible for his organization, at the lowest cost and without adding unnecessarily to the mounting volume of paper that the nation's work force now handles. Information will continue to be disseminated on paper—paper from typewriters, copiers, duplicators, and all kinds of printing equipment; but excess paper can cause as many problems as it solves.

Inexpensive mass duplicating of paperwork began with the mimeograph in 1884. To this basic process have been added high-speed copiers, spirit duplicators, sophisticated offset, and a variety of peripheral and support equipment. Capabilities to reproduce paperwork are extensive.

Office Copiers

The invention of the office copier greatly increased the convenience of communicating on paper. Though seemingly a recent phenomenon, one of the first copying processes was developed in the late 1920's. Other types of processes have since been added, and today six basic methods are available. Following is a brief summary of each, with approximate costs per copy and speeds.

1. The direct electrostatic method costs approximately $2\frac{1}{2}$ to $3\frac{1}{2}$ cents per copy. It uses coated paper and produces fair-to-good reproduction of halftones and solids. It is easy to use, and investment is moderate.

2. The transfer electrostatic method (including xerography) costs as follows: one to three copies, 4 cents per copy; four to ten copies, 2 cents per copy; eleven or more copies, $\frac{1}{2}$ cent per copy. It reproduces up to 30 copies per minute and makes dry copies in one step with minimum waste. It requires moderate investment and is fast and easy to use.

3. The heat transfer or thermal process makes four to seven copies per minute at a cost up to 5 cents each. Copies remain sensitive to heat and therefore may not be permanent. The process cannot copy all colors. It requires little skill to operate, and the initial investment is low.

4. The diffusion transfer method's costs are: first copy, 8 cents; second copy, $3\frac{1}{2}$ to 8 cents. The process makes three to four copies per minute and requires some skill in operation. The initial investment is low.

5. The dye transfer method makes up to seven copies (three to four per minute) from one multiple-copy matrix, copies all colors, and requires some manual operation. The cost of the initial copy ranges up to $8\frac{1}{2}$ cents, but the initial investment is low.

6. The diazo process makes five copies per minute at a cost of 1 cent per copy. It is primarily used in engineering reproduction and needs a translucent original with copy or drawing on one side only. Ammonia fumes must be vented. The operating cost is low, the operation is fast, but the initial investment is high.

COST CONSIDERATIONS

Despite their convenience, office copiers are the subject of some controversy. Their ease of use may lead to abuse and considerable expense. Government and industry studies show that many malpractices surround copier use, ranging from copying personal documents to using the copier as a duplicator beyond its economical length-of-run capability.

To determine the costs of machines and supplies is relatively easy; but the hidden costs, including the time of personnel traveling to and from copier stations and waiting in line to use a machine, can increase the apparent cost of copies as much as 100 percent.

LOCATION

The proper location for equipment is at the point of need; yet because of hidden costs, management control must be exercised. Thus a question of centralization versus decentralization arises. Although the answer depends on the individual situation, here are some of the considerations: (1) Will centralized copying facilities tie in with other required duplicating facilities for economy of personnel? (2) Do security requirements demand centralization? (3) Will pickup, routing, and delivery requirements cause unacceptable delays? (4) Can one central system physically serve all needs?

The advantages of centralization are as follows: the provision of copier services to the smallest office or operation; consistent maintenance; reduction of the costs resulting from overcopying and other wastes; and greater standardization.

The advantages of decentralization are these: reduced walking and waiting time, sometimes cutting the cost of copies by half; virtual elimination of delays; elimination of costly record keeping usually found in a central system; probable adequacy of floor space; and placement of control and responsibility in the local department.

The chart in Exhibit 2.19 illustrates the costs of walking and waiting time of employees. The costs shown, however, do not consider personnel delays en route and do not include basic copying costs (machine amortization, supplies, and the like). Chart figures should be added to basic costs in order to estimate total cost per copy.

Realistically speaking, 100 percent centralization of copy capability is never possible. There almost always seem to be exceptions, frequently at top management levels. Small copiers will continue to be used in local areas where their need is justified.

GUIDELINES FOR USE

There should be enough copiers in an office to minimize clerical traffic and waiting time. To keep copying costs down, however, some regulation is necessary.

Some offices hire full-time or part-time operators or limit copier use to a few selected people. Others require users to log the name or department, type of original, and number of copies made; or an automatic counter can be used. The main consideration in any of these methods is to make sure, through studies, that the controls do not cost more than the copies being made.

In any case it is helpful to establish guidelines or limits for the use of the equipment. The reason is that making copies by other processes such as mimeograph or offset may become less expensive at the 10- to 15-copy level or above it.

Before purchasing, leasing, or renting an office copier, the following checklist will be helpful: necessary copy quality; required permanence of copies; required skill of machine users; normal copy size; average number of copies per run; speed of copy delivery; form that originals are likely to be in; service factors; and master making or other systems requirements.

Among all the possible equipment requirements and considerations, industry and private studies show·that the one feature required and requested most by users (64 to 85 percent) is reliability. Copy quality and machine simplicity and speed are rated lower than freedom from breakdown and availability of service.

Office Duplicating

If the office copier is the glamor machine of the modern office, mimeographs, spirit duplicators, and offset machines are still the reliable workhorses.

A spirit duplicator accepts typed, thermal-imaged, and other masters and reproduces up to about 300 readable copies. Characters can be reproduced in several colors.

A mimeograph, despite technological advances in the copying field, remains one of the most common, economical, and convenient methods for duplicating more than 20 and up to 5,000 copies. The stencil can be typed or imaged automatically on a stencil maker from originals that are typed, drawn, or handwrit-

Exhibit 2.19

COST OF WALKING DISTANCE AND WAITING TIME

WALKING

Distance Traveled (Feet)	Employee's Hourly Rate						
	$1.50	$1.75	$2.00	$2.25	$2.50	$2.75	$3.00
50	.0056	.0065	.0075	.0084	.0093	.0103	.0112
100	.0112	.0131	.0149	.0168	.0187	.0205	.0224
150	.0168	.0196	.0224	.0252	.0280	.0308	.0336
200	.0224	.0262	.0299	.0336	.0374	.0411	.0448
250	.0280	.0327	.0373	.0420	.0467	.0513	.0560
300	.0336	.0393	.0448	.0504	.0561	.0616	.0673
400	.0448	.0524	.0597	.0673	.0748	.0821	.0897
500	.0560	.0655	.0747	.0841	.0935	.1027	.1121

WAITING

Minutes Spent Waiting	Employee's Hourly Rate						
	$1.50	$1.75	$2.00	$2.25	$2.50	$2.75	$3.00
1	.025	.029	.033	.0375	.042	.046	.05
2	.05	.058	.066	.075	.084	.092	.10
3	.075	.087	.099	.1125	.126	.136	.15
4	.10	.116	.132	.15	.168	.182	.20
5	.125	.145	.165	.1875	.21	.228	.25
10	.25	.29	.33	.375	.42	.46	.50
15	.375	.435	.495	.5625	.63	.688	.75
20	.50	.58	.66	.75	.84	.92	1.00

ten. A recent development is heat imaging of a stencil on a thermal copying machine in four to five seconds.

The offset duplicator, a high-speed, high-quality method, will produce up to 2,000 quality copies from a paper master, or several hundred thousand copies from a metal plate. Offset does not require a highly skilled operator, but many office managers err in expecting perfect results in complicated printing jobs from inexperienced operators. Convenience and quality remain the most important factors in considering offset.

Office equipment industry estimates say that offset master preparation costs can be as low as 7 or 8 cents, with copy production costs adding about .7 cents for each copy run. These estimates assume automatic master processing on readily available copiers and include cost increments for labor, machine amortization, and supplies used.

The development of the copier/duplicator is the latest in the industry's efforts to combine and automate the offset and copying processes. Since its introduction in 1965, this new device has met with outstanding success. Because the copier/ duplicator concept requires no master, it has had significant impact on the work load of in-house reproduction by handling otherwise burden-producing, short-run copies on a fast, do-it-yourself, push-button basis. Speeds of 5,400 copies per hour are possible on plain paper.

To date, no copier/duplicator can match the speed and cost of the current high-speed offset machines and quick-copy centers that utilize separate units. However, further advances are expected.

PAPER PURCHASING

Paper usually accounts for a large portion of the cost of office duplication. To avoid expensive paper loss, an office manager should pay maximum attention to the quality and performance of the paper his organization uses.

Physical properties such as fiber formation and direction, watermark, tear, fold, opacity, and weight determine paper quality. Functional quality (how the paper performs on the equipment for which it is intended) is equally important.

It is most economical to buy paper in large lots or rolls, thus taking advantage of quantity discounts. Colored paper and special papers, used creatively, can increase the attention value of printed copy.

THE DUPLICATING CENTER

The average reproduction equipment investment in a small office today is a point-of-need copier and a small duplicating machine. Most offices with 100 or more people can also justify a duplicating center as a cost-saving measure. A properly run central copying and duplicating area can respond more rapidly and economically to user demand than can a single machine in a department and tends to minimize unnecessary duplicating and wasted copies. However, the need for local area equipment will continue to exist.

A typical small center houses one or more mimeographs, offset or spirit duplicators, and a platemaker and/or an electrostatic master maker (which may also serve as a copier); one or more sorter/collators, an electric stapler, and/or other binding equipment; and often the mail and messenger system. It should handle all jobs requiring more than 10 to 15 copies (depending on situation). Work is usually turned around in two to four hours. The internal mail system should accomplish most pick-ups and deliveries, but while-you-wait service is usually also needed.

Companies using the copying/duplicating center concept report substantial drops in costs and volumes of work, as compared with local area self-service machines. For example, one company achieved a 15 percent reduction in copying costs, together with a 40 percent reduction in volume. Also, copy quality was improved.

Although while-you-wait service is important, local area needs can still be slighted if travel distance to the central center is more than a few hundred feet. This has given rise to quick-copy centers, which generally serve a large department of a company. These centers are distinguished from a point-of-need copying facility, since usually more than one piece of equipment is involved, more than 20 copies are run from the average original, and a waiting time of less than three to five minutes is desired. The usual combination is a copier with master-making capabilities and a table-top offset.

Such quick-copy centers are also being developed commercially to serve large office buildings or neighborhood areas in metropolitan centers.

In-Plant Printing

In-plant printing is growing at approximately 8 percent per year. Commercial printing is growing at about 5 percent per year. Equipment manufacturers are developing larger offset and auxiliary equipment that in-plant people can afford to own or lease and to operate; but this may be a mixed blessing. The in-plant shop manager must consider a great many factors in order to select the proper equipment and get competent operators. Lack of capital for immediate investment in necessary machines and equipment is being increasingly overcome by entering into long-term leasing arrangements with manufacturers or third-party organizations that specialize in this type of financing.

Print-shop managers cite four major advantages of printing in-house: fast response time, convenience, reduced cost (depending on product printed), and confidential information control.

Commercial printers claim the ability to produce a better-quality product at a lower cost, mainly in higher-volume runs. The administrator must resolve these questions by examining the costs and service requirements in each individual case.

Virtually all in-plant print shops send some of their work out, depending on people and equipment in-plant. Extremely long or difficult jobs, four-color specialty jobs, excess work, prepress, and some of the more complex postpress work are typically less expensive when purchased from a commercial shop. A print-shop manager should obtain two or more bids and compare them carefully before selecting the vendor for each job.

With the increased use of the computer, in-plant print-shop managers are handling more and more requests for multiple copies from computer printouts.

Managers of EDP centers, administrative managers, and controllers are discovering that computers are expensive and inefficient when used as copiers or duplicators. Many computer users are paying about 33 percent more than they should for copies of computer output.

One solution is to load the computer printer with offset masters and use them directly on an offset machine for ten or more copies. Another solution is to generate a master from one of the computer printout sheets when mass distribution of the information is required, or even to feed the master to a high-speed direct electrostatic copier/duplicator.

Computers have revolutionized the processing phase of information handling, and this has increased the systematizing of the reproduction and distribution phase.

SHOP ORGANIZATION

In-plant print shops are usually administered as part of a company's office services department. Exceptions are shops that work exclusively for one department and operate under it—advertising and/or sales promotion, for example.

The office services department manager in a small company will usually perform two or three functions and may report to top management. In a larger company he will usually report to a division head. In either case he should have a very clear definition of his authority. The more control he has over his shop, the more economical it is likely to be. He can more easily perform an efficient service without being subservient to many masters, and he can attempt to prevent high-cost, high-status, unnecessary jobs from tying up his daily operations.

In planning the work of the department the printing manager, with the approval of the administrator, must decide what to print and what to send to a commercial printer. He must plan how to print or duplicate work on the basis of acceptable quality and required speed, determine total costs, and schedule the work. Job priority is best based on a first-come, first-served method that is flexible enough to handle rare exceptions.

Scheduling depends on work load, delivery time, job time needed, length of run, and equipment speed. Installation of a "loading board" showing standard job times, individual operation times, and equipment and personnel availability will expedite this task. One shop manager requires six hours of productive, billable work from his pressman for every seven and one-half hours worked. The nonbillable one and one-half hours is taken up in makeready, clean-up, and miscellaneous work. To require more productive time than this often means sacrificing product quality and morale in the shop.

A successful method of organizing the printing operation financially is to charge each in-house "customer" directly for every job at the full cost of the service, plus extra for overtime or rush. This tends to minimize demands for unnecessary work, rush jobs, special materials, and extra copies. It enables the print shop to better plan materials and equipment and labor time. Most important, the print shop can prove its economies and often pay its own way in savings.

Most in-plant shops limit equipment size to 17½-inch by 22½-inch offset equipment. The "In-Plant Management Study" (done by Rufus C. Short of Rochester Institute of Technology for *In-Plant Printer,* August 1969) estimates that 60 to 80 percent of in-plant print shops—exclusive of duplicating centers—perform the major auxiliary operations of art, composition, camera, and plate-making.

PROBLEMS

The biggest problem plaguing the shops is labor; experienced managers and skilled pressmen are difficult to find. Many administrators suggest hiring a manager with administrative background and putting him through a graphic arts school, where he will be trained in reproduction processes, bid making, and bid evaluating. This will not make him a skilled printer, but it is believed that he can learn enough to effectively apply important management skills.

To hire and keep labor in the print shop, concentrate on finding a few highly competent people and pay them well. Wage scales in union and nonunion commercial shops average about the same, but in-plant shops tend to be lower.

Another block to the efficiency of in-plant printing is a widespread lack of people who are skilled in prepress work. This problem may diminish with the proliferation of more automated prepress equipment that produces quality copy at economical costs. Computer-prepared, magnetic tape typesetting systems are one example.

ENGINEERING REPRODUCTION

The engineering reproduction shop in most large companies is separate from the general printing shop and is administered within the engineering department. An engineering reproduction shop differs from a general duplicating center or print shop because it does highly repetitive, systematized copying work. This often requires somewhat different techniques and equipment.

Standard engineering shop equipment includes a microfilm printer-processor, aperture card duplicator, card reader, microfilm hard-copy printer and the standard hard-copy reproduction equipment, diazo whiteprinter, offset machine, and/or other duplicating equipment.

Producing engineering drawings on microfilm and microfiche saves wear on the original drawing, allows easy filing and retrieval, and provides a permanent, convenient record of the drawing that can be simply and inexpensively reproduced and mailed. Many engineering reproduction shop managers use aperture card mounting instead of microfiche or microfilm reels because a single drawing can be easily retrieved, reproduced, and refiled.

Microfilm is also used in other areas of a company or factory, especially in extended records retention and in reproducing or shipping bulky items such as sales manuals.

Cost Analysis

Careful cost analysis is the key to efficient duplicating and printing in all shops. Such analysis will provide the administrative manager with information on equipment needed, equipment available, and labor on hand to operate the equipment.

Before entering into in-plant printing, a manager must evaluate the advantages of in-plant convenience and service against the option of hiring commercial printers. Cost analysis is the only sensible approach. But there is no simple, single answer; every manager must analyze his own situation and decide on the basis of all the available facts.

The following guideline suggests a list of "factory" or direct printing costs that may be determined when evaluating the in-plant facility.

1. *Labor and related overhead:* production workers; supervision; indirect labor (plant maintenance men, for example); social security and unemployment taxes; workmen's compensation insurance; and health and welfare levies.

2. *Other fixed overhead:* occupancy expense, plant insurance, personal property tax, depreciation, and interest on investment.

3. *Other current costs:* direct materials, supplies, and related expense; spoiled work; repairs; power and light; and allocated space costs.

The general and administrative costs of a proposed duplicating or print shop must be determined and added to the total cost of the project. Depending upon the accounting theory and practices of each organization, it may be necessary to include allocations of general or administrative expense elements in job costs; these could include (for example) clerical, data processing, and general management costs.

There are many other questions that an administrator should examine. For example, a cost analysis should be made on whether to set up a centralized duplicating center; whether to do color printing in-plant or commercially; and how much total printing to do internally. The significance of each question will vary with the individual situation.

New Developments

A look at the future may be valuable because copier, duplicator, and press manufacturers are continuing to develop faster, more accurate, more automated, and—in some cases—less expensive machines.

Computers will increasingly assume a dual function in the world of reproduction. They produce information that must be communicated to users, and they are beginning to control more complex printing operations. Hard copy from computers is typically written by line printers (with up to six carbon copies), or by high-speed, computer-driven writing devices such as ink jet printers. Visual display terminals such as cathode ray tubes (TV-type monitors) are becoming increasingly important communicators. Multiple copies of computer printout or hard copies of visual display materials can be made on duplicating and copying machines adapted for that purpose.

Long-distance facsimile transmission is another communication system that is expected to gain wider use as improved technological approaches are developed.

Reaction against the paper explosion will tend to motivate many offices to control the number of unnecessary hard copies made on convenience machines, but for the foreseeable future the reproduction industry is expected to stay with words-on-paper as the primary medium.—*K. B. Marble*

BUSINESS AIRCRAFT OPERATIONS

More than 30,000 company airplanes link the ten airports that have no airline service with the one airport that does have such service. Yet the business air fleet represents, by most estimates, barely 10 percent of all companies that could use airplanes successfully. The fleet is expanding rapidly; and as it does, thousands of managers are thrust into the new and unfamiliar disciplines of aviation management.

The company plane demands a large outlay which must be justified on intangibles as well as major policy decisions affecting the well-being of corporate officers and directors. For these reasons the chief executive officer is often designated executive in charge. However, the modern trend in large companies is to assign this responsibility to the administrative services manager, who is better equipped by time and specialty to manage the operation.

Aviation Department Organization

The typical organization of a large corporate aviation department is shown in Exhibit 2.20. However, fewer than 1 percent of company plane owners reach the scale of operations indicated in this exhibit. The vast majority operate a single company plane and employ one pilot, who works under the title of chief pilot. Outside suppliers are normally engaged for such specialized services as crew training and aircraft maintenance. Scheduling is generally handled by the chief pilot and the secretary to the executive in charge.

Company Policy and Procedures

In order of importance, the success ingredients of a company aviation program are as follows, from the standpoint of safety and operational capability: (1) formulation of meaningful purpose and policy; (2) definition of crew qualifications; (3) selection of electronics and other equipment; and (4) model of aircraft operated.

The company starting an aviation program often reaches decisions in exactly the reverse order—first selecting an airplane that is already equipped, then hiring a crew, and finally establishing policy. This common failure to analyze and identify requirements can result in designing a flight department that satisfies neither present nor future needs. It manifests the emotional appeal of airplane ownership—a desire to get started, regardless of costs or future problems—and should be resisted.

The corporate policy statement normally sets forth the purpose and authorized uses of company aircraft, method of scheduling and resolving schedule conflicts, safety criteria, cost allocation, reporting procedures, and lines of authority. A detailed operating policy and procedures manual used by the flight department translates this basic policy into specific operating procedures.

Aircraft Selection

The selection of aircraft rests solidly on company purpose and policy. Prerequisites are a study of past travel, projection of future travel, and a route study

Exhibit 2.20

TYPICAL ORGANIZATION OF A LARGE CORPORATE AVIATION DEPARTMENT

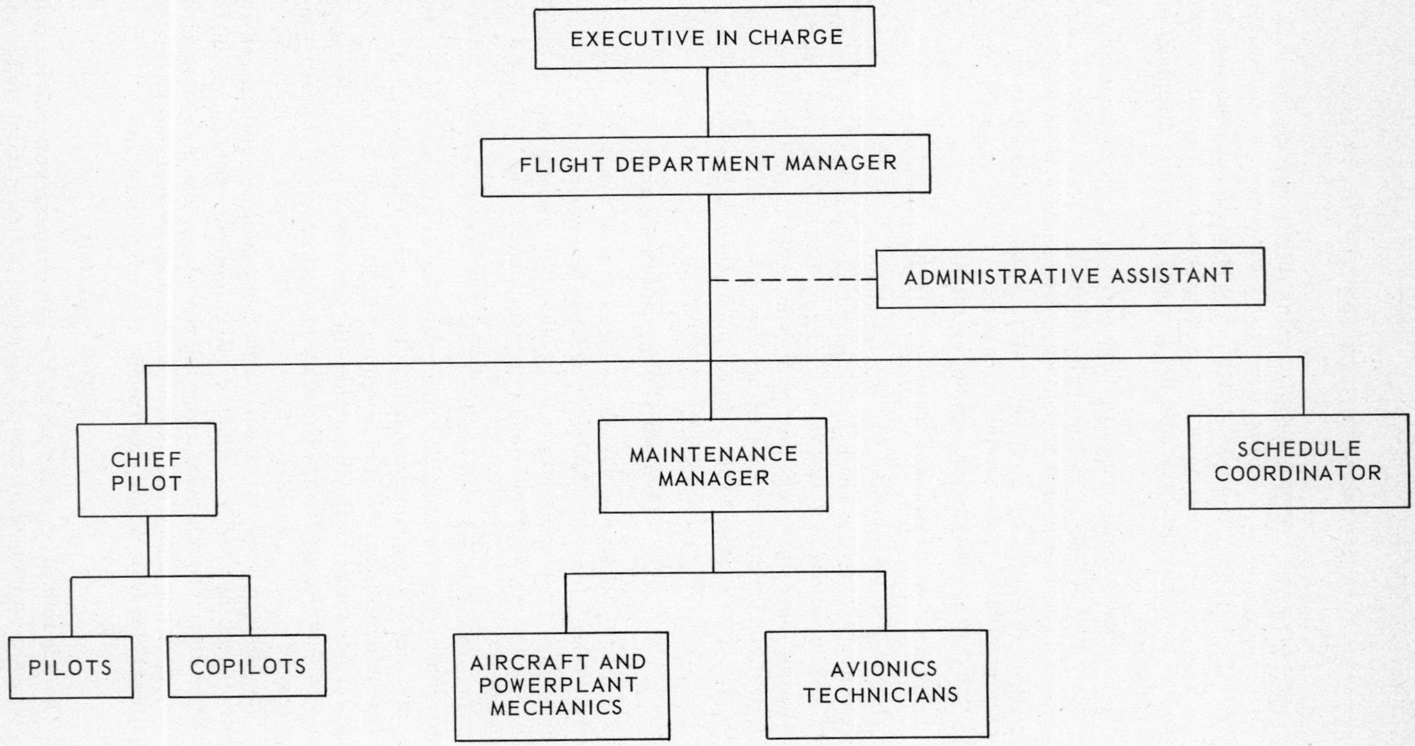

EXECUTIVE IN CHARGE

FLIGHT DEPARTMENT MANAGER

ADMINISTRATIVE ASSISTANT

SCHEDULE COORDINATOR

CHIEF PILOT

PILOTS

COPILOTS

MAINTENANCE MANAGER

AIRCRAFT AND POWERPLANT MECHANICS

AVIONICS TECHNICIANS

comparing aircraft performance and costs over the actual routes the plane will fly. With this groundwork, time savings and other factors are weighed against total cost to reach a decision.

Annual operating costs (including depreciation) should be the base for comparison, since over a period of years airplane operating costs may amount to several times the initial purchase price. The annual operating budget should be worked out by a specialist, but as a rule will range between one-fourth and one-half of the new airplane acquisition price. The smaller the plane, the larger the percentage. Typical categories of business planes are tabulated in Exhibit 2.21.

It will be noted that the tabulation in this exhibit shows no relationship between aircraft size and safety. Even a small plane that is lightly equipped can be flown to airline safety standards by establishing operating policies and limitations (weather restrictions and related considerations) that minimize risk exposure. The larger aircraft (medium twin-engine and up) are normally operated to airline weather criteria.

Few business planes rival airline cruising speeds. The company plane saves time in other ways. It reduces waiting time at terminals, offers the schedule flexibility to visit several cities in the same day, gives direct access to thousands of more convenient airports not serviced by airlines, and often enables passengers to work more productively en route. The major savings are in ground travel time.

Because of their airspeed handicap, company planes are most efficient on short and intermediate-range flights. The tabulation in Exhibit 2.21 emphasizes this by showing the approximate travel radius in which a manager can make a round trip during a ten-hour business day (8 A.M. to 6 P.M.) and spend at least three working hours at destination during the day. With a business jet a company president could leave his home in the New York area at 8 A.M., travel 1,000 miles to Des Moines, spending at least three business hours there, and return home by 6 P.M.

In any decision to acquire a first airplane, intangible factors must be weighed carefully. In particular the unanticipated application of a company plane, impos-

Exhibit 2.21
MAJOR CATEGORIES OF BUSINESS AIRCRAFT

Airplane Category	Price Range	Practical Operating Radius* (Miles)
Fixed gear, single engine	$ 7,000 to $ 25,000	300
Retractable gear, single engine	25,000 to 60,000	400
Light twin	50,000 to 125,000	400
Medium twin	150,000 to 275,000	400
Turboprop	400,000 to 750,000	600
Business jet	750,000 to 4,000,000	1,000

* See text.

sible to predict, may alone justify its acquisition. Many times, a company plane
has paid for itself in a single trip by putting a sales manager on the spot to close
a sale decisively before the competition could arrive or by dispatching technicians
and parts to remedy a costly shutdown.

Company planes supply premium transportation on demand and are used
selectively. Most companies aim for quality rather than intensity of use; thus
utilization rates are a small fraction of actual capacity. Single-engine planes
average about 200 flight hours annually, light and medium twins about 300
hours, and small jets and turboprops about 500 hours. Most single-engine planes
and many small twins are flown personally by their business owners. The larger
aircraft are flown by professional pilots or crews and reach higher operating levels by serving the travel needs of perhaps ten or 20 executives.

Dealer selection is a matter of airplane choice, since there may be only one
dealer for a particular model in an area or region. Dealer pricing is negotiable,
particularly on light aircraft, but tends to stabilize on higher-priced aircraft and
becomes virtually fixed as pricing nears the $1 million bracket.

The dealer's ability to maintain power plants, perform major inspections, and
service electronics equipment are important qualifiers. The dealer will perform
a substantial amount of warranty work and troubleshooting during the shakedown and warranty period. A dealer who is unable to furnish complete support
services should make alternate arrangements for the buyer and extend offsetting
price concessions.

Depreciation and Insurance

Aircraft depreciation practices vary widely. For tax purposes the IRS guideline
is six years. In practice some companies depreciate aircraft over as few as four
years, while others use 12 years or more. Actual replacement intervals depend on
the maturity and stability of the flight operation. The new company flight department, starting small, is likely to undergo one or two upgrading steps in the
first five years. However, the seasoned flight department that selects its equipment carefully may have a replacement cycle of five to ten years or longer, particularly if operating turbine-powered aircraft.

Aircraft insurance normally includes single-limit liability in substantial
amounts ($5 to $10 million) and hull insurance covering physical damage to
the aircraft. Many owners also carry admitted liability that pays a guaranteed
settlement (such as $50,000 per passenger seat). Normally, there is a fixed annual
premium, but larger operators sometimes negotiate more attractive rates based
on formulas that include aircraft investment, hours flown, and passengers carried.
The insurance carrier will conduct a risk appraisal and may establish such conditions as a specific crew-training program and the development of an operating
policy and procedures manual.

Financing and Leasing

Finance plans are widely used. Contracts are normally written over a five-year
term but range to ten years or longer for aircraft in the seven-figure price class.

Aircraft leasing is an accepted practice but has not reached the levels of sophistication known to computer or automobile users. Full-service leasing with guar-

anteed operating costs or leasing with large residuals is generally not available on an attractive basis. Airplane leasing invariably involves a long-term contract requiring payout of the full original purchase price plus lease charge, with a nominal purchase option.

Short-term leasing can be arranged by chartering an aircraft and crew at a fixed hourly cost. Charter produces the lowest total cost if planned usage is much below average. However, lack of availability and lack of control are obstacles that stop many companies when considering this as an alternative to purchase.

Budgets and Costs

The budget will include (1) fixed costs based on an annual estimate, and (2) direct operating costs based on an hourly cost estimate multiplied by the number of hours of expected use.

Fixed costs normally include (1) depreciation; (2) insurance; (3) crew salaries, benefits, and payroll taxes; (4) hangar and office space rentals; (5) professional services such as navigation charts, memberships, flight medical exams, and weather forecasting services; (6) crew training if under annual contract; and (7) miscellaneous provisions for telephone, supplies, and related items.

Direct operating costs normally include (1) fuel and oil; (2) line and routine maintenance and service; (3) major maintenance such as periodic inspections and repairs; (4) reserves for overhaul of engines, airframe, and equipment; (5) crew travel expense; and (6) airplane trip expenses such as landing fees and commissary. Direct operating costs are the largest expense involved in owning a company airplane. These costs deserve close study because they can vary up to 100 percent for identical airplanes, depending on the pattern of use and operating philosophy.

Regulations

The Federal Air Regulations (FAR's) fill thousands of pages but are less ominous than most managers imagine. In almost every case, compliance with the regulations is the responsibility of the pilots and mechanics who work on the plane. Procedures and controls are included in the flight department policy and procedures manual. The FAR's prescribe minimum standards, and many companies establish more stringent requirements.

The regulations directly affecting management are simple. At time of purchase the buyer sends a bill of sale and aircraft registration form to the Federal Aviation Administration (FAA) and a radio station license form to the Federal Communications Commission. Thereafter, the airplane must be inspected and proved airworthy once a year to retain its active registration. Pilots undergo an FAA medical examination every six or 12 months, depending on whether they maintain a current airline transport rating or a commercial pilot license.—*W. F. Burke*

MOTORCAR FLEET OPERATIONS

It has become increasingly apparent to executive management in recent years that millions upon millions of dollars are expended each year in the automotive transportation function of industry. Ways and means are being studied to find out how the same job can be done in a less costly manner; fleet administration is finding a new and more important niche in the organization structure.

Organization, Policies, and Procedures

There can be no set rule as to a proper departmental assignment for the fleet administrator. Surveys indicate that some companies have found the automotive function to be best situated in the sales or traffic departments, while other companies prefer purchasing or accounting department direction—proper placement being made on the individual characteristics of each case, reflecting conditions that vary from company to company. What is more important is to recognize that regardless of where the fleet function is organizationally situated for operating efficiency, the basis of the entire fleet program is a fiscal matter.

As a corollary, the centralization or decentralization of administration must be adapted to meet the peculiar requirements of the individual fleet operation. A growing concept, perhaps stimulated by the entry of professional fleet management and leasing organizations into the field, is maintenance of a strong central policy and control group with decentralized implementation of the fleet procedures so that they are better adapted to suit individual needs.

If the company fleet policy has not received the complete approval of the executive head or the policy-making group of the company, the entire program is probably destined to failure. It should be designed to permit the fleet administrator and responsible heads maximum flexibility. As a minimum the responsibility and authority for implementation of the policy should be clearly defined. Consideration should be given to the budget control requirements, the prerequisites for car assignment, the method of financing procurement costs, and the manner in which usage reimbursements or charges (if any) are to be determined.

Procedures, which are in effect interpretations of the formal fleet policy, should cover such matters as detailed administration of the program, coordination of functions, assignment and use of cars on both personal and company business, types of vehicles and equipment to be used, replacement times, insurance coverages, accident reporting, maintenance and warranty procedures, accounting and record-keeping responsibilities, and—most important—safety.

Evaluation and Selection of Equipment

The fleet car should be designed so that it will satisfy the transportation requirements of the job, will be indicative of company caliber, and will not impair the efficiency, safety, or morale of the employee. The latter requisite is extremely important, especially when experiencing a tight labor market.

Frequently, the initial cost is considered the sole determinant in the selection of the fleet car; this can be a costly, short-range view. While initial cost is a most important factor, it must be evaluated in conjunction with anticipated operating costs, estimated resale value, manufacturer's equalization programs, and pertinent intangible factors. The need for expensive optional equipment, such as air conditioning, is often a major determining factor in the selection of a suitable fleet car.

The use of compact cars in recent years has been generally reserved for company utility use and for certain low-mileage, low-speed operations; the lower-cost, standard-size cars have been utilized in operations subject to rougher usage; and the more costly cars with additional (optional) equipment have been increasingly acquired for the clean, air-conditioned operations. There is no valid reason why the entire fleet should be made up of one model of car; it should be tailored to suit the individual operation.

Automobile Ownership

The most common methods of ownership or acquisition utilized by companies today are employee ownership, company ownership, leasing, and a combination of ownership and leasing. Regardless of whether an automobile is employee-owned, company-owned, or leased, reimbursement of employee cost for company use by salaried employees is generally made on an actual or predetermined fixed-rate basis. Conversely, most companies charge the employee a sufficient amount for the personal use of company-owned or leased vehicles, if for no other reason than to avoid problems raised by the additional compensation that personal use represents. Some companies that prefer company ownership have found real value in the use of professional agencies in the procurement and resale of its automobiles; these agencies are also available to assist in the development of equitable usage reimbursements and personal use charges for all fleets, regardless of ownership.

Unfortunately, too many financial experts have unnecessarily complicated the lease-versus-purchase evaluation process. An oversimplification of this process is to consider that the lease side consists of a procurement cost, interest (generally predicated on the lessee's credit rating), and contractual fees. The purchase side similarly consists of a procurement cost, cost of money (reinvestment privilege), and administrative costs. Rarely does a company lease its automobiles as the result of a straight dollars-and-cents economic evaluation. Other considerations include, but should not be limited to, the availability of cash, relationship of assets and liabilities, depreciation versus lease expense, and professional services available. A growing concept, just as applicable to the smaller as to the larger companies, is the lease of equipment through a partially or wholly owned leasing subsidiary.

Replacement Time or Period

The same factors evaluated at the time of the selection of the fleet car must also be evaluated in the determination of an appropriate replacement time or period. Fleet administrators should always think in terms of full useful life.

The most acceptable formal fleet procedures call for the replacement of used automobiles on a given mileage and/or time basis and yet contain sufficient flexibility to enable fleet administrators to take maximum advantage of the latest manufacturers' depreciation and replacement programs, favorable resale markets, and cost avoidance measures. Generally, because of better automotive products and mandatory warranty maintenance requirements, automobiles may be permitted a longer useful life than in the not far distant past. Regardless of the results of replacement reviews, however, some fleets are required to replace their cars more frequently than economically necessary, for reasons of company image and personnel relations.

Disposal of Used Automobiles

Without much fear of contradiction it can be stated that the disposal of used automobiles is one of the most critical areas of a fleet administrator's total responsibilities. A single misjudgment in the manner in which he chooses to dispose of his cars can make the difference between a successful and an unsuccessful fleet operation.

The most commonly used methods of disposing of used automobiles are by trading on the purchase of a new car, by wholesale operations, or by sale to employees; quick turnover is the order of the day in a fleet operation. Rarely does a fleet administrator or a professional fleet management organization have the time, financial backing, or appropriate facilities to engage in the retail selling of used cars, though claims are made to the contrary.

The used-car market is constantly in a state of flux; consequently, day-to-day knowledge of both the local and the national market is mandatory in order that the fleet administrator can obtain optimum prices for his used equipment. It is not at all unusual to move a used vehicle from one market location to another in order to obtain the maximum return possible.

The reconditioning of used automobiles is probably one of the most controversial of all functions handled by the fleet administrator. Some firmly believe used automobiles should be sold "as is," some believe in "full" reconditioning, while others argue for reconditioning on a "selective" basis. All arguments bear merit. The degree of reconditioning required must be tailored to suit the individual fleet need. It is particularly important that fleet administrators who believe in "full" reconditioning have absolute control over expenditures.

Dealer Selection

Factually, the reasons why a particular dealer should be considered for selection are extremely difficult to verify from a distant point. While a dealer's cost must be reasonable, the cheapest dealer is not always the best. Dealerships are private business and in most cases are not owned by the automobile manufacturer. To this end, they are in business to make a profit; and when that profit is not there, services must be cut. If this happens, the fleet car will suffer in the long run. Manufacturer's representatives will gladly supply fleet administrators the names of reputable, fleet-oriented dealerships anywhere in the country.

The use of "drop-shipping"—the ordering of an automobile from a local dealer for delivery through another dealer at a distant (destination) point—is a highly controversial issue. In these instances the initial dealership is paid for its administrative service, and the delivering dealership is presumably paid an adequate amount for preservicing and delivering the car. Fleet administrators and professional agencies appear to be leaning more and more toward ordering cars from destination dealerships rather than drop-shipping, because the delivering dealer is thereby offered more encouragement for better initial and continuing servicing.

Maintenance

Although in earlier years there appeared to be much merit in the argument for a minimum (breakdown) type of maintenance program, the pendulum seems now to be swinging toward one of more scheduled maintenance. These facts all lend support to a greater degree of scheduled maintenance: (1) Automobiles are now generally being operated for a longer period of time; (2) manufacturers have increased the maintenance requirements for warranty qualifications; (3) there is belated cognizance of the safety problem; and (4) the fleet administrators recognize that mechanically sound and attractive-appearing automobiles bring a higher return in resale value. Full advantage should be taken of warranty repairs. For safety purposes, if for no other reason, automobiles should be continually maintained in such a condition that they can pass the most stringent state inspection. Conversely, caution should also be exercised not to overmaintain the cars and thus incur expense needlessly.

Most dealers allow a discount on parts for fleet cars, ranging from 10 percent to 25 percent. It is important to recognize, however, that this is a dealership option; the policy is not dictated by the manufacturer. Hence, this becomes a factor in dealer selection.

Budgets, Cost Controls, and Administrative Effort

The best means of getting control of decentralized automotive fleets is through implementation of a strong central budget. This is especially important in leased fleets, where the low monthly rental cost of the vehicles can be used to circumvent established appropriation procedures. The fleet administrator should be held responsible for compliance with the budget. He should not, however, be held accountable for budget approval (except for his own immediate responsibility); rather, the approval function should be reserved for those persons with direct executive responsibility in the various operations that use parts of the fleet.

Most fleets require too much paperwork, employ too many cost controls, and are overcomputerized but do not have stringent enough budget controls. In fleet administration as in any organizational function, absolutely no control is gained by receiving voluminous reports when there is no one to review them, by demanding delivery dates when the request is physically impossible to meet, and— among other things—requiring central approval of items when the control operation costs more than the anticipated savings.

Paperwork can be sharply reduced in most fleets by avoidance of the processing of duplicate paperwork, more effective design and use of forms, greater use of horizontal paths of communication, and omission of verification requirements when verification is impractical. The need for costly computerization can be virtually eliminated and verification of documentation can be greatly minimized through the judicious application of statistical sampling techniques. Less, not more, detailed categorization of fleet costs and elimination of expensive reports (prepared in anticipation of questions) will help immeasurably in reducing administrative costs. The management-by-exception principle should be implemented wherever practicable.

The "Big Problem"

The fleet administrator is constantly plagued with the troublesome fact that nearly every person considers himself a highly qualified automobile expert. Being heavily indoctrinated with Parkinson's law, these "experts" constantly advise him on such matters as automobile safety, procedures, what cars he should get, when he should get them, what extras he should put on them, how and when he should sell them, which dealers he should use, whether he should lease or purchase cars, whether he should recondition them, and how he should maintain them. Most of these self-styled experts purchase one car every other year or so; and when they do, they unquestionably accept the fleet administrator's expert opinion. Nonetheless, where the fleet is concerned, they constantly attempt to pressure the fleet administrator into costly situations.

The Fleet Administrator

The most important executive decision to be made with respect to the fleet function is the selection of the fleet administrator. His responsibility touches upon practically every activity within the corporate structure. If he makes a single misjudgment, it may happen that a salesman cannot sell his product, a job is shut down, an employee's morale is shattered, or a serious dent is put in the corporate profit picture. The administrator must be technically well qualified and thoroughly indoctrinated in the best administrative, accounting, law, engineering, safety, purchasing, selling, and personnel practices. The fleet administrator must be able to comprehend the "big picture." He must be strong, yet flexible; understanding, yet firm. He is an extremely important corporation asset.—*W. M. Wilson*

REAL ESTATE MANAGEMENT

The basic economic and market principles applicable to real estate analysis in general are equally applicable to industrial real estate. What sets industrial real estate apart from other types of real estate is the manner in which it is used, the type of user occupying it, and the processes which it houses.

Before a meaningful discussion of principles and techniques involved in achieving the most efficient use and allocation of industrial real estate can be undertaken, it is necessary to reach an agreement on precisely what is meant by the term "industrial real estate."

Defining Industrial Real Estate

The basic function of all urban real estate is to provide a location for human activity. Its value on the market is a direct function of the type of activity that may be conducted on the premises and the efficiency which the realty imparts to the performance of this activity. This is the case whether concern is with an un-improved site or with a site improved with buildings. Industrial real estate therefore includes all land and buildings (often referred to as urban space) either utilized or suited for industrial activities.

THE ZONING CONCEPT

Because zoning is a powerful land-use control that prescribes what may be done or what may not be done—or both—in substantial areas of the United States, one way to identify industrial real estate is to ascertain the kind of land uses that are permitted in an industrial zone. There are two practical difficulties with this approach, however. The first is partly terminological; many communities use the term "manufacturing" rather than "industrial" in their zoning. The second and a much more significant limitation of this approach is the fact that there is extremely wide and apparently nonsystematic variation in the range of uses that are either directly permitted in, or specifically excluded from, industrial zones. This is true even when the three most widely used categories (light industrial, general industrial, and heavy industrial) are combined for purposes of analysis. Although these precise titles are not always employed, they represent the usual bases of distinction.

The use of zoning ordinances to define industry is essentially a pragmatic guide in any given local area, but it is imprecise because most zoning ordinances permit at least some commercial activities in industrial zones. It appears that a broad conception of industry is necessary for effective administration of land use regulations.

THE BROKER APPROACH

Another way to identify the realm of industrial real estate is to discover what kinds of properties industrial brokers handle. More significantly, the exclusions from their normal activities indicate the kinds of property that normally would not be regarded as industrial real estate, such as retail, some wholesale, office, consumer service, and other commercial activities. The industrial specialist will of course assist in finding an office or retail outlet, or even a residence, for a manufacturing client. Indeed, the entire effort to define and delineate the area of industrial real estate can become bogged down in attempts to achieve too high a degree of precision. The important point is that industrial real estate encompasses land and buildings utilized for more than just manufacturing activities. Storage, transshipment, distribution, and service functions clearly associated with manufacturing are as much a province of the industrial real estate broker as are fabricating and assembly. The location and siting of these activities are functionally related to the process of delivering manufactured goods to the purchaser, consumer, retailer, wholesaler, or another manufacturer.

STANDARD INDUSTRIAL CLASSIFICATION SYSTEM

For purposes of analysis and identification, industries and industrial groupings are often divided according to the Standard Industrial Classification System (SIC) published by the U.S. Bureau of the Budget. Quite apart from any assistance it might provide in indicating what industry is and what it is not, the SIC offers assistance to the industrial real estate broker or industry representatives on two important counts. First, it helps to define and delineate the area of concern in a particular industrial real estate problem by indicating the kinds of products and processes that are (in the estimation of the compilers of the SIC coding system, at least) closely related to one another. This is extremely important when the identification of one area of interest is a central portion of a real estate problem. Second and even more important, the SIC coding system helps identify the characteristics of similar processes and related activities. The industrial real estate specialist confronted with a land-use or space-use problem thus has a means of ascertaining the range of probable and reasonable users. When a facility is available for sale or lease, or when a site is to be made available, a study of SIC characteristics can offer insights into potential buyers and/or users of the space that is to be marketed.

MEASURES OF IMPORTANCE

The relative importance of industrial activity within an area, whether a local community or the entire nation, can be measured in a variety of ways.

Number of employees and establishments. In manufacturing firms the number of employees is the most common basic guide to land and/or building area requirements. Several types of systematic relationships have been noted between number of employees and total floor area and/or total land area occupied by manufacturing plants in various industrial groups. A less common but equally simple measure of relative importance of industry in an area is the number of establishments. This has the obvious disadvantage of assuming comparability among frequently noncomparable units. However, when an analysis by number of establishments is added to a tabulation by employment-size groups, the industrial real estate specialist has a good guide to the amount and type of industrial space required in a given area. A time series of such figures indicates trends in the demand for industrial space.

Characteristics of Industrial Real Estate

The peculiar characteristics of industrial real estate indicate the significance of real estate to the industrial firm.

HEAVY INVESTMENT

As with all other types of real estate, industrial real estate represents a large commitment of funds or working capital. From the point of view of the user-occupant, the funds could often be utilized better in the productive processes of the firm, and various financing devices are utilized to minimize the commitment of cash necessary to insure occupancy of the space. This is directly related to the fact that industrial real estate is very often investment real estate, with the occupant paying rent to an investor-owner who seeks a profit from the rental of the space.

LOW LIQUIDITY

In common with other types of real estate, industrial real estate tends to be a slow-moving commodity. Generally, the more specialized the facilities, the less rapidly they will turn over. Moreover, the larger the facility, the more difficult it is to market in most instances. This enhances the investment risk and calls for special treatment in the real estate investment market.

RELATION TO PROFITABILITY

The value or contribution of industrial real estate is, typically, interrelated intimately with the profitability and inventory of the user-occupant. Indeed, it is often difficult to distinguish between plant and equipment, once the equipment has been installed and is functioning as an integral part of the capital investment of the establishment.

INNOVATION AND FUNCTIONAL OBSOLESCENCE

Technological change in industrial processes, as well as in construction or design, can rapidly render industrial real estate facilities functionally obsolescent. This both increases investment risks and requires adaptability on the part of management. It also challenges management to plan boldly into the future in an attempt to minimize these risks.

IMMOBILITY

Because industrial equipment and inventory are extremely expensive to move, most industrial organizations choose to minimize their geographic movement as much as is consistent with efficient and profitable operations. Aside from direct out-of-pocket expenses, interruption of the production process also results in a loss during the period surrounding the move. For these reasons, despite pressures from changing locational factors and from obsolescence, a high degree of immobility characterizes most industrial locations. This means that the location decision is very important—even critical—in the success of the organization. Particular care must be exercised to make sure that the location is as nearly appropriate as possible. There is a strong possibility that the firm will occupy its space for a longer period of time than may be justified on the basis of productive efficiency.

Industry's Real Estate Needs

Industry needs real estate in order to house its facilities, its operations, its offices, its inventory, and its employees. Beyond these purposes industrial organizations frequently encounter distinctive real estate needs.

CUSTOM FACILITIES

No matter how standardized the industrial process of a particular firm may appear, it has characteristics of product, process, market, or personnel that distinguish it from all other industrial operations. If the real estate that it occupies is to contribute to efficiency and profitability, it must be an integral part in the productive process of the firm. This means that the facilities, the space, and the location must be as nearly perfect as possible. The typical industrial firm—with the possible exclusion of major national companies so active in real estate that they have their own real estate or development departments—usually needs locational advice from the industrial real estate specialist.

FINANCING

Whether industrial real estate is owned or leased, the occupant's major desire is to minimize the amount of capital invested in real estate. Financing and/or leasing arrangements that offer the safe release of funds for working capital or production purposes are actively sought by the industrial firm.

LOCATION ANALYSIS

With the exception of the national or regional firm that has many facilities and relatively high turnover of locations, most industrial organizations do not enter the real estate market frequently and consequently their knowledge of this market is minimal. It may even be somewhat distorted because of an attempt to transfer their experiences and impressions from the residential real estate market. Their relative immobility underscores the importance that must be attached to the selection of the proper location with appropriate facilities for the particular firm.

FUTURE MARKETABILITY

Less often but with increasing frequency in recent years, industrial firms want to dispose of plants or other facilities being vacated. This may be the result of a move or of a decision to abandon a particular operation. If the managements of industrial firms are generally ignorant of procedures in acquiring industrial real estate, they are even less experienced in the techniques or the market through which the disposition of industrial facilities takes place. The industrial firm needs a means to dispose of real estate quickly, efficiently, and reasonably in order to minimize the financial drain of unproductive investment in idle assets. The industrial real estate broker can often perform more valuable services in plant disposition than in industrial real estate acquisition, primarily because he is filling a more pressing need.

MARKET ADVICE

The industrial firm is not usually in the real estate business. Even those organizations with active, full-time real estate departments cannot be sensitive to all regional variations or to developments in all aspects of real estate markets (finance, leasing, development, zoning, and the like). They need information and advice with respect to such developments, but even more they need insights into market conditions that assist in business decisions and their timing. Just as the industrialist turns to the financial specialist when he is seeking to raise funds or to decide on the best method for doing so, he should turn to the industrial real estate specialist when he requires assistance in a decision with respect to the acquisition, utilization, or disposition of real estate.

—S. H. Morris and Eugene Boshes

Section 3

Personnel

CONTENTS

Manpower Procurement and Placement

Development and Training

Wage and Salary Administration

Executive Compensation

Employee Benefits

The Personnel Records Function

Employee Relationships

Personnel Research

THE MODERN PERSONNEL FUNCTION

The personnel function of today cannot even remotely resemble that of 20 years ago. The expectations of the organization and of its employees have radically changed. The employee is far better informed, more articulate, and more mobile than his 20-years-ago counterpart. The large and fast-growing segment of the work force under 35 years of age knows nothing of NRA (National Recovery Administration), apple sellers, WPA (Works Progress Administration)—all the economic and social indicators of the depression of the 1930's. These people know only prosperity. And an awareness of social problems has developed in recent years to the extent that traditionally disenfranchised Americans will no longer accept the role of political, economic, cultural, and social outcasts.

The business firm finds itself in a burgeoning economy, tied to an equally burgeoning cost of goods and services (which places tremendous compression on the all-important area between the curves of sales and costs), with a geometric acceleration in the technology of product and of management processes. The firm is also faced with a serious shortage of executive talent.

All of these forces come to bear on the personnel function, requiring considerably more than keeping the people happy. In fact, it has been known for many years that although happy people are the easiest to motivate, happy employees are not necessarily productive until they are provided with the opportunity to participate to the fullest in the attainment of their employer's objectives.

All of these forces require the personnel executive, more than ever before and increasingly as time goes on, to build and improve upon the human resources of the firm and to insure long-run growth, vitality, and continuity.

The Role of the Personnel Executive

It is the personnel executive's job to relate the organization's planning to human resources requirements and to attract, train, and develop talented people within that framework. New compensation problems for the informed, mobile work force require imaginative planning within long-term growth plans for the firm. Objectives become extremely important in the planning of employee benefits rather than hit-or-miss handouts. A growing social awareness demands new patterns of relationships between and among employees and their employers at all levels. With all of these factors there is the necessity of measuring effectiveness so that clear, objective determinations can be made of the degree of effectiveness of the personnel organization.

The personnel executive has, in fact, three roles in the organization within which he works. He is (1) manager of a group of people in one part of the organization (the personnel department) and administrator of the things the department administers; (2) adviser to other managers on problems involving the human resources of the firm; and (3) a full-grown participant in the long-run growth, vitality, and continuity of the enterprise.

For many, many years the personnel executive concentrated upon the first and second of these roles, to the exclusion of the third. In today's industrial and business world, his third role demands his greatest energies, imagination, and talent. In this section of the handbook, therefore, less attention is paid to his roles of manager and adviser.

Expectations are based on experience, so that if the experience of the chief executive is that the personnel executive is concerned only with the administration of benefits, recreation, and grievances, his expectations of the personnel executive will be no greater than that. If he knows from experience, however, that the personnel executive not only runs his department well but also grapples effectively with the long-run problems of the productivity of labor, unit costs for labor, the cross-over point of labor costs and capital costs (automation), the availability of executive talent for an organization plan for the next decade, and the very design of an organization effectively to develop triple volume at optimal cost and functioning, his expectation is that the personnel executive is a contributing participant toward the attainment of the organization's objectives in the troublesome years ahead.—*J. D. Staley*

ORGANIZATION PLANNING

Organization and manpower planning is the keystone of the proper utilization of human resources in the attainment of an organization's long- and short-term goals. It assumes that all organizations exist to accomplish some worthwhile purpose. In its broadest sense, it attempts to assure that the work to be done is clearly defined and that the organization is properly structured and staffed to accomplish its goals effectively. It provides a necessary link to translate economic goals into the manpower plans necessary to develop or otherwise provide the managerial and technical expertise needed for a company to survive, prosper, and grow.

Interrelationship of Organization Manpower and Corporate Planning

In planning a company's destiny, management is continually faced with the problem of matching its short- and long-term operational plans to its current and future organization and manpower requirements. The starting point in the planning cycle is concerned with defining company goals and objectives. It involves an assessment of the organization's current operations and economic performance and considers alternative approaches designed to achieve maximum performance in the markets served and services rendered. The analysis considers the company's current products or services, financial status, technical capability, and market performance and penetration. It may redirect part of the company's available resources toward opportunities as yet unexploited. It involves corporate assumptions relative to the current and future economic and political climate and the future cost and availability of raw materials and labor. This phase of the planning cycle, conducted at periodic intervals, should result in a restatement or redefinition of the organization's short- and long-term goals or mission.

Organization and manpower planning dovetails with the economic planning phase. It is concerned, first, with identifying the work that must be done and then determining the best way to arrange human resources so that the intended consequences of the organization may be achieved. Second, considering both current and long-term goals or missions, it develops projections and plans to assure that the organization will be staffed with the numbers and types of managers, technicians, and specialists it needs to achieve maximum effectiveness.

ORGANIZATION STRUCTURE AND FUNCTION

The most effective structure—the manner in which people, activities, and functions are grouped and related—is dependent upon a variety of factors. One purpose served by a structure is to divide the activities which must be performed to achieve the organization's goals into manageable segments. The activities are grouped into individual jobs and arranged to provide efficiently for necessary internal operations that in turn will serve the organization's markets and projected growth plans. At the same time, the plan of organization must provide for necessary control and coordination between functions and activities.

Although there is no one perfect form of organization, a series of considerations can be made in determining the best alignment of activities, functions, and people at any given point in time. The first consideration involves deciding whether a functional or a divisional type of structure will best achieve the organization's goals.

Functional structure. A functional type of organization is one in which single activities are grouped together by function; thus all finance and accounting activities may be grouped under a single department head, and the activities relating to sales and marketing may report to another. Most small companies are organized along functional lines, and this technique is used to some extent in most organizations.

When a firm is being established, one of the first questions to be answered is: What work has to be done, and what is the most economical way to do it? A new computer firm—for example—would certainly describe the functions of design, manufacturing, and marketing as essential. Additionally, minimal financial and accounting services would be required. As the firm grows, the design function may logically be split between software and hardware, and purchasing and quality control may be assigned as subfunctions to manufacturing.

One of the obvious advantages of a functional organization is that it encourages specialization. For jobs at the supervisory level and higher, specialization has several benefits. For one thing, it eases the problem of recruiting or developing employees to fill the jobs. For example, it would be easier and less expensive to recruit a process supervisor for a chemical plant than to find a man qualified as a combination process supervisor and marketing expert. Another advantage is that in training a replacement for a job, specialization reduces the amount of knowledge the new man must master to perform adequately.

Divisional structure.   As companies grow, product lines and markets increase, and production and distribution facilities become more diverse, consideration is usually given to adopting a division form of structure. A divisional structure results when one man is placed in charge of some autonomous segment of the business. Divisions can be organized in a variety of ways, depending upon an organization's products or services. Classically, they are established along product or geographic lines.

Divisionalization by product line divides the work to be done according to type of products or services. Characteristically, in a manufacturing operation a division head may be responsible for both the marketing and the manufacturing of a part of the company's products. Additionally, he may be assigned other functions such as research and development, engineering, or market research if they impact directly on his division's ability to achieve its goals and objectives. This type of alignment permits a direct measurement of the division's results based on the profit-and-loss statement. Product line divisions adapt themselves readily to companies where either the products, the technologies utilized, or the markets served are dissimilar. Thus one electronics manufacturer has a product line division concerned with advanced military electronics, where both the customers and the technologies differ radically from those related to the manufacturing and marketing of radio and television sets.

The decision to organize by geographic region is frequently based on the location of major customers or markets combined with the availability of production facilities. Federal or state legal and regulatory bodies may also dictate the need for geographical divisions. For example, a major consulting firm may find it uneconomical to service its West Coast customers from its New York headquarters. It may elect to establish a branch on the West Coast, fully staffed and held accountable for profits in the area served. Similarly, a telephone system and most utilities are organized to service customers in a specified region.

(Further discussion of organization structure is presented in the General Management section, page 1·41.)

Relationships between functions. In establishing a structure, consideration must be given toward defining the levels in the organization where decisions will be made, the relationships that should exist between line and staff, and the interdependence between units of the organization.

One principle is that authority granted should be commensurate with responsibility assigned. That is to say, if a general sales manager is given the responsibility for maintaining an effective sales force, he should also be given the authority to select, train, compensate, and otherwise motivate his men. This authority should be his even though it may be necessary to temper it somewhat by other means, such as the budget or a general policy against sales meetings in Las Vegas. Policies may be established to limit a unit's activities. Thus a branch of a consulting firm might be given a mandate to sell the firm's services in a given geographic area but would be prevented by policy from taking on potentially profitable assignments outside the firm's acknowledged area of expertise.

The mission and authority of line and staff functions should be clearly defined. Line functions exist to carry out the central purpose of the organization and contribute directly to profits. Staff services provide special knowledge or services in fields essential to the organization. They may audit or evaluate the line's performance in specific areas, feeding back the results of their analysis to the line for remedial action.

Relating structure and functions to objectives and goals. The structure should be tailored to foster continuity of operations and direct human resources toward the full accomplishment of the organization's goals and objectives. Operating goals have the greatest impact on structure design. For example, if a small regional food company decides to add a line of cheese products, manufacture all its finished products, and achieve national distribution, these objectives and the activities necessary to their accomplishment will necessarily affect the structure. Classical organization rules and forms may prove valuable in the effective grouping of activities and functions; however, the organization's goals should be the determining factor in the final design.

Long-run continuity and vitality are goals within most organizations. Foresight in planning jobs and functions within the structure will aid in assuring the organization's ability to develop the manpower needed for the future.

A properly designed structure should never hinder the accomplishment of an organization's goals. Rather, it should facilitate management's direction of the organization's resources toward the accomplishment of necessary activities and functions more effectively than could be done in an unorganized fashion.

MANPOWER CONSIDERATIONS

Organizational effectiveness depends largely on the skills and abilities of the employees. This is not to imply that an organization should be structured solely around the strengths of existing personnel; if this policy were followed, overlap and omissions would occur between the available abilities and the work to be performed. It does emphasize that proper regard should be given to the proven strengths and known skills of individuals in considering any organizational change.

The structure, the grouping of jobs and functions, and the degree of specialization should be taken into account in considering the best way to achieve the organization's objectives. Temporary alterations may be desirable to accommodate special strengths or weaknesses of one or more individuals. Thus, if a treasurer's job requires a high degree of selling ability with financial institutions, along with technical expertise in finance, the job may have to be restructured if the incumbent does not possess good human relations skills.

The degree to which jobs and functions should be specialized must also be taken into account. The complexity of the product or service produced and the normal capacity of individuals to perform the necessary activities are prime considerations here. Although organization theorists point to the advantages of a high degree of specialization as a means of increasing effectiveness, behaviorists are equally vociferous in pointing out that overspecialization may lower morale and dull individual capacity for growth.

IMPENDING MERGERS AND ACQUISITIONS

Mergers and acquisitions represent one technique by which a company can achieve its growth objectives. Through this method it is possible to accelerate plans for diversifying a product line or entering new fields. Typically, management goes through a series of steps to identify and evaluate merger possibilities. Additionally, should a merger or acquisition be consummated, management must face the problem of integrating the new operation into the existing organization structure.

Organization planning is concerned in both the evaluation and integration phases. Initially, the evaluation should show whether the organization of the company to be acquired meets predefined criteria. Suppose a company has excellent capabilities in marketing and manufacturing but is consistently missing its internal growth targets through inability to develop new products: In this instance it might be prudent to consider the acquisition of a company with a well-structured research and development department and compatible marketing and manufacturing capabilities.

Organization plans must be developed for merging the acquisition with the company's existing operations. Should the acquired company be operated as a separate unit, or should it be integrated into existing operations? Decisions here are usually based on the compatibility of the line functions of the two organizations. Frequently, a synergism will result from combining compatible functions. Thus, if the parent company has extremely strong and compatible manufacturing capability but the markets and customers served by the acquired company are dissimilar, it might prove advantageous to interrelate the manufacturing and control functions to the parent company while retaining the marketing function as an autonomous sales division. In some instances, it is advantageous to maintain the acquisition as a separate entity. This is particularly true when the acquisition is designed to lead to new fields where the acquiring company has neither management nor technical know-how. The willingness of the management of the acquired company to remain and run the business is a major consideration in this type of acquisition. Acquisition of product lines without a capable organization structure can compound the problems of management.

EFFECTS OF NEW PRODUCTS

In a manufacturing operation, the design or development of a promising new product creates an additional variable in the design of an organization. Among the questions which management must answer are these: Will the new product be manufactured within the existing organization? How will it be sold? How will it be integrated into the organization? The question of "make or buy" is almost always answered by economics. If capacity exists in the organization's plants, if the new product is based on existing technologies, and if capital equipment outlays are minimal, the decision is usually to make the product and assign it to the manufacturing function. However, if the anticipated life cycle of the product is short, projected volumes are relatively low, and capital equipment outlays high, it would seem wise to assign the work of obtaining the finished product from outside suppliers to the purchasing function, assuming that a suitable manufacturing cost could be negotiated.

Some companies establish divisions to handle promising new products. One company, recognized as a leader in research and development, created a number of its divisions for new products pioneered by venture teams working out of the laboratories. Products showing consumer acceptance and economic promise were handled by separate divisions under the management of one of the venture team members.

Manpower Requirements

Although the structure provides the framework necessary to attain company objectives, the proper deployment of human resources is essential to their achievement. Personal skills and abilities, along with personality and motivation, affect job performance and may cause subtle but significant modifications to both the formal and the informal structure. The formal structure establishes, between jobs, levels of authority and relationships that continually modify behavior patterns and attitudes. A newly promoted district manager will behave differently in his relations with other district managers and have a different attitude toward the sales function than he did as a salesman.

Assigning a job or function to an employee does not mean that it will be fully accomplished. An insecure individual may refuse to delegate, to the point where his subordinates are stifled and the decision-making process brought to a standstill. In determining manpower requirements for an organization, the existing skills and abilities of the employees, along with their known strengths and weaknesses, should be considered. The problem is one of properly matching abilities and anticipated behavior to the activities to be performed.

THE LONG RUN

Although management may have a good feel for the skills and strengths of its existing human resources, it must also be concerned with the future. Most organizations have the objective of perpetuating the business and may have fairly ambitious plans for growth. Management has the continuing obligation to assure that capable human resources are available.

Over a given period of time some personnel will retire, many will be promoted, and others may die or leave. Concurrently, some jobs and functions will have to be restructured to keep abreast of changes in markets, technologies, and company growth. Automation and electronic data processing (EDP) may create a need to acquire or develop skills not readily available. Management's challenge is to anticipate these needs and establish plans to provide for the management and technical expertise needed for the future.

Structure design and planned management development are tools readily available to management in providing for future manpower needs. Many companies have made effective use of developmental positions such as "assistant to" or product manager. A product manager plans, promotes, and coordinates a single product within an organization producing a wide range of products. As he is exposed to production, finance, sales, and advertising, this type of position can be effectively utilized as a pass-through job in developing a future generalist.

If growth plans are based on acquisitions, the need for internal development may be lessened. Thus, a conglomerate may "home-grow" its financial and general management groups while relying on its acquisitions to provide and perpetuate other essential functions.

THE SHORT RUN

The immediate manpower requirements of an organization are somewhat easier to perceive. The company's objectives project what is to be done and define the necessary activities and functions that must be performed. Management's problem is to match existing human resources to jobs and provide an environment in which employees will be encouraged to act in the company's interest.

The work environment has many facets. Wherever possible, jobs should be structured to provide meaningful work and stretch employees' capabilities. A general sales manager will be in a better position to contribute to a company's profit goals if he is involved in setting prices rather than held accountable for volume alone. In the latter instance, his actions might in fact be detrimental to adequate profit attainment.

If a key employee quits and a capable replacement is not available from within or outside the company, a decision must be made either to settle for a second-best employee or restructure the job. Temporary restructuring gives a company the necessary time to develop a replacement internally or continue the external search. The assignment of an incapable employee almost guarantees that the job's functions will not be performed properly. As in considering long-term needs, developmental positions are useful in planning for near-term replacements. The "assistant to" position is especially useful here. In addition to relieving a manager of some of his responsibilities, the company gains the advantage of testing the abilities of the potential replacement through the assignment of special projects.

Study of Organization

Studies have demonstrated that there is no pattern in the frequency with which organizations make major changes in their structure. Most companies consider changes as needed to accommodate growth plans or to remedy evident and recurring deficiencies. However, a few continue to operate efficiently with a general plan of organization developed in years past.

A number of symptoms indicate that an organization study is in order. Among them are continued failure of the company or one of its divisions to secure adequate profits; the recurrence of some undesirable event such as overruns, customer complaints, or a consistent need to fill key managerial jobs from the outside; communication difficulties and slow decision making; or inability to pinpoint accountability for end results. Whatever the reason, management should consider who will conduct the study, what areas are to be analyzed, and how the results will be implemented.

RESPONSIBILITY FOR ORGANIZATION

In a sense, each executive and manager carries a responsibility to see that his subordinate organization is operating effectively. This is a continuing task requiring minor shifts in emphasis and approach to accommodate changes in technology and operating plans or to deal with evident manpower problems.

The chief executive is responsible for the design of the basic structure. His decision to centralize, decentralize, or adopt a functional or divisional type of structure depends to a large extent on the complexity of the organization and his personal management style. Additionally, for the plan to be effective, his decisions must be geared to the organization's long-range planning effort. He must assure that the structure is in readiness at all times to enable the organization to fully exploit its future plans for growth.

In the case of a major organizational realignment, top management is concerned with conducting a coordinated in-depth study of present structure and with developing comprehensive plans for change.

MANNING FOR THE STUDY

A major organization study is time-consuming. First, it "takes a picture" of the existing organization as a basis for further study. Interviews, questionnaires, job descriptions, organization charts, and manuals are usual sources of information about the current division of work. Clearly defined current and long-range growth and economic plans are essential if the analysis is to yield lasting results.

The method by which companies organize to conduct the study varies widely. A small company frequently handles a major study through a series of meetings in which the president and his key functional heads participate. If the contemplated reorganization is minor in scope, an administrative assistant to the president, the head of industrial relations, or a controller is frequently used. Larger firms often assemble a task force to conduct the study. Key employees may be drawn from all functions of the business and assigned to the study on a full- or part-time basis. Operating as a team, they bring a broad point of view in studying each function and in helping to formulate a recommended plan of action.

Organization departments exist in some companies. Generally staffed with one or a few highly trained specialists, these departments likewise draw study team members from throughout the company or from the outside.

Consultants are often brought in to assist in major organization studies, particularly if the study may result in the dissolution of part of the company. Working with the chief executive officer or a committee of the board, or as an extension of an organization department, they can bring to the work a broad knowledge of organization principles combined with multicompany experience in making studies of this type. On the negative side, however, consultants may not possess or acquire an intimate knowledge of the technologies and idiosyncrasies of the company's business that have contributed to its past growth.

CONTENT OF THE STUDY

Top management usually defines the overall scope of an organization study and the areas to be considered. In a decentralized operation the responsibility for the conduct of the study may be shared with the divisions. Many methods have been employed with varying degrees of success in developing or modifying a structure. One that has worked well requires the following five steps:

1. *Restatement of objectives.* The first step is to redefine the company's objectives. Questions (What kind of company is this? What is it trying to be? What are the opportunities and hazards?) should be considered in economic, quantitative, and qualitative terms. Redefining the objectives may help clarify misunderstandings and hitherto vague points. Committed to writing, they provide a framework that guides management and others who must make decisions in taking action.

2. *Study of existing organization.* The second step is a detailed study of the existing organization. This is a fact-finding phase designed to audit the way the organization is structured and its current effectiveness. On a smaller scale, the study might be concerned with one or more functions in the search for a solution to a specific operating problem and the adequacy to accommodate goals for future growth. It concerns itself with determining the way the work is currently divided, the degree of decentralization, the effectiveness of communications, the flexibility of the company in meeting the demands of changing markets and technology, and the balance between functions and activities.

3. *Planning ideal organization.* An optimum structure is developed by defining the essential activities and functions that must be performed in the full accomplishment of the predefined long- and short-range goals. Neither the structure nor the company's current manpower strengths are considered at this stage. Rather, the focus is on determining the most effective way to achieve the goals. The essential activities are structured into jobs and grouped under various levels of management. The ideal structure is both dynamic and spartan in nature. It

provides a workable model for directing the company's resources toward the achievement of essential activities. For the short term, it must be modified to account for existing manpower strengths and weaknesses.

4. *Manpower considerations.* The fourth phase of the study considers the ideal structure in terms of the capabilities of the manpower currently available either within or outside the organization; this is accomplished through manpower inventories and forecasts. The attempt here is to determine how closely the company's human resources match the ideal structure. Concurrently, manpower plans should be established to meet the company's plans for growth.

5. *Developing the recommended structure.* Reconciliation of the ideal structure with available personnel usually results in a compromise. This is particularly true for higher-level jobs where personal skills and abilities have a greater impact on job content. In this sense, the ideal structure represents a long-range plan for organizational improvement that may never be achieved, while the actual structure is viable and is concerned with the reality that people rather than structure make up an organization.

DEPTH OF STRUCTURE VERSUS EFFECTIVENESS

Depth of structure considers the number of levels of management between the board of directors and nonsupervisory employees. As a general rule, levels should be kept to the lowest workable number. Typically, a greater depth is found in divisionalized companies than in those organized on a functional basis.

Although five to eight levels of management appear common in most medium-size to large divisionalized companies, the trend in recent years has been toward reducing the number in an attempt to improve communications and speed the decision-making process. Ineffective communications present a major problem in most companies. As layers of supervision are added, the difficulties of communication and coordination increase. Misunderstandings are more apt to occur as each person in the chain interprets and passes along directions or information. Increased delegation has served as a partial answer to the problem; by establishing decision points throughout the hierarchy, the communication lines are shortened.

A short chain of command tends to reduce overhead, as fewer managers are needed. Conversely, a reduction in the levels of management will result in the enlargement of the remaining jobs and may require more capable managers. Each organization, then, should seek to strike a balance between organizational depth and span of control.

SPAN OF CONTROL

The number of subordinates directly supervised by an executive, as opposed to the number of employees who may have direct access to him, is his span of control. Empirical studies have shown that there is no immutable number to guide the planner in determining the ideal span. While the typical number of subordinates reporting to the president of a medium-size to large company is eight to ten, as few as one and as many as 18 have been noted in recent studies.

The span of control for any job is dynamic. It varies with the growth of the organization and is affected by the depth of the structure. The general sales manager of a small company may call personally on key customers and perform the sales planning and promotion activities while supervising all the salesmen. As the company grows, salesmen are added, and the product lines become more diverse, his span will increase to the point where physical limitations prevent him from either effectively supervising his salesmen or performing other necessary sales activities. At this point his job may be divided; he may be given an assistant; or a level of supervision may be imposed between him and the sales force. One disadvantage in the latter measure, however, is that it may build insulation and prevent effective delegation.

The similarity of the functions supervised and their complexity affect the optimum span. Homogeneity of the functions or activities supervised permits effective control over a relatively large number of subordinates. Although the executive in charge may be called upon for many decisions, the relative similarity of the functions should aid in their resolution. Conversely, if the functions or activities supervised are dissimilar or complex, a shorter span may be indicated. This is especially true in a highly technical and complex process operation where a large number of varied decisions are required continuously.

In some industries—notably retailing—the trend is toward a larger span of control with a resulting decrease in the depth of the structure. One major retailer operates with four levels of management between the president and the store clerks. The increased span forces the managers to delegate more responsibility and authority to subordinates as time limits effective supervision. This, in turn, enlarges the subordinates' jobs and forces them to learn and perform at a higher level.

In determining the ideal span of control, the planner should consider the mental and physical capabilities of the executive, the similarity and complexity of the functions supervised and their geographic locations, and the desirability of increasing delegation. For top management, the span may continue to be a function of the chief executive's desires and style of management; however, the organization planner should design and recommend the organization that best meets company objectives.

Manpower Inventory

The success or failure of an organization depends largely upon the capabilities of its key employees. Top management must optimize the strengths of current employees and identify and provide developmental opportunities for future replacements. Many companies approach the task of monitoring human resources through manpower inventories updated by periodic performance appraisals. There is, however, a great variation between companies in the extent to which the inventories are formalized.

PERFORMANCE APPRAISAL

Whatever the form or procedure used, performance appraisal attempts to assess employee performance in terms meaningful to the organization. The trend in recent years has been away from the measurement of personality traits and toward more work-centered appraisals. Management has pioneered this technique through increased attention to management by objectives, which permits measurement of performance relative to the accomplishment of short- and long-term goals. Appraisals of this type are meaningful to the employee and of practical value to the company, and have been responsible for management's increased involvement.

Other companies evaluate managerial performance against factors judged basic to any management position. One company uses a plan whose ten factors include the principal ones of planning, organizing, coordinating, delegating, supervising, and controlling. The ten factors are combined with operating results as predictors of current achievements. Additionally, this company assesses potential for advancement in terms of immediate promotability as well as defining possible promotional opportunities over the coming three years.

MANPOWER CHART

A manpower chart attempts to display the organization's human resources in both quantitative and qualitative terms. Charts of this type are fairly common in larger companies where sheer number and physical location of employees make such judgments unwieldy. Smaller firms bypass the charting stage and assess their current strengths informally. If a formal program is used, the charts define a number of variables.

Existing assets. The inventory considers the numbers and kinds of jobs within the organization and determines the capability of the company's human resources. Defining the numbers and types of jobs is a statistical tabulation. The summary of each employee's qualifications is stated in terms of age, education, current and previous experience, current performance, and promotion potential. The performance and potential considerations are factored in periodically from the performance appraisal system.

Skill levels. Some highly technical organizations, such as aerospace firms, supplement the basic data with a skills inventory listing all employees in terms of technical skills acquired at school and through work experience. When analyzed, the collective data portray the technical capability of the organization. They are especially useful when the company is bidding on or developing plans for technical projects.

Forecasting Manpower Requirements

While the manpower inventory tends to be static, the actual manpower needs of the organization are dynamic. Job openings will occur for a variety of reasons. One purpose of the manpower forecast is to define probable job openings and identify possible candidates. Additionally, the forecasts may define natural lines of promotion to each job as an aid in providing the developmental steps necessary to qualify candidates for the jobs.

ATTRITION FORECAST

An attrition forecast is a method of anticipating when vacancies will occur. The chronological age of managers provides one input. Other key employees may retire early for reasons of health. Poor performance on the job may call for early retirement in some cases, and transfer to a less demanding job in others. Some employees may die, and a high-potential manager passed over for promotion may quit. Although the forecast cannot predict every eventuality, it is a useful tool in determining probable vacancies occasioned by retirement, poor performance, and known health problems.

MOVEMENT FORECAST

A movement forecast provides a flexible timetable for planning promotions and developmental transfers. As such, it is an attempt to match qualified candidates to available openings. Some companies have complete replacement charts covering their entire management group, although most confine replacement charting to higher management positions. Still others plan movement informally by identifying and planning for the development of high-potential employees. While the attrition forecast, performance appraisals, and the manpower inventory are essential inputs to a formal system, the success of the program rests on top management's commitment and involvement.

Static performers and promotables. Some employees possess unlimited potential for advancement, while others appear to be restricted. Present job performance is not necessarily a predictor of success unless the successfully performed elements in the present job are requirements in the prospective job. More than one highly talented researcher has failed miserably when promoted to an administrative position. Although performance appraisals provide a measure of current performance quality, a well-conceived potential analysis is critical to future staffing. It should evaluate current performance in terms of performance elements adjudged to be predictors of success in higher-level jobs.

Lateral transfer. The lateral transfer is frequently employed as part of a program to ready a candidate for promotion; a highly skilled financial administrator, for example, might be assigned as assistant to the production manager to give him firsthand exposure to the manufacturing function. It is also used as a means of solving operational problems. Assume, for example, that one plant in a multiplant operation consistently carries a high efficiency rating. The manager might be transferred to a low-producing plant in an attempt to improve its efficiency. His ultimate success on the assignment would provide an additional measure of his management skills.

There are dangers in the "assistant to" assignment, however. It may be better to give the man responsibility and authority to run an operation under the guidance of an experienced boss. The "assistant to" often ends up doing "staff" work. For this reason many companies will not use this job for development.

Lateral transfers are also sometimes used to move a static performer from a position identified as a development job. This is particularly true in large companies where key development jobs have been identified.

Timing of movement. While the urgency for replacing key employees is readily identifiable, the timing of developmental transfers requires equal consideration. If a rising "young Turk" is performing well on his present assignment, his immediate superior may be reluctant to see him transferred. Top management involvement at this stage is an aid in convincing the superior of the desirability of the move. This will not be necessary, however, if managers realize that their performance is judged in large measure on how well they train top-notch promotables.

Tying Manpower Requirements Forecast into Training and Development Efforts

An organization's objectives, combined with the manpower inventory and forecast, represent the underlying requirements of an effective program for the identification and planned development of future executives, managers, and specialists.

An analysis of the inventory and performance appraisals, supplemented by economic performance data, provides a good indicator of the specific strengths and quality of the organization's human resources. As such it may point the way toward development programs geared to capitalize on the strengths of each individual. Similarly, the manpower forecast can be related to individuals who are identified as having high potential, and specific development plans can be established.

The need for coordinated planning of this type is emphasized by the challenges of an expanding economy, the acceleration of technological and social change, and the continuing shortage of qualified managers and specialists. To forecast manpower requirements and identify probable candidates is not enough. Top management must be involved and provide the leadership in establishing positive programs of training and development if the organization is to fully exploit its growth objectives.—*R. E. Wettling*

MANPOWER PROCUREMENT AND PLACEMENT

Placing people in jobs has become an increasingly complex business in two ways. First, levels and types of occupations are almost infinite in number. There are now several different sets of procedural approaches to be used in filling open positions, depending on the nature of the job. Second, heightening competition in the labor market is steadily building the pressure for more sophistication in procurement and placement technique. A programmed approach is necessary for every level, from the assembly worker to the executive.

Basic Manpower Planning

One major consequence of this new complexity is the need for the same kind of planning that is applied to other demanding aspects of the enterprise. The organization that begins to gear up on the day the job opens up will usually fill the position long after the employee is first needed, may not find the best person for the job to be done, and very likely will do less than the best hiring job relative to the long-term personnel needs of the company. The term "manpower planning" has therefore gained broad acceptance in personnel circles.

Manpower planning is the look-ahead activity that will give the organization reasonable assurance that, at any given time in the future, there will be the appropriate quantity and quality of personnel on the payroll to do the work demanded.

QUALITATIVE PLANNING

Under today's conditions closest attention must be given to the qualitative aspects of manpower planning rather than the quantitative. There are few industries where it is sufficient to provide for the right number of able bodies. The more critical (and much more difficult) chore is to be sure the organization will, at some given time in the future, have the right types of people with special qualifications. Planning for the provision of narrowly specialized scientists is a challenge. But it is no longer possible, either, to assume that tool and die makers, skilled laboratory technicians, mechanics, or clerical personnel will be readily available when they are needed.

Initially, then, manpower planning is an evolution of the best estimate of the types of employees that will be needed, and the number of each. But this is not the end point.

ACTION PLANNING

Next, the manpower planner must evaluate his manpower resources. Either enough people will become available within the organization through the normal course of events, or they are sure to be available in labor markets normally tapped for personnel—or else the manpower planner must do some creative thinking. His alternatives are to set targets for the development of the needed personnel within the company or to anticipate recruitment programs which will have to reach into new sources. In the former situation he is creating new work for the manpower development department, and, in the latter instance, for the people who handle employment. It is his responsibility to see that these down-the-road missions are brought to the attention of other departments in the proper manner.

INDIVIDUAL REPLACEMENT

At nonprofessional and lower professional levels the look-ahead is principally statistical. The planner has to figure on the numbers of properly qualified personnel who must be available from one source or another. What will be the needs for hourly workers with various occupational skills? How many accountants, engineers, and salesmen will have to be acquired?

At the top management echelons—say, for the top 10 percent of the organization—the manpower planner is obligated to engage in highly individualized contemplation of the future. Position by position, it must be determined (a) whether there is a ready replacement; (b) if there is none, whether there is someone who can be developed to be ready for the position in a reasonable period of time; and (c) what this individual's development needs are. (Here, of course, the manpower planner interlocks again with manpower development.)

When the termination date of the incumbent is known (usually because of impending retirement), or when illness or other circumstances heighten the likelihood of early replacement need, it is imperative that the manpower planner come up with an action plan. But even where the incumbency seems stable, good manpower planning will include an inventory of the replacement situation in all these higher-level positions. First, even executives are mortal. Second, if there is any degree of vitality in the company, these people are highly subject to being shuffled around. But third, and perhaps most important, the summarized results provide one overall fix on the adequacy of the executive team. If only a small percentage of the key positions is backed up, there is trouble down the road, and corrective action must start far ahead of the crisis date. (Or, if there is a surplus of talent, attrition can be anticipated.)

FOLLOW-THROUGH

Manpower planning can end with the fulfillment of the responsibilities just described. This will not be the case if the manpower planners are "on the race track" and continually involved in operational happenings.

The active manpower planner will, at least annually, update the program he laid out the year before. Equally important, he will determine whether the program which has been laid out is being followed. If replacements are not being made as scheduled, if the recruitment and development groups are not fulfilling their missions, the manpower planner is in trouble. Either his plan is inadequate, or there is not the necessary support for its implementation.

Preparing to Fill the Job

Employment is a complex business. The flow of paper is overwhelming, and calls for decisions come in a steady stream. These decisions must be made quickly, or candidates are lost to the competition. The process can be expedited to a great extent by the use of forms and form letters; they guarantee consistency in the way the process is conducted. There must be reports which tell the employment manager how things are going and pinpoint problem areas demanding immediate attention.

SYSTEMATIZATION

All these considerations mean that the operation will benefit from the attention of a professional systems man. He can install procedures that can save tremendous amounts of time and money, and insure, too, that candidates won't be lost in midstream—the most common internal failure in employment programs.

Note, however, that the systems man's work will have limitations here that he doesn't normally suffer. Though rigorous procedures are necessary, no impression of a mechanical approach can be allowed to reach the candidate. He must always feel that the attention he is receiving is highly personal and carefully tailored to his needs. This will restrict the freedom of the systems professionals, but the restriction is an absolute "must."

Related to systematization is the need for an employment manual. There are many people with a role in a good employment program, and some of these roles are demanding. There is turnover to worry about, with new management and personnel people continually brought into the problem. And in any multi-unit company there is the need for consistency from one location to the next.

The manual should spell out the procedures and include copies of all forms used in the program. Each person's role should be precisely delineated. Information of a general nature that should go to all candidates should be spelled out.

PRELIMINARY WORK

The people who coordinate employment must have the strength to do more than react when a department demands that a job be filled, and immediately, with a particular type of person. The employment manager's basic working papers are the job description and the set of candidate specifications. If the position is new, no action can be taken until these documents are prepared and endorsed by appropriate managerial levels. If the job is an existing one but the description and specifications are more than a year old, the write-ups have to be audited against the current departmental and total organizational needs.

This preparatory work is frustrating to the department with the employment need but is necessary insurance against a host of hazards otherwise likely to be encountered. These dangers include the possibilities of (a) wasted recruiting effort, when the visiting candidates find the position to be other than they thought it to be; and (b) the hiring of people who won't make the grade because they have been matched against outdated standards.

JOB DESCRIPTION

Many organizations follow sound procedures in describing higher-level jobs but perform casually at the hourly and clerical levels. Construction and use of realistic job descriptions are important at all levels. Aside from serving as a basis for setting pay levels and, in some cases, for negotiating with the unions, they are essential to the employment manager if he is to find people who will succeed on the job.

If the job description deals objectively with five key elements, it will provide the employment people with what they need. The first of these, obviously, is the job title, which deserves more attention than it is often given. When the recruiter goes out in the market, he is communicating to candidates who have definite images of title meanings. "Stenographer" will discourage the girl who wants truly secretarial work; "senior analyst" may have more connotations in a given field than "analyst"; "manager" may evoke quite different reactions than "project leader."

To maximize recruitment efficiency the title should be right on target, neither underselling nor overselling the importance of the position. The recruiter doesn't want to lose the interest of some qualified candidates because the title denotes a job below their level, but neither does he want to waste time with candidates who think there is more in the position than is actually the case.

The second key element in the job description is the outline of "purpose and scope." This is the core of the description, though it need not be lengthy and complicated: the purpose of the position (why it exists) and the scope (the degree of impact the position exerts on the plant, department, or total organization).

Third, the description must include the responsibilities and authorities encompassed in the position. Statements of responsibility include the kind of work that is done and how (generally) it is done. Authority is clarified in two ways: (a) organizationally, telling where the position fits into the structure; and (b) indicating the degree of freedom that will be enjoyed by the incumbent.

The fourth element of a good job description is an outline of the nature and degree of relationships between this position and (a) others in the organization, and (b) parties outside the organization with whom the incumbent will interact significantly. This "puts meat on the bones" for the recruiter; he gets a more familiar feel for the way the employee in the position spends his time.

The final element is a quantitative picture of dimensions. What is the required rate of production? How much dictation is required? What cutting tolerances must be observed? How many people are supervised? How much money is controlled or significantly influenced? How many plants are affected? What production volume is at stake? In this section there is little room for brilliant prose; the employment man wants hard numbers.

The description is next given to the compensation people to get the job priced out.

PERSONAL SPECIFICATIONS

Sound employment planning requires that the recruiter develop a set of specifications, including experience and training, for the person he is seeking.

The employing department plays the most important role here, since it is the department that wants the work done. But the employment man has to feed in other inputs. He may have valid personal observations about the kinds of people who survive and succeed in this organization and in this department. And, as mentioned earlier, he has guidance from manpower planning on longer-range needs. Many of those needs can be met only by bringing in people with new kinds of training and/or experience. There may be known future openings for top-level electricians, for clerical supervisors, for department heads, for scientists with rare specialties. The department head with the position opening has short-term pressures which induce him to give less attention to the longer-range problems—if, indeed, he is even aware of them. It is the employment manager who has to keep this in mind as he studies employment specifications.

Here is where the employment man has to utilize his best interpersonal skills. His larger views of employment needs are likely to complicate the hiring process and thereby slow it down. His problem is to work effectively enough with the employing department that it will go along with him.

Launching the Employment Process

Now the employment man is ready to go to work. If he has organized his job, he has a clear-cut sequence to follow.

INTERNAL SEARCH

The search begins at home. There may be an employee already on the rolls who would want and could qualify for the position.

This is an obvious consideration when the position is at a middle or higher level. However, it should not be overlooked when the job is at the entry level. There may be able people who would like to transfer laterally—or, occasionally, even take a demotion—because they would like to change their field of endeavor. The clerk might like to have a try at sales work; the laboratory technician might want to transfer to quality control; or the research engineer might have a desire to see what he could do in manufacturing. The newcomer to the labor market often takes his first job without benefit of counseling. He needs experience in the world of work to provide him with information on the activities that do—or do not—give him job satisfaction. The progressive personnel department has counseling interviews and keeps records that will bring these employees up for consideration when an appropriate position opens up.

The higher the level, of course, the more important becomes the internal search. The first check should be against the replacement charts prepared by the manpower planner. If this position is on the chart, and if there is a named replacement, this is the obvious place to start.

Organizational practice varies widely in the degree to which records are kept to provide the names of candidates for key positions. Some practices rely entirely on the personnel administrator; at the other extreme there are highly sophisticated, computerized systems. One obvious controlling factor is the size and complexity of the company.

There is one cardinal principle which should be imposed regardless of the size or nature of the enterprise: Systematize the process. There should be an understanding at all management levels that there will be no decision and no communication with any internal candidate until there is clearance through a central body—one that has a minimal vested interest in the outcome. In most cases the obvious party to hold this responsibility is the personnel department. To know employee background is its responsibility; it is integrally involved in employee progress, development, and salary administration; and it qualifies on the detachment criterion.

In any organization there are executives who love to be kingmakers, and there are others who have favored individuals they wish to see advanced. In the absence of the control described, advance commitments will be made that will result in moves not in the best interest of the total organization.

MOVING OUTSIDE

When the position cannot be filled from within, the employment group should be ready to swing smoothly into the external search for the right candidate. The first check is with the files the group already has on hand.

If the employment office is systematized, only minutes will be necessary to find files of any likely candidates. Too, if the employment shop is run as it should be, there will be files if (a) this position is one that is known to be likely to open up, and/or (b) there are openings periodically for the same or similar positions.

Normally, these will not be fully completed files, for this degree of planning ahead is hard to justify. But there will be enough information to indicate whether the case deserves to be pursued further.

If the existing files do pay out, the effort to create an input of candidates does not cease unless the files are really loaded (an unusual situation). Herein lies a principal weakness of certain employment managers. When they find one or two likely candidates, they stop looking for more and follow the ones they have right down to the end. This is foolish optimism in today's labor market. For almost any position in almost any geographic area, the competition for people is strong and constant. The employer has to start with many possibilities, since most of them will wash out for one reason or another.

EXTERNAL SEARCH

The employment manager is now a sales manager. The job he is trying to fill is the product. The employment man has to find the most effective way to bring this position to the attention of the appropriate customers and in a way that will make it seem appealing to them. Too often, he somewhat blindly goes to trade or secretarial schools, or to agencies, or to advertising, or works through professional societies or any one of dozens of other media without first going through the kind of analysis the sales manager must pursue before committing his budget.

The media that the employment manager uses to turn up candidates depend on the nature and level of the position, but more importantly, and quite simply, on where the candidates are to be found. If they exist locally, the local high school, trade school, college, or newspaper might be the most efficacious method of bringing the opening to their attention. If they are clustered in some other community, similar sources in that city might supply the best route to follow. If they are scattered across the country, there are techniques to consider.

The organized employment manager maintains data from which he can evaluate the productivity of his manpower sources. When an ad is placed, the number of returns is recorded, as well as the number of usable returns. He has numbers on the quantity of good résumés received from each of the employment agencies that he uses. He has a historical picture of success and failure at each school the company visits. From all this he has a reasonable fix on the relative efficiency of each source for various types of positions. He regards all these data as significant guideposts to his recruitment planning.

The employment man knows the relative expense of using each source. He has historical dollars-per-hire data on advertising, campus recruiting, and the like. Obviously, these too are taken into account when he decides where to launch his outside search.

ADVERTISING

In the modern labor market the newspapers have page after page of "help wanted" ads. Skill is required if the user of this medium is to get any reader attention.

To repeat an earlier statement: Selecting the appropriate job title deserves careful attention. Users of the classified advertising section, the usual medium for hourly and clerical personnel, must be precise on this point. The job seeker knows the title of the job he wants, and he zooms in on it when he opens the "classified" pages; he is not about to pore through dozens of other columns, hoping to find something in his field.

For professional and managerial positions it is now accepted practice to place a display ad in the business section rather than use the classified. In most newspapers this advertising tends to be limited to the Sunday edition, and this is known to the professional or managerial job seeker.

Many employers underutilize professional journals in their advertising programs. There are few specialized groups now that do not have their own publication. This is an ideal medium in that it zeros in on the target. The advertising rates are also relatively low.

The employer must assume that any candidate has a choice of positions available to him. Employment advertising, then, must be like product advertising: It must appeal to the customer's needs. The employer should identify those elements of his situation that will be attractive to the potential candidate and emphasize them in the advertisement.

There will be different attractive features for different types of positions. The engineer and the scientist, for instance, are usually seeking professional freedom and technical challenge. The hourly worker, normally, has a keen interest in employment security. The graduate in business administration is seeking opportunities to move up the management ladder. The skilled tradesman may be looking for an opportunity to become a group foreman.

A particular employer may have unique advantages that he takes for granted but that might attract the candidate. A particularly attractive location, a lucrative profit-sharing plan, glamorous activities, major growth—any one of these would appeal to certain types of people and, if they are present, they should be exploited.

WORKING WITH AGENCIES

Hiring through employment agencies has grown considerably in the past 20 years. The agency can be a valuable asset if selected and used properly.

One basic problem in the world of employment agencies is the ease with which anyone can get into the business. No capital is required, and licensing requirements are not always as strict as they should be; thus the people in the business have varying degrees of expertise.

The employment manager can take definite action to increase the productivity of agency relationships. First, he should select a definite group he will work with and use only these. Otherwise, particularly in a major metropolitan area, he will spend half his time reading résumés.

The best way to select them is to start with a list of "possibles," based on performance to date, and take the time to visit each. A personal discussion with the agency manager can reveal quite a bit about his method of preparation, the number and quality of candidates he attracts, and his willingness to attune his agency's efforts to the needs of the client. Just looking around his office can give the employer many clues about the caliber of the operation.

The personal visit serves another purpose. If the agency looks like one that should be utilized, this is an opportunity to establish a personal relationship with the key representatives. This can do much to expedite future communication, most of which will be by telephone.

During this face-to-face discussion the employment manager should be as specific as he can be about the company's selection criteria. The hardest job in dealing with any agency is to persuade its people to prescreen the candidates. Their tendency is to send any résumé where there is a chance of client interest. However, the agency that has the proper orientation to client relationships will respect the customer's wishes if they are made known.

When the select group of agencies has been identified, the employer might consider an additional technique for improving communication with them. If there are plans for an extensive employment operation, it will be worthwhile to bring the agency representatives to the plant or office and give them a thorough orientation. This will enrich the interviews they will subsequently have with candidates and should enhance further the quality of their prescreening.

The agencies can help best when they have an up-to-date picture of the employer's personnel needs. The employment manager should send them, periodically, a listing of open positions where he would like agency help. If it is emphasized that these are the *only* jobs where agencies are to be used, the volume of incoming résumés can be reduced.

CAMPUS RECRUITING

When there is a need for personnel with training beyond high school, the employer has the choice of hiring from other companies or going directly to the type of institution that trains such people. (Of course, there is no choice if the position requires that the person have experience beyond his formal training.) Many employers hire as often as they can from the school, and for two reasons. First, it is usually less expensive; concentrated groups of candidates, all actively seeking employment, can be reached at one time. Second, many organizations feel that the odds on their hiring a highly successful person are considerably higher at the school. They reason that the graduate who is successful in his first job is valued by his employer and that the employer therefore takes steps to keep the new employee from becoming interested in looking at other employers. Conversely, many of the people who are interested in changing jobs have been encouraged to do so or, at least, have not been given any message that they have a bright future with their present employer.

One big disadvantage in using the campus source lies in the problem of timing. Normally, negotiations are conducted months before the candidate will be available for work. The employer has to do more look-ahead planning than when he merely responds to position needs as they develop. Another problem evolves from the need to negotiate with all the candidates at the schools almost simultaneously, rather than sequentially, since they normally have a common graduation date. There is no way of knowing how many hires there will be or what the mix will be in terms of qualifications.

Selecting schools to visit. Schools should not be casually chosen for recruiting; each visit is going to require time and money. There should be a reasonable likelihood that each visit will pay out. Every school has its stronger and weaker departments; this should be researched out. The closer the school to the place of business, the higher the likelihood of success in hiring—and of success in retaining. If the company has a significant number of people with advanced training already on board, it should be determined whether there is any pattern of success or failure relative to the school of origin.

Sometimes it is better to avoid the "glamour" schools in favor of those that are less renowned, if the latter look at all likely as a source of suitable people. The big-name schools are deluged with visiting employers, and it is an uphill fight to make an impression on students or faculty. True, these schools also tend to attract a higher cut of students, but at any accredited institution there will be some well-qualified people.

Pretrip communications. Though campus recruitment has many advantages, there are special steps the employer must take if he is to be competitive. It is normal, these days, for the number of visiting companies to be several times the number of graduating students; thus the employer who expects the students to come to him seeking work is in for a big disappointment. There are things that he must do to bring his opportunities to the attention of the candidate.

First priority has to be given to establishing communication lines with the placement office, in the case of the advanced training institution, and with the student counselor at the high school level. A personal visit is the best vehicle for communicating a general picture of the employer's needs and opportunities. This should be done at a time of year—normally, the summer months—when the school is not a hotbed of placement activity. This is particularly critical on the college campus. While students' files are being prepared and when employers are visiting, the placement officer is the busiest person on campus, and he is in no mood for a relaxed discussion with an employer's representative.

The school normally provides several vehicles through which the employer can advertise his situation to the candidate. First, a file folder available to the student is usually set up for each company that visits. The employer can place descriptive information here—annual reports, product brochures, special booklets that might have been prepared by the public relations department, and so on. There should be an inventory list of items that belong in these school folders, and the contents should be checked against the inventory each time the recruiter visits the campus. Items can disappear; they can go out of date; and new items come along all the time.

The second communication vehicle for reaching the student is the bulletin board. Most advanced training institutions will use the employer's poster to announce the impending visit if he provides it. This poster can be made attractive and informative.

The third and most important vehicle is the recruitment brochure. The student whose interest has been aroused—by the file, the poster, word of mouth, or company reputation—usually wants more information specific to job opportunities before he commits himself to an interview. The brochure is the necessary means to give him what he seeks. Separate brochures should be developed for distinctly different occupations. The engineer is looking for much the same information as the stenographer, but there are also areas of interest peculiar to each.

The effective brochure is written specifically for this purpose. (Some employers use some other piece of literature they already have; student reaction to such literature is strongly negative.) Most of the content is specific information on the jobs available. Little attention should be given to company history, the financial statement, or a proud description of company products.

Some post–high school institutions provide another highly valuable vehicle for reaching students in advance of the campus visit. They allow recruiters to study student résumés and write personal letters to candidates who look particularly interesting. In some cases the recruiter has to visit the school to look through the résumés. Other institutions put them in book form and mail them to the employer for a modest fee.

This medium of communication is hard to beat. With a little effort the employer can point up in his letter the particular compatibility that exists between the company and the candidate.

Interviewer training. The candidate is probably talking to dozens of prospective employers, and among them will be many organizations that are represented by highly skilled interviewers. The company that sends out someone who can't do the job well will suffer by comparison, perhaps considerably. The candidate may not learn what he expects to get from the discussion; he may distrust the judgment of someone he feels to be incompetent; and he may feel slighted that the organization didn't care enough to send someone who could do the job better. From the company's viewpoint, a poor interviewer is not likely to get all the information he should acquire if he is to make the right decision on whether to carry negotiations to the next step with the candidate.

Many people never will make good interviewers; they just don't have the basic interpersonal skills to do this job well. But most prospective interviewers can be improved through good training. A two- or three-day training program, most of it devoted to practice interviewing, is a small investment if the employee is to make many interviewing trips.

The number of interviewers should be kept to a minimum. This is an art where nothing helps like practice. If a man goes out only once or twice a year, he will never become highly qualified.

Importance of Follow-Through

One of the principal weaknesses in employment programs is in following through. Again, the employer must keep in mind that there are plenty of jobs in the employment market. The candidate doesn't have to wait indefinitely for a given organization to respond to him.

If unsolicited inquiries are received, courtesy demands that at some point in time there be some answering communication. But if the candidate is of interest, common sense and the realities of the labor market demand that the response be immediate. The answer may only be a request for further information, though if the candidate looks very promising, an immediate invitation to visit may be in order. At any rate, he should have some early contact indicating that the organization is impressed and would like to continue the interaction.

Recruiting at advanced training schools calls for particularly keen attention to follow-through. An organization can build so poor a reputation for itself that the success of its recruiting will be inhibited for years. One of the easier ways to create a negative image is to fail to write to some of the students who were interviewed or to write a month after the visit. Every company has candidates who just drop in, particularly local people seeking hourly or clerical positions. Whether they can all be interviewed is a question of manpower resources in the employment office. Certainly, all can be given an application from the receptionist; they can either be invited to fill it in and leave it or be given written instructions on where to return it. Each of these applications deserves follow-through. One local candidate who is ignored can discourage many of his friends from applying.

Cost of Inefficiency

Recruitment becomes overly expensive when it is run inefficiently. The principal source of inefficiency is poorly directed pursuit of the quarry. If the employment people don't sense at an early stage that they are on the trail of an ideal candidate, they may lose him and have to start another search. On the other hand, if too many poor matches are given a lot of attention, time and money will be wasted and the position will continue to go unfilled.

Employment people must be directed to pay close attention to job specifications. Their own biases can make them enamored of a given candidate because of something in his background that attracts their interest; they may overlook other factors that will eliminate the person at a later point in the process. Conversely, the employment manager may reject some people who meet the specifications but have characteristics that the recruiter objects to personally.

A major expense source—often a result of inefficiency—is generated by fruitless visits from candidates. There may be travel expenses; there certainly is the expense of the time of the employment and/or departmental people who did the interviewing during the visit. The objective employment manager will ask himself a question each time a candidate visits and either (a) is not made an offer or (b) refuses an offer. The question is: "Did this happen because of something that we knew or that was readily available to us before we invited him to visit?" In some cases the answer will be, "Yes, but we decided to take a calculated risk." (If this is the answer too many times, someone should calculate the cost of the risk taking.) If the answer is, "Yes, but we didn't pay enough attention to it," an expensive error has been identified. And if the answer is "No," the cost-oriented employment manager will try to think how the information might be found in subsequent cases before the invitation has been given.

One common error is to ignore the candidate's stated salary requirement. If he is serious about a certain wage or salary goal and the pay for the open position cannot approach it, the time spent on his case is usually wasted. This may not be true, of course, if glorious advancement opportunities are associated with the position. But, too often, the employment man thinks he can use his power of persuasion to overcome a dollar differential. This kind of optimism can be expensive.

Another common source of invitations that shouldn't have been made is inadequate study of job history. A telephone discussion with the candidate can reveal (assuming he is being honest) whether he really has accumulated the kind of experience prerequisite to the position to be filled.

Overselling leads to visits that shouldn't happen. The employment manager is eager to fill his open positions, and it is natural to expect him to play up the more attractive aspects of the job when he is communicating with the candidate. The truth usually comes out during the visit, and another wasted venture is chalked up (and the company has probably lost a friend).

Many wasted visits result from poor scheduling. The causes are partly mechanical: If there are no hotel reservations, if the candidate has to hire a guide to find the plant, or if he has to fight his way through the security system at the gate, he is not going to be in a receptive mood to hear good things about the company. But the schedule itself can make the visit a waste of time. The candidate who doesn't learn what he has to know in order to make a decision will not usually accept an offer.

Structuring Selection Procedure

There is no reason for not designing the way people are selected for jobs with the same care exerted in deciding how to purchase equipment or invest capital. The employment decision is a costly one; if the wrong person is hired, there will be one wasted investment in training and another in the errors he makes—in addition to the recruitment expense. Yet, in many organizations, the process is haphazard. There should be a prescribed process, and there should be carefully defined criteria.

The process involves the collection of all pertinent background data—reference checks, samples of work done (where appropriate), academic records, and (if feasible) evidence of good health. All these data should be objectively analyzed by everyone concerned in the hiring decision. The process should also include the completion of a rating form by each interviewer. It makes him stop and think a bit when he has to record his opinions on a document that will stay on file.

The ideal candidate is seldom seen; so it is impractical to establish a rigid set of qualifications that the prospective employee must meet. But some structuring is possible.

The starting point is the set of specifications which was the basis for the employment manager's search activity. From this, through discussion with the hiring department, three types of qualifications should be established. First, there are the "must" criteria. If a candidate doesn't meet them all, he is an automatic washout. Second are the "highly desirable" criteria. Given a group of candidates who pass the "must" level, this second set enables an objective comparison of their relative merits, one with another. The third set, "desirable pluses," includes attributes that are not really expected but will enhance the candidate's present or future value if he has one or more of them. This category of criteria is necessary for two reasons. First, when a candidate comes along who has some desirable pluses, some managers can be carried away to the point where they make this the prime basis for a favorable decision. It should be clearly established that these criteria do not come into the picture until all the "musts" and probably some of the "highly desirables" are met. The second use for this category is in helping the decision when there are "ties" on the first two sets of criteria.

TESTING

There are hundreds, if not thousands, of tests that an employer can purchase to use as an assist to employee selection. Employers are fond of using them because it relieves them of some of the decision-making responsibility. The easiest ground rule to follow here is *don't*, without advice from a competent industrial psychologist. The claim that a test measures intelligence, supervisory ability, adaptability, or any one of dozens of other traits is absolutely no indication that it does so. The trained and experienced industrial psychologist knows which tests have worked well elsewhere; he knows how to evaluate the test publisher's claims of what the test will do; and he knows how to find out, factually, whether the test will be of value for this particular organization with its particular set of employment needs.

There is one area where the employer can develop his own testing program without too many qualms: the use of skill tests. These are tests that measure ability to type, take dictation, spell correctly, and the like. Even here, some tests are good but others leave a great deal to be desired, and the use of professional consultation is recommended.

Structuring the Candidate's Visit

The nature of the position to be filled obviously governs the amount of time and the level of people who spend time with the visiting candidate; procedures will be quite different for a laborer and for a prospective department head. But, in any case, the goals are common: first, to learn whether he meets specifications and therefore should be considered for an offer; second, to give him the information he needs so that he can make a rational decision if he is made an offer; third, in the event that he looks like a good candidate, to sell him on the advantages of employment with the organization. Each of these goals merits some examination.

EVALUATION

The principal responsibility for evaluation against job specifications should reside with the hiring department, not with the employment manager. The department people have to feel fully accountable for the decision to offer or not to offer, and they will not feel accountable if they let the staff people do the evaluation for them. (This creates a problem, however, in that a given manager may be hiring only infrequently, with the result that he will not acquire much practice in the art. His role therefore has to be simplified as much as possible, and he has to be given personal help by the employment manager.)

The hiring manager should have been involved (and deeply) in the development of the "musts," "highly desirables," and "desirable pluses." He must be reminded of them and advised that his role is to find out how the candidate measures up against each. He should be required to complete a rating form on the candidate. This device need not be highly complicated; it need merely call for a go or no-go on the "musts" and ask for the evaluator's overall conclusion on whether or not an offer should be made. This latter requirement is essential; the hiring manager should not be able to pass the buck to the employment manager.

This does not imply that the employment manager has no role in selection. His asset lies in his seeing most or all candidates. He therefore has bench marks which permit comparisons that the hiring department head will find it more difficult to achieve.

The employment manager has another key role in the selection process. A departmental manager who is hard pressed to fill some jobs may give the candidate an affirmative vote a little too quickly. The employment man can help maintain the necessary objectivity.

Related to the need for balance is the department man's inclination to worry more about today's needs than about the company's future manpower problems. Manpower planning has given the employment man a fix on the kinds of people that should be hired now to provide potential material for needs that lie down the road. It is a distinct responsibility of employment to audit progress toward these goals. If people are being hired who can satisfy today's needs but leave tomorrow's wanting, it is up to the employment manager to initiate appropriate corrective action.

COMMUNICATING INFORMATION

The candidate obviously has to learn such basics as hours of work, vacation policy, and benefit plan protection; these can be most efficiently communicated by preparing readable booklets on these and related subjects. A lot of interviewing time is saved, there is assurance that the story is being told consistently, and the employment man is saved a chore that becomes unbearably boring after extensive repetition.

There are less obvious communication needs which must be considered. If the position entails geographic relocation, the candidate will have a host of questions; the visit must include a planned area tour. Married men won't like to make a decision until their wives have visited and had their questions satisfactorily answered. Some organizations use employees' wives for this purpose. They are trained to do the job and are paid for it. Another convenience is a booklet describing the community, its services, school facilities, and surroundings.

The most important communication obviously concerns the job and opportunities for the future. This has to come from the employing department, and it has to be factual. The interviewer should work directly from the job description.

This discussion, however, is often not enough to satisfy the candidate's needs. He doesn't necessarily distrust the manager who is talking to him, but he usually wants a closer feel of the position than the boss can give him. It is good practice, therefore, to have the candidate spend considerable time with people who would be his coworkers. They are in the best position to tell him what it is really like in the company.

SELLING THE JOB

If the visitor looks promising, there should be a positive effort to make him want to join the organization. Everyone involved in recruitment should be well drilled on the features that make this organization an attractive place to work; people who have been in the company for some time may take things for granted that would be pleasantly surprising to the candidate. These pluses should be spelled out in the employment manual. They may include unusual benefit plans, geographic advantages, a history of rapid promotional advancement, or exciting corporate plans for growth and diversification.

One of the employment manager's responsibilities is to find out which pluses will have the most effect on a given candidate. (Does he have certain strong hobby interests? Is he keenly interested in getting into a particular type of work? Is promotional advancement most important to him?) Then the selling job can zero in on a known target.

Follow-Through After the Candidate's Visit

Again, the employment system should guarantee that appropriate action is taken after the visit. Common courtesy demands an early indication of the organization's reaction. If an offer is to be extended, speed becomes of paramount importance. A quick offer tells the man that the organization really wants him and that he therefore could have a bright future there.

Establishment of the offer amount has to be under the firm control of the employment manager. He knows the union contract and the established rates for hourly and clerical positions. He is closest to competitive salary data for higher-level jobs, and is the one responsible for assuring the proper relationship among all the offers which are extended. This points up the need for the employment and salary administration departments to work closely together. The latter group has to keep measuring the pulse of competitive salaries and wages and keep the employment people informed. The compensation people should also keep a check on the offers being extended by employment to be sure that internal problems are not being created. By bringing in people either at too high or too low pay the employment manager can build future headaches for the compensation administrator.

POSTVISIT COMMUNICATIONS

As soon as the decision is made to extend an offer, word should go to the candidate immediately, either by telephone or by telegram. It should be followed by a letter so that there will be no chance of misunderstanding the conditions of employment. If there are contingent considerations, such as the need for a medical examination, they should be spelled out in the letter. These "business" communications should be handled by the employment people, since it is imperative that there be across-the-board consistency in the way offers are extended.

At the same time the employing department should communicate with the candidate. Its job is to take a highly personal approach, to give the impression that there will be friends waiting to work with him if he accepts the offer.

If no word is received from the candidate in a week or so, the employment man should call the candidate. Besides reinforcing the impression that the company really cares, this procedure can be used to find out if there is some specific hang-up. Questions often come to mind after the visit, and the candidate may hesitate to raise them on his own initiative.

POSTDECISION ACTION

If the candidate accepts, he should not be forgotten. At this point the hiring department should take on the communication burden to make his transition as easy as possible. If geographic relocation is necessary, there is again need to fall back on an existing system. The degree of help and subsidy by the company should be precisely defined and communicated to the candidate. There should already be established arrangements with moving companies so that the transition can go smoothly.

If the candidate refuses the offer, the employment manager must do his best to find out why, since this is a critical element in the continuing audit of his program. A telephone call is appropriate if the two people came to know each other fairly well. The use of a questionnaire is also recommended, since it allows the accumulation of quantitative data that may be helpful to the employment manager in selling the organization on the need for significant changes in the employment program.

Follow-up After Hire

The employment job is not finished when the new hire comes on board. Orientation may or may not be the direct responsibility of the employment manager, but he should make sure that it is done.

The employment manager should be vitally concerned with the new hire's progress in his early months. If the department is not providing proper leadership, there is danger that the employee will leave, and the expensive employment process will have to be repeated. The new hire's department head and/or someone from the personnel department should "touch base" periodically with him. Is he having problems in relocation? Is the job as it was described to him? Is he being introduced to other people in the company who influence his job performance? Is he being given instruction and training? Above all, is he being treated like a human being? In most companies there is a probationary period, and a formal check on performance should be conducted before the end of this period. This is critically important, of course, when union contract provisions are involved.

This is another area for systematization. Periodically, during the early months, someone should fill in a form indicating that these questions have been asked and recording the answers.

The employment manager should be keenly interested if the new hire proves to be inadequate. This means that an error was made somewhere along the line. He should find out what it was, and what can be done to prevent repetition.—*P. W. Maloney*

Hiring the Underemployed

Business and industry are in the process of revolutionizing personnel policies and practices with regard to the underemployed, particularly in the minority groups. This thrust has accelerated and changed considerably since the early emphasis on integration; it more clearly recognizes the fact that certain minority groups (national or racial, or both) must be given true economic, social, and political equality. In the employment area equality of treatment is a national policy supported by law at Federal and local levels.

Of particular benefit to employers, of course, are increased human resources for a burgeoning economy, along with improved purchasing power in large segments of the population previously disfranchised.

In keeping with the sweeping social changes affecting the underemployed minorities in American culture—however belated and slow those changes may be—similar changes must take place in the hiring, training, and placement practices in business and industry. There are millions of Americans who have been relegated traditionally to the lowest menial employment, who have been denied access to skills training and promotion to skilled jobs, and who are at the lowest wage levels. These people have never seen any attainable results of hard work or initiative for themselves. The job of business and industry is to seek them out, then train and reward them in the way that their more fortunate fellow Americans have experienced. The underemployed must be brought to the full realization that it is possible to earn a living wage, to do dignified work which is personally rewarding, and to progress in the world of work in status, skills, and earnings.

Many firms have changed their hiring policy and practices in this regard and include in their employment advertisements an "equal opportunity" line. Unfortunately, changing a policy and an ad does not change the behavior of the people who actually do the hiring, placement, training, and upgrading of employees. Also, management has not really conveyed its message to the underemployed and minority groups, nor has it been able to reach out actively into the community to recruit and convince the people. When underemployed people do have the courage to apply for jobs and are hired, they may encounter the same old discriminatory practices in job assignments, skills training, and advancement.

Of course, there are not sufficient numbers of underemployed people trained and job-ready to take over the skilled, the administrative, the managerial, the technical job openings which exist today. Their heritage has been menial jobs, social service jobs (serving other underemployed people), fourth-rate education, and a long history of economic and cultural suppression. The reward system of business and industry has held no rewards for them. Therein lie the dilemma and the problem for management.

BASIC PROBLEM AREAS

The basic areas in the problem are three: recruitment, training, and the development of proper work habits in the hard-to-employ groups. The last-named of these three is related to motivation.

Recruitment. To develop unorthodox and aggressive methods for recruiting the underemployed is absolutely necessary. Some firms have sent "job-mobiles" into the inner cities or set up job centers to locate applicants. But staffing the job-mobile or job center requires caution because the typical educated, middle-class, establishment interviewer/recruiter will not be believable. The company representative must be able to relate to his prospects, must be able to "talk their language" (literally and figuratively), and must be able to convince people that *this employer means what he says.* The employer must remember that the hard-to-employ individual has had no favorable experience with business and industry; thus his expectations of business cannot be favorable. He expects the "put-on," and it requires an unusual approach to recruiting to overcome his natural suspicions.

Many other matters are to be considered. It is wise to shorten application forms to the briefest possible format; where applicants still have difficulty with the form, it is important to provide help in a warm, sympathetic manner. In many areas signs, leaflets, and other matter must be multilingual. The employer may have to purchase clothing for some candidates, and arrange car pools (or establish special bus lines, since private transportation is not readily available to the poor). The skilled recruiter will realize that the underemployed often have no knowledge at all of benefits, deductions, savings plans, or other job-related matters customarily discussed with job candidates. This is another reason why he must "talk their language."

Disadvantages of testing. Although the abuses of selection testing have been well known for many years, nowhere are they more evident than in dealing with the underemployed. Nearly all selection tests on the market discriminate against the underemployed. Coming from a deprived background, processed by an irrelevant educational system, and being without the advantage of training and experience in skills of any kind, the hard-to-employ and the underemployed have characteristics that cannot be measured against norms developed around more fortunate populations. This has been demonstrated over and over again. (It has also been demonstrated that people from a middle-class background and environment and possessing reasonably good education and training cannot pass a test which is based on the current events, language, and values of the inner-city unemployables.) There is really no "culture-free" or "culture-fair" test available for effective use by employers; however, work is now being done along these lines.

The employment test is also a threat. The underemployed individual has been denied access to employment, many times on the basis of one test or another. He therefore interprets "test" as something devised to keep him out.

A much better preparation for testing would be a careful explanation that the tests are *not* to screen him out but to screen him *in*. Then the tests are used to try to discover potential, and training can be aimed at developing that potential. Employers would also be well advised to become familiar with statutory requirements for both the application forms and the testing. Any test which has the effect, directly or indirectly, of depriving an individual of employment on the basis of race or nationality can have most serious repercussions.

Special training programs. Most companies engaged in the problem of the underemployed have had to set up special training programs. Recent studies indicate that the extra expense of such special training is repaid in productivity. Some firms have set up basic education programs for employees who are at low levels in reading, writing, and arithmetic skills, and English classes for minority groups who do not speak English. Not only do such skills pay off in job performance; the resulting satisfaction and the gain in self-confidence and self-esteem do much toward solving the fundamental problem of the disfranchised American.

Fostering motivation. Motivation and work habits have been frustrating problems for employers. Remembering that in his past experience the underemployed person could not advance, no matter how hard and well he worked, it is not difficult to see that merely having a decent job is not going to cause him to work well. The underemployed are characteristically absent and tardy. It never really mattered to an employer if they did not appear to sweep the floor; there was always another unemployable waiting for a little menial work. Through careful counseling and training the newly employed individual must be taught that he *is* important, that he *is* doing meaningful work, and that others are counting on him as a team participant with full peer status. He must be convinced that there are rewards in the offing for *him* in the work situation (despite the fact that the rewards were never before available) if he does well. Someone must take an interest in him as a person.

The underemployed individual has very little self-esteem and virtually no self-confidence. Through experiences guided by an understanding supervisor, and with follow-up counseling by people who have much practice in such cases to help him evaluate these experiences, management must extend itself to build that self-confidence until the individual, like a baby taking his first step, is ready to walk by himself. Telling him isn't enough; he must live it and believe it.

Because of the importance of the supervisor's role, management must provide thorough orientation for supervisors as well as some carefully planned and executed training in the sensitivities required in dealing with the underemployed. The most serious deterrent to the effective training and upgrading of previously underemployed people is a negative attitude on the part of supervisors. These attitudes can (and must) be overcome by seriously thought-out and applied training techniques.

Some firms have hired a specialist to deal with minority group employees, making that specialist the company's "expert" in recruitment, placement, and training. This practice does not guarantee success, since the important point is not whether the specialist is black, Puerto Rican, Mexican, or of other race or nationality—but whether the specialist can really relate to his constituents and communicate with them. The best solution is to select someone who can relate, and train him in the techniques of personnel management.

Attention must be given to longer-service employees to prepare them for an influx of people who are strange to them. With careful work these employees can be brought to understand their responsibility for treating the newcomer as they would treat anyone else and for making the newcomer welcome in his job and in the work group.

In the inner city it is commonplace for a person, however young, to have a police record; in fact, some are not considered "men" until they've been "busted." The fact that a job applicant has a police record does not mean that, if he is hired, he will steal from the company. The manager must expect that the underemployed newcomer has been fired at least once, and probably many times over. That has been his life story, but no one ever took an interest in his success, and the supervisor who does will develop a loyal and productive employee. Personnel executives look on reference checks as their bulwark against everything from pilferage to arson, but reference checks are obviously unfair to the so-called unemployables. Much judgment is required in applying standards commonly used in personnel decisions.

COMPANY ATTITUDE

Occurrences that are apparently insignificant often play an important part in the minority applicant's feeling about the company and, after he is hired, in his performance on the job. If, for example, he is "welcomed" with a lack of courtesy, this may suggest to him—however incorrectly—that he can expect little consideration in his future relations with long-time employees. The least measure of any company's goodwill is to see that all applicants—unskilled, skilled, and professional—are given the same courteous treatment.

In short, industry can profitably employ disadvantaged or minority group personnel, but success in the endeavor will require all-out effort on the part of individual companies and their long-time employees.—*R. A. Young*

DEVELOPMENT AND TRAINING

Development and training are important management tools for changing and directing job behavior toward specified organization goals. They may concentrate on improving present performance or preparing individuals for the future, depending on management's priorities of the moment.

Development and training programs in the United States come in assorted sizes, shapes, and packages. The mails are full of brochures and announcements promising cure-alls for everything, from emotional hang-ups to slumping sales. Managers of development and training put on in their own organizations, every year, many classroom programs of a similar "snake oil" type and content.

Little or no evidence exists that such programs, falling as they do outside the stream of the day-to-day life of the organization, have been effective in changing or directing an individual's behavior on the job. This fact, however, has not dampened one whit either the proliferation of the programs or the belief of management that "other people" can be trained and developed in this way. This does not mean that courses, seminars, and learning projects do not have a part to play but rather that (1) they are secondary to the work climate and work process as development and training factors, and (2) they have no impact on individual behavior unless what is taught relates directly to real life on the job.

Everyone has seen instances where an individual will role-play, in a classroom situation, a disciplinary interview observing all the principles of good practice. A short time later this same individual will attack and criticize one of his subordinates at the workplace in the presence of the whole department. An attempt to explain this about-face can lead only to the observation that intellectual understanding and even attitudinal change do not result in behavior change.

One more point of background information is vitally important to recognize. The major part of what is being done in development and training today is directly related to what is being done in the educational system of our schools and colleges. What is more natural than to assume that the method that has been successful in teaching history, mathematics, and science is the method that will be successful in teaching people how to do their jobs the right way—from operating a punch press to managing the work of others? Yet, obviously, the mere acquiring of knowledge does not guarantee its use in the context of the job and work environment.

Basic Concepts

The concepts basic to management's development and training efforts include the following: (1) The objectives of development and training must tie directly into the organization objectives of profit, sales growth, and customer service. (2) The door to behavior change is locked from within. (3) Most of what an individual learns in the work situation—about 95 percent—is learned in a job environment of superior-subordinate relationship. (4) A body of principles of learning and teaching has been validated as effective in the development and training process. (5) Criteria for measuring the success of development and training efforts must relate directly to the achievement of organization objectives.

DETERMINING NEEDS

Development and training efforts must center on problems and obstacles in achieving the organization objectives of profit, sales growth, and customer service. Implicit in this approach is the assumption that the individual charged with the responsibility for development and training is intimately acquainted with the problems in organizational effectiveness and individual performance—problems which may run the gamut from high employee turnover to lagging productivity rates and from excessive interdivisional conflict to inability to meet the executive manpower demands of an expanding operation.

Each problem requires a detailed analysis to determine its causes. High employee turnover, for example, might be found concentrated in new hires leaving the job within the first three days of employment. Further investigation might reveal that these "walk-offs" were caused by the individuals' feelings of being lost in a big, impersonal organization and by anxiety about their supervisor and their own ability to master a new job. Development and training efforts then should focus on developing in the supervisor the skills and techniques necessary to help new employees (1) to adjust to the work situation, (2) to reduce their anxieties, and (3) to become productive quickly.

The manager of development and training has a number of sources of information about the needs of individuals in the organization and the needs of the organization itself.

Performance evaluation. Individual performance evaluations are among the richest resources for determining needs. They should focus on measurable results of behavior on the job rather than the degree of presence or absence of certain character traits. An evaluation that pinpoints production or sales standards not met, costs that exceeded budget, and decisions not made is far more meaningful than one that rates vitality, decisiveness, and emotional control. It is possible to translate the trait evaluation, however, to a results evaluation by analyzing the way the presence or lack of the specific trait manifests itself in behavior on the job. A low rating in decisiveness may, under this type of analysis, confirm itself in failure to set proper priorities. Development and training can do something to help an individual in setting priorities, whereas to make him more decisive may be a completely baffling assignment.

Examining workflow. A second important source of information in determining development and training needs comes from an examination of the workflow. Bottlenecks are signaled by high rejection rates, excessive scrap, large amounts of machine downtime, an exceptional number of overtime hours, failure to meet shipping deadlines, and the like. Each of the "red flag" indicators must be researched to determine causes which may in turn lend themselves to correction via the development and training route. Machine downtime, for example, may be caused by lack of skilled mechanics—a problem which may best be overcome by the institution of a special training program to develop machine operators as mechanics.

Identifying barriers. Finding and identifying the barriers to organizational effectiveness provide another profitable source of information in establishing needs; it may come about as a result of personal participation in management problem-solving meetings or as a result of direct feedback from this type of meeting. An additional method of identifying barriers is to locate the conflict centers—especially conflicts that cross divisional lines. In any number of instances, the work to be done in an organization forces individuals and groups who report up different organization lines to work together as a team. This teamwork requirement, furthermore, may exist in the face of conflicting goals and reward systems; for example, one group may have sales growth as its objective and be rewarded for it, while the other may be striving to maintain a standardized, long-run production line output. Analysis of the cause of the barriers will lead to a determination of whether the cure is one that lends itself to a development and training approach.

Exit interview patterns. Exit interviews are a rich area for determining development and training needs. These interviews, which are designed to discover causes of turnover, may take many forms, but the following pattern of questions has been found to be effective: How did you happen to join our organization? What were your expectations on joining us? What assignments have you had? What training have you received? What increased responsibility or promotions have been yours? When did you feel particularly good about your job? Why did you feel this way? When did you start to feel particularly bad about your job? What happened to cause this? At what point did you first think about leaving our organization? What happened that made you want to quit? What could we have done differently?

The results of these interviews must be recorded and analyzed. At least one organization has received permission from its employees to tape the interviews and has found play-back to management to be an effective way to present the need for change.

One may find—for example—that a continuous theme runs through the interviews: The supervisor makes all the decisions on the job, covering what is to be done, how it is to be done, and whether it is done well, thereby leaving the employee no way to meet his own needs for independent action, creativity, growth, and participation in decisions which affect his operation. Development and training would focus on helping the supervisor restructure the job to build in the elements required to keep employees motivated for continued performance.

MOTIVATION IN BEHAVIOR CHANGE

Volumes have been written on human motivation, but the work of Dr. Abraham Maslow of Brandeis University and Frederick Herzberg of Western Reserve University perhaps best represents much of today's thinking on the subject. Maslow indicates that man is motivated by his own needs as he sees them; he has classified these needs into the following levels of importance:

Level 5: Self-fulfillment needs. The need to realize one's own potentialities, to experience continued self-development, to be creative.

Level 4: Ego needs. (a) The need for self-confidence, for independence, for achievement, for knowledge; and (b) need for status, for recognition, for appreciation, for respect of one's fellows.

Level 3: Social needs. The need for belonging, for association, for acceptance, for giving and receiving friendship and love.

Level 2: Safety needs. The need for protection against danger, threat, deprivation.

Level 1: Physiological needs. The need for food, rest, exercise, shelter.

Two points are important to recognize: (1) Once a need is satisfied, it is no longer a motivator of the individual's behavior; and (2) thwarting a need at any level tends to make that level pre-eminent. There is little sense, therefore, in designing a program to allow the individual to be creative if the company is undergoing a layoff caused by falling sales. People will be concerned with their security, not their growth.

Development and training efforts, consequently, must recognize the "what's in it for me to change my behavior" syndrome. Unless the individual can see clearly how his changed behavior will result in satisfying a personal need, he is not likely to strive to change. He may in fact drag his feet, resist stubbornly, or even sabotage the change effort.

Herzberg has developed the hypothesis that much of what management is doing today in programs to meet people's needs falls in the category of *satisfiers* rather than *motivators;* that is, things that keep employees from being dissatisfied rather than stimulating them to greater productivity and creativity. Many millions of dollars have been poured into improving the environment of jobs; into working conditions, benefit programs, security, status, supervision—the areas Herzberg refers to as making up the hygiene of the job. While these areas of course are vital in the total picture, they are not the ones that have borne fruit in terms of employee motivation.

Motivators are limited to providing in the work itself, through structured content, the opportunity for assumption of responsibility, for achievement, for individual recognition of achievement, and for individual growth and advancement. A number of large companies have tested the Herzberg hypothesis and have amassed hard data to prove its validity. Robert N. Ford, in his book *Motivation Through the Work Itself* (American Management Association, 1969), has described his company's experience in the job enrichment process.

The basic principles of this approach, according to Fred K. Foulkes of Harvard Graduate School of Business Administration and author of *Creating More Meaningful Work* (American Management Association, 1969), include the following:

1. A specific piece of work, a complete module for which the individual can be responsible, must be defined.

2. The new authority is to be given only as the individual demonstrates competence and willingness to assume it.

3. Feedback to the individual on performance results must be provided.

4. Control and inspection of work by others must be replaced with accountability by the individual for his own quantity and quality of performance.

One quick way for the manager to gain insight into this approach is to think back to a job assignment where he feels he grew most and enjoyed it most. Recalling the characteristics of that assignment and of his boss, he thinks that he liked the assignment because he was given responsibility, freedom, trust, a whole job with feedback on results. The boss just told him what was wanted and then allowed him on his own to "run the show" and make mistakes. He managed the work; the boss supported him.

LEARNING ON THE JOB

Telling people to change their behavior—even telling them how to change it—has not been at all effective. Executives, for example, could be told from now until the year 2000 about the effective ways to handle new people on the job, and the telling would not bring about a single change in the way they handle new people. Group efforts that may result in some attitudinal change on the part of individual participants, moreover, have not been too effective in getting a concomitant behavior change.

The conditions for change and growth lie in three interrelated factors: the nature of the manager-subordinate relationship, the structure of the job, and the tie-in of the reward system. Using the problem of how to get subordinates to make "good" decisions as an example, a manager has to (1) structure into the subordinate's job the need to make decisions; (2) specify both what are "good" decisions and how he wants them made; (3) make decisions that way himself; (4) discuss with his subordinates their ideas and plans on how they will do it; (5) help them do it; and (6) reward them when they have done it well.

Wallace Wohlking, of New York State School of Industrial and Labor Relations, Cornell University, notes that a major reason why development and training efforts have tended to focus on classroom programs to gain understanding and change attitudes rather than on structuring jobs and establishing management style to change behavior is that the individuals charged with the responsibility for development and training lack the power in the organization to structure jobs and set management style. In the face of this lack, they have to hope that understanding and attitudinal change will produce behavior change— a hope that has not been validated by experience.

Manager-subordinate relationship. The nature of the manager-subordinate relationship is one of the most important factors in the opportunity for growth of the subordinate. It takes many forms and is based on many factors; among the major factors are the manager's assumptions about the nature of man.

Douglas McGregor (*The Human Side of Enterprise,* McGraw-Hill Book Co., Inc., 1960) has outlined one way of classifying these assumptions in a description of his Theory X and Theory Y concepts as follows:

Theory X	*Theory Y*
People by nature:	People by nature:
1. Lack integrity.	1. Have integrity.
2. Are fundamentally lazy and desire to work as little as possible.	2. Work hard toward objectives to which they are committed.
3. Avoid responsibility.	3. Assume responsibility within these commitments.
4. Are not interested in achievement.	4. Desire to achieve.
5. Are incapable of directing their own behavior.	5. Are capable of directing their own behavior.
6. Are indifferent to organizational needs.	6. Want their organization to succeed.
7. Prefer to be directed by others.	7. Are not passive and submissive.
8. Avoid making decisions whenever possible.	8. Will make decisions within their commitments.
9. Are not very bright.	9. Are not stupid.

It is obvious that the manager who believes his subordinates conform to the Theory X pattern will reflect this conviction both in the way he manages them and in his relationship with them. He will tend to maintain tight personal control; he will not delegate; he will keep all information to himself; he will double-check on work assignments and subordinate behavior; and he will drive, push, and shove people toward the production goals he has established. Individuals managed in this way will in fact reflect their manager's perception of them by behaving as though they were indeed dishonest, lazy, indifferent, disinterested, and stupid. Development and training efforts in such a work climate will be extremely limited and certainly ineffective. A program designed (for example) to help subordinates make "good" decisions will be no more than an intellectual exercise, inasmuch as the manager has reserved all decision making to himself.

Although probably no manager is at either extreme—that is, consistently acts in accordance with Theory X or Theory Y—the opportunity for meaningful development and training efforts is greater where the manager's assumptions about his subordinates are closer to those in the Theory Y category. Many things can be done in a manager-subordinate climate that reinforces by action the effort to help people grow and develop.

Development and training efforts therefore must be tied in to organization objectives; based on the principles of individual motivation; and structured to be growth experiences—all under the guidance of an individual who not only has an effective management style but is a good teacher or coach as well.

Structuring jobs for individual growth. In a Theory Y climate of manager-subordinate relationships, structuring jobs for individual growth has proved effective. This means that built into the job itself is a series of experiences designed to foster individual development for improved performance and future increased responsibility.

Personnel researchers at one large company talk about a concept of meaningful work. If a job is to qualify as meaningful work, in their opinion, it must contain the three elements of planning, doing, and evaluating. Many jobs in industry today have been restricted to the "doing" element and do not qualify as meaningful work under this concept. Consider, for example, what would be involved in the process of making furniture at home if a man decides to do it as a hobby. He would plan the furniture, make it, evaluate it, and feed back changes into his plan as a result of his evaluation. If, however, someone else did the planning and evaluating, leaving him with just the doing, he would soon lose interest in the work as a form of fun and recreation.

Other organizations independently pursuing this approach have come up with elements of the job-structuring process that are surprisingly similar although given different titles. Foulkes (*Meaningful Work*) lists the elements cited by three companies.

| Company 1 | Company 2 | Company 3 |
Job Enrichment	Job Redesign	New Job Design
A module of work	Opportunity for	Change as a required
New authority	autonomous behavior	part of the job
Individual feedback	Useful information flow	Job identified with
Recognition	Reasonably demanding	end product
Opportunity for growth	work	Opportunity to act
	A whole task	and decide
	Respectable work	Opportunity for inter-
	Nonrestrictive conditions	action with other
	Desirable future and	people
	learning	Freedom of movement
	Absence of high stress	Opportunity to learn
		something new
		Balance between the
		mental and the
		physical
		Attractive environment

As an example of the application of the concept of structuring a job, consider the situation of a retail store that is showing a steady erosion in the profit picture. An analysis of causes pinpoints one major area as the upward spiral of sales staff wages without attendant increases in individual productivity. It is decided to focus a development and training effort on helping the individual sales clerk to sell more merchandise to more customers. Recognizing the motivational requirements for an effective program, the training and development director might take the following two approaches concurrently.

1. Work with the sales managers to enrich the sales person's job by building the motivators into the work. Does the sales person do the complete job with the customer—identify needs, relate merchandise benefits to these needs, overcome objections, and close the sale—rather than merely ring up the sale on the cash register? How much inspection of the work is done by others? What can the sales person authorize on her own—personal checks, employee discounts, customer returns and exchanges, holding of merchandise for future delivery? How much freedom does she have in her schedule? For example, if she has been working with a customer for 15 minutes and her scheduled lunch hour arrives, must she go to lunch, or may she stay until the sale is closed? What feedback does she get directly (not through the supervisor) of the results of her performance—quality and quantity? The answers to these questions will suggest ways to build into the job the opportunity for responsibility, achievement, recognition, and individual growth.

2. Involve the sales staff in a true problem-solving discussion—one where the leader has delegated responsibility for developing and implementing solutions—to identify the obstacles to sales growth. After the obstacles have been identified, the staff develops the ways to overcome them. Experience with this approach indicates that the recommended solutions will fall into one of two situation categories: (a) those where management must take action—for example, allow

employees to inspect their own work, accept customers' checks, get their own feedback on performance; (*b*) those where the sales staff must take the action—for example, learn more about the merchandise, learn additional selling techniques, and keep their own stock areas neat.

It is vital to recognize that, to preserve the integrity of this approach, a commitment must be made to accept the solutions recommended for the (*a*) category as well as those recommended for the (*b*) category.

In addition to making sure that a job contains the elements of planning, doing, and evaluating, there are a number of other ways to enrich the job experience for growth. Much of what is done, of course, has to be within the framework of individual needs as pinpointed by performance evaluation, but the following are some general actions that have been successful.

1. An individual is given, in addition to his regular responsibilities, a small piece of the operation to manage on his own; that is, the manager theoretically steps up one level to let the subordinate act in his place for this particular piece of the operation.

2. The individual is scheduled to attend and actively participate (even by making a presentation) in the decision-making, problem-solving, and information-giving meetings of his division.

3. Special projects of an analytic or research nature concerning department, division, and organization problems are assigned to be carried on in addition to the individual's regular responsibilities.

4. The individual is designated as a member of a community and organization joint project.

5. The individual is assigned to write a report on some phase of his area's accomplishments over the year.

Tying the reward system to performance. An organization's reward system consists of more than monetary increases: Promotions, titles, status symbols, participation in key group activities, recognition, criticism—all play an important role in the individual's perception of how he is being recognized for his efforts and where he stands in the organization.

The reward system, by whatever means it accomplishes its purpose, must be tied directly to accomplishment in performance and results. The subordinate who changes his behavior in accordance with his manager's direction and achieves the expected results must be rewarded for so doing. If, on the other hand, rewards are given to the subordinate who does not change his behavior or achieve the expected results, the development and training efforts are negated.

PRINCIPLES OF LEARNING AND TEACHING

If the manager-subordinate relationship is viewed as a teacher-learner relationship, the importance of all managers' gaining understanding of how people learn and acquiring skill in helping them learn becomes apparent. Much work was done in this area in the 1930's, culminating in the Job Instruction Training Program of World War II. The procedures entitled "The Four Steps of Instruction" and "Breaking a Job Down into Teachable Content" formed the basis of this program and are well known in the industrial training field.

Professor Lynn A. Emerson, in *Educational Principles and Training Manuals* (University of the State of New York, Department of Education, 1952), has summarized much of the basic body of knowledge on the learning-teaching process. Some of his more important points are as follows:

1. Performance on the job requires various kinds of learning: (*a*) *knowledge* (the information an individual has acquired that can be utilized in reacting to the needs of various situations); (*b*) *understanding* (the comprehension of the meaning of things and the ability to interpret things that occur and to see relationships between similar and dissimilar events); (*c*) *skill* (the degree of expertness in the use and application of knowledge and understanding); and (*d*) *attitudes* (feelings for or against something, based on the personal interpretation of one's own experiences as well as those of others).

2. Knowledge, understanding, skill, and attitudes, though learned in different ways, are usually interrelated in performance. Playing golf, for example, requires knowledge of rules and local regulations, distances, layout, and playing conditions; understanding of the relationship between the lie of the ball, selection of the club, and the execution of the stroke; skill in executing the stroke; and an attitude of wanting to improve both execution and results.

3. An effective learning-teaching process will be based on the principles illustrated in the paragraphs that follow.

People learn to do by doing. For example, one learns to operate a punch press by operating a punch press; to manage people by managing people; to lead a problem-solving conference by leading problem-solving conferences. This should be a guided experience, with the manager-teacher pointing out "the tricks of the trade," the conditions that will exist when the job is done well, and the possible pitfalls to guard against. Learning by doing, incidentally, does not include putting one's hand between the plates of a 200-ton press in order to learn the dangers of operating this press.

People get their new impressions through the senses (sight, hearing, touch, and so on). Many manager-teachers, unfortunately, regard this as the one and only principle in the learning-teaching process; they consider the employee's mind as an empty vessel into which pearls of wisdom may be poured through the two available holes in the head—the ears.

People learn when they are ready to learn. Think of all the children who have been locked in their rooms with their homework assignments and have still gone to school unprepared the next day. A relationship between learning and satisfying a need must be realized.

People tie their new learning to what they already know. In a class of 30 people receiving sales training on the acceptance of bank checks, for example, it was discovered that only two had ever used bank checks. The teacher had to go one step backward in the teaching process to build a foundation of understanding bank checks before teaching how they were to be handled by the sales person. Teaching must start where the learner is, not where the teacher has determined he should be.

People learn one thing at a time. How many manager-teachers have been heard to say something like this: "All right, Miss Clark, we have a big mailing to get out today. I want you to sit down at the fifth table on the left, over there, and you will find all the material you will need. Tip the edge of the stamp on the sponge; affix it to the place on the card; assemble the card, the letter, the coupon, and the brochure; insert them in the envelope, leaving the flaps up for the sealing machine; place the envelopes in the tray at the side of your table for pick-up; see me when you run out of material. Any questions?" Not only is Miss Clark unwilling and unable to ask any questions; as soon as the manager-teacher walks away, she turns to her nearest fellow employee and says, "What did he say?"

People learn more rapidly when the results are satisfying to them. The individual must be able to see accomplishment. Feedback on how he is doing, therefore, must be structured into the learning process.

People need to understand what they learn. Many manager-teachers complain about an employee's inability to adjust his behavior to small changes that occur in the work situation or setting. This may simply be a case where the employee learned by rote rather than learning the principles involved, the meaning of what he was doing, and the relationship between his performance and the total process.

People develop skill through practice. When an individual first begins to lead problem-solving conferences, his major concern is usually with the techniques of obtaining participation—the overhead question, the direct question, the relay question, and so forth. It is only when these techniques have become "second nature" that he can begin to concentrate on listening and hearing what people are really saying.

People differ from one another in abilities and background. Variations in individual ability to learn must be recognized by the manager-teacher in structuring the learning process to allow each individual to proceed at his own rate. Attention must be given, furthermore, to existing data that indicate that the high anxiety experienced by certain individuals in any new situation obstructs the learning process. Steps must be taken to reduce this anxiety before expecting the individual's performance to conform to the normal learning curve.

Teaching methods. It is almost a cliché to say today that the advances in understanding how people learn and why they don't learn have not been matched by advances in the development of teaching methods. What is done with blackboards, chalk, flip pads, and magic markers does not represent great progress over that of the teacher of ancient times who made markings in the sand for the little group of children gathered around him. Some progress is being made, of course, with the development of teaching machines, programmed instruction, video tape, and student-centered methodology such as role playing, buzz groups, case studies, and group dynamics. Many years of work and experimentation, however, would seem to lie ahead before the findings of the clinical psychologist and the psychiatrist will be applied in teaching methods.

The selection of a teaching method depends on analysis of such factors as what is to be accomplished, what the material content is, and what the situation is in regard to the number of people involved, the time factor, and the organization. Role-playing opposite sides may be most effective in developing skills in collective bargaining and grievance handling but not appropriate for gaining needed technical information. Programmed instruction, similarly, could be the best method of teaching sales-check writing procedures to large numbers of people but not as effective in developing problem-solving leadership skills. Classroom lectures, supplemented by outside reading, may be selected for inputs on social science research findings as they relate to managerial people, whereas individual coaching by the manager and structuring the work would prove best in developing or changing the subordinate's management style. Whatever the method selected, it must incorporate as many of the basic learning principles as possible.

In setting up the merchandise executive training program at a large department store, for example, the objective was stated as preparing new merchandise executives to perform all the basic and essential job elements of an assistant buyer at a quantity and quality level judged acceptable for a newly appointed assistant. A task force of experienced buyers and assistants was used to determine the basic and essential work elements and the indicators of levels of quantity and quality judged acceptable for newly appointed assistants. The program was structured to include developing skill by doing the work of an assistant buyer under the guidance of a good buyer and his assistant; classroom inputs, supplemented by outside reading, for the acquiring of systems and procedures knowledge; research questions and seminar discussions to develop and check on understanding. Exhibit 3.1, which lists the principles and characteristics of the program, gives further insights into the process of developing required job skills.

MEASURING RESULTS

Sophisticated management today has built measurement of results into almost every phase of its operations. From the telephone operators to the airline sales and reservations clerks and from the assembly-line workers to the correspondence-unit clericals, measures of quality and quantity levels of performance have been devised.

Development and training have not kept pace in this vital area. Thousands of programs, costing millions of dollars, have been inaugurated throughout the U.S. industrial complex each year, but not one shred of evidence has been obtained regarding their effectiveness. Employees at all levels are subjected to in-house and outside programs on human relations, supervisory skills, management by objectives, communications, interpersonal effectiveness, work simplification, and job instruction training but without provision for the accumulation of hard data evidencing change. Of course, in some instances, they were asked to fill out a questionnaire on how they liked the program or how they felt it could be improved—a pitiful substitute, at best, for real measurement of results.

With the approach of relating directly to the organization's goals of sales growth, profit, and services constantly in mind, ways to measure and evaluate results will develop naturally. It may be discovered that the things being done in the name of development and training may result in increased knowledge or even a change in attitude on the part of the participants but do not result in any change in behavior. This will at least give the individual charged with responsibility for the organization's development and training a clear indication of the need for program reassessment and change.

Slipping sales, declining transaction rates, excessive turnover, high error rates, dropping productivity, heavy absenteeism, inability to promote from within, increasing numbers of grievances, and increasing instances of interpersonal unrest are positive evidence of obstacles standing in the way of achievement of the organization's goals. After thorough analysis to pinpoint causes, development and training are instituted to meet only those problems evaluated as susceptible to this approach. Measurement of results will focus on determining whether what was done reduced error rates, increased sales, cut down grievances, and so forth. These efforts tie in to the mainstream of the business, foster the achievement of the organization's goals, and can be recognized by top management as an essential contribution to running the business.

It must be realized that it may not and probably will not be possible to

Exhibit 3.1

JOB ELEMENTS OF A NEW ASSISTANT BUYER

Principles

1. Trainee comes in equipped with motivation to learn, as he wants to succeed as an executive.

2. Trainee's motivation to learn is increased and actual learning is best when he sees the learning helping him prepare for the real world of sales growth and profit.

3. Trainee's motivation to learn is increased when he is actively involved in his own learning rather than passively involved as an observer — that is, rather than sitting in a classroom or following somebody around ("assistant to," job rotation).

4. Trainee learns best when there is feedback on the results of his learning and performance.

Program Characteristics

1. Heavy reliance on trainee's taking the initiative and assuming the responsibility for his own learning.

2. Program content is essentially "the job of the assistant buyer." Actual work done and problems faced are the realities of the job in retailing.

3. Program methods consist of:

   Activities

   A. Doing on the job.

   B. Thinking about the doing to gain understanding.

   C. Gaining understanding by discussing what he did and thought.

   Tools for Each Activity

   A. Checklist of work to be done representing basic work elements.

   B. Research questions to be answered.

   C. Small group seminars led by a buyer.

4. Performance evaluation by buyer and assistant, discussed with trainee. Individual help available if needed or requested.

control all the situational variables. This means that other factors besides the development and training efforts will have an impact on results. In attempting to reduce turnover caused by poor handling on the manager's part, for example, changes in working conditions, pay, and job content may have considerable impact on results apart from any development or training effort. Measurement of results will never, in the real world, be scientifically pure; but with a little ingenuity, results can be interpreted to give a clear reading on the success of the development and training process.

Essential in all development and training is an internal measure of the trainee's response to the program. Learning curves may be constructed from past experience to show where the individual should be at any point in time with regard to quantity and quality levels of performance. A key-punch operator trainee might be expected to produce 500 cards per day with a 2 percent error rate at the end of the first week, 800 cards per day with a 1 percent error rate at the end of the second week, and so on. Individual variations from the curve should serve as red flags to investigate whether special help is needed or whether some new element has developed in the learning situation.

Consider again the previously discussed situation of spiraling salesclerk wages without attendant productivity increases. An analysis of individual salesclerk statistics, shopping reports, and supervisor performance evaluations might yield the following information: (1) Many salesclerks did not even try for multiple sales; (2) many salesclerks did not attempt to trade up; (3) salesclerks with the highest multiple-sales percentage were in the bottom half of the productivity scales; (4) salesclerks with less than six months' experience were substantially below the professional level in knowledge of the merchandise and its features.

These four points would indicate the need for a development and training effort to help the salesclerks obtain the needed merchandise knowledge, gain skill in making multiple sales and trading up, and learn to identify the point at which pushing for the multiple sale becomes uneconomical in terms of individual productivity.

One approach would be to develop the salesclerks' supervisors as coaches and teachers. These supervisors would return to the job situation and work with the sales staff individually and in groups as required. The measures of results would include the following: (1) Compare sales against last year, against plan, and against similar departments in other stores where no development and training were conducted; (2) compare number of transactions in the same way; (3) compare multiple sales in the same way; (4) secure shopping reports covering individuals' sales techniques; (5) survey customer reaction in selected departments; (6) inspect merchandise information developed. These measures will give a clear picture of the effectiveness of the development and training effort.

—R. D. Frank

WAGE AND SALARY ADMINISTRATION

Even with the numerous—and sometimes exotic—compensation devices available today, the administration of wages and salaries continues to maintain a position of primary importance in any well-designed compensation program.

Role of Wages and Salaries

The principal role played by wages and salaries is the obvious one of establishing an individual's standard of living. Too often, however, their supporting roles are overlooked. Almost all supplemental compensation devices, particularly those of an incentive nature such as bonuses, profit sharing, and stock awards, relate directly to the wage or salary rate. Incentive plans are covered under "Executive Compensation" (page 3·55), as well as in the Manufacturing section of this handbook (page 6·35).

The amount of major employee benefits such as retirement income is dependent on wage and salary earnings. Furthermore, wages and salaries add an element of stability to the total compensation package, since incentive payments and even some benefits may fluctuate widely with the performance of the individual and the corporation. Conversely, it is rare indeed for individual wage and salary rates to move in any direction but upward. In effect, wages and salaries are the foundation of the total compensation house.

As can be readily seen, an inequity in an individual's wage or salary rate is compounded throughout his compensation and benefit package. This factor, coupled with the rapid escalation of wages and salaries that has occurred in this country, has caused many companies to re-examine their wage and salary programs. As a result, new emphasis is being placed on the equitable administration of wages and salaries.

Job Evaluation

Job evaluation is the determination of relative job worth. The worth of a job is determined in the light of both internal relationships among positions in the organization and external competitive conditions.

As wages and salaries are the foundation of the total compensation program, job evaluation is the foundation of wage and salary administration. The job evaluation process is also an exacting one. If an error occurs in the evaluation phase, it is mirrored throughout the entire compensation program. Comparatively speaking, the administration of wages and salaries is relatively easy once jobs have been accurately evaluated into a viable salary structure that is keyed to competitive conditions.

JOB ANALYSIS

The initial step in the job evaluation process is that of job analysis, which can be described as the fact-gathering phase of job evaluation. It is important to emphasize that job analysis is concerned with job facts—not what a job should be, will be, or used to be. Moreover, it is not the function of job analysis to measure the performance of the individual in a given job.

Sources of information. Several methods and procedures are normally employed in gathering job facts. A common method is to obtain information directly from the position incumbent himself. This is accomplished through interviewing or having the incumbent complete a job analysis questionnaire, or both. However, several other sources of information are readily available to the job analyst. The immediate supervisor is probably the most knowledgeable source, as he is responsible for the duties of the job. Organization charts, operating policies, procedures manuals, and direct observation are ready sources of data.

Job measures. The function of job analysis is to obtain a thorough understanding of job duties and responsibilities. In a relative sense, they are the qualitative measures of a job. Of equal importance is the identification of quantitative measures. For example, two supervisors may have identical functions; but a significant difference in position scope, such as the number of employees supervised, will usually result in different compensation levels.

JOB DESCRIPTIONS

The end product of the job analysis phase is the record of the job facts in a written job description. Lengthy, prose-type dissertations are inappropriate; the well-written job description contains short, factual statements that minimize the need for interpretation. The use of a standardized glossary is also effective in closing communication gaps. In brief, the job description should be written in clear, concise, easy-to-understand language that accurately describes the job.

Format. The format of the job description should be organized to facilitate both a quick understanding on the reader's part and the extraction of needed information. First, the job being described should be positively identified by a meaningful job title that reflects the job duties and responsibilities. Second, the job should be located by stating both the geographical location and the name of the particular organizational unit. Third, the level of the job in the organization should be indicated by identifying the position to which it reports and the positions it supervises. Fourth, the purpose of the job and a summary of its duties should be noted in two or three brief sentences. Fifth, the major duties and responsibilities should be listed. Finally, any quantitative measures of position scope should be indicated.

Keeping job descriptions current. If job descriptions are to be meaningful, they must be kept up to date. Whenever the duties or position scope measurements change, they should be reflected in the job description at once. As a precautionary measure, some companies audit all job descriptions every 12 to 24 months.

JOB EVALUATION PLANS

Once the jobs have been analyzed and described, the actual evaluation phase takes place. Although numerous types of job evaluation plans are in company use, all plans revolve around two variables: (1) what is to be measured (the overall job or elements of the job), and (2) how it is to be measured (against a scale or against other jobs). The many plans in use can be categorized into four basic types. The first is the ranking system, which measures the overall job against all the other jobs in the organization. In this system, jobs are simply ranked one against another until an order of magnitude is established from the lowest to the highest. The second is the job classification system, in which the overall job is ranked against a predetermined scale. The third is the factor comparison system which ranks certain elements (or factors) of jobs against corresponding elements in other jobs. Common factors used are job knowledge, responsibility or accountability, and impact on operations. The fourth method is the point system. Here, the elements of each job are measured against a predetermined scale. In this system, factors common to all jobs are selected, defined, divided into degrees, and assigned appropriate point values. Then each job is measured in terms of these factors, and the points assigned to each element are added to determine the total point value of the position.

Inherent in each of the four basic job evaluation systems are certain advantages and disadvantages. As a result, some companies have adopted variations of the single plans or have combined plans to meet their particular situation.

JOB PRICING

Although traditionally considered a separate subject, job pricing is an integral part of job evaluation. If the evaluation of a position does not correspond to competitive rates, an anomaly will exist, and, practically speaking, the evaluation is meaningless.

The primary source of competitive rates is the formal wage and salary survey. Numerous surveys are available to all companies; they range from public surveys conducted by national, state, and local governments to private surveys by associations, industry or company groups, and professional societies. Depending on the particular survey, care should be taken in accepting the results at face value. Wherever possible, published survey data should be supplemented by custom-tailored surveys in which variables can be more closely controlled. The first step in conducting such a survey is to select the positions to be studied. These bench-mark positions should have a mixture of duties and responsibilities that can be readily found in other companies. Bench-mark positions should be selected on both a vertical axis (those in different levels of the organization) and a horizontal axis (those in different functions of the organization) in order to obtain a good sampling of jobs.

Next, the companies to be surveyed are selected. These companies are usually competitors in terms of both people and product. In order to provide sufficient data, a minimum of ten companies is normally surveyed. Whenever possible, surveys of this nature should include personal visits to each participating organization to insure close position matches. Once the survey data have been accumulated, they should be analyzed closely, and any data that are suspect should be eliminated in order to obtain the highest possible degree of validity. The method used in calculating the competitive going rate will depend on the type of position and its level in the organization. As a general practice, simple or weighted averages are used for positions in the lower levels of the organization. In some cases, judgmental weightings may be applied to the data before averaging. For professional positions such as engineers or programmers some companies use maturity curves that relate level of pay to the number of years since the incumbent received a college degree. For higher-level positions, the compensation data are usually curved relative to some quantitative measure of position scope tailored to the particular position, such as annual sales volume for general managers and sales managers or value of the unit's assets for controllers.

A NEW APPROACH

In the past several years, many companies have adopted an approach to job evaluation that represents a significant departure from traditional methods. This approach uses the market value of the job as the primary evaluation criterion. This "marketplace" approach is based on the philosophy that, in the final analysis, the "worth" of a job is the rate that companies are willing to pay for it, rather than the manipulation of largely extraneous points and factors. In reference to the measurement criteria noted earlier, this approach evaluates the overall job against both a scale (the competitive market) and against other jobs. In this method, bench-mark positions are located in a predetermined pay structure according to their market value. Non-bench-mark positions are then slotted into the structure relative to the bench-mark jobs. The end result is the evaluation of jobs into a viable pay structure attuned to competitive conditions and internally balanced. The overwhelming advantage of this approach, relative to more traditional methods, is that it is highly responsive to market conditions. The volatile market conditions that have been prevalent in the past few years for many positions—such as computer programmers—have led many companies to adopt this approach to job evaluation.

Pay Structure

The pay structure is a multipurpose compensation instrument. If properly designed, it serves as both a motivational tool and an instrument of control.

CHARACTERISTICS

Regardless of the evaluation method employed, the resulting pay structures have similar characteristics. The number of pay grades within the pay structure is normally a function of the number of levels in the organization. Most companies identify three main points in each pay grade—a minimum, a maximum, and a control point between the other two that is usually representative of the going rate for positions within a particular pay grade. Many companies also identify other points within the pay grade that are either wage progression steps or performance targets. As an example of performance targets, if the control point represents the market value of a job, it will coincide with average performance, while the maximum would be indicative of outstanding performance. A point halfway between the two would be representative of above-average performance. The percent spread from minimum to maximum of each salary grade also usually varies with the organizational level. For executive positions, 50 percent or 60 percent is most common; for other salaried personnel, 25 percent to 40 percent; and for hourly positions, about 10 percent to 25 percent. These increasing spreads allow for greater movement in the pay grade by employees in higher-level positions who operate under relatively less organizational constraint and therefore have a wider latitude in which to demonstrate their performance. The percent increase from salary grade to salary grade usually varies from 5 percent at the lower end to about 12 percent in the upper levels. The smaller increase between grades at the lower end of the pay structure allows for more precision in evaluation where the number of jobs and employees is greatest. In the marketplace approach to job evaluation, it is possible to design the pay structure with characteristics that facilitate its effective use, as the pay structure is designed before jobs are evaluated.

UPDATING

The pay structure should be updated periodically to maintain its competitive edge. Most companies update the structure annually. Since individual jobs or groups of jobs move at different rates, the structure as a whole should be increased by a conservative percentage. Jobs that have escalated at a faster pace than the structure adjustment should be relocated in the adjusted structure according to their market worth. In addition to movement in the competitive market, other factors such as the cost of living, general economic conditions, and the company's financial position are usually considered in determining the overall conservative percentage movement. Some companies also project their pay structure about six months into the future by adding on one-half of the annual structure movement. The result is that the pay structure is both in advance of and behind the market for a period of six months rather than behind the market the entire year.

Administration and Control

The effective use of the pay structure requires supporting administrative guidelines and control procedures.

WAGE AND SALARY INCREASES

Most companies utilize either length of service or merit as the basis for granting individual increases. If length of service is used, increases are of predetermined amounts at scheduled intervals. Such a practice is commonly used for employees who are represented by labor unions.

Merit increases. In nonunion situations and for the majority of salaried employees, pay increases are granted according to individual merit. The merit approach implies the existence of an appraisal system that adequately determines the performance level of individual employees.

Some companies follow the practice of assigning arbitrary percentages to various performance levels, such as 6 percent for average performance, 8 percent for above-average performance, and 10 percent for outstanding performance. This practice, however, tends to perpetuate rather than resolve inequities. As an example, if an average performer who is 10 percent below the control point (which is equal to the market price and is the performance target for average performance) receives a 6 percent increase, an inequity of about 4 percent still exists. By the time his annual review again comes due, inflation and general market movement will have increased the inequity to near 10 percent again. The obvious result is that during the course of the year the individual will have advanced very little—if at all—in the salary grade and is still about 10 percent underpaid. On the other hand, some companies have adopted a different approach which does resolve inequities. If performance targets are established in the pay grade, the amount of merit increase becomes the difference between an individual's current pay rate and the pay rate established for his assessed level of performance. In today's competitive environment, such inequities should not exist for more than two years. As a general rule of thumb, gaps of 15 percent or less are closed in one increase. Inequities of more than 15 percent are usually closed with a series of increases, sometimes more frequently than annually, within two years. When an inequity of 20 percent or more exists, future salary planning must be done, since annual movements in the pay structure and possible improvement in performance will cause the inequity not to remain static. This approach to granting merit pay increases, when coupled with a pay structure that is attuned to competitive and economic conditions, automatically combines performance, market movement, and increases in the cost of living into one meaningful increase. Minimum annual pay increases normally should not be less than 4 percent or 5 percent of current pay, or they may result in a disincentive to the recipient.

Promotional increases. For promotional increases, the minimum of the new pay grade or a point in the pay grade that is near his projected short-term performance should be the pay-level target for a newly promoted individual. As with merit increases, the gap procedure can be used in determining the appropriate increase. However, for promotions, increases of up to about 20 percent are usually given all at once.

General increases. In addition to individual increases, some companies grant group or general increases. General increases are normally limited to hourly employees and nonsupervisory salaried employees. Many companies, particularly those with merit-increase programs, find general increases to be undesirable and, in well-administered programs, unnecessary.

CONTROL PROCEDURES

Some control procedures are imposed on a company, either by the collective bargaining process or by government legislation. When collective bargaining is involved, pay decisions are governed by the negotiated union contract. The Fair Labor Standards Act (FLSA) sets minimum hourly rates and establishes regulations concerning the payment of overtime. The Walsh-Healey Act regulates rates of pay for government contractors.

Beyond these measures, the pay policy of the individual company governs pay and cost decisions. The pay structure itself, with its minimums and maximums, offers built-in controls augmented by pay-increase guidelines and the pay-increase approval process; many companies use a two-level approval system. Some companies employ statistical measures that establish an overall percentage relationship of the individual pay rates in a pay grade to the control point. A similar figure is also calculated for the pay structure as a whole on a weighted basis. Some companies also compute these measures based on performance ratings. (An individual's performance level is assigned the dollar value of the corresponding performance target in the pay grade.) The percentage difference between the two measurements when applied to the total base payroll indicates the total dollars needed to correct pay/performance inequities. The compensation budget is, of course, the most widely used statistical control. Its prime function is to control overall payroll costs, since in addition to pay-increase estimates it includes allowances for turnover, new hires, and the like. Overall statistical measures, as described above, can be used to estimate total pay-increase costs; however, most companies forecast pay increases on an individual basis as well in order to estimate and control the pay-increase budget more closely.—*R. B. Carter, Jr.*

EXECUTIVE COMPENSATION

In today's world of complex communication, with its hidden nuances and perpetual ambiguity, it may be of some comfort to know that the term "executive compensation" means just what it says: the compensation—in all forms—of executives, usually the top 1 to 5 percent of a company's total work force, depending on its overall size.

The basic objective of any executive compensation program is to attract, motivate, and retain the key executives the company must have to achieve its general business goals. Since a satisfactory profit is usually the prime business goal, most companies have had to avoid the simplistic solution to the executive-staffing problem of paying more than anyone else. Instead, these companies have sought to lower the dollar costs of compensation by taking advantage of prevailing tax laws, while at the same time extracting the maximum executive motivation from each dollar.

Does compensation really motivate? Some behavioral scientists have recently said that compensation does not motivate increased performance, but can *de*-motivate it if proper pay levels are not established. On the other hand, these same academicians point to "recognition" as one of the most potent motivational forces. When properly used, compensation is most certainly an important form of recognition—and perhaps the only tangible one that the company can bestow. Recognition, however, is relative. It requires that some people get a lot more than others. There can be no winner in a race unless there are also losers.

Simple logic would indicate that if recognition motivates, and a company wants to improve performance, then that company should *recognize performance*. To repeat: That does not mean giving everyone a little something. What is required is the careful assessment of performance, followed by forceful compensation action which tangibly recognizes the significant performance differences in any executive group. Large increases must coexist with small increases, no increases, and even decreases if compensation is to fulfill its potential for recognition and, hence, motivation.

The Executive Compensation Package

The continuing search for effective solutions and maximum executive motivation has led to a profusion of executive compensation devices. The most common are base salaries, bonuses, deferred compensation, qualified stock options, nonqualified stock options, and restricted stock.

Each of these devices (and there are still others—like insurance and retirement benefits—that are applicable to all employees, including executives) is aimed at a slightly different segment of the "motivational market." Some are heavily weighted by tax considerations. Taken together, they offer the compensation planner an opportunity to maximize both motivation and after-tax compensation, while simultaneously minimizing net costs to the company.

BASE SALARIES

At once the most important and least glamorous executive compensation component, base salaries provide the hinge upon which virtually all other forms of compensation turn. Bonuses are usually paid as a percentage of base salary; stock options are often established as a multiple of base salary; the extent of retirement benefits depends on base salary. As a result, any inequities in base salary are greatly magnified in the executive's total compensation. A man whose base salary is $10,000 too high is likely to be overpaid by $20,000 from a total-compensation standpoint, and the reverse is equally true.

Societal considerations. In addition to meeting internal company objectives, base salaries must serve the broader societal goal of providing a reasonable degree of stability in people's standard of living. Unfortunately, this latter objective sometimes is diametrically opposed to the objective of rewarding performance appropriately. A cut in salary to match a slump in performance, if it resulted in the executive's having to sell his house, would do little to enhance his company's public image.

Compensation inertia. Given this social pressure, today's high demand–low supply manpower environment, and the fact that top executives have at least a modicum of human warmth, base salaries go up but rarely down. Since every compensation increase creates a new compensation floor, most executives have been understandably cautious about granting large increases lest they later discover they were overly optimistic in their assessment of performance and potential. The result has been a relatively narrow spread of base salaries which fails to recognize sufficiently a wide spread of performance.

Base-salary objectives. As a minimum, base salaries should be competitive with those paid by other companies. This objective, grounded in the concept that a job is worth what the market is willing to pay for it, requires that companies be continually responsive to the practices of their competitors (not just when someone quits). Insofar as possible, base salaries should also contain some element of performance recognition, although companies with bonus plans tend to use these as their prime means of recognizing performance.

BONUSES

Bonuses for executives are usually of two types. One involves the distribution of an overall bonus fund in proportion to base salary. The validity of this simple approach depends on the equitableness of base salaries at any given point in time. Since they normally contain a number of inequities, a pro-rata bonus plan, like a fringe benefit which depends on base salary, often aggravates rather than solves compensation problems.

Discretionary bonuses. The second type of bonus, the so-called "discretionary" award based on individual performance, is employed by most companies. Properly established, a truly variable bonus can force the total of base salary and bonus down as well as up, thereby persuading management to give freer rein to performance judgments and creating a closer relationship between compensation and performance. Making bonuses work in this way, however, requires tremendous determination on the part of top management. It is difficult to withhold a bonus from an executive who, although his performance justifies such action, has received a bonus for the past five years. It is perhaps equally difficult to double or triple an executive's bonus, knowing that such action will almost surely lead to greater expectations next year.

Bonus objectives. To confer real recognition, therefore, bonuses must be (1) related to performance, and hence variable among individuals as well as for the same individual, and (2) meaningful in size. Ranges of 15 to 40 percent of base salary for lower-level executives and 25 to 75 percent for top executives are typical. From a tax standpoint, bonuses are no different from base-salary payments, except when they are coupled with other devices.

DEFERRED COMPENSATION

Deferred compensation involves delay in receipt of a bonus (or sometimes part of the base salary). Arrangements usually fall into one of two categories: long-term deferrals (payments do not start until termination of employment) or short-term deferrals (payments start with the year of the award and are paid in three to five successive annual installments).

Motivational problems. The motivational advantage most often claimed for deferred compensation is that the individual is encouraged to remain with the company because he will usually forfeit any payments not yet made if he resigns. In fact, however, deferred compensation—unless voluntarily selected—is neither motivational nor necessarily advantageous. The individual is given, not an incentive, but a *dis*incentive. Moreover, some companies feel that such "golden handcuff" arrangements help to retain the company's mediocre performers and not its outstanding stars.

Tax aspects. Deferred compensation is said to offer tax advantages, but these are often illusory at the present time. Short-term deferrals provide a form of income averaging (both high and low bonuses may be spread over a five-year cycle), but so do the Federal income-tax laws. In addition, while the executive is waiting for his money, his deferred dollars are likely to be eroding because of inflation (investments in equities may help), and his marginal tax rate will almost certainly be rising, either because he keeps getting pay increases or because the entire tax-rate schedule, subject to congressional or tax-court revision, is continually creeping upward.

The tax appeal of long-term deferrals is related to their payment cycle, which does not begin until after the executive retires. Since the executive will presumably be earning a lot less income compared to that earned during his active career, the deferred amounts will be taxed at a lower rate.

This logic is compelling but risky. Certainly the executive's retirement benefits are going to be less than his company income immediately prior to retirement. Almost as certainly, however, his company income at the time the award was originally made also is going to be lower. Depending on the number of years' deferral, therefore, the executive's retirement benefit may very nearly equal his income during the award year. Such a situation will result in taxation of the deferred compensation at the same rate at which it would have been taxed had it been received at the time of award.

Two other factors aggravate the problem still further: (1) By the time the executive takes his deferred payments, he is likely to be receiving a good deal more outside income than during the year of the award, which may place him in a still higher marginal tax bracket. And (2) there is little valid evidence to suggest that the trend toward higher total tax rates (Federal, state, and local) will be halted—much less reversed—in the future.

The fact that deferred compensation payments cannot be deducted by the corporation until they are received by the individual tends to hinder the company's financial planning. Since such payments are usually derived from the company bonus plan, which in turn is typically based on company profits, it would probably be desirable if the payments could be deducted in the year of award. Having to defer the deduction constitutes somewhat of a lien on the company and may create serious problems if the deduction must be taken in a year in which the company can least afford it.

There is one bright aspect to deferred compensation, however. If the deferred amounts are invested, the executive can use government capital (the taxes he would have paid on the income had he received it immediately) to compound the value of his compensation. As a matter of fact, in view of the expected rate of inflation on top of all the other risks involved, deferred compensation payments *must* be invested if the executive is to avoid total disaster. Yet a number of companies do not invest deferred compensation.

Those companies which do invest the executive's deferred compensation payments usually place them in company stock. This may help to tie the executive's interests even more closely to the company's; but, since he may also be receiving company stock from options, savings, or profit-sharing plans, he runs the risk of becoming "stock poor." The problem is compounded if company stock is a dubious long-term investment vehicle from the standpoint of retirement-income stability.

A few companies have placed deferred compensation payments in mutual funds or otherwise invested them in equities of other issuers. This approach would appear to be advantageous, although top management opens itself to stockholder allegations that it has little confidence in the company's future.

Attitudes of younger executives. Since it robs them of sorely needed cash, deferred compensation is not likely to be popular among young executives. In fact, it is likely to backfire in terms of retaining younger men. An executive who is paid a base salary of $40,000 plus a $20,000 bonus in five annual installments is making only $44,000 in the first year. He may find it very appealing to go to work for a competitor who is willing to pay him the same $60,000—but all at once.

QUALIFIED STOCK OPTIONS

Qualified stock options have unique tax and motivational aspects. When an option is "qualified," the difference between the option price and the market price as of the date of exercise is taxable at long-term capital-gains rates.

Qualified-option criteria. To become qualified, an option plan must meet several criteria. Principally, the option price must at least equal the market price as of the date of grant; the option must be exercised within five years; and the stock must be held for at least three years from the date of exercise.

Tax aspects. The tax appeal of qualified stock options is directly proportional to the income level of the recipient. The tax paid (prior to the enforcement of the 1969 Tax Reform Act) was half the ordinary income rate but no more than 25 percent. In fact, qualified options may have little or no appeal for the lower-paid executive who has to borrow funds for three years in order to hold and exercise the option. Borrowing costs eat heavily into an already slender capital-gains tax saving.

Moreover, the net cost of an option to the company is inversely proportional to the income level of the recipient, since the company cannot deduct from its corporate income-tax return the amount of compensation it has given the executive (that is, the difference between option and exercise price). To illustrate, suppose the executive is taxed at a 50 percent marginal ordinary income-tax rate. Given $1,000 of option compensation, he takes home $750 after paying long-term capital-gains taxes. The cost to the company is $1,000. For a net cost of only $780, the company could place the same $750 in the executive's pocket simply by paying him an additional bonus of $1,500 (on which he would pay 50 percent tax) and then deducting the payment as an ordinary and necessary business expense (thereby saving the 48 percent Federal tax).

This is not to say that qualified stock options are never effective, costwise, to both the company and the individual executive. However, considering the current tax rates, very large income—usually substantially in excess of $100,000 per year—is required before such a mutually beneficial state can be attained.

By 1972, however, qualified stock options will no longer be cost-effective for any executive, no matter how highly he is paid. Under the Tax Reform Act of 1969 the maximum capital-gains tax rate will be raised to 35 percent in some cases. Additionally, part of the compensation value of the option may attract a 10 percent "preference" tax at exercise; and half of this value, another 10 percent tax when the stock is finally sold. Meanwhile, maximum marginal tax rates on earned income (salary, bonus, and equivalent forms of compensation) will have been lowered from 70 to 50 percent. As if all this were not complicated enough, a good part of the compensation value of the stock option will cause a reduction of salary and bonus income that can be taxed under the new 50 percent maximum provision. The upshot is that the total effective tax rate on capital-gains compensation from qualified options may actually come to exceed the rate on an identical amount of earned income. At the very least, the gap between capital-gains tax rates and earned-income tax rates will have been narrowed substantially. And all along, a company will be losing its tax deduction by granting qualified stock options. In the great majority of cases, therefore, it would seem desirable for a company to discontinue its qualified stock option plan and find a more cost-effective substitute.

Long-term incentive. Motivationally, stock options provide a longer-term, more forward-looking incentive than do such other forms of compensation as bonuses, which are usually predicated on immediate results. They therefore help to hold in check the normal tendency of many executives to maximize current operating results while rationalizing that the "future will take care of itself." Stock options also help to forge a symbiotic relationship between the executive and stockholder groups in that both are afforded common incentives.

On the other hand, stock options are sometimes a rather imprecise means of measuring performance, since the price of a company's stock, although usually responsive over the long run to company performance, is often affected by factors over which the executives have little or no control. Even if there were a 1:1 relationship between company performance and stock value, it is arguable whether that same relationship would obtain between company performance and the performance of individual executives (other than the chief executive, perhaps). Varying the option-granting pattern and the option size—and especially restricting options to a very few top managers—can, of course, help to counteract some of these problems.

NONQUALIFIED STOCK OPTIONS

Covering a wide range of compensation devices, nonqualified stock options all have a single negative feature in common: They contain one or more "defects" which prohibit them from becoming qualified. Therefore, nonqualified stock options are ineligible for the favorable tax treatment accorded qualified options. In many respects, these defects are virtues, since the compensation paid under a nonqualified stock option is fully deductible to the company, thereby making such plans very advantageous for medium- to low-paid executives. As a result, a number of companies are adopting both qualified and nonqualified option plans, the former for the highest-paid executives and the latter for the rest of the executive group.

Nonqualified option plans usually offer stock at a price less than the prevailing market price (sometimes as low as 25 percent of market price) or permit the executive a longer exercise period (usually up to ten years). These superior features often counteract the loss of capital-gains tax treatment.

In terms of motivation, nonqualified options have the same advantages and limitations as qualified stock options.

RESTRICTED STOCK

Once one of the most potent tax-minimization weapons in management's compensation arsenal, restricted stock has been defused by the Tax Reform Act of 1969. Previously, stock on which restrictions as to resale had been placed was not taxable until the restrictions lapsed. At that time the executive was taxed at ordinary rates on the difference between the value of the stock as of the date of the grant and the price (if any) that he paid for it. Any further appreciation occurring after the date of the grant was taxable at capital-gains rates only at the time the stock was finally sold.

Under the new law the full value of the stock on the *date the restrictions lapse* will be taxable at ordinary rates. Capital-gains tax rates will apply to any subsequent appreciation, but that advantage is accorded to the ordinary investor also. Thus restricted stock is no longer viable purely from a tax standpoint. It may, however, find some useful applications as a long-range motivational device.

The Trend to Individualization

How can all these diverse compensation elements be combined into a total compensation package which will have maximum motivational value? Many companies are answering this question today by giving the individual executive varying degrees of choice as to how he will be paid. This approach, called individualized compensation, is an attempt to capitalize on recent behavioral science findings which show that the value of compensation is viewed somewhat subjectively and not always in direct proportion to the actual sums involved. Therefore, if $1 of deferred compensation is psychologically worth $1.50 to a 60-year-old executive but only $0.50 to a 35-year-old, why not give the older executive a great deal of deferred compensation and find some more attractive, but no more costly, alternative for the younger man?

Giving the individual a choice is, in short, a means of obtaining more motivation at no extra cost to the company. It does present some administrative problems, but the advent of high-speed electronic data processing has largely overcome them.

In summary, a proper executive compensation package is the product of a careful blending of tax, cost, and motivational considerations. It requires custom-tailored solutions to carefully defined problems. It also requires day-to-day determination in its administration. But the reward is well worth the effort.—*G. S. Crystal*

EMPLOYEE BENEFITS

One-quarter to one-third of the compensation dollar is expended in fringe benefits. It follows that the business-related objectives of these expenditures are essentially the same as for the payment of direct compensation—to attract, motivate, and retain good employees.

In a typical company, expenditures for employee benefits are the third-largest item of expense, ranking only after payroll and purchasing. As the dollars spent for this purpose increase, it becomes each year more important to the success of a business enterprise that the money be spent wisely. In accomplishing this end, the most important single control is sound plan design. Whether the plans are for nonrepresented employees or are negotiated with unions, the utmost management attention must be given to plan design for adequacy of benefit levels and for claims control.

Plan Design

The whole of a company's benefit and direct compensation plan should be tailored into an overall design resulting in a unified program. A benefits program should never be a collection of uncoordinated, unrelated benefits.

First and foremost, there should be no pyramiding of benefits. An example of pyramiding would be weekly indemnity payments paid simultaneously with a long-term disability policy, and this on top of sick-leave plan benefits, to the extent that the total payments would be more than the employee's take-home wage. This type of integration requires careful planning so that the elements of the program fit the objectives of both income protection and claims control.

Another example of pyramiding would be a program containing a widow's benefit under the pension plan, coupled with a survivor income under the group life insurance plan.

International benefit programs are particularly susceptible to pyramiding with local government programs and require special precautions.

Use of Proven Claims Control Techniques

Sound plan design in the insurance area calls for emphasis on such time-proven control factors as coinsurance, deductibles, and coordination of benefits, thus preserving the available benefit dollar for protection against contingencies in which the employee could not possibly protect himself. Even in negotiated fringe benefits the importance of sound plan design cannot be too strongly emphasized. The more sophisticated union leaders, especially those who specialize in the benefits area, are well aware of the effects of good plan design and will cooperate in incorporating claims control features so that the employees they represent may have broader coverage from the dollars available rather than let the monies available for the negotiated package be frittered away in economically unsound coverages. No matter how good the available administrative talent or how great the emphasis on claims control, if a plan is not designed for adequate control in the first place, it will be virtually impossible to contain its cost.

Balancing Available Dollars

Business economics dictates limits on the sums of money available for payroll and benefits. There are times when a conscious decision must be made on the question of where the most mileage will be realized. This will in turn be related to the externally competitive relationship of existing wage and salary levels and to benefit levels as established by area and industry surveys. Often, as much or more employee appreciation will be shown upon the establishment of a benefits plan than upon a seemingly comparable general wage increase, although the benefits plan costs the company less. For example, a savings plan with a potential cost of 5 percent but an actual cost of 3 percent of payroll may, under the proper conditions (as when wage levels are adequate), be better received by employees than a 5 percent general increase. While various factors influence such decisions, management should always be aware of the options available in its plan design.

In short, the various elements of the fringe and compensation packages—two of the three highest areas of company expense—rate all possible attention so that they are designed into a harmonious whole in line with corporate objectives.

Sound plan design is worth all the time, effort, and money spent for it and in the long run benefits employees, unions, and employers. The payoff could often be expressed in millions of dollars.

Management of Benefits

In view of the previously stated considerations and the obvious leverage in the area of fringe benefits, it follows that employee benefits are a management responsibility and a cost responsibility as important as the control of costs in any other expenditure of similar size. It also follows that this company activity warrants the attention of an effective manager fully backed by the support of top management, to whom he should answer for the companywide design, administration, and cost of the program.

Types of Plans

The various types of employee benefit programs, although somewhat interrelated, can be broadly categorized as providing protection against catastrophic expenses; protection against interruption of income; provision for rest and recuperation; and assistance in solving employee problems.

CATASTROPHIC EXPENSE PROTECTION

A prime example of catastrophic expense coverage is the major medical insurance plan. This type of coverage helps motivate an employee to continue to be productive without adding financial worries to the family worries that could be caused, for example, by the serious illness of one of his children. These plans also fill a social need, since they are protection on a group basis that would not readily be available through the purchase of an individual policy. Because the spread of risks in a business group precludes actuarial selection, this type of protection can be purchased at a discount rate and thus is part of the "hidden paycheck" of employees of most major corporations.

Related plans. Although not strictly catastrophic coverage, base medical, optical, and dental plans also protect the employee's income against the expenses of illness or eye or dental problems. Psychiatric coverage is also provided, although most plans reimburse out-of-hospital payments for mental and nervous disorders at a lower coinsurance rate because of the difficulties of clearly defining need and controlling costs.

In recent years much attention has been given to automobile insurance purchased on a companywide basis. Although such insurance is referred to as group automobile insurance, there is no true group rate, since most of these plans make individual policies available. Nevertheless, because of mass purchasing there are considerable savings in administrative and commission charges. This, however, has been the principal cause of criticism of such insurance: the administrative load placed on the company—or on its broker—for handling the details.

PROTECTION AGAINST INTERRUPTION OF INCOME

Loss of income to the employee because of retirement and to his family because of his death or disability are covered in benefits by protection against interruption of income.

Retirement plans. A classic example of protection against interruption of income is the retirement plan. In a forward-looking program, funding for retirement begins early in the employee's career; because of the effects of compound interest, this reduces the direct expense which must be met by the company for this expensive program.

Recent studies show that retirement protection as a percentage of final pay is continually increasing. Nevertheless, because the average retirement benefit continues for 13 to 14 years (which means, of course, that many retirees will be paid benefits for a considerably longer time), mere percentage of final income may not be a satisfactory answer, especially in periods of sharp inflation. For this reason, both variable annuity retirement plans and savings and stock investment plans have been added to provide some long-term protection against inflation. In this regard, the savings and stock investment plan (in which an employee saves a percentage of his salary that is matched by the corporation and invested in a choice of funds) has become in recent years a multipurpose plan protecting the employee and his family against interruption of income from layoff, disability, death, or retirement. These plans are popular with employee and employer alike because, in addition to providing a vehicle for saving, they have the flexibility to accomplish the same objectives as severance pay plans, disability plans, supplementary life insurance, and retirement benefits. They also promote loyalty, especially where company stock is involved. They have been among the most rapidly growing plans in recent years.

Life and survivor insurance. Life insurance benefits and the newer survivor insurance benefits protect an employee's family against loss of income resulting from his death. Another kind of income protection that has become very popular is high-limit accident coverage, which protects an employee against the hazards of accident on or off the job. This type of coverage is particularly valuable to employees whose jobs require frequent travel, and it is therefore often offered to traveling executives as supplementary travel insurance.

A variation of the plan protecting against income interruption caused by death of the employee, but offering additional flexibility, is the so-called cash-value life insurance plan. Although primarily a death-benefit plan, this type of coverage provides a continued death benefit on layoff or retirement, or a source of additional cash in emergency. The growth of this coverage, however, has been somewhat limited by relatively high cost.

Disability plans. Another plan furnishing protection against loss of income is seen in the new long-term disability policies which in recent years have become a cornerstone of most up-to-date employee benefit packages. Although total disability is infrequent, its effects on the individual who experiences it and on his family can be disastrous.

Long-term disability plans provide a percentage of income such as 50 percent to 60 percent (up to a stated maximum) while the employee remains disabled, until age 65—or, in some plans, for life. Good plan design so that this benefit is integrated with others (social security disability benefits, retirement disability benefits, and workmen's compensation payments) is most important here. Too high a percentage of return from combined sources can attract malingering—or, at least, rationalization—on the part of an employee who could receive as much income for not working as for working if the plan is not carefully designed.

REST AND RECUPERATION

A third type of benefit provides for rest and recuperation. The principal plans in this category provide employee vacations and holidays. Both programs have increased in scope considerably in recent years. In many cases, forward-looking employers insist that their employees take vacations rather than pay "in lieu of," thus helping to preserve the health and productivity of their greatest asset—people. Many companies insist that a vacation must be taken in one continuous unit so that their employees can relax from the tensions of business life for a period long enough to be effective; a common guideline is two weeks at a time.

In the same thinking there is a growing tendency to rearrange holiday schedules in order to provide long weekends; and the number of holidays has increased steadily over the last decade.

Sabbatical leave. Less common among rest and recuperation plans are sabbatical leaves. Long familiar in higher-education circles, where their purpose is to refresh the mind and foster new thinking, in recent years sabbaticals have been negotiated for hourly workers, primarily in the steel and related industries. Called extended vacations, they permit longer leaves periodically—at five-year intervals, for example. The length of the vacation varies with the labor contract; in the steel industry, the combined regular and extended vacation currently runs for 13 weeks. At present, however, such plans are not widespread in industry.

Sick leave. Another benefit in the rest and recuperation category is sick leave. It varies with company policy and the labor contract. Plans for salaried employees are often somewhat flexible. Plans for hourly employees, especially if they are negotiated, are more likely to be spelled out and may include—in many instances—the payment or "banking" of unused sick leave at year's end. While this procedure may well be expensive, it has the offsetting advantage of encouraging attendance and thereby preventing costly disruptions of production.

Recreation. Not to be overlooked in the rest and recuperation category are company recreation programs, including recreation facilities. Social, physical, and educational opportunities are normal facets of a well-rounded employee recreation program and, if administered by a qualified staff, are of real assistance in attracting and retaining employees. These programs can range from bridge to football and from scuba diving to astronomy at facilities provided by the company.

ASSISTANCE IN EMPLOYEE PROBLEMS

Another benefit category is a grouping of plans designed to aid the employee in times of personal financial difficulty or to assist him in reaching worthwhile goals. They include emergency loans, grants for education and scholarships, and moving and relocation expenses. An additional service provided by some companies is employee counseling. However, care is taken in such programs not to allow the company representative to "go overboard" in trying to solve the problem. If the problem is in an area beyond the counselor's training, the employee is directed to an appropriate community agency; however, even in these cases, the counselor can be of great assistance by helping the employee to focus on his problem and steering him to the appropriate source of help.

Evaluating the Program

An employee benefit program, like a stock portfolio, should be constantly reviewed. It should be evaluated for both adequacy of plan design and claims control.

PLAN DESIGN

Much information on benefit plan design is available to the professional. Several excellent journals are published, and numerous seminars are conducted by professional associations. The professional manager has access to all these channels of information, as well as week-to-week communication with his counterparts in similar industries. In addition, if communication links are encouraged, the employees themselves form a valuable source of information if trouble spots exist in the plans.

CLAIMS CONTROL

Equally as important as evaluation for plan design is evaluation for claims control. Cost information is available, and additional information will be developed on request to the trustee on pension plans, savings, and stock investment plans and to the carrier on insurance plans.

Particular attention should be called to claims experience under the group insurance plan. Large accounts should insist that the insurance carrier furnish cost analyses no less frequently than quarterly. In these times of rapidly rising medical and hospital costs, top management should insist on a claims control program whose twofold purpose is: (1) to pay all legitimate claims promptly and cheerfully; and (2) to resist illegitimate claims to the utmost (even where this process may in some cases be more costly than the individual claim rejected). Coordination with local hospitals and physicians and close cooperation with the insurance carrier and the unions are essential parts of the program. Employees must be encouraged to question fees and insist on only necessary treatment. All levels of management must realize the amount of money involved in such programs and the real payoff that is present in a professionally administered claims control program.—*E. C. McManus*

THE PERSONNEL RECORDS FUNCTION

Managing the records of human assets as an industrial resource in the achievement of corporate and functional objectives formerly represented one of the less glamorous of management responsibilities. With today's high-level utilization of the sophisticated hardware of the computer age, the drudgery of manual paperwork and statistic manipulation has become a horror of the past. Personnel records management is more and more identified as a management function, operating the systems of control, analyzing and interpreting the dynamic statistics of human asset evaluation, and revealing the human facts that light the way to rational management decisions on effective manpower planning and utilization. Astute personnel records management can now demonstrate its contribution to the corporate objectives of profit, growth, and resources development. It can further show contributions to such functional objectives as operating production, revenue, quality control, productivity, and budget and delivery performance. If industrial relations research fails to provide these personnel records management services, it is merely duplicating the maintenance of payroll records.

By the nature of the source of these records, there is also a very human side to these data. Personnel records essentially represent the living biography of individual human beings, each of whom is not only different from all other individuals but also has his own hopes, wants, ambitions, and needs that make up his objectives. Professional personnel records management takes individual objectives into account as it takes corporate and functional objectives into account. It must serve both, and does so in a parallel manner.

Personnel records represent individual and group manpower resources. They portray statistically the sum total of an individual's or group's experience, education or training, availability, performance level, and potential for growth. Upon this record management decisions today can be made that will positively influence the successful achievement of the set objectives of tomorrow and of future years.

At the same time, professional personnel records management will recognize the needs of the individual as a dynamic entity in the industrial and social environment. It assures that each person's individuality is maintained by providing him with the means and the environment in which he can achieve his objectives, his personal growth potential, and the dignity of a mature and secure future.

Personnel Records Management as a System

Personnel records management defines a system wherein it can be shown that personnel records represent minimum input, orderly and systematic sourcing, cost-effective maintenance, and maximum contribution to set objectives on a timely basis; and that the records are refined by feedback from their operations performance.

Accuracy, Precision, Timeliness

For management decisions to be effective, they must be supported by the realities of money in the treasury, manpower availability, means and facilities of production, a salable product, and a dependable market. Faulty information on any of these resources will not support management decisions or effect positive results. Misinformation on the availability of manpower at a future date can literally stop the wheels of production. The same profit erosion will occur if manpower is overavailable at some point during the operations year.

Other real dollar losses resulting from lack of accuracy, precision, and timeliness are manifold. Poor practices in recruiting, for example, are (1) failure to use personnel records as a source for initiating referrals from employees; (2) failure to use personnel records to develop a skills inventory to fill open positions; (3) the inadvertent hiring of minors (child labor), resulting in costly legal actions and high accident rates; and (4) insufficient data for recognizing potential poor performers, accident-prone individuals, and persons who are likely to make fraudulent claims for unemployment compensation.

In the area of management development and training, increased turnover results from underutilization of employees who have been developed and trained; money is wasted in developing and training employees who do not need either activity; in some instances development and training efforts are duplicated, and in others they satisfy no company objectives.

Unfavorable consequences of poor practices in compensation include increased turnover caused by untimely or inadequate increases; fines imposed for nonpayment of overtime to nonexempt employees; union grievances arising from wage rates improperly entered in personnel records, with the result that union employees are not paid the full rates stipulated in agreements; seniority problems resulting from inaccurate hiring, transfer, and promotion dates on personnel records; and overpayment of insurance benefits.

Losses in productivity result from inept record keeping on tardiness, absenteeism, vacations, authorized time off (with or without pay), unauthorized time off taken and not recorded, discipline, grievance time, and sickness on the job.

Untold losses result from lack of record keeping, inept record keeping, and just plain carelessness when costs are being controlled under unemployment compensation, workmen's compensation, disability compensation, pension payments, and other life, health, and accident insurance plans.

Information on Human Resources

Personnel records represent the only reliable records on individuals because they have been validated at each point in their accumulation. References have been checked; college records have been verified; medical examinations have produced health profiles; results of pre-employment tests, psychological assessments, and interviews have been recorded; discharges and records from the armed services have been verified; birth certificates have been authenticated; financial and social responsibility has been investigated; and, in defense industries, patriotism and other personal attitudes have been scrutinized and recorded. These records represent base-line data, and with the exception of records of physical and mental health, they will not change. It is all past history and can influence future events only by having established a retirement date, possibly a date of induction into the armed forces, actuarial costs to the company under certain benefit programs, and an alert to the education director on expected obsolescence of knowledge.

As the employee becomes operational, he adds to his biography many kinds of data that, integrated with his base-line data, provide him with credentials to advance his own objectives. These data further provide management with the means to manage the potential he represents as a productive source, to increase his value to the company as an asset, and to assist him to achieve his recognized (recorded) potential. These additional data include records on performance level; reliability; potential level; development and training; transfers; promotion; a whole inventory of skills, talents, and abilities and the extent to which they are operational; and, finally, the carry-over potential of each. One of the most important notations, which is monitored closely in today's management revolution, concerns the extent to which the individual is developing into a professional manager—or is becoming more oriented to day-to-day matters. Personnel records must therefore be eminently susceptible to research methods and techniques in order to provide management with the individual and group profiles of the manpower resource so that this resource can be utilized in the most economical manner.

Forms Control and Records Clearance

The policies, methods, practices, and procedures that control requisitioning, recruiting, acquisition, hiring, orientation, development, training, performance evaluation, transfer, promotion, and pension termination must be designed and administered to meet the several criteria of the personnel records management system. They must (1) conform to the minimum requirements of the law; (2) contain the minimum data to profile the whole man; (3) be keyed into the management system of contributions to corporate and functional objectives; (4) serve the individual in the achievement of his potential and objectives; (5) be maintained on an up-to-date basis, at minimum cost, via a feedback procedure as they perform services to the objectives of the individual and of the organization; and (6) be compatible and responsive to the technological changes that can make them more productive.

The last-mentioned point gives the clue to the standards by which any of the numerous record systems must be judged. (Is the system productive on a cost-effective basis? Is it utilized to maximum level? Is it practical, and does it serve the objectives of both the organization and the individual?) Where authorizations are required, every effort should be made to hold to the two-level system; that is, the first signature at the point of initiation of an action, and the second signature at the next higher level for the purpose of review. Additional signatures should serve as a warning that lower-level authority is being diluted. The retention of records is normally governed by legal and financial requirements or by practical requirements such as a pool of résumés retained for recruiting purposes. Live records files should be severely limited to those that serve personnel purposes only. Payroll records should go to payroll files; security clearances, to the security files; agreements, to the legal files; minor assignments, to the department files; and awards should be recorded and returned to the individual for his personal files. Documents of almost any type should be verified, posted, and returned to the sender, to the appropriate department, or to the individual; or they should be discarded. Each personnel form should serve a distinct purpose; be authorized for use by the department head and the forms control head; be numbered and functionally described in a forms control manual; and be reviewed periodically for continued usefulness.

Legal Requirements

Federal, state, and local legislation directly affects the design, use, and retention of forms. Additionally, a company may impose certain restrictions on forms utilization to meet internal financial or security requirements or requirements in the interest of the preservation of assets. These restrictions may affect such activities as bonding, receipts for company property, employment agreements, or patent and invention agreements.

Federal labor laws are designed primarily to protect minors and minority ethnic groups and include prohibition of discrimination against individuals for reasons of religion, nationality, or color. Similar laws limit the length of the workday or workweek and govern the definition of those who are exempt from such limitations. Other laws prohibit discrimination by employers who have been awarded government contracts. State laws vary widely but in general protect the health and welfare of minors and women. They also prohibit discrimination against persons for reasons of sex and age. Other laws are always in the process of being enacted to protect the health and safety of employees in dangerous industries. Self-imposed limitations on industry are voluntary restrictions by groups of employers upon themselves to protect their employees and the public. Each law or voluntary restriction results in a flurry of paperwork, usually in the form of a new set of records and an ever increasing number of forms, instructions, and controls.

Computerized Personnel Records

The techniques of data processing are evolving into what can only be called revolutionary progress. Whether the impact of this sophistication will result in changes in basic principles or concepts fundamental to professional industrial relations is doubtful. There is no doubt, however, concerning the ability of today's equipment to turn out details in formats and combinations in such short time spans that management is presented with timely and focused fact arrays of such quality that problem spotting and decision making have been greatly facilitated. This is especially true for constructions of projections of the future in manpower planning and utilization. Models can be designed and altered to fit future expectations of other resource variables. As a result decision making has taken another step toward becoming a science.

Certainly, computerization of personnel records will make skills inventories more practical and give them wider applications in internal search which will reveal in-house talents to fill authorized openings. Wage and salary administration controls immediately take on new perspectives in relating performance to rewards and controlling turnover through timely and accurate applications of merit funds. Cost controls of benefit plans become more effective, as in wage and salary administration, with statistical printouts exposing deviations from policy and uncontrolled payouts. Input forms and control forms take on a new look, as do reporting forms to outside agencies, especially when conforming to disclosure requirements. And employees are receiving forms showing the itemized dollar value of their employee benefits, accompanied by projections to retirement showing cumulative values at that time. This information has caused many employees to think twice about changing employers.

Vital Records and Their Protection

Vital records are the documentations which—if they suddenly disappeared or if management were denied access to them or if they were put to unauthorized use—could cause a loss to the company or to an individual. Fire, strike, riot, theft, or careless handling could cause losses of vital records, resulting in loss to the company or to individuals. Theft presents one of the gravest problems because of the ease of duplicating recorded data. Tight security controls surrounding record handling are coming into wider use as industrial espionage activities increase. Personnel record keeping has reached so high a level of human assets management that serious measures must be taken to protect these valuable records—*D. K. Rowe*

EMPLOYEE RELATIONSHIPS

For many centuries it was assumed that man works almost entirely to satisfy his economic needs. There was little doubt that to most men and women work was akin to a mild form of pain, hence to be avoided as far as possible.

Until comparatively recent times, work may have indeed been pain for the overwhelming mass of people. They had to work many hours a day in an endless effort to scrape subsistence from the reluctant soil to stave off starvation for themselves and their families. Unfortunately, in many areas of the world this is still the rule today.

Under such conditions there is little doubt why man works; but once the level is reached where basic physical needs have become satisfied, if additional time is available, most men will seek to add to their basic standard of living. Their first endeavor will be to secure for themselves a continuing supply of food and clothing, and they will improve their shelter to make it sturdier against the elements. In other words, they will seek safety and security before other needs receive attention.

In a society as complex as ours, basic physical needs are taken for granted by the overwhelming majority of the people; actually, a high level of luxury (electricity, central heating, labor-saving devices, television, and even personal transportation) is enjoyed by many of those who are considered poor. In such an environment, the drives that impel men to work are much more difficult to identify.

It is even more difficult to determine why some men work harder than others. What should be done to stimulate greater effort or reduce indifference is the real question. After all, the individual improves his standard of living if he contributes his full share, and society benefits at the same time; why, then, are there such great differences in motivation?

Each person, psychologists say, is a unique bundle of complex needs, and he responds therefore to different stimuli in different ways. This is a most important principle, but it can be easily forgotten during a study of the many generalizations that make up the existing body of knowledge in this field.

Factors in Motivation

Two major concepts of motivation dominate current thinking.

According to the first concept, most people will react to influences that are considered motivators: recognition, achievement, job satisfaction, advancement, and similar rewards. It is believed that when a manager knows how to create an atmosphere in which people can find these satisfactions, they will respond favorably and strive for higher levels of accomplishment. Satisfiers, on the other hand, are those comforts or rewards that, when absent or inadequately supplied, become *dis*satisfiers and make the employee feel deprived or discriminated against; they are believed to interfere with his concentration on his task and, as a result, reduce the level of output or achievement. Besides wages, they include benefits, work environment and conditions, and similar matters.

The second concept of motivation deals with the personal development (emotional and intellectual) of the individual, and his relation to the environment in which he is expected to perform. People and organizations operate at different levels of development. At the lowest and simplest levels the individual needs clear direction and therefore responds best to an organization that treats him authoritatively. As he matures, autocratic methods seem to become less and less appropriate; more participative decision making and greater emphasis on expressions of individuality are considered more effective. However, an organization with a permissive leadership style will confuse and frustrate the individual who still needs a highly structured environment where practically all decisions, even those that directly affect him, are made by superiors.

Historical Patterns

Leadership styles and organizational patterns have followed a certain evolution of needs.

TRADITION

From ancient times down through the Middle Ages, the economic organization of man was based primarily on tradition. Each individual did as his father and forefathers had done before him. To a limited extent, nevertheless, his life was also regulated by a measure of command. On various occasions he received instructions that modified the traditional form of life and forced him into work—usually for a limited period of time—where he was told what to do, how to do it, and when to do it. During these command periods in his life he worked for his lord, or he worked in support of the armies that happened to control the area where he lived.

COMMAND

As division of labor gradually supplanted the self-sufficient organization of economic activity and industrialization and trade became more significant in the development of society, tradition became a less reliable regulator for man's activities. New occupations appeared on the scene, factories were developed, and entrepreneurs made change a major influence on the lives of most people. Tradition lost its usefulness as a guide to action. In those rugged days, when the individual was considered to have complete personal freedom over his own property, it was only natural that those who were able to control the means of production would have very great authority over those other people who worked for them. In this simple relationship, the superior gives the orders and the subordinate obeys.

This concept of respective roles in life probably was never entirely satisfactory to the worker. As society came to depend more and more on him to supply not only luxuries but also some of the necessities, he began to recognize that this state of practical servitude was not necessarily the only order. He felt, at least in part, deprived of dignity and of what he increasingly came to consider his fair share of the product of his work.

PATERNALISM

Gradually, employers either became aware that they had to satisfy the needs of workers or were forced into awareness. Pay rose from levels barely adequate to retain workers in reasonably good health, and slowly—very slowly—new philosophies evolved. First, employers came to believe that in order to create an effective, productive organization, they must see to it that their employees were happy and contented. Often, contentment was thought to be automatically assured by good pay, generous fringe benefits, and friendly supervisors who respected the dignity of employees.

SEARCH FOR MOTIVATION

Gradually it became clear that money and sympathy by themselves did not even keep people happy, much less make them exceptionally productive. Satisfied employees, it turned out, were not necessarily highly motivated to strive for high output; moreover, they often became quickly disenchanted and rebellious if their employer could not continue to increase wages and benefits to keep pace with their ever rising expectations. It was time to seek a deeper understanding of the forces that motivate people to work if business management was to create a sound base for employee relations and increased productivity.

Compensation and Satisfaction Today

Compensation, of course, has always been by far the most important reason why people work; it therefore holds the potential for some satisfaction but also for considerable dissatisfaction.

WAGES AND SALARIES

Everybody agrees that wages and salaries should be "fair." The problem, of course, lies with the definition. In the view of the employee, wages and salaries must meet many criteria if they are to be fair.

1. Compensation must meet the expectations of employees as they see them at the moment. Any discrepancy between current pay and the earnings believed to be achievable will create some level of dissatisfaction. Employees are quite ready to interpret even casual remarks by superiors as promises of some sort when pay or benefits are concerned. Take, for instance, the casual reply to a request for an increase: "I'll see what can be done" can easily be recalled several weeks later as a definite promise for a substantial raise in pay.

2. Employees at all levels compare themselves horizontally with the outside. This means that they measure their earnings against those of others who they consider are doing similar work in other companies. They also measure their earnings against those of neighbors, relatives, and friends whom they consider to be at the same social level as themselves.

3. They compare vertically with other occupations that they feel are less important or that require lower skills for their performance. Social considerations also enter here; people feel strongly that they should earn more and live on a better standard than those who, in their opinion, are on a lower level.

4. Employees compare themselves horizontally with "insiders," employees who do similar work within the same organization, as well as with those others whose work they consider to be on their level.

5. They also compare themselves vertically, within the organization, with those doing less skilled tasks. As a source of dissatisfaction, this evaluation possibly is second to none. As society has moved gradually toward greater economic equality, employees who traditionally have received higher pay have found a shrinking differential between their jobs and the more menial tasks. Probably the most outstanding examples of such inequities can be found in the pay of lower-level supervisors. These men and women frequently earn less than some of their more highly skilled subordinates, particularly when considerable overtime—for which many supervisors are not paid—is scheduled. Highly skilled artisans and professionals face the same problem.

Skilled electricians and metalworkers resent the rapid rise in pay scales of unionized industrial workers, and professional men certainly do not enjoy comparing their incomes with those of plumbers or bricklayers, whom they consider to be below their own social status and whose contribution to society's welfare they view as far smaller than their own.

6. Compensation changes in relation to changes in perceived needs are another troublesome area that employers must watch as they adapt their compen-

sation systems to changing requirements. As employees progress through their own life cycles, their real need for income varies. In general the young adult needs more and more as he marries, furnishes his home (frequently purchasing it), starts a family, and strives to maintain home and family at a comfortable and dignified standard of living.

To overcome most of these problems, large organizations and many smaller ones have established formal systems, even for their nonunionized employees, under which information about wage and salary levels of different occupations is made known to everyone. While this does not necessarily satisfy all people, it does give new employees a clear picture of what to expect, and it provides for a systematic review as workload or responsibilities change with time. At the same time, it makes comparisons with other organizations fairly simple so that adjustments can be made to keep all wages and salaries in line with area or industry practices. In short, the "simple" concept of fairness in compensation policy is an elusive one, and opportunities for dissatisfaction are many.

EMPLOYEE BENEFITS

Employee benefits have proliferated greatly over the years. The private sector of the economy now protects employees from the effects of the troublesome, sometimes even catastrophic, financial emergencies that can befall them, such as need in old age, long illnesses and accidents, time off from work as a result of the death of close relatives, and time lost for jury duty. Employees also enjoy more respite from economic activity. Companies pay for ever increasing vacations, holidays, sick leave, lunch periods, coffee breaks, and wash-up time (for shop employees), while the workweek gradually becomes shorter and shorter. (See also "Employee Benefits," page 3·61.)

Executive and professional employees often enjoy a number of additional benefits devised to hold the employee to the company or intended to enhance his after-tax income. (See "Executive Compensation," page 3·55.)

The benefits that protect employees against adversity are rarely sources of great dissatisfaction. Inadequate holiday or vacation allowances, however, or a longer workweek than is typical in the area or the industry, can be major sources of discontent.

On the other hand, for the older employee particularly it can be a source of satisfaction to know that the company's protective benefits package shields him against the hardships that bad luck or failing health can send his way. He also enjoys being able to point with pride to the benefit package his company provides.

In brief, employee benefits can add to dissatisfaction if they are substandard, but their effect on performance is rarely as important as wages, working conditions, or the psychological influences surrounding security.

WORKING CONDITIONS

Parallel to the improving standard of living at home is the desire for greater comfort within the work environment. In the modern factory, cleaner work areas, colored machines, painted walls—and, most important, an environmental system that provides even temperature during the winter and air conditioning or some form of cooling during the summer months—have become commonplace. Factories pipe fresh air into their buildings and heat it as it is brought in, so that the air inside the plant can be made as clean and as wholesome as the air outside permits. Sources of light are installed for eye comfort, and noise is reduced to an inoffensive level where at all possible. Where companies do not meet these environmental comforts, employee resentment develops against "substandard" conditions.

In the office, concepts of good working conditions have broadened to include extraordinary physical comfort, sometimes reaching high aesthetic levels in decor and design.

While the extent to which the appearance of the work environment acts as a motivator may be questioned, there is little doubt that inadequate or unwholesome conditions detract from the pride that employees take in their jobs. Where the air is inadequate or the temperature is uncomfortable, accomplishment and activity are visibly reduced. Similarly, an unattractive workplace often leads to work of poor quality. Employees assume a right to relax their efforts somewhat if the company provides a less-than-adequate work environment.

SECURITY

The term "security" has many connotations for employees; it covers job security, economic security, status security, and the security of "belonging" that accrues to members of an "in" group. While most people feel a strong drive to carve out a secure niche, there are great differences in the ways individuals strive to achieve this goal.

Job and economic security. Unions, traditionally, have labored to achieve job security for the individual through contractual agreements that reduce the effect of management influence on the tenure of the employee. The trend has been to make job security almost solely dependent on length of service, since this is probably the only criterion that can be measured objectively. For the blue-collar worker, job security and economic security are practically synonymous because protection against unforeseen circumstances is provided through the benefits package specified by the company-union contract.

The white-collar worker often distinguishes between job security and economic security, though here too, as in the case of teachers and large office staffs, many employees have turned to unions to seek both forms of security. The overwhelming majority of professional people, however, who make up the bulk of white-collar employees, look to personal competence for job security. They feel that, in the final analysis, what they know and what they can accomplish assure them their jobs and that they can sell these assets elsewhere if their current employer does not value them highly enough. This attitude requires continued willingness to improve personal knowledge and to keep pace with the ever changing technology of the field, and in a society where the demand for professional people is growing more rapidly than the supply, it is an outlook that assures considerable job stability.

White-collar workers approach economic security in part through personal insurance programs but primarily through company benefit packages. Indeed, the white-collar worker often sees the benefits offered by a company as an important reason for accepting a position.

Status security. Status is of course a very important potential source of dissatisfaction, and in many companies status symbols are coveted evidence of the rank achieved by the individual. Symbols may include such physical appurtenances as the size and location of the office, the presence of rugs, the type of decor, and even the nameplate on the door. Some observers have noticed a recent trend away from these overt displays of status, particularly in organizations where employees have high levels of educational achievement.

While the outward trappings of status may be less important, the individual's organizational level and standing in the hierarchy of the firm are becoming of greater concern to him. To the highly trained professional, achievement and the recognition of it are probably the most important rewards. When new people enter the company at a level close to his own and rise quickly to equal standing, resentment is often reflected in the performance of the senior man.

"Belonging." Identification with a group can add considerably to an employee's feelings of security, and a feeling of exclusion can be a serious dissatisfier. Psychologists who study group behavior have attempted to determine what distinguishes the effective work group from the less effective one, and they have concluded that the group which is able to align the personal goals of its members with those of the group is likely to be more successful. In fact, an accepted premise today (as a result of the work of Rensis Likert) is that an effective organization consists of groups linked to each other in such fashion that the goals of the organization can be transmitted and made compatible with the goals of the subgroups and of the individuals within each group.

Often, the mechanical aspects of security have less influence on employee behavior than those involving status and belonging. There are opportunities here for the alert manager, since he has considerable control over the latter two and can apply imagination and skill in improving conditions for his subordinates.

SOCIAL RESPONSIBILITIES

Paternalism, in the sense of direct concern with the private lives of employees, is generally and often justifiably resented. While the modern company rarely is outwardly paternalistic, most firms accept a considerable amount of responsibility toward employees. This is in part a remnant of the philosophy that the happy employee is the productive one, and in part it stems from the changing pattern of corporate management—from individual owner-entrepreneurs to professional managers who are charged with the development of an effective, loyal team. In return they must provide their staffs with a strong sense of security, and this can grow only from empathy toward employee needs. Long-service employees, for example, are rarely discarded summarily. If their performance no longer meets job requirements, the company will assign them less demanding tasks or devote considerable time and resources to help them find satisfactory alternatives. Similarly, acceptance of social responsibility has led to increasingly elaborate pension plans to supplement social security payments provided by the state.

Companies also help employees with many personal problems, through advice and counseling by competent staff members or consultants, through financial help during emergencies, and in many other ways. In general, most companies see their people as their most important asset even though they do not carry them on the books as assets; and they will extend whatever resources are required to retain and rehabilitate rather than replace. Hiring and training new employees have become so expensive, particularly at the higher levels of skill and professional competence, that it is recognized as good business practice to exert every effort to help the individual overcome his problems so that he can return to full concentration on his duties. In many instances, it is felt, employees who have had the benefit of such efforts will repay the organization through their intensified loyalty over the long run.

Participation as Motivator

Possibly the most puzzling question for any manager throughout his career concerns appropriate leadership style: Should he allow considerable or minimal participation in the decision-making process in the areas under his control?

PARTICIPATIVE MANAGEMENT

Many studies have been concluded, and more are in progress, as part of a broad effort by business and the academic world to determine under what conditions participative management will yield better results than authoritative direction. These studies have been somewhat inconclusive. What has emerged, in general terms, is a feeling that participative management offers some advantages with professional people and higher management personnel. At lower levels, particularly with unskilled or semiskilled workers, participative management is thought to be less advantageous. There, careful communication from a competent decision maker with a good feeling for human relations is considered preferable, since it usually appears to lead to higher productivity. The conclusion emerges, in the writings of Douglas McGregor, Rensis F. Likert, Chris Argyris, Frederick Herzberg, Henry Landsberger, Abraham Zaleznik, William F. White, Saul W. Gellerman, Robert Tannenbaum, Raymond E. Miles, and many others, that even at the higher levels of professional activity a leadership style that appropriately blends authoritative with participative decision making is most likely to promote an atmosphere conducive to the highest level of accomplishment. These studies suggest that the most effective environment is one where employees participate only in decisions where they feel competent and where they are able to contribute meaningfully to the outcome of their decisions.

A diagram showing the many options of leadership behavior from which the manager can and should choose was created by Robert Tannenbaum and Warren H. Schmidt ("How to Choose a Leadership Pattern," *Harvard Business Review*, March-April 1958). The choices open to the manager are not depicted as permissive on the one hand and authoritative on the other, but rather as a continuum where leadership is entirely boss-centered at one end, with decisions being made almost exclusively by the superior. At the other extreme, subordinates make practically all decisions within organizationally defined limits. Between these extremes lie many intermediate possibilities in which the manager exercises more or less of the overall decision-making function.

The ability to make good selections in this area often distinguishes the exceptional manager. He must sense to what extent the group is capable of making a decision alone, to what extent it needs or desires direction from him, and when it would prefer that he assume sole responsibility for the decision and its consequences.

INDIVIDUAL AND GROUP PARTICIPATION

The well-managed organization strives constantly to increase participation through appropriate rewards. Incentives which allow the individual or the work group to share in the growth of the organization can go a long way toward stimulating interest in accomplishment. Possibly more important, however, is the environment—the work atmosphere in the company.

Foremost among the subtle building blocks of good morale is "open" communication. If the employee is to feel that he can contribute effectively, he must know that his viewpoint will receive a fair hearing even when it runs counter to the opinion of some of his superiors. Certainly it must not work to his detriment even if it is strongly expressed or frequently stated. Employees who feel that they can influence the direction of events—to some small degree, at least— are generally motivated to contribute more fully toward helping these events take a favorable direction. An article on this subject by Raymond E. Miles ("Human Relations or Human Resources," *Harvard Business Review,* July-August 1965) discusses how, in one management philosophy, participation is thought to bring about improved satisfaction and morale. This result in turn lowers resistance to formal authority and thereby gains greater acceptance of the goals of the organization (compliance with formal authority).

Another view sees participation as a step toward improved decision making and control of the environment, which in turn brings about increased satisfaction and morale on the part of subordinates; the higher morale serves as a base for still better decision making. A cycle is thereby created. Decision making is reinforced by greater employee satisfaction, and employee satisfaction is enhanced by greater participation and resulting better decisions.

The superior who invests the effort to learn a great deal about the abilities of his subordinates can help them develop their capabilities to the fullest and, simultaneously, help them overcome shortcomings that may obstruct their growth. It is in this skill of the manager, in his ability to counsel and help his subordinates to grow and find fulfillment and achievement in their work, that the real core of effective participation lies.

MOTIVATION EFFECTIVENESS

Extensive studies on motivation by Frederick Herzberg and one by M. Scott Myers, who followed Herzberg's research ("Who Are Your Motivated Workers?" *Harvard Business Review,* January-February 1964), have discussed efforts to measure the significance of various company practices that are considered motivators and those that are regarded as dissatisfiers.

The study concludes that effective job performance depends on the fulfillment of both motivational and maintenance needs. (It classifies as "maintenance needs" the factors that have been discussed here as "satisfiers.") It also finds that companies frequently view employee benefits as more important to an effective work atmosphere than they really are: Once an adequate level of satisfaction of maintenance needs has been reached, sharply diminishing returns come from additional outlays. The results of this study suggest that much of the effort should instead be directed toward providing opportunities for genuine personal achievement and the psychological rewards that stem from a sense of personal fulfillment.

Discipline

To many people, the word "discipline" is synonymous with some form of punishment, yet its meaning goes much further. In an organization where individuals have accepted the goals of the organization and are willing to strive to achieve them, discipline exists totally without punishment. It can be said, in fact, that a high level of morale automatically implies an underlying state of good discipline. Decisions are made and are executed effectively; even the dissenter, once the die is cast, strives to get the best from the policy or direction that has been taken.

In most organizations, however, there are some individuals who do not wish to accept the fabric of the organization's behavior pattern and who consciously or unconsciously violate the rules frequently in one way or another. It is because of these violations (some of which are fully tolerable and, indeed, useful to the dynamic development of an organization) that each unit must establish, either formally or informally, a set of beliefs, rules, or standards by which it wishes to live.

REALISTIC RULES

Realistic rules are the rules that the members of an organization support, on the whole. They are consistent from department to department; they are adequately communicated; and violations are reviewed for possible punishment. Every company has its formal, written rules, most of which are contained either in the employee information booklet, in the standard management manual, or in the union contract—or in all three. Then there are the unwritten rules, which stem from day-to-day compromises between managers and subordinates. In time these gradually take on the same force as written rules. Frequently, informal practices even override formal rules because they have become deeply embedded through repeated use.

Supervisors and managers must do their share in maintaining the consistency of established rules throughout the entire organization. More important, they must see that rules are revised to remain in keeping with the general atmosphere of the company and the social environment of the community.

Many observers believe that the publication of a multitude of procedures and work rules is a requisite to "proper" behavior within the organization and to adherence to company policies. Others take an opposing stand, pointing out that every written rule raises questions about its interpretation. They further maintain that the publication of an extensive list of rules, in effect, leaves open to individual interpretation every area that is not covered. This in turn brings about still additional rules until the system becomes so unwieldy that it is no longer a meaningful guide to action. Thus there are reasons both for and against the publication of a great many rules. Every manager who has worked with a union contract knows that, no matter how detailed the writing, many questions inevitably arise for which the written word has no answer. The solution usually must be found in some combination of the written word and the unwritten customs and interpretations.

Nevertheless, most companies find that good communication requires the establishment of some fairly formal rules. These rules usually involve questions of tardiness and absence, safety practices, assignment of overtime, break periods, failure to punch the time card properly, improper parking in the parking lot, and moonlighting. Where employees are not unionized, these rules are frequently spelled out in an employee handbook; where unions exist, many rules are included in the contract.

Most companies make it a matter of principle to adhere fairly closely to the rules that they consider important and to defend their right to maintain them in the face of considerable opposition; yet forward-looking companies will also interpret the rules as generously as possible in favor of the individual employee's interest, provided the principle itself is not in jeopardy.

SYMPTOMS OF POOR DISCIPLINE

Employees indicate dissatisfaction in many ways, consciously or subconsciously.

Absenteeism. Probably the most pronounced of the symptoms of poor discipline is absenteeism. Significant increases in employee absence, late starting, and departure before the end of the workday need to be carefully investigated to discover whether they indicate that the work environment no longer provides enough motivation or that the maintenance needs of employees are not being met adequately. Frequently, it does not take too elaborate a study to obtain this information, and the manager can determine by observation or through direct contact with his subordinates where the problem lies.

Informal grievances and complaints. Another significant indicator of poor discipline is the number of informal grievances and complaints received by superiors or—when the problem is more serious—by the personnel office. Not every complaint by an employee is a grievance, however. Many companies consider that a grievance should be recognized and discussed by a manager only if there is at least some justification for the employee's feeling of discontent within the structure of the relationship between the employee and the company. Other companies take a more liberal viewpoint. They hold that any dissatisfaction felt by an employee should be brought to the attention of management and given an airing even if a resolution satisfactory to the employee cannot thereby be achieved.

Some of the most difficult personal grievances occur in this gray area. They can be questions of real or imaginary breach of promise by supervisors or management, or instances of favoritism which may have occurred accidentally, unintentionally, or as the result of a misunderstanding on the part of the employee. They can also involve some other occurrence based on the gap between a management decision and what the employee believes to be correct behavior on the part of the company.

In the more mature organization, these complaints are seen as opportunities for good communication; they are either resolved or at least explained in detail to the employee concerned, and often to others, as evidence of the company's desire to give a fair hearing to any employee who has a problem.

It is difficult for a manager to know whether his organization is generating the "right" number of complaints and grievances. Most managers have a few subordinate supervisors or managers who seem to receive too many complaints, and others who appear to get too few. The competent manager reviews enough of the complaints and grievances that are brought to his subordinates to obtain a good view of the feelings of employees on lower levels. Grievances can thus serve as excellent indicators of the leadership style practiced by subordinate supervisors.

HANDLING GRIEVANCES AND COMPLAINTS

In situations where a union contract governs the handling of grievances, several steps are generally specified.

1. In the first step, the aggrieved employee discusses his problem directly with his superior.

2. If the problem is not resolved at the first level, the employee calls his shop steward or union representative, and the matter is taken up between all three or between the representative and the superior.

3. If the question is still not resolved, it is taken to a higher level, which very often brings in the shop chairman (senior chief steward), who takes it up with a higher level of management or with the personnel department. Or it may be referred directly to the business agent, who will visit the plant to discuss the matter with these higher levels of management.

4. If the problem is still unresolved, it is sometimes taken to a still higher level of management, with a larger union representation; or it goes directly to arbitration, sometimes only after a voluntary mediation step.

For an employee who is not covered by a union agreement, a grievance procedure exists in a somewhat less formal way. He can always request permission to take a grievance to a higher level if he fails to obtain satisfaction directly from his superior. This, of course, often has its inherent disadvantages, but in a democratically organized, participative environment, it is usually an accepted practice to which the employee will resort if he feels strongly about an issue. In most cases, of course, a nonunion employee—professional or otherwise—has access to the personnel department, which acts in an advisory capacity and very often can indirectly influence the employee's superior if the grievance has some justification. The personnel officer is also generally well equipped to explain why a company cannot agree to a particular complaint if this is the appropriate response.

ARBITRATION

Arbitration is often the last legal step for the employee in a unionized shop. Some managers and unions who have worked with arbitration have found it to be a rather undesirable way to resolve an issue. Arbitration brings in a third party, who is unacquainted with the environment and practices of the organization and therefore may not perceive the fine distinctions of which the parties are aware. As a result, arbitration rulings may have the outlook of the outsider, and both parties are bound by a solution frequently less satisfactory than one they could have achieved themselves with goodwill and a willingness to keep a clear view of the equities involved on both sides. However, in many cases, where the parties are unable or unwilling to come to an amicable agreement, arbitration is the only means of resolving the issues without costly strife.—*Erwin Rausch*

Why Employees Join Unions

The first article of the agreement that a newly formed unit of a trade union will negotiate with an employer is usually entitled "Recognition." Granted that its content in today's collective agreements is a far cry from the literal meaning of the word, it is the literal meaning that forces it to the forefront of discussion between management and employees.

INOPERATIVE SATISFIERS

Virtually every employer is directly affected by unions. It starts with the fact that the employer has to recognize his employees' right to organize. This challenges his established way of managing, and the reaction creates a need for both the employer and the union to secure their respective rights to manage workers and represent members. There then follows, on behalf of the employees, the negotiation of rates of pay, benefits, and working conditions.

The whole process occurs when employees seek—or are at least receptive to— some means to accomplish a more effective dialog with their employer on matters of interest to them. In the broadest generality, however, the employer is balancing his interests across a multitude of problems, some of which may conflict with those of his employees. In their totality, the employer's interests are as engrossing and vital to him as the employees' concern for their well-being is to them.

Through collective bargaining the employer can hope to resolve only some of his problems. Certainly, there will occur a dialog that, because of the power of the collective voice, cannot but be satisfying in itself. But satisfying needs which must be bargained for, no matter by how much or how ingeniously, can and does end in frustration if there is no freestanding evidence on the part of employer and employee alike of their respect for each other's contribution to the enterprise. The "satisfier" given by management as a pacifier fails.

The record of any one of the past three decades can illustrate the point, though perhaps the sixties do it best. Wage rates have consistently risen, and with unprecedented guarantees; hours of work are breaking the 40-hour barrier; vacations have been greatly extended; and a wide range of medical and social welfare benefits is commonplace (and paid for). Notwithstanding all this, employees have reached new all-time records in days lost by strikes.

It is no wonder that management and the union become perplexed as they observe the result of their efforts, and it is equally no wonder that management and employees and their unions turn to other kinds of satisfiers to try to find the answer. It is understandable under these circumstances that employees are evolving as people with a greater respect for education and a cynicism as to the motives of both management and union; and as challengers to management, particularly for greater participation in business decision making.

THE "BANDWAGON"

Management's tools for communicating with employees are generally different from those used by a union. Few if any managements can claim a system whereby immediate feedback from employees is certain. Management is not structured in such a way that it requires the employees' mandate to function.

Union management, however, must have the voting support of its members, or it fails to meet its constitutional objectives. Thus the union relies on a political type of campaign: first, to identify employee problems; second, to suggest remedies or platforms even if they are not entirely satisfactory; and third, through the element of striving to obtain the remedies from management, to make the whole effort seem worthwhile to the employees.

Management's traditional response to this type of campaign over the years has been to attack the union to a point where legal restrictions (whose purpose is not primarily to inhibit management but rather to redirect the focus on the issues—the problems and remedies themselves) have been set. In this atmosphere the union often finds that its best approach is to create a climate where employees themselves can take action, often such action as to defy the established authority. The old maxim "If you are not with us, you are against us" forces employees into taking sides.

If management responds by attempting to improve its conditions, it is again fettered, not only by the legal restrictions but by the knowledge that the union will claim initial victory with its technique of concerted attack to force a better deal.

About the only alternative to these positions is to establish a management "bandwagon," not just because the unions start theirs but by reason of the ultimate value to the net worth of the enterprise. The phenomenon of the popular leader exciting his listeners to a pitch where they will react as one is well known. A leader within the work group may even unconsciously develop such a bandwagon attitude in his associates. If sufficient numbers of key leaders are influenced by the union organizers' sales talk for union representation, there is a good chance that, regardless of the negative votes, the employees will find that the majority has ruled.

It is essential that management understand its work groups within any potential bargaining unit and recognize who among these groups is in fact the leader.

It is not unusual to find that the person the employees really look to for direction is not the person appointed by management as their supervisor, often not even the union steward whom they themselves have appointed or elected, but another man to whom both the foreman and the union representative look to influence the others in order to assure themselves of the compliance of the group.

NEED FOR PARTICIPATION

During a recent utility strike, company supervisors performed the tasks they themselves had allotted to employees. When the strike was over, the supervisors told management that they had found the work intensely monotonous and boring. In the face of this revelation, management issued a public news release on its decision to seek new ways of making work more varied and therefore more interesting.

Few if any managers can actively do the work their employees perform, aside from the fact that they may lack the particular skills. The task of managing is in itself so demanding as to preclude such participation; yet they decide the tasks to be done and insure that they are carried out. The end result is that because neither employee nor manager is participating in the work of the other, differing goals are established—a condition that is ripe for union organization.

In the beginning, at least, the union *is* the employees; thus they are assured of a sympathetic means of reaching their goals, particularly the goal of recognition. This search for tangible evidence of recognition from the persons who supervise their work is an attempt by the employees to assure themselves that they truly belong in the organization. The fact that management so often fails to provide the feeling of belonging, in the work sense, is probably the most significant reason for the employee to establish an allegiance to a union that accepts him rather than to a company that appears only to use him.

UNION PRESSURES

The union starts organizing by establishing a small cell of employees, or a series of cells, depending on the size of the company. It must therefore persuade at least one person to join, who in turn persuades another, and in this way grow to a point where the requisite number can be counted to achieve outright representation. This activity can take years before the union knows success.

Even within the freedoms explicitly set forth in law, the union still finds it useful to begin organizing secretly so as not to stir management into action. It is difficult, however, for union organizers to make contact with employees who will dedicate themselves to selling other employees on the benefits of unionism and thereby change the existing pattern. Frequently, the union's point of contact is only with disgruntled individuals or outcasts from the various work groups for antisocial or other reasons. The union organizer must take these persons and use them as agents to attract the solid, influential employee leaders to hear his "pitch" and support his calling.

This activity is time-consuming, often tedious, and sometimes dangerous for the organizer. He cannot always carry it on during the day and must wait until the factory is closed in order to meet employees at a tavern, restaurant, or occasionally a home. As their number increases he risks the security he is attempting to maintain, and his costs increase in his attempts to find suitable meeting places for larger numbers of persons. The union agent's pitch is of course geared to appeal to the needs of employees as they see them. Thus, to some he appeals to their sense of fair play, to equal sharing, to human dignity, and to others the need to "get even." He tries to activate their acquisitiveness and excite them with the prospect of battle.

Pressure from friends. The union adds to its strength by appealing to employees on the basis of their commonality of interests, and it uses the work group in such a way that pressure on the persons in it is well-nigh irresistible. Positive unionism is a uniting factor, therefore important to the organizing of the company. Indeed, the union can identify its campaign as a veritable crusade of solidarity to enhance the value of labor, as shown in the old custom of having members address each other as "brother." (This practice, at one time continued long after the organizing campaign was over, is today somewhat short-lived.)

Management's onrushing action in these circumstances is narrowly beamed within the scope of the enterprise itself. Its intensity is directly in proportion to its end purpose, but in most industries it is required to be prepared for collision, competition, and other economic phenomena. Once set in motion, action is difficult to reverse.

Appeal of collective bargaining. The employee participates within management action under policies and procedures that are changeable mostly as a result of planning done for him, not by him. The individual worker's opportunity to add to, subtract from, intercept, or divert management's edicts is rather slim, even though modern management may recognize that channeling that opportunity may be fundamental to achieving its purpose. The employee therefore looks to a third party which has the status to do the things the individual cannot do alone. Such a party can be created by the collective organization of employees.

The organization thus formed will intercede on behalf of the individual in relation not only to the needs of the employee but also to other, similar organizations of employees. Management is now faced not only with problems that previously it alone was responsible for but also with the aspirations characteristic of all such organizations.

Union Organizing

The unfortunate circumstance in many union organizing campaigns is that management knows so little about them before, during, and after the event. It is unfortunate not so much because of their consequences, though these are of prime concern to management, or even because of the act of organizing itself, which is complex, engrossing, and intelligent behavior of a kind that management ultimately can divert to the enterprise for good purposes; but because management of an organization can be so preoccupied with its own expertise that it cannot balance its direction to enable others to work within it without having to create a countervailing force.

THE CAMPAIGN

The size and diversity of the bargaining unit determine, to a large extent, the time required to organize. Generally speaking, units of employees who are in positions closely associated with corporate management are hardest to organize, while employees farthest away both physically and by work activity are easier. Close-knit units are easier than units that work apart. In the United States, racially homogeneous groups in major industry may constitute a bargaining unit, particularly if engaged in like occupations; but similar groups engaged in services or agriculture do not seem as susceptible.

No group of employees is easy to organize if it is well managed.

Dangers of panic. If the company is unaware that employees are organizing, the news will come as a shock, since management may feel that its authority is threatened. Accordingly, it may take action in a panic framework. Small businesses with heavy labor costs, particularly in service activities, can feel that the beginnings of a union are their death knell. This attitude may affect employee job security in spite of the law's protection. Management may be tempted to threaten its employees or to attack the union as a radical, criminal, or subversive group, or to coerce individuals into revealing the extent of the campaign. These actions are unlawful, and management, if charged with them, may become panicky to the point of impotence in dealing with its work force.

Unfair labor practice. The law requires that the employer refrain from threats, coercion, or inflammatory statements. To many a management this appears to be unfair, since it may be quite evident that the union is inciting employees to organize by making inflammatory statements regarding company policy and practices. The union may give to potential members a rallying cry by creating or posing situations where they need to defend themselves against claimed "unreasonable interference" with their basic rights. In such circumstances management is likely to post a warning to employees that if they join the union, they will sacrifice a relationship that is desirable for both parties.

It is sometimes extraordinarily difficult to appreciate the difference in attitude that the threat of unionization can make between management and its employees. On one day employees may be viewed paternalistically—even affectionately—as persons who are endowed with feelings of loyalty and for whom opportunities within the organization are unlimited; but overnight this attitude can change with the knowledge that a union is successfully mounting an organizing campaign. Management may now feel that the employees have struck the hand that feeds them, that they have an unreasonable greed for more, and that their repudiation of management's granted wages and benefits is an act of disloyalty not to be forgotten.

Presenting the firm's position. Should such employee attitudes exist, management is prone to act unfairly even in law. If it attempts to buy out the employees by offering increased benefits and wages, particularly where formal certification proceedings have begun, it becomes vulnerable to attack on grounds of unfairly changing conditions of work and is liable for an examination of its practices by labor board officials. If it attempts to discharge or otherwise replace employees for joining the union, it can be charged accordingly. While management has the right to inform the employees about its attitude toward unions, in the hands of unskilled or thoughtless managers this can be risky for future relationships.

If the company being organized has not already clearly communicated its thinking, it is probably too late for management to do so effectively during the campaign. This is particularly true if it reflects an attitude different from that which prevailed beforehand.

Many large companies, on the other hand, have successfully won campaign after campaign, even to the extent of having trade unions decertified, by carefully establishing at all levels of supervision such clear-cut practices and policies that employees are assured that the company recognizes them both as individuals and as groups; that its reward system for work performed is realistically competitive; that it has the requisite satisfiers; and that organizing to get these satisfiers is unnecessary.

Need for competent counsel. During any certification campaign, competent counsel can be of great value in providing management with advice as to (1) what it can do and say, and (2) what it can't do or say to its employees. Counsel can prepare management for the possibility that the organizing campaign may be successful and that the company may have to arrange to negotiate working conditions, wages, and benefits—matters which heretofore management saw as being its own right to decide. Such counsel can assure management that it is not the first to go the route of unionism and can help it to learn the labor law; and, beyond this, can help it to acquire skills and techniques suitable for a new relationship. However, lawyers (no matter how competent) who have never specialized in labor matters and are insulated from work groups because of their professional specialization may create or reinforce management's alienation from the situation.

Labor law is becoming known to a wide spectrum of managers and employees as a result of union organizing; for many, it may be the first introduction to the importance of law in regulating the framework of industrial society. In labor law there is written, in simpler language than is used in other legal matters, fundamental protection for both groups and individuals.

ROLE OF THE NLRB

The U.S. Labor-Management Relations Act (commonly referred to as the Taft-Hartley Act) is administered by the National Labor Relations Board (NLRB). It consists of five members and general counsel and performs two major functions.

First, it conducts elections among workers to decide which particular labor organizations shall be "certified" as the collective bargaining agents of such workers. These elections are by secret ballot. Second, the board has the authority to prevent unfair labor practices or order the discontinuance of such practices.

The act applies to virtually all employment and industries involved in interstate and foreign commerce with certain exceptions, of which the most important are the employees covered by the Railway Labor Act. Section 7 provides that: "Employees shall have the right to self-organization; to form, join, or assist labor organizations; to bargain collectively through representatives of their own choosing; and to engage in other concerted activities for the purpose of collective bargaining or other mutual aid or protection."

The petition. The NLRB plays an important role in the sequence of events relating to union organizing campaigns. Prior to the actual representation election, the board must determine if a question of representation exists. It does not act on its own initiative. To determine whether a question of representation exists and an election should be held, a petition must be filed with the board. It is ordinarily filed by labor organizations seeking certification as bargaining representatives, by individuals representing the employees, or by the employer who wants to determine whether the employees have selected a representative. Usually, the union petitions. Most cases are disposed of informally. But if the company management and the union cannot agree on the bargaining unit or on election, a formal procedure providing for a hearing and report to the board is followed. The latter then dismisses the petition or designates the appropriate bargaining unit and orders an election.

Unit determination. Under the act [Section 9(b)], the NLRB has authority to designate bargaining units:

> The Board shall decide in each case whether, in order to assure to employees the fullest freedom in exercising the right guaranteed by this Act, the unit for the purposes of collective bargaining shall be the employer unit, craft unit, plant unit, or subdivision thereof. . . .

The board's discretion is, however, subject to certain limitations. Thus, professional employees may not be included in the bargaining unit unless a majority thereof vote for inclusion in the union. Plant guards are not to be included in the same unit, nor may supervisory personnel be in any bargaining unit. Note that the NLRB designates the *bargaining unit*. The employees, by secret ballot, designate the *bargaining representative* or union.

Election procedures. When the board has determined the appropriate bargaining unit as previously noted, the next step is the representation election. This may simply be agreed upon, or it may be ordered after the formal hearing. The NLRB regional director arranges for and conducts the election. Official notices of the place of the election and other details are posted in the plant. After the votes are cast, the ballot boxes are sealed and the board's representative arranges for the tally. Ordinarily, no further election will be authorized within one year following this election.

Certification. If a majority of those voting have supported the union, the next step is certification; that is, the union is certified as the exclusive bargaining agent of all the employees in the unit. Even if the union loses, the results of the election must be certified by the board. If the union does win, its status as bargaining agent is clearly established; company management and the union can enter into bargaining confident in the stability of the relationship between them.

Other procedures. There are other means by which unions may be certified and situations in which election results may be set aside or certification withdrawn. Because of the extremely complicated procedures and applications of rules, the executive should consult with a qualified attorney, one who specializes in labor law, before taking any action involving employees' rights to organize and bargain collectively. Some businesses, in fact, may not be covered by the NLRB or may be covered by state laws or other Federal laws.

Preparing for Negotiation

Depending upon the experience of the company with labor, preparing for negotiation can be either a continuing process arising out of many kinds of cooperative effort by management and the union or, at the other end of the scale, an encounter which, because it is dreaded, is put to one side until a mighty "crunch" is required. The average business organization probably heaves a collective sigh of relief when the agreement is signed at its eleventh hour, and a year or two later begins again to make ready.

DEFINING OBJECTIVES

Most precise management planning for negotiating the union contract is done for the immediate agreement to be bargained and only after the union has submitted its demands. Management is aware that the union's strategy is predicated on long-range planning for periods beyond the immediate contract.

A hypothetical example of union strategy is found in plans for an industry-wide contract that would require common termination dates for multiple units of one company in the industry in order to force a master contract, and so to parlay that position across other companies as to reach the union's ultimate goal. Such strategy requires careful planning over an extended period of time and negotiations. It also requires careful planning over the same period by management, and decision making as to the best objective for the long run. As a start for an overall objective, a company might well decide to plan the manner by which it will offset the increased cost of the forthcoming collective agreement, plus the probable increased cost of the effect of the agreement on other personnel not so covered, while still increasing efficiency and improving profit.

Short-range objectives for the contract to be negotiated vary with the level of management. First-line supervision goals are usually related to working conditions, particularly flexibility for staffing jobs. Such matters as job posting, rigid seniority, ability to revise work schedules on short notice without undue premiums, and voluntary overtime are all matters of concern.

Middle and staff management's objectives are oriented toward the operating costs of labor and the application of employee benefits. Premiums for overtime, incentives and bonuses, vacations, and welfare benefits may be of greater significance to them as they plan for the budget requirements of numbers of employees and work standards.

Senior management considerations are mainly concerned with principles and economics. They are oriented toward such matters as the union shop, the retention of management's rights in such matters as severance and contracting out, and—primarily—the maintenance of the best overall competitive position within the industry concerned.

Labor relations is one of the few areas where competing organizations willingly cooperate within the limit of the law to avoid being whipsawed. (A notable exception is in the Canadian construction industry, with the myriad problems presented by builders' exchanges, national contractors' organizations, and heavy construction agreements.)

Long-range objectives for coping with labor problems must of necessity involve planning with the unions themselves, government, and other industry—conditions which put senior management to the test. Since technology largely governs the kind of labor required and the rate of change is so rapid, it is difficult indeed to plan for ten- or even five-year periods in such matters as wage policy, numbers of employees, educational standards, and other associated areas.

GATHERING DATA

There is no lack of data to gather for negotiating a union contract. The problem is to plan the collecting properly in context and to recognize, out of the welter of information available, what is most needed to meet the situations to be encountered.

Consulting with first-line supervision. A primary source of information, of course, is found in the first-line supervisors. They can, if conditions are right, provide real information for planning. A common pitfall of labor relations, however, is to assume that the very closeness of the relation of the foreman to the worker precludes a free give-and-take of information for fear that strategic position will be lost in inadvertent exchange with employees or union representatives.

A further complication in obtaining data from first-line supervision is that, unless there is better than average communication between it and other levels of management, there will be hesitation about describing work practices that build up within the work group. Patterns of behavior between the shop stewards and foremen often develop unnoticed by senior supervisors and management. These patterns are designed to get around difficult discipline problems, and sometimes they violate principles held by both union representatives and management and specified within contracts. The selection or nonselection of certain individuals for overtime, subtle lengthening of break periods, brief unreported stoppages of work to protest discrimination or favoritism—all conspire to create on the shop floor a different atmosphere from that presumed present by the levels of management not alert or immediately responsible to the work force. The very strength of the reaction when superintendents get wind of such action tends to bury these situations even more. Studies of these conditions are mines of information on how the "system" works in reality; with care, contract language can prevent the rise of problems and contract administration can be planned to ventilate these situations.

Surveys. Survey data should cover, as a minimum, the conditions within the company itself and, if there are several plants at different locations, the conditions in each one; the conditions applicable to the competition; the community where work is done; and the general conditions of the geographic area. It is of only marginal interest, for example, if one is engaged in manufacturing, to know in detail the conditions of insurance companies or financial institutions, unless within the community these are organizations with which the plant competes for labor. It is vital to know the nature of the contracts being negotiated by the union about to be faced.

Many companies today conduct their own surveys and—depending on size, time, and money—extend them to cover the appropriate area. Public service companies, for example, draw information from numerous organizations in order to relate to balanced economies, not just to similar institutions.

Government surveys are as good as the samples they process, and since these are widespread in most cases, they can orient industries as to "going" wages in the general market.

Surveys may be designed to cover all cost aspects or only one or two significant issues. The best surveys are those conducted in a similar manner so that, year by year, interpretations of changing trends can be anticipated. It is well to know what is being looked for when data gathered by others are used. An electrical worker—for example—may be rated quite differently, as a maintenance function in a factory not making major use of power, from an electrical worker employed in an electrical utility or electrical manufacturing company. There are still situations where single industries dominate the economics of a given territory. Even so, continuing sampling by survey of the nature of change facilitates planning and assists in introducing controlled change.

Grievance and complaint settlement. Because of the conflict aspect of union-management relations, grievances require careful examination, particularly those that require arbitration and are considered "losers" by either party. So-called policy grievances (where a contract clause is in dispute) are also significant. However, a continuing grievance pattern of protest over employees' discharge, seniority "bumping," or promotion may indicate to either management or union a need to propose revisions to contract language.

It is also well for management to review actual grievance procedure carefully, since this is one of the most important clauses in any contract. Frequently, a foreman may be assigned authority for answering grievances beyond his level of responsibility, thus causing him to be bypassed entirely or unfairly charged by more senior levels of management for either making or not making decisions.

It is a common wail of labor relations managers that principles "won" at arbitration can easily be "lost" at negotiation. A case fiercely defended a year before at arbitration may be almost casually given away at the last moment in the interest of achieving a new contract. The saying, "When someone says 'it's not the money, it's the principle of the thing,' what he really means is, 'it's the money,' " is primarily true in labor relations. It therefore is well for persons engaged in this work to carefully assess the dollar impact for both short- and long-range planning of complaints, grievances, and arbitration settlements so that it can be assessed rapidly when the contract is to be negotiated.

Data on company work force. Records of productivity, absenteeism, turnover, and workmen's compensation provide important data for the negotiating team. In the computer age, with its sophisticated approach to such data, many organizations recognize and maintain accurate and current information of this type. Bonuses, whether negotiated in a collective agreement or not, establish wage levels beyond those specified in the contract and often are at levels that preclude effective incentive. Premiums for more difficult jobs or "unpleasant" working conditions have a habit of remaining or even increasing though the job becomes easier or the conditions are improved. To dispose of these situations inevitably costs money which must be allocated elsewhere. The evaluation of such cost must be made with full knowledge of the immediate and future impact.

Pay for time not worked—for example, coffee breaks and wash-up—has real value when assessed on jobs with high repetitive, monotonous, dirty, hot, or other unpleasant working conditions. However, the cost of two ten-minute breaks and two five-minute wash-ups per day can amount to 6 percent of payroll cost—enough to cause negotiators to carefully scan their allocation.

Legislation. A thorough review of current municipal, state, and Federal legislation should precede negotiations, noting particularly licensing requirements, hours of work, vacations, minimum wages, and other conditions commonly governed by such statutes. While these matters are usually well publicized when changed, management should re-examine them at bargaining time to relate its performance within the law.

Labor cost analysis. An almost limitless number of factors can enter into a company's rationale to determine its labor cost. Such considerations as the skill requirements of the labor force, the geographic distribution of the company's or competition's labor force, the urban or rural locations, prosperous or disadvantaged areas, the strength and ability of the union to negotiate, "public service" versus "private enterprise"—all affect the price that management and union decide can be paid for work.

Primarily, however, analysis of labor costs should be related and balanced to both the internal operations of the organization and the external effect—that is, the industry of which the company is a part and community industry. Both of these considerations must then be weighed against the larger economics of the current times—the going rates.

Labor cost control reports for each separate negotiation should show the company's present rates of pay and the cost of employee benefits, including both those negotiated with the union and those unilaterally granted by management and broken down into as many facets as required, plus the costs demanded by legislation such as unemployment insurance, workmen's compensation, and the like. Relevant competitive and community industry figures should also be shown so that the final document will provide a broad basis for estimating and for recommending the company's position for bargaining.

SECURING AGREEMENT OF TOP MANAGEMENT

It is imperative that persons responsible for the labor relations function maintain at all times a flow of information to senior management as a means of dispelling assumptions on the nature of problems encountered, both in negotiations and in day-to-day contract administration. Regular reporting of labor trends can assist in securing agreement of top executives sufficiently in advance of negotiations that labor cost considerations can be integrated into the overall costs for normal planned periods. Accurate cost analyses maintained on a regular basis also allow senior management to visualize the rate and amount of change. In periods of inflationary settlements, the percentage amount of a settlement required three years from the last round of negotiations may be such that it is downright unfair to present an estimate to senior management if, in the interim, labor costs have gone largely unreported in their full context.

The most difficult aspect in securing management's agreement is not normally, however, the amount of the cost but showing the results expected from the expenditure.

Practically all salaried jobs outside a bargaining unit have as a part of the salary administration plan the appraisal of individual performance in order to establish the actual amount to be paid within the appropriate range. The range may use criteria similar to those used for collective agreement negotiations, but it is the placement of the individual within the range that requires the skill and judgment of management. The bargaining process precludes this kind of assessment, so that instead of measuring what the individual employee has done by a performance appraisal, management has to assess the cost of labor as a percentage of the cost of doing business. This, in recent years, has largely meant that management has had to increase the price of the product to cover the increase in labor cost, particularly if labor represents a major portion of its total cost.

The continuing decision making that results from this spiral is not an easy one for management, particularly if the question of labor costs is avoided during the term of an agreement and arises for immediate solution at the bargaining period. Even so, what is perhaps most difficult for senior management is the ever present possibility that its decision may have to be tested by the use of labor's ultimate weapon, the strike. At such times top executives have been known to accuse the labor relations department, or others requesting authority for wages and working conditions, of bargaining as much as the unions with which they are negotiating.

Agreement may be given by top executives for terminal positions, knowing in advance that to avoid costly disruption they may have to make further concessions. These situations, if not fully and freely discussed within the executive group itself, can create a climate of misunderstanding that not only affects the instant task but spills over into other salary and compensation matters.

NEGOTIATION POLICY AND TECHNIQUES

Essentially, the basic negotiation positions are three. In the first, the company will move only as little as required to prevent employees striking to obtain their objective. In the second, the company plans to move in any direction to secure an agreement but only as far as it must. In the third position, the company plans to move according to what it believes is fair, and accordingly it assumes that the other party will negotiate from an equally reasoned decision. Companies that are organized by trade unions must bargain. The decision to establish a policy as to how and on what grounds they will bargain is largely determined by size and ability to compete.

In the first instance, companies where the style of management is more autocratic tend to assume that what they have granted must stand until they are forced to change.

In the second instance, which covers the vast majority of companies in North America, the company is open to persuasion if it can be shown that changes in working conditions and wage rates are tolerable, and it is prepared to bargain with the union for the least amount required for the given time period. It is not unusual in these cases to bargain so hard that by the end of the time period, the company may be at a disadvantage competitively in not having offered enough benefits, even though it would have offered more at the time of negotiations if pushed.

In the case of the third position, management has attempted objective reasoning which it believes to be so self-evident as to speak for itself and require only token haggling. To its dismay, management finds that the other party wants to have a say, no matter how factual and accurate management's assessment may be, to a point where such attempts to bargain by not bargaining are considered unfair by the other party.

The technique of the second position, by far the most common, contains numerous subtechniques largely depending on the skill and experience of the negotiators on both sides. There are persons in business who feel that the highest level of efficiency brings about the correspondingly highest level of satisfaction. Labor negotiations are anathema to such persons.

To "play poker" with shareholders' capital is not considered efficient, but it is without doubt "the name of the game" in much collective bargaining.

It seems to be less of a gamble, the larger the company, the bigger the union, the more skilled the players. In the final analysis, however, it still depends on the ability of one side to influence the other without knowing the other's final position.

PITFALLS

The most common pitfall that company negotiators find results from lack of information with which to influence either the union or their own senior management. The company negotiator who has briefed his committee well on all the matters pertaining to the negotiations can survive best. Overreliance on one bargaining technique can work against a negotiator: For example, if the negotiator continually holds back until forced to concede by extraordinary threats, he may find that every threat becomes extraordinary until he proposes enough to satisfy the other party. At the other end of the scale, the negotiator who assumes that his offer, particularly where it may meet a demand, will be accepted because of its very generosity and ease of offering may find that what he believes is generous may be only the floor for continuing upward bargaining.

In recent years there has been an obvious trend on the part of both parties to an agreement to go beyond independent, face-to-face negotiations so as to enter into third-party bargaining—the use of conciliators or mediators. Even this is not the stopping point for some who must consistently continue to the brink of strike in an effort to develop the final position.

Many line managers who are bargaining—particularly during the formative period of their training—may fall into the trap of underestimating the skill and ability of their employees who bargain collectively. Such an assumption almost automatically precludes any form of mutual understanding. A problem frequently encountered is management's initial inclination to resist a union demand simply because it is a demand and must, in management's view, therefore be without merit. Conversely, many unions may utterly lose management in presenting agendas which include "everything but the kitchen sink" on the assumption that at least some of the matters will be agreed to and the rest can serve as smoke screens. Under these conditions bargaining becomes difficult unless the union is prepared to back up from its position so that management can see what the union considers vital and necessary to satisfy the membership.

While there is a certain amount of unrealistic performance on the part of both parties, the sooner issues become clear-cut, the sooner and the better will be the final agreement.

CONTRACT WORDING

Contract wording must be clear to all persons using the contract. While the intent of those who negotiate may be well known to each of them, it is of no use if the management or employees not present at the bargaining table cannot understand it. Managements and unions that make use of lawyers often find that the discipline of the law provides the best basis for long-term consistent understanding. Nonlegal colloquialisms have a way of being misinterpreted.

On the other hand, since a collective agreement must sometimes set out its conditions for the benefit of a large number of persons with varying educational backgrounds, too complicated sentence structures may make the decision so complex that no one using the agreement can understand it. Much money has depended, from time to time, on a comma in a collective bargaining agreement. Punctuation, paragraphing, clause numbering, and general organization of subject matter are vital to the understanding of the persons using the document.

An increasingly frequent problem in contract wording is the desire of both parties to express the purpose of the agreement in terms that reflect the highest principles and aims. For example, the parties may preface the agreement with a statement such as: "This agreement is made to establish and maintain lawful and orderly collective bargaining relations between the company and its employees."

Although no one would doubt the sincerity of the company and the union in making such a statement, the establishing and maintaining of lawful and orderly collective relations in North America have been increasingly the responsibilities of government legislation and the labor boards and courts that it creates. Such language only opens to the persons ultimately charged with interpreting the intent of the parties a broader concept than either party probably wished to have.

There is no proven technique for assuring that the contract wording covers all the eventualities that may occur. Collective agreement language has a way of perpetuating itself, and this is perhaps its best safeguard. So-called standard clauses that have stood the test of time are in themselves the negotiator's best friends. Attempts to write new clauses, particularly if the attempt is made at four o'clock in the morning after sustained bargaining, have a way of looking foolish four months later before an arbitrator.

KEY CLAUSES

Collective agreement clauses fall generally within two types: the ones governing the relationships, and the others governing monetary matters. Key clauses in the articles governing relationships are those which establish the bargaining unit, the rights (or, preferably, responsibilities) of management, the requirements for membership in the union and the consequent paying of dues by employees, and the grievance and arbitration procedures.

In the second type of clause it is difficult to distinguish which of the multitude of clauses governing the many monetary issues negotiated are in fact more significant than others. In industry contracts, for example, seniority may be considered of prime consequence, while in craft unions company seniority may be of little significance. Basic hours of work can be commonly accepted as important in virtually every contract. So, too, are the articles governing basic wages and the premiums allowed for overtime, shift work, and other extraordinary working conditions.

Management rights. It is the article on relationships—the first group of clauses—that should and does command most attention from both bargaining parties; and in this group the most significant clause concerns management rights.

Over the years there have developed two schools of thought as to the interpretation of this article: One school supposes that the original relationship between management and labor, when it existed without an agreement, is now changed only to the extent that the agreement calls for; thus all matters not specifically set out in the contract still reside with management as being the sole authoritarian voice. The other school supposes that at the same time as the union begins to negotiate a collective agreement on behalf of the company's employees, a totally new relationship is born that establishes a sharing of responsibility between the representatives of the employees and management.

It would appear that the latter school will, with time, become more commonplace, and with it should probably come a different concept of the word "rights" when applied to management. As it now stands under the first or residual theory, management's rights are not necessarily defined but include any issue that the parties have not agreed on either in writing or in recognized practices. It would seem, however, that as both parties mature in their relationship, instead of one holding all the unused power there will resolve a kind of mutual responsibility; that there will come a time when the often-used phrase *"What* is right and not *who* is right" will be interpretable not as a slogan but as a recognized principle.

KEEPING SUPERVISORS POSTED

The kind of communications adopted during negotiations is of prime importance, both in order to reach a collective agreement and in the subsequent administration of it.

If supervisors are involved in gathering information used to establish management's agenda, it becomes a difficult problem if no immediate feedback is available until either the agreement is signed or the supervisors are informed that a strike is going to take place. Some agreements are negotiated without either party communicating anything to its principals during the negotiations. This is, of course, established by prior arrangement. It is, however, a condition that is extraordinarily difficult to support.

In a typical manufacturing plant, the employee negotiators are not continuously present at the bargaining table from the beginning of the negotiations until the final decision has been made. They come and go, and when they are not at the bargaining table, they are at their place of work. At the workplace it is practically impossible for them not to give some indication as to how the bargaining is going generally. Even the most cryptic "No comment" can be read by the listeners to mean success or failure, and the rumor that this may cause throughout the plant has in its own way considerable effect on the final outcome.

Most managements and unions find it imperative to release, from time to time, sufficient information that the people most concerned know how things are going.

Management must, of necessity, play its cards closer to its vest; after all, it is the one that gives. It would be unrealistic to advise supervisors that of the 30 cents earmarked for the negotiations, it had already given 20 and was merely waiting for the union's demand for the additional 10 cents.

In spite of these difficulties, management must find a way to keep its supervisors aware of the current climate so that it can reasonably expect to receive continuing reports from them in relation to the morale of the work force during the phases of bargaining. A pitfall in this form of communication is the temptation for management to use it for bargaining purposes. It is fairly well accepted that management messages to all levels of supervision, including the first level of foremen, become quickly known to employees. Some companies use this as a device to insure that employees will turn to them for the "true state of affairs" rather than blindly accept statements from the union that management feels may be loaded with bias.

In such battles for employees' minds, the loser is the negotiating team, for under such conditions the bargaining ceases to become its responsibility and in fact is being undertaken in the claim and counterclaim of letters and pamphlets sent by management to supervisors and by union officials to members (employees); and, worst of all, in articles in the press.

Toward the end of negotiations, should the matter be of national interest, the issues are picked up by national news media, and frequently negotiations are forced underground to try to counteract the public positions of the teams' principals.

Assessing information on morale. A great deal of conjecture has been made regarding the value of morale. While there is a kind of institutional morale, it applies only to some people. There are others, perhaps a minority, who are in a state of something other than "high" or "low" morale.

Recently, it has become increasingly apparent that a majority reaction is not necessarily the most effective. In fact, the public is now perhaps more concerned about minority group feelings and the intensity with which that minority is prepared to act in order to assure that its feelings are noted.

In the negotiating situation, supervisors' reports of high employee morale must raise some question, to thinking observers, of the validity of general statements in the matter—particularly when such reports run counter to union statements at the table. And persons who tell foremen that they are not going on strike, or that they disagree with their union's stand, or that they would support management must leave some doubts in the minds of observers that they represent a true consensus of employee thinking. Management is exceptionally responsive to such comments, however, since it wants to hear them.

To be effective, communications from supervisors to management should be dealt with in much the same way that professionals in the science of strategy and tactics find out the opposition's intentions. The point is that it takes a great deal of information, with an assessment of the reliability of the sources, to be sure that the information being received can be relied on and can therefore be used for strategic planning.

Supervisor response to prospective clauses. Supervisors appreciate any information that makes them feel as though they are true participators in the negotiating.

A royal commission in Great Britain dealing in trade union affairs recently concluded after intensive study that with the advent of big unionism as practiced in that country came the development of a relationship between supervisors and union shop stewards that was largely responsible for Britain's production problems.

The large, politically inclined union movement was not organized to cope with the multitude of problems arising on the shop floor. Insufficient union representatives meant that the union could not always advise shop stewards. Management, widely divorced from first-line supervision by compartmentalized levels of authority, also was unable to assist the foremen to any extent in responding to shop steward demands. The end results therefore were a series of negotiated deals between the foremen and the stewards that formed a far more effective base for agreement than the formal document created at the higher levels of company management and the union.

Although foremen in North American industry have perhaps not yet reached the stultifying level of their British counterparts, they are nonetheless party to similar pressures. They therefore monitor carefully the kind of response that management makes to their suggestions for changes. And if management treats such suggestions casually at the bargaining table, the foreman feels that continuing to deal with the shop steward is the only way he can achieve the kind of relationship that satisfies both his superiors and the employees for whose work he is responsible.

Contract administration at the supervisory level. A supervisor's view of contract administration is largely determined by the amount of responsibility taken by the plant personnel department in enforcing collective agreement provisions. During the many years since Douglas McGregor and Lyndall Urwick outlined the staff role for business, it has been apparent that much line responsibility is assumed by staff executives. The handling of grievance procedures in many companies where this is the case is typically as follows: The foreman receives a written grievance from a trained steward; by the terms of the contract, it demands a reply within a day or two. The seasoned foreman knows that a reply in his own words, without consultation, may implicate the company in problems which he is told are serious and far-reaching. He therefore hurries to the personnel office, where the reply to the first step of grievance is prepared with the full concurrence of management persons (who have yet to receive the grievance at the second and third stages). The foreman then returns the grievance, duly completed in such a way that his superintendent and, in turn, the manager have the pleasure of replying, "I agree with the foreman."

Under such circumstances it is a rare foreman who would trust his own initiative, and it is a rare union that does not recognize that the foreman is not in the decision-making area insofar as the collective agreement is concerned. There is even some doubt as to whether the manager is not unduly influenced by personnel and labor relations officials intent on "winning" or at least preserving the contract as written. The final outcome of grievances prepared under these procedures is of little interest to the foreman, since his participation has been of equally little significance.

Similar attitudes and practices apply to other matters relating to contract administration. If, after weeks of long argument and discussion on every clause, management assumes that foremen will absorb the nature of the argument at an evening dinner meeting or even a day's concentrated training session, it is presuming a great deal on any person's capacity.—*J. P. Chipman*

Employee Relations Programs

In the selection and installation of employee relations programs there is sometimes a tendency to "programitis"; that is to say, the company is adopting or expanding a program merely because other companies have done so. If this is the case, too little consideration will be given to the specific company's needs and circumstances. Of value in almost any company, however, are properly designed programs relating to house magazines, employee suggestions, safety, communication, food service, recreation, employee counseling, and medical services.

THE HOUSE MAGAZINE

An important tool in most communications programs is the employee magazine, which is primarily designed for communication downward to employees as the official voice of the company.

Reader appeal. The appeal of most house magazines is directed toward the employee's family as well as to the employee. In many companies the magazine frequently is mailed to the employee's home. Because of problems in mailing, however, other companies prefer distribution at work. This practice assures prompt distribution but risks loss of home readership. The tone of communication is usually objective and low-key even in describing company problems and seeking employee cooperation. The magazine offers a unique opportunity for effective employee communication. Through objectivity of content and regularity of publication, it may help to prevent the rise of employee skepticism often encountered by appeals in times of crisis (during strikes, for example).

Readability. The inclusion of a few personal reports and social items is helpful in producing a readable magazine. Photographs are used profusely. Information about the company, if written by technical experts, should be revised for greater readability before publication. Maintaining a high level of readability requires an adequate supply of suitable material always at hand. This is the point at which many house magazines meet failure. One solution is to charge one or more individuals with full-time responsibility for actively seeking appropriate material throughout the company.

Objectives and evaluation. The objectives of the magazine usually include keeping employees informed of company developments and policies. Another purpose is to promote an esprit de corps and encourage employees to identify more closely with the company. There may be collateral objectives, such as the promotion of safety consciousness by means of articles on safety achievement. The company may also strive to enhance its image by distributing the magazine to community leaders, customers, and applicants for employment.

The extent to which the objectives of the publication are attained is not easy to evaluate. One way is to conduct an employee opinion poll, with the opinions submitted in writing. Supervisors may be instructed to check systematically on employee reaction. If the questions are not carefully framed, however, the returns may be so ambiguous as to lend themselves to whatever interpretation is desired. One method of avoiding this situation is simply to find out what employees can recall of the magazine's contents after reading. This, at least, is an objective measurement.

SUGGESTION PROGRAMS

In the usual suggestion system, suggestion boxes and forms are located throughout the company. Suggestions are reviewed by the suggestion office, investigated by the appropriate department, and eventually evaluated by a committee that decides on the amount of award, if any. The award is usually 10 percent to 20 percent of the value of the first year's savings to the company from the application of the suggestion. Some companies give awards for suggestions for which no savings can be measured, such as a safety suggestion.

Engineering and cost saving. Few suggestion systems operate with formal engineering objectives; cost-saving objectives are more likely to gain acceptance. Some suggestion systems that had failed as employee relations instruments have blossomed into success when transferred to the section responsible for cost reduction. The program thus becomes an additional tool in reducing costs. The department head who ignores a cost reduction suggestion may find his performance appraisal suffering later on.

Employee relations objectives. Successful suggestion systems are expected by most companies to improve morale, further public and employee relations, improve communication, and give employees an opportunity to be singled out for promotion. Where a system is poorly administered, however, there may be an adverse effect. Resentment may be generated by delay in replying to suggestions or by rejection without a careful explanation of the reason by the supervisor. Thus it is important to have an adequate staff and constant attention to publicity on awards given. In addition, supervisors must be convinced of the plan's benefits to them; for example, that usable suggestions will improve their production records. Also helpful is a trend toward making supervisors eligible for awards for suggestions on matters outside the scope of their regular duties.

SAFETY PROGRAMS

The more successful safety programs are marked by the complete and unswerving support of top management. High-sounding policy statements alone are no substitute. Subordinates will not implement such statements if they sense half-hearted support.

Workmen's compensation objectives. The performance of a safety program is measured to a large extent by its ability to reduce workmen's compensation costs (insurance premiums, loss of time, damage to property, and compensation awards). Safety authorities have estimated that the total dollar cost to a company averages about four times the direct accident cost. The savings that can be generated make it vitally important to have an adequate professional staff to coordinate and review the safety program, evaluate progress, and make recommendations.

Safety objectives in employee relations. Safety has more than a financial aspect. An accident may take a serious toll in morale, in public and community relations, and in hardship to employees and their dependents. Company action in behalf of safe and healthful working conditions will do much to gain good employee relations.

COMMUNICATION PROGRAMS

One very successful communication program owes its origin, in part, to the discovery that employees wanted full information about their jobs and their company. Instead, they were getting incomplete information and much misinformation through rumors and other unreliable sources. Thus, a progressive company found itself deprived of the benefits expected from its enlightened policies, simply because of a failure in communication.

Communication downward. A device used by some companies to insure a continuous flow of information downward from top management is a succession of "stair-step" meetings for all levels of management within a brief period of time. The flow can then be extended to all levels of employees through either spoken or written means. The downward flow keeps any group of employees from being bypassed. The supervisor is able to amplify information or clarify points by discussion. The "personal touch" may also result in better acceptance of the communication.

Difficulties in upward flow. A major problem in securing upward flow is the unwillingness or inability of many managers and supervisors to encourage feedback of their subordinates' views and reactions. This obstacle may arise from many causes. One may be lack of empathy—inability to put one's self in the position of the other person, to see things through his eyes and his mind; or it may be nothing more than the failure of management to provide the proper training in communication values and techniques. Another difficulty is in the proper evaluation of information received. Some information reflects a tendency of subordinates to tell their supervisors what they want to hear. The supervisor himself may be a poor listener and hear only what he wants to hear.

Breaking through barriers. Perhaps the primary barriers to good communication are employee distrust and suspicion. Political propaganda and campaigns by various interests to influence men's thinking have made the average employee skeptical of both company and union messages. To overcome this obstacle, companies must communicate fully and honestly in a factual and objective manner.

It is equally important to establish communication on a regular, year-round basis; if restricted to times of emergency, it may meet little more than suspicion and distrust as a self-serving device of the company.

Feedback is essential here as in other aspects of employee relations programs, and it is a valuable means of breaking through barriers. In addition to developing the role of supervisors in this respect, companies are trying out other means. Some companies encourage employees to use a telephone service—not only to hear recorded company messages but also to give their own views to management.

In other instances trained interviewers or psychologists will periodically interview employees, especially those whom they interviewed before hire.

Face-to-face groups. Much training is given in the basic principles of behavior and motivation, and their application is tested through demonstrations and role playing. Subjects covered range from semantics (the study of the meanings of words and their uses to carry different meanings and associations to different people) to problems in overcoming blocks to intelligent listening—for example, prejudice or self-interest. Sensitivity training is also popular for helping to develop insight into the views and reactions of others. In this technique each member of a group is told frankly by the others how they react (whether favorably or unfavorably) to his remarks and mannerisms. Other training procedures employed by communication-minded companies include instruction and practice in writing clearly and directly.

FOOD-SERVICE PROGRAMS

A properly administered food-service program is one of the keys to sound employee relations. It can, however, be a major irritant if entered into without careful preparation.

Cost and operations objectives. A modern food-service program strives for the best possible service and quality at the lowest reasonable cost. It is usually advisable to engage an industrial food service because of the specialized nature of this operation. Partial subsidization may be required of the employer to keep prices low enough to encourage employee participation. In addition, the employer must closely monitor costs, employee complaints, and quality of food and service.

Employee relations objectives. A successful program provides meals that are nourishing and appetizing as well as inexpensive. A wide variety of foods should be available. If the menu is too limited, the satisfaction of individual employee needs and preferences is unlikely. Cafeteria-style operations are used by most companies to achieve the flexibility needed.

A well-run program is also designed to keep most employees on the site during meal breaks. They are likely to become better acquainted and therefore work better together. Employees who stay on company premises are also much more likely to return to their work stations on time and ready to resume work.

By insuring adequate facilities for eating, the scheduling of meal periods is also made much easier. Eliminating the practice of eating at work stations, furthermore, brings improvement in housekeeping, safety, and sanitation.

RECREATION PROGRAMS

Starting perhaps with an annual picnic and a softball team, many company recreation programs grow rather haphazardly. They may reflect the hobbies or interests of the most active employees rather than the needs of the company and the employees in general.

Extent and levels of participation. A sound program begins with company consideration of basic approaches. Decisions must be made: The program may be designed primarily for hourly employees, or perhaps a need exists for promoting relationships between the various groups. Or the program may extend beyond employees to their families or even to the community. In large cities, where employees scatter to suburbs after work, a recreational program may be limited to employees. The objective might be either to promote cohesiveness among employees or simply to encourage healthful activities.

Use of company facilities. Recreation programs often require access to company facilities for the purpose of holding meetings, social events, and athletic contests of various sorts. Problems of proper supervision and protection of company property arise. Company rules may have to be posted (and enforced) to minimize property destruction and accidents. In some cases companies permit access to on-site recreational facilities to the entire community. This promotes excellent community relations and engenders a broad-based community support for the company. Such support can prove to be an essential ingredient in developmental plans for the future.

Funding and workmen's compensation. Funding of recreation programs by the company is usually at the minimum necessary to insure success. The most successful programs are generally those where employees pay a significant share of the costs. In this way they are likely to have more voice in their programs and to take active responsibility for management and direction.

Company liability for accidents and injuries suffered by employees in recreation programs can be substantial. It is routine procedure to have such liability checked out with competent authorities and protection obtained against liability.

Family participation. Many companies provide some activities for the families of employees, thereby giving them a greater sense of identity with the company. A side benefit is that employees can become better acquainted with each other.

Evaluation. A superficial evaluation of a recreation program can be obtained by counting the attendance. However, although attendance is certainly a factor to be considered, other questions should be asked. Are there harmony and cooperation, or are cliques forming and dissension developing? Are activities coordinated to avoid overlapping and disorganization? Are employees sufficiently interested to pay part of the expense? The most important step in a thorough evaluation is probably the last: After the objectives of the program have been determined, progress made toward those objectives must be ascertained.

EMPLOYEE COUNSELING

Informal counseling exists in most companies. Much counseling, however, requires professional training, and damage can result if a member of management takes on the responsibility of counseling without adequate qualifications. Accordingly, most companies avoid formal programs for counseling. Someone in the company may be engaged in counseling executives for their growth and development, however. (One peril of this type of counseling is that the counselor may become entangled in executive-suite politics.) Medical and employee relations personnel often are approached by employees with problems and serve as counselors in these cases. A line of demarcation for an employer's responsibility in this respect might be on-the-job versus off-the-job problems, although the two types interrelate.

Supplemental services. Even companies that have a staff equipped to provide psychiatric help, treatment of alcoholism and drug addiction, and help with legal problems usually confine these services to identifying needs and referring employees elsewhere for treatment. It is obviously impractical for a company psychiatrist to attempt the extensive individual treatment needed in psychiatry. Employees can be made aware, however, of the availability of outside services such as legal aid societies, Alcoholics Anonymous, and hospital clinics.

Emergency funds for employee problems. The need for company financial assistance may have diminished in modern times. However, company facilities and assistance can be of value to employees who wish to establish credit unions in which regular saving is encouraged and loans are available at low interest rates.

Supportive counseling for socially deprived employees. Emphasis on hiring and promoting employees from minority groups has led to various counseling programs. Remedial work in education is offered through many agencies. Some companies have established "sensitivity programs" in which the supervisors and the employees from the minority groups engage in frank and open dialog concerning mutual problems. Individual counseling is also encouraged on a case-by-case basis. Companies are generally reluctant, however, to highlight such counseling programs because of the possibility that these employees might be singled out instead of integrated with the others.

Retirement counseling. Most companies limit retirement counseling to such basic functions as advising employees concerning their retirement benefits and the various alternatives such as joint and survivor options. Some start to alert employees about five years before retirement. A program may include conferences and distribution of literature on financial retrenchment and other adjustments. To take up any possible slack in normal duties, later assignments may be less demanding, but they will draw on the experience and maturity of long-service employees.

MEDICAL PROGRAMS

Medical programs are distinct from medical benefit programs. This presentation covers company medical facilities and personnel.

Objectives and staffing. Employee relations objectives in the medical program may be limited to emergency treatment for injuries or pre-employment physical examinations. In general, however, the objective extends to other purposes, such as the promotion of employee health both on and off the job.

The part-time services of a physician may be engaged by the company, or several companies may join together to share a medical staff hired in cooperation. The trend is to have a full-time medical director on company premises. He may coordinate the use of physicians at various company locations and will serve as a management adviser in other respects.

Safety objectives are promoted through liaison between the medical, safety, and production groups. In recreation, the medical program can develop activities with health value, such as calisthenics and gymnastics. Counseling is carried on by a nurse or physician because employees are likely to confide in them. Absenteeism can be reduced by care of minor ailments.

The industrial nurse. Even in a company that has only a first-aid room, the presence of a full-time nurse is important. Failure to have one (even on small night shifts) will often lead to unrest. As injuries know neither clock nor calendar, there is reason for a nurse during all working time; there is less likelihood of neglected injury if the nurse is present. Where management feels that the nurse has too much spare time, she may be given other duties, such as recording safety and absentee information and preparing statistics. Equally important, if not more so, are other functions—assistance in industrial hygiene, employee counseling, and helping the busy physician by screening out cases that do not need his attention. In addition, the nurse can be one of the firm's most important sources of information regarding employee attitudes and problems.

Preventive medicine. The physician works closely with safety and production personnel in setting up industrial hygiene standards. He also determines the nature of periodic physical examinations for employees. In many companies, annual examinations are not given to all employees; younger or short-term employees may not be examined at all. They may be asked to fill out cards in answer to health questions; the cards go into a computer to detect any need for examination. For older employees, or for middle and upper management, examinations are more common. A company that sponsors examinations should make certain they are adequate or else advise employees to have an additional examination; otherwise, an employee may be lulled into the false belief that no further examination is needed.

AUDITING EMPLOYEE RELATIONS

Perhaps the ideal test of employee relations effectiveness is in the measurement of overall company performance. Throughout all its functions the company ought to be working toward sound objectives with challenging but realistic goals and striving for high individual performance. If an organization is not performing productively and cooperatively, the effectiveness of its employee relations function deserves scrutiny. However, this type of evaluation must be supplemented with specifics.

One popular method is an employee relations audit covering all aspects of employee relations activities. Some items audited are personnel statistics, personnel procedures and records, professional activities, grievance processing, and the success of the employee relations department in promoting a people-oriented attitude on the part of management. Other typical means of evaluation include statistics on turnover, grievances, or strikes, but such figures have limitations. Low turnover may reflect the presence of long-term employees, reluctant to risk relocation but still chronically dissatisfied. A lack of grievances may result from timidity or fear. It is also true that happy employees are not necessarily productive. They may have goals and objectives that are not really challenging or meaningful.

MEASURING RESULTS AGAINST OBJECTIVES

In a company that has a management-by-objectives approach to business, there is a built-in means of evaluating effectiveness. Not only progress toward objectives but also individual performance can be evaluated. This does not mean setting goals merely in terms of quantity. Objectives should contain values accepted by management as furthering company advancement. A safety objective, for example, might be to reduce the frequency and severity rates of accidents. A communication objective could be to prepare employees to accept the elimination of a cost-of-living plan in contract negotiations.

COST CONSIDERATIONS

To promote cost-consciousness, employee relations programs should operate within a budgetary framework of some kind. Costs can escalate if not watched carefully. Excess forms and procedures can creep into activities, with resulting multiplication of staff. Duplication of functions can develop. A production group may keep the same records as those in the employee relations department. A budgetary approach will also encourage efforts to cost out programs, and the results can be most beneficial. For example, the suggestion system may be presented to management not only on a basis of total awards and savings but also with calculations to show all costs, both direct and indirect. Many executives are not really impressed by savings generated through suggestions. There is almost a subconscious feeling that all the costs are not laid on the table. If the suggestion system is costed out completely, a doubting management may see it as an instrument in cost reduction rather than as a "gimmick."

Cost data can be helpful in other ways. The hidden costs of trimming programs may be shown; for example, the elimination of orientation procedures for new employees may result in greater turnover, thus costing more than is saved.

FORWARD PLANNING

Forward planning often consists of a one-year plan and an additional long-term plan such as one for the next three years. Such planning is facilitated by the inclusion of employee relations representatives in management councils; this makes employee relations plans relate to total organization planning. Evaluations of effectiveness will require revision of planning, and goals and objectives will need adjustments. Areas needing further attention will be discovered. Changes in direction and emphasis must be made.

The timing of revision is important. To revise plans only once a year is unrealistic; evaluation of effectiveness is a continuous process, and so is the feeding of evaluations into planning. With such timely revision, employee relations plans and programs are much more likely to stay in step with company needs and objectives.—*C. E. Graves*

PERSONNEL RESEARCH

The purpose of most personnel research is to aid managers in making decisions. Because personnel expenditures are usually the second- or third-largest costs of doing business, improvements in decision making in this area can produce large dividends.

There are four types of personnel research: (1) descriptive; (2) behavioral-science-based descriptive; (3) action; and (4) basic. Most companies conduct at least the first, but very few are active in more than two areas.

Descriptive Personnel Research

Descriptive personnel research is conducted to satisfy management's need to know as much as possible about the personnel situation in its company and in competitive companies. Such research usually involves the compilation of data about a company's employees and workers who have comparable jobs in the same community or industry. Examples of this type of research are the gathering of turnover data or the conducting of a community wage survey.

The precipitant of most descriptive research is management's need to make a decision in a specified area. Management may have decided to revise its benefits program, and it needs information on the current plan, perhaps a frequency distribution of claims by education, salary, and job categories. Or it may need to prepare for an impending labor negotiation by collecting salary and benefit information on its own and comparable employees.

Another strong reason for conducting descriptive research is to spotlight areas within the company that need management's attention. Annual analyses of turnover and absenteeism by areas of the company or job category will pinpoint potential problem areas. Annual surveys are particularly effective in this role, as they provide comparative data to spot trends before the trends become major problems.

An important but relatively unused type of descriptive research concerns collecting productivity information for the entire work force, for individual units, and even for individuals. This kind of information helps management in making personnel decisions, and it is essential in manufacturing decisions involving man-machine trade-offs.

Not only does descriptive research aid management in making decisions and finding problems; it also provides bench marks by which management can evaluate the effectiveness of its decisions and programs. The efficiency of a new incentive program can best be evaluated by observing changes in productivity. Improvements in company orientation may affect early turnover. The effectiveness of a recruitment program for Negroes would show up in statistics on the ethnic background of employees. The use of research to define the benefits of a personnel program is particularly important to a company using a results-oriented management system. In planning, the company must describe in as quantitative terms as possible the results it hopes to achieve and, at the end of a period, must report on the results obtained.

In most companies, descriptive research tends to be concentrated on non-management and lower-level management employees, but there is a trend toward application at higher levels as companies become larger and the importance of decisions at that level on profits is recognized.

Descriptive research techniques are generally of the simplest variety—usually, the mere counting of individuals in specified categories. Statistical applications are usually confined to simple correlations and analyses of differences between means, but more and more companies are increasing the sophistication of their analyses. Packaged computer programs now make it relatively easy for a company to do a multiple regression or factor analysis.

DATA ANALYSIS

Far too many companies devote most of their research energy to the collection of data and very little to the analysis of the data. Information worth thousands or even millions of dollars probably lies untapped in the files of many companies. For example, one company had broken down turnover data by departments and found few departmental differences. When, by chance, the company further broke down the information by tenure within departments, they found that in some departments the greatest number of turnovers was occurring among relatively new employees, while in others more senior employees were the ones leaving. Obviously, differing approaches to the problems were needed. Productivity information almost always demands considerable analysis before it is useful. Differences in equipment, material, work area, or other factors make adjustments necessary before accurate decisions can be made.

Poor or incomplete analysis of data is usually caused by the number one problem of descriptive research—lack of problem definition. The determination of research objectives is probably the key requirement of any kind of personnel research. A manager should clearly state for his researcher the kinds of decisions he wants to make and let the researcher provide the information. When the objectives of the research are understood by the personnel researcher, he can develop a research plan that brings to bear on the problem all the resources and information available to him. All appropriate forms of analysis can be tried.

USE OF COMPUTERS

The use of the computer to store personnel data is bringing about major changes in the number of companies that conduct descriptive research. Because most of the effort is taken out of research, many studies previously impossible can be undertaken. The focus of the companies' efforts is placed on the analysis and the use of the results, not on the accumulation of data. Unusual research hypotheses become testable. One company, for instance, analyzed the performance appraisal and tenure of employees referred by different employment agencies. They found some agencies to be much more productive than others in producing stable, highly productive employees.

TECHNICAL REQUIREMENTS

Growing reliance on computers and increasingly sophisticated demands by management are leading many companies to take a more professional approach in their descriptive research operations. A specialist in descriptive research must have an understanding of statistics, research design, and computer operations. Most important, he must have a background that allows him to handle the great variations in the subject matter and methods with which he must work. A researcher must understand benefits, costing, compensation, structure analysis, seasonal projections of work force, and related areas.

COMPARATIVE INFORMATION

Most companies respond favorably to requests from other companies for descriptive information on their work force, for they know they may be needing similar help in the future. Comparative information is necessary in wage surveys and union negotiations and is helpful in interpreting many other types of descriptive information. While the Bureau of Labor Statistics (BLS) and other government agencies—Federal, state, and local—offer a variety of information about employees, it is often difficult for a company to use such information for comparative purposes. The information is seldom specific enough. Many companies use trade associations or business groups to share information or, in some cases, actually to collect the information and distribute it among the members. A caution about interpreting survey information is in order, however: If the survey is conducted professionally, it may be of much value, but in too many cases it is only a hastily drawn-up questionnaire that produces completely uncomparable data (as when the method of calculating turnover is not specified and companies report percentages by whatever method they desire).

Behavioral-Science-Based Descriptive Research

A separate type of descriptive research can be defined by the techniques used to conduct the research. An increasing number of companies are using research techniques drawn from the behavioral sciences to learn more about their employees and potential employees. Psychological tests, opinion surveys, and performance appraisals help management go beyond the mere counting of employees in various categories to a deeper understanding of their abilities, their feelings, and their performance.

PSYCHOLOGICAL TESTING

One of the most valuable, most misunderstood, and most misused sources of information about applicants is the psychological test. Tests can provide information about applicants' knowledge, aptitudes, interests, personality, and even motivation. Many companies have found that the information furnished by tests is related to performance, turnover, and other indexes of job success. They have also learned that if tests are properly used as aids in employment, costs can be reduced. The use of tests or other objective devices to aid in selection, placement, or promotion decisions is a form of descriptive research, although most companies do not realize it.

Validation. Before a company can effectively use a test, in most cases, it must conduct validation research. A test is usually validated by seeing how successful and less successful employees differ on a test score. The degree that the test predicts success indicates its validity. A form of mechanical aptitude, for instance, can be measured with a test. If a company wants to determine the relationship of this type of mechanical aptitude to success as an automotive mechanic, it will see how successful and less successful mechanics score on the test. If the distribution of scores for both groups is the same, it is not good as a selection aid. Only if most of the successful mechanics score higher (or lower) than the less successful mechanics will the test be an effective selection aid.

No matter how well constructed the test is or how frequently it is used by industries, a test has no inherent validity in itself. It is only valid in relation to a specific job situation or a specific skill. Experience has shown that, although the validity of some types of test information remains relatively constant across positions (clerical test results, for example), most test information must be re-validated for every major new use of the information. Consider the selection of salesmen: There are about as many kinds of salesmanship as there are salesman positions; thus, applicant information that predicts success in one situation may be totally unrelated to success in another. It may even be related to failure, as when the fast-talking, door-to-door salesman's qualities are found in an industrial salesman who must negotiate with sophisticated purchasing experts.

Validities are also affected by changes in the nature of the skills required by a job and changes in types of applicants for it. In a tight labor market, questions about past performance may have less validity when most of the applicants are young and have little chance to gain any kind of experience. Similarly, the quality of applicants for a specific position can vary considerably from one part of the country to another, or from one season of the year to another.

Companies that have not validated the information on which their hiring decisions are based may be guessing right, but the odds are that they are basing their decisions on some characteristics not related to success. Common examples include the company that arbitrarily demands that all applicants make above the fiftieth percentile on an intelligence test, the interviewer who will not hire applicants who wear sport coats, and the company that decides to hire only engineers in the future. When invalid characteristics of applicants are considered in hiring, the efficiency of the hiring procedure suffers; the selection costs go up needlessly; and the company's money is wasted in obtaining useless information. In the case of test information, this waste can be considerable when administration and scoring time is added to the cost of the tests. Most important, potentially good applicants may be lost to the company. In these days of high recruitment and interviewing costs, the loss may be in the thousands of dollars.

The major hurdle in validation research is in obtaining the proper criteria against which the test can be validated. If possible, applicant information should be validated against actual performance measures such as recorded output, error rate, and absences. But, for many jobs, objective measures of performance are not available, and subjective measures of performance such as ratings are employed. The problem in many cases is that ratings are not as accurate as could be desired.

Much interest in test validation has resulted from Federal Government efforts to assure that tests and other selection devices are not unfairly discriminating against members of minority groups. Research in a number of companies has shown that unintentional discrimination can exist, but it may be overcome by special interpretation of the test results based on research results. All users of tests or other objective selection or promotional devices are strongly urged to consult *Guidelines on Employment Testing Procedures* (U.S. Equal Employment Opportunity Commission, Washington, D.C., 1966). Those with Federal Government contracts should further consult the Office of Federal Contract Compliance order on testing *(Employment Tests by Contractors and Subcontractors, 1968).*

BIOGRAPHICAL INFORMATION

Another selection device that has many of the properties of a test is the biographical information blank (also called biographical history questionnaire, life history antecedent questionnaire, personal information blank, and supplemental interview form). It is an organized, statistically weighted list of questions on an applicant's biographical history.

A product of World War II, the biographical information blank is the most important new selection tool to be developed from personnel research. It is often found to be the best single predictor of future behavior where the predicted behavior is of a total or complex nature—for example, the job of a business executive.

Biographical information blanks should be constructed by a person professionally trained in industrial psychology. Interviews with successful and less successful occupants of the job under consideration provide the researcher with leads for questions. From his insights obtained from interviewing and his knowledge of biographical questions that were effective in other cases, the researcher prepares a large number of questions. These questions, which are usually multiple-choice, are administered to a criterion group so that items predictive of success can be determined. Through an often complicated statistical process, optimum weighting of the item is obtained and scoring procedures are worked out. The eventual user of the questionnaire is able to score it and interpret the biographical information blank as if it were a test.

OPINION SURVEYS

Companies are increasingly interested in the feelings and opinions of both management and nonmanagement employees. They have found that they can get far more motivational impact from their benefit plans at no additional cost if their employees' opinions are considered. Policies are more effective and more easily implemented if the desires of employees are taken into consideration.

When executives obtain feedback from their subordinates, not only is supervision improved but supervisors who need training are spotted.

An opinion survey is any organized attempt to collect information about past and present attitudes and opinions of employees. For various reasons (to save expenses, for example), the most common method of conducting an opinion survey is to distribute a questionnaire to employees. Companies faced with unusual problems occasionally collect information through personnel interviews or other methods.

Purposes. Companies usually conduct opinion surveys for one of three purposes: (1) to determine the desires of management and nonmanagement employees; (2) to determine which units or plants require special management attention; (3) to determine the company policies and operational areas that seem to be causing unusual dissatisfaction and thus warrant a study of possible changes.

Additionally, some companies conduct surveys for one or more of the following purposes: (1) to audit the effectiveness of management training programs; (2) to determine compliance with company policy; (3) to evaluate the effectiveness of various managers, particularly their ability in the human relations area; (4) to obtain information to serve as a basis for individual developmental counseling of managers; (5) to determine the effectiveness of company communication; (6) to evaluate the appeal of various benefit plans being considered; (7) to determine what went wrong when a job offer was not accepted or an employee quit.

Areas. Very few company activities and interests have not been the subject of an opinion survey somewhere. The most common topics surveyed are communication, employee benefit plans, quality of supervision, promotion, training, salary administration, company organization, safety, education and development, and transfers.

Probably the most researched area is communication. Studies have uniformly shown that well-informed employees are more satisfied; and satisfied employees are more responsive to motivators. Morale and productivity are usually related to affirmative answers to such questions as "Do you feel you know what's going on in the company?" Or this one: "How many times in the last year has your supervisor talked to you about your job?"

Most opinion surveys concentrate on the general flow of downward and upward communication and do not differentiate between the various channels. On the other hand, some companies have conducted surveys to assess the effectiveness of a specific channel of communication, such as company publications, letters sent to employees' homes, the immediate supervisor, and departmental meetings.

Industry has shown less interest in studying upward than downward communication. Although numerous studies suggest that this is a mistake, managers continue to delude themselves by thinking that they know what is going on. Too many managers assume that the announcement of an "open door" policy is all they need to achieve maximum communication.

The most common management fear about opinion surveying is that the act of asking for opinions may make employees dissatisfied. ("It may put ideas in their heads.") There is no evidence that taking a reading of employee feelings causes problems, but there is much to show that not being aware of negative attitudes and opinions can cause problems. It is important that a company be aware that the making of a survey does commit management to taking some action on the results even if the only action is showing the employees that management recognizes the problem.

Conducting the survey. There are three steps in conducting an opinion survey: (1) determining what to survey; (2) conducting and interpreting the survey; and (3) using the results. The first and third steps are the responsibility of company management and are by far the most important and the most difficult. The second step is the responsibility of the personnel researcher who conducts the survey.

1. *Determining what to survey.* While either top company or personnel department executives are responsible for determining the content areas of an opinion survey and the employees to be surveyed, they usually rely heavily on behavioral-science-trained personnel researchers for assistance. Researchers often interview departmental managers to uncover problem areas, and frequently they also interview a sample of employees to find areas of concern or dissatisfaction that should be investigated in the survey.

Executives sometimes abdicate too much of their responsibility for survey content. Questions that are not pertinent result in useless information. A good policy is to test every question by asking: "What will we do if the employees have a good opinion or answer the question a certain way, and what will we do if the employees have a poor opinion or answer the question another way?" If management's response is the same for both questions, the question is generally useless.

2. *Conducting and interpreting the survey.* Questionnaires can be mailed to employees' homes or administered on the job.

The optimal frequency of obtaining information from employees seems to depend on the company, its information needs, and both inside and outside factors that affect attitudes. Companies experiencing sudden expansion or product changes need more frequent surveys than those that are more stable.

Most opinion surveys are conducted anonymously, but research has disclosed that a large percentage of respondents will voluntarily give their names if asked to do so.

The restriction of opinion surveys to nonmanagement employees has apparently ended. Most large companies survey both management and nonmanagement. Smaller companies have less need for formal surveys of management.

No matter how carefully an opinion questionnaire is constructed, it usually ends by raising more questions than it answers. Most sophisticated users of written opinion surveys use follow-up personal interviews to further define problems and determine relationships. In addition, some companies use complicated statistical techniques such as factor analysis to reveal hidden meanings, or conduct further studies based on hypotheses derived from the initial survey. Follow-up interviews are usually conducted by professional researchers, but there are exceptions to this practice.

3. *Using the results.* Companies make various uses of opinion research findings—including just filing the results away and forgetting them. Total disregard of survey findings, which happens in a rather large number of companies, is usually attributed to poor questionnaire construction or to the fact that management had already decided what it was going to do before the survey was made. Whatever the explanation, silence on the survey findings is bad for employee morale. (The employee feels that he is getting no attention.) In most cases the survey results should be fed back to the employees, together with information on what the firm plans to do about the problems raised.

A common misconception of executives is that opinion surveys are standard multiple-choice questionnaires. The executives do not realize that paper-and-pencil techniques are not always required. Opinions can be gathered by other methods, such as conducting interviews, soliciting and analyzing suggestions, and encouraging letter writing to company newspapers.

Not only are multiple-choice questionnaires unnecessary; they are sometimes undesirable. Open-end questions are often far more meaningful than multiple-choice. Furthermore, when companies are trying to probe more elusive and deep-seated attitudes, they can achieve far greater success with interviews.

Interviews. Most interviews consist merely of an interviewer having a friendly chat with an employee about his job or some other topic. Aside from its expense, this technique always suffers from the possibility that the interviewer will misinterpret the employee's statements. Studies have shown that an interviewer's biases can easily affect his interpretation of an employee's opinions or attitudes. Bias, however, can be minimized by thorough training of the interviewer. Because interview survey techniques are flexible, they are easily adapted to the particular needs of a company.

There is usually a substantial time lag between management's definition of the information needed and obtaining quantitative results, whether the survey is conducted through a questionnaire or by means of interviews. Survey development, statistical analysis, printing, and distribution are time-consuming. For large multiplant surveys the time period often runs to six months. Yet there are times when management needs more information before it acts. To answer this type of need, a growing number of companies are developing the capacity to do "fast answer" surveys. These surveys, usually based on interviews with a sampling of the total work force, can produce answers for management within a week or ten days. In a typical situation a personnel research department or consultant might receive a request for information on Friday, conduct interviews on Monday and Tuesday, analyze the results on Wednesday, and write a report on Thursday. Within one week management has its employees' viewpoints.

PERFORMANCE APPRAISALS

Companies cannot fully train, compensate, and challenge all their employees. Not everyone can be assigned a choice job, and not everyone can be promoted. Somehow, employees who are capable of assuming greater responsibility must be identified. One of the great challenges to management today is to put its training, compensation, and developmental expenditures where they will be most effective. To help management make these important decisions, companies conduct personnel research in five general areas related to employee appraisal: (1) determining the accuracy of appraisals; (2) studying the accuracy of psychological evaluations used for appraisal purposes; (3) developing and/or validating tests and other objective measures for nonmanagement assessment; (4) developing tests and/or validating tests and other objective measures for management assessment; and (5) developing and/or validating new ways of appraising management.

RESEARCH FOR MANAGEMENT POTENTIAL

Testing for promotion in management is usually confined to predicting success in first-level management positions. Less frequently researched, but equally important, is the use of tests or other objective measures to identify early potential of executives for top management positions. This lack of emphasis on research probably has two major causes: (1) management's satisfaction with appraisals and (2) researchers' difficulties in validating tests for top management positions.

More specifically, test validation research at upper management levels has been hampered by: (1) the psychologically complex nature of the executive's job; (2) the many job, organizational, and interpersonal factors that affect an executive's job performance; (3) the great difficulty in obtaining criteria of managerial success; and (4) the small number of executives in similar positions in any one company.

It is important to remember that the same government rulings regulating the use of tests for selection apply equally to promotion. In addition, there is increasing union interest in using trade tests, which measure proficiency or even potential to learn, for promotional purposes.

Only large companies actually conduct research to determine the accuracy of appraisal or to develop new appraisal techniques, but many companies use the results of research studies conducted in large companies and government agencies. Continuing research in one large company has shown the effectiveness of goal-setting appraisals. As a result, numerous other firms have adopted this technique.

The assessment center. Currently, companies are showing interest in an appraisal approach called an assessment center, which was pioneered by the Office of Strategic Services. An assessment center supplements regular appraisal procedures in situations where especially difficult or important developmental or advancement decisions must be made. It is designed to provide appraisal information not obtainable in work situations: for example, situations where it is impossible or impractical to (1) assess all qualities needed before advancing an employee or (2) compare candidates for a position accurately and fairly because of differences in appraisers or differences in previous job assignments.

The assessment center is a standardized method that uses multiple techniques such as situational exercises, interviews, tests, and peer evaluation to evaluate individuals for various purposes. It differs from other appraisal techniques or procedures in that a number of individuals are processed at the same time; multiple, trained evaluators who, usually, are not acting in a direct supervisory capacity are used; and the procedures are not conducted on the job.

By far the largest application of the assessment center techniques is in selecting applicants for first-level management positions. In these situations, the company is primarily interested in estimating management potential, but centers may also produce training and development recommendations. In addition, assessment centers are used by companies to identify top management potential and select salesmen, and for a variety of other purposes.

In a typical center used to assess applicants for first-level management, 12 assessees participate in exercises and simulations for two or two and one-half days, after which the three to six assessors spend two or three days in coming to an assessment decision and writing reports.

Assessment centers are more effective than normal employment and appraisal procedures because all assessees (1) have an equal opportunity to display their talents; (2) are seen under similar conditions in situations designed to bring out the particular skills and abilities needed for the position or positions for which they are being considered; and (3) are evaluated by a team of trained assessors unbiased by past association who are intimately familiar with the position requirements.

Although individual company research effort in the area of appraisals should be encouraged, particularly if tests are used, most companies would do well to make sure that they are applying the knowledge that behavioral science researchers have gained concerning appraisals. Very few companies are doing so.

Training and development effectiveness. The small amount of training research that is conducted is usually on the assessment of training effectiveness. Executives want to know whether they are getting their money's worth from their training expenditures. Unfortunately, much of this type of research is superficial and probably useless. Too often, the evaluation of a training course or program is based entirely on personal comments by the participants. Considerable research has shown that participants in training programs usually evaluate courses positively, regardless of the quality of the program.

A more satisfactory method of evaluating a program is to determine how much of its factual content is retained by the trainee. One company, an automobile manufacturer, uses subject matter examinations to evaluate the effects of some of its foreman training programs.

A much more difficult but meaningful measure of effectiveness is the determination of behavioral change stemming from a training program. For nonmanagement skills training programs it is sometimes possible to determine effectiveness by measuring output or errors. For supervisory and management training programs the process is more difficult. It is possible, however, to evaluate programs by comparing the morale of employees reporting to supervisors who attended training programs with that of employees reporting to supervisors who have had no training, or by counting the number of interactions between a supervisor and his subordinates before and after training to find out if the supervisor has become more people-oriented.

The most common method of evaluation appears to be a supervisory rating of participants before and after the training program. This technique has one obvious flaw: In most cases the participant takes part in the program because the supervisor gives his permission, and the supervisor's knowledge that the participant has had training may bias his evaluation. Furthermore, the supervisor may be looking for changes. There are research designs that will minimize this problem, but they are seldom used.

Determining the effectiveness of a total development plan is even more difficult. Here, the total impact of a number of training and development activities —such as job rotation—must be evaluated. Very few companies attempt to evaluate their ongoing development programs in terms of what an employee should be able to do on the job.

Research can also provide management with information on who should be trained, an information area that should be covered in the evaluation of training techniques.

Action Research

A far less common type of research has been characterized by its practitioners as action research. It is the intent of this research to produce change, not describe it. It can best be illustrated by the handling of an employee opinion survey. The end result of a survey, in terms of descriptive research, is a report to management stating and interpreting the responses by various breakdowns such as location, seniority, and type of position. Action research, on the other hand, entails the feedback of the results—not only to top management but to individuals and groups of supervisors in a manner that triggers self-evaluative thinking and discussion. Research has shown that most supervisors think their subordinates have a higher opinion of their supervisory practices than they actually do. The "facts" as proved by an opinion survey can be a powerful stimulus to change. A bottom to top feedback of survey results to managers seems to be effective in getting supervisors to improve their effectiveness rather than react in a defensive way—as may happen if they are called in by their boss and asked to explain low morale in their unit.

TECHNIQUES

Communications and organizational climate surveys are commonly used tools in an action research program. One consultant uses tapes of top management meetings to develop data with which to generate discussion in later meetings. Several consultants survey organizational climate as both an input to training and an evaluation of training effectiveness.

An important distinction between action research and descriptive research is in the planning phase. Action research may bring about considerable management reappraisal of goals and objectives prior to the implementation of any research. In descriptive research, no follow-up is planned past the reporting of the findings. Before an action research program begins, detailed plans for the use of the results must be developed and accepted by management. A second distinction lies in the feedback loop provided in most action research plans. It is common to conduct an opinion survey, use the results to plan actions, and then conduct a second survey to show the effect of the action. Thus the survey becomes an integral part in the developmental process of the executives involved.

Only a few companies are conducting action research programs, but the number seems to be increasing as more and more companies become disenchanted with the poor usage of descriptive research findings. By combining application with research, a company is more assured of a meaningful payoff of its research investment.

Basic Research

Basic research as defined by the natural sciences is seldom conducted by industry in the area of personnel. Companies prefer leaving this type of investigation to universities and government agencies, but they show their appreciation of the need for such studies by providing funds, facilities, and subjects. Almost all personnel research conducted by industry is intended to solve immediate, applied problems.

A basic research project would include investigations such as an example in one large corporation where 400 managers are being closely followed as they progress through management. Information about the men—interview evaluations, test scores, attitude and opinion questionnaire responses, and performance records—has been gathered continually and related to their progress. The company hopes that this research will throw light on such questions as how people change over the years; the causes and results of such changes; the relationship of these changes to managerial performance and progress; and the effectiveness of the assessment center method of appraising management potential.

Basic research also concerns studies of motivation, fatigue, organizational effectiveness, group dynamics, and the effectiveness of various training techniques. In general, only large companies engage in these forms of research.

Use of Professionals in Personnel Research

Descriptive research often can be conducted by the line or staff people close to the area of research but may require professional assistance; all other areas of research should be conducted by a professional. The risk of unknowingly misusing or misinterpreting behavioral survey or research data is too great. Government regulations in the use of tests and similar objective employment or promotional devices have had the effect of requiring some professional involvement in this area. Not only do they require tests to be validated by professional standards; they suggest the use of various highly sophisticated statistical and research techniques. A number of consultants and university professors are available to conduct this type of research, but great care should be taken in their selection. The surest form of evaluation is probably found in comments from past clients.

—*W. C. Byham*

Section 4

Finance

CONTENTS

Responsibilities of the Chief Financial Officer

General Accounting and Financial Statements

Cost Accounting Methods and Objectives

Planning, Budgeting, and Forecasting

Capital Expenditure Programs and Return on Investment

Financing Corporate Requirements

Cash Management and Bank Relations

Inventory: Valuation and Control

Accounts Receivable: Credit and Collections

Internal Audit Techniques and Applications

The CPA, the Audit Report, and the Annual Report

Federal Income Tax Responsibilities

State and Local Taxes

Acquisitions and Divestments

Presentation and Interpretation of Operating Results

The Role of Finance in General Management

RESPONSIBILITIES OF THE CHIEF FINANCIAL OFFICER

The traditional responsibilities of the chief financial officer, who formerly always wore the title of treasurer, were primarily those relative to the preservation of company assets. Evolution of the function ultimately encompassed duties of accounting for all business transactions, financial planning, budgets, and other responsibilities that today are conceded to be in the area administered by a controller. (The title may be either controller or comptroller.) Most industrial controllerships actually came into existence only as recently as 1920 and were created to share the broadening executive-level financial responsibilities.

Recognition of a separation of duties between those of a treasurer and those of a controller gave rise to a third title, vice president of finance. In absence of the latter, the treasurer is recognized as the senior officer; he is usually an elected officer, whereas the controller may be elected or appointed.

Under conditions that dictate the alignment of responsibilities of the finance function in any given company, the chief financial officer may have either broad responsibilities and the relative authority, or he may be severely limited, as might be the situation in a small company, where the president often assumes many treasurership responsibilities.

Organizational Structure

As with all other business functions, the responsibilities of the finance function are departmentalized or assigned on a basis relative to the size of the company, as this factor will govern the number of individuals available in each operational area.

SIZE AND STRUCTURE

In general, and to set a framework of reference, it can be stated that companies may normally be classified as small, medium-size, or large.

Legal entity. The type of legal entity under which a company operates will often be indicative of its size: A sole proprietorship usually is a small business, a partnership may represent a larger firm, and nearly all large companies are corporations. There are, of course, exceptions, but for the most part this and the subsequent material covered in this section of the handbook will assume a corporate legal structure.

The growing company. A company which has been in the small class for a number of years and is developing to medium size is where the organizational structure is likely to be under the greatest stress. Too frequently, such companies have fitted job responsibilities to the men who were available, at times distorting duties to suit individual personalities. An older but untrained "executive" may be handling all insurance administration; cash control may be under a King Midas type of president; and some otherwise useless stockholder-employee or shirt-tail relative may be delegated to sign all checks. When new and more sophisticated executive talent is brought into the company to cope with the growth problems, frustrations develop in both the new and the older men.

The finance function is one of the first to experience the pains of growth, but alertness to impending events on the part of the president or the chief financial officer may prompt planning for an improved organizational structure which will be better prepared to meet new challenges.

The Small Company

A small company must attempt to select and employ men who are versatile—capable of handling a variety of duties and responsibilities—and simultaneously prepared to exercise wide authority. In such companies there is seldom room for specialists, and this is especially true in finance and accounting.

DUAL TITLES

The number of principals is probably limited; it is likely that most of them are directors as well as stockholders, and it is also probable that the same men serve as officers. In many cases, several of the officers will carry dual titles—president and treasurer, secretary-treasurer, vice president and controller, for example. In their simplest form, the organizational arrangements for the financial and accounting functions could follow the plan of organization shown in Exhibit 4.1.

CORPORATE SECRETARY DUTIES

In the small or medium-size companies, duties that would be in the legal department or corporate secretary's department in a larger company are frequently assigned to an executive in the finance function. This is entirely logical because of the quasilegal activities that treasurers and controllers encounter in their normal routine, such as insurance contracts, required bank resolutions, Securities and Exchange Commission (SEC) reports, leases, and local, state, and Federal tax returns.

The small corporation may wish to upgrade its chief financial officer, in which case the title of vice president–finance may be bestowed on him. In actuality, it is unlikely that any change in responsibility and authority will be granted coincident with the change in title.

The Medium-Size Company

As a company graduates into the next size group, it must begin to give recognition to the necessity and the benefits of subfunctions that must be given greater attention.

SPECIALIZATION

Other areas are often given priority of specialization before the needs of the finance functions are recognized. A vice president of engineering may be appointed, a director of personnel may be hired, and research and development will blossom as the think-tank of the company; but, eventually, what they do will require financial control.

Companies are inevitably oriented toward one profession or another, and usually according to one of two determining factors: the profession of the president or the basic technology of the business, which may be engineering, metallurgy, or any other. If the company or the president is finance-oriented, the function itself will receive recognition of the need for specialization before other functions expand and thus will be prepared to handle expanded activities of all functions. If the finance function is looked upon with the archaic view that it is "overhead," instead of enjoying its true role as the fountainhead of corporate management knowledge, it will be continually trailing other functions until full company growth is achieved.

Exhibit 4.1

BASIC ORGANIZATION PLAN OF FINANCE AND ACCOUNTING AND RELATED SECRETARY FUNCTIONS IN A SMALL COMPANY

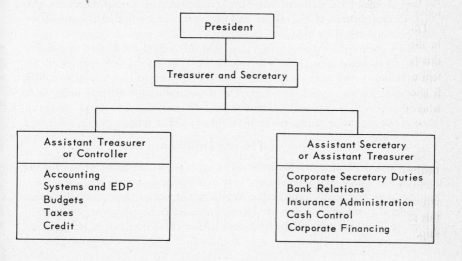

To prepare for future expansion and be organized in the best manner to cope with current activity, the medium-size company would do well to organize its finance department according to the plan shown in Exhibit 4.2.

CREDIT SHIFT

It should be noted that, while in the smaller corporation credit is more likely to be administered by the controller's office, the responsibility is shifted to the treasurer's function in a larger company. This is also apt to be true of other responsibilities that will flow to the treasurer from the controller as the former position advances from what is often an honorary title in the small company to one of full responsibility in a larger company.

The medium-size company must prepare for growth but simultaneously guard against developing too many levels of management and administration; such expansion could conceivably disturb the salary structure and unduly increase total administrative costs.

The Large Corporation

In many companies that have not attained the status of *Fortune*'s 500 largest corporations in the United States, the president may be the only officer reporting directly to the board of directors.

BOARD INFLUENCE

In the large corporation, not only may all officers report to the board; the internal audit department, the tax department, and even the administrative services function may be required to report to the board of directors.

The primary area of difference in organization of the finance department in the large company as compared with the small or medium-size company is the firm establishment of a vice president of finance as the chief financial officer.

The organization of the finance department in the large corporation may develop along several different basic lines, depending on the management philosophies and theories of the officers and directors, but a popular concept in use today is as presented in Exhibit 4.3.

The absence of the corporate secretary from this organization chart is obvious; in the large corporation there will usually be a separate office established for this function or the duties will come under a legal department, both of which will normally report to the president. The responsibility for internal audit work is another function that will be assumed by the treasurer in a large company, whereas the controller manages the function in smaller firms.

Financial Society Definitions

The Financial Executives Institute (FEI) began under the name of Controllers Institute but found that its members were experiencing an expansion of responsibilities and that many prospective members had duties that generally would fall under the treasurer or vice president of finance. In consequence the name of this professional society was changed, and with it the requirements for membership.

Exhibit 4.2

BASIC ORGANIZATION PLAN FOR THE RECOGNITION AND SEPARATION OF SPECIALIZED
ACTIVITY OF THE SECRETARIAL AND FINANCIAL FUNCTIONS IN A MEDIUM-SIZE COMPANY

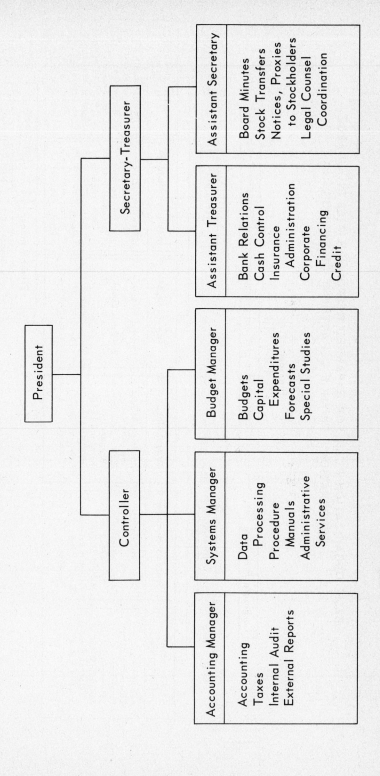

Exhibit 4.3

BASIC ORGANIZATION PLAN FOR EXPANDED RESPONSIBILITIES IN A LARGE CORPORATION'S FINANCE DEPARTMENT OR DIVISION

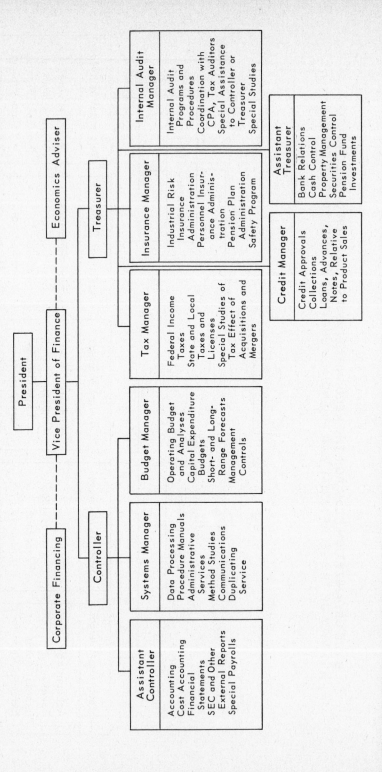

President

Vice President of Finance

Corporate Financing

Economics Adviser

Controller

Treasurer

Assistant Controller
Accounting
Cost Accounting
Financial Statements
SEC and Other External Reports
Special Payrolls

Systems Manager
Data Processing
Procedure Manuals
Administrative Services
Method Studies
Communications
Duplicating Service

Budget Manager
Operating Budget and Analyses
Capital Expenditure Budgets
Short- and Long-Range Forecasts
Management Controls

Tax Manager
Federal Income Taxes
State and Local Taxes and Licenses
Special Studies of Tax Effect of Acquisitions and Mergers

Insurance Manager
Industrial Risk Insurance Administration
Personnel Insurance Administration
Pension Plan Administration
Safety Program

Internal Audit Manager
Internal Audit Programs and Procedures
Coordination with CPA, Tax Auditors
Special Assistance to Controller or Treasurer
Special Studies

Credit Manager
Credit Approvals
Collections
Loans, Advances, Notes, Relative to Product Sales

Assistant Treasurer
Bank Relations
Cash Control
Property Management
Securities Control
Pension Fund Investments

Exhibit 4.4

RESPONSIBILITIES OF A TREASURER AND A CONTROLLER
Courtesy of the Financial Executives Institute

CONTROLLERSHIP

PLANNING FOR CONTROL — To establish, coordinate and administer, as an integral part of management, an adequate plan for the control of operations. Such a plan would provide, to the extent required in the business, profit planning, programs for capital investing and for financing, sales forecasts, expense budgets, and cost standards, together with the necessary procedures to effectuate the plan.

REPORTING AND INTERPRETING — To compare performance with operating plans and standards, and to report and interpret the results of operations to all levels of management and to the owners of the business. This function includes the formulation of accounting policy, the coordination of systems and procedures, and the preparation of operating data and of special reports as required.

EVALUATING AND CONSULTING — To consult with all segments of management responsible for policy or action concerning any phase of the operation of the business as it relates to the attainment of objectives and the effectiveness of policies, organization structure, and procedures.

TAX ADMINISTRATION — To establish and administer tax policies and procedures.

GOVERNMENT REPORTING — To supervise or coordinate the preparation of reports to government agencies.

PROTECTION OF ASSETS — To assure protection for the assets of the business through internal control, internal auditing, and assuring proper insurance coverage.

ECONOMIC APPRAISAL — To continuously appraise economic and social forces and government influences, and to interpret their effect upon the business.

TREASURERSHIP

PROVISION OF CAPITAL — To establish and execute programs for the provision of the capital required by the business, including negotiating the procurement of capital and maintaining the required financial arrangements.

INVESTOR RELATIONS — To establish and maintain an adequate market for the company's securities and, in connection therewith, to maintain adequate liaison with investment bankers, financial analysts, and shareholders.

SHORT-TERM FINANCING — To maintain adequate sources for the company's current borrowings from commercial banks and other lending institutions.

BANKING AND CUSTODY — To maintain banking arrangements; to receive, have custody of, and disburse the company's monies and securities; and to be responsible for the financial aspects of real estate transactions.

CREDITS AND COLLECTIONS — To direct the granting of credit and the collection of accounts due the company, including the supervision of required special arrangements for financing sales, such as time payment and leasing plans.

INVESTMENTS — To invest the company's funds as required, and to establish and coordinate policies for investment in pension and other similar trusts.

INSURANCE — To provide insurance coverage as required.

As set by the FEI, the definitive responsibilities of a treasurer and a controller, which have been its historical guidelines in determining the actual responsibilities of its members, are described in Exhibit 4.4.

The National Association of Accountants (NAA), the Tax Executives Institute (TEI), the American Institute of Certified Public Accountants (AICPA), and other finance-related organizations also take a serious view toward the definition of job responsibilities of their members.

Responsibility and Authority

The chief financial officer of any corporation, regardless of size, should have the scope of responsibility and range of authority that will permit the proper management and administration of all the finance functions in his company. The senior financial officer should assure himself that the duties of his department are assigned logically, that the lines of communications and working relationships are working within and between all subdivisions of his department and between finance and all other company functions, and that the staff and organization are so structured that they will always be prepared for change.

The optimum organization structure of the finance department may be modified according to personalities and strengths, particularly in smaller companies, but the large corporation must have a chief financial officer who will direct his function on a more scientific basis.—*R. A. Busch*

GENERAL ACCOUNTING AND FINANCIAL STATEMENTS

Any large accounting function is divided into various segments. The following eight segments are relatively standard separations of functions under the jurisdiction of the controller or chief accounting officer: (1) general or financial accounting; (2) cost accounting; (3) systems and procedures; (4) data processing; (5) internal auditing; (6) budgeting; (7) tax reporting; and (8) financial analysis. The key unit is general or financial accounting.

General Accounting

A clear understanding of the scope of responsibility of the general accounting unit is necessary to provide a bridge to all the other various areas of accounting. In addition, a study of general accounting leads to comprehension of the basic tenets of a general accounting system, the concepts behind the system, the chart of accounts and how it spells out the accounting system, and the philosophy behind the system indicating the trail from the development of accounting records from source documents through the general ledger.

DEFINITION AND FUNCTION

The committee on terminology of the American Institute of Accountants (now the AICPA) proposed in 1941 that the term "accounting" be defined as "the art of recording, classifying, and summarizing in a significant manner and in terms of money, transactions and events which are, in part at least, of a financial character, and interpreting the results thereof."

Interestingly, many people raise the question of whether accounting is an art or a science, or has aspects of both. Many qualified writers feel that this question cannot be answered solely by definition. Those who do take a position tend to agree that accounting should be deemed an art and not a science.

Some feel that accounting, basically, can be broken down into two major fields: public accounting and management accounting. This discussion is not concerned with public accounting. The general accounting unit is the hub of the overall accounting function; therefore, this unit is the base unit in a management accounting system. Accounting can be considered as having the primary function of facilitating the administration of economic activity. This function can be related to the measuring and arraying of economic data and communicating the results to interested persons. Accounting must therefore be considered as a service. It is a service in that it records the economic activities of persons, firms, and organizations. It carries this service further by reporting the results of the recording activities to all interested parties.

Too many people tend to think of accounting only in the sense of answering two basic questions: (1) What is the profit or loss resulting from the concerned operations over/for a specific period of time? (2) What is the financial position of the concerned operation/function at a specific time? The general purpose statements, the income statement, and the balance sheet provide the answers to these questions. These are position reports which provide value by showing status at a given time. More important, however, they provide a base of measurement when compared with prior reports of a similar nature to show trends and the results of managerial actions taken and to point out areas where new or revised managerial action is required.

In addition to preparing these general purpose reports, accountants are more and more frequently called upon to provide data for specific purposes, which are generally referred to as special purpose reports. Sometimes these reports are in the form of analyses and statistical data on information shown in the general purpose statements. More frequently, they take data from the general purpose reports and present them from different points of view to facilitate management decisions regarding the future course. Many additional reports are developed, supplying financial data designed to be useful to management at all levels in planning and administering a business operation (or personal assets, in the case of an individual). Wherever economic resources are employed, such reports are required. On a broad basis, these reports can be categorized as: (1) those useful in short-range and long-range planning where it is important to consider all feasible alternatives to evaluate them in financial terms; (2) those useful in administering operations where it is important to know deviations of current actual results from planned results; and (3) those useful or necessary to report results to persons concerned with the financial operations through ownership, taxing, or other legal relationship or a creditor relationship. While other units in the overall accounting function may be involved, the source data in large part are initiated in the general accounting unit.

It is widely recognized that accounting data are among the chief management aids. As businesses become more and more complex, the reliance on the accounting function increases. The chief accounting officer—whatever his formal title— is looked to more than any other official to provide guidance, direction, control, and protection to senior management. Gantt once stated: "There is no moral right to decide, on a basis of opinion, that which can be determined as a matter of fact." Accounting must be able to provide the required facts when they are needed to enable executives to make proper evaluation of past operations, thereby enabling them to make proper decisions, whether the facts affect current operations or changes in forward planning or action. It should be apparent that general accounting's position as the hub of the overall accounting unit places on it a tremendous responsibility to management.

INTRACOMPANY RELATIONSHIPS

Accounting is not isolated from other aspects of any business. In fact, it would appear that accounting is related to virtually every other aspect of a business.

Consider two such relationships. In relationship to law, a business must be operated within the framework of both the law and the established principles, set forth by the accounting profession, which can be deemed to be accounting law. In the first instance, the law governs the handling of records for income taxes, receivership, quasireorganization, renegotiation, form of the business organization, and other matters. In the latter instance, management must be concerned both with standards of performance for consistency in handling or recording data from one period to the next, and with conservatism indicating managerial responsibility—or recognize that deviations from these conventions can result in adverse publicity to management and/or the company.

For a second comparison, relate accounting to engineering. It is universally recognized that industrial engineering must concern itself with materials and material handling records, labor analyses, and timekeeping records and methods, as well as the numerous different approaches to allocating overhead costs. Engineering studies often must involve accounting data, and budget projections and budgetary control are areas where engineers and accountants must work closely together.

It is evident from these two examples that accounting has some relationship with virtually every other aspect of a business. The coordinator of all these accounting data moving between the accounting and the nonaccounting units should be the general accounting unit. There must be a coordinator to assure that current and complete data are exchanged with nonaccounting units. What happens when inconsistent data are passed to nonaccounting units is obvious. The entire accounting function falls into disrepute, and management in the subject functions must make decisions on incorrect and/or incomplete data.

RESPONSIBILITIES

The general accounting unit administers the general accounting records (the general ledger, accounts receivable ledger controls, accounts payable ledger controls, selling and administrative expense records, administrative and office payrolls, and general financial summaries and ledgers).

The unit assumes responsibility for coordinating all accounting work between various units of the overall accounting function, as well as with nonaccounting units.

All detailed accounting papers not normally passing through or recorded by the cost accounting function (sales and purchase invoices, cash receipts and disbursements, journal vouchers, and the like) are handled by general accounting.

Property, plant, and equipment records, including records of costs (both original and repairs or additions) and related depreciation records, are maintained by general accounting.

The general accounting unit prepares general purpose reports (balance sheet and profit-and-loss statements) and compiles other internal operating and statistical data into routine or special purpose reports as desired by management.

General accounting is responsible for maintaining appropriate records indicating differences between reporting techniques from general records, as shown on regular general purpose reports, and figures used for tax reporting.

CHART OF ACCOUNTS

The key to a system of effective accounting administration is a sound chart of accounts. The general accounting unit should be responsible for its final form, although other accounting units such as cost accounting, systems and procedures, and internal auditing should assist in its development. A chart of accounts is simply a listing of accounts systematically arranged. It should record both account names and numbers, for the numbers provide a quick reference where the chart is broad and complicated. This can be expanded into a manual of accounts by adding descriptions of the use of each account, as well as an explanation of the general operation—or, if desired, the philosophy behind the account system.

A properly designed chart of accounts is the key to effective internal check and control procedures. As such, it should be designed to reflect transactions by accountabilities and responsibilities as far as possible. This is more easily done with balance sheet accounts. Care should be taken, however, to see that the income and expense accounts also reflect responsibility for transactions by individual positions whenever and wherever possible. The total control systems concept requires that the chart of accounts design and the accounting records should be such that personal responsibility for all assets—and other accounts, to the degree possible—and transactions is clearly set forth. It is, therefore, obvious that the organization structure must be carefully articulated so that the responsibilities previously described can be identified with specific functions or positions.

While there are many approaches to the development of a sound chart of accounts, the strengths of control, as indicated, are essential. Consider now a basic numbering system and two systems approaches toward the development of a strong and effective chart of accounts as described in the next few paragraphs.

Basic numbering system. The groupings in this system are as follows:

$$
\left.\begin{array}{ll}
\text{100–199:} & \text{Assets} \\
\text{200–299:} & \text{Liabilities} \\
\text{300–399:} & \text{Equity}
\end{array}\right\} \text{Balance Sheet}
$$

$$
\left.\begin{array}{ll}
\text{400–499:} & \text{Income} \\
\text{500–599:} & \text{Expenses} \\
\text{600–699:} & \text{Special and} \\
& \text{tax items}
\end{array}\right\} \begin{array}{l} \text{Profit and Loss} \\ \text{(Income Statement)} \end{array}
$$

Within each number group, subsegments should be established as required. For example, under "Assets" six subsegments of number groupings may be established:

$$
\left.\begin{array}{ll}
\text{100–129:} & \text{Current assets} \\
\text{130–139:} & \text{Investments} \\
\text{140–159:} & \text{Fixed assets} \\
\text{160–169:} & \text{Intangible assets} \\
\text{170–179:} & \text{Deferred charges} \\
\text{180–199:} & \text{Other assets}
\end{array}\right\} \text{Assets}
$$

Systems approach. The numbers in the preceding tabulation are usually called either *primary* or *main* accounts in most numbering systems. Two basic charts of accounts with those numbers as the beginning point may be constructed:

Number of Digits	First System	Second System
		Location:
One		Area
Three		Office/Plant
Three	Primary	Main
Two	Secondary	Sub
Three	Tertiary	Item
Four	——	Detail

The use of three digits is illustrated in the basic numbering system previously shown.

Each system must be custom-designed to provide the controls mentioned earlier. Here are two examples of numbers in charts of accounts developed with the use of the two illustrated systems concepts:

First System:	Primary	100	Cash
	Secondary	–02	Payroll account
	Tertiary	–234	Second National Bank of _____

Second System:	Location:		
	Area	1	Eastern United States
	Office/ Plant	145	New Jersey Refinery

Main	100	Cash
Sub	–02	Payroll account
Item	–234	Second National Bank of _____
Detail	–3456	Confidential—salaried

A flexible concept in the systems approach will permit the administration of all data in a consistent manner providing the necessary controls, including audit trails, so that each entry can be traced from the books of entry back to the source of origin.

CONTROL SYSTEM

If the full scope of the controller's or chief accounting officer's responsibilities is understood, the basis for building a control system can likewise be better understood. The following descriptions of activities offer only broad breakdowns, but they can serve as generalized separations.

Planning includes the establishment and maintenance of an integrated plan covering both long- and short-range operational objectives.

Control includes the development, testing, and revision of standards to enable the measurement of actual performance, as well as an evaluation of the operational strengths and weaknesses of the results and the system.

Reporting covers the preparation, analysis, and interpretation of data for use by management and other concerned parties.

Accounting includes the maintenance of the general and other accounting systems and related records of entry, as well as the control system to effectively administer this function.

Other activities of the chief accounting officer are in accounting-related areas such as taxes, auditing, relationship with public accountants, insurance, systems administration, and coordination of all systems and facilities throughout the organization.

Note the repetition in this discussion of the words "establishment," "development," "testing," "preparation," "maintenance," and "control." While the chief financial officer has the broad indicated range of responsibilities, he must assure that the system of administrative controls does just that—control. Internal check and internal control techniques must be provided in the systems concept. Remember the reference, under the "Chart of Accounts" heading, to the ability to reflect transactions by accountabilities and responsibilities. Audit trails such as this, when designed in the control system, assist greatly in backing up any transaction from its last stage of recording or processing to its initial source or point of origin. For example, let us look at certain accounts:

Account	*Officer Charged with Accountability*
Cash	Treasurer (The system must be able to back up the record of initial receipt to the designated company representative or agent— as, for example, direct deposits in a lock box at a bank.)
Petty cash	Custodian
Accounts receivable	Controller (Responsibility may be delegated to the accounts receivable unit head—if the company is large enough—or to an accounts receivable bookkeeper.)

These designations of responsibility represent the overall system of internal control. In addition, provision for internal check is required. Internal control is the basic methodology by which management is carried on in an organization. Internal check is the system of transaction control providing operational and organizational protection against fraud. The attempt is to separate functions which, if in the same administrative control point (same person or locale), could too easily result in fraud if improperly administered.

The size of any operation governs the degree of success in effectively achieving the optimum separation of duties. Certain cash administration controls illustrate the need for this control approach:

1. Bank deposits should not be made up by a person who has access to the cash books or ledgers.

2. Persons who are authorized to collect cash internally (cashiers) or externally (drivers for C.O.D. deliveries) should have no access to ledgers or other basic control records relating to cash.

3. The person maintaining the cash book should not have access to any of the ledgers (receivables ledgers, account cards, voucher registers, and the like).

Separation of duties must be provided throughout the control system if it is to be effective. General accounting must assume responsibility that such controls do in fact exist.

Financial Statements

A financial statement is any presentation of financial data derived from accounting records. This definition is a bit broad to permit an approach to the subject in its proper perspective. Financial statements are classified as *primary* and *secondary*.

The four statements normally considered as the basic primary statements are the balance sheet, income statement, statement of retained earnings, and statement of source and application of funds. Each of the primary statements is discussed in later pages of this subsection of the handbook.

The secondary financial statements tend to be more functional in nature, limiting themselves in scope as a result of their formats or titles. Among these reports are the statement of cost of goods sold; the statement of selling and administrative expenses; the cash report; the accounts receivable report; the inventory analysis; the report of working capital; the capital expenditure report; and the fixed asset report.

RESPONSIBILITY FOR REPORTS

The responsibility for all accounting and financial reports is usually assigned to the controller, or the chief accounting officer. His success in developing reports which fulfill their purpose depends upon: (1) his appreciation of sound, fundamental principles of reporting; and (2) his ability to understand management's philosophy and needs. Not only is knowing the business important; it is also necessary to understand the idiosyncracies of management. This means that, in properly presenting pertinent data, the reports must recognize specific ways that management may want this information presented if they are not standard in presentation format. Many instances of nonstandard reporting formats exist because management is not adequately accounting-trained or accounting-oriented. To avoid nonstandard reporting formats, the chief accounting officer should assist the appropriate members of management to better understand the purpose of the various reports being submitted to them.

ELEMENTS OF GOOD REPORTS

The following elements are required for good reports: accuracy, appearance, brevity, clarity, completeness, intelligibility, necessity, readability, reliability, simplicity, and timeliness. From the point of view of the authority responsible for preparing and issuing financial reports, the following questions should be asked regarding each report prior to its issuance: What is the report intended to accomplish? What is the potential distribution for the report? When is the report required? Has all pertinent information been screened to ascertain the material facts? How can the material facts best be presented?

Consider these five questions while keeping in mind the 11 elements of simple, good reporting.

The first question concerns simply the act of communication—a basic purpose of a good report that is nevertheless frequently overlooked because reports often fail to accomplish their specified purpose: to present specific data with a particular purpose in mind. The second question might be rephrased as "What is the audience for the report?" Reports must relate facts to responsibility or interest: responsibility for internal purposes, and interest when they are to be distributed beyond the confines of management. The third question merely asks whether the report in question is standard or nonstandard. If nonstandard, it may be presumed to be a one-time report. If standard, however, its frequency of issue is important to establish the time framework for the development of appropriate data in time for review, verification, assimilation, compilation, and summarization for the final report. The relationship of questions 4 and 5 to the explanation for question 3 is obvious. The final format may be a standard one or a special one, depending on the nature of the data. When it is nonstandard (special), be sure the data are presented in a simple manner for the nonaccounting-trained recipient of the report.

Types of Reports

BALANCE SHEET

A balance sheet is merely a statement of assets, liabilities, and equity at the close of business for any firm, plant, office, facility, or individual, on the date specified on the report. The AICPA, in its Research Bulletin No. 9, defines a balance sheet as

> a tabular statement or summary of balances (debit and credit) carried forward after an actual or constructive closing of books of account kept by double-entry methods, according to the rules or principles of accounting. The items reflected on the two sides of the balance sheet are commonly called assets and liabilities, respectively.

Total assets should always equal the total of the liabilities plus equity (capital). Simply stated, this equation is: Assets equals liabilities plus equity ($A = L + E$).

Because claims of creditors take precedence over those of owners/stockholders, this formula can be restated as: Assets less liabilities equals equity $(A - L = E)$. A balance sheet using the first equation is called "the account form of balance sheet," while one prepared using the second equation is called "the report form of balance sheet." Examples of each are shown in Exhibits 4.5 and 4.6. The account form example is set up on a noncomparative basis, while the report form example has been set up in a comparative format. Either form of balance sheet may be used in a comparative or a noncomparative format.

The balance sheet is truly the principal financial report. However, its importance has declined of late as more and more attention has been given to budgets. It can be omitted from the report string if replaced by a trial balance of the general ledger accounts. It is better to make two separate reports (the balance sheet and the income statement) rather than submit to management a trial balance which is not as definitive because it does not provide separations of accounts into important groupings for analysis—for example, current assets and fixed assets. The account groupings for balance sheets in commercial and industrial companies, as indicated by Regulation S-X of the SEC, are listed in the following paragraphs. Additional details may be obtained from the SEC.

Assets and other debits. *Current assets* on the balance sheet include the following groupings: cash and cash items; marketable securities; notes receivable (trade); accounts receivable (trade); reserves for doubtful notes and accounts receivable (trade); inventories; other current assets; and total current assets.

Investments groupings on the balance sheet are: securities of affiliates; indebtedness of affiliates—not current; other security investments; other investments; and total investments.

Fixed assets are grouped as follows: property, plant, and equipment; reserves for depreciation, depletion, and amortization of property, plant, and equipment; and total fixed assets.

Intangible assets groupings are: patents, trademarks, franchises, goodwill, and other; reserves for depreciation and amortization of intangible assets; and total intangible assets.

Deferred charges groupings include prepaid expenses and other deferred items; organization expense; debt discount and expense; commissions and expense on capital shares; and total deferred charges.

Other assets (to be stated separately) are the total of amounts due from directors, officers, and principal holders of equity securities (other than affiliates); each special fund, including pension funds; and any other item (individually identified) in excess of 10 percent of the amount of all assets other than fixed and intangible.

Liabilities, capital shares, and surplus. *Current liabilities* on the balance sheet are grouped as follows: notes payable; accounts payable (trade); accrued liabilities; other current liabilities; and total current liabilities.

Deferred income is entered separately as warranted by amount or nature.

Long-term debt groupings include the following: bonds, mortgages, and similar debt; indebtedness to affiliates—not current; other long-term debt; and total long-term debt.

Exhibit 4.5

ACCOUNT FORM OF BALANCE SHEET

ABC COMPANY, INC.
Balance Sheet
As of ____

Assets		(000 Omitted)
Current assets		
Cash		$ 250
U.S. Government securities at cost (market value: $380)		240
Receivables (gross)	$2,000	
Less: Reserve for bad debts	80	
Receivables (net)		1,920
Inventories		800
Total		$3,210
Fixed assets		
Buildings	$3,800	
Machinery and tools	1,800	
Total	$5,600	
Less: Accrued depreciation	2,800	
Book value		$2,800
Other assets		
Cash surrender value of life insurance		130
Deferred charges and prepaid expense		
Prepaid insurance		20
Total assets		$6,160
Liabilities		
Current liabilities		
Accounts payable		$1,800
Notes payable		190
Accrued taxes		200
Total		$2,190
Long-term liabilities		
5 percent 20-year debentures (due 1982)		600
Total liabilities		$2,790
Net Worth		
Capital stock		
Common stock, no-par value (authorized 1,000,000 shares, outstanding 580,000 shares)		$ 580
Earned surplus:		
Balance, January 1, 19__	$2,500	
Net income for year	580	
Less: Dividends	(290)	
Balance, December 31, 19__		2,790
Total net worth		3,370
Total liabilities (and net worth)		$6,160

Exhibit 4.6

REPORT FORM OF BALANCE SHEET

ABC COMPANY, INC.
Balance Sheet
As of _____

	December 31		Increase or (Decrease)	
	1970	1969	Dollars	Percent
Net Assets in Which Capital Is Invested				
	(000 Omitted)			
Current assets				
Cash	$ 250	$ 135	$ 115	85.19
U.S. Government securities at cost (market value: 12/31/70 – $380	240			
12/31/69 – $125)		55	185	336.36
Receivables (gross)	$2,000	$1,750	$ 250	14.29
Less: Reserve for bad debts	80	70	10	14.29
Receivables (net)	$1,920	$1,680	$ 240	14.29
Inventories	800	900	(100)	(11.11)
Total current assets	$3,210	$2,770	$ 440	15.88
Less: Current liabilities				
Accounts payable	$1,800	$1,435	$ 365	25.44
Notes payable	190	190	–0–	–0–
Accrued taxes	200	180	20	11.11
Total current liabilities	$2,190	$1,805	$ 385	21.33
Net current assets	$1,020	$ 965	$ 55	5.70
Add: Assets other than current				
Buildings	$3,800	$3,800	$ –0–	–0–
Machinery and tools	1,800	1,700	100	5.88
Total	$5,600	$5,500	$ 100	1.82
Less: Accrued depreciation	2,800	2,725	75	2.75
Book value	$2,800	$2,775	$ 25	0.90
Cash surrender value of life insurance	130	120	10	8.33
Prepaid insurance	20	20	–0–	–0–
Total	$3,970	$3,880	$ 90	2.32
Less: Liabilities other than current				
5 percent 20-year debentures (due 1982)	600	800	(200)	(25.00)
Total net assets in which capital is invested	$3,370	$3,080	$ 290	9.42
Sources from Which Capital Has Been Obtained				
Common stock, no-par value (authorized 1,000,000 shares, outstanding 580,000 shares)	$ 580	$ 580	$ –0–	–0–
Net income employed in the business	2,790	2,500	290	11.60
Total capital invested	$3,370	$3,080	$ 290	9.42

Other liabilities groupings also include commitments and contingent liabilities and total other liabilities.

Reserves not shown elsewhere are stated separately for each major item, and the purpose indicated.

Capital shares and surplus on the balance sheet are grouped as capital shares, surplus, and total capital shares and surplus.

INCOME STATEMENT

The income statement (profit-and-loss statement) is the basic operating statement for an organization—a summary of income/revenue and expenses. It can be prepared for each operating unit or can be a consolidated presentation for several or all units of a firm. It can be prepared to show the results for a specified period alone, or to compare results with those of a prior period, or to compare a budgetary projection. Supplemental reports of a general operating nature could include such reports as these: a commodity profit-and-loss statement; a plant, office, or divisional profit-and-loss statement; an analysis of general or selling expense; and a personnel report.

The income statement can be a detailed listing of all related general ledger accounts or may be summarized into the following general categories: (*a*) operating (or gross) revenue; (*b*) cost of sales; (*c*) gross profit (*a* less *b*); (*d*) general operating expense; (*e*) other income; (*f*) income deductions; and (*g*) net income (or net loss).

As with balance sheets, there are two basic approaches to an income statement presentation. The format outlined in *a* through *g* is sometimes called the multiple-step or report form. Exhibit 4.7 is an example of this approach. The

Exhibit 4.7
REPORT FORM OF INCOME STATEMENT

ABC COMPANY, INC.
Income Statement
Year ended___

	(000 Omitted)
Net sales	$7,480
Less: Cost of sales, including depreciation	4,500
Gross profit	$2,980
Less: Selling, administrative, and general expense	1,800
Net operating income	$1,180
Less: Provision for federal income taxes	600
Net income (or loss)	$ 580

second approach, which has gained increasing popularity in recent years, is the one-step form shown in Exhibit 4.8. The purpose of this approach is to display factor costs and/or objects of expenditures that have been recorded to expense during the subject period of the report.

Briefly summarized, the segments of Regulation S-X of the SEC on income statements for commercial and industrial companies are stated in the paragraphs which follow.

Operating (or gross) revenue is gross sales less discounts, returns, and allowances. Sales to affiliated companies or organizations should be indicated separately if practicable.

The cost of goods sold is stated in accordance with the system of accounting followed.

Exhibit 4.8
SINGLE-STEP FORM OF INCOME STATEMENT

ABC COMPANY, INC.
Statement of Net Income
Year ended _____

(000 Omitted)

Sales		$7,480
Costs:		
Inventories, January 1, 19__		$ 900
Costs incurred during year:		
Purchased material and services	$3,400	
Salaries/wages	2,400	
Depreciation	400	
Federal income taxes	600	
Total	6,800	
Accumulated total	$7,700	
Less: Inventories, December 31, 19__	800	
Total costs allocated to sales		6,900
Sales (less costs allocated to sales) – Net income for year		$ 580
Profit – per common share		$2.00
Dividends		(290)
Balance of net income for year		$ 290
Balance at beginning of year		2,500
Net income employed in business at end of year		$2,790

Gross profit is operating revenues after deduction of cost of goods sold.

General operating expenses relating to affiliated companies or organizations are shown separately if practicable. Separate expenses are classified as operating expenses; other operating expenses; selling, general, and administrative expenses; provision for doubtful accounts; and other general expenses.

Other income includes dividends; interest on securities; profits on securities; miscellaneous other income; and total other income.

Income deductions are interest and debt discount and expense; losses on securities; miscellaneous income deductions; and total income deductions.

Other categories include the following items: net income or loss before provision for taxes on income; provision for income and excess-profits taxes; net income or loss; special items; and net income or loss and special items.

STATEMENT OF RETAINED EARNINGS

This statement is merely a reconciliation of retained earnings which reflects the beginning balance of unappropriated retained earnings, charges and credits thereto during the period, and the ending balance. Charges and credits during a period can include any or all of the following: (1) the net increase (or decrease, in event of a loss) transferred from the income statement; (2) transfers to and from appropriated retained earnings; (3) dividends declared; (4) reductions, if acquisitions made of the firm's own capital stock; and (5) material nonoperating charges and credits where made direct to retained earnings—dependent upon which concept of net income is adopted. The reconciliation of retained earnings may appear as a separate statement, as indicated in Exhibit 4.9, or as part of a combined statement of income and retained earnings. The latter is merely an extension of a standard income statement. Exhibit 4.8 shows a simple illustration of an identification of beginning- and end-of-year retained earnings. This, of course, can be expanded upon to become a full and detailed reconciliation similar to that shown in Exhibit 4.9.

Exhibit 4.9

STATEMENT OF RETAINED EARNINGS

Balance at January 1, 19__ unappropriated		$ XXXXXXX
Transfer from amount previously appropriated for contingencies (no longer restricted)		XXXXXXX
		$ XXXXXXX
Deduct:		
Net loss for year	$ XXXXXXX	
Cash dividends declared on common stock at xx cents per share	XXXXXXX	XXXXXXX
Balance at December 31, 19__		$ XXXXXXX

STATEMENT OF SOURCE AND
APPLICATION OF FUNDS

One financial statement of growing use—particularly with higher prime rate costs of money in recent times—and importance is the statement of source and application of funds, sometimes called the cash flow statement. This statement, as shown in Exhibit 4.10, reveals such information as the following: (1) the portion of total funds provided from operations; (2) funds provided from various outside sources; (3) the disposition of funds, including the impact (if any) on working capital; (4) the proportion of funds applied to various factors, including plant; (5) an indication of the impact of sources and application upon

Exhibit 4.10

STATEMENT OF SOURCE AND APPLICATION OF FUNDS

ABC COMPANY, INC.
Statement of Source and Application of Funds
Year ended December 31, 19___

Source of Funds	(000 Omitted)
Net income	$ 300
Depreciation	75
Reduction in reserve for future taxes on income	125
Other	50
Total from operations	$ 550
Proceeds from sale of common stock	400
Working capital of acquired subsidiaries at dates of acquisitions	180
Total	$1,130

Application of Funds	
Additions to properties, plant, and equipment	$ 250
Payments on long-term debt	200
Dividends declared	100
Increase in receivables and advances – net	175
Other	105
	$ 830
(Decrease) Increase in working capital	300*
Total	$1,130

(*) Sometimes this figure is detailed by a supplement to the statement of source and application of funds showing where an increase (if any) was put to use. For example:

Cash	$115
U.S. Government securities	100
Other marketable securities	85
Total	$300

the future of the firm, indicating its dividend-paying capabilities and/or probabilities; (6) by comparison with other companies in the industry, the capability of evaluating the financial strength of the firm (not distorted by differences in accounting techniques).—*W. T. Thornhill*

COST ACCOUNTING METHODS AND OBJECTIVES

Cost accounting is that special area of accounting which is concerned with the recording, classifying, summarizing, reporting, analyzing, and interpreting of costs regardless of cause or origin.

In the early days of cost accounting, when accountants considered themselves to be basically historians, only historical costs were considered. Accountants now consider themselves to be not only historians but also advisers to management. In line with this broadened role of the accountant, cost accounting now may be involved not only with historical costs but also with present and future costs as well.

In order that the functions and purposes of cost accounting may be carried out, the concept of cost accounting must include the development and use of systems and procedures adapted to the particular firm so that costs may be appropriately isolated by cause and origin for study and analysis.

With the need of a particular firm in mind, the cost accounting systems should be so designed and developed in such detail as to provide the greatest control and most accurate means of establishing unit costs commensurate with the cost of its establishment and operation. As a cost system is made more and more complex and detailed, better control and analysis should result; but at some point, because of the law of diminishing returns, the added costs of improving the system will not be accompanied by adequate further reductions in production costs and improved control.

Types of Cost Systems

Because of the special needs of particular firms, two broad types of cost accounting systems (methods) have been developed. They are process cost (accounting) systems and job-order (accounting) systems. Either may be used with or without standards. Often, when standards are incorporated into a job-order system, it is referred to simply as a standard cost system.

Cost systems may also be classified, according to the portion of costs charged to the product, as absorption costing and direct or marginal costing.

PROCESS COST ACCOUNTING

Process cost accounting is a method of collecting and analyzing costs of homogeneous products by divisions, departments, or cost centers. Costs are primarily identified with cost centers rather than with specific jobs or groups of units as is the case in job-order accounting.

In process cost accounting the three elements of cost—material, labor, and overhead—are first charged to cost centers and later allocated to the product.

This is in contrast to the methods used under job-order accounting, wherein the three elements of cost are charged directly to the product. The costs are recorded on the job cost sheet, which figuratively "goes with" the job as it passes from department to department in being processed. Therefore, it is often said that process costs are average costs, whereas job-order costs are specific costs.

Process cost accounting is most appropriate for firms producing large quantities of homogeneous units on a continuous basis. A few typical examples of industries using process cost systems are grain milling, petroleum refining, and chemicals.

Equivalent units. "Equivalent units" is a term used to indicate the number of completed units which might have been made with the amounts of material, labor, and overhead used in producing some finished and some partly finished units; for example, 100 units which are one-half complete are equivalent to 50 completed units. In a given process run or batch in process, the equivalent units may be different for each element of cost. Assume, for example, that 1,000 gallons of paint were started in process and that 600 were completed and that 400 gallons are still in process. Assume, further, that the 400 gallons are three-fourths done as far as material is concerned, one-half done as far as labor is concerned, and one-fourth done as regards overhead. The equivalent units of material, labor, and overhead would be 900, 800, and 700, respectively.

In process costing, the three elements of cost may be charged to a common work-in-process account entitled "Work in Process"; or each element of cost may be charged to a separate, appropriately titled account as "Work in Process—Material," "Work in Process—Labor," and "Work in Process—Overhead." Of course, it follows that since the primary basis for collecting costs in a process system is a cost center or department, separate accounts should be established for each department—for example, "Work in Process—Material: Department One," "Work in Process—Material: Department Two," and so forth.

For illustrative purposes, consider the following simplified case: A firm which produces a single product, X, through two departments has no beginning or ending inventories of work in process but incurred the following costs in producing 100 units:

Element of Cost	Department 1	Department 2	Total
Material	$1,000	$3,000	$4,000
Labor	500	400	900
Overhead	500	600	1,100
Total	$2,000	$4,000	$6,000

In process cost accounting, control and analytical data are obtained from identifying costs with departments by elements. To accomplish such identification, the following journal entries should be made:

Work in process—material: Department 1	$1,000	
Work in process—labor: Department 1	500	
Work in process—overhead: Department 1	500	
Raw material inventory		$1,000

Payroll		500
Overhead applied		500
To record charges to work in process		
for costs incurred.		
Work in process—transfer account: Department 2	$2,000	
Work in process—material: Department 1		$1,000
Work in process—labor: Department 1		500
Work in process—overhead: Department 1		500
To record the transfer of production costs		
from Department 1 to Department 2.		
Work in process—material: Department 2	$3,000	
Work in process—labor: Department 2	400	
Work in process—overhead: Department 2	600	
Raw material inventory		3,000
Payroll		400
Overhead applied		600
To record charges incurred by Department 2		
for production.		
Finished goods	$6,000	
Work in process—transfer account: Department 2		2,000
Work in process—material: Department 2		3,000
Work in process—labor: Department 2		400
Work in process—overhead: Department 2		600
To transfer the accumulated production costs		
from work in process to finished goods.		

Since all of the 100 units are completed, the equivalent units are the same as the actual units—100. The unit cost, therefore, is ($6,000 divided by 100) $60.

To illustrate the importance and use of equivalent units, the following data for a single department might be considered. At the beginning of the period, 4,000 units in process were three-fourths complete; an additional 8,000 units were received in the department. During the period, 8,000 units were completed and transferred to finished goods, and 1,000 units were lost. The ending inventory of 3,000 units was one-third complete.

The following data are available:

Cost Element	Beginning Inventory	Incurred During Period
Material	$ 2,400	$ 3,000
Labor	3,900	6,000
Overhead	3,900	6,000
Total	$10,200	$15,000

There are two generally recognized methods of valuing inventories in process cost accounting, the average method and the first-in, first-out (FIFO) method. In the rare case of no beginning inventory, the problem of which method to use would be unimportant because, without a beginning inventory, the calculations and the results would be the same by either method. Of course, it must be remembered that once a method has been selected, it must be used consistently in succeeding periods and that one period's ending inventory becomes the following period's beginning inventory.

In practice, one method would be selected and used consistently, but for illustrative purposes the previously mentioned production will be valued by both methods.

The average method. Under the average method, the units in the beginning inventory will be mingled with the units received during the period, and the costs in the beginning inventory will be added to the similar costs incurred during the period. The costs must be isolated by elements because, in most cases, the number of equivalent units may differ for one or more of the three cost elements. It follows that if only a total value is given for the beginning inventory, the average method cannot be used even though the FIFO method could be used.

	Average Equivalent Units		
	Actual Units	*Stage of Completion*	*Equivalent Units*
Completed	8,000	1	8,000
In process	3,000	⅓	1,000
Total	11,000		9,000

Elements	*Beginning Inventory*	*Added*	*Total*	*Equivalent Units*	*Unit Cost*
Material	$ 2,400	$ 3,000	$ 5,400	9,000	$ .60
Labor	3,900	6,000	9,900	9,000	1.10
Overhead	3,900	6,000	9,900	9,000	1.10
Total	$10,200	$15,000	$25,200		$2.80

The value of the goods finished and transferred is (8,000 × 1 × $2.80) $22,400. The work in process is (3,000 × ⅓ × $2.80) $2,800.

The FIFO method. Under the FIFO method, the value of the beginning inventory is kept separate from the costs incurred during the period. Therefore, the equivalent units in the beginning inventory must be kept separate from the other equivalent units.

The 8,000 units completed during the period are composed of the 4,000 units in the beginning inventory and 4,000 other units. Since the 4,000 units in the beginning inventory were three-fourths complete, only 1,000 equivalent units had to be made during this period in order to transfer out 4,000 units. Thus the 8,000 completed units represent current production of only 5,000 units. The ending inventory is one-third complete, thus representing 1,000 equivalent units. Total equivalent units under FIFO are 6,000.

The equivalent units in the beginning inventory and their costs are excluded from the calculation of the current unit costs, which are calculated as follows:

Elements	Current Costs	Current Equivalent Units	Unit Costs
Material	$ 3,000	6,000	$ .50
Labor	6,000	6,000	1.00
Overhead	6,000	6,000	1.00
Total	$15,000		$2.50

The period's production would be valued as follows:

Beginning inventory	$10,200
Cost to complete (4,000 × ¼ × $2.50)	2,500
Total cost of beginning inventory	$12,700
Units started and finished (4,000 × 1 × $2.50)	10,000
Total cost of finished goods	$22,700
Work in process	
Material (3,000 × ⅓ × $ .50)	$ 500
Labor (3,000 × ⅓ × $1.00)	1,000
Overhead (3,000 × ⅓ × $1.00)	1,000
Total work in process	2,500
Total production costs	$25,200

JOB-ORDER COST ACCOUNTING

Job-order cost accounting is a method of identifying and collecting costs with each unit or selected group of homogeneous units. This method is especially suited to firms where a number of dissimilar and separately identifiable products are produced and where it is desirable to compile separate and specific cost data for each type, group, or lot of units produced.

This system may be used by large manufacturing firms producing great quantities of dissimilar items or a limited number of large units. It may be used also to advantage by small job shops producing specific units on special orders.

Job-order costing provides a means for establishing specific costs, in contrast to average costs establishable under a system of process costing.

As in process costing, one or three work-in-process accounts may be used. In this case, however, the costs are identified with a job rather than with a department. An individual issue of material could be journalized as follows:

> Work in process—material: Job 708 $100
>   Raw material inventory $100

Of course, summary sheets may be used as a means of reducing the number of required journal entries.

Job-order costing is synonymous with job costing, job-lot costing, lot costing, batch costing, and specific-order costing.

This method is sometimes referred to as production-order costing. This is unfortunate, because "production order" is a term more commonly and properly used to refer to an order issued, usually, by the production planning department to a foreman of a producing department authorizing the start of a particular job order.

STANDARD COST ACCOUNTING

A standard cost accounting system may be built upon either a process cost system or a job-order cost system. In such cases all amounts (with the possible exception of entries to raw material and charges to work in process) are recorded at standard costs rather than at actual costs. However, the necessary records are maintained so that the differences between standard costs and actual costs can be determined, causes established, and responsibility placed.

Standard costs are predetermined costs; thus they are estimated costs. Well-developed standard costs indicate what costs should be.

Since standard costs are forecasts of what costs should be and, as such, are used in planning and decision making, they should be as scientifically and accurately determined as possible.

To be useful, standards must be developed for a particular program and through the joint efforts of the persons responsible for the operation of the program. Consideration must be given to the expected level of operation of the program or facility, and strenuous efforts must be made to determine the most effective and economical ways of utilizing men and materials.

The establishment of standard production procedures and costs should involve the firm's industrial engineers, time-and-motion study and job study persons, representatives from the personnel department, and representatives of the unions affected. In certain cases, the purchasing agent should be consulted.

Through such joint efforts should be developed the cheapest and most efficient production methods, a determination of the most economical material to use, and the cheapest labor to use commensurate with the desired quality of the end product.

Standards should be reviewed at least once a year and, if warranted, changes should be made. Affected standards should be reviewed, and appropriate changes made, immediately after *significant* changes have occurred in production methods, union contracts, or material costs. At this point, a word of caution is in order. The primary value of standard costs and standard cost accounting is to provide management with a model to be used in planning, controlling, and evaluating operations. If the model is changed too frequently, there is danger that the model or forecast may be adjusted to fit the imperfect results and thus destroy the value of the model. If the model is not changed frequently enough or in the right ways, the comparisons between standard and actual will lose meaning; and thus the system will lose value as a planning and control device.

A well-developed and maintained standard cost system, in conjunction with a well-developed and maintained budget, provides management with effective means for controlling costs.

For standard cost accounting purposes, "variance" may be defined as "a change or deviation from the established standard." The difference between the standard cost of an element or unit and its actual cost is the overall or net variance.

Such an overall variance is relatively useless in fixing responsibility. To be useful, an overall variance should be broken down as to causes. It is common practice to isolate two variances for material and labor. It should be pointed out here that in accounting presentations, when the terms "material" and "labor" are used, direct material or direct labor is implied unless otherwise indicated. In the case of overhead—because of the heterogeneous costs included in the one account—a great variety of analytical methods have been developed, resulting in the isolation of two to 29 different variances.

In the case of material, it is usual to isolate a price variance and a quantity variance. For illustrative purposes, consider a case in which 1,000 gallons of product A are purchased at an actual cost of $1.10 per gallon when the standard cost is $1.00 per gallon. Also, 800 gallons were actually used in producing commodity X in such a quantity that only 750 gallons of A should have been used at standard. The typical calculations and entries are as follows:

Price variance = (actual price − standard price) × actual quantity
Price variance = ($1.10 − $1.00) × 1,000 = $.10 × 1,000 − $100

Raw material inventory	$1,000	
Material price variance	100	
Accounts payable		$1,100

To record the liability at the actual amount and to charge the inventory with the standard price.

Quantity variance = (actual quantity used − standard quantity) × standard cost
Quantity variance = (800 − 750) × $1.00 = 50 × $1.00 = $50

Work in process	$750	
Material quantity variance	50	
Raw material in inventory		$800

To record the removal from inventory of the actual amount of raw material used and to charge work in process with the standard amount.

The calculations of labor variances are quite similar to the ones for material, except that it is more appropriate here to refer to a rate variance rather than to price variance, and to a time or efficiency variance rather than to a quantity variance. Also, in the case of labor, both variances are calculated at the same time. For illustrative purposes, assume the following cost data: The actual labor cost was $133,250 for 41,000 hours; the standard rate was $3.00 per hour; and the standard time allowed for the amount of production for the period was 40,000 hours.

Rate variance = (actual rate − standard rate) × actual hours
Rate variance = ($3.25 − $3.00) × 41,000 = $.25 × 41,000 = $10,250

Efficiency variance = (actual hours worked − standard hours) × standard rate
Efficiency variance = (41,000 − 40,000) × $3.00 = 1,000 × $3.00 = $3,000

Work in process	$120,000	
Labor rate variance	10,250	
Labor efficiency variance	3,000	
Payroll		$133,250

To relieve the payroll account of
the actual cost of labor and to
charge work in process with the
standard cost.

When management has an analysis by causes of the material variances and
the labor variances, responsibility can be fixed; and, if the variances are significant, corrective steps can be taken through consultations with or instructions
to the responsible persons. For example, the purchasing agent is responsible for
material prices; therefore, he is the one to check with if the prices are out of
line. But if too great a quantity of material has been used, the foreman of the
department where the material was used should be checked with, since the foremen are responsible for the quantities of material used in their respective
departments.

In the case of labor variances, the person or persons (usually, the personnel
manager) responsible for setting wage rates and assigning employees to jobs
should be checked with if there are significant differences between standard
rates and actual rates. But if there are significant differences between the standard hours allowed for the work accomplished and the actual hours, the foreman
of the department where the variance occurred should be checked with.

In the case of material or labor, only one class of cost is involved, and in each
case it is a direct as well as a variable cost; therefore, the variances are quite
easily and objectively analyzed.

However, in the matter of overhead, a vast variety of different expenses is
collected in one account. All of them are indirect, and they vary in type from
variable through semivariable to fixed. Thus the analysis of overhead variances
becomes more subjective and more complex than the analysis of material and
labor variances.

A common two-variance method of analysis is illustrated on the basis of the
following data:

Actual overhead	$42,000.00
Budgeted overhead for 10,000 units (normal)	$40,000.00
Budgeted overhead for 8,000 units	$36,000.00
Actual labor rate	$4.50
Standard labor rate	$4.00
Actual hours worked	11,000
Standard hours per unit of product	1
Units produced	9,500
Overhead rate, percent of labor cost	100

The amount of overhead applied to production is (standard hours worked per
unit, one hour × the standard hourly labor rate, $4 × overhead rate, 100 per-
cent × the actual units produced, 9,500) $38,000.

The overall overhead variance is the difference between the actual costs incurred and the amount applied ($42,000 — $38,000) $4,000. Since the actual cost is greater than the applied amount, the variance is said to be unfavorable. Also, the overhead is underapplied. It is this amount that must be analyzed, regardless of whether two or 22 variances are isolated. The actual costs and the applied amount have been established. To isolate two variances, only one more figure is needed—the budget at the standard-allowed level of operations. Since 9,500 units were produced, a budgeted cost for that level of production is needed. A budget cost of $40,000 for 10,000 units and a budget cost of $36,000 for 8,000 units are given. Therefore, by interpolation, a budget cost of $39,000 can be established for 9,500 units. A controllable variance (sometimes referred to as a spending variance) can be calculated as follows:

Actual overhead costs	$42,000
Budget at standard allowed	39,000
Unfavorable controllable variance	$ 3,000

A volume variance (sometimes referred to as a capacity variance) can be calculated in the following manner:

Budget at standard allowed	$39,000
Applied overhead	38,000
Unfavorable volume variance	$ 1,000

The sum of the unfavorable controllable variance and the unfavorable volume variance is $4,000, the amount of the overall variance.

DIRECT COSTING AND ABSORPTION COSTING

Direct costing, also called marginal costing, is a method of valuing production. Under this concept all fixed costs (referred to in direct costing circles as "period costs") are excluded from inventories. Only costs directly resulting from the short-run decision to produce, hence variable costs (also in direct costing referred to as "controllable costs"), are included in the inventories. Thus inventories are charged with only the additional costs of producing as compared with not producing. For this reason, the term "marginal costing" is appropriate and less confusing. Generally, the terms "direct" and "indirect" have been used to indicate the degree of identification a cost may have with production: as in the case of direct labor, which is charged directly to the product, and indirect labor, which is charged to overhead. Under direct costing, variable indirect labor is charged as a direct cost to the product.

Direct costing is especially helpful to management in decision making in cases of idle capacity and high fixed costs. It is also very useful in making decisions in the short run.

Quite different inventory costs are obtained by direct costing than by absorption costing, which is also called conventional, total, or full costing. Under absorption costing, all production costs, both fixed and variable, are charged to production.

In stressing the marginal income concept of direct costing, a distinction should be made between the terms "gross profit" and "gross margin," even though they are sometimes used interchangeably. Gross profit (used in absorption costing) is the result of subtracting the total cost—both fixed and variable—of goods sold from sales revenue. Gross margin (used in direct costing) is the result of subtracting the marginal costs (variable or controllable costs only) from sales revenue.

Under absorption costing, it is not necessary to separate the many factory overhead accounts into their fixed and variable components since all factory overhead will be charged to inventories. However, under direct costing, every account which contains elements of fixed costs and variable costs must be separated so that the variable part may be charged to inventory and the fixed part charged to expense for the period.

The following assumed data are used to illustrate and compare inventory valuations by absorption costing and direct costing.

Direct material	$ 40,000
Direct labor	20,000
Variable factory overhead	20,000
Fixed factory overhead	20,000
Total costs	$100,000
Units produced	1,000
Units sold	750

	Direct Costing	Absorption Costing
Marginal (direct) costs	$ 80,000	$ 80,000
Fixed (period) costs		20,000
Charges to inventory	$ 80,000	$100,000
Less: cost of sales	60,000	75,000
Inventory	$ 20,000	$25,000

For further comparison, a comparative income statement for the XYZ Company is presented in Exhibit 4.11.

The cost of goods sold and the inventory are less by direct costing than by absorption costing because of the exclusion of period costs. Because of the separation of the period costs from variable costs in direct costing, as indicated in the preceding comparative statement, it is possible to establish a gross margin—or marginal contribution, as it is sometimes called—and a merchandising margin. These values are not available by absorption costing. Awareness of the importance of these figures for management decision making will come when the meaning and importance of marginal income are considered.

Marginal income is the excess of revenue over the additional cost of earning the revenue—that is, the excess of sales revenue over the variable cost of making the sales.

Exhibit 4.11
COMPARATIVE INCOME STATEMENT

XYZ Company
Comparative Income Statement
For the Year Ended December 31, 19___

	Absorption Costing	Direct Costing
Sales	$800,000	$800,000
Cost of goods sold		
Material	$200,000	$200,000
Labor	200,000	200,000
Variable factory overhead	200,000	200,000
Fixed factory overhead	200,000	
Total production costs	$800,000	$600,000
Less: Ending inventory	400,000	300,000
Total cost of goods sold	$400,000	$300,000
Gross profit	$400,000	
Gross margin		$500,000
Operating expenses		
Selling	$ 40,000	
Administrative	40,000	
Total operating expenses	$ 80,000	
Variable operating expenses		
Selling		$ 20,000
Administrative		20,000
Total variable operating expenses		$ 40,000
Merchandising margin		$460,000
Period costs		
Fixed factory overhead		$200,000
Fixed selling expenses		20,000
Fixed administrative expenses		20,000
Total period costs		240,000
Net operating profit	$320,000	$220,000

The direct costing concept may be applied to either process cost systems or job-order systems and may be used either with or without standards.

When a plant has idle capacity or when prices are being depressed, management can use direct costing methods to an advantage in determining the lowest possible price to accept for additional units of production.

When there is idle plant capacity, the fixed costs of the plant become sunk costs and therefore irrelevant to decisions in regard to the additional use of the plant. The only relevant costs are the additional costs of producing the additional units. However, the possible adverse effect that a special sale at a reduced price will have on regular sales must be considered. It is better for a facility to operate than not to operate if the revenue from operations is greater than the variable costs of operating even though total costs (fixed and variable) are not recovered, because by so doing losses are reduced. At best, it is a short-run operation. In the long run, total costs must be recovered.

Direct costing is helpful to management in special pricing cases in the short run. There is danger that if direct costing is relied on too much by management for costing production, goods may be underpriced in the long run to the detriment of the firm.

Direct costing is very useful to management, but it is not generally accepted by the SEC, Internal Revenue Service (IRS), AICPA, or the American Accounting Association.

Defense Contracts

The Department of Defense (DOD) is the country's largest single customer, entering into contracts for goods and services amounting to $20 billion to $30 billion annually. Accounting for defense contracts has become a specialized area of accounting to both government accountants and industrial accountants.

Anyone who contemplates entering into a defense contract should become familiar with the special requirements and clauses of the various types of contracts awarded by the government. This may be done through consultation with experts in the area and careful study of the Armed Services Procurement Regulation (ASPR). Section XV is especially important. It is divided into six parts. Part 1 is introductory in nature, and in it the various types of contracts, as well as applicable cost principles and procedures, are discussed. In Part 2, cost-reimbursement-type supply and research contracts are treated, as well as special cost factors, definitions, and procedures applicable to these types of contracts. Part 3 deals with special problems, costs, cost factors, and special contract features occasioned by contracting with educational institutions. Part 4 deals with the cost and accounting problems and procedures, as well as special contract features applicable to construction contracts. Part 5 is concerned with cost and accounting problems peculiar to contracts for the construction of industrial facilities. In Part 6, the various types of fixed-price contracts are defined, and the use and application of Parts 2, 3, and 4 are further elaborated.

TYPES OF CONTRACTS

There are two basic types of government contracts: fixed-price and cost. Each of these classes can be further refined. Fixed-price types of contracts include (*a*) firm fixed-price; (*b*) fixed-price with escalation clause; (*c*) fixed-price with re-determination-of-price clause; (*d*) fixed-price incentive; (*e*) time and materials; and (*f*) labor hours.

Cost (reimbursement) types of contracts include (*a*) cost-plus-fixed-fee (CPFF); (*b*) cost-plus-incentive-fee (CPIF); (*c*) cost-sharing; and (*d*) cost. (Types of contracts are further discussed in the Purchasing section, page 10·23).

Care should be exercised by the contractor, as well as by the contracting government officer, in the selection of the type of contract; risks and obligations assumed will depend in general on the type of contract signed. A contractor assumes the highest degree of risk with a firm fixed-price contract. Such a contract should be used only when the contractor has thorough knowledge of production costs and reason to believe that they will not change during the life of the contract. Such a contract should be of short duration. If the contract is to continue over a long period of time, the contractor should insist on another type of contract—perhaps one including an escalation clause or a redetermination-of-price clause. The escalation clause is especially appropriate in cases where it is likely that costs will increase during the life of the contract but the amount of increase cannot be reliably estimated.

In cases where the contractor has not experienced a cost of production for the contracted item or a similar one, a cost-type contract would be much less risky.

ACCOUNTING FOR DEFENSE CONTRACTS

The government will not prescribe the accounting system to be used by the contractor. However, a contractor is expected to consistently follow generally accepted accounting principles and to maintain books, records, documents, and other evidence in sufficient detail to support all claims against the government. A major risk to the contractor in using an inadequate accounting system is the danger of loss because of the failure of a claim. A contracting officer may disallow costs which are not supported by adequate evidence. Either job-order or process costing may be used as appropriate to the type of production involved. Standard costs may be used, provided variances are adequately identified and charged to various products.

Since process accounting results in average costs for production, as compared with the specific costs developed for each job under job-order accounting, job-order accounting may be preferred if it is suitable to the particular production system. Under normal circumstances, it would be easier for the government auditors to identify costs with specific contracts when job-order accounting is used than when process accounting is used.

In the event of termination of a fixed-price contract for the convenience of the government, cost data are needed to support each item of the contractor's claim for reimbursement of the cost incurred. Special tools and equipment—that is, items usable only on the contract terminated—are charged to the contract on a unit-of-production basis. Any cost of such special tools and equipment not charged to production by the time of termination of the contract is charged to the government, according to the termination clause. For example, if a specialized piece of equipment, of value only in the production of a certain item, is required for the efficient production of the contracted item, the contractor in placing the bid spreads the cost of that specialized equipment over all of the units called for in the contract. Thus, if the contract had been terminated when only half completed, only one-half of the cost would have been charged to the contract. The balance of the cost of this equipment could be recovered under the termination clause if properly supported by evidence of its cost.

Direct costs. Any costs that can be specifically identified with a particular unit of production (contract) are direct costs. The physical association of the cost-creating item with the end product is not necessary.

Indirect costs. Indirect costs are any costs resulting from common or joint activities and of such nature that they cannot practically be assigned to production (contract) as direct costs. Consistent treatment of costs for defense contracts and nongovernment work is essential. When a given type of cost is treated as direct for contract purposes and the applicable portion is charged directly to a contract, the balance of that cost should not be charged to a pool of indirect costs which are then charged indirectly to both government and nongovernment work. Hence, all like charges must be eliminated in the computation of the overhead rate to be used in applying overhead to a contract.

Allowable costs. For costs to be allowable, they must meet four broad standards. They must be reasonable; they must be allocable; they must result from the application of generally accepted accounting principles; and they must comply with the terms of the contract.

Allocable costs. An allocable cost is any cost that can be assigned or charged to a particular cost objective, job, contract, or process. A cost is allocable (in whole or in part) to a government contract if it is incurred especially for that contract or if it is necessary to the operation of the business.

Reasonable costs. A cost is reasonable if in type and amount it is (1) necessary to the completion of the contract or for the performance of business; (2) not in excess of an amount which would have been arrived at as the result of a competitive "arm's-length" transaction; and (3) in compliance with the terms of the contract.

Costs generally allowed. Fourteen types of costs are generally allowed. They are as follows: (1) bonding; (2) compensation for personal services, except for limitations (*a*) on executive's compensation and (*b*) on wages that are discriminatory against the government, as compared with civilian work (some severance pay is allowed; under certain conditions, training costs are allowed); (3) depreciation, except for amounts improperly taken or taken on idle facilities (a reasonable use charge will be allowed on fully depreciated assets); (4) employee morale, health, welfare, and food service and dormitory costs and credits, except for unreasonable amounts; (5) insurance and indemnification, except for certain limitations; (6) labor relations costs; (7) maintenance and repair costs; (8) manufacturing and production engineering costs; (9) material costs; (10) patent and royalty costs; (11) plant protection costs; (12) precontract costs, if necessary in securing the contract; (13) recruitment costs; and (14) rental cost, if not excessive (problems arise in sale and leaseback).

Costs generally disallowed. The types of costs that are generally disallowed are almost as numerous as the types allowed. They include (1) advertising, except for recruitment of help, the procurement of scarce items, and the disposal of surplus material and scrap resulting from a defense contract; (2) bad debts; (3) contributions and donations; (4) entertainment costs, unless in connection with professional or technical meetings; (5) excess facility costs, except for reasonable standby costs; (6) fines and penalties, except those resulting from compliance with specific contract provisions or written orders from a contracting officer; (7) interest and other financial costs; (8) losses on other contracts; (9) organization costs; (10) plant reconversion costs, except the cost of removing government property; and (11) profit or loss on disposition of plant, equipment, or other capital assets.

These lists of allowed and disallowed costs are not all-inclusive, and they lack detail. They are intended only to provide the reader with a general concept of which costs are allowable and which are not. For detailed information, ASPR should be consulted.

CONTRACT TERMINATION

All defense contracts in excess of $1,000 include a termination clause. A contract may be terminated for the convenience of the government or because of default by the contractor.

The government may terminate a contract for its convenience when the need for the product is reduced or ceases to exist, or when termination is in the best interest of the government. The default clause permits the government to terminate a contract in the event a contractor fails to perform according to the terms of the contract. In case of the termination of a cost-type contract for default, the contractor shall be reimbursed for his allowable costs and an appropriate portion of the total fee. The contractor will not be allowed the costs of preparing his settlement proposal. In case of default on a fixed-price contract, the contractor may be charged with the added cost incurred by the government for acquiring the items from another source, as well as liquidated damages, if provided for in the contract, or for actual damages in the absence of the provision for liquidated damages.

A termination for the convenience of the government may be either partial or complete. A termination is complete if the termination notice orders a complete work stoppage on the unperformed portion of the contract. A termination is partial if a stoppage of performance of only a part of the incompleted portion of the contract is ordered. That part of the contract which has not been terminated is referred to as the continuing portion. Upon receipt of a termination notice, the contractor must immediately stop all work on the terminated portion. If the termination is complete, all work must be stopped at once. If it is a partial termination, the contractor is expected to complete the continuing portion of the contract.

A termination may be settled with or without cost to the government. In cases where a contractor has incurred very little or no cost on the terminated portion of the contract, the government may negotiate a settlement without cost to itself. In case of a termination, a contractor must file a termination claim with the contracting officer within a year from date of termination.

Terminated fixed-price contracts may be settled on an "inventory basis" or (with prior approval of the contracting officer) on a "total cost basis." To establish the amount of the claim under the inventory basis, the contractor may include only costs allocable to the terminated portion of the contract. All items in the termination inventory must be listed at cost. To establish the gross termination claim, an allowance for profit is added to, or an allowance for loss is deducted from, the inventory value. The inventory basis for settlement is usually preferred, but under some circumstances the total cost basis is more practical. The contracting officer may approve the total cost basis under the following conditions: (1) when production has not started (only preproduction costs have been incurred); (2) when it is difficult or impossible to establish production cost per unit of product or when the contract does not specify unit prices.

When the total cost basis is used, all costs incurred on the contract are itemized regardless of whether they apply to the completed or the terminated portion of the contract. To the total of the costs is added an allowance for profit, or an allowance for loss is deducted. The claims of subcontractors are added to the above sum or difference. From this amount are deducted the contract price of units accepted by the government, as well as all advance or progress payments. In case of a partial termination, a settlement proposal cannot be submitted on a total cost basis until the continued portion of the contract is completed.

When a cost-reimbursement-type contract is terminated, the contractor may continue to voucher incurred costs for a period extending to the last day of the sixth month after the termination date. He may elect to discontinue vouchering costs at any time during the six-month period. After a contractor has vouchered all costs applicable to the particular contract (within the six-month period), he may file a substantiated claim for his fee. The claim for fees must be submitted within one year from termination date unless he has been granted an extension.

After a contractor has discontinued vouchering costs, either because of the expiration of the six-month period or because of an election, he may present a settlement proposal. Such a proposal may not include any previously vouchered costs, any previously disallowed costs, or costs subject to a reclaim voucher.

—W. A. Howe

PLANNING, BUDGETING, AND FORECASTING

Budgeting can perform two primary functions at the corporate, divisional, and operating levels: the coordination of operating plans and the allocation of both financial and nonfinancial resources.

The coordination of operating plans involves the integration of plans not only within the divisions but also between the divisions. Thus a unity of purpose is achieved, reflecting the capabilities of the respective divisions and the goals, both immediate and prospective, of the corporation.

The proper allocation of the financial and nonfinancial resources of the corporation is crucial to the continuing growth and prosperity of the corporate whole. The allocation of these resources and the effects they engender cannot be divorced from the immediate and long-range plans of departments and divisions. The resources become the skeleton upon which the plans (muscles) of the organization are superimposed.

The budget, although expressed in financial terms, is not an accounting document but a managerial program reflecting management objectives. It is the vehicle through which senior management expresses its aims without compromising the principle of command necessary to maintain operating control.

Through the exercise of duties and responsibilities, budgeting people can, by interpreting and reporting on results, facilitate the upward and downward flow of thought and counterthought and bring the right information to the attention of the right people at the right time. Line and staff functions are coordinated, thereby giving assistance to operating management in the achievement of its goals. At the same time, accounting systems developed to adhere to generally accepted accounting principles and procedures are implemented, through the planning process, to reflect an accountability coincident with responsibility.

Purpose and Functions of Budgeting

A basic difference between budgeting and cost accounting is that budgeting is the coordination of plans for action, whereas cost accounting is measuring the cost incurred resulting from action taken. From these measured results management may change segments of the plan; but the process of developing and integrating disparate plans into a tactical exercise (the annual profit plan) or into a strategy for contending with future events (the long-range plan) is budgeting.

Thus budgeting is not to be conceived as another function of the accounting discipline with its attendant emphasis on valuation of assets and results from operations but rather as a technique to allocate resources and coordinate management ambitions to achieve the best overall results from the activities budgeted.

In recent times the planning aspects of budgeting have been delegated to a long-range planning group. This trend owes its origin, in part, to a management belief that the budget is an operational plan developed in the controller's office, whereas the long-range plan is a program for growth developed for and by senior management. Since the annual budget is a translation into financial terms of the operating plan for the first year of a long-range plan, it must adhere to generally accepted accounting principles, where applicable, and conform to recommended accounting format. But all transactions are viewed as most likely to occur, and no consideration is given to the variance analysis that is characteristic of cost accounting. The budget becomes the connecting document between the planned program and the actual performance as expressed in accounting documents. It assures a profit, provided that no uninsured catastrophe occurs, sales quotas are met, and the expected expenses at given levels of operation are maintained. Budgeting is a commitment to the "going concern" concept that presumes a continuing life expectancy of the firm. Budgeting is not planning. Planning is thoughtful, rational consideration of objectives and alternative means to achieve those objectives.

The budget is the translation into financial terms of the plan for allocating resources; it is the controlling vehicle against which actual performance is measured. Budgeting is the process of allocating the available resources of the firm in a systematic and rational manner to achieve a stated objective in a future period of time. It is a system of allocation, not valuation, of economic resources.

The purpose of the budget is to provide a system of reporting actual performance against planned performance; to provide a basis for measuring, evaluating, and criticizing actual performance through special analyses and reports on variances from planned performance; and to promote full participation by all members of management in the development of a totally integrated plan for achieving stated objectives in the current operating year and in the long term.

Much attention is being given to a budget system called the Planning-Programming-Budgeting System (PPBS), which received impetus from Robert S. McNamara when he was Secretary of Defense and Lyndon B. Johnson while he was President of the United States.

Advocates of PPBS assert that the system differs from the traditional budgeting approaches by emphasizing the output of programs rather than the input of expenditures. If the budgeting process is looked upon as a totally integrated program for allocating the resources of the firm, expenditures are merely means to achieve a stated objective or end. Unfortunately, too many companies have restricted the budgeting process to separate schedules of expenses, capital acquisitions, sales, and other company matters rather than promoting an integrated system. PPBS as a system is more akin to the capital budget (investment program) than the concept of the total budget developed in this section of the handbook.

Exhibit 4.12

PRODUCTION SCHEDULE

EXAMPLE 1				EXAMPLE 2			
INPUTS	OUTPUT			INPUTS	OUTPUT		
Units of Capital and Labor	Total Product	Average Product	Marginal Product	Units of Capital and Labor	Total Product	Average Product	Marginal Product
0	0	0	0	0	0	0	0
1.0	0	0	0	1.0	0	0	0
2.0	10	5.0	10	2.0	40	20.0	40
3.0	43	14.3	33	3.0	100	33.3	60
4.0	100	25.0	57	4.0	200	50.0	100
5.0	175	35.0	75	5.0	320	64.0	120
6.0	270	45.0	95	6.0	480	80.0	160
7.0	400	57.1	130	7.0	700	100.0	220
8.0	570	71.2	170	8.0	780	97.5	80
9.0	780	86.7	210	9.0	820	91.1	40
10.0	1,000	100.0	220	10.0	840	84.0	20
11.0	1,078	98.0	78	11.0	820	74.5	(20)
12.0	1,122	93.5	44				
13.0	1,140	87.7	18				
14.0	1,120	80.0	(20)				

Economics of Budgeting

The objective of any financial analysis program should be consistent with acceptable economic theory. The development of a corporate financial attitude reflecting sound economic theory is referred to as "financial overview." The concept of financial overview perceives rather than conceives, looks at involvement rather than being involved, instructs rather than directs, promotes divisional entrepreneurship rather than acting as entrepreneur. Financial overview is required in order to gain a perception of corporate goals and objectives and the entrepreneurial goals of the corporate divisions.

The Product Curve

The budgeting process can be better understood if the business enterprise is considered as an economic entity where attention is given to the production of goods and services by the most effective means in accordance with existing technical capability. The production of goods and services can be expressed as a function of inputs of capital and labor (Exhibit 4.12). The resulting curve is known as a product curve (Exhibit 4.13).

Exhibit 4.13
PRODUCT CURVE

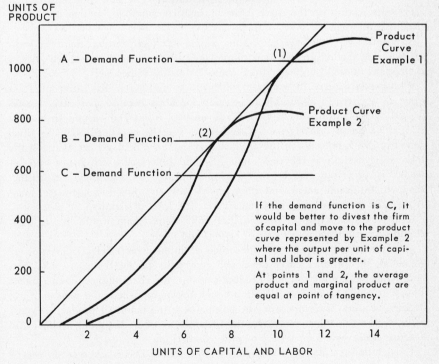

UNITS OF PRODUCT

A – Demand Function _____ (1) _____   Product Curve Example 1

1000

800   Product Curve Example 2

B – Demand Function_____(2)_____

600   C – Demand Function

400   If the demand function is C, it would be better to divest the firm of capital and move to the product curve represented by Example 2 where the output per unit of capital and labor is greater.

200   At points 1 and 2, the average product and marginal product are equal at point of tangency.

0   2   4   6   8   10   12   14

UNITS OF CAPITAL AND LABOR

DEFINITIONS

The term "capital," as used here, signifies the total of all the depreciable and financial assets of the firm that are available to management, as well as some forms of fixed labor associated with the cost of being in business. (Under certain conditions, some labor may be considered part of capital, particularly where the cost of obtaining certain skills is viewed as an investment in technical know-how.) The term "labor," as used here, means the contribution made by the total of all persons employed by the firm, with the exception of the labor included in the definition of capital.

In Exhibit 4.12, average product is equal to total product divided by total number of units of capital and labor. Marginal product is the change in total product divided by the change in the total number of units of capital and labor that brought about the change in product.

Exhibits 4.12 and 4.13 represent a three-dimensional relationship expressed in a two-dimensional form. The following assumption is made: Capital and labor are not equal substitutes. A unit of capital and labor is the optimal combination of capital and labor for that particular level of output. The combination of capital and labor can change as additional units are required to increase product output. At each level of unit input there can exist many combinations of capital and labor to produce different amounts of output. The one combination that represents a point on the curve is the optimal combination for that amount of product produced.

In Exhibit 4.12, the average product equals marginal product where the units of input are slightly greater than 10 and the units of output are slightly greater than 1,000, or slightly greater than 7 and 700 units, respectively.

The product curve shown in Exhibit 4.13 is useful for illustrative purposes only; it is virtually impossible to develop for firms because most data are reported by firms in dollars rather than in units of input and output. In Exhibit 4.13, three finance management exercises are visually expressed: (1) The planning exercise is reflected in the product curve and the demand function; (2) the forecasting exercise is reflected in the demand function, which is not only affected by price but also by the development of a need through advertising, research and development, and other promotions; and (3) the budgeting exercise is reflected in the allocation of resources at the level of required output.

The model attempts to conceptualize what management would like to do— maximize output per unit input of capital and labor.

Since budgeting is primarily concerned with the most efficient allocation of resources, the product curve developed represents the best means to a given end. After developing the best product curve in the circumstances, management would operate the firm at a level between the point where the marginal and average products are equal and the point where the marginal product becomes zero. Within this range of activity the best level is where marginal revenue and cost are equal, assuming a state of pure competition.

From Exhibits 4.12 and 4.13 it can be observed that when average product is increasing, marginal product is greater than average product. When average product is decreasing, marginal product is less than average product. Thus, when average product is near maximum, marginal product approaches average product. Restated, this means that the firm is getting increasing returns per unit of capital and labor up to the point where average product equals marginal product, and decreasing returns beyond that point. In Example 1 drawn from Exhibit 4.12, management will maximize utility from capital and labor by operating the firm within a small range of 1,000 units of input.

In real life the business manager is regularly changing inputs by adjusting labor and capital to achieve the best performance. He may do this in a number of different ways: He may substitute skilled labor for unskilled labor, substitute machines for labor, or substitute machines for machines; or he may combine any one of these three methods.

In every instance the business manager is allocating his resources in order to improve upon his marginal output of product or service per unit change of capital and labor.

The marginal concept expressed in the product curve approach to budgeting is different, therefore, from the marginal concept expressed in direct costing. In the former, the best allocation of available resources is attempted at different levels of output. In the latter, care and effort are exercised to capitalize all unexpired costs by charging into inventory only those costs directly associated with the manufacture of the product.

Budgets are generally divided into two kinds.

1. The operating budget is the allocation of available resources to achieve a stated objective in a given period of time. Generally, the operating budget covers only a single year. If the budget covers more than one year, it is considered a long-range plan. Where the budget covers more than one level of operation, it is referred to as a flexible budget. Where only a single level of operation is considered, the budget is a fixed budget. The primary objective of an operating budget is to utilize resources in the most efficient manner consistent with conditions in the marketplace.

2. The investment budget is the selection between available alternatives of those investments which, when added to or substituted for available resources, will improve upon or maintain the level of product or service.

Throughout this discussion, emphasis is placed on budgeting as an expression of plans to achieve the goals and objectives concurred in by senior management. However, many companies do not have a fully integrated budgeting system. These companies develop separate expense schedules or budgets for their major operating areas such as cash, expense, capital expenditures, research and development programs, sales and advertising, and manufacturing. Although these separate schedules may help assure control over total costs, there is no assurance that the best allocation of resources will be achieved to maximize output of goods or services per unit increase in capital and labor. Since management is constantly engaged in exercising trade-offs between the cost of doing business and the cost of being in business, the budgeting system should as nearly as possible assure that these decisions are both proper and realistic. The total budget system is also compatible with return on investment (ROI) techniques used to measure either managerial performance or the investment worth of the enterprise. However, the allocation of resources, which is budgeting, should not be confused with the evaluation of management or investment potential that is ROI.

With reference to Example 2 in Exhibit 4.12, and to Exhibit 4.13, for instance, if the demand function intersects the original product curve (Example 1) at a point low on the curve and there is little possibility that the share of market for the firm will increase or that the total market will expand, the firm may be over-capitalized. Under such conditions the firm should divest itself of capital (as previously stated, capital may include some forms of labor) and thus bring about a more efficient combination of capital and labor as depicted in Example 2, Exhibit 4.12. The converse would be true if the firm operated beyond the point of diminishing returns.

Cost-Volume Behavior Pattern

As indicated earlier, the marginal concept developed for direct costing differs from the marginal concept developed for flexible budgeting. Flexible budgeting is nothing more than developing a number of budgets, each representing a different level of output. Because marginal output is increasing, it is presumed that the total resources are combined in a manner to increase productive efficiency. However, in direct costing the primary concern is to maintain a level of profit consistent with a level of sales by not over- or under-absorbing burden by charging to inventory only those costs which are directly related to producing that inventory.

Four cases illustrate the effect on profits resulting from changes in production and sales. Following are the required data:

	Total Cost	Unit Cost
Standard volume 100,000 units		
Direct labor and material	$ 350,000	$ 3.50
Variable overhead expense	600,000	6.00
Fixed overhead expense	700,000	7.00
Profit	100,000	1.00
Total expense including profit	$1,750,000	$17.50

Case 1: Sales and production are the same; sales are 150,000 units.

	Direct Costing	Absorption Costing
Sales	$2,625,000	$2,625,000
Direct charges	525,000	525,000
Gross profit	$2,100,000	$2,100,000
Fixed overhead	700,000	1,950,000
Variable overhead	900,000	
Net profit	$ 500,000	$ 150,000
Overabsorbed overhead ($7.00 × 50,000 units)		$ 350,000

Since production and sales are equal, nothing was charged to inventory. An adjustment must be made at year end (or during the year) because of the over-absorption of overhead, under the absorption costing method, making the profit for each method the same.

Case 2: Sales and production are the same; sales are 70,000 units.

	Direct Costing	*Absorption Costing*
Sales	$1,225,000	$1,225,000
Direct charges	245,000	245,000
Gross profit	980,000	980,000
Fixed overhead	700,000	910,000
Variable overhead	420,000	
Net profit (loss)	$ (140,000)	$ 70,000

Underabsorbed overhead ($7.00 × 30,000 units) $ (210,000)

Since production and sales are equal, nothing was charged to inventory. An adjustment must be made at year end (or during the year) because of the under-absorption of overhead, under the absorption costing method, making the profit for each method the same.

Case 3: Sales and production are not equal; sales are 100,000 units and production is 150,000 units.

$$V = \text{variable cost}$$
$$F = \text{full absorption cost}$$

	Direct Costing	*Absorption Costing*
Sales (100,000 units)	$1,750,000	$1,750,000
Production (150,000 units)		
Direct charges	525,000	525,000
Overhead	900,000 (V)	1,950,000 (F)
Cost of production	$1,425,000	$2,475,000
Transferred to inventory		
(50,000 units)		
Variable cost	475,000	
Full absorption cost		825,000
Cost of sales	$ 950,000	$1,650,000
Contribution margin	800,000	
Fixed overhead	700,000	
Net profit	$ 100,000	$ 100,000

Case 4: Sales and production are not equal; sales are 150,000 units and production is 100,000.

$$V = \text{variable cost}$$
$$F = \text{full absorption cost}$$

	Direct Costing	Absorption Costing
Sales (150,000 units)	$2,625,000	$2,625,000
Production (100,000 units)		
Direct charges	350,000	350,000
Overhead	600,000 (V)	1,300,000 (F)
Cost of production	$ 950,000	$1,650,000
Transferred from inventory		
(50,000 units)		
Variable cost	475,000	
Full absorption cost		825,000
Cost of sales	$1,425,000	$2,475,000
Contribution margin	1,200,000	
Fixed overhead	700,000	
Net profit	$ 500,000	$ 150,000

It should be noted that, in Cases 3 and 4, the profit per unit of sales is always $1.00 under full absorption costing if no adjustments are made, whereas under direct costing the profit per unit of sales changes from $1.00 in Case 3 to $3.33 in Case 4. If Cases 3 and 4 were added together to represent succeeding years, total sales would be 250,000 units and total production would also be 250,000 units, or 50,000 units more than the standard production and sales for the two years. Total profits for the two years would be $600,000 under direct costing and $250,000 under absorption costing. The variance of $350,000 represents an over-absorption of fixed costs (50,000 units × $7.00 per unit of fixed costs) into the inventory. Obviously, adjustments must be made to the cost of sales. These adjustments are confusing to nonfinancial executives and have given impetus to the development of a marginal approach to both costing and budgeting.

In the cases cited, all costs incurred were at standard. The advantages of direct costing over absorption costing are more definite when sales are less than production and the costs incurred are greater than standard costs. Profits would be depressed in line with decreased sales and increased costs. In the next period, sales may be greater than production and costs returned to standard. Because of the excess costs carried in inventory from the previous period, profits would not rise in proportion to sales. To overcome this anomaly, variances from standard are charged off as period expenses. However, not all companies can develop a standard cost system—or, for that matter, a direct cost system and flexible budgets based on correlation analysis.

Marginal Analysis and Flexible Budgeting

If it were possible to develop budgets strictly on the basis of unit inputs and unit outputs, flexible budgeting would be greatly simplified. Because the budgeting process is frequently tied to financial data, a variable expense is considered the same when used in flexible budgeting as in direct costing. For this reason the method frequently used to develop a flexible budget system is the same as the method used to develop a direct cost system.

Regression Analysis

A regression analysis is a technique for establishing a relationship between two variables in which the dependent variable is expected to move in some predictable manner as the independent variable is moved.

If it can be established that the two variables move together either positively or negatively, it can be said that the two movements are correlated. How closely the correlation approaches a linear functional relationship is referred to as the coefficient of correlation. Correlation coefficients are expressed in values ranging between -1 and $+1$. The nearer the value to either one of these extremes, the better the correlation between the two variables. If the coefficient value is zero, no correlation exists. If the coefficient value is $+1$, the relationship is positive and completely predictable. The dependent variable will increase as the independent variable increases. If the coefficient value is -1, the relationship is negative and completely predictable. The dependent variable will decrease as the independent variable increases.

There are two steps in determining whether a dependent variable is correlated with an independent variable. The first step is to determine whether the two variables are significantly correlated.

COEFFICIENT OF CORRELATION

The coefficient of correlation is defined by the formula:

$$r = \frac{1/N \sum (x-\bar{x})\,(y-\bar{y})}{\sigma x \qquad \sigma y}$$

where $\bar{x}$ and $\bar{y}$ are the arithmetic means of the x values and y values; and where σx and σy are the standard deviations of the x and y distribution.

	Independent Variable	Dependent Variable
1	$x = 1$	$y = 2$
2	$x = 2$	$y = 4$
3	$x = 3$	$y = 6$

	x	y	$(x-\bar{x})^2$	$(y-\bar{y})^2$	$(x-\bar{x})(y-\bar{y})$
1	1	2	1	4	2
2	2	4	0	0	0
3	3	6	1	4	2
Total	6	12	2	8	4

Arithmetic mean $\bar{x}=2$ $\bar{y}=4$

Standard deviation $2/3$ $8/3$

$$r = \frac{1/3 \quad (4)}{(\sqrt{2/3})\,(\sqrt{8/3})} = \frac{1/3 \quad (4)}{4/3} = +1$$

FITTING A TREND LINE

The second step is to fit a trend line through the points represented by relationship between the dependent variable and the independent variable. The trend line is used to estimate changes in the dependent variable as the independent variable changes.

For example: The independent variable is direct labor dollars. The dependent variable is scrap cost. A significant correlation is computed. On a sheet of graph paper labor dollars are shown along the horizontal or x axis and scrap costs are shown along the vertical or y axis. A plot is made representing actual scrap cost incurred associated with labor dollars expended in a given period. The trend line fitted through these points gives the rate of change expected in scrap costs for a given change in direct labor.

The distribution of values of y is linear with regard to the values of x when the two quantities x and y can be related to each in the form as expressed by the equation:

$$y = a + bx$$

Two simultaneous equations are solved involving the values of a and b.

	Independent Variable	Dependent Variable
1	$x = 1$	$y = 2$
2	$x = 2$	$y = 4$
3	$x = 3$	$y = 6$
4	$x = 4$	$y = 8$
5	$x = 5$	$y = 10$

Solve for y by substituting known values of x and y.

y	x	$y = a + bx$	$xy = x(a + bx)$
2	1	$2 = a + b$	$2 = a + b$
4	2	$4 = a + 2b$	$8 = 2a + 4b$
6	3	$6 = a + 3b$	$18 = 3a + 9b$
8	4	$8 = a + 4b$	$32 = 4a + 16b$
10	5	$10 = a + 5b$	$50 = 5a + 25b$
		A.	B.
Totals		$30 = 5a + 15b$	$110 = 15a + 55b$

Simultaneous solution:

A. $90 = 15a + 45b$
B. $110 = 15a + 55b$
_____
$20 = \qquad 10b$
$2 = \qquad b$

Substituting 2 for b in Equation A:

A. $30 = 5a + 30$
$0 = 5a$
$0 = a$

THINGS TO REMEMBER

A correlation coefficient of −1 or +1 indicates that the correlation is both functional and linear. The functional relationship is the ratio of the change in the dependent variable to the independent variable. If $y = 2x$, y will increase by two if x is increased by one. The linear relationship indicates that the points lie on a straight line.

An acceptable correlation coefficient does not mean that the relationship need be one of cause and effect but rather that the movement of one may be predicted from the movement of the other.

It is not safe to predict beyond the limits of the data as given. This restriction is frequently overlooked. For example, if normal production was 1,000 units with an acceptable range of −20 percent and +5 percent, a significant correlation is meaningful only within that range of activity. Beyond the acceptable range of activity there may not exist a significant correlation.

In many instances the financial analyst can draw a line of best fit between the movement of an indirect expense (dependent variable) and direct labor costs (independent variable), but that does not give him the prerogative to extend the line to the y axis and claim that the value on the y axis represents the fixed portion of the indirect expense.

For example, given the following data, the relationship of the dependent variable to the independent variable can be shown to be a straight line expressed by the formula $y = a + bx$ where $a = \$6.00$ and $b = .36$. At 20 units of x, $y = \$13.20$ of which \$6.00 is fixed.

$$y = \$6.00 + .36 \times 20$$
$$y = \$6.00 + 7.20 = \$13.20$$

	Independent Variable	*Dependent Variable*
1	x = \$17.00	y = \$13.00
2	x = \$18.00	y = \$12.00
3	x = \$19.00	y = \$13.00
4	x = \$20.00	y = \$13.00
5	x = \$21.00	y = \$13.00
6	x = \$22.00	y = \$14.00
7	x = \$23.00	y = \$14.00

The example points up the major disadvantages from using the least-squares approach to developing a flexible budget: In most cases the range of activity in the independent variable is not great; the dependent variables do not show wide variations as the independent variables increase or decrease; and, keeping in mind the product curve, it is not likely that one can develop the fixed portion of the dependent cost by extending the line to its y axis, since going from zero production to the level under consideration is not linear.

The Budgeting Process

Budgeting is the allocation of resources in a manner consistent with objectives and conforming to policies as stated by management. These resources are more or less divided into two major classes: those resources that are related to the transformation of material, skills, and know-how into a product or service, and those resources that are related to determining what goods or services will be produced and the means used to produce the output in the most efficient manner. Such resources are referred to as capital resources and are divided into three areas: (1) research and development programs concerned with what should be produced as goods or services; (2) fixed assets acquisition programs concerned with the means used to produce or provide the goods or services; and (3) systems and procedures programs concerned with the manner in which the fixed assets are rationalized in conjunction with labor to obtain the most efficient output.

Because the budget is a translation of operating plans into an accounting language, it should conform to generally accepted accounting principles and format. However, because budgeting is concerned with the allocation of economic resources, it is sometimes necessary to depart from accounting principles primarily concerned with the evaluation of resources in order to achieve the best allocation of resources—that is, ROI versus discounted cash flow.

UNIT INPUT AND OUTPUT APPROACH

Wherever possible, the budgeting process should start with a unit output-input approach. The first constraint is the sales forecast. The second constraint is the capability to produce the forecast. Since the sales forecast establishes the requirements and inventory represented by completed or in-process units is a partial fulfillment of that requirement, it is necessary to subtract that inventory from the sales requirement to arrive at a budget requirement. The budget requirement will determine the short-run allocation of resources. It is precisely this requirement that makes the allocation of resources so difficult, since most operating statistics are financial statistics available through the accounting record. For example, factory labor may be budgeted first in units and then in dollars, as in Exhibit 4.14; but inventory represents the cost avoided in the future of material and labor cost. As long as sales and production are the same and only raw material supplies are represented in the inventory, the allocation of resources can be made on the most economic basis; otherwise, adjustments must be made.

After inventory requirements have been budgeted in the most expeditious and realistic manner, the next step is to budget the supporting functions to the major activities of the firm. Where these functions are performed by employees of the firm, the best approach is to establish tables of organization or manning tables and insist that requirements be adhered to, with changes allowed only for cause. Services bought outside the firm should be justified on the basis of least cost. (It is difficult to address remarks that have universal application to all classes of business endeavors. The difficulty is overcome in part by treating budgeting as an economic process rather than as an accounting process.)

CONTROL

The budget is increasingly being used as a control device. However, because firms are dynamic entities adjusting to changing economic forces, the budget should be self-adjusting to reflect the new conditions for operations. The self-

Exhibit 4.14

COMPUTATION OF UNIT LABOR HOURS AND DOLLARS

Manufacturing	19__	19__	19__	19__	19__

1. *Heavy Machining*

   Number of machinists x 2,080 hours
   Number of nonmachinists x 2,080 hours _____
      Subtotal _____
   Less vacation (average days___)   ( ) ( ) ( ) ( ) ( )
   Less paid holidays (number___)   ( ) ( ) ( ) ( ) ( )
   Less expense work hours   ( ) ( ) ( ) ( ) ( )
   Less time-off hours   ( ) ( ) ( ) ( ) ( )
   Available hours without overtime _____
   Add overtime hours
   Total hours this year _____
   Less hours in inventory   ( ) ( ) ( ) ( ) ( )
   Total available hours
   Less shipments this year   ( ) ( ) ( ) ( ) ( )
      Year-end inventory

2. *Light Machining*
   (same as above)

3. *Assembly*
   (same as above)

4. *Engineering*
   (same as above)

5. *Other*
   (same as above)

Summary

   Available hours without overtime
      Add overtime hours
   Total hours this year _____
      Less hours in inventory   ( ) ( ) ( ) ( ) ( )
   Total available hours
      Less shipments this year   ( ) ( ) ( ) ( ) ( )
   Year-end inventory

Convert these data into dollars by using agreed-upon rates.

adjusting budget is known as the "flexible budget." The flexible budget is a marginal approach to allocating resources and incorporates all the difficulties and disadvantages associated with marginal analysis. It is in one sense a passive approach to budgeting, as it justifies change provided the relationship of expenses is maintained rather than force a change in the composition of capital and labor to achieve a more efficient product curve. Nevertheless, the flexible budget is one of the best control devices available to management. It is an effective tool, provided it does not attempt to measure radical changes from normal operating levels. Flexible budgeting is not a substitute for recession analysis budgeting. In recession analysis an attempt is made to measure the effect on the inputs of capital and labor as the demand function is moved steadily down on the product curve.

Not all expenditures can be controlled by way of a budget. For example, a department may show that actual expenditures differed little from budgeted expenditures but performed little constructive work. A great deal of effort is expended to control direct charges; the same amount of effort should be expended to get the most return from indirect charges. One way of overcoming

Exhibit 4.15

BUDGETED DATA ON NONMANUFACTURING INDIRECT EXPENSE

	Nonmanufacturing Indirect Expense		
	1967 Actual (Dollars)	1968 Profit Plan (Dollars)	1971 Profit Plan (Dollars)
	(000 Omitted)		
Total engineering expense	300	307	382
Variable expense	(145)	(184)	(235)
Fixed expense	155	123	147
Total selling expense	293	310	400
Variable expense	(190)	(240)	(317)
Fixed expense	103	70	83
Total service expense	117	166	186
Variable expense	(80)	(112)	(136)
Fixed expense	37	54	50
Other fixed cost			
General and Administrative	540	523	600
Total fixed expense	835	760	880
Total variable expense	415	546	688
Total sales	4,230	5,400	6,800
Variable expense to sales (percent)	9.81	10.11	10.12

this drag on productive efficiency is to establish departmental goals with quarterly reviews to determine the progress made toward implementing the goals. Goals may be (a) the development of a cost control system; (b) performing product profitability analyses; (c) introducing an interdivisional pricing system; or (d) rewriting a wage incentive plan.

The Financial Model

With the increased use of the computer and the development of sophisticated programming techniques, there is a growing interest in organizing budgeting and financial data into a total system of interrelationships referred to as the corporate financial model. The model is designed to report on what has happened but also

Exhibit 4.16

EFFECT ON NONMANUFACTURING INDIRECT COST WHEN SALES ARE INCREASED FROM $5 MILLION TO $7 MILLION

Relation of Total Non-Manufacturing Cost to Sales (Percent)	Sales (Dollars)	Variable Cost 10.12 Percent of Sales (Dollars)	Fixed Cost Equals $760,000 Plus $8,500 per $100,000 After $5,400,000 Sales (Dollars)	Total Indirect Cost (Dollars)
25.32	5,000,000	506,000	760,000	1,266,000
25.02	5,100,000	516,120	760,000	1,276,120
24.74	5,200,000	526,240	760,000	1,286,240
24.46	5,300,000	536,360	760,000	1,296,360
24.20	5,400,000	546,480	760,000	1,306,480
24.09	5,500,000	556,600	768,500	1,325,100
24.00	5,600,000	566,720	777,000	1,343,720
23.90	5,700,000	576,840	785,500	1,362,340
23.81	5,800,000	586.960	794,000	1,380,960
23.72	5,900,000	597,080	802,500	1,399,580
23.63	6,000,000	607,200	811,000	1,418,200
23.55	6,100,000	617,320	819,500	1,436,820
23.48	6,200,000	627,440	828,000	1,455,440
23.40	6,300,000	637,560	836,500	1,474,060
23.32	6,400,000	647,680	845,000	1,492,680
23.25	6,500,000	657,800	853,500	1,511,300
23.18	6,600,000	667,920	862,000	1,529,920
23.11	6,700,000	678,040	870,500	1,548,540
23.05	6,800,000	688,160	879,000	1,567,160
22.98	6,900,000	698,280	887,500	1,585,780
22.92	7,000,000	708,400	896,000	1,604,400

to project what might happen, assuming certain changes in the input data. In the final analysis, it is the earning power of the firm that keeps the firm competitive and in existence.

Earning power is equal to:

Net operating profit on sales × turnover of operating assets to sales

Firms that have large amounts of fixed assets tend to have a low turnover factor but a high net operating profit. Firms with small amounts of fixed assets tend to have a high turnover factor but a low net operating profit.

Pricing mechanisms and the flow of investable funds tend to keep the allocation of resources in the whole economy in balance. For example, a manufacturer of heavy machine tools may have a turnover of operating assets of 2 and a net operating profit of 15 percent, whereas a supermarket food chain may have a turnover of 24 and a net operating profit of 1.25 percent. In both cases, the earning power is 30 percent. Identifying the market that the firm should be operating in is a marketing problem. How management responds to that market is a budgeting problem.

DEFENSIVE VERSUS OFFENSIVE MANAGEMENT

If management is thinking defensively, emphasis should be placed on a high percentage of variable cost (assuming that the material content is not inordinately high) and thus assure an orderly retreat if faced with a declining sales volume. But if management is thinking offensively, emphasis should be placed

Exhibit 4.17

BUDGETED DATA ON MANUFACTURING EXPENSE

	Manufacturing Expense		
	1967 Actual (Dollars)	1968 Profit Plan (Dollars)	1971 Profit Plan (Dollars)
		(000 Omitted)	
Total direct expense	2,552	3,335	4,125
Total manufacturing expense	391	483	603
Variable expense	(341)	(429)	(545)
Fixed expense	50	54	58
Total fixed expense	50	54	58
Variable expense	2,893	3,764	4,670
Inventory adjustment	(42)	-0-	-0-
Total variable expense	2,851	3,764	4,670
Total sales	4,230	5,400	6,800
Variable expense to sales (percent)	67.39	69.70	68.68

on an effort to substitute fixed costs for variable cost (assuming that the material content is not inordinately high) provided the marginal contribution is increased by more than the fixed charge. Thus the firm is able to take advantage of expanding sales to improve upon its net profit.

In Exhibits 4.16 and 4.18, the effect on total nonmanufacturing cost and manufacturing cost is shown when sales are increased from $5 million to $7 million, based on budgeted data shown in Exhibits 4.15 and 4.17. Variable expenses remained at approximately 10.12 percent of sales for nonmanufacturing indirect expense and 69 percent for manufacturing costs. At the same time, for nonmanufacturing indirect cost, variable cost as a percent of total indirect cost moved from 40.0 percent to 44.2 percent; and for manufacturing costs, the variable cost as a

Exhibit 4.18

PROJECTION OF MANUFACTURING COST WHEN SALES ARE INCREASED FROM $5 MILLION TO $7 MILLION

Relation of Manufacturing Cost to Sales (Percent)	Sales (Dollars)	Variable Manufacturing Cost – 69.0 Percent (Dollars)	Total Manufacturing Fixed Cost $54,000 (Dollars)	Total Variable and Fixed Cost (Dollars)
		(000 Omitted)		
70.08	5,000	3,450	54	3,504
70.06	5,100	3,519	54	3,573
70.04	5,200	3,588	54	3,642
70.02	5,300	3,657	54	3,711
70.00	5,400	3,726	54	3,780
69.98	5,500	3,795	54	3,849
69.96	5,600	3,864	54	3,918
69.95	5,700	3,933	54	3,987
69.93	5,800	4,002	54	4,056
69.92	5,900	4,071	54	4,125
69.90	6,000	4,140	54	4,194
69.89	6,100	4,209	54	4,263
69.87	6,200	4,278	54	4,332
69.86	6,300	4,347	54	4,401
69.84	6,400	4,416	54	4,470
69.83	6,500	4,485	54	4,539
69.82	6,600	4,554	54	4,608
69.81	6,700	4,623	54	4,677
69.80	6,800	4,692	54	4,746
69.78	6,900	4,761	54	4,815
69.77	7,000	4,830	54	4,884

percent of total manufacturing cost moved from 98.5 percent to 98.9 percent. As shown in Example 1, because of the large amounts of variable cost to total cost, net profit (cash flow), is not very great. Although the rate of increase is substantial, it is much less than in Example 2.

Example 1:

Sales	$5,000,000	$7,000,000
Variable cost		
Manufacturing	3,450,000	4,830,000
Nonmanufacturing	506,000	708,400
Total variable costs	$3,956,000	$5,538,400
Contribution margin	1,044,000	1,461,600
Fixed cost (without depreciation)	814,000	950,000
Net profit (cash flow)	$ 230,000	$ 511,600
Net profit to sales (percent)	4.6	7.3
Sales increased by (percent)		40.0
Cash flow increased by (percent)		122.4
Net profit to sales increased by (percent)		58.7

Net profit to sales is converted to dollars of profit per $100 of sales.

To repeat a major premise developed in this discussion: Budgeting is concerned with the allocation of the firm's resources. These resources have been referred to as inputs of capital and labor. In Example 1, the capital portion is only partially recognized because depreciation has been excluded. The variable costs remain at a given percent of sales (79.12 percent), and fixed costs are adjusted to assure the higher sales level. The marginal contribution is increased by $417,600, but fixed costs increased by only $136,000. The net advantage is $281,600.

Let it be assumed for Example 2 that an investment in capital is made that will result in a reduction of manufacturing variable expense by one-half and all other charges remain the same.

Example 2:

Sales	$5,000,000	$7,000,000
Variable cost		
Manufacturing	3,450,000	2,415,000
Nonmanufacturing	506,000	708,400
Total variable costs	$3,956,000	$3,123,400
Contribution margin	$1,044,000	$3,876,600
Fixed cost (without depreciation)	814,000	950,000
Net profit (cash flow)	$ 230,000	$2,926,600
Net profit to sales (percent)	4.6	41.8
Sales increased by (percent)		40.0
Cash flow increased by (percent)		1,172.4
Net profit to sales increased by (percent)		808.7

Examples 1 and 2 point out the two major objectives of budgeting: (1) Budgeting is concerned with increasing output by a proper allocation of total resources; and (2) budgeting is concerned with producing a given output in the most efficient manner (profits are a measure of efficiency) by combining available resources in the best way.

In Exhibit 4.19, the principle of the trade-off is visually portrayed. Variable costs are represented by the cost of doing business, and fixed costs are represented by the cost of being in business. Variable costs will increase or decrease with sales. Fixed costs will be adjusted upward or downward as required to maintain the most efficient level of operation at a given sales level. For example: A systems and procedures group may be added to the cost of being in business, provided that the group can so rationalize the inputs of capital and labor that

Exhibit 4.19

THE RATIONALE OF CASH FLOWS

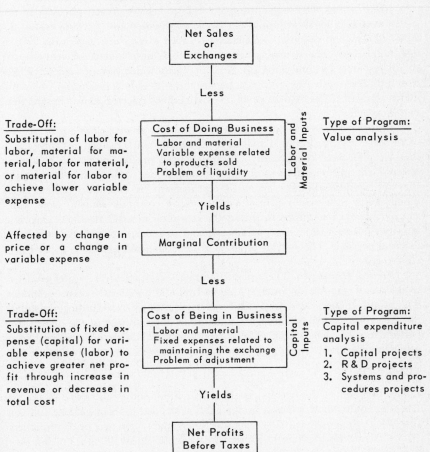

the increase in marginal contribution exceeds the cost of maintaining the systems and procedures group. In Example 2, the increase in marginal contribution from $230,000 to $2,926,000 should be greater than the cost of the investment (represented by depreciation) that was required to offset the change in marginal contribution.

Budgeting and a Computerized Systems Program

The purpose of a computerized systems program is to mechanize and integrate operations to achieve maximum performance within the capabilities of existing or justifiable computer configurations and consistent with goals of management as defined.

SCOPE

The scope of a systems program is the control and reporting of information relevant to the needs of management. The scope can be of four magnitudes:

1. *Labor saving.* The systems program seeks to achieve greater efficiency in the use of resources by substituting, for labor, mechanized unit record-keeping devices. The systems program is sometimes referred to as a first generation system.

2. *Horizontal.* The systems program seeks to achieve greater efficiency in the use of resources by combining functions or duties which have a sequential relationship. The combining process generally includes only transfer and communication activities. The systems program is sometimes referred to as a second generation system.

3. *Vertical.* The systems program seeks to achieve greater efficiency in the use of resources by integrating activities or operations with defined responsibilities that are performed concurrently. The integrating process frequently requires a reassessment and reassignment of functions and duties within and between activities. The objective of the system is management by exception coupled with economies of scale resulting from a fuller use of computer configurations. Control parameters are utilized to permit the computer to make decisions regarding activities falling within these parameters and to report circumstances requiring external decision. The systems program is sometimes referred to as a third generation system.

4. *Vertical-Horizontal.* The systems program seeks to achieve greater efficiency in the use of resources by interrelating vertical and horizontal systems programs. The object of the system is to achieve a synergistic effect regarding the fulfillment of goals as defined through a discernible improvement in the quality and performance of management. The systems program is sometimes referred to as a fourth generation system or a total systems program.

FUNCTION

The function of the systems program is to fulfill within the scope of the system the requirements imposed by the goals as defined by management and consistent with the policy so stated. The function of the system may be of two orders: (1) a total systems program in which all data produced in the firm are processed through the computer logic and decisions are rendered by the computer, with the exception of those so stated; and (2) a management information system which provides current information on any and all aspects of an activity.

In a vertical-horizontal systems program, both functions are fulfilled; therefore, the systems program and the defined goals of management must be totally aligned. The computer, in effect, becomes a major member of the team.

In a vertical systems program, the two functions are only partially fulfilled, with emphasis placed on management information systems.

In the horizontal and labor savings systems, emphasis is placed on the substitution of labor for machine techniques.

CONTRIBUTION TO MANAGEMENT

Concurrent with the development of computer hardware and programming techniques, the budgeting process has expanded to incorporate these new developments into a total program providing management with accurate appraisals of what has happened. But, more important, management can be given the opportunity to select between different alternatives based on assumed conditions and thereby contribute to the decision-making process. The utility of the computer is greatly expanded. The financial model becomes the expression of the planning, budgeting, and forecasting activities and greatly enhances the art of management.—*H. L. Clark*

CAPITAL EXPENDITURE PROGRAMS AND RETURN ON INVESTMENT

In our national economy, the key to both cyclical stability and long-term growth rests with intelligent plant and equipment decisions. Wide fluctuations in the capital investment decision, as well as erroneous decisions being made by large segments of our economy, place the entire economy in a precarious situation. It is equally true that investment decisions are the key to the success or failure of an individual firm. However, while the goals that demand investment in the economy as a whole are the same goals that demand investment in the industrial firm—future growth and prosperity—the investment decision for the individual firm is substantially different. The major differences rest with the environment in which the individual firm must make the decision. This environment typically sees rigid restrictions on available funds and only limited scope for the alternative uses for these funds.

Management's ability to operate effectively within these two restrictions, in both the short and the long run, will to a large measure determine the future success of the firm. Thus it may be concluded that the effectiveness of the capital expenditure program by a given firm may well determine the success or failure that the firm will achieve.

Program Requirements

The development of a sound capital expenditure program must consider the objectives of the firm, the many facts of long-range financial planning, and immediate operating plans. It must be sufficiently detailed to assure intelligent decisions; yet it must not burden line personnel and thus become an obstacle to creative thinking.

Authors on the subject list many different requirements and components of an effective capital budget program. Each attempts to tackle the problem from a slightly different, unique angle. However, there seems to be a common trend in the various approaches—a trend that links four major areas to be considered in a comprehensive program. These trends are as follows:

1. Effective channels of communication must be established. They must permit plans for profitable investment opportunities to flow to top management for inclusion in the long-range plans for the firm.

2. A review, selection, and approval process must be developed to evaluate the project, rank it against other projects, and act as the vehicle which will give authorization for expenditures to be made on the project. All must be consistent with the long-term profit objectives of the firm.

3. Effective control over authorized expenditures must be instituted in order to assure that the facility conforms to specifications and that the outlays do not exceed the amount authorized. A system for reporting overages will help keep estimates of investment amount honest.

4. A postaudit review and appraisal must be developed which will compare actual earnings performance against estimated earnings. A sound program of postaudits can do much to make earnings estimates more conscientious and realistic.

DEVELOPING COMMUNICATION

In a large, decentralized organization, the initiating force for most capital expenditures will come not from the central management staff but from the widespread operating units of the company. It is a difficult task to clear the channels of communication between the various general office staff activities so that they are all working toward a common goal. To accomplish this between the various operating units is an even greater task that demands more than mere lip service. A climate must be developed that will expand the scope of the managers of the operating units. Where their horizons are limited to their own operations, they must be broadened to the horizons of the firm. These men will not only need to understand the overall objectives of the firm; they must take an active part in deciding the means by which these objectives are to be attained.

The primary role that the management of the operating units will play in a capital expenditure program is one of maintaining a monitoring station which should seek out possible investments and gather data for subsequent evaluation. In seeking out possible areas for investment, the only restriction should be that the investment satisfy a present or future customer need at a satisfactory profit to the firm.

Management must not, in the monitoring process, receive only signals that indicate equipment investment potential. It must be tuned in to all wavelengths —product design and modification, new methods of distribution, techniques of financing, location of markets and operating units, and optimization of inventory balances. In essence, the operating units become the first line of defense against present and future competitors. The monitoring stations send back signals concerning the enemy's strength and weakness as well as a company's own vulnerability.

In gathering data for the subsequent analysis of the investment, the operating management will be reinforcing what have been the weakest links in the capital expenditure chain of most firms. Basically, the analysis of major capital expenditure necessitates two distinct procedures: gathering the relevant data concerned with the investment, and the rational analysis of these data. The data-gathering process, in turn, should be geared to answering two simple questions. The first question asks the cost and timing of the expenditure. The second seeks to learn the amount and timing of revenues or cost savings to be achieved.

No analysis of a capital expenditure can be better than the available and developed data on which the analysis was based. No technique for the measurement of an investment's worth, regardless of its sophistication, can improve upon faulty data.

REVIEW, SELECTION, AND APPROVAL

The review process is the analytical function that has gained much prominence in the past years. Business literature is laden with books and articles purporting to describe the most effective method of evaluating a capital expenditure. The implied panacea for the capital expenditure analysis has ranged from the simple payback method to the often complicated versions of the discounted cash flow method. There have been well-meaning analysts who, in their zeal to promote one method over all others, have turned top management against improved analysis techniques.

It seems strange that, in all other areas of business management—sales, production, industrial relations, and even accounting—it is generally understood that there are many acceptable methods of resolving problems. After reading typical articles on investment analysis, however, it is possible to conclude that the only effective technique of analysis is the "XYZ method." This is a dangerous pitfall. Management must recognize that there are many acceptable methods. Some have less precision than others but give advantages that, too often, go unrecognized. When a company reviews its existing investment procedures or when new procedures are being established, consideration should be given to the pros as well as the cons of several acceptable techniques. Whichever system is used, it must provide a sound basis for comparing the desirability of one investment with that of others. This is a critical requirement that must not be compromised.

Once a review process has been established, the selection and approval functions fall in place. The selection should be based on the relative ranking of the proposals. However, there are some exceptions to this rule. Some proposals are not quantifiable—for example, office modernization, painting, or air conditioning. These are expenditures made to maintain a standard of performance that the firm sets for itself. Management should not require that they be subject to the same analysis as other easily quantified items. The reason is not to give a blank check for this type of expenditure but to emphasize the importance of the soundness of the data furnished on expenditures where analysis and review are required.

Approval is given to a project after ranking it against other projects as well as analyzing alternates. The selection of the investment demands that management choose between two or more possibilities. The possibilities, for example, might be to purchase one large, high-capacity piece of equipment located in one producing point, or to purchase several smaller units and distribute them in several locales. These possibilities may be compared in many ways. However, the questions to be resolved are twofold: which investment will be the most profitable use of capital, and which investment is most in harmony with the long-range objectives of the firm.

CONTROLLING AUTHORIZED EXPENDITURES

The amount of control established on capital projects will be a function of the philosophy of management, the magnitude of the expenditure, and the duration of the project. While most firms have cost accounting and budgetary control systems for items of expense, very few have an effective reporting system for capital expenditures. Often, after a project has been approved, management seems to lose interest until the completion of the project. This is the wrong time for interest to wane; during the period of construction or installation of the project, much light will be shed on the reliability of data furnished in the proposal.

Progress reports on the outlay of funds on a project should be available at regular intervals. The department head, the budget director, and—if available— the capital budget committee should compare actual expenditures to those called for in the original proposal. As the work is approaching completion, it will be possible to determine whether additional expenditures are required on the project. If expenditures above the authorized amount are required, the request should be accompanied by an explanation describing the cause of the overrun. The final report on the project will provide the first formal review of the validity of the original proposal.

POSTAUDIT AND REVIEW

Capital expenditure management must not stop when a project is complete and operating. After the project has been in operation for a reasonable time, it will be desirable to determine whether it is performing in accordance with its forecast. This step is an attempt to maintain the integrity of the forecasts of profitability and to provide experience which can be used as a base for improving the reliability of future estimates. The original justification data will provide the yardstick for the measurement.

Since the early life of an investment is most important, it is advisable that the postaudit be performed after the first year. On projects with long lives, an audit may be performed several times—after the first, fifth, and tenth years, for example. In such cases, it may be necessary to adjust the results for price and labor rate changes not contemplated in the forecast.

Since no one bats 1,000, there will be projects that do not achieve the desired results. In these cases, the audit function must seek remedies through either change or abandonment. The pressures of pride and sentiment, coupled with the forces of inertia, will produce many reasons for tying up capital funds in an investment which does not produce satisfactory return. Vigilance and cold-blooded analysis in the postaudit activity will assist in keeping these noneco-nomic justifications to a minimum.

Methods of Evaluating Capital Expenditures

Many different methods are used to evaluate capital expenditures. They vary in complexity, thoroughness, and accounting treatment; however, they share a common objective: to provide a meaningful method of ranking investments.

PAYBACK PERIOD

One of the more commonplace methods of evaluating a capital expenditure is the payback method. In this procedure, the cash proceeds produced by an invest-ment are equated to the original cash outlay required by the investment, arriv-ing at some multiple of the cash proceeds that would be equal to the original investment. Measurement is usually in terms of years and months. For example: If the cash proceeds generated from an investment are constant from year to year, the payback period is determined by dividing the total original cash outlay by the amount of the expected annual proceeds. If, however, the proceeds from an investment are not constant, the expected proceeds for the successive years must be added until the total is equal to the original investment. The advan-tages of the payback method are that it ranks investments and is simple to use. Its disadvantages are that it fails to consider proceeds earned after payback date and to account for differences in timing of proceeds.

AVERAGE EARNINGS ON ORIGINAL INVESTMENT

Average earnings on original investment are the total proceeds divided by the number of years over which they are earned, and these average earnings are divided by the original investment.

In calculating proceeds, no charge is to be made for depreciation. The reason for omitting depreciation is that the analyst is viewing an original investment and not the depreciated value of the investment in making the computation. Consider the following example: The total proceeds recovered from a $50,000 investment amount to $100,000 earned over a period of five years. Average earn-ings would be $100,000 divided by five, or $20,000. Dividing by the original in-vestment of $50,000 gives average earnings per dollar of investment as 40 per-cent. Simplicity is the principal advantage of this method. Its disadvantages are that it has bias for short-lived investments with high cash proceeds, does not consider duration of proceeds, and does not consider the timing of cash proceeds.

AVERAGE EARNINGS ON
BOOK VALUE OF INVESTMENT

Average earnings on book value of investment are the average annual pro-ceeds less depreciation as a percent of average book value of the investment (essentially, half of the cost). Suppose, for example, that the total cost of invest-ment is $50,000: Average book value, therefore, is $25,000. The average annual proceeds are $10,000. Average earnings on book value are $10,000 divided by $25,000 (40 percent). The advantages of this method are that it ranks invest-ments in accordance with the typical ratio used to evaluate the firm's perfor-mance; that it is a simple calculation understandable by most individuals; and that it uses terms common to the financial statements of firms. The disadvantage is that it fails to take into consideration the timing of the proceeds.

DISCOUNTED CASH FLOW

Discounted cash flow is a method of evaluating investment opportunities that assigns certain values to the timing of the proceeds from the investment. The assumption, based on interest rates, is that a dollar earned today is more valuable than a dollar earned a year from now. There are several ways of using the dis-counted cash flow concept for evaluating capital expenditures. The two most popular are the net present value of an investment and the yield from an investment.

In calculating the net present value of the proceeds from an investment, one must relate the stream of the proceeds year by year, discounted by a selected interest rate (the interest rate usually reflects the corporate cost of capital) to the outflow of cash that is required by the investment, again discounted by the same interest rate. Should the present value of the proceeds exceed the present value of the outlays, after discounting at a common interest rate, the investment meets the accepted criterion. If the present value of the proceeds does not ex-ceed the present value of the outlays, the reject criterion is reached.

In calculating the yield from an investment, one must equate the present value of the proceeds to the present value of the cash outflow required by the investment. The procedure is to determine the rate of interest that will, when applied to the proceeds and the outflow, make these two streams of cash equal. This is usually accomplished in a trial-and-error method applying one interest rate to the two cash flows and then determining whether or not a positive or negative present value cash flow is achieved, adjusting that interest rate upward or downward until such time as the proceeds and the outlays equate. The ad-vantages of the discounted cash flow method are that it ranks investments and considers timing of investment and proceeds. Its disadvantages are complexities of computation; results that cannot be traced to published financial statements of the firm; and the implication that on shorter-life assets the proceeds can be reinvested, at the end of the life of the asset, at an equal-to or greater-than return.

Cost of Capital

In the preceding discussion of discounted cash flow techniques, reference was made to the interest rate in the present value computations and the requirement that it be set at the cost of capital for the firm, but no definition of the term "cost of capital" was stated. Unless this concept can be defined in a reasonably useful and correct manner, investment analysis techniques utilizing the present value concepts cannot be applied in a practical sense.

There are several sources of funds to finance an investment—borrowing from banks, selling marketable securities, allowing current liabilities to expand, selling other assets, issuing stock (common or preferred), and committing retained earnings. The problem now revolves around quantifying the cost of the funds provided by these various methods.

SPECIFIC COSTING METHOD

The first method is called specific costing or, possibly, could be described as incremental costing. Say, for example, that project X requires the investment of $100,000 and will provide a pretax return of 10 percent. The controller of this organization states that he can provide the funds through bank borrowings at a pretax cost of 6 percent. Thus the project maintains a positive return after considering the cost of capital to be 6 percent. It may be asked, then, whether the company should proceed to make the investment.

The strongest agreement for this approach finds its roots in economic theory. A generation or more ago, Lord Keynes made his famous economic pronouncement that businessmen would continue to invest as long as the return of one more dollar of investment (he called this the marginal efficiency of capital) exceeded the interest rate (he called this the marginal cost of capital). In general, this may hold true for businessmen in the aggregate, but whether it is valid for the individual firm is another question. As stated earlier, the concept must be reasonably useful and correct. In practice, firms do not normally approve investment yielding 6 percent or 7 percent. The reason for this departure from economic theory rests with the supply of funds available to the individual firm. Sooner or later, every firm reaches an upper limit in its supply of investable funds. Whether this is because management sets an arbitrary debt equity ratio that it will not exceed, or because the bankers say "no more," or because of some other reason, nevertheless, it does happen. When it does happen, then, one proposed investment must compete with every other proposed investment. This is an important point.

One last comment may be made concerning the specific costing or incremental approach. As stated by Harold Bierman, Jr. and Seymour Smidt (*Capital Budgeting Decision,* The Macmillan Company, 1960):

> Although there are situations in which a particular investment can be related to a specific source of financing, more commonly there exists on the one hand a group of apparently desirable investment proposals, and on the other, a variety of sources of additional capital funds that taken together could supply the financing for the increased investment. In such circumstances any procedure for assigning the cost of a particular source of capital funds to a specific investment proposal would be arbitrary and capricious.

WEIGHTED-AVERAGE METHOD

A more popular approach to the definition of cost of capital revolves around the capital structure of the firm. The weighted-average concept defines "cost of capital" as "an absolute dollar amount of cost for each type of source of funds—common stock, preferred stock, and all interest-bearing liabilities related to the total of all securities issued by the firm." If, for example, the sum of all the securities issued by the company equals $100,000 and the market value of such securities equals $500,000, the cost of capital for the firm would be 20 percent.

Cost of common stock. The cost of common-stock capital is a function of the desired return set by the owners of common stock. To measure this return, one would compare the expected future dividend with the present market value of the stock. Dividends in this sense must also include appreciation of the value in the stock. To identify the future dividends expected by the stockholders is a difficult task, one that must be evaluated on the assumption that the prudent stockholder is basing his expectation of the future on his experiences of the past. Thus this could be formularized as follows: The cost of capital of common-stock funds is equal to the current dividend rate divided by the current market price per share, plus the expected percentage rate of increase in future dividends.

Cost of long-term debt. The cost of long-term debt capital is essentially the current rate for long-term securities for any specific firm. This is only complicated by discount or premium factors that may prevail. The effective rate of interest for an outstanding issue can easily be determined by comparing the current market price for this security with the remaining application. For example, the effective rate of interest on a bond outstanding can be found by determining the rate of interest which equates the market price and the present value of the amount due at maturity, plus the present value of the interest payments.

Cost of short-term debt. The cost of short-term debt is similar to that of long-term debt, inasmuch as an interest cost would apply. However, there are short-term liabilities that do not have explicit interest charges. These, of course, are the various taxes payable, wages payable, and at any given time the normal trade payables for a firm. Attempts can be made at quantifying the cost of maintaining and enlarging upon this source of funds. One would have to quantify, in the case of short-term trade payables, the discount lost, as well as any carrying charges which may be assessed, if these liabilities are extended.

Effect of income taxes. Income taxes affect the calculations in measuring cost of capital because cost of equity capital is a distribution of income and therefore not deductible, while the cost of debt capital carries with it deductible interest charges. Depending upon the effect of the income tax rate, the after-tax effect is somewhere between 50 percent and 52 percent.

ALTERNATIVE-USE METHODS

There are many theories on quantifying the cost of capital for a given firm. The theory of the weighted average of the cost of each type of capital, as previously described, probably dominates the financial world. However, another more prevalent on the industrial scene states that the cost of capital for a firm is determined by the estimated returns on alternative investments. To calculate this cost of capital for a hypothetical firm, assume that there is $100,000 of investable funds and there exists the following schedule of investment opportunities:

Estimated Return (Percent)	Amount of Investment
26	$25,000
24	50,000
22	35,000
20	15,000
15	30,000
12	20,000

The opportunities estimated to yield 20 percent or better use up all of the available funds; hence we could say the cost of capital for this firm is 20 percent. The typical argument against this concept is expressed in the question: What if there are no investment opportunities of these magnitudes?

In the case of firms whose alternative use of capital approaches the prime lending rate, that sets the cost of capital for the firm. In reality, the alternative-use concept states that there are many investment opportunities chasing a limited number of dollars and that the firm's investment decisions should be predicated upon exhausting these funds in an attempt to exploit the higher-return projects. If the return gravitates down to a level approaching prime, in the best interest of the stockholders these dollars should be spun away from capital investments of the firm and placed in the hands of the owners of the firm for their disposition and subsequent investment.

Central Considerations

In attempting to establish a capital expenditure program, management must be totally aware of the questions that such a program seeks to answer. Frequently, management attention is absorbed in *how* a thing is being accomplished, instead of in the critical issue—*what* is being accomplished. The worth of a capital expenditure program is not found in the sophistication of the analysis technique employed. Indeed, this may be the least important aspect. Its real value is in its effectiveness in uniting the efforts of the management of the firm toward assuring that the requirements of tomorrow are provided for today.

While there are no canned programs worth their salt, there are some critical areas that must be considered by an effective program. Briefly described, these areas are as follows:

1. A climate in which innovation flourishes must be developed.

2. There must be an acceptable method of evaluating proposals. (The key word here is "acceptable.") Make sure that the method is no more complex than is warranted by the proposal.

3. Expenditures on the project must be controlled and periodically reviewed.

4. Score keeping must be conducted through a planned postaudit program. It should be geared to encourage the collection of sound data in the proposal state and to exert pressure on management to achieve the planned results.

The future success of a firm is being decided today, either by the thoughtful actions of its executives or by its competitors because of the lack of such thoughtful action. An intelligently developed capital expenditure program in itself does not guarantee future success. The lack of such a program, however, makes future success virtually impossible.—*K. A. Baker*

FINANCING CORPORATE REQUIREMENTS

The purpose of external financing is to meet corporate cash needs in excess of the amount provided by internal generation. Since cash needs form the basis of the financing decision, no financing should be undertaken without a forecast of the sources and application of funds. This forecast should extend several years into the future; the first year is divided into at least monthly intervals, and later years progress from a quarterly to an annual basis. Such a forecast permits the development of a coherent program for meeting long- and short-term cash needs in a way that will not jeopardize corporate solvency but will retain the flexibility necessary to meet unanticipated financing requirements in the future. The forecast will also indicate whether the particular financing should be long-term or short-term.

Short-Term Financing

The need for short-term financing can best be identified by looking at the duration of the need for the assets to be financed. If the need for the assets is temporary, the financing should be in short-term form. For example, a short-term bank loan would be appropriate in meeting seasonal working-capital needs, since the buildup of inventories and accounts receivable will be temporary. Long-term assets should not be financed with short-term funds, because of the risk of being unable to obtain future refinancings at an acceptable cost.

Some short-term financing is spontaneous. That is, it is available through normal business practice or operation of the law without any particular effort on the part of the company. Trade credit, payroll, and tax accruals are examples of spontaneous financing. Negotiated sources of short-term financing, on the other hand, are principally bank loans and commercial paper.

TRADE CREDIT

Trade credit arises through the purchase of materials from suppliers. If a company buys $10,000 worth of material on a 30-day open account, the vendor has in effect lent it $10,000 for 30 days. If the company buys more material, the financing will be automatically increased, subject to any credit limits imposed by the vendor. Credit terms will vary according to trade practice in the seller's industry and the credit worthiness of the buyer. While open account is the normal form of trade credit, the trade acceptance or some other form of promissory note is frequently employed in international trade. Although trade credit is usually inexpensive (or even cost-free), the failure to take offered cash discounts —or the acceptance of penalty or financing charges for stretched-out terms—can represent very costly financing.

BANK LOANS

There are three basic types of short-term commercial bank loans: casual, secured, and line-of-credit. Casual loans are made without prior negotiation and based on the general credit of the company. If the bank is uncertain of the credit, it may request that the loan be secured by pledge of specific corporate assets or endorsed by one of its officers or another company. Loans are also made against a previously negotiated line of credit in which the bank expresses its willingness to lend the company any amount up to a certain maximum at any time during a specific period—usually a year—provided that the company's financial condition remains substantially unchanged.

Banks charge their best customers a prime rate on loans—generally, a standard rate throughout the banking industry at any given time. Less desirable credits will be charged progressively higher rates of interest. In addition, bank loans usually require that compensating balances equal to 10 to 20 percent or more of the loan or line of credit be kept on deposit with the bank, thus increasing the effective rate of interest on the portion of the loan available to the company. However, to the extent that the company must maintain cash balances to meet checks and for other purposes even without the loan, the compensating balance may represent little or no incremental cost.

COMMERCIAL PAPER

Commercial paper represents the promissory notes of corporations. These notes are usually sold to investors through commercial paper dealers, although some very large companies place their paper directly with financial institutions and other corporations which have a short-term cash surplus. The notes are negotiable and represent a highly liquid investment for the holders. For the issuers, commercial paper represents a quick, convenient, and flexible means of raising varying amounts of cash, usually at a cost well below the prime rate on bank borrowings. Because assured negotiability is essential to the value of the note, however, only large, highly credit-worthy firms are normally able to issue paper in the commercial market. Even for such a firm, any indication of a change in credit status can quickly dry up the market for its paper. Therefore, to assure negotiability, most companies are required to back up their commercial paper dealings with lines of credit at commercial banks. Maturities on commercial paper normally range from one to nine months, averaging between three and six months.

Intermediate-Term Financing

Intermediate-term financing is generally long-term financing in a short-term form. As with short-term financing, the duration of the need for the asset financed is the clue. If the asset (or its replacement) will be permanently required, its financing represents long-term capital. That is to say, either the present financing arrangement must be continued indefinitely or some form of long-term capital must be substituted for it. In either event, the same dollar amount is part of the corporation's required permanent capital.

BANK TERM LOANS

Term loans are generally made by commercial banks for periods of one to five years, although in rare instances maturities of up to ten years are granted. Rates approximate those on short-term bank borrowings, and the loan may be secured or unsecured. Companies sometimes use bank loans in conjunction with construction or other major spending programs to bridge the period until attractive permanent financing can be arranged. The term loan can be taken down periodically as required by spending, avoiding the need to invest the proceeds of permanent financing short-term until needed. Frequently, companies will negotiate a revolving credit with a bank or a group of banks, under which the bank agrees to loan up to a stated maximum amount during the next few years. A commitment fee of about .125 to .5 percent is normally charged on the unused portion of the maximum credit, in addition to an agreed-upon interest rate on actual borrowings.

ACCOUNTS RECEIVABLE FINANCING

Accounts receivable financing involves the pledging of a company's accounts receivable, either with or without recourse, to a finance or factoring firm. If the finance company has recourse to the selling company in the event its customers do not pay, the financing process is called commercial financing. If it has no recourse, the process is called factoring. In either case, the sale of the receivables will be prearranged, and the finance or factoring company reserves the right to reject a certain portion or certain individual accounts offered by the selling company. Today, the bulk of accounts receivable financing is in the form of commercial financing. Receivables financing has been the traditional recourse of smaller firms unable to raise working capital in other ways or unable to support an internal credit function. Pledging receivables, often the bulk of a company's liquid assets, limits the ability to take on other financing, particularly of a short-term nature. The cost of receivables financing reflects handling costs, the cost of the funds provided, and the cost of whatever credit function is assumed by the finance company, and will tend to exceed term loan costs. On the other hand, it is an extremely flexible source of secured borrowings.

INVENTORY FINANCING

Like receivables financing, inventory financing is essentially a secured, revolving term loan. Generally, the security is administered under a field warehousing arrangement whereby inventory is released from a bonded warehouse as payments are received against advances by the bank or other financial institution. Inventory financing is quite expensive and is much less widely used than receivables financing. It retains importance in some seasonal industries like food processing, however.

LEASING AND INSTALLMENT FINANCING

Manufacturers of capital goods will often permit buyers to pay on the installment plan. Typically, a down payment of 10 to 30 percent of the price is required, and the balance is to be paid monthly over five years or less. The cost of such financing varies. A high cost might be expected, but some manufacturers occasionally use financing as a promotional device, charging barely enough to cover their own direct costs. The manufacturer will generally "discount" the receivable to a finance company or bank.

Long-term leases may be considered a form of installment financing. In fact, many "leases" are treated as installment sales for tax purposes. In a true lease, the lessee receives use of the asset without acquiring any ownership interest in the property during or after the lease period, e cept under a generally separate, arms-length transaction. The lease term must be less than the useful life of the property leased, and in no case more than 30 years. In addition to its use in acquiring new assets, leasing is also used as a means of raising cash on presently owned property by means of a sale and leaseback.

The attractiveness of leasing as a means of financing corporate requirements is a source of much debate. Logically, interposing the lessor as a middleman between the lessee and the ultimate source of the financing should add to the cost. Tax considerations often cloud the picture, however. In general, leasing does seem to expand the amount of credit available to a company but at a cost somewhat higher than traditional sources of borrowing. The remaining question is whether the company, as a matter of policy, should seek to borrow up to this expanded total.

GOVERNMENT FINANCING

Federal, state, and local governments have become increasingly involved in business financing as a means of promoting growth in the local tax base, or employment, or for other social goals. Industrial revenue bonds issued by a state or locality have been a popular means of providing low-cost indirect financing to businesses. However, the interest on issues in excess of $1 million is generally no longer tax-exempt to investors, which has somewhat cooled interest in this type of financing. On the Federal level, the Small Business Administration (SBA) has the most comprehensive program of business financing. Under a complex system of guidelines, firms which meet the SBA criteria of small business may be eligible for assistance. A number of seemingly large or at least moderate-size businesses have been found eligible under these guidelines. Loans up to $350,000 are available through the SBA's several loan programs if funds cannot be obtained from other sources on reasonable terms. The availability of SBA financing can change greatly from time to time, however, in line with changes in Federal economic and social policies. The SBA also oversees the numerous Small Business Investment Companies (SBIC's), which are generally operated as private sources of long-term debt and equity capital.

Long-Term Financing

Long-term finance is concerned with the provision of the company's permanent capital base. Long-term financing decisions should reflect a soundly conceived financial strategy whose goal should be to retain the ability to raise capital for both planned and emergency needs while maintaining the highest intrinsic value possible for the company's common stock. Three major factors must be considered in arriving at this goal: the optimum capital structure, the appropriate dividend policy, and the firm's cost of capital. "Capital structure" means the balance between debt and equity funds in the company's total long-term capitalization. An insufficient amount of debt may make it difficult for the company to earn a reasonable return on its common stock. Conversely, an excessive amount can make subsequent financing difficult or impossible and, most importantly, may substantially increase the common equity return which must be earned to compensate for the added risk. Generally, the amount a company may safely borrow is a function of the basic risk of its business: the type of business, the age and size of the company, the stability of its earnings, management ability, and so forth. Thus a public utility may range up to 60 percent debt in total long-term capital, while a well-established industrial firm will normally have to stay under 30 percent to maintain a comparable quality for its debt and equity securities. Dividend policy will influence the need for capital from external sources but can also affect the cost of capital. The cost of capital, in turn, will reflect the company's decisions on capital structure and dividend policy and will determine whether additional capital can be economically employed.

In addition to the overall strategic elements, specific financing alternatives should be evaluated in the light of seven tactical considerations: (1) *source* (private placement versus public sale of securities); (2) *amount* (how much capital to raise now in view of present and prospective needs); (3) *timing* (the condition of the debt and/or equity markets now and in the future); (4) *type* (whether debt, equity, or incentive financing is preferable at the time); (5) *cost* (both the out-of-pocket cost of the security and its impact on the required rate of earnings or cost of capital); (6) *control* (both the direct control of voting securities and the hamstringing which may be present in indenture covenants); (7) *risk* (the risk which may be added to the business by the financing, and the risk of obtaining subsequent financing when required). These tactical issues interact with one another to suggest the nature of the financing which should be undertaken at any given time.

DEBT FINANCING

Properly understood, debt financing is limited to the issue of straight debt— that is, securities without attached equity participations. Other types of so-called debt are really incentive financings. Debt financing provides a true leverage on earnings in exchange for a guaranteed return to the debt holder, whereas in combination debt/equity securities the leverage may be totally offset by future dilution. Recently, long-term debt financing has become difficult for less than major firms to obtain, as the pace of inflation has seriously eroded the value of fixed-income securities. Many commentators view this situation as a temporary phenomenon and suggest that the widely advertised death of debt financing is highly premature in announcement, although the historical rate structure may be substantially revised.

The usual route to debt financing is through an underwriting firm. The precise terms of a public offering and its cost to the company are usually determined through negotiation between the issuing firm and its underwriter. Public debt offerings are usually limited to issues of $10 million or more and generally require a quality rating of A or better. Private placements of debt are also frequently handled through an underwriter acting as agent, who will place portions of the issue with several insurance companies, pension funds, or financial institutions. Private placements are occasionally handled directly with such investors. Generally, a debenture of somewhat lower quality can be placed privately. The cost of debentures will vary according to their quality; lower-quality issues carry higher interest. The indenture covenants of lower-quality issues may also entail a "cost" to the issuer in terms of reduced financial flexibility in the future.

In addition to debentures, which are unsecured general credit obligations of the issuer, long-term debt is also raised through mortgages. The usual mortgage provides funds to build or acquire new real estate for the company. Occasionally, however, a firm with poor credit standing may be asked to secure its other long-term borrowings by a pledge of owned property.

EQUITY FINANCING

There are three basic forms of equity financing: common stock, preferred stock, and convertible preferred stock. As with debt securities, equity issues may be placed privately or sold on the public market. Private placements are usually made to investment funds or wealthy individuals, as banks and insurance companies are generally unable to invest in equities for their own account. These placements are frequently under an investment letter restricting the resale of the stock. Public sale, on the other hand, requires that the stock be registered with the SEC and/or various state securities commissions. Both public and private sales are normally handled through underwriting firms.

Common-stock financing. Additional money to share the risks of the business with the present owners is brought in by common-stock financing. If the new investors buy in at a price per share above the book value per share of the existing shareholders, the present shareholders will have their investment leveraged by the new shareholders, since the investment of the incremental amount will accrue to benefit both. The sale of common will expand or re-establish the company's borrowing base and may be easier to sell than debt, particularly for new companies with little credit standing. On the other hand, sale of common involves potential dilution of earnings and control, normally carries a higher underwriting cost, and requires a higher return than bonds or preferred.

Preferred stock. Commercial and industrial firms rarely employ preferred stock in financing because of the volatility of their earnings. Preferred dividends represent an after-tax leverage on the common which amplifies the swings in common-stock earnings to an extent that has proved unacceptable in most cases. The sale of preferred does add to the company's borrowing base, however, and a small amount may prove an acceptable financing route when the capital structure is heavily leveraged with debt yet common-stock prices are temporarily depressed.

Convertible preferred stock. This form of financing has recently become popular in acquisitions. Since the stock is convertible into common yet carries the fixed dividend of a straight preferred, it permits structuring an acquisition deal with dimensions attractive to both buyer and seller. The seller receives a tax-free exchange for his stock, a guaranteed minimum return, and a chance to participate in the future growth of the business. The buyer may reduce dilution by being able to issue fewer common shares in conversion than would be required in a straight exchange of common stock, because the preferred status of the stock when issued may cause it to be valued at a premium above its conversion value. Other benefits may also accrue to the buyer: for example, lower voting power for the selling shareholders in the combined enterprise, or maintenance of existing dividend policy for the common stock. Convertible preferreds have generally not been used for cash financings.

INCENTIVE FINANCING

Many types of incentive financing have been devised, or resurrected from the 1920's, in recent years. Basically, however, all involve the use of debentures convertible into some form of equity or debentures with warrants to purchase equity attached. The objectives of such financings are to obtain capital which would otherwise be unavailable, to sell common at a price above current market, or to lower the cost of debt. The popularity of such securities has been enhanced by the recent rapid pace of inflation, which has seriously eroded the value of fixed-income securities. To the investor uncertain about the future pace of inflation, incentive securities can be an attractive hedge, providing a guaranteed return in case of a slowdown while permitting participation in inflationary expansion if that occurs. For the issuing company, however, incentive financing can be an expensive source of capital in the long run. For example, the sale of a convertible debenture does result in a lower interest rate. However, in order to be assured of conversion rather than redemption for cash, the market price of the common stock will have to exceed the conversion price of the debentures at the time the issue is called. The cost of this discount on the then current market value is likely to vastly outweigh the fractional interest-rate saving over straight debt, even on a present-value basis. In other words, the sale of debt now followed by common in the future will probably result in cheaper overall financing. If the debentures do not convert, the company has both debt and an overhang on the common, which may impede future financings. On the other hand, if the company's stock is temporarily depressed and debt is unavailable, a convertible debenture can be a useful safety-valve source of needed funds.

Debentures with warrants can also provide an initially lower interest cost. Furthermore, if the debenture can be redeemed for part of the exercise price of the warrants, a large part of the debt may be expunged through an exchange of paper without corporate cash outlay. The warrants, however, may represent a serious future dilution of the common stock and may impede future common-stock financing. Like the convertible, the debenture with warrants is essentially a safety-valve security. It is there if needed. To plan for its use as part of a regular financing program, however, may prove costly to the holder of common stock in the long run.—H. A. Lund

CASH MANAGEMENT AND BANK RELATIONS

The balance sheet caption "Cash" represents, primarily, demand deposit balances in commercial bank accounts. The appropriate level of cash is determined by such factors as the frequency of cash transactions, the need for liquidity, and the presence of profitable investment opportunities. Cash management decisions are characteristically made in the light of many uncertainties, and it is therefore vitally important that the financial manager take advantage of every means available to remove speculation from the decision-making process.

Analysis of Sources and Uses of Funds

The significance of short- and long-range planning with respect to cash management decisions bears continual emphasis. To facilitate the financial manager's task of analyzing the masses of data from the past, present, and future which influence every financial decision, there are a number of very practical tools available.

One such tool, particularly useful in analyzing funds flows, is the preparation of the statement of sources and uses of funds, sometimes referred to as the "where got, where gone" statement. "Funds," usually very broadly defined, represent all sources (liabilities plus capital, sometimes referred to as claims on assets) and uses (assets or investments) which constitute the balance sheet of any business enterprise. "Cash," in this definition, of course, represents only a small portion of total funds. The statement of sources and uses of funds is prepared by computing the changes in balance sheet entries from one accounting period to the next and arranging the data in tabular form so that the sources and uses are viewed separately. The generating sources are reflected by increases in liabilities or net worth or by decreases in assets. The various alternate uses (the ways in which the company employs or invests these funds) are reflected by increases in assets or by decreases in liabilities or net worth.

An understanding of the counteracting flows of funds between the various sources and applications can be invaluable to the financial manager in determining whether the company's liquidity and profitability objectives are being met.

Organizing for Cash Management

More narrowly defined, "funds" represent only "cash." Many financial managers prefer this definition, since their concern is primarily with receipts and disbursements—in other words, with the cycle of cash flowing into and out of the mainstream of funds. Cash is obtained from many sources, such as (1) net income (usually reflected on the balance sheet as a component of the net increase in retained earnings); (2) depreciation and other noncash charges such as amortization of certain assets and deferred income taxes; (3) short- and long-term borrowings; (4) sale of capital stock; and (5) sale of property.

Inflowing cash from the various sources must be carefully synchronized with the many alternate uses, such as (1) payments of dividends and taxes; (2) capital expenditures; (3) investments in inventories; (4) short-term investments; and (5) other cash transactions. This is necessary in order that sufficient cash will remain in the reservoir at all times to achieve the liquidity and profitability objectives of the company.

In organizing for cash management, a primary objective should be the elimination of all conditions which impede cash flows, particularly those which are inflowing. Toward this end, it is important to free any cash that has become entrapped or allowed to remain idle unnecessarily.

Recurring periods of tight money are comparable to drought conditions with respect to the reservoir of cash. It is apparent, therefore, that the systems and techniques which help facilitate the flow of cash and improve the coordination of inflows with outflows are indispensible to the cash manager.

REGULATING CASH INFLOW

Inflowing cash can be subject to delays from mail delivery time, as well as from the many intricacies of the check-clearing process. Many commercial banks are equipped to offer valuable aid through sophisticated services that speed the inflow of cash.

Lock box plans. The lock box is a post office box maintained by a commercial bank as agent to collect receivables en route to its corporate customer. Ordinarily, a company operating a nationwide business would require its customers to remit payments some distance through the mail to the company's central accounting office. These payments would be received (possibly as much as three or four days later), processed, and deposited by the company in its central bank account. The remittance checks would be cleared through the banking system, "collected" from the drawee banks, and credited to the company's account.

The lock box plan allows a regional bank located in close proximity to the company's various customers to (1) receive remittances soon after they are mailed; (2) perform all the processing and deposit functions normally performed by the central accounting office; (3) collect the checks much sooner from the drawee banks; and (4) send the funds to the company's central bank account via wire transfer.

Lock boxes have proved to be highly advantageous in expediting cash flows and are widely used.

Concentration accounts. Many companies maintain bank accounts throughout their territory of operation which are used as branch office depositories. In the case of nationwide companies, it is not hard to imagine the difficulties encountered by the corporate treasurer in accurately maintaining several hundred accounts. The following procedures may be undertaken by a company in streamlining its flow of funds from local depository banks by means of the concentration account mechanism: (1) As local branches deposit daily receipts, depository transfer checks are mailed simultaneously to centrally located (regional) concentration banks. The checks are drawn on the local depository bank and made payable to the order of the concentration bank. (2) The concentration bank collects the checks through the clearing process and deposits the funds in the company's account. (3) The concentration bank transfers the funds to the company's central bank account by wire transfer.

In order to eliminate unnecessary delays in concentrating receipts in regional accounts, branch offices should be encouraged to deposit funds in local banks as soon as possible after receipt.

In addition to speeding the inflow of funds, this arrangement eliminates many of the headaches involved in the paperwork task of computing balances and transferring funds from various local accounts.

Data transmission. Many banks across the country are now linked by a system which allows the rapid transfer of accounting information (such as payment data derived from lock box collections) to the customer. This enables the company to update records much more rapidly than can be done by mail or otherwise.

Wire transfer. A sizable number of banks are members of a national bank wire system which provides the facilities for transferring corporate balances from one location to another in a very short time. This system minimizes delays in receipt of funds, thus allowing further maximization of cash.

Account reconciliation. For the sake of efficient cash management, companies issuing large volumes of checks—for example, payroll checks—should maintain accurate records on the number of checks issued in the accounting period, the dollar total of the checks, the number of checks paid by the bank, and the number outstanding. Many banks are able to provide account reconciliation services which save time and greatly facilitate the record-keeping task.

Payroll preparation. Companies with sizable payrolls, usually between 100 and 500 employees, may realize certain advantages from payroll accounting services offered by many banks. A few of the advantages are as follows: (1) Payroll personnel are released for more productive work. (2) Payroll accounting equipment costs will be virtually eliminated. (3) These services are normally designed to assume the company's payroll function in its entirety, providing all reports necessary for company administration.

Companies should carefully compare plans such as this with their present operations to determine which provides the greatest efficiency and economy.

Factoring and credit card services. A number of commercial banks are equipped to facilitate the inflow of cash and to eliminate the collection function through the purchase of receivables under factoring or credit card agreements. An additional advantage, of course, is the fact that bad debt risks are usually assumed by the banks.

Invoicing procedures. Company policies should be such that delays in billing customers are cut to a minimum. The receivables turnover ratio is but one measure of financial status, but it is an important one. The sooner cash is received after the sale the better, and a strict invoicing policy can aid a great deal in reducing delays.

REGULATING CASH OUTFLOW

As previously pointed out, the timing of receipts and disbursements is a critical factor in cash management. Understanding of what constitutes available cash for investment is likewise critical. One popular concept is that cash is available for investment for a period of time even after it has been disbursed—that is, while it is floating before clearing the bank. However, it should be made clear that this practice does not always fall within legal and ethical parameters. A careful review of all disbursement procedures should therefore be conducted frequently to insure their conformity to established policies.

Draft disbursements. Many companies find it to their advantage to pay by draft rather than by check. Even though a check is a form of draft, there is a significant difference. At the time a check is written, the company must legally have the balance on deposit to cover the check. Drafts need not be covered by the necessary funds until they are presented at the bank for payment. Take, as an example, a company in Atlanta issuing payroll drafts drawn on a New York bank. After these drafts are cashed or deposited locally, they are floating through the banking system until they are cleared to the New York bank account. This in effect gives the company the advantage of the use of this money for an extra period of days. When the drafts are presented to the New York bank for payment, the company simply sends the necessary balances to the account by telegram to cover the drafts.

The handling of draft systems is normally more expensive to commercial banks than check payment systems. Draft systems therefore require careful cost analysis by the bank and frequently necessitate special compensation from the company to cover the extra expense.

DETECTING HIDDEN CASH

In striving to counter the effects of the many impeding influences on the cash cycle, the financial manager should be conscious of a number of "traps" in which badly needed cash frequently stagnates.

Inventories. It is often true today that inventory on hand is in excess of operational needs. Every effort should be made to tighten inventory control (if possible, by means of computerized inventory control systems) and increase inventory turnover.

Bank deposits. Larger or more frequent transfers from local depository accounts to centralized accounts will insure that local bank balances do not build up in excess of actual needs.

Trade credit. Cash discounts should be taken even if borrowings from a commercial bank are necessary. As a general rule, cash discounts are in excess of commercial bank rates. Badly needed cash which has been uselessly tied up in trade credit may frequently be released.

INVESTING IDLE CASH

The money market instruments which lend themselves to opportunities for putting idle cash to work are numerous. With today's skillful synchronization of cash inflow and outflow, it is not uncommon to find companies with cash to invest for periods as short as one day. Securities dealers, as well as many commercial banks, are usually equipped to offer valuable advice and counseling with regard to the short-term investments which will provide the appropriate maturity as well as the desired yield.

Company-Bank Relations

Company size, location, and market territory, the nature of business, and financial status all have a bearing on a company's banking needs.

CRITERIA FOR SELECTING BANKS

In many cases, the choice of a bank may be based solely on factors such as convenience to company office location, competitive service charges, and error-free service. These are no doubt important considerations; however, there are usually many other distinguishing characteristics of banks which may not initially meet the eye.

Caliber of management. Competent and aggressive bank officers who display innovative thinking with a view to tailoring all services to the needs of the customer will contribute significantly to a beneficial banking relationship.

Philosophy of management. When banks place greater emphasis on profits than on customer satisfaction, quality of service is likely to suffer. Quality depends to a great degree on whether top management is oriented toward a true marketing approach; that is, whether all decisions are made after careful consideration is given to the actual best interests of the customer as well as to profits.

Availability of financial resources and diversity of corporate services. To a great extent, the choice of a bank should be based on whether it can satisfy the total financial requirements of the company.

The many banking services available besides the ones previously discussed are too numerous to list. However, they might be categorized as follows: credit services, computer services, investment services, corporate trust services, international services, commercial account services, and general services such as plant site location assistance, and merger and acquisition services.

Operating record and present financial standing. Past performance should have a bearing on a bank's future potential for growth and contribution to the general prosperity of its corporate customers and the community. Any developments which could affect the soundness of present operations should also be considered.

Concern for company well-being. Banks should be problem-oriented, displaying a serious interest in assisting the financial manager. Bank officers should be knowledgeable concerning the company and the industry and should offer ideas, information, and advice. Many banks establish formalized call programs which enable bank officers to visit customers and prospects frequently to become acquainted with company officials, to gain a clear understanding of the company's banking needs, and to display the various corporate services available. Whether bank representatives are qualified to discuss pertinent aspects of the company's banking needs is a consideration which no financial manager should ignore.

Other factors. Naturally, the establishment of a banking relationship will be influenced by such factors as the company's historical relationship with a certain bank, personal relationships of company and bank officials, and whether or not a bank lends status to the company. To the degree possible, however, a purely objective appraisal should be made before finally choosing the most desirable bank.

COMPENSATION FOR BANK SERVICES

The discussion of factors which constitute a mutually beneficial relationship between a company and its bank has generated a considerable amount of controversy on the topic of compensating balances. A presentation of both sides of the issue of compensating balances may be helpful in establishing their true worth.

Arguments against compensating balances. Four major arguments are advanced against compensating balances:

1. Many opponents argue that compensating balances, after all factors are taken into consideration, do not increase a bank's yield on the loan.

2. Bankers overemphasize the positive effects resulting from the reloaning of deposits obtained through compensating balances.

3. Studies have shown, with partial satisfaction, that the bank and the borrower would be better off if compensating balance requirements were eliminated and higher interest rates were charged.

4. Bankers do not have a true conception of their actual costs; therefore, compensating balances cannot be realistically established.

Arguments for compensating balances. Advocates of compensating balances offer four reasons:

1. Compensating balances typically range between 10 percent and 20 percent of a line of credit (on the basis of "collected" balances). These balances are required because the interest rate alone is not sufficient to cover the actual costs involved in holding available a commitment of funds to a customer.

2. Deposits are a bank's primary source of funds for loans and investments. As banks extend additional loans, other investment opportunities are forgone. Further loans require new liquidity, which banks obtain in part through compensating balances. As long as liquidity needs are met, additional loans will be made, and the business community will therefore prosper.

3. Compensating balances allow banks to extend more favorable interest rates to companies which would not be eligible for these rates otherwise.

4. Compensating balances are needed to offset expenses incurred in handling items paid and deposited, overdrafts, stop-payments, and wire transfers.

The relative strength of both arguments is still in question. However, the trend is clearly in the direction of increased compensating balances, and it should not be surprising to see many banks requiring balances in support of borrowings over and above balances needed to offset account activity.

In light of an ever increasing need for liquidity by both banks and corporations, it is clear that bankers and their corporate customers should each look forward to the future with a great deal of mutual respect for the other's viewpoint. In this way, each can contribute as much as possible to the attainment of a mutually beneficial relationship.—*Church Yearley*

INVENTORY: VALUATION AND CONTROL

The term "inventory" designates assets of a concern held for the purpose of sale, or conversion to products for sale, in the general course of business. For most concerns, investment in inventory is of significant size and has a substantial influence on total capital invested.

Manufacturing companies inventory raw materials purchased for conversion or incorporation in a final product of the manufacturing process. The end products of one process, of course, may well be the raw materials of another.

Work in process is raw material in the process of conversion and includes in its value the labor applied, as well as a portion of manufacturing costs which cannot be directly identified with the product; that is, manufacturing overhead (burden).

Finished goods are the end products of manufacturing processes—the completed goods held for sale. These products may serve another company as raw materials or purchased parts or may be sold to a distributor or retailer as finished goods for sale to the ultimate customer.

Inventory Valuation

The value of inventory on hand must be determined periodically, along with other assets, to enable a company to determine costs and to state its financial position. The basis used for inventory valuation has a significant effect on the costs and earnings reflected in the operating statements, and on the asset value shown on the balance sheet. The basis for valuation also determines the allocation of costs between accounting periods. In essence, the higher the costs allocated to the final inventory, the lower the cost of goods sold and, therefore, the higher the profit for the period. Since the ending inventory of a period becomes the beginning inventory for the subsequent period, these higher inventory costs may increase the subsequent period's cost of goods sold, thus decreasing the profit reported for that period.

A variety of methods can be used to value inventory. Income tax computation, accounting principles, ease of application, management reporting, and control considerations all influence the approach used. From a management point of view, the evaluation method that is selected should take advantage of benefits that may affect the operating statement but should also be easily used or converted for effective reporting for management evaluation and decision making.

The conventional accounting method for valuing inventories is known as "the lower of cost or market." It anticipates future losses during a period of declining prices by reducing actual cost to the replacement cost for inventory valuation. As used, the term "market" means current replacement cost, either the purchase price or the cost of production. The objective is to accurately represent the net realizable value in the balance sheet and conservatively value the company's inventories.

COST DETERMINATION

In the most recent practice, cost is used as the basis for valuation, with provision for the use of a revaluation allowance to reflect conservative valuation and anticipate future price declines or other changes, such as physical deterioration or obsolescence, that could reduce the value of the inventory as stated by the costing methods regularly applied.

The principal methods of cost determination are first-in, first-out (FIFO);

last-in, first-out (LIFO); average cost; cost of specific lot; standard cost; and the retail method (gross margin method).

FIFO. The FIFO method assumes that the goods are sold in the order that they were received. With the use of FIFO it is not necessary to identify lots or physically segregate items in the order of purchase. Under this method the final inventory is priced by determining the costs of the most recent purchases. Generally, this is done by working back from the most recent invoices until the quantity on hand has been covered.

LIFO. The LIFO method assumes that the last goods received were sold first. In a period of rising prices, this method reduces profits on sales by eliminating the effects of inflation from final inventory values; therefore, it has the advantage of minimizing taxes.

Although the final inventory can be calculated by keeping perpetual inventory records and historical cost figures, this method is generally not used because of the clerical work required. Instead, a simpler dollar value approach using price index levels is employed. This method assumes that all items in inventory, or a segment of inventory, are homogeneous. This assumption allows the use of price indexes to convert the final inventory priced at current prices to the same inventory priced in terms of the base year (the year in which LIFO was adopted).

Average cost. Many companies use an average unit cost to determine inventory value. Two methods are used for this purpose: an average calculated by dividing the total cost of beginning inventory and purchases by the total number of units represented; and a moving average, calculated after each new purchase is made. Where the time lapse between valuations is long or price changes are rapid, the two methods produce somewhat different results. It is important to note that the moving average requires the maintenance of perpetual records, while the weighted average may be computed periodically. In either case, the use of averaging tends to spread the effect of short-range price changes and level their effect on profit determination.

Cost of specific lot. Sometimes it is desirable to maintain the identity and actual costs of specific lots or items. This is done by recording the actual purchase price or costs and maintaining the identification of items by serial number of purchase order or invoice number for each lot or item in inventory. The application of this method is usually limited to inventories containing high-value, low-quantity items or to those situations where such records are practical or mandatory.

Standard costs. A simply administered technique for determining inventory cost is provided by standard costs. To facilitate its use, a set of standards representing expected costs of purchase and conversion must be established for materials, labor, and other expenses directly related to each inventoried unit. Those manufacturing expenses (overhead or burden) not directly identified with a product or inventory item are usually allocated to each unit of production on a reliable basis. Inventory value is quickly determined by applying these standards to each unit of stock on hand. Of course, where the actual costs are not equal to the standards, variances result and must be recorded. If these variances are substantial, they are accumulated and reallocated to all the production of the period and the inventory on hand. If the variances are minor, they are generally taken as an expense as they occur. Standard costs are also utilized in management reporting for profit performance and control of operating costs. To remain accurate and effective, standard costs must be regularly brought up to date by correcting for changes in costs and methods; otherwise, the values derived by their use lose validity either for valuing inventory or for controlling purchasing or operations.

Similarly, the practice of using only direct costs of material, direct labor, and variable overhead, at standard or actual, has been advanced as a simplified and more meaningful method of providing management information for planning, pricing, and control. Costs not directly related to products (it is argued) are a result of past management decisions and are not directly related to the type or amount of goods currently produced; they should be recognized as period expenses. This, of course, eliminates the necessity of arbitrary allocations to product cost and inventory. This procedure, commonly called direct costing, is not accepted for tax or financial statement purposes, since it tends to understate income if inventory is being increased or overstate income if inventory is being liquidated. A method of providing information for management decisions on a direct costing basis, while providing a means of converting to the full absorption accounting method for period-ending balance sheets and operating statements, is described by Robert Beyer (*Profitability Accounting for Planning and Control,* The Ronald Press Company, 1963). The transition is made by identifying the increase or decrease in inventory levels and adjusting the inventory value for the equivalent portion of fixed overhead. This method combines the direct costing advantages for management decision making with the end result of providing financial statements acceptable for corporate reporting and tax purposes.

Retail method. The retail method of pricing inventory has been developed in the distribution industries to facilitate inventory valuation by having items in inventory priced at the retail price rather than cost. Since the actual cost of each item in inventory is difficult to trace, a ratio must be determined which relates the retail value of the closing inventory with the original cost. The basis for computing this ratio is an established average margin, or mark-on, to the cost to arrive at the retail price. Assuming that the goods in inventory are representative of the mark-on of goods purchased during the recent operating period, their cost is easily determined by using the ratio to recompute the inventory value. Of course, accurate records must be kept of mark-ups over the initial mark-on, mark-downs, variations between margins on various classes of goods, and other alterations or changes so that the value of the inventory is not distorted. This does provide an easily applied method for inventory valuation, while controlling the current profit margin and identifying the effect of shortages and losses. However, because it is an averaging method, changes in mix can affect the accuracy of the final inventory value.

Selection of method. The size, age, and type of inventory must be considered in selecting the method used for valuation. The techniques chosen should provide for the requirements of financial and tax reporting as well as relate to the methods used by management for measuring its performance in inventory management and control. For consistency in financial reporting, it is mandatory that the method of inventory valuation remain constant. If at any time a change in method is made, the effect on the financial results must be clearly stated.

ASSET MANAGEMENT

One of the prime responsibilities of managers at all levels is the optimum use of assets. The dollar value of inventory represents a major capital investment ranging from 30 percent to 60 percent of a company's current assets. The investment made in inventory, therefore, is a significant portion of working capital. Investment in accounts receivable and other current or long-term assets is limited to the extent that inventory exceeds the necessary size. It is understandable that the investment in inventory is carefully watched by management and is a key factor in determining asset management performance. Recognizing that inventory reduction is one of the easiest methods of generating additional cash flow, managers often institute restrictive purchasing and production policies before any other action is taken in times of cash rationing.

Turnover. Measuring the performance of inventory planning and control is usually related to factors which indicate accomplishment of the company's objective for asset use, responsibility to the ownership, or service to the customer. Turnover is the most common measure of inventory utilization and is calculated as follows:

$$\text{Turnover} = \frac{\text{cost of goods sold}}{\text{average inventory value}}$$

The quotient represents the number of times the inventory investment was "used" during the period of measurement. Inverting the equation (dividing the inventory by the cost of goods) gives the portion of the year's sales that the inventory will cover. In either case, the measure indicates the utilization or activity of the investment. Slow turnover may indicate poor use of the asset and greater exposure to obsolescence, damage, or shrinkage. Too rapid a turnover or low coverage, on the other hand, may indicate that stock is moving too quickly, thereby increasing the cost of ordering and materials handling. It could also indicate that price discounts, based upon volume, are not being realized and that the desired level of customer service is not being achieved.

ROI. Return on investment also measures the use of assets, including inventory. Simply stated, the calculation for ROI is

$$\text{ROI} = \underset{\text{(margin)}}{\frac{\text{profit}}{\text{sales}}} \times \underset{\text{(turnover)}}{\frac{\text{sales}}{\text{assets}}} = \frac{\text{profit}}{\text{assets}}$$

It can be seen that these calculations combine common management measures (turnover and return on sales) into one factor for evaluating the profitable use of inventory and other assets. Any reduction in the value of assets will increase both turnover and return on investment.

PROFIT MANAGEMENT

Another primary measure of management performance is profitability. Inventory policies and procedures have a strong influence on the ability of a company to achieve reasonable objectives in this area. Inventory investment directly affects sales and, ultimately, profit performance, since the ability to respond to an order for products or services relates in part to the availability of required parts or finished products. Because production facilities may not profitably be left idle and serious fluctuations in production create additional problems of training and maintaining an adequate labor force, manufacturing management generally attempts to build inventory during seasonally low sales periods. This provides stock for seasonally high demand periods and equalizes month-to-month utilization of equipment and cost of labor. Thus a balance between customer service, efficient utilization of production facilities, and minimum inventory investment must be achieved as a part of effective profit and asset management.

Inventory losses represent another way in which inventory value and its control may affect company operating results, since such losses reduce profits. Several types of conditions account for most inventory losses. Obsolescence is caused by purchasing or producing products, in excess of the demand for use or sale, which are displaced by newer or more desirable goods. The obsolete goods must be disposed of at prices sometimes less than cost. The difference between the cost of inventory value and the disposal price is the loss caused by obsolescence. In addition, the investment in excessive inventory of these items generally precludes the purchase of other more desirable items, requires space for storage, and increases the effort required for taking physical inventory.

Inventory not used quickly, or stored in inadequate facilities, is exposed to damage or spoilage. A certain amount of such losses may be expected under any condition, but it can be held to a minimum by careful planning, handling, and facilities maintenance. The most effective control is the limitation of purchases and inventory to necessary quantities. Evaporation, chemical change, and spoilage must also be recognized as types of loss which may be best controlled through limiting the amount of inventory and the time the inventory is on hand.

Pilferage or theft is a special loss consideration, especially in certain industries where inventoried items are small or of high value and may be consumed by employees or easily disposed of without identification. In addition to the control of inventory areas, preventive measures include extra care to limit opportunities for access to the inventory, the number of people with access, and the routes for removal of the most susceptible items.

In many states, the value of the inventory has yet another direct influence on profit performance, since it is the basis for certain personal property taxes on corporations. This consideration usually prompts managers to plan substantial reductions in materials and finished goods on hand immediately before the physical inventory period. The ability to accomplish this effectively, however, is dependent on good planning of production and sales requirements in order that the tax savings will not be offset by losses in sales and increased expenses.

Inventory Control

To meet the requirements of customer service, production scheduling, optimum turnover, and return on investment and at the same time control possible loss through obsolescence or shrinkage, management must establish effective techniques for making inventory decisions and reporting performance.

Conceptually, there are two alternative methods of determining inventory requirements. One method uses sales forecasting techniques and bill-of-materials breakdowns to project future requirements; for instance, production requirements for new automobiles are determined in this way. The other method uses historical demand patterns and projects future requirements; automotive spare parts requirements are projected on this basis. The major problem with using historical data is that they are less sensitive to obsolescence and marketplace changes than forecasting techniques. On the other hand, the problem with using sales forecasting is that the overall accuracy that can be achieved varies greatly from industry to industry. It is important, however, to consider which concept will provide the greater effectiveness when initiating an inventory control system.

As with valuation, a number of methods for inventory control have been derived and are widely used throughout business and industry. One or more of those described here may be employed within one company to provide effective control.

MINIMUM-MAXIMUM SYSTEM

The minimum-maximum system of inventory control is based on either a forecast or a historical record of maximum demand and minimum level of stock sufficient to protect against shortage during the time required to reorder and receive stock replenishment. The minimum and maximum levels are usually related to the cycle of stock review, which may be monthly, through perpetual records, physical inventory counts, or at the time of recording receipts or withdrawals. When review shows stock at or below the minimum requirements, a reorder is placed to bring stock up to the authorized maximum requirement. A basic application of this method is the two-bin system; when the stock in one bin is exhausted, a replacement order is placed immediately. The second bin contains a sufficient quantity to meet sales or production requirements during the time that it takes to obtain delivery of the replacement order. A buffer (safety) stock is also included in the second bin to allow for a possible delay in the delivery of the replacement order.

SELECTIVE INVENTORY METHODS

For many companies the large number of items in inventory, both materials and finished goods, creates a burden in voluminous record maintenance and detailed physical counting. Although modern electronic data processing capabilities have reduced these problems, the cost of inventory control under such conditions can be greatly reduced by using selective inventory methods. It is characteristic of most inventories that a relatively small number of items account for a high proportion of activity and inventory investment. This method, referred to as ABC analysis, selects items according to their contribution to sales, profit, or inventory value. A typical mix is shown in Exhibit 4.20. The few items identified as representing the largest contribution can be given tight control at reasonable cost. Items of lesser importance may be reviewed less frequently or controlled by less demanding or less expensive methods. For instance, *A* items may be limited to one month's stock and a two-week review, while *C* items may be allowed six months' stock and a three-month review.

"Number of months' supply" and other common rules of thumb are often used for establishing maximum and minimum inventory levels, but such techniques ignore important characteristics of purchasing and stocking inventory, such as the lead time for delivery and the costs to order and the costs to carry (space, handling, and interest on investment) inventory.

ECONOMIC ORDER QUANTITY

More effective inventory management techniques incorporate these considerations in the computation of the two major control values: (1) the order quantity (the proper size and frequency of orders), and (2) the reorder point (the stock level at which additional quantities are ordered). The economic order quantity (EOQ) is one computation which produces the minimum annual cost for ordering and stocking an item. The EOQ computation takes into account the cost of placing an order, the annual sales rate, the unit cost, and the cost of carrying the inventory (interest, insurance, obsolescence, and so forth). The formula is shown in Exhibit 4.21, which also illustrates that, as the number of orders placed is reduced, the cost of ordering is reduced; however, the cost for holding (carrying) increases. The economic order quantity and order frequency occurs where the sum of the two costs is minimum. The cost of carrying inventory, it has been observed, usually ranges between 15 percent and 20 percent of

Exhibit 4.20

SELECTIVE ALLOCATION OF INVENTORY MANAGEMENT EFFORT

A TYPICAL INVENTORY MIX

Class*	Number of Items	Percent of Items in Inventory	Percent Contribution to Sales	Percent of Average Inventory	Percent of Time Out of Stock
A	156	7	51	49	2
B	835	35	38	37	5
C	1409	58	11	14	15
Total	2400	100	100	100	

* Classified here by dollar value; class may be used to segregate parts critical to production schedules or with high rate of technological change.

Exhibit 4.21

ECONOMIC ORDER QUANTITY AND REORDER POINT

HOW MUCH

Order the Economic Order Quantity, Q . . . .

WHEN

. . . When Inventory Drops to Reorder Point, P

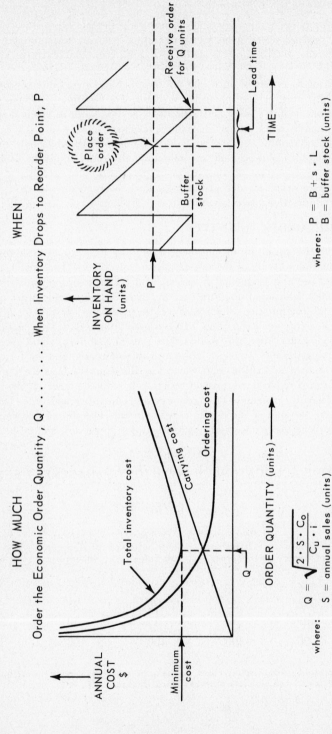

$$Q = \sqrt{\frac{2 \cdot S \cdot C_o}{C_u \cdot i}}$$

where:
S = annual sales (units)
C_o = variable cost of ordering ($)
C_u = unit cost of item ($)
i = cost of carrying inventory (percent per year of item cost)

$$P = B + s \cdot L$$

where:
P =
B = buffer stock (units)
s = average daily sales (units)
L = lead time (days)

the item's cost. Since the formula for calculating the EOQ uses the square root of the cost of carrying inventory, the EOQ is not very sensitive to this cost and the 15–20 percent range is usually considered adequate. Once determined for an item, the EOQ is not frequently changed except for changes in sales or use requirements.

The formula for calculating EOQ for production orders is

$$\text{EOQ} = \sqrt{\frac{2 \cdot S \cdot C_s}{C_u \cdot i}}$$

where *EOQ* is the economic unit lot
  S is the annual sales (units)
  C_s is the cost of production planning and set-up in dollars
  C_u is the unit cost in dollars
  i is the cost of carrying inventory (percent per year of item cost).

Reorder point (the inventory level at which the economic order quantity is ordered) is determined by the quantity of any item required to meet average demand between reorder placement and delivery (lead time), plus a safety stock or buffer stock adequate to meet heavier-than-average demand or longer-than-average lead time for delivery. Exhibit 4.21 graphically illustrates the application of the reorder point and its relation to the order quantity.

A comparison between the application of these systems and typical inventory history is shown in Exhibit 4.22. The substitution of mathematical techniques for rule-of-thumb methods tends to reduce items and dollar value in inventory. This is true because the calculations are related more closely to the actual demand and reordering characteristics of each item controlled.

The greater recognition of actual demand also tends to reduce the frequency of stock-outs and improve customer service. In practice, the buffer-stock level may be set to provide the service level desired by management.

OPEN-TO-BUY METHOD

Retail businesses have used an open-to-buy inventory control system for many years. Simply stated, under this system a department buyer is limited to a specific amount of funds that may be committed to the total of inventory on hand and on order. This amount is related to the sales expected in the immediate future, usually a month or season. To calculate the open-to-buy amount, the allowable month's closing inventory, at retail price, is added to sales planned for the month. The goods on hand (at retail) and open purchase orders (at retail) are subtracted from this total and adjusted for mark-on percentage to arrive at the funds available for purchases. Adjustments for mark-ups and mark-downs are made so that the available amount is not affected by these changes. The allowable closing inventory value is usually related to the average inventory turnover performance expected in the buyer's department and the sales expected in the succeeding month. It should be noted that this technique primarily affects budget control and does not identify the items that should be in stock or tell their number. Therefore, other procedures are sometimes used along with the open-to-buy for the selection decisions.

Exhibit 4.22

INVENTORY BEHAVIOR SHOWING RESULTS OF USING AN EOQ SYSTEM

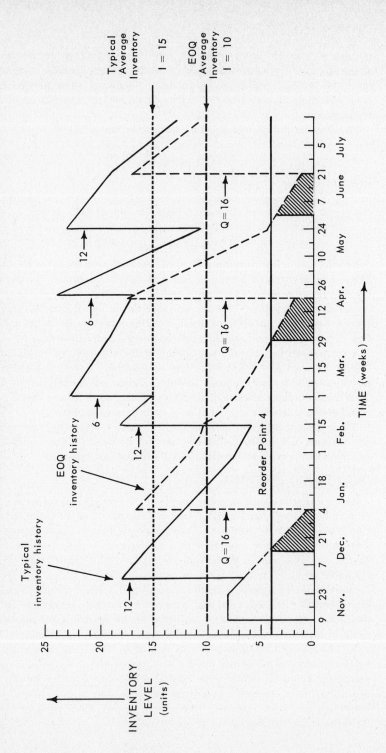

While the open-to-buy method is usually thought of in relation to retailing, it is also being applied effectively in other fields. In one application, for example, a manufacturer may establish a limit for the number of units which may be planned for production, based on the sales plan, the units in inventory, and the units already in process or planned for production. Similarly, the open-to-buy for the dollar purchase of parts and materials can be related to the production plan and the dollars of materials on hand and already on order.

Recently, retail merchants have been adapting EOQ methods to control the inventory of high-volume staple goods because the limitations of open-to-buy rules too often result in stock shortages in items of high demand. Rather than lose sales for this reason, managers are allowing EOQ purchases to override the open-to-buy restraints. This practice, however, does not relieve the buyer of responsibility to correct the "overbought" position by reducing inventory of slow-moving or overstocked items that are not controlled under the EOQ system.

PHYSICAL INVENTORY

Regardless of the care and accuracy of perpetual inventory records, the unit stock records must be adjusted periodically after a physical count for confirmation of accuracy. Of course, if no perpetual records are kept, such a count is required to determine the number of units on hand at a specific date. Since no system is flawless, the count also serves to test the effectiveness of the control systems and identify weaknesses requiring improvement.

Each company establishes procedures for counting, recording, extending, and summarizing physical inventory. The initial counts are usually rechecked—on a sample basis, at least—by different counters or clerks. These procedures are well documented in other publications and therefore are not covered here; however, certain problems recur in physical inventory counting and valuation and should be given careful management attention:

1. *Units of measure.* To describe an ounce of material as a pound, or a dozen as a gross, can seriously distort the inventory value.

2. *Liquid inventories.* Items of inventory that are not easily counted should have special procedures defined for measurement. Tank calibrations or similar methods may be appropriate. If meters or gauges are used, independent calibration prior to inventory should be performed.

3. *Goods in transit.* Goods shipped F.O.B. and assigned to a common carrier must be included in inventory even if not received at the time of inventory. A careful record of shipments to customers where title passes at time of shipment must also be kept so that these goods are not included in inventory.

4. *Damaged goods.* Products or materials of questionable value should be segregated for special valuation.

5. *Obsolete goods.* Items of excessive age or long inactivity should be segregated for special valuation.

6. *Work in progress.* If good cost records are maintained, determination of the state of completion and value is not difficult. However, if cost records are

not maintained, adequate procedures must be established for estimating the amount of cost contained in each item inventoried.

ELECTRONIC DATA PROCESSING

Inventory control procedures of some complexity have always been maintained, of necessity, but it is evident from the previous discussion that certain concessions to cost and efficiency must be made where the volume of data or the complex calculations exceed manual capabilities or economic justification. The advent of electronic data processing (EDP) equipment has greatly expanded the possibilities for utilizing scientific inventory management methods and made possible the production of timely inventory status reporting for management decisions. Applications made economically possible with EDP equipment include: (1) perpetual inventory records with up-to-date information regarding additions and withdrawals; (2) immediate inventory availability; (3) explosion of bills of material upon entry of production orders; (4) automatic allocation of inventory upon bill-of-material explosion; (5) automatic monitoring of reorder-point position and generation of purchase orders; (6) automatic computation of demand trends and calculation of EOQ and lot sizes; (7) exception reporting of inventory items out of control, production scheduling problems, and inventory age; and (8) automatic preparation of documents for taking physical inventory and comparing count results with book records.

Despite the capabilities of computer equipment to store volumes of data and reduce them to manageable forms, not every inventory system can economically use these capabilities. Where a company has many inventory items or a number of inventory locations, or must turn inventory quickly and maintain an optimum investment, computer capabilities may be very helpful in effecting efficient control and evaluation. Situations where small numbers of items, restricted locations, or other considerations limit the size and value of inventory may not require such elaborate electronic systems to maintain efficient and adequate control. Each company must carefully define the needs for inventory data and control methods before a decision can adequately be made for use of EDP equipment and systems.—*R. P. Gibbons and C. F. Stamm*

ACCOUNTS RECEIVABLE: CREDIT AND COLLECTIONS

The role of the mercantile credit manager assumes increasing importance with each passing year. The once widely held view that the credit function represented nonproductive overhead has been supplanted through relatively recent management recognition that competence in this discipline contributes substantially to company profit attainment.

Current Receivables Trends

For more than ten years, trade receivables—unlike any other asset—have risen more sharply than sales for manufacturers and wholesalers. This is reflected in increased days sales outstanding and a sharply higher proportion of total assets tied up in slower-turning receivables.

This trend is generally attributable to an increased willingness of many suppliers to accede to customers' special-terms requests, fostered by higher interest rates and a presently diminishing money supply. Also contributing to the growth pattern is laxity in enforcement of both cash discount and net terms of sale and a decline in the overall quality of trade receivables.

Business bankruptcy rates reached a 16-year low in 1969, according to Dun and Bradstreet. The fact is, however, that the last quarter of 1969 showed the first significant reversal in some time, with indications that—at least for the earliest part of 1970—this upward trend might continue.

Function of the Credit Manager

The credit manager's responsibility rests solely in the cultivation and control of the marginal account, which—depending upon his company's policies—may vary from 5 percent of total sales to 50 percent or more. "Marginals" can be defined as "accounts deficient in character, capacity, or capital—or all three." They are frequently slow in payment of obligations and universally represent a higher-than-average degree of risk.

Increasingly, credit is being recognized as an adjunct of sales; it has cast off the negative image of "the watchdog of the treasury." An unwarranted acceptance of all customer orders without restriction will lead to excessive bad-debt losses; an unduly harsh selective process will result in loss of sales. A dilatory collection follow-up system will result in ballooning receivables; stern and unrelenting payment pressure on customers will negate sales efforts. Today's credit manager must be imaginative and creative in striking the proper balance in these areas to achieve maximum profit return for his company consistent with its own financial ability to nurture the marginal client.

Value of Information

More errors in credit decision making, both positive and negative, result from lack of ingenuity in the development of facts than from the actual interpretation of data. A source exists which can provide the answer to virtually every unresolved question, and the credit manager's expertise should include instinctive knowledge of where to turn for each fact, as well as the ability to probe every source adroitly until the full story unfolds. Information should not be developed merely for its own sake, nor should investigative expense be incurred for superfluous facts. No major decision, however, need be made in a void in today's information explosion.

Aside from nominal orders, on which published ratings will suffice, or where costs for the development of even minimum data are prohibitive, the normal starting point in the evaluation of customer credit acceptability is the review of a Dun and Bradstreet report. In many cases, adequate material to obtain the proper conclusion will appear in the report, and the credit manager need go no further. Should doubt persist, however, many avenues remain to be explored, including banks, credit interchange (a service of the National Association of Credit Management), specialized industry reporting services (typified by the *Blue Book* or *Red Book* ratings and reports for packers and shippers of perishable fruits and vegetables, and the United Beverage Bureau covering the carbonated-beverage bottler), references, industry credit group discussions (both local and national), salesmen's comments, personal visits to the customer's plant, and financial statements submitted directly.

Evaluation Process

Where reliable financial statements are available, preponderant weight should be given to the story they disclose in arriving at a credit decision. Some managers rely upon cash flow analysis or various budgets and projections. Others place their faith in the interpretation of key financial ratios—and their trends—in determining the degree of financial balance represented by their marginal accounts. If problems exist, they will inevitably result from distortion in one or more of the six ratios which measure profit on sales, inventory turnover, the collection rate of receivables, the investment in fixed assets relative to net worth, the existence of either overtrading or undertrading on invested capital, or the unwarranted diversion of funds into such areas as financial support of a subsidiary or loans to officers. Should any account stray too far from industry average in these key factors, the effect will be manifest in working capital deficiency or a burdensome debt structure. The credit manager capable of interpreting his customer's financial statement properly will have little difficulty in predicting the payment pattern and the degree of overall risk present.

Where financial data are unattainable, the principal elements of customer appraisal are—in order of importance—the payment record, any evident trend, bank comment defining balances, loan experience and collateral requirements, the age of the business and its growth potential, the experience background of the principals, and personal appraisals of salesmen or others acquainted with the company.

Making the Credit Decision

Efforts are being made to determine the most important measurable factors in both financial and nonfinancial aspects of the marginal account and to assign them correct weight so that computerized answers will automatically clear most decisions affirmatively, leaving only the most difficult problems for personal study by the credit manager. Generally, regular credit terms will be arranged, but in instances where the risk is too great or excessive slowness is certain, restrictions must be placed on the account. These may include either C.O.D. or sight draft shipments whereby payment is received prior to release of the merchandise, controlled distribution is afforded through bonded or field warehousing, or perhaps cash must be paid in advance.

Risk Reduction and Payment Enforcement

Where the purchaser represents an unacceptably high risk, the way may be cleared for acceptance of orders through securing formal enforceable guaranties from responsible guarantors, through subordination of other indebtedness to the creditor's claim, or through acquiring a security interest in specific assets of the customer (the agreement to be filed in accordance with the requirements of the Uniform Commercial Code). Many firms also elect to reduce their risk through taking out credit insurance policies.

Payment agreements occasionally are firmed up through the use of notes or trade acceptances, which often carry the added psychological weight of being presented through the customer's bank for payment. Even if dishonored, they facilitate the award of a judgment in the event that suit may subsequently be necessary.

Controls

Some managers set dollar credit limits for individual accounts, and the customer is advised of the precise amount established. Others prefer credit lines or ranges for internal guidance only. Still others prefer an automatic approval or referral system whereby all orders on referral accounts only are personally reviewed by the credit staff, with no set limit on the automatic approval. The goal of all these approaches is to permit the practice of credit management by exception, thus concentrating effort in the most productive channels.

Making Marginal Accounts More Profitable

One approach gaining momentum is the service charge, generally imposed on the account paying more than 30 days beyond net terms. Commonly, 1 percent per month on eligible balances is assessed by direct invoicing. This is not primarily intended to be a revenue producer in itself but is designed to reduce days sales outstanding by discouraging delinquency. Another effective means is for the credit manager to provide financial counsel for his customer to aid the account in surmounting its financial problems. Efforts by the credit manager to develop personal rapport with the customer may also provide many opportunities to capitalize on goodwill and to educate the client regarding the seller's payment expectancy. Cash discount enforcement, too, is vital in cultivating profitability, and occasionally the holdup of pending orders provides the leverage to gain present and future compliance with terms.

Collection Procedures

The key to successful collections reverts to the information developed on the account at the time the credit decision was made. Knowing the account—the degree of risk present, its payment mannerisms, even the personality quirks of the principals—will dictate the approach best suited to bring results. Two added essentials for collection success are (1) the regularity of follow-up and (2) the negotiating skills of the credit manager in getting fast results yet still keeping the customer "working on the same side of the street." Erratic, widely spaced contact will encourage customer disregard for terms and abuse of them. Alienation of the account will lead to resistance, to argument, and probably to loss of sales or loss of the balance owed.

The medium used will vary according to the evaluation of the account and will include the use of letters, phone calls, statements, duplicate invoices, telegrams, salesmen's efforts, and personal visits by the credit manager.

Extreme Collection Measures and Insolvency

If the credit manager has exhausted all collection avenues open to him and without result, or if he has reason to suspect impending financial failure, he should waste no time in placing his claim for immediate handling with attorneys or a responsible private collection agency (one unqualifiedly recommended by his fellow credit managers), or an adjustment bureau of his local credit association. Subsequent payments, other than those made within the free demand period offered by some agencies, will be subject to fees established by the Commercial Law League.

Legal action may be required, or perhaps formal insolvency will intervene in the form of receivership, Chapter X or XI, or regular bankruptcy. If there is no evidence of fraud, the credit manager's best interests will be served through out-of-court settlements under the aegis of a creditors' committee.

Reporting Results

As a rule, a monthly statistical summary is sent to top management showing each division's or plant's individual performance and the aggregate attainment for the company. Totals and percentages are refined to portray special-terms exposures, past-due balances according to age (30, 60, 90, or more days delinquent), and days sales outstanding. Comparative figures for the preceding month and the same month for the previous two years, along with a short explanatory comment from the credit manager, provide background material for detection of trend and decision making.—*D. E. Miller*

Planning Receivables Collections

Tight money, with its increasingly high interest rates, has made management aware of the importance of foresight in planning cash requirements in advance. Cash management (or cash planning) has become a vital operation for all sizes of companies, from the largest corporations with their treasurers and money managers to the small family-owned businesses. Since accounts receivable represent a significant asset that can be converted into cash relatively easily, their timely collection is usually an integral part of any cash management program. The continuing search for improvement in the flow of accounts receivable collections can lead management from conventional cash forecasting to the use of outside financing.

Cash Flow Method of Forecasting

The cash flow method accumulates the expected receipts and disbursements for the period being forecast. When sales on credit are significant, analysis is necessary to determine the projected time when cash will be available from collections. The analysis should be prepared with the assistance of the sales and credit personnel. The method used for forecasting collections will vary and can best be determined by analysis of past experience with continuing reference to current actual results. As a minimum, however, where sales are made to differing classes of customers—government, business, or individuals—it is advisable to keep separate sales records and analyze collections separately. The segregation of sales in this or a similar manner provides data which usually lead to more accurate collection estimates.

Borrowing Against or Selling Accounts Receivable

The use of accounts receivable to obtain funds is divided basically into three areas; factoring, accounts receivable financing, and industrial time sales and equipment financing. These methods of accelerating collections are costly because of the interest expense and fees. These related costs have contributed to the downgrading of this type of financing. However, if this is the only manner through which a company can obtain the necessary cash flow from its accounts receivable, the company cannot afford to overlook it—regardless of the cost. The cost of having funds provided is as much a part of doing business as the costs of raw material, labor, plant, and machinery. A typical company usiug these financing methods might operate a business in which trade practices govern the accounts receivable collection patterns at, for example, 90 days, whereas its raw material purchases must be paid on a 30-day basis.

FACTORING

Factoring is an arrangement under which the factor purchases the accounts receivable of his client without recourse to the client as to the credit risk involved as long as the credit has been approved by the factor. The purchase of the accounts is on a notification basis. All risks (such as fraud, returned merchandise, and similar conditions), other than the client customer's ability to pay, are borne by the factor's client.

The principal advantages of factoring receivables to the company are that it protects it against credit loss and relieves the company of the time and expense of credit checking, bookkeeping, and collecting its accounts receivable. This type of financing, for which the factor charges a commission, is usually attractive to companies (1) selling to a limited number of customers where individual credit exposures are larger; (2) selling to large numbers of customers where credit information is limited; (3) with significant bookkeeping and collection cases; (4) needing greater borrowing leverage than is usually available on an unsecured basis.

Payment is made by the factor to the company at maturity of the receivables purchased, unless the company has a need for working capital on a more timely basis. In these cases, the factor may make advances against the receivables sold to him and the company will pay interest, in addition to the commission, from the date of the advance to maturity.

COMMERCIAL FINANCING
(ACCOUNTS RECEIVABLE FINANCING)

Under commercial financing the company does not "sell" its accounts receivable but instead enters into an arrangement with a bank or finance company to borrow against the security of the receivables; usually, without notification to the borrowing company's customers and with full recourse to the company for credit risks. These borrowings usually range between 75 percent and 100 percent of the net receivables assigned. Unlike factoring, all credit, collection, and bookkeeping services are handled by the company in its customary manner. The charge for this service is in the form of interest based on the average daily amount owed; and while there is a premium rate of interest charged, this can be an efficient and economical method of borrowing.

TIME SALES AND EQUIPMENT FINANCING

Financing through sales and equipment involves the sale of installment contracts covering the sales of equipment and machinery, usually with notification to the equipment purchaser. These contracts may be sold with full, limited, or no recourse to the company. The interest charge is added on to the contract or charged to the company on a discount basis. The main advantage of using this method is the quick realization of cash, together with limiting the bookkeeping and collection efforts.

Use of Credit Cards

Charge accounts have reached so great a volume that an increasingly major portion of all department store sales are not for cash. As credit use becomes greater and greater, the right to receive credit may no longer be considered a privilege that can be denied a customer. Recently, cases have been noted where welfare recipients have demonstrated against major retailers for lines of credit. Most companies have little choice but to offer credit in order to remain competitive. If a company's size or the nature of its business precludes it from having an efficient credit and collection department, its probable best approach to the problem would be to transfer its credit operations to an outside credit grantor such as a bank credit card plan. The discount paid under such plans rids the company of credit and collection problems, and the credit available gives its product wider marketability. The operators of the credit card plans are enabled by their size to utilize modern computers for controlling the credit and collection operations.

A Checkless Society?

Someday a woman may walk into a store, purchase a dress, and give an identification card to the sales person. The sales person will insert the card in a machine and punch a few keys, and thereupon the cost of the purchase will be automatically deducted from the purchaser's bank account and credited to the store's bank account.

Modern technology has brought us to consider such a system, but most people agree that considerable time and planning will be needed before checkless purchasing can be achieved. One major obstacle is that many companies—and individuals—do not want to give up writing checks, and another is that not everyone receiving checks or other payments has a bank account to be so drawn upon. The growing popularity of credit cards may offer a possible solution, but for the present the average customer is quite a long way from acceptance of the checkless society.—*J. T. Shanahan, Jr.*

INTERNAL AUDIT TECHNIQUES AND APPLICATIONS

Internal audit is an independent appraisal activity, within an organization, for the review of accounting, financial, and other operations as a basis for reporting effectiveness and adherence to policies and procedures to management. It is a control medium which measures and evaluates other controls. Internal audit has been referred to as the conscience of the company. In carrying out the function of internal auditing, the person or persons who are responsible for it should bear in mind that the purpose of the endeavor is to protect the assets of the organization and contribute to its profitability.

The internal audit function should be independent of line functions so that the individuals carrying out the function may be impartial and constructive in their approach. The auditor should be part of management and act for management. He should have authority to cross department and divisional lines when necessary. Because of his independence, he should enjoy an advantage in that he can—figuratively—stand back and see the subject under review objectively. The auditor has to do all in his power to acquire the viewpoint of management because he has to report those things in which management has an interest. His reports should highlight findings which are favorable, as well as those which require correction, and should be couched in language which will be clearly understood.

The auditor is like an ambassador without portfolio in that he has to ferret out the facts but cannot remedy any deficiencies. His responsibility is to report and make recommendations. The latter is basic because the auditor, in doing his work, has to become intimately familiar with the area of investigation and should naturally be in a position to know the remedy to effect correction.

The Internal Audit Department

The answer to the question, "What constitutes an internal audit department?" can range from "One individual" to "Many hundreds of individuals." Regardless of its size, the department is the organizational unit charged with the responsibility of checking the controls as established. Of course, the smaller the company, the fewer and less formal will be the checks and balances built into the processing of transactions. In the small, single proprietorship, the owner is really the auditor, because he is reviewing what is being done. As his business grows in size and possibly spreads out geographically, he can no longer oversee the operations personally but must rely on reports. As these reports become more voluminous, the owner may feel that he would like to be confident that the reports portray the facts. In order to have this assurance, he appoints from his organization—or hires—an individual to check on the reports. This is the beginning of an internal audit department, and it will grow as its members demonstrate that they can provide management with a meaningful and valuable service.

Banks and other financial institutions were among the first to employ individuals who were given the prime responsibility of auditing. The chief auditor in a bank is usually an officer of the company. Small banks which can't afford a full-time auditor use officers to check on tellers and senior clerks, or have employees check each other's work. The larger banks employ many auditors to test-check transactions continuously and review procedures. Where branch banking is allowed, the internal auditors travel from branch to branch reviewing all phases of the operations to insure that home office policies are being adhered to. The liquid state of the assets of a bank makes their verification at frequent intervals very necessary.

The officers of well-managed companies likewise want to be confident that their decisions are based on accurate data, and since they don't have time to personally evaluate the gathering or compiling, they depend on that arm of management, the internal auditor, to do the task of verification for them. This does not mean that every piece of data must be verified. If the system or procedure as installed is being followed, the resulting data should be accurate. This is the reason for having the internal auditor review all control procedures periodically. With the stepped-up pace of operations in many companies, weaknesses in control may develop very rapidly. The internal auditor has to be ever alert to any potential breakdown in the system of control. This is where a keen imagination is a great asset; the internal auditor must be able to mentally project hypothetical situations which could develop and to devise preventive procedures.

Important as is the protection of the cash and security in a bank, it is no more so than accounting for labor and materials in a manufacturing company, or accounting for metals taken out of the ground by a mining company. The units of measure and form are different, but the control and accountability are just as necessary. Since all companies have assets in some form, the means of controlling them should be evaluated periodically; and the control of assets includes the control of expenditures of time and money. The efforts of people can be misspent as easily as the dollars paid for commodities and services. An objective appraisal of these expenditures can prove very rewarding.

Because of the potential benefits—both measurable and unmeasurable—that can come from an internal audit department, every company should consider setting up such a department. Most companies that have had auditing departments for some time are finding that the auditors can produce good results in evaluating operations that are removed from the accounting function. The size and scope of the department can be tailored to the particular requirements of the management.

The larger and more diverse the company, the more necessary becomes the internal audit department, for the job of effective communication up and down the organizational ladder is magnified many times. This is where the auditor comes into play, as a part of management, in helping to keep clear the lines of communication. The internal auditor can help the operating people in interpreting company policies. He can also give management the assurance that policies are being adhered to.

Although a staffed internal audit department is recommended, there is another organizational approach. One fairly large company has a chief auditor who oversees the function, and when he needs to have a specific function audited in a location, he calls on individuals who are handling the same function at another location to come in and appraise the operations. This approach has specialists evaluating the things they know, but it does not provide for developing men who have both breadth of experience and management viewpoint.

Types of Audits

Accounting for the receipt and disbursement of monies was the forerunner of other financial verification and control.

CASH AUDIT

Personal financial control in its simplest form requires the reconciliation of a monthly checking account statement from a bank; this is done to insure that the entries in the checkbook agree with the charges and credits made to the checking account. In a company the receipt of monies—cash or checks—should be listed as received so that the company's record may be compared with the daily deposits as acknowledged by the bank. It is preferable that this listing be made by someone other than the individual responsible for preparing the deposit. In large department stores and other businesses with many collection points, it is usually necessary to establish a cash control function which reconciles the cash turned in with the cash slips and at the same time establishes a receivable control from the charge slips.

The operation of this cash control group is checked periodically by the internal audit department. The purpose of this audit of transactions is to uncover embezzlement of funds. The audit of disbursements is another area that deserves close scrutiny.

Most companies have procedures which call for the matching of receiving records with vendors' invoices to insure that quantities received agree with those charged for and that the prices invoiced agree with those contracted for. This function is usually carried out by clerical personnel. After the documents are matched, they are forwarded to someone else for check preparation by hand, on an accounting machine, or—in large companies—by the data processing department. Where checks are hand-signed, the signer may do much or little work in comparing the detail to the voucher detail, depending on the pressure of his work. Where checks are machine-signed, the processor may be under as much pressure and not compare the detail against the covering instrument. Besides making sufficient test verifications in this area of disbursements, the internal auditor should also make continuous reviews of the procedure to insure that personnel turnover has not resulted in a procedural breakdown. The internal auditor should occasionally perform the task of reconciling the bank account. The audit of disbursements will automatically expose the auditor to reviewing the proper authorization of purchases and the prices paid.

CAPITAL EXPENDITURES AUDIT

The purpose of the audit of capital expenditures is to insure that expenditures are proper and that the initiating party has the authority to contract for the work. Because capital expenditures are usually significant in dollar amount, they are very often sanctioned by the board of directors. The auditor may have to refer to the minutes of the meetings of the board in order to learn the true scope of the authorized project. He may also have to study actual contracts for the work to be performed by each participating contractor. When progress payments are to be made as the work progresses, he should insure that the stipulated completion estimates are properly documented. The internal auditor should trace the expenditures through the books of account to be certain that they are properly classified and documented for income tax support and that the depreciation expense is booked.

RESEARCH AND DEVELOPMENT AUDIT

As companies spend ever increasing amounts of money to find and develop new and improved products, it becomes more and more necessary to devise procedures to see that the expenditures are controlled. Because the time and money spent in this area of endeavor may or may not prove fruitful, top management should approve any project before it is undertaken. The auditor should ascertain that management's approval has been given in enough detail to enable the researchers to work toward planned goals in accomplishment and expenditures. In addition, he should review the budgeted expenditures for reasonableness and determine that the procedures for reporting are such that all time and dollars spent can be equated against the authorization. He should also ascertain that the reporting media and interval are such that the project cannot go over budget either in particular type of expense or in total. As planning is of the highest importance in research, the internal auditor can be of help by objectively evaluating all proposals in order to assist others in anticipating areas of expenditure that might be overlooked. He should make sure that the proposal as approved spells out the approval authority by class of expenditure and amount. Once the project has been approved and the various procedures for control have been established, it is the responsibility of the auditor to ascertain that they are being adhered to.

OPERATIONS OR FUNCTIONAL AUDITS

The audit of the operations or functions of an organization has been performed since the very beginning of industrial enterprise. As in the case of many other duties, it was originally performed as an adjunct to an individual's prime responsibility and in an informal way. It was also performed by an individual who was close to the operation and might not be very objective. With the expansion and growth of companies, many executives who were in top management and thus not close to operations felt a need for reports on the operations or functions within their companies; this brought about the evolution of operations or functional audits (also called management audits). This type of audit is an overall examination and appraisal of a department, division, or other corporate entity as to organization, objectives, policies, and controls (financial and operational); use of equipment, materials, and people; and method of operation. This does not mean that the auditor is to pass on the technical decisions of operating people. Basically, the audit is a measuring of controls with the intent of improving performance, eliminating inefficiencies, and increasing profits. The audit of functions or operations is as important as the audit of financial controls because there are few if any areas that are not affected by controls. Weaknesses in control of operational areas can result in dollars spent unnecessarily or income lost through inefficiency. Periodic review by an independent, objective observer who can make constructive criticisms to operating personnel should help to increase the efficiency of operations and the performance of the operating personnel, thereby enabling them to make a greater contribution to the profit of the organization. The audit should be looked on by the operating people as an assist to help them score higher. The type and variety of management audits can be as varied or numerous as the operations within the organization. When the auditor is embarking on an audit of this nature, it is very important to spell out the objectives and scope of the investigation and to make the operating people aware of the aims so that they may lend the auditor any assistance in their power in order to realize the greatest benefit for the good of the company.

AUDIT OF THE COMPUTER

With advances in technology and the ever increasing use and application of EDP in the handling of financial and operating data, data processing by human hands will diminish more and more. New concepts for gathering, transmitting, and recording information will give birth to new problems and require revised techniques of control and new approaches to the auditing function. In some industries, evolution in methods of operation may be rapid; the auditor must be prepared to keep pace by being a step ahead if he is to do a creditable job. The auditor must acquire a basic understanding of the functions of the various pieces of equipment used to process the data from input to output. The high-speed handling of input data by EDP makes necessary more exacting procedures and accompanying checks on the data. With a computer the processing functions tend to be more concentrated; hence they remove more people from the area of manipulating transactions, provided the established control procedures are adequate. The use of EDP often reduces the number of printed reports that were formerly necessary because the data are now stored in memory units to be available as required. This means that the auditor has a smaller amount of physical evidence of transactions that he may test-check, but most systems do provide for producing information as required. It now becomes the auditor's responsibility to decide when and in what detail he should request test data from the computer.

Because the possibility of misuse of the data in the computer system has to be recognized, some safeguards must be provided. The functions of operating and programming should be kept separated, and duplicate control or instructional tapes should be maintained for periodic comparison with the tapes in use by the operational personnel. Auxiliary accounting controls outside the data processing group can be established for checking the accuracy of the system.

As computer use becomes more widespread and more complicated, it will probably be necessary for the auditor to become more conversant with it so that he may program his audit checks into the system, automatically effecting more checks and balances.

In auditing an EDP system, the auditor should be alert for changing circumstances in the use and need of generated information. No matter how rapidly reports may be produced, there is always a cost for each one turned out. An unnecessary report uses up machine time which could be devoted to another, more profitable application. Since management should be concerned with the economical utilization of this physical asset, the auditor—acting for management—should work continuously to see that the installation's output is being used profitably.

Organization

The size and character of the company and the scope of audit assignments delegated by management will determine the size of the audit staff.

STAFF

Most audit staffs are made up of men with a background of education in accounting and work experience in company accounting or public accounting. This is because most companies put the main emphasis on the audit of financial statements, procedures, and controls. Some companies that have adopted a management audit approach have added individuals with other specialized backgrounds to their audit staffs; for example, industrial engineers, quality engineers, EDP experts, and many more specialty analysts. Much can be gained from the use of specialists, provided their efforts are coordinated.

Some companies use the internal audit function in order to train men for management positions; hence assignments to the group may be for varying periods of time, depending on the exposure desired for the individual. On the other hand, some companies believe that internal auditing should be a career job, and the men who join their staffs know that auditing will be a lifework in most cases. Many people feel that the auditor is in the best spot to learn the overall operations of the company, and for this reason assignments to the audit staff are prized in many companies.

LINE OF REPORTING

For the auditor to be of greatest value to his company, he should report to the highest echelon of management that will get action on the audit findings. An auditor reporting to a board chairman whose responsibility is stated merely as "future planning" probably won't get much support in effecting current changes. It is fairly common practice for the auditor to report to a financial executive, since so much of the work of the auditor requires the scrutiny and verification of accounting reports and controls. The only drawback in this line of reporting is that it may be more difficult for the auditor to be completely objective when he is reporting on an area under the responsibility of his superior. It is not uncommon for the internal auditor to report to the board of directors. So long as the board is not entirely composed of insiders, this setup can give him the greatest amount of independence.

COST OF OPERATING

As is true of any other department, the internal audit function must justify its existence. Management knows that controls have to cost money, but expenditures have to be within reasonable bounds. Although the internal audit department is not a direct producer of income, it can effect savings that are measurable and that should be netted against the gross cost of running the department. The audit staff should not attempt to cost out each and every saving; this might use up too much valuable audit time. Management should also realize that the existence of the internal audit function acts as a dissuader from wrongdoing, hence results in indirect savings.

YEAR-END AUDIT

In conjunction with the year-end audit by public accountants, the internal audit department is usually called upon to assist in many areas in order to augment the staff of independent auditors. Most public accounting firms recognize that the internal auditors have an independent status within the company, and therefore the public accountants rely on much of the work performed by the internal auditors. The use of the internal auditors in the year-end audit has a continuing value to the company in that any areas of weakness noted may be followed up at a later date. The use of the internal auditors in place of the outside staff men will probably prove to have saved money for the company when their cost is compared with the increased audit fees. This is one of the measurable savings previously mentioned. The public accountants usually make extensive use of all audit work done by the internal auditors during the year. There are many internal audit departments that include their public accountants among the recipients of all reports.

Reports

The reports prepared by the internal auditors are the culmination of their efforts; they are submitted to management to make known the audit findings and motivate action where and when required. Reports should be tailored to give management the facts in the form that will be most readily understood. Some people prefer short, narrative presentations, while others want elaborate schedules of figures or statistics; still others find charts or graphs the most meaningful forms. In any event, reports should concentrate on bringing out and evaluating the most important facts and presenting constructive recommendations.—*G. G. McConeghy*

THE CPA, THE AUDIT REPORT, AND THE ANNUAL REPORT

The CPA is unique among the persons who give professional advice to the management of a company: While most of these persons give advice as advocates of management, the CPA must maintain a certain stature of independence, expressing his opinion on the company's financial statements whether it is favorable or unfavorable to management. The CPA is bound by his ethical standards to ascertain that the report on the financial position of a company and the results of its operations to the stockholders and other outside parties is made in accordance with accounting principles commonly accepted by the business community and, more particularly, by the accounting profession. Nevertheless, management must remember that the financial statements on which the CPA expresses his opinion are entirely those of the company and its management. In view of the many changes recommended in financial reporting concerning deferred income taxes, pension plan reporting, adjustments of prior period amounts and extraordinary items, and depreciation method disclosures, management often feels that it has lost control over what is contained in statements which, it would appear, only the highly trained accountant can understand.

Rather than accept this predicament, the management of the company should make an effort to understand the underlying reasons that CPA's advocate certain methods of presenting financial statements. When changes in reporting or accounting methods are proposed by the auditors, management should obtain a full explanation of the auditors' position in order to present its financial statements to stockholders and others, explaining why certain reporting methods are used.

All too often, management's view of the CPA is that he is a necessary evil to business who must come once a year to perform superfluous examinations of company records. In the course of several weeks or months of such work, he has inquired into matters which supposedly anyone should comprehend; he has disrupted office routine; and he has not made any startling discoveries of duplications or grossly inaccurate records. Two weeks after management has been presented with the company's internal financial statements, the CPA presents his version of the same statements, embellished with footnotes but otherwise not very different from the statements that the company was capable of producing.

When management views the relationship of the CPA to the company in this manner, it shows itself deficient in knowledge of the services and functions of the CPA, who is an expert in accounting and related matters. The extent to which he serves in this function is dependent upon management's acceptance of (and desire to seek) the CPA's assistance with professional advice on accounting and related matters. Management can view the CPA as an outsider who performs a required function, or it can seek out his advice in a multitude of accounting areas such as cash and inventory planning, budgets, and relations with other advisers such as attorneys or bankers. In addition, many CPA's are conversant with tax matters and with other services which can provide management with assistance in production, data processing, marketing, and other peripheral areas of accounting. The auditor is the logical person to give a variety of assistance in accounting-oriented areas, since he has been able to view nearly all aspects of the company's business objectively during the course of his audit. The company that seeks the full services of the CPA generally finds that its financial health improves and the sophistication of management in accounting and other administrative affairs is enhanced, just as good and constant legal advice can save a company from many legal entanglements.

The Audit

The primary objective of the audit is to enable the company to obtain a favorable and reliable report on the company's financial position as embodied in the audit report and in the company's annual report to its stockholders. It must always be remembered that the financial statements are the product of the company, not of the CPA. It appears obvious that the company would desire to participate in planning the audit and constantly check with the CPA on the progress of his audit, discussing any problems which may arise and resolving these problems in a timely way.

The CPA generally views his assignment to the audit as having three stages: planning, performance, and conclusion.

PLANNING THE AUDIT

It is obvious that when a project has been properly planned and thought out, the performance and often the results are more satisfactory than if the project had been ill-planned. The audit of a company's financial statements requires involvement in many facets of the company's operations. Physical inventories often cause interruptions of production; circularization of receivables and preparation of schedules to assist the auditor require that the accounting staff devote extra time to its duties. If EDP is being utilized, plans must be made to fit timing requirements to obtain necessary schedules peculiar to year end.

Determining time requirements. The question that should be asked first is not when to start the audit but on what date management wants the completed audit report. The primary responsibility of the time when the audit will be performed falls upon the CPA, but management must inform the CPA of the due date of the audit report. Dates of stockholders' and directors' meetings should be considered, as well as the requirement to send a finished report to the printers if an annual report is prepared. In setting the timing requirements, consideration should be given to the capabilities and availability of the accounting staff personnel and the time lags that may be involved in accumulating all necessary information from offices and operations in other locations. Often, a company sets deadlines for obtaining financial statements without realizing that time is required to accrue liabilities, compile inventories, and investigate imbalances in accounts. Delays may also be caused by failure, at one or two troublesome locations, to complete work in the required time, thereby holding up completion of the financial statement. Management should therefore discuss possible problem areas either directly with the persons responsible for performing the work or through their supervisors, who must in turn discuss problems with their personnel prior to reporting to management. A clear understanding of problems and timing requirements by all company personnel who are to take part in compiling the financial statements can prevent failure to meet deadlines and can avoid errors which can result from excessive work at the last minute.

Conferring with auditors. Arrange to meet with the audit partner, manager, or supervisor well in advance of the audit date. Inform the auditor of the company's timing requirements and determine whether he feels that these requirements are reasonable. If this is a repeat audit, he will be able to point out areas that presented problems in executing the audit for the previous year, and discussions can be held to rectify the problem areas. If the company wants to receive its financial statements very close to year end—within one month after it, for example—the auditor will want to review the possibility of performing as much of his audit as possible before year end. Based upon his review of internal controls and procedures with respect to the accounting records, he will inform the management which areas of the audit can be performed early. Common examples of balance sheet work which can be performed before year end are as follows:

1. Physical inventories can be taken one to two months early in order that adjustments may be made to the physical quantities, valuation may be determined, and obsolescence may be evaluated in adequate time. For most companies, the compilation and evaluation of inventories make up the most time-consuming part of preparing the financial statements and hold up the closing of the books.

2. Accounts receivable can be circularized one or two months before year end in order to prepare an aging and evaluation of the receivables and allow time to receive adequate replies to the auditor's confirmation requests.

3. Many other accounts can be analyzed for ten or 11 months by the auditor if internal controls are adequate. Such preliminary analysis can be useful in detecting problem areas which may cause difficulty at year end.

In short, if the company employs sound accounting practices, the CPA may be able to perform practically all his detail tests of the accounts before year end and confine his tests after year end to reviews and overall tests of accounts at the balance sheet date, thus enabling rapid preparation of the financial statements. An important advantage of performing the audit in this manner is that it spreads the work of the company's accounting staff, thus cutting overtime which often results in errors and oversights.

Review of previous year's audit report. Determine whether all schedules that are included should be retained and whether any other schedules may be required. Management should define its use of the audit report and decide what improvements might be added to make the report more meaningful. In general, the audit report contains the accountants' report; the balance sheet; statements of income, retained earnings, and changes in working capital; and notes to the financial statements. These basic statements are presented, preferably, with comparative amounts for the previous year. Notes to financial statements may be required if amounts shown in the balance sheet or income statement require further explanation. Common examples of matters that may require notation are (a) principles of consolidation, if consolidated statements are presented; (b) depreciation method used for properties; (c) description of terms of long-term debt; (d) changes in capital stock and paid-in capital accounts; (e) stock option information; (f) pension plan information; (g) lease or other commitments and contingent liabilities.

Other financial information may be included, separate from the financial statements, to present details of the consolidation of subsidiaries and the parent company; sales and gross profits by product classification; details of manufacturing and selling, and an administrative summary of transactions in property, plant, and equipment; inventories; accounts receivable; and insurance coverage. When the auditor visits the company to make preliminary audit arrangements, the format of the report should be discussed so that underlying data for the schedules can be adequately obtained and will be useful to management.

Review of company changes. Review, with the CPA, any changes in accounting procedures, organization, or operations. Alternatives may be available to the company in reporting such changes or associated events, and they should be discussed to determine their effect on the financial statements. For example: A foreign subsidiary may be acquired, and the company can consider the advisability of recognizing this investment at cost (parenthetically disclosing equity) or choosing the equity method. The equity method provides for recognition of income of the foreign subsidiary each year, but it also requires the recognition of losses or devaluation of foreign assets, and the possibility of such losses should be considered. Another example might be a new product line in which alternative methods of costing may be considered.

Assistance to auditor.   Finally, arrangements should be made for the company to furnish assistance to the auditor by preparing such schedules as may be required by him. The auditor should be invited to inventory briefing conferences and should review closing instructions before they are issued to other locations. Close cooperation with the auditor will permit a smooth performance of the audit and may substantially reduce audit time.

PERFORMING THE AUDIT

The independent auditor's primary objective in performing an examination of the financial statements is to satisfy himself that the statements fairly present the financial position of the company and the results of its operations for the period under examination. To achieve this objective he must perform tests of the accounts by (a) examination of sufficient evidential material such as invoices, shipping documents, leases, or correspondence; (b) independent verification of accounts with principal suppliers and direct correspondence with customers concerning account balances; (c) observation of physical inventories to determine existence, ownership, and condition; and (d) tests of inventories, properties, and other accounts to determine that accounting principles have been consistently applied. Minutes of meetings of directors, stockholders, and executive committees and contracts in effect during the year will be read to determine that all pertinent financial matters have been considered by the auditor.

While some of the tests performed by the auditor may appear unnecessary when considered individually, they nevertheless form an integral part in obtaining an independent verification of amounts which will be presented in the financial statements.

Extraordinary items. A matter often discussed between the auditors and the management of a company is the separation in the income statement of certain income or loss items that may not reflect the results of operations for the year. Examples of such extraordinary items are as follows: the sale or destruction of operating facilities, resulting in large gains or losses; the adjustment of investment in foreign subsidiaries, resulting from devaluation; and the write-off of large amounts of inventories obsoleted by change in product line. Generally, a company should refrain from making such distinctions unless the events in question are clearly transactions which would distort significantly the results of operations for the year. A company that shows extraordinary items in the income statement, year after year, conveys the impression to the public that management is bending over backward to state the results of the company's operations.

Adjustments. During the audit, questions may arise as to adjustments which may be desirable in order to reasonably state the accounts. The CPA generally bases the importance of making adjustments on the materiality of their effect on the financial statements. Most executives are guided in their evaluation of a company's operations by the attainment of a profit plan or projection or by a goal of a certain increase in earnings per share. The CPA, while independent in his judgment of the reasonableness of the financial statements, may be agreeable to passing some of the proposed adjustments. However, he must be satisfied that by passing adjustments, (a) the company is not being inconsistent in its accounting practices; (b) the accounting practices are generally accepted by the accounting profession; and (c) the adjustments, either individually or in the aggregate, do not materially distort the financial statements.

What, then, is a material adjustment? The accounting profession does not quantitatively define materiality further than to say that a 5 or 10 percent effect on net income or on total assets may be material. More importantly, the question should be answered in the light of the effect that an adjustment would have on a stockholder, a lender, or a potential investor. To answer these questions becomes more difficult and subjective and requires sound judgment on the part of the CPA and the management. The CPA generally believes that each company (and each fiscal year of the same company) must be viewed in the light of its specific operations in determining whether the financial statements fairly present the financial position and results of operations for the period being reported.

CONCLUDING THE AUDIT

It is important that company management understand that while the financial statements are embodied in an audit report, only the accountants' report is the primary responsibility of the CPA. The financial statements, including all notes, belong to management. To emphasize its responsibility, a letter of representations is prepared for the signature of the top executive and the chief financial officer. This letter reiterates the general representation made by the company to the auditors, either orally or in writing, concerning major aspects of the accounting records. While the letter of representations is designed to place responsibility for the financial statements with management, it also defines the CPA's responsibility in performing an audit in conformity with generally accepted auditing standards and states that he has performed all work necessary to express an opinion on the financial statements. The representations made in the letter are of utmost importance to both parties and should be signed only when all obligations stated in the letter have been met.

The closing conference. The culmination of the audit is the closing conference. This is a meeting at which the audit executive and key audit personnel discuss the results of their audit with top management, generally the president and financial executives. The purposes of this conference are (a) to reiterate the company's responsibility for its financial statements; (b) to review preliminary financial statements for completeness and proper interpretation intended for outside parties; (c) to discuss operational and other matters of concern to management; (d) to discuss matters that the auditor feels warrant investigation.

At the closing conference, the format and amounts shown in the preliminary financial statements will be reviewed, and changes, additions, or deletions (where appropriate) will be made. At this meeting the partner of the CPA firm will explain the general contents of the financial statements and the reasons why disclosures should be made on certain matters. The accountants' report will also be explained. For most companies the accountants' report will express an unqualified opinion, which means that the CPA has found no significant matters in violation of generally accepted accounting principles; that the accounting principles have been applied consistent with the usage of the preceding year; and that there are no major uncertainties, such as lawsuits or contested adjustments by the Internal Revenue Service (IRS) which could materially change the company's financial condition if decided unfavorably. Depending upon the effect that such exceptions may have upon the financial statements, the opinion may be qualified, in which case the CPA expresses an opinion on the financial statements except for the departure or uncertainty in question; or the opinion may be entirely disclaimed. The decision to qualify or disclaim an opinion will not be made until the matter has been thoroughly discussed with management. A qualified opinion is not always an indictment of the company, for there are many changes in accounting principles in which the CPA concurs—changes in inventory or depreciation methods, for example—but he must bring these changes to the attention of the reader of the audit report and financial statements.

The closing conference is also a focal point for management and the auditors to discuss matters of concern to both parties. The subjects which may be discussed will vary with the circumstances of the company. The objective in discussing these matters is to give the auditors the opportunity to draw on their experience in advising management of their viewpoints regarding problem areas. Deficiencies in accounting procedures, weaknesses in internal controls, and operational areas which may need special review or improvement will be discussed. To formalize the auditor's suggestions, a letter will be written to management. The letter of recommendation is obligatory upon the CPA if, during his audit, he has found matters which should be brought to the attention of management.

The Annual Report

When considering the issuance of an annual report, management should remember that it is one of the most important statements made about the company during the year. It is distributed to a great variety of individuals—stockholders, interested bankers, brokers or other members of the financial community, potential investors, suppliers, and employees; therefore, its planning and preparation must be the responsibility of many departments of the company. As one examines annual reports issued by companies, one finds that—regardless of size of company or diversity of product line—the principal emphasis in the reports is on presenting the companies in the most favorable light. In other words, the annual report is a document of utmost importance in selling the company to all interested parties.

FINANCIAL INFORMATION

The most convincing manner in which the annual report conveys the company's status and presents its results is in the financial statements, for here the reader can see statistical proof of progress during the year. The financial statements that will be included in the annual report will be, in almost all cases, the statements on which the CPA expresses his opinion; therefore, the financial statements must be complete, and the CPA's report must be included in the annual report. The inclusion of the financial statements in their entirety requires that management consider thoroughly any alternatives available in reporting the company's financial position and the results of operations.

Generally, alternatives will relate to further elucidation of amounts shown in the statements. While the AICPA requires certain disclosures in the financial statements, companies may desire to give information in greater detail to clarify amounts. Such an expansion of financial data may be advisable for so-called conglomerates or for companies with diverse operations. Disclosure of profits and sales information by major product lines is not required by the accounting profession or by governmental agencies, but each company should appraise the advantages or disadvantages of disclosing additional information on its operations. Professional analysts find that more thorough disclosure of operational data is of great help in evaluating a company.

In addition to the financial statements, the annual report also contains, in as concise a way as possible, a message from the president; various descriptions of products or changes in the company's operations or personnel; and listings or descriptions of the officers and directors of the company. The variety of matters included in the annual report requires the coordination of numerous departments of the company in addition to the accounting and finance department. The research department must supply information on product development; the sales department must furnish prospects of the next year's sales; and the executive committee must formulate prospects for the future. A committee of departmental executives should be formed in ample time to permit a thorough review of all aspects of the work of issuing the annual report.

FORMAT OF REPORT

The format of the annual report should be discussed with the company's advertising department or outside public relations agency. Type of paper, use of color, number of pages, and arrangement of content are only a small number of the items that should be considered in selling the format to management. When the format has been determined and the financial statements have been incorporated, the CPA should be given the opportunity to read over the financial data in order to ascertain that his name can be associated with the financial statements as presented in the annual report.

Continuing Contacts

Contacts with the CPA should not cease until the next year end approaches. When questions arise concerning—for example—acquisitions, changes in the business, or tax problems, the CPA's advice should be sought just as legal advice is sought from the company's attorneys. The CPA's assistance may be needed to perform special examinations of troublesome accounting areas or to express an opinion concerning fulfillment of the financial aspects of an employment or rental contract. To implement changes in accounting or operational areas as recommended in the letter to management, assistance may be obtained from specialists in management services, who often form an integral part of the CPA firm. Continuing contacts with the CPA provide management with professional advice on accounting, taxes, and related matters—advice which will best serve management and the stockholders.—*J. H. Smith*

FEDERAL INCOME TAX RESPONSIBILITIES

Management's role in Federal income tax matters is both defensive and offensive. Defensively, the corporation must be protected against unnecessarily heavy impact of the tax law and against disallowances on the tax return because of failure of substantiation or inability to comply meticulously with the U.S. Treasury's regulations. Offensively, management may substantially achieve the subsidizing of necessary or desirable expenditures by having the costs treated as valid tax deductions. With the Federal income tax rate hovering around 50 percent for corporations with taxable income above $25,000, the government will pay about half of the costs of expenditures tailored to the conditions of the Internal Revenue Code (IRC): that is to say, deductible items. (Under the excess-profits tax which usually accompanies a major "shooting war," the tax rate may go as high as 80 percent or 90 percent, thus increasing the governmental subsidy to deductible items and weakening the corporation's urge to cut costs.)

Often, that approximately 50 percent subsidy is on a collision course with management's prerogatives in running the corporation. In his charge to the jury in a recent tax case, a veteran judge declared: "I will tell you that I have been here for almost ten years. I never knew before that the Internal Revenue Service could tell a man what his salary should be, but I will tell you that this is the law; they can do it and they did do it." (*Wynn et al* v. *United States,* . . . F. Supp. . . . D.C., E.D. Penna., 1968.) Actually, the IRS cannot tell a corporation how much a man's salary can be. But the IRS can and does tell the corporation how much of the salary is deductible (how much will be entitled to that 50 percent subsidy). This is that part of the salary which is deemed *reasonable.* And to the extent that the subsidy is not allowed, the expenditure probably will be too costly. Its after-tax cost will be almost doubled.

Management's Limitations

Management must recognize the limitations of its own ability to make decisions: that is, decisions that will be afforded tax cognizance by the IRS. These limitations cover many areas, such as what is ordinary and necessary; how much should be paid in dividends if the accumulated-earnings tax is to be avoided; what intercompany price or fee structure may be used without the IRS being able to make a reallocation of income or expenses; whether the cost of a repair is currently deductible or must be spread over the remaining useful life of the asset being repaired. Management may think that it can discontinue its qualified pension or deferred profit-sharing plan at will; for if the company devised a plan and paid for it, the company also may drop it. Technically, the company *may* do so. But if this is done without the prior approval of the Commissioner of Internal Revenue, the tax consequences will be expensive—disqualification of the tax deduction for all years not yet closed by the statute of limitations.

Management's Options

Management's role in tax matters, however, is more than the defensive one of seeing that what appears on the tax return is not subject to disallowances or reallocations. In many areas, management may make valid and acceptable decisions as to a course of action with definite tax savings potential. Among these areas are capital structure, depreciation methods, inventory methods, compensation arrangements, tax-free reorganizations, involuntary divestitures, use of affiliates based upon economic reality, and abnormal obsolescence.

CAPITAL STRUCTURE

Management may choose any original capital structure for its corporation provided the structure claimed is the same as the one actually employed and the situation is real. Inasmuch as virtually all forms of interest are deductible and dividends are not, capital structure that makes use of debentures or other bonds results in lower taxable income. Some 30 yardsticks have been used by the courts to determine whether a corporation's "securities" really are bonds or stocks for this purpose. These tests also are useful in determining whether, upon corporate insolvency, stockholder advances to the company will be treated as bad debts (deductible) or as equity (capital loss).

If the necessary tests are met, an existing corporation's capital structure may be reshuffled as a tax-free recapitalization.

The corporation may make preferential tax treatment available to the purchasers of its securities by careful choice of the language, book, and tax treatment of the certificates issued. For example: Holders of bonds that really are bonds may have them redeemed on a capital basis, whereas stock that is redeemed by a corporation at a time when there are earnings and profits will result in dividends unless it can be shown that the redemption meets one of the "safe harbors" provided by the IRC, such as a redemption to pay death taxes or the complete elimination of a shareholder.

DEPRECIATION METHODS

Assets with determinable useful lives may be written off under any consistent method that correlates adjusted cost and remaining years of useful life, such as straight line or unit of production. In the case of such assets that are acquired new and that have a useful life of three years or more, an accelerated method may be elected, such as double declining balance or sum of the year's digits. Or, if the taxpayer can keep proper records to show that its replacement policy will provide for the retirement of assets at the end of their use cycle, the generally far more liberal guidelines established by the IRS for specific industries may be used. Depreciation on the tax return is not necessarily the same as depreciation on the books: The former is what the IRS is expected to allow, while the latter (generally higher) is what management believes is the proper figure.

INVENTORY METHODS

The taxpayer may choose any consistent inventory method provided that it conforms to the best accounting practice in the industry and clearly reflects income. Thus there is a choice which is not confined to the most common methods —cost, market, or lower of cost or market.

During an inflationary period or at any time when the replacement costs of inventory exceed original cost, the LIFO method will reduce taxable income by charging out goods at current prices rather than at the lower costs of the past. But the IRS will permit the use of LIFO only if the taxpayer agrees to use this method on all financial statements, reports to stockholders, credit reports, and the like.

COMPENSATION AGREEMENTS

In straight salary arrangements, management should not be concerned solely about the possible loss of part of the tax deduction because of unreasonableness. To a high-bracket executive or other employee, higher compensation means sharply rising surtaxes, and thus salary increases or large bonuses may net little to him. But management has available a variety of other compensation arrangements with preferential tax treatment to the recipients: qualified stock options, employee stock purchase plans, deferred compensation techniques, stock purchase warrants, qualified pension and/or deferred profit-sharing plans, group insurance procedures, split-dollar insurance, and various fringe benefits.

TAX-FREE REORGANIZATIONS

Ordinarily, if there is a disposition (including an exchange) of property, gain will be taxable to the extent that the value of what is received exceeds the adjusted cost of the property surrendered. But if the exchange can meet the rigid requirements of the IRC, the transaction may be effected on a tax-free basis. This may include such situations as a statutory merger or consolidation; the acquisition by one corporation, solely for voting stock, of stock of another corporation; the acquisition by a corporation, solely for voting stock, of substantially all the properties of another corporation; the transfer of assets to a controlled corporation for stock; a recapitalization; or a mere change in form or place of organization. Spin-offs and insolvency reorganizations are among the types of reorganization that receive tax-free treatment. If management is not satisfied with the tax treatment of a reorganization, with its carryover of basis, losses, and other characteristics, there are permissible steps to take in order to prevent the transaction from qualifying as a tax-free reorganization.

INVOLUNTARY DIVESTITURES

Ordinarily, a corporation may choose the time of a sale or other disposition of property so that it will take place when it is most advantageous to the corporation's tax situation. But this is not always possible. In the case of an involuntary conversion (destruction, theft, seizure, requisition, or condemnation of property), gain is not recognized to the extent that the proceeds from the insurance company or governmental agency involved are invested in replacement property by the last day of the taxable year following the year in which the property was converted involuntarily.

Gain or loss is not recognized if securities are disposed of in pursuance of an SEC order and the necessary conditions are observed. A taxpayer may elect to have the rules relating to involuntary conversions apply where property is disposed of under a Federal Communications Commission (FCC) order.

TIMING OF TRANSACTIONS

Management may control the taxable year in which a transaction is reported for Federal income tax purposes by such devices as the installment method of reporting, use of deferred sales techniques, or adoption of the long-term contract method.

Expenses may be related to income by the use of percentage leases or contingent compensation arrangements.

An accrual-basis corporation has a choice as to the year of deduction in the case of charitable contributions which are authorized in one taxable year but are paid within the first 75 days of the following taxable year.

WRITE-OFFS

Management has considerable discretion in the taxable year to be used for write-offs for abnormal obsolescence, abandonment, or demolition, provided the necessary paper documentation can be developed.

OTHER TECHNIQUES

Other tax alternatives available to management almost defy count. Among the more popular are the sale and lease-back, the gift and lease-back, and the lease of property with option to purchase.

Business Growth

Management generally regards the growth of the business as a natural process if not a compelling objective. It should be recognized that growth brings tax problems.

If earnings are retained to finance expansion, there is an accumulated-earnings tax problem. Unless it can be shown that dividends were not paid in the taxable year (or were paid in very modest amounts) because of the existence of a specific plan of expansion at year end, the corporation will be subject to the accumulated-earnings tax of up to 38.5 percent of undistributed earnings. The mere fact that the corporation intended to expand will not avoid tax; something must have been done about it, and there must be proof that management took this into account when dividends were considered.

Where a corporation retains earnings in order to enter upon a diversification program, the accumulated-earnings tax is almost certain. Legitimate retention of earnings to avoid this tax means retention for the needs of the business where the earnings had been accumulated; needs of any other business endeavor (the diversification program) would not be characterized as a need of the business. For this reason, diversification by a corporation with retained earnings must be financed through bank loans or new capital. Most of the acquisitions by conglomerates have been effected by new stock or debentures rather than through retained earnings.

If a corporation acquires another company that happens to have a net operating loss or any other tax credit or allowance that would have been unavailable except for the acquisition, the IRS is authorized to disregard the carryover or other tax advantages of the acquisition unless the taxpayer can prove that the avoidance or evasion of taxes was not a principal purpose of the acquisition.

A corporation may consider entering upon another type of activity or even a different form of the business in which it is engaged. Any expenses for the purpose of determining whether it is advisable to enter upon this other business that are incurred prior to the time of entering that business are nondeductible for tax purposes. Thus market surveys, feasibility studies, and even such routine expenditures as salaries and travel expenses are disallowed as *prebusiness expenses* if, at the time of their incurrence, the corporation was not engaged in that field of endeavor.

Tax Planning

All corporations (except for special forms such as a regulated investment company, insurance company, Western Hemisphere Trade Corporation [WHTC], and the like) are subject to the same provisions of the IRC. But all corporations need not be equally vulnerable to taxation. This is where tax planning comes in. The U.S. Supreme Court has said: "The legal right of a taxpayer to decrease the amount of what otherwise would be his taxes, or altogether avoid them, by means which the law permits, cannot be doubted." (*Gregory* v. *Helvering,* 293 U.S. 465, 1935.) Thus, if the means used are what the law permits, a corporation may engage in extensive tax planning for the avoidance of taxes. Should the corporation operate as an entity, or should it use one or 100 affiliates? Should equipment be purchased, or should it be rented? Should a casualty settlement with an insurance company be made now or next year? In what form should contributions be made? These are only a few random instances where tax planning pays off. A recent Court decision set the emphasis: "Simply because the plan is ingenious and would, if successful, allow taxpayers to avoid some Federal income taxes should not raise the judicial hackles." (*Priester Machinery Co., Inc. et al.* v. *United States,* 296 F. Supp. 604 D.C., W.D. Tenn., 1969.)

Becoming Tax-Oriented

Ideally, management should possess great tax awareness. Usually, however, this is not possible because the company's executives ordinarily have their greatest skills in sales, production, distribution, finance, or management. Yet business decisions cannot be made without practical awareness of the tax considerations. The solution is for management to discuss all its business plans and objectives with good tax counsel who will advise specifically how and where tax planning may be applied. Constant and thorough liaison with tax counsel alone will allow management to perform its real role: decision making in business matters.

Failure to follow this obvious course can be very expensive to the corporation and to management. If excessive taxes follow from management's choice of the wrong alternative, someone is likely to accuse the directors or officers of mismanagement: A well-managed company would not have paid unnecessary taxes. And there is ample precedent for realizing that if the corporation pays taxes that a well-managed corporation would not have had to pay, the members of the management team may be found by a court to be responsible *personally* to the company for its loss. In this day of the professional minority stockholder or the disenchanted junior stockholder in a closed family corporation, that is a very real hazard which only good liaison with tax counsel can avoid.

—*R. S. Holzman*

STATE AND LOCAL TAXES

State taxation is of major concern to any business engaged in interstate commerce. Many decisions with respect to methods of selling or the location of a warehouse, a branch office, or even a stock of goods may have significant tax consequences. Before establishing an office, plant, or warehouse or making sales or soliciting business in a state, a potential taxpayer should review the local laws and regulations that determine taxability.

The factors that may render a foreign seller liable for taxation or may give a taxing state jurisdiction to assert tax liability vary from state to state. It is therefore usually desirable to obtain professional advice with respect to a specific problem. A final decision often requires thorough examination of all the facts and circumstances in the particular case, and research into all applicable statutes, regulations, and cases.

The following criteria are employed in most states to determine taxability and can be used as guidelines: maintaining an office, including a listing in the telephone directory, listing the local office on a letterhead, or placing the company name on an office door; making contracts; employing capital; owning or leasing property; delivering goods; maintaining a stock of goods; furnishing technical assistance or installation; having one or more employees, agents, or officers; qualifying to do business; entering the state to sue; and holding cash, accounts receivable, securities, or other valuables.

It should be noted that a state's ability to collect taxes depends upon its ability to obtain jurisdiction over the taxpayer. A taxpayer may be able to ignore the claims of a state so long as he maintains no property or facilities within that state. However, when such a taxpayer does find it desirable to locate within the state at some future date, he may be faced with large claims for delinquent taxes, penalties, and interest.

Types of Taxes

A great variety of taxes is used by the states and their subdivisions. Some taxes are measured by income, others by value of capital stock, and still others by gross receipts, sales price, rent paid, or similar factors. Those most frequently applied to businesses selling goods in interstate commerce are described in the following paragraphs.

INCOME TAXES

In 1959 the U.S. Supreme Court ruled in the joint *Northwestern-Stockham* case (Minnesota and Georgia cases) that a net income tax could be imposed on profits earned exclusively in interstate commerce. Subsequent decisions by the Supreme Court made it appear that almost any type of activity within a particular state would cause the income of a business to be subject to taxation by that state.

Recognizing that these new rules placed an unreasonable burden on interstate commerce, Congress enacted the Interstate Income Tax Law, which provides that a state cannot tax income derived solely from interstate commerce if the only activity in the state is the mere solicitation of orders. Simultaneously, Congress provided for a study of the whole problem of state taxation of multistate business activities.

After four years of investigation and public hearings, a House Judiciary Subcommittee concluded that the present system of state taxation creates serious problems that it would be appropriate for Congress to attempt to resolve. Some of the more important reasons given were as follows: (1) the multiplicity of nonuniform state tax laws; (2) the possibility that the same income will be taxed by more than one state; (3) the cost of compliance (often in excess of tax liability).

In 1965 the subcommittee introduced as a bill the Interstate Taxation Act. Similar bills have been introduced in subsequent years, but in each case Congress has adjourned without acting. As a counterproposal to the pending Federal legislation, which might restrict state and local taxing powers, several states proposed their own laws. Some states adopted the Uniform Division of Income for Tax Purposes Act, others adopted the Multistate Tax Compact, and some adopted both. All these proposals were under consideration by Congress at the time this book was in preparation.

The Interstate Taxation Act provides for all income to be allocated by a two-factor formula, an average of the property and payroll factors.

Under the Uniform Division of Income for Tax Purposes Act, nonbusiness income is generally apportioned according to situs, and business income is to be apportioned using a three-factor formula. This formula is commonly known as the Massachusetts formula and is computed as follows:

$$\frac{\text{Property in state}}{\text{Property everywhere}} = \underline{\quad} \text{ percent}$$

$$\frac{\text{Payroll in state}}{\text{Payroll everywhere}} = \underline{\quad} \text{ percent}$$

$$\frac{\text{Sales in state}}{\text{Sales everywhere}} = \underline{\quad} \text{ percent}$$

$$\begin{array}{c} \text{Total percent} \\ \div 3 \\ \hline \end{array}$$

$$\text{Allocation factor} \quad = \quad \underline{\quad} \text{ percent}$$

The Multistate Tax Compact provides that a taxpayer may elect to allocate in the manner provided by the laws of the state or in accordance with the provisions of the Uniform Division of Income for Tax Purposes Act. In addition, it provides for an optional "short form" computation on the basis of a percentage of sales for any taxpayer who (1) is required to file a return; (2) is engaged in the state only in making sales; (3) does not own or rent real estate or tangible personal property in the state; and (4) has gross sales in the state not in excess of $100,000.

Each state would be required to adopt rates which would produce a tax approximately equal to the tax under the conventional "long form" method, usually .5 percent of gross sales in the states that have already adopted the compact.

SALES AND USE TAXES

The constitutionality of sales and use taxes has been established beyond any doubt. The foreign seller who makes contracts and delivers goods within the taxing state is clearly liable for the sales tax. If the goods are delivered outside the state, the sales tax generally does not apply except where the order was obtained within the state. A sales tax levied by the seller's state will apply whenever delivery is made within that state. A purchaser in a taxing state can ordinarily avoid the sales tax where the order is approved by the seller outside the state and delivery takes place outside the state.

Sales that cannot be reached by the sales tax are often subject to the use tax. The use tax is usually at the same rate as the sales tax and is imposed on the storage, use, or consumption of goods within a taxing state. Ordinarily, the seller is liable for collecting the use tax; but if he fails to do so, the purchaser becomes personally liable therefor.

A problem commonly arises when a buyer takes delivery and pays a sales tax on an item which he then transfers for use in another state where he must pay the use tax. Many states have enacted provisions to prevent such a burden on commerce; for example, granting a complete exemption or granting a credit where a sales or use tax has previously been paid.

Exemptions from sales tax are often provided for goods that are sold for resale or for machinery and equipment used exclusively in manufacturing, processing, or assembling. Most states have a myriad of rules and regulations governing the enforcement and collection of sales and use taxes. Reporting requirements often result in significant expenditures by taxpayers for record keeping, training, return preparation, and professional fees. Substantial additional time may be required for audits performed by the taxing jurisdiction.

CAPITAL STOCK TAXES

Many of the taxes applied to the value of capital stock require a division of tax base among states by methods similar to those used for income taxes. Some states have both a corporate income tax and a capital stock tax and use identical procedures for apportionment. In a number of states, a capital stock tax is imposed as a minimum alternative to the income tax.

The proposed Interstate Taxation Act previously discussed would require apportionment under the two-factor formula. It also provides that a domestic corporation can be taxed on its capital so long as the measure of tax includes no element of retained earnings.

In some cases, the tax on capital may be levied annually. Other states may require payment of a tax based on capital stock at the time the corporation qualifies to do business in the state and at the time of any subsequent increases in capital stock employed in the state.

GROSS RECEIPTS AND GROSS INCOME TAXES

Taxes on gross receipts and gross income are very similar to sales and use taxes, being measured by total sales price either on an individual sales basis or in the aggregate. A "gross receipts tax" is defined as "any tax, other than a sales tax, measured by gross volume of business without the allowance of any deduction which would, in effect, convert it into a tax on net income."

Apparent overtaxation of interstate commerce results from these taxes when a tax is imposed on production activities in the state of origin and on in-shipments by the state of destination; both types of taxes are generally upheld by the courts. As a result of the tax support in these situations that produce taxation at both ends of a sale, the interstate company is subject to multiple gross receipts taxation.

The gross receipts tax is ordinarily used only in special and limited circumstances—that is, where another, perhaps more preferable tax cannot be effectuated or in a situation where the tax may be competitively and lucratively imposed on exports from the state. The primary criticism of the tax is that its burdens fall indiscriminately and unfairly. One major inequity usually stressed by critics is that variations in ratios of profits from one business group to another are not taken into account. Another criticism is that it hinders the entry of new businesses, in the sense that they tend to have lower profit margins and would be in a less favorable position competitively to shift the tax in the form of higher prices.

OTHER TAXES

Other taxes which may be imposed by the states and their subdivisions include qualification, privilege and license fees, occupancy and rent taxes, real and personal property taxes, taxes on unincorporated businesses, and taxes on the value of intangible assets.

Administration

Many states have established full-time appointive commissions charged with the administration of the tax laws of the state, such as the Department of Taxation and Finance of New York.

Most states have transferred to the administrative body all revenue functions formerly vested in elected officials. However, corporate organization or qualification fees are usually administered by the Secretary of State. All tax administrative bodies maintain offices in the state capital for the state concerned, and correspondence concerning tax matters should be addressed to the director of tax administration.

Deficiency notices resulting from audits are ordinarily issued in a manner similar to Federal procedures. The taxpayer is usually given an opportunity to file a protest, to agree with the findings, or to request a conference (frequently through a protest). When the issue is one of law rather than fact which must eventually be settled by court action, it may be expeditious to bypass the procedures for hearings with the various levels of the tax administrative bodies.

—*M. J. Gowin and R. W. Saunders*

ACQUISITIONS AND DIVESTMENTS

Corporate mobility is setting the tone for business today. The phrase states a requirement for business and also characterizes the current business scene. The requirement is for a mobility that enables a company to respond quickly and effectively to technological and economic change and to new situations in its markets—all of which are occurring at a faster rate. As a characteristic, mobility suggests today's rapidly changing patterns of corporate forms and relationships. Multimillion-dollar companies are emerging in a relatively short span of years; small companies are bidding for giants; there are marriages between companies whose interests seem 180 degrees apart; and new techniques are appearing in acquisition finance and in regulations that deserve book-length studies in themselves. Some significant organization and management problems are related to this mobility and the high rate of acquisitions coupled with it. (The most recent yearly figures from the financial consulting firm of W. T. Grimm & Co., Chicago, show 6,107 corporate marriages for 1969, with approximately this figure forecast for the following year.)

This discussion is intended as a preliminary outline for managements contemplating buying another company or selling part of an existing business. It will consider acquisitions—through merger as the commonest form—from the starting point in basic company policy to the operational phasing-in of the company acquired.

Starting Point: A Plan and a Policy

The first step toward acquisitions is the most important and the most difficult because it involves a company's self-analysis. That step is to answer the question: What business is the company really in, and what special strengths does the company contribute to that business?

A superficial answer will not serve. If a company is now making specialized metal parts for vacuum cleaners, its horizons may indeed be limited. But perhaps its business is really metalworking, or labor-saving devices, or maintenance equipment, or marketing components to appliance manufacturers. If the company's final analysis will hold up under scrutiny from directors, shareholders, brokers, and the men in the tool room, management can legitimately ask, "Where do we go from here?"

The next step—well before deciding on the role of acquisitions in the company—is to develop a long-range plan based on a solid definition of the company's business.

The long-range plan should have two aims: to set objectives for growth and to spell out how those objectives are going to be achieved.

In setting achievable objectives in sales and earnings, the results of the company's self-analysis come into play again. What are the competitive strengths in management, technology, facilities? In products, personnel, and financial structure? What are the weaknesses? Next question: What can be achieved internally in the light of present strengths and weaknesses? And then: How does this achievement from present resources compare with the long-term objectives that have been set?

The answer to that question shows the gap between the company's potential and its goals and is a possible definition of objectives for acquisition. The company still has the option of launching new development programs inside to close the gaps. But can the gaps be closed more quickly and at less cost by buying what is needed? If so, the company is in the market for an acquisition—but not just any acquisition. An acquisition policy is needed to reflect the analysis of corporate strengths and weaknesses and guide the company in whichever acquisition route it follows.

For example, analysis may point to the management depth as a pronounced strength. The company might therefore focus on acquisitions with similar manufacturing and marketing requirements but not necessarily strong, continuing management. Or—to take a second example—analysis may show that dependence on a single product is a weakness. The objective then could be acquisitions that would diversify the product base. Either situation could route the company toward horizontal mergers (acquiring similar or complementary products or businesses) or toward vertical mergers (moving into the products of suppliers and customers).

In considering the vertical route, however, a company should carefully analyze the potential antitrust aspects. The Antitrust Division of the Justice Department has been giving more concentrated attention to vertical mergers, and this is a point to explore carefully with lawyers.

Even in horizontal mergers of very large companies, the Department of Justice is challenging mergers with new concepts of "potential reciprocity of purchasing" and "potential restraint of competition through mere size alone." It may be years before the final answers to these concepts are decided in the courts. In the meantime, mergers of large companies must be carefully appraised from the legal risk point of view.

As a third example: A company's self-analysis may underscore the breadth of its management. Then, perhaps, conglomerate acquisitions (unrelated businesses brought together under the general direction of professional managers at the top) can be considered. In this case, the route is neither horizontal nor vertical. It is toward the "free-form" organization of certain well-known conglomerates created and run by managerial generalists. This kind of manager is inclined to stress innovation and strategy for widely diversified growth and is unbound to conventional methods of running a business made up of closely related parts.

Enthusiasts of the conglomerate have hailed the free-form company and free-form management as the corporate system of the future. They maintain that the conglomerate system helps to channel capital to enterprises where it can be used more profitably and to maximize the effective use of cash flow of a business to achieve growth. It helps to activate stodgy management or to supplant management that is not doing the best job in shareholders' interests. The conglomerate, it is maintained, encourages more freedom and flexibility in corporate activity and thereby promotes a more competitive business climate.

On the other hand, some conglomerates have been criticized as rapidly built "houses of cards" lacking the stability to withstand a severe economic setback. They are viewed as too complicated to be managed effectively. Their methods of acquisition have been called disruptive and unethical, and their accounting methods misleading. They have been accused of being motivated by nothing more than the desire to achieve bigness.

There is evident bias in each point of view. Suffice it to say that the conglomerates that have appeared in recent years have produced some intriguing ideas in financing and management. Some of these ideas will prove useful in the future to business in general. But a lot of testing, particularly the test of time, lies ahead for companies taking the route of rapid growth through frequent and highly diversified acquisitions.

Conglomerate-minded or not, the management that is planning an acquisition must work from the kind of policy that, laying out corporate strengths and weaknesses in relation to potential acquisitions, gives management the concept with which to approach each individual acquisition prospect. Management must approach the prospect with a clear-cut idea of what it can contribute to the acquisition over the long term and, in turn, how the acquisition will improve total performance. This concept is essential in selling the prospect on the idea of merger. Later, it is essential in evaluating the contribution of the acquired unit.

Organization for Acquisition

With plans well laid, management now needs to organize for action. First and foremost, the chief executive should be directly involved and must have a thorough understanding of all the complex steps ahead. He is the one who must sell his own board and the head of the potential acquisition. He is usually the only one who can do this effectively because he is the only executive with the authority to make the fast decisions often required and to follow through with action.

Remember that the first concern in the mind of the head of the proposed acquisition is to avoid creating shock waves that could destroy morale and disrupt operations throughout his company without any positive results. He will be interested only in talking with the top man, and talking in relative privacy. His next concern is, "What's in it for my company and for my stockholders?" This is where the chief executive draws on the homework that he and his staff will have done. Such information not only provides answers; it shows that he is serious enough to have prepared in advance.

INTERNAL SUPPORT

The chief financial officer needs to be involved at the outset; he has a continuing role as a sounding board for the president and as a source of technical information and counsel. One of his primary concerns is with the tax aspects of any proposed acquisition. The other concern is the financing of the acquisition—the right combination of cash and debt or equity securities, such as bonds and common stock. A great deal of the company's financial future is dependent on the type of securities—the commitment—involved in any acquisition of consequence.

It is imperative that the financial officer be an integral part of the long-range planning for acquisitions even before there is a prospect on the horizon. He must have the company's debt, credit, and equity situation in order well before the chief executive enters into a negotiation.

In a number of companies, the chief executive and the financial officer handle virtually all the acquisition activity, although they are assisted by outside professionals of different kinds. In other organizations, a corporate development or corporate planning vice president with a large acquisition staff has been utilized. They spend full time refining the areas of interest, researching possibilities that may fit with the company's criteria, and concluding negotiations begun by the president. Some companies have put this responsibility in their accounting or legal departments. In turn, executives in these areas will draw on other talent in the company to help evaluate the fit with the prospect's products, markets, and technology and to develop a detailed profile of its management and operating policies.

Whatever the staffing, it should always be viewed as support for the beginning and continuing participation of the man at the head of the company. He carries the responsibility for coordinating each of these efforts, weighing the findings, and establishing a final evaluation of the prospect in relation to the long-range plan he has created.

OUTSIDE EXPERTS

No matter what the exact internal arrangement, much specialized support is available from outside experts retained by the company.

Legal counsel—internal, external, or both—is essential in the activity between the announcement of agreement in principle and the signing of the contract. Antitrust implications, SEC requirements, product warranties, and patents suggest the many areas where painstaking examination and up-to-the-minute legal knowledge are required.

The acquiring company's public accounting firm should be enlisted to determine proper evaluation of the prospect's assets and liabilities. From this assistance emerges that specific accounting treatment most effective for each acquisition. Frequently, the accounting firm is also used for the audit that confirms the estimated value of the company under study.

When acquiring a business in a purchase for cash or debt securities, outside specialized appraisers should be called in to establish current market values of assets and thus establish a current basis for tax purposes. A bonus from this appraisal is substantiation of the prospect's assets and liabilities. Many acquisitions have hung fire, even after shareholder approval, because of new and disquieting information that affected evaluation.

Selection of outside counsel and service should parallel development and refinement of the company's long-range plan. Professional relationships should be established with a prolonged association in mind. The outside members of the team need to understand the route and objectives of the company as clearly as the staff executives on the payroll.

With policy, plan, and objectives set, financial tools ready for use, and an organization in place and primed, the company is prepared to undertake an acquisition.

The Process of Acquisition

It is not unusual for a company amenable to being bought to put itself on the market through discreet calls to several company presidents. What is unusual is such a company that also fits with the carefully considered plans of those presidents. The company with a well-conceived plan for acquisition is going to act and waste no time waiting by the telephone.

One excellent source for acquisition prospects lies within a company's own management. Its purchasing and marketing departments have a good feel for the strengths and weaknesses of supplier and customer companies. If they know their company's acquisition criteria, they can focus their knowledge and produce a well-screened list of prospects for future scrutiny.

Investment bankers are another excellent source for prospects. They have a very broad view of the corporate scene and should be kept apprised of a company's acquisition interests. If the investment banker can bring two companies together, some very sizable fees on consummation of the merger will have made it well worth his while.

Similarly, commercial bankers are not reluctant to add a new account. They are frequently willing to draw on their market knowledge and contacts for a transaction that could benefit both parties in the transaction as well as the bank.

For a fee keyed to the amount of the completed transaction, some acquisition consultants will step into the search. They will go further if requested and undertake the complete negotiation or be available for counsel on a retainer.

If the company is publicly owned—as most acquiring companies are—another source is found in friendly analysts, from institutions and brokerage houses, who are aware of the company's interests through security analyst presentations and interviews with company executives.

There are also acquisition brokers, a group which has multiplied in proportion to the fast rise in acquisitions. As with any new and popular service, the practitioners cover a wide spectrum of capability and ethical practice. Caution is indicated in contracting for acquisition brokerage service, especially with respect to the basis for the fee.

MAKING THE PROPOSAL

From the list of prospects produced from these sources, the head of Company *A*, who wants to buy, decides on Company *X* as the most promising prospect. If he knows the president of Company *X*, a telephone call or private lunch is a most acceptable means of broaching the subject of acquisition. If there is no personal acquaintance, the door can be opened in a number of other ways. Mutual friends, customers, suppliers, bankers, and lawyers can introduce the two in such a way that a telephone call from one president to another will not come as a complete surprise.

Personal acquaintance between the chief executives may carry an advantage that must be established where it does not exist: thorough knowledge of what makes the head of Company *X* tick. Hobbies, civic interests, magazine profiles, business and social background, his relationships with his board of directors and shareholders—all of these are homework assignments for the president of Company *A*.

He must also, from the outset, have a thorough knowledge of the proposal he would like to have accepted, the possible options, the form the transaction would take, and the reasons why all of these form a package that Company *X* should be pleased to get. Drawing on his rigorous analysis of his company's strengths, he will know where they will add to the capabilities of the company to be acquired. If, for example, he has a strong marketing organization and the courted company is weak in marketing—but is selling to the same markets—he can predict how much sales volume can be added on the acquired company's products.

The contacts between the chief executives do not necessarily lend themselves to structured interviews. President *A* must be extremely sensitive to the nuances perceived in the conversations. They will tell him which areas to press and which to avoid. They will indicate some promise or a pitfall that wasn't apparent before. Deft response to the signals from President X will establish the rapport essential when the two men start working together if the acquisition is completed; for, in most cases, the retention of existing management is a goal of the acquiring company.

President A's homework carries another important advantage besides the information and assurance it has given him. He is able to make a strong impression on President X simply because he is so thoroughly informed and genuinely interested in Company X. The man he is talking with has been busy operating his company. He has not had the time to do the research demonstrated by President A. An objective, incisive, and free evaluation of his company often comes as a revelation and a pleasure.

EARLY NEGOTIATIONS

But President X may say "no." President A's tack is to make sure that the answer is a "no" for the time being only. He has to leave an opportunity for President X to reconsider when Company A makes the first of its follow-up contacts that may continue over a period of years.

If President X says "no" and puts an exclamation mark after it, President A is only human if his thoughts jump to a tender offer. He will be well-advised to go slow. He should be especially cautious if his company has only started out on the merger route.

In a tender offer, Company A would publicly announce its willingness to buy at a specified price the shares of Company X which are offered—or "tendered"— by the shareholders of Company X. The tender offer price is set at an attractive figure above the current market price of the stock.

Not surprisingly, Company X may have a strong reaction to this, and a proxy contest may ensue. This involves competition between the two companies for the votes of the Company X shareholders, in the form of proxies, to be counted at the official meeting where the issue will be resolved. Such contests are generally well publicized, and usually to the detriment of one party or the other.

Win or lose, a tender offer and proxy contest can be expensive. They can give a cast to a company's reputation that is not always an asset in future negotiations. At the same time, a tender offer—particularly a "friendly" tender supported by Company X management—can be useful where the desired form of an acquisition involves cash. The use of cash to acquire some portion of the stock in a tender would reduce the dilution of earnings per share which would be experienced in an exchange of stock between the two companies in a merger.

It is also possible that Company X might tacitly invite a tender offer because of an internal situation or a takeover threat from another and less desirable source. This isn't a common situation. Tender offers carry pretty high voltage; they should be considered only after a careful review of Company X's value to Company A and the other options open to Company A, such as a more prolonged courtship with Company X or contact with a company that is second choice.

THE FINANCIAL PACKAGE

To return to the conversation between the two presidents: If the general idea of acquisition meets with approval, this is the point where President A lays out his proposal for the method of acquisition.

As noted earlier, the financial officer of Company A has seen to it that his president is well prepared to negotiate: Company A has head room to incur more debt, adequate shares outstanding, authorization for special types of securities that may be required, and—hopefully—a stock valuation high enough to avoid appreciable dilution from additional common shares or the conversion of preferred stock into common shares.

The method proposed for financing the acquisition must as nearly as possible serve the best interests of both parties, capitalizing on the financial strengths of each and avoiding stress on the weaknesses. Therefore, the method will vary with almost every case.

By way of illustration, here are three brief examples of typical Company A and Company X situations and methods of financing that are feasible for the circumstances:

1. Company X has a large amount of cash or liquid assets and no significant debt. Company A has a high proportion of debt in its capitalization but is blessed with a high ratio between its annual earnings per share and the current price of its stock. (The price-earnings ratio is a standard measurement that would be used by the merger parties in evaluating the stocks involved.) In this case, Company A will wish to use stock for the acquisition. First, its stock—carrying a high price-earnings ratio—is a very appealing and negotiable commodity; second, cash from Company X can decrease Company A's relatively high debt.

2. Company X is closely held, but Company A is publicly held and traded on a national exchange. An exchange of stock rather than cash might well appeal to the shareholders of Company X because the transaction would be free of capital gains taxes and because it would take them into a stock that is freely traded and thus diversify their estates over a period of time.

3. Company A has relatively little debt and a comparatively small amount of stock outstanding. Company X has good earnings and the potential for an even higher return. Company A may elect to use a debt security, such as a debenture, and pay the interest on this type of bond from X's earnings. The gain would be realized when future earnings increased over the fixed-interest commitment on the debentures.

Whatever offer is made may well be met by a counterproposal. Consultation within the respective companies and subsequent conferences between A and X may consume several weeks or more. This parleying can be trying to the patience; but it must be conducted so that even if no acquisition results, the parties involved remain corporate friends.

STEPS TO COMPLETION

When Company *A* and Company *X* ultimately come to a meeting of the minds on general terms, the practice is to announce an agreement in principle. Frequently, the news release states that "terms of the proposed acquisition were not disclosed," or that "the acquisition is for a combination of cash and stock." There is no justification for making a public commitment to an agreement that has a long way to go before final resolution.

The definitive merger agreement, or the terms of acquisition spelled out in the proxy statement for shareholders, is the end result of a prolonged effort over several months. Many of the steps taken are required by good business practice: examination of contracts in force, analysis of pending lawsuits, and the security of patents involved. There are other steps to be taken in connection with state and Federal agencies, notably the SEC filing on any securities proposed, the response to the SEC's exceptions, and an opinion from the IRS on the tax implications of the transaction.

Parallel with these steps are the continuing negotiation on matters of organization and management and the mutual education on each other's business that takes place right up to the signing. With the additional time required for proxy solicitation and shareholder approval, the acquiring company will be doing well if it completes its acquisition within six months.

A rough guess as to how many proposed mergers actually work out would be 10 percent or less. Nonetheless, the current high volume of negotiation for acquisitions would seem to be, on balance, a positive thing for U.S. business. To produce this volume of negotiation, thousands of companies have analyzed themselves and others with greater care than ever before. They have traded this information through negotiation. They have traded operating ideas and technology in the process and established ties that did not exist before. Each participant in the acquisition process knows his business better and is more confident of his future course for having had the experience. At the very least, if a company doesn't want to be taken over, it has been put on its guard; the protective measures it needs to take have been spelled out in very realistic terms. All the flurry apart, there is evidence of more muscle in U.S. business because of the exercise so many companies are taking, voluntarily or involuntarily.

Living Together After Acquisition

The final agreement signed by the parties in a merger is a mere technicality from the standpoint of operating the new, enlarged enterprise. Success of the operation depends entirely on how well the acquiring company applies what it has learned, in the course of its research and negotiation, about the corporate personality and the people of Company *X*.

COMMUNICATION

In the first stages of the new relationship, this application is essentially a matter of communication.

The primary need is for reassurance at all levels of the acquired company. The president of that company will have kept his people pretty well informed in the course of negotiations—or should have. With help from the acquiring company, he will have sold them on the merger in terms of the interests of each large group—hourly workers, salesmen, executives, technicians. But the full reaction of these groups is delayed until the marriage is an accomplished fact. This reaction must be anticipated by the acquiring company; a well-conceived program of communication must be ready for launching immediately on conclusion of the acquisition.

One aim of the program will be to spell out and relate to each group the terms of the merger that cover autonomous operation, continuation of management and general policies, handling of employee benefits, and seniority.

A second aim will be to introduce and interpret the companies to each other— how their areas of expertise complement one another, how their products and markets fit, how the combined capability of the two companies is greater than the resources of either one alone.

A third aim that underlies the whole communication program is to demonstrate the genuine interest and concern of the acquiring company for the new unit it has taken on. This may sound a little naïve in connection with the union of multimillion-dollar companies. On the contrary, communicating this attitude is even more important in the large and intricately structured company and, of course, may be more difficult to achieve. But unless a negative response within such a company is allayed, it can grow to critical proportions almost before it has been observed, and in the process other programs needed for unifying the companies can be seriously jeopardized.

Where overall communication programs have been most successful, they have involved the personal participation of the chief executive and the top operating staff. Give-and-take between these men and their counterparts, and exposure to the acquired company at large, are critical steps in establishing the mutual understanding and respect the joint enterprise must have.

PREPARING FOR CHANGE

Concurrent with the communication effort, an evaluation and melding process is under way at a number of levels. Corporate and departmental executives are matching people. Immediate financial problems are being resolved. Critical operating problems are taken in hand. Wherever possible, these things should be done within the framework of the acquired company's policies and without radical change. The object is to establish a climate in which any new operating programs that are required can be introduced and supported. This may not come for a year or more after the union. In that time, management is adding still more facts and impressions to its fund of knowledge. The operating programs proposed for the future should be periodically reviewed and refined in light of this knowledge. An example is the coordination of the distribution networks of the two companies. This area may involve long-standing relationships with dealers, an asset not to be jeopardized by abrupt change.

It can be that, at this stage, examination of the acquired company indicates problems in one of its divisions that do indeed require radical change for solution. One of the executives studying the situation suggests, "In the long run, we'd be better off to sell that division." He may have a point.

Divestments

The executive develops his point along these lines: The division's principal product is a consumer item. The balance of the acquired company's business—more than 90 percent—is devoted to the same range of industrial markets served by the parent company. Because the consumer product division has been running pretty much on its own in an industrial market environment, it has not had the necessary support to promote and distribute its product effectively; but it has kept the product up to date and maintained a modest share of market as a result of the quality of its product.

Argument comes to an end when the executive takes out the corporate long-range plan and says, "Show me precisely where that division with its consumer market assets fits with our markets, our technology, or our management capabilities." No one can show him where.

If a corporate unit is not playing to the basic strengths of the corporation, if the unit cannot be turned into a contributor without spending an excessive amount of money and management time—then a logical course is to sell that unit and put the proceeds to work in the corporation's real business.

Very likely, to sell the division will be to do it a favor. In the example used, the division had a valuable but handicapped product. Another company, geared to consumer marketing and distribution, could build that product to its full potential and would be willing to pay a fair price for the opportunity.

The process of divestment is in many respects parallel to the acquisition process. The basic decision is tied to the company's long-range plan—what its business really is, and how that business is to be developed. Internal and external aid in locating a buyer are the same sources useful in finding acquisitions. The chief executive and the financial officer and the company's attorneys and accountants must be involved for much the same reasons as in an acquisition.

There must be communication with all levels of the unit to be sold as soon as an agreement on the sale has been reached. Informing and reassuring the unit's executives and employees that their interests are protected is essential in maintaining the value of the unit through completion of the sale.

Actually, the principal difference between an acquisition and a divestment is an emotional one. A potential acquisition can generate a lot of enthusiasm within a company; it is a positive move that bespeaks much promise. A divestment *can be* just as positive a move for a company. But many seasoned executives are hard-pressed to relinquish one of their corporate children that might just still have a chance with a little more time and patience.

Emotion is about the only element that a significant long-range corporate plan cannot accommodate.

In sum, the essence of a successful acquisition and of a successful divestiture is initiative. In both cases there is a salable commodity to be presented to a carefully chosen prospect. The principles of aggressive, ethical salesmanship prevail with—most emphatically—the guidance and support of a well-conceived plan and technical expertise.—*E. W. Smith*

PRESENTATION AND INTERPRETATION
OF OPERATING RESULTS

The function of management, basically, follows in definable sequence. The manager must first obtain relevant information and employ this information to determine a course of action; make known his decision; and follow up to insure that the decision is implemented. With the exception of the decision-making portion, the sequence is almost entirely a process of communication and information handling.

Reports for Management Use

Because financial considerations permeate all areas of company operations and the success or failure of the business as a whole is measured in financial terms, it is clear that financial data are operating results. Further, one of the primary responsibilities of the financial management function is to provide a system of financial reporting so that all members of management may have a means of controlling operations and be kept informed of the company's position.

OBJECTIVES OF MANAGEMENT

Organization structure and information requirements are inherently related. Reporting for evaluation purposes cannot be at odds with the organizational structure.

With revised structures necessarily come new jobs, new responsibilities, new decision-making authority, and reshaped reporting relationships. New demands for financial information—information which may be lacking in existing systems—are created by these factors. Many firms, therefore, may well be suffering a financial information crisis without fully realizing it.

In addition to the span of control, which is the personal organizational relation between a manager and his subordinates, a new dimension is developing in management which may be referred to as the "reach of an executive." This is the ability of the manager to reach down through the management layers and diversity of an enterprise to locate problem situations. Effective reach of the individual manager is determined by the information system at his command. Again, this does not mean exclusively accounting records but rather the facts on who is doing what in the organization—that is, the current picture of the flow of action occurring within the business and the financial impact of that flow.

THE INCOME STATEMENT

Traditionally, the income statement, or profit-and-loss statement, has been considered *the* statement of operations. The statement details revenues, expenses, and net income or loss to reflect the results of operations for the defined accounting period. The income statement is presented in a number of different ways in published reports, some of which are prescribed for regulated industries. Sample income statements appear under "General Accounting and Financial Statements" (page 4·19).

LIMITATIONS OF ACCOUNTING DATA

Operating management has tended to consider financial information exclusively in terms of accounting systems and reports such as the statement of income. On the other hand, the limitations of accounting information for use in operating reports may be considerable. For example, conventional accounting reports cause confusion in the minds of many nonfinancially trained managers because of arbitrary treatment of inventories, depreciation, and allocated overhead expenses. Accounting reports in general describe what has happened within a firm and omit data such as information about the future, data expressed in nonfinancial terms such as share of market, and information dealing with external conditions. In short, inadequacy may well result from the accounting system's primary purpose of insuring the fulfillment of management's responsibilities to shareholders, the government, and other groups rather than facilitating financial planning and control of operations.

All of these specific elements, nevertheless, are essential for effective financial management. It is apparent, then, that although accounting systems exist primarily to meet company internal needs, this is often an unreasonable and unfulfilled expectation because accounting reports rarely focus on critical success factors which are nonfinancial in nature.

FLASH REPORTING

Management reporting for operating results should be limited to basic significant factors presented in a form to expedite decision making and control. Results should be presented in recognizable terms and formats in order to best communicate the information to the operating level. One effective technique is a flash (quick) status report covering abbreviated performance data. This type of report pinpoints the highlights of the current period by comparisons with past performance and future predictions as well as nonfinancial data. It may or may not include the profit-and-loss statement and balance sheet.

RESPONSIBILITY REPORTING

The operating reporting system must be closely related to the actual management process in order to effectively serve the management function of monitoring and evaluating financial results. Since the performance of people makes up the key element in this process—individuals responsible for performing tasks, incurring costs, and generating revenues—the approach to reporting operating results must be in terms of key people in the organization. In other words, the reporting system should be tailored to the actual organization and requires the fixing of individual responsibility or accountability for the results of operations.

The responsibility accounting approach recognizes that conventional reporting does not lend itself to effective control, and for evaluation and control purposes individuals are held responsible only for those operating factors over which they exercise control. In some industries the responsibility reporting concept must tie together a number of other required reporting subsystems, many of which are irrelevant for operating control purposes. In order to provide for the presentation of meaningful operating results, responsibility reporting focuses on responsibility centers and controllable revenues and costs. Basically, this approach is effective because it is people-oriented, employs computer techniques, and facilitates management by exception by specifically addressing itself to answering these questions: "Who?" "What?" "Where?" and "How much?" An example of the differences of the reporting of operating results for organizational purposes, as opposed to accounting considerations, illustrates this concept.

Organizational expense reporting. An effective financial information approach consists of reporting systems for the control of expenses and the reporting of profitability. To effectively manage expenses, it is necessary to know who is responsible for incurring various types of expenses and to evaluate whether the amounts actually spent are in accordance with management objectives. Organizational expense reporting, then, is based on the following key elements: (1) reporting of actual operating expenses on the basis of (*a*) *who* was responsible for the expense, (*b*) *where* the expense was incurred, (*c*) *what* the type of expense was, (*d*) *how much* the expense was; (2) comparison of actual expenses with planned expenses; (3) identification of significant variances for management review and analysis; and (4) summarization of expenses along organizational lines. Expenses for each management level must be identified by each cost center as well as by classification and reported to each responsibility center. (See Exhibit 4.23.)

Accounting information reporting. At the same time, in this example, accounting information pertaining to operating expenses is needed for the preparation of financial statements as well as certain external reports required for regulatory purposes. The accuracy and validity of all source reporting obviously must be controlled to insure that all accounting and management reports are reliable and meaningful for planning and control purposes. The accounting system processes all journal entry transactions for balance sheet accounts and profit-and-loss accounts as well as operating expenses, which means that the accounting reports include all financial information on a company/account level.

Accounting reporting, as contrasted with organizational reporting, encompasses (1) reporting of all accounting transactions on a sequential basis for cash receipts, cash disbursements, and journal entries; (2) reporting of all accounting transactions on a company/account distribution basis; and (3) reporting of accounting information by statutory expense classification and product line for regulated industries.

Key-Factor Reporting

Regardless of size, companies need more and better financial information to keep attention focused on the factors controlling profitability and competitive strength. In the past decade, growth, diversification, mergers, and decentralization have increased management's dependence on financial and statistical reports, trend charts, and similar forms of formal intelligence. Without such tools, management is hard pressed to know where the business is headed, how each major division is performing, and what new opportunities or trouble spots are developing.

Exhibit 4.23

ORGANIZATIONAL EXPENSE REPORTING

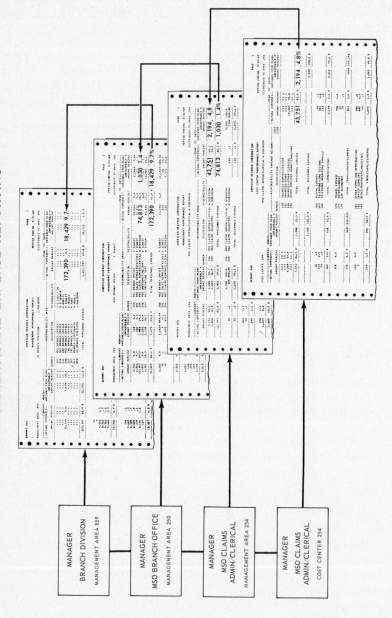

THE BASIC INDICATOR APPROACH

In the face of this need, techniques to make management's job easier and more effective are also necessary. The goal of the key-factor approach is to hammer out for each level of management a relatively few basic indicators that measure and reflect significant elements of performance simply, understandably, and forcefully.

Such control facilitates management's job in a number of ways: (1) It facilitates delegation by promoting common understanding of the key factors to be weighed in evaluating performance; (2) the information structure permits top executives to maintain adequate control of overall results without getting into day-to-day details; (3) the controls are a means of maintaining a proper balance between immediate and long-term problems by providing a mechanism to prevent short-term demands from unduly diverting managerial attention. In short, controls help management to run its job instead of being run by them.

While the need for control and its benefits may vary according to company size, small companies as well as large ones can profit from utilizing such tools as an important part of its approach to management. The heart of the key-factor approach involves thinking through overall financial planning and control needs. The process centers attention on identifying the competitive and economic forces at work in the business; determining the important jobs to be done; setting goals and standards; measuring actual performance; and holding managers accountable for results. In summary, the job of developing profit-building management controls involves identifying the key factors to be planned and controlled, setting standards of performance for each of these factors, and developing presentation techniques that make related financial information easy to use and understand.

IDENTIFYING KEY FACTORS

The first step in providing for the meaningful presentation and interpretation of operating results is to isolate the critical factors on which the success of the business depends. For most businesses, these factors will ordinarily be no more than four to six in number. They are the activities or aspects of the operation that have a major impact not only on short-term profits but also on long-term growth and competitive strength. These are significant factors, the breakdown of which for a sustained period would impair earnings or industry position, or at worst, put the firm out of business. Companies achieving the greatest advances in information analysis have consistently been those that have developed systems that are selective and have focused on the strengths and weaknesses of the firm with respect to its acknowledged success factors.

Since acknowledged success factors are key functions which must be performed exceedingly well for a company to be successful, the information developed must be discriminating and selective. Primary examples of the key-factor concept for major industries are the automobile industry (styling, efficient dealer organization, and tight control of manufacturing costs); food processing (new product development, good distribution, and effective advertising); life insurance (development of agency management personnel, effective control of clerical operations, and innovation in creating new types of policies).

The second step is to break each key factor into its profit-making components: the important elements of performance that have to be controlled individually to assure satisfactory overall results. Notwithstanding differences from company to company, a number of key control areas are common to most industries. A checklist of key areas would include (1) financial position, (2) marketing effectiveness, (3) quality of product or service, (4) cost performance, (5) creativity, (6) personnel sources, (7) payback from investment, and (8) overall performance.

SETTING PERFORMANCE STANDARDS

Effective control is built on the basis of determining how well a job is being performed. No informational tools have control value unless they contain the basis for measurement or evaluation. Following the identification of the critical elements of performance, these elements must be used to set the standards to be achieved. Goals must not be merely hopeful statements of intention or informal predictions; rather, they must represent the end results that the organization will gear its efforts toward and spend funds to achieve.

Target setting should go beyond cost-and-income planning based on the annual profit plan. The idea is to develop measurements or evaluation criteria for every important element of performance affecting short- and long-term profits. These should be expressed in terms of what is to be achieved or the conditions that will exist if performance is outstanding. A small, progressive appliance manufacturer, for example, has set standards for inventory turnover, facilities utilization, product returns, and delivery performance, all of which impact directly on financial results.

Another example is the approach to the control of personnel costs by measuring the effective hires rather than the gross number of hires for evaluating the personnel function. This measurement is derived by dividing the employment costs of hires for the period by the number of original hires still with the company a given number of months later. If the highest turnover area is in the zero-to-six-months service group, the number of hires on the payroll six months later will be used. The point is that while these measures may be difficult to establish, the elements of performance which are most difficult to measure by routine techniques may well be the very ones that have the greatest bearing on the long-term financial success of the firm.

Formalizing Financial Information Programs

Successful firms have found that information programs must be formalized. Such a program involves five steps: (1) Identify the types of financial information needed to operate the business successfully; (2) assign the information responsibility to a function or individual at an authoritative level in the organization; (3) determine the individual information needs of specific functions so that each element receives the right amount of information; (4) ascertain what information-handling and -processing equipment and personnel are available in the organization and what, if any, must be added; (5) draw up policies and procedures to establish the information program as a regular operating function.

ROLE OF INFORMATION SPECIALIST

With the exception of the decision-making portion of the management process, the sequence is almost entirely a process of communication and information handling to which EDP techniques are ideally suited. Since new and better information will be provided only when the form and kind of information are defined by management, the information specialist becomes a diagnostician. His role is to aid in the design of a discriminating reporting system which can provide relevant financial data in a form usable at the appropriate level of decision. The staff specialist, therefore, must assist in determining the measures of performance required and subsequently select and analyze masses of data and present the findings to management in everyday language and in a readily understandable form.

The location of this formal responsibility within the corporate structure may vary. Exhibit 4.24 shows an approach taken by a financial services company

Exhibit 4.24

ORGANIZATION AND RESPONSIBILITIES OF THE CORPORATE INFORMATION SPECIALIST

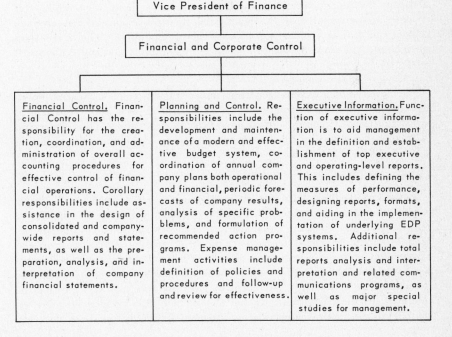

Vice President of Finance

Financial and Corporate Control

Financial Control. Financial Control has the responsibility for the creation, coordination, and administration of overall accounting procedures for effective control of financial operations. Corollary responsibilities include assistance in the design of consolidated and company-wide reports and statements, as well as the preparation, analysis, and interpretation of company financial statements.

Planning and Control. Responsibilities include the development and maintenance of a modern and effective budget system, coordination of annual company plans both operational and financial, periodic forecasts of company results, analysis of specific problems, and formulation of recommended action programs. Expense management activities include definition of policies and procedures and follow-up and review for effectiveness.

Executive Information. Function of executive information is to aid management in the definition and establishment of top executive and operating-level reports. This includes defining the measures of performance, designing reports, formats, and aiding in the implementation of underlying EDP systems. Additional responsibilities include total reports analysis and interpretation and related communications programs, as well as major special studies for management.

which includes this function within the responsibilities of its financial and corporate control section under the vice president of finance.

LINE AND STAFF REQUIREMENTS

The concept of "control" as described here helps other people in the organization control the operations assigned to them by providing measurable and meaningful analysis. Control, as used in this sense, seeks to impel action through crystal-clear analysis. The objective of the staff information function in providing clear and measurable facts showing where emphasis is needed is to bring about action by the line authorities. While one large and successful service firm, for example, defines "control" as a function, not a one-man job, it assigns a field controller full time in each regional office to function as an expert in transmitting what the figures are saying to the person who is actually responsible for making the figures go up or down. The field controller in this environment is the expert on what needs attention in order to attain control, not on taking action, which is the responsibility of the line manager.

The difference in the scope of financial information provided to line management as opposed to that provided to staff is clearly illustrated by the responsibility reporting concept referred to earlier. Line managers are specifically interested in "who," "where," "what," and "how much" for the purpose of taking direct action.

On the other hand, functional areas within the insurance management structure, for example, represent individuals having corporatewide accountability for operations of a functional nature such as underwriting, claims, and operating. Although the functional area managers do not have direct responsibility for activities at various levels of the organization, they are responsible for corporate policies and thus have influence and a secondary responsibility. These managers are interested in the performance of various responsibility and cost centers as it relates to the "whys" of variance developed, as well as the line managers' programs to deal with variances.

Functional or staff expense reporting under this concept encompasses reporting of actual expenses corporatewide for all functional areas and comparison of actual functional expenses with planned functional expenses. The relationship of organization reporting, functional reporting, and variance exception reporting is illustrated in Exhibit 4.25.

PRESENTATION TECHNIQUES

In the final analysis, the objective is to insure that the outlined process for corporate financial control really takes place. In field operations, this may be an integral part of a monthly "profit-and-loss" meeting program to review the responsibility center reports received by the field, with upward evaluation and reporting by means of a brief monthly letter. The scope and manner of conducting these meetings, as well as those invited to participate, vary considerably from company to company. At the plant level, the meetings will probably be conducted by the plant controller and may include unit foremen. In other decentralized operations, the regional management staff invited may not go below

Exhibit 4.25

RELATIONSHIP OF ORGANIZATIONAL EXPENSE REPORTING, FUNCTIONAL EXPENSE REPORTING, AND VARIANCE EXCEPTION REPORTING

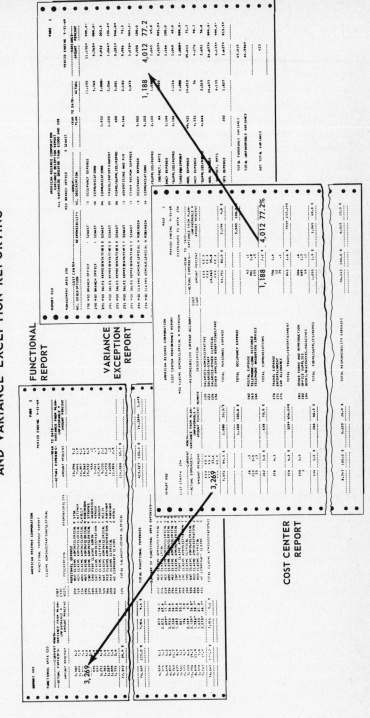

FUNCTIONAL REPORT

VARIANCE EXCEPTION REPORT

COST CENTER REPORT

the department manager level. At the corporate level, such meetings may require the presence of only the corporate staff for the purpose of evaluating field activities, which may be performed by means of a presentation by the home office executive information staff (Exhibit 4.24).

A number of advances have been made in handling information for both types of meetings. Much helpful information on arranging and conducting meetings and up-to-date presentation techniques is available from both projector manufacturers and other suppliers. Several of these manufacturers conduct courses in the development and use of visual aids for which no attendance fees are charged. Several excellent books cover financial communications programs for management. Numerous consulting firms deal exclusively with the meeting and decision-room environment, management report planning, information display systems, and graphic report development. Seminars are offered on how to make successful visual presentations using financial data.

As to the vehicle for the presentation, most studies have shown that, by reducing the information to visual form, difficulties bearing on varying degrees of knowledge, background, purpose, and interest can be more effectively overcome. In any event, determining the message and defining the audience at the outset are essential. Deciding whether the material will be a one-time presentation or is to be developed for repeated use is also of highest importance. Selecting among the categories of visuals (graphs versus tabulated figures) will aid in the choice of the proper visual medium (flip chart versus slide projector) as well as the type of presentation (free delivery versus script).

The following suggestions are made to insure that the desired communication with the audience actually takes place when operating results are presented: (1) Preview the material; make familiarity with the content certain, regardless of whether script or free delivery is employed. (2) Let the audience know what is going to be covered and what they will see and hear; thus they can alert themselves to the points that will be made. (3) Discuss the material after presenting it to make sure the basic message got through. (4) Leave some printed material with your audience; a printed reminder will reinforce the message.

IMPROVING PRESENTATION AND INTERPRETATION

The final step in the improvement of management control is to develop financial information presentation techniques to make it easy for nonaccounting operating executives to understand and use the reports provided them. The objective of those responsible for the presentation and interpretation of operating results should be the timely display of elements that effectively describe the operations of the business and permit development of the ability to adjust to changing conditions. The scope of this approach should include: (1) assembly and analysis of existing financial information to report on and control operations; (2) definition of operating responsibilities and the role of individual managers and their relation to each other; (3) development of key indicators to effectively measure and analyze performance within individual responsibility centers; (4) development of internal and external comparative context within which to evaluate key indicators; (5) development of financial information necessary to formulate short- and long-term business strategies and operating plans; (6) development of output formats to effectively display and communicate plan and performance data tailored to the needs of varying levels of responsibility; and (7) development and use of communication and information tools within cost constraints to improve the speed and comprehension of information presentations.

In brief, to improve the presentation and interpretation of operating results, keep the user in mind; follow organizational lines; emphasize important elements; interrelate the data; display significant plan comparisons; avoid allocations where possible; include significant ratios; and isolate significant trends.

Remember that every firm has a financial information system, however simple it may be. The information it provides is the basis for much management activity, whether the information is received by word of mouth or in a written report. Management success or the lack of it will in large part be a direct function of the caliber of information gathered, presented, and interpreted.—*J. L. Greene*

THE ROLE OF FINANCE IN GENERAL MANAGEMENT

In the first part of this section, the responsibilities of the chief financial officer were set forth in expanded organization charts of the finance function which implied that all activity stemmed either from the controller's office or from the treasurer. To the extent that concern is with the specifics of the function, this observation would be consistent, but not if one is to look beyond the immediate duties to the role finance should play in the general management of a large corporation and to the way it achieved its prominence.

Growth of Finance in Business

In the days of the first Henry Ford, accounting and finance were not considered to be among the prime (or even truly necessary) business functions. Marketing and manufacturing were held to be the main functions of an industrial company, and accounting was considered to be strictly overhead. Ford was said to have dismissed whole accounting departments with a wave of his hand because he could not fathom the necessity of large cost accounting departments, credit departments, or similar groups. The perseverance of a few key men, aided by the necessity of complying with government and tax requirements, eventually sustained a permanent finance function. Other companies, too, experienced the process of management evolution, and finance joined marketing and manufacturing to form the "three-legged stool" upon which business operates.

STAFF DEVELOPMENT

The necessity of improving operating efficiency and providing the data required for externally required reports dictated further expansion and specialization, which in turn created a new emphasis on staff development.

Modern corporations are selective in their employment practices, weighing education and experience against job specifications to assure themselves of a properly qualified staff. Many companies have instituted "understudy" programs wherein a newly employed member of the finance department may spend weeks or even months in various departments. The objective is to expose the new employee to manufacturing techniques and processes, marketing procedures, and various accounting activities in order to better prepare him for his position.

This type of planned personnel development has been instrumental in the preparation of financial executives for general management positions. In recent years, more presidents have been selected from financial management than from any other function. This is a direct reflection of recognition of the management knowledge accumulated by financial executives, again because of their involvement and influence in every aspect of business.

A MANAGEMENT PARTNERSHIP

The finance department of any corporation, whether large or small, is inevitably looked to for answers, and this is as it should be. Not only will sophisticated finance and accounting department personnel pride themselves on the ability to respond correctly to the many inquiries they receive; they will anticipate, recommend, and provide meaningful data on their own initiative.

In order to advance from the position of merely providing answers to questions (the informational services role) to that of management partnership, finance departments must be creative; *they* must pose new questions to other members of management, questions that have as their foundation the information of corporate activity that is recorded, separated, summarized, and analyzed in the company books and data processing equipment.

Business has long since passed the stage where the basics of recording and reporting are all that is required of accounting personnel. Financial executives must have inquiring minds concerned with the technology of business, the production techniques, and the marketing programs. Only through the satisfaction of curiosity in these other functions can finance make the contribution expected of it today.

Committee Participation

Company size may dictate numbers and types of committees; often there is but one committee, an executive or management committee, where every major function is represented. In such hands will rest the policy-making and operating responsibilities.

FINANCE COMMITTEE

If the company is large, several committees will be in operation, with a separate finance committee to supervise the corporate financial activity and develop programs for consideration by the executive committee and/or the board of directors. It may exercise all powers in the management of the financial affairs of the company up to those reserved by the board of directors or the executive committee.

The finance committee may be composed of all the department heads of the various financial and accounting subsections, but it may also include one or more directors, thus lending a degree of endorsement prior to submission of programs and recommendations to the board.

EXECUTIVE COMMITTEE

The vice president of finance will normally sit as an equal on an executive committee with other vice presidents, his peers; the president, usually, will serve as chairman.

Participation in the development of company policies and management decisions during service on this committee provides the maximum opportunity for a financial executive to exhibit general management capabilities and simultaneously to determine new ways through which the finance department may serve company management.

Intersecting Functional Boundaries

More than any other primary function in business, finance cuts across functional boundaries and is concerned with line and staff activity alike. As a consequence it should be recognized by all the other functions that finance can best provide its service if it receives full cooperation.

The marketing function frequently questions the degree of control exerted by finance over such areas as inventory, expense budgets, incentive plans, and credit. Such control is part of the system of checks and balances that should be enforced by the combined efforts of the treasurer and controller, and the success of this system is dependent upon its being understood by marketing, manufacturing, and all other functions.

Inventories, for instance, are important to the measurement of performance for several functions. The production and profit of manufacturing units may be affected by inventory controls that dictate their level of production. Marketing does not want to be in the position of selling from an empty wagon and is consequently concerned with the mix and quantity of inventory. Finance may view the inventories from the amount of money invested, the rate of turnover, the possible obsolescence, and even the personal property tax that is applicable. If the general management objectives are defined and understood by all department heads, the result should be that which best serves the company in the total perspective. It is therefore quite possible to conclude that the objectives of one or more functions may have to be sacrificed for the total good. However, such decisions should later be incorporated in the evaluation or measurement of the functions that are adversely or favorably affected. Generally, the most appropriate solutions are those that will best satisfy most of the objectives of each function.

Areas of General Management Contribution

An able financial executive will be alert to the possible contributions of finance in all other areas of company operation, some of which are as follows: the efficiency and reliability of time and motion studies specifically, and the projects and programs of industrial engineering departments generally; the costs, long-range potential, and current status of research and development projects; proposals of new employee benefits, union contract liabilities, and anticipated

settlements of labor contract negotiations; engineering changes that may ultimately affect product costs, government contracts, or capital expenditures; acquisition and merger possibilities, effect on earnings, borrowing power, and potential drain on or strengthening of cash position; employee turnover and the labor
market as they might affect pension fund contributions, forecasts, and budgets.

The part to be played by finance in general management will be subject only
to the limitations placed on it by the president or the board of directors, but
such limitations will in turn be governed by the curiosity, initiative, enthusiasm,
and performance of the financial staff.

Finance has the entrée to participation in the management and operation of
all other functions because it must necessarily cross functional boundary lines.
Beyond the point of accomplishing its own objectives, it must do a selling job
on what more may be contributed to the total effort.

The professional attitudes, competence, salesmanship, and business philosophy
and psychology of the financial executives will determine the extent to which
finance may function as part of general management.—*R. A. Busch*

Section 5

Marketing

CONTENTS

The Essence of Marketing

The Markets and Their Effects on Marketing

The Nature of the Product and Its Effect on Marketing

Competitive Forces

The Legal Framework of Marketing

Customer Buying Behavior

The Marketing Concept and the Marketing Mix

Market Research

Establishing Objectives

Product Planning

The Annual Marketing Plan

Marketing Strategy

Organization

Product Management

Managing the Marketing Operation

THE ESSENCE OF MARKETING

A company's success or failure in the marketplace depends on total commitment to marketing—on whether the organization is entirely imbued with the marketing concept or whether it views its marketing as an entity separate and independent of the other divisions. Commitment to marketing must permeate the organizational whole, from the very top through every major division. This is not to imply that a major division should ignore its primary responsibilities; it simply means that each division and department should be infused with the idea that the company is oriented and committed to a marketing concept. Each department gives support to the others to insure the company's survival and growth in today's competitive field of battle.

Too often, the concept of marketing has been limited to the sole endeavor of selling. Though selling is an integral part of the total of marketing, it does not encompass the whole of the marketing concept. The essence of marketing today is evidenced in five major areas of endeavor. To fulfill and utilize the marketing concept to serve the needs of the company and in turn increase the sales of the company, a marketing organization must be willing to do the following: (1) define its market area; (2) research consumer needs and wants; (3) develop and redevelop product and/or service to meet the demand; (4) recruit, select, and train manpower to deliver the product or service; and (5) develop its sales approach and advertising support.

Defining the Market

A man seldom begins a journey unless he first knows his desired destination; and if he is a careful traveler, he has planned his route, his stops, and his time of arrival and has determined how much it will cost to get there. The same principles apply to marketing. Basically, there are three major markets that a company attempts to woo—the general consumer market, the industrial market, and the vast, growing government market. After a company has decided where it wants to go, it needs to find out what that market segment needs, wants, and is buying.

Researching Consumer Needs and Wants

Researching consumer needs and wants is a vital step in marketing. Here the distinction—or lack of distinction—between needs and wants is encountered. Frequently, these two elements are at variance with each other, but the possibility that a need and a want may be the same is not completely excluded. A child "needs" milk; a child "wants" candy—a simple illustration of obvious distinction. A child "wants" food; a child "needs" food—a simple illustration of duplication. The company must realize, through research, the distinction or absence of distinction between the consumer's needs and wants. The product can then be so designed to fill each desire and sold to fit each element of need or want, or both. Following close on this basic research into the needs and wants of the consumer come the facts on how much the consumers are buying; when they buy; how they buy; how much they now spend; how much they can and will spend for the need and/or want. This research is, of course, planned and carried out through the company's own market research department, a vital and permanent part of the organization. This research department, along with much money, time, and effort, will yield essential information to aid in the continuing endeavor of giving customers what they want and need.

Developing and Redeveloping Product or Service

Keeping a product up to date in the latest design, with materials that are functional, attractive, and appealing, and at a production cost that is competitive with that of like products and/or services, is a continuing process. This is an essential, cooperative part of a company's development and production division, just as is the market research division. In the group life and health insurance field, for example, health coverages must be kept constantly in line with medical practices and costs to assure customers' financial well-being when service is needed. This is true of any product or service, whether it is in the field of food products, clothing, heavy machinery, television repair, banking, or other area of marketing.

Selecting and Training Manpower

It is often said that an organization's greatest strength and greatest wealth are in its people. This is certainly true in a marketing-oriented company. The function of recruiting, selecting, and training company personnel—from the president down through his executive staff—is vital to the successful fulfillment of a planned program of marketing. It must be evident throughout the various other divisions, both line and staff, down to the man who sweeps up after a production run or the girl who opens and sorts the mail. Each employee's knowledge, attitudes, and skills are important to the overall success of the organization.

There must be a planned program to enable employees to meet the company's total commitment and personal standards. A good training program gives new employees the knowledge and security they need in order to become functional, valuable forces in the organization. More than this, training should be on a continuing basis to assure that each employee can continue to function to his full capacity. All training should be directed toward the total marketing concept and aim to aid in the personal development of each individual's desire, enthusiasm, sincerity, and ambition to enable him to become and remain a successful member of the successful marketing team.

Developing Sales Approach and Advertising Support

It is often said that "nothing happens until someone sells something." This is what starts the wheels moving, the production line puffing, the shipping clerk wrapping, and the claims clerk processing. And the instigator of all this activity is the well-trained, highly motivated, hard-working salesman.

Before selling can begin, important decisions must be made. How will the thoroughly researched, highly developed, priced-right "need fulfiller" and/or "want satisfier" be sold? Will the company's own salesmen or agents do the work, or will manufacturers' representatives, brokers, or jobbers be used? Will sales be made direct, through distributors, or by some other method? What about consignment, minimum orders, restricted trade territories, and size of customers' companies or numbers of employees? All of this must be determined before that first sale of product or service is made. Until then, "nothing happens."

A further necessity in the marketing effort is advertising support. Advertising must complement the overall company image and intent. However, it must not replace the front-line salesman. Advertising can be used to whet the appetite of the defined market, to herald the good news of the arrival of the product or service, and to inform potential customers of the places where it can be seen and purchased. It should reach the vast markets of the general public or the more restricted areas of industry and government. The design, purpose, and function of the product or service should be results of the combined efforts of the advertising agency and the R&D department and marketers of the company. The company should always listen to its sales force for feedback of suggestions, praise, and criticism.

The Overall Concept

The essence of marketing is more than selling, more than researching, more than advertising, more than planning, developing, and redeveloping. It is a concept that encompasses all of these things; it is a concept that must permeate every organizational division in order to be successfully fulfilled. There are no shortcuts in acquiring and utilizing the full marketing concept. If an organization is to be groomed properly for its competitive battle in the marketplace, it must function through a sound, well-planned, and flexible market-oriented program.—*V. R. Kennedy, Jr.*

THE MARKETS AND THEIR EFFECTS ON MARKETING

The success of every seller depends upon the action of buyers. Marketing deals with influencing the action of buyers. Product characteristics, promotional efforts, and the locations where marketing action takes place—be it presenting the winning persuasion, making the purchase decision, or actually transferring possession—are all oriented to achieve the sale. Aside from the execution of the functions of design and production, the major effort exerted by the seller and his agents, from planning through implementation, is the scope of marketing.

The *job* of marketing is a different activity in almost every organization. Three key variables cause these differences:

1. *The kind of purchaser:* How does he behave? Does he act for himself or for others? How does he make his decisions?

2. *The product or service involved:* Is it a discretionary item or a necessity; a high-ticket item or a minor purchase; an item needed as an investment, a consumable, or an item used in the creation of other products?

3. *The nature of the marketing effort:* Does it involve a precise argument based on values, or an impulse-motivating inducement, or is it based on providing the most convenient system in which consumers can act?

In the following paragraphs the factors that define markets and the different approaches to marketing are examined to determine how they pair and why.

Definitions

Despite broad understanding and adoption of the marketing concept by business, much is yet to be learned about how markets are formed, how they segment or divide, and how the marketer should formulate effective marketing strategies. A major factor contributing to the problem of this knowledge gap is imprecision in the definitions of popularly used terms and hence in the understanding of the subject. The American Marketing Association (*Marketing Definitions,* 1960) has two definitions for "market": (1) "the aggregate of forces or conditions within which buyers and sellers make decisions that result in the transfer of goods and services"; and (2) "the aggregate demand of the potential buyers of a commodity or service."

The first definition is in the context of the marketplace, which is often referred to as the market. This definition denotes various environments in which buying decisions take place, such as the New England market or the agricultural market.

The second definition has significance for marketing strategy; it is concerned with potential buyers. The key point here is the identification of the potential buyers in terms that go beyond positioning them in an environment; rather, they are pointed out in terms that differentiate between a consumer who, for example, desires cold cereal for breakfast and another consumer who has a preference for bacon and eggs. This is important because it says that the bacon-and-eggs eater is not a good target for the marketing effort of a new cereal promotion.

Note also that both definitions contain the word "aggregate." This is important, for the American Marketing Association (*Marketing Definitions*) carries this underlying notion into its definition of "market potential" as "a calculation of maximum possible sales opportunities for all sellers of a good or service during a stated period."

Market potential is thus an aggregate figure, the *maximum* opportunity for *all* sellers. Therefore, a given company's sales potential is but a part of total market potential, depending upon the subgroup of potential buyers to which it directs its marketing strategy, or the segment of the market it selects as its target market. This selection in turn will depend on the differentiating characteristics the company includes in its products and on its marketing resources and capabilities.

The foregoing definitions point out that a market is defined around demands for a commodity or service, or the opportunities to sell a good or a service. That is, markets result from needs to achieve satisfactions, and it is therefore convenient to describe them in terms of the products used. There is hazard in this conceptual expediency since, at later times, these needs can find new ways of achieving satisfaction and vacate present product-defined markets. This is the point made by marketing conceptualists. Nevertheless—and pragmatically speaking—there is, for example, a very substantial market for hydraulic fluid power components today even though a new invention in subminiature electric motors could conceivably displace it at some future date.

MARKET SEGMENTS

Reference has been made here to two bases for market segmentation: the environmental basis in which buyers and sellers operate (the New England market and the agricultural market); and classifications of potential buyers according to factors that describe the varied nature of their demands or the opportunity for a seller to make the sale (the reasons that classify a person as suited to be the object of a bacon advertisement but not of a cold-cereal promotion). These two examples illustrate that markets may be segmented in several ways. The ways by which subdivisions are made are called the modes of segmentation, and they are manifold.

In earlier days of marketing, markets were segmented by market analysts chiefly according to demographic and classification modes. The factors for segmentation were geographical area, age group, company size, ethnic identity, home owner or renter, income group, political party affiliation, and the like. Although analyses on these bases permitted the improvement of marketing efforts, the reasons were more operationally than conceptually or strategically oriented. Today studies on attitudes, motivational considerations, and other decision factors reveal that a man's breakfast-food preference might well correlate with how much of a hurry he is in at breakfast time, which in turn is influenced by how late he habitually goes to bed and the starting time of his job in the morning. Thus one could propose a promotion strategy for the early-to-work market segment for cold cereal as advertising on late-evening television programs. Purchaser value criteria constitute another mode for segmentation. This factor aids the separation of the markets for high- and low-cost items within a product classification.

MARKETERS

The other party to the marketing situation is the seller. It is important to identify him in precise terms so as to differentiate among those that compete in the supply side of the economy. They comprise the organizations that conceive of the marketing strategies and also contribute largely to the dynamic character of marketing. Sellers are classified according to industry. The U.S. Government *Standard Industrial Classification Manual* states that sellers are establishments (producing economic units) which are identified by industry classification codes based on the products they produce or handle, or the services they render. Thus sellers, and in fact all industry establishments, are not classified according to what they do or the operations they perform but, rather, by the goods they produce. Therefore, precisely speaking, the metalworking industry is more like a metalworking market than an industry by the criterion of output rather than operations performed. This is an example of how markets and industries are incorrectly referred to interchangeably. Correctly, it is a matter of whether reference is to the buyer or to the seller: Buyers form markets, and sellers form industries.

The problem of distinguishing between markets and industries is more complex when middlemen are included. These organizations, too, are given Standard Industrial Classification (SIC) establishment definitions according to the services they render. The question that must be considered is this: Are middlemen markets for producers, or are they industries from which consumers buy? Middlemen—agents, wholesalers, jobbers, retailers, and dealers—constitute the extracompany elements in the channels of distribution through which a company accomplishes its marketing job. Hence, they are agents of the seller, and the answer is that they are a part of the industry structure rather than the market structure. Notwithstanding, they take title to the products they sell, and therefore they constitute a group of buyers and would appear to form a market even though they are agents. It is less confusing, however, not to refer to groups of middlemen as markets, for the reason that they do not constitute final demand, nor do they convert or integrate products into other products as do OEM's (original equipment manufacturer markets). If they were considered as markets, their purchases and the purchases of consumers would erroneously combine and thus would describe a market size twice that of ultimate consumption.

Economic Groupings

Economists are not so often concerned with the marketer's problem of defining market segments as they are with production and consumption by economic sector. These sectors subclassify according to industries and markets by major characteristic.

GNP

The combined value of the product (and service) output of all economic sectors is gross national product (GNP). This breaks down into categories of final demand, capital investment, and the purchases of government, plus certain balance adjustments. The major subclassifications of GNP and their 1969 values (*Survey of Current Business,* February 1970) are as follows:

	1969 ($ Billion)
Consumer durables	89.8
Consumer nondurables	243.6
Consumer services	242.6
Nonresidential construction	33.4
Machinery and other production equipment	65.8
Residential construction	32.2
National defense needs	79.2
Other Federal and state and local government needs	135.4
	922.0

These statistics exclude inventory changes and the net of exports and imports. When they are added to this figure, GNP shows a total of $932.1 billion. In that these classifications are based on product groups by kind of need, they describe markets.

NATIONAL INCOME ACCOUNTS

Payments for the purchase of the products and services constituting GNP accrue as income to various producing industries (the benefactors of national income). National income is equal to GNP less provisions for capital consumption (depreciation) and indirect business taxes. Also according to the *Survey of Current Business*, the industry divisions that constitute the recipients of national income are as follows:

	1969 ($ Billion)
Agriculture, forestry, and fisheries	23.9
Mining and construction	48.1
Durable goods manufacturing	140.8
Nondurable goods manufacturing	88.1
Transportation	29.0
Communications	15.5
Electric, gas, and sanitary utilities	14.6
Wholesale and retail trade	112.7
Finance, insurance, and real estate	85.2
Other services	94.4
Government and government enterprises	114.8
Other	4.1
	771.2

The economic interactions between the GNP markets and the industries that receive the national income are not at all clear from the figures given. The values don't appear to pair off. The interindustry activity that takes place within the framework of GNP and national income is a subject of more detailed study, such as the analysis of the input-output structure of the economy. This is an analysis of the manifold economic transactions that take place between buyers and sellers, plus consideration of the monies spent for value added by producers, and exports and imports.

INPUT-OUTPUT

Input-output economic data for the United States have been available in significant detail only since 1963, and even these data are exceedingly coarse for the purposes of company product and market planning. Nevertheless, there is sufficient detail to describe and show the magnitudes of the interactions of major industries and markets, and it is at this level that marketing strategies and methods take on major differences. Input-output theory holds that there are three major areas of economic (marketing) activity: interindustry transactions, industry–final demand transactions, and value-added contributions by industries.

Interindustry transactions are the buying and selling actions between industries, including industrial purchases of raw materials, components or intermediate products, energy, and services. It should be noted that, as in the SIC system of definitions, wholesale and retail trade middlemen are considered industries along with producers and suppliers of services. For the purposes of input-output analysis and also business and market planning, industries break down into five sectors by type of product or service.

1. *Final products* are products of industries that sell a large portion of their output to final demand. They are in two categories: nonmetal (furniture, apparel, drugs); and metal (machinery, appliances, and motor vehicles). It should be noted that purchases of production machinery and related durable equipment investments constitute, for the purpose of these transactions, an action of final demand. Because they are transactions entirely between industrial organizations, they are often mistakenly considered as within the interindustry activity area. Purchases included within the interindustry activity area involve raw materials, intermediate products, energy, and services.

2. *Basic products* are products of industries that sell a large portion of their outputs to other industries. They also are found in two categories: metal (machine parts and primary metal mining and manufacturing); and nonmetal (glass products, paper products, and chemicals).

3. *Energy* is the product of electric and gas utilities and of the petroleum, coal, and similar industries.

4. *Services* include government, transportation, trade, and business and consumer services.

5. *Other industries* include research and development (R&D), scrap, and secondhand goods.

These sectors constitute the broad classifications of industries that supply markets, which in turn are composed of themselves for intermediate products and services, plus a group of classifications known as final demand. The economic sectors that constitute the markets of final demand break down into the following classifications: personal consumption (consumers); producers' durable equipment investments (manufacturers, transportation companies, commercial farms, contractors, and broadcasters); construction (purchasers of residential, highway, and commercial and industrial construction); government (Federal, state, and local organizations); and exports less competitive imports.

Action in the marketplace is thus composed of the economic transactions that take place between sellers and buyers. The foregoing definitions of marketing terms and review of the major factors of national economics identify most of the participants.

The Marketing Viewpoint

From a marketing viewpoint, the viewpoint from which marketing strategies and approaches are formulated, markets may be broken down as follows: industry markets (basic materials and products industries, intermediate products industries, producers' durable equipment industries, utilities and transportation companies, construction firms, other service industries, wholesalers, and retailers); government markets (defense and aerospace agencies, public works agencies, and other Federal, state, and local agencies); consumer market; and export markets, which may be industry-, government-, or consumer-oriented.

These classifications—except the consumer market—describe markets in terms of groups that have generally common needs and require generally uniform marketing approaches.

The final demands of consumers are for a wide variety of needs, including emotional, that call for different marketing strategies and approaches. The GNP breakdown of consumer markets by product-type demand (durables, nondurables, and services) is a good first cut of this classification. The products of these market categories may be further broken down according to whether their demands classify them as necessities or discretionary purchase items.

In actuality, each supplier-and-market combination interacts in its own way, and this determines each marketing job. It is not really correct to describe this job as just a few ways of interacting, although such must be the limitation in the scope of this discussion.

The Marketing System

The marketing system has been described thus far as consisting of producers, middlemen, and buyers. Buyers can purchase as members of final demand or as purchasers of intermediate products used to make end products for final demand (requiring further continuation of the marketing process). Moreover, one more complexity must be considered in order to understand all the many variations in the marketing system.

Just as sellers have agents that are middlemen, many buyers have agents that specify and even procure for them. For example, the consulting engineer in design specifies the needs of his client, the doctor specifies the prescription of his patient, the architect specifies the materials used in the builder's building, government organizations qualify subcontract sources, and corporate headquarters often name the suppliers whose products are acceptable at the division or retail unit level. These behind-the-scene influences must also be persuaded, and therefore they too are the targets of many marketing strategies and plans. In general they enter the picture when the buyer is not qualified to properly specify or evaluate the seller's products and there is a technological knowledge gap separating the principals.

The Marketing Job

The marketing job consists of applying the elements of the marketing mix in appropriate balance, to the right extent, and at the right places. The elements that make up the marketing mix are activities that may be classified under the following headings: sales coverage and distribution, product information and application assistance, advertising and product promotion, distributor development and training, merchandising assistance and sales services, price administration and trade promotion, customer order service, and product and package design.

What is done under each of these headings differs in nearly every product-market situation. In total each set of activities describes the many different ways in which the marketing job is done. For the remainder of this discussion, the principal characteristics of the marketing job will be described for the following representative market situations: industrial products sold to industrial markets; defense and aerospace products sold to the Federal Government and its prime contractors; and consumer nondurables sold to the consumer market.

INDUSTRIAL MARKETING

Industrial markets are composed of purchasers of capital equipment (producers' durable equipment), intermediate products, and industrial construction. Without resorting to an input-output analysis of the economy for a value, the size of the overall industrial market is best appraised by examining the national income of durable-goods manufacturers. Excluding the multiplying effect of intermediate products sales on the size of the industrial sector, income for durable-goods manufacturing is the largest of the national income accounts, accounting for just under 20 percent of total national income, or $140.8 billion in 1969.

The elements of this market are corporations that have a rational and methodical approach in their dealings. The purchasing function is performed by a purchasing agent aided by buyers. Although it would appear that this function is the decision-making center, it acts in behalf of and under the guidance of others. The principal influences in the decision-making process are product engineers and designers where intermediate products are involved (components for production), production and industrial engineers for plant equipment, and facilities planners for construction. These persons establish the specifications of the purchase items and, basing selection on technical evaluation, they determine or approve the vendors who are considered as acceptable sources of supply. Moreover, even this influence is not individual action; most often it is a departmental or committee action.

The purchasing agent next negotiates and executes the fulfillment of the company's need. This activity embraces obtaining the best price and terms, an acceptable delivery promise, vendors' technical assistance where useful, a reliable and dependable source of supply, specified product quality and specifications, and flexibility to meet the company's changing requirements. For his own purposes he also seeks attentive sales coverage and responsive customer order service from his vendors.

It is difficult to pinpoint a single decision-making unit in the industrial customer organization. Initially, a number of selection criteria must be met, and different persons are assigned the responsibilities of insuring adherence to the criteria. Once a supplier and his products have been determined to be acceptable, conditions of purchase tend to be the dominant influence in supplier selection. For reasons of economy and stability in vendor-customer relations, once a source has been selected, buyers and sellers often negotiate annual supply contracts against which purchase releases are made during the year. On the other hand, distributors become involved when products are standard low-cost items and when sales are very infrequent.

In every situation, the industrial marketing job must meet the demands of the purchaser. The most critical issue is probably that of product specifications and design. Importantly, however, this must be in the context of the value considerations of the buyer. Only in very rigid situations is there no latitude for obtaining a higher price for improved dependability, performance, usefulness, or rating.

Hence an industrial vendor's marketing strategy must emphasize the following primary considerations: leadership in product planning—product specifications, design, utility, and quality; a value-derived price—a price/utility balance concurring with customer value standards; and recognized dependability and service as a supplier.

DEFENSE AND AEROSPACE MARKETING

The market for defense and aerospace products is the Federal Government, except for foreign governments, commercial aircraft, communications satellites, and the like. According to the latest available input-output estimates, Federal Government final demand less the value-added accounts of labor and capital costs was approximately $46.6 billion in 1967. Of this amount approximately $10.7 billion was purchased from industries classified as service and energy. The difference, $35.9 billion, represents products procurement of which approximately $24 billion was for defense and aerospace requirements.

The government formulates general requirements for the products needed, based on strategic posture decisions. The products themselves are not explicitly defined except for what they must do. Actual product development is left up to the supplier. Accordingly, there are several stages in defense procurement, the procurement of concept R&D, prototype development, and production. Definition of the product progresses with and parallels these stages of procurement.

The end products that are delivered to the government are fabricated by prime contractors. Suppliers of intermediate products, components, and subsystems to prime contractors are known as subcontractors. To prevent excessive economic concentration within the defense industry, the government directs prime contractors to subcontract many major components and subsystems. But, to insure meeting all intended requirements, government representatives participate in qualifying subcontractors and their product designs.

Purchase decisions, both award determinations and approval of major subcontract sources, rest in the end with the government. Such approval may be as simply achieved as getting on a qualified list of suppliers or as arduous as a full design evaluation. In nearly all instances, however, subcontractors must also be the preferred sources of the prime contractors, who must bear ultimate responsibility for final product acceptance by the government.

The marketing task in this industry is unique and complex. First, as a supplier, one must stand in good stead with both the government and the major prime contractors. Moreover, prime contract contenders often become subcontractors to their competitors after they have been unsuccessful in obtaining a prime contract. Second, one must have a well-developed market information system to be constantly informed of bid opportunities as well as the plans and unsolved needs of the government. This enables one to be prepared for opportunities and to develop, on one's own initiative, product research and unsolicited proposals directed toward perceived potential opportunity.

Because of the many levels, locations, and committees that are involved in purchasing decisions regarding defense products, and because of the many criteria that apply to successful contracting, the marketing effort that must be exerted to achieve success in this section is rigorous. In sequence, there is the initial work of becoming known and accepted as a qualified supplier, the job of being currently informed on where developing business opportunities are, the strategy of organizing or getting on the right team of prime and subcontract suppliers, the development of an extremely comprehensive bid proposal, the intense follow-up and presentation programs to achieve appropriate recognition of an offer, and a detailed program of executive selling to demonstrate top management interest and the company's overall capability. The defense contractor's marketing strategy must emphasize the following considerations: advanced product research and development capability with a record of proven success; adequate technological support facilities in terms of laboratory and testing equipment; adequate production capabilities in terms of methods and tool engineering competence, production facilities and equipment, and quality control; adequate business systems for cost control, scheduling, and contract administration; adequate manpower in all skill levels—managerial, professional, technical, and shop; and a deep concern, on the part of top management, for the contract and an approach to organization that appears effective and efficient.

CONSUMER MARKETING

The consumer market is the aggregate of all individuals acting in their own behalf or that of their immediate families. Personal consumption is the biggest figure of all in total final demand. For example, 1969 figures show GNP for consumer durables as $89.8 billion, and for consumer nondurables $243.6 billion.

In that each consumer is an individual buying unit, the market is not an organized structure. And because individuals possess all the different qualities and characteristics of mankind, and because they are free to act in whatever way they wish, they compose an extremely complex market.

The numerous population that makes up the consumer market dictates that, for reasons of economy, these buyers be dealt with in large groups, hence the designation "mass markets." It is when they are perceived and appealed to as groups that the consumer market takes on a structured appearance: That is to say, the ways in which groups differ from one another and also interrelate depend upon the basis that has been taken for differentiation. This basis is referred to as the mode of segmentation.

There are two main reasons for segmenting consumer markets. The first reason is to determine what sets of motivational and behavioral criteria can be applied to delineate different groups within the market. This analysis permits the formation of appropriate marketing strategy. The questions for which answers are sought are these: How do consumers perceive their needs? How do they perceive achieving satisfactions? Upon what bases do they make decisions? What inducements and appeals motivate them to purchasing actions?

The second reason for segmenting consumer markets is to determine other classification criteria that enable marketers to identify, reach, and serve the different members of the market. When strategic target segments have been identified and a marketing posture has been formulated, the job of marketing implementation remains to be done. The problem is, then, what descriptive and classification criteria best describe those members that make up the target segment so that they may be found? The questions for which answers are sought are as follows: How much purchasing power do the individual units that compose this segment have? What promotional communications channels best reach them? Where are they located? How may they be identified? What patterns and characteristics do they have that suggest the best ways to serve them?

A link that is unique to the consumer economic marketing sector is the retailer. Without his support the best marketing plans will come to a halt. He must be compensated and motivated to cooperate; thus trade promotion is as important as consumer promotion in consumer marketing plans. Because the population of the consumer market and its retail outlets is large, a wide variety of distributors plays an indispensable role in achieving distribution.

The marketing strategy for consumer products marketers must emphasize the following primary considerations: selecting target market segments from a motivational and behavioral analysis of the market; determining the characteristics of the population making up the target market that enable promoting to it and serving it effectively; and formulating a product design and interrelated promotion and advertising program that motivates both customers and retailers.

MARKETING APPROACH

In industrial marketing, product considerations dominate the marketing picture. In the case of defense and aerospace markets, product development and production capabilities outweigh the current state of product design in the marketing argument. In consumer markets—granted the importance of the product as the means of satisfying the need—a well-conceived marketing strategy and plan are the keys to success. These key differences in marketing approach are the result of the differences in the markets. Further differences in marketing approach are attributable to the kinds of products and the variations in strategy by marketers.—*A. John Ward*

THE NATURE OF THE PRODUCT AND ITS EFFECT ON MARKETING

The marketing concept asserts the absolute and fundamental importance of the market. Its dictum is: "Determine what the market wants, and deliver that product to the customer." The demand of commerce and industry is for positive affirmation that "*It* works, we can make *it,* and we can sell *it.*" But the individual marketer who is to sell the product musters his arguments and directs his plans and efforts to accomplish that sale, in ways that differ radically from one type of product to the next. The nature of any product category, as well as its market, very significantly influences the seller's general approach to the product's market. The intangibility and complexity of a product particularly shape that approach, as do the product's function, price, quality, and service and other after-sale characteristics.

Similar Products in the Same Market

The market's effects on marketing are indisputable. Frozen orange juice for A&P patrons, for United Airlines, or for the U.S. Army Quartermaster Corps is handled in three distinctly different ways. In each case the market dictates particular requirements related to the marketing strategy, planning, organization, research, pricing, advertising, packaging, product management, sales management, distribution, delivery, merchandising, and practically every other aspect of marketing operations. However, each market defines explicitly the manner in which *all* frozen foods are marketed; that is, the nature of all frozen foods for consumer purchase in supermarkets (for instance) dictates that they be similarly processed, prepared, packaged, advertised, distributed, and handled, right up to the time the buyer puts the item in her cart and heads for the cash register. Generally, all these products affirm their value in terms of appearance, preservation, taste, purity, and several other characteristics peculiar to such products. And, of course, a number of these characteristics differ from the corresponding characteristics of fresh fruit juice, fresh vegetables, or fresh meats; and they differ again from the characteristics of canned foods. Whether the foods are frozen, fresh, or canned, in each category their characteristics distinctly (and differently) affect their marketing.

Dissimilar Products in the Same Market

Just as the nature of frozen foods directly influences their marketing, this same relationship can be seen for every other product category. Contrast the industrial marketing of elevator maintenance service with the industrial marketing of frozen foods. Or contrast the marketing of electrical fixtures and supplies to the Department of the Navy with the marketing of frozen foods to the National Aeronautics and Space Administration (NASA). Each type of product, by virtue of its unique characteristics, must be defined, demonstrated, and delivered to the buyer in a way that is in some respects unique and peculiar to that type of product.

Factors of Differentiation

The unique quality that differentiates one product category from another may invite analysis in terms of product tangibility and product complexity. (There are many other differentiations, of course.)

TANGIBILITY

The fact that a product can be felt or tasted, or calibrated or examined in operation, or otherwise physically observed and evaluated has a direct relationship to the marketing approach for that product. The more tangible the product, the more likely it is that advertising can be used to help sell it; conversely, the less tangible the product, the greater is the need for personal selling. The more tangible the product, generally, the more important are the display and appearance characteristics and the features of serviceability, durability, and practicality of application.

At the other end of the spectrum the intangible services, such as the professional ones of psychiatry or law, or the highly specialized areas of consulting, depend almost entirely on personal relationships with potential customers: The sponsor of the product (service) markets himself directly; the "package" is expertise or authority or intellectuality, which the seller shares with the buyer. Thus the manufacturer of power tools and the admissions director at a boys' school market their products differently to the man who is a home craftsman and who also has a 15-year-old son. So do the information systems consultant and the laboratory instruments maker who face a typical corporate customer.

COMPLEXITY

A complicated, intricate product or system requires a marketing approach distinctly different from the approach dictated for a simple commodity or a basic material. Thus, the understandability of a product category, the requirement for customer education, or the need for *technical* marketing variously shape the marketing approach for that product. However, this differentiation is not a matter of tangibility in terms of the physical features of the product. For instance, both an intricate, electronically controlled machine tool and a pair of shoes have substance and dimensions; telephone-answering services and architectural-engineering services have neither. The tool, because of its complex nature, requires technical selling—perhaps of a highly personal, sophisticated type. The shoes, supported by advertising, to an appreciable degree sell themselves. The answering service also sells itself, in effect; but the architectural-engineering service must be made acceptable and understandable and be expressly particularized to each customer.

The tangibility and complexity differentiations of a product or service influence not only the marketing approach to the selling market but the approach to the service and repair and maintenance after-markets as well. And these differentiations, in addition to others such as price, quality, and competition, definitely relate to the product as well as to the markets for that product.

Managing Products and Markets

The most elementary requirements for any marketing manager are to know his markets and know his products. His astuteness concerning his products assures his appreciation of the subtle as well as the obvious effects of the nature of those products on their marketing, and this knowledge and understanding stimulate his study of similar and different effects for various other products. As a result he is able to market his own products according to established, demonstrated standards; he is also able and willing to deviate knowingly from those standards, to experiment deliberately in the marketplace, and to test unusual or special situations.

Two such deviations in the home fuel-oil business were the initiation of ten-month, averaged installment payments to stabilize buyer expense and dealer storage inventory, and the initiation of degree-day records to permit automatic delivery when needed. In both instances the nature of the market and the nature of the product accommodated these innovations that reduced costs, improved profits, and increased sales. Knowledgeable, imaginative marketing managers in every industry have employed similar adaptations; they have identified the effect of one product's characteristics on its marketing, relating this product to another in its market or in another market, and have tested the parallel.

More basic is the imperative need for the marketing manager to know first the nature of his own products. Chain saws are not outboard motors; transistors are not vacuum tubes; helicopters are not taxis; magnetic tape is not typewriter ribbon; yet the annals of postwar marketing abound with instances of marketing programs conceived by people who really didn't know the product they were marketing. They *thought* it had the same basic characteristics as some other product, and sometimes these misconceptions cost their companies millions of dollars.

The Matrix of Product Characteristics

As this brief study of dissimilar products has indicated, even within the dimensions of tangibility and complexity the nature of products and services does not affect their marketing consistently or uniformly. However, certain trends or standards can be established for broad areas or categories of products and services.

BASIC MATERIALS

Generally, basic materials and commodities have almost no differentiation; they are almost all marketed in bulk quantities, in relatively open markets, at narrow margins. Variously, tariff quotas, subsidies, and government regulatory commissions may influence a particular product's prices and markets; but these external factors in no way alter the essentially stable, fundamental nature of these products—such as minerals, wood products, livestock, and grain—and an extensive variety of first-derivative products and by-products. The cost of sales (extraction, production, processing, and so forth) is the most significant problem for companies dealing in these types of products. Historically, the marketer of a basic commodity like raw lumber, who operates rather perfunctorily—principally, managing sales—has not done very much market research, planning, testing, or advertising; and his organization is fairly simple and straightforward. He contracts or "brokers" large volumes at standard quality or condition levels, and he may have significant responsibilities for shipping and distribution.

In the shipping and distribution area, perceptive marketing managers of basic materials and commodities have successfully tested a number of new techniques. Not too many years ago, experimental pipelines were developed for gas and oil. Today more than half of the petroleum and nearly all of the gas in the United States move underground in a network of over one million miles of pipeline. Whether the idea came into fruition as a result of the oil companies' efforts or the pipe manufacturers' efforts, it was supported and nurtured by understanding of the nature of the product, of its markets, and of the technical feasibility of the system.

Similarly, a number of other handling and distribution techniques have been developed that radically affect the marketing of basic materials. Some of these might be classified as production-oriented rather than market-oriented, such as cargo-handling equipment for bulk tankers, systems for processing bulk chemicals and other materials, and computerized data systems for grading and sorting and warehousing. But regardless of who claims responsibility for this type of innovation, the idea related fundamentally to the nature of the product and impacted forcibly on the marketing of that product.

STANDARD MANUFACTURED PRODUCTS

The differentiation of products that are off-the-shelf or standard catalog items, and of certain basic standard types of services, varies from somewhat more significant to very appreciably more significant than the differentiation of basic materials and commodities.

The nature of many manufactured products, particularly those that do not change significantly from one decade to the next, affects their marketing relatively little. Just as in the case of commodities and basic materials, the simplicity and stability of this sort of product minimize the explicit effect of the product in its marketing. Rivets, sulphuric acid, or corn syrup in volume, in industrial or government markets, are all sold at generally established quality levels. Corn syrup consumer marketing is considerably different, but this results from the complexity of the market, not from the complexity of the product.

Marketing complex products—electrochemical drilling machinery, high-fidelity stereophonic equipment, or biometric centrifuges, for example—is distinctly different from marketing basic materials. The nature of these types of products, even though the products are standard, catalog, production-run, off-the-shelf items, directly influences their marketing. First, the marketing manager must have technical competence; and second, he must organize to operate across a considerable range of responsibilities. His counterpart who deals in rivets generally need not meet either criterion.

The marketing manager for complex, technology-oriented products finds himself closely involved with R&D and engineering; he variously exercises responsibilities for new product planning, technological forecasting, and commercial development; he directs a technically trained sales force and works with or directs technical services; and he may play a key role in licensing, acquisitions, joint ventures, and general business development. Threaded through all of this, the need for him to know technology is emphatically demonstrated. He must recognize and understand technical ideas long before substantial development funds are committed; follow technical progress and actively participate in the resolution of new product plans and targets; engage the customer finally, knowledgeably, and sensitively; and follow up his customers, identifying their new needs (which are technically oriented, technology-responsive) and his competitors' awareness of and attention to those needs.

His technical competence thus equips him to do the things that the product requires him to do; and in order to discharge these responsibilities, he must staff and organize his function accordingly. Overall company size will directly determine the size of the marketing group; but regardless of the number of people who report to him, he must closely coordinate with and directly relate to a diversity of functions that either do not exist or are not marketing's concerns in the company that produces rivets.

As the rate of change of technologies continues to accelerate, more and more marketing managers find their "standard manufactured" products becoming more complex.

Because of dramatic developments in materials technologies, for instance, radical changes in product composition have occurred in engineering, design, functional purpose, cost, competitive pricing, and numerous other characteristics. Technologies related to manufacturing, processing, packaging, handling, inventory, and information systems have kept the same pace. Every change in any of these technologies that serves to further product differentiation impacts directly on the marketing of that product.

The lumber industry clearly illustrates this change in the marketing man's job. The marketer of raw lumber, who has become a marketer of wood products, now deals in prefinished paneling as well as a wide variety of other new product categories. But in the area of paneling alone he must know and understand a great deal of chemistry; and he must keep abreast of changes in the state of the art as they advance toward the marketplace.

Product and brand management evolved, at least in part, because of the technology explosion and resultant greatly increased emphasis on new products that has taken place in the past 25 years. Unquestionably, market differentiations that characterized the completely new market environment that began to evolve after World War II principally stirred marketing professionals to experiment and to develop the principles and tools and techniques of product management. But there were early indications that product differentiations as well as market differentiations were important, that a particular product benefited from the direction of a highly profit-oriented, generalist manager who could view his authority and responsibility, his goals and achievements, in total function terms. Here the consideration might have been the nature of the product in relation to the company's other products or product lines, or it might have been the general differentiation of the product type.

SERVICE

The range of differentiation of services is much like the range for manufactured products. Automobile lubrication is more complex than garbage collection and less complex than television repair. But automobile repair work, sophisticated by computerized electronic "diagnostic clinic" installations, is becoming highly complex. The overall complexity, the technical features of the product serviced and of any equipment used to provide the service require the marketer to have a relative depth of understanding of those features. In some services, such as real estate, stock brokerage, or fire insurance, an understanding of the technical features of the service itself is the marketer's criterion.

Principally, the differentiation in services that in turn affects the marketing of those services is a matter of tangibility of results. Thus services are largely differentiated by the market and in the marketplace. A customer can inspect shirts that come back from the laundry to determine whether they are properly starched, or he can listen to a smoothly running repaired pump. In similar fashion he can generally evaluate the deal that he made with a real estate agent, he can always measure the worth of a broker's advice after he has bought the stock, and he quickly knows the worth of his fire insurance if he experiences a fire.

CUSTOM-MADE SYSTEMS

Nearly every standard off-the-shelf product or regular service can be obtained in some modified form to serve the user's particular needs. Some products (such as Rolls Royce automobiles) and some services (such as the installation of an office telephone system) are always custom-tailored to the buyer's requirements. At some point in the scale of modification, however, the uniqueness of the end product or service distinguishes it and thereby differentiates it from all the others generally like it. It is at this point that such a special version of a product or service approaches the custom-made category.

The truly custom-made product or service may be relatively uncomplicated, engineered to moderately particular specifications that are dictated by an express need; or it may be a highly structured, intricate complex of products and/or services. These combinations or systems have become more and more widely identified with the rapid advance in communications technologies and information management applications. Obviously, each custom-made system reflects a very high degree of differentiation; and marketing such systems requires technical competence, highly specialized customer liaison, and close personal management. The subtle implications of expertise and intellectuality impose here, for the seller is usually better able than the buyer to structure a system that balances capability and need. His consultations, however, are not offered free of charge, and his pricing-negotiating must be accomplished accordingly.

It is also characteristic of many—though not all—custom-made systems that the service market may be extremely important. In such a case, whether the sale involves a municipal sewage-treatment plant or an international credit card operation, the marketer must know the economics as well as the technology of the system intimately, and he must be qualified to furnish maintenance and service for a (sometimes considerable) period after the purchase. Simply, he must be a well-grounded student of his own company's business and technology and of any customer's business and technology. His marketing counterpart who deals in rivets, however, rarely needs to meet these criteria.

R&D SYSTEMS

The mysteries of research have never been confined exclusively to the workbench. Within a company's laboratories, scientists and engineers purposely deal with unknown, unresolved problems ranging from nondirected, so-called pure research to defined development work and application and design engineering. The other management functions' varying relationships with the research group afford them little real insight into what R&D is doing from day to day. Rather, these nontechnical types for the most part identify and evaluate what comes out of research. The more technically oriented the company's products, the more the marketing manager and his nontechnical peers must strive to comprehend R&D's work—both when it is in process and as it comes out the laboratory door. Thus, in an organization devoted to R&D systems work, the marketing manager's knowledge of science and technology is highly important; otherwise, he cannot comprehend his own organization's products, nor can he recognize and understand customers' needs in terms to which his own company can respond. However, the organization's staff includes a large number of professionals, every one of whom is potentially if not actively engaged in the marketing effort. Indeed, the technical community executes a major share of the marketing functions; thus the marketing manager's relationships with it are vital.

Much though not all systems research is done for the Federal Government, particularly for the Department of Defense (DOD) and for NASA. These customers of course affect marketing in a great many distinct and significant ways, particularly in the requirements for detailed plans and controls that they impose: proposal procedures, contractual arrangements and terms, monitoring and controls, performance evaluations, and the like. Yet, fundamentally, it is because of the nature of this type of product, as well as the nature of its market, that both the research and the development must be thoroughly planned in advance and carefully controlled in their execution.

The marketing manager necessarily plays a key role in determining what the customer wants and in shaping the plan for getting the job and for doing the job; only if his intelligence is good can the organization effectively pursue the job. He also has important responsibilities for developing additional information that may lead the firm to decide not to bid the job. In systems R&D work the stakes are high; the business strategy and marketing strategy must be sound, for an organization cannot afford many bad decisions. Good market intelligence enables the company to submit a winning proposal. This means simply that the customer finds the approach—both technical and management—most nearly what he wants; he finds it well planned and believes achievement assured.

Another aspect of systems R&D—the breadth of technology that may be involved—also affects marketing. In a custom-made system where a variety of subsystems may be needed, the marketing manager must know where and how these subsystems will be obtained, costed, and integrated into the final product system. In a major systems R&D program the marketing manager has similar responsibilities and relationships with subcontracting organizations. Inasmuch as their product, like his own, is R&D, the business-marketing judgments and decisions can be extremely difficult and highly risky.

R&D STUDIES

R&D studies are somewhat more abstract and less tangible but not necessarily more complex than systems R&D. The marketer here is almost certainly an advanced professional who is probably more a technical man than a marketing man. He may not need to relate to as broad a range of technologies as the systems R&D marketing manager, but he certainly needs to know the particular related area of technology that is his organization's or group's specialty. (Of course, he also needs to know the tools and techniques and philosophies of marketing.)

A review of the spectrum leading to R&D studies, from basic materials through standard manufactured items, services, custom-made systems, and R&D systems, demonstrates that the greater the differentiation in product type, the more personal selling replaces advertising. Systems. whether custom-made or R&D—and R&D studies even more so—must be marketed personally and directly by highly knowledgeable individuals. The understanding of business management required of marketers of R&D studies is not peculiar to their function; a high degree of management and business acumen is demanded of contracting people, R&D, engineering, finance, purchasing, and others. But the marketer frequently is—or becomes—the program general manager. He identifies and develops the market, responds in depth to the opportunity, wins the contract award, and directs the fulfillment. Most assuredly, this is not the marketer of rivets.

PROFESSIONAL SERVICES

The range and variety of professional services span a vast differentiation. The licensed certified public accounting (CPA) firm that provides a year-end audit can almost be considered in the off-the-shelf business. Its fellow specialist firm that constructs and helps to install a computerized cost-accounting profit-center control system for a multiplant company doing business around the world operates in a far different environment. However, both firms market intangible expertise. That which they deliver will not physically pump more, dig deeper, run faster, or operate at improved efficiencies or lower costs that are positively and indisputably attributable to the supplier of the service. Always, some measure of the performance achieved after the service is rendered can be blamed on or credited to the client.

The marketer of professional services must fully appreciate the ephemeral character of his product. He must explore his client's problem in the greatest possible depth in order to serve real needs and dissolve those that may be imaginary; he must demonstrate continuing sensitivity and counsel to the client while the work is under way; and he must be alert and responsive to postfulfillment problems or needs. Thus the marketer of professional services shares many of the characteristics of the R&D marketer: He is, himself, almost always a doer or practitioner; he sells a highly personalized product, himself; he must know as much as possible about his client in order to tailor his service to that client individually; and he finds that most of his business is built on reputation rather than advertising, for most of his business comes from direct referrals or in the form of repeat business.

Professional services differ from R&D in one significant respect: R&D attacks unknown elements of a problem, whereas services generally treat clearly demonstrated needs. R&D points the way to new hardware or new systems that may cause the future development of new philosophies or principles. Professional services focus on immediate, existing situations and concern interpersonal relationships, operating concepts and methods, and the health, education, and welfare of the client. Thus the marketer of professional services deals in human affairs. He must project his organization's capabilities to counsel, console, instruct, and advise, as well as to provide expertise and technical or professional understanding—all of which work toward a sound resolution to the client's problem.

Profiling Product Effects

At best, the nature of a product or service and its effect on marketing are difficult to measure in precise terms. The variations apparent in this review, ranging from basic materials and standard products to R&D and professional services, demonstrate that intangibility and complexity are often obscure, sometimes almost contradictory. The astute marketing manager, however, knows full well that the nature of the product or service does affect marketing significantly and that his study here is essential.

A decade or more before John Kenneth Galbraith (*The New Industrial State,* Houghton Mifflin Company, 1968) wrote about the "technostructure," marketing practitioners were becoming aware of the growing necessity for anticipating and dealing with change. Vast changes in technologies and in the whole order of man's social, political, and economic affairs were introducing an increasing number of new differentiations of markets and of products and services. The marketing manager, responsible for directing "the flow of goods and services from production to consumption," became a true professional whose breadth and perception enabled him to meet the demands of the new marketing environment that was evolving.

It was increasingly clear that marketing considerations would orient management strategy and marketing decisions would platform business decisions. Among the many challenges faced by the marketing manager was the requirement to understand, more than ever before, the relationship of his products to the marketing function, and the effects of changes in those products that further differentiated the products. Today that challenge is far more significant than it was in the 1950's; today he and all other managers are most certain of tomorrow's uncertainty, most certain that tomorrow will be different.—*J. L. Wood*

COMPETITIVE FORCES

Competition and competitive activity are commercial and economic realities. Because competition is something that all businessmen are aware of and in one situation or another constantly encounter, not only in business but in personal situations, it is an entity that has close personal identification and is readily understood.

Although the existence of competition and its measurable and unmeasurable influences are readily acknowledged, there is often a tendency toward overconcern or underconcern, and either a fatalistic attitude or complacency is the result. A deeper understanding of the dynamics of competition leads to a more positive and meaningful comprehension of the significance of competition; competitive forces; the influence and effects of competition, both direct and indirect; and the negative and positive aspects of competition.

Philosophy of Competition

It is sometimes valuable to pause and reflect upon the underlying principles from which psychological, sociological, and economic realities evolve. From the urge that impels individuals to excel to the collective efforts of groups to predominate, it is but a simple extension to the impulsion of corporate expansion and dominance. Although this may explain—at least in part—the origin of competition between individuals and provide a foundation for analyzing group competitiveness, there is an additional and fundamentally significant consideration in the dynamics of business competition. The means of economic survival under the free enterprise system are such that optimum opportunity exists for the exercise and application of judgments and techniques that will allow for the successful, profitable coexistence of a multitude of companies competing in the same or essentially the same markets.

Implicit in this analysis are the dynamics of the market itself. Since the market is in a state of constant change through alteration, contraction, or expansion —whether resulting from competitive or noncompetitive activities—technology and social evolutionary change itself must relate to marketability at any given time. Therefore, competitive factors prevail in varying orders of magnitude, and their influences vary significantly according to the contemporary status of the market. This is well summarized in the classic supply-and-demand concept; however, it fails to appreciate the implications of creative marketing and the effect of applying behavioral studies on the creation of demand, particularly as a comparative device.

The Market

The size, nature, and posture of the market vary depending upon the circumstances, but they are in a state of constant change. The manner and degree of competition in any given situation therefore vary. However, in considering competition and market as coexistent forces in a state of equilibrium, it is apparent that both affect each other and that a change in either one results in a change in the other; therefore, in order to fully appreciate competition and its effects, the nature and structure of the market must be considered.

Classically, the primary markets are three: the consumer, industrial, and government markets. This classification is obviously an oversimplification, but it is nevertheless cogent because the effects and influences of competition vary dramatically in relation to this market segmentation.

CONSUMER MARKET

The consumer market is probably the most competitive, volatile, and active of the three. The number of firms competing and the size, strength, and distribution potentialities of any given supplier are of vital importance in relation to his ability to compete in the consumer market. Technical evolution is a determinant, and the effects of sociological change—particularly as they relate to the psychology of consumer marketing—are additional influences. Creativity in competition as a reflection of imaginative marketing is a very important consideration in analyzing competitive activity within the consumer market. Consumer appeal, new products, product modification, packaging, price, advertising, promotion, and convenience items are all employed as active competitive strategies. In the consumer market there is deep concern with less obvious competitive strategies—for example, monetary advantages, particularly consumer credit. As the trend to deficit financing becomes firmly entrenched in consumer purchasing, the use of competitive credit techniques becomes increasingly significant.

INDUSTRIAL MARKET

There are many considerations in the industrial marketplace that parallel those of the consumer market. The differences involve the number of competitors, who are often far fewer but tend to be larger, and the elements of peripheral benefits of size prevail. The ability for sales/purchase reciprocity is not and cannot be explicit but can be and is implicit. Again, price, service, distribution, and availability are all relevant factors. New products, product development, product modification, and customer service are also important. Advertising and promotion are certainly important in the industrial market, but it is questionable that their value is of the magnitude found in consumer marketing.

GOVERNMENT MARKET

Competition in government marketing is important, despite the very distinct differences from consumer and industrial marketing characteristics. The government, in its contractual relationship with suppliers, is quite clear in its stipulation regarding competitiveness, but competition in government marketing is most directly concerned with economics and with quality in relation to price of products delivered.

Another distinction is that although in consumer and industrial markets both the nature and means of competitors are known, competitive bidding in government marketing is often done without such knowledge but merely by assumption, on initial bidding at least. This, of course, complicates entry into the government market, since the techniques in dealing with government and the nature of specific competitors can be determined only after deep study.

Competitive Techniques

The object of competition is to obtain, maintain, or improve a position in a given market; and, traditionally, the following devices have been employed for this purpose: price, quality, service, advertising and promotion, distribution, financing, supply, product and product development, and company image.

In considering these elements one by one in the discussion that follows, it is important to appreciate that the market changes have resulted in an alteration in the general approach of competitors to effective competitive maneuvers. The face of competition has changed, with the result that the elements formerly encountered as major competitive strategies have altered, by and large, to keep pace with the dynamics of marketing requirements.

Again, to put the principal techniques of competitive activity in perspective, it is essential that opportunities for creativeness, either in the use of existing techniques in combination or in approaching the development of competitive tactics, be thoroughly considered. The opportunities for imaginative competitive response are abundant, since the principal competitive activity now centers in sectors other than those of previous years.

PRICE

Price is subject to manipulation. Obviously, price concessions in a given market can result in increased sales, either temporary or long-range. There is no doubt that this is the most manifest competitive technique. However, irresponsible competitive pricing results in the imposition of forces causing some form of retaliation.

The use of price as a competitive technique has other serious ramifications. Management must always be concerned with profitability, and it is apparent that competitive pricing, if carried too far, can eventually lead to price attrition. When new products are considered, existing market price levels will impose limitations as well as provide guidelines.

The use of price was, for many years, undeniably the predominant competitive weapon. With the increasing number of competitors and competitive products, the product-value relationship has largely stabilized, thus necessitating emphasis on competitive strategies other than price manipulation. In recent years this change has been reflected in tremendous emphasis on service and service-related techniques. When the increased technical requirements are taken into consideration, this is a logical approach to improving competitive position, and either technical or commercial service assistance generates an entirely new competitive climate. This is not to say that price is no longer actively employed as a competitive tactic, but rather that it is usually now utilized as only one element in a combination of individual strategies.

QUALITY

Quality can be considered from two standpoints in relationship to competition: On the one hand, competitors may offer improved quality in a given product at the same price, thereby obtaining business; on the other hand, they may offer lower quality at a lower price with the same objective. Either technique has application that can result in restrictive, temporary gains. The response to such a technique depends essentially upon the consideration of longer-range, corporate objectives. Such maneuvers have at times resulted in the establishment and promotion of dual product lines whereby competition can be effected at equivalent quality and price levels.

Product quality has taken on added importance in recent years, particularly in scientific and government markets, where extremely high specifications and commercial tolerances are commonly encountered and the ability to compete is predicated upon technological or scientific improvement and related engineering installation and process assistance.

SERVICE

Service is multifaceted, and the levels of service required in various markets differ significantly. Customer service in consumer markets most often involves resale and maintenance; in the industrial market it is technical support; and in the government market service involves predetermined, specific arrangements. Competitors can and do offer additional services to their customers regardless of the marketplace—a definite contribution, in many instances, but one that can be quite expensive to the supplier. The determination of customer service levels as they relate either to a given market or product or to a particular product to a specific customer must be carefully analyzed from the standpoint of return on investment (ROI).

In one guise or another, service is repeatedly encountered as at least the secondary element in overall competitive maneuvers. The key to the effective application of services as a competitive device is a result of imagination and creativity.

ADVERTISING AND PROMOTION

Competitive marketing activities are of most apparent and immediate concern in two specific areas—advertising and promotion.

The effects that competition can create through advertising and promotional efforts differ in the industrial and consumer markets. Regardless of the market segmentation, the influence of these efforts is dramatic, although of questionable duration in many instances.

It is not feasible or necessary to consider here all the ramifications inherent in advertising and promotional marketing activities, since most of them are well known and established. Due consideration should, however, be given to the influence and importance of effective countermarketing measures.

DISTRIBUTION

Although distribution is not usually thought of either as an external competitive force or as a technique that can be used in competition, it can be and is effectively employed. If distribution is conceived of as being, essentially, the means of getting the product into the consumer's hands, it is evident that the competitor who can assure the consumer of his superior ability to do so has gained a competitive advantage. Conversely, inability to fill a demand with the immediacy so often required in active markets is a distinct disadvantage that can be capitalized on by competitors.

FINANCING

No longer can it be said that the customer is *becoming* credit-conscious; he is already credit-conscious. The importance of this consideration has only recently been given added significance through the introduction of new Federal legislation, the Consumer Credit Protection Act. Recognition of this factor, with proper imaginative utilization of it, provides a definite competitive tool.

SUPPLY

Though supply could be considered as a subfactor in distribution, the situation in a marketing sense is of far broader implication. Supply in the more expansive concept involves totality from inception to finalization; from earliest raw material to the last point of sales support. In this broader sense, competitors who are not in a position of strength with respect to their ability to satisfy all these requirements are not likely to be able to employ this distinct competitive factor; or, if they are able to do so, do not often fully exploit the inherent possibilities.

PRODUCT AND PRODUCT DEVELOPMENT

The competitive force implicit in the product and in product development requires little elaboration here. It is usually the first-considered and perhaps the most obvious manifestation—second only to price—of competitive activity. Product stasis is the progenitor of market stagnation. Competition recognizes this and exploits it. Product viability creates market vitality and assures the competitor of a position of prominence in the marketplace.

IMAGE-CONSCIOUSNESS

The overall image of the supplier in the market is of vital concern to initial and continuing success and growth. A definite force is associated with the image of success, and image-consciousness, not alone of product or brand but of the total corporation, is a valued asset. Modern management's recognition of psychological principles as applied to effective marketing and development of image-consciousness is of concern in this area. The constant interplay of competitive techniques creates the competitive atmosphere in which marketing functions and to which it must effectively respond.

To effectively exploit the full value of image-consciousness, it is necessary to recognize the importance of promoting the total corporation and utilizing this additional strategy as a component of the total marketing effort—more specifically, of implementing it in advertising and promotional activities.

Significance of Competition

The "whys and wherefores" of competitive significance are evident from the points already established regarding the prevailing atmosphere of competitiveness in the marketplace. The importance of competition must not be underestimated, particularly since it is clearly apparent that there is a vast increase in competitive activity in contemporary marketing and that there will be a continued acceleration of such activity, particularly as international markets expand.

The force exerted by competition through implementation of its techniques is apparent. What is essential is that the effect of the force be understood. Effective marketing and product planning require not only a recognition of competition but the establishment of appropriate countermeasures and the ability to respond rapidly as well.

It is clear that competition is a dynamic force. The balancing of situations at any time, and the shifts that occur as a consequence of competitive activity, provide the conditions in which marketing operates. Effective operation within these dynamic parameters is a basic for successful marketing.

Effects of Competition

Competition, as visualized from the seller's standpoint, has very definite controlling influences that have to be considered in the marketing activity. From the consumer's standpoint, competition carries with it benefits that are sometimes not completely understood or exploited—for example, capitalization on created consumer demand. Since the consumer is ultimately the final reduction of the market to its smallest unit, he creates the demand, the satisfaction of which is obviously used as a competitive tactic. One factor to observe and guard against, however, is overreaction to competitive activity, with the needless expenditure of compromise that can ensue, based on ill-advised or premature competitive response.

NEGATIVE ASPECTS

Management often conceives competition in its more negative aspects. There are indeed negative considerations, particularly since competition limits market share, market potential, price, and all the many factors that define total response to the given marketing effort. Viewed from this vantage point, competition undeniably has its negative side; but there is a balance in its positive aspects.

POSITIVE ASPECTS

No one will argue as to the value of competition from the consumers' standpoint. In the theory of sociological evolution, the importance of competition as a contributory force has been validated and revalidated. Visualized as a driving force in economic evolution, competition is again a primary motivating influence and as such expands the market internally and externally, thereby of itself effectively generating additional marketability through the creation of further opportunity for competitors. The most obvious positive contribution to business therefore is that, by its very nature, competition creates business.

LEGAL CONSIDERATIONS

Management, especially marketing management, when considering actions of its competitors and of its own corporation, would be very wise to evaluate such activities in the light of Federal and state legislation. Antitrust and trade regulations (the Sherman Act of 1890, the Clayton Act of 1914 and its later Robinson-Patman Act amendments, the Federal Trade Commission Act of 1914, and the Celler-Kefauver Antimerger Act of 1950), as well as local legislation, should be thoroughly considered and any contemplated competitive activities reviewed to assure that they are within the framework of existing legislation. (See the following subsection.)—*G. S. Dominguez*

THE LEGAL FRAMEWORK OF MARKETING

This discussion concentrates on situations and relationships that give rise to the legal problems most frequently encountered in marketing. Reference to the statutes and to case law is kept to a minimum. Legal problems that, although important, arise infrequently are not treated. For the sake of simplicity it is assumed that the marketing executive is engaged in marketing a product that does not require special licensing and that his company is not a member of a regulated industry.

Necessarily, the objective of these few pages must be solely to alert the marketing executive to the existence of these legal problems rather than to advise him of their solutions. The resulting legal checklist, accordingly, will inform the reader when he has need—but not how to dispense with the need—for a legal adviser.

Consumer Problems

In its relationship with the consumer, a company's advertising is usually the initial situation giving rise to legal problems. Other problem areas are labeling, warranties, and procurement.

ADVERTISING

Deceptive advertising in interstate commerce is unlawful under the Federal Trade Commission Act. There are also many state and local laws that may apply. In addition there are statutes that impose special obligations with respect to special products or services. An example is the Federal truth-in-lending law, which governs advertising of certain interest rates and financing terms.

No marketing executive need be reminded that there are legal problems in false advertising. But it is valuable to remember that there may also be legal problems where the advertising is believed to be true but no evidence exists as to its veracity, and even where the advertising can be proved to be literally true but is readily misunderstood by the careless or casual reader. In the former case a marketing executive may find that his company's legal department insists on advance documentation of controversial product claims in order to be prepared to deal with the controversy that may arise. The legal department may consider that even old-fashioned "puffing" cannot be tolerated if it provokes a competitor, a trade association, or a government agency to initiate an expensive legal proceeding. In the latter case—advertising which may be readily misunderstood although true—the trend of modern interpretation and regulation is to place on the advertiser the burden of making his message clear. This is because those most in need of the consumer protection laws may be unable to draw fine distinctions or extract the true meaning from carefully hedged advertising copy.

A host of more technical legal problems are encountered in advertising: One, for example, concerns the obtaining of releases when using others' names or likenesses (photographs or drawings). Advertising men should be encouraged to become familiar with these problems through the various texts and management courses available. The general rule of thumb in dealing with such situations is that a $50,000 advertising program should not be exposed to an injunction merely because a $50 release was not obtained or a slight change in wording was not made.

LABELING

Supplementary problems are involved in labeling products, because legislatures have generally considered that the most effective way of bringing desired information to the consumer's attention is to require the information to be placed before him when he reads the product label. Labeling is subject to extremely technical requirements. The Federal statutes on this subject include the Fair Packaging and Labeling Act and the Hazardous Substances Labeling Act. State and local labeling requirements are numerous. Since there are frequently regulations for details such as type size and location of required information, it is obviously necessary to obtain specific information on these requirements early in the course of designing packaging for a product to be placed on the market.

WARRANTIES

A further situation for the marketing executive to anticipate is the possibility of consumer claims after sale. The consumer may claim that the product has caused injury or is otherwise unsatisfactory. The extent of manufacturers' responsibility for injuries caused by the products they sell has been broadened greatly over the past 30 years. The outcome of a product liability claim may depend in part on factors under the control of the marketing executive, such as the advertising and labeling of the product and the accompanying instructional material. The result of ordinary warranty claims may also turn on advertising, and the marketing executive should take part in the decision as to the scope of the warranty and how it is to be advertised. Warranties referred to in advertising must be fully stated. The warranty given may not vary from the warranty advertised. The warranty must also be reasonable. For example, a long-term warranty may be considered improper if the product is not really expected to last for the period of the warranty. At the other extreme, an unduly short or limited warranty may be considered unlawful because it tends to mislead consumers into believing that they have protection in excess of what is offered. Obviously, a key question for the marketing executive to ask about the warranty is whether it is fair to the consumer. Another key question is whether the selling price includes an adequate allowance for the estimated cost of warranty servicing. This may reduce the possibility that the company may later be placed under pressure to skimp on warranty service.

PROCUREMENT

All these legal problems affecting consumers take on a different complexion, of course, if the consumer is not the man in the street but an industrial concern or a governmental agency. In such cases some of the laws that impose specific requirements for the protection of the public may not apply to their full extent. The Fair Packaging and Labeling Act is an example. The company's relationship with sophisticated industrial and governmental consumers is normally governed by the latter's sales contracts. It is obviously desirable to review carefully such a contract—whether it is embodied in a formal document, an exchange of order and confirmation forms, or an oral understanding—in order to determine if it protects the seller adequately as to essential terms such as price, quantity, delivery, quality, and the seller's responsibilities after sale. Occasionally, in negotiations with industrial organizations, counsel may be needed because the proposed terms are too general. Vague or incomplete contracts, especially in situations where there is no established trade custom, spawn legal problems that can often be avoided by having a proper contract prepared by counsel. In dealing with government agencies, on the other hand, the marketing executive may also need counsel but for the opposite reason. Government contracts may contain, or incorporate by reference, so many standard clauses or prescribed forms that it may be practically impossible for the marketing executive to understand his obligations under the resulting document. This makes it wise to obtain legal advice as to how much of a commitment is actually being made before determining the price to be charged.

Customer Problems

Potential legal problems in the customer area are numerous, arising chiefly from restrictions in the appointment of dealers or distributors and from pricing policy, attempts to restrain customers from buying from competitors, and attempts to control resales.

DEALER OR DISTRIBUTOR APPOINTMENT

In selecting his channels of distribution to the ultimate consumer, the marketing executive presumably will desire to sell through wholesale or retail outlets. In initially selecting the dealers or distributors to whom he will sell his products, the marketing executive of a nonmonopoly company has much latitude under the current law. Generally speaking, he is altogether unrestricted in his unilateral choice of his direct customers. He usually encounters legal problems only if he undertakes to make his dealer or distributor appointments by agreement with others, or if he terminates such appointments without adequate justification, or if he seeks to deal with his customers on discriminatory or unduly restrictive terms. One aspect of his freedom to select his customers is his freedom to determine the number of customers he will select in a particular area. To this end he may lawfully agree with a customer that he will be the sole distributor appointed within a certain area for some reasonably limited period of time, in order to induce him to devote adequate resources to marketing a low-volume product with high distribution costs.

PRICING

In dealing with his customers once they have been selected, however, the marketing executive must be aware of the laws concerning discrimination in price or promotional allowances and services among competing customers. Such discrimination is not always forbidden; but where commodities sold in interstate commerce are concerned, it is closely regulated by the Robinson-Patman Act and Federal Trade Commission Act. These acts raise extremely technical issues. Unless a seller has a uniform one-price policy, F.O.B. or delivered, and makes no promotional services or allowances available to customers, the marketing executive will almost certainly need legal assistance in the design and implementation of his pricing and promotional policy to assure avoidance of unlawful discrimination. Among the issues involved will be those of which products are sufficiently "like" to require similar treatment, when price differences may require justification, what cost savings will justify such differences, and when competition may be met.

PURCHASES FROM COMPETITORS

On occasion a seller may desire, as a condition of sale, to require his customers to refrain from obtaining goods or services from competitors. Any such attempt will raise serious antitrust problems, whether sought to be achieved by tying arrangements, exclusive dealing covenants, total requirement contracts, or franchise licenses.

RESALES

Most other legal problems in a manufacturer's relationships with customers arise from attempts of the manufacturer to control what his customers may do with his products once the products have been purchased. For example, agreements stipulating resale prices, except pursuant to Federal and state "fair trade" legislation, violate the Sherman Act and may subject the parties to severe penalties, both criminal and civil. This has been established law for many years. More recently, it has also been ruled illegal for a manufacturer to limit customers as to where and to whom they will resell products purchased by them. A manufacturer may still suggest a resale price and assign areas and markets of primary responsibility, leaving it to the customer to decide whether he will conform to such suggestions. But for a manufacturer wishing to reserve such decisions to himself, the opportunities are few. A marketing executive would be well advised to consult with counsel before discussing any restriction on resales with customers.

Competitor Problems

Relationships with competitors provide numerous matters in which the exercise of caution is essential, for this is the area most under the influence of the antitrust laws.

AGREEMENTS

The marketing executive should realize that, although the antitrust laws do not altogether forbid agreements between competitors, they tend to limit the scope and nature of such agreements so substantially that many corporations lean over backward to avoid equivocal competitive contacts. Thus corporations may, as a matter of policy, ban all business contacts with competitors except where authorized by counsel. Whether or not his corporation has such a legal policy, a marketing executive should bear in mind that the "contracts, combinations, and conspiracies" forbidden by the Sherman Act are not confined to price-fixing agreements. For example, agreements dividing markets, territories, or customers are among the many types of nonprice agreements which may violate the antitrust laws. Moreover, conduct falling far short of formal agreement has been interpreted by courts and juries to constitute a combination or conspiracy. The general rule of thumb in this area, as in the case of price discrimination, should be to check with counsel before making a move involving cooperation with a competitor.

COERCION

Like the Marquis of Queensberry rules, the antitrust laws ban not only collusion with opponents but also unfairly aggressive conduct toward such opponents. Specifically, these laws reach monopolization and attempts to monopolize as well as contracts, combinations, and conspiracies in unreasonable restraint of trade. Moreover, monopolization of a market is not solely what the term implies in ordinary usage. A company may have active competitors and yet be a monopolist in the antitrust sense if it intentionally acquires or exercises dominant power in a particular line, and if that line is sufficiently distinct to be considered a separate part of commerce. For example, the promotion of championship boxing matches was considered to be a separate part of commerce. The achievement of such a dominant position is not unlawful, of course, if it results simply from superior performance in the marketplace. However, the use of contracts excluding competitors from supply sources or outlets, discriminatory practices, and acquisitions of competing businesses are among the factors that have been taken into consideration by courts in ruling that a dominant position has not been acquired merely as a result of such superiority. Indeed, the marketing executive must bear in mind that even lawful practices such as long-term leases, if adopted for predatory or exclusionary purposes, may at some future time form part of the evidence in a proceeding directed against his company for an unlawful plan of monopolization.

ORGANIZATIONAL ACTIVITIES

From time to time it may be advisable for a company to participate in industry committees, buying groups, and trade associations. The purpose, procedures, and scope of activities of each such organization should be reviewed carefully to insure that unlawful conduct of others does not expose the executive and his corporation to attack.

PATENTS

The marketing executive must be equally on the alert, whether his company or a competitor owns patents and trademarks. On the one hand, if he possesses such rights, he may exclude others from their enjoyment or may license their use on nonrestrictive terms. On the other hand, if a patent is held by others, it is altogether possible that the manufacture and sale of a new product could be enjoined at great cost to the executive's company or that his company might be compelled to pay royalties not contemplated at the time of the formation of the pricing strategy for the product. It is essential that all patent policies be reviewed by antitrust counsel and that all proposed new products be reviewed by patent counsel. The same principle applies to proposed trademarks. A suit by a competitor to enjoin use of a trademark after an advertising program is under way can be both costly and embarrassing.

Corporate Problems

In addition to the legal problems that a marketing executive encounters in his relationships with consumers, customers, and competitors, other legal problems are thrust on him because of the management practices of his own corporation.

FORMALITIES

Normally, the legal department or the secretary will wish to keep signed copies of all outstanding agreements of the company. They will establish procedures for reviewing agreements before signature and assuring that agreements are signed only with proper authorization. They will wish to be kept advised of any changes, proposed changes, or interpretations concerning such agreements that are made by exchanges of correspondence or oral understandings, because these may create conflicts with other agreements, go beyond the authority given, or even raise questions of legality.

INTEGRATION

The corporation may also have policies requiring operating units to "stand on their own feet" without unfair assistance from other operating units. If he should fail to heed such policies, the marketing executive could inadvertently expose the company to liability. For example, if a marketing executive were to request the assistance of the purchasing department in making sales presentations to customers, or arrange for the purchasing department to maintain records on sales to potential suppliers, he could expose the company to charges of unlawful reciprocity. Or if he holds out for favored treatment of one branch by another branch of the company and this results in unfair treatment of the competitors of the favored branch, he may in some circumstances expose the company to liability. If the company has a dominant position in its field, there may even be attempts at divestiture of parts of the company.

MERGERS

A corporation is entitled to expand at will by internal growth, but it may not as freely do so through acquisitions and mergers. Section 7 of the Clayton Act must be considered before entering into negotiations with respect to the stock or assets of other corporations.

RECORDS

Management needs records to operate, and the corporate marketing executive must give attention to maintaining records that are accurate as well as adequate. Reports of sales personnel tend to contain exaggerated and colorful statements, such as a determination to "clobber" the competition or to make full use of the company's "muscle." Often, such statements are not made or taken seriously. But if the company's records are later subpoenaed, such statements may be paraded before a court or jury as evidence of an intent to stifle competition. It is advisable to have written evidence indicating that the company's actual motives were not what such salesmen's reports might inaccurately suggest. The records of a marketing department may also play an important part in assessing whether proposed mergers have been undertaken for anticompetitive purposes or may have an anticompetitive effect. For many reasons it is useful for the marketing department to work out, in conjunction with the legal department, an adequate system of records that will make it possible for the company to substantiate its legal rights, defend itself against charges of impropriety, and at the same time be useful in giving the company's other executives adequate information on which to base proposed corporate action.

The Price of Negligence

A marketing executive sometimes asks, "What risks do I incur if I should decide to ignore these legal problems?" The answer is that—if he is challenged in an administrative or judicial proceeding—he will at best incur substantial legal expenses and at worst be subject to varying legal penalties. Thus fines, jail, injunctions, and treble damages may result from antitrust violations. "There are times when fear is good."—*W. T. Lifland and J. G. Van Cise*

CUSTOMER BUYING BEHAVIOR

An understanding of the buying behavior of customers and prospects is essential to introducing a new product or service successfully and developing the full potential thereafter. This understanding must be thorough and current since behavior is constantly changing, usually gradually but at times abruptly, because of forces outside the control of any one marketer. Nevertheless, every marketer is attempting either to change behavior or, in the case of established markets, to prevent behavior from changing.

The act of buying results when internal attitudes and intentions and external catalysts combine in the absence of constraints in the environment in such a way that it seems easy and safe to a customer for him to buy. A central task in marketing is to keep the purchase as free as possible from effort and risk in the view of the buyer.

Basic Factors

Customer buying behavior is a function of six factors: (1) the nature of the marketer; (2) the nature of the customer; (3) the nature of the product or service; (4) timing; (5) availability (where and how the product or service is offered); and (6) motivation (benefits expected and received). It is helpful to think of each of these factors in terms of two dimensions. Marketers are describable in terms of size and reputation. Customers are describable objectively (by age, sex, income, education, domicile, occupation, and other demographic characteristics) and subjectively (by less apparent psychological and other intangible characteristics). Products and services are describable as to their concept and content. Timing is most usefully approached in terms of *introduction* or initial purchasing, and *continuation* or repurchase maintenance. Availability breaks down into place of purchase and means of purchase. Motivation is a matter of benefits expected and received, and the benefits can be of two kinds: primary, direct, or positive; or secondary, indirect, or negative. Adding up these items results in 12 angles from which to view customer behavior—more than most marketers actively deal with at any one time.

NATURE OF MARKETER

The marketer is a factor in customer buying behavior either directly or through the agents he selects to purvey his offering. In consumer products the name of the marketer may either facilitate or diminish purchasing activity, because of his size and general reputation, or because of specific experience of customers with other of his offerings. With this in mind, manufacturers decide whether to use corporate, divisional, or subsidiary names, especially in the case of new and revised products. In industrial purchasing the identity of the vendor, his approach to the buyer, and his capabilities are significant factors in buying decisions. In government purchasing the size of the bidder, his location, and the history of past relations all enter into the considerations of purchasing goods and services from him rather than from other possible contractors. The first task of the marketer is to prepare for his own acceptance—to insure that customer prospects will elect to deal with him at all—or, in established markets, that they will continue to deal with him.

Consumers and the marketer.   There are many examples of the varied usage of company names in retailing. A large soap company, knowing the impact of its name on housewives, allows product managers of new brands to feature the company name in introductory advertising only for a specified period of time; thereafter, the product must survive on the strength of its own image and market acceptance. A large food company knows that a subsidiary name gains more acceptance from customers for frozen foods than its own name and continues to promote that name rather than its corporate style. In contrast, a major chemical company found that consumers would accept color film bearing its name only if associated with a better-known name in photography.

Other customers and the marketer.   Business and industrial buying is no less affected by the nature of the marketer. A tobacco company buying its first computer system was less impressed by the equipment described in solicited proposals than by the number of representatives sent and the distance they had to travel, both of which were measures of installation capabilities and service intentions. A utility may divide its buying between two or three major equipment suppliers in order to insure their survival, thereby reducing opportunity for a new, smaller marketer. Many industrial and government purchasers maintain an approved list of suppliers for which the prospective marketer must qualify. There may be several lists for different products and services, each one with different standards that the marketer must meet.

In most government purchasing, suppliers on an approved list may receive some or all of the requests for quotation that the buyer sends out. However, preproposal services, including considerable personal attention in one form or another, are necessary if the marketer is to receive serious consideration from the buyer. In addition the marketer is evaluated against other bidders and prospective bidders, and the secondary effect of awarding a contract to one or the other is given weight equal to or greater than the product or service itself.

Both business and government purchasers, like the consumer, favor a marketer who has done exactly or nearly exactly the same thing before in the provision of goods and services, because the risk appears to be less. In areas where the buyer has little experience, contractors located near the work site or buyer's headquarters are favored, chiefly because of nominal cost saving; but other able marketers, including those providing R&D services, are usually given fair consideration if they persist. When the marketer is able to present his offering as unique, he may be given work as a "sole source" without competitive bidding. This is precisely the position that consumer goods manufacturers hope will be accorded to them by individuals and families. Consumers and other customers alike expect higher or lower prices to be charged by the "sole source" and are willing to pay them according to their knowledge of the marketer. Some marketers are sufficiently powerful in their respective industries to administer prices and to be price leaders. In such cases customers will not pay higher prices to smaller marketers, even for specialties, until the price leader sets the level.

In short, regardless of the marketing area, the marketer's identity affects the buyer's behavior. Many have found new sources of business from learning what people are willing to buy from them, while others have sustained losses from pushing an offering that gained little acceptance because of the nature of the marketer.

NATURE OF CUSTOMER

A customer is an individual acting for himself or as a member of a group, family, or organization. The customer for any product or service may be a reseller, gift buyer, or user of the product or service. The individual rarely purchases anything without having imagined, if not actually ascertained, the effect of his buying behavior on others, mainly people in his immediate environment. The others who are considered, even briefly, may exist in the past or in the future as well as in the present life of the individual. A consumer may be thinking of what his parents or an early mentor would say were they to learn of his purchase; he may also envision how his children would react to it in later years. An executive evaluating a buying opportunity on behalf of a corporation may look at the alternatives as he imagines the founder would, or a professor whose teachings he has always relied upon; at the same time he may be looking ahead at the effect of the purchase on those who learn of it much later—his successor, for example.

Isolated purchasing decision. The mental rehearsal of the effect of a purchase on other people may take place at the time of purchase, in the case of impulse purchasing, or, in the case of deliberative or planned purchasing, during a period of time prior to the purchase. For purchases made routinely, a customer may have gone through this process years before and closed his mind to further reflection upon it, despite the fact that in the meantime his way of life has changed in other respects. To be a prospect for some other product or service, such a customer must direct his attention to the inappropriateness of his routine habit. Customers are not necessarily loyal to their own nature but do hold to preferences for certain products and brands. Over 20 years some 25 percent of initial brand preferences may be retained. Brand loyalty is partly a function of length of use; the more something is purchased, the more likely it will continue to be purchased.

Reference groups. The other people whom the customer considers in thinking about and making a purchase may be described in terms of nonwork activities in which the customer is a participant, such as skiing or churchgoing, or in terms of class. Classes are defined by relative amounts of wealth and personal power. Education, occupation, and income are the major overt indicators of class, and many people see differences in attitudes as well. To the extent that an individual identifies with others similar to him in these respects, buying behavior can be characterized along class lines. According to one research study, in the upper class, men buy their own clothing; in the middle class, they buy it jointly with their wives; in the lower class, women buy their husband's clothes, along with virtually all the household purchases. Other habits and tastes also vary between the classes. An automatic dishwasher is distinctly an upper- and upper-middle-class product, despite the fact that the lower class purchases other appliances and household goods in the same or higher price ranges. In contrast, laxatives are a lower-class product in terms of the income of purchasers. The upper class was conservative in accepting television, but its housebound entertainment, requiring no social exposure or acceptance for enjoyment, was taken up quickly by the lower class. The lower class was conservative in adopting canasta, while it swept through the upper class. The middle class accepted supermarkets more readily than either the lower or the upper class. Reference groups strongly influence the purchase of cars, cigarettes, beer, and other products conspicuously purchased or used.

Pace setting and trend making are often functions of class. The bulk of customers in the lower and middle classes will reject the product or service that has not first been accepted by those whose taste they trust and whose behavior they emulate. Fiber-glass curtains failed to be profitable in their first years, not because of faulty manufacturing but because they were introduced in low-price lines without prior acceptance by the upper-middle class. Aluminum siding at first gained no more than an insignificant sales volume because it was placed on small development homes; as a result, it came to signify cheapness, wealthier home owners would not use it, and the middle class had nothing to emulate.

On the other hand, customers in the highest classes may deliberately adopt styles identified with lower classes as evidence of their own recognition of practical values. Consumers without much status strongly favor popular brand-named products, whereas those whose positions and fortunes are secure can afford to buy and serve cheaper private-label and off-brand products; in fact, they account for a disproportionate share of such purchases. Disadvantaged elements of society want the "best" or the "biggest" they can buy. This behavior is unrelated to personal income or to price, to actual product performance or personal service delivered, for the customers are seeking an abstract value that confers benefits beyond the mere possession of the purchased item. Each marketer of consumer products or services must determine if status or class is affecting buying behavior with respect to his offering.

Fabric converters, who buy rolls of cloth from mills and finish and print them for garment makers also make decisions in isolation; they are buying for their own positions and go through the mental rehearsal process when selecting material. In anticipating the reactions of their customers' customers, they try to imagine the ultimate consumer's reaction when approaching a rack of finished clothing. Quasitechnical terms, such as "look," "hand," and "feel," are derived directly from this mental rehearsal. The marketer must determine in each case which other groups are being considered in the buyer's decision.

Group purchasing decision. The apparent difference between the buying behavior of customers acting in isolation and the behavior of buyers acting within a group is attributable to the transfer of these considerations from the thought level to the speech level, resulting in direct information from "significant others" as to how they will react to various possible purchases. At the same time, nevertheless, all the individuals in a group are envisioning the effect of any purchase on still others who are either not present or outside the group membership entirely. How long this process goes on before the decision is made and the act of buying is performed is mainly a function of the customer's tolerance for anxiety rather than the size or implications of the purchase. People "should" spend more time in selecting and shopping for a refrigerator than a toaster, but often they do not. The decision to buy a piece of machinery must be made by a certain date, whether or not all the facts about competitive equipment are in. Pressure of time and other importunities aside, many customers end up buying a specific offer because they can't stand any further reflection or inaction.

Decision-making unit (DMU). As the proper body to which a marketer must address his efforts, the DMU itself affects buying behavior. The same individual will make different decisions and purchases, depending on the DMU he is a member of at the time, even on the same day. An individual desiring to purchase a new house or new furniture is heavily influenced by whether his children are in school or are grown and gone from home. The individual desiring to purchase office typewriters adaptable to optical character recognition is heavily influenced by whether he is on the administrative or the long-range planning committee or both. The same is true of individuals playing different roles in institutional or governmental hierarchies. The DMU takes on the character of an individual, and its members affect each other much as thoughts affect the individual in isolated buying behavior. As a result the DMU becomes personified and enters into buying considerations. This is true even of conglomerates engaged in shopping for and buying whole businesses.

Within the same DMU, criteria applied to selecting products and services may differ. Conflicting points of view also exist in commercial and industrial DMU's. In judging a new product line, the head of a department store may be concerned chiefly with net profit contribution and the store image; the division merchandiser, with gross profit and reliability of the supplier; and the department buyer, with net revenue and turnover. The marketer, however, must satisfy each viewpoint.

Price and the customer. Customers react differently to price. Some are inveterate price-shoppers, regardless of the product or service, and require some semblance of a bargain before they buy. Others feel sufficiently affluent, or desire to appear so, to give very little attention to price. The greater number of customers judge price in relation to the significance of the product or service to them. Customer awareness of, and ability to report, price is the best single indicator of its importance.

Buying power. Just as customers buy promises of benefits (offered by products and services) on the basis of expectations, they spend in advance of income on the basis of anticipated buying power. Surveys of general customer confidence are important indicators of future buying behavior, as are surveys of intention to buy specific goods because of expectations of increased income and money to spend. The rate and amount of capital expenditures by manufacturers, representing the investment of time and effort in the anticipation of profit, indicate the confidence of the productive sector of our economy. In either case, customers buy more readily when they are confident than in a period of retrenchment, when the decision not to purchase one thing leads to not purchasing others. This is true of customers in households, service firms, factories, and government agencies.

Customers in transition. About one-third of the population at any one time is in transition with respect to buying behavior because of changes induced by ordinary life experiences: moving residence, changing schools or leaving school, entering or leaving the armed services, taking a new job or quitting a job, getting married or divorced, retiring, reacting to the death of relatives, and other events that disrupt the continuity of habits and preferences. These people shortly settle into a new mode of life and re-establish a consistent buying behavior. While in the transitional state, however, their purchases may be erratic, unrelated to their prior life situation, and may reflect a trial mixture of newly possible patterns of purchasing. People in the transitional state may experiment with novel offerings, but they are not true innovators and are not in a position to influence many others. As many industrial salesmen have learned, sometimes to their confusion and dismay, the same transitional state is encountered in the buying behavior of organizations as they relocate, expand, merge, or diversify.

NATURE OF PRODUCT OR SERVICE

A benefit promised by a marketer to a customer prospect in return for money or other consideration may be in the form of a product or a service. A product may be accompanied by service or may have service built into it, as in the case of labor-saving appliances or prepared foods. A service may be accompanied by tangible goods that facilitate the performance of the service to become convertible under certain conditions, as in the case of insurance.

Buying behavior is greatly affected by the definition of the offer made by a marketer; in fact, the definition may determine whether the purchase will be made. The two aspects of an offering (product or service) that greatly affect buying behavior are its concept and its content. The concept of an offer embodies the promise of benefit and is critical in initial acceptance, while the content (what is delivered after the purchase is made) mainly determines repeat purchasing.

Concept of the offer. A compendium of information on foreign countries may fail if offered as a basic product followed by monthly updating sheets but succeed as a newsletter followed by an annual summary, even though the content is pretty much the same: Whereas the first concept requires the acceptance of a sizable reading job plus regular work in updating, the second offers a light reading task and an opportunity of obtaining a one-volume reference book. Buying behavior is triggered by the proper conceptualization of the offering. For example, a gin offered as superior because of aging may utterly fail, despite several years and several million dollars in advertising, because the concept is conveyed by a yellow color that proves incompatible with user need for a clear ingredient in cocktails that must not appear to have too much vermouth. Or an automobile advertised as "designed for the young executive on his way up" fails on a conceptual basis, when introduced during an economic recession in which the customer prospect is not sure he is on the way up.

Advertising may convey a concept that differs from the content delivered. People buy promises, however; they will change their "blind" taste ratings of beer when the labels are revealed, thus conforming to the advertised image rather than to their own senses. This phenomenon exists for products and services that provide chiefly psychic benefits; customers responding to the advertising of air-conditioned comfort are soon lost if there is no such comfort.

Content of the offer. Customers must also accept the content of an offer, either before or after a purchase, if a successful market is to be sustained. Content consists of substance and structure; structure includes all aspects of composition and presentation, from size and shape to packaging and labeling. Customers like a product or service as much or more for the way it comes to them as for the material substance provided, because therein lies the major utility of the offering in conveying benefits. And products can be made too well. Small gasoline engines must be reasonably durable, but few customers demand a 50-year life engineered into the construction. Content itself may, on inspection, influence purchase in unpredictable ways because of the absence of indicators of benefits that customers expect and insist upon prior to purchasing. Customers may select a loaf of bread because the color connotes richness, regardless of the ingredients listed on the label; a bottle of syrup because it is thin rather than pure; a small appliance because the sound of the motor connotes power, regardless of observed performance in demonstrations; or a large appliance because it has more push buttons, even though they are never used.

Packaging and labeling are part of the content of the offering and may affect customer behavior in purchasing and repurchasing by the manner in which they convey the concept and facilitate the functional delivery of the benefits promised or expected. Packaging includes the size and number of separable units in the offering. Formerly, customers were buying three or six cans of beer at a time, three or six boxes of film before vacation trips, three or six golf balls— all before packaging caught up with their preferences. When packaging is relevant to buying behavior, sales go well.

Price and the product or service. Customers have expectations based upon comparing an offering to others like it or to the cost of activities they recognize as alternatives to the offering. The key to understanding customer behavior as related to price or product or service lies in determining what other offerings are being compared and what alternatives, if any, are recognized and considered. A jar of toasted coconut, for example, may be expected by customers to cost 19 cents on the baking-ingredients shelf of a supermarket, where it is compared with the 17-cent plain, shredded coconut beside it; when the same jar is placed next to expensive dessert toppings on a shelf over the ice cream freezer, customers may expect to pay 39 cents.

Customers who shop and compare prices, or who accept bids, feel safest with a price close to what most marketers quote; they are suspicious of the lowest figures because credibility is undermined. A proportion of customers generally in any field, and specifically for any one product or service, buy on a price basis alone without considering other aspects of the concept or content of the offering. Bargain hunters and price switchers as a group form a significant number of customers when the marketer emphasizes low price. However, product quality and delivery capability are two considerations that often override the lowest price offerings to individual customers.

TIMING

There may be no more critical aspect affecting customer buying behavior than timing; the same offering in all particulars can utterly fail at one time yet reach the heights of success at another. The first step in understanding the effect of timing on buying behavior is to discard the belief that there is any possibility that timing is not important. Too often, casually deceptive comments such as "they buy all year 'round" or "a sale can be made at any time" have led marketers to a false conception of customer buying behavior. Virtually nothing in customer behavior happens evenly "all year 'round."

Seasonal buying. Men buy the bulk of their purchases of photographic film in May, women in September. More men buy watches in the first six months of the year, and more women buy them in the last six months of the year. Low-priced watches sell well in December; high-priced, in June. Toothbrushes peak in June (before summer camp) and September (before school). Educational products not ordered or budgeted for in the spring have little chance of acceptance until the following year. Most consumer products and services have cycles built around the change of seasons and the holidays.

Commercial and industrial activity cycles are also functions of these cycles but, because of variations in production and distribution volumes, develop sometimes unique patterns of their own. The heaviest sale of canned tomato products is in September, when distributors take large positions at favorable prices, even though consumption peaks later in the winter. Sporting-goods lines and toys are designed more than a year before ultimate retail sale to enable the trade to screen, order, and stock before peak consumer demand in season. Products or services offered in disharmony with such cycles have little chance of success.

Superimposed on these cycles of purchasing and use are the annual budgets of corporations. Items to be purchased in the summer for use in the fall are often inserted in preliminary budget requests the previous October, approved in December, and funded in January.

Primacy. Being first in a market affects buying behavior for a long time to come. The first filter cigarette or light scotch introduced in a given metropolitan area dominates there for many years even though latecomers may gain supremacy nationwide. But the introduction of an offering may be "before its time." For example, safety belts introduced by one auto maker in advance of public readiness to accept them cost him many unit sales one year, but several years later the same belts became a standard item on all cars.

Passage of time. The behavior of individual customers changes over the years. Customers age and either grow out or die out of the market. A sizable proportion of teen-age cola drinkers graduate to beer, and a sizable proportion of young beer drinkers go on to mixed drinks. The customers for home remedies brought out more than a generation ago slowly reduce these purchases, yet their continued usage impedes the acceptance of the product by younger prospects.

Generally, the earliest purchasers will form the nucleus of heavy users, and the bulk of those who follow will be occasional or light users of a product or service. With the passage of time, the product or service itself ages, as first more and then fewer customers have the opportunity to become aware of the offering and to purchase and repurchase it. For this reason, products have cycles of their own.

Recency. Another time-related factor that affects buying behavior is recency. Whereas primacy may have great overall impact on customers, the recency of exposure to an offering may have a greater effect on triggering the actual purchase. The reason for this is simply that people generally forget—mainly, because other matters intervene—about 70 percent of what they could report the previous day. Their attention is continually directed elsewhere. As a result customers need to be reminded of what they initially learned. Some purchases are determined on the basis of the last advertisement seen, the last store shopped, or the last salesman to call. The strongest reminder is the purchase of the offer and satisfaction with the purchase. For prospective customers the multitude of unsolicited influences impinging on them every day is the source of reminders. Marketers must determine if recency is significant in the behavior of their customers and prospects.

Price and timing. Price is closely related to timing. Customers may be willing to buy something once at a given price, but not repeatedly. Seasonal prices are recognized by customers as natural, although some price cycles are artificially induced by marketers to even out seasonal peaks and valleys in inventory or sales volume. For example, because customers came to expect tire sales at discount prices on the Fourth of July, competitors are locked into this seasonal variety of price although most tire sales are normally made at this time (prior to vacation trips), whereas in other industries sales at lower prices are usually made in the off season when purchaser volume is normally low.

AVAILABILITY

Where and how the product or service is purchasable is a major factor in customer buying behavior. To the customer, shortage or surplus of supply is significant only in his personal experience. Major effects on decisions and actions are related to place and means of purchase, which are determined by the marketer's policies in distribution and selling methods.

Distribution. For many years motor scooters had limited sales because prospects preferred not to purchase from the motorcycle dealers who dominated distribution. Then a foreign producer, heeding the repeated findings of American market research studies, set up a network of outlets with an upper-class appeal. This basic break stimulated buying behavior and opened the way for the expression of latent demand. Similarly, lottery tickets in New York State failed to meet sales forecasts until they were made available in stores where customers could feel comfortable in buying them.

Selling methods. Selling methods interact with customer behavior. Because of past habits or current situation, customers favor one form of purchasing over another. The interaction of selling method and customer behavior is demonstrated in the contrast between mail-order and door-to-door sales. People who buy by one method resist anything sold by the other method; thus a large door-to-door seller of vacuum cleaners learned that his customer lists were useless for direct mail offers. For the same reason the best mailing list for a product sold by mail is a list of those who already have purchased something by mail, preferably similar in type and price level. Customers who prefer to buy on credit, either in a store or from a route man, will be more easily sold other products on the same basis even though they may be able to pay cash. At the same time, customers who habitually pay cash tend strongly to stay with their preferred form of purchasing. Offering 28-foot inboard cruisers on the installment plan has no effect on customer behavior because such customers have the cash, expect open-account credit, or are trading in a smaller cruiser making up more than half the price of the new boat. The selling method chosen by a marketer will open some parts of the market to him and close others, even though the product or service is the same. For nonconsumer products and services, the same holds true.

Some buyers prefer to be called on; others delight in making outside investigations, either directly or through trade shows or in leisure activities. In the same way, some customers demand contact with headquarters or national representatives, while others find local agents reassuring. These preferences exist independently of size of order or account, need for service, or other factors that also influence buying behavior. In the farm product market, for example, company men often find that though they provide more personal service and information than local dealers, the customer still prefers transactions in nearby establishments to ordering direct. At times, customers may change their preferred modes of purchasing. Generally, however, the familiar has a much stronger influence on buying behavior than the unfamiliar.

Price and availability. Price acceptance by customers is related to the availability of the offer. Supply, whether surplus or short, is recognized by customers as a factor that affects price and alters their expectations and willingness to buy. The place where the offer is purchasable also influences price acceptance; the most dramatic examples are found in retail stores that have high-class or low-class images. The same phenomenon influences nonconsumer customers; often elaborate showrooms or high-caliber salesmen are necessary to sustain high-priced offerings, and without them customer price expectations are substantially lower.

Selling methods not only interact with customer behavior but induce different price expectations as well. Cost per month is the "price," rather than total cost in installment sales, and higher amounts are accepted by customers because of budget or cash flow convenience. Products sold without service features have accustomed consumers to "discount" prices. For services sold at higher-than-average prices, customers expect and usually receive tangible evidences of value in the form of gifts, premiums, or helpful aids of one sort or another.

MOTIVATION

The question of why customers are buying a product or a service is best answered in terms of the net benefits anticipated by prospects and experienced by users. These benefits can be direct or indirect, primary or secondary, positive or negative. At times the indirect, secondary, or negative benefits are the most important in motivation. Once discovered, they explain seemingly irrational buying behavior.

Primary and positive benefits. Presumably, some need is being met by a purchase, but this need may or may not be reportable by the customer or observable by others. The customer may be expecting one major benefit or a combination of benefits after accepting the marketer's offer. His motive may be to achieve economy, identity, prestige, or the indulgence of vanity. Economy is possible not only in money but also through limiting time and effort. In seeking to be provided with personal identity by virtue of the purchase, the customer may be expressing either venturesomeness or conservatism. Prestige may be conferred by indicating membership (conformity) or by signaling exclusivity for the user. Finally, in catering to the customer's vanity, a product or service may serve to demonstrate his achievement or personal qualities. It is the constant seeking by customers to fulfill these motives, in various combinations, that causes flux in the market, creates dissatisfactions that open opportunities for other marketers, and is responsible for cycles in what is fashionable.

In the initial marketing of a product or service the most important motivation of customers is that of venturesomeness. Innovators or leaders may contribute only 10 to 15 percent of the ultimate users, but they are critically important at the outset. To obtain a foothold in the market, the marketers of any product or service are well advised to seek out those among customer prospects who are unusually willing to try new things.

Secondary and negative benefits. Usually, when the customer considers others in order to obtain their approval or acceptance of a purchase, he is attempting to satisfy their expectations. In an unknown proportion of instances, however, the customer is more intent upon displeasing certain people whose reactions to his purchase he anticipates. This is a secondary benefit. A negative benefit is desired at times by individuals and organizations in order to purge themselves of unwanted feelings or possessions through the purchase of specific products or services. In the case of consumers, some buy a marketer's offering in order to punish themselves for real or imagined guilt or as a means to come to terms with their superegos or consciences. Negative motives include those mildly felt, such as simply not wanting to buy some other offer or to please someone else, and those intensely felt, such as outright defiance, hostility, or rage toward another product or service, person or group, or idea connected symbolically with the marketer's offering. Negative motives in organizations are quite varied: the desire to reduce surplus to sustain losses, to use up profit so as to avoid lower prices or rate base, to resolve tax problems, to obtain subsidies, and other means of coming to terms with the private sector's superego (usually in the form of a regulatory government body). When faced with buying behavior that does not seem to make sense on the surface, marketers may look for indirect, secondary, and negative benefits for a possible explanation. This is true of all buying behavior, from minor consumer items to major industrial expenditures and government orders.

What customers get out of a product or service is often different from what was intended by the marketer. For many years a large proportion of the packaged onion soup sold was used to make cocktail dips. When this use was discovered, direct advertising and competition to serve this customer motive opened a much broader market that included the less imaginative elements of the society. In another instance, resistance to the purchase of equipment for manufacturing intravenous solutions in hospitals was experienced by one company, despite the motivation of large cost savings and prestige for the pharmacist, because health insurance companies reimbursed hospitals for 70 percent of the high-priced bottled solutions, with an added allowance for overhead. The underlying motivation of customers must therefore be detected and provided for in relevant form before a product or service can succeed.

Combinations of benefits. Some motives are interlinked. Customers who state they selected a car because of initial price also mention style in nearly equal frequency (and trade the car in earlier); customers who state durability as a major expected benefit also mention operating-cost economy more often than expected (and trade the cars in less frequently). For any given offering, a marketer is well advised to determine which set of expected benefits his best prospects seek so as to avoid conflicts in conveying the concept. However, customers perceive selectively and believe what they want to believe; it is perfectly possible for customers with different motives to see promises of satisfaction in the same offering. In fact, satisfying many different types of customers at the same time is what creates a mass market. The real danger is that the concept or content is insufficient to confirm the hopes of specific types of customers so that they do not care if somebody else's motives are also fulfilled by the same product or service.

Belief in the future potential of a product or service can justify purchasing when it is bolstered by prestige benefits, even though economic benefits cannot be demonstrated. Most first-generation computers were purchased on this basis, and often without detailed evaluation.

Price and motivation. Price in itself, either high or low, may serve as a benefit that satisfies any or a combination of customer motives. What price signifies must be determined empirically for each situation. A relatively high or low price for a given offer may have different meaning for different customers. Expensive shoes may be justified in the working class as "more economical in the long run." Lower-priced mowers may be justified by commercial gardeners because heavy use burns out the expensive ones almost as fast, and the cheap mowers can be discarded when worn out without investing time and maintenance expense. Depending on the stage of development of the product field or service classification, a customer can be expressing venturesomeness or conservatism, membership or exclusivity, by favoring a higher- or lower-priced offering. Finally, customers unable to express personal achievement or qualities by paying a higher price may revert to the lowest-priced offering to do so. The role of price in customer motivation must be determined by each marketer for his proprietary array of offerings.

Generally, customers want to upgrade themselves in ways that are meaningful to themselves. Determining how to put together a product or service that taps this underlying motivation in a specific area is often the key to opening up a whole market.

Other Factors in Buying Behavior

Other factors in a wide array affect customer buying behavior, either directly or indirectly. The most direct and immediate is a personal salesman calling on the customer or prospect without notice or by invitation. The most indirect and remote is the environment, nationwide and worldwide, which affects the customer's outlook and orientation and the mix of products, services, and alternative activities from which he can choose. Between these extremes a multitude of influences presses on the customer, both solicited and unsolicited by him.

DIRECT SALES EFFORT

A customer buys from direct salesmen, either company representatives or agents, chiefly on the basis of familiarity: that is, the perception of the marketer's agent as similar to himself or to his self-image in important respects. Usually, the customer must consider the individual making the offering to be acceptable as a friend before he buys from him. The most significant indicator of this potentiality is that the customer thinks of the salesman as having the same education as himself, or better, and the same or higher income; or as belonging to the same political party or religion.

UNSOLICITED INFLUENCES

At times the customer is basically passive, receiving suggestions or observing the practices of others to which he simply conforms. Convention and custom are strong factors in the marketplace. The purchase of missals or prayer books is a good example of this kind of influence on individual purchases. People generally buy the missal they see others using and do not shop or make comparisons or evaluations. For this reason one publisher may have 90 percent or more of a given geographic market, and it is extremely difficult for another publisher to penetrate without waiting for gradual population changes over a long period. Similar concentrations of brand preferences are found in the outboard motor field, where one lake may be "Evinrude" and the next all "Johnson," even though the brands are manufactured by the same corporation and competitive dealers are located reasonably nearby. Attempts to break customary procedure by providing equal or better availability, price, terms, and other offers still meet resistance from those who prefer the "tried and true." In general, unsolicited influences are especially operative for products and services that are used frequently by customers or are used by many other people in an area.

Advertising. Advertising acts, in most cases, as an unsolicited influence on buying decisions and has a cumulative effect in creating familiarity. Exposures to such influences range from several hundred to several thousand daily in the life of the customer. At most, he is aware of and can report only a few dozen of them. Research has shown that he is indifferent to at least 80 percent of television advertising, for example. The effect of advertising on the passive customer is to create awareness after getting his attention. Later, in a buying situation—either impulsive or planned—the customer may recognize the product or service as familiar. In this way the sense of effort or risk in purchasing is reduced. Generalized or institutional advertising is chiefly directed toward creating attitudes prerequisite to buying decisions favorable to a marketer. It is usually inadequate for active prospects who use advertisements as they use expert opinion.

Sales promotion. Sales promotion efforts affect customer behavior by adding value to the content rather than the concept of the product or service. A customer prospect who otherwise might fail to understand or develop interest in the concept of the offering may purchase on the basis of content alone because of the added value he receives from the sales promotion, which fits into or fulfills his own felt needs. Sales promotion devices, directly or indirectly tied to the purchase, are highly varied: free samples, contests, coupons, premiums, trading stamps, and so on. Most premiums offered as sales promotion are barely suitable for their purpose. Some prove more popular than the product or service itself. A drug chain in Washington, D.C., found that discounts on purchases of prescription drugs had no value in holding or gaining customers because people do not expect or shop for discounts on medicine and few remember receiving them. Customer behavior is most influenced when the sales promotion is relevant to other aspects of the marketing task.

Customers themselves become unsolicited influences on customer prospects by spontaneously telling of their satisfactions or even of their favored expectations. Such influences are usually termed "word of mouth" and are extremely effective in creating awareness and familiarity prior to actual purchase decision situations.

SOLICITED INFLUENCES

At times, chiefly for products and services used infrequently, the customer seeks advice and relies on the recommendations of an expert or leader or the consensus of a group of persons whose approval is important. At least one and possibly as many as three out of five buyers of such an offering are likely to have done this. In these cases the role of certain individuals or organizations has a disproportionate influence in the marketplace. When this behavior is probable, the key to obtaining a good market position may lie in identifying those whose opinion is sought. An example of such a consultation is found in the individual who seeks advice on the best bank for mortgages or special loans although willing to use any convenient bank for an ordinary account. The persons asked are those whose general knowledgeability is highly regarded by the customer or by others he is acquainted with and respects.

The same seeking out of influences holds true for services and products that do not directly involve the consumer. Mechanical engineers have infrequent need to specify adhesives, for example. When they do, they seek the suggestions of the most experienced user they can find. Often this turns out to be a specialist in insulation installation. In this way, a few individuals can virtually control the preference for type and brand of a product in a large city, and the marketer who would understand customer buying behavior is well advised to identify those who influence the purchasers.

Advertising can perform as a solicited influence when the customer is "in the market" and actively seeks out advertisements as part of collecting information and advice. If an advertisement in a magazine is read by 25 percent of the readers, about 10 percent of them will be buyers or prospects; an outstanding advertisement may be read by 75 percent of the readers, of whom 20 percent are buyers or prospects. When a product is advertised in a magazine, about 15 percent more readers buy it than when it is not advertised.

In the field of construction, customers rely almost wholly on solicited influences—firms or individuals who perform design and planning services in return for a percentage of the owner investment. Architects and engineers, either in the principal organization or on the staff of professional firms, specify products and services that will be used and take responsibility for satisfactory completion of the work on behalf of the owner. Customers are so heavily dependent on these intermediaries that marketers spend the bulk of their effort in influencing them.

LIFE STYLE AND
ENVIRONMENTAL CHANGES

Buying behavior is greatly influenced by way of life, defined by stage in the life cycle and place in the social and economic sphere. This position in turn allows varying degrees of personal expression in purchasing by individuals. In consumer goods and services, innovations are introduced by those in the highest and lowest echelons of the society who have least risk (little more to gain or to lose) and, in the United States and similar countries, are validated by the most venturesome in the economically secure portion of the broad middle class. Innovators, who are the initial purchasers of new products or services, are only

2 to 3 percent of the customers; another 13 to 14 percent at most are sufficiently venturesome to be called early adopters. Later, when new modes or forms of purchasing behavior are adopted by the conservative working class and finally by the economically insecure, the process is completed and market growth is stabilized. The same pattern holds true in industrial goods and services. Growing organizations have much in common in their purchasing behavior, regardless of industry, as do firms with high earnings. Experimental or radical new designs or concepts are most quickly accepted by the largest and richest companies or by the smallest entrepreneurs, who have little established position or commitment to custom.

Young people are disproportionately represented among innovators, either because they are supported by their parents (thus resembling the upper class) or because they have nominally abandoned aspiration to membership or status in the established society (thus resembling the lower class). In both cases they have little or nothing to lose by innovating and little or nothing to gain by conforming. The extension of this period of youth portends greater amounts of change in the types of products and services purchased and a weakening of loyalties and steady habits which have sustained many marketers in the past.

Environmental changes, such as major events affecting the economy of the nation, alter customer buying behavior markedly. The effect may be direct, as with war or depression, or indirect, as with new laws, shorter work hours, longer time for education, higher interest rates, less mobility because of housing shortages, and so forth, which ultimately change life styles and living habits. Marketers are well advised to re-evaluate their offerings when overall changes are taking place in the environment.—*W. J. McBurney, Jr.*

THE MARKETING CONCEPT AND THE MARKETING MIX

In recent years no segment of management has received more attention than marketing, and few if any other management areas have developed to the extent reflected in its evolution.

Despite the remarkable advances, there is still clear need for a reassessment of marketing's position in the organizational structure, not merely from the technical standpoint of administrative delineation but also, more cogently, in relationship to the actual marketing function in the business operation and in the market.

This necessity is not inconsistent with the attention paid to marketing, since the influence of marketing has grown to its current stature through recognition of the dynamics of the market and acknowledgment that both the magnitude and rate of change have so vastly increased and accelerated in recent years that in order for a marketing-oriented business to remain competitive, marketing's function has to be constantly reassessed and restructured relative to these dynamics.

The impetus of technological change radically accelerated following World War II, and business management was quick to recognize the necessity for organizational restructuring consistent with the requirements of successful marketing in an atmosphere of constant technological, sociological, and financial innovation and change. It would be difficult to analyze the cause-and-effect relationship that prevailed at the time, and analysis is fortunately somewhat unnecessary since, regardless of the origin of the interrelationship between scientific processes, technological developments, and their sociological impact, the significance of these factors to the attitudes of the consumer and manufacturer related back to the conduct of business as it generated the marketing atmosphere.

The Marketing Concept

In reassessing marketing's position, it is necessary to analyze the marketing concept. Traditionally, marketing has been considered to be made up of those business activities required in the transfer of ownership of goods and those requisite functions providing for their physical distribution. This concept has been expanded to include those business activities involved in directing the flow of goods and services between the producer and consumer; while essentially restating the same premise, this definition extends the limits of the first one in order to include a slightly wider scope of activities.

Marketing is accomplished with the aid of two major functions: (1) planning and organizing, and (2) controlling activities. Both functions are directed toward the accomplishment of established marketing objectives.

To do this, the active marketing role has been generally structured around the concept of the marketing mix, which classically consists of product, place, price, and promotion. The product mix is the instrument of marketing employed to achieve most effectively the objectives established as representing the anticipated outcome of the marketing effort.

Marketing Activities

In the light of the expanded definitions, marketing has been responsible for eight central or key functions: marketing information, selling, finance, standardization, risk, storage, buying, and transportation.

Each of these activities—which carries with it specific objectives of its own—must be consistent with total marketing objectives as well as being directed toward meeting requirements of marketing in a given market.

The Market Itself

In order to appreciate more clearly the interrelationship of the marketing function relative to the marketing mix and the key activity areas, it is essential to have an understanding of the nature of the market.

Despite sociological and technological changes, it is still accurate to conceive of the market as consisting of three major segments—the consumer, industrial, and government markets. The significance of this segmentation lies not in the mere satisfaction of a penchant for the didactic but in its pragmatic implications. The identification of primary markets is associated with the recognition of operational techniques that can be employed optimally in the development of marketing objectives and strategies to be employed in these market segments. Since the various requirements of marketing in the segments are well founded and—by and large—remain the same, it is unnecessary to restate these techniques here; but it should be appreciated that while activities in these markets have to a greater or lesser extent remained operationally consistent, the relationship of the marketing effort and the marketing concept has changed. This will be made clear when the contemporary marketing concept as distinguished from the traditional marketing definitions is considered.

Modern Marketing and the Marketing Concept

When the definitions previously stated are compared with the needs of a modern marketing organization relative to marketing dynamics and the accelerated rate of market change, it is apparent that the definitions that have so long prevailed—although academically correct—imply limitations not consistent with the needs of modern marketing. It is first of all apparent that the classic marketing definition does not clearly identify the following factors: profit, flexibility, planning, relationship of marketing to other functional areas, product management, equilibrium of market and marketing, and market research.

Before an attempt is made to consider the totality of the marketing concept, it is necessary to evaluate these added functions more fully. Additionally, a consideration of business philosophy and the refinement of motivational and behavioral studies is essential to the proper understanding of the marketing function. In the light of the application of scientific analysis to the consumer and the market, marketing executives are now in a vastly different position in terms of understanding the market and the consumer and are therefore in an enhanced position to effectively manage marketing. It is essential to comprehend the significance of these developments because they have necessitated alteration in the conventional concepts of marketing, since marketing innovation, like technical innovation, has been vastly accelerated.

PROFIT

It is generally agreed that business functions to generate profits. Marketing, as one functional area in business administration, has as one of its preliminary objectives the same profit objectives as the corporate entity.

FLEXIBILITY

A word often heard in the marketing vocabulary is "flexibility," but despite its familiarity its meaning is not often fully considered or given the weight in practice that is necessary for marketing success. Change is often slow in coming, and many inhibiting factors—personal, financial, or mechanical—are powerful. However, with the alterations taking place in the market and marketing, as well as within other segments of the management and in manufacturing capabilities, capacity for change in a flexible organization is a prerequisite. Competitive activity, impact on imports, and product obsolescence—in an ever increasing phenomenon of curtailed product life—coupled with increased R&D lead times in many areas, require that the marketing executive constantly reassess the role of his marketing group in the context of these changes and that it be altered precisely when and where necessary. Change merely for the sake of change is confusion, not creativity. But hesitation to change when change is called for, with administrational, managerial, or market complacency in the marketplace, is certain demise.

PLANNING

Years ago few corporations engaged in formal planning—market, operational, administrative, research, or any other form. Today the exact converse is true, and few do not plan. The few who do not now plan will, in all probability, plan eventually or in due course will not have to be concerned with it. The planning function has grown in stature and importance because it has demonstrated its contribution. In a highly complex, technological, and scientific atmosphere it is hardly possible, without recourse to planning, to manage the multiplicity of functions simultaneously occurring. The vast capital expenditure and the massive commitment of men and equipment must be programmed, based on a sound analysis of the business and the company's potentials in any given market. For this purpose comes the plan, the most important element of which is the statement of objectives.

Marketing plays a vital role in the creation of the planning operation, and although the old marketing definition hardly provided for planning, the modern marketing concept does so more than adequately. It is difficult to overstress the significance of planning, which lies less in its mechanical aspects than in the conceptualization of the total marketing effort and the subsequent realistic assessments that derive from it. The marketing objectives that then follow provide the direction of the total marketing effort, providing a functional nucleus around which are generated the actual strategies, tactics, and action programs required to realize these objectives.

It is the job of the chief marketing executive and his staff to make this analysis and create the marketing plan, the objectives of which must of course be consistent with overall corporate objectives. In so doing the plan will generally be concerned with marketing, sales, finance, profit, distribution, advertising, and promotional objectives on both a short (one-year) and long (five-year) basis.

MARKETING'S RELATIONSHIPS
WITH OTHER AREAS

In the previous definitions of marketing there is a curious lack of appreciation of the interrelationships that must occur operationally between the marketing area and other functional areas. The marketing function must concern itself with the other activities within the corporation that bear a relationship—either direct or indirect—to the total marketing effort, since its success is to a large measure dependent upon them. Conversely, for marketing to obtain the cooperation and support that it requires, time and trouble must be taken to cultivate an attitude of recognition and respect for the significance of the marketing function. The product management function within the marketing operation is designed specifically to fulfill these requirements, among others.

PRODUCT MANAGEMENT

One of the newer management techniques, product management permits the integration of the marketing function in the total organization. The product manager is charged with responsibility for the product, market, forecasting, profit, planning, and coordination. In this capacity his role is essential in integrating the diverse functions existing within the marketing group, as well as correlating the activities of the marketing area with other functional groups. His position relative to the products offered is central to the marketing effort; he represents the central repository for all product data. Since his scope of activities is extremely wide and diverse, he is often charged with the responsibility for developing the marketing plan or even the total operational plan—or at least the product-planning segment thereof. The importance of product management has gained widespread acknowledgement in recent years and, despite its relative newness, it would appear to have created an established management area.

MARKET–MARKETING EQUILIBRIUM

Marketing has come to realize that it is essentially an active process functioning in an active atmosphere—the market. Neither one can truly, effectively exist without fully recognizing the other. The challenge of creative marketing clearly necessitates a full and comprehensive understanding of the nature of market dynamics. Conversely, while it may appear somewhat incongruous, the market does not exist in isolation from the effects and influences of the active marketing process. This means that although the market does create demands of its own, completely distinguishable from those created from any external sources, marketing can and does create market demand. The equilibrium existing between marketing and the market must be considered and effectively exploited.

MARKET RESEARCH

While the foregoing comments on the equilibrium of market and marketing describe the results of analysis, market research can well be considered as providing the tool whereby such information can be acquired and—upon interpretation by the marketing executive—utilized in the forecast of the marketing plan and marketing objectives. It is also of vital necessity in the establishment of long-range objectives. This is particularly the case where long product R&D efforts are required.

MODERN MARKETING CHALLENGE

The sum and substance of the marketing concept as presently envisioned is, therefore, a very substantial expansion of the narrow parameters previously promulgated in marketing definitions. The requirements of marketing as visualized in the marketing concept require these more pervasive contacts and influences. This imposes a great responsibility on marketing, since the direction it takes will, through the implementation of this concept, effectively create the direction of the business effort. With clear profit responsibility, it places the burden for the success of both the marketing effort and the company on the marketing group.

Marketing management must be sensitive, therefore, not only to the external needs of the market but to the internal needs of the marketing organization as well. It is the harmonious balance of these sometimes conflicting requirements, tempered with complete utilization of the many techniques and functional groups available to them, that will insure sucess not only of the marketing concept but of the marketing effort as well.—*G. S. Dominguez*

MARKET RESEARCH

As an organized activity, market research is about 60 years old. More than $250 million is spent yearly on it in the United States, and the amount is growing by about 15 percent per year.

The term "market research" refers to methods of finding and analyzing facts to assist in making rational marketing decisions. Market research is one of the methods used by businessmen to approach business in a systematic fashion. It can uncover facts bearing on customer interests, market potential, marketing atmosphere, competition, and the economic environment. Whether sales are made to industrial, retail, farmer, or government customers, the needs and techniques are similar. Business always needs facts, and since customer habits, competition, and the economic environment are always changing, the market research process must be a continuing one.

Goals and Limitations

Profits are gained through the assumption of risk. Market research provides facts that enable businessmen to assume larger risks and aim at higher profits.

To eliminate risk from business completely, market researchers would have to uncover—and businessmen would have to know—everything about everything. This is impossible in today's dynamic world economy. Marketing systems are changing continually. The work of market research is never done. No problems are finally solved. All that the researcher can hope to do is analyze the problem as it exists, basing his work on a number of simplified assumptions, and attempt to use the data to project the future. Even with modern high-speed computers it is impossible to cover all the facts and all the relationships between sets of facts. Fine points have to be passed over, and only the major facts and relationships can be taken into account.

Market research cannot predict the future, but it can be used to forecast the probability of future events. Market research is only one element in making business decisions. Furthermore, it is not, by itself, a basis for action. It can be used to assess the future environment and possible mutual interactions between a company and its environment. These assessments form a basis on which management can construct a plan, a structure of goals, policies, programs, procedures—the guides to effective action. Market research can be delegated; management decisions cannot be.

Market research originally concentrated on the facts alone, with a description of the marketing system. Today the emphasis is on analytical description, which not only gives the facts but uncovers and describes the relationships that exist between sets of facts. The modern market researcher follows this pattern: (1) describe, (2) analyze, (3) forecast.

All businesses do market research of some kind. In large companies the effort is usually formalized and the methods more sophisticated, but even the smallest businessman collects and uses facts. More formal market research can be obtained from trade associations, independent market research agencies, or a firm's own market research department.

Steps in Market Research

Market research has two broad functions: One is to solve specific problems; the other, to continuously scan the environment in order to anticipate and counter the effect of potential problems.

PROBLEM SOLVING

In looking at any problem, the businessman or researcher must go through a series of logical steps: (1) Identify the problem; (2) investigate alternative solutions; (3) find out what facts are needed to arrive at the correct solution; (4) decide how to obtain the facts; (5) get the facts; (6) tabulate, analyze, and report the facts; (7) decide on a solution to the problem.

After the research has been completed and before decisions based on it are made, several questions must be asked as to its validity: Have the necessary facts been obtained? Have any pertinent facts been overlooked? Have the proper techniques been utilized to gather and analyze the data?

The final research report, if one is required, should emphasize the highlights of the facts found. Charts and graphs are a valuable aid in understanding arrays of facts and their interrelationships.

SCANNING THE ENVIRONMENT

One of the most important problems in business is information. It is impossible to imagine the continued existence of a successful company that does not stay aware of information or react to it. For many a businessman, even though it is the means to the job rather than the end of it, his central concern from the moment he enters the office is to collect, evaluate, and act on information. Most of the information, from newspapers, trade journals, internal reports, phone calls, meetings, business lunches, and so on, is quickly evaluated and used. Decisions often have to be made very rapidly under today's competitive pressures.

As a company grows and enters more areas, it cannot rely on the informal collection of information. It will need a well-planned, systematized approach to gathering, screening, evaluating, and disseminating of data for use by planners and decision makers. The advantages of such an approach include more complete coverage of significant news, more effective dissemination of news, and increased efficiency through centralized coordination.

The basic concept underlying an effective marketing information system is the use of all available pertinent data, plus such additional information specifically obtained as needed for a specific decision that has to be made. This process can be best carried out when centrally coordinated and systematized.

Practical considerations in planning a formal marketing information system include the following: (1) Quality of input must be controlled; (2) retrieval must be efficient and take a minimum of time; (3) effective dissemination of collected data is essential; (4) internal cooperation is imperative; (5) management must be effective. The difficulties of appraising and storing data for appropriate retrieval are greater than the problems of obtaining quantities of data.

The marketing information system must be highly sensitive to changing company needs and objectives, as well as to the dynamics of the business environment. The manager of market research, regardless of his actual title or other activities, must have the following requirements: (1) an understanding of marketing and economics, as well as of his industry, company, and products; (2) access to relevant information; (3) appropriate personnel and facilities; (4) an appreciation of information opportunities and limitations to help decide where emphasis is to be placed; (5) an organizational reporting level that will assure effective use of the data he collects; (6) a reputation for quality of work.

Getting Facts

Facts can be derived from various sources: a company's own records; field surveys by mail, phone, or in person; trade associations; government sources; and publications. Other sources include trade shows, business meetings, brokerage houses and banks, and competitive literature. A first start is to build up a market facts file, using clippings from publications and releases from government and trade sources.

Field surveys give useful current, rather than historical, information. It requires skill to design the questionnaire, select the sample, and conduct the survey. Interviewers have to be trained and reliable. The sample has to be representative rather than merely large. Questions have to be designed to get at the facts. Field surveys can also observe consumer behavior, using mechanical recorders or human observers. These disclose the behavior of customers but do not explain the behavior.

Interviews can also be used to evaluate psychological factors in marketing (motivation research). This can be done through depth interviews or tests (word association, sentence completion, or thematic apperception, in which the subject is asked to make up a story about a picture).

Experimental research is conducted on small samples that can be kept under control. It can be used to test markets, displays, or advertisements.

Sources within the company should not be overlooked. These sources include the sales, research, patent, and credit departments. A company's own records can yield very important data on trade areas, customers, and competitive prices.

The salesman is on the firing line. He is in touch with purchasing agents; he goes to exhibitions, to sales conferences, to the customers' plants. He knows competitors' prices, plans, and new products. If he is alerted and his help is asked for, he can bring in such items as competitors' price lists, samples, and literature. Salesmen's call reports are a direct line to customers, who are the front-line contacts with the competition.

The research department can evaluate competitive products. The patent department can uncover new trends in technology by watching for early patent filings overseas. Credit departments can supply financial data on customers and competitors.

Analytical Techniques

Statistical and other mathematical techniques enable market researchers to handle and evaluate data and relationships between data, even when the data are unreliable or minor factors are omitted, or when data are obtained from small samples of the population.

Statistical techniques of value include sampling, tests of significance, Bayesian decision theory, model building, correlation, time series, and index numbers.

MODELS

A model is a mathematical description of a system. It concentrates on key factors and takes probability into account where uncertainty plays a role. The construction of a model is based on informed judgment as to the interplay of elements of the system. It is tested with actual data. It is only of value if it can be applied in the real world.

Computers help in dealing with complex models because they can be used to sort data, evaluate data, and perform many calculations in a short time. Computers can be programmed to simulate the real world by responding to hypothetical changes in about the same way as the real world responds to such changes. A simulation that takes probability and chance into consideration is known as a Monte Carlo simulation.

Models and simulation enable the researcher to evaluate alternatives, learn about the system, and verify or demonstrate new concepts. Special models can be used to solve problems of (1) linear programming (optimum allocation of resources); (2) game theory (anticipation of competitive strategy); (3) Markov chain analysis (determination of the outcome of a series of linked events, such as brand switching); (4) Critical Path Scheduling (CPS), of which the Program Evaluation and Review Technique (PERT) is an example.

The mathematical model method has the advantage of quantifying projections for broad areas of economic activity, based on assumptions that can be varied. If the forecast is wrong, the wrong assumption and judgments can be traced. The method also produces pinpoint answers, and the mathematical equations can be statistically treated. It is a way of neatly organizing a great deal of complex data of the present and the past.

The method has many disadvantages. It assumes that the past relationships between the variables are measured correctly, are significant, are largely fixed over time, and will hold in the future. The method also requires assumptions of values of the exogenous variables (variables determined outside of the system of equations). In practice, the method has not performed too well. This may be partially owing to the complicated mathematical computations and the high degree of skill required. It may also result from the fact that the method deals only with broad aggregates generally and has no place for psychological or other unmeasurable factors. Actually, even a complicated mathematical model may be too simple to adequately describe a marketing system, especially as a closed rather than an open system. If anything, the method is overprecise, using a technique more exact than the data on which the whole analysis is based. Continuing progress is being made in developing sound models.

(Mathematical and statistical techniques are further described in the Administrative Services section under the heading "Management Science," page 2·65.)

Forecasting

The end purpose of market research is not merely to describe or analyze the past or present but to give clues to the future. Generally, sales forecasting techniques may be classified as (1) nonnumerical methods based on the judgment and experience of individuals; and (2) those employing extensive numerical devices, statistics, and mathematics.

Types of nonnumerical methods used are executive consensus, sales managers' estimates, historical analogy, industry experts' composite, sampling of group opinions, simple ratio method, and Delphi method.

Numerical methods include correlation analysis, equation systems or models, end-use analysis, input-output analysis, and trend and cycle analysis.

NONNUMERICAL METHODS

Nonnumerical methods avoid the use of large masses of historical data and their mathematical manipulation.

Executive consensus. In the executive consensus method, a conference is held, and each executive states his views and gives his reasons. The chairman coordinates the various opinions. This method is practiced extensively.

Sales managers' estimate. The method of sales managers' estimates is the "grass roots" approach. The theory is that the sales managers are closer to the users of the product and thus have a better view of prospects than the executives. The information is obtained by questionnaires or conferences.

Historical analogy. A similar period with similar characteristics is examined to form a historical analogy. It is limited in use but can be employed for a new product and in some analyses of similar patterns of sales.

Industry experts' composite figures. In this method a company periodically asks experts, selected in individual fields, to submit forecasts. The forecasts are then combined and weighted.

Sampling of group opinions. Group opinions are sampled to forecast future intentions. An example is the McGraw-Hill survey of plant expenditures. The problem is in both weighting and sampling. This method is good for new products, and it can predict style shifts.

Ratio method. A naïve extrapolation of the previous year's trend is a frequently used device. It assumes that the percent of change in sales from the previous year to the current year will be the same for the current year to the coming year.

Delphi method. The Delphi method is a recent development by the Rand Corporation for forecasting new technology; it is especially useful in research planning. In this technique, experts are individually asked to state their views as to the timing and likelihood of new technology. The opinions are recirculated, anonymously, so that each expert can view the varied opinions and modify his own if he desires to do so. This eventually results in a consensus of more value than the original raw results.

Bayesian analysis. In recent years numerical and judgment techniques have been married in a technique known as Bayesian analysis. This is remotely derived from a theorem proposed by the Reverend Thomas Bayes, an eighteenth-century English clergyman who stated that it was legitimate to quantify feelings about uncertainty in terms of subjectively assessed numerical probabilities, even for a unique decision, where historical data do not exist. In practice it means that a probability can be assigned to each forecast submitted by a salesman and that combined probabilities can be used to assess numerically the likelihood of the combined forecast, and all this is based on judgment.

NUMERICAL METHODS

Some advantages of numerical methods are as follows: (1) Sales of a specific product in which only a few people are interested are linked to economic indicators estimated by many people and agencies; (2) specific direct data required for other methods may not be available; (3) the method will be reliable in estimating the "normal" trend, leaving more time to analyze the deviations from the "normal."

These methods also have some disadvantages, such as the following: (1) Seasoned specialists are required; (2) there is danger of abandoning individual and independent judgment and placing too heavy reliance on the arbitrary mathematical methods; (3) the method is often difficult to explain to executives; (4) sufficient historical data must be available to show the effect of the business cycle, both rising and declining.

Correlation analysis. The procedure of correlation analysis in forecasting the demand for a product involves measuring the relationship between certain factors or groups of factors thought to be related to the product demand. On the basis of these measurements and certain further assumptions, the future demand for the product is estimated.

Equation systems. Much attention has been given recently to the use of systems of equation, rather than single equations, in forecasting both the economy and the demand for specific commodities. Little practical use has been made of this method outside of broad economic and agricultural commodity demand forecasting.

End-use analysis. End-use analysis is a method that breaks down a commodity into its end-use pattern; studies each of these small sectors individually, using all known forecasting techniques; and recombines these elements into the aggregate.

Input-output analysis. An input-output chart is a summary of the entire national economy, arranged in checkerboard fashion with all producing sectors on the vertical axis and all consuming industries on the horizontal axis. Each figure in this table is a record of transfer of money from a buyer to a seller. The sum of the horizontal columns is the total gross output of an industry, or its total sales to all other industries and consumers. The sum of the vertical columns is the total gross outlay of each industry obtained by totaling its purchases from all other industries and suppliers. In other words, the table is a double-entry bookkeeping record of the purchases and sales of the sectors of the economy. The input-output method requires a great amount of facts and calculating. Unfortunately, little has been done to provide enough data to make the method useful for detailed forecasting. Because of their complexity, input-output tables are several years old by the time they become available.

Trend and cycle analysis. The basic fault of fitting trend lines and cycles is that time series fitted to time trends require unreasonable assumptions of the stability of long-run economic forces (that the series moves in a regular fashion with the passage of time).

SELECTING A FORECASTING METHOD

Methods available for analysis and forecasting of product demand range all the way from pure hunches to pure mathematics.

Hunches—intuitive judgments—are arrived at through personal observations of the market, its characteristics, and its reactions. The influence of changing supply-and-demand conditions is observed. The observer sees the facts, but he usually does not consciously attempt to discover or use exact quantitative relations to interpret them, even though he may be cognizant of these relations and derive valuable clues from them. For the experienced observer, hunches may succeed, in the same way that a driver can drive a car without knowing exactly how it operates. But the one who uses this method needs experience, intuition, know-how, and time for observation and reflection. Unfortunately, he usually cannot explain his methods to others in terms of methodology or principles. His learning must be by trial and error.

Pure mathematical forecasting, if carried out in a mechanical fashion, is not a substitute for common sense and thought. The analyst and forecaster cannot be content to derive a correlation equation from statistical data based on past relationships and hope to forecast by merely inserting estimated values into the formula.

The desirable approach is between these points, relying on a combination of sound personal judgment with the analysis of historical data.

The Modern Market Research Department

The management of marketing requires a vision of the future, and the vision of the future requires the management of information. Management decision making is becoming increasingly complex, with a multiplication of pertinent factors to be considered. Good solutions depend on consideration of an increasingly large number of factors and on information gathering from many different fields. The supply of data is increasing geometrically. To be useful, information must be processed to yield selected relevant data in a form usable to decision makers. The data must be related to the problem they were intended to help solve.

Managers, by the nature of their work, are generalists. They need the knowledge and ideas of specialists to make decisions. However, specialists often have certain shortcomings—limited views and one-sided inclinations. Between the specialists and management a research generalist can play a useful role as arbiter, interpreter, and coordinator. The modern market research department may be viewed as a department of research generalists. Such a generalist would not have the specific competence of a specialist. He would have a thorough understanding of each field of concern, just as an orchestra leader is familiar with each of the instruments under his direction.

The function of the market research generalist would be to gather data from the specialists and prepare it for management by reducing the volume, interpreting technology, directing the data to the proper management level, developing information for alternative recommendations, and outlining the consequences of moving in any direction.

Skills in the following techniques must be possessed by a market research department that performs generalist research functions: survey techniques, statistics, econometrics, motivation research, experimental techniques, operations research, computer techniques, secondary data analysis, library techniques, research design and supervision, and a wide range of engineering and scientific technologies.—*William Copulsky*

ESTABLISHING OBJECTIVES

The establishing of objectives is a fundamental activity for all echelons of business management. However, it is of major significance to top management, in that objectives represent the ultimate distillation of those significant aims of the corporation that, once established, represent the elements required for obtaining and maintaining its position and insuring its growth. Visualized in this manner, objectives represent statements of corporate intention that can be developed only by top management itself and that inherently require top level organizational commitment. The responsibility for establishing corporate objectives cannot be delegated to subordinate managerial levels; these objectives must be the creation of executive management.

It is also imperative that the purpose of objectives be clearly comprehended after they have been established. While established objectives do act as statements of corporate intention and thereby become operational guidelines, they simultaneously—and perhaps even more importantly—become instruments for the measurement of achievement. In effect, therefore, established objectives provide a basis for determining corporate performance, not alone in the sense of its ultimate relative position in the marketplace but as a device for the assessment of its internal performance and its ability to achieve its own stated objectives.

Clearly, then, it is essential that top management fully appreciate the implications and concerns that these objectives convey within the corporate structure, and that—once the objectives are established—endorsement and commitment by executive management are prerequisite to their successful execution. Corporate management therefore must both implicitly and explicitly endorse the objectives and recognize its responsibility with respect to their development, implementation, and promulgation. Without this top management commitment, the entire validity of the structure is undermined and the accomplishment of objectives seriously jeopardized.

Marketing Objectives

After corporate objectives have been thoroughly examined, marketing objectives can be considered more critically. Before doing so, it should be noted here that the marketing plan, whether it be short-range (one year) or long-range (five years), can be essentially one of two basic documents.

MARKETING PLAN

In many companies the marketing plan stands on its own and constitutes the total planning effort. In such cases the marketing plan becomes somewhat more expansive, and the scope of the stated objectives is enlarged to contain a greater number than would normally be found if limited to the more specific areas of marketing concern alone. It then, in effect, becomes the vehicle for the statement of most if not all the corporate management objectives.

OPERATIONAL PLAN

What is meant by the operational plan approach, whether it be called by that name or another, is the often-encountered technique of total planning, wherein separate operational or functional area plans are used as individual elements to create a total operational plan for the company. In such cases the marketing plan is only one integral part of the whole, and the statement of objectives contained would logically be limited to those specifically of marketing concern.

Regardless of the approach used, there are certain basic criteria that any objective should meet and that should be employed in testing the objective before it is established. If it fails to meet the following requirements, the objective is questionable—if not invalid—and should be reconsidered: feasibility, suitability, realism, quantifiability, and alterability. An examination of many stated marketing objectives has revealed that they do not always meet these criteria realistically. Enthusiasm is commendable, but in planning let it be tempered with the judicious application of the necessary criteria.

The most difficult of all tasks in creating marketing objectives is the consideration of how to identify and state the objectives themselves. The main reason that marketing objectives are difficult for most people to state is that they—and the market itself—are conceived of as somewhat illusive, ephemeral entities rather than as the realities—though intangible—that they are.

IDENTIFYING PRODUCT AND MARKET

Marketing is concerned with the distribution of goods—getting the material into the hands of the consumer—and with profit. This means dealing with two separate yet intimately related concerns: the product (no matter what it is), and the consumer (no matter who he may be). Simple though this sounds, it is central to the problem, for many times the seller does not really know what his product is nor who his customer is. This may seem incredible, yet how often it is the case: A situation frequently comes to light—for which the planner can be grateful—in the marketing planning preparation, thus leading to the consideration of these two factors (product and market) as they relate to the development of the plan and the statement of objectives.

To identify the product and the market would seem a simple matter; but when it involves making a dispassionate analysis of both, the degree of confusion that can exist is, more often than not, quite surprising. Additionally difficult is the identification of intention, once agreement as to present status has been obtained. There is a universal tendency to think that the ultimate areas in which the company wants to direct its efforts and objectives are known, and it is a painful revelation to find that this is not the case. While this may be an unpleasant reality, it is one with which the marketing planners must cope.

By now it should be abundantly clear that careful and complete scrutiny of all available data regarding the situation of company, product, consumer, and market—both current and projected—is necessary in order to formulate the marketing objectives. These are data on number and nature of products; manufacturing capabilities and limitations; available capital; market share; market potential; market direction; areas of attrition; competition; financial outlook (government, marketing, and corporate, and the possibilities of mergers or acquisitions); R&D (actual and potential); status of product life cycles; and opportunities and problems.

Most, if not all, of these factors are those normally considered in the development of any operational or marketing plan. But the emphasis and the perspective taken in the formulation of the marketing plan itself differ somewhat, in that the ultimate concern is the relationship with the marketing function; and it is from this viewpoint that these factors must be visualized. Upon determination of the statistical data to be used in the composition of the plan, the planner must also come to grips with the marketing "art work" of subjective analysis as it relates to the development of the marketing objectives. As has often been said, there is no substitute for personal judgment, and in the marketing area this is especially true. The resulting objectives reflect the analysis made, based on the data submitted and the individual assessment of the market, which then comprises the totality of marketing knowledge as it integrates the internal corporate positions and capabilities, present and future, with the market status and requirements—again, present and future.

FLEXIBILITY IN MARKETING PLAN

Among the most trying problems are those caused by changes constantly occurring in the marketplace. Nowhere else is the rate of change as rapid as in the marketing area, and it is not incorrect to say that every marketing plan is in effect obsolete before it is completed. This is not the result of inaccuracy in planning or of invalidity in the marketing planning concept; rather, it is caused by the evolution of the market and the prevailing dynamics, which make obsolescence inherent in the conditions of the plan. Additional elements for concern, therefore, are the flexibility and alterability of the plan. Any plan that is formulated must have the capability of change or alteration as the dictates of the market require. This can be accomplished either through formal, periodic review (an essential element in any meaningful plan) or through alteration based on the requirements of specifics as they develop. Either way, it is important that this need be clearly recognized in the planning operation. As this consideration relates to objectives, reflection must be more careful, since the necessity to alter objectives does not necessarily parallel the need to alter marketing strategies and tactics. This consideration is fundamental to validating the formulation of the plan. Objectives, if valid, represent relatively stable elements; it is the mechanism to achieve them that changes.

Identifying and Developing Marketing Objectives

As previously discussed, marketing objectives are built up from a comprehensive data base that encompasses all spheres of the corporate operation and the most thorough-going market knowledge, coupled with and subject to the evolution and interpretation of appropriate marketing management. This brings the planner to the state of knowing his position and being able to determine where to go and how to get there. However, he faces the problem of identifying the objectives that should be specifically indicated and, where possible, quantified.

In identifying the specific elements, consideration must be given to sales, distribution, profit planning, advertising and promotion, product management, and the market itself.

SALES

The sales factor is usually the most readily appreciated in identification and quantification during the planning operation. Sales on the basis of geographic area or market segment are obvious factors. Regional or specific market sales identification is important, but equally important is the estimate of potential sales. The identification and establishment of sales potential provide a mechanism for performance assessment, and in this sense the plan serves a dual function.

DISTRIBUTION

To consider sales without paying respect to the ever increasing concerns of the distribution of goods is to ignore one of the most critical marketing areas. Yet it is, unfortunately, often the case, and marketing managers tend to leave the matter entirely—or, at best, too much—in the hands of others. It is not the function of marketing to control all the channels of distribution, but distribution is so relevant to the effective marketing effort, from the viewpoint of either economics or customer service, that marketing has an obligation to itself to be deeply concerned in the formulation of distribution policies. The objectives to be sought in the establishment of clear and profitable distribution channels require identification and commitment.

PROFIT PLANNING

"Planning for profit" is an oft-heard but nonetheless expressive phrase. It is clearly the responsibility of marketing to plan the profits to be generated from the sales it creates. In instances where separate product management exists, it is customary to locate the profit-planning function with product managers. Whether profit planning is the responsibility of product management within the marketing operation or of the marketing group itself, it must again be quantified. Profit planning can be based on individual product, product line or brand, or total, by salesman, territory, region, or on a national basis. Profit planning is both short- and long-range, and the identification of profitability (both gross and net) is necessary, not only for the structure of the marketing plan, but also as an element in the overall operational plan as it relates to the assessment of the corporate position and capacity.

ADVERTISING AND PROMOTION

Effective market planning requires due attention to advertising and promotion. This is particularly the case in highly consumer-oriented enterprises. The capital expended in these areas, as well as the exact nature of the techniques and specifics of the campaign themselves, is a fit subject for consideration. To be meaningful, a statement of objectives in the advertising and promotion area is difficult and challenging. If it does nothing else, the attempt to develop such statements forces clearer consideration of the problems.

PRODUCT MANAGEMENT

At this point the consideration of product management becomes important. Where separate product management is maintained, statements of product objectives are derived from it. Consideration, of course, should be given first and foremost to profit. Additionally, product management should concern itself with product control, product forecasting, market size, penetration and potential, R&D recommendations, product life cycle, proportion, technical service, quality, and competition; and statements of objectives should reflect this concern.

MARKET

Objectives related to the market as a consideration separate from sales and profit imply consideration of market share and potential, creation or exploitation of new markets, and careful analysis of market shifts. Clearly, this implication presupposes a relationship with the assumptions that are required in the total development of the plan. In specific terms, as an element in the isolation of marketing objectives, it relates to the consideration of a statement of planned position within an identified market and a statement of action with respect to the marketing effort in any given market.

Relation to Total Business Effort

Naturally, the formulation of the marketing objectives requires a comprehensive review of the total business effort. The harmonious interpretations that must exist between marketing and other operational and functional areas are prerequisites for successful performance. The marketing concept clearly implies and is predicated on this integration of effort. In the generation of the marketing plan, the establishment of clearly defined marketing objectives affords the opportunity for clarification of these relationships and provides operational guidelines, thereby setting forth the expectations of the marketing group, and delineates the requirements for this cooperative effort.

Because the significance of objectives cannot be overstated, it is extremely important to comprehend clearly the nature of their establishment and of management's responsibilities regarding them. These considerations can be reduced to the following major elements: (1) Objectives must be established directly by top management; (2) management must indicate, explicitly and implicitly, its endorsement of established objectives; (3) in establishing objectives, consideration must be given to the primary requisites of feasibility, suitability, realism, measurability, quantifiability, and alterability; (4) objectives are used as instruments of measurement of performance; (5) objectives must be communicated within the organization.—*G. S. Dominguez*

PRODUCT PLANNING

All product-planning policies and decisions are directed toward a dual objective: anticipation of the consumer's or user's needs, and the incorporation of these needs in the products offered for sale. In order to attain this goal, it is necessary that clear and concise product objectives be set to determine the direction of policies and decisions. Product objectives direct product planning in certain directions related to the company's development of strategies, product policies, channels of distribution, type of selling, product scope, capacity utilization, and capital limitations.

As technology advances, the demand for new and improved products increases in order to meet its needs. Technological change results in more rapid product obsolescence; this compounds the pressure for innovation. Developing the capability to live with rapid change is becoming a major problem for many companies. The product-planning function is perhaps the most effective method developed thus far to meet the challenges of new product demand, shorter product life, more complicated technology, improvement of existing products, and accelerating rate of product change.

Scope of Product Planning

Although companies interpret product planning differently, according to their own needs and facilities, product planning in general involves the following factors:

1. Recommendation of product scope to include determining which products belong in the line at present and in the future.

2. Analysis of customer needs, wants, and habits, and of the factors influencing customers' choice of specific products.

3. Appraisal of products to determine the standing of a company's products in relation to competition as viewed by the customer.

4. Determination of the product ideas worth investigating.

5. Development of product specifications to indicate what products should be like and what they should do to meet customer requirements.

6. Definition of product appearance and design to determine visual appeal, style, and value added through industrial design.

7. Specification of product timing to determine the most advantageous time to introduce a new product or take some marketing action.

8. Product-line control policies for diversification, simplification, or elimination of a line.

9. Formulation of pricing to achieve maximum volume, position, and profits.

10. Development of market and product information needed for advertising, promotion, sales, and service.

Product-Planning Strategies

In addition to the implication that product planning is an integrated process, there are several other issues that influence the effectiveness of product planning. These involve strategies of responsibility, assignment, scope, and emphasis.

RESPONSIBILITY

The division of responsibility for product planning can be either centralized in one organization or divided between two organizational units—marketing and engineering. A unified product-planning responsibility establishes single accountability for product successes or failures. It also streamlines the process, avoids costly duplication of effort, and reduces the coordination requirements. On the other hand, division of product-planning responsibility forces trade-offs and assures a check and balance between the laboratory and the market. In addition it enables product planners to cope more effectively with the different managerial needs of changing markets and dynamic technology.

DIRECTION

The product-planning function can be placed organizationally three separate ways: assignment to marketing, to a technical organization, or independently in general management. Placing product planning in marketing, as most consumer goods companies do, assures that the marketing concept and marketing orientation will direct product-planning activity. It also provides greater responsiveness to customer needs and a sharper definition of new market requirements. Placing product-planning responsibility in technical departments (research or engineering) permits tighter control and direction of development and engineering projects. It also allows the incorporation of changing technologies into improvements and innovations more effectively. Placing a product-planning staff independent of marketing or technical functions balances conflicting viewpoints and risks and optimizes management decision. An independent product-planning group may involve top management more closely in key product decision, and it can manage complex marketing and technical choices more effectively. In effect, the decision as to where to place product-planning responsibility will be based on whether emphasis will be placed on market or customer needs, choosing the right technological alternatives, or product profitability.

Classification of Product Policies

When a manufacturer introduces an entirely new product, his initial strategy is simply growth. By effective merchandising and marketing he attempts to build volume as a means of achieving profit. The manufacturer's major policy is to establish primary demand for his new product entry. If he is successful, competition soon follows, requiring a shift to a new strategy of maintaining selective demand for his brand. The manufacturer now relies on superior marketing techniques to feature product differentiation, broader distribution, and production economies of higher volume. As demand broadens and the product matures, he may find product diversification strategies more important. He can then provide additional related products for the original market segments. As his options expand, he frequently branches into unrelated products. Such strategies of product growth and diversification are highly developed in American consumer goods fields, particularly in the food industry.

PRODUCT LIFE CYCLE

Closely attuned to product-planning policies is the product life cycle concept, which assumes that the life cycle of a product goes through five stages: introduction, growth, maturity, saturation, and decline. During a new product introduction, sales start off modestly and start to increase in the growth stage. Sales continue to increase during the maturity stage and level off and start to decline at the saturation stage. During the decline stage, sales volume continues downward. New products have this characteristic pattern to their sales volume. Profit-margin curves also have a characteristic pattern; they tend to start descending while the sales curve is still rising. This suggests that product strategy is better planned around the profit curve than the sales curve. Sooner or later, competition enters the marketplace, making careful product planning necessary to maintain profit margins. Each industry has its own sales volume–profit pattern, but—as a generality—the closer a company is to consumer goods and the marketplace, the shorter is the cycle of its product. Conversely, the closer a product or service is to basic industry, the longer is the cycle.

PRIMARY VERSUS SELECTIVE DEMAND

Common sense, intuition, or market studies will reveal whether the principal marketing requirement is to establish new customers who have never tried the product or to emphasize product or brand differentiation. The ideal strategy is quite clear: Endeavor to do both things simultaneously, and protect the flanks with an airtight patent or copyright. However, this strategy is seldom possible, and patent monopoly is a thing of the past.

Developing primary demand for new products. The policy of developing primary demand for new products often involves substantial economic risks and major obstacles. Classic examples of this point are color television and nylon. Four fundamental market situations present themselves when the marketer is following the policy of developing primary demand: (1) the market for entirely new products with new uses in a really new market; (2) a product new to the company but not new to its markets—essentially, a new product that is sold in markets not new to competitors; (3) a new product in a familiar market—essentially, a new product with uses similar to present products and sold in present markets or markets familiar to the company; and (4) new applications of established products or, similarly, new categories of customers for the same products and uses by virtue of fundamental changes in their buying power, leisure time, vocations, or avocations. Inherent risks, long lead times, and problems can be anticipated by following primary demand strategy, and therefore careful consideration should be given to using this policy.

Expanding primary demand for established products.   The development of markets for additional uses and applications is often a less costly and more rapid way of improving sales than simply introducing a new product. This strategy can be initiated at any stage of a product's life to extend or rejuvenate sales. An example of this strategy is a major computer manufacturer's market where there is continual marketing effort for new applications in new markets. It is feasible to follow this policy to prevent cyclical declines and to avoid the high investment and risk of new product introductions. In addition, expanded volume enables utilization of excess plant capacity and absorption of overhead expenses.

Expanding selective demand for established brands.   More defensive than primary demand development, the expansion of selective demand for established brands ultimately leads to reduced profits, higher prices, and proliferation of brands with little real product differentiation, as in the case of cigarettes and gasoline. The objectives of this policy are to capture larger market share and to establish and hold brand leadership in order to maintain strong shelf position with distributors and dealers. This policy permits entering competition later to avoid high initial costs of product development and introduction.

DIVERSIFICATION, SIMPLIFICATION, AND ELIMINATION

Certain types of product policies determine what product types and product-line scopes the company should offer. They are concerned with diversification of the product line and the related product-line policies of simplification and elimination.

Product diversification.   Planned diversification offers business certain definite advantages: (1) higher return on investment, (2) enhanced market value of stock, (3) stability of sales and profits, (4) expansion of sales and profits, (5) maximum utilization of resources, (6) more efficient marketing, and (7) profitable use of opportunity. Product diversification can extend into related or unrelated products. *Related product diversification* policy is followed when a company wants to fill out lines of related products needed by distributors and dealers and to take advantage of extra selling and distribution capacity. It also enables spreading overhead on R&D and manufacturing costs. Related product diversification takes advantage of new demand trends; it capitalizes on a family-brand "franchise" with consumers, and it results in supplementing static or declining volumes of a product line. This strategy is common in the food industry.

Unrelated product diversification is common in multiproduct companies, so-called conglomerates, which accelerate their rates of growth by stressing profitability and ROI as the main criteria of diversification. Followed extensively, this product policy often requires decentralization, which may lead to new difficulties with communication and control. However, unrelated product diversification can balance seasonal and cyclical gaps in a company's sales volume, and it can utilize idle capital. When used properly, this diversification policy capitalizes on outstanding management abilities and functional skills; it allows the application of proprietary knowledge to new areas; and it broadens opportunities for employees.

Product-line simplification. As product lines become more and more extensive, items may tend to duplicate one another, and older varieties become relatively obsolete. Thus there is opportunity for gains from line simplification. This policy is followed to eliminate unprofitable grades and variation, to reduce inventory expense, and to cull out slow movers. Line simplification emphasizes major product improvements and simplifies the manufacture and management of a product line.

Product elimination. A more extreme policy than simplification is the drastic pruning of major product types. This is done to eliminate unprofitable product lines, reduce dilution of management time, and free capital and facilities for new programs. In addition, product elimination allows concentration on prime talents and resources and specialization in prime markets.

PRODUCT PRICING AND SERVICE

In the past the use of product pricing has been a common-sense course of action in tough competitive situations, and today service policies can be structured to make a major contribution to a company's competitive effectiveness.

Leasing versus purchasing. The advantages of leasing are very apparent to every user of a computer. The policy is not new; applications have included automatic bowling-pin setters, company fleets, and capital equipment. A customer is interested in leasing because it offers a hedge against the risk of obsolescence, requires less capital, and gives more flexibility. To the marketer, leasing permits more rapid market expansion and a reduction in cyclical revenue variations, and it yields greater income over product life.

Warranties and guarantees. Used with a little imagination, warranty and guarantee policies can create a competitive advantage. Warranties have the advantage of increasing customer confidence and assurance in company products. They also assure feedback on product deficiencies, provide pressure within a company for quality engineering and control, and assure customer interest in proper use of equipment.

Expendable product policies. One of the ideal marketing situations for any business is to sell a product that is highly useful yet low enough in cost that, once its usefulness has been expended, the customer will not hesitate to throw it away and replace it. This policy has been used successfully during the early stages of primary demand by several manufacturers—most recently by the paper industry. Expendable products often take the form of refills that, if marketed with an attractively low price, expand its purchase.

"Iceberg" pricing. The selling price may include a sufficient margin to cover a variety of supporting services and functions needed to sell and maintain the product through its useful life. Like the submerged portion of an iceberg, the future need for these services is not always clear at the outset. This practice has been followed in setting prices for both leasing and purchase. Iceberg pricing assures proper care, maintenance, and use of leased equipment, provides a cushion for unforeseen contingencies, and forms the financial base for service and support manpower.

Branding

Brand identification is a necessary policy for the producer who wishes to exercise maximum control over the demand for his products and to be able to compete on a nonprice basis. Most products that lend themselves to brand identification and differentiation are branded in the American market today. The decision to use or not to use brands depends on the ability of management to truly differentiate the product; and if this differentiation is to be helpful in creating brand recognition, it must be in terms of characteristics that are important to the consumer.

BRAND TYPES

The four significant distinctions among types of brands are ownership of the brand, geographical coverage of the brand, the importance of the brand to its owner, and the number of products it covers. Brands may be owned by any manufacturer or wholesale or retail distributor. They may be sold nationally, regionally, sectionally, or citywide. Primary brands are those given major emphasis in advertising or those in which a greater portion of sales is made. Secondary or subsidiary brands may receive less emphasis or have less quality. Individual brands cover one product, and family brands cover a group of products with like characteristics or products that appeal to particular market segments. National brands are generally sold by manufacturers or can refer to national distribution of a brand. Private brands are generally sold by distributors.

OBJECTIVES IN BRANDING

Branding of goods has come to occupy a key position as the first step toward market control.

Control of demand. The assurance of a large and steady demand for a product facilitates planning and helps maintain a reasonable cost structure. By distinguishing one manufacturer's products from those of others through branding, other promotional activity becomes practicable. Branding individualizes a product, indicates its source of supply, and provides a connection between the manufacturer and the consumer.

Contact with market through servicing. Branding or other identification is a necessary condition for the administration of warranty, guarantee, or service policies. The fact of a warranty implies that there must be contact between the manufacturer and the consumer. The offer of warranties and service for promotional purposes is another means of securing and maintaining control over the market.

Greater independence in determining price. By branding, a manufacturer attempts to distinguish his products from others. He is then able to secure a quasi-independent status in pricing. Differences in product, unless readily apparent and substantial, generally do not affect price until they are brought to the attention of the buyer. However, when a buyer knows of the differences, a preference may result through which a price differential is established. The point to be made is that branding and advertising furnish the means by which a manufacturer can, at least in part, control price in his own interest.

BRAND COVERAGE

Many products may be sold under one brand, or one product in one quality may be sold under many different brands. Moreover, in order to achieve quality differentiation, different qualities of a product may be sold under different brands. Brands may be developed for specific geographic sectors or human sectors—age or nationality, for example.

Family brands. Family brands cover a group of products more or less closely connected in type or quality. The main objective in establishing family brands is to connect them in the minds of consumers so that one product will help to sell another. The family brand establishes a threshold in the market for any product that bears it, even though the product is new and untried. A major advantage in family brands is that promotional costs are incurred for only one brand. Carryover of goodwill from each product and lower promotional costs are achieved by using family brands, but no one product receives as much promotional effort as an individual product. As a result, a family brand acts as a leveler, for it implies that all products under the brand are of equal quality and distinctiveness. The criteria for selecting items included in family brands include those products that are closely associated in use, that appeal to the same buying motives, that are distinctive as a group but not individually, that are of the same general quality, and that will cause little difficulty in maintaining standardization.

Multiple brands. Multiple branding implies that the manufacturer is competing with himself, and there are times when this makes sense. Often, it is necessary to serve the market by offering different price lines and more than one quality, with differentiation through secondary brands. Usually, it is not desirable to place more than one quality of product under the same brand, especially if the difference is substantial. Companies give a simple justification for multiple branding where the markets are extremely large and widespread and where competition is actively pursuing the same business. They hope to expand primary demand for the type of product and increase the company's share of market, and thus spread management overhead and utilize excessive plant capacity. Multiple branding also stimulates internal competition in market development, takes advantage of newer technologies, and offers customers more choices favorable to the company.

Private brands. Private brands are owned and controlled by middlemen rather than manufacturers. Private-label items have contributed major volume for many years in the food and drug chains, mail-order firms, and voluntary food wholesalers. The decision to produce private brands may be affected by several factors. Commodity-type products may gain increased volume, and additional plant capacity may be utilized. Orders for private brands may offset declining demand for name brands and help realize lower per-unit sales and distribution expenses. In addition, private labels reach new customers through multiple distribution channels.

New Product Development

Much of the impetus for new product innovation stems from three interrelated needs: to match the new product entries marketed by competitors, to cope with customers' changing requirements and preferences, and to keep pace with accelerated gains in technology. But if the successful development of new products and services answers these needs, carrying out such programs and developing the capability to live with rapid change are the major problems to be encountered.

BASIC OBJECTIVES

The basic reasons for product development activities in most companies are the instability of consumer preferences and purchasing power, on the one hand, and the instability of competitive position, on the other.

Specific objectives. Specifically, the objectives of product development are: (1) to arouse customer interest and stimulate sales so as to hold or increase the company's share of existing markets; (2) to utilize idle production and sales facilities by opening new markets; (3) to keep company products and product lines in a strong competitive position; (4) to diversify product lines so as to reduce seasonal and long-term fluctuations in production and sales; (5) to replace products that, because of market saturation or intensified competition, have declining profits.

SOURCES OF NEW PRODUCT IDEAS

One of the most difficult and vital activities in product development efforts is to find sound, worthwhile ideas on which to work. Ideas come from various sources, but the number of really good ones is low indeed.

Social pressures. An extensive source of product ideas is found in the social pressures that arise from changes in manner of living or in the composition of the population. This requires developing an awareness of social pressures or social tensions and responding to them. Examples of products from this source include automobile safety glass, seat belts, garbage disposal units, and air conditioning.

The marketplace. First-hand contact with the market is always available through company salesmen, servicemen, and sales supervisors. This source provides invaluable information on buyers' needs, on inadequacies of both the company's and competitors' products, and on changes in buyers' preferences. Another source of new product ideas is in asking the user directly to express his opinion through interviews or questionnaires.

R&D personnel. The principal source of new product ideas is a company's R&D laboratories. Technically trained people in research laboratories originate product ideas and work on those that originate from other sources.

Other company personnel. Management personnel or other technical personnel within the company are a widely used source. Production, engineering, or marketing people with a keen interest and constant attention to product problems are also a fruitful source.

Inventors. Many product suggestions come to business concerns entirely unsolicited from outside inventors. Careful legal procedures are essential to avoid difficulties that often are encountered when dealing with inventors.

Other companies. The right to product ideas or processes has frequently been acquired by outright purchase from other companies or by merger.

PRODUCT DEVELOPMENT PROGRAMS

The impact of a product development program is felt throughout a company. R&D, engineering, production, and marketing departments share major responsibility for developing and introducing a product. In the course of development, the finance, market research, legal, advertising, and all other departments either take an active part in the work or are called on for advice. Cooperation between departments is of the utmost importance. Lack of proper coordination lengthens development time, increases cost, and creates a chaotic situation within an organization. A well-coordinated program permits the work to flow smoothly with a minimum of lost time and friction.

Stages of product development. Generally, a new product development program is divided into two separate activities: management and execution. Management of the project is concerned with (1) project preparation, general supervision, and obtaining top management approval; (2) coordinating action required to execute the project; and (3) reporting, including progress reports, changes in schedules, and funding. The execution of the project is handled by appropriate departments—marketing, R&D, manufacturing, sales, and so forth. To manage such a complex activity, it is necessary to break it into functions and stages that can be managed, planned, and controlled. A six-stage pattern is common: (1) exploration (the search for product ideas to meet company objectives); (2) screening (a quick analysis to determine which ideas are pertinent and merit more detailed study); (3) business analysis (the expansion of the idea, through creative analysis, into a concrete business recommendation including product features and a program for the product); (4) development (turning the ideas-on-paper into a product-in-hand, demonstrable and producible); (5) testing (the commercial experiments necessary to verify earlier business judgments); (6) commercialization (launching the product in full-scale production and sale, committing the company's reputation and resources).

Planning and controlling product development programs. Once specific objectives are established, new product development programs have certain planning and control requirements. These include the need to identify all the activities required to meet the objectives; the need to pinpoint complex interrelationships or constraints among activities; the need to predict the time and cost of all these activities; the need to optimize or allocate limited resources; the need for flexibility; the need to control the execution of the program; and the need to identify trade-offs between such factors as cost, lead time, marketability, capital, and risk. These requirements can be met by modern management techniques such as PERT/CPM, program management, OR, value engineering, and cost effectiveness. A new product venture puts the entire company to the test. Close coordination, a high degree of teamwork, and effective management can lead to new profits and opportunities for those who are successful.—*D. B. Uman*

THE ANNUAL MARKETING PLAN

The annual marketing plan is a commitment to marketing action. In form it is a written blueprint, a manager's manual of affordable methods of allocating a portion of total corporate resources and predicting their contribution to corporate profit. In *substance* the marketing plan is an information system that correlates three types of data:

1. Areas of agreement about the existing situation on which marketing action will be based; this is the plan's situation survey, and it represents the point of departure for marketing.

2. Statistical projections from the situation survey of the plan's objectives which, if achieved, will become the base of the next year's plan.

3. The ways and means by which the objectives can be achieved, outlined in the form of strategies and their controls.

Basic Marketing Planning Concepts

Four basic concepts underlie the marketing planning process: pinpointing a market as the planning base and assigning it a customer-oriented definition; isolating the market's key accounts and heaviest-using customers as the planning target; isolating a year as the planning unit; and imbedding each individual marketing plan into a harmonious relationship with the total corporate family of plans.

PLANNING BASE

A market must be the base for every marketing plan. In this context a "market" is best defined as "a group of customers who heavily share a common need." The definition of this shared need becomes the definition of the market. This means that markets cannot be categorized in terms of corporate product and service systems but according to the type of customer need that exists for them. Thus a marketing plan for an office typewriter manufacturer would be entitled, "A Plan to Market Typewriters to the Office Information Systems Market"; a marketing plan for a hydraulic motors manufacturer would be entitled, "A Plan to Market Hydraulic Energy Systems to the Construction Equipment Market"; a marketing plan for an airline would be entitled, "A Plan to Market Commercial Air Transportation to the Business Traveler Market." In this way the planning company acknowledges the nature of the markets it serves in the same terminology that the markets themselves use to describe their needs. The planning base thereby becomes market-oriented.

PLANNING TARGET

An annual marketing plan may be said to have one overriding purpose: to insure for one more year the premium pricing acceptance of a company's product and service systems. In the last analysis, there is no other reason to plan. If premium pricing is to be achieved, two conditions must be met: the product-service system must deliver pre-emptive benefits, and these benefits must be custom-tailored for the heaviest users in the marketplace. Heavy users are customers who use the greatest volume of a product-service system, who use it with the greatest frequency and continuity, and who are willing to pay a premium price to obtain its specific benefits. These key account customers are generally described by the "20-80 theory," which suggests that only about 20 percent of all customers in any market may be heavy users, yet they can account for up to 80 percent of all profitable sales volume. Heavy users, both actual and potential, must therefore be every plan's target. This does not mean that lighter users, switch-brand users, infrequent users, or specialty users will not be served by the plan's strategies. They will be. But they will not be planned for, since they may account for only about 20 percent of profitable sales.

PLANNING UNIT

A year is a convenient period of market-planning time. For the most part, it is administratively convenient. It fits budgeting and accounting frequencies, sales forecast projections, and traditional corporate reporting procedures, among other annually recurrent operations. It also matches competitive practice. But the choice of a year as the basic planning unit is an artificial convention, practical from a managerial standpoint but a contrivance from the standpoint of how markets buy. No market's needs, or preferences for product and service systems to supply them, change automatically at the conclusion of a calendar or fiscal year. A market's life-style patterns of purchasing preferences evolve throughout their own cycles, which are—except coincidentally—irrespective of "planning years." The annual marketing plan must therefore take this cyclical disharmony into consideration by engineering two controls into its management: First, the annual plan must always be regarded as a single snapshot in an ongoing motion picture, and the snapshot must continually be related to what has preceded it and what can be expected to follow; and second, the annual plan must allow for at least a quarterly review to keep it aligned with the inevitable changes in market behavior that will not necessarily coincide with the planning year.

PLANNING INTERRELATIONSHIPS

Just as an annual plan is one part of a long-term, ongoing planning process that is multiyear in duration, it must also be interrelated with every other corporate marketing plan that impinges on the same market. A company that serves one market with a variety of product and service systems needs to harmonize the plans for these various systems so that the market is addressed with a single image and so that the additive benefits of synergistic marketing can be obtained.

Each individual plan may therefore be regarded as one member of its company's family of plans for a particular market, all of which will be coordinated at the highest levels of management by a master plan for each major market. Paralleling the family-of-plans concept is the family-of-planners idea. Most plans are the product of a family approach, involving the contributions of marketing staff officers; marketing line managers—who may be known as market, brand, or product managers; nonmarketing managers, especially in R&D, engineering, and finance; and, of course, top management reviewers and approvers. Some companies prefer to combine the planning and operating functions and place them almost entirely in their line officers. Others assign heavier initial responsibilities to corporate planning staffs, then require each of the line officers to customize the basic situational information to his own needs and derive his own objectives and strategies from it. A plan must never be imposed on the man who will be responsible for its achievement. But it is a rare line operator who will conceive and execute his plan without multidisciplinary corporate assistance.

The Marketing Planning Process

The annual marketing plan is a basic information exchange system. Its inputs are composed of what has already happened in the planning situation inside and outside the company and what is happening now. Its outputs are the strategic ways and means of altering the planning situation in the company's favor. Inputs are therefore historical. Outputs, in the form of a planned strategy mix, are creative. Once put into effect, each plan's creative strategies become a part of the next annual plan's historical situation. In this way strategies exert their long-term effect on corporate marketing.

Because strategies are a plan's outputs, a marketing plan can rightfully be regarded as an instrument of change. Its objectives therefore become the plan's single most important component. Objectives quantify change. They predict what will most likely happen to the present situation if the plan's strategies are put into effect. As a result a plan is really the servant of its objectives, for they will in the short run determine its strategies, and over the longer run they will determine its success.

As a sequential system, a marketing plan has three basic components. The planning process treats these components in rank order, since each is predicated on the component which comes before it: This year's situation survey is predicated, at least in part, on last year's strategies; the plan's objectives are outgrowths of the situation survey; and the plan's strategies are suggested by its objectives. In turn this year's strategies will influence next year's situation survey.

This sequence is true for all planning companies regardless of age or size or industry. It is for this reason that the following basic outline for the annual marketing process can be suggested. Because it concentrates on essentials, it will serve all companies well. But it will probably serve no company exactly because many individual markets exert their own peculiar requirements on the planning process, as do specific corporate philosophies, organizational structures, and product-service systems. Any of these major variations can, however, easily be interwoven with the basic outline.

SITUATION SURVEY

The situation survey is composed of two parts: The first is an analysis of the external situation, and the second analyzes the internal situation.

External situation survey. The analysis of the external situation describes a company's or division's market and its socioeconomic and competitive context.

The *market situation* is covered in two sections, each of which deals with the key customer market:

1. Key customer market segmentation is described by means of key account profiles based on heaviest-using customers and their influencers, with (*a*) demographic description of age, sex, education, position, size and type of purchasing unit, and other relevant factors; and (*b*) psychographic description of needs that determine the life style of heaviest-using customers and their influencers and that underlie the specific benefits required of product and service systems and their distribution, promotion, and pricing, which are designed to serve these needs.

2. The section on key customer market segment growth and development calls for a one-year and longer-term three- to five-year projection from recent growth trends among heavy customers in terms of (*a*) their number, and (*b*) the numerical and dollar volume of their purchase commitments in product and service systems related to the plan. It includes up to ten-year long-range demand forecasts based on growth trends, as well as anticipated changes to be required in satisfaction of qualitative alterations in demand. It also identifies quantitative changes that may be required over the long range based on changes in key customer market segments' size, composition, education, affluence, purchasing options, and rank order of needs.

The *socioeconomic situation* is analyzed in four parts in the external situation survey.

1. The social environment for marketing is covered in a description of recent past and present life-style social trends which predispose, or at least correlate with, key customer market behavior; a one-year and longer-term three- to five-year projection of these trends, with documentation for assumptions of continuity or change; and a projected life-style profile of key customer markets one year hence.

2. The section on the economic environment for marketing contains a description and statistical enumeration of key economic indicators of the recent past and present which predispose, or at least correlate with, key customer market behavior; a one-year and longer-term three- to five-year projection of these indicators, with documentation for assumptions of continuity or change; and a projected economic profile of the market one year hence.

3. The survey investigates the scientific environment for marketing through a description of recent past and present scientific and technological inventions which predispose, or at least correlate with, key customer behavior, and a one-year and longer-term three- to five-year projection of these inventions, with documentation for assumptions and implications on market demand, potential product and service system innovation, and marketing system obsolescence.

4. The survey's section on the legislative environment for marketing calls for a description of recent past and present legislative trends and enacted laws which affect market behavior or marketing policy (packaging legislation; antitrust, merger, and acquisition legislation and interpretation; regulatory agency pricing policies; and consumer protection legislation) and an estimate of their degree of influence on market penetration; cost-price policies; product-service system manufacture, distribution, or promotion; corporate image; and competitive reaction.

The external situation survey's section on *competition* contains an analysis of competition, both direct and indirect, and a forecast of new competitors:

1. The direct competitor analysis is a qualitative and quantitative analysis of assets and liabilities of the company or division compared with and contrasted against existing direct competitors, showing management, fiscal, and marketing capabilities and resources; marketable product and service systems; basic promotional systems and budgets; market penetration; and corporate image profiles.

2. The indirect competitor analysis reveals the management, fiscal, and marketing capabilities and resources of existing indirect competitors—that is, suppliers of alternative product and service systems; their marketable product and service systems; basic promotional systems and budgets; market penetration; and corporate image profiles.

3. The new competitor forecast deals with the prediction of new competitors (either direct or indirect) whose entry can be anticipated within the planning year, and the marketing or scientific basis for their competitiveness; and with an estimate of degree of threat and potential maximum loss of market penetration and erosion of corporate image, together with minimum retaliatory costs and strategies required to neutralize their inroads.

Internal situation survey. The internal situation is described according to business positioning and capabilities.

The business positioning coverage provides a market-oriented charter for the business which defines its objectives, capabilities, and strategic commitments in terms of rendering a pre-emptive service to the market being planned for.

The business capabilities situation is described in terms of the basic capabilities and their supporting financial resources currently being directed against the market for which planning is being done:

1. Productive capabilities and financial resources are in two categories: established product and service systems and new product and service systems in the current year. The two categories are broken down on a per product-service system basis, by (a) investment or capital employed; (b) ROI or return on capital employed; (c) net profit after taxes; (d) sales volume in dollars, units, and share of market; (e) brand image positioning; (f) life cycle positioning; (g) marketable assets and liabilities compared against competition; and (h) cost-price relationship.

2. Promotional capabilities and financial resources, on a per product-service system basis, are described under the headings of (a) sales management capabilities, strategies, and investment; (b) distribution management capabilities, strate-

gies, and investment; (c) advertising and sales promotion management capabilities, strategies, and investment; and (d) packaging management capabilities, strategies, and investment.

3. Other capabilities and financial resources, also on a per product-service system basis, are (a) marketing management manpower capability, organization, and investment; and (b) plant and equipment capability and investment.

OBJECTIVES

Objectives are threefold in nature. First and foremost, objectives are financial. The most essential objectives of the planning process are therefore numerical, and the numbers they refer to are profit figures. A secondary denomination of objectives are the quantitative data that form the statistical basis for profit. The third category of objectives is qualitative, concerned with the image goals that are the conceptual foundation for profit. Because objectives are chiefly expressed in numbers, the objectives section of the annual marketing plan is always the shortest element in the plan. By the same token, it is the most important.

Financial objectives. Financial objectives are expressed in terms of ROI, or return on capital employed, and net profit before or after taxes.

Quantitative objectives. The expression of quantitative objectives is found in a profit-to-sales ratio and in sales volume in dollars, units, and share of market.

Qualitative objectives. Qualitative objectives are the company's overall corporate image and individual product-service systems images.

STRATEGIES AND CONTROLS

Strategies are the action elements of the marketing planning process. They represent the creative mix by which the plan's objectives are to be achieved. Each individual strategy must therefore meet one essential qualification: It must help contribute to the plan's objectives. Taken as a group, the total strategy mix must serve two criteria: The mix should be composed of the smallest number of individual strategies, and its overall investment should be the minimal expenditure required to complete the plan.

For the company as a whole, the overriding strategies will be business strategies. These top-level commitments will decide what is marketed and how and what its source of supply will be. Business strategies determine corporate growth and development and influence such major issues as growth into related new businesses by venture development or growth into unrelated, conglomerate businesses by merger and acquisition. Within corporate business strategies, there are three basic marketing strategies which must be annually planned and executed: product and service system strategies, by which the plan manipulates what is offered for marketing; promotional system strategies, by which the plan manipulates the way its products and services are offered for sale; and pricing system strategies, by which the plan manipulates the market value assigned to its products and services offered for sale. Promotional strategies and pricing strategies may be used as correlates of each other, each reinforcing the other's market effect. Or promotion and pricing may be used as alternatives to each other, with promotional strategies receiving emphasis in order to limit the need for pricing strategies, or with pricing strategies used as a replacement for promotional investments. (Thirteen fundamental strategies are discussed in the following subsection, "Marketing Strategy.")

Controls are the constraints applied against strategies in order to keep their costs in line, monitor their progress, and evaluate their contribution. There are three principal means of control: financial controls, which are largely exerted through the assignment of a budget to each strategy; information controls, chiefly the findings of sales research, market research, or technological research, which can be used to predict the market performance of a strategy or to certify its operational efficiency; and judgmental controls, which are discretionary judgments applied against a strategy in areas where an informational control would be too expensive or too time-consuming, or is simply regarded as unnecessary or impossible. In a sense, a judgmental control is a subjective information control. Either a judgmental or informational control, along with its budgetary control, should accompany every strategy.

Marketing Plan Utilization

The marketing plan should be used as a management tool for market leadership. This means that the plan must be worked as a practical guide to the three fundamental attributes of leadership: branded product and service systems, preemptive market positioning for them, and acceptance for their premium pricing. Since unbranded or commodity products and services cannot be positioned preemptively to justify a premium price, they need not be planned. Thus the marketing planning process is the basic management alternative to commodity marketing.

An annual marketing plan has, by definition, a predetermined life cycle. Its obsolescence is built in. For this reason its greatest relevance comes over the first half of its useful life. Over the last two quarters of the planned year it becomes progressively less applicable unless on-line revisions are updated into it. At any time its reliability as an action base is therefore inversely proportional to its age.

This fact helps explain why judgmental controls must always be applied to the creation and utilization of marketing plans. It is generally better to err on the side of flexible adherence to a plan by adopting a policy of loose construction toward it than to interpret or adhere to it rigidly in spite of its wear-out rate, the human fallibility that is implicit in its structuring, or the market dynamics that form its restless base. Even though a plan is designed to help marketers operate with greater economy and efficiency, no plan can ever encompass all marketing wisdom. The crucial 10 percent which can separate marketing success from failure can often be generated by the man who manages the plan. Because markets are people, only marketers—not plans—can ever serve them with sensitivity or elasticity, let alone the intuition that is the hallmark of the entrepreneur.—*Mack Hanan*

MARKETING STRATEGY

Marketing strategy is the sum total of all the individual choices that contribute to the achievement of marketing objectives. Marketing strategy is therefore a resolution of options, each one of which represents an allocated resource and therefore a cost. Of all the strategies of management, the strategy of marketing is generally the single most expensive corporate investment. It is also the single most important investment. Without a successful marketing strategy, even the most superior scientific and technological strategy—or financial strategy, organizational strategy, or strategy of any other sort—will probably be unsuccessful or certainly not as successful as it might otherwise have been. The converse is also true. A successful marketing strategy can often compensate for failings in many areas of management planning and operation.

In a facetious vein the term "marketing strategy" has often been defined as "the postmortem rationalization for why sales are down"—a remark designed to diffuse responsibility and diversify blame beyond critical evaluation. Actually, strategy must be a beforehand activity. It must be predictive in intent, forecasting an optimal mix of investments that will most economically and efficiently achieve their planned objectives. Strategy may therefore be regarded as a calculated risk: *calculated* in the sense of reckoning investments against return on investments, *risk-taking* in the sense of allocating finite and perishable resources over a committed period of the corporate life cycle.

Five Basic Criteria of Marketing Strategy

Marketing strategy is the action element of the annual marketing plan. To be truly actionable, strategy must meet certain criteria that will underwrite its effectiveness and justify its cost. Many criteria exist. Some are peculiar to specific companies engaged only in specific businesses. But for all companies at least five basic criteria form the jumping-off place for marketing strategy: pre-emptiveness, market orientation, long-range application, cost-effectiveness, and planned obsolescence.

These five basic criteria of marketing strategy can be interpreted to fit a wide range of marketing strategies that utilize a product and service system, either alone or in conjunction with promotional systems and pricing systems.

PRE-EMPTIVENESS

Marketing strategy must attempt to capture the acceptance of a market and maintain the corporate position in it against actual and anticipated competition by offering a uniquely pre-emptive product and service system. What is offered for sale must be meaningfully unique in itself, or the manner in which it is offered must be meaningfully unique, or both must be true. Strategy must therefore be distinctive, individualized by the personality of its strategists, and identifiably different from competition. "Me-too strategy" is not strategy. It is imitation, which is the absence of strategy, just as a commodity product is the absence of branding.

MARKET ORIENTATION

Marketing strategy must be based on providing a product or service system oriented to a market's needs, wants, and desires. Market-centering a strategy assures its relevance to a market's acceptance, involving the customer or end user in the strategic planning process from the beginning. Marketing strategy must therefore be a per-market approach; that is, it must cater specifically to serving an individualized segment of the total market, focusing on its needs and offering a benefit system that is optimal from the market segment's point of view.

LONG-RANGE APPLICATION

Marketing strategy must attempt to be pre-emptive, over the short run, against competition. But marketing strategy must never be so short-sighted in its near-term application that it adversely prejudices the long-range effectiveness of the corporate market image. This means that annual marketing strategy planning must be evaluated within the context of the total business life cycle. Long-term profitability should rarely be sacrificed for short-term gain. The ultimate objective of marketing strategy must be, first of all, to act as a warranty for survival of the business profit base, and then to achieve annual installments on that sum total each year.

COST-EFFECTIVENESS

Marketing strategy must be cost-effective. It must try to achieve maximum effectiveness at minimum cost. For this reason a cost-effective strategy mix is sometimes referred to as a "minimix." To plan a minimal cost strategy, the smallest number of elements—not the largest—must be included in the strategy mix, and the lowest expenditure must be assigned to each element. Strategy planning should ask, "How little do we need?" rather than "How much can we include?" This does not mean that marketing strategy must be low in cost or that it will, ideally, be cheap. At all times marketing strategy should strive for the most economical allocation of resources, whatever their actual cost, as a method of conservation of corporate assets. But to insure the effectiveness of resource allocation, no resource should be committed to the mix unless its contribution is both necessary and minimal.

PLANNED OBSOLESCENCE

A marketing strategy mix must be planned to obsolete itself; otherwise, it will be obsoleted by competition, since competition is essentially a mix-breaking counterstrategy. Every marketing strategy has its life cycle of viability. Because the combination of external and internal pressures against business stability continually alters the factual situation and the related assumptions on which a strategy rests, it must be evaluated periodically for its relevance. The same strategy will hardly ever be applicable if it is unchanged over two successive annual planning periods.

Three Basic Marketing Strategies

There are three basic classifications of marketing strategies. One strategy class encompasses the "what" of marketing: the physical, tangible product and service systems offered for sale. A second strategy class concerns the "how" of marketing: the advertising, sales, and related promotional systems by which products and services are offered for sale. The third strategy class is involved with the "how much" of marketing: the pricing systems by which products and services are endowed with a market value by correlating them with financial meanings rather than with the imagery meanings that promotional strategies confer. Thus promotion and price are correlates of each other. A premium promotional image justifies a premium price. A premium price in turn finances the creation and marketing of a premium promotional image. Conversely, commodity pricing is justified by little or no promotion, which the price both explains and reflects.

With each of the three basic classes of strategies, management has two choices. Each year at annual planning time or even more frequently, it may change one or more aspects of one, two, or all three strategies. Or it may change nothing. In either event a strategic decision is being made. A strategy of no change may be a market leader's luxury, a method of buying time to evaluate an unstable market situation, or the second- or third-year commitment of a No. 2 marketer who is successfully penetrating the competitive leader's business. Strategies of change, often revolutionary, are generally the No. 2 and No. 3 marketers' necessities at the outset of their competitive challenges. Evolutionary change is also increasingly recognized as a necessity for maintaining leadership once it has been won. In these respects strategies are often dictated, or at least significantly influenced, as much by the marketing situation that forms their external environment as by their objectives.

Individual marketing strategies within each basic strategy classification can be as numerous and as varied as their strategists. Certain fundamental strategies for all product and service systems, for their promotion, and for their pricing, nonetheless exist. As a group they comprise the great majority of marketing actions. Since they are so essential to understanding the ways in which most products and services are marketed, they are outlined in summary form here.

PRODUCT AND SERVICE SYSTEM STRATEGIES

Strategies for product and service systems may be innovation strategies, renovation strategies, proliferation strategies, market extension strategies, or market specialization strategies.

Innovation. Innovation strategies attempt to create new product or service life cycles. They are essentially developmental strategies, creating new products or services by generating them internally or by acquiring them externally. The objective of innovation strategies is to develop a new profit position. Developmental products or services may be employed to gain entry into a new market or to develop a broader profit base in an established market. Because of their innovative nature, new products and services represent the highest risk among all marketing strategies.

Renovation. Renovation strategies attempt to prolong established product or service life cycles. They are essentially product extension strategies, adding new substantive or performance characteristics on an evolutionary, incremental basis. The objective of renovation strategies is to prolong an existing profit position. Products or services are best renovated when they reach a plateau in the mature phase of their life cycle, since this is a time when a new size, shape, ingredient, performance benefit, or other additive factor can exert its most rejuvenative effect on market acceptance. Because of the simplicity, economy, and relative security with which marginal renovations can be added to established products and services, renovative repositioning is among the commonest of all marketing strategies.

Proliferation. Proliferation strategies attempt to diversify product or service life cycles across a broader market base. They are essentially image-maximization strategies whose purpose is to amortize an existing market image by distributing it across a complete line of multiple products and services offered to the same market. Proliferation strategies are also attempts to optimize advertising and physical distribution systems by creating a synergistic effect among all products and services in a line. The objective of proliferation strategies is to hedge against competitive pre-emption, technological obsolescence, or serious alteration in the nature of market demand that could erode the sales base of existing products and services, as well as to start profitable new life cycles. Product and service systems are best proliferated when their parent brand has recently entered the late stages of its life cycle's growth phase or the early stages of its mature phase. Proliferated products and services are less risky than innovative strategies but riskier than renovative strategies.

Market extension. Market extension strategies attempt to multiply the number of life cycles of a product or service by implanting it in more than one market. This allows the same basic product or service—with perhaps minor renovations—to lead several lives, often being positioned at different life cycle phases in each market. The highly profitable growth phase in one market can thereby counterbalance a declining mature phase or a high-investment introductory phase in another market. The objective of market extension strategies is similar to that of proliferation strategies: They are buffers against overdependence on a sole income source, whether such a source is a single product or service or a single market. Market extension strategies can be adopted at any time, once a base has been secured in one market. The risk involved in extending a product or service system into multiple markets can range from light to heavy, depending on the similarities in needs of the several markets and the financial and promotional capabilities of the marketer in serving them profitably. To the marketer, the ability to maximize his capabilities across a pluralistic customer base is a major incentive to market extension, since it affords the greatest economies in manufacture and marketing as well as major efficiencies in their management.

Market specialization. Market specialization strategies attempt to capitalize on a highly segmented area of market demand by producing a premium type of product or service for its specific needs. Market specialization strategies are essentially opportunistic. Their objective is to capture a small but high-value market with a high-price, custom-tailored benefit. A marketer who is able to pre-empt a specialized market can enjoy a low-risk position, since there is rarely enough premium profit for more than one supplier. This can yield at least a transiently monopolistic situation, which is the ideal expression of marketing strategy. A market specialization strategy is often accompanied by a product or service system specialization in which only one specialized product or service accounts for the totality of a business. This is the ultimate in specialization, and it generally rewards the marketer with a premium-price, specialist image.

PROMOTIONAL SYSTEM STRATEGIES

The broad categories of promotional system strategies are strategies of key account concentration, physical distribution, and advertising distribution.

Key account concentration. Key account strategies, which are also known as heavy-user or heavy-customer strategies, attempt to concentrate corporate sales resources among key proven customers and key prospective customer accounts. They direct the preponderance of sales force talent, time, and promotional and technical support against the relatively few accounts that rarely average more than 20 to 30 percent of all customers who supply from 70 to 80 percent of the sales force's profitable volume. The objective of concentration strategies is to allow the best salesmen and the best selling tools to be applied directly and consistently to the market targets whose payout offers the highest rate of return on investment. Through this type of focused selling a company salesman receives overall sales responsibility for a portion or all of one or more customers' business. If a customer is large enough, important enough, and profitable enough, the salesman may spend most or even all of his time on the customer's premises, acting as a full-range product and service account executive on behalf of his company and converting the customer into a client. Meanwhile, accounts of lesser stature can be served less intensively by the corporate sales force or by a mix of corporate, dealer and distributor, manufacturer's representative, and broker sales forces. Sales strategies that concentrate on key accounts in this way can conserve corporate resources of sales manpower and administration, improve customer servicing through the "one man—many products and services" approach, and increase long-term marketing security by establishing a close, continuing, and anticompetitive relationship with the principal sources of profit.

Physical distribution. Strategies of physical distribution are of two kinds: proliferation strategies and specialization strategies.

Proliferation strategies attempt to diversify market access to a product and service system, approaching as closely as possible the ideal of universal mass distribution. Their objective is to saturate a market, neutralize or even deny competitive access to distribution, and discount in advance the probable effects of labor problems, out-of-stock conditions, or other nullifying factors that may deactivate any single distribution channel. Distribution may proliferate into a diverse number of forms: Retail outlets such as department and variety stores, supermarkets, company-owned stores, dealers and distributor-owned outlets, agents, service stations, representatives, vending machines, and mail order are major examples of components that can be included in a multiple distribution system.

Specialization strategies are the opposite of proliferation strategies, since the objective of specialization is to concentrate distribution into one or a very small number of channels. In this way a sense of exclusivity is created for a product or service system, image control and quality control can be rigorously maintained, and premium pricing may be enjoyed. Sole distributorships, exclusive outlets such as Class A department stores, or media such as specialty shops, licensed or authorized agents, or mail order are familiar examples of specialization strategies.

Advertising distribution. Strategies of advertising distribution also employ proliferation and specialization.

Proliferation strategies for advertising are the corollary of proliferation strategies for physical distribution. Advertising impressions, rather than actual products or services themselves, are distributed through a broadly diversified array of media "outlets." Market saturation is the objective, with mass media coverage seeking to blanket a market, neutralize competition, and protect against the failure of individual media. Image transfer, the synergistic carry-over of advertising impressions from one medium to another, may also be obtained. A multimedia advertising program can include print media such as newspapers and magazines, broadcast media such as radio and television, and supplemental media such as outdoor posters, point-of-sale promotion, direct mail, catalogs, trade shows, and many pedestrian and exotic media ranging from matchbook covers to skywriting.

Specialization strategies for advertising are the corollary of specialization strategies for physical distribution. One medium, or only a small number of media, is chosen for dominance by an advertiser. Because of a combination of high-frequency, high-continuity, and high-impact advertising, a selected medium may come to appear "owned" by the advertiser who practices a strategy of specialization. A specialization strategy may be an all-television strategy with no print advertising. Or it may be an all-magazine strategy, dominating one weekly magazine with full-page or double-page advertisements throughout the 52 weeks of its publishing year. This strategy attempts to cover a single major market in great depth, sacrificing reach for impact.

PRICING STRATEGIES

Pricing strategies are of three kinds: leadership strategies, premium strategies, and price-image strategies.

Leadership. Leadership strategies are designed to pre-empt an industry image and a market image as the setter of price trends. Generally, these price trends will be upward-moving. The price-leading marketer will raise his price first; then his competitors will follow in acknowledgment of his leadership. Price leadership can operate downward, as well. Leadership strategies confirm the marketer's acceptance as the value leader, since his price comes to represent the quality standard of the industry. Connoting this acceptance is the principal objective of price leadership, followed by the objective of being able to increase profitability when necessary and to depress the market to affect competition adversely, when desired, by lowering price to the point where it will drive out marginal competition.

Premium pricing. Premium pricing strategies attempt to maximize a marketer's return on his investment. They are also useful in helping a marketer isolate himself and his product or service system from competition, imply its superior quality, and offer the customer benefits of high-status prestige and a sense of security in owning "the best." Premium pricing strategies are typically associated with a top-of-the-line product or service or with a highly segmented market specialization strategy practiced by a single product or service supplier. Premium strategies frequently depend on market acceptance of the unique benefit that may accompany a new product or service and that may be either real or simply perceived as real. The added value of the benefit may be substantive or psychological; it may be engineered into the product or service, or it may be a factor of its promotion. In either case it acts as a premium image builder for its marketer and is reflected in its price.

Price image. Price-image strategies have mass marketing objectives. They may identify an economy product or service supplier, or they may designate a premium price marketer's second line. Price lining is an attempt to diversify the sales base across the broadest possible market. A product or service may be created initially as a price item, or it may become one as it passes from the premium priced, growth phase of its life cycle into maturity; that is, as it loses its brand uniqueness and approaches commodity classification.

Strategy mix. Ability to create and execute a successful mix is the highest expression of the marketing art. Some marketers are intuitive strategists. They sense the "how" without knowing the "why" behind it. But most successful marketers are trial-and-error strategists. On a small scale, they first try many experimental approaches to a strategy mix. Then they adopt the one with the least error for full-scale application. Viewed in this manner, each year's strategy can be regarded as a modular phase of a continuing experiment. The experiment's objectives are devoted to isolating the smallest and most economical mix of variables that must be manipulated to achieve planned profit. Identifying these relatively few variables insures control over the strategy-mix investment base, reducing it to its minimal sum and thereby helping to reduce the cost of profit making. This is the basic goal of marketing strategy.—*Mack Hanan*

ORGANIZATION

When a chief marketing executive first assumes responsibility for managing the marketing function, one of his initial tasks is to decide how he will organize his group. This task often is approached by finding out how other companies—competitors in particular—that sell similar products are organized. Such research can be highly instructive; but the astute marketing executive realizes that his company is different from every other company he might examine, and that slavish copying of another company's organization plan—even that of the most successful company in his industry—probably is not his best answer.

The "Ideal" Organization Plan

In starting to design an organization plan that is truly his own and the best possible for his company, the marketing executive is well advised to develop first his idea of an "ideal" plan. In doing this he disregards completely any limitations related to availability of funds, number of people, or capabilities of individuals already on the payroll. He may go one step further and say to himself, "I'll accept any approach except what we've already tried."

Once freed from these restrictions, the marketing executive focuses his attention first on the markets in which he must sell. What motivates people to buy the products or services that he offers? How can he present his product most compellingly to prospective buyers? What is important to buyers in making their buying decisions? In short, what are the requirements for selling successfully in these markets?

A study of this kind leads naturally to some conclusions about the functions that must be performed by the marketing organization and about their relative importance. In an organization selling standardized commodities, for example, it may be that pricing and physical distribution are the most important factors in the market; thus concentration on these areas may be highly desirable. In an organization selling high-fashion merchandise it may be necessary to put the greatest emphasis on ability to detect style trends earlier than the competition. In any event the marketing executive develops a list of the tasks that must be performed by the marketing organization and the relative emphasis to be placed on each task.

With the aid of such a list, it should be relatively simple to decide how these tasks might be divided most effectively among a group of qualified individuals, assigning high-priority tasks to specialists and combining less important tasks in the job descriptions of other positions.

Rarely can a company afford the luxury of implementing the "ideal" organization plan at once. The exercise of developing such a plan is valuable, nevertheless, not only because it provides a solid foundation for developing the immediate organization plan but also because it sets a useful target for long-range building.

Need for Balance

When the marketing executive has his ideal organization well in mind, it is time for him to face up to the adverse realities that he disregarded at the outset. The ideal organization almost always is more costly in money and people than the company can afford. More significantly, the people available to staff the organization, and those the company can hope to recruit, seldom if ever match precisely the qualifications demanded by the ideal organization plan. The point of compromise has arrived.

By far the most important consideration in this compromise is that the organization plan is, in the end, nothing more than a description of how real people are expected to interact in achieving a common goal. One may hope that each individual will do whatever needs to be done in accordance with his own talents, resources, and motivation; but an organization plan so loosely conceived is more apt to result in chaos than in success. Thus it is necessary to decide in advance how responsibilities will be divided among the people in the marketing organization; but it is well to recognize that no assignment of responsibility will cause people to do things well that they are incapable of doing or unwilling to do. The first compromise is to modify the organization plan according to how the people in the organization, or those who reasonably can be expected to be brought into the organization, will work together most naturally and effectively.

In designing the ideal organization plan, it also is tempting to opt for structural purity and simplicity of control. In a multiproduct company, for example, the most comfortable choice might be either a specialized sales force for each product or a single sales force doing across-the-board selling on the entire product line. A close look at the market might suggest, however, the use of full-line salesmen in most areas but of specialist salesmen in concentrated markets or with major customers. Responsiveness to the market never should be sacrificed merely to attain either structural purity or a simple accounting and control system.

In any event, the marketing executive's objective at this stage is to strike the best possible balance between what the market requires and what he really can hope to achieve with the resources—financial, human, and others—that he has at his disposal. If he leans too strongly in the direction of the ideal organization plan for the requirements of the market, his sales expenses may be quite out of line with the sales volume realized; but if he leans too far in the other direction—toward building the organization plan around resources immediately available—he may find himself with an organization that is unable to reach its full potential and upon which it is difficult to build for growth.

Typical Organization Plans

It should be clear that there is no single approach to organizing a marketing department that applies equally well to all kinds of companies, nor even a single plan that would be equally good for quite similar companies in a single industry. Every plan must be carefully fitted to the market, the product, and the company itself. It is conceivable that two different companies might develop identical ideal plans, but even in this case they probably will end up with different actual plans because each company has a group of people with differing personalities, capabilities, and interactions.

In fact, the term "ideal plan" can itself be somewhat misleading. It is often the case that in a single company there are two or more alternatives—equally suitable and sound—to the organization of marketing. One of these may provide more stimulating interaction among the people in the organization than the others, but it should be recognized that any plan that really does not inhibit the achievement of marketing objectives may be adequate. The deciding factor may be simply, but validly, the personal preference of the chief marketing executive.

If these dangers of accepting generalizations too literally are recognized, it is useful to observe some basic differences in the typical patterns found in organization plans in various types of industries.

Probably the greatest single cause for these differences is the fact that the more intangible the product or service, the more important personal selling becomes as a key factor in the marketing effort.

If the product is highly standardized and can be compared easily with competitive offerings, personal selling rarely exercises a strong influence on a customer's buying decision. In such cases much greater weight is placed on advertising, point-of-purchase promotion, and packaging. Many such products are sold through self-service retail outlets, with the result that personal selling is virtually eliminated.

If the product is completely intangible, as in the case of personal services, the customer's buying decision often is determined solely on the basis of personal salesmanship. In fact, in many such cases the professional skills of the person doing the actual selling are the "product" being sold.

The effect of this factor can be seen clearly in the following discussion of typical organization plans in four basic types of selling operations: retail companies, manufacturing companies, contract R&D companies, and personal service companies.

RETAIL COMPANIES

A frequently heard comment is that the key to success in retailing is smart buying. The basic function of a retail store is, after all, that of displaying attractively and conveniently merchandise that is well matched to customer buying preferences. If the merchandise is truly well selected and displayed, a major part of the selling task is already done. Personal selling support may be needed for many types of fashion merchandise, but the trend in retailing over the years has been increasingly toward self-selection of merchandise. Where self-selection occurs, the duties of the sales personnel are limited essentially to keeping the display areas orderly and filled with merchandise, receiving payment from customers, and handling other procedures incident to the sales transaction. Sales people may or may not be required also to prepare inventory records.

In these circumstances it is clear that the key function is that of buying, and the organization plan is constructed largely around the buyer. In a small store this may be the proprietor himself. In larger stores, separate buyers—often called department managers—may be designated for different types of merchandise. In either case the buyers typically supervise directly the sales personnel in their departments. Thus the group of employees under the administration of the chief buyer (who often has the title of vice president of merchandising) usually is the largest group of employees in the store. The other major groups found on most retail organization charts are a financial group and an operations and personnel group. The former handles all accounting matters, including customer accounts; and the latter handles the housekeeping functions in the store and the recruitment and training of all types of personnel. Thus a simple but rather typical retail organization plan for a single-store operation is as shown in Exhibit 5.1.

In multi-outlet retail organizations, buying is commonly done at the corporate headquarters level by a number of buyers, each specializing in a particular type of merchandise. Selection of items to be offered through the stores, including decisions on such matters as style, color, mechanical specifications, and retail price, is made at this level. The quantity of each item to be carried in inventory at the retail level is determined, however, by a store manager, who is also the supervisor (often, through department heads) of the store sales personnel. Thus a highly simplified form of organization plan for a multi-outlet retail organization might appear as in Exhibit 5.2.

MANUFACTURING COMPANIES

It is among manufacturing companies that the greatest variations occur in organizing the marketing department. This is because there is such wide variation in size of company, type of product, breadth of product line, and channel of distribution.

The simplest form of organization plan for manufacturing companies involves a division of responsibility for the major activities of the company among three or four key executives, each reporting directly to the president. A common plan of this type includes a sales group, a manufacturing group, an accounting group, and perhaps an engineering or R&D group. This elementary form of organization is found in most small companies, either as shown in Exhibit 5.3 or in some close variation. The sales group is headed by a sales manager, who is responsible for all aspects of selling the product: managing the sales force or

Exhibit 5.1
ORGANIZATION PLAN OF SINGLE-STORE RETAIL COMPANY

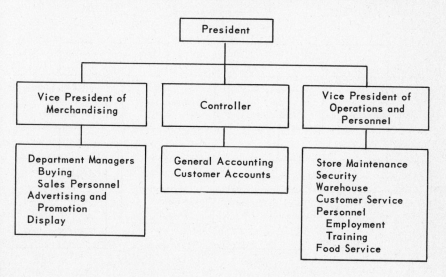

sales representatives, marketing planning, advertising, pricing, and other marketing functions.

The major difficulty with this form of organization is that, more often than not, the sales manager must spend a disproportionate amount of his time in direct supervision of the sales force and possibly in making sales calls himself. This leaves inadequate time for other marketing activities, particularly for planning. The problem can be especially severe if the company is growing rapidly.

Consequently, the commonest change from the basic organization plan shown in Exhibit 5.3, after the company has reached somewhat larger size, is to separate the responsibility for overall marketing management from that of direct supervision of the sales force. The chief marketing executive begins to spend his time primarily on planning and on managing the various indirect forms of marketing effort such as advertising; responsibility for direct supervision of the sales force is delegated to the sales manager at the next lower organizational level. With further growth it may become desirable to assign responsibility for some of the indirect marketing activities to specialists in those fields reporting directly to the chief marketing executive. Thus the company may have an advertising manager, a market research manager, a manager of marketing administration, or other specialists. This type of evolution is illustrated in Exhibit 5.4.

If the product line is relatively broad, specialization may evolve in a somewhat different direction. Instead of assigning specialists on his staff to various functional areas such as advertising and market research, the chief marketing

Exhibit 5.2
ORGANIZATION PLAN OF MULTI-OUTLET RETAIL ORGANIZATION

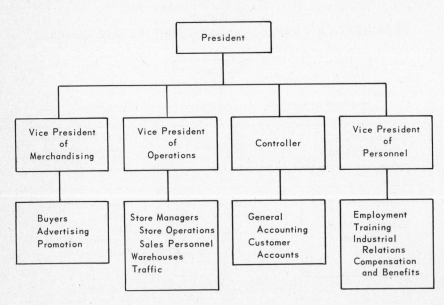

executive may elect to assign a man to handle all the functional responsibilities except direct selling for a given product or group of products. This is the product manager concept. The product manager is responsible, principally, for planning all aspects of the marketing effort for his assigned products and communicating these plans to the sales force for implementation. This form of organization is illustrated in Exhibit 5.5.

If the sales force is very large, and particularly if it is divided into a number of subgroups along product or geographic lines, two completely separate departments may be established for marketing planning and sales force supervision, each department headed by an executive reporting directly to the president. A plan constructed along these lines is illustrated in Exhibit 5.6.

The four plans discussed are basic variations in the way marketing organization can be approached in a manufacturing company. As indicated previously, the choice among them should be determined with an eye first to the characteristics of the markets being served, and second to the marketing tasks that need to be performed and the relative emphasis to be placed on each. Except in the smallest companies, it may be that the best answer is some combination of these basic forms. Perhaps the most frequent combination is the use of both functional specialists and product managers on the staff of the chief marketing executive.

R&D COMPANIES

Two characteristics of most contract R&D companies have a strong influence on the type of organization plans most suitable for them. First, the thing being sold by such companies—the collective experience and skills of a group of technical people—is intangible. Second, each prospective sale is a relatively unique situation and usually requires substantial technical analysis and tactical business planning before the sales presentation is made.

Because of these factors, the technical personnel themselves play a vital role in the overall marketing effort. It is they, much more than the marketing personnel, who can determine the feasibility of each prospective contract, decide on the technical approach to be used, and estimate the amount of technical effort required to complete the contract. These are all critical decisions in developing the sales presentation. Furthermore, the buyer's decision is often influenced

Exhibit 5.3
ORGANIZATION PLAN FOR A SMALL MANUFACTURING COMPANY

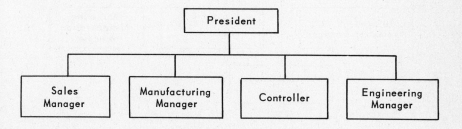

heavily by the personal qualifications of key members of the technical group; therefore, these people frequently must participate heavily in the personal selling contacts.

In a typical R&D company, there are four primary functions of a marketing nature that must be performed by some group. Whether they are performed by the marketing group or by the technical group depends almost entirely upon the relative capabilities of the two groups. In some R&D companies, senior members of the technical group have established strong professional reputations of their own and also are thoroughly articulate in both oral and written communication. In such companies the technical group assumes almost total responsibility for the marketing effort; the marketing group—if any—is responsible only for routine, essentially clerical activity in support of that effort. In other R&D companies the technical group may be less well established professionally and less articulate; in such cases the marketing group must assume much greater responsibility for the direct implementation of the marketing effort. In either situation the four functions about to be described must be performed by one or the other group or by some combination of the two, the balance being determined by the relative competence of the two groups.

Contact with buyers. Some person or group in the R&D company must maintain close contact with primary buyers of the types of services being offered, thus functioning as the eyes and ears of the company in the marketplace. Through this activity the individual or group interprets basic trends in the market and assures that the company will have an opportunity to submit contract proposals to as many qualified buyers as possible.

Exhibit 5.4
ORGANIZATION PLAN FOR A MANUFACTURING COMPANY, USING FUNCTIONAL SPECIALISTS

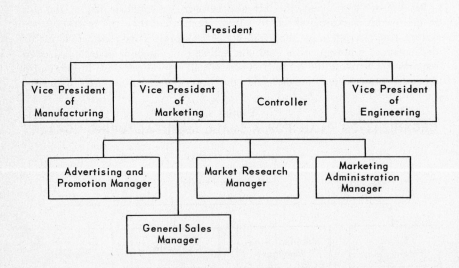

Determining marketing strategy. Some person or group must use this knowledge of the market in developing an overall marketing strategy for the company. The person or group assuming this responsibility leads the way in determining what types of work should be pursued most aggressively and what the company should do to enhance its position and image in the appropriate market sectors.

Contract proposal preparation. Someone must assume responsibility for the preparation of contract proposals. The material for these proposals is drawn largely from the technical group, but it must be shaped into the format of a persuasive selling document. If the technical group members are highly skilled and articulate in such work, they may assume total responsibility for this effort. In large R&D companies there may be a staff of technical writers and technical illustrators who can be assigned to support it. In other companies the most skilled communicators are found in the marketing group, and ultimate responsibility for preparing the contract proposal is assigned there. In this case the marketing group functions as the funnel for communications between the technical group and the prospective buyer.

Customer relations. Someone must assume responsibility for continuing customer relations after the company has been awarded the R&D contract. It is inevitable that the technical group will be involved to some extent in this effort because it is responsible for ultimate performance on the contract. On the other hand, it is often useful to have some other group in the company functioning essentially as the customer's representative, assuring that contract work is progressing productively and on schedule and that the customer is receiving

Exhibit 5.5

ORGANIZATION PLAN FOR A MANUFACTURING COMPANY, USING PRODUCT MANAGERS

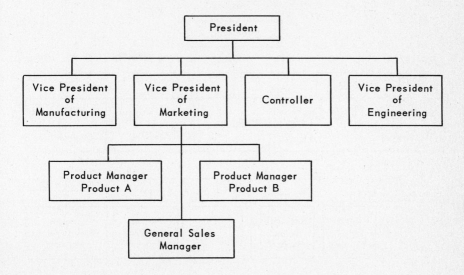

an adequate flow of information about progress and results. In such cases this responsibility often is assigned to the marketing group.

Bid committee.   Each contract proposal represents a unique marketing problem; thus many R&D companies establish a group commonly known as the bid committee. In its most typical form the members of the bid committee are drawn from the technical group, the financial group, the manufacturing group (if production is involved), and the marketing group. The bid committee may be chaired by either the chief marketing executive or the chief of the technical group, depending on the relative professional status of the two groups. Each time the company has an opportunity to submit a contract proposal, it is the bid committee that weighs the technical feasibility of the task in view of the company's resources and also the probability of capturing the contract against the expected competition. On this basis the committee makes the initial decision on whether a proposal will be prepared. If the decision is affirmative, the members of the committee agree among themselves on the part that each will play in preparing the proposal. After the individual assignments have been completed, the committee plays a major role in fitting the pieces together effectively and— most important—making the contract pricing decision. In actual practice, of course, this sometimes means that the principal role of the bid committee at this point is to assure documentation of informal commitments previously made by individual committee members. After the committee's work has been completed, the formal proposal is presented to the prospective buyer. Again the roles of the marketing group and the technical group in this process are influenced heavily by the professional reputation and skill in communication of the technical group.

Exhibit 5.6

ORGANIZATION PLAN FOR A MANUFACTURING COMPANY WITH SEPARATE MARKETING AND SALES DEPARTMENTS

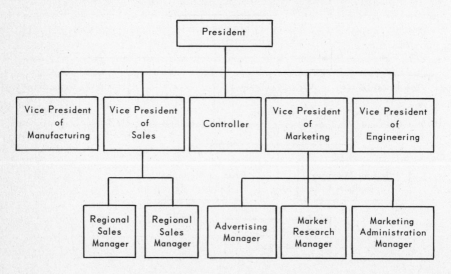

PERSONAL SERVICE COMPANIES

In personal service companies the outstanding example of marketing based on personal selling can be observed. This is true particularly among companies selling advisory services—attorneys, architects and engineers, auditors, management consultants, and the like—but it is nearly as true of companies producing somewhat more tangible services—advertising agencies, office designers, and employment agencies, for example.

In such companies the decision of the prospective buyer of services is influenced heavily by his confidence in the professional competence of the individual who will render the service personally or direct the professional personnel who do so. Consequently, it is essential that the sales effort consist primarily of direct and intimate contact between key personnel in the professional services company and the prospective buyer. In such contacts the key people have an opportunity to demonstrate their insight into the buyer's requirements and relate it to their own personal expertise and experiences, and the buyer has an opportunity to assess the degree to which the necessary intellectual and temperamental rapport would exist between himself and the person with whom he would be working. The personal selling activity may be supported by secondary tools such as brochures, proposal letters, lists of prior clients, and documentation of professional qualifications; but the success of the selling effort nearly always hinges on the effectiveness of the personal selling phase.

Personal contact is so overwhelmingly important in the marketing of personal services that the introduction of a third party, in the form of a sales representative or marketing specialist, almost inevitably reduces the effectiveness of the marketing effort. Consequently, it is relatively unusual in personal service firms to have personnel whose total responsibility is in the area of sales.

Except in very large companies that sell personal services, there is thus rarely a separate and identifiable marketing group. Responsibility for the overall marketing effort is imposed on the professional staff itself, and each key member of that staff is made responsible personally for developing some portion of the firm's total billings. The chief marketing officer is in effect the senior partner or chief executive officer of the firm. He determines the firm's overall marketing strategy and often takes personal responsibility for such matters as developing brochures and other promotional materials.

Although this approach is eminently practical for most personal service companies, it does lead to the risk that the total marketing effort will be somewhat disjointed, uncoordinated, and poorly planned. Major market opportunities may be overlooked because nobody on the professional staff has particular interest or acquaintance with people in the area of the market where the opportunity exists. As the professional personnel become heavily engaged in client work, they may subordinate their selling activities to the point that a continual inflow of new work is not maintained. Because the development of each new client situation ordinarily requires considerable time, this weakness may result in substantial peaks and valleys in the firm's billing level. Also, supporting marketing materials (brochures, client lists, and so on) may be developed hastily to meet an immediate requirement and consequently may not be prepared as well as if a more concentrated and systematic approach were taken.

To overcome these difficulties, some of the larger personal service companies have established a position for a chief marketing executive, usually with the title of director of client relations or director of development. The responsibilities of such a position are quite different from those of the chief marketing executive in any of the three types of companies discussed previously. In this case the individual is clearly in a supportive role and has little personal participation in the direct selling effort. On occasion he may accompany professional personnel in their contacts with prospective clients but in a background or coaching role only. Normally, he is responsible for seeing that a comprehensive marketing plan for the firm is developed for execution by the professional staff. Subsequently, he monitors the activities of professional personnel in securing new business and works with them to assure that the marketing plan is being implemented as it was conceived. Typically, he is also responsible for developing and directing the firm's public relations program and preparing supportive marketing materials. In some cases he may have the additional responsibility of training younger professional personnel in techniques of business development.—*R. J. Steele*

PRODUCT MANAGEMENT

Almost unknown 15 years ago, the product manager concept has begun to emerge as one of the more remarkable developments of modern marketing. Its adoption by a great number of consumer-oriented companies has substantially affected both the organization and the management of marketing operations. As planner and coordinator of all major activities related to his assigned brand, the product manager occupies a managerial post of considerable responsibility. He must generally carry out his mission without having line authority over any of the various company departments whose cooperation is essential for the market success of the product. In order to understand this difficult job, there is need to explore the product manager concept, the functions and qualifications of the product manager, and the organizational requirements for success.

The Product Manager Concept

In recent years the marketing of consumer and industrial goods has reached a state of enormous complexity. In this environment an administrative apparatus that would insure survival in an era of line diversification and product fractionalization was urgently needed. The product manager system has found overwhelming acceptance in achieving the objectives for which it was developed.

RATIONALE

Some of the specific reasons why a company may need a product manager system include the following: (1) constantly changing customer needs that make sensitivity to them essential for prompt action; (2) the need to extend greater amounts of technical service to help customers to use products more advantageously; (3) the need to monitor competition and develop strategies and counterstrategies; (4) the threat of product obsolescence as a result of the multiplication of new products and the need for alert, aggressive marketing management to maintain market position; (5) the possibility of multiproducts spread too thin, with insufficient attention given to certain product lines; (6) the problem of launching new products efficiently and successfully; and (7) the need for more selectivity in selling, concentrating on the most worthwhile prospects and opportunities for profit.

The major advantage of the product manager position is that it provides sufficient individual attention to the planning, development, and sale of each product in each market. Properly applied, the product manager concept provides an overall approach to the product as it relates to the entire company.

MARKETING MANAGER

Several approaches similar to the product manager concept exist under different names. Often these variations are found within the same industry. A close organizational and functional equivalent of the product manager is the market manager or industry manager. A market manager is oriented toward a market rather than a product. The need for a market manager may develop in companies where a particular product or group of products is sold to several markets, each of which is sufficiently differentiated from the others and important enough to the company to justify specialized staff attention. For example, a computer manufacturer may sell the same equipment to various different user industries—retail department stores, hospitals, and aerospace industries. Some companies have both product managers and market managers. In any case many features of the product manager's job and that of the marketing manager are similar.

CONSUMER AND INDUSTRIAL
PRODUCT MANAGERS

It is generally recognized that the product manager in the consumer goods field is often largely concerned with advertising and promotional matters and the product manager in the industrial products field tends to be more technically oriented. The promotional orientation of the consumer product manager is often a result of the need for extensive advertising and promotion in mass markets and the fight for shelf space in retail stores. The industrial product manager is more concerned with such activities as technical assistance, service to customers, and analysis of the implications of changes in customer requirements.

A typical product manager in consumer goods companies is usually less than 35 years old and has a formal education, often with a master's degree in business administration. His background is generally with several employers, usually in advertising, selling, or sales promotion. He tends to associate largely with advertising agency men and with marketing men in his company and is highly mobile, with a strong possibility of switching to another employer. If successful, he is highly promotable, and if seasoned, generally earns more than $18,000 per year.

A typical product manager in industrial goods companies tends to be in his 40's and has a B.S. degree in physical science or engineering. He is likely to have served his entire career with his present employer or no more than two employers. Such a product manager is experienced in laboratory or technical service work and generally associates mainly with laboratory and engineering personnel in his company. He tends to be stabilized in permanent employment with his present company, with promotions relatively slow but sure and earnings about $5,000 less than in consumer goods companies, though with exceptions. In either case a typical product manager is a decision maker and a risk taker. If he is right, he moves; if he is wrong, he is moved.

Functions of the Product Manager

Despite observable differences in the orientation and duties of product managers in different companies, there are a number of fundamental similarities in the work done by all product managers. Regardless of the kind of product they deal with, the size of the company, or their place or title in an organization, most product managers are likely to have job descriptions that use such words as "plan," "organize," "develop," "recommend," "motivate," "implement," "coordinate," and "control." A product manager basically has the following functions: to recommend sales objectives for his product; to create marketing strategy for products that are to be promoted; to develop promotional programs to be executed by advertising and field sales departments; and to coordinate all activities relating to his product.

STRATEGY AND PLANNING

At the core of the product manager's job is the marketing plan that sets the strategy and tactics for a 12-month period. Strategy means taking into consideration all marketing movements, with projections of anticipated results; tactics are the practical carrying out of that which has been directed by strategy. The product manager has complete responsibility for the development, preparation, and implementation of the annual marketing plan for the brand. It includes basic objectives, strategy, budgets, forecasts, income, and profit and generally details all aspects of a marketing program for a brand for one year, including copy, media, promotion, trade incentives, packaging changes, and research.

In developing the marketing plan, reliable background information in regard to the brand is essential. This usually requires studying the product in detail, including costs, profit margin, packaging requirements, and distribution channels; analyzing competitive products to determine their strengths and weaknesses; and obtaining information on competitive changes and technological innovations.

The product manager must also familiarize himself with every feature of the market for his product. This usually means gathering detailed market information and statistics; analyzing market trends and changing buying habits; conducting market research to determine customer needs and wants; exploring existing and possible future market opportunities for the product; and examining all marketing problems that threaten the future growth of the brand.

The next stage is the actual development of plans and programs. This usually involves developing a basic sales forecast for the product; recommending short-range and long-range objectives for the brand; producing strategies for the attainment of marketing objectives; planning sales, sales promotion, and advertising campaigns for the product.

FUNCTIONS IN OTHER AREAS

In addition to his major responsibilities for developing strategies and plans for his brand, a product manager also has important responsibilities in virtually every other major function in the company. It is up to him to utilize the total resources of the company in order to successfully market its products.

Sales. In the area of sales the product manager is usually responsible for developing a basic sales forecast on his product and reviewing it with the sales department; consulting with the sales department on product information specifications, distribution changes, and all matters of a sales nature; soliciting new customers and solving customer problems; preparing presentations and delivering them to all levels of sales meetings; and for certain product policy relating to such concerns as warranties, pricing protection, sales allowances, and returns.

Field trips. Generally, the product manager does not engage in direct selling, although in industrial product firms it is part of his duties to sell to selected accounts. A product manager generally undertakes some field trips periodically so as to get a firsthand feel of the market and familiarize himself with customer needs and the situation in the trade. In most companies the product manager spends some time with customers, sales representatives, and service personnel in order to evaluate the effectiveness of their programs and maintain an awareness of field problems.

Advertising, promotion, and merchandising. Product managers are deeply involved in all aspects of advertising, promotion, and merchandising on both strategic and tactical levels. Substantial differences exist, however, from company to company, in the authority of the product manager in these areas. A delicate relationship generally exists between the product manager and the advertising agency. Copy and media components of the marketing plan are often prepared by the agency. Even if it does not prepare the entire annual plan, the agency is often a partner in presenting the plan to upper management for approval.

Because of the enormous size of advertising budgets, other marketing management executives often become engaged in evaluating agency work. This tends to dilute the strength of the product manager system and the concept of decentralized responsibility and authority. Nevertheless, the product manager directs advertising, promotion, and merchandising effort and develops the advertising budget for higher management approval. More and more product managers are being drawn extensively into media decision making and are instrumental in media planning, selecting flexible media, developing media budgets, and directing creative effort.

In the area of sales promotion, product managers exercise more independent authority than elsewhere. However, this part of their function is generally quite sensitive because of the sometimes touchy relationship that exists between sales and marketing. For this reason, a sales promotion planning department may be established. The extent of product manager involvement in designing specific sales promotion programs varies widely. Most product managers do everything themselves, working with outside or inside promotion-planning groups. Also important is the coordination of sales promotion with sales personnel. In some companies the product group sets sales promotion objectives and timing and dollar commitments, and the promotion department recommends strategies and plans and is responsible for implementation. In other companies the product manager has complete responsibility for all sales promotion, including couponing, display activity, deals to the trade, and selecting contests, sweepstakes, and premiums.

Packaging. Another function of the product manager is to determine packaging changes and variations. His responsibilities range from developing specifications of marketing objectives, through coordinating all phases of its development, to making recommendations to higher management. The product manager rarely is involved in the technical aspects of packaging but he is responsible for the end product. These responsibilities are particularly critical during test marketing and new product development programs.

Pricing. All the critical information needed to make decisions on pricing is available to product managers. If a price adjustment is necessary, they are usually the first to realize it. Because prices are relatively stable and are often simply linked to competitive activity, only a limited amount of time is spent on analysis and recommendations. However, monitoring the competitive pricing situation is an ongoing function. Most often the product group is strongly instrumental in establishing the price and determining, with upper management approval, the actual selling price.

Market research. The product manager's role in market research is determined by several factors: the quality, strength, and experience of the company market research department, if there is one; company policy in respect to interpretation of research findings; relationship with the advertising agency, and the agency's capabilities in market research; and the product manager's expertise in this area. Three distinct types of working relationships seem to exist between product management and market research. In some companies the market research department initiates and interprets nearly all product-oriented effort. Under such circumstances the product manager is obligated to respond positively. In other companies the market research department is a service to product management. In these situations, product managers initiate research programs and are entirely responsible for their interpretation. A final approach somewhere in the middle of the road is most commonly found. Initiating and interpreting are functions equally shared by the product manager and the market researcher assigned to the brand. Generally, market research activities to be included in the annual market plan are developed jointly by the product manager and the market research staff.

NEW PRODUCTS

A typical function of a product manager is handling line extensions, modifications of existing products, and the development of new products in his line.

Otherwise, the degree of involvement in new product development depends on several factors: the strength of the new products development group, the positioning of an independent new products product manager, and the timing of the assignment of a new item to a product manager who is already handling established brands. Within the framework of new product development extensions and modifications, a product manager is generally aware of other new products and innovations within his category and is responsible for the creation and recommendation (to the R&D group) of new and additional products. He is also responsible for approving all alterations or modifications of a major nature.

In companies with a new product development group, completely new products are dealt with there. The group generally has its own staff and research personnel, who do market testing and sales testing through the company's sales organization. Once a product is established, it is turned over to the regular marketing organization and is assigned to the product manager in whose category it logically falls. In some companies the product manager becomes involved at the concept stage; in others, after test marketing is complete. It is rare for product managers to come in as late as a regional or national roll-out.

Qualifications of the Product Manager

Because the product manager's job carries such varied and exacting demands, it calls for a very special combination of personal characteristics and experience. One essential characteristic associated with the product manager is flexibility, and it is desirable that he have a broad background—as broad as possible.

EDUCATIONAL BACKGROUND

Regardless of whether the product manager is working in a consumer goods or an industrial goods firm, a college degree is almost universally required. Consumer goods firms generally look for men who have degrees in business administration—preferably, in the marketing field—but industrial goods firms seek men whose studies have been in technical areas (the physical sciences or engineering). Increasingly prevalent are product managers who have higher degrees (mostly M.B.A.'s) or who have done or are doing postgraduate work. In business areas where advertising, promotion, and selling are of paramount importance, graduate studies in marketing are regarded as excellent background to broaden an individual's experience but are not required if broad experience exists.

BUSINESS EXPERIENCE

The product manager also has to be a highly knowledgeable executive—in effect, to be able to manage his own business. For this reason many companies tend to place great emphasis on the man's previous business experience. A broad background knowledge of total company operations, as well as intimate familiarity with customer needs and opportunities for product development and market expansion, is looked for.

Sales. Most companies prefer that a prospective product manager have, as a minimum, some exposure to sales work. In fact, the sales force is one of the primary sources of supply for product managers in companies where sales work is the major route for promotion.

Advertising. A major second area of exposure for product managers is in advertising, promotion, and merchandising. This background could come through a job in an advertising agency or through the advertising department. In some cases it could be obtained through close association with advertising agencies or the company's advertising people while working on a product.

Production. In industrial goods firms, a product manager must know a great deal about the product—how it is made and what can be done with it. As a result many product managers come from the manufacturing department and are engineers, chemists, or metallurgists. Often they have worked in the plants and have been involved in making the product, which qualifies them as experts on the product.

PERSONAL CHARACTERISTICS

Personal characteristics often make the difference between the successful product manager and the one whose achievement is mediocre. The product manager must know his market, his competition, and his product. He must have the ability to create new ideas in strategy, to innovate, to utilize the total resources of his company in the marketing of his product, to communicate ideas, and to sell programs to others. He should have leadership ability, persuasiveness, and understanding. He should have administrative ability, a well-organized mind, and a great deal of drive. In other words, the qualities necessary in a product manager are much the same as those for any other responsible managerial position.

Organizational Requirements

In order to reap the full benefits of a product manager system, it is necessary to provide the product managers with support and latitude consistent with the multitude of tasks they have to perform.

The product management concept, in the 15 years or so that it has been accepted by top management in American companies, has not been without its problems. In order to obtain maximum advantage of the product management system, a number of organizational requirements must be met.

SCOPE OF RESPONSIBILITIES

Experience with the product manager concept reveals that product managers function most effectively when the scope of their responsibilities includes making recommendations for product investment, production scheduling, and participating in the total distribution process, pricing, and profit policy. They should be able to participate in new product selection, timing, and development from a market viewpoint. A product manager should be considered the most capable member of the corporate team on matters pertaining to his product lines.

ADEQUATE RESOURCES

Often it is not difficult to secure financial resources for market development. However, the assurance and allocation of selling power are quite difficult. In many cases the product manager lacks a staff and must handle many details alone. The problem is not solved by simply making available the services of inside and outside specialists. The product manager is faced with the problem of how he alone can best utilize these people and find the time to deal with them.

SIMPLIFIED DECISION CHANNELS

Decisions in developing the proper marketing strategy and determining the best mix of resources to allocate to a product are exceedingly difficult for a product manager to make. The time and communications required to transmit these decisions to higher management for approval necessitate the simplest decision channels. Simple channels clarify decision making, identify accountability, and minimize loss of communication and distortion of planning.

MANAGERIAL AUTHORITY

Unless a product manager is given managerial authority, the greatest advantages of the system are lost. The three chief reasons why little authority is generally given to product managers are doubt of their capabilities, opposition of entrenched senior functional managers, and lack of understanding of the basic organizational principles of the product management system. It is essential that product managers have the authority to plan, create, develop strategy, and marshal resources for their product lines. Their authority should include the power to command resources to implement their programs—subject, of course, to the concurrence of their superiors.

ASSUMPTION OF RESPONSIBILITY

When fully implemented, a product management system should create the means for assumption of profit-and-loss responsibility. The product manager, when provided with the proper levels of company resources and the authority to insist on their delivery, should assume the responsibility for his brands, profit and loss, sales, share of market, and distribution performance.

MANAGEMENT DEVELOPMENT

The great mobility of product managers is well known; average duration in the job is about two years. Few product managers have sufficient tenure to work their way out of difficult situations and develop their abilities. Often there is an imbalance in education, background, and experience. Competent product managers should not be expected to develop without some of the formal training that has become standard procedure for most other responsible positions. Emphasis in training should be on the compilation and analysis of data, on the specification of research requirements, and on quantitative decision making. In this way the problems of selecting and developing qualified manpower may be significantly reduced and the ultimate promise of the product management system brought a great deal closer to fruition.—*D. B. Uman*

SALES MANAGEMENT

Sales management is concerned with the development of the people who are responsible for selling and servicing the company's products or services, or both, in such a manner as to produce steadily increasing sales and profits. Good sales management can make people of ordinary ability achieve extraordinary performance—and do so willingly.

Organization and Objectives

Sales management is at the middle management level. The sales manager reports to a higher executive (the president, in a smaller company; the vice president of marketing, in a larger one). The general sales manager, in turn, may have reporting to him one or two lower echelons of sales management (regional or area sales managers and district sales managers). Finally, there is the sales force itself, or dealers or distributors. In addition sales management is often accountable for the efficient operation of sales offices, both at headquarters and in the field, and in some companies the branch warehouse also falls under sales management control. In each case the manager has the right to know—indeed, must know—from his superior exactly what is expected of him. These expectations, clearly stated and reduced to writing, become the objectives around which the sales manager plans his work. Only when he knows what is expected of him and accepts the full responsibility within his area of authority is it possible for him to function effectively. As middle management he must then assign some part of each of his objectives to those under him, making sure that they accept and understand the assignment and carry it out.

Sales management's primary concern is the development of manpower. The first step is to determine manpower needs. With his objectives before him, the manager should know what staff he must have to achieve them. The second step is to determine his present strengths and weaknesses and the gaps in manpower. Present sales personnel should be classified as (1) capable of development and therefore to be retained and developed; or (2) not capable of development, in which case they should be marked for replacement. Now the sales manager knows what additional manpower must be secured, and he can set about achieving this goal. Inherent in this operation is the development of job descriptions for all jobs under his jurisdiction.

Cost Control

The sales management function requires the expenditure of considerable sums of money: for compensation, for employee expenses, for office expenses, possibly for warehouse operations, and for special expenses incurred by contests, customer entertainment, and the like. Top management may allocate funds to the sales manager for these purposes or may ask the manager to prepare a request based upon his own estimates. In either case he must know what dollars he has at his disposal, and it is his responsibility to see that he and his people operate within the amount allowed.

Planning

Planning revolves around the achievement of the objectives that the manager has received and accepted from his immediate superior. It is his responsibility to develop a plan of action, the net result of which is the attainment of the agreed-upon objectives. The plan covers the responsibilities that he will perform personally and other responsibilities that he will delegate to those under him. For instance, the general sales manager may delegate responsibility for a specific volume of business to each of his regional sales managers; they in turn will delegate responsibility for a specific volume to each of their district sales managers, who will do the same with each of their salesmen. The sales manager may also delegate some of his responsibilities to his office manager and to his warehouse manager. In any case the sales manager is responsible to his superiors for the attainment of the objectives; he cannot place blame for failure on his subordinates. The sales manager's chief job is to help all of those to whom he has delegated responsibility to achieve their commitments and to help them get their subordinates to fulfill their commitments in turn. How he carries out this function is his own choice, but do it he must. It will be done largely through work in the field and, to some extent, by means of conferences with each key person under him. This, then, is the plan of action: Delegate responsibility to key people and work with them to help them achieve the objectives on which they and the sales manager have agreed.

Carrying Out the Plan

Involved in carrying out plans are several key matters which must be understood. First, it is impossible to help a person unless the kind of help he requires is known. Second, the only way to know of a certainty what help a person requires is to observe him in the actual performance of his job. Observation cannot be replaced with paper reports, figures, oral explanations, or even written explanations. The manager must see his subordinate perform in order to know his strengths and weaknesses and to be clear as to the areas where his subordinate needs help. Third, the manager must plan his time so that he is able to do the development job that is the key to his successful performance. He must beware of allowing desk work to overwhelm him and thus "excuse" him from necessary work in the field. The sales manager, whatever his rank, should spend most of his time in the field with those under his immediate supervision and with certain very important accounts, together with the salesmen responsible for those accounts.

The key word in pressing forward to effective results is "continuity." Each field contact must be related to the one that preceded it and the one that will follow it, and all of them should be related to the attainment of the objectives. Contacts with personnel under the sales manager's supervision should be carefully planned in advance through correspondence or long-distance telephone and should be planned with the person to be contacted. The sales manager's subordinates should feel that they are being helped, not policed, and should be aided in so concrete a manner that they welcome his coming. The manager should work to develop a team spirit; it will appear when the subordinate discusses his affairs as "our territory (or district)" and "our problem" rather than "my territory" and "my problem." When the subordinate feels that he and his manager are working together toward the attainment of common objectives, the management job is being well done.

Appraisal and Counseling

Every employee would be less apprehensive and more comfortable in his job if he knew how his superior felt about his performance; and every supervisor has the responsibility to know how each person under him is doing. Intuitively, every manager is continually appraising those under him; it is an ongoing act. Informal appraisal is valuable, provided it is done in a sound manner, without prejudice and with complete objectivity; but this is a tall order. Some time should be set aside regularly—perhaps once a week—for informal appraisal of subordinates. The appraisal should be against agreed-upon objectives, not against factors that have never been agreed upon between the manager and his subordinate. It is a good idea for the manager to set aside a period when he is to be with the subordinate for counseling him with respect to his progress or lack of it. This may be done in an informal setting—perhaps over luncheon—and occupy no more than 30 minutes. (It may, however, require a much longer period.)

It is sound practice to make a formal appraisal of each subordinate at least once a year and to require lower managers to do the same for their subordinates. Such appraisals are often set up by top management, and the forms are provided by headquarters. The results of the appraisal are frequently discussed by the manager with his own immediate superior before he reviews the results with the subordinate. The appraisal is then discussed at length with the subordinate. The success of such a counseling interview depends largely upon whether or not the subordinate recognizes that the primary purpose of the appraisal and the counseling interview is to improve his performance, not to criticize or find fault.

The end result of a successful counseling interview is agreement between the manager and his subordinate on steps to be taken to improve the subordinate's performance. Although in some cases this kind of interview also ends in some determination with regard to compensation, it is generally considered better to discuss compensation at another time and devote this entire interview to performance.

The manager may be compared to a doctor, and the appraisal may be compared to the diagnosis, while the counseling may be compared to the discussion of the diagnosis with the patient. The appraisal is valueless unless followed by counseling. The results should never be permitted to "gather dust"; they should be used as an active tool for the development of the subordinate. One caution: Personal traits are better left unmentioned unless they affect the job performance of the subordinate or the image of the company in the area in which the subordinate operates.

Motivation

Motivation of his subordinates is one of the manager's most important responsibilities. It means that he must inspire his people to want to do better—to want to grow and develop. Where motivation is concerned, the manager must concentrate his thinking on the man and for the time being forget about sales, quotas, policies, and so on. For instance, if he learns that the subordinate feels a need for recognition within his community, the manager may be able to motivate him by having an article about him or some accomplishment of his published in a local paper. Or he may motivate a man by showing him how to plan his work better so that he is relieved of tension and pressure that have been making him irritable at home and inefficient in his work.

Motivation is achieved, first, when the manager manifests to his subordinate his complete confidence in him. The sales manager is not a policeman or a social worker, but a manager, and he is not continually "breathing down the neck" of his subordinate. Second, motivation is achieved when the subordinate is given real responsibility. The assignment often involves risk on the part of the sales manager; but experience indicates that when responsibility is given to a deserving man, he seldom fails to come through. It is worth the risk to build a good man. Third, a man is motivated when he achieves success in some area and receives the congratulations of his superior. Success breeds success, and when the manager can help those under his management to do well in some one area, they gain confidence in their ability to achieve in other areas. Fourth, a man is motivated when he receives recognition in his job and in his private life. The manager should be alert to opportunities to give recognition to those under him and to give them some feeling of importance. Fifth, motivation exists when a man feels that he is "on the team" and when his boss asks his opinion and advice on various matters or otherwise indicates that he values the subordinate's judgment. Sixth, motivation is achieved when the manager and his subordinate have agreed upon objectives so that the subordinate knows what it is he is expected to do and knows that his manager is trying to help him.

Many companies have found that sales contests are strong motivating forces. However, contests at best are never substitutes for good sales management. If used, they should be planned by specialists, and care should be taken that the objectives of the contest are compatible with the overall objectives of the development of the subordinates.

Territory Design

A territory is a collection of a number of large and small accounts with a total potential buying power of a company's products or services large enough to warrant assigning a salesman, dealer, or distributor to go after the business. "Territory" is not a geographical term: Territorial coverage means account coverage, not geographical coverage.

In most organizations approximately 20 percent of the accounts in any territory make up about 80 percent of the total potential business available; it is therefore highly important that those 20 percent are sold and developed—and, of course, that they are identified and followed by sales management. Even companies that sell to supermarkets and retail stores find it desirable for their salesmen to give more time and attention to the larger accounts. Accounts are sold chiefly by "service," which in this sense means all the acts of a company and its salesmen that indicate their concern and interest in the customer and his problems. The more important accounts are sold by giving them a degree of service superior to the service they would receive elsewhere; and in order to do this, the salesman gives somewhat less service to the smaller accounts.

Sales management, in looking at a territory, must isolate the key or important accounts and locate them on a map. They are usually found in clusters, and zones of a territory can be built around them. Territory coverage is planned around an adequate coverage of these important accounts, and the smaller accounts located around and near the larger accounts are called upon less frequently, as time and convenience permit, depending upon their relative importance. Sales management has the responsibility of setting up territories in this manner and of supervising the coverage of the territories so as to insure that the business of the most important accounts is secured. In many instances sales management is involved with an important account through making calls with the salesman, obtaining contact with higher echelons that the salesman cannot reach, advising the salesman on strategy, and overcoming obstacles that the salesman encounters. The sales manager cannot keep his eye on every potential customer, but he must be alert to the progress being made with the accounts that compose the greater portion of the potential of a territory.

Compensation

The first step in a compensation plan must start with top management, for only top management can determine how many pennies out of every sales dollar are available for the functions that come under the jurisdiction of the sales manager. The sales manager can then deploy these funds to pay the salesmen, dealers, and distributors, the office personnel, and perhaps the warehouse people at branches. How much he pays the sales people depends generally upon a number of factors such as industry custom, the kind and amount of work to be performed, and the going market price for sales personnel of the kind desired. Special situations may call for differences in treatment, as in the case of a salesman who is expected to make sales only after long effort (selling bridges, for example), while a salesman in another line may be expected to obtain several orders every day. With some few exceptions it is generally felt that the best compensation plans have some built-in incentives; that is, they offer a drawing account against commissions, or a salary and commission, or a salary and bonus, rather than a straight salary with annual review for increases. Each company must determine the plan most likely to satisfy its employees and provide a sound base for their development. Generally speaking, the best kind of compensation is the simplest and the easiest to understand. If the plan is based on too many different kinds of performance, it is likely to be confusing to sales people and more likely to breed discontent.

Selecting Sales Personnel

Since it is the job of sales management to develop personnel in the sales field, it stands to reason that the sales manager must have developable people to work with, or he will be defeated in his efforts before he begins. Furthermore, as the best ball team must have good players on the bench to step out on the field when needed, a good sales organization must have people ready to step into territories when, for any reason, they become empty. Finally, it is well recognized that it is easier to employ a man than to discharge him. To separate a person from his job is always difficult, and a manager may waste large sums of money and valuable time in trying to save a man who should be discharged. Caution indicates that employee selection should be made with great care.

The first step in a personnel selection program is to find out exactly what gaps need to be filled. For each gap there should be a written job specification and a written manpower specification so that the manager is clear as to what the job requires and what kind of person is needed to fill that job.

The selection process must be a continuing one in order to avoid disruptive "panic drives" to fill vacancies that suddenly occur. Larger companies should attempt to develop a pool from which promotable people can be brought in when needed. Small companies can develop a pool of talent from people who are presently employed elsewhere but who have been interviewed and have expressed an interest in changing jobs when an opening occurs.

The best source of talent should be within the organization. The number of promotable people a sales manager has ready is often considered a measure of his ability. The ideal is to recruit and employ from the bottom and promote off the top of the organization. People should, however, be employed for a specific job; it would be a mistake to hire "potential presidents" for the sales force.

Sales managers should use all available means for recruitment. Where manpower needs are geared to a corporate recruitment plan, the job of the sales manager is much easier; but in many instances he must take the entire responsibility for sales personnel. He may wish to have recruiters scouring the field at universities, visiting employment agencies, or interviewing applicants obtained through newspaper and magazine advertising. On the other hand, the regional or district sales managers often have the responsibility for filling vacancies in their areas. Sometimes the two systems are combined. Whatever method is used, for the sake of maintaining a high standard it is desirable to bring in a large number of applicants from whom to make a final selection. When too few applicants are available, the tendency is to select "the best of the worst," and the result can be a mediocre sales organization.

Sales managers themselves should be continually alert to find desirable people in their contacts, both business and social. Above-average salesmen also are often used to "bird dog" good employee prospects for the sales managers to interview.

The selection of personnel should be made through a series of at least three interviews. In one of these it is desirable that more than one person should interview the applicant. Interviews should be conducted so that the manager does very little talking and chiefly listens to what the applicant says. References should be carefully checked in all instances, and checks should be made by personal call or planned telephone interview, never by letter. Final selection for the job—or the promotion—should be made in an extremely thorough manner so that the successful candidate knows exactly what he is moving into.

Communications

Someone has said that if the job of a sales manager were to be defined by a single word, that word would be "communicator." The sales management job has been compared to that of the switchboard operator through whom important calls are passing from the top of an organization to the marketplace (salesmen, dealers, distributors, customers), and vice versa. If the line is not plugged in, someone may be talking while no one is listening. Certainly, top management cannot do its job well without a thorough knowledge of what is going on out in the field: what customers think of the product or service, price, terms, service, and delivery; what the competitive situation is; what the morale situation of the sales organization is, and how the sales force feels about company policies, compensation, and the products it must sell; what improvements should be made in products, and what new products should be developed; which products are becoming obsolete. All this kind of information must flow upward to top management through the sales management team.

It is through this same team that salesmen and dealers and distributors are given important communications from top management: Compensation plans and fringe benefits are explained clearly so that they are accepted; product knowledge is given to the field; policies are explained to personnel and to customers so that the policies are clear and are accepted; the company philosophy and basic purposes are explained clearly; and the company image is presented in a favorable light to those in the market. It is the responsibility of sales management to perform this communication job continually and with great diligence; no man deserves a place on the sales management team if he fails to perform this function diligently.

One word perhaps needs to be said about "washing dirty linen in public." The sales manager must understand whom to go to when he is dissatisfied—certainly not to those under his supervision. The sales manager must be the champion of the company when he is in the field and the champion of his men when he is at headquarters; then he is a good communicator and an effective manager.

The Control Function

It is expected that the sales manager will be in control at all times and will see to it that the entire job is performed properly—the responsibilities that he has delegated to others as well as those he has been given. He must constantly ask himself: How is each territory going? Where are the weak spots, and what must be done to correct weak situations? Are there any weak spots in distribution? How about product mix? How about all classes of trade being sold?

The manager knows what he must control by consulting his job description, the objectives that his superior set with him, the objectives that he set up with each of his key subordinates, and the statistical material available to him. He is in control when he sees and reacts quickly to any signal that tells him a job is not being done or is not being done correctly or effectively.

The manager must set up some system that enables him to maintain control. It should be a very simple system, much like the traffic lights at an important intersection in a large city—a green light to say that all is well and everything can move forward, or a red light to say that traffic is stopped. There are many ways in which a sales manager can exercise control, but the method he works out for himself must tell him, at least once a week, where the lights are green and where they are red.

Controls need to be of two kinds: (1) controls that enable the sales manager to be sure he is performing on time all the responsibilities that he has undertaken and accepted, and (2) controls that give him the picture of the situation with respect to all responsibilities he has delegated to those under his supervision.

Sales Meetings

Almost every sales manager feels it necessary, for a variety of reasons, to bring his men together periodically. These meetings are time-consuming and costly. The men who attend are often out of production for at least a day before the meeting and a day afterward. It is therefore imperative that there be a very good reason for holding a sales meeting and that the meeting itself be well planned and its purpose clearly defined. One thing is clear: No sales meeting may be used to take the place of the field sales manager's direct work with his men out in the marketplace.

A sales meeting may encompass an entire sales organization or a large section of a sales organization, or it may be a small district sales meeting with only six or seven salesmen attending. The large sales meeting can do no more than stimulate salesmen, "pep them up," establish a good company feeling, and give men an opportunity to meet people they have been reading about in house organs and/or corresponding with all through the year. Such meetings are very costly, and they seem to be on the decline. They are held no more frequently than once a year—in many companies, every five years.

Much more valuable and helpful is the smaller district or regional meeting with no more than 30 or 35 men attending, and preferably even fewer. Such meetings, carefully planned by the sales manager, are valuable for considering regional sales problems, giving product information, discussing and explaining policies, discussing dissatisfactions, and exchanging experiences and sales techniques among the men attending. The most successful meeting of this nature is one where the manager makes the men feel that it is their own meeting. He chairs the meeting, keeps it rolling, involves those who are not eager to participate, quiets those who try to take over the meeting, keeps the meeting on its time schedule, moderates—and, otherwise, keeps quiet. The manager does not lecture, does not tell what to do, does not "throw his weight." No agreement should be forced on the men; it is the discussion that is important. These meetings are informal; they are often used when sales districts or regions are so compact that salesmen can lose no more than a single day from the field in attending, although they can be employed effectively even when salesmen must fly to attend them.

Sales management is increasingly finding a selling tool of great value in carefully planned meetings of customers and prospects in important centers. Such meetings need expert help, headquarters planning, careful use of the time of those attending, and subject matter of strong interest to those attending. The ways in which they may be conducted depend upon the kind of product and how it is used and the need for providing important information to many people in a short time. The local sales people must participate; such meetings provide excellent opportunities for them to be with their customers and prospects and to improve their relationships with them.

Distributors and Dealers

As the chief job of sales management is to develop the people for whom it is responsible, it is just as important where selling is done through dealers and distributors as it is where selling uses a direct sales force. The dealer or distributor needs much more than a call from a company representative. He needs all of the same kind of help that a direct salesman requires. The fact that he may have other lines than those of the company should make no difference. Show him how to operate more effectively and efficiently, and his results will improve, with most of the benefits accruing to the company that has worked with him helpfully.

Performance Criteria for Sales Managers

The sales manager is performing his job well when he has a plan of action for himself and for each of his key people; when he knows that his plan is being carried out and that each of his men wants to carry it out; when he knows how well he is doing with regard to every task assigned to him; when he knows the next step that he and each of his key men must take to achieve their objectives; when he constantly strives to improve his own performance and that of his organization; and when his men realize that they are doing a better job because of the help he has given them.—*Ronald Brown*

COMMUNICATIONS

The rapid expansion of markets and the need to reach them ever more efficiently have resulted in the continuous refinement of advertising and sales promotion.

Rapidly changing consumers and intensely competitive markets make flexibility and creativity a "must" for advertising executives. One need not be an expert in consumer analysis to sense rapid change in buying patterns. Today's consumer is far more sophisticated than his predecessor and is becoming more so every day. Homemakers receive increasing doses of education, not only in school but also via television, motion pictures, and printed media, and all too often today's shopper is far more knowledgeable about the product he is seeking than the retail clerk who is supposed to help him. Modern communication has expanded his range of thought and his interest in a wide variety of products but at the same time has led to considerable confusion. A proliferation of products with minimal differences causes considerable difficulty in completing sales. Note, for example, the problem of a shopper for a high-fidelity system, or for the family decorating a home. The problem is similarly confusing with low-priced products such as laundry detergents or cigarettes because of the conflicting claims designed to entice the consumer

The dynamism of the market is reflected in the changing demographic structure of society. The youth movement, with its predilection for experimentation, can easily upset the best-laid plans of a marketing campaign based upon past experience. The present is different from the past, and the future gives every evidence of becoming even more so. Consequently, communications professionals must be students in the most elementary sense, as well as marketing technicians.

The growing involvement of communications people in behavioral science developments has become obvious. These people are keenly interested in the studies being conducted by psychologists, sociologists, demographic specialists, and other types of social scientists whose findings bear directly on the planning and actions of marketing executives.

In a similar way scientific method has invaded the communications man's domain. OR techniques are ever more useful in solving problems of the market suitability of new products, probable consumer response, brand loyalty patterns, sound advertising appeals, and media selection. The application of quantitative method coupled with behavioral science offers great opportunity to marketing technicians at the present time and certainly in the future. The sharp scalpel is tending to replace the rule of thumb.

Advertising

All promotion is concerned with persuasive communication: The problem is to make sales. However, as distinguished from personal selling, advertising is nonpersonal persuasion, an indirect approach directed to masses of potential buyers. Sales promotion deals with activities that supplement advertising and personal selling, helping to integrate them and make them more effective. Sales promotion activities also tend to be short-run in nature and generally are non-recurring.

Considerable change has taken place in promotional thinking with the development of the marketing concept. Whereas it once was common for sales technicians to be concerned almost entirely with their own specialized areas, it is now recognized that all phases of marketing are interdependent and must be carefully interlocked. Salesmen, for example, are trained to appreciate the importance of profit contribution and not confine their work to taking orders. Advertising men appreciate more fully the need to assist salesmen and to be concerned with the impact of their expenditures on the profit picture. Production and promotion budgets are tightly interlocked. Individualism must be subservient to the good of the firm. This approach calls for a viewpoint much broader than in the past.

COMPANY IMAGE

Everything a firm does shapes its image. Its product line, its advertising, its salesmen, its service, its public activities—all meld into the consumer's picture of the firm. Image is not static; it changes as the company moves. This impression can help or hurt a firm and can have great impact indeed on its success or failure. A firm that has built a reputation for quality products and efficient service can depend upon goodwill to help it market new products or services. On the other hand a firm that has lost favor may find itself in serious trouble. This will be translated directly into increased marketing costs. The impact on profits is obvious.

Public activity has become increasingly reflected in image development. Large firms fully appreciate the significance of their moves in the community. Actions on the civil rights front, the kinds of products the firm markets, and the relation of these products to the public's concept of quality and propriety all have their impact on acceptance by the public. In this sense the "social firm" may become as important as its physical products in determining its economic success.

ABILITIES AND INABILITIES

It is naïve to assume that advertising is a panacea for all marketing ills. Like any other tool, it is extremely effective when used properly but of little or no value when improperly applied.

Abilities. As a mass communication tool, advertising is most effective for introducing a product or service quickly to large numbers of prospects. A new product can be presented visually and descriptively so that the reader or viewer can quickly learn what it is and how it may be used. This is far less expensive and much more practical than personal contact via salesmen, unless relatively small numbers are to be impressed.

Advertising tends to concentrate on the unique, desirable characteristics of the product or service. Product differentiation is vital in a highly competitive market. By focusing on specific characteristics, advertising concentrates attention on salable features. At the same time it may also minimize weaknesses or explain away problems.

Advertising is used effectively to open up leads for salesmen. Since personal selling is very costly, saving time in personal contact is important. Leads generated from advertising can cut down sharply the cost of exploratory contacts. Advertising may even go far toward persuading the prospect to buy, thereby shortening sales contact time.

The most effective advertising completes the sale. The advertisement may "ask for the order" or at least suggest that the prospect "go out and buy." With relatively inexpensive, mass-distributed articles, advertising can often achieve this objective. The salesman is completely eliminated, and the transaction takes place commonly on a self-help basis.

Once a product has been established successfully, it is sure to be faced with competition. Advertising, used properly, is a natural tool to maintain position and fight off competition. With older, established products this may be the most important function of advertising.

Inabilities. Advertising cannot salvage a deficient product. It is not possible to foist "just anything" on the public. It is true that initial purchases may be generated; but once product weakness becomes known, sales will plummet. Even worse, company image will suffer. Quite simply, the greater the public awareness of product difficulty, the faster the product will decline. The speed of advertising that makes for rapid sales build-up can work in reverse almost as fast.

Advertising cannot compensate for inadequate salesmen. Leads may be opened up, and the public may be interested; but poor selling technique or inordinate delay in contacting prospects will seriously hurt sales.

Advertising is not the best medium for explaining unusually complex products or services. Quick impact and direct presentation of an idea in a short period of time are what most people expect of advertising. Its educational message is easy to grasp within a short span of attention. It is true that some advertisements for complex products have been successful, but most are not. Complexities and intricate details are best left to the salesman.

PLANNING AND OBJECTIVES

There is a tendency to think that, because advertising is creative, it is not subject to the usual management principles. Such is not the case. Studies have shown that advertising efficiency is closely related to the amount of planning that precedes the advertising. Objectives can be set, the program carefully planned, and the results analyzed.

Many questions face the analytically minded marketing manager. Among them are the following: How much should the company spend for advertising? How much should be spent for each product? What theme should be utilized, and how should the presentation be made? What media are best? What is the best timing for the campaign? How can advertising results be measured?

Russell H. Colley of the Association of National Advertisers stresses four areas of information that should be developed before advertising each product line: (1) the market (who might use the product); (2) the marketing situation (status of the market at the present time); (3) the marketing goal in quantitative terms (what the marketer specifically expects to achieve); (4) the advertising goal in quantitative terms (what the advertising campaign is expected to do).

The boundaries of the problem of marketing powdered skim milk, for example, would be succinctly marked as follows by the four salient areas of information previously described: (1) the market (all adults and children); (2) the marketing situation (unfavorable image of powdered skim milk among large segments of the population); (3) the marketing goal (to increase powdered skim milk consumption 6 percent per year); and (4) the advertising goal (to improve the image of powdered skim milk 30 to 40 percent in five years).

Advertising men need clear-cut objectives and goals just as much as salesmen or production men. Unless these are carefully thought out in advance, costs may easily get out of line. And, of course, it is virtually impossible to measure results unless clear-cut objectives are laid down.

Developing the advertising budget. By far the most common method of setting the advertising budget is to relate it to a percentage of sales. From experience, the firm knows how much it has spent for advertising in the past and what the results have been. Commonly, it uses this figure as a rule of thumb for setting the new appropriation.

A second factor that usually has considerable bearing on the budget appropriation is located in the anticipated expenditures of competitors. Obviously, a firm does not wish to fall behind, and should there be indication of increased effort by competitors, it would be necessary to match the figures.

Far more desirable is the "objective and task" method. It makes little sense to establish an appropriation on a monetary basis without questioning what the sum is expected to do or how it is to do it. Certainly, introducing a new product, or breaking into a new market, or fighting off competition, or sustaining a weakening product may call for disproportionate sums. On the other hand, a well-established product with a good reputation or one that is carried along as a member of a family of products may need a relatively smaller appropriation. A dynamic market and a constantly changing economy hardly make for static decision making. It is highly desirable to lay out the problem carefully and analyze the alternatives before coming to a conclusion on the final budget. Modern quantitative methods can be very helpful here. Structuring the advertising budget in this manner sets up the opportunity for continuing and post-promotion analysis.

Classification. The starting point for planning is a determination of the intended audience and scope of the promotion. Is the product a consumer or an industrial product? Is the advertising going to be national, regional, or local? Will it be product advertising or institutional advertising? What effect is wanted—direct action or delayed reaction? These are only some of the questions that must be answered before proceeding. Each warrants analysis.

Motivation. Consumer motivation differs from industrial buying motivation. Whereas the former is more significantly motivated by appearance, initial price, and emotional appeals, the latter is primarily concerned with performance, service, and rational appeals. Whereas the industrial buyer tends to be expert and well grounded in his field, the consumer is likely to be a novice who may depend more on hearsay and information in the advertising. The dollar expenditure of the industrial buyer is almost certain to be far higher than that of the private consumer, and the media to which the two are exposed are quite different.

National and regional or local advertising. Media selection varies considerably with the "reach" of the advertising campaign. Where local or regional promotions can be directed to those specific segments and reflect the customs of the locality, national advertising must attempt to make its impact without antagonizing local or regional attitudes. To prepare national advertising that has strong impact yet avoids local irritation can be difficult. It is no accident that much national advertising concentrates on products with standard appeals or centers on subjects that are universally liked—attractive young ladies, for example.

Product and institutional advertising. Most advertising designed to generate immediate sales is built around the product. The purpose of the advertising is clear. It presents an item for immediate consideration and purchase. Firms with long lines and those with long-lived products are more likely to concentrate on company reputation. They hope to build a successful reputation in the minds of prospects so that, when need arises, the prospect will know where to turn.

THE ADVERTISING MESSAGE

Good advertising is built around a theme, and the theme depends upon the audience for whom it is intended. This is the heart of the marketing concept. Clearly, what is needed is a theme that will have the greatest emotional and rational appeal to the marketer's prospects. Preplanning is highly desirable. Market research can be most helpful in clarifying the picture so that appropriate themes and appeals are selected for presentation.

Sound creativity is highly desirable in selecting the message and preparing the advertisement. Wild flights of imagination are seldom acceptable, because they may do more to inflate the ego of the advertiser than to move merchandise or achieve the other advertising objectives. Solemn concepts, on the other hand, will probably fail through sheer inability to attract attention or excite interest. Advertising preparation in a highly competitive field is especially difficult with products or services which differ only trivially.

Once the advertising theme has been decided upon and the advertising prepared, further market testing is in order before investing large sums in the campaign. Copy, illustration, and continuity should be pretested before the final run. Even though failings may still occur, it is unlikely that major blunders will get through at this point.

MEDIA SELECTION

By far the largest portion of a company's advertising appropriation is spent on media. Media selection, fortunately, has been the subject of considerable scientific thought in recent years. Leading advertising agencies have developed highly sophisticated mathematical models to refine the media selection process. More advanced research is probably going on in this phase of promotion than in any other. For this reason it is advisable for the advertiser to select an agency, if possible, that can give him modern thinking in this area.

From a pragmatic point of view, media selection depends upon such important factors as the audience characteristics of the medium, the medium's effectiveness in presenting the product or service of the advertiser, and of course its relative cost. Audience patterns and costs are constantly changing. Note, for example, the general weakening of magazines while television has grown by leaps and bounds. Radio has come back after a period of declining years and has regained considerable but secondary stature. Newspapers, on the other hand, have maintained their strength for local, quick-impact advertising. Trade papers and direct mail have maintained static patterns. (The table in Exhibit 5.7 lists annual volume of advertising in the United States, from 1950 to 1969, by medium.)

At least as significant is the image of the individual medium. Why a magazine like *The New Yorker* should dominate its field while old, famous standbys have died out is hard to fathom. Media selection has never been easy, but the new quantitative tools should help considerably in objective selection.

ADVERTISING AGENCY

Originally a broker for advertising media, the agency has become a vital adjunct for the advertiser. Although the advertising agency has as its primary function the preparation of advertising, it has expanded its services into virtually all phases of marketing. Its services today include analyzing the client's marketing situation and offering ideas for products and promotions as well as for planning and preparing advertising. It will assist in preparing budgets and engage in a wide range of supplementary marketing services as adjuncts of the campaign.

Larger agencies maintain or work closely with marketing research organiza-

Exhibit 5.7
ANNUAL VOLUME OF ADVERTISING IN THE UNITED STATES, BY MEDIUM, 1950-1969
STATISTICAL ABSTRACT OF THE UNITED STATES
(In millions of dollars, except percent.)

MEDIUM	1950		1955		1960		1965		1966		1967		1968		1969	
	Expenditures	Percent of total	Expenditures	Percent of total	Expenditures	Percent of total	Expenditures	Percent of total	Expenditures	Percent of total	Expenditures	Percent of total	Expenditures	Percent of total	Expenditures	Percent of total
Total	5,710	100.0	9,194	100.0	11,932	100.0	15,255	100.0	16,670	100.0	16,866	100.0	18,127	100.0	19,565	100.0
National	3,257	57.0	5,407	58.8	7,296	61.1	9,365	61.4	10,176	61.0	10,250	60.8	10,883	60.0	11,460	58.6
Local	2,453	43.0	3,788	41.2	4,636	38.9	5,890	38.6	6,494	39.0	6,616	39.2	7,244	40.0	8,105	41.4
Newspapers	2,076	36.3	3,088	33.6	3,703	31.0	4,457	29.2	4,895	29.4	4,942	29.3	5,265	29.1	5,850	29.9
National	533	9.3	743	8.1	836	7.0	869	5.7	975	5.9	936	5.5	990	5.5	1,050	5.4
Local	1,542	27.0	2,345	25.5	2,867	24.0	3,587	23.5	3,920	23.5	4,006	23.8	4,275	23.6	4,800	24.5
Radio	605	10.6	545	5.9	692	5.8	917	6.0	1,010	6.1	1,032	6.1	1,190	6.6	1,270	6.5
Network	196	3.4	84	0.9	43	0.4	60	0.4	64	0.4	65	0.4	63	0.4	65	0.3
Spot	136	2.4	134	1.5	222	1.8	268	1.7	300	1.8	310	1.8	360	2.0	370	1.9
Local	273	4.8	326	3.5	428	3.6	589	3.9	646	3.9	657	3.9	767	4.2	835	4.3
Television	171	3.0	1,025	11.1	1,590	13.3	2,515	16.5	2,824	16.9	2,909	17.2	3,231	17.8	3,585	18.3
Network	85	1.5	540	5.9	783	6.6	1,237	8.1	1,393	8.3	1,455	8.6	1,523	8.4	1,675	8.5
Spot	31	0.5	260	2.8	527	4.4	866	5.7	960	5.8	988	5.8	1,131	6.2	1,245	6.4
Local	55	1.0	225	2.4	281	2.3	412	2.7	471	2.8	466	2.8	577	3.2	665	3.4
Magazines	515	9.0	729	7.9	941	7.9	1,199	7.9	1,291	7.7	1,280	7.6	1,318	7.3	1,375	7.0
Weeklies	261	4.6	396	4.3	525	4.4	610	4.0	658	3.9	651	3.9	657	3.6	660	3.4
Women's	129	2.3	161	1.8	184	1.5	269	1.8	280	1.7	282	1.7	284	1.6	310	1.6
Monthlies	88	1.5	133	1.4	200	1.7	282	1.9	316	1.9	312	1.8	342	1.9	373	1.9
Farm, national..	37	0.6	39	0.4	32	0.3	37	0.2	37	0.2	35	0.2	35	0.2	32	0.1
Farm papers	21	0.4	34	0.4	35	0.3	34	0.2	34	0.2	33	0.2	33	0.2	33	0.2
Direct mail	803	14.1	1,299	14.1	1,830	15.3	2,324	15.2	2,461	14.8	2,488	14.8	2,612	14.4	2,680	13.7
Business papers .	251	4.4	446	4.9	609	5.1	671	4.4	712	4.3	707	4.2	714	3.9	720	3.7
Outdoor.............	143	2.5	192	2.1	203	1.7	180	1.2	178	1.1	191	1.1	208	1.1	206	1.0
National	96	1.7	130	1.4	137	1.1	120	0.8	118	0.7	126	0.7	137	0.7	135	0.6
Local	46	0.8	63	0.7	66	0.6	60	0.4	60	0.4	65	0.4	71	0.4	71	0.4
Miscellaneous	1,125	19.7	1,836	20.0	2,328	19.6	2,926	19.2	3,233	19.4	3,285	19.5	3,556	19.6	3,846	19.7
National	610	10.7	1,040	11.3	1,368	11.5	1,733	11.4	1,887	11.3	1,895	11.3	2,035	11.2	2,145	11.0
Local	515	9.0	796	8.7	960	8.1	1,193	7.8	1,346	8.1	1,390	8.2	1,521	8.4	1,701	8.7

Source: Compiled by McCann-Erickson, Inc. for Decker Communications, Inc., New York, N.Y., 1950-1966, in *Printers' Ink* magazine; beginning 1967, in *Marketing/Communications*. (Copyright.)

tions and engage in media research, promotional service, and post-advertising analysis. They are doing advanced work with models in market simulation, especially in regard to the advertising field. Today's advertising agency is more properly called a marketing agency; its functions are broad and they seem to be growing every year. Because much of its service is covered by the commissions it receives from media, the alert advertising manager makes sure he receives a full complement of services from the agency. The relationship between agency and advertising manager must be close in order to achieve the maximum results.

ROLE OF ADVERTISING MANAGER

One might ask what are the functions of the advertising manager in view of his relationship with the agency. Victor P. Buell (*Marketing Management in Action,* McGraw-Hill, 1966) suggests that these fall into five broad categories: (1) to recommend and administer advertising and sales promotion policies; (2) to recommend advertising and sales promotion objectives; (3) to develop advertising and sales promotion plans and budgets; (4) to provide the communication link between the company and its advertising agency; and (5) to assure attainment of objectives through performance, measurement, and control.

MEASURING EFFECTIVENESS

Behavioral science study, always difficult, is even more so when applied to advertising and sales, and laboratory techniques in which factors can be isolated are impractical for this purpose. Nevertheless, it is possible to gain a fair insight into the effectiveness of advertising by utilizing certain recently developed techniques. It should be realized at the start, however, that advertising impact, in the sense of recognition by the prospect, should not be confused with sales impact, which may or may not result from the advertising.

Advertising impact. One acceptable technique for assessing advertisement recognition is opinion research, in which respondents are asked to describe their reactions to an advertisement. It gives some insight into audience reaction to a campaign. More exacting are memory tests, especially those stressing recognition and recall of advertisements. In these the respondent is required to recall any advertising he has seen about a product and various aspects of it. He may either be assisted by being permitted to thumb through a publication, pointing out advertisements he thinks he has seen before and commenting on them, or be unassisted in the "unaided recall," in which he will be asked to comment on advertisements that he remembers without prompting. Electronic devices have been developed to measure reactions; one such device records changes in blood pressure that indicate involuntary feelings toward an advertisement.

Sales impact. The marketing executive, as well as the advertising manager, is more concerned with the impact of sales than of advertising. Sales impact is much more difficult to evaluate. Measuring sales figures before, during, and after an advertising campaign is easy to do, but measuring the effect of a particular advertisement in a particular medium at a particular time when many advertisements are being run simultaneously in a variety of media over a period of time is another matter. Test runs in test cities under restricted circumstances are of considerable value, however, and so are consumer diaries. It is also possible to measure the response pattern generated from coupon advertising and related promotions—premiums, special promotions, and refund offers, to name but a few. But it should be realized that competitors seldom observe the niceties and are not averse to confusing the situation by meeting promotions head-on with their own campaigns.

Modern quantitative methodology has been of some help in this area, but much of the work is still too academic for utilization by marketing executives. Sales simulation can be helpful in predicting the pattern of success or failure in a projected campaign. Linear programming is an aid in selecting the best combination of media for specific purposes. Markov chain analysis (determination of the outcome of a series of linked events) can give some insight into the relationship between customer loyalty and brand shifts. Discriminant analysis can be of value in refining the view of specific promotional tactics.

Sales Promotion

For the purposes of this discussion, sales promotion consists of a wide range of supporting sales activities that supplement personal selling and advertising. It fills the gaps in marketing campaigns. It is a kind of follow-through process that picks up many loose ends and helps tie the components into a tight fabric.

The major concerns of sales promotion are dealer assistance and direct consumer stimulation. Sales promotion activities also extend into the manufacturer's marketing department, complementing the training, equipping, and motivating of company salesmen and "merchandising the advertising."

DEALER PROMOTION

To an increasing degree manufacturers have attempted to promote their products by building up their own brands, reputations, and followings. Mass production makes necessary mass distribution, and to this end increasingly large budgets are set aside for advertising and product identification.

The result has been to make the retailer more and more dependent upon the manufacturer. This builds up the manufacturer's position in the market, but at the same time it increases retailers' demands for service. The retailer expects the products to move off the floor with minimum effort. Increasingly, store traffic and sales have become the manufacturer's responsibility. Should an item not move satisfactorily, the dealer is sure to blame the manufacturer because it is his product and his image which seem to be deficient. Branded and heavily promoted lines cannot easily release themselves from this responsibility. The result has been a continuous proliferation of manufacturer-sponsored dealer services.

Self-service and sales promotion. For various reasons personal service selling has been declining. It has become inordinately expensive as salaries have risen. Any technique that would minimize individual solicitation and yet consummate sales would be to the advantage of manufacturer and retailer alike. Intensive brand development by manufacturer advertising presells consumers and decreases the need for personal contact. At the same time new generations of consumers have become accustomed to self-service purchasing. The present generation of consumers accepts and often prefers this mode of shopping, especially when the price reflects the cut in service.

Where once it was thought that minimum service distribution was acceptable only for low-priced, repetitively purchased items, it is now recognized that this method is also acceptable for higher-priced products such as clothing and major appliances. With even larger items, such as automobiles and tract houses, personal selling has been minimized and often is limited to negotiating the price and taking the order.

Impulse buying has been growing in importance. Studies have indicated that more than two out of three shoppers make up their minds in the store. If this trend is considered together with diminishing personal contact at the retail level, the need for manufacturer-oriented promotional impact at the point of sale becomes obvious. It becomes the manufacturer's concern not only to lead prospects to the retailer but also to help him complete the sale, and in order to do so, a host of promotional tactics have been developed: cooperative advertising programs, point-of-sale display, and a variety of more specialized traffic-building devices.

Cooperative advertising. Whereas manufacturer advertising tends to educate the consumer regarding a product, dealer advertising tends to lead the customer to the store where the item can be purchased. In this sense dealer advertising fills a promotional gap. Not the least important advantage of such a program is that it activates particular dealer interest in the line.

Cooperative advertising arrangements vary, but almost all of them call for the manufacturer to compensate the dealer partially or fully for his promotional efforts in the manufacturer's behalf. The typical contract reimburses the retailer for advertising the manufacturer's product, up to an agreed-upon percent of dealer purchases. At the low end, manufacturers will allow a credit of 2 to 3 percent of purchases. This may range as high as 10 percent when products carry a wide profit margin or when the manufacturer wishes to introduce a new kind of product.

Additional benefits may accrue to the manufacturer from such a program because retailers are able to buy local advertising at significantly lower prices than can the manufacturer. This differential may be as much as 50 percent. Unfortunately, retail billing processes often leave much to be desired, and the anticipated savings may never be realized. Nevertheless, the manufacturer's product receives vital support at the point of sale. This must be achieved in one way or another.

Point-of-sale display. Once traffic has been generated by advertising, it is important to attract attention and to activate the selling process. In-store display is the tool used for this purpose. Competition is intense and the battle for display opportunities is fierce. The dealer's problems must be studied carefully. His interests are vital. Consequently, displays must be designed that will fit the needs of the dealer. The physical aspects of display are best left to professionals.

How effective are displays? The answer is astonishing to the uninitiated. Increases in sales of 300 to 500 percent are common, and increases in volume of 500 to 1,000 percent are not unusual. A serious concern of the manufacturer is the extent to which residual sales effect can be expected from his display. He would like to know how many people will continue buying after the display is gone and for how long, and what this will mean in terms of extra income. Such analysis is important because it is usually necessary to compensate the retailer in order to be permitted to install a display. Obviously, if this cost is not more than compensated for by increased volume, it is not worth the effort.

To gain an objective picture of the value of displays, they may be pretested. Field studies can be set up that will measure display impact fairly accurately. It is customary to select a number of test stores and to measure sales in those which have received the display against those in which there has been no change. Careful sales records are kept for a period prior to the installation of any displays, then during the actual display period, and then after the displays are removed, to measure the residual effect. The test stores may be rotated and the studies performed again. Many variations are possible. This procedure is far superior to guesses based upon experience.

Traffic-building devices. Dealer advertising is a potent traffic builder, and many other successful devices have been developed, such as fashion shows, unusual demonstrations, and special exhibits. Demonstrators are effective traffic builders. Special services—beauty clinics, product repair services, and instruction programs, for example—are successful. The range of promotion ideas is only limited by the creativity of the marketing man.

CONSUMER PROMOTION

The intensive efforts of consumer product manufacturers to presell the consumer have led to the refinement of direct consumer promotion techniques. Such consumer promotions use sampling, premiums, consumer contests, and other more specialized devices.

Sampling. The more expensive the product, the more important is sampling. Whereas the consumer may be induced to buy an inexpensive item without pretesting, it is unlikely that he will buy a higher-priced item without prior trial. There is a tendency to think of sampling as something applicable only to the marketing of inexpensive, repetitively purchased products, but that is not the case. People do not usually purchase a radio or a suit or an automobile without at least trying out a sample of the product. They listen to the radio, try on the suit, test-drive the automobile preparatory to making up their minds.

In marketing industrial products, sampling is extremely important. Raw materials are pretested before substantial commitments are made. Office machines are often left with potential customers for extensive periods of time. Machinery is carefully studied under actual operating conditions and then purchased on a guarantee of satisfaction.

Consumer sampling techniques have been carefully refined and have undergone rapid growth. Couponing, via mail and printed media, has mushroomed to gigantic proportions. It is estimated that more than ten billion coupons offering discounts worth more than $1 billion are distributed in the United States annually. Many problems have arisen from the abuse of coupons, but their sales impact is so great that they are bound to become even more important.

Related tactics include in-store coupons, refund offers, discount sales, and bonus packs; these are commonly tied in with trade deals in which the manufacturer offers special values to the dealer if he will cooperate in extra display or other promotion tactics designed to implement the sampling program.

Premiums. A premium is something extra offered to induce a prospect to buy. For many consumers the additional value makes the all-important difference in the purchase decision. When this offer can be made at little or no cost to the manufacturer and at the same time give significant benefit to the purchaser, the promotion tactic may have great value.

Of most interest is the self-liquidating premium, which makes it possible to achieve this dual objective. With these premiums the consumer is offered a good value at a price that seems very low to him but is high enough to cover the distributor's expenses. Consumers have responded by the millions to successful premium promotions.

Industrial products have successfully used the premium tactic in promotion. In situations where items are used by employees, suitable premiums can help to generate considerable extra volume. For example, office workers look favorably on premiums tied in to the use of supplies. Working men like to accumulate premium coupons that come with products they use—hardware, for example—and thus build up strong preferences for those particular brands. Women are notorious coupon savers. Children, on the other hand, respond best to immediately available premiums.

Services also may be promoted by using premiums. Banks and personal finance firms have found premiums to be attractive business builders.

Contests. People like to compete, especially when it does not seem to cost them anything. Contests sponsored by manufacturers offer them such an opportunity. Entry usually seems free because the contestant need only submit as proof of purchase the wrapper that he would normally throw away. In many instances the contestant need not even purchase the product.

Contests are of special value to the manufacturer because they tend to force contestants to think favorably about his products. The contest often requires the respondent to say or do something favorable about the manufacturer's product. Even in the "sweepstakes" contest, in which the entrant need only enter his name and address, he is bound to develop interest in the manufacturer's product. The impact is almost assuredly far stronger than the transitory attention received by advertising in the usual media.

There are problems in contest operation, however. No one likes to lose. Every entrant secretly hopes to win, and there is disappointment in failing to win. Abuse from disgruntled losers is not uncommon, and even the honesty of the manufacturer may be impugned. Despite these drawbacks, contests are effective for promoting many kinds of products or services.

Contests are also very effective for motivating sales personnel and dealers. The classic device for generating excitement among manufacturer or dealer salesmen is to run a contest. It pulls salesmen out of the doldrums and gives management a platform from which to create new excitement. The contest may be used to focus on any one or a combination of problems: It may be designed to open up new accounts, to sell a slow-moving line, to fight off competition, or simply to expand sales. It can be tailored exactly to fit a specialized marketing problem at a particular time. In many firms the staff looks forward to contests. This is especially true when salesmen's families are informed of the program and invited to help in selecting prizes.

INTERNAL SALES PROMOTION

In addition to developing internal motivational programs such as sales contests, promotion work encompasses such projects as preparing salesmen's manuals, advertising portfolios, catalogs, house organs, brochures, and other direct advertising material. Some of this work may be done by the advertising agency, but much of it is considered an internal house activity. The range of such services will naturally be tailored to the needs and marketing program of the individual firm.—*Alfred Gross*

CHANNELS OF DISTRIBUTION

Distribution strategy essentially involves two decision areas: The first centers on the selection of distribution channels and the determination of channel strategy; the second is concerned with physical distribution.

Nature of Channel Decisions

Channel selection decisions receive major focus in this discussion. However, they interact with physical distribution strategy, and both relate to overall marketing strategy.

CHANNEL CONCEPTS

The late Wroe Alderson once defined a "marketing channel" as "a group of firms organized as a loose coalition for the purpose of exploiting joint opportunity in the market." This concept of a channel as a loose coalition implies that the marketing executive is confronted with recurring problems in coordinating channel activities.

The usual definition views a trade channel as the combination of institutions through which goods pass while en route from a producer to the next seller or ultimate consumer. The segment of the trade channel identified with a particular middleman often assumes his name; thus the reference to "wholesale channels" and "retail channels." When a producer talks of using alternative channels, he is often referring to the use of different types of middlemen. In this context, channel selection is a matter of choosing appropriate middlemen to move goods closer to the ultimate consumer.

Channels of distribution can also be viewed as organizational structures through which goods move from producer to consumer. These structures are composed of a variety of middleman-type operations. There are merchant middlemen who take title to goods as they perform marketing services. There are functional middlemen such as brokers and agents who perform distribution services without ownership. Various middleman functions are often integrated into one organization. Vertical integration comes into existence when two or more successive stages of production and/or distribution are under a common management control. Horizontal integration combines various products that might use the same channel of distribution.

Some of the more common channels of distribution are as follows: (1) manufacturer's direct sale to consumer; (2) manufacturer to retailer to consumer; (3) manufacturer to wholesaler to retailer to consumer; (4) manufacturer to chain store to consumer; (5) manufacturer to broker to wholesaler to retailer to consumer; (6) manufacturer to industrial distributor to user; and (7) manufacturer to government agency.

Channel decisions are made to some degree by all members of the channel. Producers choose among alternative channels; middlemen decide which market segments they want to reach; and ultimate consumers choose the retail stores they patronize.

ECONOMIC ROLE OF CHANNELS

Marketing channels represent a composite of activities essential to the efficient distribution of goods. A widespread belief is that the shorter the channel, the lower the costs of distribution and the lower the prices paid by consumers. Some firms advertise "Direct from factory to you," and place emphasis on the elimination of the middleman. Such claims may or may not be true. The test is not the length of the trade channel but whether the set of activities associated with marketing of the goods is performed in an efficient manner. More effective distribution may result from using not one, but perhaps two or three middlemen.

Manufactured goods are generally produced by mass production methods at locations involving minimum transportation cost to gain inherent economies of scale. Such a situation is frequently accompanied by widely scattered consumption. Middlemen can serve as the low-cost mechanism to distribute these goods because of transactional efficiency; that is, the economy of handling a number of different products results in fewer buyer-seller contacts than would be the case if all producers sold direct.

The economic function of coordinating production and consumption copes with time, distance, and the diversity of products produced in volume at concentrated points. This function is performed for most commodities by buyer-seller contact at successive stages of intermediate distribution. Middlemen survive in the channel by performing this buyer-seller contact efficiently.

Another important economic function performed by resellers in the channel is called the intermediate sort. The intermediate sort involves four activities: (1) assembling over a period of time, in a single place, like commodities that meet standard specifications for the assortment; (2) assembling over a period of time, in a single place, unlike supplies in accordance with some pattern determined by demand; (3) "breaking bulk" or dividing a large homogeneous lot into smaller lots; and (4) breaking the assortment into various types of goods for resale. Middlemen who are specialists can usually perform the intermediate sort more effectively. In any event, in a competitive situation only the efficient trade channels survive.

BASIC ALTERNATIVES

The market executive has three basic alternatives with respect to overall channel strategy: (1) exclusive distribution; (2) selective distribution; and (3) intensive distribution.

Exclusive distribution exists when a single product outlet has an exclusive franchise in a well-defined territory. Products that require specialized efforts and large investments in facilities and inventories are ordinarily marketed through exclusive dealers.

Selective distribution involves careful selection of a limited number of dealers to represent the manufacturer in a given market. Shopping goods, especially women's and men's clothing, are ordinarily marketed through selected dealers.

Intensive distribution is a policy of marketing products in many different types of outlets and in as many outlets as possible. Products such as razor blades, sold in almost every drug store, supermarket, and hardware store, are intensively distributed. These manufacturers believe that general availability is the key to greater sales volume. Most products of low unit value and high frequency of purchase require intensive distribution.

Overall channel strategy can be viewed as a continuum with exclusive distribution at one end and intensive distribution at the other. The marketing executive's decision is to select the intensity of distribution that is in harmony with the nature of his product line and his company objectives.

OTHER ALTERNATIVES

Managements of competitive firms often choose different distribution channels. Relevant decision factors are the peculiar nature of the product, sales volume that will support a particular physical distribution alternative, brand image in the marketplace, and the firm's long-term marketing goal.

Control of the distribution channel is a continuous battle. Mass retailers control the channels for many products with purchasing power and extensive use of private brands. In some instances national wholesalers are more powerful than either their suppliers or their customers. In other instances manufacturers control—especially manufacturers who do heavy advertising and offer franchises coveted by middlemen. The market institution that controls the channel of distribution is sometimes referred to as the channel commander or the channel captain.

If a producer is also a channel commander, he has the alternatives of choosing middlemen or selling direct. By using a middleman, the producer delegates certain marketing responsibilities. Transferring marketing responsibilities depends upon the producer's ability to evaluate who can best perform these services. Further, the producer's decision regarding the use of middlemen will influence the kind of sales organization he maintains and his merchandising and promotional activity.

Once a system of distribution using middlemen is in effect, the producer may come to think of the middlemen as being a part of his total marketing organization. However, Alderson's suggestion that the channel be viewed as a loose coalition comes to mind, and the marketing executive must continually strive for close coordination of company marketing programs and middlemen efforts.

Factors Considered in Channel Selection

In competitive situations the channel commander has a choice of alternative marketing channels. In exercising his choice, the channel commander evaluates trade-offs among channels by considering various factors. These factors can be classified as product factors, market factors, and institutional factors.

PRODUCT FACTORS

Four product variables must be weighed in the channel selection decision: the physical nature of the product, the technical nature of the product, the length of the product line, and the market position of the product.

Physical nature. A primary factor to be considered is the physical nature of the product. The selected channel must cope with perishability in the product— either physical deterioration or fashion perishability. If production and consumption of the product are seasonably variable, any channel used must handle the resulting inventory problem. The unit value of the product influences the channel. Generally, if the unit value is low, intensive distribution is suggested; if unit value is high, more selective distribution may be needed. Here, inventory investment and obsolescence as well as customer service requirements are considered. Finally, if the product is such that small-lot delivery is necessary to many scattered ultimate consumers, channel selection becomes restricted

Technical nature. The second factor of consequence is the technical nature of the product. Selection of a marketing channel depends upon whether the product is simple or complex. In addition, the ultimate consumer may need advice on product use. A complicating element for certain products, such as washing machines, is required final seller installation. Other products, such as industrial products, and specifically computers, may require training of the buyers' personnel by the seller.

On technical products exclusive dealers may be able to give advice; in other instances, the manufacturer will be forced to sell direct. If the product is not highly technical, intensive distribution can be selected to make the product available.

Length of product line. A product line consists of a group of products related either from a production or a marketing standpoint. The length of product line is related to channel selection. A manufacturer with a short product line is more apt to sell through middlemen than one who has a full product line. A decision must also be made with respect to using a single channel for the entire line or splitting the product and using multiple channels.

Market position. A final consideration is market position of the product. An established product made and promoted by a reputable manufacturer may have a high degree of market acceptance and can be sold readily through various channels. For example, a certain brand of lawn mower may have high consumer brand loyalty, and therefore more channels are available to it than to a lesser-known brand. Frequently, new products sell on the reputation of established brands. This type of trading may result in larger short-term sales but have greater longer-term inherent risks.

MARKET FACTORS

The consideration of market factors also enters the channel selection decision. These are the existing market structure, the nature of the purchase deliberation, and the availability of the channel.

Existing market structure. The channel commander may have difficulty in altering the middlemen's traditional modes of operation. The existing market may be highly concentrated geographically, or it may be widely dispersed. For example, industrial markets many times involve only large customers concentrated in a few large cities. Consumer goods markets—breakfast cereal, for example—relate directly to population. Consumer preference is generally the critical factor in channel selection. Manufacturers of baby food, for example, changed their channels of distribution after research revealed that mothers preferred supermarkets to drug stores.

Nature of the purchase deliberation. Some products are purchased on impulse; with others the purchase is important enough for the consumer to make a rational deliberation. The consumer who purchases a set of automobile tires, for example, has a different purchase deliberation than the buyer of toothpaste. The purchase deliberation may depend on the frequency of purchase. When consumers purchase frequently, more buyer-seller contacts are needed, and middlemen are suggested.

Formal specifications and competitive bids may be used in purchasing certain products. An illustration is the government agency that buys most products, including food, by publishing detailed product specifications and then soliciting bids from sellers who have met certain financial qualifications to be on the approved bidders list. Industrial purchases are frequently characterized by a set of specifications.

Availability of the channel. Existing channels may not be interested in adding products to their assortments, and the channel commander has the task of winning cooperation from the channel. His two basic choices are pushing the product through the channel or pulling the product through the channel. In pushing the product through the channel, the commander uses normal promotional effort and rational arguments to persuade channel members to carry his product. In pulling the product through the channel, the commander uses aggressive promotion to final consumers on the theory that strong consumer demand will force middlemen to carry the product in order to satisfy customers.

INSTITUTIONAL FACTORS

Institutional factors considered by the channel commander include the financial ability of channel members, the promotional ability of channel members, and the postsales service ability of institutions making up the channel.

Financial ability of channel members. Manufacturers may find it necessary to aid their retail dealers through direct financing, either interest-free loans or liberal credit terms. Credit terms are competitive, and willingness to extend credit influences channel acceptance. Mass retailers sometimes finance suppliers, either directly or by investing in the company. Ordinarily, government agencies are barred from making payment in advance of receipt of goods, but the DOD sometimes advances working capital for the development of special products such as aircraft.

Promotional ability of channel members. Wholesalers, by their very nature, cannot be aggressive in promoting products of a particular manufacturer. Rather, wholesalers identify with the small retailers whom they serve. Exclusive distributors, however, are able to promote or to cooperate with the manufacturer in joint promotion. Usually, it is the channel commander who finds it necessary to promote the product; in fact, his promotional efforts often establish him as the channel commander. Manufacturers assume this function in the case of national brands. The promotion of private brands usually rests on the mass retailer or wholesaler who establishes the brand name.

Postsales service ability. In many instances a warranty is associated with a product. The question arises as to which member of the channel will make warranty adjustments. In absence of a warranty, periodic servicing may be required in order to keep the product operating. The retail distributor is the closest contact with the consumer, and the consumer may expect the retailer to service the product. In other instances the product is returned to the manufacturer for service, though in some cases services are performed by independent service organizations. In any event the postsales service ability of various channel members affects channel selection.

Channel Strategy

The channel decision is not automatic. Channel commanders must use a combination of intuition and analysis and then exercise judgment in making channel decisions.

Suppose the channel commander compares Channel A with Channel B. He might find that Channel B would help make his product more available, but at the same time Channel B would result in a less desirable product promotion. The difference between the gain from a given course of action and the loss in opportunity through taking that action is termed a trade-off.

The channel decision problem is complicated by interdependencies existing among relevant factors. While it is difficult to quantify the many trade-offs associated with channel selection, certain analytical tools (some are computer-oriented) can be applied to channel decisions.

TOOLS OF ANALYSIS

Cost analysis techniques will result in reasonable estimates of each channel cost. However, the channel corresponding to lowest cost may not give the intensity of distribution that is required. Or the lowest-cost channel may not be available.

Another tool of analysis is the systems approach. One definition of "a system" is "an orderly linking of separate but interdependent components in order to achieve a given objective." The systems approach views channels as dynamic operational networks through which the product and the relevant order and decision-making information flow in a synchronized, integrated way. The given objective of the channel commander is to maximize the efficiency of the entire marketing and distribution system, not merely maximize each component within the system.

Systems analysis involves trade-offs in time, service, and costs in order to maximize profits in the long run. The channel commander makes quantitative comparisons between alternative production runs, inventory holding levels, transport modes, customer service standards, order transmission and processing systems, and the like. Because of the number of factors that must be considered, the modeling of alternatives must involve computer-oriented OR techniques. These techniques include mathematical programming, simulation, and statistical techniques such as multiregression analysis (see "Regression Analysis" in the Finance section, page 4·47).

OPERATIONS RESEARCH

Strategic and tactical planning is an essential function of today's channel commander. Marketing environment can be expressed in numbers and modeled for planning purposes.

Models. OR models have proved to be a valuable management tool by forcing the channel commander to consider all important details of the situation while eliminating those that are unimportant.

Models have been used successfully in planning and analyzing physical distribution alternatives such as warehousing, plant location and size, transport mode selection, route configuration, and safety stock levels. Models have also been employed for selecting type and location of alternative middlemen or suppliers, for pricing strategy, and for new product planning. In fact, valid uses for OR tools seem almost unlimited. Entire industry models exist; the brewing industry, for example, has been modeled by brewers to develop production and marketing plans.

Ideally, every problem should be analyzed separately and a tailor-made model developed to fit that situation. Success depends upon enthusiastic support by management, participation by the potential users of the models, and experienced and knowledgeable OR. The probability of success can be improved if the channel commander will (1) choose the model builder carefully, just as one would choose an architect or other specialist; (2) validate the model to show that it represents the system closely enough to be relied on for decision making; (3) clearly state and critically appraise all assumptions; and (4) check each essential item of information by an independent method.

An important consideration is the ease of getting the problem solved. Many excellent computer programs are available to help set up the data in the correct format, solve the problem, perform the computations, give side benefits, and report the results in an understandable way.

Network approach. A typical marketing problem is illustrated in Exhibit 5.8. The objective is to supply each middleman at lowest total cost. This, like many marketing problems, can be expressed directly as a network model and solved by a suitable mathematical procedure such as the "out of kilter algorithm." This algorithm has been programmed on the COC 6600 computer and can be solved efficiently with little or no knowledge of the algorithm.

The advantages of the network approach are its ease of formulation and its low computational cost. The disadvantages are its lack of flexibility in terms of additional constraints and its static nature, if conditions change rapidly over time.

Linear programming. This problem can also be solved by using a linear programming model, a technique that produces the minimum cost solution to a rather wide range of problems. The side benefits of a linear programming solution can be more useful than the optimal solution. The marginal profitability of adding plant, warehousing, or middleman capacity can be determined. The sensitivity of the solution to cost errors or forecasting errors can be computed. The penalty of forcing a unit of product through a nonoptimal channel is also available to the decision maker.

The disadvantage of using the linear programming approach involves size restrictions and nonlinearity. A large problem such as 1,000 distributors and 100 products would be computationally difficult to solve. Products and distributors would have to be either dropped or aggregated, and the consequence on decision making would have to be considered. Freight rates depend upon tonnages shipped in a nonlinear way, and the assumption of linearity may cause a wrong decision.

Simulation. When market channel problems are large, complex, and nonlinear, simulation may be used. Simulation programs predict what would happen if proposed changes were put in effect. Almost any problem can be simulated, and a person with only a slight knowledge of mathematics can set up a simulation model.

Several disadvantages are associated with simulation, however. The time

Exhibit 5.8

NETWORK REPRESENTATION OF THE PLANT-TO-WAREHOUSE PROBLEM

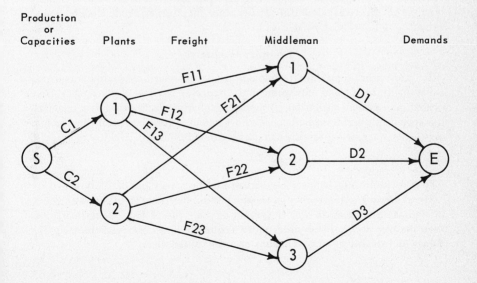

necessary to develop a simulation model is often underestimated. There are few computer programs to help in general simulation; so the simulator must often write his own programs. Factors that tend to make other approaches impractical can also make the results of a simulation unreliable. Finally, there is no guarantee that the solution will be close to optimal.

(OR techniques are also discussed in the Administrative Services section under the heading "Management Science," page 2·65.)

LEGAL CONSTRAINTS

Section 3 of the Clayton Act is concerned with exclusive dealing. It reads, in part: "It shall be unlawful . . . to make a sale . . . on the condition that the purchaser shall not deal in the goods, wares, or merchandise of a competitor . . . where the effect may be to substantially lessen competition." While Section 2 of the Clayton Act permits a marketer in free and open competition to select his own customers in bona fide transactions and not in restraint of trade, Section 3 casts considerable doubt on the practice of exclusive dealing. Thus a company is permitted to limit the number of dealers appointed to a territory and even to go so far as to grant exclusive dealerships. However, it cannot require distributors not to sell competing products; that is, it must not practice exclusive dealing if the effect is to substantially lessen competition. The *Standard Oil Company of California* v. *United States* decision in 1949 held that substantial lessening of competition was automatic if exclusive dealing was followed and a large volume of business was involved. Standard had about one-fourth of the gasoline business on the Pacific Coast at the time and about one-sixth of the retail gasoline stations.

Other legal ramifications may exist in particular industries; for example, special regulations pertain to automobile dealers. The Dealer's Automobile Franchise Act of 1956 makes manufacturers vulnerable if franchises are canceled arbitrarily. A program of maintaining resale prices by careful and systematic selection of dealers has doubtful legality since the *Federal Trade Commission* v. *Beech-Nut Packing Company* case in 1922.

Channel Dynamics

In recent years significant technological changes—such as computer-oriented management tools—and environmental changes have taken place that have focused management action on (1) managing physical distribution as a materials flow system; (2) business intelligence as a formalized function within marketing; and (3) customer service as a distinct area separate from sales activity.

ENVIRONMENTAL CHANGES

Four environmental changes are discussed in the paragraphs that follow.

Trend toward a short-order economy. With inventory holding costs generally estimated between 20 and 40 percent of the value of goods being marketed, often the best decision is to order more frequently in smaller quantities, forcing storage and related support functions on primary suppliers.

Rapid expansion of product lines. In order to maintain or expand market share, the accepted strategy is the rapid expansion of product line to secure maximum retail shelf space and thereby crowd out competitive products and minimize the ups and downs associated with the individual product life cycle. Consequently, a larger variety of models, styles, colors, packages, and price lines generates obsolescence and stock availability problems, as well as inventory imbalance.

Price differentials and discounts. According to Robinson-Patman Act requirements, price differentials and discounts must be cost-justified; therefore, a critical need exists for ascertaining actual distribution costs. Availability of reliable cost data has stimulated reappraisal of channel structure alternatives, especially in the number of stock location points.

Competitive strategies. At one time competitive strategies centered largely around product features and price. Now added emphasis is on indirect competition such as outperforming competitors on logistical planning and customer service.

FUNCTIONAL APPROACH TO CUSTOMER SERVICE

Service provided to successive buyers in the distribution channel has great impact on distribution effectiveness and market growth. This is especially true in producer/wholesaler/distributor dealings.

Channel commanders are realizing that marketing strength and stability are more likely to be secured when all critical firms in the channel make a fair profit; so the concept is developing to lend support and expertise not only in the analysis and solution of common problems such as materials handling systems but in problems peculiar to the wholesaler and distributor.

Customer services fall into two distinct classifications: service analysis and technical aid. Service analysis includes transport control through computerized car control systems, analysis of in-transit loss and damage, and telecommunication system hook-up for rapid transmission of orders and inventory data. Technical aid is specialized and is given to assist customers in areas where research and successful experiences of the firm's other wholesalers/distributors can be applied. Examples include professional consultation in warehouse layout and facilities design, forecasts, inventory control, computerized truck route analysis, fleet management programs, equipment specification, data processing, traffic management, location of capital sources, and possibly a cooperative mass purchasing plan.

The basic concept is as follows:

1. Although the channel commander and his suppliers and customers recognize that each of the above areas is the responsibility of each firm, these areas have potential cost reduction opportunities where special skills are required.

2. Specialization in these required skills, along with the one-time problem solutions, warrants that channel commander expertise be developed and applied to dependent firms.

3. About 90 percent of all customer complaints involve a distribution problem unrelated to sales and in areas where the sales representative has little

knowledge or interest. Accordingly, a customer service program including both service analysis and technical aid should be administered as a function separate from sales, preferably tied in with the firm's distribution department.

—K. U. Flood and D. L. Shawver

PHYSICAL DISTRIBUTION

Physical distribution has been a subject of management concern for relatively few years. In earlier times less attention was paid to practices and costs in handling materials and finished goods than was warranted by the opportunity for improvement in profits and customer service. Many managers have only recently found that an examination of the physical distribution area is the most rewarding program they have embarked upon.

Scope

In a very limited view, physical distribution may be considered to include only the activities that are involved in moving the finished product out of the plant and for which the producer pays the cost. More enlightened observation, however, shows that the physical distribution activities of concern to a company encompass inbound as well as outbound movement and storage, together with in-plant handling. Further, they include even activities for which others pay the cost, since in the long run these are paid for by the company or its customers.

ELEMENTS

The elements of physical distribution assume different importance for each company. Further, opportunities to modify the practices and influence the cost vary from one situation to another. The starting point seems to be in the recognition of what elements are involved. The following might be a partial list:

Inbound	In-Plant	Outbound
Transportation	Transportation	Transportation
Raw materials	Raw materials	Finished goods
Supplies	Work-in-process	Spare parts
Insurance	Finished goods	Field inventories
Receiving	Inventory	Investment
	Investment charges	Insurance
	Insurance	Loss and damage
	Loss and damage	Taxes
	Taxes	Field warehouse
	Warehouse	Labor
	Labor	Facilities
	Facilities	Inventory management
	Inventory management	Order handling
	Packaging	
	Shipping	
	Pallets	

The total cost of these elements varies widely from industry to industry and from company to company even within the same industry. For example, in the machine-manufacturing industry, physical distribution costs approximate 10 percent of sales; in the food industry, 30 percent. The transportation cost—the element frequently thought to be the only element—may be but a third of the total.

JURISDICTIONAL PROBLEMS

Because the range of elements in physical distribution is so broad and because the elements occur in a number of company departments or divisions, it is difficult for one manager to tackle the problem and achieve the optimum solution. Shipping and receiving, for example, may be found under two separate groups. What might be best for the company and its customers is for a captive truck operation to be established. The outbound trip moves finished goods, and the inbound trip hauls raw materials and supplies. Jurisdictional problems that result from the scope of physical distribution call for action by those who can bridge the gap between departments.

Historically, the traffic manager of a company has held the role of purchasing agent for transportation. Salesmen representing carriers called on him and, in one way or another, sold him on using their mode of transportation and line. Receiving and shipping departments, as well as others, expressed their preferences to him, but usually there was little economic justification for selecting one carrier over the other or even for the mode used. Keeping them all happy seemed to be the prime motive behind the traffic manager's decision. But the picture is changing; carriers are becoming more sophisticated, and the choices are becoming more numerous. Hence, the size of the problem has now far outgrown the jurisdiction of the conventional traffic manager's job.

The Changing Picture

Not only have the opportunities in physical distribution become more widely recognized in recent years; the available solutions and tools are becoming more numerous. In addition, rapid changes are occurring that affect what can and should be done. (Further discussion of the subject appears in the Manufacturing section of this handbook, page 6·84.)

IMPACT OF EDP

One of the most important tools in bringing about improvements in the practice and reductions in the cost of physical distribution has been EDP. Without it, to examine the masses of data necessary to reach sound conclusions on the methods to adopt would have been impossible. To react rapidly and properly in operational situations would likewise have been impossible in the absence of the hardware and systems skills of today. The computer can point out the optimum answer after considering literally hundreds of variables. A manufacturer with multiple plants and field warehouses spread across the country can examine whether costs would be lower and service levels proper with fewer facilities. Continuous decisions can be reached, taking into consideration all factors relating to which products should be produced and stocked at which plant and warehouse.

The improving picture in the data processing field, however, does not eliminate the need for fact gathering and decision making by skilled people. Simply feeding the computer with facts on what is being done today is not enough. A proper evaluation of a physical distribution system requires new methods and a variety of alternatives to be considered first by people and only second by the machine.

For the manager of a business, the increasing use of computers may be viewed with mixed emotions. It has given him a tool to be employed in the interests of his company. With it he can make decisions and operate systems that were virtually impossible before. On the other hand, it has given other managers the same tool, and the tool can be used against him. For example, through the use of computers the customer is in a better position to analyze the company services, including elements of the distribution package. The carrier is in a better position to know what to charge and with what company it is best to work. The wholesaler moving the company's products to market is in a better position to know how to shift the inventory responsibility back up the channel. The supplier is in a better position to price his products to reflect the distribution cost elements, sometimes including costs that were previously lost in the averages.

Welcome or not, the impact of the computer will continue to be felt in the area of physical distribution. However, its maximum benefit can be experienced only if those charged with its operation and feeding are totally familiar with all aspects of the company's distribution problem.

STORAGE METHODS

It is not unusual to see the most archaic storage methods employed at manufacturer, wholesaler, and retailer levels. The hidden costs of damage, temporarily lost inventory, and disruptions elsewhere caused by storage inefficiencies are not brought to light by the cost system; but even managers who have not adopted modern storage methods can see the rising labor costs brought by obsolete facilities and must be alarmed by them. Fortunately, storage methods for raw materials, work-in-process, and finished goods have undergone some dramatic changes in recent years. Entire businesses have sprung up just to serve the specialized needs of handling and stocking items most efficiently.

It is now possible to go the full route and have an automated warehouse. In such a facility maximum use is made of the building cube, and conventional labor is almost eliminated. Items can be placed in storage or retrieved by inserting a card in a computer.

Aside from the automated warehouse, great advances are being made in materials handling equipment, pallets, racks, and warehouse design. The key seems to be in tailoring the physical storage methods and facilities exactly to the particular situation. Naturally, as this direction is pursued, flexibility is lost; hence the potential economic risks and gains must be carefully weighed.

TRANSPORTATION

The transportation industry has come in for a great deal of criticism in the public press for failing to keep up with the times; it has also received exaggerated praise for some of its "far-out" ideas. However, the industry has moved a long way in recent years, perhaps in large measure because of the pressure of shippers who, in re-examining their physical distribution problems, have found unfulfilled needs. Through their individual and collective purchasing strength, new developments have been forced—container ships, integrated trains, special trucks, and giant cargo planes, for example.

Increasing interest in physical distribution has created markets for American suppliers everywhere. Almost every developing country has a government-owned airline (even if it consists of only one jet plane) equipped and sometimes manned from the United States. American carriers' equipment is to be seen at foreign airports and seaports and on foreign highways; for instance, 40-foot containers loaded in the United States are to be seen on the highways of Germany.

To the manager in U.S. industry, the proliferation of transportation types and alternatives can become confusing. It suggests that there should be some concerted thinking about the advantages to be gained from examining the company's own physical distribution picture.

TOTAL APPROACH

Purchasers are giving more consideration to the total "package"—product, price, availability, and reliability of delivery. In many instances, particularly in industrial markets, the product takes on the aspects of a commodity because the specifications are well established. Thus competition is based on other elements in addition to excellence of product and ability of sales force. Managers are seeking to compete by (1) reducing the delivered cost to customer, taking into consideration even shipping costs borne by the customer; (2) providing the product in the form best suited to low-cost handling by the customer (for example, shipping on pallets or in containers); (3) combining orders into lots of economical shipping quantity; (4) developing improved ways of order handling; and (5) eliminating unnecessary steps in the distribution channel, thus improving the ability to respond to customer needs as well as reducing the cost.

The means of competing with the use of an improved physical distribution approach are numerous. What is very attractive in one industrial market may very well be of little competitive value in a consumer market.

It has been possible, in the past, for a company to use the same marketing and physical distribution approach for its entire line. This assumed that all segments of the market were alike in their needs and could be served in the same manner. Unfortunately for those who failed to recognize the growing segmentation of their market and take appropriate action, opportunities were lost to competitors who were more alert.

The best approach in an examination of a company's physical distribution activity combines it with an examination of the changing marketing patterns in each of the segments of the industry in which the company competes. It can be thought of as looking at the situation from the outside in as well as the inside out. The viewpoint of the customer is an important ingredient in making any decision. Frequently, the recognition of some modest desire or need on the part of the customer can be accommodated with little expense. In doing so, the company can find that its gain in competitive edge is far from modest.

Trade-Offs

No physical distribution plan can be both the most profitable for the supplier and the most satisfactory for the buyer. Compromises must be made.

CUSTOMER SERVICE

A 100 percent level of customer service is almost impossible to obtain. It would require investment in finished inventories and create carrying costs that could not in any way be justified.

The realistic approach is to determine what can be considered competitive. Is it the delivery of 90 percent of the orders for a certain product line within a week? If so, analysis can be made to determine what this means in terms of parts, dollars, and physical space.

OUTBOUND TRANSPORTATION COST

An absolutely minimum cost of outbound transportation from warehouse to customer could be attained only by accumulating exorbitant costs in terms of warehousing and inventory. It would require maintaining stocks next door to the receiving department of each customer—an obviously impossible situation. A much more realistic approach determines the optimum situation by considering all the cost factors.

DELIVERY PROMISES

Instant delivery and 100 percent performance against promise are also beyond economic possibility. There can be no assurance that the lead time will remain constant under all conditions of peaks and valleys in terms of incoming orders. Standby costs during depressed periods would be drastic.

The need is to determine proper standards for lead time for service out of stock and provide for it in terms of inventory and handling. Perhaps even more important to competitive success than attempting to gear for the shortest lead time is formulating promised lead times that can be met with a high level of accuracy. Customers seeking to keep their inventories and yet maintain business without interruption can be impressed by suppliers who have high ratios of performance against promise.

Creating a New Physical Distribution Plan

A three-phase, ten-step program has been used by a number of managers to examine, improve, and maintain up to date the physical distribution activities of their companies.

DEVELOPMENT PHASE

Assuming that the physical distribution activity of the company has not come under recent scrutiny, the initial phase should be the careful and objective development of a complete plan.

Step 1. Form a task force to guide the development phase. Decisions must be reached as to which divisions or departments will be represented on the task force and whether outside counsel will be employed to bring in the expertise and objectivity required. As a minimum, representatives of the marketing and production departments should be included in the team. Those chosen from within the company should have company experience long enough to know where to look for the facts and should be able to look objectively at practices that have been employed for many years. In addition to having these qualifications, the task force leader should be organizationally and politically so positioned in the company that top management decisions can be secured rapidly.

Step 2. Analyze the facts on distribution in the markets in which the company competes, including distribution patterns of major competitors; demand requirements of market segments; regional differences in demand; distribution policies and practices of competitors; statistics, facts, and opinions on current practices; needs and desires of major customer groups; factors influencing shifts in current practices; and opportunities to effect change.

Step 3. Determine current distribution practices and policies of the company, and compare them with those of the competition. At the beginning it might be well to accumulate all the policy statements pertaining to the physical distribution of the company's various products. It should be no surprise to find inconsistencies; this is part of the usual problem.

A starting point might be to draw up a flow chart of the marketing channels through which the company products are sold; then chart the flow of the physical movement of goods (which may not be identical to that of the marketing channels).

Step 4. Accumulate and evaluate data on current distribution practices of the company. This frequently requires the gathering of data from basic source documents—for example, bills of lading. Data should be of distribution activity over a long enough period of time to assure the elimination of isolated practices and the recognition of significant trends. As a beginning, these data might be on the following subjects: volume (units or tons) by source and destination; volume by type of carrier; costs of transportation, inventory, and warehousing; levels of service by product class, including order cycle time and back orders; and loading and unloading costs. The question to be asked in examining these and other data should be, "Can physical distribution be managed more efficiently and with greater usefulness of time and place to the customer, and all in the light of the competitive environment in which the company operates?"

Step 5. Formulate new systems. Casting aside past practice for the time being, it is useful to prepare as many alternative systems as appear feasible. Some will be only streamlined versions of the old system, while others will adopt new concepts and require more modern hardware and practices than are currently in use. Still other alternatives that will completely restructure the distribution system can be formulated.

Step 6. Cost out the alternatives. As far as practical they should be simulated on paper, using historical or projected volumes. The simulation should include the development of investment costs of new equipment and facilities as well as of operating costs.

Step 7. Decide on the final plan. The economics of the alternatives cannot be all-powerful; certainly small possible savings cannot be permitted to influence a decision to select an alternative in conflict with marketing policy of the company. Thus, in the decision process, the task force may well consider presenting the alternatives and the recommendation to top management in a concise and written form.

IMPLEMENTATION PHASE

So many efforts fail to attain the maximum benefit of a physical distribution review that it is useful to reflect on why this happens. Principally, it seems that the development work was acceptable but the implementation fell short. The support that comes of understanding by all parties in the organization was lacking, and thus unconsciously the plan was sabotaged. This suggests two key steps, added to the seven in the development phase.

Step 8. Communicate the plan. The necessary material must be provided and meetings must be held to do the job of educating the people concerned.

Step 9. Implement the plan. Detailed procedures and the assignment of responsibilities to capable personnel are needed. Hence an organization plan, a manpower development plan, and a systems and procedures program relating to the physical distribution program are all logical parts of the implementation.

IMPROVEMENT PHASE

Conditions change too rapidly for one to expect that, once a plan has been developed and implemented, it will remain sound for all time; hence a final step is required.

Step 10. Evaluate the plan on a pre-established schedule and modify it accordingly. An information system that will give a measure of the plan's performance should be put into being. Periodically (not less often than once a year), a more formal review should be made to find out what opportunities exist for improvement.

With such a ten-step program it is possible to predict the attainment of many of the rewards attributed to a physical distribution review.—*W. J. Guyton*

MEASURING THE PERFORMANCE
OF MARKETING OPERATIONS

In this day of rapid change, swift obsolescence, and continuing technological advancement, it would be unwise to believe that marketing principles are static. Marketing today is a many-faceted process of business action.

A noted professor of marketing (W. J. Stanton, *Fundamentals of Marketing*, McGraw-Hill, 1964) believes that

> marketing is a total system of business action rather than a fragmented assortment of functions and institutions. More specifically, marketing is . . . a total system of interacting business activities designed to plan, price, promote, and distribute want-satisfying goods and services to consumers and industrial users.

> Marketing is becoming recognized as an all-pervasive part of the system of business management, and all managerial activity in a firm should be directed toward the goal of making the marketing process more effective.

It has been wisely said that all performance can be measured. To be able to measure, standards must be established. As the performance of various marketing operations is examined, it is apparent that the elements are now more numerous and complex than formerly and that measurement therefore may not be as simple as it once was.

Objectives and the Company

Knowledge of performance is insufficient. To be truly meaningful there must be comparisons on an equitable basis. To measure objective against actual performance is often a very effective comparison and an acceptable measurement.

All the people interested in a company, whether they are shareholders, officers, directors, or employees, look at the company's sales, net profits, growth, ROI, book value of stock, and perhaps other financial yardsticks, usually in comparison with those of competitors.

It is necessary to establish objectives by which the degree of goal attainment can be measured. There was a time when financial status or credit rating was considered a sufficient standard in grading a company's marketing effectiveness. Another type of yardstick is the operating statement; this is helpful in measuring overall progress but not necessarily good per se for measuring the performance of marketing operations. Under today's conditions it requires more than financial status or overall progress to properly measure; the standards used must be of a concrete nature, easily measured.

The basic foundation of a marketing program is a long-range objective; it is a road map to where the company wants to go. The word "objective" is sometimes defined as "something aimed at" or "something striven for." Other versions are "a broad aim" or "a desired end." All these definitions are loose and general. Most companies have objectives of some kind, even if only stated as "to increase sales." To be useful, specific goals should be the targets: for example, improving share of market, introducing new products successfully, selling the whole line rather than items, improving product mix, or increasing profits. Without appropriate objectives there is almost certain to be considerable wasted effort in sales, which in turn tends to create waste in other areas and departments of the business.

To set a forecast, objective, goal, or quota requires much more than mathematical computations; above all, it requires intelligent and intuitive judgment.

A forecast is a company's best estimate of what will happen. An objective is the optimum performance to be expected. A budget is the forecast for a year ahead. A goal may be either a forecast or an objective. A quota is generally used in connection with sales and is the same as a goal.

Most business firms, whether manufacturing, wholesale, retail, or service organizations, operate against a sales objective to which the profit expectation is tied. Occasionally, a business has objectives other than short-term profits; for example, investment in research or market penetration for a new product. Either of these will tend to lower profits currently and for the immediate future.

Objectives and Marketing

One of marketing's many facets is advertising—and an important one it is. The effects of advertising are often very difficult to measure. Because many companies spend vast sums in advertising, and because the cost of advertising is now approximately double what it was a decade or so ago, it is important to differentiate advertising from other marketing costs. Unless the advertising campaign has specific measurable tasks to perform, there will be no knowing what was responsible for the results, good or bad: the advertising itself, the new packaging, better selling, the weather, or general economic conditions.

For many years there has been a historical relationship between advertising expenditures and sales, and between advertising expenditures and total dollar expenditures. These factors, along with projected sales volume, can be used in evaluating advertising and will be determined in differences in degrees. Advertising can also be evaluated in terms of total impact on profits.

Because marketing policies and strategies vary so greatly in industries and even in companies within an industry, no average or norm can be formulated for objectives. Company management must determine the objectives that will best suit its purpose in reaching the goals it wishes to attain.

Standards of Performance

The most usual standard is historical—last year's sales compared with this year's. The value of this comparison may be slight; it may also be misleading. If the percent of increase in sales over a very bad year is high, the actual accomplishment may be minor if compared with an average year. However, it is better than no comparison. Standards set by engineers usually say what performance should be; marketing standards are usually set up against the performance of competition, perhaps also against industry ratios.

PROFIT

There are several factors that can affect profits, which makes the setting of standards more difficult. In almost any business the fluctuation of volume has strong impact. Usually, a strong increase in volume materially improves profits, since the greater part of the gross profit on the extra sales becomes net (most expenses have already been taken care of). If the pendulum swings the other way and there is a big drop in sales, profits fall off rapidly because the lowered volume cannot take care of the overhead.

Product mix often has a surprising effect on profits. If, normally, the product mix is 70 percent high-profit items and 30 percent low-profit items, the average profit might look like this:

Volume $60,000
70 percent or $42,000 at 30 percent gross profit = $12,600
30 percent or $18,000 at 15 percent gross profit =   2,700
                                                   ‾‾‾‾‾‾‾
                                                     $15,300
$15,300 ÷ $60,000 = 25.5 percent average gross profit

Should the product mix change to 40 percent high-profit items and 60 percent low-profit items, the picture would change materially:

Volume $60,000
40 percent or $24,000 at 30 percent gross profit = $ 7,200
60 percent or $36,000 at 15 percent gross profit =   5,400
                                                   ‾‾‾‾‾‾‾
                                                     $12,600
$12,600 ÷ $60,000 = 21 percent average gross profit

Obviously, unusual or increased expenses will adversely affect profits. A decrease in expenditures would add to profits, but this would be a rare occurrence for most business establishments. Profits can be nullified—or, at least, drastically reduced—by unnecessary expenses in branch offices, warehouses, or personnel.

A good profit ratio, although slightly smaller than in the previous year, on a high volume may divert attention from an existing profit lag. Perhaps on the high volume, profits should have gone up in greater proportion than sales.

For a standard of profit performance, some marketing people look with favor on the advertising cost to earnings (A/E) ratio. This relationship can be varied in the extreme, and it is hardly possible that there is a usable industry average. The A/E ratio has been known to run as high as $16.50 to $1.00, in the case of a manufacturer striving to establish a stable of new products. Infrequently, the ratio might drop down to $0.50 to $1.00. There are many people who prefer to pin their faith on net profit as a percentage of sales as an acceptable yardstick.

COST

Surely cost can be labeled a standard of performance. Certain costs are uncontrollable, such as taxes and insurance. There remain, however, a number of expenses that are controllable in greater or lesser degree. Total costs on an operating statement are too general to be of much value. What is needed is a careful comparison, item by item, with the industry operating ratio. Public statements rarely have an item breakdown that provides the detail necessary for such comparisons. In the case of competitors who issue public statements, a fair comparison can be gained on gross profit as a percent to sales and on net profit as a percent to sales. The general statement can be more useful if a five- or ten-year table shows the dollar expense year by year for each item and if the same chart shows the same items year by year expressed as a percent of sales.

SALES

Historically, the tendency has been to compare this year's net sales with last year's; if there is an increase, progress has been made. But sales as they are shown on operating statements may fail to portray the true situation. Many a company complacently looks at its sales and profits picture and accepts it at face value; but many times, when sales are broken down by territory, product, or some other category, glaring weaknesses come to light. The historical relationship method of comparison can entirely cover up losses in the share of the market even though an increase in sales has been achieved. A far better standard to use is the potential of sales territories by some market index, such as population, buying power, per capita income, total retail sales, or income per family.

Sales Management's annual *Survey of Buying Power* is a respected and widely used source in setting up market potential by territory, district, state, or region. The only difficulty experienced with the buying power index occurs when the salesman's territory crosses county lines, but this too can be computed. With the buying power index the optimum sales potential is determined, and performance can be easily and readily measured against it.

The traditional method of giving salesmen a percentage increase in quota over the previous year's sales is probably not nearly so fair a goal as the one based on potential. Territories have a way of varying from year to year. Too, a 10 percent increase per year for ten years may be unattainable.

Aside from the aforementioned *Survey of Buying Power,* information that can help in setting standards and also in measuring performance is available from government and trade sources.

One statistic, often not given the attention it deserves, is the individual salesman's merchandise returns expressed as a percent of sales. The problem may not always be with the salesman; sometimes a little research shows that the trouble is in distribution or production. Though returns can be a standard of performance, they should not be applied as such until a little checking is done.

MARKET SHARE

Marketing men set great store by the share of the market that their product enjoys; this is, to them, a reliable standard of performance. The percentage share of a market that a firm might enjoy on a given product has ranged as high as 80 percent, but currently not too many reach or hold that exalted position. The proliferation of high-consumption products, plus the "coat-tail riders," has long since reduced maximums by a greater split of the spoils.

One factor concerning share of the market that may be overlooked is that sales may show an increase while the share of the market has declined. A nice sales increase should not encourage the marketer until he has a knowledge of the facts.

Competition, both in products and in their promotion, is so fierce and so sustained that many changes have occurred among the leaders. For this reason some astute marketing men have preferred market segmentation to the general battle. Unfortunately, once their success is known, competition singles them out, and they are soon back in the battle.

Outside of the high-consumption, nationally advertised brands, the competition is less fierce, and a sizable share of the market is not so difficult to attain. In any case it is easier than formerly to get accurate figures, nationally or by region, on where a product stands. Firms offer their services in measuring the share of the market, the ranking of products, the evaluation of advertising, and the like.

There are also firms that, for a fee, furnish information on brand preferences, and some firms that will make periodic store inventories to tell the marketer the movement of his product in comparison with competitive items. If desired, panels of housewives will give their opinions about products, packages, and other factors. Other firms can provide product sales and distribution analyses. Occasionally, newspapers provide helpful brand surveys within their coverage areas.

Budgets

From a nonaccounting point of view, a properly prepared budget is a blueprint that guides management as management strives to reach its objective. Since practically all businesses necessarily estimate the various parts of the budget, the total budget cannot be as accurate as an architect's meticulously drawn blueprint. And because practically no entry in a budget can be considered "actual," a great deal of reliance must be put on what has transpired before. Amazingly, budgets and actual results are often close together, particularly when management is long experienced in using budgets to guide its operations.

Normally, the budget begins with the sales forecast for the ensuing fiscal year. The budget then evolves as expenses for the various departments and subdivisions are put in place. Finally, of course, an estimate is made on net profit.

The operating statement, which should be issued on a monthly basis, provides the picture of what has actually happened. When compared with the budget, which also should be broken down into months based on past history, the statement quickly shows how closely actual and estimate are to each other; it readily reveals strengths and weaknesses and shows where improvement needs to be made.

For the manufacturer and perhaps for the retailer too, the most difficult element of a budget to gauge is consumer demand; here again, however, history may be helpful in developing an accurate estimate.

Budgets can be subdivided into as great detail as desired. In some businesses— especially in the manufacture of many products in different categories—the greater the breakdown of the budget, the greater the ease of measuring the effectiveness of operations.

Industry Operating Ratios

For nearly every separate type of industry in the United States, there is an association that brings its members together periodically; generally, it also provides its members with overall operating ratios of the industry that offer excellent yardsticks to measure a company's effectiveness.

The National Wholesale Druggists' Association, for example, annually provides its members with a complete list of operating ratios on a national, regional, and sometimes state basis. The figures are highly respected, since 98 or 99 percent of the members regularly turn in their figures. The NWDA operating ratios have a historical background of many years, which increases their value as measuring devices. A great many other associations focus their members' attention on similar information at their annual conferences.

For a number of years Dun & Bradstreet has periodically issued a valuable chart of operating ratios for a sizable list of varied industries. In some industries that are government-regulated, such as the liquor industry, statistics on shipments by brand, and even by size, are easily obtainable. In such industries there is no lack of knowledge about share of the market or marketing effectiveness.

Among the operating ratios that interest top management are the following: (1) current ratio, (2) ratio of inventory to net working capital, (3) ratio of net sales to net working capital, (4) ratio of current liabilities to net worth, (5) ratio of total liabilities to net worth, (6) ratio of net sales to net worth, (7) ratio of net profit to net worth, and (8) ratio of net profit to net sales.

Obviously, when current ratios are used, the operating statement is used. It is safe to say that an accurate, detailed operating statement provides the information for current ratios of all kinds and affords the basis for many forms of comparison and measurement.

Use of Planned Performance Data

As an additional source of measurement standards, planned performance data can be very helpful. Usually, such data are objectives or goals of a very specific nature as opposed to the normal broad, general aspects. An objective of a company might be to increase sales, while its planned performance would be a 10 percent sales increase the coming year. Planned performances are specific as to time and place, within the overall objectives.

While the operating statement and much other available information are valuable for measuring effectiveness, planned performance data can greatly assist by pinpointing specifics that, as yardsticks, can help answer questions of what was accomplished and whether it was profitable.

GOALS

Typical planned performances are built around product mix, sales, profit, cost, or other goals in achieving marketing objectives.

Product mix. A company desiring to increase profits might devise a plan to achieve its goal by doubling sales of its most profitable product.

Sales. A sales goal for another company might be to reach 5 percent of the buying power index in its southeastern district. Another goal might be to achieve sales of one package of a new product to 60 percent of the families within a given area.

Profit. Part of an overall plan could be a goal of a 2 percent increase in gross profit in the territories in the mountain and Pacific districts during the current fiscal year.

Cost. One worthy cost goal would be a reduction in advertising costs in relation to sales in certain selected districts where advertising costs have exceeded the company average.

Other goals. The examples cited previously are but a few of the many specifics that may be exploited for the company's benefit. Some further suggestions are the following: (1) profit contribution by products, (2) sales to certain outlets, (3) sales to specified age groups, (4) percentage goal of a share of the market, and (5) greater distribution in certain territories.

BENEFITS

As costs continue to rise, with no relief in sight, while profits are being squeezed by a variety of causes, planned performance can offer a partial remedy for some of industry's problems. By a careful selection of specific programs based on the individual needs of a particular business, the marketing operation can become more effective, thereby making a concrete contribution to profits. At the same time it may make an appreciable contribution toward an improved share of the market. Planned performance therefore increases in value as business conditions grow more difficult.—*F. M. Truett*

MANAGING THE MARKETING OPERATION

Quality and style in managing the marketing operation are unquestionably key determinants in the success of the overall marketing effort. And the challenge to marketing management is compounded by the fact that marketing, mathematical modeling notwithstanding, continues to be part art and part science, with the probable emphasis on the former. It therefore becomes imperative that the management techniques applied address themselves simultaneously to the twofold need of (1) using management science and decision-making technology to the fullest while understanding the explicit and implicit limitations of these tools; and (2) simultaneously providing guidelines, stimulation, and encouragement for the fullest and richest use of inspiration, talent, inventiveness, and judgment. Indeed, the philosophic base for excellent management of the marketing function must necessarily be the search for balance between art and science.

Marketing Management's Responsibility

Broadly, marketing management's responsibility is to help fulfill the corporate objectives that are pertinent to the marketing function. This definition puts the emphasis on implementation rather than on initiation, with the widest latitude and discretion concerning the ways to fulfill these broad corporate objectives. Thus, if the pertinent corporate objective is profit optimizing through domination of a specific product and consumer market, it is marketing management's prime responsibility to accomplish these goals by any and all means that do not violate other corporate objectives and policies.

DYNAMIC FUNCTION

A second marketing management responsibility that is not nearly so obvious nor nearly so well accepted as the first is an implicit responsibility to provide stimulation, information, and inspiration to review, obsolesce, or alter corporate objectives as economic or market conditions indicate that yesterday's verities may be confining or out of tune in tomorrow's world.

This brief summary of marketing management's responsibility to top corporate management and to the corporation itself serves merely to indicate the fact that the most fruitful relationship within the corporate structure, whether aimed upward or downward in the organizational hierarchy, tends to contain two components that may be characterized as implementing and instigating or executing and challenging.

To interpret marketing management's responsibility in still other words: It may well be dramatized by the view that the marketing function is the function of change. It is the function of dynamic relationships and carries with it therefore the managerial responsibility to question, challenge, and stimulate, as compared with accepting or even merely assimilating.

CREATIVE PARTICIPATION

Of course, the proof that marketing management has fulfilled its responsibility ultimately lies in the development and implementation of a successful marketing strategy. Creative participation in the shaping of a marketing strategy is often best encouraged under the following circumstances:

1. Marketing management should initially pose the challenge in terms of the broadest goals constrained only by genuinely intrinsic or unavoidable limitations.

In line with this approach, the objective "We would like to develop the market for an astringent-soaked cotton pad" will encourage the creation of a broader number of alternatives than the objective "We would like to increase the use of Wash 'n Dri among young mothers."

In brief, when marketing management sees the possibility and usefulness in multiplying the number of creative alternatives to be considered, it is not only marketing management's responsibility but a matter of applying managerial techniques to encourage the available staff, or outside agency, or consulting talent to contribute as broadly, freely, and productively to the thinking as possible.

2. Marketing management should not only pay lip service to but should project a genuinely searching and open viewpoint based on management's stated objective that it must function to obsolesce its own work and strategy at any time when it is no longer optimum.

If marketing management is known to be wedded to a particular approach, enamored of a particular communications approach or medium, enchanted with a specific segment of the consumer market, or entranced with a set approach to distribution, it is inevitable that this bias will limit the creative contributions of those reporting to marketing management. It is difficult for the subordinate or the outside consulting firm to buck an entrenched viewpoint when it is obvious that doing so is tantamount to committing economic suicide within that corporate structure.

3. As open-minded as marketing management should be to the proposal of totally fresh and new alternatives, so close-minded should it be about requiring

thorough, exhaustive, systematic, and analytic written back-up. It is not the world of "blue sky" that marketing management should choose or wish to encourage but the world of constructive thinkers who carry inspiration through to the point of reasoning out and analyzing the probable outcomes of the implementation.

4. Marketing management should avoid intergroup competition, whether on its own staff or in its relationships with outside agencies and consulting firms, in order to shut noise and unproductive frustration out of the system.

Strangely enough, this particular tenet tends to divide founders and managers of commercially creative services fairly evenly down the middle. A remarkable number of extraordinarily successful managers of creative marketing departments or firms thrive—because of the compulsive dictates of their own neurotic personalities—by pitting subordinates against each other in a weird application of the concept of brand competition within the same market. In brief, they maintain their departments or marketing staffs in a continuing state of high-pitched nervous tension and interpersonal competition and hostility on the theory that this keeps them on their toes and makes them think in terms of more "far-out" creative alternatives.

There is considerable question about the effectiveness of this approach in managing creative talent, and a strong case can be made for the statement that those who operate within such an environment may be contributing at a level well below their creative capacity. Their effort is likely to be drastically reduced by their own neurotic problems, which are keeping them rooted to their artificially hostile environment, or else they are probably using their creative talents to try to get out of this environment.

Sometimes the creation of intergroup hostilities and unproductive competition is generated unwittingly by marketing management because management does not take into account the professional, judgmental, and personality differences between arty-creative executives and the predominantly mathematical-scientific intellectuals who work side by side in a marketing department or firm. The coexistence of such very divergent talents and personality types within the same function is part of the great challenge to marketing management—a challenge rather different, apparently, from that facing managements of other, more homogeneous and cohesive functions. That is the reason why this discussion of management techniques began by defining the challenge in terms of quality and style. The quality of the managing operation comes to fruition in the product of the marketing department or firm. The style of managing determines the character and nature of the executives and professional talents attracted to that department or firm, the aggregate productivity of the staff, and the climate within the organization.

Thus, while managerial style can well be highly individual and may permit—within a limited range defined by the corporate structure itself—certain idiosyncratic aberrations, its essence within the marketing function, if it is to be successful, must be its ability to adapt to the remarkably divergent needs of the arty-creative professional and the mathematical-scientific intellectual operating within the same function.

Use of EDP

The newest challenge in successfully managing marketing operations is implicit, not only in the use of computer applications, but—perhaps more importantly—in management's ability to strike an intelligent balance between the seemingly precise decision-making guidelines emanating from some marketing models and the tenuous judgmental inputs upon which the computations are based. Managerial responsibility is not fulfilled either by discounting or by debunking little-known applications or computer-based techniques, nor is it served by slavishly adhering to computer-produced decision parameters without questioning the basic assumptions that went into the original model.

EDUCATIONAL RESPONSIBILITIES

Marketing management faces a twofold challenge in considering the role of the computer within its operation. The prime challenge, of course, is the newness of many applications and therefore the difficulty of keeping as well informed about uses and developments as the fully effective marketing manager should be. It is extremely difficult to set up a system for screening out applications, technical jargon, and mathematical theory that may have only peripheral or academic value from the information that marketing management ought to have. A specific but seemingly insignificant application for solving an obscure problem in a different industry may have meaningful application to a problem in marketing management's own industry.

One technique that may aid marketing management in acquiring this essential knowledge is to assign a marketing trainee of good educational background to the editorial job of reading, sifting out, and summarizing from the literature in order to assure the marketing manager that his reading time will be well spent on the essential.

Such a full-time assignment serves the dual purpose of providing a systematic source of up-to-date information for the department and a means for developing a reference library data base from which information can be retrieved at will in the future. It assures the marketing manager that critical developments in the state of the art will be brought to his attention and that his time will be husbanded somewhat more carefully than if the entire burden for searching out current knowledge were placed upon him.

In addition and ideally, the marketing manager should take one or more courses (preferably, at a university) designed to provide him not so much with programming skills that he does not require but with insights into the potential uses and limitations of this relatively unexploited management tool. For an intelligent selection of courses, it is doubtful that the manager can rely simply on reading catalogs with descriptions of courses. He would be better served by discussing his information needs, where computer technology is concerned, with a university marketing department head or with the head of a department teaching quantitative methods or mathematics for business.

The basic point here, however, is that the changes and developments in marketing decision making have been too acute and too extreme for a marketing manager to fully live up to his responsibilities if he relies simply on reading without recourse to the updating of disciplines and factual knowledge that is requisite for the use of the computer for the purpose of solving marketing problems.

BRIDGING COMMUNICATION GAP

It is a truism that one cannot direct and supervise without knowledge or understanding. Yet a large number of executives are, in certain areas relevant to their responsibility, entirely in the hands of professional specialists whose expertise so completely outstrips the manager's own as to make a dialog totally impossible. When the knowledge gap becomes so considerable, the marketing manager has not delegated responsibility; he has abdicated it. Where the use of mathematical and marketing research techniques in marketing decision making is concerned, such abdication is a folly that can lead only to dissonance and disaster in the overall marketing strategy's development and implementation.

It is not necessary for marketing management to have programming or computer language skills or to be especially expert in multivariate analysis or the concepts of Bayesian probabilities. But management has the right and responsibility to request, challenge, and probe basic assumptions in computer models, and in crisp and strong business English. No marketing application or concept is so complex that it cannot be translated from the intimidating jargon of the OR man or the statistician or the mathematician into a common language.

By the same token marketing management, in guiding the new computer professionals, has a parallel responsibility to convey the dimensions of the problem to be considered as free from the special language of marketing disciplines as possible.

Needless to say, these objectives are easier to state than to fulfill. They are, however, essential to the intelligent management of marketing operations today.

REVIEW MEETINGS

Feedback is an essential component of management, particularly in instances where the staff to be managed is composed of relatively sensitive professional talent. Some of the feedback on quality of performance is obviously implicit in the continuing and informal relationships that are maintained as diverse skills are brought together in the development and implementation of the marketing strategy and plan. However, the complexity of marketing operations requires more systematic channels of communication and multidirectional feedback. This is the function of monthly review and quarterly planning meetings.

The purpose of each meeting dictates to some extent the degree to which the agenda should be structured or unstructured. In broad strokes, a search for reasons-why based on concrete evidence (such as historical marketing research data) can lend itself to relatively tight and structured sessions. But where the objective is the synthesizing of alternatives for future action, excessive structuring can tend to impede rather than enhance the individual contributions. At the same time, it would be a mistake to assume that the more unstructured meetings imply lack of preparation. The contrary is probably true. And it behooves marketing management to indicate clearly to all those who are to participate—in either a review or a planning meeting—what will be expected of those attending.

These expectations should be clarified in terms of the objectives of the meeting; the topics to be covered; the relevant materials available for prior study, analysis, or preparation; and the outcome or resolution that marketing management anticipates from this meeting.

An example may help bring these points into focus. If the advertising agency account group is being invited to make a presentation of an upcoming campaign to a meeting of the corporate marketing group, those invited to attend this presentation should know in advance what will be expected of them. For example, does marketing management plan to turn this presentation into a spontaneous critique of the campaign recommendations? Or is the purpose simply exposure, with a critique session planned for a later date? Is the purpose of the meeting to accept, approve, and finalize? Or is the purpose to stimulate thinking concerning new directions in strategy?

In brief, unless the ground rules for each meeting are clear to all participants in terms of expectations, preparation, and purpose, the meeting is unlikely to fulfill a useful purpose.

A LEADERSHIP TOOL

One definition that may well be applicable to all active management but has particular significance in the marketing function interprets active managing as a continuing learning and teaching process. The "learning" part of the definition underscores the manager's responsibility to combine a willingness to change, as economic, product, or marketing conditions may require it, with an ability to discriminate between temporary marketing aberrations and significant trends. Timing, that *sine qua non* of successful marketing, may well be a function of attitudes and perceptions that can be learned rather than being innate.

The teaching part of the managerial responsibility deals more with techniques of inspiration, encouragement, guidance, and planned reinforcing of good performance than it does with the transmission of substantive bodies of knowledge. It can be assumed that by nature of their levels and caliber, people managed within marketing operations tend to be sufficiently motivated to assume the quest for increased knowledge as part of their own responsibility. On that score, active management may channel or redirect in order to bring the individual's contributions to a higher level of his own potential.

A third facet of the managerial responsibility may seem passive on the surface, but it requires the most sophisticated managerial skills. This is the responsibility to act as a conciliator or—to state it in another way—a juggler between the diverse skills, talents, and performance that contribute to the marketing plan and, in making the ultimate judgment, to separate as far as possible the contribution from the personality. As the gulf continues to deepen between the broadly termed creative and mathematical aspects of marketing, this function may well be the most challenging.—*Evelyn Konrad*

Section 6

Manufacturing

CONTENTS

Organization Planning

Manufacturing Processes

Manpower Planning and Wage Incentives

Cost Reduction

Facilities Planning

Materials Management

Production Control Systems

Materials Handling and Warehousing

Physical Distribution

Industrial Engineering

Plant Engineering

Plant Safety

Industrial Security

Maintenance Management

Quality Control

Operations Research

PERT and CPM

ORGANIZATION PLANNING

Organizations are created to facilitate the accomplishment of a goal by a group of people. Since manufacturing activities have some characteristics in common, it will be useful to examine some general guidelines. However, no two factories, identical insofar as product, machinery, and building are concerned, will have the same organization. No two human beings are identical, and an individual undergoes constant change. Even without external changes, a group of people will exist within an ever changing organizational plan.

Particularly characteristic of manufacturing is the physical proximity of members of its organization; that is, many people work within one building or group of buildings. In addition, with the exception of mining and bulk processing, there is normally a major problem in coordinating a diversity of raw materials, many end products, individual shipments, and customers. The challenge to the industrial organizer is to have his management utilize its labor, material, and capital to produce a desired product at the appropriate time with minimum investment and cost.

Principles of Organization

Discussion of the principles of organization includes the areas of responsibility and authority, coordination, specialization, and line and staff functions.

RESPONSIBILITY AND AUTHORITY

In any organization, it is critical that each individual know to whom and for what he is responsible. In addition, he must be given the authority to carry out those activities for which he is responsible. Ideally, then, an individual should be responsible to only one person, and his authority should be broad enough to permit him to carry out his responsibilities. These ideal relationships are not always possible in practice.

Some companies accept the idea that certain jobs require an individual to report to two supervisors. The controller of a plant or division, for example, may report to the local plant manager and also to the corporate controller. In theory, the specific nature of this reporting may be different; the plant manager bears authority over costs and the day-to-day activities of running a manufacturing operation, while the corporate controller is concerned about reporting and financial matters. Here again, it is not always simple to categorize a given problem.

The classic example of conflict between responsibility and authority relates to a child who is injured on the street. The uninvolved passerby has no authority whatsoever to help the child, nor has he a legal responsibility to give aid. In fact, quite the reverse is true, for if the child suffers additional injury, the good samaritan can be prosecuted. Nevertheless, most of us would feel that in all conscience the passerby should rise above his lack of authority or responsibility and involve himself.

In a well-organized manufacturing plant, each member accepts responsibility somewhat broader than his authority. As a result, if there should be a gap at any time, there will be two people to fill it rather than none at all—and no organization can be planned so perfectly that there will never be a gap.

In general, the higher one's position is in a line type of organization, the greater is his authority. Authority can be delegated down, but responsibility cannot be delegated at all. The chief executive officer is responsible for everything that goes on in a company, although he may not have the authority at a given moment to act because he has delegated the specific authority.

COORDINATION

By and large, if the staff of a manufacturing enterprise is well trained in its specific activities, the real challenge is coordinating these activities to produce a given result. In essence, the object of the manufacturing organization is to enable the manager to coordinate his employees and raw materials to produce a product at the time, place, and cost required. All the details that follow are simply a means to that end.

SPECIALIZATION

Since World War II, industry has been beset by two opposing and almost equal forces: the need for specialization and the requirement to see the total picture. Equipment, processes, and products become more and more complicated and delicate, requiring increasingly specialized skills and knowledge; these tendencies generally result in increasing capital expenditures and somewhat less flexibility for a given plant than might have been the case in the past. High cost of capital and lack of flexibility require the investing company to analyze its markets, forecast economic trends, and understand future labor demands and customer requirements; in short, to have a total qualitative and quantitative understanding of the society.

Today's manager can no longer be the Renaissance man, nor can his subordinates; thus it is essential to organize the manufacturing unit to be, collectively, that Renaissance man.

LINE AND STAFF

Historically, organizations have been essentially line. In line authority there are a supervisor and a subordinate, while staff authority is advisory. The early armies had soldiers reporting to captains; captains reporting to generals; and generals reporting to the king or the commander. Each man carried his own equipment, and the commander could know all there was to know, making a staff superfluous. As technology increased, the supporting services became greater and greater; many armies now have more supporting and collateral personnel than combat troops, and many manufacturing companies have more white-collar workers than production employees. The relationship between line and staff personnel therefore becomes increasingly important.

Inasmuch as each worker must have a supervisor, the line organization is the basic unit of a manufacturing organization. The essential quality of a line supervisor is his leadership capability. Today he must also understand something of production techniques, union contracts and labor relations, cost accounting and production, his own department, and other related matters. Even if time allowed, the supervisor could not be expert in all of these activities. Thus the staff specialist becomes necessary.

Staff activities are of two types: those that support line activities such as production control or industrial relations, and those that require special knowledge not usually found in line personnel such as operations research and special or new tool engineering.

Relationships. The relations between line and staff personnel are often easier to chart than to make use of. Labor relations in a large company, for example, require centralized negotiations with the union; so it is common practice for a trained labor attorney to work with line management in negotiating the contract. But it is the foreman who first encounters the detailed problems; if he fails to solve a grievance, the staff labor-relations man will ultimately become involved. Simple though this may sound, there is a delicate human relationship involved here. The foreman needs to be the boss of his department; the labor-relations man worries about the contract and the law; the plant manager is concerned about production and precedent. To further complicate the picture, a multiplant contract will require a staff man from the home office. Each of these requirements brings with it to the total relationship a possible conflict of interest and endless complications in communication.

Advantages and disadvantages. An organization highly oriented toward staff functions can bring great expertise to a problem, which is an advantage not otherwise obtainable. In addition, staff people can take whatever time the situation demands rather than devote only the time that is then available.

A line-oriented organization has the advantage of simple lines of communication and relatively uncomplicated parameters of authority and responsibility.

In reality, an organization of combination and compromise is required. If the situation demands great technical competence and highly complex control, the emphasis will be on staff. In simpler activities, where cost and speed are important, a tendency toward line organization will prevail.

Structural Design

Factors to be considered in the structural design of an organization are the span of control, delegation of authority, departmentalization, and decentralization.

SPAN OF CONTROL

Ideally, a line factory organization will have two layers: workers and a single manager. In a small, simple concern this is not unusual; however, a single manager can supervise and communicate with only a limited number of subordinates. The actual span of supervisory control varies with the circumstances. That there is finally a limitation on the number of subordinates a man can lead creates a dilemma.

If, for example, a manager is confronted with the problem of organizing 144 men, it may be assumed that an acceptable span of supervisory control is no more than 12; then he will have 12 supervisors, each supervising 12 men. (See Exhibit 6.1.)

If, on the other hand, the acceptable span of control is limited to no more than six men, there will be a first layer of four men each supervising six men, each of whom supervises six more. (See Exhibit 6.2.)

The span of control illustrated in Exhibit 6.1 has the disadvantage of 12 men per supervisor—a number which may seem excessive under a particular circumstance but does provide two advantages over the second arrangement (Exhibit 6.2): First, and probably foremost, there is only one level between the manager and the bottom level, while in the second arrangement there are two intervening levels, thereby increasing the communication problem. The second advantage

Exhibit 6.1

SPAN OF SUPERVISORY CONTROL (12 MEN PER SUPERVISOR)

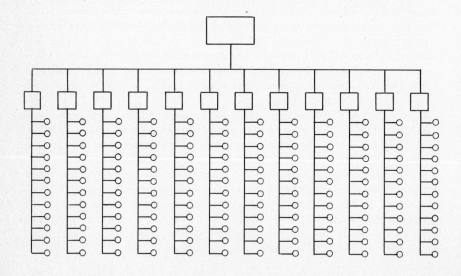

is that it requires only 12 supervisors, while the second arrangement uses 24 to supervise the same number of workers. This implies that the more effective organization will be one in which the greatest feasible number of subordinates will be assigned to each supervisor. The particular circumstances will determine what that number will be, for it depends on the type of work being performed, the amount of supervision a given worker requires, and the capability of the supervisor.

DELEGATING

Historically, the navy has proceeded on the principle that the captain of the ship is responsible for everything that happens aboard. He delegates steering to the helmsman; navigation to the navigator; running the engines to the chief engineer; and so on. That the captain may be sleeping does not relieve him of responsibility for the ship. Although a manufacturing facility may not have the formal organization associated with the navy, the basic principle remains. The plant manager cannot be everywhere in a large facility; he is forced to delegate his authority. He may do so in a number of ways, by departmentalization or by decentralization, but whatever the method, the manager is not relieved of responsibility. It is important, therefore, that the manner in which he delegates his authority be clear and unambiguous; that the subordinate clearly understand the authority that has been delegated to him and his responsibility; and that the manager maintain a continuing surveillance to be certain that actions are being carried out consistent with his desires.

DEPARTMENTALIZATION

If a factory is to be departmentalized, the problem can be approached in a number of ways.

Exhibit 6.2
SPAN OF SUPERVISORY CONTROL (6 MEN PER SUPERVISOR)

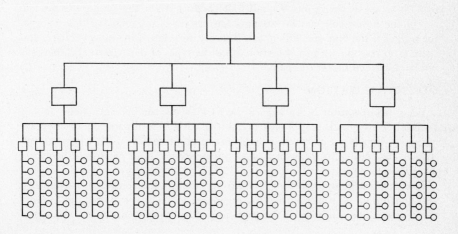

Functional departmentalization. The division of activities may be made on the basis of function (engineering, time study, industrial relations, and others). Manufacturing departments may use this same approach (milling machine, lathe, melt shop, and so forth). This system is quite common and has the virtue of keeping specialists together. It also maximizes the use of equipment or people.

Product or customer departmentalization. It is said that the National Biscuit Company once had a vice president in charge of Fig Newtons. Whether that story was true or not, it is a fact that some products can be so important or complicated that an organization must be built around them. The Department of Defense use of project management is a case in point.

The needs of some types of customers are so different from others that the company may be divisionalized by class of buyer. For example, the same automotive part may require two different plants because one is producing in large quantity for the car builders, while the other plant is making for replacement. Or a department or even a division may be set up for a specific user. Producers of gases—oxygen, for example—frequently have facilities on customers' premises, requiring an organization to cope with each customer.

Manpower departmentalization. The first, simplest, and most obvious organization delineation is by numbers of people. For every 15 workers, perhaps, there would be one supervisor. This system became less important as machines replaced common labor. Workers today are predominantly skilled or at least semiskilled, and their work is normally too diverse to permit them to be led by dividing, as was done in building the pyramids of Egypt. Nevertheless, some activities are best handled in this manner.

Geographic departmentalization. Plants in one region may be grouped as a division to achieve better communication. In some instances, combined shipping is of primary importance; appliances, for which various production facilities are clustered and operated together, are a case in point. Multinational companies often have an overseas division, which is sometimes subdivided into territorial groups.

Organizational goals of departmentalization. The objective of plant management is to make the required quality of product when the product is needed, and at the lowest cost and investment. The system of organization that achieves these goals is the best one. Often, a hybrid organization is the most effective, and there is no reason why a combination of all the types of departmentalization may not be combined in one company.

DECENTRALIZATION

When an operation is too large to be handled by the manager alone, it may be possible to take the approach of putting each subordinate "in business for himself"—that is, to make an activity into a profit center inside a department. This is not feasible in many situations, but under the right conditions beneficial results can be attained.

A company may manufacture pipe fittings, which require casting, galvanizing, and machining. The factory may be organized in such a way that the foundry manager must be competitive, and he is judged by his efficiency independently of the other activities of the factory. He may have under his control the various services required for the foundry, and therefore be a complete profit center that can, in a sense, operate independently of the total company.

This type of organization has the great virtue of putting business judgment at the very place where most expenditures are made, and it permits all levels of management to be conscious of the goals of the total business. It does, however, sacrifice some elegance of organization and often creates some redundancy and competitiveness that can be wasteful. As organizations grow in size the value of decentralization increases, and in the very large corporations it becomes almost essential. Just as efficient state planning for the total economy is beyond the reach of government, so has completely centralized planning been uneconomical for the large company. One of the great management principles of Alfred P. Sloan, Jr., was the decentralization of manufacturing management in General Motors Corporation. General Motors' foundry division is effectively an independent company competing to supply the casting requirements of other divisions of the organization.

USE OF STAFF

As a general rule, staff departments perform at least two functions. First, they provide expert advice and assistance to line managers. Second, they produce certain necessary indirect work (employee insurance records, for example) and statistics required by law or top management. Such work today is continually increasing, and as a result staff groups are becoming less able to cope with their principal mission.

To be effective, staff personnel must be constantly on guard to advise and not command. There is a human tendency for staff to feel they have the answers if only their advice is taken. If this spirit runs unchecked, the plant will be operated from the office, and hostility instead of harmony will ensue.

In a very large organization, staff work can become exceedingly complicated and interwoven in many line and other staff departments. It is here that management must carefully delineate the responsibility and authority of each supervisor to avoid conflict and permit each to accomplish his task.

Human Factors in Organization

In a capitalistic, market-directed society, a factory is established to make a profit; in a government-owned facility the situation is analogous, with the exception that the government directs what is to be made. In either case, the principal purpose of the factory is to convert raw materials into finished or semifinished goods by the use of men and machines. This simple statement expresses goals but does not include some of the limitations and collateral considerations that necessarily arise.

SOCIETAL CONSIDERATIONS

A factory exists in a geographic location and a society, and it must be compatible with its surroundings. If it pollutes the air or water or is dangerous or obnoxious for other reasons, it cannot be tolerated.

In addition to physical considerations, there are many social and economic echoes from the sound of a factory. An industry that is exceptionally seasonal may create a hardship on a community by putting an undue strain on natural resources—water, for example. In short, a factory is part of a community and must, in the long run, operate in harmony with the interests of that community. Good citizenship may not be the purpose of a factory, but it is a limitation on its activities.

BEHAVIORAL ATTITUDES

Once inside the building, a worker or supervisor becomes part of a special society. During working hours, working relationships are superimposed on social relationships. Sometimes they are consistent; sometimes they are in conflict. A manager is responsible for the creation of an atmosphere such that normal human behavior will be directed toward the goals he sets.

In a free country, people must be motivated to accomplish more than minimal requirements. Important though motivation may be at the worker level, it becomes more important and more complicated in supervisors because they must interact with their subordinates and superiors as well as their peers. For these reasons, their attitude, personality, and aspirations will constantly come into play and create an ever changing environment in the factory. Concerning the necessity for cooperation, Chester I. Barnard, in *The Functions of the Executive* (Harvard University Press, 1938), has written:

> An explicit statement on the question of free will, and certainly an avowed discussion of it, is usually to be found only in philosophic or scientific trea- tises. I must state my position because it determines the subsequent treatment in many ways. For this reason I should also add at this time that the exag- geration in some connections of the power and of the meaning of personal choice are vicious roots not merely of misunderstanding but of false and abortive effort. Often, as I see it, action is based on an assumption that indi- viduals have a power of choice, which is not, I think, present. Hence, the failure of individuals to conform is erroneously ascribed to deliberate oppo- sition when they *cannot* conform. When the understanding is more nearly in accordance with the conception of the free will . . . a part of the effort to determine individual behavior takes the form of altering the conditions of behavior, including a conditioning of the individual by training, by the inculcation of attitudes, by the construction of incentives. This constitutes a large part of the executive process, and is for the most part carried out on the basis of experience and intuition. Failure to recognize this position is among the important sources of error in executive work; it also results in disorganization and in abortive measures of reform, especially in the politi- cal field.

SATISFACTION OF NEEDS

The Declaration of Independence did not suggest that the formation of the United States of America would make one happy, but it did propose the promul- gation of an attempt at the pursuit of happiness. So, too, a manager cannot satisfy all the needs of a factory's employees, but a perpetual effort must be made to make each individual feel needed, respected, and important. These needs are often as important as wages and are probably more important than the obvious physical requirements of adequate personal facilities, safety, and heat or air conditioning. Human nature is such that a state of real satisfaction is generally debilitating or unstable, which brings the manager to the problem of change. In most cases, change is required because of outside forces such as new products, new methods, increases or decreases in production, or personnel turnover. In some instances, there is so much change that individuals cannot cope with so many new situations, but the reverse is also true. Insufficient change can create boredom, and in such cases the manager may institute some change as a stimulant; in any event the manager, while attempting to satisfy most human needs, must also create some needs in order to keep his people active and motivated.

INFORMAL RELATIONSHIPS

Any group of people will naturally form social relationships, and some personalities will dominate others. The organization chart prepared by management will rarely follow exactly the social patterns of the members of a group. A man may be selected as a supervisor for perfectly valid reasons—knowledge, reliability, or seniority—but a new, unqualified subordinate may have a stronger personality and become the social leader of the department. Such a situation may or may not create a problem, but it must be recognized for what it is. In many instances, individuals must be changed as a result, or the formal organization chart must be adjusted. One thing is clear, however: a formal organization chart rarely expresses the real day-to-day working relationships of a group.

An outstanding expression of this truth was experienced by a manufacturing vice president who had been sent to manage a newly acquired plant. After talking to the plant manager and superintendent, he despaired of any useful production arising from their efforts. In fact, he was surprised that anything was satisfactorily made, but the fact was that the products were somehow completed. In an effort to learn how this phenomenon was possible, he stopped several workers at their tasks and asked how they handled a problem when it arose. Of the first seven interviewed, six explained that they would ask Herman and do whatever he suggested. The vice president was unable to find Herman's name on the organization chart. After several inquiries he found that Herman was the laboratory assistant in the plating department. Although he had no authority, his integrity and personality made him the obvious person to ask. After eliminating the plant manager and superintendent and installing Herman, the vice president determined that in the future, if he were confronted with a new factory, the first thing he would do was "find Herman." Incidentally, he has been a very successful manufacturing vice president.

MANAGEMENT STYLE

Successful managers do not possess identical personalities. One man can lead by virtue of a deep voice and commanding personality; another because of infectious warmth; a third because of incisive and compelling logic. There are many styles of management. The important factor is not so much the style that is used, but rather the ability to follow through in that style which is natural. It is probably best, therefore, for an individual to manage in the style in which he is comfortable; but it should also be recognized that when there is a change of managers, the style of management and activities will be altered. If for this reason and none other, an organization must change as often as the individual participants change.

Communication Networks

Croesus, a king of Lydia in the sixth century, was fearful of the rise and approach of Persian power from the east under King Cyrus. He consulted the oracle at Delphi for advice and was told that if he crossed the river Halys, which lay between him and Cyrus's Persians, he would destroy a great empire. The oracle, however, omitted to say which empire. Croesus crossed the river and, in doing so, did in battle destroy an empire—his own. There was communication by the oracle, but it was inadequate. Whether it was lacking through the ambiguity of the statement or the wishful thinking of the listener is a moot question; the lesson here is that communication must be carefully handled.

COMMUNICATION CHANNELS

Channels of communication within a factory are many. There are normally standard forms such as requisitions, production orders, shipping documents, and many others. Although these represent the most organized part of factory communication, care must be taken to avoid expensive errors. It is worthwhile, for example, to introduce redundancy so that errors can be observed: A part number may be shown, along with a brief description; either would be sufficient, but if a mistake is made, the odds are that it will be caught because the reader will see an inconsistency.

Oral communication is more susceptible to error, and for several reasons. Spoken English is generally less precise than written English; accents vary, as do outside noise, velocity of speech, and the tendency to use slang. In addition, oral communication requires the hearer to depend on his memory. Nevertheless, oral communication has the virtues of low cost and high speed, and it expresses emotion and response; so it remains the major method of transmitting ideas and instructions.

Whether oral or written, an instruction may be handled as one- or two-way communication. In the first instance, an instruction is given, and the receiver acts. In two-way communication, an instruction is given, and the receiver repeats the instruction or asks questions regarding it before proceeding. The first method is fast and simple but has a fairly wide possibility for error in that it lacks feedback.

HORIZONTAL FLOWS

Although most organization charts imply that communication proceeds from supervisor to subordinate and back again, it is often essential that peers communicate. The foreman of the shipping room and the foreman of the assembly department may, theoretically, report to different supervisors, but it may be essential that they communicate with each other. It is at this point that most organization charts—and people, for that matter—operate less efficiently. The general manager must always be alert to create an atmosphere that encourages horizontal communication without interfering with proper organizational relationships.

EXPEDITORS

In principle, a well-run factory should not require expeditors. Unfortunately, a plant can become so complicated that it is necessary to give the entire system a nudge occasionally to expedite production; whether such a job is oil or sand in the machinery depends largely on the personality of the expeditor.

TYPICAL ORGANIZATION CHARTS

The remaining pages of this subsection are devoted to typical company organization charts (Exhibits 6.3 to 6.11) showing a span of control and reporting relationships for all levels of a manufacturing division.—*R. A. Pritzker*

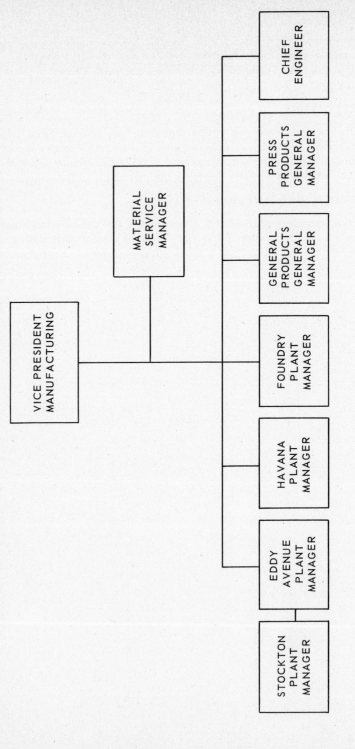

Exhibit 6.3

MANUFACTURING ORGANIZATION CHART

Courtesy of Atwood Vacuum Machine Co.

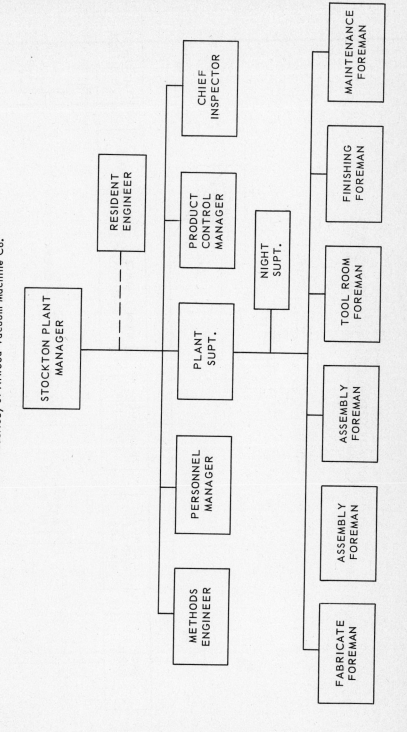

Exhibit 6.4

MANUFACTURING ORGANIZATION CHART
Courtesy of Atwood Vacuum Machine Co.

Exhibit 6.5

MANUFACTURING ORGANIZATION CHART

Courtesy of Atwood Vacuum Machine Co.

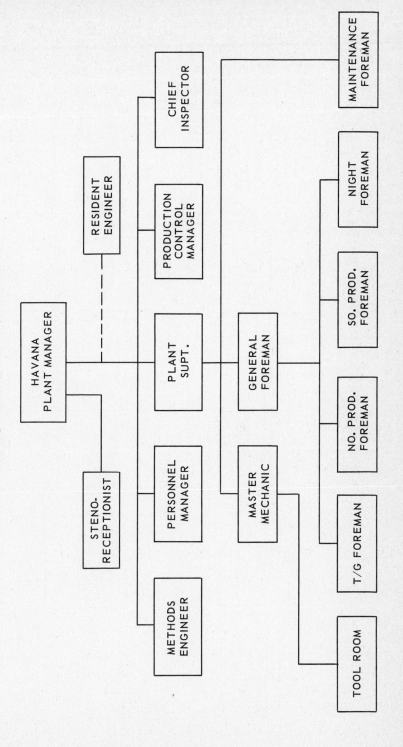

Exhibit 6.6

MANUFACTURING ORGANIZATION CHART

Courtesy of Atwood Vacuum Machine Co.

Exhibit 6.7

MANUFACTURING ORGANIZATION CHART
Courtesy of TRW Inc.

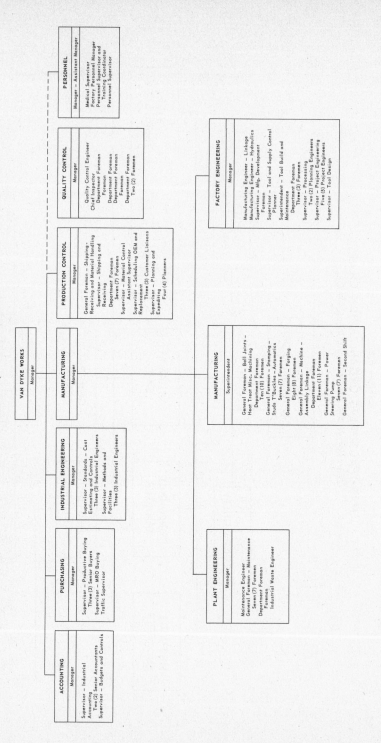

Exhibit 6.8

MANUFACTURING ORGANIZATION CHART

Courtesy of TRW Inc.

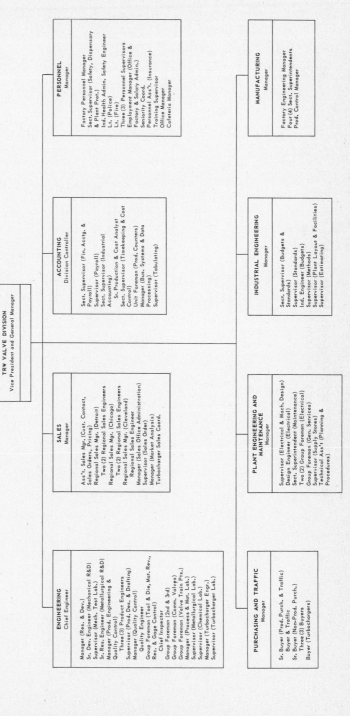

TRW VALVE DIVISION
Vice President and General Manager

ENGINEERING
Chief Engineer

Manager (Res. & Dev.)
Sr. Dev. Engineer (Mechanical R&D)
Supervisor (Mech. Test Lab.)
Sr. Res. Engineer (Metallurgical R&D)
Manager (Prod. Engineering & Quality Control)
Three (3) Product Engineers
Supervisor (Prod., Des., & Drafting)
Manager (Quality Control)
Quality Engineer
Group Foreman (Tool & Die, Mat. Rev., Rec. & Gage Control)
Chief Inspector
Group Foreman (2nd & 3rd)
Group Foreman (Comm. Valves)
Group Foreman (Valve Train Pts.)
Manager (Process & Mat. Lab.)
Supervisor (Metallurgical Lab.)
Supervisor (Chemical Lab.)
Manager (Turbocharger Engr.)
Supervisor (Turbocharger Lab.)

SALES
Manager

Ass't. Sales Mgr. (Cust. Contact, Sales Orders, Pricing)
Regional Sales Mgr. (Detroit)
Two (2) Regional Sales Engineers
Regional Sales Mgr. (Chicago)
Two (2) Regional Sales Engineers
Regional Sales Mgr. (Cleveland)
Regional Sales Engineer
Manager (Sales Office Administration)
Supervisor (Sales Order)
Manager (Market Analysis)
Turbocharger Sales Coord.

ACCOUNTING
Division Controller

Sect. Supervisor (Fin. Acctg. & Payroll)
Supervisor (Payroll)
Sect. Supervisor (Industrial Accounting)
Sr. Production & Cost Analyst
Sect. Supervisor (Timekeeping & Cost Control)
Unit Foreman (Prod. Counters)
Manager (Bus. Systems & Data Processing)
Supervisor (Tabulating)

PERSONNEL
Manager

Factory Personnel Manager
Sect. Supervisor (Safety, Dispensary & Plant Prot.)
Ind. Health Admin. Safety Engineer
Lt. (Police)
Lt. (Fire)
Three (3) Personnel Supervisors
Employment Manager (Office & Factory & Salary Admin.)
Seniority Coord.
Personnel Ass't. (Insurance)
Training Supervisor
Office Manager
Cafeteria Manager

PURCHASING AND TRAFFIC
Manager

Sr. Buyer (Prod. Purch., & Traffic)
Buyer & Traffic
Sr. Buyer (Non-Prod. Purch.)
Three (3) Buyers
Buyer (Turbochargers)

PLANT ENGINEERING AND MAINTENANCE
Manager

Supervisor (Electrical & Mach. Design)
Design Engineer (Electrical)
Sect. Superintendent (Maintenance)
Two (2) Group Foremen (Electrical)
Group Foreman (Gen. Services)
Supervisor (Supply Stores)
Technical Ass't (Planning & Procedures)

INDUSTRIAL ENGINEERING
Manager

Sect. Supervisor (Budgets & Standards)
Supervisor (Standards)
Ind. Engineer (Budgets)
Supervisor (Methods)
Supervisor (Plant Layout & Facilities)
Supervisor (Estimating)

MANUFACTURING
Manager

Factory Engineering Manager
Four (4) Sect. Superintendents
Prod. Control Manager

Exhibit 6.9

MANUFACTURING ORGANIZATION CHART
Courtesy of Borg-Warner Corp.

ROCKFORD CLUTCH DIV. – BORG-WARNER CORP.
JULY, 1966

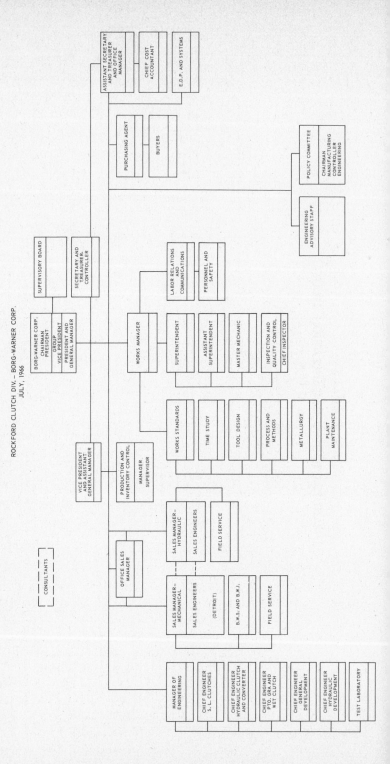

Exhibit 6.10

MANUFACTURING ORGANIZATION CHART

Courtesy of The Algoma Steel Corp., Ltd.

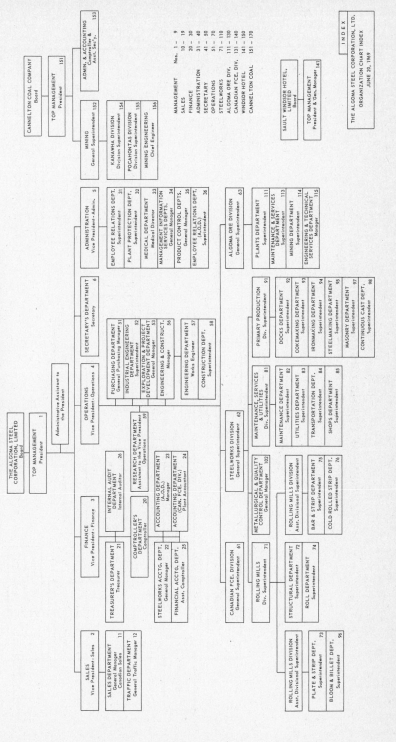

THE ALGOMA STEEL CORPORATION, LIMITED
Board

TOP MANAGEMENT
President — 1

Administrative Assistant to the President

CANNELTON COAL COMPANY
Board

TOP MANAGEMENT
President — 151

ADMIN. & ACCOUNTING
Comptroller & Asst. Sec'y. — 153

MINING
General Superintendent — 152

KANAWHA DIVISION
Division Superintendent — 154

POCAHONTAS DIVISION
Division Superintendent — 155

MINING ENGINEERING
Chief Engineer — 156

INDEX

MANAGEMENT	Nos. 1 – 9
SALES	10 – 19
FINANCE	20 – 30
ADMINISTRATION	31 – 40
SECRETARY	41 – 50
OPERATIONS	51 – 70
STEELWORKS	71 – 110
ALGOMA ORE DIV.	111 – 130
CANADIAN FCE. DIV.	131 – 140
WINDSOR HOTEL	141 – 150
CANNELTON COAL	151 – 170

SAULT WINDSOR HOTEL, LIMITED
Board

TOP MANAGEMENT
President & Gen. Manager — 141

THE ALGOMA STEEL CORPORATION, LTD.
ORGANIZATION CHART INDEX
JUNE 20, 1969

SALES
Vice President – Sales — 2

SALES DEPARTMENT
General Manager
Canadian Sales — 11

TRAFFIC DEPARTMENT
General Traffic Manager — 12

FINANCE
Vice President – Finance — 3

TREASURER'S DEPARTMENT
Treasurer — 21

COMPTROLLER'S DEPARTMENT
Comptroller — 20

INTERNAL AUDIT DEPARTMENT
Internal Auditor — 26

RESEARCH DEPARTMENT
Assistant to the Vice President
Operations — 59

ACCOUNTING DEPARTMENT (A.O.D.)
Manager — 23

STEELWORKS ACCTG. DEPT.
General Manager — 22

ACCOUNTING DEPARTMENT (CAN. FCE. DIV.)
Plant Accountant — 24

FINANCIAL ACCTG. DEPT.
Asst. Comptroller — 25

OPERATIONS
Vice President – Operations — 4

ADMINISTRATION
Vice President – Admin. — 5

EMPLOYEE RELATIONS DEPT.
Superintendent — 31

PLANT PROTECTION DEPT.
Superintendent — 32

MEDICAL DEPARTMENT
Medical Director — 33

MANAGEMENT INFORMATION SERVICES DEPTS.
General Manager — 34

PRODUCT CONTROL DEPTS.
General Manager — 35

EMPLOYEE RELATIONS DEPT. (A.O.D.)
Superintendent — 36

SECRETARY'S DEPARTMENT
Secretary — 6

PURCHASING DEPARTMENT
General Purchasing Manager — 51

INDUSTRIAL ENGINEERING DEPARTMENT
Superintendent — 52

EXPLORATION & PROJECT DEVELOPMENT DEPARTMENT
General Manager — 53

ENGINEERING & CONSTRUCT.
Manager — 56

ENGINEERING DEPARTMENT
Works Engineer — 57

CONSTRUCTION DEPT.
Superintendent — 58

ALGOMA ORE DIVISION
General Superintendent — 63

PLANTS DEPARTMENT
Superintendent — 111

MAINTENANCE & SERVICES DEPARTMENT
Superintendent — 113

MINING DEPARTMENT
Superintendent — 114

ENGINEERING & TECHNICAL SERVICES DEPARTMENT
Manager — 115

PRIMARY PRODUCTION
Div. Superintendent — 91

COKEMAKING DEPARTMENT
Superintendent — 92

IRONMAKING DEPARTMENT
Superintendent — 93

STEELMAKING DEPARTMENT
Superintendent — 94

MASONRY DEPARTMENT
Superintendent — 95

CONTINUOUS CAST DEPT.
Superintendent — 97

MAINTENANCE, SERVICES & UTILITIES
Div. Superintendent — 81

MAINTENANCE DEPARTMENT
Superintendent — 82

UTILITIES DEPARTMENT
Superintendent — 83

TRANSPORTATION DEPT.
Superintendent — 84

SHOPS DEPARTMENT
Superintendent — 85

STEELWORKS DIVISION
General Superintendent — 62

METALLURGICAL & QUALITY CONTROL DEPARTMENT
General Manager — 102

ROLLING MILLS DIVISION
Asst. Divisional Superintendent — 98

CANADIAN FCE. DIVISION
General Superintendent — 61

ROLLING MILLS
Div. Superintendent — 71

STRUCTURAL DEPARTMENT
Superintendent — 72

ROLL DEPARTMENT
Superintendent — 74

BAR & STRIP DEPARTMENT
Superintendent — 75

COLD ROLLED STRIP DEPT.
Superintendent — 76

ROLLING MILLS DIVISION
Asst. Divisional Superintendent — 98

PLATE & STRIP DEPT.
Superintendent — 73

BLOOM & BILLET DEPT.
Superintendent — 96

Exhibit 6.11

MANUFACTURING ORGANIZATION CHART
FENESTRA, A DIVISION OF THE MARMON GROUP, INC.

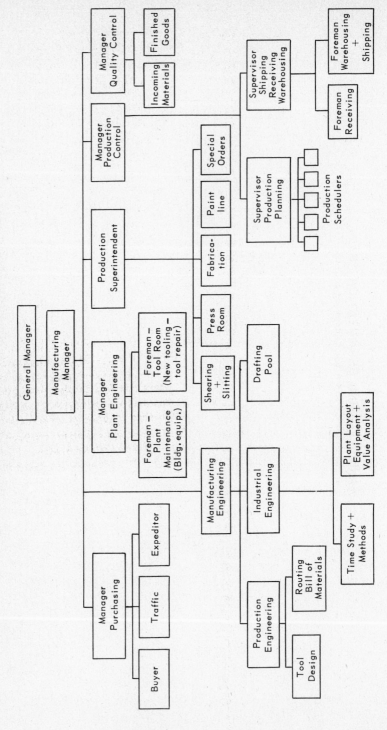

MANUFACTURING PROCESSES

Manufacturing is the organization of productive resources—employees, plant, and equipment—to produce goods. There are three generally classified types of manufacturing: job order, intermittent or serialized, and continuous or automated.

In job order manufacturing, production is in lots as ordered by the customer. This is the work of a jobbing machine shop, for example.

Intermittent or serialized manufacture produces items on internal company order; railroad cars are in this category.

In continuous or automated process manufacture, production is carried on 24 hours a day, and usually, once the item is started into the production flow, it must be completed. Glass and cement are examples of continuous or automated process manufacture.

Each type of manufacture requires different organization and costs as scheduling, paperwork handling, and the like vary from industry to industry.

Production processes fall into two broad classifications: metalworking and non-metalworking.

Metalworking Processes

Metalworking includes casting, forging, forming, machining, heat treating, joining, and surface treating.

CASTING

Casting is the production of a desired shape by the introduction of a molten material into a previously prepared cavity or mold and allowing it to solidify. It is one of the oldest methods of producing metal products, particularly intricate pieces. It is almost as easy to make complex shapes as simple ones. Metals most commonly cast are iron, steel, aluminum, brass, bronze, magnesium, and zinc alloys. Five common factors are encountered in casting.

1. A mold cavity, allowing for shrinkage of the molten metal as it solidifies, must be produced. The mold material must not be too greatly affected by the flow of molten metal into it, and a suitable melting facility providing an adequate temperature and the means of satisfactory quality production at low cost must be available.

2. A satisfactory method of introducing metal into the mold and assuring the escape of all air or gas must be used; trapped air or gas would cause holes in the casting (porosity).

3. Provision for shrinkage without the excessive restraint that causes cracking must be made.

4. It must be possible to remove the casting from the mold. There is no problem when sand molds are used, because the sand breaks away from the solidified metal; but serious problems occur with some other types of molds—permanent molds, for example.

5. Finishing operations must be performed on castings, which adds to the cost.

Sand casting. Of the six major types of casting processes, sand casting is the most widely used and accounts for by far the greatest amount of the total tonnage of castings produced.

Sand casting utilizes sand as a mold material. A new mold must be prepared for each casting. Gravity causes the metal to flow into the mold, and the finished casting varies about 1/16 inch in one foot.

To produce a mold, sand is packed around a pattern in the shape of the desired casting. After the sand has been firmly packed, the pattern is removed, leaving a cavity of the desired shape. A sprue hole is cut for the entrance of the metal into the cavity. After the solidification of the casting, the sand mold is broken up so that the casting may be removed.

The design and selection of patterns are vital to the finished quality and cost of the sand casting. The volume determines whether the pattern should be of wood or of metal: High volume requires metal (aluminum, magnesium, or brass); low volume calls for wood (sugar pine or Honduras mahogany). Wood patterns must be protected by coats of shellac. Metal is much more expensive because finishing work and a master pattern are required. Plastics are being used as pattern material because they are cheaper than metal.

The shrinkage of various metals varies, causing the need for special patterns for each metal. Cast iron, for example, will shrink 1/8 inch per foot, steel 1/4 inch, aluminum 5/32 inch, magnesium 5/32 inch, and brass 3/16 inch. The pattern maker uses special shrink rules to incorporate the desired shrink allowance in the pattern. Master patterns used to make a metal pattern must have double the shrinkage allowance for the metal that is to be poured into the mold. Draft is a taper provided on the pattern to allow drawing from the sand. The draft must run to the parting line where the two parts of the pattern come away from each other. Hand drawing requires more draft than machine drawing because the machine will pull directly away from the sand repeatedly, whereas a hand draw needs more allowance for error. The draft is not usually less than 1 degree or 1/8 inch per foot, with a minimum of 1/16 inch on any surface. The draft should be kept at a minimum to save excessive machining. A finish allowance must be provided on the casting where machining finishes are required. Usually, 1/8 inch is provided, but the allowance may be more or less, depending on the size and type of casting. Sometimes draft alone may be ample machining stock.

Rap allowance may be considered; the pattern may be rapped to loosen it if there is not ample draft, and in such a case it will need to be made smaller in order to allow for rapping before removing it from the sand.

The types of patterns depend upon the number of duplicate castings to be produced and the complexity of the part. A one-piece or solid pattern is the cheapest and simplest to make but produces the most expensive castings. Loose or split patterns are used to produce moderate quantities and usually have doll pins to insure the two halves' matching. The upper half of a pattern is called the cope, and the lower half is called the drag. Matched plate patterns are used to produce large quantities. The cope and drag sections are matched on opposite sides of a plate, and the gate and runner system is integral with the plate. Cope and drag patterns are sometimes mounted on separate plates to achieve high production of small or large castings, since two molders can work on the mold.

Loose-piece patterns are used when it is impossible to provide draft. Loose pieces can be used on any of the other types of patterns also but, of course, would slow the production of units. A pattern with a follow board to form the parting line is used on loose patterns only.

Generous fillets of 1/4 inch or 1/8 inch radius are necessary where sharp corners occur, to prevent shrinkage cracks and stressed intersections. The use of leather or wax for radius filler material is common.

Sometimes metal chaplets need to be used. Their purpose is to cause the thicker sections of the casting to solidify at the same time as the thinner sections. Holes in castings can be cast there by the use of cores. Green sand cores are a part of the mold. Dry sand cores are set in place by the utilization of core prints.

Dry sand cores must possess special properties in order to function properly. They must be hard enough; strong enough for handling while green; permeable; collapsible, to prevent cracking and permit easy removal; highly refractory; smooth-surfaced; and constituted to generate a minimum of gas. Core-making equipment includes dump boxes, split core boxes, metal rods for strengthening thin cores, plates for drying flat cores, dryers for drying intricate cores, vents to allow gases to escape, and core-blowing machines in which the sand is blown in. In this case, the box must be vented to allow the trapped air to escape. Cores are baked in batch ovens or continuous ovens, or even with dielectric. They are then finished and assembled. Sometimes they are baked in half and pasted or wired together and scraped so that the parting lines are smooth; then they are daubed with a refractory paste to fill up any irregular surfaces on the core. Some cores are even dipped for a smoother surface, using a graphite, silica, or mica dipping solution.

Shell molding. The shell-molding process is used for better dimensional accuracy and control. In this process, sand and a plastic binder are dumped into a heated pattern so that a 1/8 inch plastic shell can be cured. The excessive sand is dumped off, and the pattern and shell are placed in the oven for additional curing. The hardened shell is then stripped from the pattern. Two half-shells are clamped or glued together, and the shells are placed in a pouring jacket packed with sand or shot ready for pouring. The metal flows into the mold by gravity, and a new mold must be made for each casting.

The shell process has the advantage of being more accurate because of the use of metal patterns; .003 to .005 inch accuracy can be achieved on small castings. It gives a much smoother casting and is relatively inexpensive equipment for molding, and very complex castings can be made. Low machining costs are the results of the close tolerance casting.

Permanent molding. The necessity of making a new mold for each casting is eliminated through permanent molding. A metal mold is used over and over. Of fine-grain iron or steel, this mold is made in halves and hinged or mounted with a linear motion to open and close. The majority of castings produced from permanent molds are nonferrous, but some are cast iron. Before the molten metal is poured in, the mold is heated to slow the cooling of the molten metal. Usually, a thin refractory coating is placed in the mold. A carbon black coating is added by a torch for cast-iron castings. Dry sand cores can be used.

The advantage of a permanent mold is its low tolerance of 1/64 inch per foot. The necessary special venting and the ability to produce only simple parts are disadvantages.

A variation of permanent molding is slush casting, in which a shell is allowed to solidify inside the slowly rotating mold and the excess molten metal is poured out. There are variations in the wall section, but this type of casting is suitable for ornaments and similar items that do not need a uniform wall section.

Die casting. This is another variation of permanent molding in that a metallic die is used over and over. Only nonferrous metals are used; the metal is forced into the mold under pressure and held during solidification, resulting in very fine sections and detail. The dies are made of alloy steel with one or more cavities. The die is sometimes made of multiple pieces with complicated cores of steel. The dies are expensive, but the parts are inexpensive in volume runs.

The die-casting cycle consists of closing and locking the die, forcing metal into the die, maintaining the pressure, permitting the metal to solidify, opening the die, and ejecting the casting.

Both gooseneck and cold-chamber machines are used. The gooseneck machines are used for materials of low melting point; the gooseneck is submerged in molten metal. The cold-chamber machines require ladling molten metal for each casting, and higher pressures are used and denser structures gained. Bearings, studs, and the like can be placed in the dies and the metal cast around them.

Aluminum, magnesium, and zinc die castings can be held to plus or minus .003 inch per inch, and .025 to .050 inch wall section can be cast.

Centrifugal casting. This method utilizes centrifugal force to thrust molten metal against the surface of the mold. The mold is rotated at 300 to 3,000 revolutions per minute while the metal is being poured, creating a uniform, dense metal structure. The mold is metal, but is without cores. A sand lining is normally used for ferrous metals.

Horizontal or vertical pouring is possible. Horizontal pouring creates a cylinder, and vertical pouring creates a paraboloid.

Pipe, brake drums, and similar products are produced by this method.

Investment casting. The investment-casting process is very old, but it became an industrial production process during World War II. Hundreds of years ago, jewelry was the most common example of investment casting: The ring (or whatever the form to be made) was produced in wax; sand was packed around this wax master pattern; and the metal was poured on the wax so that the wax would melt and run out the bottom of the sand mold and the metal would replace the wax cavity. In modern times, the procedure is more complex because of higher volume, lower cost, and high precision parts. A master pattern is first produced and from it a master die. Next, wax patterns or frozen mercury patterns are made and assembled to a common wax sprue. The assembly, called a cluster, is coated with a thin coat of investment material that is a slurry of a finely ground refractory. The final investment is poured around the coated cluster, and the flask is vibrated to remove the entrapped air and settle the investment material around the cluster. The investment is allowed to harden; the wax is melted to run it out of the mold; the mold is preheated to 1,000° to 2,000° F. to help the metal flow; and the metal is poured, cooled, and removed from the mold.

Some of the advantages of investment casting are as follows: very thin sections (as thin as .015 inch); exceptionally smooth surface finish; .005 to .010 inch casting tolerance can be obtained; and only .015 to .040 of machining stock is required. Most investment castings are less than three inches and under two pounds, but much larger parts are possible.

FORGING

The strength of metal decreases as temperature increases, with the result that metals are easier to form when hot; thus they require less massive and expensive equipment. The grain structure is also refined and improved by hot working at higher temperatures, in which the grain fiber changes to give greater strength in some parts. And hot working allows a desired shape to be obtained. Forging, the most common method, is the localizing of compressive forces to alter hot metals to the desired shape. Hammering or smith forging is the mechanical hammering of a heated part; the accuracy depends on the operator's skill. Drop forging uses closed impression dies in which the excess metal flows out the parting line and the resulting flash is trimmed off. Drop-forging dies contain multiple cavities which involve the edging, fullering or bending, blocking, and the final shape. Steam hammers or board hammers are used in drop forging; an impact forging machine drives the hammers together, catching the piece between them. The drop-forging dies are made of alloy steel and are expensive. To make a part for drop-forging design, the parting line must be in a single plane and at the center of forging. There must be at least 7 degrees draft on the vertical portions of the die, and generous fillets and radiuses with low and wide ribs are required.

Press forging employs a slow, squeezing action to produce much larger forgings. Less draft is required than for drop forging. Press forging is a more accurate method than drop forging, and extremely heavy equipment, such as 50,000-ton presses, is in use. Upset forging increases the width of bar while decreasing the length; cap screws are an example.

Roll forging is used to draw out sections of bar stock in which semicylindrical rolls are used.

Swaging is hammering metal while it is partially confined. Cylinders can be necked down by this method.

FORMING

Rolling is a forming process, as are forging, welding, piercing, drawing, extruding, and spinning. It is used for making such products as plates and bars; some are the end products, but most pieces need further processing. Hot rolling is most used and requires very massive and expensive equipment. In this process, two rolls revolve in opposite directions and are closer together than the metal to be formed, causing a squeezing action. The metal must be uniformly heated for rolling—normally, in a soaking pit in which carbon steel can be heated as high as 2,200° F. It is then finish-rolled at 100° to 200° F. above the critical temperature to prevent cracking.

Continuous mills can run finished plates, bars, and the like, in which each successive roll must turn faster to accommodate the elongation. A speed of 70 miles an hour may be reached at the last roll.

A 3 percent dimensional tolerance in the size of a finished rolled product is normal for hot-rolled products. More or less tolerance is needed, depending upon the type of metal and the size of the piece.

The heating of the metal to make it workable creates the problem of oxidation when it cools. The resultant scale must be removed for some products but is left on as a rust inhibitor for others.

Powder metallurgy. Another means of forming is powder metallurgy; a cold metal powder is pressed into a die and then heated (sintered) at a high temperature. Large quantities of parts can be made economically with this process, and some very difficult pieces can be produced.

Oxide reduction is commonly used to prepare the powders; they are afterward mixed and blended to obtain uniform distribution, coat particles with lubricants, and mix powders of different materials. Water or a solvent may be used to mix better, reduce dusting, and lessen explosion hazards, but powders can be mixed dry. Graphite or stearic acid lubricants reduce die wear and improve flow characteristics.

The powder is pressed by a press of up to 50 tons pressure per square inch. Powder is usually measured into the die by volume but can be weighed to control the quantity of powder, or preformed tablets can be used. Powder flows reluctantly; the compaction of the powder should be uniform over the entire surface to make the pressed part uniformly dense. A double plunger press, which gives a more uniform density, has become the workhorse of the powdered metal industry.

One hundred pieces per minute can be pressed and ejected from a die mechanically, but the dies wear quickly and are expensive to maintain and replace.

Sintering is done in either a batch-type or continuous oven at 70 to 90 percent of the basic metal's melting temperature to diffuse the powdered particles into a single mass. The time period varies from half an hour to several hours. During the sintering process, volatile materials are driven off, leaving a porous part. The porous openings in the metal can be controlled by introducing volatile material and impregnating them with lubricant, thus creating a permanently lubricated bearing.

The sintering atmosphere must be controlled to avoid combustion of the powder or oxidation of the part. Partial sintering is sometimes done to give the piece enough strength to be machined before the final sintering. This practice is useful for metals that are hard to machine.

Sizing and finishing are performed on some parts by coining, a method in which the part is placed in a die and hit with a press to press it to size.

On a powdered-iron part which has a 20,000 tensile strength (in pounds per square inch), an additional 12,000 psi can be achieved by coining. Products made by powdered metallurgy are porous bearings and filters, complex gears, carbide which is difficult to machine, motor brushes, and electrical contacts. The bearings are largest by volume, in which 10 to 40 percent of the volume of the bearing itself is oil.

The advantages of powdered metal are elimination of machining, high production rates, elimination of scrap, production of complex shapes, and wide variations of composition. The disadvantages include low strength, high die cost, high raw material cost, and design limitations.

MACHINING

Desired shape, size, and surface finish can be imparted to metal by metal cutting (machining). Up to 50 percent of the work piece may be removed in machining. Interrelated variables in this process are properties of work material, properties in geometry of tool cutting, and interaction between the tool and the work during the cutting. Work material properties are important because high strength of material causes increased tool and work deflection. Chip formation is most important. This is a shearing action that creates heat through friction. Tool geometry is concerned with chip formation. Direction of cut, cutting-edge position, and tool taper to prevent rubbing are some of the problems. Cutting-tool materials are commonly tool steel, high-speed steel, cast nonferrous stellite, sintered carbides, and bort (industrial diamonds).

Machining is a science that requires much knowledge to shape the myriad of materials now available. Machines, tools, and materials are changing rapidly. A basic knowledge of each of these and their relationship with each other will serve only as a foundation for orienting the many swift developments taking place in the metal-cutting field.

HEAT TREATING

It has long been known that the properties of metals can be changed by heating and cooling the metal. The stability of the metallic properties at various temperatures and rates of cooling can be predicted, and the study of this field has become a science because the physical properties of metals are extremely important to the engineer.

The hardening of steel is the most common form of heat treating. The metal is heated to a high temperature and then rapidly cooled by a quenching material, which may be water, brine, or a hydroxide such as sodium or potassium. The method is to dip the piece into the quench medium or spray the medium on the piece to be quenched. Spraying assures the absence of air pockets, giving a more uniform quench. Oils with a high flash point are used to obtain milder quenches.

Tempering is accomplished after a piece has been hardened. Once the piece is cooled, the hardness is reduced by reheating the part between 400° and 1,200° F. and cooling it again in a controlled atmosphere. A wide range of properties is obtainable by the hardening and tempering process, making possible varied products such as spring steel, dies, and tooling. It is important that the engineer understand the properties obtainable by the heating and cooling of metals so that processing can be achieved without changing the properties—or, if desired, so that processing can be achieved to change the properties for the desired product.

Annealing operations are employed to remove stresses, induce softness, or alter toughness, ductility, or other mechanical or electrical properties. The temperature and cooling rate employed are determined by the purpose of the annealing treatment.

The stress-relieve anneal is often employed to remove stresses from welded structures or castings. This is done by heating for several hours at temperatures from 1,000° to 2,000° F., followed by slow cooling.

Surface hardening is achieved by various treatments. In one treatment, carbon is added to the surface so that the steel will be hard on the outside when heated and cooled yet the interior steel piece will still be soft and tough. Another surface-hardening process is nitriding, in which special steels containing aluminum, chromium, molybdenum, or other metals that will form nitrides are used. In still another method, the surface of the metal is heated by electricity or oxyacetylene flame so that only the surface temperature is raised. The work is then quenched rapidly so that the surface is hardened but the core remains soft.

JOINING

Metal joining is done by welding. A weld is a uniting of two pieces of metal into a single piece. Heat and pressure are used together or separately, depending upon the metal properties and end use of the part.

Forge welding is an ancient method in which two pieces are heated and hammered together as the blacksmiths do it. Die welding is useful in the production of pipe manufacture; the flat stock is heated and drawn through a die which forms the pipe and provides pressure on the two butted edges, causing a weld. Cold welding is a process that uses high pressures to bond small parts.

Gas welding came about when oxyacetylene gas was developed to produce a temperature of 6,300° F. This temperature is easily adjustable downward, making it easy to melt thick or thin metals so that they fuse together. Gas welding melts the metals at the point to be joined; pressure is not necessary. Disadvantages of this method are contamination and distortion created by localized heat and flame.

Electric (arc) welding employs an electric arc maintained between the work and an electrode. Alternating or direct current is used. A carbon arc is used for cast iron, copper, and galvanized steel in a process for which the arc is solely a heat source and a filler wire is used when needed to fill a void between the two metals. Metal arc welding uses a metal rod and supplies heat and filler material. The rods, normally, are coated with a flux material.

Inert gas metal arc welding is done by shielding with an inert gas such as helium or argon. Nonconsumable metal electrode welding utilizes the tungsten rod and inert gas shield for welding materials such as magnesium. Atomic hydrogen welding utilizes an alternating current arc between two tungsten electrodes. Hydrogen is fed through the holders so that it is disassociated in the arc, combining with the base metal to give off a high heat. This method is well suited for high-alloy steel welding.

Submerged arc welding maintains an arc beneath a granular flux. The flux is put on just ahead of the copper-coated electrode to give good shielding and, consequently, quality welds achieving up to 30 inches per minute of welding in a one-inch plate.

Inert gas shielded tungsten arc spot welding utilizes inert gases to keep the arc from being consumed.

Thermit welding does not generally employ pressure but a chemical reaction in which the liquid metal supplies the heat and filler. One part aluminum and three parts iron oxide are burned at a temperature above 5,000° F. This method is rarely used, but it may be the only way of welding a very large casting that has been cracked or broken.

Soldering is another form of joining in which coalescence does not take place. Soldering is achieved at below 800° F. The solders are alloys of tin and lead. The higher percentage of tin, the greater the fluidity. The surfaces must be very clean for soldering; must be lapped, not butted; and a flux must be used. The greatest strength achieved with solder is 250 pounds per square inch.

In all welding and soldering, fluxes aid the joining by dissolving surface oxides, preventing oxidation during heating, and promoting the flow by lowering the surface tension of molten metal. Residual flux remaining after the use of flux must be removed from the work piece to prevent corrosion. Cleanliness of the metals before and after welding is essential to good products.

COLD WORKING

Cold working is the plastic deformation of materials below the recrystallization temperature. Squeezing, bending, and shearing are common cold-working methods; they require expensive equipment but give better accuracy, smoother finish, and better productivity than hot working, and without requiring additional finish. Extrusion, riveting, staking, peening, burnishing, hobbing, coining, and cold heading are all squeezing processes.

Bending is plastic deformation about a linear axis.

Shearing is a method of cutting sheet or plate without burning or chips. Deformation is severely localized, and when 10 to 40 percent of metal thickness is deformed, it exceeds the shear strength. Slitting is a shearing action, as are piercing and blanking. Piercing and blanking also include lancing, perforating, notching, nibbling, chafing, trimming, cutoff, and dinking.

SURFACE TREATING

Cleaning and smoothing methods include abrasive blasting for removing sand or scale; 60 to 100 pounds per square inch of air is used for ferrous metals and 10 to 60 pounds per square inch for nonferrous. Clean, sharp-edged silica sand or steel grit makes less dust, cleans faster, and rounds the edges considerably.

Tumbling is a means of removing dirt, fins, and other contaminants by placing slug, sand, or sawdust in with the parts and rotating. This is inexpensive, and it may be done wet, which will improve the smoothness of the finished product.

Belt sanding gives a smooth flat surface; wire brushing with a high-speed rotary brush gives another type of finish; barrel rolling is a cutting-down operation using acid, sawdust, or slugs and actually cuts down the part. Buffing is a means of polishing surfaces with a ferrous oxide rouge to improve the sheen. A similar finish is achieved by barrel burnishing, using rounded pins, balls, and the like, rotating them with the parts to peen surfaces.

Vapor degreasing is a method of cleaning by solvent vapor. Alkaline cleaning is used extensively; emulsifiable solvent cleaning is used where alkaline cannot be. Pickling is the use of heated diluted acid to remove oxides only.

FINISHING

Painting is done by dipping, spraying, and brushing; adequate ventilation is needed because paint is a fire hazard. Paint is applied in coats of thousandths of an inch thickness per coat. When parts are atomized by air or dipped, a superior finish is achieved. Drying time may be decreased by baking.

Hot dip coatings—galvanizing and tin plating—are other means of finishing, as are phosphate coatings. One such coating is parkerizing, which produces a corrosion-resistant coating .0015 to .0030 inch thick.

Blackening is done to make steel rust-resistant. The part is heated to 1,200° F. for one and one-half hours in a spent carburizing compound and quenched in oil. There are several electrolytic finishes also that add a coating of some non-ferrous metal to the surface to improve appearance, reduce corrosion, or inhibit rust.

Nonmetalworking Processes

Pieces produced from all types, sizes, and shapes of materials usually pass through an assembly area where the pieces are put together into the final product.

ASSEMBLY

The assembly department layout is either for batch, continuous, or automated assembly. Movements of materials to and from the area, storage at the area, and movement of the finished product away from the area must be carefully planned for in the assembly area layout.

Most assemblies are made with hand tools that require skilled labor. More and more automated assemblies are being made, however, as product volumes increase and new assembly machinery technology is available.

PROCESS INDUSTRIES

There are several plants—primarily chemical—that convert basic materials into other, usable forms; they are known as process industries. The basic materials are heated or cooled or mixed with other materials until the final product is achieved at the end of the process and is packaged for transporting and handling to its end use. Most plastic resins are produced in a process industry.

Plastic molding. Most plastics are organic substances containing hydrogen, oxygen, carbon, and nitrogen in resin form that can be rolled, molded, extruded, or cast. The properties of plastics can be altered by adding fillers, colors, lubricants, and plasticizers. Some of these materials aid the molding process; others improve the physical properties of the finished part.

Thermoplastic plastics can be reheated and reused, but thermosetting plastics cannot be.

Injection molding is a low-cost, common method of molding thermoplastic materials. The material is mixed, fed into a heater (gas or electric), and injected into the mold cavities in a molten state but under high pressure. The mold halves are then cooled rapidly with water, and the solidified plastic form is ejected from the mold. Excess flash is removed, and the part or product is ready for use within seconds. Thermosetting materials can be injection-molded for some applications.

Blow molding of thermoplastic materials is done by extruding a cylinder of material between two mold halves, clamping the halves together, blowing air into the plastic cylinder through a needle to force the plastic out against the mold halves, cooling the molds, and unclamping and trimming the finished part—also completed within seconds. Plastic baseball bats are commonly produced by this method.

Plastic films and sheets are rolled on a calender to the proper gauge, cooled, cut to size, and rolled or stacked.

Plastic tubing and other cylindrical shapes are extruded by forcing heated material out of a die onto a table or conveyor, where it is cooled by air or water spray.

Transfer molding, cold molding, casting, and machining are other methods of forming plastics to desired shapes for special uses.

Woodworking. Wood is a soft natural material to be shaped into a useful piece. Machinery is employed for high-production items, but many useful items can be produced with hand-powered cutting and shaping tools.

A wide range of hardness and toughness is provided by the many varieties of wood. Each type of wood has a grain which must be considered when working it, because wood tends to split with the grain.

Sealers provide a surface for varnish, paint, or other final finish.

Adhesives bond layers of similar wood together (plywood) or bond dissimilar woods for decorative pieces.

PACKAGING

Packaging is increasingly important to all types of products, whether they are intended for a consumer or an industrial customer. Consumers want their purchases to look new when they receive them, and a package serves this purpose. An industrial customer wants special packaging for convenient handling in its plant. Whatever the reason for its use, packaging is necessary; ideally, it becomes part of the assembly line, where the package can be added with minimal additional handling.

Repackaging is also necessary when packages have been damaged or opened for inspection.

Tools, Jigs, and Fixtures

Each industry, whether chemical, refining, paper, pottery, or textile, has its own variety of tools for its own kinds of production. Each of these industries will have common tooling used in the maintenance of plant and equipment. Different industries may have basic machine tools—lathes in the metalworking industry, for example. However, the arbors, cutting tools, drill bits, and other parts required by a basic machine tool are the subject of discussion here, rather than the machine tools or productive pieces of equipment.

CLASSIFICATION

Tools are difficult to classify because of their many possible uses. A jig is a tool that clamps the work and guides other tools in performing a cutting operation. A fixture is a tool that holds work while machining operations are being performed on it. General classifications are in use among industries. However, each plant will probably have its own classification system, depending upon its tool storage and control practices. Measuring gauges are often included with the tool categories, or they may be excluded.

STANDARDIZATION

Tool standardization is increasingly important in consequence of the complexity of industries. Standardization reduces the number of tools stored; it also reduces the clerical and engineering work required to maintain drawings and records of the various tools. As a plant grows, tool standardization becomes more desirable and will support an intensified tool standardization effort at some point in its growth.

STORAGE AND CONTROL

The location, quantity, and condition of tools are important to efficiency. Planned storage and control of tools can raise efficiency. First, a tool room should be maintained that will control the location and condition of the tools as they are moved from one location to another and as they are used for different operations. Each operation should have specific tools called for, and the tool room should be informed before the job so that the tooling will be ready prior to its need on the shop floor. The tool room should hold the workmen responsible for all tools allocated to them and used by them. Maintaining tool records of each tool also assists in developing historical costs and performance of tools which will aid in future standardization decisions.

Production Systems

An ideal production system will have the right material at the right place and the right time, and the right number of man-hours and the right number of machine hours to meet the completion schedule. The thinking through of all the detailed steps necessary to achieve this end, with a communication network to relay the thought-through information to all parties concerned, is vital to an efficient operation. The degree of success with these two essentials will determine to a large extent the degree of success of the plant. The thinking through is reduced to the communication tools of written factory orders, work-in-progress information, and the end-of-the-line report on completed units produced. The finest plant building with the newest, most modern machine tools may be extremely inefficient if it has no adequate production system. Some very old and antiquated plants are competing with new and modern ones because the antiquated plants do have adequate production systems.

FACTORY ORDER

The factory order tells operating personnel which items are required and at what time. Written information is used to avoid possible errors. It contains information regarding the drawings, tooling, and so forth that are needed to produce parts or complete assemblies satisfactorily.

WORK-IN-PROGRESS INFORMATION

Feedback on all shop operations should be handled as quickly as possible. Feedback every hour will help production scheduling personnel to adjust their planning, and it will help production supervision to take action before serious problems arise. Work-in-progress information can be fed back through various communication media—telephone, TelAutograph, loudspeaker call-in systems— or merely by word of mouth from the foreman to the scheduling personnel. Information must be accurate so that action can be taken with minimum delay.

IN-PLANT COMMUNICATION

Communication and understanding are interdependent. A myriad of details must be understood by the workers at all levels.

Written instructions are issued in many forms to communicate the requirements of each task. Blueprints, shop orders, route sheets, set-up cards, job descriptions, and methods sheets are only a few of the written means of communication used by most manufacturing operations. Oral orders are often used successfully in small plants; but as operations become more complex, written information is needed to reduce errors and insure repeatable performance.

—R. E. McCoy

MANPOWER PLANNING AND WAGE INCENTIVES

The objective of manpower planning is to achieve the most effective and economical use of employee skills, efforts, and abilities in accordance with present and planned operating conditions.

Manpower Planning

Two basic factors in regard to manpower planning must be known in advance. They are the human skills required and the human skills available. Each must be measured in terms of the time available for productive use.

REQUIRED ABILITIES

The skills and abilities required are determined by the nature of the manufacturing operation itself. There must be appraisal of available equipment, job methods, quality requirements, normal working conditions, and man-hours required to meet varying production schedules established from volume requirements and product delivery dates.

AVAILABILITY OF SKILLS

The skills and abilities available must be determined by evaluating and appraising the employees in terms of available skills, knowledge, physical abilities, and job responsibilities.

MAN-HOURS REQUIRED

The man-hours of abilities required are determined from job process sheets, productive job standards, measured nonproductive work, labor variance data, production requirements (per order and per period), available equipment, and delivery schedules.

Job process sheets describe the operations sequences on the tools and equipment required.

Productive job standards, when multiplied by the volume requirements, establish the productive labor time needed. The addition of the predictable measured indirect labor hours (such as set-up, machine maintenance, and so forth) and the percentage of time required for nonproductive labor variances resulting from waiting for work, training, temporary methods allowances, and similar factors will determine the expected man-hours required at a normal performance level.

The required man-hours can be established by operation, cost center, department, or machine. These in turn can be easily expressed in terms of required skills and abilities to the same degree of accuracy.

MAN-HOURS AVAILABLE

The man-hours of skills and abilities available are described in the job evaluation plan, payroll earnings efficiencies, and employment records.

The job descriptions of the job evaluation plan should describe the job requirements, provide an employee performance efficiency list, and state the potential improvement to be expected over and above the schedule developed from the job standards. Employment records will indicate available skills not in active use which may be saved for emergency or peak periods.

The man-hours of available skills can be determined by multiplying the number of employees who have the required abilities by the working hours available on the particular machine or in the work center, department, or plant.

PROBLEM ANALYSIS AND SOLUTIONS

Planning and administering a manpower plan and schedule are carried out as in operating a straight-line, paced conveyor system. But here it becomes apparent that perfection in balance can never be achieved; it can only be approximated. In scheduling manpower, there is always a bottleneck or critical position which limits or restricts every other phase. The major bottlenecks encountered in manpower planning and scheduling are a critical machine or process, a limited number of specific job skills, limited facilities and space, and uncontrollable production requirements. It is obvious that a manpower scheduling plan designed to improve the complete function must concentrate on minimizing the effect of any bottlenecks indicated by preplanning and analysis.

MINIMIZING BOTTLENECKS

The most common methods of minimizing the effects of manpower bottlenecks are overtime; extra shift operations; scheduling of longer runs to minimize lost productive time caused by set-ups, job change-over, and the like; provision of relief operators; methods and job improvement; and wage incentives. Decisions as to which of these solutions is most effective are based on tangible economic considerations, available personnel, and—in some instances—labor-management agreements.

The additional cost of overtime can be readily calculated and evaluated in terms of its effect on product cost. The addition of an extra shift can be considered in terms of the available personnel who are capable of handling the operation and in terms of the increased operating expenses caused by extra supervision and staff personnel required. The use of longer runs per job order can be evaluated in terms of added inventory costs, additional storage space requirements, and the increase in invested capital requirements. The use of relief operators to provide greater use of productive machine time necessitates consideration of the available qualified personnel and the added labor cost. Increased job efficiency and performance created by means of job methods improvements and an effective wage incentive plan are obvious answers to the improvement of productivity and the operation of manpower planning and scheduling systems. If an effective wage incentive system is in operation, the major portion of the technical details necessary for the development of a sound system is already available.

Many manpower bottlenecks are caused by unique operations or machines requiring long learning times. These are inevitably long, complex operations. Frequently, such operations can be broken into a series of less difficult operations which are easier to learn and require simple tools and machines. While the ultimate labor cost for the series of operations may be greater than that of the original complex task, the effect on productivity and reduced unit cost may be sufficiently great to justify the increase in direct labor cost.

In many seasonal industries, the characteristic job skills are required for only a portion of the year. To hire skilled help for seasonal work is difficult under most situations and almost impossible during periods of labor shortage; furthermore, such practices usually involve major expense for hiring and training. Careful consideration should be given to evaluating these costs and comparing them with the costs of maintaining a stable, year-round force that may on occasion be called upon to perform make-work duties. Properly planned, these make-work occupations can produce results valuable in the overall administration of the business.

Wage Incentives

A wage incentive plan is a wage payment system that offers employees an opportunity to increase earnings by better-than-expected performance.

ECONOMIC VALUE

The economic value of incentives to management and labor is widely recognized. The accompanying tabulation summarizes the production increases that can be expected from the application of a sound and effective wage incentive system to work currently paid on a nonmeasured day-work basis. (These findings apply to labor-controlled operations only.)

Type of Production

	Highly Varied (Percent)	Varied (Percent)	Mass-Produced (Percent)
Average expected production increase	105	80	47
Average reduction in unit direct labor costs	40	30	20
Average reduction in unit overhead costs	80	70	60

It is of course equally important to consider the losses that will be suffered by improper operation of a wage incentive system. Actual appraisals of more than 50 wage incentive plans currently in use indicate the following losses caused by such improper operation. (These are indexes only but highlight areas for investigation and improvement in existing wage incentive systems.)

1. Seven cents out of every direct labor dollar is lost through improper rate setting.

2. Three cents out of every direct labor dollar is lost because of faulty timekeeping, inaccurate piece counting, and similar errors.

3. Twelve out of every 100 documents necessary to pay incentives contain arithmetical errors. These costs average .2 cent out of every dollar.

4. Unmeasured work performed by incentive operators costs 25 to 250 percent more than it would if it were properly placed on incentive.

5. Fifty to 80 percent of labor grievances are owing to improper control of incentive plans.

Where a moderately effective wage incentive plan has been in use, its abandonment in favor of a nonincentive wage system has been found to have the effects shown in the following tabulation. (These figures are applicable only to labor-controlled operations rather than those controlled by equipment or processes or where wage limitations on incentive earnings have been in effect.)

	Expected Loss of Production	
Type of Work	With Measurement and Control (Percent)	Without Measurement (Percent)
Highly repetitive	36	43
Semirepetitive	44	58
Nonrepetitive	47	59

MOTIVATION

The key words in the definition of wage incentives are "opportunity" and "motivate." An incentive system that, on the contrary, is based on real or imagined penalties rather than opportunities is usually ineffective, for it is rarely accepted and operated with the full cooperation of the employees. In fact, a major problem in gaining the acceptance and use of wage incentive plans is the widespread opinion that incentive systems penalize and restrict rather than offer additional opportunities.

To motivate employees, an incentive system must meet the following criteria: (1) the earnings opportunities must be sufficiently attractive; (2) the basis and the methods used for determining the rewards must be understandable and acceptable to the employees; (3) the rewards must be considered as commensurate with the extra efforts and abilities expended by each employee; and (4) the employees must be protected against conditions beyond their control. Unless every aspect of the wage incentive system meets these criteria, it will not function properly.

OPPORTUNITY

The attractiveness of the wage rewards is inevitably measured by employees in terms of possible addition to their total pay; therefore, the earnings opportunity must exist in (1) the performance standards themselves and (2) the percentage of incentive opportunity available during the total pay period.

The average earnings opportunity for a good incentive performance based on measured standards should be at least 25 percent over the day-work earnings level. Thus an employee working completely on measured standards could expect to increase his pay by that percentage by providing a good incentive performance for the full period. It should be emphasized, however, that 25 percent is the average expected opportunity. As individual skill and effort vary, so will individual earnings potential.

No limits should be placed on incentive earnings; limited opportunity will result in limited performance. Exceptional operational skills exist in many people; these people should be encouraged to use their talents to their fullest capacity and should be rewarded for them.

Adequate incentive opportunities must also be available. Even though the performance standards themselves offer a provable 25 percent incentive opportunity, the total earnings potential for a pay period may be insufficient to motivate the employee if too few hours of incentive work are available. For example, if only 20 percent of the hours worked by an employee offer incentive opportunity, his potential payment earnings through the incentive plan will be only 5 percent greater than his guarantee.

EMPLOYEE ACCEPTANCE

Each incentive employee must fully understand the principles, policies, and practices of the incentive system if he is to accept it, have confidence in it, and be motivated by it. Lack of understanding will result in unavoidable malpractices, earnings inconsistencies, and operational errors which, in turn, will destroy confidence in the incentive plan and lead to its inevitable destruction.

An employee who works on the incentive system must thoroughly understand how his incentive standards are set; the method to be followed in order to meet and surpass the standards and produce a quality part; and the responsibilities and activities covered by the standards, as well as those that are not included. And, finally, he must be able to calculate his incentive earnings in order to verify the accuracy of his incentive pay.

Each of these requirements is of vital importance. For example, the incentive standard is usually based on a specified job method that must be followed if the standard is to be valid. If the proper method is not followed, the standard may not be achievable and/or the quality may be improper. In either event, the employee's earnings will suffer.

Job incentive standards seldom—and should not—include allowances for unpredictable, substantial variations. When such variations from normal conditions occur, they must be compensated for, over and above the established standard. If they are not, the employee's incentive earnings will be adversely affected. If the employee knows what is and what is not included in the incentive standard, these variances can be brought to the supervisor's attention when they occur, and temporary allowances or adjustments can be made to compensate for the unavoidable condition. Hence the incentive opportunity will always be available and the motivation provided by the incentive system will continue to exist.

It is equally important that the employee be able to determine, by personal calculation, how effectively he is operating and earning. He is thus in a position to check and verify the pay he receives and to determine how well he is doing at any particular time during the pay period. This, in turn, lends further stimulus and motivation to increased performance.

INDIVIDUAL PERFORMANCE

The incentive opportunities offered by a wage plan must be understood and accepted as being commensurate with extra performance. This relationship can be easily recognized if the incentive system is applied to individual performance, for an employee working on an individual incentive fully realizes that his earnings are a direct and personal reward for his own efforts and are not shared with or provided by others. Consequently, the greatest incentive pull exists when the incentive is applied to the individual employee.

PRODUCTIVITY STANDARDS

The most widely used incentive plans are based on productivity. For such plans, a standard of productivity is established that can be met by a qualified operator working at a normal or day-work level of effort. Performance standards are usually expressed in terms of money, time, and/or number of units produced. Standards so established can be exceeded when the operator exerts better than normal skill and/or effort.

Piecework. If money standards are used, the incentive system is known as piecework. Under a piecework system, the standard of performance is expressed as dollars or cents per unit produced, such as 2 cents per piece or $2 per 100 pieces. The employee is paid this fixed amount of money for the total number of units produced in one day's time. Under a piecework plan, the employee's earnings increase in direct proportion to his production. The unit labor cost is constant for normal or better-than-normal performance.

Standard hour system. A variation of piecework is the standard hour system. Here the basis for performance is the standard hours or time allowed to produce the unit or product. To calculate incentive earnings, the units produced by an employee are multiplied by the standard allowed hours per unit. The result is the standard hours earned by the employee. These hours are then multiplied by the employee's hourly rate of pay, thus determining his incentive earnings. The standard hour system, like piecework, provides a fixed unit labor cost for normal or above-normal performance. Thus an employee's earnings increase in direct proportion to his productivity.

There are many variations of the basic standard hour incentive system; usually, they have been designed and installed to compensate for measurement and/or incentive control problems or to provide a strong incentive to meet and surpass the normal performance level. The Halsey and Rowan plans are typical of the first of these variations. They are used primarily where the time standards are estimated and unrefined or where close control of manufacturing variance cannot be maintained.

The Gantt task and bonus plan and the standard time performance plus plan are variations of the basic piecework and standard hour systems. Both offer a strong additional incentive to meet the established performance levels at which the direct incentive begins.

Halsey plan. The Halsey plan shares the time saved between the employee and the company; hence, excessive earnings resulting from very liberal standards are minimized. Earnings are calculated according to the following formula:

$$[\text{Time Taken} + F\,(\text{Time Allowed} - \text{Time Taken})] \times \text{Hourly Rate} = \text{Earnings}$$

F, the incentive factor, is usually .5, but other values can be and are being used.

Rowan plan. The Rowan plan offers a bonus on the amount of time saved. The theoretical maximum saving in time is, of course, 100 percent or twice the guaranteed earnings. The formula used is as follows:

$$\left[\text{Time Taken} + \text{Time Taken}\left(\frac{\text{Time Allowed} - \text{Time Taken}}{\text{Time Allowed}}\right)\right]$$
$$\times \text{Hourly Rate} = \text{Earnings}$$

Gantt plan. Under the Gantt plan, a low guaranteed rate is offered for substandard performance. Upon achievement of the normal performance level, a higher hourly rate of pay is awarded, becoming the basis for the calculation of all above-normal incentive earnings.

Standard time performance plus plan. A higher hourly rate of pay is offered under the standard time performance plus plan than under the Gantt plan. The minimum rate is usually the going rate for the proper class of work in the area. A more moderate bonus, up to 10 percent, is offered for achieving and surpassing the standard. Once standard performance is achieved and surpassed, incentive earnings are calculated at the higher day rate. In both systems, unit labor cost is calculated at the higher of the two rates.

These plans and various modifications of them have been employed where a substantial increase in productivity is required in order to meet the properly established performance standards. The additional bonus makes such plans more appealing to employees because it rewards them for the initial increase in productivity necessary to reach the level at which the incentive pay begins.

It should be emphasized that an infinite number of mathematical formulas can be used; most of the existing formulas have been tailored to meet a particular set of conditions. However, with the increased accuracy and availability of new and effective wage control techniques and procedures, the administrative and technical shortcomings of the past that made necessary these variations to the basic standard hour incentive system have been eliminated or at least minimized.

GROUP INCENTIVE SYSTEMS

The various wage incentive plans previously described are most often used for individual wage incentives. However, operating conditions frequently make the use of individual incentives impractical. Where this is true, a group payment plan may be advisable or necessary. If so, it is equally applicable.

A group incentive system is a system applied to a group of employees working in a common geographical location, on a related type of work, or on an interrelated activity. Its basic purpose is to enable those participating in the group to pool their efforts and performance and then equitably share the incentive earnings of the group.

One such application is made to paced conveyor lines or machine-controlled operations in which the production is controlled by the equipment. The group system gives employees on such work an opportunity to share the work and share equitably in any incentive earnings. A second instance in which a group incentive system is useful is in its application to activities, such as heavy maintenance or construction tasks, where a group of craftsmen may handle a major assignment collectively. In such instances it is impractical—if not impossible—to specify, measure, and control the individual job assignments; hence, the total job must be measured in terms of labor content, and the detailed sharing of the work is determined by the employees on the job. A third instance is a short-run machine group, in which the greater part of the work of each employee is composed of set-up time, machine attendance, troubleshooting, and the like, making it impossible to establish and control a specific method and a precise standard for each individual job for each individual employee.

The determination of efficiency (incentive) earnings is the same for a group system as it is for an individual incentive plan. The time earned by the group is determined by multiplying the established standards by units produced. Extra allowed time, such as waiting for work, is added to the group incentive time earned. The total earned hours thus determined are divided by the hours worked by the group members to determine a group efficiency. Each group member's pay is calculated by multiplying his individual hours worked by his individual hourly rate and multiplying the result by the earned group efficiency.

Wherever possible, groups should be limited to 15 or fewer employees in order to make the individual incentive motivation direct and recognizable to each and all. Under the proper conditions, the group system will provide a highly practical and effective method, satisfactory to employees and company alike, for paying labor incentives.

OVERALL BONUS PLANS

There is an infinite variety of overall bonus plans based on productivity, profits, savings, and/or combinations of the three. Examples are the well-known Scanlon plan, the Kaiser plan, and similar systems which are, in effect, profit-sharing arrangements. (Excellent source material describing many of these plans in detail is available.) It is imperative, however, that a plan of this type truly reflect the problems and conditions in the plant or company to which it is to be applied.

PROBLEM AREAS

Contrary to popular belief, incentive systems do not police themselves. They must be carefully established and even more carefully maintained by constant audits and checks if they are to remain effective. If these precautions are not taken, the systems will quickly deteriorate, and as a result serious labor relations problems and equally serious cost problems will result. The major problem areas encountered in wage incentive operations are inconsistency of standards, improper control of job variances, and inadequate incentive coverage. Each of these problem areas contributes to the deterioration of the others; unless they are constantly policed, the incentive system will deteriorate. When deterioration occurs, its effects on other important areas of management can be—and usually are— more serious than the obvious labor relations problems created.

If the incentive standards are inconsistent, their use for machine scheduling, departmental manning, production planning, inventory control, and the like will create serious errors. The standard costs of given products (if based on inconsistent production standards which are part of the incentive system) will be equally inconsistent, resulting in equally serious effects on pricing, profit determination, and marketing policies. They will also result in erroneous decisions in purchasing, equipment selection, plant layout, and the like.

A wage incentive system properly established and maintained is one of management's best assurances of the validity of the basic information it must use in most of the management functions and activities. Since employee earnings are directly in question, a constant check of standards and variance control is maintained throughout the organization. Hence wage incentives properly used are a most valuable tool of management, serving many other activities as well as employee motivation.

STANDARDS MAINTENANCE

To develop and continue to maintain consistent standards, the following factors must exist: a consistent technique for setting all standards; production standards based on specific, predescribed job methods and quality standards; an established, acceptable procedure for changing standards that are affected by creeping methods changes and employee job improvement suggestions; and a sound wage structure based on an acceptable and consistent job evaluation or job-ranking system.

Predetermined motion times and proven standard data developed from accurate, individual time studies are by far the most effective techniques for establishing production standards. Both methods require the predescription of the method and quality conditions, and the standards developed from them are based on massive data which more truly represent the so-called normal or average performance level.

Regardless of the rate-setting procedure used, the production standards themselves should cover only the predictable conditions and variations of the task. Any attempt to broadly average unpredictable variations into the published standards will result in a wide fluctuation of earnings, depending primarily on the existence or nonexistence of the variances which have been averaged into the rates at a particular time.

Proper definition of the method and quality standards on which the production standard is based is mandatory, for productivity variations resulting from methods changes and/or short-cutting quality requirements are the major single cause of variation extremes in performances and variances. When such extremes occur, the employee's concept of a fair standard is inevitably based on the highest figures. If tangible evidence of the basis on which the standard was set is unavailable, mutually agreed-upon solutions are difficult if not impossible to achieve.

The part played by creeping methods changes in the destruction of wage incentive systems is well known. Merely minor changes may be insufficiently important to warrant immediate changes in the existing standard. However, a series of such minor changes caused by working conditions, minor material changes, equipment improvement, and the like over the years create loose or inconsistent standards—or both—and an ineffective wage incentive is the inevitable result.

The production standards and related incentive administrative procedures may be established with accuracy and consistency, but an incentive system will still not function properly unless equally accurate and consistent controls for variations in manufacturing conditions are in existence. Such variances (which may come from a multitude of causes—temporary material variations, waiting for work, temporary methods, and the like) must be measured and allowed for, over and above the published standards. To control such variances it is imperative that an equally factual measurement procedure be available so that time standards can be set for these unusual conditions before or during their occurrence. Variances that are unpredictable (waiting time, for example) must be measured and controlled by an accurate timekeeping system that will enable the time variances to be measured and allowed for with equal accuracy. A third and final control required is accurate piece counting or production determination. These activities must be established as simple, verifiable procedures accurately reflecting the true amount of work done. If they are not, the wage incentive system will fail.

Making the Decision

A decision to introduce a wage incentive system, modify an existing wage incentive system, or abandon a wage incentive system must be predicated on a tangible, factual appraisal of existing productivity, costs, and administrative considerations. Such an examination (audit) must be an in-depth study that considers the specific details rather than a broad overall evaluation of productivity and costs.

The audit should begin by establishing tangible and provably consistent production standards for selected operations. These standards may be developed by any accurate and accepted system of industrial work measurement. Predetermined motion time standards and provable standard time data derived by time study are usually the most effective work measurement tools for this action.

The operations selected for the evaluation should statistically represent the distribution of operations and skills applied in the factory.

By the use of accurate test standards, a direct comparison can be made between existing productivity and actual production studies taken on the floor with a consistent norm. The deviations will indicate the degrees of difference between actual and expected normal production and unit labor costs, where they exist, and in most cases the causes of the variations.

The production and time variances over and above those allowed for in the production standards can be determined by several methods: ratio delay studies or examinations of company records of downtime, lost time, waiting time, losses due to defective material, and the like.

APPRAISING ADMINISTRATIVE TECHNIQUES

Equally important are the evaluation and appraisal of the administrative techniques used or required and the acceptance of the wage incentive plan by supervision, the bargaining unit, and the employee. An in-depth appraisal of this phase would cover the following areas:

1. The technical aspects of establishing time standards would be studied with the objective of determining the adequacy and consistency of this basis for the most critical controls of management.

2. The qualifications of the personnel responsible for the time standards would be appraised to determine their ability to use the required techniques properly.

3. The acceptance of wage incentives by labor and management would be weighed to determine existing or potential sources of labor relations problems and evaluate possible solutions.

4. Wage incentive controls would be appraised to determine inconsistencies which might result in disrupting time standards, costs, earnings, or management controls.

5. Management control data would be appraised to determine the quality and quantity of information available to the management team for its assistance in maintaining a sound and effective wage plan, and to determine the effectiveness with which these data and reports are used to control costs, to utilize equipment effectively, and to fairly and equitably administer the wage plan.

Each of these areas should be subjected to thorough investigation through a cooperative study by all who are engaged in the wage incentive operation. An evaluation or ranking procedure should be developed and applied in order that the appraisal be conducted as a fact-finding and educational procedure.

The audit, properly developed, will indicate the problem areas, their magnitude, and the steps necessary for their correction; the course of action which should be pursued for the mutual advantage of management and employees; and the economic justification for the necessary actions.—*J. L. Schwab*

COST REDUCTION

It is essential, in this age of intense foreign and domestic competition, that every manufacturing organization reduce costs in order to survive and prosper.

Cost reduction is a creative, positive program aimed at profit improvement by reducing labor, material, and manufacturing overhead costs. It is accomplished by systematically re-evaluating and reanalyzing work methods, material usage, manpower requirements, work layout, machine utilization, tools, fixtures, and basic product design.

Developing a Profit Improvement Philosophy

Many managements speak in terms of profit improvement rather than of cost reduction, because of the resistance that the term "cost reduction" has encountered in the past. A profit improvement program is quite different from the periodic command to operating management to "chop heads" and "cut costs across the board," which only encourages the hoarding of employees, equipment, and supplies. It should be a continuous, well-planned, companywide program that begins with top management and moves downward, strengthened by the force of example. Thus successful cost reduction is rooted in a profit improvement philosophy that covers guidelines for (1) the introduction of the cost reduction program; (2) the manpower, methods, and techniques that will be used to reduce costs; (3) the method by which people will be retrained or replaced; and (4) the evaluation method for eliminating or replacing obsolete equipment and processes.

EMERGENCY AND LIMITED OBJECTIVES PROGRAMS

Crises such as drastic competitive price reductions or technological breakthroughs often demand emergency action for the survival of a company or product line. Although the methods and tools of the long-range program generally apply to emergency situations, the pace and method of implementation are greatly accelerated, and less time and effort are given to overcoming employee resistance because time is so important. In a limited objectives program, the focus is on a specific substantial cost area such as indirect labor or a cost item such as heat, and efforts are concentrated on it. This is often a short-range program, but it frequently results in substantial savings.

HANDLING RESISTANCE

Successful implementation of a profit improvement program depends primarily upon the enthusiastic cooperation and creative ideas of every member of the organization, from top management to the porter, but especially the first-line supervisors and production workers. Every program must include provisions for dealing with their fear of job loss, which is one of the main causes of failure in many programs. One method of gaining support is to refer to the program as profit improvement rather than cost reduction; this will create a positive rather than a negative image. Since the first-line supervisor directly controls job assignments, downtime, raw material usage, waste, and labor efficiency, he must know how labor and material standards are established and how to analyze these standards. Above all, he must be trained in how to improve profits by eliminating unnecessary jobs, improving methods, and reducing waste. One way to gain his enthusiastic support is to make him a part of the cost reduction team in the early planning stages. If the supervisor does not want to reduce costs or does not understand the importance of his part in the effort, the plan will either fail or require an indefinite period to implement. Another possibility leading to cooperation is to make the workers part of the program by offering cash awards for suggestions. Most important is proper communication with the supervisors and workers, which will prevent rumor and panic and will create an atmosphere in which the basic outlook and attitude toward profit improvement are everyone's job, not just the job of those members of management who are working on the program at the time.

Organizing the Profit Improvement Program

Long- and short-range goals should be established. Long-range goals are based on anticipated external and internal conditions five to ten years in the future. External conditions (which are difficult to foresee) include changed international relations, social conditions, labor shortages, and government controls or market conditions (such as competitive price reductions and product improvements). Internal conditions include such elements as anticipated increased labor costs or obsolescence of equipment. Short-range goals, which usually run no longer than two years, should fall within the framework of the long-range goals except in emergency and limited objectives programs. Short-range goals are easier to establish because they are usually based on present unsatisfactory conditions such as high labor costs, low inventory turnover, or poor deliveries. Goals should be established by the profit improvement team in terms of both anticipated dollars saved and specific objectives. The purpose is to force the profit improvement team to (1) establish a well-thought-out program with achievable dollar goals, (2) initiate a realistic overall plan for implementation, and (3) accept the responsibility for the results of the program.

COST DATA

Cost data on labor, material, and manufacturing overhead must be made available to the cost reduction team for analysis so that major opportunities for cost reduction can be determined. After that, major product lines and major individual products can be analyzed in depth to further pinpoint cost reduction opportunities. Both of these analyses are frequently made, since not only does every company have different cost factors; even within the same company, product lines have different factors making up the individual costs of manufacturing.

In order to further evaluate costs, statistical analyses of cost trends, breakeven charts, marginal income forecasts, flow charts, organization charts, quality control procedures, prior cost reduction programs, organizational studies, plant and equipment studies, operational analysis studies, and efficiency studies of material and labor must be carefully analyzed. Each should be viewed as an opportunity to improve profits. The study of the cost data should be viewed as an aid to decision making. It should be recognized that accounting information is often developed in a form geared to financial statements and tax reporting. When these data are used for decision making, they should be viewed through the perspective of the company as a going concern, taking into account sunk (irretrievable) costs and opportunity (future) costs. For example, in the case of the classical make-or-buy decision, the use of the average manufacturing cost may lead to a "buy" decision, while the correct alternative may be "make" because of idle capacity.

ADMINISTRATION

The overall administration of the profit improvement program may be a function of either the line or the staff organization, depending upon the size of the company, the scope of the program, the availability of competent personnel, and the nature of the problem. The work on the program itself can be done by outside consultants or inside personnel, depending upon the same criteria. The success of every profit improvement program, however, depends upon the close cooperation and active support of line, staff, and outside consultants (if they are used). Responsibility for the overall administration of the program is frequently determined by the results of an organizational study.

COST VERSUS SAVINGS

Profit improvement programs cost money to establish and implement. However, after the initial expenses, a well-thought-out and successful program can make a considerable contribution to profits. In order to assure that the expenditures are justified, the potential savings should be carefully estimated and evaluated by an audit team of outside consultants or an internal team reporting directly to the overall administrator of the program.

Major Cost Reduction Areas

Labor, material, and manufacturing overhead are major cost reduction areas, but mounting operating expenses (caused by inefficient or obsolete equipment and machinery) and slow inventory turnover must also be taken into account.

LABOR

Direct labor costs are costs directly attributable to a product. They are frequently reduced through work methods analysis by individuals trained in time and motion study. The intent is to mechanize, eliminate, simplify, and standardize each individual operation in order to reduce costs.

MATERIAL

Direct material costs are those directly attributable to a product. Material costs can be lowered by instituting proper controls at key points before manufacturing begins: (1) At the time the items are designed, costs can be cut by using the techniques of value analysis and by good machine design aimed at establishing a machine capable of maintaining a desired quality level. (2) At the time of purchase, material costs can be reduced by locating new and less expensive sources of supply and by using the techniques of value analysis. (3) At the time of receipt, good incoming inspection permits defective parts to be discovered before they reach the manufacturing area. This reduces in-process waste and permits the return of the parts to the vendor within the allowable time period.

After manufacturing operations have started, proper control of material by the supervisor is the key to reduced material costs. Good, close, daily supervision can reduce waste by means of clear and complete work instructions; by not permitting further processing of substandard material; by verifying that tools and fixtures are in good repair; by salvaging reparable material; by training new workers properly; by storing goods carefully; by discouraging pilferage; and by careful use of operating supplies.

MANUFACTURING OVERHEAD

Overhead costs are frequently broken down into fixed, semivariable, and variable categories so as to focus attention on specific cost areas. Fixed overhead such as taxes or depreciation does not vary directly with changes in production volume. Semivariable overhead such as supervisors' salaries does increase or decrease with volume but not in direct proportion. Variable overhead such as material handlers and operating supplies changes in direct proportion to product volume. Fixed and semivariable overhead are scrutinized periodically rather than continually because they usually do not change appreciably from day to day. Variable overhead, on the other hand, changes rapidly and should be constantly reviewed because it offers a prime opportunity for considerable cost savings. The responsibility for controlling these variable expenses should be in the hands of the area supervisor who is directly responsible for the costs at the point where they occur. However, the area supervisor should be held accountable only for those costs he can directly control.

PLANT AND EQUIPMENT REPLACEMENT

Establishing a replacement program requires a commitment from top management that an organized, systematic, and continuous replacement program is necessary and that it is an integral part of corporate policy. Top management must issue clear guidelines for the basis and system that are to be used in determining plant and equipment replacement; the procedure that is to be followed; and the persons specifically responsible for the successful implementation of the program. Some advantages of a continuous program include reduction of expensive crash expenditures, lower maintenance costs, less waste, and less downtime.

Determining guidelines for replacement of equipment is a complex procedure because actual, presently known factors as well as future unknown factors must be considered. For example, predictions of the future for sales, technology, and the value of money force individual value judgments. The issue is made more complex because various methods and techniques can be used to choose between alternatives. The essential point is that, although replacement analysis is complex and is based on many unknowns, it is most necessary that a systematic mathematical analysis be made, not just a guess based on past experience and intuition. Several methods for evaluating alternative proposals include the MAPI (Machinery and Allied Products Institute) method, the annual cost method, the present worth method, and the rate-of-return method. Although each method has its advantages, the one best fitted to the specific company and situation should be used.

Manufacturing Operation Analysis

In order for a realistic and meaningful evaluation of the overall manufacturing operation to be made, information must flow freely and willingly between the individual or team making the organizational study, the people in charge of the manufacturing process being studied, and the administrator.

ORGANIZATIONAL STUDIES

Policies, procedures, and responsibilities in an organization are constantly undergoing change. For this reason, many companies make a comprehensive audit of the entire manufacturing organization before embarking on profit improvement programs. Audits can be conducted by outside consultants or corporate management, depending upon the size, circumstances, and availability of competent personnel in the company.

UTILIZATION STUDIES

Overall plant layout, including machine utilization records (taking into account peak periods), storage facilities, individual work areas, material handling, and material flow, is carefully analyzed to determine whether present plant and equipment is properly utilized or whether a new layout would increase capacity and efficiency. After the study has been completed, a managerial decision is made to determine whether to plan requirements for present sales volume (including seasonal peaks) or for expected sales volume. If requirements for future volume are to be planned, the period of time (one, two, five, or ten years) and expected sales levels at that time are projected. Next, an economic decision is made as to whether it would be less expensive to utilize present plant and equipment better (by redesigning the plant layout, by transferring operations from one machine to another, or by adding a second or third shift), or whether the company should subcontract or add additional space and buy additional equipment. By this type of careful evaluation of alternatives, present plant and equipment utilization as well as future needs can be determined systematically.

INDIVIDUAL OPERATIONAL ANALYSIS

Individual operational analysis is the systematic reduction of each of the methods used to produce an item into its simplest component parts. Every facet of the individual job, including all the tools, fixtures, equipment, tolerances, work layout, and waste, is carefully examined. The reasonableness and necessity of every detail of each individual job is questioned; nothing is accepted without careful examination. Next, every necessary facet of the operation is further broken down into its simplest parts with the intent of further elimination, simplification, and study. Individual operational analysis charts are frequently used on complex jobs to make certain that every detail is questioned and investigated. Depending upon the complexity of the operation and the potential savings, these chart checklists can either be formally filled in or informally used as a guide.

WORK METHODS ANALYSIS

Methods analysis is one of the main tools used in reducing labor costs. To use it effectively, it is necessary to analyze procedures, operations, and systems; establish standards of accomplishment; and control performance. Methods analysis involves the systematic study of each job with the intent of eliminating unnecessary operations; standardizing equipment, tools, methods, and working conditions; and measuring the time required to perform each operation.

To determine which analytical tool to use, a comparison is made between the anticipated return and the costs involved in applying the various techniques. Depending upon an evaluation of costs versus savings, process charts, man/ machine charts, operation charts, or other techniques may be indicated.

Standardization. In order to control performance, it is important to establish an accurate measurement of the time required to perform each job; this necessitates the standardization of equipment, production material, tools, and fixtures. Methods also should be standardized in all parts of the plant. This will help assure that labor standards will be uniformly and fairly established, thereby reducing grievances and facilitating the rapid introduction of improvements in all areas of the plant with a minimum of time and effort.

Labor standards. To effectively control manufacturing labor costs and obtain a fair day's work from employees, labor standards must be established throughout the company. To assure accuracy (which will help reduce labor problems), labor standards are normally established on the basis of work measurement. Standards are best established by an individual trained in work measurement techniques who is not directly responsible for the jobs being studied. These labor standards can then be effectively enforced, controlled, and used as a basis for manpower planning and wage incentives.

COMPUTER SCIENCES

Many different industries have begun to use the computer in order to achieve cost savings. The computer has made notable contributions to profitability in job shops through the effective use of numerically controlled machines. In assembly shop operations, the computer has reduced overall costs by relating and controlling customer orders, inventory, and production scheduling. Moreover, the process industry has profited by using the computer for optimum blending, which results in fewer errors and more consistent quality. Additional opportunities for cost savings by the use of the computer include the reduction of distribution costs, maintenance costs, scrap costs, and inventory carrying costs.

Value Analysis

Value analysis (sometimes referred to as value engineering) basically consists of (1) analyzing and evaluating the fundamental use of a product; (2) systematically attempting to build greater value into the product without reducing its performance or interfering with its function; and (3) simultaneously reducing its cost. The principles of value analysis are applied at the drawing board when a product is initially designed (sometimes referred to as "first look"), and are continued all the way through each of the operations to final assembly. In the past, the techniques of value analysis were frequently used not on new products but primarily on existing products. When these same techniques are applied to existing products and product lines, they are referred to as "second look." "Second look" should be used as a supplement to—not a substitute for—"first look." Although specific techniques vary from industry to industry, the goal is to increase the difference between the product worth and product cost, thereby increasing the value to the customer. Some companies use value analysis as a sales tool by training their own salesmen in the technique to help them make more knowledgeable sales presentations.

NEED FOR VALUE ANALYSIS

The need for wider use of value analysis has never been greater, since competition is growing fiercer and customers are demanding better quality products at lower prices. Because value analysis attacks the cost-and-value problem from a functional standpoint, thereby getting to the root of the problem, it is well suited to helping solve the customers' needs. Although the concepts and techniques used in value analysis have had their greatest application in companies doing government work, they have been successfully used in diverse industries to achieve greater value at lower cost.

ORGANIZING

The goal in organizing the value analysis program is to bring the right people together at the right time on the right product. Participation and endorsement by top management are vital because the program is based on teamwork which crosses many department lines, including the purchasing, marketing, design engineering, manufacturing, cost, and field service functions. One technique is to gather experts from many different disciplines, utilize their combined creative ideas, and end up with a lower-cost, superior product.

The organization of the function depends upon many factors such as the type of product and customer and the size and organization of the company itself. Reporting should be to a key individual high enough up the chain of command so that the corporate viewpoint is maintained, prompt decisions can be made, and implementation can be rapid. When value analysis is a centralized function, the overall responsibility often rests with a corporate officer who is frequently chosen because of his specialty and the overall orientation of the company (for example, a vice president of engineering if the company is engineering-oriented). When value analysis is a noncentralized function, the overall responsibility often rests with a divisional manager.

AID TO PURCHASING

Since materials frequently make up the highest percentage of the total cost of an item, value analysis can be particularly valuable in purchasing. The cooperation of suppliers can be encouraged by the use of incentive contract clauses that enable them to share in any savings that result from their recommendations on such things as standard parts, loosened tolerances, design changes, or the substitution of less expensive material.

EVALUATING RESULTS

Value analysis programs are difficult to measure quantitatively. One method of measurement compares the estimated savings in labor and material with the estimated cost (including costs of redesign, tooling, and analysts' time). However, there may be additional intangible savings, such as increased reliability or improved quality, which cannot be quantified. Any evaluation of the overall effectiveness of the program must be done carefully and objectively, taking into account all related factors.—*J. J. McCrea*

FACILITIES PLANNING

By outlining a concrete method for facilities planning, it is hoped to make tangible what is inherently a rather nebulous task. Although the accent may appear to be on the method of planning, it should be understood that the quality and intensity of thinking used in preparing and executing the basic plan are more important than the precise procedure employed.

The Planning Team

Any program aimed at the planning and expeditious completion of a new facility or major improvements to an existing one should be thoroughly organized and should start with selection of the planning staff or team. This should be an integrated team that would include individuals having experience in such areas as plant layout, processing and packaging, equipment selection, materials handling, inventory control, and efficient warehousing. An additional distinct advantage will be present if the group includes experience and abilities in the development of new equipment and modifications to existing equipment, assuring that the new facility will be capable of operating at maximum profit and be sufficiently flexible to permit economical response to the dynamics of future product demands.

Ideally, all members of the planning group—but especially the leader—should possess additional attributes. The leader should be imaginative, with an analytical flair; he should have a proven affinity to the broad viewpoint (not merely expressed interest) and have the ability of objective judgment based on sound evaluations.

In this age of constant change, intense competition, and ever increasing complexities, such primary attributes are the extra insurance against obtaining a facility that is just a duplicate of an existing operation rather than one capable of meeting today's technological challenges.

Charting the Program

Although the tasks and activities to be performed will vary among companies and industries, the planning and programming remain a vital function of the planning team. The initial task should be the development and arrangement of a master guide which will cover the sequence of steps that must be undertaken in performance of the entire program.

The work tasks in each of the guide steps should be grouped together on a phased project basis. The advantages of well-defined steps and phases are that they provide pre-established checkpoints at which progress can be formally measured and present and future objectives reassessed in light of the latest findings, costs, and schedule projections; efficient utilization of technical personnel to assure maximum depth of project coverage at minimum cost; savings in time and money in nonproductive areas such as orientation, communication, administration, and coordination; optimum sequencing and scheduling of work in performing the planned tasks to avoid duplication of effort and unnecessary stoppage and delays.

The factors that should be covered in the overall plan and included in the master guide are as follows: (1) statements of the company's objectives in determining that a facility is to be established; (2) a program of developments or activities to be undertaken to attain these objectives; (3) a summary of the requirements generated by these developments; (4) a time schedule and assignments of responsibilities for accomplishing the various segments of the planning; (5) a plan for accomplishment, including a means of measuring progress; (6) calculations of cost (capital and expense) and return on investment; (7) a means of evaluating overall performance.

Stating the Objectives

The starting point of an effective plan for a new or improved facility is the development of comprehensive statements of management's objectives as to the kind and scope of manufacturing that will be undertaken; the required production capacity in terms of units of products to be produced per given period of time; the limitations, if any, to the size of the investment; and the time allotment within which the facility must be planned, procured, set up, and put into operation.

Organizing the Tasks

Once the objectives have been clearly documented and accepted by management, the second step in the master guide can be undertaken. This requires determination and organization of a series of tasks and actions that will be necessary to obtain the objectives. These too will vary by companies and industries as to details; however, the basic tasks will be similar.

A very helpful means of setting up the program of tasks is to develop a network diagram showing the sequence of activities and events required to achieve each of the planned objectives. Such a network provides not only an excellent means of programming but also of controlling the entire project. Two modestly sophisticated systems used extensively by many companies for planning major projects are PERT (Program Evaluation and Review Technique) and CPM (Critical Path Method). There are other systems equally useful, although somewhat more sophisticated, which combine features of CPM and a Gantt chart. Substantial published information on all these systems is readily available to those who are not already familiar with them. The use of such methods as network diagramming of the tasks to be performed permits development of factors 2, 3, and 4 of the master guide in combination. If CPM is used, factor 6 can also be included. As an alternative to any of the standard systems, the planning group may devise a method for organizing its program of activities. Many planning groups prefer this approach.

The reasons prompting a need for the facility can be many and varied. There will, very likely, be a need to make some alterations in the planning program as the execution of tasks takes place; but these alterations will generally be in the minority in relation to the essential tasks that must be part of any facilities planning program. These changes, additions, or deletions in total tasks will be almost automatic—or, at least, they will be obvious when the project motives are known.

Facility Location

The area location of the plant and the selection of a site should be early considerations as performance is initiated on the programmed tasks. If the primary reason for a new facility is—for example—expansion for increased capacity or the consolidation of several separate operations into a single efficient plant, a location that can best serve the whole market area or a specific segment of it must be the first concern. The plant must be economically accessible to the supply lines of raw materials and be centrally located within the area to be served in order to minimize distribution costs and time. The necessary facilities and means to effect the distribution must be readily available or easily obtainable. Local availability of services such as light, power, water, and the like must be investigated and evaluated. Of major importance will be the local labor market and any of its conditions that might have a bearing on plant potential: the type, amount, and availability of labor; local union conditions, favorable or unfavorable, that could affect the operation; the possibility that this plant will be required to expand at a later date, and the adequacy of the site for expansion; and the zoning restrictions and local or state tax laws that could be beneficial or detrimental to the operation. And don't neglect the need for employee parking facilities—a "must" in this motorized age. These are but a few of the items that must be considered, investigated, documented, and evaluated. There will, however, be others, depending on the individual company's requirements and objectives.

Product Analysis

The kind of manufacturing that is to take place in the facility will have a significant bearing on the layout. It is therefore essential that the planning team have complete knowledge of all products to be produced in the plant and a thorough understanding of each operation to be performed on these products, both current and future. Look closely at all operations, with the aim of finding the ones that can be modified to simplify the work or the equipment required. Also look for instances where two or more operations can be done in combination to reduce manpower needs and machinery. The starting point in this portion of the program should be with the products to be produced: their number and variety; variations within each type of product line, and their extensiveness; and any items so different that separate production equipment must be made available. To cite a case in point: To obtain satisfactory marketing volume, a conveyor manufacturer must manufacture various types of equipment. Some types, such as gravity rollers and wheel conveyors, will utilize a minimum of manufacturing space, equipment, and worker skills. Items such as belt or slat conveyors, vertical conveyors, overhead chain systems, and other types of powered units require greater skills as well as more and different types of production equipment. The volume in numbers of units produced would usually be greater in the gravity line than in the powered line. Both are needed, in the conveyor company's case, to meet market demands for combinations of both. Under such circumstances, greater efficiency can be achieved if the layout is designed to provide separate areas for each type of production. Such a requirement, however, will make it more difficult to plan the layout around straight line flow principles. Fortunately, with today's advances in handling techniques and the great variety of handling devices and means of application, the problems of staggered departments and operations within a system can be greatly minimized.

Plant Capacity Requirements

Before finalizing the product analysis, consider the projected volumes of each product. Determine whether there are any seasonal variations that could affect production or any styling problems that would require flexibility in the producing areas to permit such changes as can occur—for example—in a garment or sporting goods plant. Determine whether the finished products are made of separate components treated individually as subassemblies to be finally joined to other subassemblies into a finished item at final assembly. What is the make-up of materials that go into production? What are their forms? Are they solid, liquid, or bulk? Can the materials be easily handled both into and out of the various operations? What manual labor is necessary, or can automatic handling means be employed for the movement between operations? Detailed process flow charts should be prepared for each product line; they should include both the operations sequence and the average time period spent by the product or part at each stage.

There is a basic reason for beginning plant layout development with an analysis of the products to be manufactured. The findings of the analysis, when documented in orderly fashion, will outline the basic departments and areas that have to be provided for in the layout. It will remain for the planning group to determine the amount of plant space the separate departments will require and the relative position of each that will contribute most to a smooth flow of production through the facility. At the conclusion of this task, a clear picture will emerge as to the capacity assumptions on which the new facility is to be based.

All product information should be documented for each product—preferably, in detailed process chart form; from these records decisions can be made regarding both flow of work through the plant and production machinery requirements.

Production Flow

The ideal flow arrangement is one where raw materials are received at one end of a plant, are fed directly to the first operation, and proceed in a straight line through successive operations until the finished product goes directly out of the plant to the customer. Such a manufacturing manager's dream will not be readily located, but an approach to it as a target will be helpful in the consideration of work flow.

Most manufacturing operations have a variety of raw materials that must be received in quantities and held in raw materials inventory storage. Similarly, finished products are rarely shipped directly from the final operation but usually go into finished goods inventory storage from which shipments originate. One of the early considerations must be concerned with this procedure as work flow is analyzed.

Determine the size of the inventory of manufacturing materials that must be carried. Study its space requirements and the size of lots and their frequency of reception. Are the materials easily handled, and can standard materials handling equipment be utilized to receive and place them in accessible storage, easily retrievable with a minimum of manual labor? How much truck dock or railroad siding space will be needed? Can warehousing be in the open, or must it be in an enclosure? Must it be heated or cooled? These and similar questions in connection with the finished products warehousing requirements must be answered and the findings analyzed. Is the movement of goods, both in and out, sufficiently infrequent and staggered to permit utilization of common receiving and shipping facilities? Are the storage and handling such that the same personnel can perform both functions without undue congestion? For reasons of economy, if for no other, this is preferable; but it is not always attainable.

If the findings permit common facilities for the warehousing chores, considerable initial investment savings can be made in plant construction and utilization of available site area. If the findings indicate a marginal condition, an exhaustive investigation should be made of available handling and storing equipment, as well as scheduling flexibilities that might assist in overcoming the objectionable features of a common receiving and shipping department. Under no circumstances, however, should a compromise be made in the hope that future changes in movement patterns or equipment will permit the desired arrangement. While initial investments will be lower, any savings will quickly vanish if congestion in the warehousing departments causes production limitations and delays to finished goods delivery.

If the original objectives assumed separate processing equipment for each of the product lines, review the reasons behind these objectives. Perhaps considerations of interchangeability of machinery (packaging equipment, for example) between product lines should be included as a consideration. Very often, substantial economies are made possible by planning joint use of equipment; thus evaluations of these interactions, after the basic requirements and process flow data have been obtained, can be desirable. While the planning and procurement time may be lengthened somewhat to accomplish the additional investigations, the results in many cases can be of major significance.

Facilities Layout

Once plant location has been determined, a site established, and the products to be produced thoroughly analyzed, the next activity on which to concentrate is plant layout. Resist the natural tendency to simplify the job by duplicating an existing facility, even if the facility has a good record for efficient operation. Strive for improvement; it is a rare case where improvements cannot be effected. Find the weak points and areas in an existing plant that need correction; then copy only the good ones when and if they fit into the plan.

If careful consideration is given to all pertinent matters applying to the facility, several alternative plant layouts will be formulated. These general layout concepts should initially be illustrated in block area layout drawings. The layouts will provide a basis for the general evaluation of the various concepts for analysis of flow process requirements, general operating economics, and potential capital cost.

In the course of developing layouts for the facility, consideration must be given to whether the planning will proceed along lines of a functional, process, or product-line layout. A product-line layout may require duplicate equipment for separate product lines, thus leading to increased capital investment. On the other hand, the functional type of layout will frequently introduce operational problems associated with the scheduling of different products through a common department. This can become a serious problem if one or more of the products are subject to rapid and extreme fluctuations in demand or have product characteristics that will restrict the allowable size of inventory. There is thus the possibility that a combination of functional and product-line layouts may be most appropriate, especially in the packaging areas.

Materials Handling

In association with the planning functions for the type of layout concept being developed, the incorporation of proper materials handling must be considered. This subject is covered under "Materials Handling and Warehousing" (page 6·74).

Automation

In the planning program, include allowances for investigation into the possibilities for automation of processing operations. Each year sees major advances in the techniques of making operations that traditionally have been manual completely automatic. In addition to the labor-saving potential possible through automation, there are many times when quality control, higher production volumes, and improvements in customer service resulting from automation within manufacturing can produce profit improvements of major magnitude. Consider also the improvement possibilities in semiautomation, especially in those functions that will not show economic justification for complete automation. In many instances, providing mechanical or electronic assists to an operator will maximize that operator's performance to such a degree that full automation could not be justified. Such items as automatic positioning and holding devices, parts feeders, and inspection devices in an assembly operation are assists that often permit one operator to control a production process formerly requiring two or more people.

Warehousing Requirements

One overall consideration to be kept in mind is the growing tendency of customers to insist on smaller shipments of merchandise delivered at more frequent intervals. This minimizes their need to provide warehousing facilities and reduces long-term investment in merchandise. It does, however, place a responsibility on the manufacturer to compensate with larger storage facilities and more complicated scheduling of outgoing products. Here again, the nature of the company's operation and the industry will have a major influence on decisions.

Planning Modifications

Frequent reference to the objectives developed in the first step of the master guide should be made in order to be certain that any decisions reached in the various stages of overall planning meet these objectives. This also serves another purpose. Very often, findings and conclusions in any of the planning areas will show sufficient advantages, either economically or functionally, to make changes in earlier decisions—and even, under some circumstances, in the objectives— worthwhile. For example, one company, faced with increasing demands by customers for smaller and more frequent shipments while the firm was still under the handicap of having to produce its products in large quantities because of the heavy cost of manufacturing change-overs, brought in the marketing department for consultation. A resulting alteration in marketing policy made it sufficiently advantageous to customers to order in large quantities and accept less frequent deliveries.

Final Plant Layout, Equipment, and Building Specifications

Allow provision in the program of tasks for the preparation of reports outlining the conclusions reached for each planning function. These reports will form the summary of recommended actions that can be taken and provide a basis for the final evaluation.

The most attractive of the alternate plant layouts should now be compared and evaluated in considerably greater detail. More precise cost estimates should be developed. Equipment and structural costs should be based upon price information from equipment manufacturers and construction firms. Explore also the ability of each of the alternate layout concepts to meet any probable future contingencies.

The actual selection of equipment for processing, warehousing, and packaging should be based upon a comprehensive study of economic and utility factors— cleanliness, safety, minimum machinery downtime, potential for product breakage if the products are fragile, ease of maintenance, and operational flexibility to meet possible future production requirements.

From the information developed in the summary reports, a detailed rating and evaluation of the most attractive plant and equipment layouts can then be prepared. Capital and operating costs, flexibility, ease of operation, cleanliness, and adaptability to expansion will be among the factors considered. On the basis of these findings, the final recommended layout can be developed. It may be one of the original alternates or a combination of the better elements of several. The report should include a discussion of the reasons for the selection and, after it has been finalized, should be presented to management for review, comment, and approval.

With approval from management and appropriations for construction and procurement, the final facilities layout can be detailed to define the equipment to be procured and the building specifications to house the operation. If the project is of major size and includes a great number of operating segments, a further in-depth analysis of each segment should be made in an effort to maximize the possibilities for cost savings. Develop such information as the following: optimal concepts of equipment and method for each segment of the operation; an economic appraisal of each optimal concept in relation to present practices; detailed specifications of the selected concept in terms of equipment and operating requirements; an analysis of reaction time of source vendors or raw material suppliers (in some instances, on-hand inventories can be kept at absolute minimum if vendor reaction time is short and dependable); and a review of the company's attitudes toward production leveling and inventory size. Here the trade-offs between a stable production force and inventory size will be tempered by considerations of such items as investment in products, product shelf life, and cost of storage facilities.

Procurement and Installation

In the summary report covering the final facilities layout, the equipment needed for operation should be listed with emphasis on items that need long lead times for delivery. Procurement efforts should be started with these items to minimize delays in final plant completion. In some instances, certain items may be ordered even before determination of the final layout.

This final phase of the program will include the procurement of all materials, equipment, and facilities and their installation in accordance with the preferred layout. Wherever possible, all elements of the plant should be tested and any required corrections made before turning them over to the operating department. Ideal conditions permit putting the entire plant into trial production operation before final acceptance. This procedure serves two purposes: It permits the training and evaluation of operating personnel and also provides a period of time to review the concepts in operating form and make changes or corrections that appear to offer improvements. A well-planned program will include in its time schedule such a period for run-in and testing.

Exact procedures for each step in the procurement and installation phase would be very difficult to set up. Much depends upon the industry, the nature and volume of products to be produced, the services to be provided—whether the items produced are finished products or just components, and many similar considerations. The general overall actions, however, are covered in the following areas of work effort: the purchase of capital equipment, including building; the design of modifications to standard equipment and processes, plus supervision of the modifications; the supervision of equipment installation and testing of operation in accordance with acceptance test specifications; the start-up and debugging of the equipment and system; the completion of operating and maintenance manuals and spare parts lists; and continued liaison with plant operating management during the early periods of production.

Frequently, during this period, assistance can be given to plant operations on such topics as inventory control and optimum transportation arrangements and facilities for finished goods.

Upon the completion of the planned facility, when all equipment and processes are in operation and have been thoroughly debugged, a summary report should be prepared. It should include an outline of all actions taken and tasks performed, with an explanation of any·major or unusual decisions. The report can provide a source of reference in the event of future changes to plant or products. It will also serve as a guide in planning any new or additional facilities and thus expedite the planning function by minimizing the initial work.

—*J. F. O'Hora*

MATERIALS MANAGEMENT

Materials management is a concept that has been developed and implemented in recent years. It represents an attempt to reach a balance between conflicting interests through the planning and control of materials from acquisition through manufacturing to the finished product available for sale.

Objectives and Organization

The primary concerns of materials management are adequate supply to maintain satisfactory customer service levels, economic utilization of plant equipment and labor, and optimum dollar investment in materials.

As materials costs in many operations account for approximately four times the labor costs of converting these materials to finished product, it becomes increasingly important to maintain a high degree of control over investment in materials inventories.

FUNCTIONS

Materials management is often looked at as an opportunity to organize related functions under one manager to provide increased control and avoid wasteful overlapping of activities. It is natural that a number of functions are found within the organizational structure. Some of the areas falling within this responsibility are planning, production control, inventory control, scheduling, purchasing, stores, receiving, warehousing, shipping, materials handling, value analysis, statistical analysis, traffic, operations research, make-or-buy decisions, distribution control, forecasting, and materials control. Actually, few if any organizations include every one of these functions.

The classical approach to materials management today would include under the materials manager's direction the following functions: production planning; materials control; purchasing; traffic; receiving, handling, and shipping; and distribution control. There has been much controversy between production and inventory control, purchasing, and physical distribution over the question of which of them is the most important and should dominate the materials management function. The answer seems to be more in the nature of the business itself than in the individual function.

PLACE IN CORPORATE STRUCTURE

If materials management is to provide top management with the control of materials supply, inventory investment, and flow-through operations that are its primary opportunities, it must have authority commensurate with responsibility. Materials management should be considered one of the major functions within the operation. It is generally a part of the total operations responsibility. It should be structured at the same level as manufacturing, quality control, and production engineering.

ORGANIZATION

Before the organizational structure can be developed, specific decisions must be made on the functions to be included. A number of factors will undoubtedly influence this decision. Some of them are the complexity of the business, the importance of various functions within the present organization, the recognition of simple resistance to change, and the competence and availability of managerial talent. Other influences are the need for improved cooperation between functions, a requirement for tighter inventory control, and anticipated improvements in communication, coordination, and control.

One of the most controversial points, usually, is the question whether purchasing should be a part of materials management or separate and on the same organizational level. When purchasing is a part of materials management, basic conflicts between purchasing and materials control are reduced. Purchasing has a strong interest in buying at the lowest price. The lowest price, naturally, is a result of buying larger quantities. Materials control is responsible for the availability and turnover of inventories. When the two functions are able to appreciate each other's problems and operate as partners seeking a common objective, an opportunity to reduce conflict and achieve optimum costs and results is provided.

A distinct disadvantage may appear if purchasing is subordinated to the production planning or materials control function. Purchasing will quickly become overly concerned with the day-to-day pressure of specific production requirements and fail to accomplish its own most important task of vendor selection, buying, and negotiating.

In many industries, the purchase of materials accounts for more than half the money spent. Obviously, the purchasing function is an important aspect of cost control. Through close contacts with many other companies and supplier representatives, purchasing is in an ideal position to keep informed on general market conditions, changing business legislation and regulations, and improved or new materials introduced to the marketplace.

INTERDEPARTMENTAL RELATIONSHIPS

The nature of the activities involved with materials management implies that the function will have frequent contacts with almost all areas of the business. One of its major responsibilities is the coordination and timing of activities between many unrelated areas. Because of this broad involvement, it is important that materials management personnel exercise authority to go with their responsibility. At the same time, it is equally important that they become proficient in communicating with a variety of persons concerned with specialized functions.

Production Planning

"Production planning" is defined as "the function of setting the limits on levels of manufacturing operations in the future" (*Dictionary of Production and Inventory Control Terms,* American Production and Inventory Control Society,

Chicago, 1966). The production plan establishes the ground rules that will be followed within the limits of previously determined corporate policies. The development of a plan will provide a forward look at inventory levels as they relate to inventory turnover and investment and cash flow requirements, the degree of customer service that can be anticipated (based on planned stock positions), and the need to begin stockpiling inventories early to overcome seasonal sales patterns and limits in manufacturing capacity. Forward planning will determine the need to increase or decrease the labor force or attempt to maintain level employment through inventory planning. It provides the basis for authorization of actual manufacturing activities. Advance planning permits the orderly procurement of raw materials and components. It allows time for purchasing vendor selection, negotiation, and make-or-buy decisions.

THE SALES FORECAST

The sales forecast is the foundation on which all plans are based. The relative accuracy of the forecast will have a direct effect on future capital investments, inventory turnover, efficient utilization of equipment, and customer service. Unless the forecast provides a firm foundation for planning, much time, effort, and money will be misdirected.

Types of forecasts. Forecasts fall into three general categories: (1) long-range, projecting out five years and used for equipment planning and plant expansion; (2) medium-range, projecting out two years and used for the examination of seasonal patterns and the procurement of specialized production materials requiring long lead times; (3) short-range, projecting out six to 18 months and used in the development of master plans and the procurement of production materials.

Forecasting responsibilities. Certain basic functional responsibilities with regard to forecasting should be considered.

1. Preparing the forecast is the responsibility of marketing, with advice from production planning and market research.

2. Developing the master plan is the work of production planning.

3. Monitoring the forecast for deviations and trends is the responsibility of production planning.

4. Interpreting the deviations and making forecast corrections is done by marketing.

5. Regulating materials flow to accommodate changes in the forecast is the responsibility of production planning and materials control.

6. Alerting management of developing problems that result from forecast deviations and changes is the responsibility of production planning.

To fulfill these responsibilities there must be a high degree of communication and cooperation between marketing and production planning. Marketing should think not only in terms of dollars of sales but also of units to be sold. Variations in unit prices can have a decided effect on the relationship between dollars and units. Production planning should provide marketing with guidelines to use in changing the forecasts and developing promotions as they relate to changing manufacturing conditions and lead times.

Approach to forecasting. In developing a forecast, the first consideration is normally given to the overall business forecast; this provides an overall look at the anticipated climate of the future as it applies to the particular business or perhaps to a specific group of products within the business.

The next step is to begin looking at each item within the product group. This will be necessary if correct materials planning and scheduling are to be achieved.

At this point, historical data, statistical trends, seasonality patterns, and changing promotional plans must be considered. Also, new product introductions and their impact on existing products will need to be examined. Numerous advanced statistical techniques can be applied to the development of forecasts.

Forecast evaluation. Proper forecasting requires a specific procedure for routinely evaluating the forecast. Deviations from forecast must be examined and changing trends recognized. Statistical techniques can be utilized to establish control limits that indicate the significance of forecast deviations. There are two basic reasons for revising forecasts: (1) recognition of changing trends and patterns in the marketplace because of customer preference, competition, or other uncontrollable factors; (2) planned changes in promotional plans. Forecasts should be revised as soon as the first of these two conditions is recognized to be of significance; to ignore the condition and fail to begin rescheduling manufacturing activities to actual sales conditions can only lead to excess inventories or out-of-stock conditions.

Before changing forecasts under the second condition, it should be determined whether manufacturing lead times will permit timely support for the new promotional plan. Otherwise, a planned promotion may end with an out-of-stock condition, considerable customer dissatisfaction, and wasted promotion money.

THE MASTER PLAN

Periodically, a master plan or schedule is prepared from the most recently updated forecast. Because production planning activities are always looking ahead, the master plan becomes the information that will be used to develop more specific plans in many areas. The relative accuracy of the plan is important, since the total manufacturing operation will accommodate itself to the plan. Errors in the plan will result in false commitments and lead to changes and confusion at a later date. How far out the master plan is projected will be determined to some extent by the type of industry. Generally, because of manufacturing cycles and purchasing lead times, master planning should project forward at least a year. It must be accepted that changing conditions will undoubtedly change the forecasts to some degree. A method of revising master plans must be available. Revisions are often prepared monthly or quarterly; only very unusual circumstances should require revisions more frequently.

Preparing the master plan. Certain steps should be considered in preparing the master plan.

1. Determine how far forward the master plan should project.

2. Establish the frequency with which the plan will be updated.

3. Establish the minimum inventory level acceptable for each product. This is the quantity below which desired customer service levels cannot be met.

4. Establish some common measurement of products, units, and families of products. This will be necessary in order to relate production requirements to facilities and labor requirements.

5. Be certain that the sales forecast is stated in the unit of common measurement and broken down into time intervals. The forecast for production planning should be in units of each item to be sold during each time period. A forecast in dollars on an annual basis will not suffice.

6. Basing the calculation on inventory at the starting period and desired positions by month or quarter, spread the production requirements over the planning period. At this time, production leveling and capacity limitations by groups of products are taken into account and problem areas identified in a general way. This plan will also provide a projection of inventory position and turnover rate throughout the year.

7. Analyze the data and determine the corrective action required to avoid potential trouble areas.

8. Establish controls that will identify variations between plan and actuality for sales and production. These controls should operate by exception so that only deviations of significance justifying changes to the plan will be highlighted.

DETAILED PLANNING AND SCHEDULING

From the master plan detailed plans and schedules can be developed; they must provide for the implementation and control of the master schedule in each of the various phases of manufacturing. Requirements for economic production quantities, a production authorization system, the development of machine loading data, and dispatching procedures will be set up.

Inventory policy. Inventory policy is essentially the balancing of investment in inventory against a desired customer service level. Too little inventory will cause out-of-stock conditions. Too much inventory will tie up funds that could be used for other purposes.

There are four basic types of inventory.

1. *Safety stock* is inventory planned to take care of fluctuations in sales demand and manufacturing lead time.

2. *Anticipation stock* is inventory built up in advance of planned seasonal selling peaks, special promotions, or plant shutdowns. This planned buildup recognizes the capacity limitations of the manufacturing facility. This type of buildup should be planned to occur as close to the time of need as possible.

3. *Economic order quantity (EOQ) stock.* Mathematical formulas have been developed to determine the most economic order quantity for any item to be manufactured or purchased. The use of this analysis provides an answer to the question of how much and how often to produce. It provides a balance between set-up costs, manufacturing costs, and inventory carrying costs.

4. *Distribution stock* represents the amount of inventory that must be available to provide time for distribution of the stock from the manufacturing plant to the warehouse and the ultimate consumer.

Inventory categories. Manufacturing companies generally classify inventories in four categories.

1. *Raw materials.* These are the materials that will be converted or combined during the manufacturing process.

2. *Components.* These are the parts, subassemblies, and packaging materials that will become a part of the final product.

3. *Work-in-process.* These are the materials worked on at various stages of the manufacturing process.

4. *Finished stock.* This is the final product ready for sale to the customer.

A useful practice in establishing inventory policy is to apply the ABC principle to each of these categories of inventory. This principle simply recognizes that, as a rule, 20 percent of all products represent approximately 80 percent of inventory investment. Each category of inventory can be broken down into three or more groups based on their value. Different inventory policies and procedures can be applied to the A (high dollar) group and to the C group, which represents very little value. The most important products should be controlled more closely because they represent a greater dollar investment.

Machine loading and labor. The production plan must be examined to determine whether sufficient labor hours are available and whether machine capacity is adequate.

Labor requirements can be determined by multiplying the units of each product to be produced in each time period by an established labor standard. A summary of the labor hour requirements for all products can be compared against the available labor force. Projected forward, this comparison will indicate need for hiring, firing, and overtime commitments.

Machine loading compares the quantity of work to be done on a machine or group of machines with the capacity and availability of the equipment. Short-term overloads on machines can be overcome by overtime or rerouting of work to other machines. Long-term overloads can be solved only by procuring additional equipment, changing production methods, or purchasing the item from an outside source.

Dispatching and marshaling. Dispatching is the job of seeing that the plans and schedules are followed in the manufacturing area. This is done through the release of job or production orders. The manufacturing departments should produce only those items for which they have been given an order. The dispatching group will determine priorities and materials routing between departments, see that work is forwarded from one area to another, report idle time of machines and operators, and request action on delays. In some cases, timekeeping is also a responsibility of the dispatching function.

The marshaling and movement of materials from the warehouse to the first process operation and from one operation to another are performed by the dispatching group. This frees the manufacturing supervisor from concern about materials availability and permits him to concentrate on efficiency of operation and quality of product.

Materials Planning and Control

To support the planned and scheduled manufacturing operation, it is essential that raw materials and components of the right type and quantity are available when needed. At the same time, excess inventories of these materials tie up dollars, reduce turnover, and present potential obsolescence problems.

MATERIALS ORDER SYSTEMS

The type of order system used will depend to some extent on the size and complexity of the business. Frequently, several different systems are used concurrently for different types of materials that present distinctly different problems. One universal application is the ABC analysis of all materials; it provides the basis for setting up inventory policy on each category of materials. When this ranking of materials, based on dollar value, has been completed, the correct emphasis can be placed on each group of items and inventory investment can be controlled. For example, a commonly used screw representing an annual purchase of only $1,000 will be purchased once a year, while a specialized raw material representing annual purchases of $50,000 will be purchased on a monthly basis. Dollar investment, clerical control, and order costs are used to the best advantage.

In any order system, the lead time necessary for procuring additional supplies of an item must be considered.

EOQ analysis should also be completed, along with the determination of price break points based on purchase quantities, to determine how much of each raw material or component should be procured at each reordering point.

Some of the order systems in use today are briefly described as follows:

The two-bin system. This is a simple system whereby a determined amount of stock is set aside (frequently, in a separate bin or sealed bag). When all other stock has been used and this separate stock must be opened and used, an order is placed for replenishment stock.

The visual review system. Stock levels are checked visually and replenishment orders placed when a predetermined minimum level is reached. This is a common application for tank-held items where it is important that a new order not be placed for tank wagon delivery until there is sufficient room in the inventory holding tank.

The order-point system. This system is based on perpetual inventory records; when an item reaches a predetermined order point, a replenishment order is placed.

The materials control system. This system is the most sophisticated and in medium-size or large businesses is generally handled on electronic data processing equipment. In this system, orders for materials are based on a production plan. Quantities and delivery requirements are predetermined on the basis of safety stock factors, production requirements, economic order quantity analysis, and procurement lead times. Common materials for different finished-stock products are collated and summarized within specific time periods.

SAFETY STOCK

The decision on how much safety stock to maintain for any category of materials is difficult and requires the attention of corporate management.

Too much safety stock and poorly defined limits will result in excess inventory.

It is a natural tendency—at all levels—never to run out of stock and thus be safe. Most businesses cannot afford the luxury of never having an out-of-stock condition. Conversely, too frequent an out-of-stock condition will result in manufacturing interruptions and poor customer service. The determination of reserve stock is based on the accuracy of forecast demand; the size of the economic order quantities; the length and accuracy of lead times for procurement of materials; and the service level demanded.

A number of statistical techniques can assist in the determination of safety stocks. Two of these techniques are the estimation of forecast error and the calculation of reorder point by product based on probability of out-of-stock conditions.

LEAD TIME

The time to procure or manufacture an item must be identified. Lead time becomes a part of the planning and controlling activity if inventories are to be kept within required limits and materials are to be available on a timely basis to avoid work interruption. The introduction of new plant equipment can have a dramatic effect on lead times and consumption requirements. Changes in suppliers, general industry backlogs, and supplier operating problems and strikes can cause lead times to change. Through frequent contacts with supplier representatives, purchasing can identify changes in lead times for procurement. These changes must be communicated to the materials control function so that requisitions for materials will be placed on a realistic basis.

PHYSICAL INVENTORIES

The common practice is to take a complete physical inventory of all production materials once each year. As a supplement to this and in some instances as an eventual replacement for the annual physical inventory, rotating or cyclical inventories are taken. When rotating inventories are taken, their frequency should be established on the basis of the value of various items. An ABC analysis should be made for all items. Those items representing the top 80 percent in value may be checked every three or four months. Those with very little dollar value would require checking only every two years.

The physical inventory provides an opportunity to verify and correct inventory records. Normally, two counts of each item are made by different people. The warehousing, stores, materials control, and accounting personnel generally conduct the count. An auditing team should also participate in the physical inventory.

New Versus Established Techniques

Most of the methods and techniques discussed herein have already been tried and proved and are in general use today. The dynamic evolution of rapidly increasing business complexity, the introduction of advanced computer technology, and the application of mathematical analysis have brought to the area of materials management a dramatic future. The potential applications of new methods must constantly be explored.

Some of the techniques that should be examined for their value to the business are described briefly here.

LINE OF BALANCE

A simplified technique developed to assist in the monitoring of various defense projects is line of balance. The concept is one of control by exception. Although related to PERT, it deals only with the main checkpoints that pertain to the overall project schedule. A basic reporting system rather than a detailed planning system, it simply attempts to monitor a project's progress as related to its planned goals. This technique is a simple monitoring tool to replace the knowledge and follow-up in a total situation that was once handled in a less complex situation by the line supervisor.

Line of balance is established in three phases and committed to graphic presentation for tracking.

The first approach is to establish the basic delivery schedule. On this same chart is plotted the actual performance on a week-to-week or monthly basis.

The second phase is to establish the time and unit schedule indicating how each major part of the total project will be completed.

The third stage of the program is the plotting of the progress of the manufacturing activity (taking into account purchased items and subassemblies) as of a certain date.

The result is then compared to the original objective to determine the line of balance. The analysis provides data on portions of the plan that are ahead of objective, as well as those that are late.

CRITICAL RATIO SCHEDULING

A technique for continuously re-establishing production priorities based on the latest information is critical ratio scheduling. It is of particular value when lead times are long, since there is increased opportunity for change in the lead time intervals. The development of critical ratio scheduling generally indicates that production orders will not be released to the manufacturing department until required. This probability is based on the premise that 50 percent or better of these requirements will change in priority.

The critical ratio or priority for scheduling is developed from a factor based on available stock, reorder quantity, standard lead time to manufacture, and manufacturing lead time remaining. It is a technique for precisely putting first things first.

PLANNER PERFORMANCE

Through the use of electronic data processing and the detailed explosion of requirement techniques against an established plan, it is now possible to determine individual planner performance.

By the use of an input of predetermined criteria such as safety stock, lead time to manufacture, test time, forecast, and inventory position, it is possible to prepare a theoretically ideal production plan. This plan can be modified by the individual planner proceeding from knowledge he possesses regarding anticipated changes in capacity, component delivery, or other factors. This exploded plan (broken down into finished stock, raw materials, and components) can be shown in terms of a dollar variance from the ideal plan. It will indicate dollars of inventory overcommitted or potential out-of-stock conditions. This technique will be of great assistance to management in monitoring individual planner performance.

SIMULATION THEORY

Through the use of computer programs, it is possible to simulate the consequences of planning and inventory decisions in terms of dollar investment in the future or potential out-of-stock conditions. When these techniques are fully developed, they will permit management decision experimentation before actual commitment. Ultimately, this should be an extremely useful tool in determination of the best decisions for the business.

Materials Handling

Materials handling as a part of the materials management function generally consists of the receiving, warehousing, and shipping operations. Support for this area in the form of engineering studies and major equipment analysis is provided by the industrial or plant engineering departments. This subject is covered under "Materials Handling and Warehousing" (page 6·74).

Evaluation of the Function

To properly evaluate the materials management function, objectives must be established and understood by all levels of operating management. Many of these objectives in the area of inventory management and customer service are shared with other functional areas of management. These objectives must have the approval and support of corporate management if they are to be effectively attained. They should provide a good measurement of performance, and to do this they must be realistic and be thoroughly understood.

TECHNIQUES AND CONTROLS

A number of techniques and controls are available in measuring the attainment of materials management objectives.

Inventory investment. A plan for the level of inventory investment should be established. This plan should project forward at least one year and take into consideration all special plans (buildups, major purchases, forecasted sales, and production demands, for example) that are known. A monthly reporting system should be established to provide comparisons with previous years and projected plans. These reported data should be broken down by plant location, product groups, and types of inventory. The types of inventory covered should include raw materials, components, work-in-process, returned goods, and finished stock. This detail is necessary if problem areas are to be identified and the necessary corrective action taken.

Inventory turnover. Turnover data relating inventories to cost of sale and cost of materials used in production, for all categories, must be provided monthly. These data should be compared with a projected planned turnover rate by month and on a cumulative basis.

Budget control. A majority of costs associated with the materials management function are associated with fixed personnel costs. Comparisons should be made periodically with industrywide surveys to determine whether organizational staffing is reasonable. In recent years, the introduction of computer-oriented systems has provided an opportunity for reduction in clerical effort.

Customer service levels. Precise data should be accumulated in the area of customer service. Common goals in this area are expressed as a percent of customer orders shipped incomplete and the percent of line items that are backordered. Total backorders should be analyzed item by item, including not only the number of items and the dollars of backorder but also the length of time the item has been backordered. The operational area responsible for the backorder should be identified so that the necessary corrective action can be taken. This is extremely important, since many different areas of the operation can directly influence backorders and ultimate customer service levels.

Manufacturing efficiency. Frequently, manufacturing efficiencies and costs are affected by planning and scheduling activities. A detailed analysis of changeovers, idle time, and materials delays can indicate a need for improved planning and materials control activities.

Number of months of stock. The determination of the number of months' coverage of finished stock is a frequently used indicator of adherence to inventory plans.

Comparison of actual with planned production. Information on how well planned or theoretical planning is being followed in actual practice is provided by this comparison.

Timeliness of promotions. A constant review should be made of the availability of stock to support special promotional plans and new product introductions.

Forecast performance. Forecast versus actual sales should be regularly reviewed. This review should make allowance for required manufacturing lead times. For example, last month's actual sales should not be compared with a forecast introduced last month. These sales should be compared with a forecast introduced several months earlier, which allows time for manufacturing to react.

Disposal of assets. Obsolete and surplus materials that result in a disposal of assets cost should be monitored. An analysis of such costs should be kept by category of material, dollars to be disposed of, number of items, and reasons.

Stability of labor force. Frequent hiring and firing of the labor force add costs through training costs, operating inefficiencies, employment costs, and compensation costs. Wherever possible within the limits of inventory policies, effort should be made to maintain a level work force through scheduling adjustments.

Warehousing costs. Failure to maintain proper inventory levels and dispose of obsolete materials regularly will soon add significantly to warehouse costs. This result is particularly noticeable when warehouse space is being rented.

Slow-moving items. Production planning should routinely identify, for marketing management, those products that are moving slowly and indicate potential obsolescence. This will provide an opportunity for special promotional plans for disposing of such materials.—*L. F. Edelblut*

PRODUCTION CONTROL SYSTEMS

Many types of production control systems provide effective means of correlating information necessary to the planning and materials control functions. Such systems range from simple graphs to intricate control boards and, finally, to complex electronic data processing systems.

Control Charts

The relationship between two or more factors can generally be more clearly understood if some type of visual presentation is used. Some of the control charts employed to show relationships when the information to be presented is not too detailed are as follows:

1. Line and bar graphs, drawn on a single horizontal and vertical axis, are normally used to indicate progress against a plan on something, such as the number of automobiles built each month during the year.

2. Gantt charts (named for Henry L. Gantt, who invented them), although simple in design, offer the distinctive ability to show quickly and precisely the relationship between several different factors—time, labor, and others—that occur concurrently. When they are all parts of a final product, it becomes possible to readily identify a factor that presents a potential problem for the product because it is falling behind others in its progress through the manufacturing cycle. This permits corrective action before it is too late.

3. Assembly charts are a series of plottings over a time period, indicating when various parts of a total job are to be started and completed in order to fit in with the schedule for other parts. Charting the sequence of operations in terms of time intervals is a simple method of predetermining which subassembly (for example) is behind schedule.

Control Boards

Control boards are, to some extent, related to charts, for they also are visual means of determining the status of an activity, making comparisons against a plan, and quickly identifying problem areas. Boards are generally mounted on the wall of the planning office and kept up to date by hour or day so that all concerned can quickly see the progress of any particular activity. To be effective, they must be kept current. There are several commonly used types of control boards.

POCKET AND HOOK BOARDS

These boards have several pockets for each line or machine. The pockets represent work not yet ready but assigned a priority, work ready to go on the line, and work on the line. For those items not yet ready there may be a color-coding system whereby attached clips indicate the component that is required before the job can be moved to the ready pocket. This simple board gives an immediate indication of work reserves and backlogs.

STRIP OR MAGNETIC BOARDS

Mounted on these boards are horizontal strips or channels along which labels on tags can be moved. The board may have a product or component list down the left side and different machine numbers across the top. If the tags are moved across the board, the immediate status of work can be determined visually.

PEG BOARDS

This type of board has many pegs attached to multicolor strings. The pegs are moved across the board, pulling the string with them as the item progresses through the manufacturing process. These boards are frequently used for production plan monitoring.

Card Files

Vertical card files consist of a series of card racks mounted on a wall, arranged so that several racks are side by side. Cards representing a particular job are maintained with job progress data and moved from rack to rack as the work is completed. This visual tool quickly indicates capacity bottlenecks and individual job status. Matching boards are sometimes kept in the manufacturing area and the production planning office, thus providing an excellent communication tool.

Visible Index Files

Many types of visible index files are readily available from suppliers. They consist essentially of a series of cards in flexible holders that overlap either vertically or horizontally to permit quick identification of items. A variety of control indexes or flagging strips can be utilized to identify special requirements or important review dates. These cards are used in manually operated perpetual materials control systems.

Electromechanical Systems

Electromechanical systems provided the first significant departure from purely manual control systems and others utilizing common office equipment—calculators, bookkeeping machines, and paper-tape controlled calculating equipment. Today many businesses have progressed beyond basic electromechanical systems to more sophisticated and complex equipment.

Electromechanical systems are capable of handling the calculations necessary for many of the reports and documents required in the planning and control operations. The basic elements of such a system are three:

1. The punched card, which records through perforations in the card itself, is a record of data specifically related to a transaction. These data are recorded in alphabetical or numerical form.

2. Perforating or keypunching equipment is used to put the information onto the card. It is similar in operation to a typewriter, except that it punches holes in predetermined positions on the card. The operator of this equipment transfers information from operating documents, such as receiving tickets, onto punched cards. There are also devices which will automatically transfer electronically sensitive pencil marks onto punched cards by perforating the card.

It is universal practice to run the punched cards through another keypunch machine, called a verifier, to be certain of the accuracy of the data. This is essentially a duplication of the process of keypunching, which was performed initially.

3. A great variety of processing equipment is used to produce required data from the prepunched cards. This equipment is capable of collating and sorting the cards in order to arrange the data in a required sequence for further processing. Other electromechanical equipment uses the data from the cards by adding, subtracting, dividing, and multiplying to prepare the necessary planning and control documents.

APPLICATIONS

These same systems are frequently used to prepare statistical operating reports. They provide information for the planning of the manufacturing operation, materials control, inventory planning, labor and capacity planning, and detailed scheduling and dispatching activities. As the business becomes more complex, the systems provide the opportunity to prepare data in more detail, on a much more timely basis, and with a significantly lower amount of clerical effort.

Electronic Data Processing

EDP equipment has already progressed through several generations. This type of equipment is the most sophisticated and expensive. It is commonly rented rather than purchased. In some instances where the cost to rent or buy an entire operation is prohibitive, use-time on someone else's equipment is purchased. Because of its high cost, it is frequently utilized on a 24-hour basis. This type of equipment provides extremely versatile applications, and extensive data can be prepared, stored, calculated, analyzed, and printed out in a very short period of time. Printing speeds of 1,100 lines a minute are possible. Complete calculations on national sales analyses for large organizations can be prepared in a matter of minutes. Data storage facilities permit the storage on tapes and disks of millions of pieces of information that can be used at a later date. This information can be retrieved for use in a matter of seconds.

The mathematical ability of this equipment to handle extremely large numbers of additions, subtractions, and multiplications quickly has made its application to planning and materials control a true technological breakthrough. Complex production plans, materials explosions, purchase-order preparation, inventory analysis, and shop scheduling programs are being produced through EDP today.

Electronic data processing systems permit data preparation and analysis that simply could not have been made manually within a reasonable time and cost. Probably most significant of all is that management can now be given status reports of an exceptional nature, based on extensive data, that are timely enough to use for future decision making.

A more detailed discussion of electronic data processing is presented in the Administrative Services section of this handbook (page 2·72).

Duplication Systems

It is inherent in control systems that many of the documents used are required in a number of copies. It is essential for all the different functions using these documents to be informed correctly and to have a written record of activities to be performed and the critical timing involved in schedules.

FORM DESIGN

One of the most important aspects of the duplication and distribution of information is the design of the form used. The form should lend itself to the easy preparation and clear interpretation of the data. It should be of handy or suitable size for the persons who use and file it. In effect, the form must satisfy the criteria for presenting information in a readily usable manner.

METHODS OF DUPLICATION

The methods of making duplicate copies include carbon paper, offset printing, Ditto masters, Addressograph duplicating plates, and Xerox. Each method has its own special features. More than one duplication system is used in most operations.

Communication Systems

The production planning function relies on a rapid exchange of information and instructions between various separated locations.

Points of communication may be scattered throughout the plant or office and frequently are even situated in different plant locations. To provide the necessary coordination between locations and functions, a rapid and convenient communication system must be available. Some of the systems commonly used are the telephone, Teletype, TelAutograph telescriber, closed-circuit television, two-way radio, and integrated reporting equipment. (See Administrative Services, under "Telecommunications," page 2·129.)

For using the telephone, planning personnel frequently are given direct lines and private wires to speed up the communication.

The Teletype consists of a teletypewriter on whose keyboard the operator types a message. This same message is reproduced exactly at another location on a similar piece of equipment. The Teletype gives the distinct advantage that both parties to the message see it in writing. Messages that go to several points can be prepared on perforated tape in advance and fed into the typewriter automatically.

The TelAutograph telescriber transmits handwritten messages from one point to one or more other, separate locations.

Closed-circuit television is rapidly increasing in industrial use. It provides an opportunity for personal contact without the normal traveling time that would otherwise be necessary. It is an ideal instrument for contact between the planning office and the shop floor.

Two-way radio is frequently used in the area of materials handling. Through the use of a radio system, personnel can be located as they are performing their jobs in various areas of the warehouse, and many hours of searching for these people will be eliminated. Two-way radios on mobile equipment can provide for a dispatching system.

Integrated reporting equipment is rapidly coming into wide use. This type of equipment permits input to be processed into the computer from remote stations. This information provides a constantly updated data base for consultation to determine job progress.—*L. F. Edelblut*

MATERIALS HANDLING AND WAREHOUSING

Materials handling has been aptly described as the logistics of industry. It encompasses the movement of raw materials to the plant and through the processing cycle, and the delivery of finished goods to the customer through distribution channels. Whether the work-in-process material moves in a box, on a conveyor, or in a pipeline, the activity is still materials handling.

The manufacturing process may require hours or years, but at every stage—even when materials are stored between operations—the handling of materials should be performed by the best techniques possible. Although there have been many advances in processing machines, until recent years very little was done to recognize, analyze, and reduce the costs of the indirect labor of materials handling. Since handling adds nothing but cost to the product, the first goal is to eliminate handling whenever possible.

Good materials handling is imperative throughout the distribution system, for here the product is at its highest manufactured cost—completed, inspected, and packaged. If damage caused by poor handling occurs, the product must be returned and reworked at the factory or reworked, reinspected, and repacked in a less efficient field operation. If damage occurring in distribution is ignored or undetected, the worst penalty of all is applied—customer dissatisfaction. These are all cogent reasons for the development of the best handling and distribution system that can be devised.

Basic Handling Principles

It is basic to any handling operation that the movement of the material must keep pace with the needs of the operation (quantity) so that an out-of-stock condition never occurs. It must be done, however, with the least amount of damage and at the lowest practical cost.

Wherever possible, the force of gravity is used to move the material through the stages of processing. Liquids and granular dry materials are frequently stored in a vertical silo so that mixing, blending, or treating may proceed at stages of a natural flow from top to bottom by gravity. The goal is to keep materials at each stage instantly available for movement when needed without incurring further handling costs. This in-flow storage principle may be utilized in many other kinds of systems.

When high-volume movement, heavy loads, round-the-clock operations, or hazardous or unpleasant working conditions are involved, an automated mechanical system may be a good investment. If the payoff will not justify an automated system, a mechanical system with people at key points may be justifiable. Where short runs or variety of product or processing may preclude the use of all but the simplest of handling devices, carts, containers, universal conveyors, or general utility trucks and racks may suffice.

In terms of return on investment, a high-priced, automatic system may be the best buy if it eliminates enough labor. The cost of eliminating labor by mechanical operation varies greatly with the complexity of the handling operation. Usually, mechanical handling is cheaper, causes less damage, and is much safer than manual handling.

LAYOUT

The layout of facilities is generally dictated by the dominant factors in any materials handling system—the materials, the building, the method, the available funds. If a system is being created from scratch, the receiving department should be planned so that truck or rail movement will not interfere with employees' or visitors' access to parking lots or buildings.

A "quality hold" storage area adjacent to the receiving station must be adequate to permit the retention of incoming materials long enough for sampling, testing, and palletizing or preparing the stock for movement to the storage areas.

Ideally, the stock would now be in suitable containers and in typical quantities to serve the production line so that it could be moved to a position adjacent to the area where it would be used. Storage of incoming materials *at the point of use* does more than just eliminate waiting-for-stock downtime. It minimizes handling labor and helps to monitor overordering while serving as a visual reminder of depleted stock at the reorder point.

If floor storage is decided upon, both raw stock and in-process storage may be allocated to the wall areas that will be moved out in the event of plant expansion. If such storage is along the expansion wall, many entrances and handling innovations may be added to keep pace with technological changes. If plant expansion occurs, it usually provides the best way to expand without shutting down production lines.

At the end of the production lines, there are usually an inspection area for quality testing and a packaging area. If packaging is done mechanically, the area should be large enough to allow for the newer, faster—but larger—machines which are the trend of the times. An adequate storage area for packaging materials should be planned adjacent to the point of use in the packaging area.

Loading facilities for rail and truck should be so planned that they provide ready egress from the plant area without creating traffic problems for personnel and vehicles. If the volume is high, a trailer park for both empty and full trailers should be provided so that tractor jockeying and other movement will not inhibit the loading cycle.

In the layout of a new facility, the process, equipment, storage, and handling are all planned, and then an architect is instructed to "wrap a building around it."

When a layout is planned for an existing building or process, compromises must be made. Frequently, the objective of having the best materials handling system must give way to some other dominant factor such as space requirements, building limitations, or process demands.

EQUIPMENT

Materials handling equipment is offered in a wide variety of designs and capacities at, of course, wide variations in price. It is most important that its selection be properly made. Dependence on a salesman's word alone is not the best criterion for the selection of equipment that must fit the job. Errors at this point can be disastrous later on. If price is a great consideration, certain calculated risks can be taken, or a leasing plan may be considered rather than the purchase of basically unsuitable equipment.

If no one with sufficient handling-equipment background is available within the company, by all means employ a consultant of known skill in the area being considered. A consultant has usually studied the particular usage in depth and can bring to the problem the wisdom of broad experience with almost any aspect of every handling job.

If new and untried designs are being considered, they may frequently be purchased with a performance guarantee whereby the risk in trying new equipment may be reduced.

If the performance of handling, packaging, or unitizing equipment is crucial to the production level, it is wise to provide for an alternative path and equipment (sometimes rental equipment) to maintain the flow if serious problems of any duration develop.

METHODS

Handling methods are determined mainly by the type of material, the volume to be handled in a given time segment, and the percentage of return expected from the expenditure; but there are other considerations.

Marketing considerations can supply the ground rules as to whether the product will continue at high volume or whether design changes will be required to hold the sales volume. Engineering may be able to anticipate design or process changes that will influence the methods of handling to some extent.

If the process seems to have a long period ahead without change in design or volume, a high degree of mechanization or even automation is in order. If the trend is toward change, or if extreme versatility is one of the requirements, the methods are more likely to be simple, even manual. If equipment is used, the payoff must be scrutinized carefully. Versatility and adaptability are likely to rank higher than efficiency in the selection of methods and equipment when change is imminent or likely.

In such cases, people will probably dominate the operation, and there will be more reliance on human judgment. Controls will be more manual, and dependence on skilled personnel a greater factor.

In such a simple system, controls may account for only 25 to 30 percent of the cost of the system. A sophisticated, highly automatic system can easily involve additional control costs of 50 to 75 percent of the cost of the mechanical system.

Production efficiencies for some expensive production machines may decline markedly for reasons of inefficient feeding or lack of materials. Some high-cost equipment is dependent upon operation 24 hours a day to provide an adequate return on the investment, and human failure may prevent an adequate return.

Pacing the machine feeding or other operations by the insertion of mechanical conveyors can often restore the feed rate needed. To hitch the human being to the machine pace may require some orientation, but it frequently results in greater employee satisfaction because the pace is more rhythmic. Many conveyors are supplied with variable speed controls for just such reasons.

MANPOWER

To determine manpower requirements, an analysis must be made of the flow of raw materials, work in process, and finished stock through the manufacturing operation. This analysis should include volumes and scheduling patterns. Common techniques such as time study and work sampling can be applied to determine manpower requirements. The number of units or pallets moved per hour is a meaningful measurement in evaluating manpower requirements.

Materials Handling Equipment

The range of materials handling equipment includes conveyors and vehicles of many kinds for the horizontal movement of materials; cranes, hoists, and elevators for vertical movement and storage; and containers and supports.

CONVEYORS

Conveyors are frequently used to move loose powdered, granular, and solid materials as well as packaged materials in containers. A few years ago, many of these were "specials" designed to fit a specific need and were not available except on special order. Today their proliferation is extended to accessories and modular unit design that permits the insertion of added sections so that the conveyors can grow with the layout.

Some equipment manufacturers specialize in package conveyors, others in bulk material conveying; it is worthwhile to seek vendors who have experience in what the problem requires.

CRANES, HOISTS, ELEVATORS

Cranes are made mobile for outdoor use on almost any kind of terrain and are made very versatile for yard storage and handling by the accessories available. They may be equipped with magnetic or mechanical grabs that make random pick-up or rack stacking very simple. Counterbalanced reach forks enable steel bars, pipe, lumber, and other materials to be stacked or retrieved from vertical racks for very efficient storing and picking. Cranes for inside use are made mobile and sized to fit almost any need.

Overhead rail cranes are offered in a great variety of sizes and capacities and can be operated from the floor by a control pendant. Wireless controls are also available; they operate the crane by radio signals from a small box on the operator's belt. Such controls have increased the hours of effective use and provide better crane service with safer operation.

Hoists have been so updated in design that continuous operation without operators is a reality and vertical movement can be almost as simple as horizontal movement. These are available in sizes and capacities from small cartons to full pallet loads.

Where large shaftways were formerly required, hoists (vertical conveyors) are now available which, by ingenious design, require space not much larger than the loads to be carried. Formerly, reciprocating movement limited speeds because the return trip was empty; but now there are vertical conveyors that are continuous in operation and can convey at speeds matching that of horizontal conveyors. Such equipment needs no operator to ride the car and can be loaded and unloaded without additional labor by automatic conveyors. The elimination of operators has drastically reduced the cost of vertical materials handling.

When, in the course of horizontal materials flow on the factory floor, an aisle or other conveyor intervenes, the new design of continuous-flow vertical conveyors permits movement up and over the aisle without the penalties of slow speed and operator involvement.

A built-in feature of every multistory factory building in the old days was the freight elevator. Slow, with cumbersome safety gates and requiring an operator, such vertical movement required in addition a man to load and a man to unload the car. The waiting time created a further waste of man-hours, thus making elevators a very expensive kind of vertical materials handling.

Freight elevators can now operate at higher speeds with automatically operated gates and other refinements that reduce operating costs. Some require only the deposition of pallet or other loads at a loading station adjacent to the elevator. The entire operation can be automatic and the loads unloaded on run-out conveyors which accumulate material loads on the proper floors.

A study of the load data and the direct and related costs of vertical materials handling will usually indicate the kind of equipment to buy.

VEHICLES

Vehicles for the horizontal movement of materials range from straddle carriers, that can pick up 50-foot trailers or stacks of lumber of the same size, to single battery-operated scooters for personnel and materials.

Powered vehicles are available to move rail cars on a siding without waiting for the railroad locomotive. Personnel carriers have been improved to carry firefighting and maintenance equipment to the point of use. Telescopic ladders extendible to 60 feet or more are now moved to required locations through doorways and passageways no more than eight feet high.

Pushcarts and other manual traveling containers are now available for easier and even automatic dumping. Aluminum and magnesium are widely used as materials in their construction, which increases the volume per man while lowering the fatigue and accident factors.

CONTAINERS AND SUPPORTS

The movement of quantities of goods and materials from factory to customers and from plant to plant has been the subject of keen investigation. Starting with the Conex containers of World War II, the problems of protection from damage, weather, and pilferage have repeatedly found no better answer than containers.

Forty-foot trailers with built-in legs for support and removable bogey wheels and running gear are available. Suitable for rail, highway, air, and sea traffic, they are extremely versatile and can even be separated into 20-foot units. They can be stacked for storage in a yard or the hold of a ship and can be equipped with heating or refrigeration units.

Since road taxes are applied only to the wheel section (bogey), these storage boxes have possibilities for real economies. Taxes on inventory in many places are applied at a specific calendar time. Storage in containers that can be made mobile overnight represents the possibility of minimizing this form of taxation.

The savings in packing material, particularly in overseas shipment, are truly amazing when containers are used in lieu of the very expensive unit carton packing usually done. Packed and sealed in the factory, the container can be shipped overseas, and the next access to its contents will be by the consignee in some foreign country.

Similarly, domestic shipments of parts and subassemblies can be made plant to plant, obviating the need for much of the packing material and labor now required. In many instances, special containers can receive the parts in an oriented manner and feed them back in like manner to automatic machinery at their destination.

Specialized types of racks and racking are now obtainable "off the shelf" because their use is so general. Readily available are racks for cradling tires and storing coiled materials, steel drums, rugs and carpeting, and innumerable other unusual types of materials. The main purpose of such racking is to make easily available every separate type of article stored.

Racks to store pallet loads have reached a high stage of development; some rack systems are even being built first, and the building that will enclose them is added later. Racks are made that permit trucks to drive through the storage space to reach the distant filled spaces. Such racks will materially reduce the space wasted on aisles for access to stored materials.

Racks and racking systems are quite sophisticated; again, if there is no one on the staff who is proficient in this area, call in a consultant to design and plan the system.

Materials Handling Systems

Modern industrial systems are very complicated; they are usually conceived and operated by teams that possess the skills of industrial engineers, production and inventory control specialists, production specialists, and materials handling experts. The system must be conceived in its entirety and consideration given to the impact of each specialty on every other phase of the production plan. Omissions and errors in the early planning show up as expensive obstacles to efficient production later.

Simulating the actual operation and its response to problems that normally arise is frequently performed on a computer to test the ability of the system to meet all obstacles and variations. By this technique the actual dollar cost of out-of-stock conditions, delayed shipments, and similar problems may be assessed in advance, and some prediction of their probability may be made before investment in a particular system is made.

INDUSTRIAL TRUCKS

Many handling systems are based entirely on material movement by fork truck only. Such a trucking operation is very versatile, especially if it is coordinated and controlled by two-way radio mounted on the trucks.

Industrial trucks equipped with forks are the workhorses of industry, roughly nine times as efficient as the manual lifting and carrying of single-case loads. They are available with a remarkable array of special attachments to handle unusual loads with ease. Loads can be lifted by squeezing or hooking, by vacuum, by being pulled onto and pushed off forks, and can be rotated, compressed, and weighed while in transit. The possibility of damage to materials, however, is greater with fork trucks than with conveyors, and labor and maintenance costs are higher.

The ability to convey large, heavy loads with speed and versatility makes the fork truck method the most widely used in handling, particularly in warehousing.

CONVEYOR SYSTEMS

Conveyor systems are usually designed to connect fixed positions with the most appropriate type of conveyor (belt, roller, troughed belt, pan, plate, oscillating, air, and so forth), operated by gravity or powered. The speed at which they convey can be critical if the production line they feed is closely integrated. Frequently, the conveying speed is used to pace the production machine operators to obtain higher production rates.

In a closely integrated system, several slower production machines may be needed to keep up with a higher-speed machine in the next operation. The conveyors may be branched out to feed the multiple set-up and converged again to feed the higher-speed equipment.

When a production machine is temperamental or has critical adjustments that tend toward excessive downtime, alternative paths through duplicate machinery should be built into the system.

Many methods are available to accomplish the switching of product flow through these conveyors—air, hydraulic, electrical, controlled by sonic or optical sensors.

A production system keyed to automatic conveying will usually be totally nonproductive if the conveyor system fails. If preventive maintenance is scheduled regularly, such failures will be very unlikely to occur.

Overhead conveyors. Manufacturing space is usually high-priced; it is natural to look overhead for the location where conveyors can connect floor-mounted equipment. Frequently, in older plants, it is the only remaining clear space where conveyors can be located.

When planning for overhead conveyor runs in a new building, it is wise to have all piping, ductwork, bus duct, or other overhead impediments run parallel to the production line or to the proposed conveyor line. The use of "air rights" within the plant may offer great returns because of the straight paths that are offered and the use of otherwise wasted space.

Overhead conveyors may be of many types similar to floor-mounted designs, with the exception of oscillating conveyors. These are not usually used overhead, because of the extra steel required to support and balance them as well as the live load they can create. Overhead monorail conveyors are uniquely suitable, because of their versatility, for carrying large or small objects of many shapes. Designs are available which permit raising and lowering the material loads; storage banks with automatic pick-up and discharge; powered and free sections to rationalize out-of-phase production equipment; and automatic dispatching and pick-up.

Overhead conveyors can be enclosed with safety screens that are easily released for conveyor servicing while completely protecting personnel and equipment below. Maintenance can be simplified by automatic lubrication systems and by automatic signaling systems that pinpoint troubleshooting problems. Some processes, such as washing, drying, painting, heating, cooling, seasoning, and storage, can often be included in a good overhead system.

IMPACT OF VOLUME

Generally, large-volume, continuous handling in a process industry can be done so much more cheaply by a handling system that the savings can pay for sturdy, well-designed equipment replete with controls and maintenance provisions that mean low-cost, trouble-free operation over a long time period. In fact, the system may dictate the shape of the building and layout. Materials handling provisions not properly organized can raise costs to a prohibitive level and can even destroy production scheduling.

Large-volume production systems dependent upon manual handling and feeding run the risks of labor shortages, sickness epidemics, labor problems, and oversupply of labor during downtime. Virtually all of these risks can be eliminated by automatic conveyorized handling.

In a low-volume processing industry, simple gravity conveyors may have to suffice with in-process storage before each successive operation. This usually requires more floor space and better production scheduling and increases the investment in in-process materials. Sometimes, specialized containers are needed to make the system work or to prevent damage to the product.

Such conditions are typical of a job shop operation. The versatility of the equipment is usually accompanied by a loss of efficiency and a higher labor content. Preservation of batch identity requires more record keeping.

Planning the Warehouse

In addition to the problem of locating the warehouse where transportation costs, land investment, taxes on stock, and labor costs are minimal, many other considerations are important. Hazards of weather such as high winds, flooding, tornadoes, and the like must be considered.

The degree of mechanization or automation of the warehouse facility is a most important decision, for it determines the design of the building. Many existing buildings are totally unsuited to mechanical warehousing because the column spacing and truss height (optimum, 35–40 feet) do not permit economical spacing of the aisles and mechanism.

If the volume is high and a single modular size (unit load) will accommodate most of the products, it will be worthwhile to consider a mechanized system. Most mechanized systems are basically a set of racks to store the modular loads with a storing and retrieving device that gives access to all loads. The system may also have a unit load make-up device (palletizer) and feed conveyors, strapping equipment, and so forth.

In general, the cost of constructing a high building is less than the cost of spreading out the greater area (two to three times greater) of a conventional warehouse. Labor savings are made in the automatic or mechanical storage and retrieval of product.

The alternative to this is, of course, the use of fork lift trucks or other handling devices suitable for stacking loads (optimum, 21–24 feet high).

To minimize long runs by fork truck, some warehouses have a circulating tow-cart system powered by either an overhead or in-floor tow line. Fork lift trucks then do the handling of loads into trucks and rail cars from the tow-line carts. Electronically guided, self-powered tractors are also used to tow trains of carts. Automatic dispatching and guidance are a feature of most of these systems.

Warehouse Layout

Warehouse buildings are usually located adjacent to a rail siding and a good service road for trucks and trailers.

Sales offices and visitors' parking are usually located in the front of the building; the front entrance is as imposing as costs permit. Employee parking is usually at the sides or back to lessen confusion. Rail siding and out-shipment truck dock are usually located at right angles to the rear or sides of the building. This provides for minimum distance when some loads are transferred directly from one shipping mode to another.

If possible, rail sidings are extended beyond the building to provide more car capacity with the use of some car-moving device. If the rail siding is indoors, it removes the problem of "spotting" the cars with their doors at the warehouse doors. Truck docks are usually external, with weather-sealing door pads and mechanical dock boards to adjust to tail-gate heights. Roll-up doors minimize heat and cold interchange during loading and unloading. Staging areas are arranged in a clear space before the rail and truck dock areas. Aisles are usually laid out in the direction of the longer axis of the building, with cross aisles at intervals for convenience. Sprinkler controls and lighting panels should be located at aisle ends for easy access without waste of space.

BULK AND RESERVE STORAGE

Stock that is received or shipped in bulk can be stored in orderly piles on the floor or in piles separated in usable stacking height on pallets. Usually, access from one aisle is provided with stacks of a size that permits shipment within a reasonable time to approximate first-in, first-out shipping. Reserve storage may be similarly "brick stacked" for periodic feeding up to an order-selection area as required.

INTERNAL MATERIALS FLOW

Basically, the flow of materials within a warehouse should be planned so as to minimize movement and handling. An analysis of previous orders will yield data on the quantity and frequency of each product; these data can be used to arrange the stock. The national average indicates that 15 percent of the products account for 85 percent of the traffic.

The 15 percent of products in high demand should be stored in closest proximity to the out-loading points. The quantities contained in unit loads should approximate the typical order quantity, if possible. Products in high demand could be received by truck or rail and reloaded directly in one move for out-shipment. Sometimes they can remain in the same conveyance with other products added to the load. Such treatment will definitely minimize handling.

Operations

In planning for the operations of a warehouse, consideration is given to the location of the order-filling area, methods of stock selection, shipping techniques, shipping and receiving docks, administrative offices, and service areas.

ORDER-FILLING AREAS

The section most convenient to the order-staging area should contain a variety of the 15 percent of stock most frequently ordered, in ample quantity for picking small-lot and single-carton orders. These may be arranged in shelving or palletized in pallet racks for quick access. The next adjacent area should contain the unit loads and bulk stock of the items of highest frequency in quantity orders. Slow-moving items should be stored peripherally in quantities appropriate to their historical ordering quantity. Small-sized cartons of high frequency can be stored in pick racks (supermarket slide racks) that permit wide selection in a small frontal area to reduce walking. They do require labor for stock replenishment to be effective. Order-picking fork lift trucks make upper levels of pallet racks easily available for order picking also.

STOCK SELECTION METHODS

Orders printed by computer frequently have the stock location printed out at the same time. The location of break bulk stock, at least, can be so indicated.

Because break bulk stock selection is time-consuming, it is frequently the starting point in order filling, leaving bulk and unit loads to be picked last.

The location of highest-frequency stocks may be changed by reason of seasonal demands, making permanent location of bulk stock impossible. Such changes should be posted to avoid confusion.

Labeling and other identification methods have much to do with speed in order picking. Large numbers, legible to a man with ordinary vision at a distance of 20 feet, will be very helpful. Product-numbering codes that give a clue to the classification of the product will aid in locating stock. This practice can also reduce the number of digits the stock man must remember, thus reducing errors in stock selection. Adequate lighting (minimum, 20 foot-candles), particularly in the aisles, will speed up order picking and reduce errors.

SHIPPING TECHNIQUES

Unit loads are frequently loaded first because the empty vehicle provides more space to maneuver. Side shifter forks are valuable in loading a tight load with minimum voids.

Manual loading should be done in such a manner that dunnage (space fillers) will be minimal if needed at all. Careful loading will prevent much of the transit damage, particularly in rail traffic. Mechanical dunnage, load restraining devices, and special types of cars will do much also to insure safe delivery of products. Obviously heavy loads should be placed at the bottom when loading, and frail packages or cartons at the top.

SHIPPING AND RECEIVING DOCKS

The physical facilities for receiving and shipping from truck docks should have padded weather seals on the doors, mechanical dock levelers, and in-car lighting from the door frames.

Truck-leveling devices to raise or lower truck and trailer bodies are very useful and save time. (Some fork trucks have small floor clearance and cannot enter a truck body until it is almost level with the dock.)

Rail docks are usually at the same height as the floor of the car, and the open space is bridged with a dock board. Aluminum or magnesium dock boards with raised sides and gridded surface will make car loading easier and safer. Use of lightweight materials may prevent a hernia or crushed foot in the course of moving from one location to another. A mechanical rail car door opener is a "must" for safety reasons. In-car lighting can be accomplished conveniently with a variety of fixtures now available. Car loading is not only safer in a well-lighted car; damage to the product is usually lessened as well.

ADMINISTRATIVE OFFICES

The administrative offices should provide a view—from a picture window, if necessary—of a broad area of the warehouse such as the out-loading or order-marshaling area. A view down one aisle is not of very great help.

SERVICE AREAS

A fork truck or conveyance-repair area should be provided, usually close to the battery-charging area if electric trucks are used. If liquefied petroleum gas trucks are used, check the insurance company's safety requirements for the storage and changing of gas cylinders.

An area near the truck docks, if provided with a toll phone, coffee machine, and rest room, will alleviate the problem of truckers' using company phones or wandering around in the warehouse.—*G. C. Stryker*

PHYSICAL DISTRIBUTION

Distribution expense has become a significant part of the total cost of goods supplied by manufacturers: The costs of distribution range from 15 to 40 percent of the total cost of goods manufactured. The number of employees engaged in distribution has increased at a faster rate than for those in production. Paul W. Stewart and J. Frederic Dewhurst point out in their book *Does Distribution Cost Too Much?* (Twentieth Century Fund, 1939) that "for every 100 workers engaged in producing goods in 1870 there were 271 in 1930, and these workers were turning out nine times the total volume of goods produced in 1870. Employment in distribution increased from 100 to 877 or nearly nine times—almost as large an increase as the volume of goods distributed." Little more evidence is needed to understand the current emphasis on distribution in the management of American industry.

The Concept of Physical Distribution

In concept, physical distribution is the grouping of activities, both line and staff, that are concerned with moving a product to a customer after manufacture. Physical distribution is, quite simply, the management of customer service.

First popularized in business literature in the late 1950's and early 1960's, the concept advanced slowly at the beginning but in recent years has gained in popularity until today it claims a rightful place with manufacturing and marketing as an organizational center of the line activities of a manufacturing concern.

Rationale for Physical Distribution as an Organization

The need for a formalized distribution organization was an outgrowth of the inability of management to responsibly control its customer service without it, coupled with unrealized areas for profit improvement. Distribution tasks and costs are interrelated in a complex way. Scattering distribution activities throughout a company creates a lack of cohesiveness and direction in approaching distribution cost reduction. When responsibility and authority are placed in one individual for the full range of distribution operations, companies find themselves able to develop comprehensive programs for cost reduction that neither over- nor underemphasize customer service.

CONFLICTING OBJECTIVES

As in so many business situations, distribution cost reduction presents a series of conflicting objectives and opportunities. Multiple warehouse locations improve the speed of service to customers and reduce freight costs to the customer —but at increased fixed cost of operation for the additional locations; increased need for inventory to stock these added warehouses; increased freight costs for plant-to-warehouse shipments; and, finally, significantly increased need for inter-company communications.

BALANCED OBJECTIVES

When all the proper activities of distribution are grouped into a physical distribution organization fairly reflecting its complex interrelationships, a company realizes a balancing of objectives. In the decision-making process, all considerations are weighed, and the lowest total cost becomes the only valid yardstick.

ORGANIZATIONAL CONSIDERATIONS

A typical distribution organization structure draws together the functions directly associated with the movement of goods from the factory to the customer. These functions usually include, as line activities, warehousing and shipping, transportation, order processing, and inventory control. The distribution staff group generally encompasses materials handling engineering, planning and analysis, and coordination.

REPORTING STRUCTURE

Historically, the distribution function before the physical distribution concept has been a part of the marketing organization and usually included only the actual warehouse and order-processing operations. When the broader concept of physical distribution is implemented and other functions such as transportation, inventory control, and materials handling engineering are brought into a total distribution organization, a new structure which places physical distribution on an operating par with manufacturing and marketing becomes the more favored arrangement. This is necessary if physical distribution is to operate in an environment of balanced objectives in which one organizational group can achieve its goals at the expense of other groups as long as the lowest total cost results.

MARKETING STRATEGY AND DISTRIBUTION

In many industries, physical distribution can be a vital if not a decisive factor in marketing success. Customer service can be sold, just as product design, quality, and price are sold. In a very competitive situation where products frequently offer little to choose from, service can determine where the business goes. An organization that wishes to incorporate its distribution service into its total marketing strategy must define the type of service it is prepared to give; must be certain that the level of service presents a competitive advantage; must sell the service concept to its customers; and must establish the necessary performance control systems to measure and evaluate actual performance against standard.

Physical distribution is also discussed in the Marketing section of this handbook (page 5·138).

Elements of Physical Distribution

Although the nature of the physical distribution function will vary among different organizations, it is basically made up of four elements—warehousing, transportation, inventory control, and engineering. Not all companies include all these operations in the physical distribution organization; but if they do not, they run the risk of being unable to apply the advanced techniques needed to analyze and minimize the total of all costs involved. Now that physical distribution has been recognized as the last frontier for major cost reduction opportunity, this would seem a high risk to take.

WAREHOUSING

The foundation around which the distribution organization is built is usually the warehousing function. Branch warehouses are the major operating element in distribution, much as production departments are in manufacturing.

It is the branch warehouse function that physically stores, handles, and ships finished goods from the plants to the customers. Commonly associated with the warehousing function is the order-processing function responsible for turning a customer order into an invoice with allied documents for shipping and customer accounting. Order processing is normally located at the branch warehouse site and generally is part of the branch organization.

TRANSPORTATION

The transportation function is the second most important element in the distribution operation. Freight costs can be a very significant part of total distribution expense, being dependent on the type of industry, product, and service offered. In many cases, freight costs are the equivalent of branch costs. The transportation function determines the routing of shipments both from the plant to the branch warehouses and from the warehouses to customers. Because of the technical expertise required in this function, routing for inbound freight to the plants (raw materials and the like) is frequently handled by this department.

INVENTORY CONTROL

Inventory control at the factory level, although a complex situation dealing with production planning, plant capacity, and the like, differs in nature from that in distribution. While some plants deal with the same item at more than one warehouse, this is not normally the case. In distribution, however, this is almost always the case. Distribution inventory control has been classed as a multilocation, multistage problem wherein inventory of the same item is stored at more than one location and, frequently, in multistages. A multistage inventory is one that flows through a series of locations before reaching the final user. This flow, called cascading, is typified by the problem that small changes in demand at the ultimate user level trigger larger variations up the inventory chain, producing an effect of instability and erratic demand that is not truly representative.

Even without multistage complications, the multilocation problem makes inventory control more intricate as it multiplies the number of stock-keeping units to be accounted for.

DISTRIBUTION ENGINEERING

This function serves many vital purposes in the distribution operation. Many companies organize a distribution function without including a specialized engineering staff; this practice can have serious consequences. The engineering demands in distribution are heavy, and it is unrealistic to depend on the existing manufacturing engineering groups to serve both functions properly or fairly.

The distribution engineering group is usually called on to provide engineering service for materials handling methods and equipment, warehouse layout, order-picking systems, packing optimization, order-processing systems and procedures, office and warehouse work standards, and branch warehouse location studies.

Warehousing Considerations

The questions of number, type, and location of warehouses are some of the most significant to be answered by a company's distribution function. The final answers will reflect in the level of service that can be provided to customers and the costs that will be borne by the organization.

MULTIPLE WAREHOUSES

Branch warehouses usually are established for one overriding purpose: to improve the level of service in the consumer market areas they serve. Since inventories are stocked at each location, transit time to customers is shorter than from more distant, consolidated warehouses. A network of small warehouses in many locations can also reduce the order-receipt and processing time and result in a less remote approach to customer service operations such as credit control, merchandise complaints, requests for special handling, and the like.

Impact on inventory, cost, and order processing. Subtle relationships with other service elements are drawn into the question of multiple branch warehouses. Additional warehouses do generally result in faster delivery, but the dispersion of inventory required to stock all the locations has a deleterious impact. Either the inventory will be too thin to provide safety stock adequate to protect against unexpected demand, or the total company inventory will have to be increased to cover the safety stock required for the additional locations.

The cost considerations of multiple warehouse locations are especially significant. Each warehouse location has an overhead expense for rent, utilities, warehouse management, and other fixed costs. As a rule, the overhead for a consolidated warehouse is lower than the combined overhead of the smaller warehouses it replaces.

Another cost element likely to be higher when dealing with many small warehouses is the cost of shipping inventory from the plant to the branch. Because of the dispersion of inventory, it becomes more difficult to achieve shipping loads which move at the best transportation rate.

A less obvious disadvantage of the multiple small warehouse concept is the difficulty of supporting the many locations with order-processing systems of the same sophistication as is possible with fewer, larger warehouses. This is particularly true when dealing with computer systems. The smaller order volume at each branch makes it difficult to justify the introduction of a computer system and commonly results in the installation of less expensive equipment—such as for punched-card or even manual operation.

Reduced freight costs. In addition to reasons cited for setting up multiple warehouses, there is a major cost advantage in reduced cost of freight to the customer. In the total cost of freight, the segment dealing with delivery from warehouse to customer is the largest by far. In some instances, this portion can be ten times the freight cost for plant-to-warehouse shipments. The nature of the shipments causes this imbalance in the distribution of costs. Plant-to-branch shipments move at the most favorable rate, generally in truckload quantities. Most customer shipments are in relatively small quantities and require a premium freight rate. For many customer shipments there may even be a minimum charge which, on a pound-for-pound basis, is many times the weight-based full (or even less) truckload rates.

BALANCING COSTS

Exhibit 6.12 shows the conflicting cost curves for warehouse and freight expense as the number of warehouses increases. The total cost curve is the sum of the customer transportation cost curve (which decreases as the number of warehouses increases) and the warehouse operating cost curve (which increases as the number of warehouses increases). The point at which the sum of these two curves is lowest shows the lowest total cost and therefore the optimum number of warehouses.

PUBLIC WAREHOUSES

After a company decides that it will operate through warehouses and has established the number and locations, it must determine if the warehouses will be private (company-operated) or public.

Public warehouses are in business to provide warehousing service to others. They receive, store, and ship goods and perform many other related services.

There are five generally defined types of warehouses: (1) commodity warehouses handling specific commodities such as cotton and grain; (2) bulk storage warehouses for storing tanks of bulk liquids; (3) cold storage warehouses for

Exhibit 6.12

DISTRIBUTION COSTS VERSUS NUMBER OF WAREHOUSES

Reproduced, with permission, from *Journal of Marketing*, published by American Marketing Assn.; Wendell M. Stewart, "Physical Distribution: Key to Improved Volume and Profits," Vol. 29, Jan. 1965.

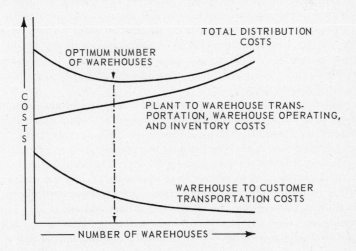

materials requiring controlled, low-temperature conditions; (4) household goods warehouses for storing furniture and other household items; and (5) general merchandise warehouses.

Transportation

The goal of the transportation function in physical distribution is to achieve the service level requirements set by policy at the lowest possible cost. Management's interest in this area has grown increasingly over the past few years because of rising freight costs and intense marketing competition. A buyer of transportation services has the opportunity to contribute substantially to a cost control program while playing a vital role in securing marketing advantages from effective delivery operations.

TRANSPORTATION SERVICES

The basic methods of moving freight are five: rail, motor carrier, water, air, and combination. Water transport offers the most attractive rates but of course is characterized by long transit times. Air is the most rapid method of shipping, and its rates are commensurately higher for the service offered. Rail and motor carrier rates and transit times occupy the middle ground between water and air.

Rail. Rail shipping offers many distinct advantages not available in other modes of transport. The smallest box car has 50 percent more cubic capacity and two to three times the weight-carrying ability of the average highway trailer. It is therefore the ideal method for moving large masses of freight at attractive rates. Of course, there are offsetting disadvantages in rail movement. Rail shipping generally takes longer in transit, particularly for shorter hauls. Furthermore, minimum load requirements for rail shipment are higher than for motor carrier service, and despite a lower rate, higher total charges can result if the minimums cannot be met.

Motor carrier. Motor carrier service has been the fastest-growing segment of the transportation industry. Speed and flexibility characterize its operation. Although motor carrier rates are higher than rail, the motor carrier has the advantage of being able to place the load at the destination point without off-loading.

Water. Water service has diminished in importance with the advent of rail and motor carrier services. Water service is generally slower, less frequent, and less flexible than the others; of course, these disadvantages are compensated for by substantially lower rates.

Air. Air freight began operations as a rapid-transport medium for emergency shipments; however, over the years it has developed as an important segment of the transportation industry. Many shippers now use air carriers as standard routing, especially where the short transit time represents a significant marketing service that is worth the premium freight cost. The introduction of jumbo-size jet planes is expected to revolutionize approaches to the use of air freight, particularly as the trend of air freight rates, already downward, declines even more sharply and reduces the spread between surface and air.

Combination. Over the past 15 years an increasing blending of basic transportation methods has been developed, producing combinations of motor carrier and rail, rail and water, and motor carrier and water. These hybrid methods have met with significant acceptance, since they offer the shipper the inherent advantages of both methods—the flexibility of the motor carrier to provide point-to-point pick-up and delivery, and the economy of mass rail or water movement at greatly reduced labor costs.

RATE STRUCTURE

The subject of freight rates (tariffs) is highly complex. Added to the factors of distance, type of material, and volume shipped are the many government regulations promulgated by the various regulatory bodies concerned with intrastate and interstate commerce.

Generally speaking, rates have been established by freight class of material. For each freight class, rates vary from point to point, depending on distance, and there are ranges of volume for which varying rates apply.

The basic volume breaks are the truckload and carload versus the less-than-truckload (LTL) and less-than-carload (LCL). However, even in the LTL and LCL movements there are ranges: for example, under 1,000 pounds, 1,000 to 3,000 pounds, 3,000 to 8,000 pounds, and 8,000 pounds or over. For each range, of course, a separate rate would apply.

SPECIALIZED SERVICES

The basic transportation methods are well below the total of the services available to move goods. When shippers are dealing with less than mass movement, there are many specialized services available.

Parcel post. The small-package service operated by the U.S. Post Office is subject to regulations on the weight and size of the package. Complete information on parcel post regulations is outlined in the *United States Postal Manual.*

Railway Express Agency. REA is a service, formerly owned and operated by the railroads, which includes pick-up and delivery service.

United Parcel Service. UPS is a small-package delivery service operating in many metropolitan areas. It provides fast and efficient local delivery service, including pick-up at the shipper's dock.

Freight forwarder. The freight forwarder is a consolidation agent who picks up freight from many small shippers and consolidates it into economical shipments to be moved at the best rates by regular rail and truck carriers. The freight forwarder arranges for delivery at the destination point.

Contract carrier. Another type of service is based on a private contract between the shipper and the carrier. The operations of the carrier may be regulated or unregulated. Unregulated contract carriers generally operate within a city. Intercity and intrastate operations are normally regulated.

Order-Handling Systems

One of the major determinants in the operating efficiency potential of a branch warehouse is the order-handling system. Many automated devices are available, and others are in advanced stages of development for the efficient processing of large quantities of orders; these devices can yield economies not only in processing orders through the office but also in the physical handling operations.

ELECTRONIC DATA PROCESSING

Recent years have seen the successful introduction of powerful, small-scale computers priced low enough to permit deployment at a manufacturer's branch warehouses. These computers depend on the storage and rapid recall of repetitive data regarding the customers and products and can produce invoices from a minimum of input information.

Capabilities in invoicing. In preparing the invoice, the computer is able to determine from the permanent customer master record the customer's name and address, credit status, special order-handling instructions, special prices quoted, and shipment routing.

From the product files for those items being ordered the individual items can be priced, weights determined, and discounts applied where applicable.

By-product data. As by-products of the invoicing operation, various sales reports can be produced, input generated to accounts receivable, and inventory files maintained.

Warehouse benefits. Warehouses can be planned to take advantage of the computer capability. Frequently, case-lot picking is segregated from less-than-case-lot picking, and the invoice can be produced to show all items from a group or zone together and within the group so as to sequence the items in exactly the order they are stored within the zone.

INVOICE FORMAT

One of the more interesting recent developments in standardizing practice is an attempt by the National Retail Merchants Association to develop a standard invoice format. The results of a three-year study by the association's standardized vendor invoice committee were published in October 1967.

Exhibit 6.13 represents the format established by NRMA for the payment copy. Additional copies may be designed to vendor specifications to incorporate shipping labels, accounts receivable information, and the like. The vendor need use only those boxes on the invoice that apply to his needs and the retailer's, as per agreement.

The size of the invoice ($8\frac{1}{2} \times 11$ inches) is dictated by overall conformity in the industry for the following reasons: ease of filing, handling, and processing; compliance with the requirement of standard register invoice machines; readability by optical scanning devices; and conformance to the size of standard folding and inserting machines and window envelopes. Vendors who require a larger invoice because the body area is not sufficient for stock listing or for data processing requirements must adhere to size and layout standards for the heading and summary areas as illustrated on the pro forma invoice.

It should be noted that NRMA is primarily concerned with the standardization of the invoice heading (boxes 1–17 in Exhibit 6.13) and the summary (boxes 26–36). The body of the invoice (boxes 18–25) has been designed in order to

Exhibit 6.13

STANDARD INVOICE FORMAT
Courtesy of National Retail Merchants Assn.

V ①	*Vendor's Name Co., Inc.* 123 Westfield Road, New York, N. Y. 10016 D*U*N*S Number 123-456-9	► PAY THIS INVOICE TO ◄ ② PAYEE FACTOR OR VENDOR WHEN DIFFERENT D*U*N*S Number 129-062-6

		3-STORE	4-DEPT./DIV.	5-CUSTOMER ORDER NO.
⑯ SHIP TO	SUBURBAN STORES CENTRAL SHOPPING CENTER HEMPSTEAD, N. Y. 11550	2	183	12631

6-INVOICE DATE	7-TERMS	8-SPECIAL DATING
2-20-67	8/10 EOM ROG	

		9-DATE SHIPPED	10-SHIPPED FROM	11-SHIPPED VIA
⑰ SOLD TO	DOWNTOWN STORES, INC. 5TH AVENUE NEW YORK, NEW YORK 10016	2-18-67	FOB NEW YORK	UPS

12-CUSTOMER ACCT. NO.	13-NO. OF CNTS.	14-OUR REFERENCE NO.	15-INVOICE NO.
123-438-4	2	4428	**12345**

18-STORE USE	19-STYLE OR LOT	20-MODEL	21-DESCRIPTION QUANTITY BREAKDOWN (OR OTHER DESCRIPTIVE DETAIL)	22-TOTAL QUANTITY	23-UNIT	24-UNIT PRICE	25-EXTENDED AMOUNT
	9422	13	LODEN	6	ea	23:75	142:50
	9424	14	BLACK	3	ea	12:60	37:80

26-	27-SALESMAN	28-PAGE NO.	29-TOTAL NUMBER OF UNITS →	30-SHIPMENT	31-SUB-TOTAL MDSE. AMOUNT	
	H. WILLIAMS	1 OF 1	9	COMPLETE [X] PARTIAL [ ]	180:30	

36-		32- SALES TAX	5:40
FOR INSERTION OF LEGAL STIPULATION OF CONTENTS OR TERMS OF SALE, OR OTHER INDICATIVE INFORMATION.		33- INSURANCE	1:80
		34-	
		35- GRAND TOTAL	187:50

THIS IS YOUR INVOICE (PAYMENT COPY)

illustrate the concept of a complete invoice and is optional with the vendor. The small triangles on either side of the invoice are line-up points for easy two-way fold for insertion into a standard window envelope.

The wording, "This is your invoice (payment copy)," at the bottom of the invoice has been standardized; since many vendors are preparing several copies of an invoice simultaneously, the original is not always the retailer's copy. Additional information can be obtained from NRMA.

Inventory Control

Inventory control in distribution represents the lifeblood of the system. Many retail businesses have turned to computers to control their inventories, resulting in a general trend toward more frequent buying and smaller orders. In addition, the highly competitive markets have led to increasingly larger product lines and variations. The net result of these factors, combined with the usual multiple-warehouse environment, creates inventory management problems of staggering proportions.

MULTISTAGE, MULTILOCATION

An inventory control system designed to handle multiple locations and multiple stages can be extremely complicated when the inventories are considered to be interrelated. When the inventories are independent, the problem is simplified greatly. However, in a warehouse distribution system this is not usually the case. The interreaction problem is one of determining how the inventory at one location affects other locations' inventories and whether inventory is permitted to flow between warehouses. The best approach is to attempt to treat the plant and warehouse inventories as a total when determining plant manufacturing requirements. Once inventory is manufactured into stock, this becomes the pool from which outlying branches draw stock to meet current requirements.

Inventory shortages at one branch location should not trigger manufacturing at the plant. An improperly balanced inventory should be rebalanced by trans-shipping between branches rather than requiring new production.

—*R. M. Goffredo*

INDUSTRIAL ENGINEERING

Since the time when an early industrialist first established a sequence of work operations as a planned activity, industrial engineering in some form has been in operation. With the assistance of formal curriculums in colleges and universities, industrial engineering is a valuable scientific management discipline.

The single most descriptive phrase applicable to industrial engineering activity is found in the definition used by the American Institute of Industrial Engineers: "Industrial engineering is concerned with the design, improvement, and installation of integrated systems of men, materials, and equipment. It draws upon specialized knowledge and skill in the mathematical, physical, and social sciences together with the principles and methods of engineering analysis, and evaluates the results to be obtained from such systems."

A manager constantly evaluates the performance of his personnel. For a given industrial event, the manager must know what should happen, how it should be accomplished, how long it should take, and what it should cost. The manager's appraisal of the performance of his staff must be against an established norm so that deviation from the norm can indicate better than, equal to, or poorer than expected performance. Setting such standards and establishing systems to measure performance is a key function of the industrial engineer.

Methods—Motion and Time Study

The role of the industrial engineer is to provide a technical service to plant management in a variety of tasks.

METHODS ENGINEERING

Methods engineering is the scientific study of an operation being performed, or planned, that utilizes the techniques of detailing each section or subsection of the operation with the intent of reducing or simplifying the work content. This task is accomplished by eliminating wasted motion, reviewing the immediate work area to place parts used in the operation in an optimum position, and planning and prescribing a specific sequence of operations for the operator to follow in performing the task.

The industrial engineer may utilize standard data tables for work element evaluation of the operator's movements of hand, foot, or shoulder, or review motion picture film of pictures taken during the operation so that the work cycle can be studied and replayed in slow motion or at a stopped-still frame of any portion of the task.

OBJECTIVES AND TOOLS

Low job costs are predicated on doing things well. The industrial engineer's objective in studying an operation is to make adjustments in operator work pattern, machine selection, material compatibility, and work area layout, with the result that the task is performed efficiently. A typical industrial engineering study result reduces job costs from 5 to 15 percent.

Five tools are used in a typical industrial engineering job study: job area layout review, standard time data reference tables, the stopwatch, repetitive run data, and the motion picture camera. Each of these tools adds a depth of understanding of the variables influencing the job being studied.

Job area layout review. In the study of job area, study elements may include measurements of the reach distance of the parts bin in relation to the operator's work area; a review of lighting to achieve proper intensity or color tone; and a review of location, labeling, and variety of controls for equipment used in the operation.

Standard time data reference tables. The standard time data tables show typical operator work times for such movements as reach, move, grasp, position, disengage, release, and hold.

If a graphic chart of each movement required in the operation is set up, estimates of standard time for that motion are obtainable from the standard time reference tables.

The stopwatch.   The stopwatch is a most valuable aid in gathering job information on a task. By dividing the task into subsections, the stopwatch readings can provide valuable time data on method A as compared with method B and on the difference in recorded time results of operators A, B, and C; and they can show variation in total operation time from one day's sample compared with another day's sample. The stopwatch is also used to verify information by taking time study samples from a process in which the original time standards were set by simulation, using standard time data reference tables.

Repetitive run data.   Where the task being performed occurs again and again, information gathered on the time required to perform the task, the review of data recorded for measured values of key parameters of the product being produced, and the variations noted in equipment, materials, and methods used to manufacture the product can provide a valuable data base for analyzing the process variables. An example would be an operation, running on a two-shift basis, where historical data show greater productivity on the second shift. Many questions such as the following arise: Is more work done on the second shift because of less interference? Does greater output in quantity on the second shift mean that a lower quality is being produced? Is there some know-how in method or project knowledge that is greater on the second shift? Is the supervision better on the second shift?

Through analysis of the repetitive run data, answers may be obtained that, potentially, could boost first-shift production by adoption of some of the second-shift improvements; or, conversely, the answers might provide evidence that the "better" second-shift performance was not a valid judgment because of shortcuts or unauthorized trade-offs of the prescribed work methods.

The motion picture camera.   The industrial engineer utilizes the filmed operation as a captive process where, in either fast or slow motion, the operation can be studied in a calm, objective manner. Through the replay capability of a filmed operation, individual details of the operation can be subjected to close scrutiny: the physical movements used by the operator in loading and unloading a fixture, physically awkward storage arrangements, possible safety hazards, evidence of fatigue, and similar work area characteristics. In a further valuable capability, the motion picture camera projects an enlargement of small areas of the task in order to define and illustrate minute physical details that may be missed by the eye during the operation. Through the replay capability of filmed operation, a number of mechanical problems have been solved by physically viewing on the enlarged screen such actions as a roller riding over an eccentric cam, hydraulic shock absorbers impacting under the load of a severe bump, or a die forming a part under the pressure of a deep draw of a metal material. With modern cameras using improved optical systems, a relatively low light level is required to take good action pictures inside the plant.

A second purpose in using the camera is to study the flow of factory operations. The planned operation is set up, and the camera shoots several runs of it. The film results are often startling in review, when what happens to a paperwork plan under industrial application is observed. Many times, problems not recognized at the time of establishing the original plan become graphically clear when viewed on the screen. Examples are traffic congestion blocking efficient use of a lift truck; poor overhead lighting, requiring the operator to move to another area to properly read a gauge; and operators inventing new ways of doing the job without administrative coordination with the area foreman and the industrial engineer.

JOB ANALYSIS AND JOB STUDY

To plan in depth requires a review of all aspects of the total task to be accomplished. The industrial engineer often uses an evaluation check sheet in the survey of a task so that the more important characteristics can be highlighted to receive major attention. (See Exhibit 6.14.)

With this information on the important factors, the industrial engineer will establish support programs for the major portions of the task, such as training programs for servicing industrial equipment at regular intervals. By grouping similar tasks together, he can set up standardized formats making it possible for other tasks of the same type to be readily assessed for equipment needs, materials needs, skills required, type and intensity of light required, and other factors related to a given job area or type of job to be performed.

Many plants set up talent banks, after an industrial engineering job study, wherein each skill is cataloged by name, department, service date, and specialty. Talent-bank information is used in planning manpower for new business projects or setting up "tiger teams" of specialized skills to solve persistent or troublesome problems.

With this organized information on plant skills and manpower availability, major manpower-planning activities can be accomplished with speed and accuracy. In larger plants, the results of job studies are necessary to optimize the use of equipment, floor space, and skills.

MOTION STUDY

The early pioneers of motion study—Frank and Lillian Gilbreth, Professor David Porter, Henry L. Gantt, and many others—had a common goal: to study a task with the objective of making the operation simpler or physically easier.

Exhibit 6.14

EVALUATION CHECK SHEET

	Survey No. 1604			
Job Analysis Rating Check Sheet	Date 6/19/69			
Job No. 8251	Area-Supervisor R. Smith	Contract 6-1203A		
Element		Major	Minor	No Factor
Operator Skill		√		
Equipment Maintenance			√	
Area lighting				

In accomplishing this goal, operations were eliminated, fatigue was lessened, and the combination of these factors reduced the time required to perform the task. As time went on, industry relied more and more on specialists (whose titles at various periods included "motion engineer," "work simplification engineer," "efficiency engineer," "motion and time study engineer," and "industrial engineer") to provide expertise in the best way to accomplish a given task.

Progressing from classroom theory utilizing chalked distances for work travel, motion picture films, stopwatch data recordings, and other theoretical system approaches to reducing work content, trained industrial engineers in the practical world use work simplification techniques for laying out new buildings to minimize movement of product storage and distribution; for establishing paperwork documentation for material control, quality control, and accounting records; and for coordinating planning and factory costs for typical standard operations used to measure factory work performance.

TIME STUDY FUNDAMENTALS

Time study provides a factual method for recording the elapsed time for a given industrial event to occur. By repetitive readings for different operators, different shifts, and different work methods, variables adversely affecting work efficiency can be measured and analyzed, and solutions can be applied to the causes of work delay or work variation. The scope of the technique is not limited to a given type or series of operations. Applications of recording by the time study technique may include such as the following: the number of letters typed per stenographer; units produced per hour on (for example) factory operation No. 20; the delay factor in loading four machines per operator in contrast to loading three machines per operator; and establishing a time cycle for normal activities against avoidable delays.

The key benefit of measuring work elements or sections of a work cycle is that, with relatively little effort, factual information can be obtained that will allow a management evaluation of what is actually happening in contrast to what was planned to happen.

Limitations. While much factual data may be obtained, judgment must still be exercised in making allowances for such factors as percent worker effort, work area morale, and worker fatigue. One skilled industrial engineer studying work area efficiency with the use of a stopwatch will agree quite well with the independent observations of another industrial engineer as long as some common ground is agreed upon for allowances applicable to worker efforts, fatigue, and morale.

MAKING A TIME STUDY

In performing a time study, it is good practice to view the area to be studied, meet the supervisors of the area, and become reasonably familiar with the flow of material and the work cycles of the task to be performed.

Tools. The industrial engineer will use a stopwatch and a recording sheet mounted on a board holding the watch. The stopwatch may be timed in either fractions of a minute or fractions of an hour. The watch that records fractions of a minute utilizes a large sweep hand which makes one complete revolution per minute, with a smaller hand recording the movement of one space with each sweep of the large hand. The watch that records fractions of an hour has a large sweep hand that makes a complete revolution in 1/100 of an hour (0.6 of a minute).

Since many operations are very rapid, the watch using 1/100 of an hour is more widely used; this scale permits segments of the dial to be read to increments as low as 1/10,000 of an hour.

Allowances. When an operation is studied by the stopwatch method, the period of making the time study usually measures relatively short intervals of the observed operations which may not include all the day-by-day work variations. A typical study may be of one to three days' duration. Allowances must be made for potential factors affecting the work activity of the day-to-day task. Some examples are adjustments to the machine tooling, changes in the machine tools, accidents, faulty tools or material, machine breakdown, fatigue, and personal needs of the operator.

The industrial engineer is working toward the objective of setting a time standard that will be fair to both the company and the worker, and an allowance will be established. This allowance factor will be factored into the elapsed time total computed by the stopwatch data recordings.

Rating. Performance rating is an evaluation, during the time study, of skill level and of work effort expended by the operator during the performance of the task. For workers with a high degree of skill who perform the task rapidly, the recorded work cycle time will be shorter than for a less skilled operator performing the same task. A second factor for consideration is the work effort generated by the operator: In performing the task, one operator may work very hard, while another operator works with reduced effort. Typical evaluations used in industry rank the operator's performance according to work effort (excessive, excellent, good, average, poor, or unsatisfactory) and skill (highly skilled, excellent, good, average, fair, or poor).

To these judgments of performance is assigned a percentage which adds or subtracts from the actual data performance time. The technique of judging skill and work effort is called leveling. This evaluation of operator performance for the degree of skill exhibited and work effort expended during the time study is often re-evaluated by viewing motion picture films made of the operation. By the use of the replay of specific portions of the task, individual operator differences can be reviewed and a reassessment made of the leveling factors of operator skill and operator work effort.

Setting standards. The data recorded as observations during the performance of the task are subjected to a number of conditions which may not be representative of the task. Some of these are as follows: unusually long or short times differing widely from other observed times; allowances for delays—interruptions, fatigue, or personal time; rating evaluations of a very rapid worker with a high degree of skill, in contrast to a slow-moving worker with little skill; and a learning curve of time improvement as the worker becomes more familiar with the work cycles of the task.

With the help of judgment, a balance among these factors will produce a set time standard for a given task. It is to the advantage of the industrial engineer to set a fair standard so that the worker output required to meet this standard is attainable by the average worker who may be assigned to the task. A standard that is too relaxed or loose will allow less productivity than should be expected from a fair day's work. A standard that is too restricted or tight will create poor morale and prevent satisfactory agreement between the worker and the supervisor on what constitutes a fair day's work.

If an inequitable standard—whether tight or loose—has inadvertently been set, an immediate review should be made so that a wholesome time standard, fair to the worker and the company, can be set. Adjustments to standards for corrective purposes include the following: establishing a longer period of observations to include more of the day-to-day variables; noting avoidable delays and correcting them where possible—late stock deliveries, poor product or material quality, and excessive tool breakdown; training operators to better cope with the skills required to perform the task; and standardization of the method used by the operators so that a uniform sequence of process steps occurs in performing the task.

Standard times need periodic maintenance and review. New methods, new tools, new materials, and changes in work area layout may have an influence on the original time required to perform the task. Good management dictates a constant review of standards to maintain time standards that are fair to the worker and the company.

SYNTHETIC STANDARDS

As a necessary part of business, jobs are often bid before the product has ever been made. To accomplish the dual task of setting a standard time to evaluate productivity and of providing a cost estimate based on a known rate for each productive shop hour, standard element time data tables offer a source of information. By matching the fundamental motions of the operator in performing the task to the standard element time data tables—which are based on fundamental motions—a predetermined time value is obtained. In setting time values with synthetic standards, the industrial engineer very carefully analyzes each basic motion. The information tables give data on motions such as moving, turning, grasping, positioning, disengaging, and releasing. Factors such as the weight of the object being moved (heavy or light) and the size of the object (large or small, long or short) are selected from the appropriate data table.

By establishing each basic functional movement required to perform the task in a flow diagram, a total time can be calculated as a synthetic time standard for the operation. Many industries use synthetic standards to cross-check or supplement actual time studies where it is difficult to achieve portions of the actual stopwatch analysis because of production schedule, machine downtime, or other cause.

Several of the newer synthetic time standard data table systems are based on short-run operations of less than one minute's duration. These tables include a small number of fundamental motions which cover a large percentage of typical manufacturing applications. Through seminars and company training courses, supervisory personnel can learn to make satisfactory estimates of synthetic time standards in only an eight-hour training session.

FLOW PROCESS CHARTS

In studying the sequence of progressive operations on a given piece of material, the industrial engineer uses symbols associated with each task to be performed. As shown, each symbol has a graphic meaning denoting the action taking place at that point in the process flow.

Activity	Symbol
Operations	◯
Transportation	⟶
Inspection	☐
Storage	▽
Delay	D

Two elements of information—time and distance transported—are often added to the chart.

In making a chart of the operation, three aspects are continually in focus: (1) Is there any operation that could be eliminated or combined? (2) Is there any transportation that could readily be automated by conveyor, chute, or moving belt, or be eliminated by a relay out of the area? (3) Is there any delay that can be converted to activity?

An example of a flow process chart for material is shown in Exhibit 6.15.

Another type of flow process chart shows the relationship of the operator who is running the equipment and the equipment itself; a running, side-by-side record is kept of what the operator does and what the equipment is doing. This charting is of great value when an operator is running more than one machine, since the graphic picture quickly points out idle equipment or idle operator time that may be converted from idle time to activity time.

WORK STATION ACTIVITY

Where work flows progressively through a series of operations, improvements in work efficiency can often be achieved by studying how the various work stations are interrelated one to another. Where interdependence negates improvements made in one work station because the next work station has not also made a comparable improvement, a work station activity time chart quickly points up this bottleneck.

The following factors for each work station are recorded: number of production units per day; material usage and storage volume; operator output per day; average lost time per tool and equipment; specific cost breakdowns; and similar productivity information peculiar to the station. Through a review of these factors a clear understanding can be obtained of the impact of unbalanced loadings between work stations, the effect of operator absenteeism or sickness, and problems caused by lack of material storage or equipment capacity. This management tool is widely used by industrial consultants, who often produce startling savings in a plant where the individual work station is in control but an optimum productivity has not been achieved between the work stations. In a plant that is growing, work station activity charts are especially valuable in pointing out limitations in equipment capacity, production inefficiencies because of lack of storage in the work area, and idle time created by imbalance in man and equipment utilization.

Work Sampling

Work sampling, also called the ratio-delay method, is most commonly used as an audit check on procedures and practices already established to evaluate opera-

Exhibit 6.15
SAMPLE FLOW PROCESS CHART

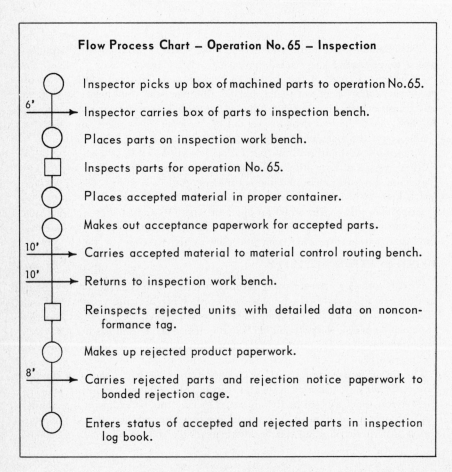

Flow Process Chart — Operation No. 65 — Inspection

Inspector picks up box of machined parts to operation No.65.

6' Inspector carries box of parts to inspection bench.

Places parts on inspection work bench.

Inspects parts for operation No. 65.

Places accepted material in proper container.

Makes out acceptance paperwork for accepted parts.

10' Carries accepted material to material control routing bench.

10' Returns to inspection work bench.

Reinspects rejected units with detailed data on nonconformance tag.

Makes up rejected product paperwork.

8' Carries rejected parts and rejection notice paperwork to bonded rejection cage.

Enters status of accepted and rejected parts in inspection log book.

tional consistency with the original plans. When used for this purpose, key elements of the process, with productive cycle times, are set up as percentages of the total task. Random and intermittent visits are made to the work station where the work is being performed. Careful recordings are made of the events occurring at the time of the visit. In the same random-time manner, many visits are made to the same area and observations are noted, after which the results of these work samplings are compared with the planned activity.

For new and original task analysis, the work sampling technique can cover a broad physical area with good results if sufficient samples are taken and if the area is relatively stable in its operation from day to day. Evaluating activity time in a department store would be one example: The analyst could move to a given station, observe occurrence, and move on to the next station. In a three- to five-day period, a valid and useful analysis could be made of work activity in the store, pinpointing avoidable delays and noting which unavoidable delays require an investigation for long-term correction.

DEFINITION AND APPLICABILITY

Work sampling is the industrial sampling of a process or work area on a random observation basis with a careful recording of activity, avoidable delays, and unavoidable delays so that a synthetic total work activity in functions performed and relative time cycles for the functions being performed may be estimated.

The work sampling approach may be applied to any repetitive task for which a planned result can be evaluated against the observed result.

UNDERLYING THEORY

Work sampling is based on the statistical theory of sampling where a random proportional series of observations of a stable process will predict the proportionate occurrences with the same relative frequency as a 100 percent observation of the process. Should the variables in the process cause it to vary widely where it no longer predictably will have task functions performed at the same frequency of occurrence as the 100 percent observation, the work sampling observations will reflect this lack of process stability.

Sample adequacy. Since work sampling is based on statistical consistency in the process, it is also affected in its accuracy by the number of observations made where the number of observations is limited. Thus the accuracy of duplicating, in a few observations, what is going on 100 percent of the time becomes limited. Two methods are used for judging sufficiency of observations.

In the first method, a predetermined number is arbitrarily set; it is based on the work cycle, the cost of each observation, and the distance traveled to and from the work area to make the observation. When data are collected, they are tallied by normal work activity, avoidable delays, and unavoidable delays. These proportionate results are then monitored against a second set of observations, generally one-third fewer in number. In a similar manner, these observations are tallied into the three categories of normal activity, avoidable delays, and unavoidable delays. If the second set of observations is reasonable to the proportional distribution of the first set, the process is stable and sufficient samples have been obtained. If a good correlation does not exist, either more samples are needed to cope with the process variability or it is evident that biasing factors are influencing the process variables of men, machines, methods, and materials; and further detailed investigation of the causes for variation is required.

A second method utilizes statistical probability in which a given risk of error is established, and through calculation of the binomial theorem, a calculated sample size is achieved. This method requires a deep understanding of statistics and enough knowledge of the process variation to establish a good estimate of normal activity.

Statistical tests for accuracy. In using the work sampling approach, the industrial engineer must constantly balance the economics of making the study with the probability that the results are workable and practical. Where more sampling observations give a refinement in data information that leads to an increased cost reduction, more sampling observations pay their way. In some instances, data obtained by work sampling may show the normal activity of work performance as 70 percent of the time, but a 100 percent check might show 67 percent; however, if the missing 30 percent made up of avoidable and unavoidable delays can be investigated and corrective action instigated that raises normal activity to 80 percent of the time, the small error in estimating by work sampling may have no effect.

A rule of thumb frequently used for determining work sampling accuracy is that if the reported observations show results that are plus or minus 5 percent of the expected occurrence, no further observations are required.

ADVANTAGES OF WORK SAMPLING

To attain the prime objective of business—profit—on a day-to-day basis requires control. A major activity in maintaining control is to maintain production efficiency—that is, to assure that what was planned to be done was done within the expected time standards. If confidence exists that the plant time standards are set fairly, a periodic monitoring to assure compliance with standards is good insurance of continuing efficient and profitable operations. Work sampling, when used by the industrial engineer, can provide this audit capability at relatively low cost.

WORK SAMPLING PROCEDURE

Three basic activities are recorded in a work sampling procedure.

1. *Normal activities* exist where the planned sequence of work is occurring in an orderly and timely manner.

2. *Avoidable delays* represent the interruption of the normal activity because something did not happen as planned, such as a delay in stock delivery, the exhaustion of storage space because earlier production did not move to the stockroom, or defective material that arrived at the work station because it had escaped from the incoming-material inspection screen. Avoidable delays are correctable by better planning and improved supervision.

3. *Unavoidable delays* are the category for limitations of equipment, area layout restrictions, or one-time occurrences such as power failure, equipment break-

down, or labor strikes at a vendor's plant. Although some of these unavoidable delays may be correctable on a long-term basis—by dealing with several suppliers of a vendor item, for example—for the purpose of the specific work sampling study made for the immediate operation on one day, they would be classified as unavoidable delays.

A tally is recorded, as shown in Exhibit 6.16; when the observations have been tallied, a percentage breakdown is compared with the planned event workflow. If reasonable agreement is achieved, confidence exists that things are running as planned. If the percentages of planned events and random, intermittent sampling results differ—generally, by more than plus or minus 5 percent—further investigation will be conducted to correct the sources of variation.

For a new area where no established standard exists, the work sampling observations would be reconstituted into a process flow chart, discussions would be held on the results, and the results would be evaluated as satisfactory or unsatisfactory. If they were judged unsatisfactory, closer attention would be given to the suspect work areas.

Methods Improvement

Industrial engineering approaches methods improvement from two directions: (1) improving the present method; (2) introducing a new or better technique to replace the old method.

ANALYSIS OF WORK

A decision to work within the existing process may be a very realistic assessment of the situation where certain factors exist: a short run left on the present production contract; appropriations restricted momentarily for capital equipment; or physical limitations for establishing an improved work area layout in the allocated physical work area. The industrial engineer in this situation would

Exhibit 6.16

WORK SAMPLING OBSERVATION SHEET

ACTIVITIES	FREQUENCY OF OCCURRENCE	TOTAL FREQUENCY
(A) Normal activities	~~HHT~~ ~~HHT~~ ~~HHT~~ ~~HHT~~ ~~HHT~~ ~~HHT~~ ~~HHT~~ ~~HHT~~ ~~HHT~~ ~~HHT~~ ~~HHT~~ ~~HHT~~ ~~HHT~~ ~~HHT~~ ~~HHT~~ ~~HHT~~ ~~HHT~~ ~~HHT~~ ~~HHT~~ ~~HHT~~ ~~HHT~~ ~~HHT~~ ~~HHT~~ II	117
(B) Avoidable delays	~~HHT~~ ~~HHT~~ ~~HHT~~ ~~HHT~~ I	21
(C) Unavoidable delays	IIII	4
Total		142

record in a step-by-step manner every variable affecting the operation—such specifics as tools to be used, tool replacement cost, material to be used, inventory parameters associated with material, quality standards in AQL's (average quality levels) and descriptive criteria, review of operator skills, and key functions dependent on area supervision. Armed with this process flow chart of every element entering into the process, the industrial engineer would review in microscopic detail ways to make the process more efficient. In an organization large enough to have tool specialists such as training directors or area layout specialists, the industrial engineer would pose to them searching questions geared to provocative stimulation to find a better way.

In the case of a more open climate to purchase new equipment, tear down walls for physical changes in layout, or introduce a totally new technology, the industrial engineer gathers his flow process chart information but opens his horizon to introduce new and better techniques to replace the older ones. The industrial engineer may be the leader in a brainstorming session; he may deliberately play devil's advocate in reviewing the way things are presently processed. He may draw on his technical reading or attendance at industrial seminars or technical conferences to bring to the industrial team new ideas generated by universities or industrial competitors. Working from the flow process chart, with patience and determination he reviews each and every detail for the possible elimination or combination of operations, the introduction of technological methods changes to the process, and similar activities to reduce costs.

PROPOSED METHOD DESIGN

At times the designer of a machine sequence of operations, the designer of a fabrication process, or the designer of an assembly or subassembly process may arrive at his end results by virtue of a fixed set of parameters defining the task as originally established. Through the inclusion of industrial engineering principles in the design review, the process often becomes more flexible in the tools that can be used, less restrictive in the skill specialties required, or more realistic in product cost ratios to finished parts. A primary tool in the industrial engineering approach is the flow process chart, which forces a disciplined approach to defining the operation. It is often the result of design review conferences that two or three alternate plans for production may evolve, and their merits can then be considered for growth or product volume capabilities, comparison of return on investment percentages, comparison of product cost ratios, economics of capital equipment modernization, and similar long- and short-term profit considerations.

REVIEW AND TESTING PROCEDURES

The industrial engineer can assist in employee skill training, making learning curve predictions on familiarization of the operators with the task work cycle, setting up instructions and procedures as associated with the work method, and setting time standards for work accomplishment. Another key task of the industrial engineer is keeping initial cost data on predicted costs in contrast to actual costs. An early effort should be directed toward placing the process on motion picture film. By the detailed review and playback of the film, judgment can be exercised in adjustments to the requirement of operator training, equipment capabilities, material storage area locations, and time standards used for task performance evaluation.

Examples of Industrial Engineering Activity

Within the industrial activity, it is rare that a static condition exists. Growth, expansion, and diversification establish the criteria for a dynamic climate. An examination of the role of the industrial engineer in a typical plant problem gives an insight into the value of the planning capabilities of the industrial engineering function.

PRODUCTIVITY INCREASE

Suppose the problem to be the expansion of production volume in the same physical area. The industrial engineer would examine all the factors and make the following recommendations: to make a detailed flow chart of the existing product line; to mechanize, where possible, operations currently being accomplished by hand labor; to provide jigs, fixtures, and holding tools wherever possible to free operators' hands for a work cycle; where required, to provide operator training, visual standards, and work instructions; to evaluate present tooling and equipment, making equipment-life cost charts for recommendations with justification for any upgrading of present equipment or where new equipment is considered; to review equipment maintainability to assure that the preventive maintenance concept is in force; to review layout to evaluate if a shift of benches, equipment, walls, partitions, or doorways would improve product flow; and to make a new product flow chart with recommended changes.

Once these functions were evaluated, a planned, detailed proposal would be made for increasing productivity. Several alternatives would be prepared to allow for flexibility in the ultimate decision. After a favorable judgment was made on a given plan, the industrial engineer would coordinate the other functions of the plant by setting a milestone plan for task accomplishment.

TIME STANDARDS

The margin for profit and loss can often be measured in volume production by a constant review of the planned operating time performance versus the actual operating time performance. To achieve an understanding of the elements that make up a work cycle, the industrial engineer divides the task into logical segments of activity. He amplifies areas requiring close management attention by reports related to individual cost centers.

The problem, in this case, might be to establish factory time standards for a four-part assembly. The industrial engineer would initiate the following activities:

1. For each segment of the work cycle, he would familiarize himself with the item being worked, the equipment required, and general criteria for an acceptable item at the end of the task. Where an apparent mismatch, extra handling, inefficient tooling, or the like was observed, he would make a mental note to

make recommendations that would lead to improvement of the noted inefficiencies.

2. Once the task was defined in measurable incremental sections by a planned
workflow chart, a typical operator or operators representing average working
effort would be selected to run through the work cycle. With the use of a stopwatch or by observations, typical times for a segment and/or sections of the work
cycle would be recorded. Variations in the recorded times would receive close
attention to evaluate if the equipment, the material, the method, or the operator
represented the variable. In this instance, attention would be focused on shorter
performance times and longer performance times so that a related and under-
standard cause-and-effect relationship could be obtained.

3. With a background of information on what was occurring during the work
cycle, judgment would be placed on worker effort and anticipated delays, with
some adjustment for the possibility of unavoidable delays. By means of the stopwatch recorded data coupled with judgment, a standard time would be projected.

4. The standard time thus projected would serve as a norm for operators performing the same task. Data would be collected for evaluation of the time standard over varying conditions of operators, materials, and equipment performance.
Where this norm indicated achievement levels representative of a fair day's work
for a fair day's pay, continued performance measurements would be established
by such yardsticks as pieces per hour, units per day, and total hours per unit.

5. By periodic reassessment, the standard times would be updated where new
equipment was installed, labor-saving jigs and fixtures were made available to
the operator, or operations were combined.

6. In some instances, tasks must be forecast without an actual operator performing the task—for example, new business proposals for which specific materials or capital equipment may not be available. The industrial engineer would
lay out each segment of the task and study the movement and work cycle involved. With a clear understanding of the effort required, standard data tables
containing the typical time values for moving a hand, finger, arm, leg, or shoulder through an estimated distance while reaching, lifting, grasping, pushing, or
pulling a given part of known weight can be used to achieve a time standard for
the simulated task function.

COST STANDARDS

The role of the industrial engineer in working new business cost projections,
keeping track of current cost statistics related to specific tasks, and providing information on operator learning curves where volume production occurs is of
ever increasing value to the profit-minded company.

Assume, for example, that the industrial engineer's problem is to project costs
at the two-hundredth unit of a 500-piece run. He would gather the necessary
data and coordinate them into a graphic cost curve. (See Exhibit 6.17.) In doing
so, he would (1) establish a time standard estimate for first piece produced;
(2) evaluate training time for the operator to become familiar with parts, methods, equipment, and operation sequence; (3) evaluate process improvements
likely to be initiated during the progress of production run—for example, im-

Exhibit 6.17
COST PROJECTION FOR VOLUME PRODUCTION

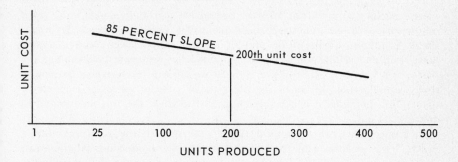

proved handling tools, automation where applicable, and combined operations; (4) evaluate task complexity for possible subdivision of task to multioperators, each performing a portion of the task; (5) evaluate possible motivation influences such as group bonus and individual incentive plans.

With these data, a cost projection could be made of average cost throughout the production run. As the complexity of the task varied and the unit time cycle varied, differing slopes of experience could be utilized.

The industrial engineer today is entering new fields where his skills in planning, evaluating, and executing programs for progress, cutting costs, shortening work cycles, and utilizing modern technologies make a valuable contribution to the industrial team. Examples of the versatility of industrial engineering principles are found in supply problems for ships of the line; airport congestion and facility planning; logistic planning in a major hotel chain; contractor performance appraisals in government purchasing; optimizing warehouse storage and routing flow; scheduling and planning for naval ship maintenance; and coordinating computerized performance evaluations of daily production.

These and many other applications are evidence that, to both the large and the small employer, the function of organizing, planning, evaluating, and optimizing performance is a prime task for the industrial engineer. And among the principal sources of personnel for higher management positions are the ranks of the industrial engineering function. The requisite objective and analytical training provides a good foundation for firm decision making.

—*W. A. MacCrehan, Jr.*

PLANT ENGINEERING

No area of plant operation better typifies the rapid advances of modern technology than plant engineering. Relegated to a position in the boiler room a few short years ago, this function has emerged as a professional task that grows more sophisticated and is more depended upon by management with each advance in automation or other productive innovation.

Background of Plant Engineering

Plant engineering is intimately connected with all the tangible aspects of modern plant operation. It is that form of engineering discipline whose emphasis is placed not on the product or even the production machinery design but, rather, on the control of the production environment. The environment includes atmospheric conditions (temperature and humidity); illumination; sound control; floor, wall, and ceiling construction; equipment layout; plant landscaping; employee comfort area accessibility; and decor. Modern management recognizes that a considerable portion of the plant dollar is spent for plant engineering operations; therefore, it is management's need to study the area, understand it, and control it.

In former times, when operating units were smaller, the plant engineering function was performed by the chief mechanic, the maintenance supervisor, or the design engineer. Today, many companies capitalize on the close relationship between plant engineering and maintenance by placing the two groups in a single department where they reinforce each other's abilities.

IMPACT ON MANUFACTURING

Probably no other service function has as direct an impact on manufacturing operations as plant engineering, which is responsible for properly supplying adequate housing and facilities for the variety of production processes that result in a product. If properly defined, originated, and installed, production tools and equipment operate with minimal disruptive maintenance at a predictable rate and with few rejects. If tools and equipment are improperly conceived and installed, the result is unreliability and uneconomical or even lost production.

COORDINATION WITH MANUFACTURING

Of primary concern in translating manufacturing requirements into plant engineering output is a mandate from management. This is the plant engineer's charter which enables him to actively and effectively help determine the optimum facilities needed for successful production—present and future.

The plant engineering staff must define manufacturing requirements and determine how plant engineering can most effectively perform its function. However, plant engineering must realize its abilities and limitations. The point where facilities design ends and production equipment design begins is sometimes hard to discern.

Of great assistance to plant engineering is a manufacturing coordinator who understands the production cycle thoroughly yet is capable of understanding the difficulties of supplying facilities for a plant. The coordinator should be the funnel through which manufacturing requirements can be transmitted to the plant engineering staff.

In plant engineering is found the "generalist engineer," capable and willing to engineer many tasks. Such an engineer will become drawn into the manufacturing universe and will plan projects with drawings and specifications, whether one machine or a factory complex is involved.

Some of the manufacturing requirements will be best determined by information from tool and equipment manufacturers. In some cases, soil analysts, structural engineers, sanitary engineers, and others will have to be called on.

Plant Buildings

The structures that house the manufacturing operations are of primary concern to plant engineering. Without a well-conceived shelter to support and reinforce operations, proper attention cannot be given to maximum production effectiveness. A sophisticated electronic assembly cannot be made in a coal yard. Buildings should as far as possible be tailored to production needs.

It should not be thought that only a new plant will fit the custom needs of production operations. Much can be said for multiple-purpose buildings, which are flexible and adaptable to many operations. At any time, of course, older construction may be more readily available, lower in cost, more centrally located, and may have other attributes that make it more desirable than new construction. In plant engineering circles, it usually takes more courage and imagination to make proper housing out of existing buildings than is the case with new ones.

MULTISTORY VERSUS SINGLE-STORY CONSTRUCTION

Early in the design of a new plant, the question of multi- or single-story construction must be answered. The decision depends on several factors. Land value is of maximum importance. The type of operation to be housed is another variable. Foundries are seldom more than one story high. However, first-floor plant space can be serviced by second-floor offices and even third-floor penthouses. The use of second-floor or rooftop equipment rooms is now common.

In general, multiple stories cost less per square foot to build—up to 50 percent savings on basement areas and 25 to 33 percent on upper floors. Consideration must be given to transportation of people and materials in multistory buildings. Elevators, dumbwaiters, inclined conveyors, escalators, hoists, and other materials handling devices become of importance.

The primary advantage of the single-story building is, of course, the limiting of transportation motions to horizontal travel.

CONSTRUCTION MATERIALS

That this is the day of latitude in the use of building construction materials cannot be denied. First-class plant construction, a few years ago, called for masonry units with brick facades and steel framework. First-class construction now can include concrete spandrel units, sandwich curtain walls of steel or aluminum, built-up fiber glass roofing with plexiglass skylights, and other modern materials. Class of construction is also related to fire protection capabilities, including fire-rated interior walls, stairwells, water supply, and sprinkler coverage. Plant engineering would be well advised to consult with insurance carriers to be sure of obtaining the desired outcome—a building constructed within financial parameters and having the lowest ongoing insurance rates.

EXPANSION PLANNING

Seldom is a building constructed that will never have growing pains. The plant engineering department has a major obligation to insure that building growth potential is possible. The quality of preliminary planning is readily apparent when floor space becomes tight and relief steps must be taken.

Architects will not usually plan growth or building expansion unless directed to do so. However, even if growth is not expected at the location, the extra attention required to make it feasible will be well worth the planning and expense. The basic consideration is to identify fixed facilities and locate them where they will not be in the path of future growth. Another possibility is to locate a fixed facility in such a way that growth occurs around it, making it more central as time goes on. An example is an electric substation, located outside an expansion wall, that becomes centrally located as the plant grows. This has the advantage of optimizing copper distribution wiring. Other examples of fixed facilities include rail sidings, compressor rooms, boiler rooms, plating rooms, furnace operations, air conditioning equipment, toilet and locker facilities, entrance lobbies, high-grade office space, elevators, and shipping and receiving platforms. In general, fixed facilities are difficult and expensive to relocate.

BAY SIZE

The bay size (horizontal spacing between columns and/or walls) is another consideration which must be decided very early in the design stage.

Bay size is dictated by several factors such as economics, product size, production equipment size, and material handling considerations.

Formerly, a 20 by 20 foot bay was considered the most economical in terms of steel costs. Many 40 by 40 foot bays were also built. Today it is not uncommon to find 100 to 400 foot clear spans and 40 to 100 foot side spacing of columns. The major problems in long spans have been the high steel cost and the excessive depth of the roof-supporting trusses; however, structural designers are continually finding methods to lower costs. Examples are high-tensile-strength alloys, cantilever construction, and multiple-hinge truss design.

The elimination of columns is obviously desirable: Flexibility of layout is enhanced, material handling is simplified, and product flow is facilitated. Air conditioning duct installation is eased by fewer intersection problems, and this holds true for wiring, lighting, and piping. Plant cleanliness is enhanced by limiting horizontal overhead surfaces and ledges.

When considering bay size in relation to product and equipment size, both present and foreseeable future should be borne in mind. Products can change; and production equipment, through automation and transfer devices, is becoming larger. Remember that production machinery must be moved into, out of, around, and inside the building.

CEILINGS

As in the case of bay sizes, ceiling heights should fit the product, equipment, and budget.

Product size is of great importance. Small units make mandatory excellent lighting, a high degree of temperature and humidity control, and dust control.

These requirements are best accomplished in a small cube, which produces a low ceiling. Where the product or equipment is medium or variable in size, a 12 to 14 foot height is common. As the roof deck or ceiling becomes higher, lighting becomes a problem.

Office areas are usually ceilinged at 10 feet. This is a practical height which simplifies air distribution and lighting. Ceiling areas must usually be sprinklered "over and under" according to fire laws. Newer "drop-out" plastic panels can be used without underside sprinklers and are practical, though in general the cost is similar to that of an "over and under" sprinklered ceiling.

PREFABRICATED WALLS

As in the case of private home construction, plant buildings are fair targets for prefabricated sections, particularly walls. Much of this construction is spandrel or reinforced, precast concrete sections, from one to several stories high, which lock together and are mortared to form an impervious shell. A similar procedure is the "tilt up slab" method in which slabs are tilted into an upright position where they are steel-fastened to structural framework. The result is a dense, monolithic masonry structure with rough window openings ready to accept sash. This is less expensive than conventional block and brick construction and much faster where completion time is imperative.

A further advance is in sectional panels of sandwich-type curtain wall. These have steel framework, batt insulation, and skins of steel or aluminum. Usually, they come in a variety of colors through baked enamel or anodizing. The panels have an advantage over masonry in insulation, and by being lighter they do not require so heavy a steel structure.

Glass is another material used extensively in prefabricated facades. It comes in many types, including heat-reflective, glare-absorbing, multicolored, and thermal-insulated glass.

The trend is clear: Prefabricated construction will increase still more rapidly in the future. Prices are dropping through mass production; speed of erection is phenomenal; lasting qualities are comparable to those of conventional methods; maintenance costs are low; and repair is inexpensive. Prefabricated construction may provide a partial answer to the high cost of skilled construction labor.

INTERIOR SURFACES

A plant's appearance and utility, maintenance costs, and the morale of employees may well be affected by the choice of interior surface materials for floors, walls, partitions and panels, and the like.

Floors. By far the best approach is to base the flooring-material decision on a multifactor analysis that will include product sizes and types, employees, cleaning costs, and other factors. The best floor will probably be a compromise. The use of tile is widespread, and the vinyl-asbestos group is preferred because of its resiliency and elasticity. It does not crack or deform permanently, as does asphalt tile, when loads such as desks or bench legs are imposed. Prefinished tiles are to be specified where possible. Vinyl-asbestos is easy to work with, and the colors are many, varied, and pleasing. A word of warning: Never put pure vinyl or rubber tiles directly on "slab on grade," as lifting will undoubtedly occur.

Considerable attention is being given to epoxy floor toppings, which are especially useful in areas of high chemical activity. They are expensive—three to five times more than tile—but where special operations indicate their use, they are worth the money.

Acid-proof brick is another time-tested special floor but is giving way to epoxies because of its high cost.

Carpeting is the latest trend. For many years restricted to "executive row," carpeting is now found throughout plants, from cafeterias to rest areas and production floors. This is possible with synthetic fibers, which are easily cleaned and immune to many chemicals and soils. Studies indicate a maintenance cost lower than that of vinyl-asbestos tile, but usually the crossover point of maintenance savings and initial cost differential is not realized for five to seven years. Appearance and comfort index should be highest with carpeting, and acoustic noise control is a desirable side effect.

Walls. Interior walls are in two categories—fixed and movable. In the interest of plant flexibility, as much construction as possible should be movable.

Fixed walls are those required by function—for example, walls around toilets and rest rooms, boiler rooms, chemical storage, and compressor rooms. The basic reasons are noise control, safety, privacy, security, and decor. These features can best be achieved with fixed masonry walls.

Most common fixed-wall construction is of masonry units which come in a variety of sizes. If designs are based on modular principles, the work goes fast.

Fixed walls, however, may be made of other materials. Wood stud and gypsum board sheathing can be used to advantage. When they are used, there is less mess; they fall into clear expense categories; and, of course, they are much easier to fasten to. Insulated walls of this type give a high degree of acoustic damping. The gypsum sheathing is an excellent bonding surface for modern paneling or for acoustic blocking.

Partitions and panels. Movable partitions are of three basic types: wood, mineral board, and metal, with increased prices in that order. Great flexibility is their principal attribute; and they can be used over and over. Ordinarily, they are used in an unceilinged manner. The degree of sound damping is usually lower than with fixed walls, but newer movables have desirable acoustic properties. Erection labor costs are low compared to those of walls, but the initial cost of panels must be considered.

Panels, framed doors, and windows are produced in stock sizes. The products of different manufacturers are seldom compatible. Management will do well to choose a manufacturer carefully and plan to stay with him for some time. Layout planning should, where possible, be on the basis of stock panel units, eliminating custom panels. There will always be some custom work, but it is expensive and contrary to prefabrication principles and should be minimized.

ROOFING

Roofs are composed of decking and, over that, the built-up roofing. Decking can be of preformed metal, wood planking, poured concrete, gypsum, and numerous other materials.

The choice of roofing material will be based on building use, including possible hazards, bay sizes, availability of material, and climate conditions. The primary problem in design is the control of expansion and contraction. Old roofs with monitors had built-in construction or expansion points; the vast, flat roofs used today do not. It is imperative that expansion joints be included at regular intervals and that the roof be properly anchored along outside walls. Even a flat roof must be adequately pitched—usually, to interior roof drains leading to a storm drainage system. Sags or pockets will cause untold problems.

Roof decking is covered with insulating materials, usually in the form of fiberboard and/or fiber glass. Proper insulation will result in thermal conductivity ("U" factor) low enough (.15 to .25) to slow the transfer of heat between the building and outdoors and to inhibit condensation.

Over the insulation is laid the ply roofing. A hot mopped, 40 to 45 pound asbestos fibered base sheet, followed by two additional plies of 15 pound asbestos felts overlapped properly and mopped in place, completes the plies. The surface can be of two types, "bald" or graveled. "Bald" is a smooth top covered with a layer of "steep" (high-temperature) asphalt and—hopefully—a water emulsion coating which retards leeching of the bitumens by sunlight. This surface is used for steep inclines and flat surfaces that receive minimum traffic. Its desirable feature is that leaks are easily spotted.

Gravel surfaces are used on so-called flat roofs subject to wear from traffic. Gravel surfaces tend to reflect heat better than bald roofs but result in difficult leak detection and decidedly more work when the surface must be renewed. Reflective coatings are of questionable value after the second or third year. Surface oxidation and dirt films greatly reduce their reflective capacity. Ponding and roof sprays to aid interior cooling are not as popular as they once were, because of the demands they place on the plies. Flashing is of great importance in sound roof design. Copper is still the main choice, and sheet lead is important where some motion is unavoidable and a "limp" material is needed. Wood stripping made of cypress is desirable for its rotproof and fastener-holding properties.

Little or no reliance should be placed on roofing "bonds" (10-, 15-, or 20-year); they usually turn out to be difficult or even impossible to collect against. By far the best protection is the choice of an experienced, reputable roofing contractor who will give a two-year full guarantee that includes prompt service as a major point. A good contractor will automatically dam off each day's work, "envelope" the edges, nail off at close spacing, and use the proper bitumen at the correct temperature and in the prescribed quantity. A relatively small extra amount of money spent at the outset will usually save great amounts through the years of expected roof life.

PARKING AREAS

The design and layout of parking areas make up a morale factor important to all employees. Nearness to the work station is the main criterion. The problem is small when the number of employees is small. Extremely large plants arrange for their employees to park in remote, supervised areas, transporting them by bus to and from the plant. Parking can take place near the plant when effective use is made of natural or synthetic screening. Indeed, some plants have underground or roof parking to achieve proximity.

Parking areas should be laid out with central driveways 22 to 28 feet wide. Spaces should never be less than 8½ feet wide—preferably, 9 feet. Diagonal parking helps control one-way traffic flow and makes for ease of parking, though it is somewhat space-consuming. Parking standards information is available in *Architectural Graphic Standards,* by Charles G. Ramsey and Harold R. Sleeper (John Wiley & Sons, Inc., fifth edition, 1956). Landscaping is a "must" around parking areas. Trees are functional for screening and shade but must be protected from salt run-offs, which kill maples (for example).

Parking lots should be as open as possible and accessible for ease in cleaning and (in northern climates) snow removal. Snow stockpiling areas should be planned to reduce snow removal costs by eliminating "pick ups."

Large lots must usually be policed and require adequate lighting. This usually means a minimum of one-fourth to one-half footcandle. Mercury vapor lamps with a 22,000-hour life expectancy are a fine investment.

EMPLOYEE FACILITIES

Plant planning must include ever larger portions of employee facilities—cafeterias, picnic areas, rest rooms, lounges, locker rooms, libraries, and even chapels. It is not uncommon to find barber shops and facilities for automobile repair.

All these take bold, progressive management and imaginative plant engineering. They directly affect employee morale if they are properly provided. Excesses in either direction—too lavish or too little—will be criticized. Employee facilities should be attractive and functional, planned for hard use and easy maintenance.

MAINTENANCE FACTORS

Usually, plant engineering, the department charged with building design, is closest to plant maintenance, which must maintain the facilities. By involving maintenance in the design concepts, future upkeep costs can be minimized. An example is "back-up system reliability," which requires extra valves, motors, switch gear, and transformers but will result in the practical elimination of emergencies that bring resultant downtime and high repair costs.

Servicing catwalks should be provided around overhead equipment such as air-handling units. Rooftop equipment—condensers, compressors, and the like— should be located in enclosures so that maintenance is a year-round procedure not hampered by weather conditions. Good entrance design will materially reduce the amount of winter dirt "track in" and additional cleaning cost. Floor surfaces are extremely important to low maintenance costs. Proper design of lighting and ceilings will result in easy access and reduced operating costs. The use of an adequate number of the proper valves and electric switches will result in easy "cutting in" of added equipment or rearrangement of existing production areas without hindering production.

The design of an environmental system that will keep the plant under a positive pressure with regard to the outdoors will result in fewer rain leaks, fewer drafts, considerably less airborne dust and dirt, and greater employee comfort, resulting in fewer "environment complaints" later.

There are innumerable ways in which building design and planning can reduce or eliminate future maintenance costs. Let the maintenance department help reduce the nuisance problems that can be eliminated during design.

Plant Office Construction

Many of the criteria for manufacturing construction do not hold true for offices. Appearance and esthetics may rule over such standbys as production flow, access, and premium use of space.

BASIC CONSIDERATIONS

Before the plant offices are designed, there should be a clear-cut space policy relating size of office or space to job level or job requirements. Conference or interview areas, conveniently located, can help reduce private office size. Most office buildings favor private offices on the perimeter with general offices in the center. Many times, the center core is used as a service section for stairwells, elevators, air conditioning and plumbing equipment, and service rooms, toilets, and rest rooms.

Of great importance is flexibility. Office groupings are forever changing size and needs. Private offices should be flexible, to a degree, but not as much so as the general space. Modular construction is in order. This includes outside walls and inside partition intersection spacing, lighting layout, air conditioning, and heating plans. Floors should be uniform in materials and color to make partition movement easy and unrelated to flooring.

Power and telephone services should be in underfloor raceways where they can be provided at two-foot intervals. Nothing is as damaging to office appearance as a forest of wires dangling from the ceiling. Lighting quality should be high—100 to 150 footcandles. Window glare and sun load on air conditioning become important factors. "Eyebrows" or building overhangs, heat-reflective glass, or sun shading may be in order. Care should be taken to provide adequate elevator service for both freight and passengers if multiple floors are used.

Noise control is considerably more important than in the plant areas. Acoustic ceiling tile is a "must." Carpeting and drapes are usual for private offices. Frequently, over-the-ceiling voids between offices must be baffled to avoid sound transmission. Lead sheeting is a newer baffle material that is very effective. Ductwork can be acoustically baffled.

Environmental control is particularly critical here because of the sedentary nature of office work and the type of employee. Every effort should be made to result in "small area" control and system flexibility to accommodate layout changes. Perimeter heating is necessary to eliminate wall and window "chill radiation" effect. A double duct system or its equivalent should be used to allow extreme variations between offices or on opposite sides of the same floor.

Care should be taken to provide adequate service space adjacent to or inside of offices serviced: janitor closets, ladder storage, maintenance space, and "staging" area. Wastepaper disposal is fast becoming a major office design problem involving efficiency, cost, and safety.

In general, office construction must be handled differently from that of the plant in view of the type of personnel, visibility to frequent visitors, and the type of mental work performed. The solutions to the special problems are worthy of the extra time and energy that should be expended in design.

Building Services Installations

The success of plant operating functions depends to a high degree on the excellence of installation design. When it is realized that future years of operation will depend on decisions made at the outset, the scope of the task and its importance can be glimpsed.

PLANT UTILITIES

In the plant utilities—electric power, water, sewerage, and natural gas—is the plant's lifeblood.

Electricity. Electric power is vital to every second of operation. As such, capacity—or available quantity—and reliability are the main criteria. Shortly after World War II, industrial power consumption doubled every six or seven years. It is obvious that future growth capacity must be included when distribution systems are designed. Product forecast, equipment needs, and available money should be considered, but it must be remembered that extra electric capacity added later is extremely expensive incrementally and results in less than a "clean" system.

Reliability is the second criterion which must be addressed. All plants should have a minimum of two main electric feeds housed in separate conduits or separated in every way so that a failure in one does not jeopardize the other. This is the only way to reliable power. The concept of redundancy should be carried throughout the primary and secondary distribution systems. The switch gear should be cross-tied so that all critical loads at least can be fed from either incoming main. Automatic tie switches and selective drop-out switches will result in minimal downtime or none; they are to be preferred over manual switching. Breaker switch interrupting capacity should be sized according to anticipated fault currents, and care must be taken to avoid cascading effects where a series of interrupting devices trip out.

Switch gear should be centrally located to reduce distribution copper costs. In large plants, several area load centers may be indicated. Proper metering of both energy usage and demand should be included, and an accounting basis for deciding meter location should be used.

Multiphase systems (as nearly all systems are today) should be monitored to insure equality in phase-to-phase loads. Ground fault indicators should be installed initially to warn of potential hazards.

Water, sewerage, natural gas. Other common utilities are water, sewerage, and natural gas. The criterion of capacity is ultraimportant, while reliability is of less importance because of the low incidence of supply failure. Here again, historical usage growth is the guide. Size piping and equipment for future needs. Frequently, on-property water wells can be used advantageously.

Pollution control dictates methods of water disposal such as sanitary and storm sewerage, and requirements vary widely among plants, communities, and states. In view of present and pending legislation, it is wiser to overtreat waste disposal now than to be forced to do so later. Industry should show the way, as it does in so many other segments of public life.

HEATING, VENTILATION, AIR CONDITIONING

The importance of excellent heating and ventilation and air conditioning systems on the output and morale of today's employee cannot be overemphasized. However, an aspect of diminishing returns must be guarded against. Employee comfort cooling must not be allowed to merge with process air conditioning.

Systems should always introduce enough fresh air to avoid odors, stuffiness, and negative interior air pressure. Adequate filtration will produce a more healthful environment, easier to clean and keep dust-free. Product contamination can be controlled more readily with filters. Heating and cooling should use the most economical fuel available in terms of initial installation, fuel costs, and maintenance requirements. Systems can be central, as in the case of large, central water chillers and heating boilers; or they can be of a package type—independent cooling and heating units strategically located. Perimeter heating should be a "must," and air curtains used at large glass areas. Low-velocity intake air—not more than 500 feet per minute—should be insisted on to minimize the intake of snow and rain. Economizer cycle systems use outside air when it has cooling value, thus eliminating the cost of mechanical refrigeration in spring and fall.

Systems should provide for cooling and heating simultaneously for greatest comfort. Double ducts, multizone units with "hot and cold decks," and modulating dampers are methods used for combination heating and cooling systems. Care should be taken to provide for water treatment in chilled water, condenser water, and heating systems. Proper treatment prolongs equipment life and inhibits scale formation that reduces heat transfer capabilities.

Control systems should actually control system operation based on sensed conditions in serviced areas. Freeze protection must be positive, and fail-safe procedures should be designed into the systems.

Humidity control can be realized at extra cost through dehumidification, by supercooling and then reheating and rehumidifying to desired limits.

LIGHTING

Plant and office lighting should above all be suited to the seeing tasks involved —both present and future. This requirement is usually expressed in terms of footcandles intensity. The most noticeable of advances in lighting technology in recent years have been the recommended intensities. Requirement increases of 200 to 300 percent are common. Twenty years ago, an intensity of 30 to 40 footcandles in a machine shop was usual; now, a minimum of 100 and an average of 130 are common.

"Footcandles maintained" is the definition that should be specified; it refers to the light-meter reading in footcandles at table height from average soiled lights one-third to one-half through average anticipated life.

Other factors require design attention. The quality of light can be more important than the quantity. Paperwork and the inspection of glossy surfaces require glare-free light; this can best be obtained by the use of "egg crate" or prismatic plastic or glass diffusers. Benches or desks should be at right angles to the light centerlines. Desk tops frequently need covering with a light absorptive material to eliminate reflected glare.

Plant lighting may be fluorescent, incandescent, or mercury vapor. Fluorescents are more popular than incandescents because of their longer life, lower electric power requirements, less heat load, and better natural diffusion over their length. Incandescents are used where color is a problem; they can be intermixed with fluorescents—to bring out the natural color of foods, for example.

Mercury vapor and incandescent combinations have been used for high-bay lighting. Mercury lamps give up to 22,000 hours' life; and if color correction is successful, they will be used universally. Mercury vapor lighting is highly desirable for exterior illumination.

Lighting maintenance is an important factor. The accessibility of fixtures from the floor, the difficulty of removing and replacing lamps, ease of cleaning, average lamp life, and ballast cooling design are all parts of the analysis.

The trend is toward general area lighting, with spot lighting used only where absolutely necessary. It is wiser to plan lighting layouts with ultimate use in mind than to add rows of fixtures later. Areas with low seeing tasks, such as warehouse space, can be laid out with fairly close rows but with "skip fixtures"—troffers where light units are replaced with blank plates until the fixtures are required. The best procedure is to bring in a lighting engineer or manufacturer's representative, early in the design, and take advantage of his experience and specialty.

NOISE CONTROL

As other factors of industrial environment are becoming more controlled, noise is emerging as one of the most fatiguing and potentially dangerous problems. Employees exposed to high noise levels—80 to 120 decibels over a long period—frequently suffer serious loss of hearing.

The design of a modern plant or the adaptation of an older one demands serious consideration of noise factors and diligent design to minimize disruptive sounds. The use of acoustic ceilings has helped immeasurably to deaden sound. Acoustic wall materials, draperies, cork facings, and any wall material that can deaden and absorb (that is, not reflect) sound are on the rise.

Enclosures made of sheet lead or acoustic gypsum materials around noisy equipment can keep the sound in and relieve surrounding areas of the problem. If the sound cannot be confined, confine the people in acoustic booths. This is the answer at engine test stands.

Some novel sound problems involve the use of random background noise to mask offensive sound.

Public address systems and "canned music" are methods of introducing harmonious sound to relieve monotony and lessen fatigue. Care should be taken, however, to initiate "quiet breaks" to again break the monotony chain!

COLOR

Modern living is definitely a world of color. Bright tones, the mixture of previously "bad taste" colors (blue and green), and departure from somber tones are the order of the day. If management requires an unusual color scheme, the wise choice is to hire a known color consultant. This person should have a good reputation and should be able to show examples of industrial work.

If plant and office colors are to be chosen by the staff, a few pointers will be helpful.

First, choose a standard set of "area tones" through the use of a paint manufacturer's color sample book. These should be pastel, neutral tones that look well together, at least in pairs. The general relaxing neutral appearance can be spiced with bright, contrasting-color doors or panels. Paint colors should be primarily attractive, but surfaces must be functional to be well designed. Door framing and doors should never be light-colored; they receive heavy wear and will soon become soiled.

Color coding. In recent years, the use of a safety color code has become prevalent; it assigns colors to specific tasks—for example, "fire engine red" and "traffic yellow." Information on the color standards can be obtained by writing to the American National Standards Institute, 1430 Broadway, New York, N.Y. 10018, and requesting Code Z53.1.

An outgrowth of this system is color coding of pipes and plant equipment to indicate usage. A further development is the use of periodic stripes or stick-on bands explaining—for example—which utility is being carried in a pipe.

—*W. L. Sykes*

PLANT SAFETY

To provide safe working conditions for employees was recognized long ago as a moral responsibility of plant management. However, as in many other areas of life, direct and indirect benefits accrue to those who fulfill their responsibilities creditably. Employee well-being, including physical and mental security, results in improved production and profitable operation, further enhancing investor ownership as well as employee security. Lowered workmen's compensation insurance rates are another benefit, the result of minimum accident experience.

Organization

Every plant has a safety program of some kind, and its effectiveness is directly related to organizational support. Usually, safety receives less attention in medium-size and small plants. Commonly, the least busy personnel or industrial relations manager is given the responsibility for safety measures in addition to his primary duties. Ideally, the chief of a plant safety program reports high enough in the organization to be assured of backing and cooperation at every level of management.

An improvement on the usual organizational slot assigned to safety is the inclusion of the task in the plant engineering charter. The logic behind this recommendation stems from several circumstances. Most of the tangible work accomplished by safety is through the efforts of plant engineering and maintenance.

Maintenance is recognized as a first line of defense in times of emergency or disaster. Safety is important in the daily routine of maintenance where men are dealing with high voltages, explosive gases, power tools, ladders, scaffolds, and other utilities or equipment that demand constant respect.

Owing to the advisory nature of its task, plant safety does not itself require an extensive formal organization or staff. Usually, one or two engineers and a combination clerk-secretary will suffice. There is need for functional organizations including a safety inspection committee, evacuation group, and fire brigade. These organizations perform the action portion of a safety program. They should be advised, directed, and guided by the safety staff and should be so organized that their functioning is automatic and spontaneous, especially in time of need.

Safety Program Administration

The results of a safety program bear a direct relation to the effort expended.

MANAGEMENT COMMITMENT

Maximum effectiveness requires a commitment from the highest level of plant management. This entails active participation, for lip service to safety is easily spotted by employees. Commitment requires becoming involved with practice sessions of the fire brigade; acquiring a knowledge of serious shortcomings; and studying reports and statistics.

Safety authority must obviously be blessed from the top, but it should be a function of the safety engineer to seek out authority and proper backing and—once they have been gained—to nurture them and use them wisely. There is nothing wrong in requesting an executive to become an active member of the fire brigade or safety committee. On the contrary, his participation may well catalyze a complete plant safety program.

FORMAL PROCEDURES

Proper safety administration will require the formalization of safety procedures, forms, and reports (all of which are readily available from neighbor companies and—very importantly—from the company insurance carrier's accident prevention department).

The proper and frequent use of procedures and standard forms will help ingrain desirable safety habits, make possible expert investigation and analysis, and result in fruitful reports. Unfortunately, the degree of accident investigation, reporting, and follow-up is tied to the severity of the accident. Many times, this has the result of underrating a minor accident that has serious future potential. This is an understandable human failing; it can be corrected, however, by the proper use of detailed investigation and report forms. The proper use of such forms requires a "stop and look" analysis of various factors that, many times, will make apparent the semihidden potential for future tragedy.

First aid stations and all other medical aid facilities, even to a band-aid kit in a shop, must be in the safety program control loop. Each must feed back to the safety staff promptly so that analytical and corrective action can be taken. Care must be exercised to make safety action as unthinking as possible—that is, to make it automatic through force of habit. The actions are repetitious, and proper proceduralization will save time and misspent energy. Major attention is demanded for analysis and corrective action, not for retracing steps to arrive at a "full story." One method of "follow through" analysis and reporting is the use of a line-oriented operating safety committee which periodically hears cases and arrives at conclusions and recommendations which the committee will help implement.

LINE SUPERVISION

The most day-to-day influential and hardest to involve segment of the plant population is first-line supervision. Supervisors operate from a clear-cut priority plan that they have evolved through experience. Safety will normally have a low priority unless its position on the priority chain is moved up, which is accomplished by various means.

One way of advancing priority is by edict or command. A better method calls for the participation and personal involvement of higher management in an active program. A stimulating use of the latter method will require the full resources of the safety staff. Participation on safety inspection committees is effective. Supervisors who inspect each other's departments periodically under a formal system will shape up their own departments.

Participation in accident analysis studies will also result in keener interest in the complete safety program. Frequently, in the course of first-line supervisor involvement, a man will stand out for his interest, enthusiasm, and ability; this man should be used to convey the message to others in his sphere.

It should be clearly understood that the first-line supervisor is the key man in a safety program that includes his own department. His basic responsibilities are expressed in three principles: (1) engineering (determining the safe methods); (2) education (instructing his employees in the methods); (3) enforcement (making certain that his instructions are being followed).

SAFETY TRAINING

Education is essential to safety effort because safety is a man-made condition; merely to work safely is not instructive. The education of employees can be achieved through a well-prepared and well-executed training program. Because the supervisor is in closest touch with the new employee during his introduction to work, he obviously plays an important role. The supervisor must be educated in the techniques he will use in training his employees, from their first day on the job, regarding safe working practices. (Many new supervisors have had no previous safety training.) Employee training, as opposed to safety orientation on the job, depends upon accident frequency and severity as determined by accident reports. Safety training is also made necessary by unfavorable comparisons of the company's accident records with those of competitors or of industry as a whole and by the importance of proper accident investigation.

Safety training must stress individual responsibility; it should be conducted continuously at the lowest level and integrated with on-the-job training.

Newly hired personnel should be briefed on the company's safety record and given safety orientation before being placed on the job. Appropriate general training should be given as deemed necessary by the safety and training specialist or safety engineer.

Safety contacts should be made through the employee's supervisor. The staff nature of safety should be lost sight of only in emergencies when precipitate action is demanded. The proper reporting of hazards or minor accidents is a voluntary action by employees that must be stimulated; only as a last resort should it be made the subject of disciplinary action.

Safety grievances can be of two types. One is the result of a sincere desire on the part of an employee to seek the remedy of a dangerous condition or prevent a possible incident. Frequently, a safety grievance points up the lack of a proper procedure for reporting, and many times it indicates inability to get prompt action in a voluntary manner from management. This is a deplorable condition that requires correction. Unfortunately, many companies wait for the union to force them into corrective action. This strengthens the union's position; and management, instead of capitalizing on the morale factors present in the situation, is further weakened. Inaction is the surest way to stop the flow of suggestions and recommendations by employees. Another type of safety grievance has the purpose of finding work for the union steward when grievance activity is low. This type of complaint should be recognized as harassment and dealt with accordingly.

Developing Employee Attitudes

Safety requires the continuous selling of a little-appreciated commodity. Many programs operate only on a demand or crash basis. This is haphazard management at its worst. When only a serious accident can arouse interest in safety, the whole program needs an overhaul. The key word in safety selling is "continuous," and here the safety engineer or staff will be hard pressed to keep interest at a high level. All the tools of modern advertising have been used. Posters such as the National Safety Council distributes may be ineffective unless tied in with a complete program or related to employee interests by other supplementary means. Safety contests are effective and popular means of spurring interest; but they must be of limited duration, or the impact will dribble away.

Use has been made of the visible results of accidents—dented hard hats, shattered safety glasses, crushed shoes, broken grinding wheels, and other easily understood hazardous results. Costs of injuries can be posted. Contests between departments can be fostered for best safety records.

A proper employee attitude toward safety can be inculcated by convincing employees that (1) accidents are caused and can be prevented; (2) safety is a mark of skill and common sense; (3) the company is sincerely interested in safety and is willing to invest time, money, and whatever else it costs to prevent injuries to workers; (4) safety is a personal responsibility.

Activities to foster safety attitudes are of three general kinds: cooperative work, in which the employees actively participate in the safety program; training or educational activities in which formal teaching is performed; and general safety advertising or propaganda. New equipment and approaches must be continuously sought by the safety staff, and demonstrations become very important as the most easily understood form of visual aid.

Recent studies indicate that more than 80 percent of an individual's perception is by sight and 11 percent is by hearing. People retain 50 percent of what they see and hear simultaneously, but only 30 percent of what they perceive through hearing alone. It is apparent that visual aids are a necessity in safety training.

Wherever possible, groups of employees in the same department should be trained to avoid hazards peculiar to the department. This sometimes results in a "brother's keeper" attitude that can be highly effective.

Auditing Results

The effectiveness of a safety program can be tested only by the results observed, and results are in the form of accident experience. The most expensive program, if it is coupled with continuously high accident rates, is not a successful program and should not be so regarded.

Data on accidents and illness must be accumulated and analyzed. An excellent source is the plant nurse or medical department, using the customary accident report form and sending one copy to the injured employee's supervisor and one copy to the safety engineer. Some forward-looking companies utilize data processing equipment with storage capacity to file each employee's accident and health record. Most plants keep manual records, as safety has not as yet attained a high priority on the computer programmer's list.

Other sources of data for evaluation and subsequent action are Federal and state government reports and insurance carriers' inspection reports. The carrier's itemized statement of workmen's compensation losses (quarterly and annual) is an excellent source to establish dollar loss directly attributable to an accident injury.

Additional loss information may be in the form of repair costs of damage to plant or equipment. Lost production is an immediately available cost. Retraining—or the training of a new operator—is a usual cost incurred as a result of an accident. The effect on morale and subsequent production output as the result of an accident in a department is intangible, but it is a cost.

Record keeping is an integral part of a well-organized safety program. It is used to test the program's effectiveness and to compare the plant's safety records with those of other plants in the same or a similar industry. Audits tell how the company stands and how it is likely to stand if trends continue. Record keeping must be formalized and reduced to habit-forming procedures in order to be effective.—*W. L. Sykes*

INDUSTRIAL SECURITY

By the very nature of the times, the scope of industrial security starts with a company's owner, president, and manager and continues on down through every level, department, or section, including vendors and suppliers, to the man on the street: the visitor, the passerby, the neighbor, the rioter, the vandal, or the trespasser. Industrial security programs, through the professional application of controls or calculated disciplines (including psychological deterrents), must either directly or indirectly persuade, dissuade, or discourage in an overall safeguarding effort for the protection of the organization—its assets, its property, its proprietary interest, and its people.

Supporting and Safeguarding

Business exists to realize the stated objectives of its charter. It organizes itself to attain these goals with economy of effort, time, and money and operates to produce an end item or service that is attractive, timely, and competitive at the marketplace. Today, more than ever, business is faced with many complex "people problems" and threats to profitable operation: thefts of property, supplies, products, proprietary interest, and money; disloyal employees, riots, business espionage, overall crime increase, labor unrest, emergencies, and disasters that disrupt or endanger the very existence of the business enterprise. At best, the enterprise loses valued time and direction and profit margins suffer a downward trend. A continuing industrial security effort has as its purpose to identify or uncover such threats and correct them. It also exists to prevent situations that might cause a breach of employee integrity. Security strives to reduce the conditions in and around a facility or business office that expose it to costly and unnecessary risks. The proverbial ounce of prevention is assuredly worth a pound of cure; it makes the security role both supporting and safeguarding.

Security Organization

The first requirement in establishing a security effort is to set up a program organized by section or department. There must be a positive point of reference for the program in order to serve the interests of the company. The assignment can be full-time with staff, or part-time as dictated by the size of the firm; but it must be positive in designation, action, and support. In order to put support in the correct frame of reference—for top executives as well as employees—the unit should report to a vice president or manager of industrial relations or finance, who in turn reports directly to the president or owner.

STAFFING AND ACTIVITIES

A formal organization for a security department is usually under the direction of a security director or manager. This position is designed to coordinate the various interrelated security functions. It provides a professional security sounding board for top management and, through surveys and research efforts, gives the firm security in depth—a complete series of controls for its present and future requirements. The security director's staff is organized to meet the day-to-day operational needs of the department efficiently and economically.

Physical security or plant protection. Usually under the direction of a chief security officer or inspector, the physical security activity includes all uniformed security personnel and is responsible for perimeter and interior activities of the security effort, including closed-circuit television systems, alarms, fire fighting, and fire prevention; it also participates, under direction, in emergency and disaster planning.

Emergency planning. This activity is designed to meet emergencies stemming from human failure, equipment failure, or so-called nature failures—explosions, cave-ins, fire, riots, bomb threats, labor disturbances, transit strikes, blackouts and power failures, heavy snow, wind or rain storms, and so forth. Before emergency planning can be organized, a study must be conducted in all phases of the company's activities in order to identify needs and set priorities and standards of criticality.

Government security. One section of an industrial security department acts as liaison with representatives of the government agencies that have security interest in the firm. It assists in government-conducted inspections and performs company-authorized inspections to assure continuous compliance with security regulations. This section is also responsible for writing and updating the company's security standard practice instructions, a document based in part on the Department of Defense industrial security manual. Government security requires security badges for employees. The government security program's many other requirements include personnel background investigations, which are contractual inasmuch as the government manual is made a part of each defense contract.

Investigation. Another phase of the security organization's operations is the investigative workload. This section of the program deals with pre-employment, in-plant, and incident investigations; conducts business and industrial espionage surveys; and monitors labor-management climate. Under a government defense program it also administers requests for personnel access; authorizations; and classified visit clearance coordination.

An outside investigative agency can be used to perform pre-employment and special personnel investigations. This possibility should be considered if the demand for such a service is not sufficient to justify hiring an in-house investigator.

SECURITY PROGRAMS

After the functional areas of the security department have been organized, the next step is to set up and develop the programs necessary to deal with the identified areas of the company's security vulnerability. (The assessment of vulnerability can be made by a professional security organization, by a government industrial security survey when classified government contracts are involved, or by an experienced security professional.)

Security programs vary with each individual company but usually include the ones described in the following paragraphs. Today's security challenges cannot be met with yesterday's programs, and tomorrow's security challenges will not be met and controlled with today's security programs. Therefore, like any other professional management effort, it must keep up with the times in approach, thinking, and equipment—or fail in its mission.

Security employee orientation. The program of security orientation sets the scene for new employees and continues to remind longer-term employees of the security programs.

Physical security. Keys, locks, fences, caged areas, doors, windows, screening, safes, electronic alarms, security lighting, closed-circuit television installations with audio capability—all these are controlled by physical security programs. These controls can also reduce security costs and improve overall security.

Money controls. Cashiers' areas, transportation of money to and from banks, expense accounts, petty cash, and payroll checks are protected by a money controls program.

Embezzlement controls. Fictitious accounts, payroll checks for nonexistent employees, fraudulently raised checks, payments to nonexistent companies for purposes of fraud, and the like are covered under an embezzlement control program.

Inventory controls. If an inventory problem exists, the areas of control should be reduced if possible; this approach makes it easier to detect problem areas and institute corrective action. Every internal and external shipment or transfer of the product should be documented.

Identification. Employees, visitors, and vehicles require identification. Visitors and vehicles should be recorded as they enter and leave the plant premises. Positive controls of this nature give a facility a needed air of discipline that has many side benefits.

Pre-employment investigation. This type of investigation program has proved its worth in reducing business risks resulting from bad hires. Curtailing employee turnover reduces costs and improves morale.

Communication security. Mail rooms, telephones, meeting rooms, and all other vulnerable areas require security monitoring.

Sensitive and/or confidential information control. Continual security thinking is required to protect the company's patents, new products, packages, ideas, new marketing programs, and new manufacturing processes. Establish positive "need to know" practice regarding confidential information. (The "need to know" concept requires that certain kinds of information be discussed only with people who need to know because they must act on the information or contribute in some manner to its sophistication or development.) One caution in this regard: When vendors, consultants, or suppliers are on the "need to know" list, advise them strongly of the company's protective thinking for this type of information. Information along these lines can be the lifeblood of a company; shred sensitive or confidential notes, letters, memos, and so forth when they are no longer required. Industrial espionage is a threat to industry; reduce the risk with tighter controls. This action will make the firm a more difficult target.

Psychological deterrent programs. A spot check of various functions from time to time lets employees know that the company is interested in their work and at the same time creates a psychological deterrent to wrongdoing. It also provides an opportunity to check on whether work requirements are realistic; if they are overburdensome, it is possible that the workload can only be carried by dishonest means. This type of problem is at the base of many security problems. It breeds discontentment and disloyalty and allows for unhealthy rationalization against the best interests of a firm. Thus a "conflict of interest" program is sometimes initiated.

Security programs tend to create an atmosphere of discipline within the company both inside the facility and outside. They breed respect with all its related benefits.—*J. C. Burke*

MAINTENANCE MANAGEMENT

As manufacturing processes in all industries have been modernized by automation, higher speeds, larger single-train operations, and electronic controls, the man-hours of productive labor per pound or piece (or any unit) have decreased, while the size of the maintenance force has necessarily increased to maintain the additional machinery. This trend will continue. The emergence of maintenance as a larger item on the cost sheet and thus a greater factor in profitability brings maintenance into focus as a major force in the success or failure of a business. It is imperative that today's maintenance effort be directed by modern managers using modern methods.

The goal of good maintenance management might be stated as *achieving optimum maintenance level at minimum cost in a safe manner*. This immediately poses the question of what is "optimum." "Optimum maintenance" might be described as "that level of maintenance which permits the unit to produce in quantities and at quality required by sales demands."

Creating an Effective Organization

The top maintenance position—manager, superintendent, chief, by whatever title—should have equal rank with the top production job. (Production people are usually not maintenance oriented and are unable to manage for maximum service at minimum cost.) Lower ranking or submergence in the operating organization is not recommended. It must not be inferred, however, that maintenance should become a separate empire, since it is strictly a service function. Rather, the top production man and the top maintenance man should display the ultimate in cooperation while dealing with each other as equals. A company is fortunate if it has a top maintenance man who has had production experience or at least has a good "feel" for production problems. Extensive previous maintenance experience up through the line is probably not necessary; it may even be a detriment. Today's maintenance demands a fresh, new look unhampered by "the way we have done it in the past."

It is recommended, first, that the top man have an engineering background; the particular discipline is not important, as there are many successful managers from mechanical, civil, electrical, and chemical engineering disciplines.

Second, he must be a leader, since the maintenance effort is not particularly adaptable to the driving technique. The maintenance manager does not make repairs himself; the output of the department is the result of his working with and through people.

The good manager needs one or two subordinates who have potential for the manager's job and whom he is training. Such men might appear on the organization chart as assistant manager, general foreman, planning supervisor, plant engineer, or other. The surest way to promotion is to have a replacement trained and ready. Middle levels of maintenance management are not discussed in detail here, since the number of levels and number of people vary widely. In most cases, the managers of tomorrow will come from these middle levels; thus the middle level of today should include the type of person, with appropriate background, that is needed in the manager's position.

The first-line foreman is, perhaps, the forgotten man in the maintenance organization. He bears the brunt of union push-pull activity while being pressured from above by his superior for greater productivity and lower costs. He deserves more attention. Many first-line foremen are promoted craftsmen and still retain the ideas and prejudices they had as hourly workers.

It is strongly recommended that, when promotion is from the hourly-rated group, psychological testing be used to supplement performance records and foreman recommendations. While not cheap, the cost for testing is miniscule compared with the money a poor foreman can waste. A new foreman should be given opportunity to take management development courses, encouraged to read books germane to his field, and offered opportunity to further his education with tuition assistance (if possible), since most first-line foremen do not have the educational background to permit much advancement in today's maintenance organizations.

An effective maintenance organization needs the related departments that will make it effective: planning and scheduling, plant engineering, and maintenance storeroom. An extremely useful adjunct is industrial engineering, but this group would more logically report to the plant or works manager.

Appraising the Existing Organization

Appraising an organization is most effectively done by evaluating results rather than studying organization charts, procedures, and people to see if they conform with modern management theories. The chief function of all levels of management is to produce profits or contribute to profits.

By definition, to measure is to compare with a standard; with maintenance, the difficult problem is to find the standard. A number of indexes can be used; some are absolute and factual, and others are indicators only. The first comparison is total maintenance expenditures: this year versus last year; this month versus last month; comparison of total costs over, say, a ten-year period. While widely used, these comparisons are of doubtful real value because they give no effect to important variables such as production level or changing wage rates. A better yardstick is cost per unit of production expressed as dollars or percent of total unit cost. This type of evaluation gets into the profit statement, since total profit is the product of unit profit and volume.

The comparison of maintenance costs per unit on a calendar basis gives the maintenance manager and his superiors a powerful tool to determine maintenance contributions to increased or deteriorated profits. A favorable trend whets management's appetite for more; unfavorable results demand corrective action. If action is indicated, there are several areas to probe.

1. Wage rates are continuously increasing in all areas of operation; therefore, increases in maintenance rates should not have too great an impact, particularly on a percentage basis.

2. An increase in maintenance hours per unit of production means a possible decrease in maintenance labor efficiency.

3. An increase in the labor-to-material ratio is another indicator of decreased labor efficiency.

4. A sharp increase in maintenance material, both per unit of production and total, may indicate the need for replacement of old equipment. The cause must be determined.

5. An increase in emergencies and overtime orders indicates reversion to breakdown maintenance or insufficiently controlled operations.

The probe areas are symptoms that merit continuing attention to possibly forestall unfavorable maintenance costs. Many other comparisons, such as maintenance as a percent of fixed capital, can be used; but their validity must be checked for the individual situation.

Planning and Scheduling

Maintenance may be classified as *breakdown* or *planned,* with many gradations between the two. Few companies run on a strictly breakdown basis because of the high cost and limitation on production. Most organizations use at least rudimentary planning and scheduling. Conversely, there are few companies that could not profitably improve or enlarge their planning and scheduling effort.

OBJECTIVES

Planning and scheduling contributes to the goal of achieving optimum maintenance at minimum cost by decreasing machine downtime, utilizing manpower more effectively, adjusting work force to demand, planning for major jobs, and anticipating repetitive jobs.

WORK ORDER SYSTEMS

A work order system is the first step in setting up planning and scheduling. Work orders may be simple or complex, but the simplest form that will fulfill the local needs is probably the best. As a bare minimum, the following information must be included: description of work requested; location; urgency or priority; name and code number of department for charging; signature of originator and space for approvals if required; a number for identification and collection of charges. As an organization becomes more sophisticated, more data can be included to permit processing and analyzing by EDP.

With a work order system, it is possible to take the first step from breakdown maintenance toward planned maintenance by preparing daily work schedules, one day at a time. The effect should be apparent immediately, since each craftsman will know at the start of a workday where he is expected to be and what machine he is to work on. Work schedules, even the most simple, are a strong force toward real maintenance management. At this point, it should be emphasized that work schedules, whether crude or sophisticated, will always be broken to handle true emergencies.

A weekly schedule is recommended after some experience with daily schedules. This is prepared at a joint meeting with operating supervision. A further logical extension is the monthly schedule, handled in much the same manner as the weekly—by conference with production supervision. In the daily schedule, practically all the workforce will be committed (scheduled). The weekly schedule might commit 75 percent to 80 percent of the force, and the monthly no more than 50 percent. This is done to permit orderly scheduling of unanticipated work. The longer-term schedules permit the scheduling of preventive maintenance and repetitive jobs which might be overlooked in day-to-day scheduling.

SHORT- AND LONG-TERM PLANNING

A logical extension of work orders and scheduling is planning, both long- and short-term. A schedule must make at least a rough estimate of the time required for a job, but estimates of this type are usually too liberal. The planner is expected to make a more realistic time estimate. In addition, there is the problem of materials: Are they available, or must they be purchased? Where more than one craft is involved, the job needs to be sequenced. Production should be consulted on how the job would fit in with production schedules. With a planner in the picture, the scheduler receives a "package" instead of a bare work order. Savings in time resulting from having the necessary materials on hand or even delivered to the job site will often justify the salary of a planner. Closer estimates of time required and sequencing in a multicraft situation allow the scheduler to prepare more meaningful schedules.

Longer-range planning on weekly, monthly, and annual bases follows in logical order. The problem of necessary materials, spare parts, and the like is of great importance in longer-range planning. Since some parts call for deliveries up to one year apart, the position of a job on the long-range schedule is often dictated by their delivery date. Long-range planning also provides an opportunity for leveling manpower. It is also a vehicle for noting—for example—the annual state inspection of boilers and the annual (or less frequent) inspection of machinery. Once on a long-range plan, items recorded will not be overlooked; furthermore, such records help fill the gap when key people leave the organization through promotion, transfer, or another reason.

MANPOWER REQUIREMENTS

On a daily basis, the scheduler can schedule only the man-hours that he knows he will have available for the next day. The same principle applies to weekly and monthly schedules; however, with these longer-period plans it becomes possible to start leveling manpower.

Work order priorities. Many priority systems are available, some very complex. A simple system of four priorities will suffice in many situations: (1) emergency (do now, no scheduling); (2) urgent (do within 24 hours, scheduled but not planned); (3) schedule (as implied—planned and scheduled); and (4) shutdown (as implied).

On a daily basis, the scheduler first schedules his urgent orders and then fills out available manpower with schedule orders.

Backlog. A symptom of shortage of manpower, owing either to actual lack of hands or to poor utilization, is a gradual buildup of schedule orders. This backlog is the most potent indicator available for adjusting the workforce. Conversely, a decrease in backlog is an invitation to reduce the force. Short-term changes in backlog have little significance, but longer-term trends—say, several weeks or a month—definitely require action. If a rising backlog is noted but thought owing to poor manpower utilization, it may still be necessary to temporarily increase the workforce, since the improvement of manpower utilization and worker efficiency cannot be accomplished quickly. Again, maintenance is a service department and the machines must be kept running.

TIMEKEEPING PROGRAM

Timekeeping serves two purposes: The worker must be paid for the hours he works, and the time he spends on a job must be charged to the proper department or cost center (in some systems, to the individual machine). The first is usually recorded on an individual weekly time card by a punch-type time clock. The question of charging the worker's time to the right "customer" is more complex. A clerk-type timekeeper is sometimes used; he circulates through the plant, noting jobs being worked on and time chargeable. This is not an efficient practice. With a work order system, the foreman may keep the time by noting the hours on the work order before he turns it in as completed. This system works very well, and there is only one possible objection: It makes paperwork for the foreman. A third system being adopted in many plants is to have the worker note his own time on the work order. Bear in mind that the worker is being paid according to the record on his time card. He has nothing to gain from a false entry on the work order. If there is a problem of low productivity, it must be solved by other means than the distribution of his daily time to job orders. Further, in the normal industrial organization there is little to be gained from accuracy to the minute in charging time to a work order.

SCHEDULED AND UNSCHEDULED SHUTDOWNS

An unscheduled shutdown is usually an emergency. As such, the normal daily schedule is broken to provide the necessary manpower. Even in this emergency situation, the planner and the scheduler can be of invaluable assistance. The scheduler can pull manpower from noncritical jobs in other areas to make up the required force. The planner, from prior knowledge of the area, can locate necessary parts and get them delivered; he can dispatch special apparatus such as welding machines, burning outfits, impact wrenches, and portable air compressors; he can alert the machine shop for any special parts to be made or repaired. Companies that have a well-organized planning and scheduling function will attest that unscheduled or emergency shutdowns are definitely shortened by its efforts even though the job obviously could not be planned and scheduled in the usual manner.

Planned shutdowns are one of the shining areas where planning and scheduling really pay off. In a well-structured situation, the planner would be accumulating individual work orders (priority-shutdown) as the production people see the need. These work orders would be individually processed, labor estimated, material availability checked (or ordered), and special tools noted. When the shutdown is scheduled, the planner and scheduler assemble the pertinent work orders and may plot out a bar graph or even prepare a critical path chart. This furnishes the necessary data for manning. The savings possible with this method —in both dollars and time—over a nonplanned, hit-or-miss style are tremendous.

Material and Labor Cost Controls

Controls over labor, material, and overhead are necessary if maintenance is to make its contribution to profitability and profit improvement. True costs, by areas or departments, must be known in order to control them. The work order system will allocate direct labor to the proper cost center. A system must also be devised to charge materials to the proper user.

MATERIAL AND INVENTORY CONTROL

All maintenance organizations have some sort of storeroom. If raw materials are disregarded, 80 percent or more of the storeroom is used specifically for maintenance. The storeroom exists for the purpose of having on tap the repair parts and materials that may be required to minimize machine downtime. On long-delivery spare parts where lead time can be up to a year or more, there is no alternative but to have an adequate supply on hand. A typical store may have items with individual values from a few cents to $100,000. Stores management has undergone changes in recent years. Several areas that contribute to decreased total stores inventory while maintaining adequate supplies to expedite maintenance are as follows:

1. *Decontrol of low-cost items.* Many companies no longer require requisitions for these items ($1 limit), which are charged to overhead when received and are placed in free-access bins. A few companies have raised the limit to $2. Minor losses in these items have been found to be far less than the accounting expense for processing requisitions.

2. *The ABC system of inventory control.* This takes into account both the cost of possession and the cost of acquisition. It concentrates stores and purchasing effort on the high-cost items. Considerable economies can be achieved under this system.

3. *The stockless storeroom.* This is chiefly applicable in populous areas. A supplier of bearings, for example, agrees to hold in his stock a certain number, size, and type of bearings for the customer. This is covered by a blanket order. He will ship any designated bearing by a release against this blanket order, using his own truck, common carrier, or taxicab, depending upon urgency.

Requisitions. Normally, a stores requisition is required for any item taken from stores. This requisition should show the work order number. The use of the work order number ties together material and labor on a job for later evaluation and application to the proper cost center. The stores area should be enclosed, with limited access, and in general out of bounds except to stores employees.

Quantities. Quantities of any item carried are a function of usage and lead time for replacement. Many plants function with a perpetual inventory system, using a maximum-minimum set-up or reorder point in case of ABC. In order for this to function, there must be a feedback from the requisition; a card system is often used with clerks posting withdrawals and pulling a card for purchasing when minimum or reorder point is reached. This function is also compatible with EDP. Additionally, an inventory check system (continuous or cyclical) is needed where one-twelfth of the stock is inventoried each month. On a maximum-minimum set-up, the limits should be constantly reviewed to see if they can be decreased—again, aiming at decrease in total inventory. A good rule of thumb is that inventory (dollar value) should turn over once every three to six months (for chemical plants, once every one or two years is considered more reasonable). Periodic reviews should be made of slow-moving items showing no transaction in one to three years, depending upon the industry, to see if they cannot be removed from inventory and put on an on-request basis.

Carrying charge. The cost of stores inventory is considerable. In one plant, it has been estimated as 23 percent of the value of the inventory per year; higher costs have been used but they are unusual. It is made up of such items as the cost of capital; local and state personal property taxes; salaries of personnel; cost of warehouse facilities; and inventory insurance, theft, damage, and obsolescence.

LABOR STANDARDS

Standards systems and controls for labor are necessary to secure optimum maintenance at minimum cost. A work order system is mandatory for any program of labor standards.

Historical standards. Relatively simple to install, historical standards are widely used. The method consists of accumulating the labor hours for repetitive jobs, starting at any point in time. Each repetitive job is recorded on a separate sheet of multicolumn paper. As the job is repeated, an entry shows the date, the hours required, and any special conditions. After a few entries, an average is taken for all normal occurrences; this becomes the standard time to be allotted by the planner. Average or standard is updated from time to time. If on any job the time is found in excess of standard, questions can be asked, thus furnishing a measure of control. If improvements are made in planning, scheduling, material delivery, supervision, or other areas, they quickly show up by "beating the standard," thus providing a measure of the effectiveness of the improvements. There is much to be said in favor of historical standards. Their principal disadvantage is that they are comparative rather than absolute. In other words, a company's performance might be so bad that even a considerable improvement as measured by historical standards might still leave it far below an acceptable level.

Engineered work standards. Engineered work standards apply a standard time to a job. Most consultants have a system of engineered work standards that they generally recommend. A standards book is supplied that contains tables for various mechanical acts. In developing a standard time for a particular job, the planner breaks it down into its smallest components, looks up the standard time for each, and adds up the segments; this becomes the standard time. Though this process may appear to be excessively time-consuming, it need be done only once for each job. Standards so obtained are realistic in that the job can be accomplished in the stipulated time by a good mechanic.

In practice, the actual time is generally greater; figures of 60 percent to 80 percent efficiency are common. Furthermore, in most plants no more than 80 percent of the work orders are susceptible to engineered standards. The engineered standard does, however, provide a solid base line against which performance can be measured. As with historical standards, improvements in techniques are readily apparent in increased percentage efficiency.

Improved scheduling. Use of standards is bound to improve performance by permitting tighter scheduling. In the absence of standards, the planner is usually too liberal in the time allowed, with the result that the worker either uses Parkinson's law ("The job expands to fill the time allowed") or is idle. Standards plus improved or tighter scheduling will result in lower labor costs and better manpower planning.

BUDGETS

Maintenance may range from 5 percent to 15 percent of total production costs; thus it swings considerable weight in cost-profitability studies. The budget must be tight enough to contribute to profitability yet be attainable. In most plants, the new budget leans heavily on previous years' experience, particularly the current year's. In its simplest form, the new budget is the current year's experience adjusted to compensate for increased wage rates, known major repairs, improvements in efficiency, and level of operations. The attempt should be made to identify as many jobs as possible for the coming year, both for cost and timing. Identification of major portions of the budget money as separate, discrete jobs is of great assistance in manpower leveling. It also permits a greater degree of control. Preventive maintenance may be shown as a separate budget item.

Appraising performance. The first yardstick used to appraise the maintenance effort is usually budget compliance for both labor and materials. While this comparison used in a vacuum is not a particularly valid measuring device, it is the way maintenance costs appear on the cost sheet and bears directly on the cost-profitability picture. Obviously, materials and labor for individual jobs should be continuously compared with the estimate, and tabulations prepared on a weekly, monthly, and annual basis. EDP is of great assistance in this effort.

Improving and Appraising Maintenance Performance

Improved maintenance performance is not confined to costs; it is equally important to increased operating time on machines, modifications to increase output, and decreased operating labor. These items may actually increase overall maintenance expenditures but will pay off in increased productivity.

PREVENTIVE MAINTENANCE PROGRAM

Preventive maintenance is practiced to some extent in every organization; it is a potent contributor to profitability. In its simplest form, it might be defined as "detecting and repairing a fault in a machine before it actually breaks down." There is a popular belief that a PM program will reduce maintenance costs. This is not true, in most cases. A PM program will pay off chiefly in increased availability of machines, leading to more production and attendant benefits: improved scheduling of workers, better utilization of workforce, and possible elimination of major equipment repairs.

Equipment. A PM program can be started on any scale, applying it to even one piece that may be troublesome but is vitally important to an operation. Even with an elaborate program, not all equipment is covered. If a company goes into a program on a piecemeal basis, equipment will be added to the PM list as such pieces are identified as production deterrents.

Schedule. The PM program normally consists of four parts: lubrication, inspection, adjustment, and repairs. A schedule is set up for frequency, based on lubrication requirements and known or estimated frequency of repair. The PM inspector handles the first three items, noting repairs needed, and the repairs are scheduled in the normal manner according to urgency, machine availability, and manpower. Records can be simple or elaborate. A master PM schedule is necessary for the schedulers so that they can set up the PM work on the appropriate day. One way of handling work orders is a yearly PM order for each cost center. EDP can be used to good advantage in developing schedules.

Cost allocation. The allocation of costs is not difficult for an organization that has a work order system plus planning and scheduling. The costs for PM would go to the proper cost center, and the actual repairs would also be charged properly by the regular work order.

Evaluation. Evaluating the results of a PM program is often difficult. The availability of a machine or process and the frequency of breakdowns or emergency shutdowns can be compared with previous conditions; improvements in each of these categories might be expected. Total maintenance costs also should be evaluated, although little or no improvement may be noted. In any event, total maintenance costs are an unreliable yardstick for maintenance effectiveness. Maintenance on a unit basis—cost per unit of production—should show improvement after the program has been implemented.

DEVELOPING PERFORMANCE DATA

Meaningful performance data should be developed so that improvements can be evaluated qualitatively and, hopefully, quantitatively. The simplest comparison (total maintenance this year or month against the same period last year) is of little real value; many other variables may be working to cloud the issue. A more accurate measure is the comparison of actual against standard time by job or of maintenance costs per unit of production for various periods. A significant decrease in this unit cost, for example, is honest added profit and a measure of effectiveness.

Worker efficiency. If work sampling is used, the performance index will show improvement, particularly as a result of planning and scheduling. The difference in the index before and after the installation of modern methods is often startling. The labor-to-material ratio is another tool; a decrease in this ratio generally indicates improved manpower utilization. A decrease in emergency orders is a measure of PM effectiveness. A decrease in the backlog of work orders indicates improved maintenance efficiency. Although no single measure of work efficiency exists, these several tests should add up to a valid picture of trend.

Adherence to budget. Budget compliance is an unreliable tool to use in measuring a department or a manager, particularly on a month-to-month basis. A budget overrun is not necessarily bad, nor is an underrun always good. The evaluation of a monthly cost sheet to determine true position requires considerable study; mere comparison of budget against actual cost is of little value. The actual cost must be corrected for jobs canceled, jobs postponed, jobs done early, and unbudgeted jobs in order to arrive at a true position for an individual month. In such a comparison, it is a great advantage to have as large a portion of the budget as possible in identified jobs.

Timely job completion. Timely job completion is principally a function of the planning and scheduling effort. Very often, production runs are scheduled on the basis of the completion of a maintenance job, and considerable dollar losses can accrue if a job runs over. Maintenance promises on job completion and the production statement of the date required must be realistic, since chaos results if each group applies its own liberal safety factor.

Training. Increasing complexity of machinery, rapid technological change, increased size and speed of machines, and new construction materials all dictate that the knowledge and skills of the maintenance section be continuously updated. This means the training of all levels in new methods and techniques, plus additional education for supervisory levels through night classes, college extension courses, or other means. Many forces are at work to make training ever more important: technological change, early retirement, greater mobility of people, the expansion and addition of new facilities, and more.

For reference in training programs for salaried employees, the use of a replacement table is suggested. Such a table indicates replacements for all levels on the organization chart and contains columns for "years to get ready" and "training required." Adherence to the training recommendations will be of great help. An adjunct is a chart showing supervision, age, general estimate of health, any known data on early retirement, plans to move, and the like.

The old apprentice programs for hourly personnel appear to be losing favor; some of the newer techniques—programmed instruction, for example—might be used with young, intelligent new hires to develop them into good mechanics.

Staff requirements. The staff should also be periodically reviewed, asking such questions as: Is the type of organization adequate for the future? Has it been compromised to hide incompetents? Do authority and communication flow in short, straight lines? The answers to these and other questions will indicate the changes necessary to meet the future head on. Only the maintenance manager can make this study.

These several suggestions could result in a sound plan for the future. If the plan is sound, it must be implemented to be of value and cannot be compromised for expediency.—*G. A. Coleman*

QUALITY CONTROL

The function of quality control is to assure a satisfactory relationship of product performance to standards. Standards of performance are set by management and are based on management's interpretation of the demands of the marketplace. Increasing attention is being given to the relationship of quality level to cost of product. If the quality level is unreasonably high, the product will be priced out of the market; if too low, it may not find customer acceptance.

Role of Quality Control Director

The concept of quality control as an analytical laboratory reporting to the plant manager is a matter of history. The quality control director now reports to higher management rather than to the production manager. He is involved in other responsibilities than those of testing, rejecting, and approving. His responsibility extends to participation in planning new products, production facilities, and manufacturing methods. He must also inform management of the long- and short-term impact of decisions affecting product quality.

Reporting to Management

Management support of a "nonproductive" function such as quality control depends on the quality of the reporting of objectives to management. Lengthy reports in excessive number are less acceptable to a busy manager than shorter, well-organized reports. The best approach to reporting is the use of highlights. This is reporting by exception; detailed backup information for each item highlighted should be available if called for. High-level management is frequently more interested in how its products compare with competition than it is in standards or specifications per se. Tools useful for this evaluation include periodic examination of competing products and of frequency and type of customer complaints. Reporting quality actions to management will gain better acceptance by relating the impact of defect prevention on product cost. Visual presentations, including charts, graphs, and pictograms, are more easily understood by a busy manager than is a lengthy report.

Organization for Quality Control

The quality control function has operated successfully in many organizational positions.

ORGANIZATION CHART POSITION

Currently, most companies are not in favor of having quality control report to the production manager; reporting at this level is workable only if the production manager is sufficiently sold on the importance of quality and has unswerving confidence in the judgment and ability of his quality control director.

Many highly successful companies consider that quality control is basically a scientific discipline and have it report to the research director. This policy has the danger of insulating quality control from day-to-day plant problems and making multilevel cross-communication with plant supervision more difficult. Another reporting method which has been successful in multiplant operations will be discussed under that heading.

STAFF REQUIREMENTS

The multidisciplinary nature of quality control allows the utilization of people of diverse skills and backgrounds. Depending on the industry and the product line, quality control staff may include chemists, engineers, inspectors, statisticians, pharmacists, and physicists. In specialized industries, quality control staff members may have backgrounds in pharmacology, physiology, bacteriology, biochemistry, or other sciences. People hired for their technical qualifications are candidates for training in quality control philosophy and management techniques. On the other hand, a quality control man hired for his management ability may require additional training in one or more of the specialized fields. In addition to on-the-job training, many universities and management training organizations offer excellent courses in the philosophies, objectives, and techniques of quality control.

IMPROVING PERSONNEL PERFORMANCE

The most important key to improving the performance of quality control personnel is a searching, realistic, and regularly scheduled performance appraisal. In conducting performance appraisals the objective should be that of improvement rather than merely measurement.

MULTIPLANT OPERATIONS

In a large corporation operating at many locations or comprising many organizational units at one location, a choice must be made for a centralized quality control division or for decentralization of quality control in each operating unit. Many successful large companies have recently taken the latter approach, appointing a quality control manager for each operating unit and placing the responsibility for policy with a manager of corporate quality control. To assure the adherence of decentralized quality control units to corporate policy, periodic audits of each unit are made by the staff of corporate quality control.

Control of Vendor Quality

The best motivation for a realistic, closely controlled program to obtain satisfactory raw materials is to prevent the addition of "cost extras."

INCOMING MATERIAL

Poor incoming quality of a part, raw material, or container can generate increased costs to the purchaser in many ways. The first and most frequent result is an increase in inspection cost. If a sequential plan is used, an excessive number of defects will result in the inspection of a larger sample and may require 100 percent inspection. If the inspection is complex, and particularly if chemical, physical, or biological analysis is required, the cost of the inspection skyrockets. The inspection may bring about the destruction of the sample; in this case, 100 percent inspection becomes an impossibility. Poor vendor quality may force the buyer to carry a large inventory to compensate for increased inspection time, rework, or on-line rejections. Also—since no inspection is 100 percent effective— some defects will get through to the final product, causing scrap, rework, or (if not caught in time) customer dissatisfaction.

PURCHASING RELATIONSHIP

Major benefits from the control of vendor quality arise only from a close, day-to-day working relationship between purchasing and quality control. This is accomplished either formally or informally; in either case, it is important to remember that other functions in the purchaser's organization are involved. These include departments engaged in developing and setting specifications— package development, process engineering, and the operating departments.

It is purchasing's responsibility to see that each vendor has complete specifications for each item; negotiations with the vendor on specifications should be conducted by purchasing with the advice of quality control and other groups concerned.

VENDOR QUALITY PROGRAMS

A recent development from the close cooperation of purchasing and quality control is the evaluation of a vendor based on his quality performance. This is part of an overall program that includes the vendor's price and delivery performance. Vendor evaluation, the first step of this program, is a joint effort by purchasing, quality control, and the materials manager. When the evaluation has been completed, vendors are rated on quality and ability to meet delivery dates. This rating is subject to revision to reflect significant changes in vendor performance.

Vendor certification is a formalized extension of vendor rating. Often, material from a vendor whose performance can be certified is accepted with abbreviated sampling and testing. Another useful application of cooperation between purchasing and quality control is known as tailgate sampling. This procedure is especially useful for bulky items purchased in large quantities—for example, glass containers. The vendor is given the purchaser's sampling plan and samples during the production run. The sample is kept separate "on the tailgate of the truck" from the rest of the run. The purchaser uses this sample for the required testing, saving the labor of sampling the entire shipment.

Controlling In-Process Quality

The complex nature of the products of industry today makes it increasingly difficult to assure that the product will be satisfactory if the only testing is on the final product.

ORGANIZING CONTROLS

Meeting the specifications for the end product is the result of a well-controlled program. This is the target which must be hit, and in-process control is the best means of increasing the probability of hitting it. Complexity of product design generates increased necessity for precision in testing. If quality judgment is based entirely on the final product, complete disassembly or destructive testing may be required.

In complex assemblies, one department may be the supplier to another who acts as the customer; in this instance, in-process controls must be used to determine the suitability of a part or an assembly for the next production step. In-process controls must, therefore, be developed for the whole process so as to test critical properties at critical points. Poor planning of in-process quality control may result in meaningless measurements taken at inappropriate points in production. A smoothly functioning quality engineering function must specify not only the measurements to be taken and the limits on them but also the specifications for each measurement device. The accuracy and sensitivity of the device must be keyed to the dimensions to be measured and the limits placed thereon.

LINE RELATIONSHIPS

As part of the planning and in-process quality control, once the parameters and specifications have been set, the decision must be made whether enforcement is the responsibility of quality control or of production. Depending on the situation, either system can work satisfactorily, but responsibilities and authorities must be clearly defined at the outset. Since controlling in-process quality is a production tool, it is most often the responsibility of the production unit. This is usually the case in mechanical and continuous-process industries, since there is no batch or other cutoff point where production can be halted and samples taken for examination by quality control.

PROCESS CONTROL CHARTS

Graphic representation of quality characteristics is a time-honored method of presenting information on in-process quality. Recent progress, which has increased the sophistication and information content of process control charts, has been greatly stimulated by sophisticated automatic equipment for acquiring, logging, analyzing, and plotting quality characteristics. Computer programs are available to handle in-process control data, whether in terms of variable measurements or attributes. If attributes are used, established methods for classifying defects are available, as are statistical methods for determining the significance of deviations from the norm. These techniques have been developed because of the recognition that visual presentation of quality information is much more easily assimilated than numerical presentation.

INSPECTION REPORTS

The dissemination of information obtained by in-process quality control is the key to its success. The type and extent of reporting used must be keyed to the recipient of the report. While detailed reports in tabular or graphic form may be required by those closely involved with production, the interest of management—including quality engineering and process development—is more likely to be in a brief summary of the current status. One very useful type of reporting is the exception report, which covers only the phases of the operation that are out of control. If in-process control is the responsibility of the production unit, exception reports to quality control, quality engineering, and process development serve as an indication that troubleshooting is required.

DISPOSING OF LINE DEFECTS

The most usual fate of defective production is scrap, rework, or limited use. The choice among these three is made on the basis of economics. For example, if the cost of rework is higher than that of producing additional units, the logical decision is to destroy. The decision for limited use (also known as "restricted approval" or "approval with warning") may be an alternative if the defect can be corrected later in the production process.

FINAL TESTING

From a theoretical standpoint, if in-process control is 100 percent effective, there will be no need for inspection or testing of the final product. If the final product is a "single use" item, such as a rifle bullet or an intercontinental ballistic missile, final inspection and testing often cannot be done without destroying the product; complete reliance must be placed on in-process testing. Fortunately, the nature of many consumer products allows the testing of an adequate representative sample of the final product. If this is possible, the final inspection and testing confirm that the control of in-process quality has been effective.

Customer Feedback Information

Since the success of any product depends upon customer satisfaction, prompt attention must be paid to feedback of customer reaction to the product. There are many forms of customer reaction; it is important that they be recognized, properly routed, promptly evaluated, and answered. The most common form of feedback is a customer complaint, which may come directly to the company or may be forwarded by salesmen or field representatives.

FEEDBACK FROM THE FIELD

Salesmen are, without doubt, the best source of customer reaction and of the product's relationship to competition. Analysis of customer complaints and reply to them are an important function of quality control. This is often supplemented by purchase and critical evaluation of the products of competition. Competitive evaluation is most effective when regularly performed but may require additional attention when a problem arises.

The sales force must be given detailed instructions on handling customer complaints; the importance of prompt communication through established channels must be emphasized. The staff in quality control charged with the responsibility of handling complaints must be instructed in the importance of a rapid reply to the customer. A copy of the reply should always be sent to the representative handling the account. If replacement, refund, or credit is necessary, the proper people should be informed so that the adjustment can be made quickly and customer dissatisfaction dissipated.

PRODUCT IDENTITY SYSTEM

The system used to identify the product must be adequate to insure thorough investigation of customer feedback. Such information as the model number, the serial or lot number, and the production date (the latter often keyed to the serial or lot number) are extremely important. If the complaint originates with a salesman, he must realize the importance of submitting as much specific information as he can obtain.

FAILURE ANALYSIS

Failure of a product at the consumer level may be of several types. The product may be defective when received by the customer, or there may have been a weakness in design or construction that caused it to become defective in routine use. Another possibility is misuse by the customer.

If the product was defective when it reached the customer, it must be determined whether there was design failure or faulty manufacture. If design failure is to blame, correction should be instituted, since additional failures are likely. If manufacture was faulty, a weakness in the inspection system or the application of an unrealistic specification is a possible cause. If the complaint resulted from customer misuse, attention should be given to the directions for use of the product; these must be written so as to minimize misuse. Another important aspect of the analysis of customer feedback is the evaluation of possible liability on the part of the manufacturer; if this is a possibility, the company's legal department should be made aware of the situation promptly.

DATA REPORTING SYSTEM

In reporting information to management on customer feedback, the incidence of customer dissatisfaction should be related to the number of units produced; this is necessary to determine the severity of the problem. If a significant upward trend exists, the need for corrective action should be examined. The classification of customer complaints often reveals geographical and seasonal differences, particularly if the product is adversely affected by extremes of temperature or humidity. Geographical differences in complaint incidence, particularly if the product is sold throughout the world, may reflect different uses (or misuses) of the product in different areas or different countries. Reports to top management should be limited to exceptional situations where management action or decision is required. Visual presentation should be used wherever possible.

CORRECTIVE ACTION

Many types of corrective action may be taken in the light of customer dissatisfaction. These range all the way from a simple increase of the inspection effort to complete redesign of the product or the production facility. Wherever possible, quality control should include a recommendation for action in its report.

New Design Quality Assurance

The requirement of designing and building quality into a product has long been recognized. One of the oldest axioms in the field says: "You cannot test quality into a product; you must build it in." Progress toward meeting this requirement was slow until the concept of total quality control and the part played in it by quality engineering was developed by A. V. Feigenbaum.

BUILT-IN QUALITY

Quality engineering works with quality control, design engineering, and manufacturing engineering to plan product development. Its objective is to design a product that will be as free as possible of defects prior to the start of production.

In the absence of a quality engineering function, the key to satisfactory quality control of new products is constant communication among all groups involved in new product development. These may include research, process development, research engineering, production engineering, analytical research, production, marketing—and, of course, quality control.

INTERDEPARTMENTAL COORDINATION

Quality engineering can act as a catalyst in obtaining required communication and interaction among all the groups involved in new product development. It is most important to prevent the omission of important points and to resolve hang-ups quickly, and it is easier to take such action as product development proceeds than to go back and attempt to fill in gaps later. CPM is a very useful tool for planning and scheduling product development. This method, correctly applied, serves as checklist, road map, schedule, and reporting system. It should be developed to show not only what needs to be done, and when, but to indicate clearly to whom each responsibility is assigned. Programs are available for the use of computers as a follow-up and report system for CPM. The computer is programmed to print out regular progress reports, which raise a flag if a point in the path is missed or behind schedule. These periodic reports can often point out potential trouble before it becomes actual trouble.

NEW PRODUCT TESTING

The determination of the take-over point where responsibility for quality shifts from research and development to quality control can be programmed as part of CPM. Usually, research and development or quality engineering develops specifications and tests for each new product. If this is done carefully and thoughtfully, the take-over by quality control can be made smoothly at the start of production. Quality control must be included in all planning and discussions to assure that the specifications are suitable, that methodology is compatible with existing or obtainable skills, and that suitable instrumentation is either available or obtainable. Some companies appoint a standing specifications committee composed of representatives from all groups involved in getting the product into production.

NEW TESTING EQUIPMENT

It is evident that as the complexity of products increases, a parallel increase in the complexity of testing equipment is to be anticipated. In the electronics industry, for example, the ability to develop a complex product may be entirely negated if equipment sufficiently sensitive to test its reliability is not available or cannot be developed. The production of space hardware provides another example of this phenomenon. Requirements for environmental control in the spacecraft industry have brought an entirely new approach. A professional group, the American Association for Contamination Control, has been set up to accumulate and disseminate the methodology required to achieve and evaluate facilities which are not only free of particulate matter but also biologically clean. This points up the fact that a company or an industry must meet increasing demands for sophisticated test equipment and production facilities in order to survive.

IMPROVING PRODUCT RELIABILITY

Early in the space program of the United States, an astronaut responded to a press inquiry about the state of his nerves before a space flight by asking the reporter how he would feel if he were about to orbit the earth in a machine consisting of several hundred thousand parts, each of which was made by the lowest bidder. The success of the space program is a monument to the ability to improve reliability to whatever degree the circumstances require. Improving reliability depends on improvements in precision of measurement. Improved precision may, of course, be used to detect defects in the final product. However, its best application is the upgrading of in-process testing to prevent defects rather than detect them. Newly developed measurement devices with automatic read-out, analysis, and feedback can check a critical operation minute by minute without waiting for many units to be produced, sampled, and tested. Almost instantaneous detection of an item which is "out-of-spec" often allows rapid correction so that the number of defective items produced is minimized.

Analyzing Quality Assurance Costs

Quality control costs must be considered as a part of the overall cost of production. As such, they are an important consideration in planning the most economical way to produce a marketable product.

ENGINEERING FUNCTION

Quality control techniques, particularly those of statistical quality control, can be of great assistance in product planning. The objective of this planning is to develop a product that will function according to the user's requirements and that can also be produced without excessive scrap, rework, or downtime. Many statistical quality control techniques (such as fractional or complete factorial designs) can be adapted to study the effect of changes in specifications or operating conditions on the quality of the product.

INSPECTION LABOR AND EQUIPMENT

The design of the product as it relates to its producibility exerts a major influence on the amount of quality control effort that must be expended to achieve a satisfactory quality level. A specification set tighter than necessary may strain production facilities and require increased sampling and inspection. Surprisingly, it is often forgotten that tight specifications should be reserved for critical characteristics.

SCRAP AND REWORK

When scrap and rework become excessive, the real cause must be found. The areas that should be searched include faulty design, unrealistic specifications, poor production methods, inadequate production equipment, and inadequate instruction of production personnel. Quality control must examine its own operation to be sure that it is not contributing by using an incorrect test method, inadequate sampling, or poor test equipment. All instrumentation, from the simplest gauge to the most complex electronic testing device, should be regularly checked (preferably against a standard material) to be sure that it is giving correct information. The maintenance of complete records on performance of test equipment is as important to quality control as the records of production capability are to the production department.

DEFECTIVE MATERIALS

Defective materials may not all originate with a vendor but may come from within the production complex. One department often produces a material or a part to be used by another unit within the same company. The problem of defective materials within a company involves the same considerations that apply to materials received from vendors. The classic solution of this problem, particularly if production is discontinuous, is to call on quality control to sample and test each part or material before the next production step. This is not the best solution; the necessity for it can be minimized or avoided by instituting meaningful in-process controls during production. In either case, strict attention to and complete understanding of specifications and test methods by both the producing and using departments are required.

FIELD SERVICE

The familiar slogan, "We service what we sell," can result in a significant cost to a company that produces a defective product. Service, repair, or replacement during a warranty period can be costly. Whether this service is provided by the company or the dealer, its cost is an important factor in the overall profit picture. Consumer service organizations publish ratings of automobiles and television sets based on their record for frequency and cost of repair. As this type of information becomes increasingly available to consumers, sales may be lost as a result of poor quality. One industry has recently been criticized in the public press and before Congress for depending too fully on its customers for quality evaluation. There is no doubt that governmental and consumer pressures to eliminate defects will increase, particularly where public health and safety are involved.

CUSTOMER COMPLAINTS

The receipt, evaluation, and analysis of customer complaints, together with the replies to them, make up a real part of the cost of quality control. On first examination it might seem that this cost is not controllable by quality control. However, if quality control can communicate effectively with management and raise the quality level, the number of complaints and the cost of processing them will diminish.

REBATES

The assignment of the cost of rebates, refunds, adjustments, and replacements resulting from the distribution of defective units is sometimes considered a quality control cost. This practice is not uniform within industries or companies. Many attempts have been made to assign the cost of field adjustments to a "guilty party," but the controversial nature of such an assignment makes this extremely difficult.

Appraising Quality Control Performance

Probably the greatest contribution that quality control can make to increasing the sales and profits of a company is to establish and sustain a favorable quality image.

MAINTAINING QUALITY IMAGE

Because the image of quality is, by definition, intangible, its impact on the success of the company is hard to evaluate in terms of dollars. The quality image can be promoted and communicated to the public by the company's public relations department or as part of its institutional advertising program. It is a serious mistake to promote a quality image unless it can be backed by quality performance.

BUDGET COMPLIANCE

Modern accounting procedures and long-range forward planning require a realistic forecast of operating expenses and capital requirements for each operating unit. Yearly budgets are required as long as six months in advance of the start of the year, and management often needs a realistic forecast as far as five years ahead. Each significant variance must be explained. Examination of the reason for variance can aid in generating realistic forecasts of future operations. One usual cause of variance is overtime. This may result from increased workload, insufficient staffing, or the necessity to meet production schedules. Overtime may indicate decreased efficiency in quality control; this can be determined only if a realistic method of measuring output per man-hour can be established. The methods used by industrial engineering to set work standards and evaluate performance can be applied to quality control.

Improving Quality Performance

The quality achievement of a company depends on the attention given at all levels of management to short- and long-range planning for quality. If quality is recognized as a prime company objective, with constant involvement by all of management and with the responsibilities for quality input clearly defined, the quality goal can be reached.

PERSONNEL MOTIVATION

Effective upgrading of the abilities and dedication of people is another important facet of the search for quality improvement. The dedication to quality improvement must be from the top down. If the boss can demonstrate his involvement in improving quality, he can involve others. If he gives only lip service, he cannot expect others to do more. "Zero defects" programs have been highly successful only where there was demonstrable involvement by top management. Dismal failure occurs when this involvement is absent.

MANAGEMENT RESPONSIBILITY

The achievement of quality is a management responsibility, and all systems of product planning, facilities design, and data feedback must be keyed to achieve optimum quality at minimum cost.—*R. S. Cowles*

OPERATIONS RESEARCH

In present-day usage there is very little distinction between the terms "operations research" and "management science." Either can be defined as "the application of the methods of science to decision making in the management of complex systems of men, money, machines, and materials."

Operations research is a philosophy, a way of looking at decision problems—not merely a bag of mathematical tools, as it is often represented. Unlike finance, production, and marketing, it is distinguished not by the kind of problems it studies but rather by the way in which it approaches problems, not only in these fields but in many others as well. Basically, it is concerned with optimization: that is, the selection of that alternative policy or procedure that will lead to the maximization of profits, the minimization of costs, or the optimization of some other appropriately stated objective. It is future-oriented and is primarily concerned with planning, policy formulation, and decision making.

Russell Ackoff, in his book on the fundamentals of operations research (*A Manager's Guide to Operations Research,* John Wiley & Sons, 1963), names three characteristics that describe the OR approach to a decision-making situation. These are the systems point of view, the use of interdisciplinary teams, and the employment of mathematical modeling techniques. Basic material on the nature and philosophy of operations research/management science is covered in the Administrative Services section of this handbook (page 2·65). In the present discussion, several examples will be presented to illustrate their application to manufacturing and inventory control problems.

Techniques of Operations Research

A huge literature exists on the many and varied types of models that have been developed; the scope of this presentation does not permit an exhaustive picture. The examples offered here can be illustrative only, but it is hoped that they will give some notion of the flavor and power of OR analysis. Of necessity, for expository purposes the problems have been kept relatively simple, but the reader should be able to see how these basic concepts could be extended to more realistic and complex decision situations.

LINEAR PROGRAMMING

Mathematical programming models are concerned with the efficient allocation of scarce resources among competing activities. If the total available amount of the various resources is constrained and there are various ways to allocate these resources to the activities that may be undertaken, and if it is desired to optimize some function of the activities (such as minimize costs of production or maximize profits resulting from manufacturing), an analysis of the decision problem by mathematical programming may be considered. In the case where all the relationships can be stated as linear (straight-line) functions, the linear programming model may be employed. This model has been successfully applied to such diverse problems as aircraft maintenance scheduling routine; hospital menu planning; advertising media selection; gasoline blending; capital budgeting; multiplant, multiwarehouse production and transportation scheduling; inventory control; manpower allocation; and many others. CPM analyses are also based on linear programming methods.

Problem data. To illustrate the approach, consider a manufacturer whose product line consists of only two products, called product X and product Y. Each unit of product requires certain amounts of machine capacity and labor input, and at least in the short term, the availability of these resources is constrained. Also, each unit of each product returns a certain profit to the manufacturer. Representative data might be expressed in tabular form as follows:

Product Resource	X	Y	Available
Machines	1	2	100 hours
Men	3	1	100 hours
Profit	4	3	

This means that each unit of product X requires one hour of machine time and three hours of labor, and returns a profit of $4. For product Y, two hours of machine time and one hour of labor input are required to produce a profit of $3 per unit. One hundred machine-hours and 100 man-hours are available to be scheduled. The numbers in the tabulation, called input-output coefficients or technological coefficients, would typically be developed by work measurement techniques, and the profit figures would be determined by standard cost accounting procedures.

Further, assume that the sales department has already accepted orders for ten units of product Y and has determined that the maximum number of each product that can be sold is 60 X's and 45 Y's. The manufacturer must determine how many of each product he should make in order to maximize his profits subject to his capacity constraints and the sales considerations.

The model. The first step in constructing the linear programming model would be to write a linear equation that expresses the profit to be maximized. This is called the objective function.

$$P = 4X + 3Y$$

Then, other linear equations of detailed balance, called constraint equations, must be developed to express mathematically the conditions of limited resource availability and marketing restraints. For example, whatever the decision as to the values for X and Y, the total amount of machine time used will be $1X + 2Y$, and this total must be less than or equal to 100, the maximum amount of machine time available. Mathematically, then,

$$1X + 2Y \leqq 100, \text{ or } 1X + 2Y + S_1 = 100$$

where S_1 is a so-called slack variable representing the amount of machine idle time, if any, that will result from a particular choice of X and Y.

Similarly,

$$3X + 1Y \leqq 100, \text{ or } 3X + 1Y + S_2 = 100$$

where S_2 will represent the unscheduled labor hours. The marketing constraints can be expressed as $Y \geqq 10$ to represent the fact that at least 10 units of Y must be made, since orders have already been accepted, and $X \leqq 60$ and $Y \leqq 45$ to represent the maximum market availabilities.

The manufacturer's problem is now to choose a value for X between 0 and 60 and a value for Y between 10 and 45 so that the objective function is maximized and the constraint equations for machines and men are satisfied. Since there are only two products, the optimal answer may be found by graphical methods. A more realistic problem might involve several hundred or even thousand potential products, with the solution limited by 100 or more constraint equations. Such a problem would have to be solved by algebraic methods (the so-called Simplex Computational Method), the description of which is beyond the scope of this introductory exposition but can be found in many texts on linear programming. (See, for example, George B. Dantzig, *Linear Programming and Extensions,* Princeton University Press, 1963.) In any case, canned computer programs are available to solve such problems and are also available through many computer service bureaus.

Graphical solution. Mathematically, the solution of a linear programming problem can be described as finding that solution, out of a great many possible ones, to a system of linear equations that optimizes some linear function of the unknowns. For this problem, the solution may be found graphically by plotting all the linear constraints and the linear objective function as straight lines on an X, Y coordinate space. (See Exhibit 6.18.)

Solution space. Theoretically, any positive values for X and Y could possibly be considered for the optimal solution, but the various production and sales constraints limit the search for the optimal solution to the crosshatched area in the diagram. For example, the constraint on labor availability restricts the solution point to below the line labeled $3X + Y = 100$; the constraint that no more than 45 Y's can be sold restricts the solution to the left of the line labeled $Y = 45$; and so on. Since all constraints must be simultaneously satisfied, the solution is constrained to the crosshatched area, called the feasible solution space.

Locating optimal solution. From geometrical considerations, if a profit of $100 was desired, any solution (pair of values X, Y) lying on the dotted line labeled $4X + 3Y = 100$ would suffice. This line is called the isoprofit line; that is, at any point on it the profit is equal (in this case, $100). An isoprofit line for any other profit value would be parallel to the one shown. Since it is desired to maximize the profit, the isoprofit line is moved as far from the origin as possible, the limit being reached when the line no longer passes through any part of the feasible solution space. Here the profit-maximizing solution is thus obtained at the point circled, giving an X value of 20, a Y value of 40, and a profit of $200.

The mathematics of the solution methodology guarantees that this solution is

Exhibit 6.18

GRAPHICAL SOLUTION OF A LINEAR PROGRAMMING PROBLEM

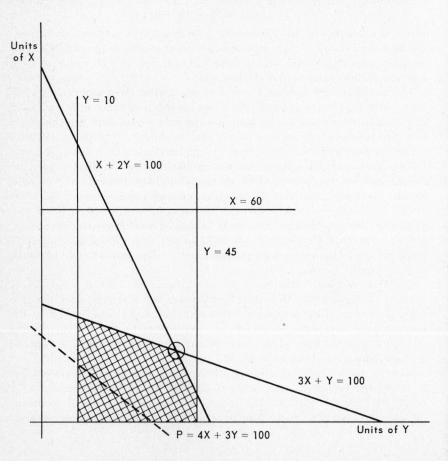

the true optimum, and no other production schedule can be found within the stated constraints that will produce a larger profit.

Sensitivity analysis. Often, not only the optimal solution is desired; a researcher also wants to know the effect of changes in the input data on the developed solution without having to solve the problem all over again—a major issue for large-scale problems. These changes might represent real changes that could or must be made; or they could be simulated changes to reflect uncertainty in the basic data. Algebraic techniques are available, making use of the so-called shadow prices of the resources, to conduct these investigations. Typically, five types of changes are of interest: (1) changes in the resource availabilities; (2) changes in the profit, or cost, coefficients; (3) changes in the input-output coefficients; (4) the addition of new variables (products); and (5) the addition of new constraints.

QUEUEING THEORY

Many operational problems in manufacturing and elsewhere can be formulated and solved with a certain type of stochastic model called a queueing, or waiting-line, model. Such problems are characterized by an input population of discrete units, called customers, who require service at some facility, the design of which is typically under management's control. Because of the random nature of customer arrivals to the facility, and because the time to perform the service is not perfectly predictable, a queue or waiting line forms. The behavior of this queue as a function of the service system design is of considerable interest. Management can often use these mathematical models to optimize the design of the service system in the sense of cost minimization, profit maximization, or optimization of various probabilistic measures.

Basic structure. A service system consists of one or more facilities which can provide service, the duration of which can be described by a probability distribution. Customers arrive at the service system from the input source according to another probability distribution and may or may not enter the system to join a queue (which could be of length zero) awaiting service. The service facilities select customers from the queue by some priority system and provide the service, after which the customer leaves the system. (See Exhibit 6.19.)

Some examples of problems that can be formulated and solved with queueing models are shown in the following list, with their types of customers and service facilities.

Problem	Customers	Service Facilities
Machine breakdown maintenance	Machines	Repair crew
Supermarket checkout	Housewives	Checkout counters
Hospital clinics	Patients	Doctors
Airport design	Airplanes	Runways
Accounts payable	Bills	Accounting department
Tool crib operation	Mechanics	Clerks
Assembly line design	Units of production	Work stations
Insurance adjusting	Motorists	Claims adjusters
Port development	Ships	Docks
Organization design	Subordinates	Superiors
Bank operations	Customers	Tellers

Operational characteristics. Management would typically be interested in controlling some or all of the characteristics that are functions of the design of the service system, the rate at which it can be made to operate, and its scheduling. They are also functions of the arrival rate, but this can usually be influenced by management only in the long run (say, by advertising or market development activities). These operational characteristics are as follows: length of queue; number of customers in the system; waiting time for a customer; total time of a customer in the system; idle time of service channel; percent of balkers (potential customers turned away); number of customers discharged per unit time; probability a customer will have to wait longer than some given time period.

Decision making. Theoretically, the decision maker would like to so design and schedule the system that total costs would be minimized or profits maximized. This, however, requires the determination of the "costs of waiting," which are extremely difficult to evaluate in many operational problems. In such cases the decision maker usually wishes to design and schedule to keep some or all of the previously listed characteristics within acceptable limits.

A simple example where such costs can be determined is that of optimizing the rate at which a repair department can service machine breakdowns. (See Exhibit 6.20.) The faster the service rate, the more expensive the maintenance department costs because of more men and equipment; but downtime costs in the production department are lower because of shorter queue lengths and waiting time for service. If the service rate is slower, maintenance costs are lower but downtime costs are higher. At what service rate would the sum of these costs be minimum? Without going into the mathematical details, it could be found that $R^\star$ is the optimal rate that minimizes the total system costs.

Input data. Typically, the following input data are required: the probability distribution of arrivals to the system; customer attitudes toward queue length and waiting time; the probability distribution of service times as a function of the facility design and configuration; the service discipline—priority system (for example, first-in, first-out, random access); and relevant costs.

Exhibit 6.19

A SERVICE SYSTEM ILLUSTRATING
APPLICATION OF QUEUEING THEORY

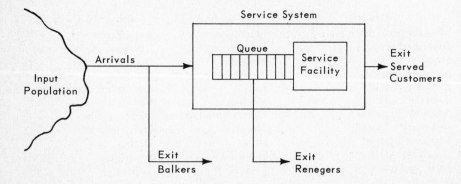

EXPERIMENTAL METHODS: MONTE CARLO SIMULATION

In many problems, analytical solutions to the mathematical models developed are extremely difficult or even impossible, and the researcher turns to simulation techniques for problem solving and policy formulation. Such procedures have been called the experimental part of operations research, where experiments are conducted with a mathematical model of the real world rather than run the risk and expense of experimenting in the real world itself. The following example, drawn from inventory theory where commodities are perishable, is simple enough to be readily solved analytically but will serve to illustrate the Monte Carlo approach.

The newsboy problem. Consider the problem of a newsboy who, wishing to maximize his long-term profit, purchases the daily newspaper for 3 cents a copy and sells it for 10 cents if there is a customer demand for it. If the newspaper is not demanded, it has no value and must be thrown away (salvage value = 0). On any given day he does not know how many papers he will be able to sell, but he does know, on the basis of forecasting from past records and market research, a probability distribution for the number of papers that will be requested. Since he must purchase the papers in the morning before he knows what he can sell, he wishes to develop an ordering policy that will lead to a maximization of profits. Several possibilities come to mind. (1) Order the same number (yet to be

Exhibit 6.20

OPTIMIZING RATE OF SERVICING MACHINE BREAKDOWNS

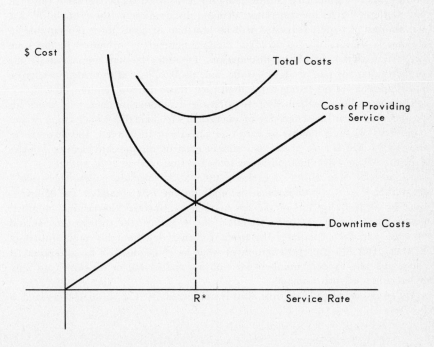

determined) every day. (2) Order whatever was demanded the previous day. (3) Order the average of the past week's daily demand. (4) Order whatever was demanded the same day the previous week. Many other possible policies could be considered. Rather than try each of these in the real world and run the risk and expense of experimenting with nonoptimal policies, he decides to analyze his problem with Monte Carlo simulation.

Letting x be his decision variable (how many papers to buy), he first develops a mathematical expression for his daily profit.

$$\text{Profit} = \begin{cases} (10 - 3)x, & \text{if } d \text{ is greater than or equal to } x \\ (10 - 3)d - 3(x - d), & \text{if } x \text{ is greater than } d \end{cases}$$

where d is his (unknown, except in a probabilistic sense) demand for that day.

He then develops, by means of forecasting techniques, the probability distribution for his daily demand shown in columns 1 and 2 in the following tabulation:

Column 1 d = demand	Column 2 Probability that demand = d	Column 3 Probability that demand $\leq$ d	Column 4 Random number assignment
3	.10	.10	00–09
4	.15	.25	10–24
5	.20	.45	25–44
6	.30	.75	45–74
7	.18	.93	75–92
8	.07	1.00	93–99

For the sake of simplicity, the distribution is assumed to be the same for each day. Column 3 gives the cumulative demand distribution, or the probability that the number of papers requested will be less than or equal to d, the number in column 1. He then assigns two-digit random numbers in column 4 in the same proportion as the cumulative distribution. Two-digit random numbers have the property that any pair of digits has the same probability—in this case, one chance in a hundred—of occurring if the digits are drawn from a random process.

He now needs a random process to choose a random number, and hence his demand, for each simulated day of operation. He takes 100 poker chips, writes a different two-digit number on each one, puts them all in a hat, and mixes them thoroughly. He is now ready to simulate each of his possible reorder policies with the Monte Carlo method for as long a period of time as he wishes.

Suppose he first wishes to evaluate the policy "buy six papers every day." Therefore, $x = 6$. To determine his profit for the first simulated day of operation, he pulls a chip out of the hat at random, observes the random number, determines the demand from columns 1 and 4, returns the chip to the hat and remixes, and then computes the profit for that day from his profit function. Actually, this is a conceptualization of what he could do with his computer (it could generate random numbers for him automatically); or he could use published tables of such numbers.

For example, suppose the first chip is numbered 79. The simulated demand is thus equal to 7, and since $d \geq x$, the profit for the first day is $(10 - 3)x = 7(6) = 42$ cents. If the second draw produces a chip numbered 32, demand is equal to 5, and since $d < x$, the second day's profit is $(10 - 3)(5) - 3(1) = 32$ cents. He proceeds for a large number of days, keeping track of his total profit. In this way he may evaluate each proposed purchasing policy and choose the best to implement. The Monte Carlo process has precisely modeled his business environment and enabled the optimal policy to be selected.

Limitations and Evaluations

These issues are discussed more fully under "Management Science" (page 2·65). Suffice it to note here that although the models and examples presented here are simplified, they should serve to give some idea of the power and generality of the operations research approach. Many other models and techniques could have been chosen for illustrative purposes. A great many large-scale, complex planning and operating problems have been successfully solved by the techniques and philosophy of operations research. The applicability of mathematics to management no longer requires proof, but it is well to keep in mind a warning from Henry Scheffé in his book, *Analysis of Variance* (John Wiley & Sons, Inc., 1959).

This [subject matter] is *not* a cookbook of formulas and rules—to be blindly applied and the answers ground out. It is a subject matter requiring the highest order of invention, ingenuity, and imagination to successfully tackle operational problems.

Scheffé was writing about certain statistical techniques, but the point is equally well taken for the entire field of operations research.—*G. M. Parks*

PERT AND CPM

Operations research techniques for the planning and control of operating systems can be conveniently divided into three general types—those for continuous operations, those for job-shop type problems, and those for the one-at-a-time, or project, situation. The project management concept is presented in detail in the Administrative Services section of this handbook (page 2·59), and application areas are discussed. A great many management techniques have been developed to assist in the scheduling, planning, and control of such projects. These are all based on more or less the same principle: that of a network model of the interrelated project activities that enables explicit time and/or cost trade-offs to be made to obtain adherence to schedules. Two of the more popular techniques are PERT (Program Evaluation and Review Technique) and CPM (Critical Path Method). Although a great many variations are possible, the basic ideas are representative of the various approaches.

Applicability

Although these techniques were originally developed for the planning and control of large, complex industrial and defense projects, they have proved equally valuable for helping management set and keep project schedules on smaller-scale programs. They have been successfully applied to such diverse endeavors as new product introduction, house building, book publishing, construction of a supermarket, theatrical production, computer installation, preparation of legal briefs, and many others. It is often assumed that large, expensive computer facilities are required to implement these techniques, but in point of fact reasonably large projects—consisting of up to, say, 200 separate activities—can be readily analyzed by manual computation. Many users claim that most of the advantages of employing such planning and anticipatory control methods come from the carefully detailed planning necessary to construct the network itself, which is really a schematic model of the entire project, even if no formal mathematical analysis is carried out. The model shows the many interrelationships between the project's individual activities in such a way that potential trouble spots can often be highlighted in advance by simple inspection of the network; potential deviations from plan can be significantly increased; and the possibility of extensive cost overruns can be reduced.

The Model

The underlying mathematical structure, which is of the linear programming type, does permit extensive computational manipulation to provide management with a great variety of planning and control information. Predictions can be made on estimated schedule completion dates; resource allocations can be made to project activities to minimize costs subject to schedule dates; manpower can be planned and scheduled; and critical activities can be identified for special management attention. As with most mathematical models constructed for management problems, the primary use is to provide guidelines for management decision making, but in certain applications they are true optimization models in that they can determine the best course of action subject only to stated operational constraints.

Network Fundamentals

The basic concept is that of a network of interrelated activities necessary to achieve prescribed events. Activities are represented by arrows, which are defined by predecessor and successor events. Events, represented usually by circles, signify the completion of all activities whose arrows lead into that event.

The most important notion is that of establishing the appropriate precedence relationships among the various activities. This is equivalent to determining which activities can be accomplished concurrently, which must be done sequentially, and what the interrelationships among them are. The basic topological ground rules are as follows: (1) Each activity must have a predecessor and successor event, but an event may have more than one preceding or succeeding activity. (2) No activity may start until its predecessor event is completed. (3) No event may be considered completed until all activities leading into it have been completed. These conditions portray the real restraints on project completion and were not explicitly stated in previous scheduling techniques.

A path through the network is a sequence of activities (arrows) from start to completion, indicating activities that must be performed in that sequence. A given network will contain many such paths, differing in the time required for completion. The critical path is the path through the project network that takes the longest time to complete. It is this sequence of activities that management is most anxious to determine, shorten, and monitor, since a delay in any of these activities will cause a corresponding delay in the entire project. In general, other activities, said to "have slack," can be delayed at least for a certain (calculable) period of time without affecting the scheduled completion date.

PERT Time Estimating

Since PERT is often applied to research and development activities where precise time estimating is impossible, the method provides for the determination and use of probability distributions for projected activity duration. These usually take the form of three time estimates for each activity, designated "optimistic," "most likely," and "pessimistic." If we let a, m, and b stand for these three estimates, and further assume the beta distribution for activity completion times, we can approximate the expected activity duration by

$$t_e = \frac{a + 4m + b}{6}$$

and its variance by

$$\left(\frac{b - a}{6} \right)^2$$

A representative data input work sheet is shown in Exhibit 6.21.

PERT Output

It is then possible to compute such quantities as the following:

1. The earliest time a particular event can be expected to occur, and the probability that this value will be realized.

2. The latest time a particular event, or milestone, can occur if the scheduled final completion date can still be met.

3. The probability that the entire project can be completed by a particular date. This is accomplished by summing the expected activity completion times and the variances along the critical path and using the normal distribution assumption to get the expected value and variance for the completion date. If any of the necessary probability theory assumptions are violated, Monte Carlo simulation methods may be employed.

4. Allowable schedule slippages for any activities (or events) not on the critical path.

5. Any of the previously mentioned quantities, and others, at any point in time as the project proceeds. Trouble spots can be detected in advance.

Many additional inferences useful for management decision making can also be made from these computations. For instance, if slack does exist, it may be possible to reallocate resources to reduce total project time. Also, management can determine where and—just as importantly—where not to buy attractive time reduction opportunities if the whole schedule must be expedited. Such proce-

Exhibit 6.21

A DATA INPUT WORK SHEET

PROJECT MANAGEMENT WORK SHEET

Project No.: _____

Project Name: _____

Date of Last Update: __/__/__ Page ____ of ____

Project Manager: _____

ACTIVITIES			TIME (T_e) IN TERMS OF								COMMENTS
No.	Name	Predecessor(s)	FORECASTS			Slack Time	Elapse Time	Start Time	Stop Time	Responsibility	
			a	m	b						

dures can contribute significantly to the avoidance of "management by crisis." It is also possible to simulate a change in any activity duration time and compute the effect on all scheduled event times. It further can tell a manager where not to make impossible delivery promises or expect impossible performance. If a computer is used, a wide variety of control reports can be easily generated to suit individual needs and preferences.

CPM Cost Considerations

CPM typically refers to those network planning and control techniques that are primarily concerned with time-cost trade-offs in meeting or expediting scheduled completion times. For each activity in the network, the following function is defined. (See Exhibit 6.22.)

The basic notion is that an activity can be completed in a *normal* time equal to t at a *normal* cost equal to c. This cost cannot be reduced, no matter how long the activity completion time is extended. At additional expense, the time to completion can be shortened as shown. The shortest possible time, called the *crash* time, is equal to t' and can only be accomplished at a *crash* cost of c'. In-

Exhibit 6.22
TIME-COST PLANNING AND CONTROL WITH CPM

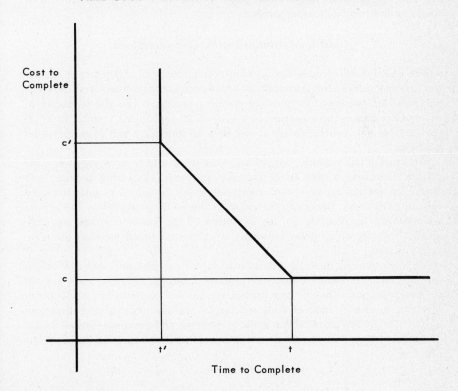

creased expenditures on this activity cannot further reduce the time for completion.

Management would, typically, be interested in computing the total cost and time to complete the project if all activities are scheduled for their normal completion times—that is, computing the critical path. It would then want to know how to shorten this completion date to any desired value at minimum cost. Initially, if it is desired to shorten the project completion time, the activity on the critical path that can be expedited at minimum cost will be shortened. Eventually, however, either that activity will be reduced to its crash time or some other path will become critical, and one or more other activities will have to be expedited to obtain further schedule reductions. This trade-off process becomes computationally quite complex, and a computer is often required for even relatively small projects. The process does, however, precisely pinpoint for management the activities that should be expedited with the application of additional resources when schedule reductions are necessary, rather than follow the common procedure of attempting to expedite everything when difficulties arise. The shortest possible time to complete the project will result when all activities on whatever path becomes the critical one are scheduled for their crash completion times, and that path is still the critical one. In general, there will be many other activities that need not be scheduled for crash times; hence, crash costs can be avoided. The optimum allocation of resources and the least cost program can be found for meeting any feasible target date.

Additional Administrative Considerations

The PERT/CPM process can be used on any new idea or product as soon as the idea has germinated. Although its advantages are maximized if all levels of personnel are concerned early in the planning process, it can also be employed at any time during the execution of a project. Its replanning features make its use valuable as a control device at any stage to anticipate and avoid potential problems.

Personnel at any concerned organizational level should be encouraged to make realistic estimates; if only "safe" estimates are made, the wrong activities will appear on the critical path, and management will be forced to take increased risks in other areas. Generally, the estimates should be generated by the personnel ultimately responsible for the execution of the work. This has the additional advantage of involving personnel at all organizational levels in the planning function.

Although some of these procedures may appear complex and time-consuming, they are no more complex than the problem itself. In addition, many canned computer programs and project control systems are commercially available to effect the implementation of these techniques. Standardized input routines and output formats are provided for initial structuring and planning, as well as updating capabilities for network restructuring and progress reporting for in-process projects.

Problems in Applying PERT and CPM

Some problems that have been encountered in the application of these techniques are the following: (1) Psychological problems have resulted from resistance to being forced to conduct such explicit initial planning and replanning, as well as resistance to the application of such a dynamic control system; (2) cost analyses have shown these procedures to cost as much as twice the cost of more conventional planning methods; (3) top management backing and understanding are vital—the system is neither automatic nor rigid; (4) the work breakdown is usually not equivalent to the existing organization structure so that interface and coordination problems develop; and (5) established precedence relationships may not be real but merely established for convenience or reduced cost.

Benefits from PERT and CPM

The benefits of successful application are impressive.

1. All activities necessary to meet end objectives are identified and planned in advance, and there is better visualization of the individual tasks to be accomplished at all organization levels. All personnel can see where their contribution fits into the whole.

2. Planning and performance are closely associated.

3. Control procedures can be pinpointed and are anticipatory in nature.

4. Interim schedule objectives and meaningful milestones can be established and coordinated.

5. There is a clearer delineation of responsibilities and results expected.

6. Resource management and decision making are improved. Optimal trade-offs can be made.

7. Outcomes in terms of time and costs can be predicted with reasonable precision.

8. Participation in initial planning is increased, and flexibility in replanning is provided.

9. Ultimately, total project costs can be reduced and schedule overruns avoided by proper planning and control throughout the duration of the project.

—G. M. Parks

Section 7

Research and Development

CONTENTS

Definitions

The Role of R&D in Corporate Growth

Measuring Return on Investment in R&D

R&D Budgeting

Financial Control in R&D

Project Management

Technical Service

Organization of the R&D Function

Facilities and Services

Test Engineering

DEFINITIONS

Since World War II, industrial R&D has progressed from what might well be described as a "back room" operation existing on a financial thread to a multi-billion-dollar financed, almost untouchable corporate function. The research function in particular has risen in acceptance to the point where, in many companies, it has assumed separate divisional stature. However, during this entire period of unprecedented buildup there has been a constant gnawing doubt in top management minds concerning the worth and contribution of R&D to the company. It is interesting to speculate on how corporate management could have allowed such growth in expenditures to occur while harboring doubts as to its return on investment.

This question can be partially answered by first defining certain technical activities which go to make up the R&D function. Too often, the definitions are formulated by technical professionals defining the subclasses of their scientific and technological professional activities, and do not necessarily reflect what management wants from the R&D function. An equivalent set of definitive statements setting forth what is expected of the R&D function within the corporate structure is seldom available. Where a set is available, there is no inherent conflict. In the few cases where conflict arises, it can be traced to confusion between statements concerning *what* R&D should do and *how* R&D should do it. The former is the prerogative of corporate management, the latter that of R&D management.

The following definitions represent a composite of the many that have been proposed. It should be particularly noted that they interrelate R&D.

Research

The term "research" refers to those technical activities which include (a) all efforts directed toward increased knowledge of natural phenomena and the environment, and (b) efforts directed toward solutions of problems in the physical, behavioral, and social sciences that have no obvious product or service application. It thus, by definition, includes all so-called fundamental and basic research. It does not include efforts directed toward proving the feasibility of solutions of problems of immediate product or service importance or time-oriented investigations and developments.

Exploratory Development

"Exploratory development" is the term applied to those technical activities which include all efforts directed toward the solution of specific problems. The type of effort may vary from applied research to quite sophisticated breadboard hardware study, programming, and planning efforts. It includes feasibility investigations. The defining characteristic of this effort is that it is pointed toward specific corporate problem areas with a view toward developing and evaluating the practicability of proposed solutions and determining their limiting parameters.

Advanced Development

"Advanced development" is the term applied to those technical activities which are directed toward potentially salable products, processes, or services, and a degree of program control is exercised on a project basis. A further descriptive characteristic is that the design of such items is directed toward hardware for testing and potential market exposure, as opposed to items designed and engineered for direct sale.

Engineering Development

"Engineering development" refers to those technical activities which include all efforts directed toward a workable process or a product suitable for manufacturing and marketing. This activity is characterized by major new product-, process-, or services-directed projects, and continuous program control is exercised through review.

Proceeding from the definition of research to that of engineering, the length of the definition decreases. As the product or service can be more precisely described, the type and amount of effort can be more clearly and briefly defined. More importantly for the manager, the terms "project," "program," "review," and "control" become more evident as the development and engineering stages or functions are reached.

On the basis of this progression, it might be well to consider research (fundamental or applied) as "nonprojectizable" and noncontrollable in the conventional managerial sense—that is, in terms of time-orientation and profitability. Research may be regarded as the activity which yields results upon which future product objectives and planning are based. Development and engineering are activities undertaken to augment predetermined or preplanned product objectives.

Quality Control

The term "quality control" includes corporate activities directed toward the minimization and eventual elimination of the causes of defective production, thereby to assure that the product will comply with all requirements as established by the seller and/or the buyer.

Equally important to defining quality control and its functional responsibilities is the enumeration of the results expected from it. Joseph M. Juran, in his *Quality Control Handbook* (McGraw-Hill Book Co., Inc., 2nd ed., 1962), has done an excellent job in listing them: (1) scientific inspection planning; (2) coordination of quality problems; (3) channeling of quality information through the total organization; (4) data on machine capability; (5) control of processes; (6) development of quality consciousness among operators; (7) assurance that quality is built into the product.

It should be particularly noted that the quality control inspection activity has not been emphasized. Inspection is merely the physical examination subprocess which can be likened to the routine experimental or analytical methods used in R&D. Scientific planning of the inspection process and correct interpretation of the results of the examination are the keys to success.

In recent years the term "reliability engineering" has entered the industrial vocabulary. To a remarkable degree the defined responsibilities of this function parallel those of quality control. Upon analysis, it might be said that, whereas quality control concerns itself primarily with an existing product and its manufacturing process, reliability engineering concerns itself with the new product and its design and development. Additionally, if only the classical definitions of these activities are applied, the former deals with product performance at the time of producing it, whereas the latter is concerned with performance over the projected life of the product. The fact that all new products, if successful, become existing products would suggest that these two functions be combined.

A more detailed discussion of quality control is presented in the Manufacturing section of this handbook (page 6·139).

Technical Service

Technical service, as a separate corporate organizational entity, has two principal and separately definable functions. The first of these has to do with the technological relationship between the company and its potential customers as it pertains to the products or services involved. It may include the development of product standards, the development of technical product literature and its dissemination, and the maintenance of a technical service facility designed to permit potential customers to evaluate the company's product; and it may include or train field service engineers. In this capacity, it performs the technological liaison function between the company and its customers.

Technical service, in some cases, has a second set of functions which are exercised primarily within the company. They may include the operation of an environmental testing facility, process trouble-shooting in the plant, statistical engineering, internal standards, the operation of the computer center, or the maintenance of engineering records (drawings and the like)—to name but a few.

By combining these activities in a single organization, a considerable reduction in equipment and number of professional and skilled personnel can be realized. Generally speaking, this type of organization exists in companies where, although there is a multiplicity of operating divisions, the products are all based on the same broad technology. Where widely differing technologies exist between divisions, this centralization of technical services is difficult and offers little if any economic advantage.

Innovation

Whereas the definitions previously stated cover discrete professional activities or industrial organizational functions, the term "innovation" is far wider in scope.

The simplest dictionary definition of the word is "the act of introducing something new or novel; also, a novelty added or substituted." Its most common usage in industry is to describe the process of discovery (whether by design or accident) of products or services, and in this context it is used somewhat interchangeably with "creativity" and "invention." This usage is incorrect.

Individual steps of innovation are dynamic components of the process normally labeled "advancement of technology." According to George L. Bata (*Corporate Growth Strategies*, Isay Stemp, ed., American Management Association, 1970, Chapter 8), innovation is a technological-social phenomenon. It changes the status quo, thus it entails an element of risk. It involves a change of the environment, thus it has to be in contact with it. As it alters existing ways and means, it has to involve new concepts. New concepts being the manifestations of the human mind, it involves inventions and their application. An invention alone is not innovation. The embodiment of the invention, which is probably based on some scientific principles, has to be carried to the point of manufacture, distribution, and utilization. The difference between invention and innovation is the same as the difference between the verbs "to conceive" and "to use."

Although innovation is (or should be) a principal concern of the company, it is the most difficult action to bring to successful conclusion. Successful innovation includes market acceptance of the new product; therefore, the successful solution of the "need" and "means" relationship must be found. The company must invent (application of means) that which, when it is introduced into the market, will be accepted (satisfaction of need) to the extent required to realize the projected growth and profit.—*B. G. Ryle*

THE ROLE OF R&D IN CORPORATE GROWTH

This subsection presents a discussion of how the activities of the technical staff of an industrially oriented company are integrated into the totality of the company's functions; what is expected from them; and how their contributions can be evaluated.

Corporate Objectives and R&D Goals

Whereas R&D personnel spend considerable time discussing the relationship between corporate objectives and R&D goals, this matter is seldom discussed at the corporate planning level. There is evidence to support the statement that

R&D goals become a topic of discussion only under emergency conditions—that is, when sales growth and profits are down.

An awareness of corporate objectives is essential for the establishing of R&D objectives. Seldom, however, are they spelled out in the form of specific statements. Too often, R&D management must develop its own interpretation of corporate objectives based upon previous corporate actions.

Where there is inadequate understanding of corporate objectives, serious errors may occur in establishing R&D goals. One of the most common of these is misdirecting R&D efforts into technical areas which are outside the company's capabilities to finance, manufacture, or market. Valuable technical manpower, time, and dollars are wasted. This portion of the total R&D availability is nonproductive.

Another negative result of mismatching R&D goals and corporate objectives— one which probably results in greater long-range problems—is the creation of too large a technological gap between the R&D function and the rest of the corporate structure. This gap can be one of either depth or kind of technology. There is a strong tendency for the R&D function to develop the kind of technical professionalism (basic research, applied research, or development orientation), professional discipline (chemical, physical, metallurgical, electronic), and technical area (solid state electronics, polymers, metals, and so forth) in which the R&D management is most knowledgeable and proficient. Though the R&D effort may be eminently successful under these conditions, the probability of realizing total company success—*successful innovation*—is extremely low.

There is, on the other hand, something to be said against issuing a set of corporate objectives upon which the R&D function *must* establish its goals. Rigid and narrow criteria may stifle R&D to the extent that nothing new is accomplished which will form a basis for company growth.

A good set of objectives issued by corporate management to R&D supervision first cites the overall company objectives, generally in the form of desired or anticipated dollar growth and profit margin. These guidelines are extremely important to R&D supervision in that they point to the selection of technical work areas which will lead into markets judged to be sufficiently expanding and profitable. Furthermore, they force the technical function to forecast which technologies are in the ascendancy and which are lagging or being replaced, and the rate at which these changes are taking place. This might be called technical market forecasting.

Second, the corporate objectives should state in as broad terms as possible the scope of the business area that management wishes to exploit. As an example, consider "pollution" or "antipollution." These are probably the broadest definitions of the area. Depending upon the desired corporate objectives, the area may be limited to air, water, or soil pollution. Further limitations might spell out control of air pollution by vehicular exhausting. Still further, the objectives might consider only improvements in internal combustion engines and their fuels.

It will be noted that as the scope of the corporate objectives is narrowed, they tend to include not only *what* the objectives are but also *how*, or by what route, these objectives will be attained. When this emphasis on *how* something will be done is injected too early in the innovative process, the probability of success is reduced or risk is increased. By sharing the responsibilities in the following manner, an adequate set of statements relating corporate objectives and R&D goals can be generated.

1. To establish economic objectives, both short- and long-term, is the responsibility of corporate management.

2. What to do to meet them is the responsibility of corporate management, and the technological input of R&D management plays an important part in their development.

3. How to accomplish these objectives technically and technologically is the responsibility of R&D management.

Relationship with Market Research

The results of industrial R&D must help lead to acceptance of the company's goods or services in the marketplace. This holds true whether the idea for a new or improved product comes from the R&D entity, whether it is developed by R&D, or whether R&D participates only in a consulting capacity. Market research has the primary role of establishing the existence of a reasonable market. In this capacity it can either test the need for a preconceived product or locate a need prior to conceiving it. We have then two bodies: R&D geared to generating the "means" to satisfy a market, and market research geared to finding or testing a market "need." Based upon these capabilities, a close and continuous relationship between the two is one of the keys to successful innovation.

This important interplay can be enhanced if technological surveillance is included in the scope of the market research function. Awareness of the R&D programs on the part of the market research team, coupled with continuous monitoring of the competitive technical activities in these areas, can lead to pre-empting that particular market. On the other hand, this technological market research can lead to the cancellation of certain R&D efforts, thereby avoiding prohibitively expensive competition.

Relationship with Other Functions

Historically, the R&D activity has been designated as a staff function to the operating organization—the manufacturing, marketing, and auxiliary groups. This implies that R&D is "available when called upon"; that it is a pool or source of technical competence to draw upon as required.

Under this type of corporate organization, the relationship of R&D with other functions varies considerably from company to company. Little evidence of a set pattern exists. There is strong evidence that such a relationship is determined by the existing dominant company function—marketing, manufacturing, engineering, or finance.

In technologically progressive and science-based industries this staff function image is less prevalent. The R&D function in such organizations is the member of a partnership of equals with manufacturing, sales and marketing, and engineering. This position is understandable, as a substantial percentage of the profit dollar is reinvested in the R&D function in companies of this type.

The working relationships between R&D and the other functions can be classed in two major categories: the informal and the formal. In the informal relationship, R&D acts as a technical consulting body and is called upon when its expertise exceeds that of the operating divisions' staffs for solving a problem that arises during the development and engineering phases.

The formal relationship exists in those instances where the new product or service is initiated within the R&D organization, either through self-generation or by assignment. The work is formally projectized and carried through the early innovation stages and then transferred to the operating function. The transfer point varies both as to stage of development into product and as to methodology of transfer. Again, these depend to a large extent on the particular company and its philosophy of organizational responsibility.

Looked at from one point of view, the separate R&D entity acts as a staff function in the informal relationship with other functions and as a line function in the formal relationship.

To maintain the informal relationship, daily and continuous personal interplay between operating divisional and R&D group personnel must occur. R&D operates as a kind of liaison with the total bulk of technical and technological knowledge within or outside the company, judiciously selecting and communicating that knowledge which will most completely and rapidly solve the technical problems as they arise.

The more progressive companies look upon their R&D organizations as a source of new technology upon which the expansion of existing product and service areas and entrance into new ones can be based. The organizational title—research and development—implies this. Technical and technological "creativity" is expected. Where this broader scope of responsibility is placed on the R&D group, it becomes a potential *source* of innovation in addition to being an *assisting* body to innovation. It is forced to consider the practical application of newly generated technical knowledge. It has a more direct and definable stake in growth and profits. R&D becomes peripherally involved in time and dollar scheduling as its work moves into the design, manufacturing, and market planning stages. This creates two important conditions: It gives R&D personnel firsthand knowledge that the results of their work are being used and therefore meaningful to the company, and it gives corporate management direct knowledge of the contribution of R&D's efforts to the company's growth and profit.

Technological Planning

Until relatively recently, a company developed its technical plans within a single technological area. For example, a company in the basic raw materials area started and remained in that area. Furthermore, in most cases it chose to remain within a narrowly defined area—a certain class of polymers, a particular metal (copper, iron, lead), or a single fuel (coal or oil). Where a second technology was involved in the product, the company looked to outside suppliers. The extent of its expansion planning was generally limited to taking advantage of all the technical possibilities within that particular technological area. Companies could be characterized as being technically or nontechnically based but only in a single technology.

With the advent of the recent technological revolution, many completely new areas have suddenly appeared: oceanography, cybernetics, bioelectronics, space exploration, housing, mass transportation—to name only a few. Companies are now realizing that entrance into these new areas offers excellent opportunities for increased growth and profits—in many cases, far greater opportunities than lie within their existing technological fields.

For an established company to enter a new technological area has proved difficult. The number of recorded failures far exceeds the successes. This situation may be largely the result of failure in overall technological planning.

Technological planning can be regarded, in the final analysis, as the technical phase of diversification planning. If taken in this frame of reference, each new technological area under consideration must be evaluated on a financial, operational, marketing, and technical basis. With respect to technical evaluation, the following questions should be objectively answered.

1. Is the technology under consideration sufficiently new that a technical position can be established?

2. Does the general level of required scientific and engineering skill in the new technology (including the potential market) fit that now available in the company?

3. Do the technical disciplines (chemical, electronic, mechanical, and so forth) invoved in the new technology fit those now in the company?

4. Does an adequate degree of personal interest in the new technological area exist in the current technical staff?

5. Can the new area be entered with the current size of the technical staff?

6. Do the manufacturing methods and types of machinery match those available within the company?

7. Will the investment in new equipment be on the same level as that required for the current technology?

If the answers to all of these questions are affirmative, the new area is a candidate for exploitation. However, the probability of this happening is slight, and therefore it is advantageous to weigh the questions as to their significance in arriving at the final decision. Based upon the experience of companies which have successfully (or unsuccessfully) used these criteria, the questions have been listed in their order of significance.

The foregoing statements assume that the exploitation of the new technological area will be undertaken by the existing corporate entity. Acquisition or merger with a company possessing either all these attributes or those which are missing is a powerful method for closing the gaps and making the venture successful; however, these approaches fall outside the scope of this discussion.

The next stage in technological planning is the selection of specific research and advanced development projects designed to yield products or services needed in the new area. In essence, this planning stage involves the generation of the innovative process within the new technological area.

Contribution to Growth and Profit

In a well-managed company, all the organizational functions are developed in size and scope of responsibility to fit plans for the company's perpetuation,

growth, and profit. The contributions of each subdivision are regularly monitored, and changes are made according to the evaluation results. The R&D function is organized for the same purpose. It appears, however, that management has
difficulty in evaluating R&D or is reluctant to evaluate it with the same criteria.
To overcome these difficulties, a number of different evaluation schemes have
been proposed; some of them are discussed under the heading "Measuring Return on Investment in R&D" (page 7·10). The present discussion concerns itself
with how R&D must contribute.

Since the company's growth and profits come only from the profitable sale of
goods and services, any evaluation of R&D performance must be related to
these goods and services. To define the output of the function in terms of the
quantity of research and development performed and attempt to balance this
against the R&D budget is impossible and would be useless. Only the definable
and economically measurable products and services which are a result of the
R&D activities can be classed as contributions. Research and development are
methods, not results, in this evaluation procedure.

R&D personnel will attempt to refute this approach by stating that only a
small part of their efforts results in marketable items, or that it is impossible—
or, at least, difficult—to trace R&D efforts to final products, or that research is
not product-oriented. All these statements are true; however, they do not negate
the validity of this method of evaluation. A successful industrial R&D group will
be able to enumerate specific products and services to whose success they have
contributed and to state the cost of their contribution. Equating these costs to
the return on the products and services to the company will demonstrate R&D's
contribution to growth and profit. If this cannot be done, one or more of the
following deficiencies will be found to exist: (1) The R&D activities do not fall
within the company's technological plans, or such planning has not been accomplished; (2) the results of the R&D activities have not been translated and
communicated to the rest of the company; (3) research (nonproduct-oriented)
alone is being conducted, without adequate provision for applicational support
(development) either in the R&D group or in the total company structure.

The first of these deficiencies can be corrected by establishing corporate technological objectives—that is, broad technological areas which the company wants
to exploit. It will avoid the generation of technical information, concepts,
products, or processes which the company is unable to market for financial,
operational, or marketing reasons. The second error can be corrected by generating formal and informal liaison between R&D and other company divisions.
The third can be remedied by staffing the R&D and operating divisions with
personnel skilled in the various technical phases (applicational research, product
and process development engineering, and so forth) required to bring the product into being.

Finally, it should be realized that the research and development expenditure
is a *risk capital investment.* The probabilities of success (in terms of eventual
dollar return to the company) of each R&D project are small. However, the
probability of profit on total R&D expenditure over a sufficient period of time
is high.

The Innovation Process

If the process by which innovation occurs can be recognized, the possibility of assisting it to a successful conclusion is enhanced.

The initial stage is the simultaneous recognition of a "need" and a "means" for fulfilling that need. This correct matching of recognition of demand in the marketplace with realization of a technically feasible approach to meeting that demand is essential. Without it, the total innovation process will not lead to an economically successful conclusion. Misjudgment of the potential demand may seriously reduce or eliminate the return on program investment. Not to recognize a technically feasible approach obviously negates the total program.

Assuming that this simultaneous recognition phase has occurred, the second step is the coupling of "need" and "means" with a definite idea or concept— a design concept.

The third stage is the difficult task of bringing the design concept to reality. Where the necessary knowledge or experience is available to overcome problems as they arise, the time involved to complete this step is relatively short. Where new technical knowledge must be generated (research), the time to completion can be greatly prolonged. It is in this stage of innovation that the R&D activity plays its major role: bringing the total of applicable technical knowledge to bear on the problem. The degree of "newness" in the design concept generally dictates the amount of R&D required to find solutions to all the problems.

The successful solution of all the problems arising during the research and development phase results in a new product. If the product or concept is new and not a modification of—or improvement on—an existing product, a strong patent, market, or know-how position can be gained. At this stage there exists a proprietary product developed to meet a previously determined market demand.

The innovative process is not, however, completed until the manufacturing facility is built and operating and the product is successfully marketed. This stage completes the cycle by proving the validity of the initial recognition stage through realization of the return of investment.

The innovative process is the pump of the economic cycle in which the company realizes growth and profit.—*B. G. Ryle*

MEASURING RETURN ON INVESTMENT IN R&D

There are always a number of uses to which money may be put. Since R&D is an investment area, it is logical to compare the returns from this type of investment with others to which the same money could be applied. Even merely having an R&D establishment in order to support the proper company image can be measured by placing some estimated value on having such a capability. The ever increasing expense of R&D makes it mandatory to direct scrutiny to the results of this activity and the monetary return from new products or new processes. This subsection is devoted to the discussion of methods of measuring this return.

R&D Expense as a Type of Capital Investment

Capital investment approval procedures recognize the long-term impact of a capital investment; depreciation charges remain on the books for many years. In a similar sense, R&D expense is a commitment of personnel and material. Translated as an investment, it normally implies a continuing project expense; later, pilot expense; and, eventually, prototype manufacturing expense. Management attention to the initial project is imperative in view of the continuing expenditure normally required. Some companies actually capitalize R&D expense, but generally the tendency is to expense R&D as the work progresses.

R&D expense should be considered as risk investment, together with other possible uses of available risk money. It must be recognized, however, that total R&D effort should show stability; it cannot fluctuate from year to year if it is conducted in-house. The means of obtaining new products or processes may be provided by in-company R&D. Alternatives are acquisition of product lines from outside, licensing of products or processes, and purchase of outside R&D.

The concept of R&D as capital investment implies the concept of recovery. It requires a forecast of total project cost, pilot cost, and manufacturing cost, together with sales and an estimate of the break-even date. Total estimated investment and its return can be compared with alternate R&D project investments and their rate of return, permitting the choice of the most probable project. The concept also permits comparison with other investments such as advertising, acquisition, plant automation, and so forth.

Discounted Cash Flow Method

The term "present value" means today's value of future expenditures and receipts at specified rates of compound interest. For example, at a 10 percent interest rate $1.00 received one year from today is worth only $0.909 now, as it could have been earning interest in the meantime. The present value of current and future capital investments and future net profit or net loss arrived at is discounted at some assumed percentage to give present value figures. The present values are added for all the years, recognizing that in the last year the results of the operation have a sales value which should be considered as an asset. This also should be discounted to present value. The object of the game is to find out, by trial and error, what assumed value percentage return makes the negative figures (obtained from capital investment and net loss) balance out with the positive figure (obtained from net profit). This percentage value is the return on investment (ROI). When this procedure is applied to various projects in the preliminary stages, it is often possible to compare projects by means of their individual ROI in order to arrive at a priority rating.

Computer programs are available to carry out this type of trial-and-error calculation. Advanced programs of this nature also can take into account estimated probabilities of success at various stages of progress.

New Product Introduction Rate Measurements

The limitation on the introduction of new products to an organization is the capacity of the receiving organization to fully develop and take advantage of the new products. If operating divisions can handle only one new product at a time, the rate of new product generation should be geared to this time period. Bringing new products to the operating function too soon after the most recent new product has been transferred out will cause dilution of attention to earlier new products and general decrease in probability of success for both. The rate of new product introduction will also depend on the company's markets and field of activity. Some operations will demand a high rate of new product generation, while some others cannot tolerate a fast pace of innovation.

Annual or semiannual review of R&D projects permits the display of new products developed by the R&D organization. Top management participation in such meetings will insure that proper attention is being given to new products and that new product projects are not proceeding where present information indicates a lack of market or impractical manufacturing costs. Failure to explain why new product ideas have been discarded can cause a negative impact on the morale of R&D personnel and even result in their leaving the company.

Negative Measurements

It is possible to assume that the competition will come out with a product which, because of cost or improved characteristics or some completely unusual product characteristic, will reduce the market for the present products considerably. In such a case, the lack of an R&D effort to prepare for this competition would result in a loss of sales and profit. This can happen, even though it is sometimes possible to assess the probability of such an occurrence and thereby determine the impact of not making a certain R&D effort. This procedure is usually difficult to follow in assessing the importance of an R&D effort, but it is not uncommon.

It is important that the assessment of the losses which would have been suffered without the R&D effort be made by sales and marketing personnel, although suggestions by the R&D people should be taken into consideration by them.

A large portion of the investigative research in the area of a product line is basically defensive and is used to reduce the time lag to take into account some competitive action. Product improvements that may result from such investigative research can take place on a continuing basis but are very difficult to measure specifically as a return on a financial investment. The funds for R&D should be considered along with other risk funds of the company, and R&D is generally only one means of implementing the growth of the company. Utilization of the equivalent of R&D funds in other efforts, such as acquisition, should be given top management attention before the establishment of a major R&D activity.

Spin-off

New products or new processes may at times be licensed or sold outright to another company. In these cases, the return on the R&D investment is easy to calculate. Naturally, the only fact that can be taken into account when a new product or process is licensed is the market value of the innovation, and the return on investment required cannot be used to determine license rates. Spin-off generally involves products, not related to the product line, that have been developed as a result of R&D devoted to the product line of a company. These new products do not relate to the company's interest, and the licensing or sale of these inventions is a return on investment that is a "plus."

Other Measurements

There is a great deal of published literature on various other measurements, all of which have limited applicability. Various indexes of return and relative profitability have been proposed, as well as measurements directed toward the efficiency and wisdom by which R&D funds are spent. These latter indexes include space per scientist, research-to-technician ratios, man-year costs, and the like. One of the best qualitative methods appears to be the one based on the opinion the management of the company holds of the R&D function. The fact that an R&D budget is approved and spent is in itself a semiconscious qualitative appraisal that the function does make a worthwhile contribution to the profitability and growth of the company. (See Robert E. Seiler, *Improving the Effectiveness of Research and Development,* McGraw-Hill Book Co., Inc.. 1965.) —*D. G. Wilson*

R&D BUDGETING

It is generally accepted that research and development activities are accomplished within the framework of a budget prepared in advance. It is increasingly important that this type of budgeting be done in order that the total company requirements for investment may be properly reviewed and balanced. In many organizations, R&D budgeting is similar to operational budgeting, since sales in the form of government contracts may be expected. In this type of activity, R&D management must maintain a certain flexibility with respect to its total expense structure to adjust to variations from budget in government contracts. R&D budgeting can be of value to the technical supervisor, helping him better understand the viewpoint of management in appraising technical results. Personnel charged with keeping within a budget should participate in the formation of that budget.

Priority of R&D Goals

The total budget requirements for an R&D program must be placed together with other requirements that are on the order of risk investments. Additionally, it must be recognized that the total R&D capability needs stability so that personnel are not employed and dropped as sales and profit goals change. This requirement for a longer-term stability has an impact on the priority of R&D investment when it is compared with other types of risk investment. Long-range forecasts of total risk investment are valuable in helping anticipate where major changes in R&D investment—either increases or decreases—may be needed. Within the total R&D budget there is a responsibility to assign the money so as to maximize the possible return. This leads to a requirement to establish priorities for various projects or programs, which can be done in advance of budgeting and is often used to determine—in part, at least—the size of the total budget. Projects which are lower on the priority list and would be dropped for specific R&D budget totals have an influence on decisions when management is arriving at final R&D budgets. The priority of individual R&D goals should rest with the top management of the company. Particularly, the operating head and the R&D head must mutually recognize the priorities assigned to various goals and be ready to change priorities as circumstances warrant during the period of the budget. Where R&D is pointed primarily to product lines already in existence, the operating heads of these divisions or companies will be involved in the selection of priorities, making their recommendations to their company operating head. Normally, such priorities will be accepted by R&D, although R&D should retain the privilege in certain instances of establishing specific changes in priority if R&D feels they are dictated by staffing, previous capability, or the likelihood of achieving goals. There are R&D goals that are established for the long-range future of the company, perhaps in the area of products completely new to the company or in terms of investigative research that supports the present product line. Recommendations in these areas should be sought from operating personnel, but generally the priority should be the responsibility of the R&D head so that he may later be measured by the results of these decisions.

Sources of Funds

Sources of funds can be internal or external or a combination of both.

INTERNAL SOURCES

Internal funds may be supplied from a total company fund or may come from the operating divisions, or there may be a combination of the two procedures. When the source of funds is a corporate fund, the probability of long-term stability of the R&D effort is enhanced; there is less likelihood of rapid fluctuations in the amounts of money available for R&D over the period of a year or from year to year. When the funds are completely based on division contributions, the contribution may either be at the complete discretion of the division or be assigned to the division by the corporate function on some basis such as sales or profits. When the funds are coming from the division for projects approved there, it is highly likely that the projects will be near-term, with a decrease in the possibility of R&D projects that protect the long-range future of the division or company. Short-range fluctuations in profitability for the division, or fluctuations from year to year, can have a severe impact on funding in the R&D organization. This can lead to problems with respect to personnel and consequent long-range effect on the capability of attracting good personnel. On the positive side, funding of projects by the divisions may increase their total interest in the R&D effort and make the transition from feasibility to production easier. The authority for funding, naturally, can bring with it the desire on behalf of a division to direct the manner of technical activity as well as the personnel staffing. Such action by the division can lead to serious problems in the R&D function, bringing decreased authority and responsibility and lowered morale. Unless the division is accustomed to receive charges over which it has no control, this type of accounting can have more disadvantages than advantages.

Often used is a combination of these two methods of funding, wherein certain projects are supported by a corporate or independent fund and other projects are supported directly by the divisions. However, here again is the opportunity for short-term fluctuations in business to cause the division to terminate the R&D project that it has been supporting. This creates a problem with personnel who must be either absorbed by the R&D function or dropped from the staff. Where division funding is utilized, there should be a commitment for some mutually agreeable period of time for the project, with a guarantee that it will not be abruptly terminated.

Where encouragement needs to be given to an operating function to do R&D for the protection of its long-term future, arbitrary allocation of the costs to corporate overhead is worth considering.

EXTERNAL SOURCES

Government funding, funds from other commercial companies, and fees from the licensing of inventions are external sources of funds. Government funds are especially useful where the R&D effort is in line with the technological growth objectives of the company. Government funding of projects that are not related to the company's goals leads to the effort of research for the sake of research. This lack of requirement for output useful to the company can have a negative effect on the remaining project activities and personnel within the R&D organization. Where government funds are utilized, it is often the case that any patents resulting from such work will not be wholly owned by the company. In such cases government funds should be sought only after considerable attention has been given to the impact of possible resulting patents on the company's future position.

Some companies fund their basic R&D activity with company funds, and after innovation government funds are sought for further development and improvement and preparation for manufacturing. Where the government has rights for its own use to any patented result but leaves the commercial rights with the originating company, the market for the possible new inventions should be weighed, and the relative balance between commercial and government use should play an important role in the decision to seek government funding.

R&D for other commercial organizations is not practiced to a great extent by organizations that are not in business for R&D alone. When projects are accomplished for other companies, care must be given in advance to define the type of information that will be exchanged and the assignment of any patents that may result. One source of funds to R&D may be the license fees that result from inventions licensed to other companies. This type of funding should be shown separately as income to the R&D organization. Where great financial dependence is placed on this source of income, there must be monitoring by management to insure that projects under way are not all being established to maximize license fees rather than as projects that will result in new products or processes for the company. The display of license income in accounting for the R&D organization can add to internal appreciation of the effort.

Short- and Long-Range Budget Planning

Long-range planning of an R&D budget must be accomplished in conjunction with the long-range planning of the total company. The relationship of R&D investment to the total sales of the company and the relationship of R&D programs to the specific elements of the company that they support are alike important. Long-range planning should be accomplished within the R&D organization, resulting in a total long-range plan with broad as well as specific objectives with respect to new products and new processes. This long-range plan must then be placed together with the total plan of the company, and as a result of management study it should be compared with the long-range financial investment plan. Some understanding should be shown within the company with respect to the stability of R&D funding so that there is mutual understanding on the stability over two years. The first year of the long-range plan can be considered as the short-range budget plan; this plan should be specific with respect to the investments planned in specific projects. In some organizations the planning can be based on requirements for personnel and material, whereas in others the dollars for labor, overhead, and material will be estimated. In addition to the budget for projects, a budget based on individual expense items is often required. The breakdown of the budget into individual expense items such as travel, recruitment, and salary permits future forecasting by R&D management of specific expense components. Naturally, the total of the expense budget should be the same as the total of the project budgets. Not all the projects need be or even can be defined in advance. The R&D management requires some flexibility during the year to either add to or subtract from projects, as well as to establish specific new projects on a temporary basis. The latter can determine sufficient technical information to permit proposing new projects. This type of flexibility can be attained by establishing projects without specific goals but primarily funded at the discretion of the R&D manager for use during the year. A report on the use of this fund should be made by R&D management, either quarterly or annually.

Normal short-range budget planning is established in the latter part of the preceding year. The information leading to this budget is based on projects, although in some companies it is purely on the basis of manpower. Corporate planning of projects means that objectives should flow from any corporate planning function to the head of corporate R&D. There will also be a communication line from divisions to corporate R&D leading to suggested products from the corporate R&D function. The R&D head will prepare a list of projects and estimated expenditures for the year, obtaining justification for projects and including market information where it is available. Division project budgets should give the same kind of information, including market information. R&D budgeting for a company, both division and corporate, needs to be looked at in one package. Where divisions are autonomous, there is less opportunity to modify division development projects than where the corporate R&D office has authority for total company expenditures.

In some cases the short-range or one-year budget is a rolling type of budget with revision taking place each quarter or each half-year and still spanning a year in advance. Project screening should be accomplished by corporate R&D, utilizing review procedures with the divisions to insure interest in later transfer of completed projects. The long-range budget may encompass a five-year period and will have some relationship to the sales growth of the company. Corporate R&D programs can often be built up from a program of subpieces, each related to specific division areas and their respective growth pattern. Long-range budgets are useful in arriving at stability for R&D personnel.

Budget Cutbacks

It is important to try to keep the professional staff when a budget cutback is expected to be of short duration. Certain expenditures may be sacrificed during a temporary cutback—travel, materials purchases, and the like. If the budget cutback is expected to be more or less permanent, personnel reductions have to be made. It is often better to drop certain projects and keep the manning level up on the remaining projects than to reduce manpower across the board on all the projects. Where outside R&D is contracted for, it is possible to use this practice as a means of absorbing cutbacks, since outside R&D expenditures may be adjusted while internal staffing is held constant. Even in these cases, attention must be given to priority of technical projects to insure that work continues on high-priority developments.

Budget Overruns

A monthly review of the expense structure of R&D should avoid any major overrun in the R&D budget. Monitoring staffing level alone is useful in avoiding later budget overruns. There are times when a budget overrun is the result of a deliberate management decision in order to accomplish certain objectives that have been newly set during the year. Such budget overruns should be documented and meshed smoothly into the total R&D budget system to aid in monitoring R&D project expenses.

Budgeting for Rapid Growth

Where established R&D budgets envision a rapid growth in the technological capability of the company, there may be a rapid expansion internally, or there may also be an outside purchase of R&D work to permit the more rapid growth. The rate of internal expansion is often controlled by the rate at which manpower may be practically added to the system and trained. Long-range planning is needed here to insure that the maximum rate of additions for R&D personnel is matched by the availability of required items such as space and equipment. Outside-purchased R&D can be useful for rapid growth, permitting the rapid acquisition of R&D capability with a phasing-out of the external or contracted research as the internal capability grows.·

Budget Revisions

Corporate R&D needs a certain flexibility inside the total budget. Where major R&D programs are affected, the original review procedure should be repeated. Revisions inside a technical program should be accomplished with the approval of the R&D head and need not be reviewed by total management. The need for revisions should be properly communicated to R&D personnel to prevent them from drawing a mistaken conclusion regarding the reasons for such changes.

Contingencies

Flexibility is needed within R&D to take into account added requirements in certain project areas of personnel or material, or the need to tackle new projects that were not considered at the beginning of the budget year. A fund for such contingencies is often placed within the R&D budget and charged against it. This avoids the necessity of doing that work at the expense of established development projects. The requirement for a contingency fund should be recognized by management. As special projects funded by this fund demonstrate future promise, new projects should be defined with proper budgeting to carry on the work.—D. G. Wilson

FINANCIAL CONTROL IN R&D

The principle of financial control in R&D requires the provision of financial information to the R&D head to aid him in operating his facility. Financial information permits him to follow the costs of his projects and provides a means of comparing the level of activity on that project against budget. R&D personnel who are concerned with the supervision of individual projects should have financial information made available to them also, so that they can recognize their progress against budget in a financial sense. Management should always take care to see that financial control is not interpreted as a means of directing R&D by management but rather as a service offered to R&D management. The intensity of control should be proportional to the magnitude of the expenditure.

Project Control

The budget year should have a month-by-month accounting of labor and materials for each project. In many cases internal and externally charged overhead is also shown separately on the monthly and yearly accounts. It is important that information collected each month be displayed during the following month so that there will not be too long a time lapse between expenditures and the reporting of expenditures to the project leader and management. R&D management must be concerned with overhead reporting to keep large variations in expenses not directly tied to a project from creating project overruns beyond the control of the project leader. Overhead charges are different from industry to industry in respect to details of expense applied directly against the project. Precaution must be taken to insure that the cost of obtaining the financial information is a practical one and that too much detail is not requested at the expense of time and labor in collecting the information.

Cost Control

A basic method of controlling costs is to control manpower. Since merit increases are placed in the original budget, they should not be a contributing factor to variation from budget. Occasionally, the loss of professional personnel and the consequent replacement lead to a salary level different from that originally planned. Certain costs such as rent or its equivalent are not susceptible to change unless major square footage becomes available and can be subleased or utilized for other purposes.

At times there is need to monitor—very strictly—certain expense items such as travel and telephone, when departure from budget is observed. This type of correction should not be made too radically because of its impact on the communication of R&D information to others within the company. These types of expense components are more significant in their totality than individually. It is conceivable that, in case of travel controls, long-distance telephone and telegram costs will increase. At times the purchase of certain items, such as material or operating supplies, can be delayed in order to bring costs into temporal line with budgets. It should be recognized that budgets are very useful guides, and expenditures should always be compared with budgets. Some flexibility in underspending or overspending should be allowed. Major unexpected expenses should not be permitted to have major impact on technical project work but should be separately reviewed and approved by management. Major R&D groups may have administrative managers to help technical management control costs. Such a procedure can relieve the technical manager of much routine and permit more time for technical supervision.

Budget Control

In establishing the budget for a future period, a beginning estimate can be made by using the total manpower costs, the material costs, and an overhead figure. In preparing and reviewing a detailed expense budget, a comparison of items can be made with a previous year in order that variances may be noted and discussed. Generally, experience will indicate an overhead figure for the R&D group which will be quite accurate for estimating future budgets. When changes in methods of charging to project are accomplished, a review of overhead structure must be made. Supervision in one type of R&D facility may individually charge its time to projects, thus contributing to labor and decreasing overhead, or it may charge its time to overhead, creating a reverse effect.

Control by Business Objectives

Estimates of the eventual use of R&D projects can be made, including future sales and future expenses, thus arriving at a break-even period of time as well as return on investment. Estimating and re-estimating such a plan for a given development project can yield an investment plan for R&D that is practical on the basis of the assumptions. If technical management feels that project effort can come to fruition within that estimated amount of money, it can be feasible to proceed. Total plan may show that the R&D investment permitted is insufficient to yield a high probability of success. In such cases the development project may not be initiated, or a lower return on the product may be accepted in the future.—*D. G. Wilson*

PROJECT MANAGEMENT

A discussion of project management should begin with the definition of "project" and proceed to describe the methods of project selection. A project is an action or series of actions having a specific goal or end product. This means that there is a quantitative way to define the end point of the project.

A project may be called by other names—research objective, program, business (or market) research—but what is all-important is that projects must be defined with specific attainable goals or end points. In today's competitive business and political climate, the R&D activity is required to pay its way. If the research director's objectives and goals are nebulous or ill-defined, he will find that a major portion of his time will be spent in justifying the existence of the R&D activity. The pressures will be sometimes very severe. Thus the generation, evaluation, and selection of projects form one of the most important phases of project management.

Several projects may be integrated into an overall program of study on continuing effort in a general scientific, technical, or business field of interest to the organization. The management of a program is more in the nature of general direction, encompassing an integration of the resources of the corporation, the corporation philosophy, and the delegation to subordinates of the responsibility for establishing and executing projects within broad guidelines. In this context, the head of the R&D function would be responsible for this aspect of program direction, and his subordinates would be in charge of the establishment and execution of the projects.

Idea Generation and Selection

Ideas for projects come from diverse and sometimes unexpected sources. Sources from outside the R&D organization should not be ignored. Customer problems may indicate shortcomings of existing products that merit serious consideration at the R&D level rather than being relegated to the technical service organization.

GOVERNMENT PUBLICATIONS

Various government publications cite required products. Some of the requirements or desired products appear at first to be outlandish or impossible, but many a profitable business has been built on products developed in pursuit of something to satisfy these requirements (for example, radar, infrared mapping, anti-ice coatings). Partial funding can also be had from government sources if it is within corporate policy to accept R&D funding from such sources. In some defense-contract-oriented industrial organizations the entire research program is based upon support from these idea sources.

Response to a published need can be to an RFP (request for proposal) or can be submitted to an appropriate agency as an "unsolicited proposal." Few truly unsolicited proposals receive response in days of government austerity. Informal exploration of the subject matter before preparation of the proposal will go far to prevent useless and expensive proposal preparation and will result in a faster response. There is no substitute for efficient communication with the decision-making level (not necessarily the top) of the agency. It is in exploring this avenue that a good marketing department can be of invaluable assistance in finding the right person in the right agency to respond to an unsolicited proposal for R&D effort.

OUTSIDE INDIVIDUALS

Some R&D organizations accept ideas from individuals outside the organization. The acceptance of these ideas on an unsolicited basis is very dangerous from a legal standpoint. Before any information is accepted or even allowed to be heard, the cognizant attorney in the corporate legal department should be consulted, and precise legal arrangements should be settled before the communication of any information is permitted. Many companies have standard practices and systems under which unsolicited ideas can be received and evaluated. The possibility exists that an outsider's suggestion would duplicate an idea on which work is done at present or will be done later. Whether the outsider's idea is rejected or accepted concerning this same product, process, or method, a damage suit by the suggester would receive sympathetic consideration by a court. It would be very difficult to document the contention that the idea would have been generated internally in any case. Without proper documentation of meetings with suggesters, there is danger of loss of R&D investments already made in product development programs; at best, a payment of royalty to an independent inventor might be the result.

Accepted on the proper terms, however, information of this sort can sometimes be of mutual benefit to both the outside individual and the research organization. The most convenient form of such idea submissions is a granted patent or a patent application. Such documents have a well-defined legal status, and this minimizes the risk in later litigation for both parties. Several well-known large and profitable businesses were originally based upon such unsolicited ideas—the self-developing camera and electrostatic reproduction equipment, for example.

The generation of useful ideas for the initiation of projects is by no means an easy task. The greatest source of ideas is the organization itself; its people have a better knowledge of resources, capabilities, and fields of interest and needs than any outsider could have.

INTERNAL SOURCES AND TECHNIQUES

Every R&D organization has some group, committee, or person charged with the responsibility of selecting the projects to be worked on. In most organizations the function is served by a project review committee or a planning committee. Their recommendations must then be sold to corporation management before funding is available.

Normal sources of ideas are customers' problems; logical extensions of existing projects; advanced planning and market research; top management directives; and manufacturing problems. To be of most use to the organization, R&D must utilize as many sources of ideas as practicable.

Reward systems. Formal systems are usually set up for presenting ideas of people in the organization for consideration. When monetary reward is promised for ideas used, the number of ideas presented increases, but unfortunately the quality of ideas does not always improve with the quantity. Financial rewards are controversial, as instead of fruitful competition they may bring about an atmosphere of internal secrecy and jealousy. Increased prestige is usually a safer encouragement to potential inventors.

Brainstorming. Another technique for increasing the input of ideas is the brainstorming session. In general, brainstorming requires at least two meetings. At the first meeting no idea is rejected, regardless how far-fetched. After all the ideas presented have been recorded, a second meeting is held to rationalize them. It is a difficult technique, but it can lead to projects, concepts, or approaches that would never have been considered in traditional ways of problem solving.

Customers' problems. As an important source of ideas, customer contact is not to be overlooked. Discussion of problems or complaints often yields positive results in that it opens up new areas for possible exploration.

Logical extensions of existing projects. The easiest source of ideas for projects is in already existing projects. The danger, however, is that the R&D group may find itself "beating a dead horse" or, if successful projects result, may become ingrown and increasingly specialized and thus lose some of its value to the organization as a whole. Logical extensions are generally more readily sold to management. This ease of acceptance, combined with existing expertise and equipment, makes it very easy to fall into the trap of using the logical extension of a project as the *sole* source of ideas.

Advanced planning and market research. As an adjunct to rational corporate planning, the company will have a formal or informal group whose job it is to map out the road ahead. The R&D function must be closely coordinated with these activities to have meaning for the future efforts of the parent organization. In fact, R&D is almost always represented on such long-range planning groups or at times even given the responsibility for organizing and directing the function. In this way, programs and projects can best be integrated into the orderly development of the corporation as a whole.

Top management directives. Sometimes a project idea will be generated at top management level and directed to the R&D laboratory for development. The success—or failure—of such projects varies widely, depending upon the ability, insight, and intuition of the manager to whom the project is entrusted and, to some extent, the esteem which he personally commands. His position gives him a horizon wider than that of most other members of R&D, and this is a great asset in defining long-range project objectives and ideas.

Manufacturing problems. An often overlooked source of fruitful projects is found in minor manufacturing problems that some intuitive or otherwise resourceful supervisor has solved unknown to R&D or even engineering management. These "little tricks" contain the seeds of real progress, many times in completely unexpected or unrelated areas. The lesson here is that there is no substitute for having in the R&D activity some personnel with current manufacturing experience. To rephrase an old adage: "R&D manager, know thine own products."

Project Evaluation and Selection

Various criteria can be used in project selection and evaluation. It is often difficult to prevent emotional selection. Pet projects, thesis or dissertation extensions, "gut feel," and similar subjective considerations are certain to influence the ultimate selection of a project. Regardless of the scientific, systematic, financial, or other criteria established, the weighing of various factors tends to be emotional.

FINANCIAL METHODS

Four of the financial methods used in project evaluation are discounted cash flow (DCF), return on investment (ROI), return on assets, and marginal income. This is by no means an exhaustive list, but it should give an impression of the variety and complexity of the selection process. As an R&D organization matures, the system and procedure that work best in that organization will be developed for selection and evaluation.

DCF. Probably the most dispassionate method for evaluating a project is DCF. Basically, the DCF calculation asks the question: "Would the money that is to be spent on this project bring a greater or lesser return than the same money spent, with the same timing, on another project or even deposited in a savings and loan association?" The method involves fairly detailed and accurate knowledge of the amount of money that must be spent and when it must be spent. Estimates of the market share and projected selling price, manufacturing cost, and related factors are needed. To overcome some of these difficulties, M. L. Anderson, J. Eschrich, and R. C. Goodman developed a series of parametric curves whereby the impact of the inaccuracy of these estimated elements on the project's worth can be gauged. ("Economic Analysis of R&D Projects," *Chemical Engineering Progress,* July 1965.) The study is probably most useful for the comparison of one project with a similar project rather than as a "stand alone" calculation of worth. This limited applicability is caused by insufficiently accurate estimates of available market, served market, and share of market, as well as estimated time to completion. The technique is useful when product life is as short as development time, or nearly so.

ROI. Although similar to DCF, the ROI method of project evaluation is usually calculated with "equal magnitude dollars" as if the investment were instantaneous. It is usually satisfactory when the project is short in duration and the life of the product fairly long in comparison. The return required to make a project profitable is usually a preset parameter.

Return on assets. For projects in which building and installation costs are by far the greatest expense, the return-on-assets method may be used. Again, the exact magnitude of the return for a "go" or "no go" decision is a preset parameter.

Marginal income. The marginal income measure of worth of a project may be useful when investment and development time are small. It is most often used when the "new" product or service is a natural outgrowth of the present business. The assumption is that only a small or at least accurately predictable increase in fixed cost will result and that the predominant "production cost" is volume-dependent. The income is then compared with the cost of the project.

NONFINANCIAL EVALUATION

Obviously, no one method gives all the answers. The method used will probably be a combination of all those previously mentioned and others. Remember, however, the results are only as good as the data used for the calculation.

Many objective factors other than the purely financial must be considered in project selection. What is the relationship between this project and the existing business of the company? Is the project of such a nature that the present product will be made obsolete? It is sometimes necessary to develop a product but keep it secret until the competition approaches, as was the case with stainless steel razor blades and square color television tubes. Or it may be that if one company does not develop it, another will do so. Does the organization have people of demonstrated ability in the fields required? If not, can such people be easily hired in time to be of value to the project? How has the organization fared on similar projects in the past? Sometimes, for political, managerial, organizational, or other completely nontechnical reasons, certain types of projects fail in one environment but may flourish in others. Is the project really too large for the R&D organization to undertake? Perhaps it should be divided into smaller segments—or, if this is not practical, left until a future time.

Now, what if the project is successful? Is the marketing force geared to handle this type of product? If not, does management understand that a change will be required? Will an entirely new or different type of production facility be required, and if so, is this fully comprehended by management? Is the economic atmosphere such that a project of this magnitude should be proposed at this time? Is the product of so compelling a market potential and so closely related to the company's business that almost any reasonable investment is worthwhile? The utilities' experience with the fuel cell is a case in point.

Thus it is clear that the criteria for project selection are not simple, straightforward, "can we do it" considerations. They must be integrated into the whole system of the business policy and planning of the company.

Project Initiation and Management

Getting a project started on the right foot is the second most critical stage in the life of the project. (The most critical stage is the "progress plateau"; that is, the period during which first approaches to solutions of the problems appear to be stifled.) The best time to select a manager for a project is before the project becomes a project. Sometimes this is not possible, but in any event the manager should be chosen as early in the project life as possible. If the project is predominantly technical in nature, the manager must be technically strong. In most cases, however the manager should be chosen for leadership ability rather than technical expertness. A high degree of skill in a technical field does not guarantee management skill. Will the project need a champion other than the manager? The champion should be at as high a level in the organization as possible—preferably, on the board of directors. He is important for large projects and is almost indispensable during the most critical, progress plateau phase. He must be completely convinced of the value of the project during the project's early life.

PLANNING

Once the manager is selected, the next important action is thorough planning. A project of large size cannot be thoroughly planned as a whole. It must be broken down into phases or stages, and these must be further defined until workable segments are identified. One technique used in this process is the Program Evaluation and Review Technique (PERT). This technique is described in the Manufacturing section of this handbook (page 6·157).

Other techniques are covered in various project-planning publications. Each technique is used to break down the project into easily visualized segments, estimate the needs of the segments, and resynthesize the whole project. In the process the manager will see: (1) where the pitfalls are; (2) how long the process will take to complete; (3) what the most critical stages are likely to be; (4) what facts need to be reported to keep him informed of progress; (5) what controls are likely to be needed to maintain progress.

The resulting synthesis can be used as a progress chart and serve as a basis for reporting. The dangers the manager faces in establishing his reporting and controlling system are, on the one hand, reporting so informal or so little that he has no real idea of the extent of progress and thus loses control; or, on the other hand, so much reporting that the only progress made is the writing of progress reports.

REPORTS AND PROGRESS MEASUREMENT

Provided the preplanning and organization of the project have been done properly, the measurement of the progress of a project is a matter of course. Means must be established beforehand for performance to financial plan, adherence to schedule, and attainment of technical progress.

Financial reporting. Generally, the simplest data to gather and report are on financial performance. This is often used as the sole criterion for performance. However, though it may be a good measure for a manufacturing function, it is a poor—and, at best, misleading—criterion for R&D performance. This is not to say that R&D should be devoid of financial responsibility or control, but rather that blind and forced adherence to a pre-established budget may stifle or even prevent real technical progress. Deviation above or *below* the pre-established budget by some agreed percentage or dollar figure should be cause for a review outside the ordinary reviewing cycle. It may be that progress is more rapid than anticipated (below budget) or that some unforeseen barrier has developed. On the other hand, the deviation from the financial plan may be merely an expenditure that occurred out of planned sequence, such as early delivery of equipment, payment for contracted work to be performed over an extended period of time, accruals and reserves, or other peculiarities of the financial data gathering process. It is well to establish an understanding with the corporate comptroller on this vagary of R&D finance; otherwise, the project manager will find himself spending a disproportionate amount of his time explaining away an overexpenditure that is really "within experimental error" of the forecasting process. (Strangely enough, the project manager never seems to be under the same pressure when the error is in the other direction, even if it is ten times greater.) The obvious result is that projects are overplanned and their salability compromised under the criteria previously discussed. The financial reporting system is only an indicator, not in itself a measure of progress.

Adherence to schedule. A better criterion of progress is adherence to schedule. It has been said that technical breakthroughs are not made on schedule. Perhaps not, but the experiments during which these breakthroughs were made were performed on schedule. Consider, for example, a hypothetical project that has to do with the development of a product involving (*a*) two reaction products; (*b*) a possible range of temperature and pressure for reaction; (*c*) an unknown catalyst to be determined; (*d*) a distillation separation; (*e*) a recrystallization purification.

During the preliminary phase of the project preparation, the manager or one of his chemists has determined the general range of pressure and temperature, the general types of reactants required, the generic type of catalyst needed, the most probable boiling range of the product and impurities, and the approximate recrystallization temperature expected. With this general information in hand, available experimental design techniques will allow a somewhat detailed plan of the number of experiments to be performed. The optimum concentration ratios, pressure, and temperature can be related to reaction rate and catalyst in a time-phased program consistent with personnel and equipment available. The breakthrough that is being sought is a catalyst to enhance the product formation at a sufficient rate to make the whole process practical. The time constraint on the project is that the distillation column cannot be designed until a "typical mixture" is available. In addition, the design and delivery time required for the column is a major item in the duration of the whole project. The result: panic!

This example has been intentionally set up as a classic illustration of the "you-can't-do-research-on-schedule" theme. The point is that, although breakthroughs are not scheduled, the amount of resources expended up to the point where they may be required for success is accurately known and controlled. At some point in the experimentation, the discovery of the crucial catalyst becomes the rate-determining step in the project. The subsequent expenditures of money and manpower can then be deliberately made with knowledge of the consequences. At this point a reassessment can be made if the DCF, return on assets, ROI, or whatever measure of project value is chosen. The impact of the additional expenditure can be calculated and based upon work to date, an estimate of completion, or a revision of PERT or other schedule system performed.

Technical progress. Of all the indicators of project performance, technical progress is probably the most difficult to assess objectively. The best indicator is improved accuracy of attainment of the forecast schedule. Here again, the very early achievement of a milestone is a negative indicator; it may be caused by either technical progress or the padding of a schedule because the technology is not well in hand. Both overdue and very early achievement must be signals for detailed review by management. Although not always possible, major report-writing time should be spent in the preparation of technical reports, technical memorandums, seminars, and other technical communications. There are three major reasons why this desirable goal is not often achieved.

1. Management is always thirsty for weekly, monthly, quarterly, and other time-phased reports on the status and progress—or lack of progress—of the various projects in process. After the agony of preparation of these not necessarily technically related reports, the scientist or engineer at the bench is loath to spend additional time collating his results and priming a good technical man to publish "unfinished" work.

2. There is a tendency not to report anything until all avenues are explored and all areas of doubt adequately explained. Owing to the pressure of the project schedule, these perhaps unrelated avenues may never be explored, and thus a valuable amount of work will be left unreported.

3. The individual may feel that he has discharged his responsibility for communication within the company by the inclusion of a paragraph or two in the monthly reports during the course of the work. The difficulty, however, is the matter of retrieval for later use by someone elsewhere in the organization who did not follow the work while it was in progress.

For the foregoing reasons, the monthly report might be better directed toward financial status, achievement of milestones, and other semiquantitative indicators of progress, leaving all technical matters to technical communications that are work-phased rather than time-phased. If the project is unsuccessful or is cancelled—and even if it is not—the technical reports generated can be a lasting resource to other, perhaps unrelated, projects and programs.

Decision Making

With all the planning preceding a project and the copious reports on status during the course of the project, it would appear that making decisions about a project should be an easy matter. This is rarely the case.

During the assessment of the various progress indicators, the project manager must be alert to changes in the market climate, the ever changing financial situation of the corporation, and technical breakthroughs in other projects inside and outside the company that may make his project obsolete or, on the contrary, even more important than when first planned. If the decision is made to scrap or terminate the project, care should be taken that real progress made is not lost through hasty elimination of nearly complete portions of the project. Projects have a way of being resurrected after a time. If this occurs, the maximum benefit from previous studies in the area should be sought, if for no other purpose than to show what not to do.

If the project seems to be successful, the decisions revolve about such considerations as the time to move into pilot production, the size of the pilot plant or pilot line to be employed, the time and method of transfer to production, the project people who should go with it, and the method of maintaining liaison between R&D, pilot production, and manufacturing.—*S. S. Baird*

TECHNICAL SERVICE

The technical service function of R&D is employed in various ways, depending on the nature of the business and the history of this function within the company. In most cases the primary duty of the technical service group is to communicate and, to some extent, filter information between two groups. In science-based and technologically progressive industries, technical service should be physically located together with the R&D laboratories regardless of its reporting structure. The resultant cross-fertilization of ideas will tend to make the whole organization more innovation-oriented. The problems of the plant and of the marketplace will be thus more realistic to the research scientist, while the technical service engineer will be better exposed to the scientific method in problem solving and will be somewhat slower in his rate of scientific obsolescence.

R&D and Manufacturing

A technical service group becomes all-important to the success of a new project as the project transfers to manufacturing or production. It is very important, in the final stages of pilot work and the early stages of production, that the technical service group be intimately concerned. This function is often served by the project manager and his team, especially when the company's philosophy on R&D includes following through to production. However, when another project is waiting in the wings for the R&D team, the follow-through approach may dilute the strength of the R&D effort. Each decision in this area should probably be handled on its merits without a hard-and-fast rule. A very new or complicated process may require the continued attention of the original project team to properly execute the critical production shakedown phase. Process troubleshooting is another important aspect of technical service to manufacturing. It is important for the R&D function to have a proper appreciation and feel for the problems of the plant. Such appreciation will insure the improved practicality of new ideas and the ability to do improved process development. It will also enhance the solution of day-to-day plant operating problems as a result of improved access to varied skills from the laboratory.

R&D and Marketing

The assistance of a technical service group may be required by marketing when the field application of the company's product is technically complicated. Companies whose product is computer software, for example, require technical assistance to enable the marketing group to adequately apply the systems knowledge of R&D to the customers' applications. This is the practice in other business areas as well; concrete additives, oil-well drilling mud modifiers, and electronics are examples. In some highly competitive tonnage chemical businesses, management wants to keep the marketers away from the R&D scientists so that the scientists' efforts are not diluted by minor problems and also to prevent information leaks on new developments still a year or two from production.

R&D at the Customer Site

The position of the technical service group at the customer site differs from its service to marketing only in degree of direct contact with the customer. In such areas as construction work, seismic exploration, and specialized machinery application most of the technical service work is performed at the customer site. In such instances the prime R&D input is attributable to the skill of this group in setting up technical and scientific information in an organized and efficient manner. Such services reduce the feeling of isolation for the field man—and also help to minimize the development of a "prima donna" attitude.

Coordination Among R&D Groups

When decentralized R&D is being performed, there is always need for a group aware of the work at two or more sites to maintain some degree of coordination and communication. If such a group is not officially established, it will usually spring into being informally if any work of similar or related nature is carried on at the separate sites. If it does not exist, the probable result may be compared to an endless series of reinvented wheels; the R&D groups might just as well work for entirely different companies.

Pool of Technical Experts

A technical service group is used for placing exceptionally competent technical personnel at the disposal of project managers in many of the larger and more diversified companies. Thus, when the services of the expert are no longer required, the project manager is not forced to find a slot for a highly paid technical person who may have no further interest in the project as a whole. In addition, the pool provides a way for competent individuals who have widely ranging interests and talents to be utilized most effectively by the company. Highly skilled scientists who are not especially skilled in management or interested in it can thus contribute profitably to projects and programs and still be paid salaries commensurate with their value.—*S. S. Baird*

ORGANIZATION OF THE R&D FUNCTION

Specialization, here to stay, is also here to grow. This is a consequence of the impressive rate of technological progress during the past 25 years. Today one-man research work has a very limited probability of success. Research work in a range from space travel, electronic computers, and nuclear fuel to the design of a new automobile (or any other kind of item) requires the coordination of efforts of scientists who specialize in various fields. They should work together and understand one another, but they cannot replace one another.

The problem of effectively organizing the R&D function is further complicated, in most companies, by a recent and continuing trend toward more and more diversification and the growth of companies through mergers and acquisitions.

The experience of several companies where entirely new procedures have been introduced in recent years has clearly indicated that the adequate organization of the R&D function makes it possible to operate successfully. This can be achieved by reconciling the need for the company to keep its position on the market—to spend enough money on research but not to waste it on ineffective research—with the need to avoid interference with the freedom of thinking of the scientists involved in the research.

Director of Research

The position of the director of research, who is often called vice president of research, research manager, or director of technology, will depend on the organizational structure of the company. In cases where an entirely new R&D function is being organized, it is highly desirable that staffing should begin with the selection of the director. This is the single, most important decision which will largely determine the success or failure of the R&D function (B. E. Noltingk, *The Human Element in Research Management,* Elsevier, Amsterdam, 1959).

NONDIVISIONALIZED COMPANY

The director of research in a nondivisionalized company is in a position similar to that of the other executives in charge of specific functions. He works in close touch with them under the leadership of the president.

DIVISIONALIZED COMPANY
WITHOUT RESEARCH CENTER

The director of research of each division in a divisionalized company that has no research center manages the research work under the leadership of the general manager of the division, following the policy decisions of the corporation's top management. However, a corporate director of research is needed; he will be kept informed of what is being done in the research laboratory of each division and will give special attention to long-range planning. He is not, of course, the administrative superior of the general managers, but it is his responsibility to call their attention to such problems as the following:

1. The risk of duplication of effort, which may cost a great deal of money if one division plans to start a research project which was recently completed or will soon be completed by another division.

2. The risk of failing to start a research project if it is needed to keep the division's position on the market in the years to come.

3. The need to avoid expense and undue delay—or even idle time of other scientists—when a division's laboratory does not have the skills needed in a special field while another division has the scientists and equipment and may make them available.

DIVISIONALIZED COMPANY
WITH RESEARCH CENTER

The cost of building and operating a research center and the complexity of the relationship with the plants of the divisions, which are dispersed throughout the country, are obvious obstacles to this approach. The benefit of using the specialized talents of well-selected scientists for several divisions is, however, a great advantage. One survey (reported by Raymond Villers, *R&D Planning and Control,* Financial Executives Research Foundation, 1964) has indicated that during the past several years more and more companies have recognized the advantages of a corporate research center.

The corporate director of research will not only orient the research work conducted at the research center but will also stimulate communication between the research center and the divisions.

Selecting the Type of R&D Organization

Whether the corporate research center, the division's research laboratory, or the research center of the nondivisionalized company is under consideration, the selection of the best type of organization involves the same kinds of problems.

FIVE TYPES OF ORGANIZATION

A recent survey indicates that five different types of organization are being used in industry (Alexander O. Stanley and K. K. White, *Organizing the R&D Function,* Research Study 72, American Management Association, 1965).

1. *The subject/discipline structure* groups together the specialists, thus creating either an electronic engineering department, a metallurgy department, or others.

2. *The product-type structure* groups together the various specialists who work on the research related to the development of one or several categories of products.

3. *The project/problem structure* brings together a team of specialists working on a specific research project.

4. *The process-type structure* is used in exceptional cases. For instance, in a petroleum company one group is involved in exploration, another in production, and still another in refining.

5. *The stage/phase structure* attempts to separate the scientists in basic research from those in applied research, product development, and product engineering.

Much has been said both in favor and against each of these five structures. The selection of the optimum solution requires, of course, a review of the condition of the operations of the company, and special attention should be given to preventing three adverse factors: conflict of leadership, instability, and loss of time.

PREVENTING CONFLICT OF LEADERSHIP

It is a well-recognized principle of management that an employee should report to only *one* superior.

If the scientists are reporting to only one project manager, the product-type structure and the project/problem structure can be considered. More often, however, a specialist is involved in several projects. Such a case indicates the appropriateness of the subject/discipline structure under which each scientist reports to his department manager.

In at least one instance, a large company (chemicals) has organized its R&D function as part of a business team structure where key employees are reporting to *two* superiors (*Corporate Growth Strategies,* Isay Stemp, ed., American Management Association, 1970, Chapter 8).

PREVENTING INSTABILITY

When a project continues for a substantial period of time and requires the full-time assignment of each scientist working on it, the leadership of the project manager may be adequate. If, on the other hand, the project requires only a few weeks' work, the scientists will dislike being transferred so soon from one boss to another. When this is the case, the subject/discipline structure is advisable.

PREVENTING LOSS OF TIME

The subject/discipline structure has the great advantage of grouping together specialists who report permanently to a manager who is a specialist in the same field. Not only do they understand each other very well and thus exchange ideas which stimulate their thinking; they can also replace each other temporarily in case of sickness or family problems. Opinion unfavorable to the subject/discipline structure has pointed to the fact that much time may be lost if one or several specialists needed for a specific assignment to a project are not available. This problem can be alleviated by an adequate scheduling system.

Auxiliary Functions

Another new trend related to the impressive increase of specialization is the recognition of the need for bridging the gap between the research people and other functions. The experience of many companies has indicated the advantage of creating three new functions which usually report to the director of research but may also report to other executives.

VALUE ANALYSIS

The value analysis function will assist scientists by giving them the information they need to avoid designing parts which cannot be made on available equipment and also to avoid purchasing too expensive material or designing new parts when current parts can be used for a new item.

A more detailed description of value analysis is presented in the Manufacturing section of this handbook (page 6·49); and *Techniques of Value Analysis and Engineering* (L. D. Miles, McGraw-Hill Book Co., Inc., 1961) is an exhaustive work by the inventor of this technique.

RELIABILITY ENGINEERING

Statistical techniques and electronic computers make it possible to detect the risk of failure of a new product before it has been produced, thus protecting a company's reputation for quality and preventing the financial loss that would be incurred in redesigning an item after tools and equipment had been bought, material spoiled, and labor wasted.

Reliability engineering requires, however, the services of a new function which not only pays attention to the design of a new product and the material selected for it but also studies how this new product is expected to be used. The reliability engineer is responsible for: (1) evaluating the probability that the environment in which the product is used will reach a certain state, such as excessive pressure, humidity, temperature, and so forth; (2) evaluating the probability that one or more parts may fail to function in such a case; (3) relating these probabilities to the consequences of such a failure.

If—for example—the probability of failure of a new spark plug is 5 percent, it may not be unreasonable to introduce it on the market; but if the probability of explosion of a new airplane is 0.1 percent, 150 passengers might be killed, and the airplane should definitely be redesigned.

NEW PRODUCT DEVELOPMENT

The need for a new product development function is clearly indicated by the experience of several companies visited during a recent survey (Villers, *R&D Planning and Control*).

The new product development function should be responsible for conducting a market analysis for a new product. The marketing people—even those who have proved their ability to conduct effective market research for a reliable sales forecast of the next year's sales of current products—should not be expected to evaluate the sales of a product which is not yet clearly defined and will not be produced until a few years have passed.

Communication

Besides the well-known formal means of communication, informal means are also required. The need for adequate frequency of meetings attended by the top executives who represent all the functions of the company is well recognized. Two approaches—periodic discussion and unscheduled review—have proved successful in specific cases.

PERIODIC DISCUSSION

The research people are the audience at the periodic discussion. They are addressed by various employees who speak about their own problems, which may be related to marketing, production, financial control, or still other functions. A two-way conversation is encouraged and has proved its value in assisting the research people to become more familiar with the other activities.

UNSCHEDULED REVIEW

Research people too often feel committed to complete a research project exactly as it was approved at the beginning. It should be expected, however, that after several years of research new ideas may be discovered or unexpected problems detected. A good approach in dealing with this possibility is to make clear to the research people that they should feel free to request the review of any kind of change at any time. They may, for instance, ask the marketing people to indicate to what extent a more expensive but more efficient product should be considered or, in other cases, to what extent a less satisfactory product selling at a much lower price would be received.

Motivation and Supervision

To operate effectively, it is necessary to coordinate and control the activities of all scientists and engineers. For this reason it is increasingly recognized that the principles of scientific management should be applied to R&D operations, but it is also well known that the principles should be adjusted; the way a research scientist works cannot be compared to the activities of production.

The need for making a profit for the company and for being ready on time, either to meet competition or to meet the deadline accepted for a contract, has to be reconciled with the need for operating without affecting the freedom of thinking of talented scientists.

FUNCTIONAL DECENTRALIZATION

A practical approach which has proved effective applies the concept of functional decentralization to the scheduling of research work.

The well-known and often-used PERT network provides the overall picture needed for scheduling a complex project. But it does not show the names of the individuals who will work on the project.

An advisable approach is to use the PERT network as step one for complex projects—which include thousands of events—but not for projects that are less complex. Then a Gantt chart should be prepared, either alone or as step two, to analyze in great detail the activities of the PERT network (if used) and assign duties to each individual.

If the concept of functional decentralization is applied, the project manager is not the boss of the scientists who will work on the project (Villers, *Dynamic Management in Industry,* Prentice-Hall, Inc., 1960.

Compensation

That research people are paid regardless of the number of hours they actually work is a well-accepted rule. The controversial issue is whether or not incentive compensation should be added. The usefulness of incentive systems in R&D is very questionable. Scientific workers are primarily motivated by a feeling of accomplishment, a challenge, advancement, working conditions, and the possibility of contributing. While compensation is a very important consideration, it should be built into the basic salary structure.

A serious objection is that it is often impossible to identify the scientist whose idea was the reason for the selection and successful completion of a project. It is, in fact, the experience of some companies that a reward often interferes with research work because some scientists who were involved in the research think that they should have received the reward allotted to others.

Successful compensation plans are based on accomplishment and contribution to corporate objectives rather than only on administrative position and seniority.

Appraisal of Professional Performance

The appraisal of professional performance should be based on understanding between superior and subordinate. There ought to be an agreed-upon standard of performance, established beforehand in the form of a position description outlining the accountability, objectives, responsibilities, and authority of the position filled by the researcher. Specific mention should be made of the areas in which he is expected to maintain expertise. Such a position description should be the foundation for establishing the value of the position in a salary range.

As to the performance of the scientist: He should be measured against the objectives outlined in the position description. He and his superior should reach agreement on the strong and weak aspects of his performance.

Salary increases within the range defined by the position description should be governed by the results of periodic appraisals conducted in accordance with the aforementioned principles.—*Raymond Villers*

FACILITIES AND SERVICES

The purpose of this discussion is to identify the key matters in the area of R&D facilities and services that should concern management and to explain briefly why they are important. The unique function of R&D is to generate departures from the existing order. Accordingly, good R&D facilities are characterized by versatility and flexibility. They are primarily the tools of people who are expected to be creative, and they are more effective if scientists and engineers are satisfied with them and have been permitted to influence their design or selection. The image of a company is significantly affected by its R&D facilities.

Location

No location is perfect. Trite though this statement is, it suggests accurately that many factors determine whether an R&D facility is in the right place, and very seldom are they all favorable.

If possible, R&D should be located where scientists and engineers want to be. Regional preferences are becoming less pronounced, but opportunities for professional advancement and for satisfying social, cultural, and recreational experiences are important for employees and their families. Scientists and engineers abhor intellectual and professional isolation. Proximity to universities, libraries, and other laboratories is preferred.

Central research groups are usually located near corporate headquarters for good and fairly obvious reasons. The independent action expected of a corporate research facility can be adversely affected by too close proximity to other technical groups. However, R&D should not get out of touch with other parts of the corporation.

The selection of an R&D site must of course take into account special service or environmental factors which derive from the nature of the work to be done;

for example, unusual demands on the public utilities, or extreme sensitivity to vibration, noise, or pollution. Proximity to certain related features or to a related industry may be indicated.

Transportation facilities for goods and material are much less important than transportation of personnel. Acceptable commuting distance varies considerably from one locality to another and according to available highways, but clerical and other indispensable support personnel are penalized if the only mode of transportation to a remote location is the individual automobile.

Building

Although unimpressive buildings seldom drive away employees who are otherwise satisfied with their lot, quarters that are comfortable, well designed, and well kept signify a successful enterprise both to employees and to outsiders who have occasion to see them. The company that is oriented to technology should not overlook the "sales value" of a well-ordered, attractive research laboratory; it can serve effectively to enhance the company's reputation for technological strength.

Exclusive of buildings designed for very special purposes, the average cost of laboratory space varies from $25 to $40 per square foot; air conditioning, which is becoming universal, adds about $4 per square foot. The part of the building that is devoted to management and support functions can be built at lower cost. If such features as high load-bearing capability or special air conditioning are needed only in certain locations, provision for them only where needed may be feasible.

Most companies find that significant changes in buildings are needed within five or ten years after construction; most commonly, these are additions to existing structures. Flexibility and provision for growth are essential, since R&D (particularly "R") is inherently unpredictable. User input is very desirable during the planning stage. Features that facilitate convenient modification or enlargement, such as movable walls or oversize utilities, increase the original cost but may reduce the long-term cost. Probable expansion and local codes determine how much land is needed.

Communities are becoming less tolerant of obnoxious effluents. Along with other industrial buildings, R&D facilities will have to collect and dispose of wastes acceptably regardless of location.

An R&D building should have conference rooms of assorted sizes, and if the number of scientists or engineers is fairly large—say, 250 or more—an auditorium is needed. The size of the auditorium depends upon other factors such as the proximity of alternate meeting places and the policy of the company in entertaining technical societies, customer groups, and the like. The auditorium should be designed for good acoustics and clear visibility and should make provision for adequate audiovisual equipment. The building should be designed for good housekeeping and provide adequate space for storage.

Some dangerous or at least obnoxious fumes are usually generated even if the laboratory is not used for chemical or biological processes. Careful attention to ventilation is essential.

Instrumentation and Computers

Science and technology advance only as fast as the means are developed to compute, measure, and analyze the functions performed by instruments. Powerful instrumentation characterizes modern industrial laboratories; it is needed for successful competition at the technical level. Adequate instrumentation relieves the manpower shortage, but it raises the standards for technicians.

In high-energy physics, instrumentation expenditure amounts to 75 to 80 percent of the total R&D costs; in agriculture, 3 percent. Aerospace spends 25 to 30 percent. Costs are diminishing in petroleum but are going up in the life sciences (Zola Bronson, "Instrumentation and the Management of R&D," *Research/Development,* August 1966).

The reasonableness of a proposed instrument purchase is frequently difficult to establish, largely because the dollar value of the observations derived from it is uncertain. The opinion of an informed user and the cost of alternate approaches are about the only significant criteria for resolving the matter—in addition, of course, to the pressures to apply available funds to other uses. Requests for performance capacity in excess of what is needed for the immediate application are frequently very valid. For computers, an excess as high as 100 percent may be in order.

Computers not only save time; they make possible some jobs which would otherwise be out of reach. Computer simulation is a particularly valuable technique in R&D. If the mathematical model has validity, simulation enables the scientist or engineer to obtain solutions quickly for many values of the variables.

The first step in applying a computer to an R&D facility is to get at least one person who knows how the users' problems can be most advantageously solved with computer help. The questions of ownership, rental, or some form of subscription service must be weighed and decided. Samples of typical work should be run on the candidate services before a commitment is made. In most cases both variety of problems and volume of work expand as the users gain experience. For that reason, excess capacity should be considered. Fortunately, the use of a computer now requires less specialized skill, thus enabling scientists and engineers to deal directly with the machine with less help from intermediaries.

Most laboratory instrumentation is in some way electronic. A strong electronics capability is needed in every laboratory even if the company's products are not electronic.

Libraries

The typical R&D organization can generate only a small fraction of the information it needs; the rest must come from other sources. Most of it exists *somewhere*; the problem is to get it. The library is an important agent in the acquisition process. (See *Special Libraries,* published monthly by the Special Libraries Association, 235 Park Avenue South, New York 10003.)

The conventional library is a repository for books, journals, and other documents identified by someone as being needed sometime by the people it serves; from this repository, material can be drawn when needed. This is a facility that supplies textbooks, handbooks, directories, dictionaries, and encyclopedias. Such a library is equipped by acquiring items which the librarian and the users declare to be necessary, up to the limit set more or less arbitrarily by management. Typically, industrial R&D libraries use approximately 1 to 2 percent of their companies' total R&D funds.

Certain developments are modifying the library's method of operation. The prodigious rate of information generation and the rapid rise in book and periodical prices are making the inventorying of all relevant material in each R&D library physically and economically impossible. However, copying systems and computerized methods of information acquisition are making it possible to get information quickly and as needed from central information "warehouses." The circulating library is becoming a distributing agency and may eventually become predominantly so.

Librarians need to be qualified in modern search and retrieval methods as well as knowledgeable in the areas of technology that are important to the company. Where the technologies are few but intensive, it may be feasible for the information manager to be a specialist in technology who has become acquainted with library procedures. However, the virtual revolution in library practice favors specialization in library science. It is evident that library techniques are becoming more complex and specialized. (See *Annual Review of Information Science Technology*, American Society for Information Sciences, 2000 P Street, N.W., Washington, D.C. 20036.)

Machine Shops

Nothing comes in stranger forms, is made of a greater variety of materials, or is expected to perform more unconventional functions than research equipment. The keynote for the shop, therefore, is versatility.

The work of such a shop is best accomplished when the scientist or engineer and the man who actually fabricates the equipment collaborate on the design. Rough sketches should not only suffice; they are preferred, because the craftsman is encouraged to contribute his ideas. A corollary of this, of course, is that personnel in the shop should be highly skilled and versatile.

Basic machine-shop tools and glassworking facilities should be provided.

Pilot Plants

To scale up the research experiment to a large, profitable, commercial plant in one step is usually too much of a gamble. For this reason, to have a pilot plant is standard practice. Specifically, a pilot plant generates design data for the large plant, provides a laboratory for modifying the processes by which existing products are made, and makes small amounts of product during the start-up of a business. It operates under pressure because it adds considerable expense and delays the payoff; but it reduces the risk if the job does not take too long.

Pilot plants are predominantly chemical or metallurgical. A pilot plant is designed in accordance with the plans for the full-scale production plant for which it is expected to get useful answers. The larger it is, the better the answers—but the more it costs and the longer it takes to build. The full-scale to pilot capacity ratio may be hundreds—perhaps thousands—to one. Each component must be examined to assure faithful simulation of performance.

Among the factors determining location is the expected dominant interface during operation. If the process is very complex, a location near the research laboratory is indicated.

Flexibility, versatility, and the requirement for high-salaried personnel make both the original cost and the operation of a pilot plant expensive. The cost of delaying production (presumably, with good reason) may be the most important factor. There are strong incentives to complete the pilot-plant phase as quickly and inexpensively as possible. Toward this end, the method of statistical analysis and the use of computers are significant. Careful analysis and planning, using PERT charts, will optimize the usefulness of data from experiments. Computer simulation can make some experiments unnecessary; in fact, with its use the construction of a pilot plant might be avoided altogether. The applicability of computers should most certainly be investigated.

Safety in a pilot plant may receive less than adequate attention because of the transient nature of the pilot plant and the pressure for quick results. This should be avoided.

Accounting

The administration of R&D involves the disposition of a substantial part of the corporate profit; while inherent uncertainties should be given due consideration, there must be accountability. (See *Accounting for Research and Development Costs*, Research Report 29, National Association of Accountants, 505 Park Avenue, N.Y. 10022.)

Costs are controlled by (1) determining how much should be spent on a project and (2) careful reporting to insure that the money is spent as intended. Accounting provides the tools to perform these functions.

The first step is the more difficult of the two because it deals with the estimated future effectiveness of the research effort and the worth of the expected results if they are achieved. It is basic to good management to commit a calculated expenditure before the work starts. Techniques have been developed for doing this, and while it is clear that opinion affects the magnitude of the factors, the formulas are usually valid and the whole process at least sharpens the manager's intuition. By such methods, also, decisions can be made about allocation of funds among candidate projects.

The allocation of R&D investment funds entails other important and sometimes overriding factors of a corporate policy nature, such as the relative emphasis to be put on exploration, new product development, and maintenance of the present business. Other determinants derive from the relative importance of new ventures as suggested by major sociological, technological, or economic trends, including the military-civilian consideration. R&D is usually expensed, not capitalized, because neither the value nor the time of arrival of the results can be predicted accurately.

R&D costs should be classified in a way that recognizes the purposes for which management wants the data, and the reporting should be done accordingly. Questions to be answered are these: How much was spent? By whom? For what?

The professional judgment of research personnel must be relied upon to a considerable degree in determining whether funds are being used effectively.

Desk Facilities

Every employee must have a work "home," whether it is a corner of a bench or an elegant office. The decision on placing a desk in the laboratory or in office space must be made on the basis of the work to be done and the local factors, some positive and some negative, that affect it. With regard to desk location or any of the other elements that constitute an employee's personal domain, the key requirement is that management be aware of what the employee considers important.

Miscellaneous Services

In varying degrees depending upon size, technology, and proximity to alternate sources, every R&D facility needs to provide essential miscellaneous services.

1. *Safety measures.* There should be an active safety committee with permanent and rotating members and strong management support.

2. *Emergency procedures and devices.* Showers, eye washes, gas masks, fire extinguishers, quick-acting and remotely controlled shut-off valves for flammable gases should be available at all times.

3. *Medical services.* Everyone should know the location and access route to the nearest doctor and hospital. First aid should be available in the laboratory.

4. *Call system.* This avoids unnecessary disturbance of others.

5. *Copy and reproduction.* Inexpensive methods for routine memos and a facility for making more permanent copies are needed.

6. *Printing.* This calls for frequent generation of material for wide distribution. Commercial printing may suffice; larger companies have in-house presses.

7. *Photography.* Pictures are needed for documentation of accomplishment, publications, illustrated talks, proposal preparation, and public relations. All common forms are needed.

8. *Drafting.* A standard type of drafting is employed by the R&D function.

9. *Maintenance of meters and gauges.* Secondary standards may suffice. Comparison with Bureau of Standards references may be necessary.

10. *Calculators.* Standard types of calculators may be used in R&D work.

—*R. O. Anderson*

TEST ENGINEERING

The philosophy and practice of test engineering are highly dependent upon the nature of the manufacturing activity of the business. It is obvious that, for a product for which testing results in destruction or in damage to such an extent that it cannot be sold, a different system must be established than for a product whose testing involves a practical method of proving performance. Techniques of statistical approaches to testing are discussed in the Manufacturing section under the heading. "Controlling In-Process Quality" (page 6·141). The basic principle of test engineering as a tool for gaining detailed knowledge about the product is the same in R&D as in manufacturing.

The Testing Program

When a product is approaching finalization, full consideration should be given to the testing program to assure that the product will meet expectations. Design or process changes may be required, and it is less expensive to do them as early in the development cycle as possible. The program should be so designed that any inherent deficiencies will be revealed. Conditions other than ideal should be considered so that the range of performance of the product can be adequately assessed. The field trials should be carried out with the aid of R&D personnel (of the project, if possible) so that there can be no doubt of the validity of the results.

In R&D the test engineering function is often a part of the project team. Rapid feedback of results is thus achieved, and shortcomings can be quickly corrected.

Testing Problems

Some products require the complete testing of each one before being certified as salable. All aircraft, for example, must be test-flown before delivery. Electronic components are tested as many as four or five times before shipment. To design testing methods and systems that adequately categorize a complex product into the multitude of types suitable for sale is by no means an easy task, and if these tests are to be made on millions of parts per month, the task is even more complicated. Accurate information on the expected distribution of the product should be at hand or obtainable through sampling. If the number of attributes is large, automatic equipment is almost mandatory. In this situation "go, no go" testing is generally used rather than measuring the magnitude of the attribute and then making the categorization decision separately. Test equipment for electronic components is commercially available; it can not only make the categorization decision but can also mechanically sort the parts into separate containers through computer-controlled testing. The critical control problems here are (1) verifying that the machine is performing as instructed by the program, and (2) determining that the program is what is desired for the testing operation.

In any categorization of this type there must be overlap between the desired limits of adjacent categories, especially if the "demarcation line" is in a populous part of the distribution. If adequate overlap has not been allowed in the design, there will be a large amount of product on which a decision cannot be made because of slight inaccuracies in the test equipment. In spite of best efforts to calibrate, the testing of some portion of the product will be inconclusive. Coordination of test engineering, manufacturing, and marketing is essential to assure that the overlap and subsequent "guard bands" do not overly restrict the distribution of one of the types from the product or, on the other hand, make the attribute variation so wide as to make the product useless for the customer.

Certain types of products do not allow for complete testing of every unit because the test may damage or even destroy the product (flash bulbs, photographic film, paint, and many similar perishables). In these cases product testing must be done on a statistical basis. Additional testing is often used to verify that these tests still define the desired degree of reliability and quality. Unfortunately, most of these tests require a great deal of time. This emphasizes the need for developing short-term "accelerated" tests that can predict with some degree of accuracy the field performance of the product. The search for the "time compressor" is probably the most widespread endeavor of test engineering in all industries, from steel to toys. The desire, obviously, is to obtain data on reliability or performance within the production cycle time so that the next batch or next unit can be modified to improve that attribute. The customer dissatisfaction that can result from lack of performance may be reflected far beyond the sales price of the product.—*S. S. Baird*

Section 8

International Management

CONTENTS

Multinational Management Planning

Financing International Trade and International Monetary Relations

Multinational Marketing and Product Strategy

International Pricing

Environmental Factors

International Managerial Resources and Compensation

Taxation and Repatriation of Income

Legal Factors in International Operations

MULTINATIONAL MANAGEMENT PLANNING

Planning is the recognition of the need to investigate and gather, review and evaluate, and—finally—filter data, leaving only those that represent the salient factors of information. These factors are then ranked and priorities given, resulting in a master blueprint for the planning endeavor. This process is as applicable in international or multinational as in domestic management planning, as it refers to any method of thinking out acts and purposes beforehand or to a scheme of action or procedure.

The purpose of planning as a management tool is twofold: first, to maintain objectivity during the investigation as in the formulation process; second, to relate, search, and make a definite statement on the issue at hand. These are the simple but firm rules of planning, and their application is universal.

Planning has been a golden principle of American enterprise, and to mark its advent and trace it in company history might position a milestone in corporate growth. Of late, planning has acquired a sine qua non status; however, this has not always been the case.

The early entrepreneurs managed intuitively; they served their purpose as executives for a limited period during which they mainly "filled a vacuum." Later, with the coming of complex operations, growth, the pressure of diversification in products and services, and the geographic expansion of business, the next breed of managers required a better alternative: This was planning.

Objectivity and realism charted the course for the expansion of products and markets that has occurred in the past half-century. The movement from local to regional and then to nationwide operations was achieved primarily by three factors working toward one goal: people, planning, and product. Companies that perished during the transition had major deficiencies in one or more of these three. Companies that survived benefited by the lesson and adopted professional management and planning as their stock in trade.

A similar stage of advancement characterizes American business—depending on the size, products, and management of corporations—as it enters the race toward "one world of markets." This stage thrusts stateside management into multinational management planning. Consider the following statistics: U.S. investment abroad increased from $10 billion in 1949 to an estimated $70 billion in 1968; worldwide international trade moved to approximately $230 billion in 1969 from $34 billion in 1946; foreign investment in the United States stood at over $60 billion in 1968, as compared with a figure of $18 billion in 1950; during 1967, one-fifth of all U.S. industry plant and equipment capital was invested abroad.

The effect of these achievements should be a response to challenge and opportunity. However, international trade must be entered from strength if it is to be successful; mediocrity in operations as in planning can only yield unsatisfactory results.

Moving Toward International Operations

Top management has a number of primary responsibilities—to the stockholder, to the perpetuation of the company, to the satisfaction of consumer demand, and to the growth in product, markets, and profit that is necessary for corporate growth.

Although it is acknowledged that the first demand on management is to be profitably operating nationwide, it is not equally accepted that management's subsequent responsibility is to steer the company to multinational operations. This is a singularly shortsighted approach to an overwhelming reality. That the traditional, protective geographical boundaries will, in the next 20 years, be effective commercial walls is an assumption that has already been totally discredited.

There is an absolute and unpostponable need to awaken board rooms to this fact before the combined effect of shrinking profits, foreign competition, and stockholder demands makes precipitous changes in management and/or unsophisticated foreign involvement a reality.

In U.S. corporate life there is nothing that corresponds to the Oriental's respect for seniority nor the European's disciplined response to top management infallibility. Senior executives in this country have scaled the position by being better than their peers and without much regard to age, family background, social prominence, or the marriage bond. However, such a singular atmosphere for advancement also allows for swift and sweeping change when the greatest error of all—the error of omitting to seize an opportunity—is committed.

Reaching the Initial Decision

Once the need for multinational involvement is realized, the next move is one of recruiting opinion among those of influence in corporate affairs. "Marshaling the troops" for this effort is a primary objective. There has to be widespread understanding of factors that exert pressure, a common measurement of their meaning, and agreement on the purposes of action. This may call into play the human relations skills that are part and parcel of top management, as some members will be better informed than others.

After understanding is achieved and a strong and united commitment has been reached, it becomes necessary to draw up and present a position report on "the state of the art" that will serve as the base for planning.

The Research Study

The investigative process is never quite so important as at this point, and the time, cost, and effort expended will be self-rewarding. A major objective of this fact-gathering step is not only to report the natural findings, but to continuously relate them back to the specifics of the company. To do this is anything but simple; it requires a well-qualified source to investigate the facts and an experienced source to relate them without molding them to fit personal interests.

Guidance of the highest quality must be given those who are assigned to the reporting function. A profile of objectives must be carefully brought together, detailing all areas of interest for which specific answers are sought. If this is superficially covered or not comprehensively stated as a major objective, the resulting presentation will be unauthoritative and incomplete.

Limits should be placed on any activity, however, and on this one the areas of interest should be clearly designated—geography, finance-export, license, equity participation, time schedule, manpower resources, products, profit objectives, and the like. This will provide concentration of effort within all the possibilities and produce a report with greater depth and perception for the outlined needs.

AUTHORSHIP OF RESEARCH STUDY

The next decision is also crucial: Who will author the study? On this issue opinion is divided, and the various viewpoints should be reviewed.

The research company. The expertise and professionalism that a qualified international research firm can provide are indisputable. They have been verified by a list of satisfied corporate clientele, and this vehicle may be the wisest choice if there is agreement on the following: (1) clear and specific instructions from the client on the purpose, depth, length, and presentation of the study; (2) transmission of company and product information to the researcher so as to insure the proper perspective and adherence to the client's needs at this particular point of development; (3) mutual respect, common interpretation of the research, and (not least) rapport between the client and research firm coordinator to minimize confusion in communication and maximize cooperation during the period of the study; and (4) agreement on a fee that will enable the research firm to completely fulfill the client's expectations. The client must approach the program as an investment rather than as a short-term recuperative cost.

The in-house research group. The in-house method is highly valued by many. It has proved so successful as to warrant the formation of a research department in some companies. However, success per se does not necessarily qualify it for a specific study. If the research department has been working on regional or even national domestic projects and its experience does not lie abroad, serious thought should be given to using it in a way other than as a contributing and coordinating function.

The company executive. A seasoned and competent senior executive can be used to conduct the study. The intimate knowledge of the company, product, and direction that he possesses are the basic qualifications, but there are other special considerations as well.

1. The executive must be detached from his regular duties for an appreciable amount of time to concentrate entirely on the study.

2. Time must be spent at the grass roots of the markets, which means going to unfamiliar countries that have different languages, business approaches, and philosophies. Obtaining reliable data and understanding the idiosyncrasies of the market can at times be an elusive goal, one that is not easily reached by an American businessman traveling on a tight schedule and given only limited introductions.

3. The sheer difference and novelty of many aspects of foreign business, when mirrored against a solid and extensive business background directly related to American conditions, can have a mirage effect.

4. The "detachment factor"—the ability to exhaust the sources of information, weigh their meaning rationally, interpret relative importance and position, and express the various aspects of business in any one area while remaining bound to realism and the facts—is something that can be better afforded to a "contract professional" than to a closely related party who of necessity will have some personal conceptions.

Most companies, realizing that this particular position study can be better conducted by an unrelated party, use this approach and supplement it by designating a top executive with the responsibility for its progress and completion, and avail the research company of the assets of the house research group and/or a knowledgeable manager to be the information and data flow supervisor on the client's part.

When the research has been completed and presented, the first cycle is completed. It began with recognition; progressed through explanation, acceptance, and acknowledgment of its importance; and ended with the choosing of an investigative vehicle.

The next step is one of understanding and evaluating the report. Its major corporate advantage is to bring all the members to the same knowledge level and obtain the benefit of their questions and reasoning. The effect is to surface the decision-making alternative.

Putting the Decision to Work

The company is now faced with the need for decision: whether to move on to planning its multinational operations or to shelve the study and agree on inaction.

At this particular point in time the depth, accuracy, and currentness of the reported facts place the company in the enviable position of knowing where it stands in relation to a large number of areas. This is most worthwhile, as quality input to planning governs the firm base of the decision.

The planning function in international is quite similar to planning in domestic operation once the "special factors"—distance, language, customs, manpower, and nature of business—have been recognized and their proper weight established. Sound business practices have universal validity and application and require only minor modifications to tailor them to the particular market; however, the newness of the venture and the effect of its potential success on future international efforts warrant scrupulous attention to the mechanics of setting it in motion. This means that, whereas under more familiar circumstances top management involvement would culminate at the acceptance of the plan and the decision to proceed, in new ventures in a less comfortable frame of reference and with dissimilar environmental pressure factors the vigilance of top management will produce at least two desirable effects. First, it will provide counsel and guidance to the operation, thus maximizing the potential for success. Second, it will follow through the application of the plan and cross-check the reliability of the method and input.

In a situation such as described, the traditional subject areas are of course dealt with in detail, but there is also a need to cover matters that are directly related and react to the peculiarities or differences of the new environment. It is wise not to underestimate these special considerations and to include distinct checkpoints and measurements to gauge their effect on the plan. This foresight should be based on accepting that once a major ingredient or factor demonstrates in operation that it has a different grade of importance than that which was estimated, a "red flag" must automatically emerge and a thorough reappraisal of that factor and all others should follow. This is the "danger light" warning in planning, and it is not a sign of failure but, on the contrary, a built-in mechanism of change.

To be a living document, the plan must be understood by all. As such, it will rise to meet new challenges, but it must lead the operation while adapting to it.

A word of caution is in order. Once a program has been initiated and the pressure of other activities is mounting, time is demanded by the international operation. This must be accepted. In order to deal fairly with all the issues, it is wise to appoint a top executive, preferably a board member, to oversee and report. The resulting channel of communication to the top and the ability to obtain speedy action contribute greatly to the success of multinational operations; management involvement makes the vast difference between growth abroad and disenchantment and failure.

Form of Company Organization

A look at the result of international involvement on the part of American companies reveals that a change is taking place in both the depth of the activity and the view of it by headquarters and senior management.

Although no time cycle is applicable to each stage, the general progression began with limited exporting, advanced to licensing and equity investment, and currently appears to be inclined to full or majority ownership wherever practical or possible. Another important evolution is occurring in the management philosophy through which international operations are organized. U.S. business has no patent in this area, as some of the more internationally oriented companies of Europe have pioneered the movement and led in the field until the more massive participation of American industry.

THE INTERNATIONAL COMPANY

The international company is a company that is active abroad through (usually) more than one of the following activities: exporting, licensing, management contracts, joint ventures, and wholly owned subsidiaries. The accepted management definition of such a company is that its headquarters are in the United States, it sets policy for its overseas activity, and it controls through a divisional or international entity.

THE MULTINATIONAL COMPANY

The multinational company accepts the higher relative position of its affiliated companies abroad and grants a greater degree of policy making and decision making to each. Thus every one of the affiliated companies is self-contained, with some duplication in certain areas and some inflexibility. The American parent is a coordinator; it exercises overall authority in major planning and arbitrates in matters of dissension.

THE WORLDWIDE COMPANY

The worldwide company is composed of separate legal entities but acts as one. This maximizes efficiency, interchange, mobility of personnel, and ideas. Policies are for the whole company because the company operates as one; however, the management at each location continues to fit policies to the local situation and retains profit responsibilities.

A Look at the Future

These profiles are not exact, nor do they reflect every operation described here. A company is what it is, regardless of what it calls itself; the majority operate as in the definition of the international company. While this may not be the most advantageous method, the reality is that American industry is today involved abroad as never before in its history, and operations in several countries, even if in varying degrees of involvement, do thrust it into multinational operations. These cannot succeed without multinational management planning.

It is certain that in the years to come, U.S. corporations will become more active, concerned, and challenged outside the North American continent. That there will ever be a full world of free markets is questionable, but what is not questionable is that the half of the world that can be considered available from a market viewpoint will be exposed further to international competition.

American business will not be remiss in recognizing this opportunity; American enterprise is at its best with competition and has an amount and quality of expertise that may be challenged but by no means surpassed.—*H. L. Aizcorbe*

ORGANIZATIONAL DYNAMICS

This discussion of organizational dynamics in international trade is concerned with the export-import process and the institutional structure of international trade; the multinational corporation; and the nature of joint ventures and foreign licensing as alternatives to other means of international business organization.

International Trade and the Export-Import Process

International trade, in its simplest sense, is a purchase or sale in which the merchandise exchanged crosses national boundaries. It is not as simple a matter now as it was in an earlier and less complicated era when the merchant would load his ship with the goods he wanted to sell, sail to his market, and sell or barter his goods there. Today the necessity for more sophisticated marketing techniques and the restrictions imposed by almost all countries make foreign trade a greater challenge. One factor remains constant, however: The merchant in earlier times had to have a knowledge of his market and a desire to expand it, and this remains a responsibility that the businessman must bear if his business is to prosper.

There is a good possibility that any company could sell its products in an overseas market. Whether or not it chooses to exploit that market is dependent on many factors. The government, through export controls, may discourage entering some markets, but in general the desire to ease the balance of payments fosters government encouragement of foreign trade. Unsolicited foreign inquiries may arouse the interest of management, especially if domestic demand is not keeping pace with production capabilities. Whatever the reason, once a company has chosen to export, it commits itself to work within a framework of institutions that interact to accomplish the distribution of the company's merchandise.

One of management's first decisions on exporting is on the form the company's efforts will take. If a market must be created, marketing strategy must be planned. Various media are available through which potential customers can be reached: trade fairs and exhibitions at which products are displayed; visits to countries and to specific potential customers within those countries; publicity campaigns with news releases and presentations at international conferences; and advertising campaigns in newspapers and magazines, on radio and television, or through direct mail efforts. It is up to management to craft the combination that best suits its products and the market sought.

The company has now to choose whether to export indirectly, through the use of middlemen (see page 8·16), or directly. Many factors, chiefly the extent of the export activities planned and the tax advantages that might accrue from the adoption of one plan over another, influence the decision.

DIRECT EXPORT

If the manufacturer chooses to export directly and if export volume warrants it, some sort of entity can be organized to handle foreign sales. Direct exports can be managed through a "built-in" export department or a wholly owned export subsidiary. Both forms of organization are discussed under "Export Structure" (page 8·15).

FREIGHT FORWARDER

At an early stage of the export planning, the services of a freight forwarder should be secured. The freight forwarder oversees the movement of export cargo at the port of export, acting as the agent of the exporting firm. Depending on the breadth of his experience, he may be consulted on broad questions such as the product's market potential, sales terms, details of shipping and packing, channels of distribution, and the export price quotation. His most common assistance to the exporting firm is in booking space on an ocean carrier; preparing export declarations, bills of lading, consular documents, and insurance; sending the documents to the bank, the shipper, or the buyer; and arranging for the acceptance of the goods on the dock and seeing that they are transferred to the vessel.

HANDLING INQUIRIES

Now that he has formed an export organization and implemented a marketing plan, the manufacturer is ready to deal with inquiries. On receipt of an inquiry the actual process of exporting begins, and dozens of factors must be settled in their proper places. One of the manufacturer's first concerns on receipt of an inquiry is whether he can supply the type and quantity of goods specified. If the merchandise in question is manufactured wholly by the would-be exporter, the problem is less; but if materials have to be obtained from a supplier, an option to buy them must be obtained to assure that the requirements of the expected contract with the importer can be met.

PREPARATION FOR SHIPMENT

Exporters quickly discover that containers suitable for domestic trade are seldom adequate for export purposes. Containers for export are subjected to greater handling, pressure from other cargo in the hold of a ship, salt air and variable temperature, and exposure in port areas to adverse weather conditions.

Since marine rates are determined by gross weight or volume—whichever means more revenue for the carrier—it is the exporter's concern to maintain a balance between these two factors when packing goods for export. Packing for export requires varied techniques and specialized materials.

By employing the more popular method of containerization, savings in packing costs, handling, travel time, customs clearance, and insurance are effected. In the case of insurance, however, rates may vary depending on whether the container is shipped unopened from the domestic warehouse to the foreign warehouse or the goods are transferred to a local container at the port of entry.

TRANSPORTATION

If it seems likely that the inquiry will lead to an order, the manufacturer obtains an option to ship from the ocean carrier. To do this, he makes an estimate of the tonnage, time period, and destination of the goods and in turn is given a quotation on the freight rate by the carrier. This option is left open for the period of time needed to complete final negotiations with the buyer.

An understanding between the buyer and the seller early in the negotiation stage will have decided the terms of the transportation, the insurer of the shipment, and the kind of insurance necessary. The options open are five: ex factory, F.O.B., F.A.S., C&F, and C.I.F.

Ex factory. The ex factory price applies only at the point of origin; the seller agrees only to put the goods at the disposal of the buyer at the agreed place (the loading dock of the factory) at or within the time stipulated.

F.O.B. The F.O.B. (free on board) price quoted includes the costs and charges of placing the goods on board a specified carrier at a specified point. This could mean placing the goods on a railroad car at an inland point or placing them on board the ocean carrier at the point of exit.

F.A.S. The F.A.S. (free along side) price includes the cost of placing the goods alongside the vessel or on a dock specified by the buyer.

C&F. The C&F (cost and freight) price includes the cost of transportation to the named point of destination.

C.I.F. The seller's C.I.F. (cost, insurance, and freight) quoted price includes the cost of the goods, the marine insurance, and all transportation to the point of destination named in the contract.

As a rule, it is more helpful to the overseas buyer if prices are quoted C.I.F. overseas port than, for example, F.O.B. factory. This practice should be followed whenever possible, as it is usually more difficult for the importer to obtain accurate cost figures on insurance and freight within the borders of the United States.

FINANCING

Arranging for the financing of an export transaction is usually accomplished through the international facilities of a commercial bank. The methods used for collecting payment for goods sold abroad are essentially the same as those for domestic sales. Every exporter uses one or more of several basic methods unless the goods are paid for in advance. The choice is dependent on such factors as the credit standing of the buyer, the capital position of the exporter, and the competition that the exporter faces.

Affording the least risk to the exporter is prepayment (goods shipped have been paid for). This method will be used if the credit standing of the foreign buyer is unknown and to acquire this information is deemed too expensive. An open account exposes the exporter to the greatest risk. Goods are shipped to the foreign buyer, the account to be settled by a predetermined date. In effect, the seller has loaned the price of the goods to the buyer. This type of transaction would be allowed only to a firm which engenders trust and whose credit standing is impeccable. Between these two extremes there are methods of collecting payment which offer compromises; they allow the exporter to be a bit more lenient in regard to terms of payment without exposing himself to the risks inherent in an open account.

Drafts. A draft is a legal instrument transferred from the seller to the buyer ordering the buyer to pay a specified third party a certain sum of money at a certain time. There are two types of payment by draft.

A *sight draft,* accompanied by the necessary documents for export, is sent by the seller's bank to its correspondent bank in the buyer's country with instructions to release the documents only against payment. When payment has been made, the buyer receives the documents entitling him to the merchandise.

A *time draft* is collected in a similar way except that the buyer is allowed more time to make payment. By writing or stamping the word "Accepted" across the draft and adding his signature, the buyer agrees to pay the amount of the draft on the date it comes due. Documents are released to the buyer on his acceptance of the draft.

In each case, unless arrangements are made to the contrary, the exporter must wait until the buyer has paid the draft before his bank will reimburse him. To avoid tying up his money, the exporter can negotiate with the bank for an advance on the draft, or the bank may discount the draft for him. In the first method, the exporter is advanced all or part of the face amount of the draft at the time it is deposited with the bank after he agrees to subsequent adjustment for charges and interest upon the bank's receipt of the funds. When the bank discounts a draft, it deducts estimated bank charges and interest and advances the remainder to the exporter.

Letters of credit. The importer abroad can initiate the financial arrangements by opening with his bank an export letter of credit, which is a commitment by the bank to pay the exporter a certain sum of money dependent on his compliance with the terms of the letter. The exporter benefits from this type of financing in that he is relieved of many of his credit worries because he is relying on a bank's credit rather than that of the importer. Also, funds are immediately available to him at the designated paying bank without the deduction for interest or bank charges that would be the case with a draft.

A letter of credit is issued in either revocable or irrevocable form. The irrevocable form offers the greater degree of protection for the exporter. The issuing bank may cancel the revocable letter of credit at any time, but an irrevocable letter is valid until its expiration date unless all parties concerned agree to cancel it.

As an extra guarantee of payment the exporter should arrange for an irrevocable confirmed letter of credit. The less desirable irrevocable unconfirmed letter carries a notation from the exporter's bank that the letter is to be considered solely an advice of credit opened at the importer's bank and that the exporter's bank assumes no obligation regarding payment of the letter. The obligation of the irrevocable confirmed letter, on the other hand, is assumed jointly by the foreign and the American bank. The exporter is thus assured of payment because the act of confirmation by his bank is legally binding and payment will not be contingent on the solvency of the foreign bank.

To secure payment of the letter of credit, the exporter presents to his bank the shipping documents proving that he has acted in accordance with the terms of the letter and then draws a draft on the bank for the amount due him. If the draft is to be drawn at sight, the bank will make payment immediately; if it is to be drawn on a time basis—that is, if the importer has specified that a specified period of time must elapse before payment—the bank will accept the exporter's draft and pay it on maturity.

(Methods of financing are further discussed under "Financing Foreign Trade," page 8·44.)

GOVERNMENT CONTROLS

It is essential that the government controls of both countries involved in a transaction be ascertained at the time other preparations are being made. The exporter would be in an embarrassing position if he discovered, after accepting an order, that he was not allowed to ship the merchandise by one of the countries.

Almost all exports from the United States and its territories and possessions are subject to the regulations of the Office of Export Control of the Department of Commerce. Goods under the licensing authority of this office are listed numerically by export control number on the comprehensive export schedule published by the Department of Commerce.

Licenses. The Office of Export Control issues two types of licenses: general and validated. A general license, for which no application is needed and no document is issued, permits export within general limitations prescribed by the office and accounts for about 95 percent of U.S. exports. A validated license is issued in document form and authorizes the export of certain goods within specific limitations delineated within the document.

The type of license required depends mainly on the commodity being exported and its destination. Denial of strategic goods to Communist countries is a specific aim of the export regulations, though the controls have been relaxed from time to time to promote the expansion of trade with some Eastern Bloc countries. Controls are applied to foreign countries in accordance with the best interests of the United States.

Foreign import restrictions. Foreign import restrictions must also be considered in any foreign transaction. Quotas, tariffs, duties—all can complicate the import-export process and figure in the assessment of the profitability of the transaction. Information as to restrictions in effect is available from the consulate of the country concerned.

TERMS AND CONTRACT

After accumulating all the information needed on transportation and the expenses which might be imposed by any regulations of the country to which the goods will be shipped, management must combine that information with knowledge of its own manufacturing costs, desired profit margin, cost of special packing, and insurance. In many cases the export price is determined by adding these costs to the domestic price structure of the merchandise. This method may lead to a price that is not competitive in the foreign market.

Terms. The form of payment must be decided on. Does the exporter want payment to be effected with a draft? If so, what kind—a sight draft? A time draft? Would he prefer payment through a letter of credit opened by the foreign purchaser? The exporter may, depending on business conditions, have to offer some leniency in payment terms. He must decide if he wants the business under those conditions.

Once the terms of sale have been determined, the exporting firm drafts a statement of the terms and transmits it to the prospect by the most expeditious means. The importer weighs the offer against his knowledge of his market to determine his chances for profit; he either accepts the offer, rejects it, or offers a counterproposal. If the two parties reach an agreement, the export-import process will proceed; the exporter's acceptance of the order means that he has entered into a contract to supply the named merchandise at the named price and under the terms specified.

Contract. A written export contract formalizes the agreement. It is generally considered the responsibility of the exporter to have a lawyer draw up the contract. Care must be taken that all terms and conditions of the transaction are spelled out in unambiguous language and that the legal requirements of each nation are observed scrupulously. If copies in two languages are necessary, extra precaution must be observed to insure that the sense is in agreement in both versions, since the parties are committed irrevocably to the terms of the contract after signing.

The exporter must now take the step of exercising his freight contract option for transportation of the goods within the agreed-upon time period and to the port specified by the importer. Arrangements with the bank for the financing of the trade are completed.

DOCUMENTS

Proper documentation of a shipment for export will depend on the terms of the sale, the method chosen for shipping the goods, and the legal requirements of the countries of the exporter and the importer. The basic documents for most shipments include a commercial invoice, bill of lading, insurance certificate, and U.S. Government export declaration. Certificates of origin and consular invoices are often required by the country of the importer.

Commercial invoice. The seller's commercial invoice must identify completely the shipment being undertaken; it will serve as the source of information for filling out all the other documents necessary for the movement of the goods from one country to another. Included on the invoice will be a complete description of the goods; the gross, net, and legal weights, together with the cubic dimensions of the containers; shipping marks and numbers of containers; the name of the ocean carrier and the sailing date; the name and address of both the exporter and the importer; the price per unit and the total price; and the terms of the sale.

Bill of lading. The principal functions of the ocean bill of lading are that it (1) indicates receipt of the merchandise by the ocean carrier; (2) serves as a contract between the shipper and the ocean carrier; and (3) may, depending on the form it takes, serve as an instrument of title to the goods involved.

The form of a bill of lading determines the extent to which an exporter retains control of the merchandise; and thus it determines the extent to which he can protect his interests. The nonnegotiable (straight) bill of lading is used when the merchandise is consigned directly to the customer. Title to the merchandise remains with the seller until the buyer properly lays claim to the goods. The buyer, however, can usually obtain the merchandise by simply identifying himself as the consignee; in this respect the seller is offered little protection. The seller can consign the merchandise to a third party in the buyer's country, the third party to act as the seller's agent, and can thus gain greater protection for himself.

The maximum protection and ease of transfer of the goods are achieved by consigning the goods "to order of" the seller or "to order, notify buyer." In the case of this negotiable bill of lading, title to the merchandise is transferred to and borne by the shipper until it is transferred to the next bearer of the bill of lading by endorsing it on the reverse side in blank. The buyer must pay or accept a draft and surrender a properly endorsed original of the bill of lading in order to secure possession of the merchandise.

Insurance certificate. The insurance certificate fully describes the type and quantity of goods, origin and destination, marks and numbers of packing cases, value, vessel, and all other identifying information. Shipments should be protected by adequate insurance at all times. The minimum coverage that should be purchased is the C.I.F. value of the goods.

A policy for an individual shipment can be negotiated with an underwriter if the export transaction is on a one-time basis. An open marine policy is desirable for continuing shipments of goods. The protection of the open policy remains in force until the policy is canceled; individual shipments are declared as they are made. Protection begins when the shipment leaves the warehouse named in the policy.

Marine insurance does not cover every loss that occurs in shipment: Hazards such as theft, pilferage, nondelivery, damage from fresh water or oil, and breakage usually have to be especially provided for, and an additional premium must be paid. An "all risk" policy that covers many such risks can be obtained, but even it does not cover strikes or riots.

SHIPMENT FROM PORT OF EXPORT

At this point the manufacturer has shipped his merchandise to the port. Upon arrival of the merchandise, the freight forwarder examines its condition and checks it against the commercial invoice to determine if there is any irregularity. He makes out a dock receipt or a bill of lading as proof that transfer of the merchandise from the inland carrier to the ocean carrier has been effected. The dock receipt covers the merchandise before it is loaded on the ship; when loading has been completed, the bill of lading is made out to replace the dock receipt.

After the freight forwarder is sure that the shipment is safely under control and when he has gathered all the necessary documents, he forwards the documents to the exporter, who presents them with his draft to the commercial bank handling the financial arrangements.

If the exporter is shipping on the basis of a letter of credit from the importer, the presentation of the documents proves that he has complied with the terms of the letter. If the exporter is to draw payment from a draft, the documents are attached to the draft by the bank and are forwarded to the importer's bank. The importer must either pay or accept the exporter's draft before he can obtain possession of the documents (and, by extension, title to the merchandise). The exporter's interest in the transaction effectively ends when he presents the shipping documents to his bank for payment.

RECEIPT BY IMPORTER

The importer—or, more likely, his customshouse broker (the import equivalent of the freight forwarder)—usually receives the documents before the merchandise because of the difference in speed between air mail and ship travel. If the merchandise has been shipped under a negotiable bill of lading, as is most likely, the importer presents the documents he obtained from his bank and the ocean carrier transfers the title of the merchandise by surrendering the bill of lading and releasing the cargo.

The merchandise now belongs to the importer, but it must remain in the custody of the customs officials of the country of import. The importer must fill out the necessary forms and attach the required documents while the customs officials appraise the merchandise and determine the import duties. After paying the duty and complying with any other requirements, the importer is allowed to take physical possession of the merchandise and carry out his plans for marketing it.

The export-import transaction is not a cut-and-dried one; each side must be flexible in negotiations if the transaction is to be executed efficiently. Details are all-important; the utmost care must be taken to insure that documents are complete and accurate. If the extra trouble necessary in foreign transactions is taken, a valuable new market will have been opened.—*L. G. B. Welt*

Export-Import Institutional Structure

Ever since the early thirties, the U.S. Congress has been deeply concerned with seeking ways to help American industry increase its overseas business. First to follow the Webb Pomerene Export Trade Act of 1918 was the historic Reciprocal Trade Agreements Act of 1934, which in turn was followed by the creation of the Export-Import Bank (Ex-Im Bank), the General Agreement on Tariffs and Trade (GATT), the Western Hemisphere Trade Corporation (WHTC), the export exclusions to current taxation in the 1962 amendments to the Internal Revenue Code (IRC), and finally the Kennedy Round, lowering tariffs still further.

As U.S. exports skyrocketed from the depression-year average of $2 billion to approximately $36 billion, a far-reaching evolution occurred not only in the composition of exports but also in their method of distribution. When the Common Market, or European Economic Community (EEC), was created in 1957, approximately 90 percent of the overseas business of American companies was accounted for by exports; but recent surveys show that direct sales abroad now contribute only 65 percent of U.S. business with foreign countries, while nearly 30 percent depends on overseas operations and about 5 percent on licensing. Fewer than half of all companies involved in international business report that their foreign activities are exclusively devoted to exporting. Moreover, only 35 percent of American firms anticipate that the greatest expansion in their future overseas business will be in direct exporting.

EXPORT STRUCTURE

It is obvious to the businessman approaching a foreign market for the first time that he must be careful in selecting the best of the many alternate methods for him to penetrate the foreign market. Because of the innumerable factors, from politics to tariffs to exchange fluctuations, that influence sales abroad, the U.S. company about to begin selling overseas should choose the easiest and most flexible route. Generally, this is the company export department; however, it is assumed that no structural plan is adopted until the company has examined its objectives and the future potential based on its present assets and facilities.

Company export department. Establishing a built-in export department to handle the corporation's foreign sales activities is a relatively simple matter. This form of direct export is an integrated part of the regular sales organization, using the same personnel assigned to the domestic operation but usually hiring an export manager or assigning a sales executive to supervise its activities divorced from domestic sales. Some companies prefer to have the general sales manager also direct the foreign transactions, adding the export-related duties to his other responsibilities. Credit, accounting, advertising, traffic, shipping, and all other activities necessary to export are handled by the regular departments devoted to these functions in the domestic business.

The principal function of the export manager or other official delegated to handle the foreign business is to coordinate the activities of all departments as they relate to each individual export sale. He is also responsible for developing new business, handling correspondence, and maintaining overseas contacts, as well as carrying out company policy in regard to exports.

Separate export department with divisions. When a company's overseas sales have grown to sufficient volume, it generally becomes feasible to establish a separate export department within the company, headed by an export manager responsible for all export functions. It should be staffed with export salesmen who are specialists in overseas business. It may sell directly to the importer abroad or through middlemen in the foreign market—commission houses, purchasing agents, resident buyers, brokers, auction houses, jobbers or independent agents, and distributors.

An export department consists of a number of divisions; each is usually headed by a manager in charge of one function—sales, credits and collections, traffic, advertising, or accounting. The manager of a sales division, for example, is responsible for hiring and training his sales staff and selecting his foreign distributors if this is the method of sale. A separate department does not have to be located at the company's main headquarters or manufacturing facilities. It usually operates from a major seaboard city.

Export sales subsidiary. Frequently, large companies find it more advantageous to handle their overseas business through export sales or trading companies, which may be established either in the United States or in a foreign country. Although relatively few domestic sales companies of this nature exist today, there are many operating as a subsidiary or a branch operation in a foreign country. These are usually created by the parent corporation in one or more countries to serve a specific overseas market or area.

Since the adoption of the 1962 amendments to the IRC, the sales trading company is less important because its earnings from foreign operations generally are taxable currently in the United States, whether or not they are distributed. The sales trading company (also known as the tax-haven company) has taken on such other functions as servicing, financing, or insurance. Many such companies have been converted into manufacturing subsidiaries or branches.

An export sales company handles all the foreign business that ordinarily would be conducted by the parent U.S. company. It usually buys goods from the parent company or other unrelated exporters, pays for them, and makes its profits from the mark-up after deduction of all expenses. As a separate entity located in a foreign land, the sales trading company does its own merchandising, extends credit, collects payments, keeps its own books, and pays taxes, if any, to the foreign government.

Earnings from foreign sales of domestic sales trading companies (but not of foreign corporations) may be consolidated with those of the domestic operations. Profits of foreign branches are included in the parent's earnings. The selling entity has its own officers and directors if it is a subsidiary, or a manager if it is a branch. A principal function of a U.S. sales company is to coordinate all the foreign sales of one or more factories of the parent company manufacturing products. If it is a foreign subsidiary, it may be responsible for coordination in a specific country or area. When the manufacturer's overseas business consists of foreign factories, branches, or assembly plants, a separate sales trading company is of particular help in handling the foreign distribution.

Domestic or foreign subsidiary export sales corporation?　Because of the many complexities of operating in world markets, it is vital to have the best-suited organizational structure. Whether a sales company should be domestic or foreign depends on such factors as (1) demand for new products, (2) degree of saturation of U.S. market, (3) foreign tariffs and other trade obstacles, (4) competition in regional markets, (5) foreign government attitudes, and—most important—(6) available channels of distribution.

Once the parent organization decides to operate abroad, the next step is to determine whether it will be more advantageous to conduct selling through (a) branches of the domestic company (or of a domestic subsidiary), or (b) foreign subsidiaries organized under the laws of the individual countries in which they are located. Both methods have pitfalls as well as benefits, but the advantages of a subsidiary usually outweigh those of a branch. However, if a sales trading entity expects a sizable operating loss in the first year, the branch method is generally preferred because the loss is deductible for U.S. tax purposes.

INDIRECT EXPORTER

An exporter with no previous experience often sells his goods abroad through a middleman. The most common of these are the combination export manager, the export merchant, the export broker, and the export commission house.

Combination export manager. The combination export manager acts as a firm's department. Often using the stationery and official documents of the manufacturer and signing them as export manager, he formulates foreign sales contracts, negotiates prices and terms, selects distributors, and handles the shipping and insurance. Sales are billed and financed by the manufacturer, who maintains control over pricing and credit policies. The combination export manager, however, has some latitude within the guidelines set by manufacturers.

Export merchant. The export merchant buys and sells for his own account. Since he gains title to the products on purchase from the manufacturer, the latter's role in exporting activity is nil. (Concomitantly, the manufacturer has also relinquished his control over final sale in the foreign market.)

Export broker. The export broker's service consists of bringing a domestic seller and an overseas buyer together. If a contract follows, he collects a broker's fee from either the buyer or the seller.

Export commission house. The export commission house acts as a representative in the United States for a foreign buyer. It locates American goods in which the foreign buyer is interested, and the buyer pays the commission house for this service.

Export house. The operations of the export house are similar to those of the export merchant; the export house buys for its own account and sells to overseas companies. It continually investigates the U.S. market for goods that meet overseas companies' specifications. Its primary duty is to fill orders for the foreign buyer, and its secondary function is to handle the transaction in the interest of the seller. The manufacturer or producer receives cash for the merchandise in the United States, from the export house, which is paid by the foreign firm.

Trading company. Another form of export merchant is the trading company, which also buys from manufacturers or producers and sells to foreign customers. The trading company also works for a profit, not a commission. It is quite similar to a pure trader, who buys and sells for his own account. Both the trading company and the pure trader are classified as general exporters.

Pure trader. The pure trader knows his foreign buyers abroad and, after scanning the U.S. market thoroughly, buys goods for them which he believes their customers have a good market for and will have no trouble in selling.

International desk jobber. The international desk jobber is a version of the pure trader, buying and selling odd lots for his own account but frequently picking up surplus commodities and other bargains. He is a one-man organization, usually operating from limited office quarters.

Purchasing agents. Operating in the United States to obtain goods for export abroad are government or company purchasing agents, usually established to buy merchandise—principally capital equipment or raw materials—in large quantities for their foreign clients. Foreign government purchasing missions and development corporations are among the most widely known. Many large private utility, mining, steel, and transportation companies located abroad also create such offices in the United States to supply their needs.

Piggybacking. A new type of indirect exporting has come to the forefront recently. Called "piggybacking," this is a voluntary cooperative program supported by the U.S. Department of Commerce. It is designed to help newcomers to international trade find export-experienced American companies that distribute compatible and noncompetitive products of other firms as a means of filling out their own sales lines abroad. Using a computer, the Department of Commerce matches "riders" and "carriers" according to their interests.

Piggybacking is not confined to Department of Commerce supervision; recently, another version of the practice has become a major technique of international marketing. It is being used more as a process through which one firm markets products manufactured by another firm through its own distribution channels. An increasing number of companies now buy portions of their product lines from local suppliers in foreign markets or in neighboring countries.

EXPORT ASSOCIATIONS AND CORPORATIONS

In an effort to bolster U.S. exports, Congress has from time to time enacted various laws that offer special privileges to export organizations.

Webb-Pomerene association. The oldest of the institutional forms resulting from laws enacted by Congress is the export trade association, also known as the Webb-Pomerene association because of the 1918 Webb-Pomerene Export Trade Act. This act permits competitors to combine in "Webb" associations for export purposes by exempting them from antitrust provisions against (1) illegal acts of price setting and (2) dividing export territories. Export trade associations fall under the jurisdiction of the Federal Trade Commission (FTC) and are subject to annual reporting. Some associations act as central agencies for their members, handling all sales and shipping operations. Others allow members to write orders and operate through their established foreign agents. A few have been created to buy the products of their members and resell them abroad.

Today there are fewer than three dozen Webb associations, accounting for about 3.5 percent of all U.S. exports. They are principally in chemical, raw materials, paper and wood products, textile, motion picture, and television industries, and in various agricultural products. Four of the largest export corporations are in sulphur, textiles, potash, and rubber. Since so few firms have taken advantage of the Webb-Pomerene provisions, the Justice Department has been urging repeal of the act. However, surveys show definite advantages in operating through an export trade association: product standardization, stabilization of credit conditions, selection of foreign sales agents, joint storage and surplus disposal, consolidation of shipments, joint advertising programs, lower bidding opportunities, larger orders, and the two original objectives of Congress (price setting and division of markets).

Western Hemisphere Trade Corporation. The WHTC, created in 1942, is a domestic corporation operating in the Western Hemisphere at a tax rate approximately 29 percent lower than is applied to other corporate income. Under the IRC, the WHTC is allowed a deduction from pretax income of the percentage resulting from a fraction whose numerator is 14 and whose denominator is the normal income tax rate. Assuming the 10 percent surcharge applies, the effective tax rate is 17.14 percent on the first $35,294.10 of income and 37.4

percent over that amount, as compared with the 52.8 percent corporate income tax and surcharge.

To qualify as a WHTC, a domestic corporation must operate within three basic requirements: (1) All of its business other than "incidental purchases" (considered to be no more than 5 percent) must be done in North, South, and/or Central America and/or the West Indies; (2) more than 95 percent of its gross income must be derived from sources outside the United States; and (3) more than 90 percent of its gross income must be derived from its active conduct of a trade or business.

According to Internal Revenue Ruling 58–56, dividends, interest received on money loaned, and gains from the sale of capital assets are regarded as passive income, not active. Therefore, if a business had more than 10 percent of its gross income from dividends, interest, and gains from sales of capital assets, it would not qualify. However, Revenue Ruling 65–290, issued in 1965, indicates that interest received by a domestic corporation on obligations owed to it by its Western Hemisphere customers for products exported by the corporation to such foreign customers is active income from foreign sources.

Two other points must be observed closely if the WHTC is not to be disqualified from the 14 percent tax differential by the Treasury Department.

First, the courts have determined that the "source" of income from the sale of goods purchased by a corporation in the United States and sold by it outside the United States depends upon where the title (with risks and all benefits of ownership) passes from the seller to the buyer. Thus it is necessary only that title to goods sold be passed outside the United States (but within the prescribed territory of the Western Hemisphere) in order to establish that the resulting income is from sources outside the United States. The Internal Revenue Service (IRS) now abides by this decision. It is important that all WHTC's insert on the bill of lading a "reservation of title" clause stating that the selling corporation retains title until the arrival of merchandise at the destination point. This "reservation of title" clause is absolutely required in the event that payment for the merchandise is made prior to the arrival of the merchandise or prior to the endorsement of the bill of lading. Even so, payment prior to the arrival of the merchandise might very well disqualify the WHTC transaction and is therefore not recommended.

Second, there is the vital problem of determining the fair amount for charging goods, services, or other items between related parties. (Frequently, the WHTC domestic corporation conducts its operations in the parent company's headquarters office and with the latter's personnel, for which the parent company charges the WHTC.)

When the WHTC merely buys from the parent company for resale, a serious pricing problem may be created. There is considerable uneasiness among American corporations over pending controversy with IRS agents concerning the criteria that tax examiners apply to prices charged in intercompany transfers. Under the "arm's length" section of the IRC, the tax authorities will disallow a pricing system that displaces profits artificially to the WHTC. A taxpayer may justify a price by comparison with a similar transaction between unrelated parties or, in cases in which the WHTC is basically a distributor, by comparison with the price it charges on resale less a distribution profit. Where these criteria are not applicable, the taxpayer may justify his price on a cost-plus basis. If none of these three standard methods can be claimed, the taxpayer may choose another method of justification if he can convince the Treasury that it is more accurate than the three designated in the regulations.

Export trade corporation. A third type of export organization relates to the most widely criticized provision of the Internal Revenue Act of 1962, which in practice does little to help U.S. exports. This is the special exclusion from foreign base sales income (so-called tainted income, which is taxed currently in the United States) for export trade income realized by an export trade corporation (ETC). The objective of this provision is that, if a controlled foreign corporation in a certain country invests in export trade assets, some income from the sale of exports of a U.S. parent corporation to unrelated customers in their countries may enjoy tax deferral in the United States if there is an increase in such assets during a taxable year. The U.S. parent company becomes taxable once there is a decrease, within certain limitations, in the investments in export trade assets.

Briefly, if 90 percent or more of the gross income of a controlled foreign corporation is derived from sources outside the United States and 75 percent or more of the gross income is derived from export trade income, Subpart F income or "tainted" income is reduced by an amount equal to 1.5 times the export promotion expenses or 10 percent of the gross receipts, whichever is less. Export trade income is income from sales to unrelated persons, outside the United States, of export property or from commissions, fees, or other services in respect of the installation or maintenance of such export property. It also includes commissions and fees or other income from industrial, financial, technical, managerial, or other services in connection with the use of patents, copyrights, franchises, and the like, in respect of which export trade income is earned or attributable to the use of export property. The usual procedure in some companies is to have the ETC make the sales to the world, and a foreign trading-holding corporation sell, manage, or service for the ETC as well as handle the sales exclusively to the country in which it is located, be it Switzerland, Panama, or the Bahamas. A principal goal is to put all possible legitimate income of the ETC and the foreign trading-holding company into the latter and to transfer as much of the legitimate expense of the foreign trading-holding company as possible to the ETC by billing the ETC for servicing and handling sales.

IMPORT INSTITUTIONAL STRUCTURE

The institutional structure covering imports into the United States from foreign countries is practically the same as the export structure, except that the transactions are handled in reverse. For instance, the import merchant usually buys goods outright from abroad, on a nonexclusive basis, and resells them in the United States for his own account.

Import representative and commission house. An import representative or resident buyer is the direct representative of a large foreign firm, for which he deals directly with the U.S. importer. The import commission house is a buyer or purchasing agent for U.S. companies, investigating foreign markets for goods and filling orders for the American importer; his secondary interest is the foreign producer.—*W. H. Diamond*

Multinational Corporations

The multinational corporation is a business phenomenon that many people discuss but very few have ever clearly defined. To some extent, then, discussions that have taken place in the past about the organization, operation, and staffing of multinational corporations have been vague and general. Some corporations have assiduously denied that they are multinational corporations (because they feel that the name has a negative connotation), while others have staunchly defended the fact that they are multinational corporations (because of the benefits which they feel derive from the designation).

In reality it would seem that, depending on one's definition, a multinational corporation could be of many kinds, from a corporation widely owned by the public throughout the world, and conducting operations in most countries throughout the world in the form of its own controlled subsidiaries, to a company which merely has extensive worldwide licensing agreements and is based in, and owned by people from, one country. The writer's preference in this regard is that the one essential element of the multinational corporation should be a wide range of ownership of the company throughout the world, since a company owned by the residents of one country, although it may have an extensive overseas operation, still relates itself too thoroughly to the dimension of size (as opposed to diversification of ownership) to be considered truly multinational. If this criterion is applied, certain internationally owned companies (for example, Shell and Unilever) would be considered more multinational than some of their major counterparts in the United States. However, in the realization that the label "multinational" is in fact applied by businessmen throughout the world to companies that do not meet this strict criterion of diversified ownership, for the purposes of this book the discussion will be concentrated less on ultimate ownership than on the organizational structure of a company with wide-ranging foreign operations. In this regard, also, it should be noted that where the term "multinational corporation" is used, it could quite as easily apply to the plural, depending on whether the organizational structure at the top level of the complex is in the form of a joint ownership of companies (for example, U.S. Time–Timex) or whether the entire organizational structure pyramids up to one company.

MULTINATIONALS VERSUS CONGLOMERATES

In studying the make-up of a "multinational" operation it appears that the term is properly used whether the operations themselves follow a distinct line of products or whether the complex would meet the definition of what the U.S. business public calls conglomerates. It is safe to say that the element of multi-product lines, when added to the dimension of foreign operations, tends to multinationalize a company to a greater extent. In fact, when the overseas operations of such companies as International Telephone and Telegraph Company and Gulf–Western Industries are considered, it appears that the multinational label might apply there to as great if not greater extent than to some of the larger U.S. corporations that deal in one product line but have historically operated abroad directly only in that product line. The main point, however, is not to engage in a discussion of conglomerate versus nonconglomerate structures but rather to observe that the conglomerate aspect often serves to accelerate the pace at which a company group will be considered multinational.

OBJECTIVES OF FOREIGN OPERATIONS

One of the better ways of analyzing the way a multinational operation functions is to review the objectives of the particular company in organizing for overseas operations. The primary considerations are to create the maximum demand for the company's products, to organize the functional as well as the corporate structure in order to maximize the company's ability to fill that demand, and finally to do these things in such a way as to produce an adequate return to the various operating units in the company as well as to any independent parties the company may be using for manufacturing, distribution, or financing. These simply stated objectives are the underlying considerations which permeate the organizational and developmental decisions that must be reached by a multinational operation if it is to advance properly. They are accomplished by considering the manner in which a multinational operation grows, the manner in which that growth is reflected in organizational development, the advantages which this type of multinational operation provides, and the disadvantages stemming from this type of operation.

GROWTH OF A MULTINATIONAL OPERATION

Over the years a standard procedure has developed whereby companies establish a growth pattern in a foreign market. The market penetration begins through a direct export approach based on the goods manufactured in the home country. (In this regard it must be remembered that the term "multinational" does not apply exclusively to companies with essentially U.S. backing.) A direct export operation generally is expanded by the use of a local distributor, appointed for a particular market, whose activities consist of carrying a line of products for the manufacturer, handling the duties of importing the goods into his country, and perhaps providing some after-sale servicing.

The use of a distributor in turn can often lead to the appointment of a local licensee to manufacture the product. This development will normally occur when the market has been developed to a stage where the use of a purely independent distributor is inefficient in terms of properly servicing the market. The use of a licensee also helps to combat the immediate problem of customs duty barriers, a matter which has become particularly important with the growth of the EEC, the European Free Trade Association (EFTA), the Latin American Free Trade Association (LAFTA), the Central American Common Market (CACM), and the Caribbean Free Trade Association (CARIFTA). Finally, the operation will often reach a point where the markets and manufacturing capabilities abroad are such that it becomes clear to the parent company that additional profits can be realized through the establishment of a local sales and/or manufacturing subsidiary. This growth pattern tends to reflect itself in differing organizational structures.

ORGANIZATIONAL STRUCTURE

To achieve multinational sales volume, companies export, use wholly owned manufacturing subsidiaries, form joint ventures, license manufacturers, have world trade associations, use foreign corporations, and resort to the WHTC. To a great extent, the organizational structure results from participation in individual country programs and manufacturing in the regional groupings previously mentioned. While, in many cases, companies might prefer to operate without a grouping of foreign subsidiaries, for strictly nationalistic reasons this eventually becomes their method of operation. Furthermore, internal company politics plays a heavy role in that, in many cases, to be president of a foreign subsidiary is preferable to being merely a branch manager.

Many multinational corporations begin their overseas operations through the use of an international division. This is generally an outgrowth of the export manager's department.

The general staff and operating divisions concept. A newer concept of organization is the choice of a number of multinational corporations (Caterpillar Tractor, for example). The concept embraces two separate areas; a general staff and operating divisions. The general staff is organized to serve worldwide needs and has worldwide responsibility for the functioning of its category of activity. The operating divisions are largely groupings of profit centers which are complete organizations. Interestingly enough, the staff and operating people are equally responsible for total results although the concept of joint responsibility is contrary to one of the commonly recognized principles of management theory. In one company at least, there seems to have been no great difficulty in having two areas (one staff, one operational) jointly responsible for the accomplishment of identified goals.

Strategic location in expansion. Given complete freedom of choice with no artificial barriers or other inhibiting considerations, companies would generally prefer to supply a market from an already existing source. Normally, less expense is involved in increasing production in an existing plant. However, when the product goes farther from a factory source, multinational companies become increasingly concerned with the time factor in providing the essential back-up of parts availability to service equipment. While dealers maintain stocks of parts to service equipment, there are practical limits to the value of parts or depth of support which can be given by an individual dealer. This factor has caused many multinational companies to establish factory depots strategically located for the distribution of service parts. In locating these new parts depots, tax matters are to be considered, since in certain instances the company is thus established as doing business in the country where the depot is located. Duty-free zones, for obvious reasons, have become attractive to this function because of the flexibility they provide. In using the depot approach, an overall worldwide strategy can be utilized by planning marketing and manufacturing to meet the requirements of areas most strategically placed so as to serve economic groupings on the most efficient basis.

Wholly owned manufacturing subsidiaries. The impact of the foregoing factors on organizational structure results in company preference for the wholly owned subsidiary when ultimate manufacturing is required. Most major companies have manufacturing and/or marketing activities in the United Kingdom, Canada, Australia, South Africa, a country in the EEC, a Far East country such as Japan or Hong Kong, and a country in the LAFTA area (serviced out of Argentina or Brazil), with perhaps an overriding WHTC set up to handle Latin American exports. Finally, the organizational structure for a multinational corporation is often sprinkled with subsidiaries in Switzerland, Hong Kong, Panama, the Bahamas, or other so-called tax-haven countries.

Tax planning and manufacturing subsidiaries. Despite the existence of tax treaties between the United States and many other countries, double taxation is a very real problem for multinational corporations because of the imprecision with which profits are measured by various taxing authorities around the world. Thus many companies are currently evaluating their intricate foreign subsidiary organization to see if they can simplify the structure to minimize double tax exposure. This is a change from tax planning in the 1950's, which was geared rather to keeping the overall tax burden at a minimum level. This type of tax planning is particularly germane when companies engage in programs to determine the harmonization of their production facilities within the regional trading groups. For example, several multinational corporations are studying the possibility of doing away with multilocation manufacturing facilities in several countries in Europe with a view to substituting one manufacturing location with satellite marketing subsidiaries in the various individual countries. While organizations of this type are being encouraged by the European merger laws, such exercises could have significant U.S. tax consequences and must be evaluated in a rational manner not influenced to any great extent by internal power struggles.

An alternative to the wholly owned subsidiary is the joint venture with a local partner. In such countries as Japan and India there is a fair amount of pressure brought to enter into a full 50–50 partnership. However, it goes without saying that if the joint venturer is not a wholly cooperative partner, the partnership is doomed to trouble in any event. In underdeveloped countries a local partner rarely can contribute a skilled work force, since there is generally no sizable float of skilled technicians. Furthermore, the U.S. practice of plowing back considerable earnings into a business is one which is not shared to a great extent in many foreign operations. Consequently, foreign partners tend to desire more sizable cash flow out of the earnings of an operation than would be expected by U.S. parties.

Another organizational feature of multinational companies is the use of licensees. While not strictly a part of the internal organization of the firm, it is definitely an aspect of the "organization" in the broad sense. Licensees are often used when the market is not sufficiently large to warrant construction of a plant for the purpose of producing the particular product to be manufactured. A licensee becomes particularly attractive where the import duty situation is such that export into the country is not a realistic alternative.

ADVANTAGES AND DISADVANTAGES OF MULTINATIONAL OPERATIONS

As companies multinationalize, research and product development are supported by a greater sales volume and economies of scale become increasingly important. This is particularly true where basic product design can be utilized the world over. The widespread distribution of greater numbers of the same product provides more thousands of hours of experience faster, which improves the product mix. Furthermore, a more efficient distribution system can be developed through multinationalization. All of these factors result in a back-up organization for continued servicing of the product on a multinational scale. The greater production population tends to attract better dealers and, being in more markets, spreads the risks of economic recession. These advantages attract investors abroad as well as in the local country, and as mentioned previously, the broad investor population tends to generate the real multinational outlook of the country.

Notwithstanding the advantages, there are a number of disadvantages in operating on a multinational basis: tariff barriers; restrictions on imports of products; shortages of hard currencies; local competitive manufacturing, necessitating the finding of ways to cope with such conditions or suffer restricted markets; nationalistic tendencies on the part of certain countries to protect local industry; shortage of capital combined with the restriction on foreign investment imposed by certain countries (for example, the U.S. Foreign Direct Investment Program and the United Kingdom Bank of England restrictions). In addition, there are the normal frictions of one company, based in one country, rubbing against the local economic fabric of another country which is the recipient of an investment.

—W. F. O'Connor

Joint Ventures

Joint ventures in overseas operations have many attractions. Entering into a joint venture may reduce the risk of operating in an uncertain economic environment; facilitate business where cultural problems may exist; allow a company with limited resources to engage in foreign business; or accelerate entry into overseas markets, forestalling competition from pre-empting opportunities. Where government concessions are necessary or regulations limit the entry of business foreign to a host country, a joint venture may be the only way American companies can penetrate certain foreign markets or gain a position in low-cost production facilities.

For companies engaged in manufacturing, joint ventures represent an attractive alternative to patent licensing or know-how agreements. A joint venture can result in an enterprise which outlasts the life of key patents. However, forming a joint venture is considerably different from a royalty agreement based upon patents, know-how, or trademarks.

NEGOTIATIONS

The intent of a foreign joint venture is the establishment of an independent enterprise by two or more partners, each of whom supplies certain ingredients needed for the initial success of the new enterprise. If the American management insists upon forming a joint venture and contributes only valuable technology, the resulting joint venture is in essence a royalty agreement. The foreign partner, no doubt, would have wished to have a licensing or know-how agreement. Except in unusual circumstances, the intent of the foreign partner is such that American management should not expect more authority in the venture operation than would be possible in a royalty agreement. Anything an American company receives in the long run that is better than royalty payments should be viewed as payment for the risks assumed. Any performance that is less than what would have been expected from a royalty agreement should be viewed as the effect of the risks involved.

On the other hand, if a joint venture is based upon an alliance more subtle than technology alone, it requires more effort from both partners and presents more difficulties during negotiations and afterward. At the outset very frank discussions should be carried on between potential partners, particularly regarding each partner's objectives and intent. Farsightedness and wisdom should be exercised with skill and candor in the beginning. After agreement is reached, patience, understanding, and very clear communication should be maintained at all times. If this style of management cannot be maintained, difficulties may arise.

Before negotiations are started, policies regarding share of ownership should be made clear. A minority stockholder position is not an enviable one if misunderstandings arise. In order to avoid problems, it is well to spell out respective areas of responsibility for each partner or to retain veto rights over certain decisions. Or, if local laws permit, election to board membership can be arranged to provide a balance of representation regardless of stock ownership. It is also well to provide a mechanism for a change in ownership if the parties so desire.

PROBLEMS

Most often, the difficulties that arise after a joint venture has been formed can be traced back to misunderstanding in intent and limited discussion of future plans during the period prior to the time the venture was established. The legality of an agreement does not guarantee success if the interests of the parties to the agreement are not in harmony. For example, a joint venture that relies upon production in the plant of a foreign partner can easily result in eventual misunderstanding regarding transfer pricing. If the success of the joint venture is dependent upon a keen marketing program but marketing strategy, plans, and policy direction are not clear, clashes with regard to these matters can arise.

Personnel. Problems common to many joint venture operations tend to originate in the personnel area. A foreign joint venture, unless it is very large and important to an American company, will most often be manned at the top by foreign nationals. Initial transfer of technology should not present problems, since it is usually readily recognized by foreign management that American firms will be superior in this regard—and, after all, this is most often the basis for a joint venture. However, in the area of management technique a foreign partner and the foreign management of a joint venture will probably be less likely to accept suggestions. The reason given will be that Americans are insensitive to cultural differences, even though the Americans in the partnership may be simply suggesting new concepts that should be adapted to the foreign scene. However, since the personnel assigned to a joint venture are not invariably equipped with broad experience overseas, such subtleties can often be lost; and Americans are not always skilled at communicating with others who have a different frame of reference.

It is usually wise at the outset to reserve the right to review and veto the assignment of personnel a foreign partner might wish to assign to a venture. It is also wise to invest considerable time and expense in bringing foreign top management personnel to the United States for intense exposure to American operations and management training before they assume positions in a joint venture. Such exposure in an American company should consist of a responsible work assignment—for example, as a member of a task force solving a key problem that has both short- and long-term implications. In this way, the joint venture top management should become more objective and flexible and more independent of a foreign partner in thinking and action.

Marketing. A variant of the personnel problem that may be viewed by American management as a separate issue concerns marketing. If the product or service offered by a joint venture depends upon astute marketing, cultural differences will be accentuated. The greater the dependence upon marketing, the more likely it will be that a joint venture form of operation will not succeed. American management much prefers to make its own mistakes in marketing because it is used to experimentation in this area. Foreign management often doesn't understand this principle and, viewing the United States from afar, imputes ulterior motives to Americans in general, basing this opinion upon Americans' supposed insensitivity to foreign cultural differences.

Ambiguity of intention. Another kind of difficulty can arise if the joint venture is founded with the intention of expanding its activities into new product or business areas which at the outset are not clear. Such an intention, without a commitment by both parties as to their respective roles, can lead to future difficulties. In addition, if the intent of the joint venture is to have an existence of its own, a limited capacity of foreign management to develop long-range plans is a difficulty often encountered.—*F. V. Fortmiller*

Foreign Patents and Licensing

Millions of dollars are spent every year by American inventors and corporations in seeking and maintaining foreign patents, yet—largely because foreign patent practice is little understood—few of these patents are ever converted into profits.

INTERNATIONAL TREATY

Most of the developed countries reward the inventor or owner of an invention with patent protection for a limited period of 15 to 20 years. In 1883 the principal industrial countries agreed to an international convention for the protection of industrial property providing equal treatment for national and foreign inventors. The treaty gives an inventor who has filed an application for patent in any signatory country a period of one year in which to file such application in any foreign member country and thereby obtain priority from his first filing date.

CHIEF USES OF PATENTS

To formulate a patent policy for foreign markets requires a knowledge of the major uses of foreign patents. The foreign patent permits the owner to profit in the following ways: It protects his rights to export sales and foreign manufacture and allows him to engage in foreign licensing and patent exchange.

Protecting export sales. When the foreign patent covers the product or the principal method of making the product, it may be used to protect export sales by not granting licenses to foreign competitors. This policy causes no conflict with the antitrust laws because the patent grant expressly states that the owner may exclude all others from making, using, and selling the patented product. However, some members of the international convention require that the foreign patent be "worked" by manufacture or by licensing within the country within three years of its effective date. To ascertain which countries have this requirement the export sales manager should consult patent counsel.

Protecting foreign manufacture. After developing substantial export sales, the patent owner may find that a larger return can be produced by manufacture abroad. Since the establishment of the EEC and the EFTA, tariff barriers between member nations have been gradually lowered, while a high duty has been maintained on imports from nonmember nations. If foreign patents of proper scope have been obtained in a foreign country, manufacture in that country is justified because the production may be protected from unlicensed competition.

Foreign licensing. In some foreign countries, the environment of business is not favorable to outside capital investment. This situation may arise from unstable government, government regulations, higher taxes, or labor problems. On the other hand, trade deficits and currency restrictions make exports to some countries very difficult. The Near East, India, Pakistan, and countries behind the Iron Curtain are markets not capable, in many cases, of being tapped by direct exports from the United States. But when a license is granted to a European firm, the licensee is frequently able to sell in these closed areas because the licensee is able to accept payment in soft currencies instead of dollars. In this way the patent owner, in effect, can use his patent to profit from larger export markets.

Patent exchanges. Foreign-owned U.S. patents can be used in cross-licensing agreements in which each party gains rights to patents in its home country which the other party may own. Where there is little export competition between the parties or where the patents relate to different products, such exchanges may not affect the competitive situation between the parties but advance the technical knowledge of each.

OBTAINING PATENTS

To reduce costs and obtain the best protection, the following steps should be taken:

1. Carefully screen the inventions to be filed abroad.
2. Select only basic inventions that have been reduced to practice; preferably, only those that have achieved commercial use.
3. Carefully select the foreign countries with regard to customs, habits, and the need for the invention in the country.
4. File in the five principal countries of EEC.
5. File all European patents through a single European patent firm so that all translations will be identical and claims can be unified in scope.
6. File the foreign applications within the convention year (within one year of the first filing in a member country).
7. Publish the invention *after* filing the first application. Premature publication will invalidate patents in many foreign countries.
8. Combine related patent applications. Several foreign countries permit the combination of two or more applications by the same inventor if the applications relate to common subject matter and if they are initially filed within one year of each other.
9. Protect improvements by filing "patents of addition."
10. To avoid premature publication, never file the first application in one of the "nonexamining" countries (Italy, Belgium, or France, for example), since publication will take place within a few months.

LICENSING DIRECTOR

If the domestic patent owner has substantial export sales or holds equity interests in foreign-based subsidiaries, the licensing function should be an integral part of the company's international department or division. The reason is that licensing in such a company is a middle course between exporting and foreign manufacture. In such a company, licensing should be the full-time assignment of a competent person, with the title of licensing director, who has technical and legal training and will be aided by competent patent counsel and technical personnel. The execution of all foreign licenses should be delegated to the director or officer in charge of international operations. It should be the responsibility of this director or officer to check proposed licenses with the domestic sales and production managers.

SCREENING

The patent owner should be aware that (*a*) not every invention that is a success in the United States will be profitable overseas; (*b*) foreign patents are expensive to get and maintain; and (c) taxes on foreign patents increase with the life of the patents. For these reasons, careful screening of the inventions to be filed abroad is essential. The selection should be made by a committee composed of the chief patent counsel, the production manager, the director of the international department, and the person charged with foreign licensing. During the screening only those inventions are selected which receive affirmative answers to the following questions:

1. Is it practical? Was it reduced to practice? Is it a feasible approach to solving a problem? Is it in use or very likely to be used by the company?

2. Is there a need for it? This means, will it satisfy an existing need within Europe? Does it run counter to some established method of European operation? Is it contrary to an established custom?

3. Can it compete? Is it more or less expensive than products now in use? Are there facilities in Europe for its production? Can it produce a profit? To cite an example that must take into account all these questions: A small motor for attachment to an ordinary bicycle will encounter much competition and a falling market in Europe; therefore, the new motor must be cheaper or use cheaper fuel that is readily available.

4. Will the patent protect? Is it likely that basic or strong claims will be obtained in the U.S. Patent Office? If not, the chances of obtaining claims under the stiff patent examinations in the Netherlands and Germany will be remote. Will the claims as issued protect the capital invested or to be invested? Will patents owned by others be required to commercialize this invention?—*Worth Wade*

LICENSING ARRANGEMENTS

One overriding rule should always be followed in dealing with a licensing situation: Think of the ultimate consequences and get the corporate attorneys to examine every issue involved.

No attempt is made here to oversimplify this complex subject, but there are some fundamental points to be checked off when considering a license arrangement. Bear in mind that many foreign companies may approach a firm with a licensing proposal and even back it with the statement that it is the only means of overcoming local hurdles to sales of the product. In this case, as in many others, merely to take their word for it is not enough. If the company has genuine interest in the market, investigate means of penetrating that market if import duties, economic controls (import license or availability of hard currency), or government protection for local competitors preclude exporting in volume. Often such a study will show that licensing is not the only alternative.

Transmission of property. A license agreement may cover many different aspects, but the heart of it is the transmission of corporate property. It may also encompass the use of patents and/or trademarks, the availability of tooling, the use of improved techniques developed by the licensor, and manufacturing and sales assistance. At times these interests are covered by separate but parallel agreements for the life of the license or a shorter period. Truly, the issue is clear, regardless of the trimmings. The licensee wants the corporate property developed over a period of time and is willing to offer in return a royalty based on units produced or dollar volume, and even an initial lump sum as an inducement for relinquishing the property. The rationale is basic: With a royalty payment the licensee obtains all the techniques necessary to go into business with a winning product. No research and development expense, no market failures, no "if," "when," or "but"—just an almost sure thing. This is not to say that the licensee will not have problems with production and sales; but if he possesses the building, personnel, equipment, and resources, the rest is almost a "master key" operation.

The licensee will usually want protection from the export of the licensor's product into his market, exclusivity as a licensee, and a guarantee that the licensor will not enter his market with an equity position. He will want as much as he can possibly get for as little as he can pay. This is good business on his part, therefore understandable, but the licensor must beware of being shortchanged.

Protecting the licensor. The main pitfall for the licensor is in making available prints, manufacturing techniques, and processes (for example), and there are properties that will not be returned to the licensor upon the expiration or cancellation of the agreement. Most countries have a limit on the length of an agreement; it may be in a range from five to 15 years. This situation poses distinct problems for the licensor in that the licensee may object to the renewal of the license (and payment of the royalties) once the technique has changed hands and the term of the agreement has expired. There are ways of solving this problem, but they are mostly related to the type of product rather than the written license. If the product is highly tooled and the tooling is made available through leasing, the control of the licensee rests with the licensor through the tooling. On occasion the product will be highly sophisticated, with certain key components available only from the licensor. There are even cases where the product has a very short life and the continuous feeding of the replacement is available only through the U.S. company.

In sum, the successful licensing agreement is based on de facto control by the licensor of the licensee rather than on any written agreement binding them, and much less on years of acquaintance or business relations. Licensees tend to question the wisdom of a continuing flow of royalties for a static technique that from their point of view has been paid for many times over. Also, an attempt to obtain a cease-and-desist order from a foreign court of law against a former licensee, who is a national of the country and usually a prominent businessman, is not only expensive but at times difficult. As pointed out, licensing is not for every company or every product. The dangers to a company in granting its know-how to others are numerous and so real that many companies will not license. However, some companies have the "right" products for licensing, and those that do have an impressive array of licensees throughout the world; their coffers are swelling because of developed processes and products that have been underwritten by U.S. demand and are producing, in addition, foreign profits. When this is the case, then by all means license. Prepare the basic program of what the U.S. company will make available, for how long, and under what conditions; then scout the markets and tailor the presentation for each one.

Quality control. One of the basic issues in a license where the use of patents and/or trademarks is involved pertains to quality and workmanship. This is also very important to the overall product image worldwide; it is a decisive point in any litigation with the licensee, as one of the services the licensor should provide continuously is supervision through quality control of the product.

Licensing should also be utilized when the company adopts an equity position, be it partly or wholly owned. Here again, the license agreement will be separate and enable the U.S. partner or parent to receive some revenue from the foreign company under an independent contract. This is quite commonly done; it provides additional leverage, especially when the U.S. company has a minority share in the ownership.—*H. L. Aizcorbe*

FINANCING INTERNATIONAL TRADE AND INTERNATIONAL MONETARY RELATIONS

The fact that each country has its own monetary system creates problems for those who buy, sell, or invest abroad. Residents of foreign countries desire to be paid in their own currency for most shipments or services sold abroad or investments made in their country. Foreign purchasers of these items must exchange their own money for the currency of the country of sale.

International Currency Systems

The international exchange of different currencies creates the need for an international currency system or an international payments mechanism.

GOLD EXCHANGE STANDARD

As World War II drew to a close, monetary authorities recognized the need for a restructured international payments system. This conclusion was made effective during the summer of 1944 at Bretton Woods, New Hampshire, when representatives of many nations met to discuss these problems and prepare an acceptable solution.

The international payments mechanism that emerged, and that in a somewhat modified form is still in effect, is the gold exchange standard. Under this system, international reserves consist of both gold and foreign exchange. The mechanism has as its center the International Monetary Fund (IMF), the charter of which was drawn up at the 1944 meeting. The IMF provides for a system of fixed pars of exchange and the limited movement of exchange rates. In addition, it grants considerable freedom for nations to pursue domestic economic policies without subordinating them to the vicissitudes of balance of payments surpluses and deficits.

Exchange rates and pars. Each of the members of the IMF adopted, in agreement with this institution, a fixed par for its currency expressed in terms of both gold and dollars. According to the IMF articles of agreement, the market rates of exchange of the members could not vary either upward or downward from this par by more than 1 percent. Most industrial nations now maintain their market rates of exchange within .75 percent of this par.

The system of fixed pars mutually links gold, dollars, and national currencies at defined and consistent rates. It also makes for exchange stability where foreign traders and investors abroad are able to avoid the risks of excessive exchange rate fluctuations.

The suspension of currencies' free convertibility into gold broke the link between the size of a nation's money stock and its gold reserves, thus mitigating the harshness of the former gold standard balance of payments automatic adjustment process. Under the modern gold exchange standard, the balance of payments adjustment mechanism is no longer automatic but must be set in motion and implemented by the government itself.

International reserves. To support the system of fixed pars and narrowly fluctuating exchange rates, the trading nations require a supply of international reserves. These reserves, which grow as a country runs balance of payments surpluses and decline as it runs deficits, serve two purposes: They enable a deficit country to continue to import at higher levels than it would without them, and they enable the country to protect its rates of exchange. As the rate of exchange declines in deficit countries, the central bank or exchange stabilization institution supports the rate by buying its own currency with these reserves.

Slightly more than half of these international reserves consists of gold; almost 40 percent is in holdings of convertible foreign currencies, principally dollars; and about 10 percent consists of drawing rights on the IMF. The drawing rights entitle a member to draw foreign currencies from the IMF and are divided into two parts: the gold tranche, which is virtually an automatic right and amounts to about 25 percent of a member's quota or subscription (with certain adjustments); and the credit tranche or drawing rights above this amount, which are not automatic but conditional.

Role of the dollar. Since the end of World War II the dollar has constituted an increasing part of the world's international reserves. The annual increments of monetary gold (total gold production less amounts hoarded and utilized by industry and the arts) have been insufficient to sustain the desired increase in these reserves, and the main burden of this growth has fallen on the dollar.

The dollars required to meet these needs have come—and can only come— from U.S. balance of payments deficits. Between 1950 and 1969, the United States ran deficits on its balance of payments in every year except 1957 and 1968 —deficits which totaled, during this period, over $30 billion. These balance of payments deficits have had two untimely effects.

First, under the Gold Reserve Act of 1934, foreign *official* holders of dollars have been able to exchange their holdings of dollars for gold on demand. In this way, the U.S. monetary gold stock, which stood at almost $25 billion in 1947, had declined to $11.9 billion in January 1970. If the gold drain were to continue, this country might be obliged to abandon the convertibility of foreign official dollar holdings into gold, undermining confidence in the dollar. Second, the growing foreign supplies of dollars have tended to make this currency somewhat redundant, prompted a loss of confidence in it, and made it easy prey to speculative attacks.

On the other hand, if the United States were to balance its external accounts or run a surplus on its balance of payments, the trading nations of the world would experience a crisis of liquidity where the growth of international reserves would fail to keep pace with the growth of world trade. Difficulties such as these were brought to a head by the devaluation of the pound from $2.80 to $2.40 in November 1967 and by the speculative attacks against the French franc in 1968, which threatened the international stability of this currency as well as that of the German mark and which later led to their devaluation and upward revaluation, respectively.

REFORM OF GOLD EXCHANGE STANDARD

After about four years of intensive study, discussion, and negotiation, a group of interested governments hammered out a new reserve asset—special drawing rights (SDR's) on the IMF, which are sometimes called paper gold. The IMF and the Group of Ten (the ten most highly industrialized nations) endorsed these SDR's in 1967 and 1968, respectively; the plan was approved July 28, 1969, by three-fifths of the members, representing four-fifths of the total rating power of the IMF, and it went into effect immediately.

SDR operation. SDR's are separate and distinct from all other drawing rights on the IMF. They are to be distributed among the members that participate in the plan in accordance with each member's IMF subscription or quota.

Participants will be assigned a quota of SDR's. Should a participant require additional foreign currency because of balance of payments deficits, it can instruct the IMF to draw down its SDR balance in exchange for an equivalent amount of convertible foreign exchange. When so instructed, the IMF will designate one or more participants to transfer their currencies to the deficit country in exchange for an equivalent increase in the designated countries' holdings of SDR's. With the SDR plan now in effect, international reserves consist of gold; foreign exchange, principally dollars; IMF drawing rights; and SDR's. A total of $9.5 billion in SDR's was available as of mid-1969 for the following three years.

Other reforms. Many government financial authorities as well as students of the problem feel that the creation of SDR's will not solve all the problems faced by the international payments system, and a number of additional reforms have been advanced. Some of these plans advocate restructuring the IMF to make it perform the work of a central bank for government central banks. Others propose freely floating or flexible exchange rates in the place of the narrow-band fluctuations of the IMF-determined rates. A very small number apparently favor a return to the old international gold standard.

Although central bankers are wary of contrived solutions, many of them appear to be leaning toward a widening of the permitted exchange rate fluctuations. Under these proposals the rates would be allowed to deviate by, say, 5 to 20 percent of par. The need for international reserves would be reduced by the adoption of a wider band, and the crises resulting from speculative pressures against national currency would be mitigated.

Other reforms or changes in the present international gold exchange standard are under consideration; they are among the important items of international business and economic cooperation that lie ahead. As long as these reforms are in the hands of the world's central bankers, however, changes in financing methods are not likely to be extensive or radical.

Black markets. Although not an exclusive result of the gold exchange standard, black markets in national currencies tend to develop under this standard where the official par of exchange overvalues the currency in question. In such cases, a black market in this currency develops with an exchange rate somewhat below the official rate.

Thus, at one time after World War II, the official par of the French franc was 350 francs to the dollar. This rate overvalued the franc, and its price on the black market was more accurately quoted at about 420 to the dollar. Later this black market became a sort of gray market with partial official recognition given to the rates of exchange that prevailed on it.

Between the end of World War II and 1958, black markets developed in many countries (some countries still have these markets) and often the black market rates became the basis of new official pars of exchange when currencies were devalued. Although dealings on the black market were generally illegal, enforcement in many countries was lax, and some legitimate foreign traders employed the facilities of these markets.—*M. J. Wasserman*

Foreign Exchange

Foreign exchange may be simply described as the purchase or sale of the currency of one nation with the currency of another nation. It follows that a foreign exchange rate is the ratio of one currency to another; ideally, it would represent the purchasing power of one currency unit compared with the other. Exchange rates are quoted in a variety of ways depending on the custom in various countries, but the end result is essentially the same. Thus a rate obtained for the deutsche mark (DM) in New York might be $0.27 (which is its approximate parity); but in Frankfurt the same rate might be expressed 3.70, meaning 3.70 DM per U.S. dollar. The relationship of one currency to the other is also *sometimes* known as the cross-rate; for example, the cross-rate for the deutsche mark to the Canadian dollar might be 3.40 DM per Canadian dollar in Frankfurt, but in Canada it would be Canadian $0.294. An important variation on this theme is the practice of quoting the Canadian dollar in discount terms in New York, while in Canada the same transaction is quoted as a premium on U.S. dollars. Thus the exchange rate in New York could be U.S. $0.925 or a discount of 7.5 percent (which is parity per Canadian dollar), while at the same time the rate in Canada would be 8.08 percent premium on the U.S. dollar. These two rates are identical, since a premium of 8.08 percent (actually, 8.080808 percent) on one currency is the same as a discount of 7.5 percent on the other. (It should be noted that the various examples used are based on markets at the time of writing and are accordingly subject to change.)

BID AND OFFER

In the previous examples only one rate, for the purpose of simplicity, has been employed in comparing the relationship (exchange rate) of one currency to another. Parity arrangements under agreements with the IMF are established in the same way, and maximum permissible trading ranges are set above and below this figure; but in the marketplace there are two exchange rates. The first is the bid side, the price which a buyer has expressed willingness to pay for a given currency; the second is the offer side at which a seller of the same currency is willing to sell. The difference between the two rates, known as the spread in the market, is by nature the same as in any other market.

INTEREST FACTOR

The purpose of this discussion is not to analyze supply-and-demand factors that influence foreign exchange rates, but the use of the ideal yardstick of purchasing power is, unfortunately, an oversimplification. Many qualifications have a bearing on exchange rates, other than the relative purchasing power of the two currencies; the effects of interest rates and confidence most readily come to mind. Favorable investment returns by way of earnings, profits, or capital appreciation will automatically attract foreign funds and place the currency of the receiving country in demand, thereby increasing its exchange rate, as long as the anticipated return is higher than available on a domestic basis—but only provided the investor has confidence in the safety of his investment. Conversely, when confidence is lacking, investment funds return to a relatively safer haven, and the currency of the "host" country becomes heavily offered and in relatively less demand; thus its exchange rate declines.

TYPES OF EXCHANGE

There are three actively traded types of exchange transactions, all of which have the bid and offer sides. These are (1) a "spot" deal, which is for immediate delivery or at least for delivery in a day or two; (2) a "future" or "forward" contract, which calls for delivery at some future date—from a very short period of days up to (in most cases) one year—supported by a contractual agreement between the customer and his bank; and (3) a "swap" transaction, which involves both a purchase and a sale, although one may be for spot delivery and the other forward, or both spot or both forward. Thus an exporter may sell his foreign exchange proceeds of sales as they are received (spot), or he may sell forward in anticipation of his receipts (future contracts). Similarly, an importer might purchase his exchange requirements on a spot or forward basis. Or an importer from Mexico who exports to Canada might swap his Canadian dollar receipts (actual or anticipated) against his Mexican peso requirements (spot or forward). As will be readily apparent, the variations are endless.

FUNCTION OF TRADER

The function of the foreign exchange trader is, basically, to meet the requirements of his customers in these various time periods and currencies and to do so without assuming undue risks for his own account as to either timing or currency fluctuations. In the final analysis this means matching the buyers against the sellers, for the various dates, either internally among his own customers, in domestic markets close at hand, or in international markets around the world.

HEDGING

One of the dictionary definitions of the word "hedge" is "to secure oneself against loss by compensating transactions on the other side." An exporter, in effect, "buys" a foreign currency when he transfers title to his merchandise in return for foreign currency. Suppose he ships on a 90-day term arrangement: He has accordingly bought the foreign funds for 90-day delivery, and if he wishes to hedge against a possible loss from exchange rate fluctuations, he enters into a compensating transaction on the other side by selling his 90-day receivable on a future-contract basis to his bank. He then knows categorically what payment in his own currency he will receive in 90 days' time, and he will be in a position to establish his profit. The exchange rate for 90-day futures could be at a premium over or a discount under the prevailing spot exchange rate, in which case the exporter will either receive a bonus or pay what in effect is an insurance premium.

Another very common form of hedging relates to investments in foreign currencies. Assume that the 90-day treasury bill in country A is .5 percent higher than in country B. If such considerations as risk and exchange restrictions are disregarded for the time being, investment funds will tend to flow from B to A. Many investors are unwilling to assume the exchange risk of converting their funds to a foreign currency and will accordingly enter a swap transaction to hedge their investment. They therefore purchase spot foreign exchange (using the funds to buy the foreign treasury bill) and concurrently sell the 90-day proceeds of the maturing treasury bill on a future-contract basis. As long as the applicable swap cost is less than the .5 percent interest differential, the investor will have a net yield higher than is available through a purchase of treasury bills in his domestic market.

While other factors influence forward exchange rates, this one of interest rates is of prime importance. Ideally, the future exchange rates between any two countries or currencies will reflect the prevailing interest rate differential in the various time periods, with the currency of the high-interest-rate country at a discount and that of the low-rate country at a premium; both tend to offset the advantage or disadvantage of moving investment funds from one country to the other.

MARKETS

From a trader's point of view, it is naturally desirable that buyers and sellers be matched up on his own book so that he repeatedly buys exchange on the bid side of the market and sells on the offer side; thereby he not only makes a profit of the spread in the market rates but also has a balanced position, both spot and forward, enabling him to sleep soundly without worries about fluctuations in rates, tie-up of capital, or such other considerations as revaluations or devaluations.

Time and cash problems. The problems arise when customer A of an American bank is a buyer of Canadian dollars spot (delivery Thursday), customer B is a seller of deutsche marks 90 days forward, customer C is a buyer of sterling for 30-day delivery, and customer D wants to swap spot Canadian (delivery Friday) against a four-month purchase of Canadian dollars. As can be readily appreciated, the ramifications are legion. The trader may say, "I'll use D's spot Canadian to deliver to customer A," but here he has a problem: A wants his Canadian dollars on Thursday, but D doesn't deliver until Friday. The trader must therefore either have the necessary Canadian dollars on hand (which ties up U.S. dollar capital in acquiring them), be overdrawn overnight on Thursday (and pay overdraft interest), or swap U.S. dollars against Canadian Thursday over Friday, whereby he buys Canadian for delivery on Thursday and sells Canadian dollars for delivery on Friday. This last course balances his receipts and deliveries for those two days but will have a price in the market (a one-day "roll over" price), which can be either absorbed (it could be advantageous or disadvantageous), or paid or charged, as the case may be, to the customer. Since this price, translated into an exchange rate, can be extremely fine, it is not hard to see why rates may vary fractionally from bank to bank.

Services are sometimes provided to customers that are not available to the banks themselves in the interbank market. For example, a customer may be provided with an option period for delivery under a future contract. No such facility exists in the interbank market, and the trader must buy or sell his forward positions for specific dates without knowing when he himself will receive payment from his customer. This causes cash problems and gives rise to many swap transactions to adjust cash flows in various currencies.

Obviously, traders around the world will develop exchange positions for various currencies and delivery dates. They then have access to domestic and international markets to enter into whatever transactions are required to tailor their positions—that is, to program their receipts and deliveries of various currencies to attain approximate balances on a day-to-day basis and also so far as their future commitments are concerned.

BROKER'S ROLE

Foreign exchange markets exist in most of the large money-market centers of the world—New York, London, Frankfurt, Montreal, Toronto, Paris. In each of these markets there are foreign exchange brokers operating privately on a brokerage basis or perhaps as salaried employees of a national banking association. In either event their role is to provide a centralized service to the interbank market to receive and disseminate bids and offers of the various types and ultimately to service the requirements of buyers and sellers. In addition the brokers provide a method of placing bids or offers anonymously. (The names of the respective bidders or offerers are given only after a transaction has been agreed to.) Thus a trader's position is not unnecessarily revealed to all and sundry, many of whom would have no interest in the specific proposal but might—for example—reduce or remove their own bid in the local market if they saw a certain currency heavily offered on a direct basis and accordingly anticipated a decline in the exchange rate.

RESIDUAL DEMAND ADJUSTMENT

The market thus far described is the interbank or "wholesale" market in which any bid or offer must be for a minimum amount (usually $250,000 or

£100,000), and very often transactions for the equivalent of many millions of dollars take place when the rate is acceptable to both parties. The prevailing rates in these interbank markets are, of course, the governing factor in establishing exchange rates in any country, since it is through this medium that any residual excess of supply or demand will be adjusted after each individual trader offsets his own sources against his requirements. Similarly, the domestic market will to a large degree offset purchases against sales, as will the international market. Thus the exchange rate will move upward in the event of overall residual demand, and downward in the event of overall supply. Thus also, the exchange rate at any given time could be only fractionally different in (for example) New York and London and Frankfurt, because otherwise it would be only too easy to buy in the low-rate city and sell in the high—which, with today's communications, can be done very quickly and economically.

RETAIL RATE STRUCTURE

Many transactions between banks and their customers take place every day in amounts far smaller than the stated minimums. In addition, business is often transacted after all markets are closed; this is particularly true with reference to European currencies because of time-zone considerations. Finally, at branch offices transactions will be consummated which will become part of the bank's exchange position only at a later date. For all these reasons, there will exist a "retail" rate structure fractionally different from the interbank market. The differential will also usually vary according to the amount of money, since (for example) amounts greater than $100,000 may warrant telegraphic advice to the exchange trader, who will then immediately take the transaction into his position and act accordingly to avoid losses, providing in return an up-to-the-minute market rate by telephone or telegraph. Such a procedure is obviously not economically justifiable for a $1,000 sale of travelers' checks. Thus the exchange rate applied to the sale of the travelers' checks will not be as fine a rate as the larger transaction. It should be remembered, however, that the rate could be in fact a better one. Assume that the head office trader had authorized a branch office to sell Canadian dollars up to a set limit at a certain rate. Before a revised rate was issued to the branch, the Canadian exchange rate has moved upward. The branch may then sell the travelers' checks at a rate more favorable to the customer than would have applied had he obtained up-to-date information by telephone or telegraph. Obviously, the reverse situation also applies; these are the perils of the game for both bank and customer. However, an elaborate communications system within any bank—Telex or private wire—is designed to minimize these risks for both the bank and its customers.

EXCHANGE INSTRUMENTS

Foreign exchange is bought and sold in many forms. Various types of payment may be proffered, and although they may all be in one currency, they have in fact different values.

Cash (banknotes). Consider a situation where Canadian dollar banknotes were used in New York as payment for a cashier's check or for a telegraphic remittance in U.S. dollars to Miami. The American bank would be confronted with a disbursement on the same day or the following day at latest. The bank can pursue one of four courses with the Canadian banknotes: It may ship them to Canada to be credited to its Canadian dollar account; ship them to a correspondent bank; hold them until enough have been accumulated to warrant making a cash shipment; or retain them in anticipation of selling them to customers who may be traveling to Canada. In all cases the bank is faced with shipping costs or loss of interest through holding a nonearning asset, or a combination of both. Accordingly, a lower exchange rate may be accorded to offset these costs.

Mail transfers, drafts, or checks. A bank receiving payment for an exchange transaction will in no case receive credit in its account until the payment instructions or the drafts or checks have physically reached their destination by mail, air courier, or other delivery method. Here, again, there will be an interest loss unless the bank's payout on one side coincides with its receiving credit on the other.

Cable or telegraphic transfers. Transfers by cable or telegram are executed immediately upon receipt and consequently are the most satisfactory method of settlement to the recipient. Particularly when large amounts are involved, the loss of interest for even one day can be substantial, and exchange rates will accordingly be geared to the type of payment being received in relation to the type of payment the bank will be asked to make.

MONETARY AREAS, BLOCS, AND ZONES

As noted previously, many countries use the U.S. dollar in their international trade and finance, but there is no "dollar area" in the strict sense of the term. A *monetary area* is comprised of a center (metropolis) and several member nations which employ the currency of the metropolis for international financial transactions. Such centers provide their members with a widely used money, the facilities of their well-developed financial institutions, and a money market. The areas or zones also make it possible for member nations to pool their reserves, institute and enforce more or less uniform import and exchange controls, and establish common administrative regulations relating to monetary, credit, and fiscal policies.

The three most important monetary areas are presently the sterling area, the franc zone, and the escudo area. Of lesser importance are the Dutch guilder area and the Spanish peseta area. A ruble area is sometimes referred to because the ruble is widely used in international transactions within the European Communist bloc. But it lacks the basic characteristics of the other monetary areas just mentioned: reserve pooling, a common unit for international payments, and uniform monetary regulations.

The sterling area. The largest of the several monetary areas as here defined is the sterling area. It has its origins in the mercantilist period of economic development. Its members were bound together through the years by the common use of the pound, with London as the financial center, for international transactions. The sterling bloc was organized in 1931 when the United Kingdom dropped the gold bullion standard. In 1939 the bloc was supplanted by the sterling area. It was through the use of some of the pooled reserves of scarce foreign exchange, earned largely by member countries, that the United Kingdom was able to finance needed purchases during World War II.

The area's metropolis (center) has subsequently arranged for similar use of the exchange earnings of members to finance international transactions. That is, members have permitted the United Kingdom to use their scarce currencies in exchange for sterling credits. The following are presently members of the sterling area: Australia, Barbados, Botswana, Ceylon, Cyprus, The Gambia, Ghana, Iceland, India, Irish Republic, Jamaica, Hashemite Kingdom of Jordan, Kenya, State of Kuwait, Lesotho, Libya, Malawi, Malaysia, Malta, New Zealand, Nigeria, Pakistan, Western Samoa, Sierra Leone, Singapore, South Africa, South West Africa, People's Republic of Southern Yemen, Tanzania, Trinidad and Tobago, Uganda, Zambia, together with all British Dominions, Protectorates, Protected States, and Trust Territories not previously mentioned, except Canada and Rhodesia. The Maldive Islands are administratively treated as being within the sterling area. (*Nineteenth Annual Report on Exchange Restrictions,* International Monetary Fund, Washington, D.C., May 1968.)

The franc zone. Although not so widely employed as the pound sterling, the French franc also is a leading international currency. The franc zone is a highly organized institution with relatively uniform administrative and budgetary policies in effect among the members. The zone presently consists of (1) the countries of the West African Monetary Union (Dahomey, Ivory Coast, Mauritania, Niger, Senegal, Togo, and Upper Volta); (2) the countries of the Central African Customs and Economic Union (Cameroon, Central African Republic, Chad, Congo [Brazzaville], and Gabon); (3) three North African countries (Algeria, Morocco, and Tunisia) and two other countries (Malagasy Republic and Mali).

Although local currencies are employed by some of the members for domestic business, the franc is used for international transactions. The banks of issue of several members are under the general control of the Bank of France, and such banks keep their reserves in the pool of metropolitan France (Caisse Centrale de la France d'Outre-Mer).

The existence of the zone, together with tariffs and other trade regulations, has tended to channel the trade of overseas members to metropolitan France. In contrast to the situation in the sterling area during long periods, it is the members of the franc zone who have very often had to draw on the foreign exchange earnings of metropolitan France in order to sustain their international trade, rather than the other way around.

The escudo area. A distinctive feature of the escudo area, whose metropolis is Portugal, is that it has resulted in a greater degree of economic integration among the members than has resulted in either the sterling area or the franc zone. At the same time members have some autonomy in administering their own financial affairs. Although several different currencies are used within the area, each has a fixed par in terms of the Portuguese escudo, and the latter is generally used both in transactions among members and between the area and outside nations.

Portugal has been heavily dependent upon the foreign exchange earnings turned in by the overseas provinces to support her foreign trade, since the metropolitan area often experiences a deficit on its balance of payments.

International transactions with countries with which Portugal has bilateral payments agreements are settled through clearing accounts maintained in U.S. dollars for Greece, Israel, and Turkey; in pounds sterling for Poland; and in escudos or currency of the partner country for Czechoslovakia, East Germany, and Hungary. In exceptional cases, payments to nonresidents may be made by expediting escudos to the nonresident account.

Significance of monetary areas. From the point of view of the exchange trader, the existence of monetary areas tends to promote uniformity in the exchange system because of the wider use of common regulations and practices. Too, the trader has less often to deal with unimportant currencies. From the broad perspective of international commerce the pooling of foreign exchange has enabled Portugal and, to a lesser extent, the United Kingdom to maintain a volume of international trade that probably would have been impossible otherwise. In contrast, it has been possible for exchange-rich metropolitan France to support the trade of franc zone members and utilize zone arrangements for the distribution of government aid to these members.—*C. E. Lawson*

The Eurodollar Market

The Eurodollar market came into existence in its modern form during the 1950's and grew rapidly to $40 billion at the end of 1969. It is an international market not restricted to Europe, although its center is more or less in London. The market is composed of other currencies besides the U.S. dollar, despite the fact that the dollar accounts for over 80 percent of the volume of the transactions. A Eurodollar deposit is created when banks accept deposits in foreign currencies. The transaction, if in dollars, is based upon a deposit in a U.S. bank. The ownership of the U.S. deposit changes from the original owner to the accepting bank, but the deposit does not disappear. Foreign banks, including U.S. branches abroad, stand ready to accept dollar deposits and to make loans with a small spread between bids and offers. Rates are published daily for call money and for deposits with maturities up to one year. Longer-term deposits are negotiated.

Borrowing rates in the Eurodollar market are generally more favorable than those in the European currency markets but somewhat higher than comparable U.S. rates, although arbitrage operations keep the rates relatively close. The purposes for which Eurodollar loans are made vary; financing trade is one of the most important. Only firms with excellent ratings and a sufficient cash flow in dollars or convertible currencies for repayment are eligible for Eurodollar credits. The market for Eurodollars is affected by international credit conditions, confidence in various currencies, the U.S. balance of payments position, and restraints on international transactions, among other factors. Recently, official monetary institutions have operated in the market to promote its stability.

The Eurodollar market increased the role of the dollar in international transactions and strengthened it in the exchange markets at a time when dollar claims resulting from the large U.S. deficits had become difficult to manage. It has allowed U.S. foreign branches and affiliates to obtain funds in excess of the amounts which would otherwise be available in the markets of the host country. The Eurodollar market has also helped integrate European money and capital markets and stimulate the growth of international trade by easing the transfer of money to alleviate conditions in particular areas. Nevertheless, the size of the flow of funds between countries has caused some official concern and has led to restraints by certain monetary authorities.

BALANCE OF PAYMENTS

The balance of payments is a statistical summary of the transactions of the residents of one country with those of the rest of the world during a specified period. The balance of payments, unlike the balance sheet of a business firm, does not reflect cumulative values. The term "resident" also has special meaning in balance of payments statistics. The residents of a country are not only the individuals residing there but also the branches and subsidiaries of foreign companies.

The most important classifications of accounts in the balance of payments are goods and services, unilateral transfers, capital accounts, and official reserves. Goods and services are further classified as merchandise, transportation, travel, fees and royalties, income on investments abroad, and a miscellaneous category for other services. Only the remitted portion of earnings on foreign investments is included in income. The balance of goods and services accounts becomes a part of the gross national product (GNP).

Unilateral transfers include private remittances abroad and government grants, pensions, and other transfers. This account is debited or credited to offset the real or financial resources transferred to or received from foreigners and is necessary because there is no quid pro quo for these transfers.

Direct and portfolio investments of the United States in other countries and foreigners' investments in the United States are shown in the capital accounts. Direct investments are those which give a controlling interest in a foreign firm; usually, 10 percent is considered sufficient. Portfolio investment includes all other private long-term claims. The long-term claims of the U.S. Government arise primarily from various foreign assistance programs. Short-term claims other than official U.S. reserves reflect largely banking claims.

U.S. official reserves are composed of gold, foreign exchange holdings of the government, and the gold tranche position in the IMF. The gold tranche position is calculated by subtracting the IMF's holdings of a member's currency from the member's quota. The member has virtually an automatic right to borrow from the IMF up to the extent of its gold tranche position. The United States has maintained extensive holdings of convertible currencies since 1961 and participates in a swaps network that can provide additional exchange when needed. Gold remains the primary reserve asset and the ultimate means for the short-run settlement of international accounts.

Recording methods. The balance of payments always balances, since accounts are maintained in accordance with principles of double-entry accounting. The official summary of the U.S. balance of payments is presented in this manner and shows no surplus or deficit. Nevertheless, surpluses and deficits may be calculated by grouping certain accounts for analytical purposes. At the present time, the United States uses two of many possible measures—liquidity and official reserves transactions. The deficit on the liquidity basis is the change in official reserves and the change in liquid liabilities to all foreigners. Liquid liabilities are short-term claims maturing within one year. The official reserve transactions basis differs from the liquidity method mainly by the inclusion of changes in short-term liabilities to official foreign agencies, for only these institutions may buy U.S. gold. The remaining short-term liabilities to foreigners are grouped with other capital transactions.

Balance of payments equilibrium. Since there are numerous ways to calculate surpluses and deficits, there is no clear relationship between surpluses and deficits and equilibrium. However, the transactions reflected in the balance of payments affect various assets and liabilities, and these changes must be sustainable over time. In the case of the United States, which is often called the world banker, indication of equilibrium may be found in the relationship between its reserve assets and liquid liabilities. If outflow of gold together with a build-up of short-term liabilities is incompatible with the position of the dollar in international finance, the balance of payments may be said to be in disequilibrium. Despite consistently large deficits, the United States has rapidly enlarged its net foreign investment position; that is, its total assets abroad have grown faster than its liabilities even though the reverse is true in the case of short-term assets and liabilities. Nevertheless, the balance of payments must reflect sustainable relationships among all the transaction accounts to be in long-run equilibrium, and this has not been the case in the United States for almost two decades. Only a large initial reserve and the underlying strength of the U.S. economy have permitted the situation to continue.—*R. M. Ware*

Financing Foreign Trade

There are four basic methods of financing international transactions: the commercial bill of exchange; bank financing or the commercial letter of credit; the bank draft; and the open or book account. Each method has many variations.

COMMERCIAL BILL OF EXCHANGE

The use of the commercial bill of exchange or draft can be illustrated by an example. Assume that an American manufacturer of men's clothing decides to purchase some British tweed. The cost of the tweed is £100,000, and the terms provide for payment in 90 days.

Documenting the transaction. When the tweed is ready, the British mill prepares its invoice, obtains a consular invoice from the nearest American consulate, places the agreed insurance, and receives a bill of lading (B/L) from the steamship company forwarding the shipment. These documents, together with any others required, are attached to a 90-day draft drawn on the American importer.

Collecting the draft. The British mill delivers these documents to its bank with instructions to collect the draft. The British bank forwards the draft and the documents to its American correspondent or branch bank, which presents the draft to the importer. If the transaction was on a documents on acceptance

(D/A) basis, the importer is given the B/L and other documents when he accepts the draft, and he can claim the goods when they arrive. If he does not accept the draft, the documents are not transferred to him and the exporter retains title and possession of the tweed. In some transactions, however, the documents are transferred only when the draft is paid (D/P). Had this transaction been made on a C.O.D. basis, the exporter would have drawn a sight draft on the importer, payable when the importer had seen the draft. The B/L and other documents would have been delivered to the importer as soon as he saw and paid the draft.

Ninety days after accepting the draft, the American importer must find £100,000 to meet his obligation. He can purchase the required pounds from his own bank or any large commercial bank or from a foreign exchange dealer.

The British mill is the owner of the accepted draft and could do any one of several things with it. It could hold the draft until maturity and collect its face value from the importer. It could sell the draft to a bank or dealer in the United States, the United Kingdom, or any financial center. The purchaser of the draft would pay its face value less the discount at the going interest rate for a draft of this type for the number of days the draft had to run.

Hedging the transaction (forward exchange). The rate of dollar-pound exchange could have either risen or fallen during the 90 days that separated the importer's acceptance of the draft from its maturity date. When he accepted the draft, the rate might have been, say, $2.40 to the pound, but when the draft matured, the rate might have stood at $2.42. Under these conditions the tweed would have cost the importer $242,000 instead of $240,000; he would have lost $2,000 through the change in the exchange rate. Had the pound fallen in terms of dollars, the importer would have stood to gain.

The importer could have avoided being an unwitting speculator in foreign exchange by hedging the transaction through the purchase of forward pounds for delivery in 90 days. The importer's bank or any large commercial bank would ordinarily have sold the importer the pounds for future delivery at the time that the importer accepted the draft. The price of these forward pounds would have been the spot (immediate) rate for pounds plus or minus the short-term interest rate differentials prevailing between New York and London. If the interest rates were higher in London than in New York, the forward rate would probably have been at a discount, or lower than spot, in New York; if higher in New York than London, the rates would probably have been higher than spot or at a premium. Other factors, principally the demand and supply for forward exchange, could also affect this rate. Once the importer had purchased pounds for future delivery, he need not worry about fluctuations in the rate of exchange, for he had already hedged, or covered, his exchange risk.

LETTER OF CREDIT FINANCING

When the exporter has doubts about the importer's credit-worthiness, he is likely to employ a financing method that offers greater protection. The most widely used method employs bank financing through the commercial letter of credit.

Utilizing bank credit. The American importer, if he lacked available funds to pay for the tweed, would first have established a line of credit at his bank sufficient to enable him to cover the cost of the tweed. His bank would then instruct its London branch or correspondent bank to issue a letter of credit in favor of the British mill, authorizing the mill to draw drafts on the branch or correspondent for a total of £100,000 payable 90 days after sight. A summary of the principal conditions of the transaction would be incorporated in the text of the letter of credit.

When the tweed had been shipped, the British mill would go to the London bank that issued the letter of credit and, armed with the required documents, draw a draft which this bank would accept if the documents corresponded to the conditions set forth in the letter of credit. The mill would then turn the documents over to the bank, which would forward them to the American importer through its parent or correspondent bank in the United States, and the importer would be able to claim the tweed upon its arrival.

A frequently used credit arrangement between the bank that issues the letter of credit and the importer involves a trust agreement. Under such an agreement the bank takes title to the imported goods financed by the letter of credit but releases the merchandise to the importer under stipulated trust conditions. As the importer sells the goods, he reimburses the bank.

Collecting the draft. The British mill now has a bank acceptance that could be discounted at a lower rate of interest than a commercial acceptance. The mill could either hold the draft until maturity or sell it for cash to a bank or a dealer in foreign exchange. Upon maturity, the holder of the draft would present it to the accepting bank for payment. This bank would debit the account of its American correspondent, branch, or parent for £100,000 and forward the draft. The American bank would either debit the account of the importer for the dollar equivalent of the face of the draft or make arrangements for him to pay for it under his line of credit.

To avoid the risk of exchange rate fluctuations, the American importer should have arranged to buy forward pounds for the amount of the transaction at the time that he consummated his arrangements. Had this transaction been on a cash basis, the British mill would have drawn a sight draft on the London bank and presented it for payment at the time that it turned over the required documents to it.

Other uses of bank acceptances. Banks often make use of bankers' acceptances to raise or borrow short-term money in foreign markets. Thus, if a New York bank needed French francs, it could draw on its Paris branch or correspondent bank for the amount and for the number of days for which the francs were needed. This draft, when accepted by the branch or correspondent, could be sold (discounted) on the Paris market and the drawing bank would then have the use of the francs for the tenure of the draft.

BANK DRAFT

Much of the trade in unilateral transfers (gifts), services, and capital, as well as in some merchandise shipments, is financed by the use of the bank draft.

Use of bank draft to make payments abroad. Large banks that do a substantial volume of foreign trade financing maintain deposits denominated in the local currency in correspondent or branch banks located in foreign financial centers. In return, the foreign branches or correspondents generally maintain deposits in these large banks.

If a resident of the United States wanted to send money to family or friends abroad (unilateral transfer or gift), he could go to one of these banks, which would then draw a draft on its branch or correspondent bank in the country in question for the amount of foreign currency demanded. The bank would furnish this draft to the American donor at its selling rate for the foreign currency.

The donor would mail the draft to his recipient; after clearing, it would be debited to the account of the American bank on the books of the foreign branch bank or correspondent. A similar procedure could be followed when paying for services purchased or an investment made overseas.

Receipt of foreign currencies. The larger banks usually stand ready to buy foreign currency from their customers who receive it. Thus, if an American resident is paid in Italian lire, he could sell them to one of these banks at its buying price for lire. The bank in question could deposit these lire in its account with its Italian correspondent or branch bank and thus build up its lira holdings for future sale to customers.

Foreign currency holdings and the rate of exchange. Thus a bank's holdings (deposits abroad) of foreign currencies depend upon its sales and purchases of foreign currencies. These holdings increase with receipts and decline with payments abroad, and the bank's buying and selling rates for foreign currencies are a function of the demand and supply for the currency in question. The rate of exchange of a country tends to rise, in terms of other currencies, with a balance of payments surplus (excess of receipts from abroad over payments) and to fall with a deficit (excess of payments abroad over receipts.)

OPEN OR BOOK ACCOUNT

Formerly, but a very small fraction of international trade was financed on the open or book account method, but today more and more foreign trade is financed in this way. When payment of such an account falls due, the debtor frequently settles by use of a bank draft.

The open or book account method is widely used in financing transactions between parent firms and their overseas subsidiaries. Such firms frequently buy and sell from one another and carry these reciprocal purchase and sales transactions on their books. At agreed intervals the accounts are settled, with the debtor remitting the net balance due the creditor firm.

INSURING FINANCIAL RISKS

In addition to the usual commercial risks of nonpayment that characterize domestic trade—and that are substantially greater in international trade—foreign trade is subject to the political risks of inability to obtain payment as a result of currency inconvertibility, war, or nationalization of property.

FCIA and Ex-Im Bank policies. Insurance against political risks is obtainable in the United States from two sources: the Foreign Credit Insurance Association (FCIA) and the Export-Import Bank of Washington (Ex-Im Bank). The FCIA insures both credit and political risks. The organization consists of a group of some 60 private casualty insurance companies and the Ex-Im Bank.

Credit risks up to 180 days' duration are called short-term and are insured jointly by the private insurance companies, which are members of the FCIA, and the Ex-Im Bank. Credit insurance in excess of 180 days and up to five years, as well as political insurance, is underwritten by the Ex-Im Bank. Both commercial credit and political insurance may be obtained usually for 90 percent of the sums involved. When a firm has obtained insurance on invoices payable from 181 days to five years, it can assign the FCIA policy for a loan on a nonrecourse basis from its bank.

Ex-Im Bank loans. If a foreign buyer contemplates the purchase of a substantial amount of capital equipment from U.S. suppliers and ordinary commercial bank financing cannot be obtained, the Ex-Im Bank will frequently aid in financing the transaction. In some cases the loan is made directly to the foreign purchaser of the capital goods; in others, the American exporters' drafts on the foreign purchasers are discountable on a nonrecourse basis by the Ex-Im Bank.

AID Investment Guarantee Program. U.S. firms making certain *new* direct investments overseas (in branches, subsidiaries, and affiliates abroad) can purchase insurance, at a nominal cost, guaranteeing the payment of both the income and the principal of the investment against expropriation or nationalization, impediments to currency convertibility, and war. Such guarantees are not available against ordinary commercial risks. This program is administered by the Agency for International Development (AID). Investment guarantee insurance is limited to investments in countries with which the United States has investment guarantee treaties.—*M. J. Wasserman*

U.S. Government and International Agencies

Numerous institutions and agencies have been created, for the most part since the end of World War II, to assist in solving problems with respect to the international movement of short- and long-term capital. Of particular interest to the U.S. businessman are the programs conducted by the U.S. Government and by the United Nations (UN) through its affiliated institutions.

UNITED NATIONS INSTITUTIONS

Four institutions with a major interest in world financial affairs have been established under the auspices of the UN. Membership in these organizations has been widespread among the countries of the free world. Two of the institutions, the International Monetary Fund (IMF) and the International Bank for Reconstruction and Development (IBRD) were established in the mid-1940's; the International Finance Corporation (IFC) came into existence in 1956; and the International Development Association (IDA), in 1960.

IMF. The problems associated with financial chaos in the 1930's and exchange controls during World War II convinced the governments of most countries of the need for cooperation in international monetary matters. The IMF, with a membership of more than 100 countries, is designed to promote stability in the foreign exchange markets and to develop a multilateral payments system free of quantitative restrictions.

The IMF has advocated fixed pars of exchange in the belief that stable exchange rates induce certainty and confidence in world trade and investment. According to the articles of agreement of the IMF, member countries are to peg the market rate of exchange within 1 percent above and below par. If a country experiences difficulty maintaining a given par of exchange and finds its own foreign exchange reserves diminishing, it is able to borrow a certain amount of reserves from the IMF.

If a country's payments disequilibrium persists, the assumption is made that the existing exchange rate is unrealistic. Under these circumstances the IMF assists in providing an orderly adjustment to a new par of exchange.

During almost 25 years of operation, the IMF has provided balance of payments loans amounting to about $15 billion and has helped avert crisis in the world financial system. Despite improvements in the structure and operations of the institution, there is some feeling that the system is vulnerable to serious disturbances. Accordingly, there has been discussion among monetary authorities of the need for alterations in foreign exchange markets and in the IMF itself.

IBRD. The IBRD or World Bank, with a current membership in excess of 100 countries, was established to provide long-term credit for purposes of reconstruction and development. During almost 25 years of operation, it extended loans equivalent in value to about $12 billion, in its early years largely to European countries and in more recent years to the developing countries.

The IBRD extends credit for worthwhile projects to member governments and to private firms able to secure a guarantee from their governments. The bank is not allowed to undertake projects which might otherwise be financed by private enterprise; it is not to compete with private investment. Actually, the fact that the greatest share of the bank's loans has been used for the development of electric power and transportation has probably stimulated private investment in contiguous areas requiring such facilities.

IFC. The IFC, with an authorized capital stock of about $100 million and a membership of approximately 80 countries, was designed to promote the expansion of productive capacity through direct investment in conjunction with private investors. It provides funds to business firms in member underdeveloped countries through the purchase of nonvoting securities in such firms. These funds, which supplement resources the firm must already possess, are usually available in amounts of no less than $100,000. After a time during which the firm has an opportunity to become firmly established, the IFC sells its holdings to private interests. In effect, the corporation possesses a revolving fund for continued use in promoting private enterprise. The IFC also serves as an intermediary to bring together private capital, management, and investment opportunities.

IDA. The IDA was also designed to provide financial assistance to developing countries. It is unique in that the terms of its loans are more favorable than those specified by most lending institutions. Credit is sometimes extended for a term of 50 years, repayment may not begin for as long as ten years, and there may be no interest charge.

Development loans can be extended either to governments or to private enterprise; they are extended only in instances in which projects would not otherwise be undertaken by private firms because of an anticipated low rate of return.

During its first eight years of operation, IDA extended development credits equivalent to about $1.8 billion. About two-thirds of the total was for projects in Asia and the Middle East, largely for transportation and industry.

U.S. GOVERNMENT AGENCIES

U.S. Government operations have become increasingly important in the movement of short- and long-term capital. Particularly significant are the Ex-Im Bank, the FCIA, and activities now conducted under AID (see also page 8·47).

Ex-Im Bank. The Ex-Im Bank was created in 1934. Its major function is to promote the exportation of U.S. commodities by making loans to American firms to facilitate foreign sales and to foreign borrowers seeking American goods.

In the period following World War II, a large share of the bank's loans financed exports for European reconstruction. Loans in recent years have been employed more frequently for exports for development in low-income countries. The bank serves as an agent for the U.S. Government and assists in securing a variety of international political objectives.

FCIA. The FCIA was created in 1962 to promote U.S. exports by offering insurance to exporters against credit and political risks. The association, which consists of a number of private U.S. insurance companies and the Ex-Im Bank, will provide reimbursement if nonpayment by the foreign importer arises out of insolvency, inconvertibility, war, or nationalization. The policies available are either short- or medium-term in nature; in order to qualify an exporter must provide certain evidence and information.

In comparison with the export credit insurance systems of other countries, U.S. export credit insurance was started relatively late. Interest in FCIA has increased significantly during its years of operations.

AID. The U.S. Government has maintained a program of foreign assistance since the end of World War II. Bilateral assistance now provided under AID is either economic or military in character and has ranged in amount from $3 billion to $3.5 billion in recent years.

Assistance is currently provided to about 75 countries, in some instances in the form of grants; in other instances, in the form of loans. Virtually all assistance is "tied"; the proceeds must be used for the procurement of U.S. goods and services.

The U.S. aid program reflects a number of objectives: the promotion of the economic development of low-income countries; the development of export markets for U.S. goods and of a source of supply of essential imports; the containment of communism; and the enhancement of the military security of the United States.

The Investment Guarantee Program is also administered by AID. Under this program the private U.S. investor can secure insurance on new foreign direct investments at a nominal cost against the risks of inconvertibility, expropriation, and war loss.

U.S. FIRMS AND THE FINANCIAL INSTITUTIONS

Although the various U.S. Government and UN institutions are important in world financial markets, it is apparent that they do not compete with or substitute for the operations of private business firms. In fact, the aggregate operations of these institutions serve to expand profit opportunities for U.S. trade and the U.S. investor by providing a framework for certainty in financial transactions, providing capital for basic development projects, and extending short-term credit and guarantees for export trade.—*C. W. Hultman*

Foreign Investment Analysis

U.S. industry can move its skills and products abroad in any one of three ways. It can export, license, or make a direct investment in a foreign country. Of all these methods, a direct investment more permanently commits a company to a certain locality and scale of operations. This limitation is true for any investment, but with the many differences and uncertainties of overseas operations, these considerations are particularly critical in foreign investments. It is not surprising, therefore, that the analysis and evaluation of overseas investments are among the most crucial aspects of international business management. Generally, this important process involves three basic steps: (1) an assessment of the overall investment climate of the country where the investment is being considered, (2) an analysis of the estimated profitability of the specific investment proposal, and (3) a close evaluation of the funds flow aspect of the proposal.

INVESTMENT CLIMATE EVALUATION

A foreign investment, like any other, must be justified by the earnings to be created over its life. Also, the resulting return must be proportional to the risk. In a foreign investment a country's investment climate is often the most important consideration in determining this risk.

One of the key elements in a country's investment climate is its general attitude toward private foreign investment. With a domestic investment there is little question on this point, but this is not necessarily the case for a foreign investment. Political as well as economic nationalism besets the world, and many a foreign nation still holds skeptical, Marxian views of capitalism. The foreign investor should realize that these negative attitudes can take their most extreme form in acts of nationalization and expropriation of foreign investments. Ideally, guarantees against expropriation will exist in any foreign country where an investment is being considered. When this is not possible, a country's history on this issue as well as any current attitudes should be carefully studied. A related but less extreme hazard can be found in state-owned and -operated industries which abound and flourish under favorable treatment in many foreign economies. The prospective foreign investor is equally well advised to learn in advance to what extent they may be his competition.

Other key factors that need to be included in an evaluation of a country's investment climate are its political maturity and stability, its economic plans and prospects, its balance of payments, and its foreign exchange outlook.

When all these considerations are taken together, it is not the total presence or absence of favorable investment climate that is important but rather the balance between risk in the investment climate and the potential profits of the investment under consideration.

PROFITABILITY OF PROPOSED INVESTMENT

The process of estimating the earnings that will provide the anticipated return on investment is the second critical step in the analysis of a prospective foreign investment. Forecasts of revenues and costs will be required for this purpose. However, the heart of the process involves the development of bases for these projections, which realistically take into account the differences and complexities that can be expected in foreign operations. For example, in most foreign countries inflation is greater than in the United States. In many countries there is also the threat of devaluation. To maintain long-term profit margins in the face of these conditions, frequent price increases will be necessary to keep pace with inflation and/or devaluation. Revenues should not be projected under either the assumption—implicit or explicit—that this will be possible unless competitive price pressures and/or the possibility of outright government price controls have been appropriately assessed.

Cost estimates for an overseas project can also present problems. One of the frequently advanced reasons for an overseas investment is to obtain lower costs of operation, but the foreign investor always needs to be sure that these cost advantages are not overestimated. For example, labor savings (the most frequent economy) can be eroded away by such factors as extensive social and fringe benefits that must be paid for by employers, hostile and belligerent labor relations that bring about lost time through work stoppages and strikes, and less skilled and trainable work forces.

Nonoperating costs such as interest can also differ significantly in a foreign operation. Foreign interest rates almost always reflect the significantly higher rates of inflation in other countries and for this reason raise the cost of any local capital that may be used to finance the investment.

FUNDS FLOW ANALYSIS

Once all the assumptions and projections for an investment have been developed, some sort of quantitative technique will be used to translate them into a return on investment. It is important to note that, whatever the method, earnings in terms of cash will be the primary criterion for measuring return. Furthermore, these so-called cash flow methods implicitly assume that funds to be generated by the investment will flow freely and in dollars to the investor. In a foreign investment this basic premise is not necessarily true, because the investor's return primarily accrues through profit remittances to the United States that can be limited in the following ways: (1) Profit remittances or dividends may be limited by law to a certain percentage of invested capital; (2) exchange controls which restrict the repatriation of earnings altogether can be imposed.

It is evident that the free flow of funds cannot always be taken for granted. When this is the case, the foreign investor should make certain that the real facts of the situation do not become distorted by the quantitative techniques that he uses for investment evaluation.

Although these comments touch on some of the key problem areas in foreign investment analysis, they are far from a comprehensive checklist for the foreign investor. They do, however, suggest the type of analysis that should serve as the basis for a foreign investment decision rather than superficial or simplistic assumptions regarding the real but challenging business opportunities in foreign operations.

Protecting the Direct Foreign Investment

More and more international business undertakes its commitment to a world enterprise in the form of direct foreign investment; in other words, the establishment and permanent operation of a business entity, usually as an affiliated company in a foreign country.

As is the case with any prospective business venture, the profit incentive in this particular approach carries with it certain risks. One of the greatest and most common risks is the adverse financial effect that devaluation can have on the earnings and capital of such a direct foreign investment.

THE DEVALUATION PROCESS

Although devaluation has always been a major concern of the foreign investor, the dramatic fall of the British pound and the currencies of 20 other major countries in late 1967 has highlighted its relevance and prevalence to the international businessman.

The process of devaluation is relatively simple: A government modifies the official rate of exchange between its own currency and U.S. dollars or gold. In the British devaluation, the government devalued the pound from $2.80 to $2.40. From November 18, 1967, therefore, 0.42 pounds were required to purchase one U.S. dollar, rather than 0.36.

FINANCIAL EFFECTS OF DEVALUATION

In general terms, the financial effect of a devaluation on the direct foreign investment is dependent upon the following factors: (1) the foreign affiliates' local-currency, working-capital position at the time of devaluation; (2) the level of current dollar assets or liabilities held by the foreign affiliates at the time of devaluation; (3) pricing strategies to protect dollar margins on goods in inventory at the time of devaluation; and (4) longer-term pricing strategies to insure adequate recovery of depreciation expenses relating to original dollar investments. Some simple, hypothetical figures will more clearly illustrate these statements.

Working capital. To explore the financial effect of devaluation on working capital, assume that the EZI Corporation, as shown in Exhibit 8.1, has current assets (exclusive of inventories) and long- and short-term liabilities in local currency in the amounts shown in the first column. The equivalent U.S. dollar values at an assumed exchange rate of 10 to 1 are shown in the second column.

At this point, assume further a devaluation of 16.7 percent. The third column shows the revised dollar value of local currency, taking into account the effect of devaluation. The fourth column shows that the dollar value of assets has deteriorated. On the other hand, the dollar equivalent of all liabilities in local currency has been reduced. In this particular illustration the proportion of assets to liabilities is such that the loss on assets is greater than the reduction in liabilities. There is a net loss in dollars to the company. If the proportionate relationship between assets and liabilities had been reversed (liabilities in excess of assets), a gain would have occurred.

Dollar debts. Exhibit 8.2 illustrates the effect that the level of dollar assets or liabilities has in this situation. In this case the value of all balance sheet items and the rate of devaluation are identical to those shown in Exhibit 8.1. It will be noted, however, that the bank loans are now assumed to be in U.S. dollars. Consequently, the corporate liability in dollars for this item remains unchanged despite devaluation. This, in turn, lowers the overall reduction in liabilities that can be used to offset the loss arising from the deterioration in the equivalent dollar value of assets. Thus the foreign exchange loss is greater. The loss would have been less had there been assets in U.S. dollars. The level and kind of dollar items on a company's balance sheet at the time of devaluation are obviously of great importance.

Exhibit 8.1

EZI CORPORATION
FINANCIAL EFFECT OF DEVALUATION ON WORKING CAPITAL
Courtesy of *The Financial Executive.*

	1	2	3	4
		U.S. Dollar	U.S. Dollar	
	Local Currency	Value at 10	Value at 12	Gain/Loss
Assets				
Cash	1,000,000	100,000	83,333	(16,667)
Accounts receivable	3,000,000	300,000	250,000	(50,000)
Other current assets	500,000	50,000	41,667	(8,333)
Total	4,500,000	450,000	375,000	(75,000)
Liabilities				
Current liabilities	750,000	75,000	62,500	12,500
Bank loans	1,000,000	100,000	83,333	16,667
Reserves and other	250,000	25,000	20,833	4,167
Total	2,000,000	200,000	166,666	33,334
	Loss on assets		(75,000)	
	Reduction in liabilities		33,334	
	Loss resulting from devaluation		(41,666)	

Exhibit 8.2

EZI CORPORATION
IMPORTANCE OF DOLLAR ITEMS
ON FINANCIAL EFFECT OF DEVALUATION
Courtesy of *The Financial Executive.*

	1	2	3	4
		U.S. Dollar	U.S. Dollar	
	Local Currency	Value at 10	Value at 12	Gain/Loss
Assets				
Cash	1,000,000	100,000	83,333	(16,667)
Accounts receivable	3,000,000	300,000	250,000	(50,000)
Other current assets	500,000	50,000	41,000	(8,333)
Total	4,500,000	450,000	375,000	(75,000)
Liabilities				
Current liabilities	750,000	75,000	62,000	12,500
Dollar bank loan	1,000,000	100,000	100,000	-- 0 --
Reserves and other	250,000	25,000	20,000	4,167
Total	2,000,000	200,000	166,666	16,667

Loss on assets	(75,000)
Reduction in liabilities	16,667
Loss resulting from devaluation	(58,333)

Inventory values. The effect of devaluation on the value of a company's goods in inventory and the implications for short-range pricing strategy are explored in Exhibit 8.3. As indicated, it is assumed that at the time of devaluation the EZI Corporation had on hand inventories with the total value shown. The equivalent values in dollars before and after the assumed devaluation of 16.7 percent are indicated. The last item indicates the potential loss as a result

Exhibit 8.3

EZI CORPORATION
FINANCIAL EFFECT OF DEVALUATION ON INVENTORIES
Courtesy of *The Financial Executive.*

	Value of Inventory
Local currency	18,000,000
U. S. dollar value at 10	1,800,000
U. S. dollar value at 12	1,500,000
Potential loss*	(300,000)

* Loss can be avoided by increasing local currency prices for products in inventory to the extent necessary to maintain previous dollar margin.

of devaluation. It will be noted that at the time of devaluation the loss is only a potential one, inasmuch as the effect of devaluation can be offset by selling price increases. If the sales margin in dollars that existed prior to devaluation can be maintained, the loss can be avoided altogether. (In some instances, an even greater margin may be required than before to compensate for a higher tax bite.)

Long-range prices. The implications of devaluation in relation to long-range pricing strategy are examined in Exhibits 8.4 and 8.5. Exhibit 8.4 shows figures relating to a simplified case of investments in fixed assets for the EZI Corporation. In the first column the dollar investment and the associated annual depreciation charges are shown. The second column indicates the local-currency equivalents of both these items at an assumed exchange rate of 10 to 1 existing prior to devaluation.

In Exhibit 8.5, a simplified profit-and-loss statement of EZI Corporation is shown. Local-currency revenues and operating expenses, excluding depreciation, are shown and translated into dollar equivalents at an exchange of 12 to 1, the exchange rate that exists, as in the other case, after the assumed 16.7 percent devaluation. It can be seen by looking at depreciation charges that if the amount for this expense in local currency is translated into dollars at the devalued rate of 12 to 1, an inadequate amount of depreciation cost will be taken in this period to recover the full amount of the company's original dollar investment. Over the long term, failure to recover the dollar investment can spell disaster. The problem can best be identified by accounting for financial results in both local currency and dollars. The problem can be offset only by continuing efforts to increase local-currency revenues. These increases must maintain the relationship of dollar depreciation costs to sales revenues in dollars contemplated at the time the investment was made.

PROTECTIVE MEASURES AGAINST DEVALUATION

The foreign investor can take action to protect himself from the adverse effects of devaluation. The necessary measures are of two general kinds: The first kind is of a financial nature, and the second is additional protective strategy of an overall corporate nature.

Financial defenses. Financial defenses primarily protect the foreign investor against the adverse financial effects of devaluation on local currency, working

Exhibit 8.4

EZI CORPORATION
FINANCIAL EFFECT OF DEVALUATION
Courtesy of *The Financial Executive.*

	U.S. Dollar Value	Local Currency Value at 10
Assumed investment in fixed assets	5,000,000	50,000,000
Depreciation at 10 percent a year	500,000	5,000,000

capital, and dollar items that were illustrated in Exhibits 8.1 and 8.2. Financial defenses consist of the following activities:

1. They keep cash balances low and intensify efforts to reduce cash float throughout an affiliate's operation.

2. They maintain a bank account in dollars or some other stable currency when possible.

3. They pay import or other types of dollar obligations promptly.

4. They maximize local-currency borrowing and, as a general policy, keep the company in debt. (Note that the classical ratio of $2 of current assets to $1 of liabilities may have little application overseas.)

5. They obtain extended terms from suppliers and from the government for the payment of taxes.

6. They contract in local currencies for future obligations.

7. They purchase forward against short-term hard-currency obligations. (In essence, the purchase of exchange "future" bets company funds on the rate and timing of a devaluation. This is risky but can be profitable. The better the company's information on the key indicators of a devaluation, the less the risk.)

8. They implement accounting policies that frequently translate profit-and-loss statements and balance sheets into dollars. Failure to reflect the effect of devaluation in financial reporting can lead to an overstatement of profits and disguise decapitalization. Failure to understand these effects can foster corporate inaction and confusion.

Exhibit 8.5

EZI CORPORATION
EFFECT OF DEVALUATION DEPRECIATION COSTS

Courtesy of *The Financial Executive*.

Depreciation Effects	Local Currency	U.S. Dollar Value
Gross operating margin	36,000,000	3,000,000
Less:		
Operating expenses, excluding depreciation	24,000,000	2,000,000
Depreciation charges*	5,000,000	500,000
Profit before tax	7,000,000	500,000
Taxes	1,200,000	100,000
Profit after tax	5,800,000	400,000
Dollar equivalent of local currency profits	$\frac{5,800,000}{12}$	483,333
True dollar profits -- relating depreciation costs to original investment in dollars		400,000
Effect of devaluation		83,333

*The dollar equivalent of local currency depreciation charges at the new devalued rate of exchange $\frac{$5,000,000}{12}$ equals $416,667, an inadequate charge in relation to original investment of $5,000,000 to be depreciated over ten years.

Corporate protective policies. As examples for the EZI Corporation further suggest, protective measures beyond those of a peculiarly financial nature will be necessary. These measures consist of corporate policies which in six strategic ways assist in defending the company against the adverse effects of devaluation.

1. They reduce the levels of the company's local-currency accounts receivable and, when warranted, foster the use of devices such as cash discounts and keep them low.

2. They keep selling prices adjusted to levels that will offset devaluation. As Exhibits 8.3 and 8.5 indicate, this is a necessary but often difficult step because of competition or price controls. It can sometimes be accomplished by means of long-term sales contracts in dollars or geared to dollar indexes.

3. They return earnings quickly and promptly to the U.S. shareholder by means of interim dividends.

4. They encourage selling efforts in hard-currency export markets.

5. They encourage the rapid investment of any long-term excess funds in property that tends to increase its value in local currency in proportion to devaluation. Classic examples are land, buildings, and automotive equipment.

6. Policy is to review periodically the local-currency book value of fixed assets. Devaluation rapidly and dramatically "obsolesces" fixed-asset values carried at their original cost in local currency. This is also true, as shown in Exhibit 8.5, of local-currency earnings, which can very likely be overtaxed. A formal accounting revaluation of fixed assets can provide a solution to this problem. Formal asset revaluations, although not allowed in the United States, are sometimes possible in other countries. At best, such a revaluation may be acceptable for tax purposes and eliminate a company's tax payments on overstated profits. Even when this is not possible, revaluation can be used as a device to make a company's official local-earnings reports reflect a more accurate picture of its real profitability.

The implementation of protective measures against devaluation is not always suitable or possible. The effort should be made, however, for the company that fails to creatively manage the risks of devaluation seriously jeopardizes the profit potential of its foreign investment.

(The material on protecting the direct foreign investment has been adapted from an article that appeared in *The Financial Executive,* January 1968.)

—*H. W. A. Sweeny*

MULTINATIONAL MARKETING
AND PRODUCT STRATEGY

Before a company can expect to establish meaningful criteria for selecting a foreign market, and whether it plans to operate by exporting, licensing, building its own facilities abroad, acquiring an established firm, or acting under a joint venture with an overseas company, it should ask itself these questions: "What business are we really in? What are we attempting to do? How did we get here? Where do we hope to go?"—and the ultimate question, "Why should international operations fit into our picture?"

Selecting and Researching Foreign Markets

By arriving at agreement on mission and scope, however preliminary, a company automatically limits the number of options it can pursue abroad. Such an agreement may be stated in detail or may be merely an understanding that a minimum return on investment will be sought, a specific share of market desired, and specified rates of growth for sales and profits pursued. Having thus made a delineation of the nature and extent of objectives, the company will be in a position to select market opportunities through the use of criteria that fit in logically with its goals and resources.

SIMILITUDE OF MARKET

The most common method of identifying overseas markets is to seek out those whose characteristics conform reasonably to the milieu within which the company currently operates. In the case of industrial products custom design is a major factor, and mass-market principles are less apt to apply than for consumer items. To develop data that will supply rationale for comparisons, the executive will wish to examine the size and diversity of the industry, the size of the major customer or customers, the geographical extent of the customer's operation, the position occupied by the customer in the country's distribution network, and the overall distribution system itself. The marketer of consumer products will be concerned with demographic considerations and geographical, climatic, and related conditions.

Economic profiles. The quickest way to assess the degree of market similitude is to collect data which will enable the researcher to build comparative economic profiles for a number of countries. Sources of these and other data are described in the latter part of this discussion. Helpful initially will be basic information on the following: size of population and its rate of growth per year; number of households; national income; GNP; and private consumption in total, per capita, and as a percent of GNP. Other general economic indicators that can be included in the overall market similitude table are number of passenger vehicles, telephones, radio and television sets, and refrigerators; and indexes of industrial production, wholesale and retail prices, and wages in manufacturing can be studied. A five-year experience record should be prepared for these data.

With a rough idea of the market thus obtained from the foregoing exercise, the manufacturer or service company will wish to collect more data to refine the picture. Some of this information will cover the urban and rural make-up of the population and major areas of concentration; it will include specifics on housing, as well as food habits and consumption; the distributor system and buyer shopping habits will be evaluated; and the relative use, importance, and coverage of advertising media will be particularly important. The analyst will also be interested in comparing imports of the products in question with local production and determining tariff and nontariff barriers and tariff rates; local and foreign exchange regulations and controls; labor availability, wage rates, and regulations; and taxation and incentive factors. Finally, the prospective host country's attitude toward foreign imports, investment, and related forms of activity should be scrutinized and evaluated. While such qualitative information is difficult to quantify and is subject to sudden changes in direction, early appreciation of its possible effect on a venture can be a useful exercise in achieving a realistic picture of market similitude.

PREFERENTIAL TREATMENT

Although preferential treatment is less commonly considered as a deciding factor in market selection by companies just starting out in the foreign field than by firms already active abroad, it is perhaps the most attractive one (often deceptively so) used by American manufacturers in choosing the "best deal" available. Not surprisingly, most of the industrialized countries (with exceptions, such as Switzerland) and virtually all the developing countries recognize the value of laws granting tax and financial incentives and exclusive production or importation rights to qualified foreign investors.

Investment incentives. Generally, investment incentives include tax incentives, loans and grants, duty-free imports of raw and semimanufactured materials needed in the production process, export aids, and protection against competitive imports or similar foreign investments. Tax incentives range from "tax holidays" of from two to as long as ten years, in the case of some developing nations, to corporate tax levies well below the roughly 50–55 percent imposed in the industrialized West and Japan. A popular form of incentive in some foreign states is to exempt from tax 50 percent of the net income of enterprises qualifying as "productive." One of the snares that confronts a researcher lies in trying to determine whether his business qualifies in this respect. Regardless of the country's state of development, officials and written law are sometimes vague on these key points. Tax incentives tend to be higher in the developing nations than in the industrialized ones. However, the prospective investor will wish to look carefully for other levies in force. Some countries, for example, impose taxes at various levels in the production process, and their net effect can be devastating in high prices for the consumer and low profits for the investor. Aids to export are another form of preferential treatment. They can make an investment look profitable overall, particularly in countries that have a limited domestic consumption potential. Such conditions in the host country, however, generally mean higher production cost because of small volume, with end prices to the consumer greater than export markets can reasonably pay; hence the export subsidy can be meaningless in practice. An important area of preference is found in government loans or grants offered to new enterprises: special subsidies which reduce borrowing costs, interest-free loans on a percentage of the total capital outlays for research and development of new processes, special grants for construction costs, and even machinery and equipment. Loans and grants are usually more easily obtainable from the industrialized than from the less-developed nations.

Exclusive rights. Government offers of an exclusive right to manufacture or import free from competitive pressures are most commonly available in countries that least resemble the American market and require greater commitment of resources and fortitude to succeed. The surface advantages are evident: primarily, the absence of competition and hence the time to develop an effective managerial and marketing organization, debug and refine production operations, and generally integrate the company into the economy, grow with its progress, and attain an impregnable position. The problems that can arise should be anticipated by the market analyst so that adversity will not come as a surprise after the investment has been actually undertaken. Very simply, what is given can be taken away—or at least altered. Countries granting such preference expect in return higher wages from a foreign-origin manufacturer than from a domestic firm, attractive prices to the consumer despite often small markets, and a healthy income for the government on taxes levied on the enterprise—to name a few. With the very effective threat of loosening import restrictions on competitive products and encouraging other foreign investors to initiate an additional venture in the same industry, the host nation can bring onerous pressures to bear. Both the attractions and the drawbacks of preferential treatment as a criterion for the suitability of a foreign market opportunity should be fully appreciated in advance of commitments.

OUTLET FOR SURPLUS PRODUCTION

Foreign markets are frequently thought of as a convenient means of disposing of manufactured or processed items which may be below standard, or of acceptable quality but out of style or behind the style, or merely available in such embarrassingly large quantities that disposal on the domestic market would cause price dislocations. From time to time it is inevitable that certain of these goods will find their way into overseas markets on a legitimate and planned basis by an alert company faced with a surplus of production. It is clear, however, to every intelligent foreign trader or executive responsible for foreign operations that such policies, pursued indiscriminately, will result in disruption of the normal economics in the company's established markets or make later entry into new markets extremely difficult. What has not been clear even to some major U.S. marketers is that disposal of surplus production—for example, in certain segments of the food and chemical industries—has been the real though unstated rationale for foreign involvement from the beginning. Aside from the risks in dumping, the danger of such a reason for market selection is that, within the company itself, overseas operations receive overemphasis one year and no emphasis the next year. Thus when foreign markets are recognized to have more than spasmodic potential, the company will find that it has built neither an organization nor a philosophy that can cope with a normal competitive environment. As a yardstick for the desirability of foreign involvement, dumping is the least reliable.

OTHER CRITERIA

Some companies in the "billion-dollar club" perhaps feel that they can justify operations in some areas over the foreseeable term on the basis of shutting out their competitors or, over the longer term, on the basis of "we should be there." Both justifications raise knotty problems, not the least of which is the danger of stretching too far any company's most valuable resource—its people.

RESEARCHING FOREIGN MARKETS

The most rewarding task to be performed initially in preparing for international operations is a thorough search and evaluation of the sources and information available on foreign countries and markets in the United States.

Sources in the United States. Within the major international centers of New York and Washington the executive has a myriad of available sources. Beyond the agencies and departments of the U.S. Government, the commercial and economic units of foreign diplomatic missions, and the major international organizations, the researcher should cover such specialized sources as trade and industry associations, various magazines and other publications, U.S. and foreign chambers of commerce, major international banking institutions, private management consulting and market research firms, and—where welcomed—private companies, active in overseas markets, which have no objection to sharing or recommending sources or data known to them.

U.S. Department of Commerce. Less use is made of this major source than is deserved by the range and excellence of material that it provides. Through its Bureau of International Business Operations in Washington or by contacting the many regional field offices of the department, the researcher will gain an introduction to the available material. A valuable statistical measure of potential are Report FT 410, *U.S. Exports of Domestic and Foreign Merchandise—Commodity by Country of Destination,* and Report FT 420, *U.S. Exports of Domestic and Foreign Merchandise—Country of Destination by Sub-Group.* Schedule B, "Statistical Classification of Domestic and Foreign Commodities Exported from the United States," should be used in conjunction with these reports. General economic conditions, special characteristics, and particular opportunities abroad can be followed by subscribing to *International Commerce,* the weekly publication of the department. The World Trade Information series supplies detailed reports for most countries of the world and covers basic economic data, establishing a business, market factors, and other analyses pertinent for the exporter or investor. Trade lists of prospective agents, dealers, and distributors abroad can also be obtained. U.S. Foreign Service personnel make and have on file in Washington confidential reports (*World Trade Directory Reports,* WTD), available at a nominal charge, on overseas companies' business activities, trade relations with U.S. firms, and general and financial responsibility. Beyond the foregoing, there is important bibliographical material such as *A Guide to Foreign Business Directories, A Directory of Foreign Organizations for Trade and Investment Promotion,* and *A Directory of Foreign Advertising Agencies and Marketing Research Organizations.* The bibliography of the department's own publications is entitled *Checklist of International Business Publications.*

U.S. Department of State and agencies. While less active than the Commerce Department in publishing reports, the State Department does issue valuable analyses of some countries and areas; they are available from Washington and other strategically located outlets in the United States. AID has published the *Catalogue of Investment Information and Opportunities,* a comprehensive listing of published economic and feasibility studies in the underdeveloped countries. Additionally, staff members of AID in Washington can be helpful sources.

Other Federal and state agencies. The Departments of Agriculture, Labor, and the Treasury, together with the departments of commerce of some states (New York, for example) are further sources of published data on foreign trade matters and opportunities.

International and diplomatic installations. The UN and subsidiary units such as the Food and Agriculture Organization (FAO), the World Health Organization (WHO), and the International Labor Organization (ILO) publish general and specific data that the researcher may consult.

OECD, EEC, IBRD, Ex-Im Bank, and others. The thorough investigator of foreign markets should familiarize himself with these key international organizations, the publications of which are available through U.S. distributors or directly from the institutions themselves. The Organization for European Cooperation and Development (OECD) is particularly informative. The Inter-American Development Bank and the IMF also should not be overlooked.

Chambers of commerce, and industry and trade groups. The U.S. Chamber of Commerce in Washington has published *A Guide to Foreign Information Sources* and *Doing Import and Export Business,* among others. The U.S. Council of the International Chamber of Commerce may also be contacted. All the industrialized countries and many developing nations maintain chambers of commerce and other units in the United States which are among the best sources of information in this country on their economies, consumers, industries, and the like. Some have excellent and extensive libraries. The National Foreign Trade Council and the International Executives Association are important forums and publishers on overseas trade and investment. Finally, the National Industrial Conference Board (NICB) and the National Association of Manufacturers (NAM) have also become active in this field.

Banks and private firms. The larger international banks publish periodicals and reports on economic conditions and supply credit data on foreign firms. A final major source of information lies in the experience of American firms with operations abroad. Cultivation of knowledgeable personnel within these companies and perusal of some of the periodicals they distribute can be rewarding.

Sources overseas. If the company has done its homework thoroughly before setting foot in a foreign country, the field investigation abroad can consist primarily of researching the most crucial sources of all: the consumers, the various levels of trade (retail, wholesale, distributors, and agents), and the manufacturers.

U.S. sources. As a starting point, the researcher might visit the U.S. Embassy, the U.S. Trade Center, and AID to obtain introductions to key local officials and businessmen. Discussions with executives of American firms operating locally should be the major effort.

Foreign sources. The various government industries and statistical offices in the host country and the international organizations mentioned previously may be able to supply back-up or fill-in data still needed. Trade and industry associations, trade fairs, and industry periodicals, however, should be key targets of the researcher. The marketplace itself (the customers, the distribution system, and the producers of the product or service) should take precedence over all other sources contacted during the actual field research.

Outside and professional assistance. In carrying out the industry survey, the company may wish to supplement the efforts of its own personnel by obtaining additional help from other sources. The U.S. Department of Commerce will conduct a trade contact survey at a price of $50, using U.S. Foreign Service personnel abroad to contact prospective local buyers or business partners for the U.S. firm. U.S. commercial banks, through their own foreign branches or correspondents, offer a similar service to established customers.

The major U.S. management consulting firms with offices abroad and professional personnel experienced in the country's markets and problems can be extremely valuable. Where there is a mutual understanding of the information and objectives sought in the study, such professional assistance may bring the benefits of expert knowledge of the country (and, often, of the pertinent industry); extra manpower to gather and evaluate the local facts required; an impartial outsider's view; and, where the American firm does not wish to expose its interest in a product, industry, or foreign firm, complete confidentiality of source.

PROBLEMS IN SELECTION AND RESEARCH

Most of the difficult problems that arise in the process or at the conclusion of seeking out and evaluating foreign opportunities arise from failure—sometimes technical but more often managerial—to understand or even fully investigate the subtle differences that exist between the domestic market and the overseas market.

Technical problems. At some point, particularly when evaluating consumer product potentials in a foreign country, most analysts will wish to use statistical techniques in their research efforts and apply proven sampling methods. Regardless of the procedure followed—unrestricted sampling, stratified sampling, quota and area sampling, or proportional or disproportional sampling—the same measurement problems that occur in the domestic market will occur abroad: the standard errors that arise from the validity of the estimates. Overseas, as here, the validity of the estimates will depend on the extent of bias present in the sample estimate and the expected range of error within which the estimate may vary because of the random sampling elements. However, researchers often tend to believe that the strangeness of a foreign market is the primary force affecting their estimates, and a tendency to overreact or underreact follows in consequence. Behind this problem is often the fact that few firms abroad are experienced in conducting reliable consumer surveys. Client supervision must be close.

Attitude problems. Managerial attitudes are perhaps the principal reason for shortcomings in selecting and researching foreign markets. Prime among these is unpreparedness—the too early trip abroad to "get the feel of the market" before any significant attempt has been made to gather and assess the substantive information already available from the wide range of sources in the United States. The result of this approach is that hard-core data never become acquired to the extent necessary, and the venture is begun largely on "feel." A corollary attitude, equally dangerous, is the tendency to oversimplification implicit in the statement, "People are much the same everywhere." It is true that some of the industrialized markets of Western Europe are becoming "Americanized" in their tastes as a result of the enormous strides in communication and personal contact over the past 20 years. However, these similarities in taste are more limited than is realized and are still difficult to quantify. Cultural biases of custom and tradition or of religious and racial nature do continue to play a significant role in the success or failure of any foreign venture.

A final error of attitude lies in the human tendency to believe that there is nothing new about any particular market, only variations of characteristics standard to all world economies and distribution. For example, analysis of a marketing organization chart of a Japanese firm showing branch offices throughout the country might lead the researcher to conclude that the Japanese marketing structure is the same as that of typical U.S. firms; but it would be discovered later that sales in Japan are indirect, the branch offices functioning only as a liaison between the head office and the local distributor or sales agent. Failure to gauge distribution, to make the product suit the market, to recognize opportunities in countries because of political systems incompatible with one's own bias, to appreciate language differences, or to utilize foreign nationals in key management positions—these and the other errors commonly met in the field of foreign operations can be largely avoided by doing a proper measure of homework first, utilizing experienced outside advice on appropriate occasions, and—above all—retaining a firm grip on one's own bias throughout every aspect of selecting and researching an overseas market.—*D. P. Adams and Masaaki Hotta*

Product Strategy

With the ever increasing complexity of business management, the product strategy becomes increasingly important to effective marketing. This is especially true in international marketing, not only because of the subjective considerations inherent in a relatively unfamiliar market area but additionally because of practical requirements in product modification or adaptation.

PLANNING CONSIDERATIONS

Effective product strategy is based on comprehensive market analysis. To collect and analyze market information is difficult enough in a well-known, established domestic market. It is obvious, however, that the difficulty is vastly greater when the market is distant and relatively unfamiliar. The need, therefore, for accurate and comprehensive data for examination and analysis is fundamental to the market plan, the product plan, and the development of a product strategy.

The following major factors should be documented and analyzed: the market, as shown in ethnographic, demographic, and economic studies; and all ascertainable facts on the product and product line (existing products, product modifications, product life cycle, style, packaging, multipurpose/multimarket products, and distribution).

Eventual product strategy will involve three principal product areas: (1) new products created for the international market, (2) existing products marketed in the new market, and (3) modified products adapted to the requirements of a particular international market. A further subdivision of these three major classifications is possible—for example, marketing an old product for a new use on a new market—but it would in reality be little more than an extension of the second category.

In considering market strategies, therefore, it follows that once the data have been accumulated, analyzed, and interpreted, the identification and selection of the product to be marketed will place it within one of these three categories. The strategy to be employed is directly related to the socioeconomics of the intended market.

THE MARKET

Numerous considerations are required in market analysis. Aside from the obvious concerns—population, population density, economic indexes, sociological characteristics, and marketability—less obvious factors should also be considered. Political as well as legal aspects must be reviewed, and existing or potential competition carefully scrutinized. Once these considerations have been evaluated, more specific product-oriented aspects—for example, product need, style, packaging, competition, pricing, and durability—must be examined.

The total product strategy can be effectively made known only in the context of the total marketing situation. While the analysis of the market can be visualized as a summary of sociological, economic, and general environmental considerations, there must in actuality be a close interrelationship between these factors and the product or products themselves. The analysis therefore deals with a single entity wherein the market is visualized in relation to the suitability of a particular product, while the product is taken into consideration in relationship to the market. It is the harmonious interrelationship of these two dominant factors that allows for a logical interpretation of both and, upon completion of the decision-making process, the effective implementation of the determined product strategy.

THE PRODUCT

The following factors of concern in product strategy analysis must be thoroughly considered: climate and local area conditions; transportation and storage; packaging; product life cycle; competition and competitive activity; license, patent, and trademark considerations; pricing; and multipurpose and multimarket products.

Close familiarity with an individual product or series of products in an existing major market may present a challenge to clear-sighted visualization of the problems that may be encountered in the marketing of the same product in another market. This, of course, holds true with respect to the marketability of a new product in a new market. And the same challenge relates to the development of an additional new product for the market, a modification or adaptation of an existing product, and the ability to offer an existing product for new uses in the new market.

The most obvious examples of foreseen difficulties are variations in available energy sources (differences in European electric voltage from voltage in the United States), the language barrier, weights and measures, and the like. But other factors less apparent may be involved: climatic conditions; transportation; storage, license, patent, and trademark considerations; tariff or trade restrictions;

and a myriad of other factors. It is essential to cultivate the attitude of total review and cautious search.

Climate and local area conditions. It is evident that products subject to deterioration by heat will be adversely affected in areas of excessively high temperatures and that items subject to freezing will not be stable without protective precautions in areas of extremely low temperature. From a technical standpoint, some less obvious physical considerations are the effects of humidity, atmospheric gases, and pressures resulting from high altitude.

Photographic equipment provides an excellent example of both the direct and the indirect influence of weather and climate. The direct effects on lens and lens coatings are well known, but the less obvious concerns—humidity and thermal variations that create mechanical failure or interfere in mechanical function, creating inaccuracies in shutter aperture and speed—are extremely significant. The influence of an arid climate on local power sources or auxiliary requirements for a specific product is also well known. While these situations present problems, they are in many instances not unsolvable, and they provide an opportunity for product modification or the development of new products to meet the individual market's needs. The development of the voltage transformer packaged with traveling electric razors is a classic case of adaptation.

Transportation and storage. Due consideration must be given, when utilizing exported products, to the possibility of prolonged or delayed transportation as well as storage and handling problems. Some of the difficulties encountered in storage and handling are related to shipping and packaging, but product durability from a physical and chemical standpoint is of more significant concern in the ability of the product to withstand the unusual stresses of international transportation. It is apparent that close cooperation between product management and the corporate traffic function will be required.

Packaging. There are two areas of concern with respect to packaging in international marketing: The first is the physical container in which the product is to be shipped, whether a bulk container for bulk chemicals, an individual drum for a chemical product, or a carton or "multitainer" for individual prepackaged product units; the second is the necessity to modify the package because of a consumer need or appeal that is different from that of the home country.

The problems of transportation/packaging are primarily related to durability. Since the stresses to which the package and products are exposed in rail and ship transportation differ radically from the stresses of trucking, the construction of the package is important. Breakage, leakage, or container damage can be extremely expensive, not only from the point of view of direct replacement but, still more seriously, from the psychological standpoint of inability to supply. Materials flow abroad is obviously more protracted and complicated than in the domestic situation; therefore, replacement is more difficult. Size and weight of container are additional but most important aspects of packaging (many foreign markets have regulations restricting the size and weight of containers). Again, coordination with company traffic and export groups is essential.

In considering consumer packaging, thought should be given to the alteration of the existing package, based on psychological considerations or style (size, shape, color, or design) and assessment of the market as it relates to consumer acceptance of the product. In many foreign markets convenience packaging, which is costly, is not nearly as prevalent as in the United States, and more economical and less complicated packaging may be both necessary and desirable. Sometimes, however, packaging innovation may prove successful. The number of units per package relative to family size and distribution patterns is of concern as are, in some instances, the physical restrictions of size and proportion. Language problems are manifest in multimarket products, but many of them have been easily solved through multilanguage descriptive literature printed on or in the package or product itself.

Product life cycle. A product is expected to have a given longevity in a given market. However, the domestic life cycle does not necessarily correspond to the life cycle in the foreign market. Individual life cycle analysis is required in every market area. It is possible by judicious timing to prolong the life cycle of the individual product greatly through successive introduction on various markets. The scrutiny of ascendant and descendant sales and distribution curves can provide significant data in the formulation of the strategic approach. The examination of such documentation is the key to two very important aspects of individual strategy—control and timing.

Competition and competitive activity. It is manifestly a mistake to assume that the same competitive situations or practices prevail in different markets. Inability to successfully market a product in a given area, predicated upon competitive situations, may be totally nonexistent in another market, thereby permitting the successful introduction of the product. Competition should be carefully analyzed in each market and given appropriate weight in determining strategy.

When considering competition in this context, the planner of market strategy should reflect upon the elements of competitive analysis; it is not sufficient merely to identify competitors and competitive products. It is naturally of importance that consideration be given to market size and market share, market share distribution, competitive capability, market receptivity, and a number of other closely related factors; but one factor often neglected is a thorough understanding of prevailing competitive practices.

The practices of a given competitor are germane to strategy development in that they may dictate marketing tactics. For example, where bulk shipments are employed as a basis for volume purchase agreements, preparation must be made to either market similarly or offer other offsetting inducements. In a highly price-sensitive area, pricing policies of competitors are obviously of concern, but deeper analysis should be attempted so that, based on a knowledge of the competitors' approaches to the market, future action and reaction can be anticipated. Provisions predicated upon such expectations are reflected in the evolved strategy. Contingency planning—as it relates to competition, at least—is largely based on this kind of forecasting.

Licenses, patents, and trademarks. The feasibility of improved capital return through intercompany licensing arrangements, whether for manufacturing or marketing, can be an important consideration. External manufacture for direct or indirect sale constitutes another source of revenue with minimal capital investment. These alternatives should be studied.

Thorough investigation must be made regarding the existence of patents or trademarks covering products to be marketed abroad. International patents should be considered, both in regard to application for a patented product to be marketed and with respect to possible contravening patents already existing in the foreign market. Where trademarked products are being sold, similar problems with registration arise, and due caution should be exercised to protect an existing trademark or expansion thereof.

Pricing. Price is a strategic weapon. In many existing product markets, competition dictates price; but in areas of new products or modified products, market price establishment is more subjective and is a basic strategic determinant. Since market price in either circumstance is subject to controlled variation, it can be utilized as a factor in the development of a product strategy.

The obvious relation between selling price, cost, and profit is of the utmost importance in the establishment of market price. And price levels, as they relate to the appraisal of the market and the distribution of the product, represent significant criteria. The ability to sell in a particular market may well be predicated upon the cost, selling price, and profit ratio and can lead to the future option of local direct or indirect manufacture or agency sales.

Initial strategies of product sale at break-even, or even slight profit loss, to establish the market would obviously relate to long-range manufacturing capability in concert with long-range profit goals.

Pricing should be analyzed in product strategy and planning for both immediate and long-range objectives. It is insufficient to consider only immediate price and not allow for possible competitive maneuvers (if competition exists), market changes, new products, and similar external influences. The usual influences of product life cycle and economic dynamics as they affect pricing must be considered even if they may be subject to uncontrollable factors.

The effective utilization of the fundamental strategy of pricing can be applied only within the realistic assessment of these characteristic elements. While many of these influences are not subject to direct quantification, wherever they can be quantified, they should be; but, more importantly, the exercise of executive judgment must be employed for the establishment of the longer-range price and profit goal and strategy.

International pricing is discussed further in this section of the handbook (page 8·74).

Multipurpose and multimarket products. From a strategic point of view, the possibility of marketing the same product in many markets is most desirable. In some instances, this would be feasible and would provide the multimarket product rather than the multipurpose product. Multipurpose products are familiar to everyone, representing as they do one product that serves many divergent needs, but the multimarket product in international transactions is more the exception than the rule.

Product strategies developed upon logical and accurate assessment of interrelated market and product concerns will enable effective statistical determinations applicable to either the elusive multimarket product or, individually, to the product that is oriented to a specific market.—G. S. Dominguez

Merchandising, Sales, and Promotion

Merchandising a product overseas is similar to merchandising a product in the United States; but it has important differences, slight though they may be in some cases, that can span the distance between profit and loss, failure and success. These are dissimilarities in such activities as distribution, advertising, packaging, and possibly in patent problems.

Most companies enter merchandising overseas via the export route. That is, they usually package and crate a product, currently being sold in the United States, for shipment overseas to an importer or distributor who in turn handles the distribution or sale of the product. Though in some cases the product, package, and label may be changed somewhat to meet what are considered the needs of the market, these needs are seldom researched to any great extent. Also, responsibility for the merchandising of the product usually ends with shipment. Whether the market is thereafter effectively penetrated is often a moot question. Worse still, whether markets exist that could be penetrated is seldom considered.

The potential for merchandising a product overseas is considerable. Preparation for merchandising may include setting up an international division with responsibility for establishing overseas markets, including extensive market research; establishing an overseas sales force; hiring the services of an advertising agency familiar with the customs and needs of the market; and even setting up plants overseas for the purpose of assembly or manufacture. How far a firm should go in merchandising its product or products overseas, however, will depend upon a number of things. Chief among these are the potential (resources of talent and money) that exists within the firm for expansion overseas and the seriousness of commitment on the part of top management.

If utilizing the services of an importer is the initial approach to merchandising overseas, the next step is normally an attempt to take over the import functions. But this calls for on-the-spot investigation—often lengthy—of the foreign market in question and requires close examination of the distribution channels currently used or available. The channels used by the importer may have been best for his own profit and convenience but not necessarily best for the firm.

DISTRIBUTION

The distribution question is one of the most important in merchandising a product in a foreign market. If the distribution channels being used are outdated or outmoded or in danger of becoming either of the two, the firm can be in trouble at the outset. The available distribution channels must be analyzed carefully and compared to determine which is best for the firm, product, and market.

Working with a distributor. There are two alternatives to working with a distributor. The firm can set up its own overseas sales force, or it can work through agents or representatives. If to work with a distributor is the choice, there must be a decision on how far the company is willing to go in working with that distributor. That is, what kind of contribution can and should the firm make in merchandising its product overseas? At the very least, the company should investigate pricing, selling methods, promotion, the use of trademarks and brand names, and servicing.

Pricing. When a firm abdicates responsibility for merchandising its product, pricing abuses can be one of the results. It is not unheard of for the distributor to price a product too high or too low, for his own quick profit, rather than price it for the long-term gain of the manufacturer. Any arbitrary action on the matter of price, however, should be out of the question. First, some flexibility is called for in meeting competition that may arise. Second, pricing policies in the market being penetrated call for considerable study (see page 8·76).

Selling methods. The amount of help that can be offered the distributor overseas will depend to a considerable extent on the distributor chosen and the firm's familiarity with the selling methods being used. If they are similar to methods used in the United States, perhaps a great deal of help can be offered. It may be possible to offer sales training materials and direct sales training help—with allowances, of course, for differences in the market. If the selling methods are dissimilar, close study may be called for to determine where help can be most effective. In either case the firm may want to consider monetary assistance to develop more effective selling methods. Such involvement is particularly important if the firm contemplates ultimately setting up its own overseas sales force under its own management.

Promotion. Generally speaking, the more sophisticated the markets being penetrated, the more important the promotional techniques become; but here again, close study of the market and of the techniques being used by foreign competition is called for before money or help is offered. Where markets are similar, it may be that the firm will want to project the same kind of company and brand image as in the United States; or it may be that slight differences are appropriate. These questions are important to work out. In any event, because of the long-term impact of promotional activities, it is essential that the firm be concerned and exercise control.

Trademarks and brand names. For the firm that desires to maintain long-term control over its product and market, trademarks and brand names are of crucial importance. It is important that the firm's brands and marks be used, and that they be used correctly, to protect the firm's right to the product and in accordance with the government regulations of the country in question. If they are not so used, it is possible that, after capturing a good share of the market, the company may lose it to an unscrupulous distributor or competitor.

Servicing. Unless the firm's product is of a one-time, throwaway kind, the area of after-sale servicing is apt to be of major concern. There is no quicker way to lose a market than failure to provide the servicing necessary to keep a product operative, particularly where warranties are concerned. Too often, this area is neglected or cared for only on a make-do basis to the detriment of long-term profits. What the distributor is currently doing should be carefully examined, and the needed help or money—or both—for servicing should be provided.

ADVERTISING

In developing a program of advertising for a foreign market, a firm can work cooperatively with the distributor or develop its own advertising program. In either case, care must be taken to work closely with an advertising agency that knows the market in question. Customs, tastes, and appeals vary widely from country to country, and only an expert can steer a firm through the shoals toward maximum effectiveness.

Cooperative advertising. To provide the distributor with an advertising allowance and let it go at that may seem an easy and natural thing to do, but this approach has its pitfalls as well as advantages. At the very least, although it is assumed that the distributor will create and place advertising to the best advantage, there is a loss of control that does not insure this result. Frequently, the distributor will view the advertising allowance as a concession and cut back on his own advertising efforts; and, while the firm can demand that the distributor spend matching amounts, there are ways of getting around this requirement. In any event, the distributor is apt to place the advertising to suit his own profit needs rather than those of the manufacturer.

Methods of control. There are methods of controlling cooperative advertising, but they are not always satisfactory. One method is direct control: The manufacturer takes full responsibility for the creation and placement of the advertising, working through an overseas advertising agency. But, since the distributor is being asked to commit money, he must be consulted—and, indeed, it is advisable that he be consulted in any event. However, the distributor may be less than enthusiastic about this method and make less of a commitment than he would otherwise.

A second way of controlling overseas advertising is the fixed-sum method, whereby the distributor matches the amount and is permitted to control the advertising. While the distributor may like this arrangement better, it has the disadvantages already noted.

Distributor cooperation. If the distributor route for merchandising overseas has been chosen, consultation with the distributor in the matter of advertising is all-important. If anyone knows the market, the distributor does. In addition, his commitment to the firm's advertising program is essential. This consultation is best conducted person to person. In fact, in merchandising overseas there must be frequent contact with the distributor who handles the product.

The advertising campaign. In drawing up plans for sales and advertising overseas, it is wise to consult with the distributor before submitting even tentative plans to him. In this way his own thinking is not inhibited or restricted in any way. (There is a danger in applying U.S. thinking to foreign markets.) At the same time the distributor should not be allowed to think that his views will necessarily prevail; for while his expertise may be in the market and the local media, the final content of the advertising is something else.

In planning an advertising campaign for an overseas market, the same considerations must prevail as in advertising in the domestic market: determining the advertising objective, determining the consumer market to be reached, picking the most effective approach, selecting the media, producing the advertisement (production problems), and managing the campaign. Seasoned judgment and expertise are called for in each of these areas, particularly when advertising overseas.

Creation and placement of advertising. The problem of the creation and placement of advertising in an overseas market would seem to be solved by utilizing the services of an international advertising agency. To find an agency with true capability in the market the firm is trying to penetrate is not always easy, however. Usually, a company has two choices. It may deal with an agency that has contacts with agencies overseas and works through them, but such an agency is apt to offer little in the way of personal services itself. Or the company may try to engage the services of one of the larger domestic agencies with international competence, but the large agency may not want to handle the smaller account. Fortunately, this situation is being eased as more and more U.S. agencies develop foreign departments or connections in response to the demand from multinational firms for international advertising.

Media selection. In selecting media for advertising to foreign markets, it is well to keep in mind their breakdown into three broad groups: media that transcend national boundaries, such as top-circulation consumer magazines and certain professional or business journals; media that are primarily national in scope and distribution; and media that are strictly local. The first group tends to reach an elite of the educated general public, but the intranational and local media are of greater significance in penetrating a specific market. They also present more difficulties in selection. For example, many foreign magazines grossly overstate their circulation (there is no Audit Bureau of Circulation to rely upon), and a hodgepodge of broadcast regulations in different countries complicates television and radio advertising.

Maintaining control. One modest course to take for maintaining control of an advertising program is to create the advertising in the United States but leave placement to the distributor overseas. If this is done, however, thorough consultation with the distributor is mandatory, for the problem is to create the firm and brand image one wishes to maintain but at the same time meet the needs of the local market, keeping legal, ethnic, cultural, and other restrictions in mind. Particularly important is the language barrier. The translation should be made by someone who knows not only the language but also the local idioms, including current slang. It is too easy to make a bad mistake in this respect. In any event, when advertising overseas, it is even more important to maintain control and follow-through than it is in the domestic market, for more can go wrong.

Advertising appeal. The appeal to be used in advertising in a foreign country is a particularly delicate subject, for what works in the United States is not necessarily successful abroad. Ads or commercials in poor taste can boomerang in many countries—which is also the case with American humor, hard-sell, and pseudoscientific appeals. To determine the best appeal requires a fairly exhaustive knowledge of the culture and mores of the people one is trying to reach. To try to impose one's own values or—through sheer ignorance—one's own way of looking at things, however widespread it may be in Western culture, can be fatal to business. Basic, too, is the choice of words and phrases; this can be as important as the themes and appeals.

PACKAGING AND LABELING

The package and label of the product are, of course, part of the total advertising message and as such are subject to the same difficulties and restrictions as space advertising. Not only are there the usual linguistic difficulties; straight translation is seldom adequate, and the domestic name of the product may have unpleasant connotations for a foreigner and may need to be changed. Color and design can also be extremely important. A color that is attractive to the consumer in this country may be considered ugly in a foreign culture, and the consumer may have different needs in package design, depending upon the national or local situation.

TIE-INS

Finally, if there are to be any tie-in promotions accompanying the advertising program—premiums, discounts, trading stamps, giveaways, and the like—they must be thought out very carefully and local customs observed. It may be also that the firm will want to exhibit its product at one or more of the numerous trade fairs that are held annually throughout the world and will use advertising that ties in with its exhibits. Trade fairs are much more important abroad than they are in the United States. If the product is to be shown at such a fair, it is best not to make the distributor responsible; a top executive of the firm should be involved and attend the fair. Not only is this a way of getting to know the market; if opportunities arise for further promotion or distribution of the product, the firm will be in a position to take advantage of them. This also holds true for other activities that fall into the category of public relations; top executive involvement is essential.—*J. G. Cowley*

INTERNATIONAL PRICING

Price is the vehicle through which costs are recovered and profit flows to the company. This is as applicable in international as in domestic pricing.

When pricing for domestic operations is to be done, there are historical company pricing data and competitive reasoning to consider plus the pricing components of manufacturing cost, overhead, R&D amortization, sales and advertising, and profit margin. All these factors, however, have been used in a certain mix or progression in previous years; they have provided the correct price for the unit volume and have insured market acceptance.

In pricing for international operations there is need to review the objectives and the pricing method to be used. The method varies according to the objective. Pricing is done for export to independent parties, export sales to related companies, market penetration, depletion of excess inventory or production, and profit in each individual sale.

Pricing for Export to Independent Parties

The domestically manufactured product reflects prevailing domestic costs, including the higher wages and fringe benefits in the United States and the engineering and machinery amortization, and this product must still bear transportation costs, duties, and foreign distributors' sales costs and profit margin.

In pricing to independent third parties abroad there is theoretically little danger of incurring government disapproval, since the company will simply try to interpolate in the price a profit factor acceptable by American standards. This profit will be made domestically and taxes will be paid on it, because the relationship with the foreign customer is not a "preferred" one but rather a free-market supply-and-demand affair. Therefore, an acceptable means of establishing export prices is to take the U.S. price, subtract American advertising and selling costs, and add foreign advertising and selling costs. Nevertheless, even this simple approach may present complications when the product is modified in order to insure foreign acceptance, for in such cases it might have to bear pyramiding R&D, engineering, and production costs.

At times additional problems can arise in pricing to an independent third party. Assume that, while researching the market for its product in Country X, the company finds a good distributor who will import on his own account, maintain inventories, service customers, advertise, merchandise, and so on. But in the preliminary negotiations the distributor proves that because of insurance, freight, duties, customs-clearing expenses, and currency conversion—as well as his own costs incurred in the distribution of the product—the resultant price to his domestic customers is exceedingly high. Assume also that he can demonstrate that locally manufactured competitive goods are sold for less and that some American competitors are selling in his market at a price that meets or only slightly exceeds that of the domestic producers. What will the company's price be?

If the company does not reduce the price, it will be undersold even by American-produced competitive products exported to Country X (a fact which indicates that, assuming the distributor's costs are correct, American competitors are selling to their distributors at a lower price). But if the company does lower the price, it runs the risk of engaging in pricing practices contrary to U.S. and foreign government regulations. One widely used method is to adopt the pricing policy deemed appropriate, bearing in mind that profits should be made in the United States, taxes should be paid on them, and the company must be prepared to explain and defend the policy to IRS and to the customs authorities of each foreign country.

These authorities will generally request that prices be related to what some of the domestic customers pay for the product. It is good practice to maintain an up-to-date file on the prices paid for a product by domestic buyers who order in roughly the same quantities and perform similar functions. These domestic prices should be established not only as a reference but also as minimum figures that cannot be undercut without special review and approval.

Pricing for Export to Related Companies

Pricing for "preferred" relationships—that is, for transactions with companies that are not independent third parties but licensees or affiliated companies (minority, majority, or wholly owned)—is often much more complex. Here, again, the "arm's length" position is applicable, and deviation from it may entangle the company in charges of dumping, dumping penalties, and the problem of value for duty purposes. Furthermore, sales to a related concern may involve not only finished parts and products but also semifinished parts, incomplete subassemblies, and completed central components that must be integrated with other parts. The major hazard in pricing to related companies, however, stems from the risk of exporting profits. The IRS takes an extremely hostile view of this because most foreign companies are located in countries that provide a corporate tax structure construed as favorable in comparison with that in the United States. Of course, the tax differential is eliminated upon repatriation of profits, but while profits remain outside the country they yield in essence a higher return on investment (ROI). From the host country's position the liability of preferred pricing is lower duty collection and possible dumping.

Pricing for Market Penetration and for Depletion of Excess Inventory or Production

The two pricing situations—market penetration and depletion of excess inventory or production—have several things in common. First, they are normally short-term, as market penetration pricing cannot be maintained throughout many years because it does not provide the necessary profit margin (or, in some instances, full cost recovery), while inventory depletion is in itself a terminal situation once the objective is achieved.

The second common factor is that where government is concerned, the "arm's length" criterion is fundamental. For two reasons both the U.S. and foreign governments are interested in any instance where this has been overlooked: (1) They wish to prevent dumping, which can be detrimental to local industry and in general offends nationalistic feelings; and (2) it is to their advantage to secure as much revenue as possible from import duties. Normally, the duty is figured on the value that appears on the invoice (the duty rate is usually applied on the CIF price); and if the price is unduly low, customs receipts will be low. The U.S. Government is sympathetic toward effort directed at increasing exports, for exporting provides a host of assets ranging from improvement of the balance of payments, job creation, increased plant utilization, reduced costs, and balancing of cyclical industries to improvement of the national image abroad and the strengthening of people-to-people ties. However, the government does not accept dumping or exporting of profits. In this connection the IRS is conducting more extensive investigations of foreign operations in general and pricing to foreign customers in particular.

Pricing for Individual Sale Profit

The only acceptable as well as viable pricing structure that can be used on a long-term basis is pricing for profit on the individual sale. It includes all the necessary pricing requirements, such as full cost recovery, profit percentage, the "arm's length" criterion, tax generation, and ROI.

Pricing Methods

Pricing on a full-cost basis is quite generalized, and its application is usual in U.S. industry; thus for that reason it does not require specific comment here, as its implementation for either export sale or foreign manufactured product is well understood.

This may not be the case with incremental pricing, however, which is being used to a greater degree nowadays in export sales. This method, in actuality, is a way of subsidizing international prices and is relatable to price leadership in that neither is usually a full-cost price. Incremental pricing is based on a business logic that assumes that a certain increase in unit production over a given production run does not need to carry the same burden, overhead, and other nonmanufacturing costs as the original production-run quantity. Thus the rationale goes that on a certain unit quantity (normally required for domestic users) the overhead and administrative cost is fully absorbed, and any additional quantity added to the original run (for export) should only have to provide the direct manufacturing cost and a modest percent contribution to overheads. With this lower "cost" the resulting price is consequently lower, as it is not bearing full operational cost and profit.

The major distinction between incremental pricing and price leadership is that the latter is a market price concept which in essence proclaims that the product is the lowest-priced item within its range of competition. Price leadership generally requires a subsidized cost price when the product is of American origin and sold abroad. This is not to say that price leadership is always based on incremental pricing, but it may be on many occasions. However, incremental pricing is a method used at the manufacturing facility to compute the price, and it does not necessarily follow that the end price at the market will not have a profit margin or full recovery of sales cost; it only addresses itself to selling the product to a distributor or marketing arm at less than normal price when compared to its total production output.

Effects of Pricing Decisions on Quotas, Duties, and Taxation on the Transfer Price

While the effect of pricing decisions on each question may be different, depending on their definition in each country involved, there are several common results.

First, if a country has a quota system for imports, it is usually expressed in terms of a net amount of money rather than units; thus a lower transfer or import price will yield more unit volume. If tax is accrued on the imported dollar amount (the usual method of assessing duty and transfer tax), again a lower per unit price will elicit a smaller per unit tax or duty burden.

Second, unless one is dealing in the capital equipment and/or durable goods area, it is more tolerable to the host countries' nationalistic feelings to view a lower price—although their duty income is lessened—as they feel that no cost penalty is being pressed on them because of low volume demand.

Third, if the marketing arm that sells the product in a host country is related to the manufacturer, additional and obvious advantages are present. If, however, the distribution is conducted by an independent party, he will be in a position to devote more effort to it because of the profitability involved.

Fourth, lower prices are a tool to the marketing group but not necessarily an end in themselves. This, at least, is the case in most industries. Marketing has to operate within its company framework, and low prices are by no means a unique or even spectacular advantage. Competitive prices, when part of a marketing plan and coupled with other sales tools such as delivery, service, part availability, and advertising, are a welcomed and cherished advantage.

Fifth, pricing is a crucial part of any new product introduction, but ultimate success cannot and should not depend on price but rather on product, marketing, and the people responsible for marketing.

Top Management Responsibility

It is quite apparent that the decision of the pricing method and pricing objective falls in the senior management area.

The overall planning for international operations has to include a policy statement on pricing and even a review date for that decision if subsidized pricing is used. There is a vital need to have pricing objectives (as well as methods) understood, and once a given one is chosen, its computation and application can be provided by a directive. Review of price objectives should be an annual requirement regardless of which method is decided upon.

The secure and sensible approach is to comply with the written legal precepts even though these sometimes price the product out of the foreign market. If the international manager can determine a pricing policy that will allow the company to compete, he should ask the attorneys and auditors to provide a written opinion of it; make adjustments when necessary; and proceed to comply with it thereafter. In addition to maintaining a reference file on related pricing to U.S. customers, it is recommended that the corporation practice continuity in foreign pricing by applying the same basic guides to the different international situations.—*H. L. Aizcorbe*

Illustrations of Incremental Pricing

As noted previously, incremental pricing is an important concept in export sales. Ideally, export pricing should be established on the basis of the largest profit return while still remaining competitive. But an export price may be somewhat lower than the U.S. domestic price and still produce a better profit margin in spite of higher sales costs.

An example will demonstrate this fact. A factory that is producing at 100 percent of capacity in turning out goods for domestic markets is not likely to be interested in meeting a competitive situation abroad which will involve a lower return of profit than can be obtained in the U.S. market. But the prospect will be different if the producer is operating at 80 percent of capacity and another 10 to 20 percent of output would bring in large additional profits.

The incremental pricing method should be explored. Manufacturing costs, fixed charges, and burdens must be broken down, and those not applicable to exports should be removed. An export price that is competitive may well result. It may be 5 to 30 percent lower than the domestic price and make possible increased output and profits even in the face of higher sales costs in the export market. These costs usually result from the need for extra service beyond the F.O.B. point—specialists in traffic, documentation, correspondence, and so on. A higher selling commission may also be involved.

To take a further example in illustration of possible advantage in incremental pricing: A factory produces 1,000 units at a cost of $300 each. Suppose direct labor and material costs constitute only 60 percent of total costs, the remaining costs constituting fixed charges that will be incurred whether 1,000 or 2,000 units are produced. If the additional 1,000 units are produced for export, their price can reflect a reduced portion of total overhead expense. The export price can accordingly be lower than the domestic price in order to meet a competitive situation, with export sales increased and without upsetting domestic prices.

—*David Coe*

ENVIRONMENTAL FACTORS

Isolation and its companion, protectionism, have long had an effect on U.S. trade with other countries. With the current trend away from protectionism, however, business environmental factors in the United States and abroad have taken on a more contemporary aspect through common markets, free trade associations, and regional integration concepts tending to foster the freer movement of trade.

Isolationism

The concept of isolationism includes a desire for economic self-sufficiency; a belief in protectionism in foreign trade; a refusal to participate in alliances and joint or cooperative ventures with foreign powers; a disinclination to aid underdeveloped nations in their economic reconstruction; an unwillingness to succor other countries threatened by invasion, aggression, or subversion; and a desire to eliminate foreign influences from the thinking and activities of the people. Isolationism is a peculiarly American phenomenon distinct from the extreme nationalism existing in some other nations.

There was a strong upsurge of isolationism during the 1920's, following American disillusionment with World War I and the results of that war, but it has been on the decline ever since. Isolationism is not dead, however, and some of the objections voiced against U.S. foreign policy today have their roots in isolationist sentiments.

ECONOMIC SELF-SUFFICIENCY

The concept of economic self-sufficiency is based upon the idea that, in time of war, a successful enemy blockade could bring the country to its knees without a military defeat. From this original meaning the term has been expanded to include self-sufficiency in time of peace as an offshoot of the individual virtue of self-reliance. Opponents of this theory contend that, with modern transportation and an increasingly fine division of labor, self-sufficiency is of far less importance to the economy now than formerly.

PROTECTIONISM

Protectionism consists of the employment of the tariff and other devices to restrict the entry of foreign-made goods in competition with domestic products. This doctrine holds it desirable to preserve the American market for American-made goods and protect the standard of living of American workers against the competition of foreign labor.

Since the adoption of the Hull Reciprocal Trade Agreements Act of 1934 and the gradual decline in protectionism in most industrial nations, this doctrine has lost much of its former luster and many of its advocates.

ALLIANCES

Antagonism toward participation in foreign alliances and joint or cooperative ventures is based on the notion that Americans tend to become too deeply involved in international intrigue and that they often come out the worse while their foreign partners reap most of the benefits. The assumption is that Americans are no match politically for the diplomats of Europe and Asia and are thus easily outmaneuvered. This notion is no longer supported by the facts, and modern American diplomacy is held to be the equal if not the superior of that of any foreign country.

UNDERDEVELOPED NATIONS

Disinclination to aid the underdeveloped countries is an adaptation on the international front of the Puritan ethic which holds that nations as well as individuals should reap as they have sown. It is the responsibility of each nation, according to this doctrine, to attain self-development through its own proper efforts. Opponents of this policy point out that poor nations are poor customers and that the funds which the United States spends in the improvement of poorer nations return many times over in future trade possibilities.

AID AGAINST AGGRESSION

Largely prompted by American intervention in Korea and South Vietnam, some people hold that the United States cannot and should not play the role of world policeman. They maintain that it is up to each nation to protect itself and that the lives of Americans cannot be equated with those of the natives of the distant lands where life is held to be but of little value. Proponents of American efforts to resist the spread of aggressive communism point out that each aggressor victory in "small" wars whets the appetite for larger conquests. The defeat of aggression, they maintain, must take place wherever it occurs to avoid a far greater and costlier global conflict at a later date.

FOREIGN INFLUENCES

According to those who want to eliminate foreign influences, the United States has developed a unique economy, ethic, and culture far superior in many respects to those found abroad. In this view these attainments are peculiarly susceptible to foreign influences and could easily be unfavorably modified. The conclusion is that the United States should isolate itself as far as possible to conserve, consolidate, and advance its gains. Against this position it is argued that America's economic and cultural gains are hardly delicate hothouse plants to fear contagion from abroad. Opponents of this doctrine believe that this country should not only expose its virtues abroad but should export them so that less fortunate countries can share the benefits.

EFFECTS OF ISOLATIONISM

In the short run and especially in the past, whenever isolationism has prevailed in the United States, this country has failed to play the role in international affairs to which its economic, political, and military power entitles it. In the long run and especially since the outbreak of World War II, isolationism has been of declining importance and has not served to prevent the United States from playing a leading role in international affairs. However, the memory of past periods of isolation-inspired periods of withdrawal from international affairs has served to cast a very faint shadow of doubt on the continuity and future of America's international policies.

THE TARIFF

The import tariff is employed for two broad purposes: (1) to raise revenue and (2) to protect domestic industry, agriculture, and labor from foreign competition. In recent years the tariff has lost ground in favor of other taxes as a source of government revenue, and today it is largely employed for purposes of protection. Technically, the tariff is a form of excise tax on commodities imported into a country from abroad. A few countries employ an export tariff, or an excise tax on exported goods. Used by itself, however, the term "tariff" usually refers to the import tariff and is so used in this section of the handbook.

TYPES OF TARIFF

Although there are differences between them, all national tariff systems have certain characteristics in common.

Ad valorem tariff rates or duties are based on the value of the imported goods; specific duties are calculated on the weight, measure, or count of the imported items; and combined duties utilize both value and measure. Thus an ad valorem duty on textiles might be 10 percent of their value; a specific duty could be 5 cents per yard; and a combined duty might be 5 percent of the value plus 1 cent per yard.

Behavior among these three systems is quite different. The receipts from ad valorem and combined duties increase and decrease with movements in prices, and the protection they afford is constant regardless of price movements. The specific rates afford less and less protection as prices rise and more and more as they decline.

A single-column or unilateral tariff is one in which equal tariff treatment is given to all countries. A multicolumn tariff is one in which a country applies certain rates to one group and other rates to other groups of nations. Preference or preferential tariffs consist of two-column duty schedules with a set of lower rates applying to certain countries and higher rates applying to others. The British imperial preference tariff, with one column of rates applying to members of the British Commonwealth and another column of higher rates to nonmembers, is an example of this type. Customs unions, free trade associations, and common markets usually apply one set of tariff rates, or no rates, to members of the organization and other and higher rates to nonmembers.

Countervailing duties may be imposed on certain imports where they have been subsidized by foreign governments. Antidumping duties may be levied upon imports from countries where the exports are being dumped in other countries at prices substantially lower than their costs of production or than the prices at which they are commonly sold on the domestic market.

Some nations maintain free ports (ports in which imported goods may be entered free of duty). The goods so entered may be re-exported to other national destinations without the payment of any duty. Tariff duties are assessed only when the goods are withdrawn from the free port and entered into the national customs territory.

The American equivalent of the free port is the foreign trade zone. Goods may be entered into these zones free of duty, and the merchandise so entered may be exhibited, mixed with other goods, or utilized in assembling and manufacturing processes in the zone without the payment of any duty. The duty on this merchandise is due only when it enters the customs territory of the United States either separately, mixed with other goods, or as a manufacturing component.

DECREASING IMPORTANCE OF TARIFF

The tariff today is less important and is not considered a certain means of protecting domestic industry against foreign competition. Industry in the United States and abroad has learned to cope with tariffs by means of increased efficiency, lower costs, and innovation. Industrial protection is now much more effectively attained through the use of other devices such as import and exchange controls; import quotas; and domestic excise, sales, and border taxes, as well as administrative procedures.

Partisans of protectionism and high tariffs have advanced a variety of arguments to support their positions. The "infant industry" argument, long a favorite, was based on the notion that an agricultural country can industrialize only when its new or infant industries are protected from foreign competition by high tariffs. The home-market argument maintained that this market should be exclusively reserved for domestic industries. The "pauper" or "coolie" labor argument contended that American high-priced labor should be protected against the low-paid labor of other countries.

The "free-traders" countered these and other protectionist arguments by an appeal to the doctrine of comparative advantage, which affirms that a nation should produce and export those goods for which it has a comparative advantage in production over other nations and import those for which it is at a comparative disadvantage. In this way, the optimum utilization of the resources of all countries is obtained and the levels of world trade and standards of living are increased. In addition, partisans of this doctrine state that unless a nation is prepared to accept the exports of other countries, those countries will lack the currency needed to purchase exports of this nation.

U.S. TARIFF HISTORY

The tariff has a varied history in the United States, for at times the rates were increased and at times lowered. Over the long term, however, the trend of U.S. tariff rates from 1791 to 1930 showed an increase. In 1916 the U.S. Tariff Commission was created to serve as a fact-finding body to study and make reports on various aspects of the tariff in an effort to render it less a political issue than it had been in the past. In 1930, at the beginning of the Great Depression, the Hawley-Smoot tariff raised the duties to the highest levels in American history in an effort to stem the ravages of the national catastrophe. As a counterdepression measure this tariff was a failure.

The reciprocal trade agreements program. In 1934, after the passage of the Hull Reciprocal Trade Agreements Act, U.S. tariff policy was reversed. Under this act, which has been renewed each time its term expired, the United States undertook tariff negotiations with other countries, reducing its tariff duties in exchange for reciprocal tariff reductions on the part of these other nations.

At first this country negotiated tariff reductions with other nations on a single-country basis. In 1947, however, the trade agreements program moved into high gear and negotiations were conducted simultaneously with groups of nations. At the same time the GATT was established to police the trade agreements program and to establish a set of ground rules for international trade.

Since 1947 there has been a series of multilateral trade negotiations between the United States and relatively large groups of countries, all of which substantially reduced the tariff barriers to international trade. The negotiations under the Kennedy Round that took place between 1962 and 1967 resulted in especially substantial reductions in the tariffs on industrial products.

U.S. tariff reductions under the reciprocal trade agreements program can be removed under two different sets of circumstances. The first of these is the escape clause and the second the National Security Amendment to the Reciprocal Trade Agreements Act. Under the escape clause the President of the United States is authorized to raise tariff duties that have been reduced by trade agreements negotiation, provided serious injury is threatened to any industry.

Under the National Security Amendment the President is authorized to raise the tariff duties reduced by trade negotiations if he feels that national security is endangered.

TARIFF PROTECTION FEATURES

Two important differences are found in the several national tariff systems. One deals with the valuation of goods for the application of ad valorem and combined duty rates, and the other with the classification of merchandise for the purpose of ascertaining the appropriate tariff duties to be applied.

Valuation of merchandise. Section 402 of the Tariff Act of 1930, the last tariff act, provided five different methods of evaluating goods for the application of duties: (1) the foreign value, (2) the export value, (3) the U.S. value, (4) the cost of production, and (5) the U.S. selling price.

The duties are assessed first, if possible, on the foreign or the export value, whichever is higher. If neither of these values can be satisfactorily ascertained, the customs appraiser is to apply the U.S. value. If none of the three can be determined or applied, the appraiser is to use the cost of production. Under certain conditions, and especially where there are substantial differences between U.S. and foreign costs of production, the U.S. selling price is used as the base price for the assessment of tariff duties. However, since the passage of the Customs Simplification Act of 1956 there has been a tendency to utilize the export value whenever possible.

Different countries apply various methods of evaluating merchandise for the imposition of ad valorem and combined tariff rates. The valuation methods under the Brussels Convention are different from those utilized by the United States, as are those employed by several Latin American and other countries.

Classification of merchandise. Products are divided into classes for the purpose of assessing tariff duties, with a different duty rate applicable to each class of goods. Some nations utilize many minute divisions and subdivisions of products rather than a small number of commodity groups. The classification system is further complicated as new products are introduced and an effort is made to group them under classes established earlier.

Because of the wide range of tariff rates applicable to different imports, the classification assigned to a product may be crucial. Importers are often faced with unpredictable product classifications and rates, and the classification procedure may involve considerable delay. Zealous customs appraisers often tend to assign to imported merchandise the classification utilizing the highest rates which could conceivably be applied.

REGULATIONS AND ADMINISTRATION

The regulations that interpret a customs law, as well as the attitude of the officials who administer it, may be almost as important as the duty rates themselves in determining the protection which the tariff affords domestic industry.

The invisible tariff. The customs regulations, as well as the administration of the customs acts, are often exceedingly complicated and have been held to constitute an invisible tariff. In addition, other legislation—the U.S. Food,

Drug, and Cosmetic Act; the Plant and Quarantine Act; the Federal Seed Act; and other so-called sanitary acts originally designed to protect the health of Americans and American agriculture against disease and pests—has been used to exclude foreign commodities from domestic markets. The "Buy American" acts of the Federal Government and some state governments have served to reduce the public purchase of imported goods and services and to impede their use in public contracts.

Customs simplification. In response to considerable pressure from abroad, the United States has endeavored to reduce the complexities of its customs administration by the passage of the Customs Simplification Acts of 1953, 1954, and 1956. These acts have done much to reduce the impact of the American invisible tariff and to render customs procedures and administration less cumbersome, more easily understood, and less subject to arbitrary interpretation. These acts have simplified valuation and classification of imports, tariff paperwork and accounting procedures, and marking of imported goods, among many other tariff procedures. The regulations of the Customs Bureau have been streamlined, in addition, rendering importation much easier.

Although the complexities of the U.S. customs tariff have received much attention, this country is not the only one whose tariff administration has been designed to exclude imports or to make them more costly and less competitive with domestic products. The tariff administration of most other countries constitutes an important manifestation of protectionism and a barrier to international trade.

Border taxes. The United States tends to favor direct taxes such as the net income tax as a primary source of revenue, whereas many other industrialized countries favor indirect levies such as sales and transactions taxes as the main source of government revenues. The most modern form of the transactions or general sales tax is the tax on value added (TVA).

The transactions or general sales tax has a tendency to pyramid because it is applied every time the merchandise changes hands. Under these conditions a 10 percent transactions tax where the goods move from the factory to the wholesaler, then to the retailer, and finally to the consumer, adds not 10 percent to the price of the goods but approximately 33 percent. To avoid this pyramid effect, the TVA levies a tax on the mark-up, the value added at each step of the distributive process, thus avoiding adding taxes on taxes.

To equalize the burden of this tax between domestic and imported goods, the TVA is generally levied, in addition to the tariff duties, on goods imported into the country. To place their export industries in a strong international competitive position, many nations exempt goods destined for export from the payment of this levy and, according to the rules adopted by GATT, this is an acceptable and legal procedure.

However, the GATT rules provide that exported goods may not be exempted from the payment of direct taxes such as the corporate net income tax employed by the United States. Thus American exports to countries using the TVA must pay the TVA tax when imported by many countries but cannot claim exemption from the U.S. corporate income tax. American exports are thus placed at a competitive disadvantage with those of many other industrial nations.

Future of invisible tariff. Analysts who have followed the several reciprocal trade agreements negotiations, especially those of the Kennedy Round, have concluded that future negotiations are likely to concentrate on the reduction of the invisible tariff as well as border taxes.—*M. J. Wasserman*

International Economic Integration

A major development in the international economy since World War II is regionalism, the economic integration of two or more national states. The major regional groupings include the European Economic Community (EEC) and European Free Trade Association (EFTA), composed largely of advanced, industrialized countries, and the Latin American Free Trade Association (LAFTA) and Central American Common Market (CACM), composed largely of underdeveloped nations. These arrangements are designed to encourage a greater flow of commerce among participating countries; in some instances, social as well as monetary and fiscal policies of member countries are being integrated, coordinated, or harmonized. In general the regional arrangements will effect and promote a better use of land, labor, and capital in member countries, but the policies instituted also have important implications for the U.S. trader and investor.

EEC

An early effort at economic integration was the EEC, popularly known as the European Common Market. Established in 1957 by the Treaty of Rome, the EEC includes six full member countries: Belgium, France, the Federal Republic of Germany, Italy, Luxembourg, and the Netherlands. The significance of the arrangement is reflected in part by its size—a population of about 185 million and aggregate gross national product of about $300 billion.

Perhaps the most important feature of the arrangement is the elimination of trade barriers among member countries; this was undertaken on a gradual basis and completed ahead of schedule for industrial products by mid-1968. A uniform external tariff has also been established to enable member countries to develop a unified commercial policy with respect to all other countries.

Other features of the EEC include the development of a common agricultural program; provisions for a relatively free movement of labor and capital among member countries; the development of common antitrust legislation and transport policy; the establishment of patent, copyright, trademark, and industrial property legislation; and the harmonization of monetary, fiscal, and social policies.

Although the EEC had a number of setbacks, it has made significant progress in implementing the provisions of the Treaty of Rome, with the possible exception of an acceptable agricultural program. It would appear, however, that further economic integration will require a degree of political integration.

The Treaty of Rome makes provision for additional full or associate members. Greece and Turkey participate as associate members. The more important question of additional full membership has yet to be resolved. Great Britain has applied for admission but has been unsuccessful, largely as a result of past French opposition. Should Britain finally secure membership in the organization, applications from other members of the EFTA are likely to be accepted.

EFTA

In 1960 the EFTA, which is composed of Austria, Denmark, Norway, the United Kingdom, Portugal, Sweden, and Switzerland, came into existence. Finland, at a later date, agreed to participate and is well on the way toward becoming a full member. The EFTA arrangement, representing a population of 100 million and an aggregate gross national product of about $200 billion, is a less ambitious undertaking than the EEC. The key feature is the elimination of internal trade barriers on industrial commodities; each country will maintain its own external barriers with respect to imports from nonmember countries. These provisions have been completed, and since 1967 industrial commodities have moved freely within the region.

The EFTA does not contain many of the integration provisions that characterize the EEC. The major reason is that the member countries generally hope to participate in the EEC and thus facilitate a much broader integrated structure within the European community.

LATIN AMERICA

Regional integration has come to be considered a useful technique for accelerating economic growth in a large number of less developed countries. The regional arrangements of greatest immediate significance to the U.S. trader and investor are composed of countries of Latin America.

LAFTA. Well over three-fourths of the population and income of Latin America is represented in the LAFTA. Its membership includes Argentina, Bolivia, Brazil, Chile, Colombia, Ecuador, Mexico, Paraguay, Peru, Uruguay, and Venezuela. In addition to gradually reducing internal trade barriers (to be completed in the early 1970's), efforts are being made to promote and finance new regional industries and thus achieve a degree of industrial diversification.

CACM. Costa Rica, El Salvador, Guatemala, Honduras, and Nicaragua comprise a regional integrated group that began operations in 1960. The five countries, which represent a population of about 14 million, have with a few exceptions created a system of free internal trade and a common external tariff applicable to nonmember countries. Institutional arrangements have also been created to promote industrial growth in the area. However, because of recent disturbances in the area, the future of the CACM remains unsettled.

Latin American common market planning. In 1967, 19 Latin American countries signed an agreement pledging themselves to work toward the creation of a common market which would encompass all of Latin America. It is expected that the arrangement will be in operation by 1985.

The regional arrangements in Latin America are not expected to provide the degree of economic integration characteristic of the EEC. The conditions and problems of the two areas are extremely different. For Latin America, regional integration is considered to provide the essential framework within which a new structure of production and trade will be created and economic growth will be promoted.

IMPACT ON U.S. BUSINESS

The regional arrangements in operation in Europe, Latin America, and the rest of the world represent both a challenge and an opportunity to the U.S. trader and investor. It is likely that, for certain types of commodities, the U.S. exporter will be placed at a competitive disadvantage with respect to firms located within a given trading bloc. If the regional import barriers are sufficiently restrictive, intraregional exchange may expand at the expense of interregional or international trade. Although regional arrangements cannot impose barriers more restrictive than those previously in force if their operations are to be sanctioned by GATT, there is still a possibility of trade diversion working to the disadvantage of nonmember countries.

The overall impact of regionalism need not be restrictive, however. Much depends upon the willingness of member countries to participate in the liberalization of trade barriers worldwide. The European countries negotiated in the Kennedy Round of GATT and have demonstrated a willingness to reduce tariff barriers on industrial products on a reciprocal basis. Latin American and other developing countries, however, in seeking internal industrial diversification have sought to retain protection for domestic firms.

Regional arrangements may create greater opportunities for U.S. exporters and firms wishing to invest abroad, to the extent that they contribute to increased productive efficiency and an improved allocation of land, labor, and capital. Broader markets, opportunities for mass production, and access to factors of production from a wide geographical area contribute to a better allocation of resources and a higher level of income. Higher levels of income, in turn, contribute to improved investment opportunities and broader markets for U.S. exports.

The member countries of existing regional arrangements are dependent upon the rest of the world as a source of raw materials, capital goods, and investment funds. The trading blocs are too small by themselves to provide member countries with completely adequate resources and product markets. On an overall basis, regional integration is likely to prove advantageous to U.S. firms, although some firms exporting certain kinds of commodities may find they are unable to compete in foreign markets.—*C. W. Hultman*

INTERNATIONAL MANAGERIAL RESOURCES
AND COMPENSATION

The equitable treatment of overseas managers occupies a place high on the list of chronic problems for nearly every international company. Struggling with the cultural, language, and distance gaps that yawn between the home office and its international managers is one part of the problem. Weaving through the legal technicalities and status differentials surrounding the hard-to-identify third-country national is another. Even its own trusted personnel—the native expatriates, weaned on familiar business methods and knowledgeable regarding the company—pose their own set of problems to corporate management. As if this were not enough, the consternation often felt in considering these groups at home is fully reciprocated in the way they see things from abroad.

The International Manager

There are three general categories of international managers with which most companies are concerned. The first is the expatriate, the employee who is a national of the country of his parent company. The second is the local national, the overseas employee who works in his native land. The third is the so-called third-country national, the employee who is a citizen of neither the country in which he currently works nor the country in which his parent company is based. Each of these types of international manager has his distinct characteristics, considerations, and problems.

A fourth group—possibly a hybrid group combining two or more of the other categories—is emerging as a part of worldwide management. This group, which might be called an international cadre, consists primarily of younger managers interested in an international career. In many respects they are like the third-country national, but their increased mobility and exclusive internationality make their remuneration problems somewhat different.

THE U.S. MANAGER ABROAD

The U.S. manager on overseas assignment has leaped on the international scene with the tremendous expansion of his country's foreign business activities since World War II. Typically, his overseas assignment is for him only a step up the corporate ladder. Unlike his counterparts in most other countries, who are trained to spend their entire careers serving their companies internationally, the U.S. manager can expect to step back into stateside company life after what may be a very brief stint abroad. This characteristic has a pronounced effect on the way the American manager is selected, trained, and compensated for his foreign duty—and the way he performs it.

Recruiting and selection. The recruiting or internal selection of U.S. managers for assignment abroad is often handled with little attention to the added considerations that differentiate the foreign assignment from an organizationally similar position at home. A man qualified by knowledge and experience to manage a plant in Denver is not infrequently thought capable of handling the same job for his company in Liège. The misunderstanding that leads to such conclusions continues to be a symptom of many of the basic difficulties of American management in its international personnel relations.

His qualification for the job in question is, of course, a major consideration in selecting an international manager. He must be even more qualified than his domestic equivalent if he is to bear up under the added strains of adjusting to foreign working and living conditions, not to mention withstanding the extra scrutiny he will get from his foreign workers. Careful investigation of a candidate's record is essential. If it reveals difficulty in adapting quickly to change, lack of initiative and resourcefulness, or inability to work independently and under pressure, his qualifications should be seriously questioned.

One way to reveal whether a candidate is not only qualified but suited to overseas assignment is to discuss the job and its conditions candidly with him and his wife and review the background of each. This may do much to reveal potential obstacles, particularly in the absence of previous international experience. The personal flexibility, openmindedness, and self-sufficiency that are so important in adjusting to a foreign assignment can often be uncovered only through careful interviewing and psychological testing of the candidate and his wife.

Facility in the local language is of course highly desirable, since it will greatly ease the task of adapting to local conditions. However, care must be taken not to make linguistic ability the primary consideration in selecting a man for overseas assignment. A language can be learned much more easily than technical and human relations capabilities.

Training. Aside from any technical training required, the preparation of a manager for his overseas job amounts to little more than a hasty language course in many cases, and sometimes conditions surrounding the assignment prevent even that. The average company often feels itself ill equipped to prepare the manager for the social, cultural, and other changes he will experience in his new assignment, and there are few outside agencies to turn to for help. Instead, heavy reliance is placed on the adaptability of the individual—perhaps too heavy in a start-up operation or other circumstances that would be trying even in a domestic assignment.

Ideally, a period of adjustment is allowed for the new overseas manager and his family; during this time he is freed from many of his work responsibilities. If this is impractical, an initial period of separation of the manager from his family may be considered desirable. Such a period allows him to concentrate on adjusting to his job without having to lead his family at the same time through a separate adaptive process that can be just as difficult.

Motivation and human relations problems. Motivating the U.S. manager in his overseas work is a process that begins even before he leaves the country for his job abroad. This is the case, at least in part, because of the attitude shared by many—and often fully justified—that assignment overseas is at best a step sideways in a career. Talk and actions in convincing a manager of the importance of a foreign post—both to the company and himself—sometimes imply a degree of comprehension by his U.S. superiors that does not exist. If his fears of recognition are quieted long enough to get him to the foreign post, once he is on the job the communication problem and others that are common between the home office and its foreign operations often quickly convince the overseas manager that he is performing a thankless and forgotten role.

The U.S. manager outside his native land is faced by what can be a vast and often frustrating array of unfamiliar problems. Most of these have to do with human relations—the most critical part of a manager's job anywhere. If he feels that his problems and accomplishments are not understood at home, he will inevitably feel deprived of much of the recognition that is essential to motivate him. This is fundamentally why many U.S. expatriates complain loudly of the communication gap between themselves and headquarters. The complexities involved in bridging that gap, with the seeming uniqueness of many of the related problems, account for the small amount of corrective action that often seems to be taken at headquarters. The solution begins with developing greater understanding at the home office—understanding of the conditions that put the overseas manager's problems in a class by themselves and of how their solution fits into the company's overall plans and objectives. From greater understanding come more effective selection, training, and motivation of the U.S. expatriate.

Effectiveness. The effectiveness of the U.S. manager abroad is more than a function of his personal qualifications, motives, and sensitivities. Outside forces over which he may have little or no control also influence his performance. Most U.S. companies follow a policy of staffing overseas management posts, wherever practicable, with local nationals. The reasons for this, quite apart from the more obvious shortcuts in training and the costs and other problems of relocation, are largely tactical. The fact is that the U.S. expatriate, regardless of his qualifications, is not as well suited for most managerial slots abroad as his local national counterpart. Part of the reason has to do with local acceptability.

Despite the familiar image of the "ugly American," diminished U.S. prestige abroad, and widespread suspicion of American business expansiveness, the U.S. manager can win the degree of local acceptance necessary for him to perform effectively. Vital, however, is the quality of the expertise he brings to the job. The man who could clearly be replaced by a local national will have difficult sledding in winning local acceptance. Also, as international understanding of U.S. methods and organization increases, internal justification of U.S. managers in positions that might otherwise be occupied by competent local nationals becomes more difficult. A large part of the *Défi Americain* is the challenge to U.S. business to be responsive to the changing international business environment.

THE LOCAL NATIONAL

Few U.S.-based international companies are truly multinational in outlook and planning. As a result the local national manager is often discriminated against in two key areas: promotion policy and compensation. His resentment of such treatment focuses not only on the company whose policies forget him but also on his American associates, who are a daily reminder of his disadvantaged status.

Yet the situation is changing. As competent local nationals increase their understanding of U.S. companies and their business methods and as more are brought to the United States for temporary or perhaps permanent assignment, traditional differences in their opportunities and compensation are gradually disappearing. It is a two-way educational process. As local nationals accept—and often offer improvement to—American techniques, so is American management accepting them. Increasing numbers of European nationals are occupying key posts in many U.S. subsidiaries in Europe, and in some European countries, such as West Germany and Belgium, the gap between U.S. and local management compensation is rapidly narrowing.

Selection. The recruitment and selection of local national managers follows in many respects the same pattern as the selection of U.S. managers for overseas assignment. Personal qualification ranks first, closely followed by demonstrated ability to adapt to many situations which in a worldwide company will be foreign to them. Evidence of such flexibility may be hard to come by in the absence of related actual experience, however.

Formal educational facilities—a major proving ground for young managerial talent in the United States—still generally cling to the traditional liberal arts curriculum abroad. There does not yet exist anything approaching the number and quality of U.S. business schools, and management is not a subject generally offered at either undergraduate or postgraduate levels. However, many universities in Europe are developing well-based business administration courses, and growing numbers of young foreign nationals are supplementing their liberal arts education with business courses at American universities.

Versatility in other languages is usually much less important in the selection of local national managers than is the case with their American counterparts. At least one foreign language is now required in many primary educational systems in Europe and elsewhere. As English is entrenched as the universal language of international business, it is the usual second language of the young man or woman interested in a career in industry.

Training and development. Local national managerial personnel in international companies are now offered access to many of the same internal development programs historically provided for U.S. managers. Through the fairly recent growth of management associations, university seminar programs, and seminars sponsored by industrial groups, they can also obtain this kind of condensed or specialized management training in most parts of the world. The principal reason for the growing availability of such programs is a shortage of trained management talent that in many places overseas is even more severe than in the United States.

This increasing capacity for developing local national managers, however, can create its own set of problems for the international company whose advancement and compensation practices do not make room for such developed managers. The problems are felt most in attracting, retaining, and motivating the emerging group of highly qualified internationalists. Add to the competitive advantage of these internationalists the resentment toward any sort of discriminatory practice and the nationalistic pride felt by many local national managers (especially a factor in many developing nations), and the often parochial corporate policies toward local national and third-country national managers become even more vulnerable.

Compensating the International Manager

Just as they do in their home countries, most international companies rely heavily on their compensation package (more appropriately termed "remuneration" abroad) to attract, retain, and motivate their overseas personnel. Each category—expatriates, local nationals, and third-country nationals—presents a distinct set of compensation requirements and problems, each of which is further complicated by the fact that there are practically as many sets of requirements and problems as there are countries in which a company operates. To maintain order in the face of such confusion, the multinational company must view its compensation programs in their totality.

TOTAL COMPENSATION

In order to meet the varied requirements of one or more types of overseas employees and the often sharply differing standards of living, compensation rates, social security programs, tax structures, and cultural patterns that exist from country to country, a company must adopt the total compensation approach to management remuneration. This means developing an international package that includes both direct and indirect forms of remuneration. These elements—wages and salaries, benefits, allowances, and perquisites—when considered as interrelated factors, form a total compensation program. This approach enables the company to establish its remuneration objectives in a manner that is exportable throughout the world even though the mix or balance among the elements of the package will vary substantially from country to country.

Well-formulated compensation objectives take into account the basic requirements and principles of any international compensation program; the framework of the many economic, cultural, and legal influences which affect such programs; the results of comparative international total remuneration surveys; and the overall international objectives of the company.

Major elements. The international program must provide ways of administering each part of the total package. A typical program consists of the following major elements:

1. *Base salary* is the cash compensation; it reflects competitive market levels, internal consistency, and individual responsibility.

2. The *incentive or bonus* is extra pay for above-average performance or results. If the effective communication with headquarters that provides other forms of individual recognition is lacking, incentive remuneration takes on added importance with overseas employees and creates the need for a well-defined program of individual or position objectives as the basis for determining the incentive bonus.

3. *Stock option and ownership plans* provide a long-term incentive and an opportunity for estate building through a share in the ownership of the business. This long-standing American concept is rapidly gaining popularity in other countries where the tax laws and currency exchange controls permit the adoption of stock acquisition plans.

4. *Employee benefits* range from pension and profit-sharing plans to company automobiles and from group insurance to club memberships—plus such other benefits and perquisites as vacations, subsidized housing, and periodic medical examinations.

The specifics, including the blend of elements of the total package, will of course vary with local practices from country to country. What is important is that they be formulated under a universal compensation policy.

WORLDWIDE COMPENSATION POLICY

The main objectives of a total compensation program in any country should be to satisfy overall corporate objectives, meet individual operational needs, be compatible with local practice, and represent reasonable costs.

To illustrate the adaptability required, consider that in Europe alone the country-to-country variance in direct versus indirect remuneration practices is tremendous. In the United Kingdom wages and salaries comprise over 80 percent of total compensation, whereas in Italy direct pay is just about half of the total labor cost.

Three key considerations are taken into account in developing a worldwide compensation policy.

Internal equity. Managerial compensation must maintain internal equity for reasons of motivation and mobility—not only within each plant but regionally, nationally, and throughout the worldwide organization.

Such factors as local taxes make it difficult to maintain equity in simple monetary terms on an international scale. The impact of an increase in compensation from $10,000 to $20,000 on the individual will be much more in the United States, where it would mean a boost in taxes of only 5 percent, than it would in Holland, where the manager's taxes would jump 15.5 percent to a rate of more than 40 percent annually. In many situations it is apparent that imaginative devices other than cash must be used to provide incentives for managers and maintain an equitable total compensation program.

Competitive program. Another important factor in applying an international compensation policy is the need to be externally competitive within the geographic region, the industry, and the technical, trade, or professional specialty. This need holds reasonably true for each major element of the total compensation package although the emphasis for a competitive program must be placed on the total package, since the internal requirements may dictate variations from standard practice in some of the major elements of compensation (for example, the ratio of bonuses to base pay).

An example of the need to recognize the competitive compensation requirements of the technical and professional specialty is the distinction between engineers in Belgium. There are two distinct kinds of engineers: the civil engineer, who is university-trained in engineering theory, and the technical engineer, who has received his training in trade schools and on the job. Regardless of a frequent edge in practical knowledge, particularly in his earlier years, the technical engineer is at a decided disadvantage in his expectations of advancement, pay, and other opportunities throughout his career.

Regional adaptability. A further requirement of international compensation is that it provide total remuneration which guarantees appropriate living standards and social benefits, meets the company needs economically, supplies performance incentives, and promotes identification with company goals. Regional considerations introduce one of the major variables in the total compensation package. In some European countries, compensation increases are tied to increases in cost of living; the basis for bonuses also varies from country to country.

Index-related wages. It is required in Italy that salaries and wages be increased whenever the official cost-of-living index rises. Index-related increases are also required in Belgium, France, and Luxembourg but only for hourly personnel. In Germany and Holland index-related compensation is relatively uncommon.

The extra-month bonus. The thirteenth-month bonus is required by statute or by most collective bargaining contracts for both salaried and hourly personnel in Italy and Luxembourg. It is usually provided privately for all personnel in Belgium and Holland and sometimes in Germany, but seldom elsewhere in Europe.

Vacation bonus. In Belgium a vacation bonus is mandatory for both salaried and hourly personnel; this bonus, however, is often privately provided by Dutch companies and occasionally is found in Germany.

Latin America. Executive remuneration in Latin America is rapidly approaching the levels found in North America. However, because of tax laws and statutory benefits favoring the lower-paid, special remuneration and perquisites play a significant role in a manager's total remuneration.

SPECIAL PROBLEMS

Compensation programs should be designed to remain flexible and sensitive to changing corporate requirements and international conditions, yet they must be simple to administer and easily communicated. They should help provide management control of individual and group performance and take advantage of corporate and personal tax incentives.

Statutory requirements and customs within individual countries can be significant barriers in achieving the goals of compensation programs for native managers. These goals can be even more difficult to reach with respect to managers employed abroad and living outside their native lands—that is, the U.S. expatriate and third-country national.

The U.S. expatriate. The American expatriate is the source of some of the greatest problems in the entire area of international compensation. He not infrequently resembles the stereotype of the overpaid American living luxuriously in some romantic foreign clime. Paradoxically, he does more complaining—audible complaining, at least—than any of his foreign colleagues. Many a promising overseas assignment ends prematurely in resignation or early repatriation. Compensation is often an undeserving scapegoat for the expatriate's unhappiness, for it is more easily identified than many of the communication problems and others that probably account for most of the trouble. However, sometimes compensation does deserve the blame.

Most U.S. companies pay a bonus for overseas service, plus allowances intended to permit the expatriate to retain his accustomed living habits at no added cost to him, but such devices—or the attitudes behind them—tend to reinforce the alienation of U.S. nationals from the foreign community in which they live. They are in theory encouraged to integrate but in practice discouraged from doing so; and they resent the inconsistency, often without knowing why.

There are some indications that corporate philosophy regarding the methods of compensating U.S. employees living abroad is changing. Historic "sacred cows" of the expatriate compensation package are being re-examined with some questioning of the necessity of a cash inducement in the form of a premium to live abroad, particularly in the metropolitan areas of Europe and Central and South America. The cost-of-living allowance concept has also come under some scrutiny, both in its methods and long-term need.

The third-country national. Some of the problems of both the U.S. expatriate and the local foreign national are combined in the third-country national. Not only does direct remuneration present difficulties; employee benefits become a special problem. Emergence of the cadre of career international managers mentioned previously makes this problem one of growing concern. It is nearly impossible to predict where these internationalists will be when they retire, become ill, leave the company, or die.

To provide up-to-date group insurance coverage is thus a complicated, demanding task. Retirement benefits pose even more difficulties, since types and levels of funding contributions that are tax deductible and appropriate in the country to which the manager is assigned may be inapplicable in his eventual retirement site.

One frequent answer to the problem of funding retirement benefits is the "offshore trust," usually located in an area with comparatively free currency exchange and low taxes such as Curaçao or the Bahamas. However, firms adopting the offshore trust approach must take care to protect the tax status of both the company and the employee in the country of employment, as well as to watch for possible statutory changes in the offshore trust location.

In developing compensation programs for third-country nationals and other internationalists, care must be given to individual employer or employee group situations. At the executive level, complete individual treatment may be unavoidable. But in many situations, such as where groups of foreign nationals are imported, or where employment is near national boundaries and employees may daily commute from one country to another to work, more economical group practice may be possible.—*S. D. Stoner*

TAXATION AND REPATRIATION OF INCOME

A U.S. company engaged in international operations should consider the overall effect of both U.S. and foreign taxes and make a study of foreign government regulations and other restrictions governing repatriation of income.

Taxation of Multinational and International Operations

The emphasis here is upon taxation of U.S. companies and their foreign subsidiaries or affiliates rather than upon wholly unrelated foreign companies engaged in business in the United States.

Foreign taxes can be as important as U.S. taxes in determining the form of organization for international operations. Corporate income tax rates abroad are generally comparable to or slightly lower than U.S. rates and usually apply uniformly to closely held as well as public companies. However, in many countries there are sales, turnover, and other indirect taxes that constitute a greater source of revenue than income taxes. Many countries grant tax exemptions or reductions in connection with operations that replace imports, increase exports, or use a substantial amount of local materials and labor, especially if located in less developed areas of the country.

The United States generally taxes a domestic corporation on all its income on a current basis, whether the income is derived from U.S. or foreign sources. A U.S. company may also be subject to foreign taxation with respect to income derived from the conduct of its business in the foreign country; therefore, a major objective is to avoid double taxation by the foreign jurisdiction and the United States. Since profits from foreign operations are normally subject to taxation in the foreign country when earned, often at rates below the U.S. rate, it may be advantageous to conduct operations in foreign countries through separate subsidiaries. It may be possible to postpone U.S. taxation of the profits of such subsidiaries until they are actually remitted to the U.S. parent company in the form of dividends.

FOREIGN TAX CREDIT

The U.S. tax system provides a basic mechanism for avoiding double taxation. A credit is allowed against U.S. income tax for income taxes paid to foreign governments on income considered, by U.S. concepts, to be from foreign sources. Foreign sales taxes and other indirect taxes do not qualify for the tax credit and are merely deductible in computing U.S. net income. Foreign income taxes can also be deducted in computing U.S. taxable income rather than credited, but this seldom results in a lower U.S. tax.

In addition to a credit for foreign taxes paid directly by a U.S. corporation, a credit may be available for a portion of foreign taxes indirectly paid by it through its affiliates or subsidiaries. If a U.S. corporation owning at least 10 percent of the voting stock of a foreign corporation receives dividends from the foreign corporation, the domestic corporation is deemed to have paid a portion of the foreign taxes levied on the profits out of which such dividends were paid. This results in an overall tax rate equal to the foreign or the U.S. tax rate, whichever is higher. However, a distinction is made with regard to income from corporations in less developed countries that can result in an overall rate lower than the U.S. rate. The amount of foreign tax credited can never exceed the amount of U.S. tax attributable to the foreign-source income, but in computing the credit the U.S. company can elect to combine taxes paid to low-tax countries with taxes paid to high-tax countries.

SOURCE OF INCOME

Rules for determining the source of various types of income are set forth both in the IRC and in several tax treaties and are important both in determining whether such income is subject to foreign taxation and whether it qualifies for the foreign tax credit. The source-of-income rules are not uniform under all treaties, and the taxpayer may elect to follow either the code or applicable treaty rules.

TAX TREATIES

Bilateral income tax treaties are another means by which double taxation is avoided. As of March 31, 1970, the United States had in force income tax treaties with 21 countries: Australia, Austria, Belgium, Canada, Denmark, Finland, France, Germany, Greece, Ireland, Italy, Japan, Luxembourg, the Netherlands, New Zealand, Norway, Pakistan, South Africa, Sweden, Switzerland, and the United Kingdom.

The tax treaties typically define the circumstances in which a company formed in one of the countries which is a party to the treaty will be regarded as conducting business in the other treaty country and therefore subject to taxation in that country on its profits. The treaties also usually provide for tax reductions or exemptions for dividends, interest, and royalties paid by a resident of one country to a resident of the other and for administrative cooperation and exchange of information between the governments. A reduction of the dividend tax can be important where otherwise total foreign taxes would exceed the U.S. tax and not be wholly creditable. Most recent U.S. treaties closely follow the format of the OECD model treaty.

TYPES OF FOREIGN OPERATIONS

Relevant U.S. tax considerations depend upon the nature and extent of foreign business operations. These operations typically follow a progression from exporting U.S. goods to ultimate users or foreign distributors, through use of foreign sales subsidiaries and the licensing of foreign manufacturers, to the U.S. company's manufacturing abroad through branches, subsidiaries, or joint ventures, and eventual development of truly multinational corporations.

Exporting. A U.S. company is usually not subject to foreign taxation on income derived from export of its products unless it conducts business in the foreign country through a branch, office, or other fixed place of business or through an agent who has general authority to conclude contracts on its behalf or to draw upon a stock of inventory maintained in that country.

Income received by a U.S. company from sales to foreign customers is normally subject to U.S. taxes at the regular corporate rates. However, in limited circumstances a reduced rate of U.S. taxes may be available through the use of a WHTC (see page 8·18) for business done exclusively in North, Central, and South America or the West Indies, and an exemption applies to so-called possessions corporations for business done within a possession of the United States.

Licensing. The licensing of a foreign company to manufacture a U.S. company's products may give rise to royalty income and technical assistance fees. Royalties paid for the use of patents, trademarks, know-how, and other similar industrial property in the foreign country usually constitute foreign-source income subject to taxation by the foreign country but often at rates reduced pursuant to treaty and qualifying for the foreign tax credit.

Technical assistance fees may not constitute foreign-source income to the extent that services are performed in the United States. All such income, consisting not only of any lump-sum payment or advance royalty but also of periodic payments based upon sales of the licensed products, is subject to U.S. taxes but may qualify for capital gains treatment where the licensee is not controlled by the licensor and the licensor has transferred substantially all of its interest in the property rights involved. Some countries may impose sales or turnover taxes on license agreements or royalty payments. These do not qualify for the foreign tax credit but by agreement can often be transferred to the licensee.

Selling or manufacturing through a branch, subsidiary, or joint venture. As a result of both tax and nontax considerations, most foreign sales or manufacturing operations are conducted through a separate foreign subsidiary rather than through a foreign branch of the U.S. company. The income of a branch is combined with the other income of the domestic corporation for U.S. tax purposes. This can be disadvantageous where the foreign operation is profitable, where the applicable tax rate in the foreign country is lower than the U.S. rate, and where the imposition of the U.S. tax could otherwise be successfully deferred until the profits of the foreign company were paid to the U.S. company. Where a branch is used, it is also necessary to determine what portion of the corporation's income is derived from foreign sources. The foreign government and the U.S. Government may not resolve this question uniformly, with the result that the foreign tax paid may not be fully creditable against U.S. taxes. The losses of a branch can be offset against the other income of the U.S. company. However, if the foreign corporate tax rate is comparable to that of the United States and if its tax law permits a net operating loss carry-over, essentially the same tax benefits may be obtainable through a foreign subsidiary. The conversion of a branch into a foreign subsidiary after the foreign operation has become profitable may require an advance ruling from the IRS.

Foreign countries sometimes impose a tax rate on branch profits that is different from corporate tax rates, and a tax in lieu of dividend withholding taxes may also be applied. The effect of these taxes could result in a significant advantage or disadvantage from the use of a branch.

A company can conduct foreign operations through either a domestic or foreign subsidiary. However, unlike the case of a domestic subsidiary, a foreign subsidiary's income cannot be consolidated with that of the parent company; dividends from a foreign subsidiary do not qualify for the intercorporate dividend deduction; and the tax-free organization, reorganization, and liquidation provisions of the IRC do not apply unless a prior ruling is obtained from the IRS that the avoidance of Federal income taxes is not a principal purpose of the transaction. On the other hand, the income of a domestic subsidiary is taxable on a current basis in the United States, whereas U.S. taxation of the profits of a foreign subsidiary is normally deferred until remitted to the U.S. parent in the form of dividends, royalties, or otherwise.

U.S. tax treatment of a foreign corporation depends upon whether the foreign corporation is considered to be resident or nonresident. The distinction is whether the foreign corporation is engaged in trade or business within the United States. The IRC does not define what constitutes engaging in a trade or business within the United States, but a tax treaty may do so. A nonresident corporation is taxed at the rate of 30 percent on most income from U.S. sources calculated according to U.S. source rules, which may be modified by treaty. However, a foreign corporation can buy goods in the United States and resell them abroad without incurring U.S. taxes. A resident foreign corporation is taxed on income "effectively connected" with the conduct of a trade or business within the United States at regular corporate tax rates applied to net income after deductions.

Prior to 1962, companies often formed so-called foreign base companies in tax havens (low-tax countries) and avoided paying any substantial income tax on a current basis. The base company would accumulate profits, often using them to invest in expanded foreign operations or to make loans to the U.S. parent or foreign affiliates. Such a company also frequently served as a holding company and as the source of technical know-how for affiliated companies, so that it also received dividends, royalties, and technical assistance fees. Eventually, the company could be liquidated and its profits taxed at U.S. capital gains rates.

The Revenue Act of 1962, however, substantially curtailed this practice. The act taxes U.S. shareholders on the Subpart F income of controlled foreign corporations (CFC's) even though it is not distributed by the foreign company. A CFC is a foreign corporation in which U.S. shareholders own more than 50 percent of the stock, either directly or by attribution. A U.S. shareholder is a U.S. person or company owning 10 percent or more of the stock of a CFC. Subpart F income includes passive income, such as dividends, interest, rents, royalties, and gains on the sale of securities, which is received as a result of investment of funds or ownership of property rather than the active conduct of a business. It also includes profits, fees, and other income that is earned by a foreign corporation from business activities having no substantial economic or business connection with the country of its incorporation and which results from purchases from or sales to related parties or the performance of services for related parties.

It is still possible, however, for a U.S. corporation to conduct foreign operations through a wholly owned foreign subsidiary and to defer U.S. tax on the subsidiary's earnings until remitted to the United States. The CFC provisions do not apply to foreign joint venture companies in which U.S. shareholders own 50 percent or less of the shares. Subpart F income does not include sales income if neither the U.S. parent company nor another related company is involved in the purchase or sale of products by the CFC; or even if a related company is involved, where the products are sold by the CFC in the country of its incorporation or manufactured by any party in that country.

Various exemptions also apply, including the following: If the Subpart F income constitutes less than 30 percent of the subsidiary's gross income, none of it is taxed currently; conversely, the entire income of the subsidiary will be taxed currently if more than 70 percent is Subpart F income; and Subpart F income from qualified less developed country investments is exempt if reinvested in other qualified less developed country investments.

If the subsidiary has Subpart F income which is not exempt, current U.S.

taxation of such income can be limited by distributing a portion of the subsidiary's earnings to the U.S. parent in accordance with an IRC schedule. The amount required to be remitted is in inverse proportion to the rate of foreign tax paid on the earnings. The ETC provisions of the code permit the exclusion of limited amounts of Subpart F income from current U.S. tax in certain circumstances where U.S. exports are being actively promoted and increased by a foreign subsidiary.

The act also provides for the filing of information returns in connection with the ownership of an interest in a foreign corporation (Forms 959, 2952, and 3646).

A U.S. shareholder is subject to ordinary income taxes rather than capital gains on the sale of shares in a CFC or the receipt of distributions upon its liquidation. Gain from the sale or exchange of a patent and other similar property to a foreign corporation by a U.S. person owning more than 50 percent of the stock of such corporation also constitutes ordinary income.

The foreign personal holding company provisions of the IRC also result in current taxation of U.S. shareholders on earnings of foreign corporations but apply only where more than 50 percent of the stock of the foreign corporation is owned by five or fewer U.S. individuals.

Multinational companies. Since 1962 the use of foreign holding companies has decreased considerably, and the legal form of foreign operations has tended to become decentralized. However, holding companies and regional administrative companies can be useful management devices and can still avoid current U.S. taxation under the CFC provisions where U.S. shareholders own no more than a 50 percent interest in the foreign company, where it is used for the coordination of operations in less developed countries, or where it also is engaged in active business operations and less than 30 percent of its gross income is Subpart F income. However, even if the CFC provisions do not apply, the use of a holding company can lead to increased overall taxes if dividends are required to be paid through a chain of companies and are subject to withholding tax in more than one country.

It is customary for a U.S. parent company, as the originator of proprietary products and know-how, to charge its related companies a fee for the use of such products and know-how. This approach avoids the tax problems otherwise inherent in the parent's contributing its know-how and intangible property rights to the capital of the subsidiaries, which can either result in taxation to the parent on the appreciation in value or necessitate its obtaining an advance ruling from the IRS. It also provides the U.S. parent with a source of income which is normally deductible by the subsidiary; serves as a reimbursement to the parent company for research and development expenses which benefit the subsidiary through improved products; and can eliminate possible tax problems under Section 482 of the IRC, which permits the IRS to allocate income, deductions, and credits between related companies in order to prevent evasion of taxes or clearly to reflect the income of the various companies involved. This section has been used frequently by the IRS in recent years as a device for taxing the maximum amount of income from within a group of related companies in the U.S. on a current basis, and detailed regulations have been issued with respect to licensing of intangible property, leasing of tangible property, performance of services, making of loans, and pricing of sales between related companies. Related problems can arise, under foreign laws and income tax conventions, where subsidiaries may be denied deductions for payments to related companies if they are excessive. The administrative provisions of the IRS for mitigating double taxation resulting from different treatment of the same transaction by the U.S. and foreign governments are not always satisfactory.

Tax problems can also arise in connection with intercompany loans. Loans from one foreign subsidiary to another may be regarded by the IRS as a dividend from the first subsidiary to the U.S. parent and a contribution to the capital of the second subsidiary. It is also important, in a U.S. company's investment in foreign companies, that a proper ratio between debt and equity be maintained so that loans from the U.S. company are not reclassified as stock under the so-called thin-incorporation doctrine, pursuant to which repayments of the loan by the subsidiary would be regarded as dividends to the parent company.

U.S. EXCISE TAXES

An interest equalization excise tax aimed at improving the U.S. balance of payments by discouraging foreigners from raising funds in the U.S. capital market is imposed at rates up to 11.25 percent, as of March 31, 1970, on the acquisition by a U.S. person of stock or debt obligations of a foreign company. Exclusions apply for acquisitions of 10 percent or more of voting stock; for investments in less developed countries; for certain new and original issues, including Canadian issues; and for debt obligations with maturities of less than one year, securities acquired from a prior American owner, and obligations connected with certain export transactions. The tax is generally not deductible but increases the basis of the acquired security.

Section 1491 imposes an excise tax upon the transfer of stock or securities by a U.S. person or company to a foreign corporation as a capital contribution, equal to 27.5 percent of the excess value of the stock or securities transferred over the transferor's basis. This tax is designed to correspond to the U.S. capital gains tax which would otherwise be payable on a sale of the stock or securities.

—*M. A. Olson and Michael Prichard*

Repatriation of Income

The major reason for undertaking overseas investment is the hope of securing a higher income return than that available in the home market. The extent to which a firm repatriates its interest and dividend income instead of reinvesting in the host country during any given period of time depends upon a variety of factors: exchange controls in the host country; tax laws in both the United States and the host country; and the risks associated with increased overseas holdings.

Funds are also transmitted to U.S. firms from overseas affiliates in the form of royalties, license fees, rentals, management fees, and services. The inflow received in this fashion has increased steadily in recent years and is expected to continue to expand.

EXCHANGE CONTROLS

Many countries of the world, especially the low-income countries, impose restrictions on the purchase and use of such hard or convertible currencies as the U.S. dollar. Typically, the local currency is overvalued, and at the official rate of exchange the quantity of hard currencies demanded exceeds the quantity supplied. Under such circumstances the U.S. investor receiving interest and profits in the currency of the host country may be restricted in the amount of local currency which can be converted into dollars during any given period of time. The Chilean government, for example, in the past has not permitted repatriation of invested capital until two years after entry; the amount repatriated annually could not exceed 12.5 percent of the original investment.

The Brazilian government levies a progressive supplementary income tax on remittances of earnings on foreign capital if their average over a three-year period exceeds 12 percent of the registered capital and reinvestments. In addition, overseas firms producing goods or services for luxury consumption are limited in profit remittance to an amount equivalent to 8 percent of registered capital each year.

Significance of inconvertibility. The policy established by governments with respect to income repatriation varies considerably from country to country, although for the majority of countries controls are either absent or only slightly restrictive. For countries that do employ controls the degree of restrictiveness depends upon such factors as the type of currency in which repatriation occurs, the kind of investment project, the amount of income to be repatriated, the length of time the original investment has been in the host country, and related factors. Many countries simply place an upper limit (usually some percentage of the company's contributed capital) on income that can be remitted each year.

Control over repatriation of income represents a compromise that many countries reach in developing an appropriate balance of payments policy. A foreign exchange market free of controls generally encourages an inflow of outside capital. However, during some periods, governments find the demand for foreign exchange (including that for repatriation of income) so great that some kind of priority system and rationing become necessary. Under such circumstances the external investor may be unable to use the proceeds of his earnings as freely as he would like.

Inability to remit earnings affects many aspects of a firm's operations. For example, the firm with blocked currency may find it advantageous to use the currency to purchase local raw materials and other inputs even though the cost of imported items may be lower. It may be added that exchange controls may hamper a firm's operations not only by limiting the extent to which profits are remitted but also by controlling the volume and composition of its purchases from sources in other countries.

Guarantees against inconvertibility. It is believed that the risk of inconvertibility is a major deterrent to U.S. investment abroad, particularly in many of the countries of Latin America, Africa, and Asia. In order to minimize this risk with respect to overseas investment, the United States initiated the Investment Guarantee Program (IGP), under which a U.S. firm investing in certain countries can secure insurance against the risks of inconvertibility, expropriation, and war. If the firm is unable at a later date to repatriate its income because of restrictive exchange controls by the host country, it submits a claim and is reimbursed by the U.S. Government. The annual premium for each type of guarantee is .5 percent of the coverage; in addition, the program is limited to certain specified less developed countries (about 80 in number).

Firms insure against the risk of inconvertibility more frequently than against the other two risks. The procedure followed with respect to this type of risk is specific. Assume, for example, that a U.S. firm invests in one of the covered countries with the understanding that it can remit its earnings but finds, at a later date, that this is not possible because of new regulations or policies, or finds that remittance is possible only at a discriminatory exchange rate. Under these circumstances the U.S. Government will pay the U.S. firm, in dollars, an amount equivalent to 95 percent of the currencies the firm wishes to transfer. This program does not insure against devaluation, only that a transfer can be made at the applicable nondiscriminatory rate.

IMPACT OF TAXES

Tax laws of the United States and foreign countries have an impact not only on capital movements but also on the repatriation of earnings and principal. Tax laws and regulations are not only complex but also vary considerably from country to country and from one time period to the next. Accordingly, only generalizations are possible here. Particularly complex (and beyond the scope of this study) are tax laws pertaining to the transfer of funds from foreign subsidiaries to parent companies through such other forms of remittances as management fees, royalties, trademark licenses, and interest expense. Under some circumstances, these methods of transferring funds to the parent company may provide a tax advantage or be useful for a related purpose.

It is also possible that the prices charged in commodity exchanges between related companies be established in such a way as to reduce the tax burden. Generally, however, the IRS prohibits price quotations which differ significantly from those of an unrelated company.

When an overseas firm pays taxes to the government of the host country, the amount is a credit against the firm's tax liability to the U.S. Government. In most instances, the foreign tax rate is lower than that in the United States.

Taxes and the form of business operation. A major factor affecting repatriation of income with respect to tax laws is the form of overseas operation. In general, an overseas branch plant (not established as a corporation) is regarded by the IRS as a part of the U.S. parent firm. Its profits are combined with those of the parent firm and taxed at the applicable rate regardless of whether the profits are remitted to the U.S.

The situation with respect to an American subsidiary, incorporated abroad, is not altogether clear. Such a firm is regarded as a foreign residual by the IRS and until 1962 its income was generally not taxed until it was repatriated. Although the tax liability was only deferred, this technique was widely used by firms to conduct overseas operations in an advantageous fashion.

Provisions of the Revenue Act of 1962 were designed to prevent the practice. Accordingly, unless a subsidiary can prove that it is principally an operating company with legitimate manufacturing or distributing functions, its profits are taxed even though not repatriated to the United States. Nevertheless, the complexity of tax regulations still enables some firms to manipulate their operations and thus achieve a tax advantage.

The legality of taxing unremitted earnings of overseas subsidiaries has been questioned by some persons. It is argued that the U.S. Government has no jurisdiction over profits of an enterprise incorporated abroad, since the profits are not earned in this country. Finally, it is pointed out that it will be extremely difficult to enforce or administer these provisions of the Revenue Act of 1962.

Tax havens. Numerous countries and areas have established arrangements to set themselves up as tax havens and to attract the incorporations of foreign firms. Some of the tax havens are the Bahamas, Bermuda, Liechtenstein, Luxembourg, and Switzerland. Some of the inducements offered include a low income tax rate, sophisticated banking and legal systems, and a communication and transportation system which facilitates close contact with the industrial countries of the world. Other requirements include political and monetary stability and currency convertibility.

Western Hemisphere Trade Corporation. Under some circumstances a firm, such as one that qualifies as a WHTC (see page 8·18), is also able to secure a tax advantage.

ENVIRONMENTAL FACTORS

A wide range of factors within the host country influences the extent to which a company repatriates dividends and capital. In 1967 retained earnings (income not repatriated to the United States) accounted for about 20 percent of new U.S. private investment abroad. The figure was considerably higher (about 40 percent) for foreign-incorporated affiliates. Environmental factors influencing the repatriation policy include the risk of devaluation or inflation, conditions in the local capital market, and tax laws.

Devaluation. A key consideration is the threat of devaluation, which induces the firm to transmit funds out of the host country as quickly as possible. If a company decides to retain earnings in the firm abroad and the exchange rate is altered later, it will find the dollar value of earnings reduced to the extent of the devaluation of the foreign currency. Some firms partially avoid the risk of loss associated with devaluation through the forward purchase of foreign exchange. To be effective, the overseas firm must be able to predict its foreign exchange requirements relatively accurately. In addition, a cost is associated with a forward-exchange contract.

Appreciation of the foreign currency would, of course, enhance the value of retained earnings; few countries, however, correct balance of payments disturbances in this fashion.

Inflation. A closely related factor affecting the policy on income repatriation is the degree of inflation in the host country. Where inflationary pressures are severe, profits should be converted to dollars as quickly as possible. Devaluation is usually inevitable if inflation continues over an extended period of time. In the event that local currency cannot be converted into dollars because of exchange restrictions, a firm should hedge against inflation by converting its cash holdings into some other form, usually a real asset.

The capital market. The interest rate and availability of local capital will affect the decision to repatriate earnings and capital. All other things remaining equal, a low interest rate and ready access to the local capital market will encourage a firm to finance planned expansion from borrowed capital rather than retained earnings. The existence of inflationary pressures is also an incentive for borrowing local capital.

Tax structure. The tax structure in the host country is also a relevant factor. In some European countries, for example, the corporate income tax rate depends upon the extent to which earnings are distributed. Typically, the tax rate is higher in instances where earnings are retained than when they are distributed. In some countries these regulations apply to foreign corporations.

—C. W. Hultman

LEGAL FACTORS IN INTERNATIONAL OPERATIONS

Certain of the more important legal considerations in international business transactions are discussed in this section of the handbook.

Antitrust Laws

The U.S. antitrust laws are found mainly in two statutes: the Sherman Act, which states general prohibitions against contracts and combinations in restraint of trade, monopolies, and attempts and conspiracies to monopolize; and the Clayton Act, which contains more specific prohibitions against corporate acquisitions and mergers, tying arrangements, and (under the Robinson-Patman amendments) discrimination in price, services, or allowances.

THE SHERMAN ACT

The Sherman Act is applicable to transactions abroad that produce a restraint on or monopolization of "foreign trade or commerce of the United States." An agreement performed abroad that would prevent a foreign party from exporting its products to the United States would be within the scope of the Sherman Act even if permissible under the laws of the foreign country. Restraints or limitations on a U.S. company's freedom to manufacture in the United States or export from the United States into foreign markets would also be covered. Similarly, an act of a U.S. company abroad aimed at maintaining or enhancing a foreign monopoly would be subject to the Sherman Act if that monopoly limited the availability of products for importation into the United States.

In some circumstances even agreements between corporations related by stock ownership (such as a U.S. parent and its foreign subsidiaries) may be subject to the Sherman Act if their effect is to limit the corporations' freedom to compete with each other with respect to imports into or exports from the United States.

A U.S. parent may be subject to the Sherman Act if it causes its foreign subsidiary to act outside the United States to create or preserve a monopoly or trade restraint which affects U.S. trade or commerce.

There have been suggestions, but on no direct authority, that agreements to refrain from or restrict investment of capital into or out of the United States might be subject to the Sherman Act even though such restrictions would not necessarily restrict the flow of commodities into or out of the country.

THE CLAYTON AND ROBINSON-PATMAN ACTS

The jurisdictional bases for the application of the Clayton Act and Robinson-Patman Act are somewhat different from those under the Sherman Act. With respect to corporate mergers and acquisitions the test is whether the acquisition might tend substantially to lessen competition "throughout or in any section of the country" (the United States). Thus a merger between a U.S. corporation and a foreign corporation, or the acquisition of one by the other, would be subject to the Clayton Act if the two corporations were potential competitors in the United States—as, for example, where the foreign corporation had been actively planning to enter the U.S. market either by production in the United States or by exports to the United States.

The Robinson-Patman Act prohibits discrimination in price between two purchasers of commodities sold for use, consumption, or resale *within the United States*. The provision of the Clayton Act prohibiting tying arrangements in sales and leases of commodities also applies only to commodities sold for use, consumption, or resale *within the United States*. The language of these statutes seems clearly to be inapplicable to sales made in foreign commerce. However, price discrimination in favor of foreign buyers over U.S. buyers may be subject to the dumping laws of the foreign country. The Robinson-Patman provisions dealing with brokerage payments and discriminatory merchandising services and allowances appear to be applicable to any sale in U.S. or foreign commerce.

STANDARDS OF LAWFULNESS

Most cases involving foreign commerce arise under Section 1 of the Sherman Act, which prohibits contracts and combinations that *unreasonably* restrain trade. To determine what is reasonable, the adverse effect on free competition of a restraint is weighed against its commercial justification. For example, limited restraints preventing a foreign licensee of know-how from using the licensed know-how in competition with the licensor may be lawful if it could not reasonably be expected that such know-how would be used in the particular part of the world except by license or that such a license would be given without the protection of such restraints. However, if protection of the licensor's rights in the know-how is really of less importance than a desire to divide world markets, or if the restraints are broader than reasonably necessary to assure the confidentiality and properly limit the use of the know-how, such restraints will be illegal.

Restraints that might sometimes be clearly illegal if they occurred within the United States may be reasonable in international transactions, particularly if—

owing to economic conditions, governmental restrictions, or other barriers—there would be no U.S. commerce into the particular foreign area but for an arrangement (such as a joint venture) that requires certain restraints. On the other hand, a restraint may violate U.S. antitrust laws and be held invalid by U.S. courts even though a foreign court might enforce the restraint.

Illegality under the antitrust laws can result in criminal penalties; in civil injunctive action by the government that may restrain the defendant's freedom to conduct its future business; in a refusal by courts to enforce a contract, patent, or trademark in whole or in part; and in liability for treble damages to any person or company injured as a result of the antitrust violation.

THE WEBB-POMERENE ACT

The Webb-Pomerene Act exempts from the antitrust laws U.S. companies which associate together or cooperate for the sole purpose of engaging in export trade. The exemption does not apply if the participants restrain trade within the United States or restrain the export trade of any of their domestic competitors, or if the foreign purchaser is financed in whole or in part by U.S. Government funds.

FOREIGN ANTITRUST LAWS

A number of foreign countries have now enacted antitrust laws. However, such laws are typically much less stringent than the U.S. laws, often prohibiting only monopolies or abuses of market dominance, and their enforcement is generally less vigilant. Moreover, unlike the U.S. laws, they sometimes provide a procedure whereby a restrictive agreement or practice may be determined in advance to be *exempt* from the statutory prohibitions if it contributes significantly to the improvement of production or distribution of goods or the promotion of technical or economic progress within the country.

Of particular importance among foreign antitrust laws are provisions of the Treaty of Rome, which provides the legal basis for the Common Market. Although some European countries have traditionally fostered the development of cartels, Articles 85 and 86 of the treaty establish the basis for a viable antitrust policy that supersedes the national laws of the member countries to the extent that they are inconsistent. Article 85 is directed toward the elimination of practices that affect trade between member countries and are designed to prevent or restrict competition within the Common Market or have that effect. Article 86 prohibits the use of a dominant position within the Common Market to engage in certain restrictive business practices. A company that violates these provisions can be subject to substantial fines, and an agreement contravening Article 85 is null and void.

Exemptions from the treaty provisions may be available either on an individual basis, by filing the proposed agreement with the European Economic Commission, or on a class basis if the agreement comes within the scope of regulations issued by the commission. For example, exclusive distribution contracts, which have been subject to extensive surveillance under Article 85, are exempt without being filed with the commission if drafted and administered in compliance with the conditions set forth in Regulation 67/67. The treaty does not restrict contracts with commercial agents, who, unlike a distributor or independent merchant, sell for the account of the manufacturer.

The Stockholm Convention establishing the EFTA also contains general statements of intention renouncing restrictive business practices. However, unlike the Treaty of Rome, it does not encroach upon the sovereignty of the signatory countries, which are solely responsible for enforcement of its provisions.

Japanese industry is marked by a high degree of cooperation among competitors, and collective action is often permitted and even encouraged by the Japanese government as a means of strengthening the international position of Japanese industry. Japan's investment restrictions normally compel foreign companies to conduct business in Japan by means of joint ventures in which the foreign company owns less than a majority share interest. U.S. firms should be aware of potential liability under the U.S. antitrust laws that may arise from their participation in such a joint venture where the Japanese firm may be engaged in such collective action.

Termination of Contracts with Commercial Agents

Many countries compel a manufacturer who, without justification, terminates an arrangement with a commercial agent or sales representative to compensate the agent or representative in an amount intended to indemnify him for the resulting loss of profits. The public policy of protecting such representatives against a manufacturer's confiscation of their customers and goodwill without fair compensation overrides the principle of freedom of contract, and normally the statutory benefits cannot be effectively waived by contract. The applicable laws vary from country to country and must be checked in each case. They usually do not apply to independent distributors who sell for their own account, but exceptions to this rule have been established in a number of countries either by statute or judicial construction. Although various provisions can often be included in the agency contract to reduce the manufacturer's exposure under such statutes, frequently none completely insulates it from such liability.

Protection of Industrial Property Rights

Industrial property rights are protected in foreign countries by patents, trademarks, and copyrights. Unpatented technical know-how should be safeguarded by a binding agreement.

PATENTS

A patent provides its holder protection only in the country granting the patent; therefore, companies engaged in international business must consider in which foreign countries to file. Filing is often done only in major industrial countries. Many foreign countries require the payment of annual taxes or fees and the actual use of a patent within a designated period of time to maintain a patent in force.

Generally, a foreign patent application must be filed prior to the publication of any writing describing the invention or before its sale or public use, although

a U.S. or Canadian application can be filed within one year after the first published disclosure, sale, or public use of the invention. If a U.S. application has
been filed, a corresponding foreign application filed within a period of up to
one year thereafter will usually be accepted in the foreign country as if filed on
the same date as the U.S. application, under a provision of the International
Convention for the Protection of Industrial Property ("Paris Union"), to which
most industrialized countries, including the United States, adhere. Unless a
prior license is obtained from the U.S. Patent Office, a U.S. inventor cannot
file an application for a foreign patent on an invention made in the U.S. until
at least six months after the filing date of the corresponding U.S. application.
Foreign filing of certain inventions or in certain countries may require a U.S.
State Department or Commerce Department license.

As of this writing, a patent cooperation treaty has been prepared for submission to a diplomatic conference of the member states of the Paris Union. The
proposed treaty, if it is enforced, would significantly simplify the procedure for
obtaining patent protection outside the inventor's home country. It does not,
however, provide for an international patent.

TECHNICAL KNOW-HOW

Unpatented technical know-how is frequently sold, transferred as a contribution to capital, or licensed to foreign firms by U.S. businesses. As a matter of
practice, valuable know-how should normally not be disclosed to a licensee until
a valid and binding license agreement has been executed by the parties and
approved by the foreign government, if necessary. However, where a potential
licensee wishes to evaluate the know-how in advance, a special disclosure agreement is sometimes used, pursuant to which the licensee pays the licensor a
substantial advance payment and also agrees to keep the information confidential. Disclosure of technical know-how to a foreigner is subject to U.S. Commerce Department, State Department, or Treasury regulations.

Protection of the confidential nature of know-how may be wholly dependent
upon the terms of the license agreement or general contract law, for a number
of countries do not have specific laws protecting trade secrets. Both patent and
know-how licenses are frequently subject to special taxes, foreign governmental
regulations and approval, and other foreign legal considerations. Special precautions should be taken in licenses of know-how and patents in combination.
Restrictions upon the licensee's manufacture, use, or sale of a patented product
may be legal because of the national character of a patent, but similar limitations may violate antitrust laws when unpatented know-how is also in question.

TRADEMARKS

Trademark rights, like patents, are national in character. In contrast to U.S.
practice, in most foreign countries these rights depend on priority of registration
rather than priority of use; therefore, early consideration should be given to a
foreign trademark program. Where a trademark license is granted, the licensor
must control the nature and quality of the goods on which the licensed trademark is used, and in many countries the license or a registered user agreement

must be submitted to a national trademark office. The manner in which a non-controlled foreign business is permitted to use basic trademarks should be carefully defined.

Most European countries (but not the United States) are members of the Union of Madrid, an international trademark agreement. The union permits a business establishment in a member country to obtain a national registration and then obtain protection in all member countries by making a single additional registration with the international bureau of the union. If operating subsidiaries of U.S. corporations are located in member countries, they can register marks under the union. However, most parent companies prefer to retain full ownership rights in their basic trademarks and merely license their use to subsidiaries. Under Section 526 of the U.S. Tariff Act of 1930 the owner of a U.S. trademark registration can, under some circumstances, prevent the importation of foreign items bearing that trademark, but not where the trademarks are affixed by a licensee of the registrant or a company related by stock ownership.

INTERNATIONAL COPYRIGHTS

Most of the major countries adhere to the Universal Copyright Convention or similar treaty. The use of the symbol © for copyright on all published copies of a writing, together with the name of the person claiming to be the owner of the copyright and the year in which the copyrighted writing was first published, if in the proper place and form, will normally provide the basis for protection in all member countries. Sales brochures, advertising programs, contract forms, and other documents are often copyrighted.

Contracts, Foreign Litigation, Enforcement of Judgments, Arbitration

A number of special problems can arise from the international nature of transactions and from the influence of civil law systems and concepts.

CONTRACTS

Almost every international business transaction involves one or more contracts. Special emphasis must be placed upon clarity and comprehensiveness of the contract itself, particularly where the parties themselves are not bilingual and the unfamiliar laws of a foreign jurisdiction are potentially applicable. It is often preferable to stipulate that the English version of the contract will be binding upon the parties.

The ultimate test of a well-conceived contract is its enforceability. Much uncertainty can be eliminated by expressly providing that the contract will be interpreted under the laws of a particular jurisdiction, and most courts will give effect to a choice-of-law provision if the jurisdiction selected by the parties has a reasonable relationship to the execution or performance of the agreement. If, as sometimes happens, neither party will agree to the application of the laws of the jurisdiction in which the other party resides or has its principal place of business, the contract may have to be silent on this point, with the practical result that the applicable law will be determined by the court where a lawsuit is entered. Many courts purport to apply the law of the jurisdiction where the contract was made in determining questions of validity of the contract, and the law of the place of performance in determining the manner and sufficiency of performance. However, owing to difficulties in proving foreign law—as well as determining the place of execution or performance of a contract where more than one country is involved—as a practical matter the laws of the jurisdiction where suit is brought are frequently applied. In many foreign countries, a contract cannot be enforced unless it has been recorded in a public registry. Such recordation may be subject to significant notary fees and stamp taxes, which are often calculated as a percentage of the value of the contract.

Contracting with foreign governments. Contracting with foreign governments or their agencies presents special problems. Care should be exercised to insure that the governmental party has complied with all applicable procedures and regulations before entering into the contract, and it should be recognized that the foreign government may be immune from lawsuit under a doctrine of "sovereign immunity" unless a valid waiver has been obtained.

FOREIGN LITIGATION

In the absence of an agreement to submit to the jurisdiction of a specified court, a determination must be made under court rules and statutes as to whether a court can properly exercise jurisdiction. The concepts of jurisdiction exercised by foreign courts may differ markedly from U.S. concepts, permitting— for example—jurisdiction over any party contracting with a national of that foreign country if that party has received notice of the lawsuit. U.S. courts have traditionally been more reluctant to exercise jurisdiction over a foreign party and have typically required that the foreign party either be present in the jurisdiction, conduct business therein, or at least own property situated therein, in which case jurisdiction is limited to the property itself; but in recent years U.S. courts have asserted jurisdiction over parties on the basis of extremely limited contacts with the jurisdiction.

Discovery and evidentiary procedures in foreign courts also differ substantially from those to which U.S. litigants are accustomed. Evidence is typically presented almost entirely in written form, and the parties to the dispute may not be permitted to offer testimony, either written or oral. The losing party frequently is obliged to pay the legal expenses of both parties. Language differences and the expenses and difficulties inherent in carrying out investigations, transporting witnesses and exhibits, researching foreign laws, and working with foreign lawyers can make a lawsuit with a foreign party even more expensive and disruptive for a U.S. company than a domestic suit.

ENFORCEMENT OF FOREIGN JUDGMENTS

Even after a judgment has been obtained, its enforcement may be difficult and uncertain. If the judgment is entered by a court in the losing party's country, enforcement difficulties may be limited to the customary ones of finding sufficient assets, but the delays encountered in foreign countries can also be extraordinary. It may be necessary to begin a new lawsuit in the losing party's country to enforce a judgment entered by a court outside that country, and that party may be permitted to raise its defenses anew. Some countries have agreed by international treaty to enter judgment by means of a summary proceeding in such circumstances, and courts in some other countries not a party to such treaties may do so as a matter of practice if certain minimum standards are met. The manner in which foreign judgments can be enforced in the United States usually depends on the law of the state where enforcement is sought. Such enforcement is a matter of comity and may require a showing that the courts of the particular foreign country would grant enforcement on a reciprocal basis. It may also be more difficult to obtain equitable forms of relief in foreign countries, such as injunctions and specific enforcement of contractual provisions; the only remedy is more likely to be the payment of damages.

ARBITRATION

An agreement to arbitrate international commercial disputes may enable the parties to a contract to settle such disputes privately, more quickly, perhaps less expensively, and by submission to a person or persons and laws or principles familiar or acceptable to the parties.

At present, the enforceability of clauses in international contracts providing for arbitration of future disputes must be considered on a country-by-country and state-by-state basis. They are currently not enforceable under the laws of most Latin American countries but are enforceable in most industrialized countries and most states of the United States. However, unless agreed to the contrary by international treaty, an arbitral award entered in a country other than that in which enforcement is sought may not be recognized, or if recognized may be subject to enforcement in the same manner as a foreign court judgment.

The U.N. Convention on the Recognition and Enforcement of Foreign Arbitral Awards, dated June 10, 1958, provides for the general recognition of the validity of arbitral clauses in contracts and for simplified enforcement of awards made thereunder. As of March 31, 1970, 35 countries had ratified the convention —including, however, only Ecuador and Trinidad and Tobago in the Western Hemisphere. The U.S. Senate has approved accession to the convention, but the accession will not become effective until uniform recognition and enforcement of foreign arbitral awards within the United States itself has been established by changes in the Federal Arbitration Act.

A comprehensive arbitration clause may include not only agreement to arbitrate a dispute if not otherwise settled within a specified period of time but also agreement as to the place of arbitration; the number and manner of appointment of the arbitrators; the portions of their fees and other costs of arbitration to be borne by each party; the laws, if any, to be applied by the arbitrators in reaching their decision; and the rules of arbitration to be applied with respect to matters not otherwise agreed upon. Parties to a contract frequently stipulate that the rules of the International Chamber of Commerce, the American Arbitration Association, or some specialized trade association are to apply to any arbitral proceeding thereunder. The parties may want to expressly exclude certain types of disputes from arbitration, particularly matters in which a decision is apt to be clear, such as the validity of patents, trademark rights after termination of the contract, and amounts due on intercompany accounts; and they may wish to limit arbitration to disputes involving amounts less than a stated dollar value.

An agreement to arbitrate should not be looked upon as a panacea. When the arbitration has taken place in a foreign country, many parties have encountered nationalistic prejudices and have been compelled to accept procedures to which they are not accustomed. Moreover, expenses of arbitration often are not substantially less than expenses of litigation itself. Many parties do not agree in advance to arbitrate future disputes but prefer to attempt to reach agreement on arbitration at a time when a dispute has actually arisen.

UNIFORM LAWS

The dire need for more uniform laws and more widespread acceptance of such laws by the United States and all industrialized countries, whether in the area of arbitration and enforceability of foreign arbitral awards or judgments or in the areas of commercial laws relating to the sale of goods, the manner of payment in international transactions, and the like, is becoming more widely recognized. It is a particularly acute problem for multinational companies, which are in a unique position to urge progress on such matters and to assure that such laws, when adopted, reflect not only a workable compromise of diverse legal traditions but also practical and acceptable commercial and business practices.

U.S. Restrictions on Foreign Direct Investments

The Foreign Direct Investment Regulations are a part of the U.S. balance of payments program. They limit the amounts which a U.S. individual or company may invest in foreign entities or business ventures in which it owns at least a 10 percent interest. (They complement the interest equalization tax, which is aimed at portfolio investors and has no application where a 10 percent or greater interest is owned.)

The regulations may require repatriation of foreign earnings as well as restricting new transfers of capital. Moreover, they do not apply just to "capital investments" in the normal sense but also to the extension of open accounts to related companies, even when on normal business terms, and in some circumstances to the transfer of shares of stock and other noncash assets. Among the major exclusions are investments in Canada, guarantees of loans obtained by foreign affiliates (although repayment of the loan by the guarantor would be an investment at that time), and investments made from funds borrowed on certain terms from foreign sources.

The burdensome effect of these regulations for small and medium-size companies has been substantially reduced by the increase (up to $1 million) of the annual amount which may be invested without specific authorization from the Office of Foreign Direct Investments and without relation to prior years' investments. An additional exemption of $4 million per year for investments in developing countries has now been proposed.

The regulations also limit severely the amounts which a U.S. direct investor may maintain in foreign bank accounts, commercial paper, and other short-term paper and foreign government securities (except where such paper arises from the export of U.S. goods or services); currently, the limit is $25,000 for most investors. Special record-keeping and the filing of reports at least annually is also required

Role of U.S. and Foreign Lawyers

Both U.S. and foreign laws normally apply to an international transaction in which a U.S. company is engaged, and frequently both U.S. and foreign lawyers must be consulted. A U.S. lawyer specializing in international business matters should be contacted initially, for he may be in the unique position of knowing the applicable U.S. laws; knowing the foreign legal problems likely to be encountered and being at least generally familiar with the applicable foreign laws; having well-established correspondent relationships with skilled foreign lawyers, notaries, or doctors of economics, whichever may be appropriate to consult on the particular matter; and, if he is a member of the law firm acting as general counsel for the U.S. company, being able to readily coordinate the foreign venture with the corporate and domestic policies of the company.

—*M. A. Olson and Michael Prichard*

Section 9

Risk and Insurance Management

CONTENTS

The Problem of Risks

Risk Management Objectives

Risk Management Organization

THE PROBLEM OF RISKS

As a consequence of its activities and properties, a company is exposed to various risks of accidental loss—for instance, damage to a factory by fire, liability for injury or death caused by an automobile, loss of goods by shipwreck or embezzlement, or theft of trade secrets. Such risks, inadequately controlled, can be a threat to solvency or a needlessly high and unpredictable cost.

This section of the handbook discusses the management of such risks. Employee benefit insurances are treated in the Personnel section (page 3·61). The text is formulated in terms of a business venture, a company whose objective is profit, but the principles apply to any organization that is concerned with its operating costs.

Risks of Accidental Loss

It is not possible to make a complete list of the risks of accidental loss. They vary with operations, place, and time. They are not all insurable. Moreover, their identification depends on how they are analyzed: for example, fire, as opposed to fire caused by war, by riot, by earthquake, or by other causes; and direct or material damage by fire, loss of rent, loss of earnings from use of property, or liability for fire damage.

Scope of Risk Management

The work of managing a company's risks of accidental loss requires up-to-date information on company operations present and planned, perception of the risks incident to the operations, and appreciation of the risks as to probable frequency and possible severity of losses.

The risks can be controlled by various means. Measures can be applied to reduce the frequency and severity of losses. Risks can be transferred by insurance and other contracts. For some losses, a plan of risk retention (noninsurance) is advisable. In rare cases, a risk can be avoided entirely by operational means.

The administrative function of risk management involves records, statistics, communications, and reports.

All risk management functions must, then, be managed—planned, organized, directed, and controlled—toward defined objectives.

Definition and Terminology

Risk management is the control of the risks of accidental loss to which a legal entity is exposed, by avoidance, transfer, reduction, and other means, coordinated to the efficient protection of the assets and earnings of the entity and the furtherance of its objects.

The term "risk management" is rapidly replacing "insurance management," which earlier replaced "insurance buying." Evolutionary changes in function rendered the old terminology misleading and an impediment to communication and cooperation within companies.

The term "insurance management" was appropriate when the job done was, above all, the programming and buying of insurance, and when loss prevention measures were justified primarily by premium saving. But there are several lines of attack on risks besides insurance; some insurable losses should not be insured; premium saving is as often as not an inadequate test for loss prevention; and, finally, the various costs and control measures have to be coordinated. The function so conceived extends beyond insurance and premium-justified loss prevention; it requires dealing with other company departments in matters beyond the scope indicated by the "insurance" title. Since it is important that job titles, position descriptions, company organization charts, and manuals be communicative, it is recommended that appropriate changes be made to reflect the corporate need for risk management, not just insurance management.

The essence of risk management, as a practical concept, is coordination of the means of control toward a defined integral objective and organization appropriate to that end.

In a later part of this section an objective for risk management is formulated. Its basic principle is expressed in terms of the cost to a company of risks during a given period. This cost, briefly stated, is the sum of the cost of loss prevention, insurance premiums, losses sustained net of indemnities from third parties and insurers, and financial and management expense.—*Douglas Barlow*

RISK MANAGEMENT FUNCTIONS

To facilitate the explanation of the respective components of risk management, it is assumed that the company has in its employ a risk manager, a person with prime responsibility and authority for managing its risks of accidental loss.

Information About Company Operations

Operations, meaning activities and properties, entail risks. A risk manager must be fully informed about the operations if he is to deal effectively with the risks. The information needed is extensive, and here only a few illustrations can be given.

The risk manager must get a general picture of the company's structure, operations, and finances. He must learn whether each location is owned or leased and, in the latter case, he must see the lease. He must learn the work done at each location and its relation to that at other premises. (It may be a factory that makes components for another, with resulting reciprocal dependency.) He must also learn the replacement and actual values of buildings and machinery, sources of supplies, principal takers of products, servitudes, and pertinent building codes.

He must examine construction contracts; contracts with governments; license contracts; and standard contracts of purchase and sale, including finance contracts. The possible list is long. The sources include financial records and reports, and visits to locations. A skilled risk manager should know where to look for information, when to stop, and when to dig more deeply; but even a skilled one, if he is newly in a company, would do well to use a checklist, of which several exist in the literature. One such checklist, entitled "Risk Analysis Questionnaire," is published by the American Management Association.

The risk manager must have timely information of plans for significant changes in operations. If the company is considering the purchase of a certain building, the site and the building ought to be inspected by a fire prevention engineer, for there may be hazards that would be costly to correct (for example, a roof presenting special hazard, a deficient water supply, or inadequate access). If the construction of a building is being considered, fire prevention engineers should be consulted on the plans for it. If another company may be purchased, its risks, incurred but unsettled liabilities, loss prevention, and insurances should be examined.

Timeliness of information is important, for usually control measures planned early are more effective and cheaper than those applied late.

Perception of Risks

A company's risks of accidental loss must be known if they are to be controlled. To perceive them in the company's properties and activities is a prime responsibility of the risk manager. It is a technical function, in which imagination, inquisitiveness, study, and experience count. Some risks seem obvious after a loss but fail to attract attention beforehand (mudslide risks, for example); and there are indeed accidents and losses that in retrospect must be conceded as unforeseeable, but the risk manager should not relax in anticipation of such an excuse.

The common risks—fire, riots, automobile accidents, injury to employees, and the like—are evident. But others are likely to be missed except by a person whose duty it is to perceive them. For example, it has not been unusual in the past for the top management team of a company to travel together in one airplane; and the practice is still not unheard of, despite widely publicized disasters. These executives ignore—or dismiss from their minds—the possible great loss to the company and their families, balancing the small probability of accident against what they can accomplish by traveling together.

In like manner, a company launching a new product arranges a trip by chartered airplane for a large group of its dealers and thus risks a substantial part of its sales. Or models, patterns, dies, and molds are shipped by rail or truck, entailing a risk of loss of earnings.

Appreciation of Risks

Estimating the probable frequency and probable and possible severity of losses from a given risk is called appreciation of risk. These factors figure in the assured's decisions on risk retention, the amount to be retained and the financial arrangements back of it, and on insurance and the amount of it.

As to probable frequency of losses, it is usually not hard to form an opinion that is accurate enough for practical purposes. In the case of a sizable company, the loss record of the past few years is the most significant guide.

"Maximum probable loss," which is synonymous with "probable severity," is a term of art in insurance on property and earnings from it. It is taken into account by an insurer in fixing the amount of insurance he will grant. The direct damage figure is estimated by loss prevention engineers. A figure for loss of earnings is developed on data and opinions from procurement, production, personnel, accounting, and sometimes other departments. It is accepted that there is an element of conjecture in both figures and that good faith must prevail.

"Possible severity," for which the term of art is "maximum possible loss," bears upon the amount of insurance to be carried. Experience shows that unexpectedly high losses happen. In the matter of the fire risk in respect of a building and contents, for instance, one should first postulate conditions that inhibit or handicap fire fighting by employees and the fire department, and then—in estimating the possible earnings loss—a period of reconstruction that may be prolonged by difficulty in getting replacement equipment.

Intelligent and diligent management can usually reduce the probability of extraordinarily high losses to a very small fraction of a percent, but not to zero.

In the matter of legal liability toward third parties for damages on account of injury, death, and property damage caused by automobiles, products, aircraft, and many other hazards, the possible loss is beyond the company's control and knows no absolute limit.

When estimating loss potentials, the possible ramifications of an accident should not be overlooked. For instance, in a complex of mutually dependent specialized factories, the destruction of one may close them all or add much to production cost. A fire in the factory of a supplier may interrupt or reduce company operations. An accident to an automobile driven by a salesman can result in destruction of the car, third-party liability, workmen's compensation claims, group insurance claims, bad publicity, and lost sales. Such ramifications have particular bearing on decisions on loss prevention.

Uninsured Consequences of Insured Losses

The loss possibilities of all risks of accidental loss should be appreciated—those that are insurable and those that are not, or that, though real, are not measurable. As a rule, insurance is patterned to pay obvious, easily measurable losses resulting from specified perils. In practice, there are also secondary loss consequences that do not get identified or measured and are not covered by the insurance, and they may range from insignificant sums up to multiples of the insured loss.

In the case of industrial accidents, there are many possible consequences not insured—the interruption of work in the vicinity or the training of a replacement, for example—and for most companies they amount to several times the insured loss.

In the case of risks to life and health, a potential consequential loss is present in the effect of accidents upon relations with employees, customers, or the public. This kind of loss cannot be predicted or measured, but it is real and not insured.

When a factory is put out of operation by fire, insurance may cover the direct damage and replace the earnings from production during a certain period, but in some cases there can be longer-lasting effects for which insurance is not adapted; such effects would include a loss of market to competitors, including the loss of dealers and distributors.

Such uninsured consequences of insured losses are an important consideration in making decisions on loss prevention. If a proposed measure of loss prevention is rejected only upon the test of the premium saving it will produce, and in disregard of the uninsured consequences of losses, the company may not be making the best decision.

Risk Avoidance

Company operations may be planned or changed in order to avoid or eliminate a risk. A department store may stop selling fireworks because of the special fire and explosions hazard to its property and the danger to customers and employees. To cite another instance: In some places, in accordance with local custom, wages are paid in cash at a company office, and for that purpose the company sends a car to a bank for the money; the hold-up risk can be eliminated for the company by hiring a special contractor to pick up and transport the money and even to deliver it to the employees.

Risk Transfer

The transfer of risk is accomplished by contract when, ancillary to the prime stipulations of the agreement, there are others that shift risks from a party who otherwise would bear them. Thus a contract for the lease of a building may provide that the lessee will, to the relief of the owner, bear such liability as would fall upon the latter for third-party injury and damage—for example, by collapse resulting from defect.

Loss Prevention

Measures may be taken in anticipation of losses to reduce their frequency and abate their severity. Common examples are sprinkler and fire alarm systems, good housekeeping practices, and welding-permit procedures, to control the fire risk; car inspections, driver training, and seat belts, to control automobile risks; safes, burglar alarms, watchmen, and accounting checks, to control the theft risk; the maintenance of duplicate or ancestor tapes, to prevent or minimize the loss of computer data; inspections of boilers, pressure vessels, and electrical devices, and consequent repair or renewal, to avert explosions and breakdowns.

In practice, most loss prevention methods are in the domain of established specialties such as fire prevention engineering, safety engineering, law, and accountancy.

Loss prevention measures are one of the factors in risk cost. For risk management planning, the cost of a proposed measure should be estimated as closely as is practical; and the cost of most preventive measures can be estimated to a useful degree of accuracy.

The cost of a fixed installation such as a sprinkler system can be closely forecast. The capital cost will be a contract price or equivalent; and if the system is installed on premises that are already occupied and in use, one may or may not choose to take into account the cost of disturbance of operations by the work of installation. The annual cost will be that of amortization, possible real estate taxes on the value the system adds to the building, weekly inspections by an employee, and maintenance.

For some measures there is justification outside loss prevention; thus good housekeeping practices in a factory, garage, warehouse, or the like serve efficiency as well as fire prevention.

Risk Retention and Insurance

Relative to an assured, insurance is a contract under which, in consideration of a fixed or determinable price in money known as a premium, another party who is known as the insurer and who is in the business of making such contracts undertakes, subject to conditions and limits, to indemnify the assured in money in the event that, during a certain period, he suffers a defined loss that, at the time the contract is made, is uncertain of occurrence, amount, or time. The contract may also stipulate that the insurer will provide services to prevent losses and to abate those that occur.

Risk retention means bearing losses without insurance, a practice sometimes called risk assumption. It may be accomplished by not insuring a given risk, such as loss and damage to automobiles, or by using a deductible (loss payable in the measure that it exceeds a certain figure) or a franchise (loss payable in full if it reaches a certain figure).

The motives for risk retention are as follows: First, it may be assumed that the premium for a given type of risk is adequate or that, over the years at least, the insurer will break even or make a profit. However, on the average, the premium dollar paid by a commercial or industrial assured includes 35 to 45 cents for the insurer's expenses (including commission to the agent or broker, or corresponding sales and service expense), the remainder being for the loss fund; and the smaller the loss, the higher the expense ratio. Therefore, to carry insurance against losses that are small in proportion to a company's means will normally add unnecessarily to risk cost. Second, in some circumstances, risk retention can evoke greater care and so reduce losses; and this factor in turn may induce an underwriter to accept a risk that he would turn down were the applicant not sharing it.

A company's interest is to be served by a planned pattern of risk retention in respect of accidental losses which it can economically bear, and insurance upon those it cannot. A first-thought ideal pattern would be a single insurance contract covering "all insurable risks" or "all risks of accidental loss," to pay the excess of the aggregate of the losses during a year over an agreed amount. This is not only impossible; it would need exceptions if it were possible. The pattern will be affected not only by a general objective for risk retention and the needs for insurance but by the fact that certain risks should not or may not be retained, by the circumstances of the insurance market, and by the reputation and skill of the assured and of those who negotiate for him in the market.

RISKS NOT TO BE RETAINED

A deductible is not usually desirable in liability insurance when it would involve the company in setting up its own organization and procedures for investigation of accidents and negotiation and defense of claims, for insurers' organizations can normally do the job better.

Parenthetically, it may be noted also that a company (or private person, not an insurance company) may not legally "retain" risks of other parties—loss and damage to goods under financed sale, for example—beyond reasonable warranty obligations, for to do so would be to practice insurance without a license and might exceed the company's charter powers.

OBLIGATORY INSURANCES

In some jurisdictions, the law requires insurance of certain risks such as workmen's compensation, automobile liability, or direct-damage fire insurance on buildings in certain countries.

Contracts also may require insurance—for example, some leases and most construction contracts.

THE INSURANCE MARKET

Insurance market conditions are a principal factor in determining a pattern of risk retention and insurance.

By experience-based customs and laws and regulations, insurance is divided into classes such as life, annuities, fire (including certain other perils), general liability, automobile, aircraft, marine hull, and marine cargo. These in turn are divided into subclasses. The classifications differ in some degree between states, provinces, and countries. Thus a portfolio of insurance will have a number of separate contracts; and furthermore, they will not automatically mesh and some cannot be made to mesh.

Laws, regulations, and tariff agreements exist that restrict freedom to buy where and what one wishes.

There are hundreds of insurers, domestic and foreign, differing in classes of insurance written, financial risk-bearing capacity (including reinsurance), services, preferences, methods, skill in underwriting, and attitude in interpreting the contract when a loss occurs.

The term "services" refers in practice to the organization, personnel, and skills for preventing and abating losses. In the case of boiler and machinery risks, the inspection service accounts for more of the premium than do loss indemnities. In the case of the fire risk, insurers conduct research and provide skilled inspection and advice in planning through their associations. Insurers covering workmen's compensation provide prevention and rehabilitation services. There are analogous services for other risks.

Skill in underwriting means the ability to size up a risk and appreciate the loss possibilities in it, produce ideas to improve it, help draft a contract to cover it, and—except as restricted—name a fair rate. A further test of a good insurer is that bizarre losses do not upset him.

Among insurers there is diversity in attitude when interpreting the contract, particularly if there is a heavy or borderline loss. The prime legal evidence of the meaning of a contract is its written words, and interpretations of them can differ. Furthermore, an assured can inadvertently violate policy conditions. The assured will wish to deal with an insurer whose mind is open to unprejudiced discussion and for whom the concept of the spirit and intent of the contract has meaning.

For some high-loss or especially hazardous risks (for example, some of those to which aircraft operators, petroleum companies, and pharmaceutical manufacturers are exposed) it may not be possible to buy the amount of insurance needed, even in the entire world market. And a desired deductible or franchise may be refused; or it may be offered at a premium reduction so low, relative to the probable retained losses, that it would be uneconomical to accept.

THE ASSURED

Apart from the previously mentioned factors, the degree to which the pattern of risk retention and insurance approaches the optimum for a company will depend on the reputation of the company, its risk manager, and the insurance broker (if any) who negotiates for it—their reputation for good faith and fair dealing in negotiations on coverages, premium rates, and claims. Without such a reputation, the company will not get concessions, and it may not be able to get all the insurance it needs.

The pattern will depend also upon the knowledge of the market factors possessed by the risk manager and the broker (if any), and their technical skill in dealing with those factors.

RISK RETENTION LIMIT

To risk retention there must be a limit according to the company's means; the pattern of retention must not be such that the uninsured losses will embarrass it.

If a company's finances were run on an accounting cycle of 50 years rather than one year, and if it had plenty of surplus funds or unused credit, it could follow a policy of very high risk retention. An abnormally large aggregate of uninsured losses in some years would be offset by a small aggregate in others. But company finances are run on a one-year cycle; so the risk retention pattern must be such that the aggregate of uninsured losses in one year, the company's financial year, can be safely borne.

Predictability of losses depends on spread of risk. With more cars, buildings, employees, sales, and so forth, the loss pattern becomes more predictable. For any company, there is a probable minimum aggregate of accidental losses in a year; and in principle that aggregate at least should be borne uninsured, as being essentially inevitable. But the figure so produced will contain no margin for real risk bearing—that is, the acceptance of variance from year to year in the aggregate of the uninsured losses, and risk cost saving on that account; so a higher figure should be sought.

In the matter of pushing upward the level of risk retention, mention should be made of one line of reasoning that can be misleading. It goes like this: "If we can stand a four-month strike, as we did last year, we can certainly bear uninsured losses up to. . . ." In equally practical terms, the answer is that shareholders will accept a strike as an excuse for a shortfall in company earnings because the risk is uninsurable, or insurable only on terms so onerous that to accept them would be reproachable. In other words, if the risk to earnings by strikes were insurable as are, say, fire and automobile accident risks, the insurance would be carried.

An acceptable approach to establishing a permitted maximum for the aggregate of retained losses sustained in a year is to ascertain from top management what amount could be lost per share without so significantly affecting earnings as to evoke criticism by directors or shareholders, and multiply that amount by the number of the shares. Under one reservation, the resulting figure is the permitted upward variance from the probable aggregate of retained losses, and the total of these two figures is the permitted maximum of the uninsured losses during the year. The reservation is as to cash availability for repairs or replacements, and the said total may be reduced on this account.

The program of risk retention under the various insurances must then be so set up that it will be a practical impossibility for the aggregate of the retained losses sustained in a year to exceed the permitted maximum; this is a matter of technical skill and judgment.

Add that it is practice in many companies not to claim upon the insurance for very small losses that are in fact covered; they apply a voluntary franchise. This is sound practice, justified either by avoidance of time cost within the company, by the effect on loss prevention at profit centers, by premium rating considerations, or by the fact that picayune claims give an assured or a risk an unfavorable reputation in the insurance market, particularly if they are frequent.

RISK RETENTION FINANCES

When risks are retained, accounting/financial procedures should be set up for the losses that will be borne. The issues for decision are the following:

1. Should the losses be absorbed by the respective profit centers (facilities, services, or as desired) whose properties or activities occasioned them, or by the head office? (If by the former, the questions following do not arise.)

2. If the losses will be borne by the head office, should a reserve be set up for them? (If not, the questions following do not arise.)

3. If a reserve is set up: (*a*) Should quasipremium charges be made to the profit

centers, proportionate (in principle) to their risks? And (b) should the reserve be funded?

In the vocabulary of risk management, risk retention with a reserve (funded or unfunded) is called self-insurance.

Decision on the accounting/financial pattern is for the finance division, taking account of information from the risk manager about probable losses; and it should issue the implementing procedures.

As to a fund in a business enterprise, the writer is not aware of any justification for one, but in some cases there may be justification for a subsidiary insurance company.

A reserve without quasipremium charges is a device for budgeting and controlling the annual aggregate cost of the retained losses, and one should be set up if it is so justified in the interest of finance and risk management, account being taken of the cost of any added bookkeeping.

A reserve with quasipremium charges is a device for budgeting and controlling the annual cost of the retained losses, both aggregate and per profit center (or facility, service, and so forth), and it thereby contributes to costing and may act as an incentive to loss prevention. Again, the interests of finance and risk management are served, but to greater degree.

Broadly, a company should set up a reserve if the annual aggregate of probable losses from the retained risks is significant in the scale of its profit and loss figures, or if it desires the refinement of costing and (saving an alternative course open when a reserve is not used) the incentive to loss prevention, both mentioned in the preceding paragraph.

If a reserve is adopted, and if quasipremium charges are made to the profit centers, it is for the risk manager to determine the amounts, which he will do by reference to the premiums saved (actual and estimated) and the record of past losses.

In final word upon reserves, note that income and capital gains tax rules do not recognize them. In other words, the effect of an uninsured loss upon income and capital gains taxes is not changed by the existence of a reserve, and whether or not it be funded.

If a reserve is not set up, the question is whether the retained losses should be absorbed by the head office or by the respective profit centers (or facilities, services, and so forth) whose properties or activities occasioned them. The latter procedure would not serve costing but would provide an incentive for loss prevention, and for that purpose it is an alternative to quasipremium charges. However, if the loss retention is at a high level in relation to the finances of the respective profit centers, to charge the losses to them might impose a burden both disproportionate to their means and unfair as an index of the quality of their loss prevention—but, if desired, some ad hoc relief could be granted.

As compared with the considerations that operate in a business enterprise, those in a local government are quite different, and in practice the main issue there is whether to have a fund. Some local governments have one, some have had one, and some have not. There is a good deal of experience in the matter—part happy, part otherwise—and any government looking into the idea of a fund should get acquainted with the record.

SUBSIDIARY INSURANCE COMPANY

Decision regarding the formation of a subsidiary or captive insurance company as a risk management tool (as opposed to a measure of diversification) involves consideration of many factors. Readers who are interested in looking further into the subject are referred to AMA Management Bulletin 102, *Captive Insurance Companies,* and the bibliography noted therein.

RETENTION OF REMOTE RISKS

So far, the discussion of risk retention has postulated the carrying of insurance, adequate in amount, upon all insurable risks that present possibility of high loss (with deductibles or franchises when practical). However, when a high-loss risk is of extremely low probability and the premium to cover it is exorbitant, a company may not unreasonably decide to take its chances on it.

An example is earthquake or flood damage to property in a zone considered safe from such perils. (But the insurance market should be sounded at intervals, and it would be reasonable to carry insurance to pay damage up to a certain fraction of the value.) Another example is the risk of liability over and above an insured limit indicated by caution in awareness of the widening exposures to liability—for instance, an automobile can derail a train carrying explosives or cut a gas pipeline—and the expanding concepts of legal duty and quantum of damages that the courts are developing.

Potential losses from risks so retained should not be taken into account in fixing the limit to the aggregate of uninsured losses. A decision to retain such a risk should be approved by top management or the board of directors, and the risk manager should review it from time to time to take account of changes in the motives. (The probability may have increased, or the premium cost may have dropped.)

RECOVERING LOSSES FROM THIRD PARTIES

Many companies have procedures for recovering losses from third parties who are responsible for them—procedures that operate regularly in the case of uninsured losses, such as collision damage to automobiles; and in some companies in respect of relatively small insured losses, such as damage to goods in transit. The motive in the case of insured losses is to keep the insurance record clean of small claims that, in the case of experience rating, are unduly expensive in the form of premium.—*Douglas Barlow*

RISK MANAGEMENT OBJECTIVES

If the risk management function is to be performed satisfactorily, it must be directed to an established objective or, in other words, by formulated company policy on risk management.

Risk Cost as Basis for Objective

An objective should be a guide to action and a test of it. But the questions that arise in risk management are many and diverse, as also are needs and means of control; and with changes in a company's operations and in technical and economic conditions, new questions arise. So, while the objective should not be specific as to means, it should as far as possible be definite as to ends.

Such an objective can be formulated if risks are regarded as a cost. The cost of a risk during a given period would be the sum of the cost of loss prevention; insurance premiums; losses net of indemnities from insurers and third parties; and relevant managerial, administrative, and financial expenses—all incurred during the period and in respect of the risk concerned. Like any other cost, that of risks should be minimized; and this should be the basic objective of risk management planning. But the upward variability in risk cost introduced by risk retention must be ceilinged, and the basic objective must be qualified accordingly.

INTERDEPENDENCE OF RISK COST FACTORS

If the factors in the formula were independent of each other, a reduction in one would reduce the total, but they are reciprocally interdependent. Money well spent on loss prevention will reduce losses, including their uninsured consequences, and will usually reduce premiums. In the matter of the marine cargo risk, for example, improved packaging may save premiums and reduce retained losses (including such consequences as customer discontent because of delay for repair or replacement).

Risk retention means less cost in the form of premium and more cost in the form of uninsured losses, but through the psychological effect of the retention the losses may be fewer and smaller than they would be if covered by insurance.

Certain insurances may require considerable expense by way of administrative work in assembling information (on values, for instance), when a repatterning of the insurance, though involving more premium, might produce a net saving by eliminating such work.

APPLICATION OF RISK COST FORMULA

Because risk cost is the sum of interdependent factors, the process of developing a pattern among them that would produce minimal cost over the years and insure a limit to upward variance in one year would ideally be a purely mathematical one; but that is not possible.

The probable and possible secondary consequences of losses can, as a rule, be only bracketed; and premium rating formulas to take account of loss prevention measures are, unavoidably, both empirical and, as mathematical formulas, "noncontinuous." So the application of the risk cost formula becomes, as a rule, a comparison of risk costs based on specific alternative risk control measures.

In practice, it is in deciding upon measures for loss prevention that the formula is most often consciously applied; and then it is not uncommon that a recognition of possible serious uninsured consequences of large insured losses will turn the scale, with little actual fine calculation.

In summary, the risk cost objective is sound in principle; and it is a recommendable guide in practice, in that it requires all relevant factors to be taken into account, and in that—by quantifying the factors as far as possible—it restricts the scope for error in judgment.

Political or Social Basis for Objective

In some countries, mainly the developing ones, a company's practices in buying insurance can affect its relations with government and financial interests. The risk manager must take this into account, lest he prejudice the prime objective of the company.

Activities and property can cause injury and damage to others; and transfer of money under insurance or law of liability does not undo loss or restore the economy. Moral duty to prevent loss can go beyond risk cost interest.

Company Policy on Risk Management

In the light of the foregoing discussion, company policy on risk management may be formulated in accordance with the three broad rules that follow:

1. The aggregate cost of the risks is to be kept to a minimum and, in each financial year, below the point at which, by reason of uninsured losses, the company's assets or earnings would be significantly reduced, the cost of the risks being defined as (a) the cost, direct and consequential, of measures for loss prevention; (b) plus insurance premiums; (c) plus losses sustained, including consequential effects and expenses to curtail the losses, net of indemnities from third parties and insurers; and (d) plus expenses of relevant management, administration, and finance.

2. The prime objectives of the company are not to be prejudiced.

3. The life, health, and property of others are to be respected.

—*Douglas Barlow*

RISK MANAGEMENT ORGANIZATION

Responsibility for risk management is part of the overall responsibility of directors to manage a company to the advantage of the shareholders and conserve its assets; in practice it is part of the directors' general mandate to the chief executive officer, but at the next stage of delegation the function is divided.

Although the objectives of risk management require that the function operate as an integral one, it is usually divided in organization by reserving to manufacturing, finance, marketing, and other company functions the line authority (the power to decide and act) for loss prevention measures within their respective fields of action, and to the legal department the line authority over legal proceedings stemming from risk management. The risk management department then has staff responsibility (to study and advise) in these domains, line authority in the rest of the risk management field including risk retention and insurance, and general responsibility for seeing that company policy on risk management is implemented; and it is as having this organizational content that the term "risk management" is used in the rest of the discussion.

Comparison of the function with, say, manufacturing or purchasing will show that risk management is not an essential or necessary part of finance or any other of the more or less standard major functions into which companies are organizationally divided. The delegation from the chief executive officer should therefore be specific.

In practice the function, with the reservation mentioned, is delegated by the chief executive officer to a person charged with another function—the corporate secretary or the head of finance, sometimes the head of the legal department. This person either retains the function and would properly be called the risk manager (though this title would usually be eclipsed by his major one), or he delegates it to a subordinate, designated here as the risk manager.

The Risk Manager

For any company or group of companies under one control, there should be one person with express general responsibility for risk management. Central control is essential. There may be risk managers in subsidiaries or conglomerate members, but they should function as a team with a captain. Insurance buying power can then be used to best advantage, interdependencies covered, and money for loss prevention spent where it will accomplish most. In brief, company policy will thus be better realized.

An executive charged with organizing the risk management function for his company is well advised to get an idea of the work by looking over programs (not merely titles) of recent annual conferences of the American Society of Insurance Management (an association of companies that have risk or insurance managers). Advice upon the matter can also be obtained from the American Management Association, from managers of companies that have a risk manager, and from insurance consultants and brokers who serve such companies.

PLACE IN THE ORGANIZATION

Practice differs as to the place of the risk manager in a company organization. The important points are that he answer to an official who can give him the support he needs to do his job and can review his work against company policy; that he have access to information about company operations and plans; and that he have a status conducive to cooperation on the part of other departments.

QUALIFICATIONS

Ideally, a risk manager should have special and general skills. Possession of the risk management diploma of the Insurance Institute of America or the Institute of Insurance of Canada would be an indication of special skills. Otherwise, or in addition, experience in insurance brokerage or in a risk management department should be sought. Although the work is upon a special problem, the risk manager will find use for any knowledge he has of law, business organization, engineering, and accounting.

To be borne in mind in selecting a risk manager is the fact that, to accomplish his task, he will have to deal with people outside the company—insurance brokers, consultants, engineers, adjusters, and insurers; that these people will be of diverse skill, from highest to indifferent; that the risk manager is responsible for getting good service from them; and that, whatever their self-orientation and good faith, their service will usually be improved in the measure that the risk manager is capable of checking it.

One technical aspect of risk management should be emphasized: The risk manager should cultivate his sensitivity to risks. To perceive them is a prime responsibility. In practice, he will have help from insurance brokers and others, but outsiders cannot fully relieve him of the burden.

One nontechnical aspect should be noted: The risk manager's work requires contact with all parts of a company's operations and, consequently, skill in getting cooperation from people over whom he does not have authority.

The risk manager works against a basic handicap. His duty is to foresee possible losses and then, in many cases, to get other people to change their methods so as to reduce the hazards. But this obligation runs against human nature. People in production and marketing, for instance, think positively in terms of producing and selling, and subconsciously they reject thoughts of possible fires, explosions, and accidents, particularly when the probability is very small; and, in defense of the positivism that makes them valuable, they may tend to regard the risk manager as a Calamity Jane. The risk manager should be an able salesman.

In the case of a company where means compel a compromise, better performance would usually be expected from part of the time of a generalist (company secretary, treasurer, or controller) than from the entire time of a lower-paid employee without special qualifications (young, promising executive material excepted).

CONTINUING EDUCATION

The risk manager should take the risk management course previously mentioned if he has not already done so; it is a home study course. He should also consider joining the American Society of Insurance Management, through a local chapter if there is one, otherwise by membership-at-large. If through a local chapter, he should attend its meetings and participate in its activities. Attendance at the society's annual conference is recommended as highly instructive. He should receive an insurance magazine. He would profitably attend a four- or five-day course in fire loss prevention soon after his appointment, and again after, say, five years.

RELATIONS WITH SUPERIOR

The official relations between the risk manager and the officer to whom he answers will be within the following areas:

1. The risk manager must count on his superior for timely information about company projects so that he can plan the risk management for them.

2. The risk manager will look to his superior for advice and support in case of difficulties in his relations with other departments—for instance, in getting information or in getting acceptance of loss prevention recommendations.

3. The risk manager should keep his superior informed upon matters of importance such as serious losses, departmental action of which the superior might wish to inform top management or about which he might receive comment or inquiry, and changes in law or in the insurance market that might necessitate substantial changes in the company's risk management patterns.

4. The risk manager will have occasion to seek instruction or confirmation of

proposals on changes in organization or procedures of the risk management department, and on important changes in the insurance program.

5. The superior will occasionally check with the risk manager upon progress or action on particular matters.

6. Periodically, the superior should hold a meeting with the risk manager and the broker to check performance against company policy, discuss problems, and make plans. The meeting should be structured by an agenda. The frequency of the meetings will depend on the size and complexity of the company and the changes in its operations, but twice a year should be regarded as a minimum.

7. The superior may require an annual report showing premiums, aggregate losses, important losses, and significant events and accomplishments.

Risk Management Staff

The size and responsibilities of the risk management staff depend chiefly on the size, operations, and complexity of the company but also on external organization—relationships with insurance brokers and others; no practical directives can be given.

In very few cases is there justification for having one or more loss prevention engineers on staff. Such services are available from consultant firms, insurers, and the larger brokers, with usually some saving in cost and the further advantages of wider experience and the fact that different engineers with differing perception will be doing the inspecting from time to time.

In the matters of record keeping and the compilation and analysis of loss statistics, there is potential duplication of work between the risk management department, the insurer, and the broker, and some of the work can be left to the insurance broker.

Some risk management departments do the relevant accounting as if they were a subbranch of the controller's department. This practice is debatable.

Establishing the Risk Management Function

Because the risk management function requires the cooperation of all departments, and in particular because loss prevention is divided as to responsibility but must be coordinated with other means of risk control, it is necessary to establish the right of the risk manager to get information and to be heard when he offers advice. To that end, a formal organization text is advisable, and the following (or an adaptation of it to company format and style) may be used.

Risk management means the management of the risks of accidental loss to which the Company is exposed, comprising the perception and appreciation of such risks and the control of them by measures of avoidance, elimination, loss prevention, risk retention, insurance, and loss recovery, coordinated to the objectives of Company policy; and it is organized as follows:

1. The position of Risk Manager is established, and it may be held by a person having other functions in the Company.
2. By delegation from the Chief Executive Officer to the Secretary (or other designated executive), and in turn by the latter, the Risk Manager is charged with line authority and responsibility for risk manage-

ment save that, as to the matters mentioned in the following paragraph, and legal proceedings relevant to risk management, he has staff authority and responsibility.

3. All officers and employees of the Company have authority and responsibility for loss prevention and avoidance and elimination of risks, within the scope of their respective functional authority.

4. Company policy as to risk management will be most fully implemented when the following conditions are present:

   a. There is organization that establishes responsibility and authority for the management of the risks and insures the availability of the skills needed to that end.

   b. Those having special responsibility for risk management are aware of Company operations, actual and planned, including contracts, and perceive the risks and appreciate them as to probable frequency and possible severity of losses.

   c. There is coordinated action to control the risks by avoiding or eliminating them, retaining them wholly (noninsurance) or partly (deductibles, for example), insuring them, and recovering losses from third parties and insurers.

   d. Mutual understanding of functions and cooperative relations exist between those having special responsibility for risk management and those from whom information, decision, or action is needed for the realization of the risk management objectives.

   e. The function is kept under critical review by those responsible for it, and reviewed periodically by higher authority, to test its service of its objectives and to ascertain that it responds appropriately to changes in operations and in available techniques of risk control.

   f. Records are kept as necessary to the foregoing.

In many companies, circulating an organization text and an appointment bulletin is not enough to establish the function effectively, and the subject should be put on the agenda of a meeting of division heads, where an announcement can be made and explanation given with particular reference to objectives and the need for cooperation.

The Insurance Broker

An insurance broker (usually a firm, but the third person singular is used here for convenience) is an intermediary between assured and insurers who, by his title and otherwise, holds himself out as having special skill in patterning and negotiating insurance and as being oriented to the service of the assured alone and free of obligation to favor any insurer. Generally, his income is in the form of a commission that is an integral part of the premium for the insurance bought, but exceptionally, for a fee paid by the assured, he may act as adviser only and not place the insurance, or he may negotiate insurance on terms that do not include a commission.

Should a company use one broker, or more than one? Should it ask competitive quotations of brokers? Among companies practice differs, and these questions are debated; but at present they are brought to no compelling conclusion. The reason for this is the diversity in quality of brokers' services, and the following notes must be regarded as reflecting the personal opinions of the author.

Insurance brokerage is undergoing a marked evolution, by way of clarification of objective, to acceptance by many of the brokers of the idea that, at least regarding industrial and commercial accounts, their future lies in service oriented unreservedly to the risk management objectives of their clients and of professional quality; this evolution will gradually put the broker's remuneration on the basis of fees paid by the client rather than commissions from insurers.

This development permits the recommendation that a company select a broker not by quotations on premium rates but on his reputation for service of professional quality and his ideas about service; that it appoint one broker only; and that it have an explicit understanding with him that his function is risk management directed to company policy. It may then be left to the broker to get competitive quotations when, in his opinion as an expert, it is in the company's interest to do so—for an assured's interests can be hurt by unsophisticated shopping.

As to the appointment of one broker only, a company that appoints more than one reduces its buying power, the broker's legal professional responsibility, and the interest and challenge that conduce to good service.

Organization for Loss Prevention

It is for the risk manager to provide or procure expert advice on loss prevention. Regarding such perils as fire, explosion, automobile accidents, and industrial accidents, he has access to expert services provided by insurance brokers, insurers, safety associations, and others. There are also consultant services in these fields and for the control of data processing risks, crime risks, and industrial espionage. For practically all risks, there is literature.

The risk manager's responsibility for providing advice on loss prevention extends to all risks of accidental loss and is not confined to those that are insured or insurable. Thus, for example, he may properly discuss, with the head of research and the head of the personnel department, the risk of industrial espionage —which is not insurable—and inform them of the available consultant services and get them the relevant loss prevention literature.

In the majority of companies, it is in the matter of fire prevention that the risk manager can accomplish most. Because he has provided the inspection of facilities and the consequent recommendations, it is his duty to provide to management concerned a judgment appreciation of the importance of the recommendations in the light of company policy; and if an important recommendation is rejected or neglected by local management, it is his duty to follow it up and, if necessary, get a review by higher authority.

The most important single factor in loss prevention is interest on the part of top management, and in duty to the company the risk manager will take opportunities to nourish that interest, particularly through the officer to whom he is responsible.

SPECIAL PROCEDURES

Certain risks need special procedures or practices. Following are two examples. For many companies, the products liability risk is particularly dangerous. It is recommended that a committee be set up to develop awareness of the risk and a concerted program of action to control it. Such a committee would include high-level representatives of research, engineering, manufacturing (including quality control), marketing (including advertising), law, and the risk manager, and be chaired by the risk manager or the representative of the legal department.

In regard to the fire risk in a metalworking industry, welding and cutting outside the booths set up for the purpose—in maintenance work, for instance—are a prime fire hazard and should be done only with permission of the fire chief and under conditions established by him.

It is for the risk manager to identify the cases where special procedures should be set up and to take the initiative in getting them established.

LOSS LESSONS

The risk manager, with help as needed from the brokers or loss prevention engineers, should examine all loss reports or, in the case of a very large company, see a periodic analysis of losses. The purpose of this practice is to identify trends and dangerous areas and practices and to institute corrective measures. In a company with many locations, the risk manager can use circulars to let location managers know of lessons drawn from losses.

Manuals

The use of a risk management manual is advisable. Such a manual should cover (1) policy; (2) organization, including an outline of the functions of the risk manager, his superior, and the broker, and the responsibility of other departments for loss prevention and legal proceedings; (3) practices (explanatory development of policy); and (4)(a) procedures considered advisable for routines within the risk management department and between it and the brokers, and (b) procedures for the governance of other departments in such matters as notice to the risk manager or the brokers of changes in risks, value reports, procedure on inspections and inspection reports, and procedure on the occurrence of loss.

Copies of the manual should be distributed at management levels, and copies of part (4)(b), with a brief explanatory introduction, to others as instructed by respective department heads.—*Douglas Barlow*

The Risk Management Consultant

Independent risk management consultants, usually called insurance consultants, are compensated by fees paid by their clients. Corporate executives use them for a range of services, from occasional special studies to continuing full-scale insurance management. With the exception of salaried risk managers, independent insurance consultants are the only professional insurance people whose income is derived directly from the insured corporations. This is in contrast to the situation of brokers, agents, and employees of insurance companies, who are compensated by salary or commission from the insurance companies. Consultants are not in competition with agents, brokers, and salesmen for direct-writing insurance companies, as they do not sell insurance. They undertake to provide their clients with an objective view of insurance problems that those more directly dependent on insurance markets cannot be expected to adopt. Although they are not in competition, it is nevertheless the function of consultants to review the work of agents, brokers, and insurers and to inform management what can be done to improve the insurance program.

Corporations large enough to have their own insurance departments and risk managers do not normally dispense with them by substituting an independent consultant. Smaller corporations might prefer to use a consultant to manage the insurance program rather than to hire a manager whom it could be difficult to attract and hold. Even large corporations, however, find value in having their insurance programs reviewed by unbiased experts. AMA Research Study 68, *Auditing the Corporate Insurance Function,* reports that risk managers showed a decided preference for insurance consultants, as auditors, over such other outside sources as agents and brokers or general management consultants. This study clearly indicates the importance which risk managers place on objectivity and competence.

Corporate executives, even more than their risk managers, have a vital interest in the objectivity and competence of the consultants they engage. Risk management is much less subject to quantitative and more subject to qualitative analysis than most corporate executives seem to imagine. Accordingly, the attributes of professionalism and integrity are more important than if the task were simply to measure whether standard coverage X is obtainable more cheaply from insurer A than insurer B. If coverage X were boiler and machinery insurance, for example, and the client corporation were a paper manufacturer, the choice of insurer A based on price alone could be the first step toward disaster.

Since they are compensated by their clients, rather than receiving compensation from the insurers, independent insurance consultants have no interest in maintaining premiums at high levels. Therefore, they feel free to recommend every legitimate technique and to suggest the employment of every responsible insurer in the market place. They also feel that their freedom from obligation to any segment of the insurance market enables them to perform nonpremium-producing services for their clients which premium-oriented producers might find unnatural. An example of such a service would be a study culminating in the establishment and staffing of a corporate insurance department. Another example would be a study resulting in the acceptance of a higher level of deductibles with concomitant premium savings, or a program of self-insurance.

When a large loss has occurred and it becomes apparent that the loss will be complex and difficult to adjust, the interest of a commission-minded producer may flag. He can be uncomfortably squeezed between his interest in the insured's problem and his continuing financial interest in selling insurance. He may even find, in case of dispute, that he is torn between the interests of the insured and the insurance markets, particularly at a time when insurance capacity is limited and the producer may be in dire need of markets for his difficult accounts. In such circumstances, the advisory services of a consultant could prove invaluable.

Reputable consultants recognize when agents, brokers, insurers, and corporate insurance managers perform creditably and are pleased to acknowledge such performance. Consequently, there is an increasing degree of respect and cooperation among the technically competent practitioners in these areas.

Critics of the insurance consultant tend to base their criticisms on fear of loss of income or displacement from the insurance picture; fear that the consultant will find fault without regard to fact; resentment that performance is being reviewed by outsiders; concern that the audit will be (or even must be) superficial; and the possibilities of sheer opportunism. Qualms of this type will be familiar to every corporate executive who has considered the employment of a consultant in any facet of his business. They do not, of course, constitute a valid argument against using consultants. They do, however, imply the importance of engaging technically qualified firms with broad experience, unquestioned integrity, and no financial interest in the placement of coverage.—*D. W. Berry*

Section 10

Purchasing

CONTENTS

The New Top Management Viewpoint of Purchasing

Purchasing Responsibility and Authority

Purchasing Controls

Purchasing Analysis and Planning

EDP and the Purchasing Function

Formal Purchasing Arrangements

Systems Contracting

Source Development and Selection

Negotiation

Legal Aspects of Purchasing

Internal and External Relationships

Evaluation of Purchasing Performance

THE NEW TOP MANAGEMENT VIEWPOINT
OF PURCHASING

The industrial purchasing function has evolved through many phases since the turn of the century. Two major wars, a long-term depression, and a number of business recessions and booms have all made their impact on the purchasing man and changed the manner in which he plays his role in the industrial business world. His role today is that of manager, not agent. His ability to operate effectively in this new role is based primarily on two factors: his management's attitude toward the purchasing function, and his own ability to manage a business relationship with his suppliers.

Historical Development of Purchasing

The responsibilities of the industrial purchasing man and his role in his company's operations have changed greatly over the past 50 years. In the early days, the owner or chief executive of the company generally handled important purchases. This is still true today in many companies where a purchased raw material or product represents, to a large extent, the final product sold to the customer. The purchasing department, for example, usually does not buy raw tobacco leaf used in the manufacture of cigarettes. The growth of business during the early 1900's gradually forced management to delegate some of the buying of key goods and commodities to the purchasing department. It was a slow and selective process, however, because growth was minimal at best, particularly during the depression of the '30's.

THE PURCHASING "AGENT"

In the early industrial organization, the purchasing function was not generally considered part of the internal operations of the company. The term "agent," commonly used as the title of the top purchasing man, signified an individual who served the company as liaison with the supplier. The company made its plans, generated its requirements, and turned over to the agent the list of items to be purchased outside the company which were needed to support (or "service" —the term generally applied to purchasing's operations) the internal operations of the company.

The World War II period saw the first major change in the role of the industrial purchaser. Shortages, priorities, rated orders, and related matters made the job of dealing with suppliers a highly complex one. The purchasing man became important, if only for his ability to scour the country for raw materials and parts to meet the company's production schedule. "Cost" was a word that was temporarily erased from the company's vocabulary. If the purchasing man could get what was needed—at almost any price—he had, in most cases, done his job to the satisfaction of his management.

The end of the war did not change the situation to any great extent. A consumer market that had gone without goods and services for five years was eager to buy and had the money to do so. The purchasing man continued to be viewed primarily as a developer of sources of supply, and the word "cost" continued to be heard but seldom. A couple of minor downturns in business did not change the environment appreciably, and the Korean conflict in the early '50's merely brought back most of the shortages, priorities, and other industrial troubles of World War II.

During this entire period, the techniques and responsibilities of the purchasing man changed very little. His activities fairly well reflected his title of "agent" ("one who represents someone else"), and the definition of the word "purchasing" ("exchanging money for goods"). Someone else told him what to buy, how much to buy, and when to have it delivered. In general, both he and his management were satisfied to leave things this way. The purchasing activity, sitting in the corner and handling paper, was generally considered as a necessary overhead by management, while the manufacturing man and the engineer thought of it as a function to be bypassed whenever possible.

COST CONSCIOUSNESS

The first indication of a change in the role of the industrial purchasing man began in the recessionary period which, for many industrial concerns, began in 1957 and extended through 1962. For the first time since the '30's, management became seriously concerned with cost. Profit margins began to shrink in the highly competitive marketplace as the consumer found himself, for the first time in many years, in the driver's seat. Management now began to seriously explore ways of reducing the costs of production. In so doing, it became aware that the purchased content of a product represented, in most cases, at least 50 percent of the total product cost. A quick financial look at the company's business easily showed that $1 saved in the purchased cost would have the same effect on profit as a $10 or possible $15 increase in sales. It soon became apparent that the purchased content of the product was virgin territory for cost reduction if one knew how to exploit it.

EXPANDING RESPONSIBILITIES

The enlightened purchasing agent reacted to the challenge of cost reduction and began to expand his responsibilities and develop the techniques which would lead him away from being an agent for his company and make him a manager of outside business relationships.

The change from agent to manager did not come easily. The mortality rate was high. A study of the men appointed to top industrial purchasing jobs during this period would probably show that at least half of them had nonpurchasing backgrounds. Just what did this change from agent to manager entail? First, it required recognition on the part of company management that the purchasing function, because of its tremendous impact on cost, had to become an integral part of the company's operations. Once this had occurred, the purchasing man was asked to accept the responsibility for managing the total relationship with suppliers—a responsibility which included far more than just "exchanging money for goods" and which, if effectively implemented, would assist the company in meeting its business objectives. Second, the change from agent to manager required the recognition and acceptance of his new role by the purchasing man himself.

Many managements in recent years have recognized the importance of the purchasing function within the company's total operations and have taken various steps, organizational and otherwise, to indicate their recognition. Although this new attitude has created an environment in which purchasing can operate more effectively, the primary responsibility for the implementation of his managerial role must fall directly upon the purchasing man himself.

PROCUREMENT FUNCTION

To fill this new role, the purchasing manager has to place particular emphasis upon two areas. First, proper support to purchasing from the other functions—such as engineering, quality control, and production control—which have an impact on buying decisions and supplier relationships must be established. The directing of all of these functions—including purchasing—toward the support of the buying relationship represents a relatively new functional concept (originally introduced in government buying) called procurement. Procurement expands the role of working with suppliers from one of merely exchanging money for goods to one of total responsibility for acquiring goods. Second, a procurement organization equipped with skills and experience necessary to perform the function at an excellence level must be developed.

The Procurement Organization

In order to balance more effectively the many functions which affect the buying relationship and assure their continuing support, companies should consider combining them organizationally to form a procurement function. The functions generally included are manufacturing engineering (known as procurement engineering when it is related strictly to purchased requirements), production control, quality assurance (not receiving and inspection, however), traffic, financial analysis, and estimating. Although management opinion generally agrees that all these functions must play a part in the supplier relationship, disagreement exists as to whether they should be grouped together organizationally and report to one man or operate as separate departments. To cite manufacturing engineering as an example: Many management people feel that it should be a separate organization, outside both purchasing and manufacturing, and providing services to both areas as required. Experience has shown, however, that two general problems result from such a separation. The first arises when both the manufacturing and purchasing groups require assistance from manufacturing engineering at the same time. The usual result is that the manufacturing group's requirements are met first. This is only to be expected, since the manufacturing group is made up of the company's own employees and the solutions to problems in one's own company are generally easier to implement than those of an outside source. This problem, nevertheless, can often be solved if the manufacturing engineering manager fully accepts his continuing responsibilities to suppliers as well as to in-house functions and distributes his manpower accordingly.

The second problem, probably the greater of the two, is created when an attitude of "service when requested" exists in the manufacturing engineering area.

SUPPORT FROM OTHER FUNCTIONS

The real benefit to the procurement concept is the establishment of a continuing and full-time responsibility to support purchasing on the part of other functions—manufacturing engineering, for example. When a manufacturing engineer is assigned full-time to outside relationships, he develops strong feelings of responsibility toward the supplier relationship. If the relationship is effective, he feels that he personally helped make it so. This type of continuing responsibility covers more than handling problems on a service-as-requested basis; it includes the initiation of such activities as technical cost reduction programs, improvement in the manufacturing processes, and the introduction of new and improved tooling programs. These are the sort of cost reductions the purchasing man cannot implement on his own; rather, they require the continuing support of the manufacturing engineer.

MAKE-OR-BUY DECISIONS

The ability to combine effectively all the functions which impact the buying relationship into a single organization hinges primarily on the make-or-buy picture within a particular company. If the make-or-buy decisions are fairly static so that the items that are purchased remain constant over a relatively long period, it should be possible to combine these functions into a single procurement organization. On the other hand, if the make-or-buy decisions are fluid so that the source decisions for items change back and forth, the personnel problems connected with shifting skills in and out of the procurement organization may negate the advantages to be gained. Such a shifting of sourcing decisions does not, however, change in any way the need for acceptance by the other functions of a continuing responsibility to the suppliers. If a separate procurement organization is not practical, employees in the other functions should be assigned on a full-time basis to support the purchasing organization.

Although we have discussed only the pros and cons of the procurement concept as related to manufacturing and engineering, the same points are valid for quality assurance, production control, and the other functions that support purchasing.

Purchasing Excellence

Regardless of the organizational approach used, the responsibility for meeting the company's objectives of cost, quality, delivery, and supplier relations must remain with the purchasing department. Only by handling all the areas effectively can an excellence level of performance be achieved. Effective handling is reached through no one skill but rather through the use of many skills applied in a professional manner by the purchasing department. Company management and the purchasing manager himself must recognize that only through the proper marrying and balancing of the skills can excellent performance be attained.

SKILLS

Among the more important skills that must be found and developed are proficiency in managing the various functions which affect a purchasing decision and the supplier relationship; ability to conduct effective negotiations and provide the supporting skills which are necessary for effective negotiation; and ability to understand and analyze all aspects of the business relationship with the supplier and to reach business decisions which properly consider these aspects.

These and all other required skills in purchasing are primarily acquired through continuing professional buyer training.

TRAINING PROGRAMS

The primary objective of any buyer-training program is to provide the buyer with the tools, techniques, and knowledge which will allow him to manage a business relationship effectively. The term "professional" applies because a great deal of the material can be taught within an academic environment. Few colleges or universities, however, offer more than a single general course in purchasing; therefore the responsibility for the development of the curriculum has fallen primarily upon the companies themselves. A partial listing of training subjects would include negotiations, including such areas as cost and price analysis; value engineering; contracts; industrial economics; and business ethics. Through these subjects, the buyer in his new role of manager of a business relationship gains the capability of evaluating all factors (both the buyer's and the seller's) which can affect the buying-selling decision. This type of training supports a fairly new concept: that the buyer and the salesman are not in direct conflict, each attempting to outdo the other in getting a "better deal" for their respective companies, but rather that the buyer accepts a role of manager and attempts to develop a relationship which utilizes the strengths and minimizes the weaknesses of both the buyer and the seller in a total business relationship.

The industrial purchasing man of today should play a basic part in his company's operations. When he does, he can, through his skills and knowledge, play a major role in the success of his company.—*H. J. Moore*

PURCHASING RESPONSIBILITY AND AUTHORITY

Consider the situation of the manager of a large industrial manufacturing company which produces a variety of products. As a profit-oriented business manager, he recognizes that procurement commitments control a significant proportion of the total operating budget; 50 percent of his production costs are for purchased materials and services. Furthermore, unplanned changes in the cost of purchased items could dramatically affect his budget. He cannot tolerate lack of control or of information on the status of purchased material costs or on progress accomplished against long-range plans. In fact, he needs more and better controls, more and better information. The traditional responsibility of purchasing to obtain a continuous and adequate supply of raw materials at reasonable prices is no longer adequate to meet company needs and must be expanded. The manager must be as well informed on planned purchased materials costs as he would normally be informed on the comparative costs of competitive manufacturing methods, distribution techniques, or marketing strategies. Effective control of such costs can no longer be regarded as a casual goal; it has become a vital necessity.

The paper-processing clerical function of purchasing is obviously not adequate to meet the company's information needs. What is needed is a single reliable source of advance information on cost of purchased materials, availability, long-range market trends, alternate sources, technological developments, and a host of other factors so that plans can be modified in time to prevent losses or take full advantage of possible gains. Equally essential is solid evidence that current and known future requirements will be met by competitive and competent suppliers.

If purchasing is to provide the expanded services required of it, purchasing must become a management function responsible for establishing goals, developing profit potential, providing essential information to management, and exploiting and directing market potential to achieve management objectives.

Coordination and Control

In seeking positive assurance that all requirements for purchased materials and services will be met and that the costs of these items will be within the limits available under the budget, management can consider making purchasing responsible for the development of standard unit prices for all major budgeted purchased materials and services, in the same manner as production is required to develop and forecast manufacturing unit costs. Standard unit purchase price forecasts could be incorporated into the budget, and performance could be measured by monthly variance reports in the same way as labor or other variable costs.

DELEGATION OF PLANNING

Recognizing planning as the key to effective control, the manager may elect to assign to purchasing the responsibility for developing long-range plans and specific recommendations for the systematic procurement of all required purchased materials and services. If the plans are prepared in writing well in advance of planned commitment and indicate the time period to be covered, quantity requirements, suppliers considered, suppliers selected or basis of proposed selection, unit price, terms, type of contract, estimated total commitment, and a comparison with the budgeted standard unit price, using-department managers and plant management can review and comment on, or approve, such plans with minimum research. Having the written plans on hand would at least provide assurance that adequate arrangements could be made to secure all requirements for purchased materials and services. If the manager is concerned about premature commitments or possible unilateral action by purchasing, he can make purchasing's authority to commit contingent upon prior written approval of the plans by selected persons responsible for production and for profitable operation of the using departments.

COMMITMENT RESPONSIBILITY

If purchasing is to be assigned responsibility for control of purchased material unit costs, purchasing will also need authority to control all commitments made for the company. Assuming that grants of commitment authority are issued only from a single source such as purchasing, management can look to that single source for positive control. When it is considered that "back door" commitments, whether made by several departments or by management, can tend to disrupt approved long-range plans, exceed budgetary limits, cause duplication of effort, demoralize purchasing personnel, and confuse the vendor's representatives, the need for an effective single source of control becomes more apparent. A management policy establishing purchasing as the function responsible for coordinating and controlling all purchasing activity, including the presentation of pertinent information to other departments and the securing of necessary management approvals, would assure the reception, assembly, and evaluation of all information in one place and prevent critical data from being overlooked or discarded.

Assigning to purchasing the responsibility for control of commitment authority should not be interpreted as a requirement for purchasing personnel to examine, evaluate, and "sign off" every purchase transaction that occurs. On the contrary, major emphasis would probably be on concentrating available purchasing manpower on the big-dollar items, where minor cost improvements would have a major impact on total costs and profit because of high volume. Purchasing commitment responsibility can be organized so that small things can be handled in a small way, leaving the greater part of time and talent available to concentrate on major items representing significant cost areas. Such techniques as national contracts or blanket orders can be utilized to establish the specifications, source, and price for certain repetitive items, and the using departments can be allowed to authorize delivery of these items as needed. During the effective life of those master contracts purchasing will have no further need to become involved in the day-to-day transactions unless the vendor fails to perform or prices have to be changed. Meanwhile, relieved of the routine paper processing, purchasing will have more time to work on the high-cost items.

YARDSTICKS FOR VENDOR PRICES

Authority to select sources and establish prices is, of course, essential in obtaining control of purchased material unit prices. However, it is false economy to establish so-called low prices if those prices are obtained at the expense of quality, delivery reliability, or other valuable considerations. If purchasing is given all commitment authority, the plant can be protected from such an occurrence by various methods. One device, often used in the construction industry and in equipment fabrication plants, is to prepare an independent engineering estimate of the cost and probable selling price for use in evaluating vendor prices. An alternative method would be to assign to purchasing the responsibility for developing and maintaining key information on major commodities used by the company. Reference to these files would enable purchasing to construct a profile covering current prices, availability, long-term market trends, alternate sources, potential new sources, and acceptable substitutes. Such a profile would give a reasonably accurate picture of the market in the commodity in question and provide a suitable yardstick for use in evaluating quoted vendor prices. Information of this type is readily available from market and specialty publications, government agencies, and vendor representatives. Recognizing that so-called competitive bids do not always produce the lowest or best prices, since all bids received may be overpriced or out of line, the company manager may wish to assign purchasing the responsibility for developing and maintaining profiles on major purchased commodities.

Many vendors maintain expert technical personnel to assist customers or potential customers in working out acceptable solutions to production equipment problems. Normally, there is no charge or obligation for such service and, properly handled, it can be effectively utilized. However, activities associated with or immediately following such arrangements can easily lead to extensive and unplanned purchase commitments. Often, the potential customers are unaware until after the fact that they have led the vendor to believe that he has been authorized to furnish materials or extra services. Obviously, management approval for commitment of the funds would not be obtained in advance. Perhaps such problems could be avoided by establishing relatively simple controls which would limit vendor access to the plants and clearly define the authority to make commitments. Under such conditions, purchasing would be ideally situated to serve as the principal contact and primary control agency for such projects.

Reporting to Management

Most managers are too busy to read and evaluate voluminous and repetitious reports on purchasing statistics such as numbers of purchase orders or contracts issued, purchase requisitions received, and number of vendor representatives interviewed. Although it may give some indication on the volume of paper being handled, such information is relatively meaningless in terms of management objectives and accomplishments. Even dollar commitments have little meaning unless they are measured against some predetermined standard. It would be far more meaningful, as well as convenient, to have reports emphasizing change— deviations from the planned accomplishment—with brief but comprehensive statements defining the cause of deviation.

REPORTING BY EXCEPTION

If purchasing is to be responsible for the development of standard unit costs for purchased materials, and if these standards are incorporated in the budget, the result will be an acceptable basis for reporting the actual cost experience against the standards. Only costs that deviate substantially from the standard will need to be reviewed. (A minimum reportable deviation can be established to avoid getting reports on minor discrepancies.) Such reports will automatically identify any existing problem areas. Ranking the problems in order of importance becomes a simple matter of listing dollar amounts in declining order.

Important as it is to maintain current control of purchased material costs within the budget, it is equally important to be fully aware of outside technological developments and changing market conditions that may affect future costs, particularly if such information can be accurately forecast and measured against some recognizable standard that will permit projection of total impact. In the event that purchasing is made responsible for the preparation and maintenance of commodity profiles on major purchased items, there will be available a source file of up-to-date market information that can be periodically summarized, interpreted, and reported by purchasing as a forecast of specific variances from standard unit prices for purchased materials. Both negative and positive variances can be quickly evaluated, and—where appropriate—corrective action can be initiated before the forecast event actually occurs.

Since a $1 reduction in the cost of purchased material from the standard would increase profit by an amount roughly equivalent to a $10 or $15 increase in sales, it is highly desirable to establish some method of forecasting such possible actions and of estimating their impact on cost. Assuming that purchasing personnel are to be kept fully informed of the company's products, manufacturing processes, and long-term production plans, purchasing can reasonably be expected to recognize situations where consideration of new sources of supply, changes in specifications, or substitute materials may have an economic advantage. Further, with regular access to outside information, purchasing may become aware of technological developments or other changing market conditions that can be exploited and directed to achieve company objectives. By assigning to purchasing the responsibility for recording each such opportunity as it occurs, the basis can be established for a careful review and evaluation by the using department and other responsible personnel. Items which appear to have potential can be assigned to purchasing as specific profit improvement projects. Periodic reports on progress accomplished against such projects, when reviewed on an exception basis, will provide a quick summary forecast of profit improvement.

TECHNOLOGICAL DEVELOPMENTS

Fresh ideas from the manufacturers, from the suppliers' research, or from the expert technical representatives of either source may help keep the company abreast of new developments and technological changes. A further spur to investigation of these sources is the possibility that the competition may take full advantage of such services.

The vendors' normal competitive desire for business, as suppliers, could provide a strong motivating force for the development of service innovations that might be translated into cost savings. Suppose a vendor could be persuaded to maintain part of the company's inventory at his plant, ready for shipment on call; the company's investment in inventory would be reduced with no sacrifice of raw material supply protection. Or perhaps the company's purchasing people could suggest alternate design or materials for use by a vendor, permitting manufacturing cost savings that could be translated into reduced selling price. Similar results might be achieved by encouraging vendors to farm out complex subassemblies and highly competitive components to reduce their cost of production. The responsibility for performing these functions could be assigned to purchasing people, provided that they were not bogged down with mountains of nonproductive paperwork. Equipped with the knowledge and experience gained from observing production techniques at vendors' plants, purchasing would also be in a good position to make positive contributions to the buying company's own make-or-buy studies, well beyond the usual information on cost or availability of materials.—*D. E. Howard*

PURCHASING CONTROLS

No management function is performed today without some element of control. Government regulations, corporate structuring, and management philosophy by their very nature impose some degree of regulation on the function being performed. The procurement function does not escape these restrictions.

The real question to be considered is the degree of control. Overcontrolling this function imposes on the upper levels of purchasing management a morass of paperwork, while undercontrolling may result in a very loose and ineffective operation. The objective of purchasing management is to strike a fine balance between these two extremes.

Authorization Limits

Purchasing management often considers the dollar authorization limit as a restrictive device whose purpose is to permit the manager to analyze all purchases over a given dollar value. In essence, limitations should not be considered restrictive but informative.

In a large purchasing department with a competent buying staff, senior buyers may review purchases of buyers and assistant buyers exceeding a stipulated dollar value. Senior buyers may forward to management contracts comprising significant sums, performance or service contracts, or contracts of a highly complex technical or legal nature.

The question always arises as to what the dollar limitations should be in a typical organization. No hard-and-fast rule can be drawn. The purchasing manager must equate the review function against the number of orders or other formal purchasing arrangements being issued by the department in relation to the amount and frequency of paperwork that he wants to flow daily across his desk. Too stringent limitations will bury the manager in paperwork, but too lax limitations will not let him review contracts that are significant to his operation.

Dollar limitations should not be considered cast in concrete. A newly appointed top purchasing manager may want to impose very restrictive limitations for a period of time to serve as an informational or training device for himself. This practice enables him to learn what is being bought and how it is being bought. After the informative period, dollar limitations may be raised by the manager so that his paperwork is equated to a reasonable daily volume.

Purchasing Policies and Procedures

Much has been written about purchasing policies and procedures. Policies are general corporate or departmental guidelines defining the broad limitations within which the procurement function is going to be performed. Procedures, on the other hand, tell specifically how, when, by whom, and with what the procurement function is going to be accomplished. The item of greatest significance as it relates to purchasing policies and procedures is a systematized approach.

Many purchasing organizations produce a continuing stream of policies and even more procedures in memorandum form. They are duly noted by concerned buyers and then filed. Procedures continually revise previous procedures until the buyer's files bulge with changing operational detail. Reference to these files for up-to-date information soon becomes chaotic.

Policies and procedures must be handled on a systematized basis. A specific manual must be established for holding this information. New procedures should be assigned specific serial numbers; if they supersede previously written procedures, a statement should be made as to which serial-numbered procedures should be discarded. Procurement manuals must be continuously up to date and so organized as to serve as a ready reference catalog for the new trainee as well as the old-time buyer.

A well-conceived and current manual also provides the best possible basis for annual audits of purchasing by professional auditors. The annual audit is still one of the best control devices, particularly if the audit group is capable of seeing "the big picture."

Centralized Versus Decentralized Purchasing

Large corporations seem to move a complete 360 degrees on the subject of centralized versus decentralized purchasing. The corporate headquarters purchasing staff will analyze in detail all purchases of the local plant level and institute national contracts for almost all common plant requirements. Five years later it will be found that corporate headquarters has almost completely relinquished the procurement function back to the local plant purchasing agent.

Centralized procurement is as good and as effective as the feedback from the local releasing activity. Contracts negotiated on a national basis for local plants can result in strangulation at the plant level. Price and quality may be defined on the national level, but service is another problem. Late deliveries, substitutions, and poor paperwork processing on the part of the vendor can all but destroy the effectiveness of a national buy. It is mandatory that the local plants feed back to the corporate headquarters continuing information on the adequacy or inadequacy of national contracts.

Corporate headquarters should never consider national contracts as a static situation. Contracts for services, supplies, and components must be continually evaluated on the basis of information received from the local level. Items once procured very satisfactorily on a national basis may suddenly become impossible to obtain at the local level. New sources must be sought, or the responsibility for procurement again delegated locally.

Sourcing Approval

Selection of the source of supply is the responsibility of every purchasing department. In making such selection, management should consider the following questions:

1. What is the relation between the physical location of a supplier's plant or warehouse and the company's use points?

2. Is the supplier capable of producing the company's requirements on a best *total* value basis?

3. Is the supplier financially sound, on the basis of definitive information obtained from banks, *Moody's,* Dun and Bradstreet, and other creditable sources?

4. Has the supplier's plant been inspected by qualified personnel from the company?

5. How has the supplier handled company requirements in the past—or, if new, how is the supplier evaluated by existing customers?

Management should exercise sustained control in the vital area of source selection—equal in intensity to the controls over in-house manufacturing.

Central Maintenance Contracts

Many corporations spend a great deal of time and money to determine the economics of having equipment covered by full maintenance contracts. However, there are situations when the decision is not made on an economic evaluation but on the basis of other factors deemed more important to the corporation.

A case in point is that of a large retail chain which owns many specialized machines for measuring yard goods to be sold to customers. The corporation maintains that the accuracy of these machines must be maintained because it has a significant impact on the corporate image. In addition, the manufacturer of these machines has a very small maintenance staff that travels throughout the United States, and it is wise to have the equipment checked while the mechanic is visiting in a particular town. The same retailer established national contracts for floor-care chemicals that have been approved by its laboratory. The use of these products is mandatory in the stores; as a result, customer accidents (slipping and falling on the floor) are held to a minimum. Thus it can be seen that national maintenance contracts are often negotiated on factors other than the pure economics of the situation.

Selection and Training

Perhaps the predominant subject on the minds of current purchasing management is that of personnel. Because 40 to 60 percent of a company's revenue dollar is probably being expended by purchasing, the following stipulations should be made:

1. Job specifications should be accurate and current. The dollar decision aspect of professionally performed purchasing must be delineated. Purchasing performed at the clerical level is expensive.

2. Qualified persons, once hired for purchasing, must be properly trained, motivated, and rewarded with the same care and intensity as the sales force. A dollar saved in purchasing usually equals $10 to $15 of new sales; yet it is a fact that many purchasing people are ill equipped to cope with highly trained sales personnel.

In addition, management should insist that its top purchasing man play an active role in the process of selecting, training, motivating, and rewarding good performance.

Fulfillment of Responsibility and Authority

Annual audits of purchasing performance against the purchasing policies and procedures manual is not enough; the purchasing function must continuously be directed toward profit, and management must implement the controls needed to determine whether or not purchasing is contributing to improved profitability and service. Some vital controls are as follows: (1) ample evidence of careful short- and long-range planning; (2) a record of actual expenditures versus approved budgets; (3) a record of actual prices paid versus standard unit prices; (4) evidence of close liaison with user departments prior to the execution of costly long-term commitments; (5) tight controls over all major commitments; (6) reasonable controls over the multiplicity of small dollar value transactions, for overcontrol by purchasing in this area is expensive; (7) clear evidence that purchasing is furnishing management with information on the current commercial happenings of concern to the company.

In short, management must exercise those controls necessary to assure that purchasing is contributing to increased profits by reducing unit costs.

—*R. K. Fusselman*

PURCHASING ANALYSIS AND PLANNING

Analysis and planning are the management tools that keep a company competitive and sensitive to the changing needs of its customers. In order to make meaningful contributions to the specific goals and objectives of the company it serves, purchasing must be proficient in its use of these tools. The function of planning is to deliberately seek ways to advance the effectiveness of purchasing; and planning itself must, of course, be based on careful analysis.

The experience of most large companies indicates that an organization group reporting to the director of purchasing is needed to assure that planning is accomplished. This group functions as the general staff does in the military for planning operations. Men in this activity should be seasoned and experienced purchasing people who have developed convictions concerning methods of realizing more effective performance.

Whether or not a company can justify a full-time purchasing planner or planning group, the principles are the same. Managers, in any function, who "fail to plan—plan to fail." Time must be budgeted for this purpose, particularly for a function such as purchasing in which 40 to 60 percent of the revenue dollar is probably being expended.

Focus of Effort

The focus of the purchasing analysis and planning effort should be on the management decisions needed to improve performance. Such issues as purchasing policy, organization, procedures, controls, interaction with other functions, more advanced techniques of decision making, staff support in essential material decisions, training, and personnel planning should be thoroughly studied. From this effort, specific plans of benefit to the particular company should evolve.

One of purchasing's prime responsibilities is to fulfill general management's urgent need for advance information concerning both short- and long-term aspects of the cost of purchased materials, availability, market trends, new processes or materials, and the like. Effective planning must be preceded by selective analysis of worthwhile opportunities. Some of the major sources of the required information should therefore be reviewed.

Sources of Information

Many progressive companies commit their forward plans to writing one, five, or even ten years ahead of anticipated events. These plans and the resultant capital and expense budgets should be made available for careful study and analysis by the purchasing function. Under ideal circumstances, purchasing should contribute to the formulation of these planning documents, particularly in view of the ever rising percentage of the revenue dollar that leaves the average manufacturing company by way of the purchasing function.

Purchasing must stay abreast of the forward plans of principal suppliers of materials, supplies, and equipment essential to the continued profitability of the company. This information is readily obtainable through effective communication with supplying companies' general management, sales personnel, and marketing analysis and research groups, as well as government and trade groups. It must not only be sought; it must be carefully analyzed and thoughtfully interpreted in terms of the company's special needs. Thus purchasing can be a valuable source of commercial intelligence to the key personnel of a company by furnishing information on what the firm's competitors are doing in terms of new materials and manufacturing processes.

Another source of information is a carefully recorded history of the past purchases of a company. However, analysis of the past is important only if coupled with a realistic viewpoint of the future.

Intelligent use of all three major source areas by purchasing is needed. Just as in any other management activity, meaningful data must be analyzed, worthwhile opportunities selected and planned out, and plans committed to writing so that they can be carefully evaluated by knowledgeable people from many functions. Purchasing should be required to operate in this manner.

Planning for Excellence

In planning for excellence within the purchasing function, management must consider both buying and nonbuying responsibilities.

BUYING RESPONSIBILITIES

Specific areas that must be analyzed and planned if a company's purchasing function is to be effective will be obvious from the questions that follow.

Flow of purchasing expenditures. How is your company's money being spent *now?*

Corporate interest materials. What reasoning should be advanced on the methods of selecting materials of corporate interest? In a particular business, which specific materials should have the strongest corporate focus? Which materials are better purchased at the local level? Is sufficient attention being paid to these essential items by general management?

Future needs. What are these needs? What systems are needed to enable management to make imaginative decisions regarding future material requirements sufficiently far in advance?

Markets. Is purchasing alert and sensitive to the markets in which it buys, so that it can make better decisions than its competitors? Will essential items be available in the right quality, quantity, and place—and at the right price— one, three, or five years from now? Is the technology changing? Will new materials or equipment lessen or heighten the company's competitive thrust? What is happening to the supplier's markets for his raw materials? Should the company shift its policy to make rather than to buy? When is the best time to buy? Purchasing should acquire sufficient knowledge in this area to accurately predict the future direction of key markets.

Value decisions. How can purchasing make more effective value decisions beyond the arrangement of supply at a certain price? General management can help in at least two main ways. First, it can encourage the participation of purchasing as a team member in planning the development of new products; and, second, it can insist that purchasing make judicious use of value analysis and cost-price analysis.

Value analysis. Purchasing's search for the best total values must be endless. In this context, "value" can be defined as "the lowest overall cost that must be paid to have a useful function or service performed reliably"; "value analysis" can be described as "an organized method of systematically evaluating the materials and services which are purchased." To be fully effective, value analysis must be a team effort of which purchasing is a vital member.

Cost-price. The purchasing function should, on a selective basis, continually analyze supplier costs and prices. This is necessary in order to accurately determine whether or not the company is paying fair and competitive prices for essential items. In this context, the terms used can be defined as follows: "price analysis"—"a comparative technique to facilitate choosing the best price, with or without competitive quotations"; "cost analysis"—"the process of developing a breakdown of vendor cost, verifying it, evaluating specific elements of cost against value to the company, and projecting these data to determine the probable effect on price." The application of this technique is difficult and time-consuming. Its use is normally resisted by purchasing people, but it is justified and in fact necessary on a selective basis.

Source development. Is purchasing actively seeking new technologists and new sources with definable improved skills? Management should consider purchasing as a link between the company's needs and an endless variety of outside resources. Purchasing should be expected to ferret out suppliers who are leaders in new ideas, new processes, new materials, and overall management.

Negotiation. Effective negotiation is preceded by considerable analysis and planning. Each important negotiation session should, similarly, be analyzed and planned for by the development of definitive answers to questions such as the following:

Does this subject warrant the time required to properly plan for and conduct a negotiation session?

What are the company's objectives? How important a customer is the company?

What will the supplier's position probably be?

What concessions should the company consider? What concessions should be solicited from the supplier?

Should the company use a team? Who should be represented on the team?

What facts must be assembled and verified in advance of the session?

Can this subject matter be negotiated? Does the supplier agree?

What subjects should be included on the agenda? Who should participate? What are the time and location of the meeting? Does the supplier concur?

Should a "dry run" or simulated session be held?

Supplier selection. Is purchasing choosing suppliers on a rational basis for the long-run needs of the company? Long-term capabilities must be accurately assessed, following the critical analysis of supplier strengths and weaknesses: financial, managerial, innovative, technical, process, logistical, and geographical factors as they apply to the company's precise short- and long-range needs.

In selecting suppliers, purchasing should use many or all of the other "planning for excellence" approaches. For example: Through the use of value analysis and cost-price analysis, purchasing can often imagine better ways in which a supplier can design and manufacture the improved materials that the company needs.

NONBUYING RESPONSIBILITIES

Individuals carefully selected, highly trained, and motivated toward excellence are, of course, the key to the ultimate success of a company's purchasing function. This requires careful analysis and planning effort within certain broad areas which, again, will be obvious from the questions which follow.

Policy decisions. What general objectives should purchasing have for the company? What specific policy decisions will help corporate buyers and purchasing men in decentralized operations make better decisions in the future?

Procedures. What procedural changes are needed to simplify the flow of paperwork?

Controls. What controls are needed to satisfy internal auditing needs and assure top management that needed, decentralized decisions are being properly made?

Organization. What plan should be made to design the organization so as to assure that the general objectives of purchasing are realized and that the emphasis with regard to company needs is correct?

Manpower. What specialist skills are needed?

Training. What training will be effective in developing the specific skills needed?

Decision making. What techniques and specific staff support will lead to more competitive decisions in essential materials?

Interaction with other functions. What plans can be made to effect better interaction with other groups in decision making, especially in the material design stage?

Measures of performance. What measures of performance can be devised to provide top management with purposeful insights to purchasing results?

Succinctly stated, management should expect its purchasing function to identify problems which limit optimum purchasing performance and to create plans and programs which will convert these weaknesses into strengths. The effective management of purchasing deserves the same careful attention as is normally given to other functions which are directed toward profit. Purchasing should be seen as an activity that can be used by planning to "brew" business decision makers—an ideal training ground for general management. Virtually every decision made by purchasing is a dollar decision. These dollars should be wisely invested to increase the capital available for profit-seeking opportunities. Purchasing, in any large or medium-size company, generally requires staff people specifically assigned to nonbuying responsibilities; otherwise, these forward-planning activities of a general but essential nature are done poorly or not at all.

Results of Planning

The principal measure of effectiveness in planning is the general competitive edge of purchasing performance. Realistic measures may be reduction in the unit costs of essential purchased materials, standard costs lower than projected for new products, or lowered costs of products from an acquired facility. More important may be the confidence of top management and, as a result, the participation of purchasing in top management decisions.

Among the outputs of planning may be the following: definable policy and general objective statements from the director of purchasing; carefully thought-out controls in a variety of forms; analyses of the flow of purchasing expenditures, with recommendations for management action; the projection of forward needs for essential materials; staff support in essential material decisions; cost and market studies of essential materials; suggestions for improved organization; and definition of training objectives and advancement of specific programs.

To emphasize: Analysis and planning can lift the purchasing function into a viable position from which to optimize its contribution to the company's planned, profitable growth.—*D. L. Murphy*

EDP AND THE PURCHASING FUNCTION

The increasingly extensive use of computer-oriented systems by business management has resulted in numerous opportunities for improved performance—and, in doing so, has created many serious organizational and operating problems. Most of these difficulties have been caused by a general ignorance of computer capabilities and limitations and a lack of understanding of the extent of involvement, on the part of the functional manager, that is needed to insure the success of such systems.

Computer Capabilities

A computer system can store vast amounts of data and process them at an inconceivable speed. It has a high-level analytical capability. Assuming that the information provided to it is accurate and usable and that its processing instructions are correct, it can provide decision-making information to management and eliminate clerical and record-keeping activity. For the purchasing function, this means that the buyer will have more time available for vendor selection and better information on which to base his decisions.

Computer Limitations

The computer is incapable of thinking for itself and requires that the processing instructions be put in analytical terms. Incomplete instructions are very common. Even an experienced professional will often regard some steps in operation as too obvious to mention, forgetting that he is communicating information to an "idiot" who has no understanding of any subject and is incapable of converting what the professional *says* to what he *means*. There are also unnecessary operations; numerous tasks that an experienced and intuitive manager can perform much more effectively are given to the computer. And many decisions cannot and should not be put in mathematical form, for the problems contain too many intangible or constantly changing factors.

The economic justification for the proposed application also should be considered. Computer time, systems design and installation, and programming cost very significant sums.

Purchasing Applications

The vast majority of systems applications and reports create and maintain a permanent computer file of all open purchase orders from the information used.

The file is created by the placement of the purchase order. It is processed and maintained by receipt, invoice, inspection, disposition, notification of shipment, and order change data. Closed-out purchase orders are used for vendor evaluation, and a history of transactions should be maintained for inquiry purposes. The more valuable uses of such a system are described briefly here.

AUTOMATED ACCOUNTS PAYABLE

In many businesses, much time is wasted by skilled buyers and financial analysts in posting receipts and invoices against purchase orders and correcting discrepancies. These routine reports are easily mechanized. It is not difficult for the computer to take discounts, apply taxes, check for double billing, close out all purchase orders if the receipt and invoice quantity is within 5 percent, and reject discrepancies of more than 10 percent overshipment on other than blanket order items.

OTHER FINANCIAL APPLICATIONS

Other common requests include cash flow information on money needed to cover current and anticipated purchases; automation of the materials variance calculation on price and quantity; and a vendor cost rating on every material, based upon recent purchases. These choices require material and vendor coding, standard costs, and due dates on all purchase orders.

OPEN-ORDER STATUS

The most useful method is to give each buyer a list of all of his purchase orders that are overdue, due within the next two weeks, or require special expediting because of inventory shortages. This report is generally supplied in buyer-vendor-material order so that all follow-up with a vendor can be grouped together and handled with one phone call. Finance will probably want it in either accounting number or buying source sequence to evaluate actual purchase against budget, and inventory control will want it in material-vendor-purchase order sequence to determine how to best expedite a critically needed item.

MATERIAL INQUIRY

Under manual systems, buyers are forced to maintain accurate records on all activity against every purchase order in order to be able to explain discrepancies.

If a transaction history file is available, all the buyer has to do is make an inquiry request for the desired information; he can receive it almost immediately.

VENDOR EVALUATION

Typically, vendor evaluation reviews the current performance of all vendors of a given material on cost, quality, and timeliness. This information can be obtained by a mechanized calculation, but not easily. On all items to be evaluated, it is necessary to determine how much weight to give to cost, quality, and timeliness and the specific analytical techniques that will be used to measure them. The results of the vendor evaluation are displayed in two action reports, by material-vendor and vendor-material. This procedure makes it possible to rate all vendors on a specific material and individual vendors on all items that they supply.

Other useful information on these reports includes latest-price, year-to-date purchases by vendor and material; lead time; and year-to-date activity. All ratings are kept in a vendor-information file with inquiry capability.

PURCHASE-ORDER WRITING

This application is of trivial value, for a computer is a very expensive printer and has numerous systems options more valuable than this one. The computer can generate orders on one vendor—EOQ (economic order quantity), order-point items automatically bypassing purchasing. It can also write orders, given all specifications information.

BUYER EVALUATION

With the use of a vendor evaluation system, it is possible to rate the buyer on the overall cost, quality, and timeliness performance of all orders he has placed. It is also interesting to note whether his performance on "A" items indicates that these items received special attention. Other measures are orders placed and total dollars purchased.

PURCHASING PLANNING

In this application, purchase requirements are determined by an explosion of the anticipated production schedule and netting it out against available inventory. The result is a time-phased report for each buyer, stating what is needed and when.

In a sophisticated system, actual orders and their due dates are compared to requirements, and an exception report is generated on shortages.

QUALITY CONTROL

It is quite possible to perform an extensive quality evaluation, including defect analysis, and make it part of the open-order control system. This is a very useful application, especially when reports are given the vendor that show not only the quantity rejected but also a penetrating analysis of the reasons for rejection.

Selection Criteria

There is no neat formula for determining the purchasing system's needs. Special applications are often needed. A brief list of the factors that a professional consultant might review would include order volume, number of vendors, dollar volume of purchases, contractor volume, materials controlled by purchasing, centralized buying, product life, and sophistication in quality control.

—Jerry Cantor

FORMAL PURCHASING ARRANGEMENTS

Formal purchasing arrangements are contracts that bring the management ability of suppliers to bear on attaining the objectives that the purchasing manager seeks for his organization.

The choice of the appropriate type of contract is important in achieving purchasing's objective: to purchase supplies and services from responsible sources at fair and reasonable prices calculated to result in the lowest ultimate overall cost to the organization. Considerable flexibility is needed in the purchase of the many varieties and the various volumes of supplies and services; as a result, a wide selection of types of contracts has been developed and made available for use by contracting organizations.

Contract types vary according to the degree and timing of responsibility assumed by the supplier for the costs of performance and the amount and type of profit incentive offered the supplier to achieve or exceed specific standards or goals. Types of contracts can be arranged in order of decreasing supplier responsibility for the costs of performance. At one end of the spectrum is the firm fixed-price contract, under which the parties agree that the supplier assumes full cost responsibility. At the other end of this spectrum is the cost-plus-a-fixed-fee contract, where profit rather than price is fixed and the supplier's cost responsibility is therefore minimal. Likewise, the risk of successful performance is shared in relative amounts by the supplier and the purchaser. Between these extremes are the various incentive contracts which provide for varying degrees of supplier cost responsibility, depending upon the degree of uncertainty involved in contract performance. One type of contract deserves special mention. This is the type known as cost-plus-a-percentage-of-cost, which for people involved in U.S. Government or U.S. Government-related business is an illegal contract, and its use for this purpose is prohibited. For purchasing managers in all other areas of business, this restriction does not apply. However, because the incentive for the person performing under such a contract is to relax controls on costs, the higher the project cost, the greater becomes the supplier's profit.

The basic principle for selection of contract type is profit. Both the purchasing manager and his suppliers should be concerned with harnessing the profit motive to work for the truly effective and economical contract performance required in terms of their mutual interests. To this end, the parties should seek to negotiate and use the contract type best calculated to stimulate outstanding performance. The objective should be to insure that outstandingly effective and economical management performance will result in high profits; mediocre management performance, in mediocre profits; and poor management performance, in low profits or a loss. Profits are wages earned through the use of management methods, and proper contracting can and will encourage good management methods. Success in harnessing the profit motive begins with the negotiation of sound performance goals and standards. The management objectives should be such that the selection of the contract type results in the supplier's either benefiting or losing in relation to achieving or failing to achieve realistic targets.

Where an award is based on effective price competition, there is reasonable assurance that the contract price represents a realistic pricing standard including a profit factor that contains an appropriate return to the supplier for the financial risk he assumes. Where there is a lack of competitive forces in either large or small degree, the contract type selected should provide a profit factor that will tie profits to the supplier's management ability to control costs and meet desired standards of performance, schedule compliance, and reliability of product.

Factors in Selection of Contract Type

Good judgment must be exercised and sound analysis employed to determine the type of contract best suited to each transaction. Consideration should be given to such factors as the nature, complexity, and state of development of the material or system to be purchased; the urgency of the need for the requirement; the period of the contract performance, length of the production run, and the amount of money involved; and the degree of competition. (In addition to price competition, also to be considered are engineering technical ability, reliability, and manufacturing as well as overall management ability.)

Equally important in contract type selection are the following factors: the difficulty of estimating performance costs because of a lack of firm specifications or a lack of production experience; the availability of comparative price data and the lack of firm market prices; prior experience with the supplier; the extent and nature of subcontracting contemplated by the supplier; the assumption of business risk; the technical capability of the supplier; the financial responsibility of the supplier; the costs of administering the contract; the degree of confidence in the supplier's estimating and accounting system; the type and requirements of the contract the company has with its customer or customers; and the degree of risk to be assumed by both parties.

In many procurement situations, particularly in research and development work and sometimes in production, objectives other than cost control may be significant. They may be performance with a view toward a better or more reliable product, delivery when supplies or services are urgently required, or a combination of any of the objectives of cost, performance, and delivery. A contractual arrangement can be used to provide incentive to obtain these objectives in addition to effective cost control. Thus, by providing for increased profit for exceeding predetermined target levels and decreased profit for failing to meet target levels, an additional incentive is created for maximum effort on the part of the supplier. When additional objectives are made a part of the various types of incentive contracts, particular care must be taken by the purchasing manager to maintain an appropriate balance between the various incentives by weighting incentive objectives to apportion the total incentive profits or fee in accordance with the emphasis and maximum benefit desired. Without proper balancing of the incentive objectives, the purchaser may receive—at unwarranted expense—a product of greater quality than desired or a delivery before needed.

Types of Contracts and Where to Use Them

The selection of a contract type is generally a matter for negotiation on high dollar procurements and the exercise of judgment on all procurements. The type of contract and pricing are interrelated and should be considered together in negotiation. Because the type of contract affects the resulting price, the use of an appropriate type is of primary importance in obtaining fair and reasonable prices. In this connection, it is good practice to include documentation to show why the particular contract type was used, as well as the reasons for the selection of the supplier and the justification for the price paid.

FIXED-PRICE CONTRACTS

The fixed-price contract provides for either a firm price or, under appropriate circumstances, a price subject to revisions based on limitations established in the purchase-order provisions.

Firm fixed-price contract. This type of contract is such that both parties are bound by the agreed price for the duration of the purchase order. The price is not subject to any adjustment by reason of costs experienced by the supplier in the performance of the contract. Unless otherwise provided, no adjustment of the price is possible except as stipulated under the "changes" article, or partial termination under the "termination" article, as provided in the standard terms and conditions on the reverse side of the purchase order. Under this type of contract, the supplier accepts maximum risk and assumes responsibility for efficiency in performance, since he retains any resultant savings. This type of contract is preferred by organizations over any other—circumstances permitting —since the firm fixed-price arrangement imposes a minimum administrative burden on both the supplier and the purchaser. The criteria for its use are as follows: (1) Definite specifications are available to achieve fair and reasonable pricing; (2) competition produces reliable initial quotations; (3) a reasonable price comparison can be made against prior purchases of the same or similar supplies and services; and (4) experienced cost information or sound estimates of anticipated costs are available for analysis during negotiation of the contract price.

The firm fixed-price contract is particularly suited to the purchase of catalog or "off the shelf" commercial products and to purchased labor transactions. It also lends itself to transactions calling for the construction of new facilities, alteration and relocation of existing buildings and facilities, and the modification and relocation of machinery and equipment.

Fixed-price contract with escalation provision. The fixed-price order with escalation provides for the upward or downward revision of the stated price upon the occurrence of certain contingencies which are specifically defined in the order. The management risks in a firm fixed-price order are reduced by including an escalation provision in which the parties agree to revise the stated price after the occurrence of a prescribed contingency. This type of order should be considered only when serious doubt exists as to the stability of market and labor conditions which will exist during an estimated period of production. Escalation provisions do not allow for price changes resulting from failure of the supplier to estimate accurately the hours, labor rates, or quantity of material required to produce an end item.

Fixed-price incentive contract. This form is a fixed-price type with provisions for adjustment of profit and establishment of the final price by a formula based on the relationship which final negotiated total costs bear to total target costs. The incentive enables suppliers to receive more profit if their performance surpasses the objectives set forth in the targets. Fixed-price incentive contracts should not be used unless the supplier's accounting system is adequate and permits the satisfactory application of the profit and price adjustment formulas. Fixed-price incentive contracts should be used only after it has been determined that (1) such a method is likely to be less costly than other contracting methods, or (2) it is impractical to secure supplies or services of the kind or quantity required without the use of such a contract.

Fixed-price contract with redetermination provision. This type of contract provides for a price ceiling and for retroactive price redetermination upon the completion of the contract. It does not provide the supplier with an incentive to control costs, except to the extent that final costs do not exceed the price ceiling established in the contract. This type of contract is appropriate when it is established at the time of negotiation that a fair and reasonable firm fixed price cannot be negotiated and the amount involved is so small, or the time of performance so short, that the use of any other type of contract is impractical.

COST-PLUS CONTRACTS

Cost-plus contracts are based on the reimbursement of allowable costs plus a fee. The fee may be fixed under the terms of the contract; or it may be determined under an incentive agreement using the relation of total allowable costs to target costs; or it may be based on an award for excellence in contract performance.

Cost-plus-fixed-fee contract (CPFF). This type of contract provides for the reimbursement of allowable costs plus a fixed fee which does not vary with actual costs and which may be adjusted only in accordance with the terms of the contract. Its use is discouraged, since it provides the supplier with only a minimum incentive for effective management. This type may be considered under the following circumstances: (1) The work to be performed is in the nature of research, preliminary exploration, or study, and the level of effort required is unknown; or (2) the work involves development, test, or prototype effort where the use of a cost-plus-incentive-fee contract is not practical. Rarely will this type of contract be employed in a transaction amounting to less than $100,000.

Cost-plus-incentive-fee contract (CPIF). The CPIF contract is a cost-reimbursement contract with a provision for a fee adjusted by formula in accordance with the relationship which final total allowable costs bear to target costs. In the event that performance characteristics are included, the relationship of actual performance to target performance will influence the final total costs. Under this type of contract, there are negotiated initially a target cost, a target fee, a minimum and a maximum fee, and a fee-adjustment formula. The formula provides for increases or decreases in the target fee, within the prescribed maximum and minimum limits, to the extent that actual performance is greater or less than target performance. This type of contract is suitable for use in undertakings involving development and test and initial production when a cost-reimbursement contract is found necessary and when a target and a fee-adjustment formula can be negotiated which are likely to provide the supplier with a positive profit incentive for effective management.

Cost-plus-award-fee contract (CPAF). This is a cost-reimbursement type of contract with special fee provisions. It provides a means of applying incentives in contracts which are not susceptible to finite measurements of the performance necessary for structuring incentive contracts. The fee consists of two parts: (1) a fixed amount which does not vary with performance; and (2) an award amount, in addition to the fixed amount, sufficient to provide motivation for excellence in contract performance in areas such as quality, timeliness, ingenuity, and cost effectiveness.

LETTER CONTRACTS AND WIRE AUTHORIZATIONS

When it is necessary that a supplier proceed with work before a definitive purchase order can be completely negotiated, the purchasing manager may enter into contractual arrangements by means of letter contracts or wire authorizations. These contracts contain limitations and are used primarily to authorize a supplier to begin performance of a specific task. Letter contracts and wire authorizations are employed only in emergencies; they may anticipate either a fixed-price type or cost type of definitive contract.

TIME, MATERIAL, AND PURCHASED-TIME CONTRACTS

Time and material contracts provide for the purchase of supplies or services on the basis of (1) a composite hourly rate or rates which include all elements of cost, factory burden, general and administrative expense, and the supplier's profit; and (2) material at cost. In the purchased-time contracts, the supplier also furnishes labor or services at a composite hourly rate or rates but does not furnish materials which may be required in the performance of the contract. These contracts generally contain a "not to exceed" limitation on the total contract amount. When it is necessary to use such contracts, provision should be made for proper administration control, including appropriate surveillance to assure that inefficient or wasteful methods are not used.

PURCHASED-SERVICES CONTRACTS

It is necessary at times to contract for consultant and other services, the nature of which may vary from technical engineering to maintenance. Skilled personnel from the architectural, structural, civil, electrical, and mechanical engineering professions may be needed from time to time to supplement work of the production, industrial engineering, maintenance, and other departments.

BLANKET PURCHASE ORDERS

This system of contracting provides standby procurement coverage in anticipation of need for material, equipment, supplies, or services. Such orders are appropriate for use when there is a continuing requirement for the same items or services, or when it is known that occasional recurring requirements may arise in circumstances that would not allow sufficient time to solicit bids. This system is used to reduce the time to obtain materials, to effect price savings, and to reduce supplier negotiations and document processing. Blanket purchase orders are intended to cover families of items rather than individual items.

Procurement support to the organization can be increased when authorized requesters are established in departments where the materials or services are used. When a proper contract has been established, the requesters can call for delivery of materials or services as needed. One such program is described under the heading of "Systems Contracting" in the following subsection, and another variation is called RAM (readily available materials). In this system, all items on the blanket purchase orders under the responsibility of an authorized requester are listed in a catalog distributed to personnel in that department. Standardization of materials is promoted, inventory investment is kept low, paperwork is almost eliminated, and the organization's needs are taken care of in minimum flow time.

The blanket purchase-order category covers many contracting techniques that are similar but have different names. Some of these are open-end contracts, requirement contracts, indefinite quantity contracts, definite quantity contracts, and indefinite delivery contracts. The terms "basic agreements" and "corporate agreements" are used to establish a procurement understanding in multidivisional organizations. Generally speaking, the basic agreement is not a contract but an instrument of understanding. It contemplates the coverage of a particular procurement by the execution of a formal contractual document such as a blanket purchase order or a purchase order.

BAILMENT AGREEMENTS

The term "bailment" normally applies to the consignment or loan of property by a supplier to the buying organization, or the loan of property by the buying organization to the supplier—tooling, for example. All property furnished under such circumstances should be covered by a bailment agreement setting forth the responsibilities of the parties for the care of the property and for liability in case of damage, loss, or destruction; the use to which the property can be put; and other pertinent provisions.—*A. G. Pearson*

SYSTEMS CONTRACTING

Simply defined, "systems contracting" is "a purchasing technique that enables a company to acquire repetitively used materials and services from outside vendors so that the cost of these items is at the absolute minimum at their point of consumption." Whether the agreement is written or oral, the understanding between both parties is called a systems contract.

Objectives of Systems Contracting

Virtually every company is confronted with a small-order problem. The 80-20 theory that 80 percent of all orders issued account for 20 percent of the dollars committed still holds true. An in-depth analysis of this concept will also confirm the fact that these orders are not only small in value but also repetitive.

Where properly implemented, systems contracting will greatly reduce the amount of paperwork normally associated with the acquisition-retention cycle and will virtually eliminate the partial-delivery back-order problem and emergency orders. Additional benefits include the reduction of obsolescence, improved expense control, reduction of inventory shrinkage, reduction of inventory levels with a corresponding gain in usable floor space, and a significant reduction in true costs of items covered. The main objectives of systems contracting are, therefore, to (1) improve service, (2) reduce costs, and (3) improve profit.

Purchase-Order Method

Most companies use a standard purchase-order method in acquiring their materials from outside vendors. A brief analysis of this method will immediately show that at least ten individual multipart forms are associated with this method.

FORMS

The ten forms commonly used in acquiring materials from vendors are material requisitions, inventory stock cards, departmental expense controls, traveling requisitions, requests for quotation, vendor quotations, purchase orders, shipping papers, invoices, and checks. This multiplicity of forms is the chief cause of the avalanche of paperwork confronting most purchasing departments.

SERVICE

Of even more concern than the multiple forms, perhaps, is the considerable length of time that the purchase-order method requires for the completion of the entire cycle. For example, a material requisition spends an entire day in moving from the requisitioning department to the purchasing department through the intracompany mail system. A second day is usually required for the purchasing department to process the papers necessary in issuing a purchase order. A third day will be required by the vendor to process the order for shipment—assuming, of course, that the materials are available for immediate release—and the fourth and fifth days of the process will be used by the shipper and the internal delivery mechanism necessary to move the materials from the receiving point to the point of consumption or storage. Hence, even in this era of instant communication, five days or more are required to purchase materials from local vendors.

INVENTORIES

The time lag in materials purchasing is primarily responsible for the internal establishment of formal and informal storage areas. Whether or not the materials stocked on the corporate premises are classified as formal inventories or as expense items, they represent a cash investment in unconsumed materials. Perhaps the most dramatic result of systems contracting has been the drastic reduction—in many cases, elimination—of both controlled and expensed inventories.

TRUE COST

It is recommended that a brief survey be conducted to determine the kind of materials stocked and the true cost of controlling these materials. Most company storerooms contain such high-volume use items as pipe, valves and fittings, fasteners, cutting tools, electrical supplies, and stationery. Generally speaking, these are the MRO (maintenance, repair, and operating supplies) items that are used repetitively by the company. They are also the easiest supplies to acquire from good industrial vendors and are, in general, the lowest in value.

If the total cost of operating these corporate storerooms is compared with the value of materials being processed, it is not unusual to find overhead values of 30 to 80 percent. Additional costs are generated by the following factors: interest lost on dollars invested in inventory; annual obsolescence expense; annual inventory shrinkage; taxes; insurance; heat, light, and power; rent; and salaries. (When the salaries are considered, all personnel associated with the operation must be included. For example, a steel storeroom would require stock handlers, saw men, delivery men, inventory control clerks, expediters, and perhaps an MRO steel buyer.)

Systems-Contracting Method

The first step in establishing a systems contract is the selection of a category or categories of material. It is recommended that any initial attempt at this kind of program be confined to nonproductive materials so that minor problems which may arise during the learning phase will not adversely affect any sensitive areas. It is suggested, therefore, that office supplies, fasteners, cutting tools, plumbing and heating supplies, and general industrial hardware be considered as potential first-time categories.

Consideration of categories of material for a systems contract must also include the value necessary to insure vendor interest in such a program. For smaller companies, the necessary dollar value can generally be met by combining several basic categories that fall within the capability of the supplier.

VENDOR SELECTION

Once the categories have been determined, the vendor who is most acceptable to the company should be contacted. This is perhaps the most important decision in systems contracting. It is not enough to select the vendor who offers the lowest price. On the contrary, it is very often advantageous to pay a premium price under systems contracting. Consideration of the following factors is important.

1. Experience indicates that vendors in close geographical proximity offer a better potential from the standpoint of on-time delivery of materials than vendors located several hundred miles distant.

2. Vendors who represent quality branded merchandise, compared with those who sell second-rate materials, will be the cause of fewer rejections in the using area.

3. Is the vendor a stocking supplier or a broker?

4. Obviously, price must be considered when selecting a vendor; but this should not be the sole determining factor, in view of the previously mentioned points. It has been well substantiated that price differentials between competitive suppliers on repetitive materials of comparable quality are generally less than 5 percent. This is perhaps the strongest reason for selecting a vendor on the basis of a complete capability analysis rather than on competitive price bidding.

Once a vendor has been selected, it will be necessary to convince him that systems contracting will be advantageous to him. One of his more obvious benefits will be that, as a supplier under systems contracting, he will be in a better position to invest his capital in inventory. Not only will he know what items will sell; he will also know how many will be required, and this will help him determine the proper inventory levels. In the same fashion that systems contracting can greatly reduce paperwork for the customer, it also reduces paperwork for the vendor. For example, systems contracting will eliminate the problem of answering quotations for the successful vendor, and here alone a tremendous amount of paperwork can be eliminated.

CATALOGING THE MATERIALS

The first step in establishing the agreement is for the vendor to determine exactly what items will be covered. This is generally accomplished by allowing vendor personnel to examine the customer's existing records. The objective here is to let the systems contract vendor know exactly what materials are required so that he can decide for himself if these materials can be properly supplied by him. The vendor can gain the necessary knowledge from inspecting stores materials, stores records, closed purchase-order history, traveling records, and invoices.

The result of such an analysis will be the establishment of a listing of materials called the systems contract catalog, which is next submitted to the requisitioning areas for their approval. In most instances, brand preference will no longer pose a problem, and corporate standardization can be accomplished by concentrating the material requirement through a systems contract supplier. Only one vendor is normally required for most companies when systems-contracting office supplies, and this is probably true of industrial mill supplies. Occasionally, especially where parts are involved, more than one vendor is required. However, each vendor should be responsible for specific materials and should not be competitive as an alternate source.

In effect, the concept of a single source of supply for a systems contract vendor is being applied. This should not cause concern; in the area of major production capacity there is usually only a single source of supply for electric power, major machine parts, or patented commodities.

Once the catalog of materials has been approved by the requisitioning areas, the vendor is responsible for developing a priced catalog. The price will relate to the EPQ (economic purchase quantity) but will be at the EOQ (economic order quantity) level. The catalog price, therefore, will be shown as the price "per each," and the "each" quantity will be the least amount the vendor is willing to sell and deliver.

A price catalog should be made available to the accounting department for verification of material costs. Unpriced catalogs are made available to the requisitioning areas for order entry purposes. In the event of price changes, only the accounting and vendor catalogs will require updating. Every effort is made to limit price changes, and generally they will occur quarterly.

ORDER PROCEDURE

The actual order procedure for acquiring materials under systems contracting begins with the creation of a four-part material requisition by the requisitioning area. This document is essentially the same type of form used to order supplies from a company storeroom. It is controlled by the charge numbers; the signature of the requisitioner; and the signature of the requisitioner's superior (normally referred to as the purchase authorization point). Once the four-part requisition has been approved, the fourth copy is separated from the set and retained by the requisitioning department as its record of the transaction. The original and copies 2 and 3 are forwarded to the vendor, usually by mail.

Most vendors in a local geographical area will receive requisitions on the morning following mailing. Upon receipt, the vendor will assign each three-part set of requisitions an order number in numerical sequence for control purposes. The vendor will also price each item according to the prices indicated in the priced catalog. Each item will be extended to a total, and the total value of all materials required will be indicated on the original and copy 2. The second copy will be retained by the vendor as his record of the transaction.

The original and copy 3 will be returned with the merchandise and will serve as shipping papers. The two documents can be stapled or taped to the outside of the package. When the shipment arrives in the company receiving department, the receiving clerk will remove the original document from the package and forward the package and copy 3 to the requisitioning area. The requisitioner, therefore, becomes the ultimate point of verification of the acceptability of the transaction. He is responsible for inspecting the materials received and insuring that the count is accurate. This is essentially the same responsibility that the requisitioner would assume if he had received the supplies from a company-controlled storeroom. The receiving clerk signs the original document, verifying that the transaction has been received by the company, and the original is forwarded to accounting. Accounting checks the item prices with the pre-priced catalog, checks the mathematical extensions and additions, checks the signatures, and expenses as received the total value of the transaction against the charge number shown. In effect, the material requisition order also serves as an invoice. Rather than pay each transaction individually, accounting will accumulate transactions for a specified period of time (usually 15 days) and will then issue a voucher referring to the requisition numbers in sequence so that only one check will be required. When the vendor receives the voucher, he will make a tabulation of values by the corresponding order numbers for verification. The fact that the original document resides in the company's accounting department eliminates the possibility of duplicate payments.

This, then, is the basis of systems contracting; if the method is properly imple-

mented, a company can acquire 80 percent or better of its repetitive requirements from outside sources in a matter of 24 to 36 hours.

Special Situations

Occasionally, quantities of material greater than those established for a vendor's inventory are needed, and the vendor and the customer must reach an
agreement on the amount that will be acceptable in partial fulfillment of the
order. Similarly, the customer may experience an emergency need for material
outside regular delivery schedules.

PARTIAL DELIVERIES

The chief reason that partial shipments exist is that most companies order
large quantities of materials only infrequently. Under systems contracting, the
quantities required will be considerably less and will be ordered "as needed."
Most vendors attempt to turn their inventory six times annually, and they should
therefore have ample stocks to take care of daily and weekly requirements.

In the event that the inventory is not sufficient to permit a complete shipment,
the vendor must notify the requisitioner immediately. If the requisitioner agrees
that the quantity available for shipment is acceptable, the quantities indicated
on the requisition are adjusted accordingly. The transaction is therefore considered as "shipped complete," and no back order will be required.

EMERGENCY SHIPMENTS

Most vendors will agree to provide emergency deliveries, regardless of the time
of day, under systems contracting. When an emergency delivery is required, the
requisitioner simply telephones the vendor, giving his charge number and specifying the material required. The vendor is permitted to add to the cost of materials shipped on an emergency basis all additional charges incurred by him. The
total value of the transaction will therefore be charged against the requisitioner's
charge number—a fact which tends to decrease the frequency of emergency
orders.

Writing a Systems Contract

Essentially, systems contracting is a management-to-management technique,
and therefore the agreement between the parties should be well defined. Caution
is recommended, however, in that both parties should be in a position to discontinue the agreement in the event of nonperformance. Systems contracting is definitely a two-way street, and if either the vendor or the customer feels that he is
not being treated fairly, service will deteriorate and the program will fail.

—R. A. Bolton

SOURCE DEVELOPMENT AND SELECTION

Because every purchasing transaction involves a source of supply, the methods
and techniques applied to the proper selection of such sources are fundamental

to the purchasing function. Proper source selection has been described—and not without reason—as the acid test of good purchasing. From the common, commercial, shelf-type items whose possible suppliers are practically unlimited to the highly complicated and sophisticated space-age requirement where no known suppliers exist, the exercise of this all-important prerogative of the procurement function is almost a science in itself.

General Objectives of Source Selection

In most industrial and commercial enterprises, the purchasing or procurement function concerns itself with achieving the objectives of quality, service, and price (not necessarily, but usually, in that order) for each of the materials and/or services it is required to buy. In the fulfillment of this threefold objective, it is essential that the source eventually selected be capable of satisfying the quality demands of the requirement; that it be able to meet the service needs in respect to timely delivery, integrity, prompt adjustment of defects, and competent sales and technical personnel; and, finally, that these demands be met at a price consistent with the sound economic goals of both buyer and seller. While on occasion other factors may be involved in source selection where specialized situations occur, they will in all probability relate to the general objectives of providing the right material or service at the right time, the right place, and the right price.

Objectivity in Source Selection

While it is and rightly should be the prerogative of the purchasing agent or buyer to be the final authority in the selection of suppliers, it is his obligation to do so without undue regard for personal preference, prejudice, bias, or pressure from other sources either within or without his company and to apply himself to the task of vendor selection with complete objectivity. Although, on occasion, there may be instances where suppliers will be suggested or specified by others for purposes of expediency, trade relations considerations, highly technical requirements, single-source situations, or other good and sufficient reasons, the buyer nevertheless will not relinquish his vendor-selection prerogatives; and when such an outside recommendation is in violation of sound selection principles, it is his responsibility to bring the matter to the attention of the proper authority.

Tools for Sound Source Selection

It is essential that the buyer be equipped with certain informational tools which, if properly understood and used, will greatly assist him in selecting his sources wisely. These tools include (but are not necessarily limited to) the following: (1) a general knowledge of the commodity or commodities to be purchased; (2) possession of at least some general specification information; (3) a knowledge of and familiarity with the marketplace in which the buyer must deal; (4) a comprehensive knowledge of the end-use application of the product or service to be procured.

KNOWLEDGE OF COMMODITY

Certain essential facts must be known about the commodity to be purchased before any basic steps can be taken toward selecting a source. Knowledge of the type of industry which produces the product can immediately eliminate certain enterprises from any consideration and narrow the field of potential suppliers to a classified industry group. Knowing whether the commodity is a standard or special product will assist in determining whether it can possibly be purchased from a distributor or if it must be specially produced by a manufacturer. A brand name or other commercial designation may provide a clue as to its potential source or sources.

SPECIFICATION INFORMATION

It is most desirable that some information on specifications be available to the buyer if he is to select an adequate source of supply. For raw material components, detailed specifications are essential. For other raw materials, descriptive data in as much detail as possible will enable him to better judge the potential field of suppliers. In addition to knowing such basics as type of material, size, shape, composition, and similar academic information, the buyer must be aware of the quantities required and if needed on a one-time, intermittent, or continuous basis.

KNOWLEDGE OF MARKETPLACE

As important as the knowledge of the commodities to be procured is a comprehensive knowledge of the marketplace in which the commodities are sold. This includes information on trade practices (terms of sale, reciprocity, direct sales or sales through dealers, and the like); type and availability of labor, union affiliations, and bargaining practices; competitive aspects of the supplier situation; broad location of the procurement activity (domestic or foreign markets, or both); government or other regulations restricting the market for the commodity; and, finally, the firmness or softness of the market at any given time, including seasonal factors which may relate to advantages or disadvantages of purchasing from any specific supplier at those times.

END-USE KNOWLEDGE

It is of the greatest value for the buyer to be completely familiar with the end-use characteristics of the materials he is expected to procure. This information is helpful not only in the selection of possible suppliers; it is also extremely useful in judging the acceptability of any substitutes or alternates which potential sources may suggest in the interest of reducing cost or improving service. Additionally, such information will often define the scope of the procurement activity needed to satisfy the demand: for example, information on sources (single or multiple); size of supplier; amount of research or technology required on the part of the supplier (much, little, or none); the possibility of an existing supplier's qualifying; and so on. If the buyer does not know the application or end use of the materials he procures, his effectiveness will be considerably impaired. This knowledge is critical in relation to all basic procurement procedures.

The Selection Process

The actual process of source selection can be difficult and time-consuming. Nevertheless, whatever effort is applied to this most relevant detail of the procurement function can be very rewarding to the buyer and his company by assuring satisfaction in this primary area of his responsibility. Additionally, much of the work becomes automatic after constant practice by experienced purchasing personnel.

THE FOUR-STAGE METHOD

Normally, good source-selection techniques follow a series of basic steps or phases which can be classified in four general categories. These are the phases of preliminary exploration, inquiry or solicitation, analysis and selection, and review and re-evaluation. Every purchasing transaction, however routine, passes through one or more of these phases. The more sophisticated transactions pass through them all, and the careful and efficient purchasing man proceeds deftly through each step.

Preliminary exploration. This phase begins as soon as the need for the commodity or service has been determined and conveyed to the purchasing man. The buyer's first step is to review his available resources, which are generally found in two broad categories—published sources and his own personal experience.

Published sources of vendor information include trade registers and directories such as the Thomas *Register of American Manufacturers,* MacRae's *Blue Book, Sweets Catalog,* and the yellow pages of telephone directories. Most or all of these should be available in the library of a good purchasing department. This category would also include trade papers, magazines, periodicals and journals, catalogs, and advertising literature.

The seasoned purchasing man will probably draw more heavily on his personal experience in his initial consideration of potential sources. His recollection of previous transactions of a similar nature may provide immediate direction to the situation at hand. His store of personal experience may be enhanced through the regular exchange of information with associates, both inside and outside the company. Great value in this regard is attached to membership in professional societies, attendance at trade shows, frequent visits to vendors' plants, and similar outside activities. One of the most prolific sources of information is found in the buyer's many interviews with sales representatives—an activity of inestimable value to sound purchasing.

Regardless of the category the buyer chooses—and probably he will use a combination of both—the purpose to be served by this review is to enable the buyer to develop a list of potential suppliers. The number of such potentials will add weight to the considerations of the value of the purchase, the quantity required, the complexity of the specification, and the time element in question. It is at this stage of the procedure that knowledge of commodity, specification information, knowledge of marketplace, and end-use knowledge will come most prominently into play.

Inquiry or solicitation. Once the list of potential suppliers is available, the selection process then moves into the second phase. It is at this point that the preselected potential suppliers are apprised of the requirement and invited to submit proposals for supplying it. This invitation may take several forms, including direct contact through meetings or phone calls, or it may be made in writing. The usual and preferred method is for the buyer to submit to each potential bidder an "invitation to bid" or "request for quotation" form. This spells out in as much detail as possible the exact requirement, including the requisite quantity, complete specifications, time and place of delivery, deadline date for bids to be submitted, and in most cases the terms and conditions which will apply to any purchase orders that may result from the offer. Although there is, normally, no limit to the number of such requests that can be sent out, it is considered poor purchasing practice to solicit quotations from sources with whom the buyer does not intend to do business. In other words, all bidders should be considered as potential suppliers.

These invitations to bid are frequently sent out in duplicate so that the potential supplier can use the same form in replying, although in some cases this may not be practical because of the complexity of the bid. In other situations, some vendors may elect to use their own form for bidding, specifying thereon the terms and conditions under which they are quoting and according to which they will accept any subsequent order.

Regardless of the form used, the bidder should be requested to submit his proposed price; his expected terms of payment, including any prepayments and their schedule; the F.O.B. point and any unusual delivery terms; the lead time which will be required to deliver the goods or services following receipt of any subsequent purchase order; and, where applicable, the costs of any tools, dies, or fixtures which may be required. Some buyers also regularly solicit their bidders to recommend any changes which may result in lower cost, a better product, or other possible improvements.

Analysis and selection. When all the proposals have been received, they should be analyzed in detail to determine which is most favorable to the situation at hand so that a selection can be made. This phase is undoubtedly the most difficult and delicate in the entire process of source development; it requires sound judgment, a good sense of values, and the responsibility to assure the best possible acquisition for the purchaser. In some of the more sophisticated situations —buying military hardware or aerospace requirements—the analysis of bids is so complex as to require the use of computers to determine the best proposal. However, in the vast majority of cases, this analysis is normally conducted by the buyer or someone else in a staff function who assists him.

In the process of bid analysis, many factors must be considered. Among the more important are the vendor's geographical location, financial considerations, quality of vendor's management, labor factors, and legal considerations.

Geographical location is important from the standpoint of modes and costs of transportation, access to supplier personnel and facilities, and availability of re-placement parts.

Financial considerations, in addition to the actual price quoted, are concerned with such matters as terms of payment, cash discounts, applicable sales taxes, tooling costs (if any), preparation and/or installation costs, and—for orders re-quiring long-term delivery—policies on price protection or cost escalation which may apply.

Evaluation of the prospective supplier's management involves a careful judg-ment of his financial stability and an understanding of his general credit rating. Depending upon the commodities being purchased, it may also be desirable to weigh his capabilities in the areas of research, engineering, and design know-how and experience. The profitability record of the potential supplier is a good meas-ure of his management acumen and a significant key to his dependability as a good supplier.

Labor factors take into consideration such matters as available labor supply, type and reputation of the bargaining unit (if any), and the relationship which exists between labor and management in the plant or operation of the potential supplier.

Legal considerations give due weight to such essential propositions as compli-ance with local, state, and Federal laws on statutes; warranties; cancellation clauses; matters pertaining to patents; applicable insurance considerations; and a full understanding of any potential reciprocal arrangements.

Depending upon the type of commodities being purchased, additional factors may be considered in the bid analysis. Such factors may include the supplier's capacity; an evaluation of his production equipment; his purchasing capability, which could have a direct reflection in his selling or quoted price; any possible advantages of a favorable product mix or combined production process; the technical and/or personal ethics of the potential supplier; the competence of his sales and technical staff; and his possible attitude in respect to cost-price analy-sis and/or renegotiation.

Once the analysis is complete, a tabulation of the various applicable factors should be made so that the differences between the bids are readily apparent. Most buyers use some formal type of tabulating procedure; as previously men-tioned, some even resort to computers. Whatever method is used, it should be able to inform the buyer adequately about the differences between bidders on all important factors of the quotations, thus enabling him to make a sound judg-ment in respect to the subsequent award of the order.

At this critical point in source selection, the objectives of quality, service, and price must be most carefully and seriously considered, because the source which is finally selected must assure their attainment in a degree sufficient to satisfy the best interests of the purchaser.

Review and re-evaluation. In many instances, source selection and develop-ment end with the final placement of the purchase order. It is, however, fre-quently advisable to retain the bids and all records pertaining to them for a period of time—certainly, at least, until the order has been received and in-spected. A review of the entire process can be undertaken at that time and a determination made of its effectiveness in the light of the final results. Depending on the results, a re-evaluation of all or part of the procedure can then be undertaken where indicated, thus refining it for future use.

If questions arise in regard to any portion of the transaction, the review and re-evaluation documents can be valuable in resolving them, thus providing another good reason for their retention. They are also frequently necessary in substantiating matters pertaining to audits, renegotiation, and related activities. Finally, they may serve as valuable resource material in future vendor location and selection.—*V. E. Huether*

NEGOTIATION

If one single choice had to be made as to the most important attribute separating average from professional purchasing, it would be the art of contract negotiation.

Russell T. Stark, then president of the former National Association of Purchasing Agents, in an article entitled "Professionalism Through Negotiated Purchasing" (*Connecticut Purchasor,* November 1962), wrote: "Negotiating skill may be the critical asset for the buyer of the future, regardless of the size of his company. It is the most advanced form of purchasing skill."

What is negotiation? The U.S. Air Force defines the term as follows: "Purchasing by negotiation is the art of arriving at a common understanding through bargaining on the essentials of a contract such as delivery, specifications, prices, and terms. Because of the interrelation of these factors with many others, it is a difficult art and requires the exercise of judgment, tact, and common sense" (*Air Force Procurement Instruction,* Government Printing Office, 1968).

Negotiation, then, is a method of procurement under which the purchasing executive has considerable discretion in selecting and dealing with suppliers. He must give careful consideration to all factors affecting a particular purchase in order to negotiate contracts which will best serve the interest of his company.

When to Negotiate

The use of negotiation is not intended to preclude competition. The result of negotiation is the same as receiving quotations on which to base purchases. A sound contract is beneficial to the purchaser's company. The extent to which this objective is attained is determined by the experience, judgment, and initiative of the persons who have the responsibility for making the purchases.

The great advantage which negotiation has over formal bidding as a method of procurement is its flexibility. In receiving price quotations, the order or contract is usually awarded to the lowest responsible bidder, with little or no weight given to other factors. Therefore, when the free interplay of various factors such as price, quality, business reputation, and delivery will result in a better purchase, negotiation should be used.

Certain guidelines can be used to enable the negotiator to reach a decision whether to negotiate or request open bidding. Situations commonly require negotiation when one or more of the following conditions are present: (1) when there are only a few sellers in the market; (2) when the specifications of the item to be purchased are not available or are not clear; (3) when new items require experimental and research work; (4) when the items to be procured are perishable (foods); (5) when purchases are outside the United States; (6) when personal or professional services require an individual contractor; (7) when price is not the only determining factor; (8) when special tooling or additional facilities are required; (9) when the items are classified or of confidential nature; (10) when the items are such that the negotiator has an option to make or buy.

To be a competent negotiator requires considerable research and study. To some extent, negotiation is an art. A successful negotiator has a background of professional knowledge which he must display in the face-to-face discussions of the negotiation conference.

Objectives in Negotiation

There are at least five major objectives in the negotiation process: (1) to select a contractor or supplier who can perform under the contract; (2) to establish fair and reasonable prices; (3) to develop sound relations with contractors; (4) to obtain information which will be useful in subsequent negotiations; (5) to reach a complete agreement with the supplier on price, delivery, and other contractual terms.

Negotiation is more than a matter of knowledge and logic. In order to receive fair prices, the negotiator must often utilize the full strength of his bargaining position and display sufficient skill to obtain concessions from contractors. The negotiator should recognize that price is only one factor and that the primary objective is to assure delivery at the proper time and place required.

Preparing for Negotiations

After the negotiator makes a thorough study of the contractor's proposals, he will be able to measure the reasonableness of these proposals and will be in command of the facts needed to place the burden of proof on the contractor to justify prices on terms which appear to be out of line. Of equal importance is the negotiator's ability to anticipate the issues which are likely to arise during the conference and to plan an effective presentation of his position on these issues.

The negotiator is not adequately prepared to enter the negotiation discussions until he has carefully sized up the prospective contractor's bargaining position, which is usually dependent on three important factors: (1) how much the contractor wants the contract; (2) how sure he is that he will get the contract; (3) how much time is available to reach full agreement.

Often, the negotiator will have no difficulty in determining that the contractor is anxious to get the contract. The contractor will ask for assistance in keeping his plant operating at full capacity and will make it clear to the negotiator that he wants to get the contract. On the other hand, if suppliers are operating their plants at or near capacity, they may be willing to quote only on long delivery dates. In this type of situation, the contractor usually does not need a contract and therefore may be unwilling to make concessions during the negotiations.

If the contractor is a sole source or if he is told that his price is low, he will probably feel assured of the contract. This position may lead him to refuse to make concessions during negotiations. In some cases of this kind, there may be nothing the negotiator can do but accept the contractor's terms.

If early delivery is an urgent requirement, the contractor knows that the negotiator has to accept the contractor's terms in order to obtain delivery when needed. The contractor, therefore, may delay negotiations to force acceptance of his terms, especially if he is a sole source.

Conduct of Negotiations

There are many ways in which negotiations can be conducted. The following order is recommended: (1) Select the important contract issues; (2) establish position on important issues; (3) recommend alternatives in the event of disagreement; (4) reach agreement on all contract terms.

One of the most important aspects of the negotiations is the need to confine the discussion to the important issues and avoid unimportant matters. In determining the important issues, the negotiator should attempt to find out why the contractor wants certain contractual terms and wishes to avoid others. The contractor may be unwilling to consider the logic of the negotiator's position until he has explained his own side of the issues. For this reason, the negotiator should attempt to hear the contractor out and avoid stating his own position until the contractor has fully explained his case. The negotiator should not weaken his own bargaining position by making concessions to the contractor without obtaining concessions from the contractor when they are appropriate.

After learning the contractor's position, the negotiator should establish his own on the most important issues. He should not take a definite stand unless he intends to adhere to it. By explaining his position in a broad manner the negotiator is not committed to any single provision but can indicate to the contractor that his position is a matter of policy. This action puts the burden on the contractor to find a way in which he can comply with the policy or justify the exception. It is essential that agreement be reached on the most important issues. Afterward, the lesser issues can be discussed.

In case of disagreement, the negotiator should explore alternate courses of action which may be acceptable to both parties. Often, it is wise to have the contractor suggest a solution.

The best way to assure agreement with a potential contractor is to avoid argument. Try to give him a choice between "something and something" rather than "something and nothing." It is often said that, within limits, negotiation is a matter of horse trading. It is important to make sure that a common understanding has been reached before terminating negotiations, or the contractor may refuse to sign the contract. It is always desirable to put the essential terms in writing before concluding the negotiations.

Pursuit of Price Advantage

The pursuit of price advantage is one of purchasing's prime responsibilities, and it does not necessarily involve ethical considerations. The purchaser should not allow himself to be confused by the misuse—usually by salesmen—of the term "ethics." There is nothing immoral or unethical about negotiating for a price advantage if it is done in a fair and impartial manner.

Ethics of Negotiation

All persons engaged in purchasing occupy a position of company trust. This places a direct responsibility upon them to act according to the highest standards of personal conduct in their relationships with contractors and suppliers.

The acceptance of entertainment or gifts should be avoided, as it may embarrass everyone concerned and impair confidence in the integrity of business relations between the parties. Purchasing actions must be governed by the highest ethical code as outlined by the National Association of Purchasing Management in "Principles and Standards of Purchasing Practice."—*L. M. Caras*

LEGAL ASPECTS OF PURCHASING

A purchasing executive need not be a lawyer to properly handle his responsibility of procurement; however, a general knowledge of business law and the current acts, codes, and taxes of the national, state, and local governments is necessary. The purchasing excutive must be aware not only of the legal obligations to which he commits his company but also of the areas in which he can be held personally liable. He should be familiar with the legal aspects of titles, warranties, rights of rejection and inspection, order cancellations, and patent rights; and, in general, with the terms, conditions, and ramifications which normally are considered as part of a formal purchase order and acknowledgment.

No longer is the age-old doctrine of *caveat emptor* ("let the buyer beware") the basis on which business is transacted. While, frequently, warranty may be merely implied, it is becoming more and more important—because of the complexity of items manufactured and purchased—that the items be clearly described in a manner which is legally termed as an "expressed" warranty—one where all details and performance are spelled out.

Purchasing personnel should limit their application of legal principles to the area of preventative law and the recognition of problems and situations that should be referred to legal counsel. Familiarity with basic concepts will provide a means of avoiding pitfalls and enable purchasing personnel to recognize areas in which to seek legal guidance.

Liability

In purchasing, the individual—whether his title is "buyer," "purchasing agent," or "director of purchasing"—serves as an agent in carrying on the business of buying to which he has been assigned and to which, for each transaction, he makes his employer legally responsible under contract law. The actual authority under which he operates may be express, implied, or apparent, depending on whether or not it is spelled out by his employer. The purchasing man must be completely aware of his limitations as they exist so that he may enter into only those transactions which are within the scope of his authority. There can be cases where a purchasing agent would become personally liable if he were to obtain personal gain or give aid to a competitive company.

The Uniform Commercial Code and Standard Practices

The most recent legal code which affects purchasing-sales transactions, the Uniform Commercial Code (UCC), is a compilation of many commercial laws. It was developed by the American Law Institute and the Conference of Commissions on Uniform State Laws. Since the law is relatively new, managers should make certain that their purchasing personnel understand its implications.

The code is re-examined every five years. However, it should be noted that the code does not take the place of accuracy in a purchase order, care in negotiations, or scrutiny of the seller's offer or sales material. It is not a substitute for definitive contractual language, nor will it override the seller's clear terms.

TELEPHONE AND WRITTEN PURCHASE ORDERS

An order placed for less than $500 need not be confirmed by a purchase order. Orders issued for $500 or more require written confirmation including specific details of the transaction. Exceptions may be made in this area, however.

TERMS

Terms on purchase orders are binding, provided that the order is acceptable to the seller and/or that delivery is made. If the terms of the buyer and the seller are conflicting, terms agreed to in writing are binding. The UCC will usually supply many of the terms. These will be fairly reasonable, middle-ground terms unless the buyer or seller protects himself by specifically stating, in writing, that his terms are to prevail and are acknowledged by the other party.

PRICE

It is preferable that a firm price, to be in effect for a specified period of time, be established on the written purchase order.

MATERIALS AND EQUIPMENT
FOR SPECIFIED PURPOSES

The seller must be advised of the specific use for which the purchase is intended. The purchaser should provide for details on specifications, performance expected, liability to be assumed, and delivery. Inclusion will insure that material can be rejected if not delivered on time; that material can be rejected if specifications have not been met; and that material can be rejected because of damage, nonperformance, or delayed or inadequate performance.

TITLE

Risk of loss passes at the time of title passage, which is usually F.O.B. There is no reason, however, that the parties cannot decide on another time and place.

INSPECTION AND REJECTION

Qualified personnel should inspect material within a reasonable time, and inspection should be followed by notice of rejection when necessary.

Rejected material should not be used except to minimize damages.

Rejected material should be protected, since the seller is entitled to receive the material if he is to return the purchase price.

Specific Federal Laws and Acts

There are two specific Federal laws and acts common to purchasing activity, and the purchasing man must have some understanding of both.

THE SHERMAN ANTITRUST ACT

This act pertains primarily to contracts and agreements which tend to monopolize or restrain trade. A triple-damage clause may be awarded to the person or corporation injured in the violation of the act.

THE ROBINSON-PATMAN ACT OF 1936

This act, which is a further refinement of certain aspects of the Sherman Act and the Clayton Act, is under the jurisdiction of the Federal Trade Commission. It is designed to prevent discrimination in price between different purchasers of commodities of like grade and quality where competition may be lessened and a monopoly created. Most important is the fact that the buyer and his employer can be held liable under the act if he knowingly is a party to such discrimination.

The purchasing man should also be familiar with other laws, such as the Federal Trade Commission Act, the Unfair Trade Practices Act, and the Defense Production Act, so as to avoid situations which could result in legal entanglements for both himself and his employer. Legal counsel should be sought whenever a doubt exists concerning the legality of a purchasing transaction.

State Laws and Taxes

Federal laws are a guiding influence in the operation of the purchasing function. There are, however, local municipality and state laws which must be of concern. Sales, excise, personal property, and inventory taxes vary. Multiplant operations are frequently complicated by such variations and must be reckoned with in interstate as well as intrastate activities. Purchasing awareness is most important here in the proper management of the expenditure of company funds. Taxes are considered as part of the ultimate cost of material or services purchased. If a tax that should have been paid has not been paid and an assessment is made by the state against the taxpayer, additional costs in the form of penalties and interest are incurred by the taxpayer. Such assessments may equal 36 times the amount of the tax due. It is logical, therefore, that purchasing people obtain some knowledge in the tax area and consult their tax administration departments for guidance.

Warranty

Warranties can be expressed or implied. If—in the absence of expressed warranties of quality, fitness, or performance of a product by a seller—the buyer makes known to the seller the particular purposes for which the goods or equipment are required, relying on the seller's judgment and skill, there is an implied warranty that the goods will be reasonably fit for that purpose. The inclusion of an expressed warranty covering quality, fitness, or performance renders the implied warranty void, because the implied warranty cannot exist if the seller expressly guarantees his merchandise.

The Purchase Order: A Legal Contract

Every purchase order or other formal arrangement can be a legal contract and will be considered by the courts as such if it contains four basic elements: (1) agreement based upon offer and acceptance; (2) consideration or obligation; (3) competent parties; (4) lawful purpose.

Such contracts, which are consummated by authorized purchasing personnel, commit company funds and make the company legally liable.

Purchasing people must use the same caution in their verbal commitments as in written orders, for there are situations in which a verbal agreement will stand up in the courts as the fulfillment of the basic elements of a contract.

—A. E. Carney

INTERNAL AND EXTERNAL RELATIONSHIPS

General company policies as well as purchasing policies influence relations with other groups both inside and outside the organization. Within the company, purchasing serves other groups and receives support from them. Outside, purchasing's relations with vendors, government agencies, and the community enhance the profits and reputation of the company.

Internal Relationships

As a staff department responsible for the procurement of materials, goods, and services required by other departments, purchasing has a continuing service obligation to these internal groups.

In turn, the purchasing function depends upon certain services from other internal groups, as well as communication and, in some instances, participation from those requiring purchasing services. All these areas of interdependence are necessary and significant in properly carrying out the purchasing function.

Differences in industry practices or nomenclature may lead to variations in responsibility assignments. For example, an engineering department in some organizations may control construction, or vice versa; in others, planning and scheduling may be a part of production. Nevertheless, the relationships and interaction between purchasing and other departments in all organizations are essentially the same.

CORPORATE PLANNING

The support that purchasing provides to production and other company functions is more effective when purchasing participates in corporate and divisional planning, such as the development of new product lines or new manufacturing facilities, or even acquisition of other companies.

Arranging for coordination of any new requirements with existing requirements necessitates a purchasing review of source, supply, and price factors. These activities may lead to the development of alternate sources or to price renegotiation or the use of substitute materials. Clearly, purchasing should be involved in corporate planning and prepare well in advance of need for the impact on its own area of responsibility if it is to provide the most effective support of the corporate goals and objectives.

RESEARCH

In addition to meeting current production needs, purchasing must be aware of research programs and projects which may influence future trends of sales or production within its own company. This requires knowledge of general company interests as they expand or change, and the options in the marketplace which will support and foster those interests.

Consequently, a real need exists for continuing knowledge of supplier research and development projects that may relate to the company's research efforts. Within the limitations of patent disclosure or other internal security requirements, information on such suppliers' projects should be obtained by, or with the assistance of, purchasing for its own company's research staff. In cases of significant value to its company, purchasing may be in a position to assist in obtaining exclusive patent rights or licensing agreements.

Purchasing also may be persuasive in directing supplier research efforts into channels which offer potential advantages to both organizations, but this can be effective only if purchasing is aware of what its own company's research staff is thinking about. Particularly in companies producing highly technical products, purchasing activities related to supplier research and development may have strong influence on the ultimate market position and profit achievement of the company. This area of purchasing profit making is less easily measured but potentially quite as significant as formalized cost improvement programs.

FINANCE

Since purchasing commits a very substantial portion of the company's income, purchasing should work closely with the company finance function. This is particularly important when negotiating terms of payment on major commitments or in the development of leasing programs.

Purchasing must assure that corporate financial policy is adhered to in the purchasing area and that any unusual expenditures are properly planned with the finance function.

Just as is necessary in the materials marketplace, purchasing has a responsibility to be aware of conditions in the financial marketplace. When money is more costly or when specific company programs necessitate assistance, purchasing should contribute by recommending leasing programs or similar approaches to assist in bridging exceptional periods and in making better use of corporate funds.

LEGAL DEPARTMENT

The intricacies of modern business necessitate legal department review of many activities within a company. Major purchase contracts fall in this area. Review of such documents should verify the legality of proposed contracts under bond indentures or credit agreements, determine accuracy of legal content, check that business and policy aspects and consequences of the proposed contract have been analyzed and understood by those negotiating and signing for the company, and insure that remedies or safeguards in event of default by the other party have been considered.

In addition, the legal department should participate in many other purchasing activities such as approval of purchasing forms as well as special or standard terms and conditions, settlements of disputes, the legal aspects of insurance matters relating to purchasing, and the provision of legal advice respecting proper compliance with local, state, and Federal laws and regulations.

ENGINEERING

The association between the engineering and purchasing departments often involves areas of very significant expenditures which necessitate the maintenance of excellent communications. Engineering may issue bills of material or purchase requisitions including specifications for the procurement of equipment, new facilities, product subassemblies, or raw materials.

With the actions of both departments closely bound in fulfilling company objectives, purchasing and engineering must work together in coordinating technical data from sources of supply. Engineering personnel should continually maintain a neutral attitude with vendors to avoid compromising the company's purchasing position prior to commercial negotiations. Purchasing, in turn, must provide the fullest support to engineering so that the company's aims and programs are effectively and expeditiously implemented.

PRODUCTION

In most industrial business, production is the principal function which purchasing serves by procuring required materials, supplies, and services in time to provide optimum rate and continuity of production operations. Purchasing also has a continuing responsibility to recommend new products, more practical quality, and more economical quantities to the production department and to keep production informed of supply conditions likely to influence future production schedules and operations.

Both departments share an obligation to management to obtain maximum value per dollar expended in determinations relating to value components such as quantity, delivery, and price. Thus the development of a harmonious relationship is vital to achieving corporate profit objectives.

PLANNING AND SCHEDULING

Regardless of position in the organization structure, the planning and scheduling department must assure that material for production operations is requisitioned in ample time to permit purchase and delivery to meet production schedules. Therefore, the responsibilities of the purchasing department to planning and scheduling are similar in large degree to its responsibilities with regard to the production department.

TRAFFIC

Traffic department services and participation are a necessary ingredient in the attainment of purchasing department objectives. Chief among the many significant services provided to purchasing by the traffic department are the cost reductions which traffic effects through its specialized knowledge of freight rates, classifications, and routings relating to purchased goods and commodities. It is the responsibility of purchasing to solicit the cooperation of traffic in all such areas.

STORES

When the stores function is under the supervision of the purchasing department, purchasing usually has responsibility for control of inventory levels. Irrespective of the organizational responsibility, when electronic data processing is the control method for maintaining proper inventory levels and initiating shipping releases to suppliers, the accuracy of information generated by the stores department is vitally important to purchasing. Much of the information generated and documented by the stores department provides computer data to aid purchasing in evaluating vendor and buyer performance and measuring control of inventories as well as usage of materials in production and maintenance operations. The basic actions which are triggered by stores information are the release of orders for purchase and the expediting of delayed deliveries. The necessity for stores and purchasing to work closely is self-evident.

OTHER DEPARTMENTS

Throughout the organization structure there are other departments with which purchasing has interaction from time to time, some more frequently than others. These include such departments as maintenance, construction, and public relations. However, most of these associations are not as significant and demanding as those with the departments previously listed.

LINE MANAGEMENT

When major commodity purchases are under centralized headquarters control, the headquarters purchasing group should recommend appropriate levels of inventory and should maintain the levels authorized by line management. Consistent with requirements established by management, purchasing must assure the most advantageous supply arrangements and procurement costs.

In single or multiplant companies with purchasing groups at each location, plant managers should expect purchasing performance which complies with company purchasing policies and procedures and fully supports objectives and programs of the plant. Purchasing should provide leadership in developing plant purchasing profit improvement programs. Plant management must support such programs and also coordinate purchasing activities with other plant departments to insure the proper climate for most effective purchasing performance. The interaction in all of these areas can be highly significant in profit potential.

Vendor Relationships

Today, business recognizes that supplier goodwill is as important a company asset as customer goodwill. One frequently begets the other since, regardless of the managerial skills of the buyer, production emergencies occur from time to time which only a cooperative supplier can help the buyer's company to overcome. Supplier goodwill results from purchasing's motivation of suppliers to participate in a mutually profitable buyer-seller relationship. This means that the seller will be exposed to the buyer's manufacturing, inventory, receiving, and other operational problems related to the supplier's products. If a continuing relationship is developed, the supplier can reduce his selling effort and devote more time to the study and solution of mutual problems. The ultimate objective of the buyer is to have the seller's production line become an extension of the buyer's production line.

Since vendor capability is really what is being purchased, although it is in the form of products, the ability to motivate the vendor is extremely important. This ability is enhanced by the manner of dealing with vendors. A company with a good reputation in vendor relations is likely to do well in meeting the basic objectives of maximum value and assurance of supply.

Reputation is the sum total of public opinion resulting from all favorable and unfavorable personal and corporate experience. Vendor personnel react in accordance with their personal experience. Integrity and reliability are evident to the salesman if purchasing is fair and honest in its dealings and lives up to promises made. Cooperation is the effort to meet the vendor halfway. The buyer is far more likely to obtain maximum contributed value through new ideas, suggestions, and extra efforts to meet the buyer's special needs in an atmosphere of friendly understanding rather than in that of a cold, forbidding reception.

Community Relationships

Good community relations result when a company or a plant spends its money locally. Purchasing can often develop excellent local vendors by working with them in defining the company's needs and pointing out how they can go about meeting such requirements.

Plants often sponsor junior achievement activities, and in such cases it is rather common for members of the purchasing department to participate actively in the guidance of such groups.

Purchasing is also in a good position to open the door to minority group businesses which make small dollar value products but do not know how to market their products and services.

Active participation in local trade and professional associations as well as civic organizations also contributes to the company's reputation as a good citizen of the community. In each of these activities, purchasing can make its contribution.

Government Relationships

Purchasing departments in most companies have no direct contacts with governmental agencies in the normal course of business; but exceptions exist in the areas of government procurement, ranging from minor construction contracts to major defense contracts. Government procurement regulations are specific as to the obligations and responsibilities of the purchasing department of the supplier company. Thorough knowledge of the requirements of such regulations and adherence to them are essential to the maintenance of good relationships with government personnel. Contracting officers and other government procurement representatives can be most helpful, and their counsel and assistance should be sought.

Companies that depend upon the purchase of government stockpile materials for use in production operations often assign responsibility to the purchasing department for handling the submission of competitive bids for the purchase of these materials. In still other instances, purchasing works with representatives of the corporation's Washington, D.C., office in processing such bid documents.

There are numerous regulatory bodies whose rulings can affect purchasing performance through limitations imposed upon either the buyer or the seller, or both. Generally, any relations with these entities generated by purchasing activities or connected with them are handled by the company's legal department; thus relations between such governmental regulatory bodies and purchasing usually are indirect.

Competitive Advantages

Many areas of competitive advantage accrue to a company through the effective performance of the purchasing function, and both internal and external activities must be considered.

INTERNAL ACTIVITIES

Purchasing must be staffed with men who have technical and administrative training, intelligence, imagination, and enthusiasm. They must exercise initiative, judgment, and tact, and have the ability and willingness to assume responsibility. A buyer need not be an engineer to buy engineered products, a cost accountant to understand the meaning of cost, or a lawyer to write or interpret contracts; but, in integrating activities of his own internal operations, he must understand the principles of each of these as well as other areas. Only with such understanding and background can he effectively cooperate with departments inside his own company and effectively negotiate with suppliers.

The quality level of a company product is usually established by engineering or production. If the buyer has a broad and deep knowledge of the materials required and actively participates in establishing quality levels, he can substantially influence the cost of the product to the competitive advantage of his company.

Quantity and delivery decisions usually are made by the production group responsible for inventory control and scheduling. Their job is to bring together the men, materials, and machines to accomplish the desired production objective. However, through minor modifications in quantity and delivery schedules, there may be great opportunities to enable the vendor to produce the required materials at considerably lower costs and to sell them to the buyer's company at lower prices. This type of participation by the purchasing man in planning and scheduling decisions which result in more efficient use of the seller's facilities can also create competitive advantages through lower product unit cost for the buyer's company.

Technical assistance is available to every company from its suppliers. It is an important responsibility of a purchasing organization to obtain technical assistance in terms of highly specialized knowledge, research and development, and product application effort. This can be done only if purchasing is working closely in its own organization with product development or engineering to stay abreast of company plans and objectives. Purchasing can then effectively communicate with suppliers who are strong in research and development and are the innovators, the people who believe in progress.

Finally, if a purchasing man has participated in the other significant decisions concerning quality, quantity, delivery, and level of technical assistance required, he is in an excellent position to handle price negotiations. If he has the authority to make modifications in quality, quantity, and delivery through cooperation with and knowledge of the programs and needs of other internal departments, it enhances his ability to bring competition to bear on the requirements. It should be clear that price can never be successfully separated from the other important elements of value in the buying decision. Therefore, if the buyer participates substantially in the other significant areas, he has great negotiating leverage.

EXTERNAL ACTIVITIES

Good buyers recognize that the maintenance of sound vendor relations enables them to secure valuable advance information concerning price movements and availability of materials. Such information is essential to the competitive position of their own company.

Good relations with the vendor, and particularly with his sales representatives, provide a real opportunity to develop new ideas, new techniques, and better application of existing materials and supplies to the mutual benefit of both the buyer and the seller. The development of such a relationship takes place over a period of time and results in a gradually increasing exchange of information about the business of the buyer and the seller that brings out savings and profit opportunities for both parties.

The buyer-seller relationship should be held within the context of a business association; if it is extended into the social area, such a relationship can easily be self-defeating. Other potential suppliers will learn of it and tend to withhold helpful information, in the belief that it will not get business for them but merely contribute to the improvement of their competitor's position by being passed along through the buyer.

Good vendor relations with a broad range of suppliers in all the important categories of materials used in any business will enhance competition. There is no real substitute for true competition between suppliers for a company's business. Good vendor relations which maximize that competitive situation will inevitably create lower costs and greater profits for the buyer's company.

Effect on the Corporate Image

With the possible exception of the sales department, no department sees more people from outside the company than purchasing. The fact that vendor representatives are required to call on purchasing in order to sell their products should not inhibit purchasing's opportunity to enhance its company's image through friendly reception, courteous treatment, promptness in keeping appointments, and a fair hearing.

Salesmen are usually realistic. They know that no salesman can get every order. Even so, a salesman naturally feels disappointed when he fails to get an order, particularly one on which he has worked very hard. He will, however, bear no ill will toward a purchasing department that has a record for fairness to all vendors. But if he feels that he has been given a brush-off or that he is the victim of unfair treatment, the purchasing agent and his company will suffer damage to their reputations everywhere salesmen meet to compare notes.

Although a reputation for fairness does not appear on the balance sheet, it is a valuable asset to any company.

Effect on Sales

Good internal and external purchasing relations contribute to more efficient operations and more effective purchasing. Both of these favorable effects will show up in an end product that meets the corporate objectives on quality and cost. As a result, these favorable characteristics should place the company in a better overall competitive position to generate a sales volume that also meets the corporate objectives.

Most large multiproduct companies will find some of their best customers in the ranks of their suppliers. This will be true particularly where the supplier is itself a large multiproduct company. Under these circumstances a buyer's fair dealing will provide an extra dividend in opening the door for his own salesmen.

Equally important in its effect on sales and the ability to sell its product is the company's reputation throughout the trade for being fair, impartial, progressive, and yet considerate in its dealings with vendors.—*D. S. Gregg*

EVALUATION OF PURCHASING PERFORMANCE

Since the days of Taylor and Gantt, few elements of management have been as intriguing as that of measuring employee performance. Top management and purchasing executives alike would welcome some universal and reliable method of evaluating individual and departmental efficiency. Nearly every purchasing text has a chapter on the topic, and the serious student of the subject would be well advised to consult the literature if only to review the diversity of opinions expressed.

An easy error that must be guarded against in measuring purchasing performance is that of oversimplification. The task is difficult even in the most fundamental cases because so little can be adequately appraised in quantitative terms. It is true that in the supporting clerical activities, where much of the work may be repetitive in nature, it has not been too difficult to develop workload data and performance criteria. Work standards have been set for tasks such as typing purchase orders, filing, processing various documents, and so on. But on the buyer level and within the areas of administrative responsibility, performance is not so easily appraised. When the work of an individual or a department is complex, largely of a mental nature, and involves a high degree of personal contact, it becomes far more difficult to measure levels of proficiency. Like salesmen, purchasing personnel must be highly effective in the area of interpersonal relations. When evaluating those who deal with people rather than things, the dangers inherent in subjective evaluation become apparent because of the attempt to measure psychological matters in physical terms. Despite some similar difficulties, and as a result of substantial interest and effort, a few general performance yardsticks have been developed and applied to finance, marketing, and manufacturing functions in many of the larger companies. Purchasing may now be approaching that level of sophistication. The apparent ambiguity and difficulty in evaluating purchasing performance may not have proved to be a hindrance, after all, but rather a stimulus to the pursuit of a solution.

Why Evaluate?

There can be only one reason for evaluating purchasing performance: the desire to improve it.

Progressive management, with proper concern for the future, must continually monitor departmental effectiveness and efficiency. However, a summary or report of past performance can no longer be considered sufficient. What management needs to know is what a department *can* and *should* be doing in order to be better prepared to react administratively to future developments and assure optimum performance. If this is true of most departments in the company, it certainly must apply to purchasing, where good or bad performance may have a greater impact on profits than any other functional area.

The major objective of evaluating purchasing is to record how the department is being run. To do this is the essential first step in establishing a plan for the future. Without permanent data on past performance, we have no way of knowing if the present is better or worse; it would be like a ball game where no one kept score and neither team could win. But it is possible that some of the most beneficial results from an evaluation of purchasing will be as intangible as the factors undergoing measurement. Although difficult to precisely identify and define, they can be very meaningful if improvement is the goal. In large companies, many costly gaps can exist in the coordination and control of purchasing activities. Occasional conflicts over the utilization of talents, facilities, and personnel may be brought forth and resolved as a result of an overall investigation and evaluation. There may also be other desirable results, such as a clearer understanding of the function itself by both the evaluator and the evaluatee. However, these results are not primary but secondary.

What to Evaluate

The factors that are to be evaluated are a direct product of management's expectations for adequate purchasing performance. There are the well-known "rights" of purchasing—right quality, right quantity, right price, and right delivery. Although they are somewhat ambiguous, they can help direct attention to areas of responsibility that must be evaluated. Or management may expect purchasing to buy competitively, to have alternate sources of supply, to maintain effective inventory levels, to help in the selection of materials, and to maintain appropriate vendor relations. If this is the case, these elements must be evaluated in some way. From this it is clear that an imperative prerequisite to the decisions of what is to be evaluated is a thorough understanding and analysis by top management and purchasing management of personal and departmental responsibilities. If an order of importance or priority can be established, the list will be of even further value. Certain additional factors will assist in developing such an analysis: conformance with departmental budget; variances from standard costs; scrap and salvage sales and recovery; frequency of small, rush, and emergency orders; production delays attributable to purchasing; traffic costs; discounts achieved; adequacy and accuracy of records; value analysis participation; interdepartmental cooperation; cost reduction accomplishments; timeliness and acceptability of reports; and suitability of training programs.

All these elements of purchasing management require subjective as well as objective appraisal. What is important to note at this point, however, is that no single element is likely to be adequate. Perhaps a few may be satisfactory, but frequently a greater number would be better, and each company should select those that seem practical and sufficient within the context of its own experience and requirements.

How to Evaluate

"How to evaluate" might be interpreted as "who will do the evaluating," or perhaps "how it can be initiated." This remains an arbitrary choice of management, but it is most commonly performed by the purchasing management group itself, particularly in smaller companies. Many companies may also use an internal audit staff, if available, and others may turn to independent auditors or management consultants. Ideally, there should be self-evaluation by the purchasing department, supplemented by evaluation by another independent party. Both approaches in the long run seek the same objective of setting appropriate goals, relating accomplishments to them, and then devising means of more nearly reaching those goals. The extra benefits of departmental self-evaluation should not be readily dismissed. The very fact that matters of administrative concern are under constant surveillance has a way of shortstopping problems before they occur. Furthermore, administrative reaction time is shortened when the evaluator is responsible for the effective operations of his department.

Whoever assumes the responsibility for evaluation will be looking at three things: an appraisal of purchasing efficiency, an appraisal of purchasing proficiency, and an appraisal of purchasing managerial effort. And he will be looking at these matters in three ways, comparing them as to past performance, planned or budgeted performance, and known performance standards in other departments or companies.

EFFICIENCY

Appraising purchasing efficiency pertains somewhat to the dispatch with which the regular work load is handled. A variety of statistics are typically used to reflect buying efficiency. Most common is some combination of the following: dollar value of expenditure, number of orders placed, average dollar value per purchase order, average number of purchasing employees, cost of the purchasing department, cost of purchasing as a percent of purchases, number of interviews conducted, and telephone expense.

Data such as these, when accumulated on a current basis, can be conveniently compared with past performance. Although there can be no assurance that past performance occurred at an optimum level, such a comparison does indicate a trend and quickly highlights deviations. If planned levels of activity are established, comparison with expectations also becomes possible. Of course, every purchasing executive wants to maintain an optimum level of departmental operating efficiency while stimulating outstanding purchasing proficiency.

PROFICIENCY

Purchasing proficiency pertains to the control of prices, quality standards, quantity and inventory levels, and timeliness of deliveries. The problem in evaluating these factors is that they are difficult to measure in absolute terms. Furthermore, improvement in one may induce deterioration in another; the statistics must therefore be examined carefully if their true meaning is to be properly assessed.

MANAGERIAL EFFORT

The appraisal of purchasing managerial effort is the least tangible but very possibly the most meaningful to top management. Such an appraisal may include a study of procedures, policies, personnel, organization, records and reports, planning, and management controls. What the evaluator seeks is evidence of a well-planned program. Effective purchasing performance is no accident.

SETTING STANDARDS

Every well-managed purchasing department has some standards of performance against which it evaluates current levels of activity. The level of sophistication of the evaluation system and top management's interest in its application are frequently an indication of purchasing's importance to a company.

Setting standards and then measuring performance against them can have a very stimulating effect on the purchasing department. This management technique can be used by the purchasing department administrator himself to monitor performance and induce improvement, and it can similarly be used by management service personnel or independent consultants. Often, the justification and review of activities help spot deficient practices, and the psychological effect alone is frequently beneficial.

Any department or functional area is likely to benefit from analysis and evaluation. Improvement is always possible. But management probably has most to gain from appraisal and subsequent improvement in purchasing. Although it is inherently difficult to evaluate and often regarded as an expense or nonproductive factor, purchasing can produce a greater impact on profit than any other functional area of management. Management expects this impact to occur, and purchasing must accept this responsibility.—*J. E. Ahrens*

Section 11

Public Relations

CONTENTS

The Corporate Role of Public Relations

Establishing the PR Program

Internal Public Relations

Public Relations and Specific Groups

Maximizing PR Benefits

Evaluating PR Benefits

Public Relations in the Future

THE CORPORATE ROLE OF PUBLIC RELATIONS

Few terms used as widely as "public relations" are so poorly understood. The confusion is understandable, however, for the term—whether correctly or incorrectly employed—is one in multiple usage. In part, the problem arises from the fact that public relations is both a concept and a function of management.

In a conceptual sense, public relations is an intrinsic element of management. Whether organized or haphazard, sound or poorly conceived, active or passive, public relations figures in any corporate policy or decision involving people within or outside the company. As has been so often said, every company has public relations—whether it wants to or not.

In a functional sense, public relations encompasses the varied activities undertaken to advance and achieve corporate objectives—for example, opinion research, booklets, films, speeches, publicity, advertising, and employee and shareholder communications. Taken together, coordinated, and unified by well-defined goals, activities such as these constitute a public relations program.

In less precise usage, public relations becomes an expression of public opinion. Thus a person who thinks well of a company and approves its actions may say it has "good public relations." Conversely, and as a consequence of suspicion born of misunderstanding, he may disparage something he disapproves of as "just public relations" or a "public relations gimmick."

Definitions and Objectives of Public Relations

The difficulties of succinctly explaining the function, methods, and goals of corporate public relations have prompted some broad definitions—"doing good and getting credit for it," for example. While valid enough, these definitions summarize to such an extent that they give no hint of the increasing ubiquitousness of public relations as the role of the corporation in society changes.

Among the definitions included in Webster's *Third New International Dic-*

tionary is this one: "the art or science of developing reciprocal understanding and goodwill." "Goodwill"—akin to "getting credit for it"—is present in the definition; precedence goes to "developing reciprocal understanding," a much larger assignment. But "understanding" with whom? Who is the public?

"PUBLIC" VERSUS "PUBLICS"

There is, in fact, no single public. What is commonly called the public is actually the composite of many smaller publics grouped together by such common denominators as occupation, geographical location, interests, political leanings, religious affiliations, age, education, or income. It would be a serious mistake to assume a homogeneous audience in which each person would respond in the same way to identical circumstances. Nor will a company's public be the same for every one of its activities; in each case, it will attempt to direct its efforts to people who are likely to be interested in the subject and with whom the company would like to communicate.

In a product publicity effort for a consumer item widely used by both men and women, the audience comes close to being the general public; most people, regardless of occupation, politics, or education, would be grouped by a common denominator—use of the product. But far more typical of corporate public relations is the need to select carefully the groups with which a company might realistically seek to develop reciprocal understanding. And as our social, economic, and business environment changes, corporate objectives and publics are being more precisely defined. Examples are found in the following relationships: (1) with scientists, governmental agencies, and conservation groups increasingly concerned about pollution and environmental health; (2) with shareholders, investors, and the financial community, to counter the threat of possible tender offers and take-over bids by corporate raiders; (3) with youth, as a population of younger average age translates its expectations into a broadened concept of corporate social responsibility; (4) with community leaders, social scientists, government agencies, and religious groups, as the nation presses for solutions to the problems of its cities and its minorities; (5) with those within and outside government who are evaluating the need for consumer protection legislation; and (6) with officials and a full range of special publics in other countries, in keeping with the growing internationalization of business.

THE PUBLIC INTEREST

An effort to develop reciprocal understanding must of necessity be a two-way street. Not only must it take into account the point of view of the audience; it must address itself to the audience's interests if it is to gain acceptance and achieve understanding. In a changing society, this means that a company must be fully responsive to the environment in which it functions if it is to interpret itself in meaningful, effective terms. It goes without saying that its policies and objectives must be in the public interest as well as its own. The corporation exists only to serve the needs of the public; to attempt to achieve acceptance and understanding for anything not in the public interest would be foolhardy and, in the long term, a lost cause.

PR RESPONSIBILITY

Good public relations cannot be made out of bad policy. And since top management bears the responsibility for sound policies, in the interest of the public as well as that of the company, it is ultimately responsible for corporate public relations.

In turn, top management looks to its public relations people to function in a number of capacities: (1) as counsel, to contribute to policies and decisions with public relations implications; (2) as tacticians, to anticipate, evaluate, and recommend on public relations situations that may require top management decisions; (3) as planners, to develop, for management approval, corporate objectives and the platform on which management will seek understanding; (4) as technicians, to develop and execute programs that will contribute to the attainment of objectives; (5) as ready reserve, to be sufficiently familiar with the company's activities to be able to render prompt, effective public relations support to any department whenever it is needed or desired.

WHAT MANAGEMENT EXPECTS

Among the various capacities in which public relations serves the corporation, the technical and mechanical functions are pretty much taken for granted. Ability to get publicity for the company, or skill in handling routine programs, falls short of the broader involvement increasingly expected by management. More and more, management looks to public relations for a greater contribution to corporate policy and planning and for a longer-range perspective in its thinking.

Public relations also should be familiar with activities throughout the company and alert for developments in any area of the business that could have companywide effects. At the same time, public relations should be attuned to the world of education, government, and other segments of society so as to be able to advise management regarding trends which could have significance for the company. Public relations' contribution to corporate success is enhanced to the extent that it can anticipate circumstances, thereby permitting the company to plan for—rather than react to—problems and opportunities.

GENERAL AND SPECIFIC OBJECTIVES

If a company's public relations effort is to be effective and fully productive, there must be well-defined objectives for the overall program and for the individual activities by which it will be implemented.

Corporate goals are usually couched in broad general terms covering such points as what the company seeks to achieve, the attributes for which it wants to be recognized, and the policies which give it special character. Once agreed upon and approved, the statement of corporate goals gives public relations people guidance as to the way in which the company is to be projected.

The objectives of individual programs and projects will be much more specific, but each should contribute in some measure to overall goals. For example, a shareholder relations program designed to achieve wider understanding of management's targets for earnings growth would also advance an overall objective calling for wider knowledge and understanding of the company and how it operates.

Typical objectives for programs directed toward various publics might be the following: (1) the plant community (company shown as a responsible neighbor concerned about pollution control); (2) employees (mutuality of interests between company and its people); (3) customers (close manufacturing controls assuring quality that gives added value to products); (4) financial community (diversity of operations, making company different from other companies with which it is usually grouped); (5) consumer groups (competition among companies as consumer's guarantee of full value).

THE PR GROUP AND OTHER FUNCTIONS

As both a staff and an operating unit, the corporate public relations group frequently finds itself working for and with other departments. Indeed, a major function is to provide public relations services to other parts of the company.

Thus typical corporate public relations activities might include helping recruiters meet their goals for scientific and technical personnel; working with product development people on a professional relations problem caused by a new product; preparing a statement for a congressional hearing on tax-law changes; developing, with the legal department, a stand-by publicity plan for an antitrust suit; preparing a program and materials for the introduction of a new product; consulting with the government relations group on appropriate responses to new legislative proposals.

In bringing its skills and techniques to bear across the breadth of the company's activities, the corporate role of public relations is becoming more and more that of a generalist among management functions.—*V. N. Gannon*

ESTABLISHING THE PR PROGRAM

Management must establish ways to plan, organize, and implement its public relations program objectively, just as it applies objectivity to such other functions as production and marketing. There is no valid reason why objectivity cannot be applied to this service function.

The *concept* of public relations as a corporate activity may be less well defined than some of the others; it covers more ground than most, as psychology involves a broader area than pediatrics. But, for operational purposes, the same principles of professional management used to plan, organize, and carry out other corporate work can be used in connection with the public relations program.

The vital first step in planning a public relations program is to set public relations policy; this should be done jointly by the chief executive and the public relations executive if the program is to be successful. It is the chief executive who conceives and shapes the corporation's overall objectives and policies. He consults with the public relations director to arrive at policies that are clearly in the public interest. The public relations director has the responsibility of presenting them in the best possible light to many audiences—customers, shareholders, labor unions, government, and the rest of the public.

Setting PR Policy

In establishing an operating public relations policy, the following checklist will be useful.

1. *Clearly define company goals.* What are the major market targets? Growth objectives over the next five years? Short-term objectives? Ambitions concerning diversification? Financial plans? Hopes for legislation affecting the industry?

2. *Decide on the public image to be projected.* Does the company want to be characterized publicly as adventurous, or conservative? Is the company's talent for innovation a quality to be stressed? Or is solid, year-in, year-out earnings achievement the strong suit? Does the company want to capitalize on youthful management? On progressive social involvement? Or on a straightforward business philosophy and continuity of executive strength?

Self-analysis is simpler for a corporation than for an individual. The kind of personality the corporation has developed should be reasonably clear. If the corporate personality is not the kind that should be projected, it will have to be changed. Do not hope to project what does not exist.

3. *Commit to writing management's views, philosophy, and goals.* It is important to document them as useful points of reference that can be checked occasionally against current public relations programs. It is easy to lose sight of fundamentals. Write them down and make them available for continuing guidance. Many companies find it useful to have a basic document of this kind reproduced and distributed in a form that can be displayed in company offices.

4. *Decide on a definite communications policy.* This should include internal and external audiences. Typically, internal audiences include hourly rated employees, professional employees, sales personnel, middle management, and executive management. External audiences include shareholders, government, the financial community, and the press; that is to say, the general public. The customer public generally is reached through advertising, although in some cases communication with customers—where the intention is to tell rather than to sell—becomes a public relations function.

Decide what each of these groups logically wants to know and should know, and how much should be disclosed to them. If the organization is publicly held, the disclosure of certain information is regulated by law; and the company will be governed by regulation as well, much as it is guided by good sense.

5. *Provide for advance considerations of the public relations impact of major company developments.* Establish a system for two-way access between top management—where such developments originate—and public relations management. The chief executive should obtain the counsel of his public relations director on major corporate policy decisions before those decisions become final. The experienced public relations executive can evaluate the public relations aspects of important decisions and offer recommendations which will help implement new policies and carry out new objectives.

The assumption here is that the public relations executive is a professional in whom management has the same confidence it extends to its legal, financial, and other specialists. If this confidence does not exist, any public relations program will be undermined from the start.

6. *Set up a system for top management availability in news breaks and crises.* It is not always possible to hold formal conferences before corporate developments of public interest are announced. There are circumstances in which top management approval of public announcements is needed quickly. Plant accidents, surprise labor walkouts, and natural disasters affecting the company and its employees are such occasions. An emergency system of communication between public relations and top management should be arranged.

Since contingencies of this kind do not always occur during normal working hours, the system should provide for off-hour access. It should provide for the distribution of travel itineraries each week so that all concerned can be reached wherever they happen to be.

7. *Establish a public relations clearance system.* Implicit in the establishment of a public relations policy is the understanding that management will accept public relations instruction and guidance as willingly as it accepts counsel from other areas of expertise. This understanding becomes explicit when management makes it clear that public relations is to act as the clearance center for all speeches, news releases, and public announcements affecting the company.

In many cases, of course, material of this kind originates with the public relations department and clearance is not a problem. If it does not originate in the department, it should be cleared with public relations people before it becomes public.

Formal clearance procedures should be established. Instructions concerning such procedures should emanate from top management and be issued to all those who might conceivably be affected.

Constructing a PR Plan

The development of a public relations plan should flow logically from the establishment of public relations policy.

When policy is established, the company's goals are defined and agreement is reached on the desired public image. The desired image takes on different shadings and emphases depending on the audience to be reached. It follows that a public relations plan must actually take the form of one central plan with several subplans.

The central plan will aim at making the corporation's major long-range policies, objectives, accomplishments, and problems clear to all audiences. Subplans will deal with specific objectives and specific audiences. To put it another way, there should be a corporate public relations plan and as many others as are needed to satisfy specific goals.

The corporate plan, typically, provides for executive speaking engagements at which broad company or industry activities are discussed; the release of general news concerning such things as plant expansion, recruitment plans, contract awards, and labor negotiations; the publication of quarterly reports to shareholders, and an annual report; the dissemination of corporate news to employees.

Subplans, typically, aim at specialized audiences like the financial community, the government, community groups, and educational groups.

In either the corporate or the specialized program, the following should be considered as the basis for planning:

1. What are the public relations objectives in terms of public persuasion? What message is intended?

2. Who is the audience? Where can the message be most effectively taken?

3. What are the appropriate media? Will newspapers reach the audience? Trade magazines? Financial publications?

4. Is time a factor? Is the audience to be reached continuously over a long period (usually the case in a corporate program)? Or is there a specific time period in which public relations efforts will be most effective (because of seasonal considerations, perhaps, or in support of or opposition to pending legislation)?

MARKET-ORIENTED PLANNING

The case of a large company that manufactures luggage is an example of the kind of planning that may be done. This company decided that it needed a market-oriented public relations plan to (1) broaden consumer awareness of its product line, particularly among selected target groups whose travel schedules were known to be heavy; (2) promote the line to retail merchandisers and distributors; and (3) promote the use of vinyl luggage as the most popular modern travel accessory.

General objectives were first established to tell the company's story to specific buying influences and to the merchandising organization.

It was recognized that hand in hand with direct sales benefits from such objectives go less tangible ones: strengthening distribution channels; building an image of a lively company in the mind of the general public and the business community; and lending support to the company's overall corporate and financial public relations program.

The public relations program was planned in three parts, each with its particular objectives. A basic, continuing program was organized in the first two parts, one covering communications to the retailing trade and the other covering communications to the buying public. The third part included special projects to strengthen the basic program.

The overall objective of Part 1 (communications to the retail luggage trade) was to position the company as a manufacturer of the most complete line of high-quality luggage in America—a line with demonstrated consumer appeal, strongly supported by an aggressive marketing program designed to increase store traffic. The specific objectives were to increase allotments of floor space; promote use of special displays; educate retail personnel in product advantages; strengthen dealer force; and attract new merchandising-oriented outlets.

The overall objectives of Part 2 (communications to the buying public) were to position the company as the manufacturer of America's most complete line of luggage in the mind of the general public and to make the company's name synonymous with high quality, rugged dependability, and up-to-the-minute styling. The specific objectives were to obtain a larger share of the executive travel market; increase sales in the vacation travel market; increase sales to women travelers; develop the youth market, particularly college students and campers; and obtain a larger share of the gift market.

Part 3 outlined market-oriented special projects outside the realm of the basic product publicity program. Its objectives were to build an image of the company as a helpful source of travel-planning information and to make the image show the company to be as concerned with its products' use as with the number of products sold.

To meet objectives set forth in Part 1 (communications to the retail luggage trade), a program was established that included product publicity in the retail trade press; tie-in publicity releases for use in local papers; feature articles and case histories in the retail trade press; and quantity reprints of articles in the consumer press.

The objectives outlined in Part 2 (communications to the buying public) were met with a program that included feature articles placed in a wide range of magazines devoted to the varied special interests of today's men and women on the move.

These publications included men's and women's fashion magazines as well as books in the fields of travel, shelter, and sports. It was planned that many stories developed for those magazines would also be placed widely with the corresponding feature sections of the nation's daily and weekly newspapers, resulting in a substantial extension of coverage. All these stories were "service" articles designed to be helpful to the consumer. Sample titles included "The Art of Packing a Suitcase"; "How to Avoid Losing Your Luggage"; and "Things Most People Forget to Pack."

Broadcast media were deemed ideal for this consumer-targeted part of the program. The large numbers of women's "talk" shows on daytime television offered opportunities for publicity placements which had the same themes as those used in publications, but they were rewritten in the style of the broadcast media and supplemented with necessary props.

Finally, new product stories were scheduled for distribution to all appropriate publications in the fashion and travel fields.

As special projects for Part 3 of the public relations program, the following were proposed: a point-of-purchase display graphically outlining correct methods of packing luggage; a series of clinics, to be held by retailers in their stores, to teach packing to interested customers; local publicity releases about the clinics, for dealer use; and ad mats for dealers, announcing clinic times and dates.

Also planned was a five-minute film for television syndication, covering the essentials of packing as developed for the clinics. The film would provide company identification and project a service-oriented image in a light but informative script ideally suited to fill open spots in daytime television. Such a film also would be suitable for showing to civic groups, women's clubs, travel clubs, and others. It would be made available to retailers for their use in community affairs programs.

Organizing for Implementation

Three considerations are paramount in the organization of a public relations program: the budget, the staff, and individual staff responsibilities.

THE BUDGET

Over the years, any number of formulas have been worked out to arrive at "proper" public relations budgets. Some of these involve percentages of sales; some are based on percentages of the advertising budget. Neither system makes real sense. Nor does any pat formula for public relations budgeting.

The public relations budget should be predicated on a realistic balance between what the corporation hopes to accomplish and what it can afford to attempt.

"Balance" is the operative word here because the possibilities for public relations activities are almost unlimited. A well-rounded program could include everything in a range from a four-color quarterly publication for stockholders to a heavy annual schedule of movies for school groups. Not every company, however, can afford either the lavish publications or the film production. Common sense must dictate the limits of ambition. The budget should grow out of a sensibly delimited program whose potential costs have been carefully investigated. In other words, decide what must be done; then find out what it will cost to do it. The budget, ideally, would be the total figure of those costs plus salaries and overhead.

STAFFING AND RESPONSIBILITIES

The matter of salaries leads naturally to the matter of staff.

Again, there is no workable formula for the composition or size of a public relations staff. Many small companies employ one person who is "the public relations staff." The very largest corporations use hundreds of professionals who have such specialties as speech writing, audiovisual communications, or governmental affairs. The scope of the program will dictate the size of the staff, and the staff's size will in most ways dictate its composition—that is, the division of activities among the people on the staff.

The one rule that should be held inviolable is this: Hire the most professional, best-qualified people the company can afford.—*Elias Buchwald*

INTERNAL PUBLIC RELATIONS

It is generally accepted that sound corporate public relations must be based on good performance. A company's relations with its various publics are ultimately shaped by what it does, not what it says it does. None of its publics, normally, is more important than its own employees, and no amount of rhetoric can create positive employee attitudes out of slipshod corporate practices.

Assuming basically good corporate performance, a thoughtfully conceived, diligently pursued internal public relations program can go far toward reaching several objectives. Fundamentally, internal public relations seeks to bring each employee the maximum understanding of his company and an appreciation of its problems, plans, and achievements. This kind of understanding is essential if employees are to have any basis for a sense of involvement that will insure satisfactory productivity on the job and a positive attitude toward the company off the job.

Establishing a favorable working climate has other positive effects as well, not the least of which is the impact on recruiting efforts; word moves swiftly that a given company is—or is not—a good place to work. Internal harmony is reflected, too, in the manner in which employees are disposed to treat customers, suppliers, and each other. Thoughtful security analysts probe for indications of employee attitudes, and union negotiations are obviously influenced by them.

Putting the House in Order

The public relations business is committed both internally and externally to the concept of two-way communication. If a company is to win public support, someone in the company must make it his business to determine whether existing corporate policies and practices are acceptable to the public. Taking the public pulse is generally accepted as a responsibility of the public relations director. It is not the kind of job he can handle alone; however, he can approach it by systematically arranging for key employees to alert him promptly to danger signals.

In some circumstances such an informal system will be inadequate, and the public relations director will elect to go after specific areas of information in a more structured way. For example, he may launch an employee attitude study by an outside organization to bring to the surface possible areas of employee dissatisfaction such as poor supervision or work environment or to find evidence of a communication breakdown. Results of such studies can, depending on the circumstances, be made known to selected employees with productive results.

PREACHING AND PRACTICING

For some years, American business has increasingly broadened its definition of corporate responsibility. The company that publicly expresses its concern about the nation's educational system, rising medical costs, or racial problems is no longer pioneering. Moreover, its employees will regard these expressions as synthetic if the company has done nothing internally about these same issues. Does it, for example, have any sort of scholarship program for employees' children? Does it have a program for matching contributions to educational institutions? Does it provide training opportunities so that employees can advance through on-the-job training? Does it offer adequate group medical insurance? Does it have a meaningful charitable contributions program? Does it, indeed, pursue fair employment practices inside its own organization? A company with any understanding at all of internal public relations will know that it cannot gain employee support if its practices don't square with its public posture.

ESTABLISHING A COMPANY POLICY

A useful but frequently overlooked internal public relations tool is a written statement of corporate objectives. On first thought, it seems to some people that a recital of such company aims as "a quality product at a fair price" or "fair wages and agreeable working conditions" would simply result in a parade of platitudes. Experience has shown, however, that in itself the process of articulating corporate objectives requires more soul-searching and brings about a greater perspective than most of the people taking part initially expect.

The process of stating the objectives is an education for the participants because it brings them as close as they can get to the overriding concern of the company's chief executive officer. His principal problem is to balance contradictory pressures that beset him from all sides. He must, for example, weigh union pressures for higher wages against stockholder demands for higher dividends and sales force pressures for lower prices. Putting corporate objectives in writing requires all who share in that task to face up to the problems of the chief executive.

The main purpose in the public relations area, however, is to provide those who are specifically involved in internal public relations with a set of themes on which they can base their in-house communications. These themes help give a unity and sense of direction to internally directed messages and indeed will do the same for external communications.

Many companies post these policies conspicuously so that management and supervisory personnel are, in effect, on record—publicly and permanently committed to the stated policies.

The Base for Internal Public Relations

If employees are to be expected to perform effectively and to become advocates for their company, they must be fully and accurately informed about their company. Yet the communications process probably gets more lip service than any other single function of management. "Nobody ever tells me anything" may be the most frequent complaint among American workers at all levels.

There is a great gulf between management's ability and willingness to provide operating information and its ability to provide the kind of information that builds interest, enthusiasm, and a sense of participation. The employee communications challenge has long been to keep a job from being "just a job." Although many factors enter here, of course, the root of the problem is in communications.

COMMUNICATING WITHIN

The first requirement in structuring an effective internal communications program is to determine who needs and wants what kinds of information, and what kinds of information serve management's purpose in dissemination. Obviously, a given employee's place in the ranks governs what he needs and wants to know. The turret-lathe operator will have little interest in the company's banking connections, but he may very conceivably have a deep interest in his company's investments. He may be one of America's 22 million investors.

Similarly, the chief executive officer need know little about lathe operation but may have more than passing interest in learning that one of his lathe operators is the commander of a local Veterans of Foreign Wars post. And salesmen—to take another example—have their own needs for being kept informed about new facilities, product innovations, what the competition is up to, and so on. Variable, complex needs for information run strongly through organizations of every size, and sorting out these needs is a perpetual challenge to the internal communicator.

No house organ or other single technique can conceivably cope with the task; for this reason, some organizations depend on a dozen or more plant or departmental newsletters supplemented by regular executive staff meetings and departmental meetings. The constant problem, of course, is to balance the productivity of meetings and company publications against budget considerations and daily work requirements.

COORDINATING COMMUNICATIONS

Company practices in coordinating written employee communications differ widely. The need for a uniform expression of corporate policy is obvious, and where responsibility is fragmented, such uniformity can be difficult to obtain. It is made more difficult when a company seeks to create a "family resemblance" in all its corporate publications, but uniformity in expressing policies and practices should take precedence over format and design. Generally speaking, the public relations department has a broad-based knowledge of corporate affairs and is in a competent position to act as the clearance point for all internal publications.

EMPLOYEES AS PR REPRESENTATIVES

A public relations director is reminded regularly that he alone cannot do his company's public relations job. Ideally and potentially, everyone in the organization can and should serve as a public relations representative for the company; however, scores of factors influence an employee's ability or desire to act as a company spokesman. Many of these factors are beyond the control of the public relations director, but he can control the amount and kinds of corporate information disseminated to employees.

But to educate an employee about his company is only the first step; it is quite another matter to make him so interested in off-the-job activities that his knowledge and support of his company can be brought to bear in useful ways.

As with most corporate efforts, this kind of program has the best chance for success if it enjoys the sincere, energetic support of the chief executive. He can best show his sincerity by his own involvement in community, industrial, and civic affairs and by encouraging other top management members to follow suit.

Some people, of course, are natural joiners; others simply do not know how to get started. Handbooks prepared by some companies tell employees how to become active in politics, local educational affairs, or civic or fraternal groups. Success stories in house organs, including personality pieces about employees who have taken leadership roles, can also be helpful in assuring other employees that they too can become more active in their own community.

Two major returns are to be gained from employee participation programs. First, there is the reward the employee himself feels in terms of recognition and his own satisfaction for having made an extra contribution to his community, his party, or his church. Second, the exposure that the company indirectly receives because of its identification with the employee can also be beneficial. In critical situations, for example, employees may well be in a position to help defend their company against legislative attack, community harassment, or any of the unforeseeable local problems that can threaten a national organization.

—*Lee Hirst*

PUBLIC RELATIONS AND SPECIFIC GROUPS

The human environment in which a business or a nonbusiness institution must operate is composed of people who have varying relationships with the business. The expectations of customers, for example, are different from the expectations of investors. The government and the press exert an influence on every business, though in different ways.

Thus business success depends on maintaining a favorable web of relationships with a variety of groups and institutions. If these relationships are favorable, the business can prosper under intelligent management. If they are unfavorable, the businessman will find his plans thwarted, his achievements stunted, his costs distorted, his operations hampered, and his customers gone elsewhere.

Management of Relationships

A favorable human environment is not an accident. It is achieved by creative management of the human relationships required to run a successful enterprise.

The key man in the management of relationships is the chief executive, whose strategies, actions, and statements determine the posture of the business in its relationships with other people and groups. A public relations officer who specializes in understanding and communicating with the various publics can provide expert counsel and manage much of the work required. But the personal leadership of the chief executive is essential to assure relationships that serve the needs of the business.

Structure of Relationships

Exhibit 11.1 is a chart showing the generic structure of the relationships required to operate a profitable business. Using this systematic way of identifying the groups that affect the business, the manager can establish relations priorities, objectives, and programs that grow directly out of the real needs of the business. Two of the groups shown in the chart—the direct interest groups and the press —are discussed in detail later in this subsection.

Start reading at the center of the chart: a circle representing a company. What does the company absolutely need to operate at a profit? As shown in the second circle (reading outward), it needs income, capital, labor, supplies and services, and a favorable structure of laws, regulations, and public policies that will enable it to operate without undue restrictions. These necessities must be provided for the company by the people in the third circle in Exhibit 11.1, the direct interest groups: customers, share owners, employees, vendors, and governments (national, state, and local). These are obviously the most important relationships in the business, but sometimes it is forgotten that they determine, to a large degree, whether the general manager will make the business grow and earn a profit.

Relationships with customers determine the size of income. And costs are largely determined by the other four direct interest groups. If employees and suppliers want too much money for their services, or if any of these groups impose costly restrictions or delays on operations, costs go up and profits are squeezed out. Hence the manager must maintain cooperative, mutually profitable relationships with these direct interest groups, reasonably meeting their needs and expectations so that they will reasonably meet his own.

These are not the only relationships needed to operate profitably. In the fourth circle of Exhibit 11.1 are the direct influence groups. Dealers, distributors, consultants, and original-equipment manufacturers steer their customers either to the company's products or to competitors' products. Investment counselors advise potential share owners where to invest. Unions and colleges influence the expectations and demands of employees. Government agencies and purchasing

Exhibit 11.1

BUSINESS RELATIONSHIPS

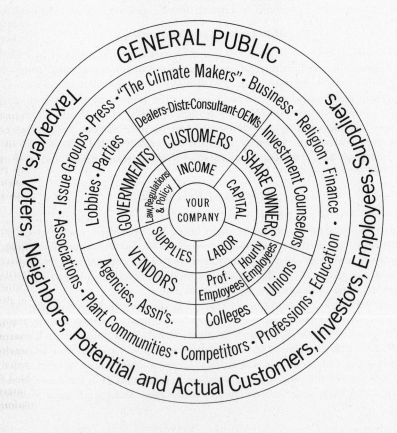

associations affect vendor relations. Lobbies and political parties influence government actions for or against business.

In the fifth circle of the chart are the climate makers—the groups and individuals who determine the climate of opinion in which a business will grow or decline. There are the various opinion-leader communities, including the business, religious, financial, educational, and professional communities. There is that vociferous institution, the press—newspapers, news services, magazines, radio, and television. There are groups pushing particular issues—civil rights or consumer protection, for example. There are associations advancing the interests of their members. There are plant community leaders. And even competitors are busy making or unmaking the climate of opinion. What all these people think, say, and do can enhance or injure the basic relationships and raise or lower the costs of the business. They can support the business in common objectives or make things very difficult.

Finally, in the outer circle of the chart, there is the general public: all the taxpayers, voters, neighbors, potential and actual customers, investors, employees, suppliers, and the like—the body social. Today the general public expects of business not only good economic performance but also the advancement of personal and national aspirations. A business must demonstrate that it serves the public interest, or it will find itself criticized, isolated, and unable to obtain what it needs to prosper.

Direct Interest Groups

Among the direct interest groups, of first importance to the company on its road to sales, and through sales to profits, are the customers.

CUSTOMERS

Management of customer relations is primarily a marketing responsibility, but public relations can help maximize sales and assure sound customer relations.

Institutional advertising. Public relations can increase brand preference for the company's products by helping to build an understanding of "the company behind the product." This is one of the functions of institutional advertising, which sets forth the identity, character, and competence of a company. Surveys and market tests indicate a strong correlation between information about the company and purchase of its products. Individuals who have a specific, informed, favorable understanding of the company have also, by a considerable margin, a greater ownership of the company's products than those who possess only a blurred, uninformed picture of the company. Hence many companies maintain a program of institutional advertising as a continuous backdrop behind their product advertising program, or they present a mix of institutional and product advertising in the media they use to reach their customers. Institutional advertising should illustrate the characteristics that distinguish one company from other companies and should present a consistent and of course truthful pattern over the years.

Product advertising is covered in the Marketing section of this handbook (page 5·117).

Executive speeches. Every industry has its conventions and association meetings where a business executive has opportunities to address his customers. While heavy-handed commercialism would of course be inappropriate here, the executive's perceptive grasp of industry issues and his leadership tend to personify the competence of his company and the excellence of its products. Distribution of speech reprints further builds the reputation of the company and its products.

Product publicity. Customers read and believe product information they see in the editorial columns of their favorite magazines perhaps more readily than they believe advertising; hence the company should provide the press with solid, newsworthy information about its products and their application. The normal mode is a press release, written as a journalist would report on the new product, telling what, who, where, when, and why it is important. Avoid puffery and exaggeration. Be ready to provide additional information if editors should request it. For really important announcements, the press conference may gain added attention. But the conference must be worthy of the reporters' time and attention, usually including product demonstrations, question-and-answer discussions, and a press kit of quotable, newsy facts, pictures, and background.

Product safety and use information. Public service literature, objectively presenting facts on how to get maximum value out of company products, how to avoid accidents or misuse, and how to shop for values, is an excellent way to build customer relations and prevent criticism from the active consumer-protection movement. Variations of this method include seminars and teaching materials for home economists and other people who are close to consumers.

SHARE OWNERS AND INVESTORS

Management has an obligation to provide sufficient corporate and financial data on which the investing public can base intelligent decisions. Adequate and timely disclosure also fosters a broad and active market for the company's securities at fair price levels.

Continuing share owner communications. The annual report is the principal means of reporting the company's progress, plans, and financial results to the investment community. It provides an opportunity to present not only the required financial data but also a verbal and pictorial perspective answering the perennial questions of the investor: How's business? What's new? What are the company's plans and prospects? Many companies supplement the annual report with quarterly reports accompanying the dividend check. The annual meeting, in addition to electing directors and transacting such other business as may be legally required, is also frequently used as an opportunity for the chief executive to offer a report on company progress and answer questions about the business.

Adequate and timely disclosure. Corporations are expected to make adequate and timely disclosure of news that would materially affect investment decisions or have a substantial impact on the market price of the stock. A company does not have to release news that it needs to keep confidential for sound business reasons. As long as such news is kept secret, those privy to the information—the "insiders"—may not trade in the stock and derive special benefit from the secret information. But if important news leaks, a prompt public disclosure is advisable whether or not this appears advantageous to the management. Because the stock market is an auction market, timing is very important. The number of persons who have to know or review important information, especially earnings information, prior to public release should be kept to a minimum. When information is released, it should be distributed simultaneously to a broad range of media reaching the investing public, such as the Dow Jones service, news services, and major brokerage firms, to assure that all investors have equal access to important corporate information.

Security analysts. The primary role of the security analyst is to provide the investing public with in-depth studies and recommendations on particular stocks and industries. If previously unpublished important information is to be given to an analyst, it should be done only if an adequate public disclosure is made simultaneously. A common approach is to address formal meetings of security analysts' associations, issuing a press release coincidental with the presentation. Interviews with individual analysts or small groups of them are also helpful to the investment community, but the manager should be careful not to reveal important confidential information to such an individual or group, thus giving them and their clients a significant advantage over other investors.

Take-over bids. If management is threatened by proxy fights, tender offers, or other forms of take-over bids, it had best seek professional financial relations counsel.

EMPLOYEES

The role of employees in company public relations is discussed earlier in this section under the heading "Internal Public Relations" (page 11·9).

SUPPLIERS

Because suppliers are an important link in the production chain, management should strive for supplier relationships that are mutually profitable and avoid relationships in which either side exploits the other.

As a general rule, the manager should not demand terms and conditions of his supplier that he would not accept from his own customers.

GOVERNMENT

The policies of government—local, state, and national—deeply affect what a company can or cannot do, and they also influence the cost of operations. Hence business has the responsibility of participating in the democratic process of government policy making.

Acquaintance with government leaders. The manager should know personally his representatives in Congress and in the state legislatures, as well as local officials and members of agencies which affect his business. He should keep them informed about his company and offer his opinion—including formal testimony where it would be helpful—on legislation or policies in which he has some relevant experience.

Political use of funds or facilities. Company funds and facilities may not be used, directly or indirectly, to support a particular party or candidate for political office. This does not preclude offering opposing candidates equal opportunity for plant visits or gate rallies—for example—or encouraging employees to support, as individuals, the candidates of their choice.

Nonpartisan programs. Many companies conduct programs to encourage employees to register and vote and to support the parties and candidates of their choice. Such programs should be nonpartisan and voluntary, and they should be conducted in a manner which will permit each employee to choose freely whether to participate and will protect the confidential character of his action.

Speaking out on public issues. The public expects company officers to speak out on issues that affect the business community; to remain silent implies consent in decisions that may not serve the public interest. But the manager must respect the right of employees to dissent from the managerial viewpoint, so long as they make clear that they are not speaking for the company.

The Climate Makers

Of the outside groups and institutions that determine the climate in which a company will thrive or decline, one institution—the press—more than any other has access to the public ear.

THE PRESS

Magazines, newspapers, wire services, radio, and television constitute a major continuing element in the formation of public opinion. The company manager should constructively utilize these channels of communication with the public. But it is important to recognize that the press is not simply a transmission belt for company messages. Journalists are independent reporters and interpreters of events, looking for news and its underlying significance. They should be objective. Companies that want regular and favorable press coverage must respond to these basic needs of the press.

Working relationships. The manager and/or his press relations man should cultivate the media and the editors most important to the company. Personal friendships, however, are not as important as a reputation for providing prompt, trustworthy, and newsy information. This reputation must be earned.

Providing information. Conduct a steady program of positive news, interviews, and interpretive material for the press; otherwise, the company will be in the newspapers only when it is in trouble. If working relations with the press are favorable, reporters will contact the company manager or public relations man when the company is being criticized, and an opportunity will be given to offer a rebuttal in the same article. A simultaneous response to criticism is more valuable than a detailed response 24 hours later.

Timing and availability. If other pertinent factors are favorable, the company that gets out news and photographs well before press deadlines will be given more press coverage than the company that holds its news to the last minute. Company officers should be available for interviews from time to time and should allow themselves to be quoted directly; save the "no comment" or the "anonymous spokesman" position for times of genuine need.

Interpretive function. Management cannot be passive in its relationships with the press or any other groups affecting the business. Rather, with the help of its public relations professionals, it must make a positive effort to anticipate and respond to the expectations of those who provide what the business needs to operate profitably. And it must follow these actions with interpretive communications that set forth the company's character, standards, and achievements.

—*R. L. Fegley*

MAXIMIZING PR BENEFITS

Even a company that has no formally planned public relations program or activity will generate goodwill when its operations are conducted in a reasonably businesslike and well-ordered manner. If management tries to satisfy its customers and treats its employees with the consideration that attracts and retains competent people, it will more or less automatically develop fairly good public relations with these groups, or at least with large segments of them.

Most corporate managements, however, regard good public relations as too important to be left to chance or improvisation. Sophisticated managements expect their public relations staffs to generate maximum goodwill in areas of maximum importance to the company at minimum cost. Careful advance planning is essential to accomplish this aim, because of the necessity for controlling prime factors in public relations work—content, timing, and emphasis.

The content of public relations activities must be coordinated with management policies. For example, if management plans to close an obsolete plant and employee dismissals will be an unavoidable result, the public relations program must try to minimize the damage to the company's reputation as an employer. If, on the other hand, the public relations program currently emphasizes job security, severe damage will be done to the company's reputation for credibility when the closing of the plant is announced.

Public relations timing must be coordinated with the management goals. If capital investment in a new plant community, for example, is scheduled for two years hence, community support must be developed in the meantime to insure a favorable climate when construction, hiring, and operations begin. Careful public relations preparation will enable management to adhere to its calendar without the costly delays that can result from community hostility.

A dozen or more publics, ranging from suppliers to stockholders, may be important to the company. But no corporation can afford unlimited funds to communicate with and influence all these groups in equal proportion. The public relations program must reflect management's emphasis in terms of its current problems and objectives. If a major product introduction—whether a new fluoride toothpaste or a new computer—is the big event of the corporate year, the public relations plan must allocate sufficient resources to provide adequate support.

The Objective of the PR Program

The objective of a public relations program, simply stated, must be favorable public relations; yet management does not always see the whole picture. In 1966, a study of *Fortune* magazine's 500 largest companies by the New York

University School of Commerce found that 77 percent of the 500 companies measured the success of their public relations only by the number of clippings— published publicity items—they obtained from their media placements. And a 1968 survey of 45 companies in the business equipment industry showed that 21—most of those which responded to the query—used the same yardstick: number of clippings resulting from publicity stories.

Publicity alone, however, may not be enough to produce the best public relations results. A good public relations program lists the specific techniques that will be used to reach each specific public and describes the impression the company wishes to make upon that public. Of course, publicity will be one of the major techniques.

A well-managed, operating public relations program should always be in written form. Prior to its adoption the corporate director of public relations should secure the approval of other appropriate management executives to whose areas of activity the program is related; and, finally, he must obtain acceptance of the program by the president or chief executive officer. In the process of securing such approvals, there are often delays and complications. But experience suggests that the management group, if it has participated in preparing the program, will support it with greater understanding.

A typical corporate public relations program will summarize the major proposed areas of activity and explain why each is being considered for action. Current attitudes regarding employees, plant community, and customers should be summarized for management, if possible with substantiation for the statements. The public relations director's evaluation of community opinion may be acceptable, but many managements will insist on a professionally conducted opinion survey. The larger the company and the more important the problems, the less likely it is that management will accept subjective judgment in this area.

How Publicity Is Obtained

Publicity was for many years the basic tool of the public relations man, and it will remain a major part of any public relations program today.

An effective starting point for maximizing publicity results is the simple technique of reading carefully the target publication (or watching the particular television program) for a few issues. Every newspaper has a particular style. It likes long feature stories or short "filler" items. It likes corporate news, or it doesn't. It likes news of constructive activities in the field of urban and racial affairs, or it doesn't. These editorial preferences reflect the policies of the media —or, at least, their judgment as to what their readers want to read. A company public relations man may convince an editor that the editor's judgment is wrong, but this rarely happens.

ADAPTING TO MEDIA PREFERENCES

The public relations man has the best chance of getting his corporate news into print if he reflects the known editorial attitudes of the editors in style, format, and content. This practice, in turn, will determine how the public relations man can create news within his company.

If, for example, a local television station is highly sports-minded, the chances for news coverage of a company story may be increased if sports celebrities are invited to participate. A national news service may ordinarily relegate a merger story to a few paragraphs on the news wire, but if the editor has a special interest in racial problems, and if the acquired company has successfully hired and trained minority applicants, the story will perhaps receive major coverage. The public relations department should be alert to such editorial preferences.

ADAPTING TO COMMUNITY INTERESTS

In other words, maximum favorable publicity is generated when the company relates its activities to community, regional, or national interests. The company cannot expect the community to be especially interested in it as an entity.

Newspaper, radio, and television news editors often show little enthusiasm for corporate news releases. They regard business news as somewhat less important than world events, national politics, human-interest stories, or even a fire down the block. Furthermore, few newsmen today (except those on the staffs of business and industrial publications) have sufficient familiarity with business to evaluate the importance of a corporate story.

Even if they did consider the corporate story important, news writers would have little space to tell it. Outside the major metropolitan areas, most newspapers devote less than one page daily to business-related news, aside from the stock market reports. There are also fewer newspapers to report the news. More than 1,500 U.S. cities, at this writing, have only a single newspaper; if that one editor doesn't like a story, it simply will not get into print.

The nationally circulated magazines show similar disinterest in business or product-oriented stories. Magazines such as *Life* and *Look* have upgraded the intellectual level of their content to keep pace with their new readership. The so-called press-agent stunts which often made their pages in earlier years now seldom appear; instead, there are features on artists of the Renaissance, intimate problems of marriage, the psychological impact of discrimination on preschool black children, and so on.

The publicity activities of the company must, therefore, reflect these realities. There is little sense in committing major energies to seeking a new-product story in *Life* magazine if *Life* hasn't run that type of story in years. There may be a notable exception, but the odds are against it.

DISSEMINATING COMPANY NEWS

The technical side of publicity activity is the easiest. Here are seven basic guidelines:

1. Information should always be given to the press in writing to prevent errors or misunderstanding. Emergencies are an exception.

2. The local media should know where to reach company officials at all times, and all company releases should indicate from whom additional information is obtainable.

3. Misleading statements, much less deliberately untruthful ones, should never under any circumstances be made to the press. They may be accepted as the

truth and published, but when eventually the full truth is known, the editors will never again trust the company.

4. Where unfavorable or damaging news occurs, minimize damage by releasing it, in full, immediately. It will be published quickly and forgotten almost as quickly.

5. Give the press any information it requests if it has a legitimate interest in the information. If legal or competitive reasons prevent disclosure, say so immediately and frankly. Don't be foxy.

6. Don't play favorites among the press. Those not favored may try to damage the company in the future.

7. Don't try to buy the press, whether with free lunches or with advertising. A steak dinner for a reporter won't guarantee publication of a story. On most—but not all—newspapers, the editorial department is completely insulated from the advertising department. Companies buy advertising because the newspaper provides them with an efficient channel of communication to their markets. Influence is not for sale in the editorial columns. Sending the company's advertising manager to the newspaper to complain of unfair editorial treatment would not only be unwise; it might even make the situation worse.

"FREE ADVERTISING"

Suppose that the company's story is published and favorable publicity is received. How valuable will it be to the company? If the article is essentially "free advertising" in the sense that its message could have been told equally well in paid advertising space, the likelihood is that management did not get much of a bargain, considering the time and effort required to prepare and place the story.

THE CREDIBILITY PROBLEM

If, however, the news story deals with a matter in which the company has self-interest and there is a possible credibility gap, editorial news coverage can bestow enormous benefits on the company. After one such occurrence a number of years ago, one cigarette brand suddenly climbed to first position in major markets because *Reader's Digest,* after independent tests, had reported that it was lowest in tar and nicotine content. The reference to the brand was made in a single paragraph of a single article in the magazine; yet it had more sales impact than the entire four-color, full-page advertising campaign of the same brand. The reason was that, although the public distrusted cigarette taste-and-health claims in advertising, it trusted the editorial integrity of *Reader's Digest.*

In this particular instance, no public relations man influenced, directly or indirectly, the *Reader's Digest* test. This story therefore illustrates not the power of the public relations man but the power of the independent third-person endorsement when credibility is a major company problem.

For a soft-drink company, a public relations objective might be to convince dentists that its carbonated beverages do not create caries. Parents would tend to reject this message as self-serving if the company made the claim; but if their family dentist told them the same thing, they would tend to believe it.

For the corporate treasurer, a public relations aim might be to secure favorable analyses and "buy" recommendations from leading brokerage houses and investment advisory services. Such recommendations have greater impact on investor decisions than the earnings and growth statistics in the company's annual report.

Finally, for the personnel manager, employees who spread the word around town that the company is a good place to work will bring more applicants to the factory gate than a dozen recruitment ads.

PERSONAL CONTACTS

A company public relations staff will find it easier to generate goodwill if it systematically cultivates personal relationships with those whose opinions are important to the company's growth. These personal contacts need not be made by the public relations staff; indeed, often they would be better made by other executives of the company. But they should be planned and coordinated by the public relations department. For example, the plant manager might regularly visit the mayor to better understand municipal problems and acquaint him with the company's activities. In this case, of course, the plant manager and the mayor might meet socially anyway at the local country club or Rotary club. But elected municipal officials have been known to appreciate the deference implicit in a more formal visit.

The public relations staff will appropriately invite editors and local newsmen to lunch, from time to time, particularly when they have no news to release. The purpose of these meetings is to get to know each other better. Other company people may meet similarly with ethnic-group leaders. These meetings are often most successful when the company executive does more listening than talking.

Another effective public relations technique is close liaison between the public relations staff and the company executives who are in direct contact with customers. In retailing, the executive will be the store manager. In a company manufacturing home appliances, it may be the service manager who handles customer complaints. From these people can come vital clues on sources of customer dissatisfaction. For most companies, customers are their most important public; yet, too often, public relations people have ignored them instead of being concerned with their complaints about poor service, inaccurate billing, or failure to make delivery on the date promised.

These customer-oriented areas, of course, may be regarded as outside the realm of responsibility of the public relations director. Yet, if he works jointly and cooperatively with the corporate executive who has been assigned primary responsibility, a sound public relations program can generate many solutions.

Psychological Considerations

The astute corporate public relations staff pays careful attention to psychological considerations in planning its programs. This practice may generate particularly good results in employee relations.

To cite one prevalent situation: While company benefits, pension programs, wage rates, and job security are greater than ever before, many companies face increased labor unrest. Traditionally, the relationship between the industrial relations director and the union business agent has been good. ("We fight each other once a year but get along fine the rest of the time.") This relationship, however, is being disrupted by the union members' frequent refusals to ratify wage agreements reached by their own leadership. Since the industrial relations director and the union business agent cannot solve the problem in the traditionally effective way, public relations directors are increasingly involved in reaching the union rank and file directly. The public relations techniques they use are old: mailings to employees' homes, ads in the local media, articles in the house organ, and the like. But public relations maximizes their impact by changing the content.

Public relations men who have an understanding of the behavioral sciences recognize that, while employees appreciate generous benefits, they simultaneously resent their dependence on the employer's paternalism. So, instead of emphasizing the company's generosity, the wise public relations man takes a more down-to-earth attitude that says, in effect, "We're giving you these benefits because we need you to stay with us." Instead of ridiculing union demands and union leaders during a strike, the public relations director suggests an approach calculated to win the goodwill instead of the hostility of the striking union members: He recommends expressing sympathetic understanding of their needs and their demands, with quiet explanations of why the company can't grant them.

This illustration suggests that the right content is more important than the right form in generating good public relations. Every professional public relations man has at his disposal a wide variety of communications techniques, but his greatest strength should be his ability to understand the viewpoint of the target audience and to prepare communications whose content is most likely to influence it.

LISTENING

Listening, in its broadest sense, is essential to generating positive public relations results. It can take the form of opinion sampling, or attendance at meetings, or reading. However the input is obtained, the public relations director must be well-grounded and up to date in an understanding of his target audience's current thinking.

BEHAVIORAL SCIENCE

The public relations director will be assisted in developing effective public relations programs by an awareness of human and social behavior. Psychologists and social scientists have formulated many conclusions on why people act as they do in many situations, and additional data are constantly being published. If the public relations director knows how and why people are likely to act in certain situations, he will increase the chances for successful communication.

—*Chester Burger*

EVALUATING PR BENEFITS

In the media-influenced society of today, the reach and scope of public relations make it a meaningful and profitable instrument of corporate policy, providing it is structured properly and evaluated realistically.

Return on Investment

The term "public relations" has many meanings and shadings of meaning. If corporate management is to be able to gauge the effectiveness of this function, it must (1) measure the specific form meant by the broad term "public relations"; and (2) project the results to be expected from the dollar and labor investment in it.

COMPETITION FOR FUNDS

Public relations must compete with manufacturing, sales, research, advertising, and other company elements for its share of available corporate funds. It is an instrument of management policy and style and thus should be subject to the same objective standards of performance and evaluation of achievement as any other unit of corporate operations.

Public relations is a program initiated to project either a total corporate message or a part thereof; to convince one public or a variety of publics; and to result either in persuasion or in the initiation of specific action. Thus it encompasses a greater totality than advertising and sales promotion; is more of a broad-gauged program of communications; and often may include or extend any or all of the others. Yet, in terms of dollars budgeted and expended, public relations usually compares favorably on an activity-cost basis with its affiliated disciplines, primarily because the major share of public relations expense is usually attributable to direct labor and supplemental services without including media costs. (The printing and postage costs per reader unit and the media costs of print, radio, and television advertising, on the basis of per interested individual reached with the company message, can be expected to require higher budgets than a public relations budget normally does. Nevertheless, some public relations budgets may include both, although the target publics will usually be smaller, more select groups.)

Establishing a public relations budget may be approached from any one of several ways. These would include: (1) lump-sum approach, whereby the budget allowable is set first by management, usually as a portion of expected sales or operating income, and a program is developed to fit this pre-established dollar figure; (2) overall program approach, a method under which the ideal program is established first, then the budget request is initiated on a total-need basis; and (3) project method, which is basically a segmentation of the program approach under which funding requirements are set up by specific single projects, thereby creating greater flexibility and allowing for adoption of individual projects.

The most successful public relations budgeting works out realistically as a combination of all three approaches—considering the needs of the program, structuring projects and priorities, establishing the final overall program cost, and negotiating with management for funding.

A tenuous, often misunderstood segment of corporate operations, public relations nevertheless must be capable of measurement by the same basic yardsticks of profitable management that pertain to all other aspects of the company.

COSTS AND BENEFITS

Priorities for public relations, as with other corporate functions, must be set up on a basis of variable factors, among which those that give promise of greatest progress toward specific goals receive the most sympathetic hearings.

A realistic approach of dollar return on dollar invested must be utilized. However, public relations evaluation seeks to measure public attitudes and so does not lend itself to the usual corporate performance measures such as units sold or units manufactured.

Research and dollar value. It should be understood that public relations measurements are more valid when they establish a dollar value for a given program objective. For example, the very element of transferring cognitive knowledge of information, as is done in a financial public relations program, in itself must have a dollar value that can be established in relation to the overall impact of its effect for corporate good.

Of prime importance in developing substantive and profitable public relations is the first move: analyzing the situation. Next, realistic objectives that coincide with management's specific goals must be outlined, after which a program to achieve them can be evolved; standards of performance created; and a viable, regular check on results maintained.

Defining corporate problems for public relations and developing realistic objectives (the important foundation for successful public relations program investment) requires early in-depth analysis to probe factors able to influence results, help define objectives, set up a base for future measurement, and establish a dollar value for proportions of achievement.

Should a distortion or an invalid premise be integrated into the objectives of a corporate program, the program itself can become sharply out of balance and create a resultant error factor which could militate against attaining the desired objectives.

Analysis requires knowledge and comprehension of the program and the techniques of program implementation. For example, in a project program involving the opening of a local branch or facility, the type of neighborhood and people, objectives of the branch, market and type of customer to be attracted, style and image of the corporate entity, employee programs, local civic and social environment, time of year, and all other special elements of the area should be considered, along with creative elements and cost, in enunciating objectives. Just as with a sales program, the market capabilities with short- and long-term potential should be weighed as a major factor in deciding the budget for the project. It should also be appreciated that the creative capabilities of the company's public relations professionals and the acceptance factor of their product (whether outside publicity, brochures, or in-house literature) bring added benefits often beyond the purely local and immediate results of the program.

Input-output analysis. To select the best program to achieve the best results with a specific budget requires comprehensive understanding of the factors involved and the techniques that influence public attitudes.

This body of knowledge is crucial in establishing realistic program budgets and goals. For example, the selection of a broad-spectrum, million-dollar public relations program, however ideal to accomplish a desired end, would be impractical and relatively nonproductive for a company whose operating public relations budget can be only $100,000.

Conversely, to aim for a minimal-dollar program when the achievement of corporate needs requires a figure several times as great and the capital is available, can be a penny-wise, pound-foolish attitude. Essentially, then, public relations expenditures should be judged on their own merits within the scope of predetermined capabilities.

Similarly, without a sound evaluation of results actually achieved against objectives originally set up, there can exist no valid way of deciding the degree of success a program has reached toward attaining a stated goal.

It becomes important, therefore, that postprogram evaluation set up valid yardsticks to define the amount of the program that was successfully implemented. Postprogram appraisal highlights the faults of a program as well as the successes, permits a pragmatic appreciation of the benefits or deficiencies of the objectives themselves, and provides a working base for future activities in the same area. This is because, in public attitudes, nothing really remains static, and every situation usually leads to another which will likewise require education, stimulus, and a program of its own.

MEASURING PROGRAM RESULTS

The best way to judge the progress and results of an individual public relations program is to lay out and graph the objectives at the beginning; set the specifics of the program to be used; establish a timetable; and coldbloodedly and analytically weigh the results at the end of the budget period to learn how much progress was made along the predetermined path.

In public relations, where results must be measured in terms of changes in public attitudes, it is considered difficult to set up accurate measurements on a per dollar, per result basis. Yet the structuring of budget, analysis, objective, program, progress, and final—or periodic—appraisal does set up a basis of comprehensive measurement for determining performance percentages per dollar budgeted.

The key to control in a public relations program rests with the realistic creation of the before-the-fact plan. Optimum results may be undermined because objectives initially established were unrealistic in terms of capability to achieve. The classic example occurs all too frequently in publicity, when companies attempt to interest a national news medium in what is essentially a trade-paper or local story.

The input-output infrastructure of a public relations program rests, basically, upon the development of the corporate story or "case"; a proper application of the analysis and evaluation of the publics that are to be reached with this story; sound employment of the channels of communication to these publics; and creative but businesslike investment of available funds to achieve results. The input of time and money must result in returns productive to the corporation just as with sales, advertising, or manufacturing programs.

To measure this productivity, standards of performance—particularly in view of the intangible and sometimes esoteric nature of the public relations function—must be enunciated as clearly and simply as possible. Performance should be evaluated for both the short and the long term and measured critically against established criteria.

If publicity is a major thrust of the program, the original scheduling should include specified stories (or story approaches) and media according to a predetermined time schedule. Then the achievement or nonachievement of these standards can be appraised in businesslike fashion.

Many practitioners view publicity clippings as a major, tangible measure of success in public relations. One of the techniques such advocates use is to measure clippings linage and compare it against the cost factor that would be involved in buying a similar amount of advertising space. Opponents of this technique point out that it does not provide value consideration to intangible benefits that accrue from publicity space but not from paid advertising messages, such as greater inherent credibility, higher-impact reader ratios, and a more focused market segmentation.

MEASURING RETURN ON INVESTMENT

The difficulty of attributing direct dollar return from the intangibles of public relations has unnecessarily deterred many corporate managers from attempting to quantify their corporate efforts in this field and caused many to rely on instinct rather than on actual measurement.

A realistic approach is to set up tangible goals and gauge the percentage of attainment of these goals on a regular and continuing basis. If the objective of the program is to shift public attitude regarding a company or a project or to create acceptance of a product, program appraisal of results must be measurable against the predetermined set of standards. At these times, the main measure may well be clippings; at many other times, it will not.

The capability of improving return on investment rests basically upon establishing what the initial return should be and whether the standard is being met—and, if it is not being met, pinpointing and analyzing the reasons for failure. The reasons may be varied: perhaps an overreaching program or an underreaching one; an unanticipated lack of response on the part of the market public to a given company story; a new sociological or psychological situation; or circumstances unanticipated and beyond anyone's power to control. Similarly, the program may be more successful more rapidly than planned; this will be pinpointed by early appraisal, with attendant increased return on investment— which might well raise the question, "Should the program be accelerated or expanded?"

PR Benefits in Individual Categories

A corporate public relations program can be segmented into six general categories: internal, public media, community, financial, shareholders, and customers and dealers.

INTERNAL PUBLIC RELATIONS

Investment in this category can best be appraised when intercompany communications channels are open and free and information moves swiftly through them. Internal programs include bulletin boards, information racks, house organs, employee brochures and mailings, pay-envelope stuffers, company meetings, extracurricular activities, and the like. Feedback through internal channels of communication is the major gauge of success—although, in plant operations, climate of union negotiations and employee turnover rates are good indicators. Internally, there is often an overlap between labor relations and public relations. This part of the program, like all others, must be evaluated strictly by the yardstick of whether it accomplished what it sought to do. If it hasn't done so, reappraisal of input factors should be initiated as quickly as possible so that a more meaningful program can be implemented.

PUBLIC MEDIA

This category deals mainly with publicity elements such as corporate announcements, product stories, and the climate of public attitudes, and involves communications elements such as newspapers, magazines, radio, television, newsletters, and others which serve the general public under third-party ownership. It encompasses media that educate, enlighten, and entertain. In this category, print clippings and appearances or mentions in audiovisual media are the truest gauge of message projection. Here, too, the same basic standard should be applied: Did the public relations program do what it was supposed to do? Were the stories sent out and the appearances scheduled as programmed? Sometimes there are tangential benefits. A story may appear and "take off" far beyond expectation. At another time, a story just as good may shrivel and die. Only analysis of the factors influencing each one of them—timing, other stories breaking at the same time, creative elements, or methods of dissemination—can provide the truest measure of performance and highlight any inadequacies or deficiencies in the original premise.

COMMUNITY PUBLIC RELATIONS

This category is usually associated with the local physical environment in which the company, plant, or facility exists. It has recently come to include much of the corporate sociological involvement program in a broader sense than tradition had established. Local civic activity, extracurricular participation by employees and management, and now minority affairs and concerns are included in this category. Local plant stories, disaster programs, personality pieces, fraternal and civic organization participation, as well as corporate contributions and management "good neighbor" activity, are an integral part of a well-rounded community program. Once more, the measure of success depends upon programmed expectation. Since much of this area deals with corporate-neighborhood relationship, an element weighing heavily in measurement is found in corporate style and traditional and past relationships, which may take a long time to change.

Again, it is the realistic original expectation and the dollar value allocated to it that define the return on investment in this area of public relations.

THE FINANCIAL COMMUNITY

The financial community is one of the few areas in which, to a great degree, public relations success or failure may have an almost immediately measurable impact. A financial relations program, which involves corporate contacts, meetings, and literature directed to the total financial community—security analysts, investment bankers, investment letter writers, institutional investors, and a highly specialized financial press—is generally measured by the price/earnings ratio of the company's stock and the opinion of a relatively small group of influential executives across the country, dominated by New York's Wall Street but extending, ever more so, through the key financial communities of the nation and even the world. The corporation and management are constantly under appraisal in the financial community; the financial relations program must therefore capitalize upon utilizing the varied media, literature, and contacts that project sound and accurate appraisal of the company as an investment medium. Unlike other programs, financial relations places a legal responsibility upon management to report facts accurately. The importance of the financial community is that it encompasses the major channel of communication to the investing public and the sources of investment capital which corporations must approach for financing. Similarly, the price/earnings ratio of a company's stock is an important factor in such matters as corporate acquisition and expansion and executive recruiting. Here again, the daily stock quotations do not necessarily provide the most accurate gauge of return on investment to the company, and only a sound, planned program, appraised periodically and flexible enough to change to meet new and important situations, can provide the best return on investment. Financial relations is a highly complex, rigidly structured, legally vulnerable area and is best approached by specialists in the field.

SHAREHOLDERS

Shareholders are a public closely associated with the corporation. In fact, they are considered its owners, with management responsible to them for the operation of the company. Management makes a report of its stewardship annually to the shareholders in a public meeting. Through the literature of its annual report and interim reports, it provides financial information for the edification of this public. The relationship between management and its shareholders is established, to a large extent, by the requirements of the various securities laws. In addition, shareholders as owners vote their stock for or against corporate proposals. The techniques of shareholder communication extend from highly complex programs, for companies with hundreds of millions of shares outstanding, to small-budget, minimal communications from firms in a more minor category. Evaluation here depends upon shareholder views. Loss of support, in some companies, can mean replacement of management or take-over by another firm. Only solid analysis, realistic programming, and regular appraisal can define the quality of the return on investment here. With a built-in feedback situation—since shareholders often write to their management and, at least each year, either vote or do not vote their proxies for or against management—an ongoing evaluation relationship and early information about shifts in attitude are reasonably easy to maintain.

CUSTOMERS AND DEALERS

The customer-and-dealer category can well be the most important element of public relations because upon this area, seemingly, hinges the success or failure of the entire company and its operations. Yet this may not be so, and the public relations role may be much less significant. Sales departments maintain strong and ongoing relationships with company dealers, and marketing divisions evolve programs to sell company products.

In many firms, this category is called trade relations and is an extension of the overall marketing program. It is, in fact, generally in the purview of marketing and sales departments. Media dealings here are with a specialized trade press, in many instances composed of highly competent professionals who are fully informed about the industries they cover and have exacting requirements for stories and articles. The trade press is an important communications channel, as can be company-sponsored literature. Relationships may also be subject to more influences outside the public relations field, depending often upon such things as the company's style in reference to its trade customers and dealers, particularly in such bread-and-butter areas as contracts, supply capabilities, interpersonal relationships, and product or service quality, as well as a whole spectrum of dealer-supplier relations.

Evaluation of dollar return per dollar invested hinges most directly upon the distribution relationships, since these programs basically are the extensions and support of other ongoing activity.—*S. A. Krasney*

PUBLIC RELATIONS IN THE FUTURE

To some people, the term "public relations" conveys a curious ambiguity, as if it implied a difference between an organization's private affairs and the image the organization seeks to create. It may also seem to suggest that what goes on in the business is different from what goes on in the rest of society. It is the intention of the following discussion to dispel both impressions.

The History of Public Relations

Over the past 60 years, as business has matured, public relations has gone through several phases: a fire-fighting function in the early years; puffery and stunts; a more subtle formula, explaining rather than selling business performance; and, finally, the emerging function of today. The public relations man's new task is one of sensing the needs of the environment, feeding them into his organization as key factors in policy and planning decisions, and using effective communications inside and outside the organization to help achieve its goals, long-term and short-term.

Business now recognizes that it has many publics and that none of them can be excluded from consideration in the sphere of normal corporate operations. They are, in fact, essential to every aspect of corporate existence.

Capital, the lifeblood of an enterprise, increasingly comes from the savings of many, rather than from one or two very wealthy individuals, and the modern company needs well-informed investors who are willing to support it in order to foster its growth and prosperity.

Customers are the essential element of any business, and a public relations program that helps to create a more responsive environment for marketing is of major value to every enterprise.

The ability to exist and continue to do business is dependent on the continuing willingness of the government and of society to let individual businesses, and business as a whole, continue. This means that business must act responsibly and in the interests of society.

These and similar considerations have made public relations today almost a public responsibility function.

In the next ten years, the public relations—or public affairs—specialist has an unparalleled opportunity for accomplishment. He can contribute to service and progress to a degree that he has not yet approached and perhaps has not yet begun to think about seriously. To fill this role, however, he must learn how to lead, discover the advantages of risk taking, and be willing to follow some paths that may seem very unpopular in the short term.

The Current Status of Public Relations

American society is living through one of the most revolutionary and chaotic periods in its history. (An old-time public relations man might describe it as "creative.") And the hard job of reintegrating and reorienting the national life on a new plane of values has scarcely begun. All the time-honored institutions and organizations find themselves reaching farther and farther out into the world—striving desperately, at the same time, not to lose sight of any man among their members. Old boundaries, old beliefs, and old shibboleths are tumbling to the ground.

But balance should go hand in hand with change, if new ways are to be better than the old ones. In the desire to be modern, it is easy to throw out substantial, lasting values. The public relations man is, more than most people in the business world, in danger of erring on the side of "going along with the crowd." Too often, the public relations man of the past has been the advocate, within the organization, of simply riding along with the current surface mood of society. This is the essence of "followership," and it can result only in a decline of public relations' role as a relevant and major contributor to progress.

Today, it is too easy to be complacent and convinced that public relations has arrived—that everything that should be done is being done. But is it? Are all the available tools being used? Is public relations goal-oriented, and is the total organization kept in mind when public relations sets out to solve a problem? In planning a modern marketing approach, does public relations really go all the way in sensing customer needs or regarding this step as the first stage in designing a new product?

Public relations needs to become more customer-oriented, more knowledgeable about "what's out there," and less functionally oriented. Concentration should be on the needs of the publics served, not on the communications empires that may be building. These publics should be studied and listened to, and public relations organizations geared to serve them better.

Public relations men must be the social scientists—perhaps the social conscience—of business, learning the historian's skill but refusing to relive all the errors of the past.

Businessmen, as well as educators and leaders in religion and governments, recognize that they must take part in shaping the future; for it is their future, along with everyone else's, that is taking shape. Increasingly, businessmen are becoming aware that their own creativity and thought are essential in shaping the future of the community.

Present-Day Problems and Opportunities

The businessman of today and tomorrow faces two major challenges: (1) to understand and redefine his own business mission; and (2) to understand, and thus be able to function successfully in, the new business environment. In both these formidable tasks, the public affairs specialist ought to play a major role.

Some of business's new problems and opportunities are briefly stated in the following paragraphs.

WORLD TRADE

All business is now involved in world trade, whether or not a given company actually sells or produces goods abroad at present. Markets today are worldwide, and most of them attract substantial international competition. Trade among nations is a common bond, and it ought to be one of the freest of our international associations. The truly international organization can plan and operate on a global scale, and this means planning and thinking beyond its natural cultural associations.

MODERN ELECTRONICS

Business must learn to use its new electronic tools better. The computer, rapid long-distance data transmission, closed-circuit television, and the rest of the electronic package that makes this a world of instantaneous communication and information retrieval will become as common to the manager as his telephone and dictaphone are now. The use of these tools must be learned in order to make men more productive and, at the same time, to enable them to lead more satisfying lives. Programs that teach new skills and—equally important—the *acceptance* of new skills are part of the new challenge confronting the public relations expert.

THE AFFLUENT SOCIETY

The businessman of the future will need a deeper understanding of the change from a subsistence-oriented society to a society which emphasizes the quality of life. Most Americans save part of their income, and record numbers of people have chosen to invest, to some degree or other, in the productive resources of the nation. They have, in short, become part owners of the capitalist system. Most employees of today will retire with substantial retirement incomes, good health programs, and a desire to make the most of their leisure time. The generation that follows will tend to spend less of its lifetime in work and more in education, leisure, and other personal activities. The needs and desires for goods and services in both groups will be of increasing concern and interest to business in general and to the public relations specialist.

OTHER SOCIETAL CONSIDERATIONS

The businessman ought to be fully aware that public attitudes about business are undergoing marked change. The public not only expects business to provide jobs, income, goods, and services; it also expects business to contribute to the solution of pressing social problems. Business needs to help in such activities as job and training programs for the underprivileged and the dropouts. Business's aid is also needed in the development of technical skills and products to work on the problems of urban decay and congestion, air and water pollution, and natural blight. The public affairs professional will be called upon, as never before, for advice and counsel.

DUAL ROLE OF PUBLIC RELATIONS

In addition to all these new considerations, the businessman must manage his company as a growing, profitable enterprise. He is quite willing to accept the idea that business purposes must be in step with those of the rest of society, and thus he needs to participate in all the functions of society to a greater extent than ever before. But the participation must be that of a businessman managing a business enterprise. While the businessman must learn to be a better citizen of the community (not to pollute the environment, for example), it is equally important for the community to understand how essential business is to society's continued healthy existence. Businessmen must work to develop responsible public attitudes as they themselves display responsibility. This is an important two-way job for public relations.

Integration of Business and Societal Goals

In all these areas of change, the investor relations man and the public affairs and public relations specialists can contribute mightily to the organization's understanding of what is happening, to the efforts to integrate the organization with its new environment, and to the reorientation of the organization to its new purposes. These specialists can help create the new programs and functional apparatus through which business can solve its internal organizational problems and take a greater part in the more integrated community of our time.

The businessman in our society has never before been so influential and so well regarded—and, at the same time, so closely scrutinized by society. His base of operations has never been so broad. He is a leader whose counsel is sought on every side and on every subject.

In spite of this generally favorable climate of opinion, there are indications (found in some surveys) that a dishearteningly large percentage of college students do not plan to seek a career in business. In the minds of many of these students, business is a faceless institution—a place where initiative dies and individuality is stifled. Nevertheless, business can turn ideas into reality. It can create, and it offers that chance to the creative individual. In this area is a great gap that the public relations professional must work to close.

The public relations function now has better tools available to it than ever before—better opportunities to serve, and a better understanding of how to serve. With all these, will it be able to make the most of its new environment?

In the past, some institutional communication has been bad. Organizations talk to themselves about themselves, and not enough to the customer or the public. What is needed is a return to first principles: "Effective communication is not what I say—it is what you hear."

The challenge this poses to public relations is enormous. From now on, the public relations man will be narrow indeed if he sees his task as only that of an image maker or product promoter.

Never before have the requirements of business so closely coincided with the broadest and best goals of society; and rarely, if ever, has there been a time when business skills and talents so closely matched society's broader needs, when the best interests of business and all its publics were so completely intertwined.

The problems are being solved on a massive scale, one that requires more massive organizations than ever before. Business offers creative ways of solving these problems without going toward a welfare state.

To do this, and do it effectively, will require a great deal of new thinking on the part of the professional; he must re-educate himself before he can begin to create and operate the new programs and create and maintain the new relationships his company must forge to successfully engage the future.—*O. Glenn Saxon*

Section 12

General Index

(Figures in boldface indicate section numbers.)